# Christianity in Roman Africa

# Christianity in

WILLIAM B. EERDMANS PUBLISHING COMPANY

# Roman Africa

## The Development of Its Practices and Beliefs

J. Patout Burns Jr. *&* Robin M. Jensen

*In collaboration with*

Graeme W. Clarke

Susan T. Stevens

William Tabbernee

Maureen A. Tilley

GRAND RAPIDS, MICHIGAN / CAMBRIDGE, U.K.

Published 2014 by
Wm. B. Eerdmans Publishing Co.
2140 Oak Industrial Drive N.E., Grand Rapids, Michigan 49505 /
P.O. Box 163, Cambridge CB3 9PU U.K.

Printed in the United States of America

20 19 18 17 16 15 14      7 6 5 4 3 2 1


**Library of Congress Cataloging-in-Publication Data**

Christianity in Roman Africa: the development of its practices and beliefs /
    J. Patout Burns Jr. & Robin M. Jensen; in collaboration with Graeme W. Clarke,
    Susan T. Stevens, William Tabbernee, Maureen A. Tilley.
        pages        cm
    Includes bibliographical references and index.
    ISBN 978-0-8028-6931-9 (cloth: alk. paper)
    1. Africa — Church history.
    2. Church history — Primitive and early church, ca. 30-600.
    I. Jensen, Robin Margaret, 1952-

    BR190.C49   2014
    276.1'01 — dc23

                                                    2013038812

www.eerdmans.com

# Contents

# List of Illustrations

*Unless otherwise noted, all photos are by the authors*

**BASILICAS, BAPTISTERIES, AND SHRINES**

1. Ammaedara (Haidra), Melleus basilica
2. Ammaedara (Haidra), Melleus basilica *(Plan after Baratte and Duval [1974], p. 51, fig. 19. Drawn by E. Brown)*
3. Ammaedara (Haidra), tomb inscription of Cresconia, from nave, Melleus basilica
4. Ammaedara (Haidra), detail of reliquary emplacement in nave, Melleus basilica
5. Belalis Maior, basilica I, phase II, baptismal font
6. Belalis Maior, basilica I, phase II *(Plan after Lassus [1970a], p. 222, fig. 2. Drawn by E. Brown)*
7. Belalis Maior, basilica II (cathedral?), phase II, baptismal font
8. Bennafa (La Skhira), mosaic pavement from baptistery, near Gabès, Tunisia, now in the Sfax Archaeological Museum
9. Bennafa (La Skhira), mosaic pavement from baptistery, near Gabès, Tunisia, now in the Sfax Archaeological Museum
10. Bulla Regia double church (basilica I) — looking toward apse
11. Bulla Regia double church *(Plan after N. Duval [1989], p. 356, fig. 5. Drawn by E. Brown)*
12. Bulla Regia double church, baptismal font
13. Bulla Regia, baptismal font steps

## Carthage

## Castellum Tingitanum (Orléansville)

## Hippo Regius

## Sufetula (Sbeitla)

## Thamugadi (Timgad)

## FUNERARY INSCRIPTIONS AND MOSAICS

## OTHER

# Preface

This project originated in conversations at the annual meeting of the North American Patristics Society in May 1994. By November of that year, William Tabbernee and Maureen Tilley had joined us in planning. Graeme Clarke and Susan Stevens accepted our invitation to join the team. The National Endowment for the Humanities approved and funded our application for a multidisciplinary and collaborative study. In June 1996 we spent three weeks in Tunisia, exploring the archeological evidence of Christian practice and attempting correlations with the literary sources.

Beginning in November 1996, we arranged seminars at the national meetings of the American Academy of Religion and the North American Patristics Society. Each of these was dedicated to exploring a particular aspect of the practice of Christianity in Roman Africa. The original NEH funding, a grant from Florida State University, and a grant from the AAR for collaborative research supported these seminars and additional meetings of the central team. The research was enriched by the contributions of specialists in the topics of the seminars: William Harmless, David Hunter, Thomas Martin, Andrew McGowan, Jane Merdinger, Claudia Setzer, Alistair Stewart, and Jonathan Yates. The papers and images prepared for each of these sessions were made available through the Christianity in Roman Africa (CHROMA) Web site, now hosted by the Augustinian Institute of Villanova University. In April 2001, we joined Maureen Tilley as participants in the international colloquy "Saint Augustin: Africanité et Universalité," organized by Le Haut Conseil Islamique of Algeria in collaboration with the University of Fribourg and the Institutum Patristicum Augustinianum; it provided an unusual opportunity to visit the ancient city of Hippo Regius and other significant Christian sites in Algeria under the guidance of local scholars.

This project was designed and executed as a collaborative investigation engaging different disciplinary resources. Members of the central team and the seminar participants contributed to the resulting study. No element in this final report is the work of a single individual; team members reviewed and commented on the drafts of the chapters. Maureen Tilley prepared an extensive initial bibliography. Graeme Clarke drafted the first historical chapter, Maureen Tilley the second, and Robin Jensen the third. Robin Jensen organized both the survey of archeological evidence in the fourth chapter and the deployment of this evidence elsewhere in the book. Drawing upon the contributions that participants made in the seminars, we prepared the studies of the various Christian practices. Patout Burns drafted the concluding chapter. The manuscript was reviewed by the central team and others who had contributed to its individual parts.

As the book neared completion, we turned to other specialists. Our daughter, Elizabeth Brown, prepared the architectural drawings of sites and buildings, with supplementary work by Ralf Bockmann. Nathan Dennis, Michael Flecky, and Annewies van den Hoek contributed photographs not in our collection. Robert McFadden assembled the tables outlining the history of African Christianity. The text was edited by Andrea Thornton. Jeffrey Harris assisted in setting up the indices. Sarah Porter and Mark Ellison contributed to the final proofreading. Through the good offices of Tracy Miller of the History of Art Department and Dean Carolyn Dever, Vanderbilt University's College of Arts and Science provided a subvention for the use of color plates.

From the beginning of this project until his death in January 2011, Henry Y. K. Tom, executive editor at the Johns Hopkins University Press, provided advice, encouragement, and regular prodding. As the manuscript grew beyond the limits he had set, Jon Pott welcomed it to William B. Eerdmans Publishing Company. There, Mary Hietbrink undertook the task of editing and Klaas Wolterstorff of designing the present volume, a process that required two years of regular, if not constant, work and consultation. Kevin van der Leek designed the cover. They responded creatively to our requests, initiated proposals of their own, established consistent usage, and graciously accepted updates of the final proofs up to the time the project was passed to the printer.

Through the years in which this project took shape, our principal collaborators and many other colleagues offered suggestions, responded to questions, and provided insistent encouragement. May the result justify their generous contributions. Appropriately, this work was completed on the feast of the African matron whose son devotedly described her Christian practice.

ROBIN M. JENSEN & J. PATOUT BURNS JR.
*August 27, 2014*
*Feast of St. Monica*

# Abbreviations

| | |
|---|---|
| AnBoll | Analecta Bollandiana |
| CCSL | Corpus Christianorum: Series latina |
| *CIL* | *Corpus inscriptionum latinarum* |
| CSEL | Corpus scriptorum ecclesiasticorum latinorum |
| *DACL* | *Dictionnaire d'archéologie chrétienne et de liturgie*, ed. F. Cabrol |
| GCS | Die griechische christliche Schriftsteller der ersten Jahrhunderte |
| *ICUR* | *Inscriptiones christianae urbis Romae Septimo Saeculo Antiquiores*, ed. J. B. de Rossi |
| *ILCV* | *Inscriptiones latinae christianae veteres*, ed. E. Diehl |
| Loeb | Loeb Classical Library |
| *MA* | *Miscellanea Agostiniana*, ed. D. G. Morin and A. Casamassa |
| *MGH* | *Monumenta Germaniae Historica* |
| AA | Auctores Antiquissimi |
| G. Pont. | Gesta pontificum Romanorum |
| Musurillo | Herbert Musurillo, ed. and trans., *The Acts of the Christian Martyrs* |
| PG | Patrologiae cursus completus: Series graeca, ed. J.-P. Migne |
| PL | Patrologiae cursus completus: Series latina, ed. J.-P. Migne |
| PLS | Patrologiae cursus completus: Series latina: Supplementum |
| *PSI* | *Papiri greci e latini* |
| *P.Lips.* | *Griechische Urkunden der Papyrussammlung zu Leipzig*, ed. L. Mitteis et al. |
| P.Mich. | Michigan papyri, Ann Arbor: University of Michigan Press |
| *P.Oxy.* | *The Oxyrhynchus Papyri*, ed. B. P. Grenfell, A. Hunt, et al. |
| *RB* | *Revue bénédictine* |
| *SB* | *Sammelbuch griechischer Urkunden aus Aegypten*, ed. F. Preisigke et al. |
| SC | Sources chrétiennes |
| SPM | Stromata Patristica et Mediaevalia |

# ANCIENT AUTHORS AND WORKS

| | |
|---|---|
| *Act. Abit.* | *Acta martyrum Saturnini, Datiui, Felicis, Ampelii et Ceterorum* (Studi e testi 65 [1935]:49-71) |
| *Act. Cass.* | *Acta Cassiani*, ed. T. Ruinart (*Acta Martyrum*, p. 345) |
| *Act. Marc.* | *Acta Marcelli* (Musurillo, 250-59) |
| *Act. Max.* | *Acta Maximiliani* (Musurillo, 244-49) |
| *Act. Procon.* | *Acta Proconsularia Cypriani* (CSEL 63.3:cx-cxiv) |
| *Act. pur. Fel.* | *Acta purgationis Felicis episcopi Autrumnitani* (CSEL 26:197-204; Maier, 1:174-89) |
| *Act. Scil.* | *Acta Scillitanorum* (Musurillo, 86-89) |
| *Act. Thec.* | *Acts of Paul and Thecla* (Lipsius, *Act. Apost. Apoc.* 1:235-72) |
| *Act. Zeno.* | *Acta apud Zenophilum* (CSEL 26:185-97; Maier, 1:214-39) |
| Ambr. | Ambrose |
| *Exc.* | *De excessu fratris sui Satyri* (CSEL 73:207-325) |
| *Fid.* | *De fide* (CSEL 78) |
| *Sac.* | *De sacramentis* (CSEL 73:13-85) |
| Aug. | Augustine of Hippo |
| *Adult.* | *De adulterinis coniugiis* (CSEL 41:347-410) |
| *Agon.* | *De agone christiano* (CSEL 41:101-138) |
| *Anim.* | *De anima et eius origine* (CSEL 60:303-419) |
| *Bapt.* | *De baptismo contra Donatistas* (CSEL 51:145-375) |
| *Bon. coniug.* | *De bono coniugali* (CSEL 41:187-231) |
| *Catech.* | *De catechizandis rudibus* (CSEL 46:121-78) |
| *Ciu.* | *De ciuitate Dei* (CCSL 47-48) |
| *Coll.* | *Breuiculus collationis cum Donatistis* (CCSL 149A:261-306) |
| *Conf.* | *Confessionum libri XIII* (CCSL 27:1-273) |
| *Cons.* | *De consensu euangelistarum* (CSEL 43) |
| *Corrept.* | *De correptione et gratia* (CSEL 92:219-80) |
| *Cresc.* | *Contra Cresconium Donatistam* (CSEL 52:325-582) |
| *Cur.* | *De cura pro mortuis gerenda* (CSEL 41:621-60) |
| *Doct. Chr.* | *De doctrina christiana* (CCSL 32:1-167) |
| *Don.* | *Post collationem aduersus Donatistas* (CSEL 53:97-162) |
| *Dulc.* | *De octo Dulcitii quaestionibus* (CCSL 44A:253-97) |
| *Emer.* | *De gestis cum Emerito* (CSEL 53:181-96) |
| *Enchir.* | *Enchiridion de fide, spe et caritate* (CCSL 46:49-114) |
| *Ep.* | *Epistulae* (CSEL 34, 44, 57, 58; CCSL 31-31B) |
| *Ep. ad cath.* | *Epistula ad catholicos* (CSEL 52:231-322) |
| *Ep. Divj.* | *Epistulae a Divjak editae* (CSEL 88) |
| *Ep. Io.* | *In epistulam Iohannis ad Parthos tractatus* (PL 35:1977-2062) |
| *Eu. Io.* | *In euangelium Iohannis tractatus* (CCSL 36) |
| *Faust.* | *Contra Faustum Manichaeus* (CSEL 25.1:251-797) |
| *Fel.* | *Contra Felicem* (CSEL 25.2:801-52) |

| | |
|---|---|
| *Fid.* | *De fide rerum quae non uidentur* (CCSL 46:1-19) |
| *Fid. et op.* | *De fide et operibus* (CSEL 41:35-97) |
| *Gal.* | *Expositio in epistulam ad Galatas* (CSEL 84:55-141) |
| *Gaud.* | *Contra Gaudentium Donatistarum episcopum* (CSEL 53:201-74) |
| *Gen. litt.* | *De Genesi ad litteram* (CSEL 28.1:3-435) |
| *Gen. Man.* | *De Genesi contra Manichaeos* (CSEL 91:67-172) |
| *Gest. Pel.* | *De gestis Pelagii* (CSEL 42:51-122) |
| *Haer.* | *De haeresibus* (CCSL 46:286-345) |
| *Hept.* | *Quaestiones in Heptateuchum* (CCSL 33:1-377) |
| *Iob* | *Annotationum in Iob liber* (CSEL 28.2:509-628) |
| *Iul.* | *Contra Iulianum* (PL 44:641-874) |
| *Iul. op. imp.* | *Contra secundam Iuliani responsionem imperfectam opus* (CSEL 85.1:3-506; PL 45:1337-1608) |
| *Mag.* | *De magistro* (CCSL 29:157-203) |
| *Maxim.* | *Contra Maximinum Arianum* (PL 42:743-814) |
| *Mor. eccl.* | *De moribus ecclesiae catholicae* (CSEL 90:3-156) |
| *Nat. et grat.* | *De natura et gratia* (CSEL 60:233-99) |
| *Nat. et or.* | *De natura et origine animae* (CSEL 60:303-419) |
| *Nupt.* | *De nuptiis et concupiscentia ad Valerium comitem* (CSEL 42:211-319) |
| *Parm.* | *Contra epistulam Parmeniani* (CSEL 51:19-141) |
| *Pecc. merit.* | *De peccatorum meritis* (CSEL 60:3-151) |
| *Pecc. or.* | *De peccato originali* (CSEL 42:167-206) |
| *Pelag.* | *Contra duas epistulas Pelagianorum ad Bonifatium* (CSEL 60:423-570) |
| *Perf.* | *De perfectione iustitiae hominis* (CSEL 42:3-48) |
| *Perseu.* | *De dono perseuerantiae* (PL 45:993-1034) |
| *Petil.* | *Contra litteras Petiliani* (CSEL 52:3-227) |
| *Prax.* | *Adversus Praxean* (CCSL 2:1157-1205) |
| *Psal.* | *Enarrationes in Psalmos* (CCSL 38-40; CSEL 93.1A–95.5) |
| *Qu. eu.* | *Quaestionum euangelicarum libri II* (CCSL 44B:1-118) |
| *Quaest.* | *De diuersis quaestionibus* (CCSL 44A:11-249) |
| *Reg.* | *Regula*, ed. Luc Verheijen |
| *Retract.* | *Retractationum libri II* (CCSL 57:5-143) |
| *Rom. inc.* | *Epistulae ad romanos inchoata expositio* (CSEL 84:55-141) |
| *Rom. prop.* | *Expositio quarundam propositionum ex epistula apostoli ad Romanos* (CSEL 84:3-52) |
| *Serm.* | *Sermones* (PL 38-39; CCSL 41, 41Aa, 41Ba) |
| *Serm. Arian.* | *Contra sermonem arianorum* (CSEL 92:47-113) |
| *Serm. Caes. eccl.* | *Sermo ad Caesariensis ecclesiae plebem* (CSEL 53:167-78) |
| *Serm. Cail.* | *Sermones a Caillau editi* (*MA* 1:243-64) |
| *Serm. Casin.* | *Sermones in bibliotheca Casinensi* (*MA* 1:413-19) |
| *Serm. Denis* | *Sermones a Denis editi* (*MA* 1:11-164; CCSL 41:203-11, 218-29, 378-80, 418-22) |
| *Serm. Dolb.* | *Sermones a Dolbeau editi* (Dolbeau, *Vingt-six Sermons*) |

| | |
|---|---|
| *Serm. Dom.* | *De sermone Domini in monte* (CCSL 35:1-188) |
| *Serm. Etaix* | *Sermones ab Etaix editi* (*RB* 86 [1976] 41-48) |
| *Serm. Frang.* | *Sermones a Frangipane editi* (*MA* 1:212-37) |
| *Serm. frg. Verbr.* | *Sermonum fragmenta a Verbraken edita* (*RB* 84 [1974] 253, 265-66) |
| *Serm. Guelf.* | *Sermones Moriniani ex collectione Guelferbytana* (*MA* 1:450-585) |
| *Serm. Lamb.* | *Sermones a Lambot editi* (PLS 2:744-840) |
| *Serm. Liver.* | *Sermo a Liverani editus* (*MA* 1:391-95) |
| *Serm. Mai* | *Sermones a Mai editi* (*MA* 1:285-386; CCSL 41:231-34, 303-6, 321-23) |
| *Serm. Morin* | *Sermones a Morin editi* (*MA* 1:289-664; CCSL 41:341-45) |
| *Serm. Wilm.* | *Sermones a Wilmart editi* (*MA* 1:673-719) |
| *Simpl.* | *De diuersis quaestionibus ad Simplicianum* (CCSL 44:7-91) |
| *Solil.* | *Soliloquiorum libri II* (CSEL 89:3-98) |
| *Spir. et litt.* | *De spiritu et littera* (CSEL 60:155-229) |
| *Symb.* | *De symbolo ad catechumenos* (CCSL 46:185-99) |
| *Trin.* | *De Trinitate* (CCSL 50-50A) |
| *Unic. bapt.* | *De unico baptismo* (CSEL 53:3-34) |
| *Util. iei.* | *De utilitate ieiunii* |
| *Vid.* | *De bono uiduitatis* (CSEL 41:305-43) |
| *Virg.* | *De sancta uirginitate* (CSEL 41:235-302) |
| *Bru. Fer.* | *Breuiatio Ferrandi* (CCSL 149:287-306) |
| *Bru. Hipp.* | *Breuiarium Hipponense* (CCSL 149:30-53) |
| *C.Just.* | *Corpus Iuris Ciuilis*, ed. P. Krueger |
| *C.Th.* | *Codex Theodosianus*, ed. T. Mommsen |
| *Cau. Apiar.* | *Canones in causa Apiarii* (CCSL 149:101-49) |
| *Chron. Gall.* | *Chronicum Gallicum a. CCC* (*MGH* AA 9:615-32, 646-62) |
| *Col. Auel.* | *Collectio Auellana* (CSEL 35.1-2) |
| *Col. Carth.* | *Gesta Conlationis Carthageniensis* (CCSL 149A) |
| *Con. Arel.* | *Concilium Arelatense* (CCSL 148:3-25) |
| *Con. Carth.* | *Concilium Carthaginense* (CCSL 149:2-19, 69-77, 149-63, 169-72, 255-83) |
| *Con. Hipp.* | *Concilium Hipponensis* (CCSL 149:20-21, 250-53) |
| *Con. Mil.* | *Concilium Mileuitanum*, Aug. Ep. 176 (CSEL 44:663-68) |
| Constantine | Emperor Constantine I |
| *Ep. Const. Zeu.* | *Epistula Constantini Zeuzio et al.* (CSEL 26:213-15) |
| Cypr. | Cyprian of Carthage |
| *Demet.* | *Ad Demetrianum* (CCSL 3A:35-51) |
| *Dom. orat.* | *De Dominica oratione* (CCSL 3A:90-113) |
| *Don.* | *Ad Donatum* (CCSL 3A:3-13) |
| *Eleem.* | *De opere et eleemosynis* (CCSL 3A:55-72) |
| *Ep.* | *Epistulae* (CCSL 3A-B) |
| *Fort.* | *Ad Fortunatum de exhortatione martyrii* (CCSL 3:183-216) |
| *Hab. uirg.* | *De habitu uirginum* (CSEL 3.1:187-205) |
| *Laps.* | *De lapsis* (CCSL 3:221-42) |

| | |
|---|---|
| *Mort.* | *De mortalitate* (CCSL 3A:17-32) |
| *Pat.* | *De bono patientiae* (CCSL 3A:118-33) |
| *Sent.* | *Sententiae episcoporum de haereticis baptizandis* (CCSL 3E) |
| *Test.* | *Ad Quirinum testimonia aduersus Iudaeos* (CCSL 3:3-179) |
| *Unit. eccl.* | *De catholicae ecclesiae unitate* (CCSL 3:249-68) |
| *Zel. et liu.* | *De zelo et liuore* (CCSL 3A:75-86) |
| Cyr. Jer. | Cyril of Jerusalem |
| *Cat. myst.* | *Mystical Catechesis* (PG 33:1065-1128; SC 126) |
| *Didache* | *Didache,* Loeb 24 |
| *Didasc. apol.* | *Didascalia apostolorum,* ed. F. X. von Funk, *Didascalia et Constitutiones Apostolorum* |
| Eus. Caes. | Eusebius of Caesarea |
| *Hist. eccl.* | *Church History* (GCS 9.1-3; SC 31, 41, 55) |
| Evag. Sch. | Evagrius Scholasticus |
| *Hist. eccl.* | *Church History* (PG 86.2:2115-2886) |
| Fac. | Facundus |
| *Def.* | *Pro defensione trium capitulorum* (CCSL 90A:1-398) |
| Ferrand. | Ferrandus |
| *Vita Fulg.* | *Vita Fulgentii* (AnBoll [1982]: 277-89; PL 55:117-50) |
| Fulg.-R. | Fulgentius of Ruspe |
| *Psal. Ab.* | *Psalmus abecedarius* (CCSL 91A:877-85) |
| Greg. Mag. | Gregory the Great |
| *Ep.* | *Epistulae* (CCSL 140-140A) |
| Hieron. | Jerome |
| *Iou.* | *Aduersus Iouinianum* (PL 23:221-338) |
| *Vir. ill.* | *De uiribus illustribus* (PL 23:603-720) |
| Hipp. | Hippolytus of Rome |
| *Dan.* | *On Daniel* (GCS 1:1-340; SC 14) |
| *Hist. Aug.* | *Scriptores historiae augustae* (Loeb 139-40, 263) |
| Idat. | Idatius |
| *Chron.* | *Continuatio chronicorum hieronynianorum* (PL 51:873-90; SC 218, 219) |
| In. Chry. | John Chrysostom |
| *Cat.* | *Catechetical Homilies* (PG 49:223-40) |
| Innoc. | Innocentius I |
| *Ep.* | *Epistulae* (PL 20:463-608) |
| Iord. | Jordanes |
| *Get.* | *De origine actibusque Getarum* (PL 69:1251-96) |
| Isid. | Isidore of Seville |
| *Hist.* | *Historia de regibus Gothorum Wandalorum et Sueuorum* (*MGH* AA 11:241-303) |
| Julian | |
| *Ep.* | *Epistulae,* ed. J. Bidez et al. |
| *Kal. Carth.* | *Kalendarium Carthaginense* (PL 13:1219-30) |

| | |
|---|---|
| Lact. | Lactantius |
| *Inst.* | *Diuinae Institutiones* (CSEL 19:1-672) |
| *Mort.* | *De mortibus persecutorum* (CSEL 27.2:171-238) |
| *Later. Wand.* | *Laterculus regum Wandalorum et Alanorum* (*MGH* AA 13:458-60) |
| *Lib. Gen.* | *Liber Genealogicus* (*MGH* AA 9:154-96) |
| *Lib. Pont.* | *Liber Pontificalis* (*MGH* G. Pont. 1.1) |
| Liban. | Libanius |
| *Ep.* | *Letters,* ed. Richardus Foerster, 10-11 |
| *Or.* | *Orations,* ed. Richardus Foerster |
| Marcellinus | Marcellinus Comes |
| *Chron.* | *Chronicon* (*MGH* AA 11:60-108) |
| *Mart. Hieron.* | *Martyrologium Hieronymianum, Acta Sanctorum,* Nou. 2.2 (PL 30:435-87) |
| Minuc. | Minucius Felix |
| *Oct.* | *Octauius* (CSEL 2:3-56) |
| *Mirc. Steph.* | *Miracula sancti Stephani* (PL 41:833-54) |
| *Not. Africae* | *Notitia prouinciarum et ciuitatum Africae* (CSEL 7:117-34) |
| *Nou. Afr. Ecc.* | *Nouella de Africana Ecclesia* (Krueger, 1989) |
| *Nou. Val.* | *Nouellae Valentinianae* (Mommsen, 1990) |
| Optat. | Optatus of Milevis |
| *Parm.* | *Contra Parmenianum Donatistam* (CSEL 26:3-182) |
| *Orac. Sibyl.* | *Oracula Sibyllina,* ed. Aloisius Rzach (Vindobonae: F. Tempsky, 1891) |
| *Pas. Crisp.* | *Passio Crispinae, Studi e Testi* (1902):32-35 |
| *Pas. Don.* | *Sermo de passione sancti Donati episcopi Abiocalensis* (PL 8:752-58) |
| *Pas. Fab.* | *Passio S. Fabii Vexilliferi* (AnBoll 9 [1890]: 123-34) |
| *Pas. Fel.* | *Passio Felicis Episcopi* (AnBoll 39 [1921]: 214-76) |
| *Pas. Isa. Max.* | *Passio martyrum Isaac et Maximiani* (PL 8:767-74, 778-84) |
| *Pas. Mar. Iac.* | *Passio sanctorum Mariani et Iacobi* (Musurillo, 194-213) |
| *Pas. Marc.* | *Passio benedicti martyris Marculi* (PL 8:760-66) |
| *Pas. Max.* | *Passio ss. Maximae, Donatillae et Secundae* (AnBoll 9 [1890]:110-16) |
| *Pas. Mont. Luc.* | *Passio sanctorum Montiani et Lucii* (Musurillo, 214-39) |
| *Pas. Perp.* | *Passio Perpetuae* (Musurillo, 106-31) |
| *Pas. Pion.* | *Passio Pionis* (Musurillo, 136-67) |
| *Pas. sept. mon.* | *Passio septem monachorum* (CSEL 7:108-14) |
| *Pas. Typ.* | *Passio S. Typasii Veterani* (AnBoll 9 [1890]: 116-23) |
| Pont. | Pontius |
| *Vita Cypr* | *Vita Caecilii Cypriani* (CSEL 3.3:xc-cx) |
| Possid. | Possidius of Calama |
| *Vita Aug.* | *Vita sancti Augustini* (PL 32:33-578) |
| Proc. Caes. | Procopius of Caesarea |
| *Aed.* | *De Aedificis,* ed. J. Haury (Teubner), vol. 4 |
| *Anec.* | *Historia arcana,* ed. J. Haury (Teubner), vol. 3 |
| *Hist. bel.* | *Historia bellarum,* J. Haury (Teubner), vols. 1-2 |

| | |
|---|---|
| Prosp. | Prosper of Aquitaine |
| *Chron.* | *Epitoma Chronicon* (*MGH* AA 9:385-485) |
| Quodu. | Quodvultdeus of Carthage |
| *Prom.* | *Liber promissionum et praedictorum Dei* (CCSL 60:1-223) |
| *Symb.* | *De Symbolo* (CCSL 60:305-63) |
| *Temp.* | *De tempore barbarico* (CCSL 60:421-86) |
| *Rebapt.* | *De rebaptismo* (CSEL 3.3:69-92) |
| *Reg. Carth.* | *Registri ecclesiae Carthaginensis excerpta* (CCSL 149:182-228) |
| Salu. | Salvianus |
| *Gub.* | *De gubernatione dei* (CSEL 8:1-200) |
| *Serm. Arian.* | *Contra sermonem Arianorum* (CSEL 92:47-113) |
| Sid. | Apollinaris Sidonius |
| *Carm.* | *Carmina* (*MGH* AA 8:173-264) |
| *Sirm.* | *Sirmondian Constitutions* (Mommsen, 1990) |
| Soc. | Socrates |
| *Hist. eccl.* | *Church History* (PG 67:29-872) |
| Tert. | Tertullian |
| *An.* | *De anima* (CCSL 2:781-869) |
| *Apol.* | *Apologeticus* (CCSL 1:85-171) |
| *Bapt.* | *De baptismo* (CCSL 1:277-95) |
| *Carn. Chr.* | *De carne Christi* (CCSL 2:873-917) |
| *Cast.* | *De exhortatione castitatis* (CCSL 2:1015-35) |
| *Cor.* | *De corona militis* (CCSL 2:1039-65) |
| *Cult. fem.* | *De cultu feminarum* (CCSL 1:343-70) |
| *Exst.* | *De exstasi* (CCSL 2:1334-36) |
| *Fug.* | *De fuga in persecutione* (CCSL 2:1135-55) |
| *Idol.* | *De idolotria* (CCSL 2:1101-124) |
| *Ieiun.* | *De ieiunio aduersus Psychicos* (CCSL 2:1257-77) |
| *Marc.* | *Aduersus Marcionem* (CCSL 1:441-726) |
| *Mart.* | *Ad martyras* (CCSL 1:3-8) |
| *Mon.* | *De monogamia* (CCSL 2:1229-53) |
| *Nat.* | *Ad nationes* (CCSL 1:11-75) |
| *Or.* | *De oratione* (CCSL 1:257-74) |
| *Paen.* | *De paenitentia* (CCSL 1:321-40) |
| *Pat.* | *De patientia* (CCSL 1:299-317) |
| *Praescr.* | *De praescriptione haereticorum* (CCSL 1:187-224) |
| *Prax.* | *Adversus Praxeam* |
| *Pud.* | *De pudicitia* (CCSL 2:1281-1330) |
| *Res.* | *De resurrectione mortuorum* (CCSL 1:921-1012) |
| *Scap.* | *Ad Scapulam* (CCSL 2:1127-32) |
| *Scorp.* | *Scorpiace* (CCSL 2:1069-97) |
| *Spec.* | *De spectaculis* (CCSL 1:227-53) |
| *Test.* | *De testimonio animae* (CCSL 1:175-83) |

| | |
|---|---|
| *Ux.* | *Ad uxorem* (CCSL 1:373-94) |
| *Val.* | *Aduersus Valentinianos* (CCSL 2:753-78) |
| *Virg.* | *De uirginibus uelandis* (CCSL 2:1209-26) |
| Theophanes | |
| Chron. | *Chronographia* (PG 108:55-1009) |
| Theo. Mp. | Theodore of Mopsuestia |
| *Lib. bapt.* | *Baptismal Homilies,* A. Mingana, Woodbrooke Studies 6; Studi e Testi 145 (1949) |
| *Trad. apos.* | *Traditio apostolica* (SC 11bis) |
| Tyc. | Tyconius Afer |
| *Reg.* | *Liber regularum,* Texts and Studies, 3.1, 1894 (reprint, 2004) |
| Vict.-Ton. | Victor of Tunnuna |
| Chron. | *Chronicle* (CCSL 173A) |
| Vict.-Vit. | Victor of Vita |
| *Hist. pers.* | *Historia Persecutionis Africae Prouinciae* (CSEL 7:3-107) |
| Zosimus | Zosimus of Rome |
| *Ep. Tract.* | *Tractate* (CSEL 57:159) |

# Summary of Events

| | |
|---|---|
| July 17, 180 | Carthage: Scillitan Martyrs are executed. |
| 197–c. 220 | Tertullian writes in Carthage, starting with *Apologeticum*. |
| c. 202–204 | Carthage: Perpetua and Felicitas are martyred. |
| c. 207 | Tertullian supports the New Prophecy. |
| 211-213 | Sporadic persecution continues in Carthage; Tertullian writes *To Scapula*. |
| c. 220–240 | The Council at Carthage (70 bishops): Bishop Agrippinus upholds rebaptism of heretics. |
| c. 245 | The Council at Carthage (90 bishops): Privatus of Lambaesis is removed from office. |
| 248 | The millennium of Rome is celebrated. |
| 248/249 | Donatus of Carthage dies; Cyprian is elected bishop. |
| December 250–January 251 | The Decian Edict is issued, requiring sacrifice. Bishop Fabian of Rome dies as a martyr. Cyprian goes into voluntary exile. |
| March 251 | Cornelius is chosen Bishop of Rome; Novatian is chosen in opposition. |
| After Easter (March 23), 251 | Cyprian returns to Carthage. The Council of Carthage requires penance of sacrificers; the certified are reconciled. |
| June 251 | Decius dies; Gallus becomes emperor. |
| After Easter (April 11), 252 | Council at Carthage (66 bishops): The council reaffirms penance for sacrificers and affirms infant baptism. |
| After Easter (April 3), 253 | Council at Carthage (42 bishops): In anticipation of persecution, all penitent sacrificers are readmitted to communion. |
| Spring-Summer 253 | Cornelius of Rome dies in exile; Lucius is elected. |

| | |
|---|---|
| 253 | Emperor Gallus dies; Valerian and Gallienus secure control. |
| March 254 | Lucius of Rome dies; Stephen is elected bishop. |
| After Easter (April 8), 255 | Council at Carthage: The council focuses on the rebaptism controversy in Africa. |
| After Easter (March 10), 256 | Council at Carthage: The council revisits the rebaptism controversy, decides schismatic clergy may not be received into communion in office, and informs Stephen of Rome. |
| September 256 | Council of Carthage: 87 bishops affirm the rebaptism of heretics and schismatics against Stephen. |
| 257 | The Valerian persecution begins; clergy and the corporate life of the church are targeted. Stephen dies; Sixtus II is elected; Cyprian is exiled. |
| September 14, 258 | Cyprian returns to Carthage; he is tried and executed. |
| Summer 260 | Valerian is captured in Persia, and persecution ends. |
| 284 | Diocletian becomes emperor. |
| 293-303 | Diocletian establishes the Tetrarchy (Diocletian, Maximian, Galerius, and Constantius Chlorus), reforms the army, and restructures provinces. |
| 303-304 | The Diocletian persecution is active in Africa. |
| c. 305 | The Episcopal synod is held at Cirta. |
| 305 | Galerius and Constantius ascend; Severus II and Maximinus are added. |
| 306 | Constantine gains Britain and Gaul; Maxentius rules Italy and Africa. |
| 311 | Galerius rescinds edicts on the persecution of Christians; Caecilian is elected Bishop of Carthage. |
| 312 | Constantine defeats Maxentius and rules the Western Empire. He restores confiscated property to churches. The Roman Synod supports Caecilian over Donatus. |
| 313 | Emperors Licinius and Constantine issue an edict of religious toleration. |
| 314 | The Donatists appeal to Constantine; the Council of Arles validates Caecilian. |
| 316 | Constantine unquestionably supports the Caecilianists. |
| 317-321 | Imperial attempts are made to force the unity of the African church. |
| 321 | Constantine goes to war with Licinius and tolerates the Donatist party in Africa. |
| 324 | Constantine defeats Licinius and becomes sole emperor. |
| c. 336 | Caecilian dies; Rufus becomes Bishop of Carthage. A Donatist council accepts converts without rebaptism. |
| c. 342 | Gratus becomes Bishop of Carthage. |
| c. 345–348 | The Council at Carthage is held under Gratus. |

| | |
|---|---|
| 347-348 | Constans sends Macarius and Paul to appease the Donatists, then exiles Donatist bishops. Donatus dies in exile. |
| 354 | Augustine is born at Thagaste. |
| 359 | Restitutus becomes Bishop of Carthage. |
| 362 | Julian recalls exiled Donatist bishops. Parmenian becomes the Donatist bishop of Carthage. |
| 364 | The Rogatist schism forms among the Donatists. |
| 387 | Augustine is baptized by Ambrose in Milan. |
| 390 | The Council at Carthage (under Genethlius) begins reform of Catholic clergy. |
| c. 391 | Primian becomes the Donatist Bishop of Carthage. |
| June 393 | During the Donatist Council at Cebarsussi, Deacon Maximian revolts against Primian of Carthage. |
| October 8, 393 | During the Catholic Council at Hippo, Augustine preaches as presbyter to bishops. |
| April 394 | The Donatist Council at Bagai suppresses the Maximianist schism. |
| 394-396 | Theodosius I outlaws traditional Roman religion and gradually withdraws funding. |
| 395 | Augustine is elected Bishop of Hippo. |
| 395-398 | The revolt of Gildo, Count of Africa, is supported by Donatist Bishop Optatus of Thamugadi. |
| August 28, 397 | Council at Carthage: The *Hippo Breviary* (reform of clergy) is formally ratified. |
| 399 | Imperial officials close traditional Roman shrines in Africa. |
| September 13, 401 | Council at Carthage: A plan is developed to accept Donatist bishops who join Catholic unity. |
| August 8, 402 | The Council at Milevis continues the reform of Catholic clergy. |
| August 25, 403 | Council at Carthage: Catholic bishops call for public debates with Donatists. |
| June 16, 404 | Council at Carthage: Catholic bishops petition for protection against Donatist violence. |
| February 15, 405 | Emperor Honorius decrees the unification of the African church. |
| June 13, 407 | Council at Carthage: The council makes provision for the assimilation of Donatist congregations and clergy. |
| August 22, 408 | Stilicho, guardian of Honorius, is overthrown and executed. Donatists and traditional polytheists expect the withdrawal of suppressive legislation. |

| | |
|---|---|
| October 13, 408 | Council at Carthage: Bishops send a delegation to Honorius to secure the enforcement of laws against the Donatists. |
| January 409 | Honorius reaffirms legislation against the Donatists. |
| August 410 | Alaric sacks Rome. The wealthy seek refuge in Africa. |
| August 410 | Pelagius arrives in Africa after the sack of Rome. |
| Winter 410 | Caelestius — disciple of Pelagius — seeks ordination in Carthage and is condemned for heresy. |
| May 18–June 8, 411 | In an imperially sponsored meeting between Catholics and Donatists in Carthage, Flavius Marcellinus rules against the Donatists. |
| December 20, 415 | Synod at Diospolis: Pelagius is examined and declared orthodox. |
| September-October 416 | Provincial Synods at Milevis and Carthage condemn Pelagius and appeal for support of Innocent of Rome. |
| May 1, 418 | Council at Carthage: Pelagius is condemned and support of the emperor is sought. |
| 429 | The Vandals invade Africa. Boniface, Count of Africa, retreats to Hippo Regius. |
| August 28, 430 | Augustine dies during the Vandal siege of Hippo. |
| 435 | The treaty with Geiseric cedes Numidia to the Vandals, with Hippo Regius as the capital. |
| 439 | Geiseric attacks Carthage; he persecutes Nicene Christians and exiles bishops. |
| 441 | Theodosius II and Valentinian III attempt but fail to reverse the power of the Vandals. |
| 442 | Valentinian III recognizes the Vandal state as an independent kingdom; it includes Tripolitana, Byzacena, Proconsularis, and eastern Numidia. Western Numidia and Mauretania revert to Rome. |
| 454 | Deogratias is elected Catholic Bishop of Carthage after a fourteen-year hiatus. |
| 455 | Valentinian III is assassinated; Geiseric rescues his family and sacks Rome. |
| 457 | Geiseric forbids future ordination of Nicene bishops around Carthage after the death of Deogratias. |
| 468 | Emperor Leo I fails to recapture Africa. |
| 475 | Emperor Zeno negotiates a peace settlement with the Vandals, guaranteeing the safety of Byzantium. |
| 481 | Huneric allows Eugenius to become Nicene Bishop of Carthage in exchange for toleration for Arians throughout the Empire. |
| 484 | Huneric calls Nicene bishops to a conference with the Arians; they are compelled to cede property to the Arians. |

| | |
|---|---|
| 487 | Felix I, Bishop of Rome, gains readmission of Nicene bishops to Africa from Gunthamund. |
| 504 | Thrasamund prohibits episcopal elections of Nicene bishops. |
| 525 | Hilderic allies with Byzantines and recalls Nicene bishops. Bonifatius is elected Nicene Bishop of Carthage and holds a council. |
| 530 | Gelimer imprisons Hilderic. Justinian fails to restore Hilderic. |
| 533 | Byzantines invade Africa; Belisarius retakes Carthage on September 14th, the feast of Cyprian. |
| 535 | Justinian restores the rights of the Nicene church, and persecutes Donatists, Jews, heretics, and pagans. |
| | Council at Carthage: The Nicene bishops refuse to recognize Arian orders. |
| 543-544 | Justinian orders Nicene bishops to accept condemnation of the *Three Chapters.* |
| 543-546 | Byzantine rule provokes Mauri uprisings. John Troglita, installed as new magister militum, restores Byzantine control to Africa. |
| 550 | Council at Carthage: There is opposition to the *Three Chapters* and Roman collaborators. African bishops are summoned to Constantinople. |
| 551 | Facundus of Herminae writes *The Defense of the Three Chapters,* asserting episcopal independence. |
| 630 | Maximus the Confessor flees to a Carthaginian monastery because of the Persian advance. |
| 645 | In the debate between Maximus and Phyrrus, defender of monothelite doctrine, Phyrrus recants. |
| 646 | Episcopal synods condemn the monothelite doctrine in each African province. |
| 648 | Gregory I, Exarch of Africa, dies in battle against Arabs at Sufetula. |
| 649 | Pope Martin I and Maximus seek condemnation of monothelite doctrine at the Lateran Synod in Rome. |
| 655 | Maximus the Confessor is arrested and tried in Constantinople. |
| 698 | Carthage falls to Arab advance. |

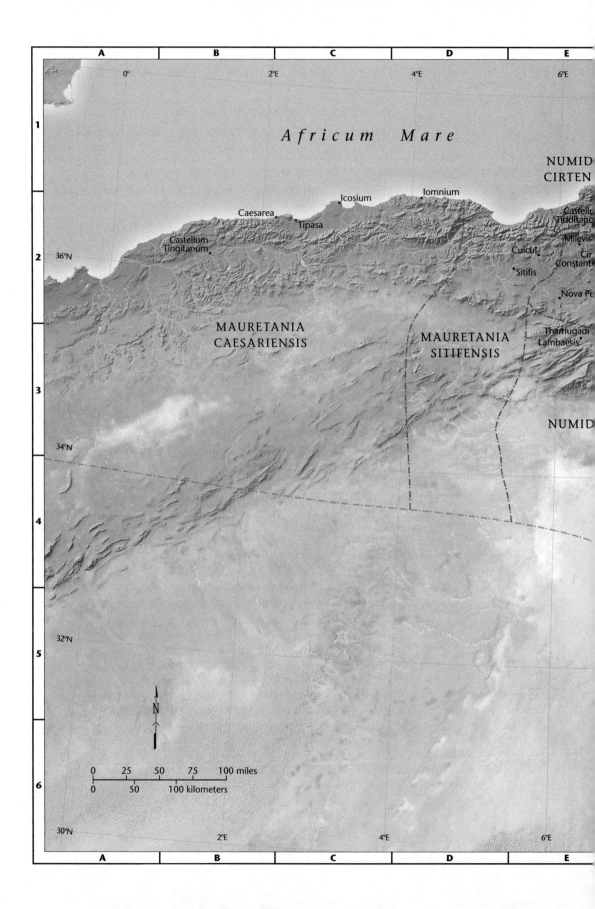

Africum Mare

NUMID
CIRTEN

MAURETANIA
CAESARIENSIS

MAURETANIA
SITIFENSIS

NUMID

Castellum
Tingitanum

Caesarea

Tipasa

Icosium

Iomnium

Castell.
Tidditano

Milevis

Cuicul

Cir
Constant

Sitifis

Nova Pe

Thamugadi
Lambaesis

36°N

34°N

32°N

30°N

N

0    25    50    75    100 miles
0         50        100 kilometers

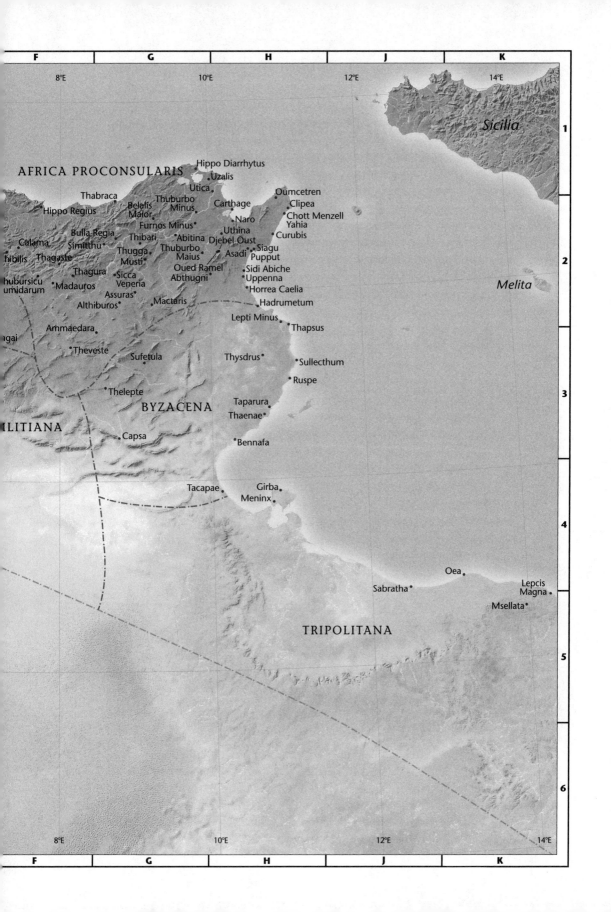

F      G      H      J      K

8°E      10°E      12°E      14°E

*Sicilia*

1

AFRICA PROCONSULARIS

Hippo Diarrhytus
Uzalis
Utica
Thabraca
Belalis   Thuburbo    Carthage    Oumcetren
Hippo Regius   Maior   Minus     Clipea
     Furnos Minus    Naro    Chott Menzell
Bulla Regia       Uthina     Yahia
Calama   Simitthu   Thibari   Abitina   Djebel Oust   Curubis
hibilis   Thagaste    Thugga   Thuburbo   Asadi   Siagu
      Musti   Maius      Pupput
  Thagura      Oued Ramel   Sidi Abiche
hubursicu    Sicca   Abthugni   Uppenna
umidarum   Madauros   Veneria      Horrea Caelia
     Assuras
   Althiburos   Mactaris     Hadrumetum

2

agai   Ammaedara      Lepti Minus
   Theveste       Thapsus
    Sufetula    Thysdrus   Sullecthum
ILITIANA        Ruspe
  Thelepte   BYZACENA
      Taparura
      Thaenae
  Capsa     Bennafa

*Melita*

3

Tacapae    Girba
     Meninx

4

      Oea
   Sabratha     Lepcis
      Magna
      Msellata

TRIPOLITANA

5

6

8°E      10°E      12°E      14°E

F      G      H      J      K

# Key to Cities and Provinces in the Map

| | | | | | |
|---|---|---|---|---|---|
| Abitina | G2 | Hippo Regius | F2 | Simitthu | G2 |
| Abthugni | G2 | Horrea Caelia | H2 | Sitifis | E2 |
| Africa Proconsularis | F2-H2 | Icosium | C2 | Sufetula | G4 |
| Ammaedara | G3 | Iomnium | D2 | Sullecthum | H3 |
| Asadi | H2 | Lambaesis | E3 | Tacapae | H4 |
| Assuras | G3 | Lepti Minus | H2 | Taparura | H3 |
| Bagai | F3 | Lepcis Magna | K5 | Thabraca | G2 |
| Belalis Maior | G2 | Mactaris | G3 | Thaenae | H3 |
| Bennafa | H3 | Madauros | F2 | Thagaste | F2 |
| Bulla Regia | G2 | Mauretania Caesariensis | A2-D4 | Thagura | F2 |
| Byzacena | G2-H4 | Mauretania Sitifensis | D2-D4 | Thamugadi | E3 |
| Caesarea | C2 | Meninx | H4 | Thapsus | H2 |
| Calama | F2 | Milevis | E2 | Thelepte | G3 |
| Capsa | G3 | Musti | G2 | Theveste | F3 |
| Carthage | H2 | Naro | H2 | Thibari | G2 |
| Castellum Tidditanorum | E2 | Nova Petra | E2 | Thibilis | F2 |
| Castellum Tingitanum | B2 | Numidia Cirtensis | E2-F3 | Thuburbo Maius | G2 |
| Chott Menzell Yahia | H2 | Numidia Militiana | E2-G5 | Thuburbo Minus | G2 |
| Cirta/Constantina | E2 | Oea | K4 | Thubursicu Numidarum | F2 |
| Clipea | H2 | Oued Ramel | H2 | Thugga | G2 |
| Cuicul | E2 | Oumcetren | H2 | Thysdrus | H3 |
| Curubis | H2 | Pupput | H2 | Tipasa | C2 |
| Djebel Oust | H2 | Ruspe | H3 | Tripolitana | G4-K6 |
| Furnos Minus | G2 | Sabratha | I4 | Uppenna | H2 |
| Girba | H4 | Siagu | H2 | Uthina | H2 |
| Hadrumetum | H2 | Sicca Veneria | G2 | Utica | H1 |
| Hippo Diarrhytus | G1 | Sidi Abiche | H2 | Uzalis | G1 |

# Introduction

This study of the Christian church in Roman Africa intends to track interactions between its changing social context, its practices of life and worship, and its theology. Religious devotion and doctrine are here judged to be interactive; thus, a change in Christian thinking both responded to and resulted in new forms of Christian living. The practice and thought of Christian communities engaged and sometimes even determined the social culture in which they operated. To achieve a correlation of context, practice, and thought, this study attempts to access and coordinate the literary and material remains of the Christian church in Africa. In some instances, only one type of evidence has survived or been discovered; both types are used whenever they are available.

Christianity in Roman Africa is particularly well-suited to the objective and methods of this project. The principal theological production of the Christian culture of this region was an understanding of the church and its rituals, along with an elaborate set of rules for performing the rituals and fulfilling the duties of that church. Thinking about the other major themes of Christian belief — God and Christ, sin and grace, life and afterlife — was either defined or strongly influenced by theoretical commitments related to the nature and structures of the community. The practices that defined this community — incorporation and exclusion of members, differentiation of roles by marriage, consecration and ordination, care for the dying, and commemoration of the dead — were themselves embedded within and reacting to the changing political and cultural context of that part of the Roman Empire.

## PRACTICE AND THEOLOGY

Three of the most influential theologians of the early Christian period — all of them decisive for Latin Christianity — were Africans. Tertullian was the first to write in Latin and left an extensive body of work that covered nearly the entire creed and many practices, both ritual and ascetic. Cyprian's justifications of the sacramental practice of his church and the role of its officers set the terms of debate for the following millennium. Some of his writings were appreciated in the Greek church as well. A century later, Augustine drew upon both of these predecessors to develop a theology characteristic of Western Christianity.

Not only did Christians first begin to speak Latin in Africa, but there the translation of the scriptures into Latin began. On July 17, 180, a Christian from Scilli, Speratus by name, appearing before the Proconsul Saturninus, responded to a demand to identify what was in his carrying case; he replied, "Books and letters of a just man named Paul."[1] By the end of the century, Tertullian was using a complete Latin bible.

### A Theological School

These major theologians are the more prominent members of a broader group of thinkers whose work they drew upon or influenced. Their work bears the twin characteristics of African Christianity: a concern with the holiness of the church and its performing the sanctifying work of Christ. Minucius Felix and the anonymous author of *The Treatise on Rebaptism* worked in the third century. In the late fourth century, Optatus of Milevis and Parmenian of Carthage responded to the writings of the great exegete Tyconius. Petilian of Constantina and his colleague Cresconius challenged Augustine, whose work on baptism Quodvultdeus of Carthage continued. Later in the fifth century, the chronicler Victor of Vita and the theologian Fulgentius of Ruspe upheld the orthodox tradition under the Vandal occupation. Even in the Byzantine period, the Africans influenced the development of Christology by resistance to Justinian's *Three Chapters* proposal, an opposition anchored by Facundus of Hermiane, Liberatus of Carthage, and Fulgentius's disciple Ferrandus. In their last defense of Chalcedon, articulated by the Greek exile Maximus, the characteristic African insistence on the full humanity of the Savior, which had first been articulated by Tertullian and elaborated by Augustine, can still be discerned.

Like the disciples of Origen, though in a radically different way, these African theologians formed a school. Whereas those Greeks focused their concern with salvation on the nature of the Godhead and its manifestation in Christ, these Latins worried about the adequacy of human organizations and ministers

---

1. *Act. Scil.*

to mediate the divine life. The Greeks studied the interaction of divine and human in the Savior; the Latins attempted to discern the standards which would guarantee divine operation in the rituals of the church. Theologians read, developed, and even subverted their predecessors, usually without calling attention to the acceptances and rejections. For centuries, they dealt with the same practices of Christian living, especially the efficacy of the rituals, the role of ministers, and the regulation of marriage. Jerome's citation of the report of an eyewitness to Cyprian's daily consultation of the writings of Tertullian reflects the judgment of his contemporaries who had read both authors.[2] Some of Cyprian's treatises are reworkings of his master's writings; for example, his *On the Lord's Prayer* is obviously dependent on Tertullian's *On Prayer*. Cyprian's innovative explanations of the unity of the church and the role of the bishop in guaranteeing the efficacy of its rituals themselves provoked questions and rebuttals from his contemporaries, which are found in his own correspondence as well as in the anonymous *Treatise on Rebaptism*. A century and a half later, Augustine's *On Baptism* framed the Donatist controversy as a conflict between the roles of purity and unity in Cyprian's theology. A major part of his work was rescuing Cyprian for the Catholic cause by demonstrating that, in practice, Cyprian had preferred unity. In this and other treatises on the church, Augustine developed Tertullian's identification of the church as the whole body of the faithful to balance (or even displace) Cyprian's insistence on the primary role of the bishop. Yet he never explicitly cited his predecessors against one another. Augustine was no less influenced by Tyconius, whose exegetical principles he employed to demonstrate the unity of Christ and the church, and then recommended to all preachers in his *On Christian Doctrine.*

African theologians not only dealt with the influence of their predecessors but engaged their contemporaries. Cyprian's actions and explanation were challenged in both Rome and Africa. A century later, Parmenian of Carthage condemned the work of Tyconius. Optatus of Milevis responded to that letter of rebuke. Augustine challenged Petilian of Constantina by reviewing a letter he had written to his own clergy. When Petilian responded, Augustine launched yet another attack. Petilian promised a longer riposte which either was not written or did not survive.

African Christianity developed a distinct and distinguished school of theology. For more than three centuries, its teachers sustained an investigation and argument over a closely related set of problems. As their communities grew from a persecuted minority to a dominant but conflicted majority, each generation of theologians developed the theories of its predecessors to justify adaptations in the practice of the Christian life.

---

2. Hieron. *Vir. ill.* 53.

African theology focused on the role of the church as the medium of Christ's salvific work and therefore on the church's holiness and the efficacy of its rituals. Concern over the qualifications of the ministers for discharging their offices drove conflicts over the practices of congregations. The earliest writings of Tertullian witness to debates over avoiding the pollution of idolatry and maintaining fidelity to Christ. The primary concern of these arguments was the necessity of excluding certain kinds of sinners from the membership, the eucharistic communion, or the leadership of the local and universal church. This debate can be traced from the end of the second through the middle of the fifth century. In the fourth century, disagreement over the proper means of maintaining purity divided the African church into two factions named for their leaders, Caecilian and Donatus. The conflict between these two parties — now known as the Donatist controversy — was no less fundamental and persistent for Africa than the Arian and consequent Nestorian controversies were for Egypt and Syria.

The African understanding of the church was influential or even decisive for the development of other doctrines. This is most evident in the theology of Augustine. His techniques of scriptural interpretation and his peculiar incorporation of the faithful into the Whole Christ depended upon his elaboration of the Pauline identification of the church as the body of Christ. His firm belief in Christ as the only Savior and the church as the sole mediator of that salvation was the foundation of his doctrines of original sin and inherited guilt, of the necessity and the efficacy of divine grace, and thus of the limitations of human freedom. His teaching on the gratuitous predestination of the elect startled most contemporary — and subsequent — Christians, but it met little opposition among his fellow Africans, who understood its ecclesiological basis.[3]

Thus the preoccupation with the nature and role of the church as the continuing presence of Christ on earth resulted in the development of a distinctive African theology that regularly puzzled and even alarmed Christians in Italy and Gaul. Yet it became the dominant theology of Western Christianity.

## Correlation with Practice

The doctrinal development carried forward by the African theologians was driven by dissent over the practices through which Christian communities

---

3. See J. Patout Burns, "The Atmosphere of Election: Augustinianism as Common Sense," *Journal of Early Christian Studies* 2 (1994): 325-39. Robin Jensen's suggestion that the methods used in this essay be combined with her own use of material evidence for studying practice led to the investigation reported in this book.

worked out their identities and their fidelity to Christ. The dialogue between theory and practice was constant in the African church.

The difficulty of responding to post-baptismal sin is already evident in the New Testament, where the stances reflected in 1 Corinthians 5 and Hebrews 6 diverge. An interpretation of Acts 15 identifying adultery, idolatry, and murder as the only unforgivable sins was assumed in the late second century but was contested early in the third by the innovations of the Bishop of Carthage and the pronouncements of the New Prophecy. The debate over reconciling adulterers was no sooner settled than the Decian persecution forced a consideration of idolaters. Cyprian and his colleagues could find in the scripture no decisive answer to the problems they faced. Cyprian's creative explanation of the role of Peter and the responsibility of the bishops for guaranteeing the holiness of the church allowed readmitting repentant sinners among the laity but entailed a practice of rejecting baptism performed outside the unity of the church. These decisions divided African bishops among themselves and from the overseas churches. In the aftermath of the Diocletian persecution, Cyprian's system of maintaining church purity provoked a full schism in the African church: his standards of episcopal fidelity and ecclesial purity simply could not be applied. The intervention of the overseas bishops only worsened the conflict because they insisted that the Africans recognize baptism — and ordination — performed by openly sinful ministers, even outside the unity of the church. African Christians on both sides of the divide struggled to develop understandings of the church's holiness and enforceable regulations that could guarantee its role as the effective mediator of salvation. Augustine's solution was theoretically sound, but its lowering of the religious status of the clergy was so alien to the assumptions of Donatists and even overseas Catholics that it did not succeed in uniting the African church.[4] The problem endured, it seems, until the church itself was absorbed by Islam.

## ARCHEOLOGICAL AND LITERARY EVIDENCE

The correlation of archeological and literary evidence is hardly a new method of investigation. W. H. C. Frend's influential book *The Donatist Church*[5] used archeological remains to support hypotheses of ethnic and economic differences in North Africa that could help explain the division between the parties in the

---

4. To the invitation to bring their congregations into Catholic unity, an unnamed bishop — probably Gaudentius of Thamugadi — responded: "If I have sinned against the Holy Spirit by schism and rebaptizing, how could you let me serve as a bishop in your church?" (Aug. *Ep.* 185.11.48). The bishops of Rome and Milan refused to support the practices based upon it (*Reg. Carth.* 68).

5. W. H. C. Frend, *The Donatist Church: A Movement of Protest in Roman North Africa* (Oxford: Clarendon Press, 2000).

Donatist schism. The objective of this study is to correlate these two forms of evidence in the investigation of the forms of worship and other practices of Christianity. Reconstruction of rituals based on literary evidence, such as those of Wunibald Roetzer and Frederik van der Meer[6] using Augustine's works, are here brought into dialogue with archeological reports on the buildings in which the Christian rituals were performed, such as that of Erwin Marec for the Christian quarter in Hippo Regius.[7] The dialogue between these different kinds of data can yield a richer understanding of the rituals themselves and their impact on the faithful. In some instances, such as Augustine's distinction between the bishop's role as *episcopus* and *sacerdos,* an understanding of the differentiation of space within the basilica in which he was speaking and offering can reveal the meaning and power of his argument. The presence of multiple churches and baptisteries in a small city suggests the intense, local competition between the Caecilianists and the Donatists. The large, extra-mural pilgrimage churches built in the Byzantine era indicate the continued vitality of the cult of the martyrs and the desire of the faithful to be buried (and perhaps baptized) near the relics, and under the protection, of a saint.

## Second and Third Centuries

Few archeological remains have survived to provide evidence of Christian activity in the second and third centuries; however, literary evidence indicates that Christians did own buildings and already controlled cemeteries or burial areas prior to the Constantinian emancipation. The absence of an archeological record can be accounted for in various ways: the destruction of church buildings during the Diocletian persecution, the extensive renovation and rebuilding projects sponsored by Constantine during the fourth century, and the expansion of the Christian church itself. For the second and third centuries, therefore, the literary evidence must suffice. Fortunately, the extensive treatises of Tertullian and the eighty letters associated with Cyprian's episcopate yield as much information on Christian life as can be gathered in any other region of the Roman world in this period.

6. Wunibald Roetzer, *Die Heiligen Augustinus Schriften als liturgie-geschichtliche Quelle: eine liturgie-geschichtliche Studie* (Munich: M. Hueber, 1930), and Frederik van der Meer, *Augustine the Bishop: The Life and Work of a Father of the Church,* trans. Brian Battershaw and G. R. Lamb (London: Sheed & Ward, 1962).

7. Erwan Marec, *Monuments chrétiens d'Hippone, ville épiscopale de saint Augustin* (Paris: Arts et métiers graphiques, 1958).

For the fourth and fifth centuries, archeological evidence is available, though not in the same abundance as in the Byzantine era, when renovation and new construction once again reshaped or even displaced earlier structures. Very few full structures have been recovered, but foundations, columns, portions of walls, and other parts that indicate the shape and size of many Christian basilicas survive. Shrines and pilgrimage sites can be distinguished from the urban basilicas that were used for the regular worship of a congregation. Altars and episcopal chairs were made of wood; though they are lost, their stone footings show how they were placed in the basilicas, even at different times. Many baptismal fonts survive because they were set into the ground, protected from earthquakes and other hazards. Some have even retained their decorations.

In the cemeteries, grave monuments were also often at ground level. Many of their stone inscriptions can still be read. Stone mosaics cover burials cut into the floor of basilicas. These offer a rich variety of information about the persons honored with such locations: portraits, pictures, clothing, indications of status or office, length of life and time of death, church affiliation, and hope for a future. Small domestic and personal items — such as decorated lamps, bowls, and gems — also survive.

For this same period, the literary evidence is also remarkably extensive. Some documents detail the working of the imperial government as it attempted to regulate the activities of the churches and resolve conflicts. The imperial and ecclesiastical records that the Catholics gathered to make their case against the Donatists are extensive, though they were not presented systematically; instead, they often were included in or attached to controversial works.[8] The legislation by African episcopal meetings surviving in various collections covers a great range of issues. The decisions recorded in them reveal problems that the church leaders faced and their attempts to regulate practice. Augustine's surviving sermons and letters enable the reconstruction of the rituals of worship and occasionally a glimpse of how the participants responded to what he said or did. His theological writings, particularly of the Donatist controversy, demonstrate his attempts to explain and justify the practices of his community.

In some instances, practices and rituals described in the literary evidence can be mapped onto the archeological remains in Carthage, Hippo, and other cities. In other cases, the archeological evidence has no literary match. For example, large pools and baptisteries are found in cemetery and pilgrimage churches that were not episcopal seats and in which performance of the baptismal ritual is not witnessed by ancient texts.

---

8. The *acta* of the Donatist Council of Cebarsussi that deposed Primian of Carthage in 393, for example, survive in Aug. *Psal.* 36.2.20.

## The Vandal Era

After the third decade of the fifth century, the literary and archeological record becomes sparse; because it is found in Carthage and its environs, however, it can be better coordinated with the equally meager literary evidence. Victor of Vita and other chroniclers of the Vandal regime provide biased information on the distribution of church buildings between the Arians and the Nicenes. The Vandals seem to have taken over existing basilicas within the city and used them as they were, without significant modification or repair. The buildings used by the Nicenes were largely outside the city itself and had to be modified to convert them from use as cemetery churches to congregational worship.

## The Byzantine Period

The Byzantine government placed its stamp on the African church by extensive renovation and decoration of existing buildings that had fallen into disrepair under Vandal use. It also undertook construction of new basilicas. Most elaborately decorated baptismal fonts, such as the one at Clipea, are from this period. The arrangement of space within the churches was modified to fit the Byzantine eucharistic ritual: the altar was moved closer and sometimes connected directly to the apse in which the bishop and presbyters sat. Large and elaborate pilgrimage churches, such as that at Bir Ftouha, were constructed. Unfortunately, the literary evidence for Christian practice is more limited than it had been in the early fifth century.

This attempt to coordinate archeological and literary evidence must therefore proceed under a significant handicap. The eras of greatest archeological remains and fullest literary evidence are not well matched. In the seven decades beginning with the episcopate of the Donatist Parmenian of Carthage (361) and ending with the deaths of Aurelius of Carthage (429) and Augustine of Hippo (430), the method of correlation can be most fully employed.

## THE STRUCTURE OF THIS BOOK

This study proceeds in three unequal stages. The first offers an overview of Christianity in Roman Africa and provides a foundation for the detailed investigations of practices and the corresponding theologies in the second part. The third focuses attention on the religious and theological contribution of the African church to Latin Christianity.

Chapters one through three review the history of Christianity in Africa. The second and third centuries are treated together in the first chapter. The next period begins with the Constantinian liberation and continues to the Vandal conquest. The third chapter chronicles the Vandal and Byzantine occupations. The fourth provides a survey of the archeological remains of Christianity in Africa, focused on basilicas, baptisteries, and burials. It reviews in some detail the evidence for Carthage, Sufetula, Hippo Regius, and Thamugadi. The subsequent chapters build upon this foundation and refer back to the archeological evidence collected here.

Chapters five through twelve are the heart of the book, dealing with the practices and social structures for which sufficient evidence has survived: baptism, eucharist, penance, orders, marriage and consecrated life, death and burial, the cult of martyrs, and practices of individual piety. Certain practices, such as pilgrimage and the monastic life, are omitted because the available evidence is inadequate to achieve the objectives of this project. Each of these chapters reviews chronologically the development of the practice and the accompanying theology, usually proceeding from Tertullian through Augustine. Each chapter ends with general observations in two categories: the first summarizes the significant points of contact between archeological and literary evidence; the second reviews the interaction of practice and theology in the particular subject of the chapter.

The final section considers the development of a particularly African contribution to theology. It shows the way that concern for the holiness of the church dominated not only sacramental theology but scriptural interpretation, Christology, and the practices of piety.

# CHAPTER 1

# Christianity in North Africa to Diocletian

......................................................................................................................

## BACKGROUND

By the early third century of the Common Era, the Roman provinces of North Africa were filled with "cities." Quite literally hundreds of towns of various sizes and pretensions, but urban centers nonetheless, stretched from the Atlantic coast of the Mauretanias eastward all the way to the olive lands of Tripolitana.[1] In addition to these centers, villages, and hamlets, farmsteads and the growing villa-culture spread over the countryside. Transhumant pastoralists worked on and beyond the fringes of the provinces. Fortified farmsteads were established in the pre-desert zones near the limits of Roman control. But when one's focus is narrowed to the spread of Christianity in the African provinces, this fundamental rural background fades largely from view, as the evidence for the early Christian period is almost exclusively urban. Indeed, it tends to be for this period elsewhere as well: what evidence does survive elsewhere suggests that the spread of Christianity into the countryside was both slow and irregular, albeit with some notable exceptions (e.g., in Phrygia, especially in the Upper Tembris Valley and in Eumeneia and its surrounding district).

Those African cities are often remarkably well-preserved and, by the beginning of the third century, already equipped in large part with their full tally of monumental urban facilities and elegant town houses with brilliant mosaic floors. These urban amenities might include a colonnaded forum bordered by porticoes and shops or furnished with a market pavilion, a basilica for law

---

1. This chapter is, in part, an abbreviated version of "The Third Century" in "Third Century Christianity," in *The Cambridge Ancient History.* Vol. 12, *The Crisis of Empire,* A.D. *193-337,* 2nd ed., ed. Alan Bowman, Averil Cameron, and Peter Garnsey (Cambridge and New York: Cambridge University Press, 2005), 589-671.

courts, a curia for the town council, generous baths and palaestra with the occasional plunge swimming-pool. More wealthy cities might have had a library, nymphaea and public fountains, and other luxury facilities for public entertainment (odeon, stadium, theater, circus, amphitheater, hippodrome). Port cities like Carthage could be equipped with harbor installations, warehouses, and arcades. The paved city streets might boast an imposing and commemorative archway. Above all, there were temples, frequently more than one and — especially those fronting on the forum — often raised high on an artificially elevated podium. These temples were often lavishly embellished with variegated marble — unmistakable and dominating from any angle. All around were other signs of religious sentiment: altars and dedications, statues and shrines, inscriptions testifying to promises made and fulfilled. Urban Christians who worked and walked daily among these monuments must have been made acutely aware of the religious traditions and pious practices of their fellow townspeople, practices their Christian faith specifically repudiated. Indeed, many contemporary Christians regarded these rituals not just as idolatrous but as positively diabolical.

The surplus wealth that funded all these urban embellishments came from the flourishing agriculture of the countryside. Cereals and grains came from the rich, broad river valleys of Tunisia and the great plains stretching through Northern Algeria westward. Other produce came from cattle-ranching, orchards, viticulture, and bee-keeping. Garum (fish sauce) was prepared in coastal towns; dates and olive oil came from further inland in the drier regions and above all from Tripolitana to the east; timber and fine woods were extracted from the mountainous regions. The trans-Saharan caravans brought ivory and slaves, as well as exotic animals, for the export market (ostrich, leopard, giraffe, bear, tiger, rhinoceros, hippopotamus, elephant). The short sea-lanes from the African coast to the ports of Italy, especially Ostia, helped supply an insatiable Italian and specifically Roman market. In addition, luxury materials, like colored marbles from the Numidian mines, were in high demand; there was a thriving industry in African red-slip pottery popular throughout the Mediterranean.

All this agricultural industry and urban development had been greatly advanced by a network of roadways and bridges that opened up the countryside. The construction of aqueducts and reservoirs supplied water for the towns, and the skillful management of the intermittent rainfall in marginal regions extended the area for viable agriculture. While many of the engineering projects were carried out by personnel from the resident legion (III Augusta) — based by the third century at Lambaesis in Numidia — the legionary soldiers and their detachments were still required for intermittent guerilla warfare, to protect the developed areas from periodic raids and marauding skirmishes by belligerent border tribes.[2] The Fossatum Africae was also in place, a dry moat

2. Cypr. *Ep.* 62 illustrates the endemic dangers by its arrangements for ransoming of captives.

with occasional crossings, designed to control and funnel the annual migration of the flocks and herds of transhumant pastoralists in these border regions. The southern frontier system also included a series of fortified farms, watchtowers, and fortresses.

The indigenous population — and previous immigrant groups, including Punic and Greek — had by now been supplemented by the steady influx of entrepreneurial Italians, Spaniards (especially in the west), and wealthy Romans investing in lucrative African estates, and the establishment of a series of veteran colonies of discharged soldiers. While other languages were clearly spoken — and persisted — Latin had begun to dominate as the language of administration, education, and high culture.

The initial evidence suggests that there was a Greek-speaking component in the African church of the early third century just as there was in contemporary Rome. In the vision reported by Saturus, Perpetua addresses the Carthaginian bishop Optatus and the presbyter-teacher Aspasius in Greek, and they hear the angels in Paradise intoning the Sanctus in Greek.[3] Their contemporary Tertullian went to the trouble of composing a Greek version of several of his works.[4] That Greek element is quickly lost from view, nor does any hint of a Punic element appear throughout the century. On present testimony by mid-century, a Latin-speaking church emerged with its own accepted Latin version of the Bible and its liturgy conducted in Latin. While earlier in the century Tertullian was prepared on occasion to criticize the Latin version of the biblical text he had before him, Cyprian simply accepted his scriptural text as it stood. One cannot tell whether the contents of the *capsa* of the Scillitan martyrs ("books and letters of a just man named Paul") were in Greek or already in Latin; this will be discussed below.[5]

........................................................................................................

## GEOGRAPHICAL SPREAD

Knowledge of the presence of Christianity in North Africa comes fully formed, as it were, not in an account of evangelization but in those *Acts of the Scillitan Martyrs* ( July 17, 180), twelve martyrs (seven men and five women) arraigned in Carthage before the proconsul. The location of the hometown of these martyrs is obscure. It must be technically within the province of Proconsularis, falling within the jurisdiction of the proconsul at the time, but inscriptional evidence from Simitthu (Chemtou) — an epitaph with the ethnic *Iscilitana* — suggests that the location of Scil(l)i should be, broadly, somewhere towards

3. *Pas. Perp.* 13.4, 12.2.

4. Tert. *Spec., Bapt., Virg., Cor.,* and cf. Hieron. *Vir. ill.* 53 on the *Exst.*

5. Libri et epistulae Pauli uiri iusti. *Act. Scil.* 12, Herbert Musurillo, *The Acts of the Christian Martyrs,* Oxford Early Christian Texts (Oxford: Clarendon Press, 1972), 88.15 [180 C.E.].

the upper reaches of the Bagrada (Medjerda) River.[6] The implication is clear: there was a well-established spread of Christianity already by 180 C.E., not just within the confines of the conurbation of Carthage and its immediate territory. And it is highly unlikely that, hailing from such a location, the twelve *Scillitani* should be skilled in Greek as well as in Latin: those scriptures they carried with them had, therefore, probably already been translated into Latin. By what means and on what timetable Christianity had reached the African coastline and then penetrated well inland can only be conjectured. However, it would be reasonable to conjecture that some Christians had reached Africa a good half-century or more before the report of the Scillitan martyrs. A large seaport like Carthage would attract visitors and immigrants from all directions, but this would be particularly true of Rome and Italy, given the short traveling distance and the strong economic ties. The African church, while clearly aware of the Roman church and its policies, was quite independent: it was no mere Roman daughter-church. Yet it had no pretensions to a (legendary) apostolic foundation.

Equally startling is the literary output of Tertullian (fl., 197 C.E.–220s C.E.). Beginning late in the second century, this Carthaginian Christian shows himself fully aware of contemporary ecclesiastical issues and currents, ready to debate the major theological questions of the time, often while attacking perceived heretical teachers (e.g., Marcion, Hermogenes, Valentinian, Praxeas). He was not concerned just with local issues: as the third century began, he represented an ecclesiastical community neither isolated nor unsophisticated. He showed that he and his fellows were open to the international pull of Montanist revivalism, the New Prophecy.

Tertullian was notoriously triumphalist in his claims of the spread of Christianity (e.g., "Such are our numbers, amounting to almost a majority in every city"),[7] and he attested to Christians in Numidia and Mauretania as well as in the proconsular towns of Thysdrus and Hadrumetum[8] and in Uthina.[9] The closest statistics available are for three councils of bishops. Cyprian reported a meeting had convened under Agrippinus, Bishop of Carthage (220s or 230s), and later sources specify seventy participants.[10] Cyprian also referred to the ninety bishops who met under Cyprian's predecessor, Donatus, in the earlier 240s[11] to

6. The evidence is fully discussed by Serge Lancel, *Actes de la conférence de Carthage en 411,* SC nos. 194, 195, 224, 373 (Paris: Éditions du Cerf, 1972), 4:1456. The area is some 150 km. west of Carthage and 60 km. south of the nearest port. It was, however, the site of an important marble quarry which served Rome and other markets beyond Africa.

7. Cum tanta hominum multitudo, pars paene maior ciuitatis cuiusque, Tert. *Scap.* 2.10 (CCSL 2:1128.42-43).

8. Tert. *Scap.* 3-4.

9. Tert. *Mon.* 12.3.

10. Aug. *Unic. bapt.* 13.22; *Cresc.* 3.3.3; cf. Cypr. *Ep.* 71.4.1.

11. Cypr. *Ep.* 59.10.1.

condemn their fellow bishop Privatus, along with his episcopal supporters. The minutes of the council meeting held in the autumn of 256 record the opinions of eighty-seven bishops. These were bishops loyal to Cyprian's stance against recognizing heretical baptism; the correspondence preceding the meeting indicates other dissenters who were prudently absent.[12] Each bishop is identified with the name of the city whose Christian community he represented.

While this evidence is striking enough to give a notion of the numbers of those prosperous African small towns and centers that had a Christian *conventiculum* by mid-century — well in excess of one hundred is a very safe conjecture — that unfortunately tells little of the relative size of such communities despite Tertullian's stridently iterated assertions. By contrast with, for example, the ecclesiastical organization of the contemporary Egyptian church, most Christian communities in Africa appear, on the evidence, to have been led by a bishop, irrespective of size. The distribution of those communities, however, is relatively clear, thanks to the minutes of the council of 256:[13] sparse in the Mauretanias as well as in Tripolitana, but clustered closely in the fertile tracts of Africa Proconsularis and the populous centers of Numidia (where at least twenty-five locations have been identified by modern researchers).

Tertullian and Cyprian certainly demonstrated a high level of literary competence — indeed, brilliance in the case of Tertullian. The delicately mannered and cultured apology of the *Octavius* of Minucius Felix (c. 230) in all probability reflects the polite literary and educated circles of Cirta in Numidia (though its literary setting is Rome and Ostia). But these three writers seem to have had few Christian peers. Certainly some of Cyprian's correspondents reveal much lower standards of literary competence.[14] It was to be another half-century before the rhetorically trained and articulate Arnobius and Lactantius emerged from the African church in the early fourth century. The grounds are missing for positing too sanguine a picture of the social levels to which Christianity may have reached generally over the century in the region, despite its remarkable geographical spread. The description of Perpetua at the beginning of the century (a well-educated Roman matron of good family)[15] seems to carry a studied emphasis on her exceptional status. In mid-century, Cyprian's personal wealth (suburban estate) and elite social standing (to the end he enjoyed old friends among the high-born local pagan aristocracy)[16] appear to be without parallel among his contemporary African Christians: he was, self-consciously, a *persona insignis*,[17] a figure of eminence; ultimately he went to his martyr's death

---

12. Cypr. *Sent.*
13. Cypr. *Sent.*
14. Notably *Ep.* 21, 22, 26, 78, 79 and some of the *sententiae* of *Sent.*
15. honeste nata, liberaliter instituta, matronaliter nupta, *Pas. Perp.* 2.1, Musurillo, 108.5-6.
16. plures egregii et clarissimi ordinis et sanguinis, sed et saeculi nobilitate generosi, qui propter amicitiam eius antiquam. . . . Pont. *Vita Cypr.* 14; CSEL 3.3: cv. 22-23.
17. Cypr. *Ep.* 8.1.1.

with the capital punishment appropriate for an *honestior,* by beheading instead of condemnation to the mines or the beasts. Nevertheless, this was a highly organized church, with a strong metropolitan leadership based in Carthage (though regional councils could also be held), with a structured and salaried clerical hierarchy, and an elaborate system of charitable support.

The nearest snapshot we have of a typical African Christian community — the congregation at the major Numidian town of Cirta — comes right at the beginning of the fourth century embedded in a record of court proceedings.[18] The clergy consisted of a bishop and at least two presbyters, two deacons, four subdeacons, seven lectors, and in excess of six gravediggers, as well as elders *(seniores):* there was a church-house[19] which also had a well-equipped dining area. There was also a cemetery *(area martyrum)* which had a large cottage. The church paraphernalia, in addition to chalices, lamps, lampstands, candelabra, and other gold, silver, and bronze items, also had in store eighty-two women's tunics, thirty-eight veils, sixteen men's tunics, thirteen pairs of men's shoes, and forty-seven pairs of women's shoes, and nineteen rustic *coplae* (cloaks?), all presumably donations for charitable distributions. This congregation also possessed as scriptures one unusually large bound book, which might have been a lectionary, as well as thirty other books, two smaller books, and four fascicules.[20] The professions of two of the lectors are given: one was a marble cutter; the other was a teacher of Latin letters whose father was a local decurion of indigenous descent.[21] One of the gravediggers describes himself as an artisan. In the court proceedings we also hear of a successful fuller (definitely not an approved upper-class profession) named Victor, who could afford a donation of twenty *folles.* The Carthaginian Lucilla, a wealthy and influential woman of the highest class *(clarissima femina),* also figured in the narrative through her contribution of no fewer than four hundred *folles.*[22] Throughout, such gifts to the church are assumed to be intended for distribution to the poor, little old widows, or simply to the people — and not to be pocketed by the clergy as bribes.[23] This type of ecclesiastical establishment, with this sort of (modest) social mix and these sorts of resources, partly to meet the needs of a significant body of indigent followers, may reasonably be assumed to have been duplicated — scaled proportionate to population — throughout similar urban centers of Africa by the end of the third century.

---

18. *Act. Zeno.*
19. domum in qua christiani conveniebant, *Act. Zeno.* 3; CSEL 26:186.20.
20. *Act. Zeno.* 3-5.
21. origo nostra de sanguine Mauro, *Act. Zeno.* 1; CSEL 26:185.12-13.
22. *Act. Zeno.* 6; CSEL 26:189.4-8. For a valuation of these sums, see p. 43, n. 41.
23. *Act. Zeno.* 18.

This first section provides a quick summary but minimal analysis of the known clashes between Roman authorities and the Christian communities in Africa in the first half of the third century.

"Persecution" of Christians by Roman officials through the course of the second century had been sporadic and unsystematic, basically local in range. It is best seen in the context of the occasional harassment of many of the other exotic groups that were regarded as equally deviant (astrologers, soothsayers, and magicians, for instance). However, Christians had been considered troublesome enough to have been brought to the attention not just of Roman provincial governors, or of the Roman urban prefect, but on rare occasions of Roman emperors themselves (Trajan, Hadrian, Marcus Aurelius). This was common enough that early in the third century the jurist Ulpian was able to demonstrate the punishments deemed appropriate for Christian adherents by drawing up a register of imperial responses to referrals by provincial governors and to complaints or queries by provincial councils.[24] By that date, the accumulation of case histories with imperial authority was adequate to merit systematic description. Even so, the intermittent and regional nature of the outbreaks needs to be emphasized. Christians were *ipso facto* potentially on the wrong side of the law, but some local circumstances were required to realize that potentiality: especially popular agitation arising from religious fervor or from superstitious fear occasioned by earthquake, drought, flood, plague, or famine, or, occasionally, in response to Christian enthusiastic provocation. Pressure from below gave rise to troubles, rather than imperial initiative breaching the limits of the generally prevailing, but nevertheless fragile, Roman tolerance. The official attitude was passive until forced to confront particular cases, and its activation was normally confined to the local and provincial level. As the heroization of the past age of martyrdom gained pace in the post-Constantinian era, the Christian literary sources have a strong tendency to universalize these local outbreaks. No solid grounds can be found, however, for the conclusion that the second-century pattern of local conflict did not continue into the first half of the third century.

Throughout the first half of the third century, this intermittent trouble is casually evidenced: the sources being so fitful, allowance must be made that they provide only a sample of what Christians may have experienced elsewhere. Thanks to Eusebius of Caesarea, a fundamental source, moreover, the record is notoriously biased towards eastern evidence. Additionally, victims belonging to other Christian sects may well have been crowded out of that imperfect

24. Lact. *Inst.* 5.11.19.

record. With martyrdom valued as the supreme sign of the elect, memory of these sectaries was promptly erased in what emerged as the orthodox tradition. The orthodox solemnly and consistently argued, in their attempt to lay claim to the spiritual high ground, that there could be no true martyrdom outside the church. Thus in the latter half of the second century, Montanists, Marcionites, and other non-orthodox groups could lay claim to "innumerable martyrs,"[25] but knowledge of individuals comes typically through efforts to discredit their spiritual credentials.[26] A century later, the martyrdom of Pionios (250) casually — but significantly — includes (without elaboration) a Marcionite martyr and a Montanist confessor.[27] Such sectaries, generally suppressed, have to be added mentally to the register of Christian victims. In all this, the frequent occurrence of confessors (that is, released Christians) as distinguished from perfected martyrs is noteworthy. The discretionary powers of provincial governors, who wielded the authority to order capital punishment, could be crucial to the outcome of a confrontation. A period of imprisonment after an initial hearing (with pressure to recant) appears to have been standard procedure. In the earliest surviving African record of a trial of Christians, "The proconsul Saturninus said: 'Take a reprieve of thirty days and think it over.'"[28] This delay would be followed, in a significant number of cases, by eventual release of the Christian as hopelessly recalcitrant — or as a renegade.[29] Thus, arrest for Christianity did not inevitably lead to a martyr's death: adventitious circumstances such as the hostility of a crowd or the strength of the religious sentiments of a governor could be determinant.

Under Septimius Severus, the spotlight fell on Egypt and Africa, but that focus may be due to the vagaries of the surviving documentation.[30] When the procurator Hilarianus was acting proconsul in Africa Proconsularis,[31] a group of five youthful catechumens and their teacher were condemned to death by fighting the beasts in the amphitheater of Carthage[32] at games celebrating the birthday of Geta, the emperor's younger brother. The condemned were two slaves, Revocatus and Felicity, Saturninus, and Secundulus (who actually died in prison before the public execution of the others),[33] along with the twenty-two-year-old Perpetua highlighted in the account as being "of good family,

25. Eus. Caes. *Hist. eccl.* 5.16.20-22.

26. For example, in Eus. Caes. *Hist. eccl.* 5.18.5-10 (Montanists), Tert. *Prax.* 1.4.

27. *Pas. Pion.* 21.5-6, 11.2.

28. *Act. Scil.* 13: Saturninus proconsul dixit: Moram xxx dierum habete et recordemini. Musurillo, 88.16-17.

29. Tert. *Scap.* 4 provides, among many other instances, some pertinent illustrations.

30. Eus. Caes. *Hist. eccl.* 6.1-5 and Tertullian's writings especially *Cor., Scorp.,* and *Scap.* and the *Pas. Perp.*

31. 203, but 202 or 204 are also possible: the date is traditionally remembered as March 7.

32. Though the location is not actually attested in *Pas. Perp.,* the shrines commemorating the martyrdom are found in Carthage.

33. *Pas. Perp.* 14.

well-educated, and a married Roman matron."[34] Their teacher, Saturus, was not arrested with his catechumens but voluntarily surrendered himself to join them.[35] The dream account of Saturus adds four named others, seen to be already in the garden of Paradise, "Jucundus, Saturninus, and Artaxius, who were burned alive in this same persecution, together with Quintus, who had actually died as a martyr in prison."[36] The visionary also recognized in Paradise "many of their brethren, including martyrs."[37] The extraordinary document of their trial preserves the record of their imprisonment written by Perpetua herself; it includes four of her dreams[38] and Saturus's account of his vision.[39] This account offers a remarkable insight into the contemporary mentality of such martyrs: their sense of privileged spiritual access (a prophetic dream, on request, to determine whether they would indeed suffer or be reprieved),[40] their sense of spiritual powers (Perpetua's deceased brother Dinocrates was released from his sufferings by her prayer),[41] their sense of spiritual superiority (they act as mediators of the contention between their bishop Optatus and their presbyter Aspasius),[42] and their sense of immediate election to Paradise.[43] Apart from graphically perceiving the stark realities of their periods of imprisonment (awaiting formal trial before the acting proconsul and, then, after condemnation, awaiting the games at which they would be executed), the reader also notices conflicts within Perpetua's family: her father attempted to dissuade her ("I grieved for my father's sake because he alone of all my kindred would not be rejoicing at my suffering"),[44] but one brother was also a catechumen (her younger brother had died, it seems, unbaptized),[45] and both her mother and her (absent) husband were presumably already Christian. Other-worldly aspirations are highlighted by her preparedness to abandon her infant son at the breast (as well as by Felicity's abandonment of her newborn child). The crowd

---

34. "honeste nata, liberaliter instituta, matronaliter nupta." *Pas. Perp.* 2.1; Musurillo, 108.5-6.

35. *Pas. Perp.* 4.5.

36. Iocundum et Saturninum et Artaxium, qui eadem persecutione uiui arserunt, et Quintum, qui et ipse martyr in carcere exierat. *Pas. Perp.* 11.9; Musurillo, 120.11-13.

37. Et coepimus illic multos fratres cognoscere sed et martyras, 13.8; Musurillo, 122.9-10. Tert. *Scorp.* 1.11 may refer to them: "Some Christians the fire has tested, others the sword, others the beasts, while yet others are still hungering in prison, having had in the meantime, through clubs and claws, a foretaste of their martyrdom." Alios ignis, alios gladius, alios bestiae Christianos probauerunt, alii fustibus interim et ungulis insuper degustato martyrio in carcere esuriunt. CCSL 2:1070.11–1071.14.

38. *Pas. Perp.* 3-10.

39. *Pas. Perp.* 11-13.

40. *Pas. Perp.* 4.

41. *Pas. Perp.* 7-8.

42. *Pas. Perp.* 13.

43. *Pas. Perp.* 10-14.

44. Et ego dolebam casum patris mei quod solus de passione mea gauisurus non esset de toto genere meo. *Pas. Perp.* 5.6; Musurillo, 112.17-19.

45. *Pas. Perp.* 7-8.

in the amphitheater is variously shown to be sympathetic and hostile.[46] The grounds for condemnation are importantly and unequivocally reported by Perpetua: "The procurator Hilarianus . . . said: 'Have pity on your father's white hairs, have pity on your infant son. Perform sacrifice *(fac sacrum)* for the well-being of the emperors.' And I replied: 'I will not.' Hilarianus said: 'Are you a Christian?' And I replied: 'I am a Christian. . . .' Then Hilarianus pronounced sentence on us all and condemned us to the beasts."[47] The sequence of official thinking is clear: so long as Perpetua was prepared to conform to accepted public Roman ritual ceremonies, she could go free (whatever the beliefs — and indeed practices — she might privately continue to maintain). The exclusivity of Christian worship was the sticking point. That avenue refused, condemnation followed precisely on the grounds of her persistent Christian adherence. Had it emerged during the questioning that she was Jewish, for example, her refusal to sacrifice would not have resulted in condemnation.

Many have attempted to link the apparently unrelated incidents in Egypt reported by Eusebius and those in Africa recounted by Perpetua with a compressed and confused passage in *Historia Augusta*. It has Septimius, with Caracalla, journeying from Syria through Palestine on their way to Alexandria (in 199) and "on their way he established many privileges for the Palestinians. He forbade under severe penalty that people should become Jews. He also decreed the same concerning Christians."[48] However, if such a linkage is to be made, there are clear chronological difficulties: the purported imperial embargo does not find any resonance elsewhere in the surviving sources. Indeed, Tertullian, in 212, could wax eulogistic on Septimius's favorable personal relations with Christians (including imperial protection of Christian men and women of senatorial status). Moreover, not all of the known victims fall into the envisaged category (perhaps of converts and their teachers).[49] The *Historia Augusta* passage is best regarded as spurious, an invention reflecting its author's late fourth-century preoccupations and prejudices, and the temptation to link these incidents should be resisted accordingly. They can be considered as typical of the perils that potentially could befall any openly enthusiastic converts and staunch Christian adherents alike. The charged atmosphere in which Christians found

---

46. For example, *Pas. Perp.* 17, 18.9, 20.2, 21.7.

47. Et Hilarianus procurator, qui tunc loco proconsulis Minuci Timiniani defuncti ius gladii acceperat, Parce, inquit, canis patris tui, parce infantiae pueri. Fac sacrum pro salute imperatorum. Et ego respondi: Non facio. Hilarianus: Christiana es? Inquit. Et ego respondi: Christiana sum. Et cum staret pater ad me deiciendam, iussus est ab Hilariano proici et uirga percussus est. Et doluit mihi casus patris mei quasi fuissem percussa; sic dolui pro senecta eius misera. Tunc nos uniuersos pronuntiat et damnat ad bestias. *Pas. Perp.* 6.3-6; Musurillo, 112.27–114.7.

48. in itinere Palaestinis plurima iura fundauit. Iudaeos fieri sub graui poena uetuit. idem etiam de Christianis sanxit. *Hist. Aug.* Septimius Severus 16.8–17.1.

49. Leonides, Origen's father, Eus. Caes. *Hist. eccl.* 6.2.2, 13; Tert. *Scap.* 4.6.

themselves living was guaranteed to generate eager talk about the coming of the Antichrist and perfervid millenarian expectations.[50]

However, Tertullian's *On the Crown* (datable to a time before late 211)[51] focuses on a soldier, who may be a Carthaginian, brought to trial,[52] imprisoned, and awaiting the largesse of martyrdom.[53] He had ostentatiously refused to wear the ceremonial laurel crown, which drew the complaint of pusillanimous Christians for "jeopardizing for them a peace so long and so good."[54] This would indicate that not many incidents like that of Perpetua, Felicity, and their companions in the interim, since c. 203, were known to Tertullian and his audience.

Under early Caracalla, it was no different. Tertullian bore incidental testimony to lethal danger in Numidia and Mauretania,[55] as well as continuing stress in Africa Proconsularis itself.[56] One martyr, Mavilus of Hadrumetum, was condemned to the beasts.[57] Likewise again for Africa, Cyprian in early 251 incidentally mentioned the illustrious martyred forebears of the young military confessor Celerinus: his grandmother, Celerina, and his two uncles (paternal and maternal), Laurentinus and Egnatius, both also soldiers.[58] We must assume that their deaths occurred in the reasonably distant past, though within no more than two generations, and presumably in Carthage, because their anniversaries were annually commemorated there. Cyprian, in *On the Lapsed* (251), could blame the long peace for its lulling effects in stultifying the faith of those who had recently lapsed in the Decian persecution.[59] Such scattered incidents were endemic, liable to occur anywhere at any time: though these incidents may have become infrequent, Christians still had to live out their lives against a background of insecurity and some peril.

That pattern of peril was quietly changing. There is much less evidence of outbreaks of popular hostility against Christians in the thirty-five years or so before 250. This may have been the result of Christianity becoming a more familiar part of the kaleidoscopic religious landscape, thereby less secretive and less feared. In parallel, fewer Christians are known to be arraigned for trial. But appearances can be deceptive and perception distorted by the tyranny of the sources: scant

50. At this season, Eus. Caes. *Hist. eccl.* 6.7 (the writer Judas); Hipp. *Dan.* 4.18 (Syria), 4.19 (Pontus); Tert. *Marc.* 3.24 (Palestine).

51. A work of Tertullian's Montanist period, dated to the time of a military donative by joint Severan emperors, *Cor.* 1.1.

52. reus ad praefectos. Tert. *Cor.* 1.2 (CCSL 2:1039.14).

53. donatium Christi in carcere expectat. Tert. *Cor.* 1.3 (CCSL 2:1040.21).

54. tam bonam et longam pacem periclitari sibi. Tert. *Cor.* 1.5 (CCSL 2:1040.29).

55. Nam et nunc a praeside Legionis, et a praeside Mauretaniae uexatur hoc nomen, sed gladio tenus. Tert. *Scap.* 4.8 (CCSL 2:1131.51-53).

56. Tert. *Scap. passim*.

57. Tert. *Scap.* 3.5 (there are textual uncertainties).

58. Cypr. *Ep.* 39.3.1. Celerinus himself was not yet old enough to qualify for the presbyterate, *Ep.* 39.5.2.

59. Cypr. *Laps.* 9.

western evidence survives for the period between Tertullian and Cyprian, and much of what does exist (e.g., *via* the papal calendars) is unreliable.[60]

Origen, writing towards the end of the 240s, confirms the general impression of the peace of this period for Christians, though he anticipates a return of imperial suppression in response to recent turmoil.[61] Likewise, writing with hindsight after the devastation of the persecution of Decius, Dionysius of Alexandria also refers to the preceding principate of Philip as having been "more kindly" towards Christians.[62] Overall the record of persecution, as it survives, would indicate an increasing acceptance of the Christian presence in the empire as the first half of the third century progressed and a corresponding reduction of the physical molestation of the Christian communities.

## Persecution under Decius, 250/251 C.E.

A summary account of the course of the persecution will be followed by detailed analysis justifying the construction of that summary. Sources are abundant, comprising principally the correspondence of Cyprian[63] and his treatise *On the Lapsed,* the letters of Dionysius of Alexandria,[64] the *Passion of Pionios,* and the forty-five extant Decian *libelli* from Egypt.

### SUMMARY

By autumn 249, Emperor Decius was securely in power after his usurpation. Not very long afterwards, orders went out from Rome to all the provincial governors of the empire that a universal sacrifice was to be offered to the gods of empire. This proclamation might have been scheduled for January 3, 250, at the public civic ceremony of the *vota solemnia,* the annually celebrated sacrifices for the emperor's personal welfare.[65] Victims are attested before the month of January 250 was over.[66] On the face of it, this gesture was decidedly old-fashioned, modeled on a *supplicatio:* in times of public distress in the distant past, the people of Rome were bidden to come forward as a body to throng all the temples and shrines of the tutelary deities of the state. The scale of the Decian operation, however, was entirely unprecedented: it was to be a religious rally by the inhabitants of the

---

60. *Lib. Pont.* 16-20.

61. *Contra Celsum* 3.15. This reference may be to the revolt of Pacatianus, which was put down by Decius in 248.

62. Eus. Caes. *Hist. eccl.* 6.41.9.

63. Especially *Ep.* 5-41.

64. Largely preserved as extracts in Eus. Caes. *Hist. eccl.* 6 and 7.

65. Though attractive, this connection is an entirely speculative setting.

66. Fabian, Bishop of Rome, Jan. 19 or 20, *Lib. Pont.* 21, *Mart. Hieron.* XIII Kal. Feb.

entire empire to win the favor of its protecting gods and their support for the new emperor. His dynasty was to inaugurate Rome's second millennium (the millennial games and pageants having been celebrated with much pomp and fanfare the previous year, 248). So far as the evidence goes, which gods were to be honored was left unspecified; variants in local civic divinities were allowed, such as the Nemeseion in Smyrna, the Serapaeum in Alexandria, the Capitoline triad of Jupiter, Juno, and Minerva in the more Romanized cities, or indeed some more personal cult. In a revealing vignette of this persecution, the proconsul of Asia vainly urged the Christian Pionios to offer the sacrifice to whatsoever deity he cared to have in mind — to the air, if he liked.[67] Some publicly accepted gesture of religious obeisance had to be performed by pouring a libation and tasting sacrificial offerings.[68] The emperor cult was involved only insofar as it had always been used, as a means of testing Christian obstinacy or proving apostasy: Pionios was urged to sacrifice at least to the emperor.[69] Honor to the gods was the object of the action; it did not necessarily entail abjuration of private beliefs or local cult practices, which were legion throughout the length and breadth of the empire, Christianity included. Decius's edict, however, provided a foretaste of that autocracy which would mark fourth-century imperial government. Directives were being issued from above that affected the lives of the entire population as the central authorities grappled with the problems of commanding and controlling an unwieldy and extremely diverse empire. The Decian edict is a presage of those centralist pressures for conformity and homogeneity. Christians, certainly, would have experienced it as a dramatic — indeed, drastic — departure from the more tolerant attitude towards their religion that had characterized the previous years; the preceding regimes now appeared benign by contrast, and Philip was credited with Christian sympathies.[70] For a significant shift had occurred: henceforth, the religious sentiment of the imperial court — rather than that of the local populace — would determine the well-being or suffering of Christians. Decius's decree marked a watershed. The sources are repetitious in declaring the suddenness and unexpectedness of the outbreak of persecution for Christians.

Still, an attack on Christianity as such was clearly not the object of the legislation. By this date, however, bishops could be figures of prominence, especially in the major metropolitan cities where they were known to command sizeable congregations. They were promptly put under pressure to lead their followers to the pagan altars. Christians, therefore, quickly became victims by their refusal to comply. Jews appear to have been exempted, as was by then traditional in Roman governance.[71] As the year 250 progressed, local officials and governors regularly imposed various pressures to conform, such as tor-

---

67. *Pas. Pion.* 19-20.
68. Or burning incense, Cypr. *Ep.* 55.2.1.
69. *Pas. Pion.* 8.4.
70. Dionysius, in Eus. Caes. *Hist. eccl.* 7.10.3; 6.34; *Orac. Sibyl.* 13.88.
71. *Pas. Pion.* 3.6; 4.2-11, 13-14.

tures, confiscations, exile, and periods of imprisonment with varying degrees of deprivation; the death penalty was rarely used. As before, the patience (or piety) of the governor and the variable mood of the local populace, which he prudently assuaged, could still be determining factors. Though incontestably a period of intense anxiety and extreme apprehension for most confessing Christians, the Decian persecution — the first of the "General Persecutions" — was in fact less lurid than later accounts of martyrdom and even many modern accounts might lead a reader to believe.

One of the remarkable features of the Decian orders was certification — the issuing of certificates *(libelli),* signed by official witnesses, bearing testimony to the recipients' having complied with the orders, and no doubt protecting them from further harassment. This process was not unlike the issuing of taxation receipts. Copies of forty-five such certificates have been recovered from Egypt.[72]

There are no good grounds for believing that only Christian suspects were required to acquire and produce such documents. The implications for the imperial government must have been immense and, in many less urbanized or bureaucratized districts, nearly insurmountable. Still, the process indicates that Decius's intentions were far from idle: the depth of traditional piety involved in imposing and enforcing the edict ought not to be underestimated. To issue those certificates and to supervise the sacrificial actions, panels of local commissioners were established, varying in size and composition from place to place.[73] A fixed date[74] was also set locally by which the inhabitants were to have presented themselves; thereafter the commissioners would have had to deal with latecomers, defectors, or defaulters drawn to their attention. The recalcitrant were left to languish in prison, awaiting trial before the higher magistrate to whom their cases were referred. All indications are that after a lapse of twelve months from the date set for the sacrificial rites, the various commissions were dissolved, Christians still imprisoned were released, and exiles were recalled. Refugees began to return, and those who had lain concealed in hiding were free to emerge. By March 251, bishops were planning to hold post-persecution council meetings. By that date all danger had clearly passed, though Decius did not die until May or June of that year.

Decius might have been surprised by his posthumous reputation in the Christian tradition; Lactantius called him an execrable animal.[75] Matters of state more pressing than the fate of a relatively few Christian recusants had claimed his attention. He may even have regarded his religious program as generally

---

72. See John R. Knipfing, "The Libelli of the Decian Persecution," *The Harvard Theological Review* 16, no. 4 (1923): 345-90. Nos. 35-36 were re-edited at P.Mich. III.157-58, with further five published in *PSI* VII.778, *SB* VI.9084, *P.Oxy.* XLI.2990, *P.Oxy.* XVIII.3929, *P.Lips.* II no. 152 (2002).

73. Cyprian identified a group of five commissioners for Carthage. *Ep.* 43.3.1; 56.1; 67.6.2.

74. *dies . . . praestitutus,* Cypr. *Laps.* 3 (CCSL 3:222.49).

75. Lact. *Mort.* 4.

successful. After all, so many pagans as well as lapsing Christians throughout the empire had honored the empire's gods, difficult though it may be to understand that the gods were honored by lapsing Christians' patently false declaration that they had always respected the gods and practiced their cult.

Attention is now directed to a fuller analysis of Decius's orders, their implementation, and their victims.

## THE ORDERS

The wording in several passages of Cyprian's letters certainly leaves the impression that all inhabitants, regardless of sex, age, and citizen status, were probably enjoined to perform the sacrificial rites involved. One of his letters reveals that entire households, having lapsed, sought re-admittance to communion "up to twenty and thirty and more at a time who claim to be the relations, in-laws, freedmen, and domestics of the person holding a certificate of forgiveness" (issued by one of the martyrs).[76] Freedmen and domestics could well encompass the servile classes. A similar inference could be drawn from a later letter: the case of a Christian who sacrificed in person but as proxy "for his entire family, thereby protecting his wife, his children, and his entire household."[77] Even babies were not exempt.[78] This was a religious rally on the grandest of scales.

The Egyptian certificates that have been published were issued between mid-June and mid-July 250: that was a good six months since the promulgation of the edict, at least in some other parts of the empire.[79] Might certificates, then, belong to a second and more intensive stage in Decius's persecution when documentation was required? The evidence for Rome indicates that certification was required there by at least March: Numeria, in bribing her way out of actually sacrificing before Easter (April 7, 250), had thereby committed a sin entailing her exclusion from communion.[80] She must have acquired an incriminating certificate,[81] an action regarded by many (at least in the west) as tantamount to apostasy. Similarly, by May 250, Cyprian could mention grades of apostasy (i.e., *libellatici* vs. *sacrificati*)[82] and later explain "those who had stained their hands

---

76. Late enim patet quando dicitur "ille cum suis" et possunt nobis et uiceni et tirceni et amplius offerri qui propinqui et adfines et liberti ac domestici esse adseuerentur eius qui accepit libellum. Cypr. *Ep.* 15.4 (CCSL 3B:89.67-70).

77. Qui ipse pro cunctis ad discrimen accedens uxorem et liberos et domum totam periculi sui pactione protexit. Cypr. *Ep.* 55.13.2 (CCSL 3B:271.217-19).

78. Cypr. *Laps.* 9, 25.

79. The earliest known Decian victim is Pope Fabian in Rome in late January 250. See note 66 above.

80. Cypr. *Ep.* 21.2.1, 3.2.

81. Compare the description in Cypr. *Ep.* 55.14.1-2.

82. Cypr. *Ep.* 15.3.1.

and lips with sacrilegious contagion or had none the less contaminated their conscience with impious certificates."[83] That he mentioned this casually, not as a recent new wave of perils for Christians, suggests a significant and importunate group of purchasers of certificates in Carthage by May 250. Certification was part of the routine of this persecution in his experience.

It is possible, given the locality of the known Egyptian *libelli* (Theadelphia, Alexandru Nesus, Philadelphia, Oxyrhynchus, Arsinoe, Narmouthis, Thosbis),[84] that it took some time for Decius's orders to penetrate into these up-river areas and for a local date then to be set for their implementation. Parallel delays in the promulgation of Diocletian's first edict against Christians are attested: February 23, 303, in Nicomedia; June 5, 303, at a town near Carthage.[85] If this was so, Christians in this locality may well have had advance warning of the coming trial from their brethren down on the coast, and may have been able to make themselves scarce. This would reduce considerably the likelihood of finding any apostate Christians among the finds of the Egyptian *libelli*.

IMPLEMENTATION OF THE ORDERS

The sources provide a glimpse of the workings of local commissions. The appointed magistrates were flocked by crowds anxious to prove (correctly or not) their religious loyalties;[86] at times Christians of prominent station were pushed forward, urged on by pagan inciters to demonstrate their own compliance.[87] Smoking altars were set up around the forum to help cope with the numbers, but characteristically, in the larger and Romanized town centers, long and slowly moving processions wound their way up to the altars set before the Capitoline temples.[88] When the pilgrim reached an altar, he (or she) placed on it a portion of ritual meat in offering, poured there a little wine in libation, and tasted a morsel of the sacrificial meats provided. Some apostates were so eager to establish their pagan loyalties that they brought their own offerings and victims with them.[89] The pilgrim then would present a certificate to the commission; it was often prepared by a notary for the illiterate and the speaker of only a native language. It was read out,[90] the petitioner acknowledged it as his or her

---

83. Item cum conperissem eos qui sacrilegis contactibus manus suas atque ora maculassent uel nefandis libellis nihilominus conscientiam polluissent. *Ep.* 20.2.2 (CCSL 3B:107.25–108.27).

84. See note 72 above.

85. Feb. 23, 303, in Nicomedia: Lact. *Mort.* 13.1; June 5, 303, at Tibiuca near Carthage: *Pas. Fel.* 1.

86. Cypr. *Laps.* 8, 25.

87. Dionysius, Eus. Caes. *Hist. eccl.* 6.41.11.

88. Cypr. *Ep.* 8.2.3; 21.3.2.

89. Cypr. *Laps.* 8.

90. Cypr. *Ep.* 30.3.1.

own,[91] and one or more of the commissioners then duly signed it as witnesses in the appropriate place on the document.

The sources also provide evidence of clandestine evasions of the orders. Many Christians did not perform the actual pagan rites enjoined upon them but bribed the official or officials concerned and purchased their certificate. They could thereby secure immunity from the edict's penalties, and, they thought, retain their Christian faith unimpaired.[92] Writing a good generation or so earlier, Tertullian testified that bribing one's way out of the clutches of a persecutor was common and acceptable practice for Christians, though one which, with his rigorous temperament, he personally disapproved.[93]

In the minds of the *libellatici,* or purchasers of certificates, during the Decian persecution, passing money over to a commissioner or to an intending informer in order to secure freedom from threatened molestation (as Tertullian testifies Christians had done in the past) differed in no significant way from passing over money, either in person or through a deputy,[94] to a local official in order to secure a certificate and thereby exemption from offering sacrifice. But to the legally minded ecclesiastical authorities, at least in the west (the eastern sources are comparatively meager), the purchase was significant. For Christians the statement in the certificate was tantamount to a formal declaration of apostasy; any Christian who acknowledged a certificate was, technically, guilty of denying the faith. They joined the ranks of the *lapsi,* the fallen.[95]

Other Christians took flight in order to escape detection by authorities or delation before a commission. Even bishops fled from distant provinces to be lost in the crowds of Rome;[96] and, for example, sixty-five refugees from Carthage were cared for by the two sisters of Celerinus in Rome.[97] Christians also hid among the crowds in Carthage; they required special funds for their needs[98] and might find shelter in Christian homes, where they were protected, with some irony, by the *libellatici.*[99] Elsewhere, Gregory Thaumaturgus took to the safety of the Pontic hills,[100] and many Egyptians fled to "the Arabian mountain" for refuge, but faced other perils.[101]

When the persecution died down, Cyprian could muster a "copious number of bishops" for his African Council, held in the first half of 251, and these

---

91. Cypr. *Ep.* 30.3.1; 55.14.1.
92. Cypr. *Ep.* 55.14.
93. Tert. *Fug.* 5.3, 12-14.
94. Cypr. *Ep.* 30.3.1; 55.14.1 for deputies.
95. So, firmly, Cypr. *Laps.* 27-28.
96. Cypr. *Ep.* 30.8.1.
97. Cypr. *Ep.* 21.4.1.
98. Cypr. *Ep.* 7.2.
99. Cypr. *Ep.* 55.13.2.
100. Relying on Gregory Nyssa, *de uita b. Gregorii Thaumaturgi,* PG 46:945.
101. Dionysius, in Eus. Caes. *Hist. eccl.* 6.42.

bishops were "whole in soul and body."[102] The charity of hospitable Christians had ensured that even the main figures in the church, the bishops, had managed to escape in safety and to avoid spiritual compromise. Little evidence suggests that any systematic search had been made for them. The authorities appear to have relied on delation as the main weapon for subsequent detection. If inhabitants were poor, insignificant, and unobtrusive, they were unlikely to be the victims of delation. Even if they were delated, their few goods and personal insignificance hardly justified the expenditure of resources in dealing with them. Very many Christians were poor and insignificant, and thus many escaped. These were the *stantes,* the steadfast; they were the silent, and characteristic, heroes of the persecution of Decius.[103]

### THE VICTIMS

When a recusant was detected by or reported to a commission, when a well-known Christian was arrested by searching soldiers or was hounded by neighbors to sacrifice and publicly refused, when an enthusiastic Christian defiantly flaunted a refusal to comply, or when persons who had initially sacrificed subsequently presented themselves voluntarily in order to repudiate the earlier actions, then the task of the local officials was clear. After verifying the facts, and possibly putting some pressure on the recalcitrant to relent,[104] they referred the case to the local governor to deal with as he came on the rounds of his assize *conventus.* For however tempted they may have been to act beyond their authority, the matter was strictly beyond the legal competence of such minor magistrates; the penalties liable (which the edict may not have specified) could be capital. After an initial ordeal and confession, the Christian could face a period in prison, awaiting trial, that was followed by appearance before the governor's tribunal. At the trial, the judge might exercise his rightful discretion and dismiss the case,[105] or he might sentence the accused to some form of exile and confiscation of property. Because the empire preferred apostates (who honored the gods) to martyrs (who defied its authority), torture and further periods of imprisonment under conditions of varying stringency might also be employed. Under such circumstances, obstinacy might be repaid in the end by death in prison,[106] or, in relatively rare cases, by a death sentence, or by eventual dismissal as a hopeless case. Defiant Christians were not automati-

---

102. Copiosus episcoporum numerus, quos integros et incolumes fides sua et domini tutela protexit, Cypr. *Ep.* 55.6.1 (CCSL 3B:261.79-80).

103. Cypr. *Laps.* 3.

104. *Pas. Pion.* 15-18.

105. For some African instances see Cypr. *Ep.* 29.1.1 (Optatus); 38.1.1 (Aurelius); 21.4.2 (Saturninus); and for Rome, Cypr. *Ep.* 39.1.1-2 (Celerinus).

106. For example, Mappalicus, Cypr. *Ep.* 10.

cally punished with death. Christians were not being extirpated, but induced by variable means and at variable levels of intensity to conform, and, even then, some of those apprehended were simply dismissed in despair or contempt.

Cyprian's writings provide rich details that illuminate these events for Africa: flight, trials, exiles, confiscations, imprisonments, tortures, and a mob lynching.[107] All were there, to be sure, with their attendant fears and horrors; but deaths were relatively few, and none can be identified with certainty as the consequence of a legal condemnation. The best commentary is found in *Letter 22* in the Cyprian collection, which supplies all of the named victims (seventeen in total) except for the pair Castus and Aemilius, who died undergoing tortures and probably at this period.[108] Two of the prisoners are said to have died while being interrogated, and thirteen were starved to death. The writer, a confessor named Lucianus, expected to share the same fate.[109] This letter remains a humbling reminder of the haphazard nature of the evidence: had Cyprian not had occasion to include a copy of it with his correspondence, no detailed and personalized knowledge of the harsh realities of the sufferings being endured in Carthage would have been possible.[110]

To judge from the list of the victims provided, by no means can one say that all Christians "died in prisons dark, by dungeon, fire, and sword." Yet the memory of the nightmare, if not of the details of this persecution, lived vividly on, and understandably so.

Churches everywhere were left with the devastation of the fallen within their ranks. For Cyprian "the wild tempest had overwhelmed not only the majority of our laity," but "it had included in its destructive wake even a portion of the clergy."[111] In Smyrna not only had the bishop apostatized[112] along with many of the Christian brethren,[113] but Pionios was urged to obey and offer sacrifice like everyone else,[114] and the proconsul could declare that many others had of-

---

107. Cypr. *Ep.* 40.1.1.

108. Cypr. *Laps.* 13.

109. Et ideo, frater carissime, saluta Numeriam et Candidam, quas secundum Pauli praeceptum et ceterorum martyrum, quorum nomina subicio, Bassi in pignerario, Mappalici in quaestione, Fortunionis in carcerem: Paulus a quaestione, Fortunata, Victorinus, Victor, Herennius, Credula, Hereda, Donatus, Firmus, Venustas, Fructus, Iulia, Martialis et Ariston, qui deo volente in carcerem fame necati sunt; quorum et nos socios futuros intra dies audietis. Iam enim ut iterato reclusi sumus sunt dies octo in die quo tibi litteras scripsi. Cypr. *Ep.* 22.2.2 (CCSL 3B:118.32-41).

110. The letter was a response to Celerinus's petition that the confessors intercede for his two sisters, who had failed in Rome. It may have been provided to Cyprian by Celerinus himself, who later supported the bishop's rejection of the very privileges he was seeking. Cypr. *Ep.* 39.

111. Sed quoniam infesta tempestas, quae plebem nostram ex maxima parte prostrauit, hunc quoque addidit nostris doloribus cumulum ut etiam cleri portionem sua strage perstringeret. Cypr. *Ep.* 14.1.1 (CCSL 3B:79.4-7).

112. *Pas. Pion.* 15.2.

113. *Pas. Pion.* 12.2.

114. *Pas. Pion.* 4.1.

fered sacrifice and were alive.[115] Alexandria in turn saw many defections, especially among the more socially eminent, including those in official employ.[116] Smyrna and Alexandria might have been typical of the cities in at least the eastern empire. In Italy and Africa, whole communities were led by their bishops into apostasy,[117] and apostate bishops subsequently fought for reinstatement[118] or joined schismatic groups.[119] Decius's religious rally had left behind a long-lasting legacy of disorder and disarray within the Christian ranks. Bitter dissension over the proper conditions for readmitting the fallen divided the churches everywhere, and bishops were challenged for spiritual leadership by the surviving (and, by definition, inspirited) confessors.

## Persecution under Gallus

Dionysius, writing from Alexandria in the early 260s, addressed a festal (presumably Easter) letter to Hermammon and the brethren in Egypt. This was penned during "the peace of Gallienus."[120] It expanded on the congenial (but rhetorically unexceptional) theme that emperors enjoy peace, health, and prosperity (as, currently, did Gallienus) while they engage the favors and prayers of Christians but are beset with wars, plagues, and disasters when they persecute them.[121] Dionysius illustrated this interpretation of imperial history not only from the recent reigns of Decius, Valerian, and the Macriani, but also from the reign of Gallus, Decius's immediate successor (mid-251 to mid-253). Gallus was blessed — tendentiously — with an initial period when his reign progressed well and affairs went as he wished; subsequently he was unwise enough to drive away the "holy men" who were mediating before God for his peace and well-being. Consequently, when he banished them, he also banished their prayers on his behalf.[122]

After carefully clearing Egyptian Christians of any taint of complicity in the (by then defeated) cause of the Macriani, Dionysius concluded his whole argument that Gallienus had not persecuted like his predecessors and as a result was successfully completing his ninth year as emperor.[123]

Unfortunately, Dionysius left entirely unspecified the identity of the holy men and what precisely Gallus did to them when he is said to have "hounded

---

115. *Pas. Pion.* 20.3.
116. Eus. Caes. *Hist. eccl.* 6.41.11.
117. Cypr. *Ep.* 55.11.1-2 (Trofimus, in Italy); 59.10.3 (Repostus, in Africa Proconsularis).
118. Cypr. *Ep.* 65; 67.
119. Cypr. *Ep.* 59.10.2.
120. Eus. Caes. *Hist. eccl.* 7.22.12.
121. Eus. Caes. *Hist. eccl.* 7.1, 10, 22.12–23.4.
122. Eus. Caes. *Hist. eccl.* 7.1.
123. Eus. Caes. *Hist. eccl.* 7.23.4.

them out" and "banished" them. While such vagueness is not untypical of the panegyric mode in which his festal letters were couched, some named identities might have been expected if these heroes were Egyptian. Two candidates from overseas Rome can be supplied.

Cornelius, the Bishop of Rome, was exiled to Centumcellae (Cyprian did not know of his confession until late spring 253), and there he died while apparently still in office, at least before June 25, 253, which was the commencement date of his successor's pontificate. That successor, Lucius, was also promptly relegated upon his election to office, sharing his punishment with companions.[124] Cyprian could write not too long afterwards congratulating them on their release.[125] Their recall may possibly lie behind Valerian's much exaggerated reputation for initially regarding Christians with favor.[126] No information survives about the circumstances that gave rise to these relegations, but the periods of exile of these "holy men" would indeed have coincided with the collapse and downfall of Gallus's principate and would have lent credence to Dionysius's loaded version of history.

Elsewhere, in a letter written in the summer of the previous year, 252, Cyprian addressed Cornelius (at that time still in Rome) as leading a church he regarded at the time as greatly flourishing — i.e., not threatened with difficulties.[127] Yet Cyprian had this to say of himself: "In recent days, also, just as I am writing this letter to you, there has been once again popular outcry in the circus for me to be thrown to the lion: this has been occasioned by the sacrifices that the people have been ordered by a public edict to celebrate."[128] Obviously Cornelius (the addressee) and the Roman church were not affected in the troubles, which were a local outburst, and the edict was presumably proclaimed by the local proconsul. The order might have been for a public expiation against the plague, at a ceremony in the circus. The notable absence of the leader of the Christians, who were popularly blamed for the visitation of the plague through their failure to worship "Roman gods," enraged the crowd.[129]

The following year, 253, the Christians of Carthage had anxious premonitions of a threatened persecution, manifested by frequent ominous signs and minatory visions,[130] but, so far as we know, these apprehensions were never actualized. The letters in which the warning was given are datable to May 253, ·

124. Cypr. *Ep.* 61.1.1.

125. Cypr. *Ep.* 61.

126. As witnessed by Dionysius of Alexandria in the same — tendentious — festal letter to Hermammon, Eus. Caes. *Hist. eccl.* 7.10.3.

127. Cypr. *Ep.* 59.19.

128. his ipsis etiam diebus quibus has ad te litteras feci ob sacrificia quae edicto proposito celebrare populus iubebatur clamore popularium ad leonem denuo postulatus in circo. Cypr. *Ep.* 59.6.1 (CCSL 3C:347.165-67).

129. See, for example, Cypr. *Demet.* 2, 5.

130. Cypr. *Ep.* 57; 58.

at the onset of another summer, bringing with it the threat of further deaths in Carthage by the devastating plague — and the prospect of similar terrifying scenes in the circus of Carthage.[131]

No other church reported similar troubles. Lactantius notably failed to dilate on any "persecution of Gallus," though it would have been congenial to his theme.[132] There are no indicators of a "persecution of Gallus," or a continuation of Decius's edict. Instead, the evidence reflects the intermittent local troubles and isolated incidents to which especially prominent church leaders were constantly liable under the stress of local circumstances, especially at a particular season of social and political instability and insecurity. Because of their unnerving experiences under Decius, however, this was a time of heightened apprehensions for many Christians, and particularly so in Africa.

## Persecution under Valerian and Gallienus, 257-260 c.e.

So far as can be judged, Valerian and Gallienus started off their principate with a tolerant attitude towards Christians. This was probably not a delicately modulated policy but simply the consequence of other and more pressing matters of state commanding their attention.[133] That did not mean, however, that Christians were assured of going unmolested. They were still individually liable to hostile attack. For example, a papyrus of February 28, 256,[134] reveals orders to arrest from the Egyptian village of Mermertha one "Petosorapis, son of Horus, Christian." That wording could mean that the man's Christianity provided the grounds for his arrest. In the course of the following year, as the regime approached the completion of its first quinquennium, that laissez-faire imperial attitude was modified. The date is summer of that year, 257; the orders conveyed to the proconsul in Africa by imperial *litterae* were implemented on August 30 in Carthage.[135] While the precise and immediate circumstances that may have triggered the dispatch of these *litterae* remain unknown, two precious documents convey more generally the official reasoning that lay behind them.

### DIONYSIUS OF ALEXANDRIA

Dionysius, Bishop of Alexandria, in the course of defending his actions under persecution against defamation from a brother bishop named Germanus, had occasion to quote the official court records of his trial before Aemilianus (at the

131. See the contemporary descriptions in Cypr. *Mort.* 14; Pont. *Vita Cypr.* 9.
132. Lact. *Mort.* 4-5.
133. See Dionysius in Eus. Caes. *Hist. eccl.* 7.10.3.
134. *P.Oxy.* XLII.3035.
135. *Act. Procon.* 1.1.

time vice-prefect of Egypt) in Alexandria. He was accompanied by a presbyter, three deacons, and a visitor from Rome. Dionysius claimed for Christians the right to worship only the god in whom they believed. Aemilianus exiled the group to Cephro in Libya and forbade them to hold Christian assemblies or to enter the cemeteries.[136] The official concerns were two: that worship be given to known gods who preserved the empire; and that public conformity in religion be displayed as part of the process of winning that preservation of the state. The "unnatural" gods and "unnatural" religious assemblies of Christians were, as a corollary, to be forbidden. Dionysius's attempt to sidestep the imperial demands is telling: Christians were already praying without ceasing for the continued security of the empire, and to the one God that mattered. Thus both sides understood the underlying objective to be maintaining peace with the divine. Both sides also appear to have agreed in closely interpreting the course of contemporary history theologically.

### CYPRIAN

The court records (dated August 30, 257) of Cyprian's appearance before the proconsul in Carthage are also preserved. The proconsul Paternus demanded that Cyprian participate in the Roman religious rites. Cyprian refused to do so but explained that he did pray to the one, true God for the well-being of the emperors. He was ordered into exile at Curubis. When asked to name his clergy, Cyprian explained that Paternus would easily find them himself: Roman law prohibited informers, and Christian practice forbade voluntary surrender. A general warning not to hold meetings or enter the cemeteries concluded the proceedings.[137]

The same stress on public conformity in acceptable ritual action can be discerned in the proconsul's statements. Cyprian's defensive insistence that Christians pray without ceasing for the well-being of the emperors' persons indicates what he too perceived to be the imperial motivation behind that stress on ritual conformity. Only the higher clerical orders, those involved in performing the "unnatural" Christian rituals, were targeted, and Christians' ritual assemblies themselves and their sacred grounds were proscribed. The imperial administrators seem increasingly concerned that Christian rituals, far from being merely harmless aberrations, were positively offensive to the "natural gods."

The implementation of these orders is exemplified in Africa by the exile of Cyprian (to Curubis) and of the bishops Agapius and Secundinus in Numidia.[138] Much will have depended on the initiative and zeal of the individual governor,

136. Eus. Caes. *Hist. eccl.* 7.11.6-19.
137. *Act. Procon.* 1.
138. *Pas. Mar. Iac.* 3.

the eminence of those local clerics too much in the public eye to allow them to be overlooked, and popular hostility against Christians in a particular area, which led to the reporting of Christian law-breaking or the whereabouts of Christian clergy. Numidia again reveals the hardships and ordeals that could confront clergy and laity as a result. Cyprian's correspondence discloses the exile and condemnation to the mines of nine named bishops, along with presbyters and deacons, together with laity (including women and children):[139] deaths had already occurred.[140] The surviving version of Gallienus's rescript of toleration also implies that Christian places of worship and cemetery grounds might have been subject to sequestration.[141] The imperial attack had shifted from individuals to the corporate life and property of the Christian communities.

### FURTHER IMPLEMENTATION

Subsequently the Roman senate appears to have written to Valerian, then in the East, requesting clarification and guidance in the implementation of the imperial orders. Cyprian summarized the contents of the imperial reply. Christian bishops, presbyters, and deacons were to be executed immediately. High-ranking laymen were initially to lose their status and property, and to be executed if they persisted. Matrons were to be dispossessed and exiled. Members of the imperial staff were to lose their property and sent to work as prisoners on agricultural estates.[142]

The fact that the Senate had written to the emperor requesting guidance in dealing with prominently recalcitrant Christians (whether notables of the church or of society and of Caesar's own household) suggests that conscientious enemies of Christianity could be found within the conservative upper social circles of Rome: Valerian himself need have been no different. The virulence is reflected in orders requiring the recall and retrial of clergy already sentenced in the first stage. Thus the African bishops Agapius and Secundinus were brought back from exile to their execution,[143] as was Cyprian himself. Harsher treatment was meted out to already confessed (and presumably sentenced) members of the imperial staff. The emperors and their agents had decided that Christian religious leaders should be extirpated and that Christians in positions of prominence must not appear to repudiate "Roman ceremonies" with impunity. The proconsul in Africa, putting into effect the new ordinances on September 14, 258, in Carthage, may have echoed some of the phrases in the preamble of the imperial rescript itself. He denounced Cyprian for leading

139. Cypr. *Ep.* 76-79.
140. Cypr. *Ep.* 76.1.2.
141. Eus. Caes. *Hist. eccl.* 7.13.1.
142. Cypr. *Ep.* 80.1.2.
143. *Pas. Mar. Iac.* 2.5–3.7.

a conspiracy in opposition to the "Roman gods and to their sacred rites." Since the emperors had "been unable to bring him back to the observance of their sacred rituals," he was ordered to be executed immediately.[144]

For the Roman governing circles, at least, it still remained incomprehensible that Roman citizens should fail so conspicuously in their civic duty of honoring their Roman gods and observing their sacred rites. The traditional mode of thinking focused on "civic duties" rather than "civil rights." Cyprian, himself of the local curial aristocracy but now a Christian bishop, highlighted this clash of perceived duties and theological stances. So Cyprian confronted his executioner on September 14, 258, and became the proto-episcopal martyr in Africa (as his biographer, somewhat tendentiously, claimed).[145]

Unusually rich testimony for the implementation of Valerian's rescript elsewhere in the African provinces has survived. For Africa Proconsularis, the *Passio* of Montanus and Lucius records the deaths in prison of two recently baptized Christians;[146] of a presbyter, Victor;[147] of Quartillosa, her husband and her son;[148] of Bishop Successus, Paulus, and their companions;[149] as well as of Lucius, Montanus, Flavianus, Julianus, and Victoricus (presumably all clerics). For Numidia, the *Passio* of Marian and James reports many in prison (in Cirta) to be sent on eventually for trial (and death) before the governor at Lambaesis: altogether there were the bishops Agapius and Secundinus;[150] the deacon James, the lector Marian, along with others of the clergy;[151] lay martyrs,[152] including Aemilianus, an equestrian, and Tertulla and Antonia.[153] If the "titles of glory" annotated against the names of the African bishops in the *Judgments of the Eighty-seven Bishops* from a year earlier are to be trusted, five subsequently became "martyr," seven "confessor and martyr," and no fewer than twenty-four "confessor."[154]

The terms of Valerian's rescript to the Senate in 258 gave rise to a deeply divisive and bloody conflict. Eusebius reported how that division and conflict was

---

144. Diu sacrilega mente uixisti et plurimos nefariae tibi conspirationis homines adgregasti et inimicum te diis Romanis et religionibus sacris constituisti, nec te pii et sacratissimi principes Valerianus et Gallienus Augusti et Valerianus nobilissimus Caesar ad sectam caeremoniarum suarum reuocare poterunt. *Act. Procon.* 4; CSEL 3.3: cxii.23–cxiii.5.

145. Cyprianus . . . sacerdotales coronas in Africa primus imbueret . . . ex quo enim Carthagini episcopatus ordo numeratur, numquam aliquis quamvis ex bonis et sacerdotibus ad passionem venisse memoratur. Pont. *Vita Cypr.* 19; CSEL 3.3: cix.18-23.

146. Primolus and Donatianus, *Pas. Mont. Luc.* 2.

147. *Pas. Mont. Luc.* 7.2.

148. *Pas. Mont. Luc.* 8.

149. *Pas. Mont. Luc.* 21.8.

150. *Pas. Mont. Luc.* 3.

151. *Pas. Mont. Luc.* 10; 11.3.

152. *Pas. Mont. Luc.* 5.10; 9; 10.

153. *Pas. Mont. Luc.* 11.

154. On the "titles of glory," see G. F. Diercks, "Les tituli gloriae," in CCSL 3E:xli-xlii.

resolved: Valerian was captured and enslaved by barbarians; his son, Gallienus, immediately put an end to the persecution.[155] Valerian's ignominious capture is best dated to early summer 260. Eusebius certainly placed the imperial edicts revoking the previous orders against Christians as an immediate reaction to the disaster. This theological reading of the dire event by the imperial authorities may have been Eusebius's own interpretation. No doubt prudential counsels were also proffered against exacerbating internal strife and divisions (as Valerian's second rescript had been doing) in an empire that must have seemed at the time perilously fragmenting.

Too much might be made of Gallienus's ordinance: in strict legality Christians were only returned to their status before Valerian's orders were issued — that is, they were still potentially liable, as Christians, to fall foul of the law. In revoking those earlier orders and by that very act positively permitting unmolested Christian worship, however, Gallienus in effect also conceded a major degree of official tolerance: some forty years of relative peace for the churches then followed from this significant move. To those minds inclined to read the events of 257-260 theologically, the Christians' god may finally have appeared to be a god of vengeful power, a power to be treated with the same caution due Rome's protectors. The realities of the civil place of the Christian churches within the social organization of the empire had at last come to be officially recognized: a growing church would be a familiar, if still minor, presence in very many communities (especially urban) in Africa, as elsewhere.

## DISCIPLINARY AND DOCTRINAL DISPUTES

Civil peace did not ensure internal peace within the Christian communities. In 251, when the persecution of Decius had died down,[156] the churches everywhere were faced with the vexatious issue of penitential discipline. How were they to treat the large numbers who had apostatized in one way or another under the persecution? Working guidelines had been drawn up, where circumstances allowed, for dealing on a temporary basis with the urgent cases of the dying[157] until collegiate resolutions were possible. The remarkable feature discernible in many churches of the time, though, is the habit of conciliar consultation, which the stirring ecclesiastical events of the 250s disclose everywhere. It was a reflex that must have become habitual over the preceding half-century or so.

Only tantalizing glimpses can be caught of earlier conciliar decisions taken in North Africa itself. They dealt with a wide spectrum of issues: the treatment

---

155. Eus. Caes. *Hist. eccl.* 7.13.
156. Cypr. *Ep.* 55.6.1.
157. For example, Cypr. *Ep.* 20.2-3.

of adulterers,[158] the question of "re-baptism,"[159] down to quite minor general regulations.[160] Though the view is partial, it makes clear that a pattern of regular consultation and conciliar resolution over major issues of discipline and doctrine had been well-established in North Africa before the 250s.

Before Easter of 251, invitations had gone out to North African bishops to attend a council in Carthage.[161] No doubt the bishops were given some indication in advance of the major items to be discussed and were themselves given the opportunity to raise questions for resolution.[162] Cyprian, as Bishop of Carthage, appears to have been in charge of arranging such matters.[163] After celebrating the great Easter festival with their own people,[164] bishops set out on their journey to Carthage, accompanied perhaps by one or two of their presbyters and deacons.[165] The attendance figures are unknown, but on a number of occasions Cyprian stressed the generous tally of venerable bishops who gave their approval to the resolutions passed in this year.[166] Absentees would receive copies of the conciliar resolutions after the meeting itself was over.[167] And while it is clear that the bishops were the ones who sat in debate and passed those resolutions,[168] their attendant presbyters and deacons and a large body of the laity were present as well.[169] The assemblies could run into the several hundreds. The physical and financial resources of the church in Carthage must have been significant to house and care for the delegates.

The bishops so assembled in Carthage were faced with pressing and urgent questions. Some were disciplinary: they confirmed the excommunication of the party of Felicissimus and the five rebel presbyters in Carthage who had admitted the lapsed to communion without requiring formal repentance;[170] they expelled two lapsed bishops who had allied themselves with the heretical church of Privatus of Lambaesis in Numidia;[171] and they confirmed the removal of a lapsed bishop who refused to submit to penitence.[172] The central issues of penitence for apostates (in their various grades) most exercised the bishops. Cyprian's *Letter* 55 helpfully rehearses those resolutions and the reasoning that lay behind them

158. Cypr. *Ep.* 55.21.1.
159. Cypr. *Ep.* 70.1.2; 71.4.1; 73.3.1, the heretical church of Privatus, Cypr. *Ep.* 59.10.1.
160. Cypr. *Ep.* 1.1.1, 1.2.1 — clerics not to be nominated as legal guardians or trustees.
161. Cypr. *Ep.* 43.7.2.
162. Cypr. *Ep.* 56.3; 64.
163. Cypr. *Ep.* 56.3.
164. Cypr. *Ep.* 56.3.
165. Cypr. *Ep.* 59.15.1.
166. Cypr. *Ep.* 55.6.1; 59.1.1.
167. Cypr. *Ep.* 55.6.1.
168. Cypr. *Ep.* 59.14.2.
169. As later, *Sent. proem.*
170. Cypr. *Ep.* 59.1.1, 9.1.
171. Cypr. *Ep.* 59.10.2.
172. Repostus of Satunurca, Cypr. *Ep.* 59.10.3.

for an African bishop who was not in attendance. Cyprian makes clear the nature and the outcome of the debate: it was a "healthy compromise"[173] between the extremes of unrealistic rigorism and polluting laxity. The debate itself was no mere formality: its quality, earnest concerns, and high seriousness emerge clearly and impressively from the summary presented in *Letter 55*. Cyprian, for one, would appear to have changed his mind significantly as a result of it, moving substantially away from the severe program he had announced only weeks earlier in his formal tractate, *On the Lapsed*. There he had provided no hint of the special concessions to the *libellatici* that were approved as a major resolution of this council.[174] Indeed, in *Letter 55*, he was obliged openly and at length to defend that shift in stance, by then plainly visible and under criticism.[175] Copies of these important resolutions were promptly communicated to Rome.[176] It would be reasonable to assume that copies would also find their way to churches in Spain and Gaul that would later communicate with Cyprian about implementing similar policies.[177] All the churches there were confronted with the identical problems. Cyprian could later claim the support of the Italian council meeting under Cornelius: its resolutions on the penitential question harmonized with those of the Africans.[178] Cornelius, in turn, included in the dossier he dispatched over to Fabius in Antioch copies of the minutes of both the Italian and the African councils of 251.[179] In this way the findings of this African council would have been disseminated widely in turn among the eastern churches, since Fabius was in active communication with the major churches there.[180] Despite the tyranny of long distances and the delays in hazardous communications, the churches everywhere were busily seeking to keep in close contact and, if possible, harmonious step with one another. They freely exchanged their own views and passed on those of others, putting especial weight upon resolutions that had been approved by bishops meeting together in council.

In the following year, 252, an African council was certainly in session at Carthage on the Ides of May.[181] It firmly rejected Privatus's attempt to have his case reconsidered, and a list was drawn up of the orthodox bishops in North Africa (tainted neither by lapse nor heresy) that was sent over to Cornelius in Rome for his guidance and information.[182] As likely as not this council was attended by sixty-six bishops, who resolved on two matters drawn to their atten-

173. Cypr. *Ep.* 55.6.1.
174. For details, see pp. 321-22.
175. Cypr. *Ep.* 55.3.2–7.3.
176. Cypr. *Ep.* 55.6.2.
177. Cypr. *Ep.* 67; 68 — he has received a copy or synopsis of at least one conciliar document from Gaul in *Ep.* 68.1.1.
178. Cypr. *Ep.* 55.6.2.
179. Eus. Caes. *Hist. eccl.* 6.43.3.
180. Eus. Caes. *Hist. eccl.* 6.46.3.
181. Cypr. *Ep.* 59.10.1.
182. Cypr. *Ep.* 59.9.3.

tion by Bishop Fidus, who was unable to attend. These were a violation of the new penitential regulations drawn up the previous year and the propriety of baptizing newborn infants before the eighth day. The bishops resolved these matters; they were both plainly conscious of the weight of their collective authority and fully aware of their powers to police the regulations they had established in council.[183]

Fidus had signified in a letter to his fellow bishops points that were disturbing him and thus would become, he expected, items on the council agenda of 252. In a similar way, six bishops wrote to Cyprian about an anomalous penitential case and requested that he discuss the matter fully with many of his colleagues.[184] Cyprian promised that a firm ruling would be reached at the meeting of bishops that was to be convened after the Easter celebration was over. This would have been the Council of 253, attended by forty-two bishops drawn heavily from proconsular sees and largely from districts not too far distant from Carthage.[185] Haste and apprehension may have limited the size and distribution of this attendance. The question of relaxing penitential rigor for the lapsed demanded quick and urgent resolution in the face of a feared renewal of persecution.[186] Carthage was a city doubly to be avoided: it had not only persecution but plague hanging over its crowded alleyways. The smaller assembly of bishops manifested no sense at all of any diminution in the authority of their collective decisions. They wrote *Letter* 57 to inform Cornelius that they had profoundly modified the agreed policy by readmitting to communion all remaining penitent lapsed. No further matters that were discussed are known: after reaching this conclusion, the bishops may have dispersed promptly in order to get back to their own threatened flocks and to prepare, if need be, for battle or for flight. Cyprian himself proceeded to cancel his planned trip to Thibari so as not to be any distance or length of time away from his own people.[187]

Councils were proving themselves to be a vital instrument for reaching settlement on vexatious disputes. Up to this point, meetings in different parts of the empire had reached — independently or by consultation — similar decisions on the most pressing issues. A question still remained to be faced: What was to be done when such regional councils came to sharply divergent conclusions?

This conflict arose shortly afterwards over the question of "re-baptizing" heretics and schismatics. By the year 252, Cyprian had to face the affront that in his own city, as a consequence of conflict over the penitential regime, two rival bishops had been installed, one rigorist, the other laxist. Over in Rome, Cornelius had to contend with a rigorist anti-bishop, Novatian. The two rigorist groups, moreover, were coordinating their attacks on the concessions made

183. Cypr. *Ep.* 64.
184. Cypr. *Ep.* 56.
185. Cypr. *Ep.* 57.
186. See above, pp. 20-22.
187. Cypr. *Ep.* 58.1.1.

to the penitent lapsed. It was not long before the question was to be raised: Did converts from these sects, when they wished to join the "mainstream" church, stand in need of its efficacious baptism? This question raised a series of fundamental issues: the location of the Holy Spirit, who was empowered to bestow that Spirit, the boundaries of the church as an exclusive source of salvation, the essential purity of the church preserved free from pollution, and the role of local church traditions in determining common discipline.[188] The high seriousness and intensity with which this issue was debated is revealed in a veritable flurry of correspondence[189] and the calling of no fewer than three African council meetings to discuss the matter.[190] In opposition, Stephen of Rome staunchly defended his own church's hallowed traditions against African innovation. His tactics managed to estrange not only Egyptian[191] but also eastern bishops.[192] Stephen abused Cyprian as being "a bogus Christ, a bogus apostle, and a crooked dealer."[193] Regional church councils had indeed reached sharply divergent views.

## CHRISTIAN LITERATURE

Documentary and literary evidence proves the existence of third-century church-houses, meeting halls, *areae* (burial grounds), and *martyria* (shrines) in Africa, but they are all lost. Church buildings would have been razed everywhere during the Great Persecution.[194] Lost as well was the evidence for practices that might have been read from the nature and appearance of Christian building complexes, cemeterial structures, and martyrs' shrines, along with their decorative schemes and symbols, from baptisteries and the liturgical spaces, from episcopal *cathedrae,* presbyter seating, the lector's raised pulpit, ecclesiastical altars, liturgical vessels, and vestments. The *realia* of third-century Christian life in Africa are beyond recall. What does survive, in compensation, is a remarkable body of literature that illuminates the rich intellectual and spiritual lives of third-century African Christians.

One category of church writing continued from the second-century tradition and can be construed as a process of self-definition as Christians endeav-

188. For details, see below, pp. 187-89.

189. Witnessed by Cypr. *Ep.* 69-75.

190. See Cypr. *Ep.* 70; 72 and the special muster of 87 signatories at the meeting of September 256.

191. Dionysius, in Eus. Caes. *Hist. eccl.* 7.5.3-6.

192. Cypr. *Ep.* 75 from Firmilian of Caesarea in Cappadocia.

193. Cyprianum pseudochristum et pseudoapostolum et dolosum operarium dicere. *Ep.* 75.25.4 (CCSL 3C:603.508-9).

194. For the evidence, see L. Michael White, *The Social Origins of Christian Architecture* (Valley Forge, Pa.: Trinity Press, 1996).

ored to delineate their own particular identity with all its attendant ambiguities. They wished at the same time to be distinguished from and to participate in their Greco-Roman society. They wished to inherit as part of their patrimony the Jewish scriptures but at the same time to distinguish themselves from their Jewish brethren with whom they shared these same texts and this same past. They wished to define their ("orthodox") doctrine and practice in opposition to myriad Christian variations they represented as breakaway sects and deviant heresies — with most of whom, however, they shared a great deal in common.

Achieving this identity in separation was the task of apologetic writers, well represented in Africa across the century by Tertullian, Minucius Felix, Cyprian, and then Arnobius and Lactantius. Their writings show an increasing tendency to represent Christians as morally ideal members of Greco-Roman society, attaining in practice the philosophically approved virtues to which pagans merely aspired in theory. While they uniformly rejected crude polytheistic idolatry, they asserted a theological monotheism with which, philosophically, many non-Christians might have had much sympathy. It nevertheless remains unclear how far these works merely satisfied the sense of self for a Christian readership — or reached beyond, to a non-Christian audience. It may be significant that in the Greek East, where Christianity appeared as the century progressed increasingly more established as an accepted constituent of society, no urgent need was felt to produce this particular category of literature beyond the middle of the third century (after Origen's response to Celsus). Methodius revived the genre in responding specifically to the polemic of Porphyry (now lost) and Eusebius of Caesarea to both that of Hierocles as well as that of Porphyry (in several voluminous works).

This apologetic endeavor can also be viewed as part of a wider movement towards the cultural accommodation of Christianity to its Greco-Roman setting and away from its Semitic origins. Re-formulating and re-presenting Christianity in Hellenic terms and in acceptable Greco-Roman rhetorical discourse was a process vital for the long-term survival of Christianity in its adopted setting. The Christian literary output of third-century Africa ought to be regarded, therefore, not so much as separable from the mainstream of the contemporary Greco-Roman rhetorical culture but rather as a significant constituent of that culture, itself in the process of transformation.

Another type of literature continued from the second century was the *Adversus Judaeos* genre, again represented in Africa by works of Tertullian and the anonymous *Against the Jews*.[195] Less was written on this theme in the contemporary Greek East, possibly because there the Jewish Diaspora was more comfortably integrated into its social setting and may have been perceived by Christians less as a dramatic threat. Even so, Christians felt a manifest urge to establish a separable identity and to lay claims to the inheritance of the bib-

---

195. CSEL 3.3:133-46.

lical past. In both regions the output in the *Adversus Haereses* genre showed no diminution. It was most voluminous against individual leaders, doctrines, and sects, whether in specific treatises (Tertullian being particularly prolific) or in the flurry of epistolary exchanges and conciliar debates and resolutions, which were richly documented in the corpus of the Cyprianic correspondence, *Judgments of the Eighty-seven Bishops,* and the anonymous *On Rebaptism.* Such polemic and controversy was frequently the vehicle for arriving at dogmatic definition — this was a religion in which (right) *belief* was a crucial feature. To judge by the literary output, this activity would seem to have been much more an obsession with Christian writers than martyrdom or persecution ever was. The chance survival of Origen's *Discussion with Heracleides* provides a particularly illuminating and lively vignette of this characteristic preoccupation of the third-century church. Africa was no exception.

To be sure, the potential threat of persecution, under which Christians lived their third-century lives, clearly waxed and waned, given the record of what can be reconstructed of events, but it is difficult to assess in what way such a threat (erratic or not) may have psychologically impinged on Christians' daily consciousness. Here and there, particularly after the 250s, there would be surviving confessors — especially enrolled among the clergy — to remind communities of the stark realities of persecution. Certainly the output of protreptic literature on martyrdom can be traced to periods of actual or perceived persecution. Indeed, they are often the major source of information, notably the works of Tertullian at the beginning of the century and Cyprian in the 250s. Even if the theology of martyrdom scarcely progressed beyond that of the second century, the supreme religious valuation placed on confession and martyrdom produced other forms of popular literature. Heroic martyr-acts, some much closer to the forensic protocols than others, circulated widely. In this, Africa was peculiarly productive. While there are non-Christian predecessors to this genre, much stimulus was gained by the self-awareness of the confessors themselves. They were alert to the fact that they would be remembered liturgically on their anniversaries and that their inspirited dreams, words, and deeds would be popularly recalled as models of Christian heroism year after year. Out of Africa also came the first Christian biography, Pontius's *Life of Cyprian,* which was stimulated precisely because the subject was, as the work proudly proclaims, the proto-episcopal martyr of Africa. Soon this genre would spawn fourth-century narratives of ascetic lives, the mirror image of third-century martyrs' lives. Persecution may well have loomed larger in the mind than the historical phenomena may seem to have warranted, but this literature should nevertheless be read against a background of many other activities.

All those tracts and homilies directed towards the moral life and spiritual guidance of Christians that occupied so much of the literary effort of Tertullian and Cyprian (exemplifying the strong pastoral bent of western churchmanship) were not the productions characteristic of a beleaguered church, panicked before persecuting demons. In all their pages of exhortations, injunctions to go out and preach to the heathen are conspicuously absent; this was a church driven not by a missionary imperative to incorporate those outside, but rather by the urge to build up the moral probity and spiritual status of the Christian assembly.

Finally, it must be recalled that so much ecclesiastical life was conducted around the Mediterranean by means of correspondence, whether by routine letters of communion (and excommunication), letters recognizing new bishops, encyclical reports of synods and councils, the exchange of ideas (and disagreements), and (at least from Alexandria) regular festal letters announcing the date of Easter. So much has been lost. For example, Eusebius was able to compile a collection of over a hundred letters by Origen:[196] only two are now extant, one to Gregory Thaumaturgus, and one to Julius Africanus. Of Gregory's own correspondence,[197] only the *Canonical Epistle* survives; and of Julius Africanus's letters but two examples, one of which is fragmentary. Thanks to Eusebius's *Church History,* books six and seven, there have been preserved fragments of most (but not entirely all) of the great epistolary output of Dionysius of Alexandria and one brief letter. Thereafter, for example, there still exist only scraps of all of the papal correspondence throughout the century, one letter of Firmilian of Cappadocian Caesarea, in Latin translation,[198] three letters attributed to Novatian,[199] one brief letter and some fragments from Peter of Alexandria, and the letter of the four Egyptian bishops. These few remains make all the more precious the collection of over eighty documents associated with Cyprian of Carthage to remind us both of what has been lost and of the vigor of life in this level of ecclesiastical society. It is a sobering thought that the historical understanding of third-century church life would be transformed were other decades illumined in the same lively light as the single decade of Cyprian's life as a Christian in Carthage.

It distorts perceptions of third-century Christians to leave them in constant fear of persecuting dungeons, fire and sword. Other serious matters also preoccupied their minds and engaged their energies.

196. Eus. Caes. *Hist. eccl.* 6.36.3.
197. Hieron. *Vir. ill.* 65.
198. Cypr. *Ep.* 75.
199. Cypr. *Ep.* 30, 31, 36.

# CHAPTER 2

# The Christian Imperial Period: Diocletian to the Vandals

This survey of Africa under the Christian Roman Empire does not begin with the accession of Constantine but rather with that of Diocletian in 284. Diocletian's tenure was the bridge uniting the political and religious past with the events of the early fourth century. His reign, especially the persecutions of 303-305, provided the impetus for many of the events and disputes of the fourth and fifth centuries; thus, this portion of the history of Christianity in North Africa begins with a summary of Diocletian's reforms of the late third century. This part of the story covers the end of the persecutions, the establishment of Christianity, the internecine rivalries of various Christian sects, and the arrival of the Vandals, which resulted in Arian persecution of Catholics. The period ends with the Vandal Geiseric's gaining control of Carthage in 439.

## FROM DIOCLETIAN TO CONSTANTINE

### Diocletian's Reforms

Diocletian inherited a vast empire, stretching from Hadrian's Wall in England and the coast of modern Portugal in the west all the way to the Black Sea and Syria in the east, from the Rhine to the upper reaches of the Nile. In an effort to stabilize such a large area, he initiated fiscal, political, and religious reforms.[1] First, in the area of finances, he reformed taxation systems, put a lid on inflation, and instituted price controls. Politically, he labored to enforce Roman hegemony at the peripheries of the empire. The frontiers were a source of concern for Rome.

---

1. For a survey of Diocletian's reforms, see Stephen Williams, *Diocletian and the Roman Recovery* (New York: Methuen, 1985), chap. 6.

During the late third century, Mauri, Baquates, Gaetuli, and other tribes pushed northward into Roman Africa.[2] In response, Rome committed more troops to the *limes* (i.e., the frontiers), and tried to enlist native tribes of the area as allies. Unlike the northern frontiers along the Danube or the Rhine, however, the frontier south of the African provinces was never completely stable.[3]

Second, in order to facilitate fiscal reforms, Diocletian restructured the empire's internal boundaries by reforming the political structure. He divided the empire into halves, each governed by a senior emperor titled Augustus and assisted by a junior called Caesar. This four-person arrangement, dubbed the Tetrarchy, was designed to lessen the burden on a single person, provide closer control of affairs in East and West, and provide for a smoother transition of power, with a Caesar serving an apprenticeship before becoming an Augustus. Mirroring the division of the entire empire was the redistricting of provinces into smaller entities which would be easier to manage. A century earlier under the Severans, Africa had been divided into the central province of Africa Proconsularis, with Numidia split off in the west and Cyrene to the east. Under Diocletian, the territory was divided into seven provinces. The two provinces of Africa Proconsularis and Cyrene were divided into three: Africa Proconsularis, Byzacena, and Tripolitana. Numidia was broken into two: Numidia Cirtensis in the north and Numidia Militiana in the south. Mauretania Sitifensis and Mauretania Caesariensis formed the western flank of Africa, though they remained a single ecclesiastical province until 393, when Sitifensis was accorded its own primate bishop. The westernmost portion, Mauretania Tingitana, was attached to Hispania for ease of administration.[4] In 314 Constantine reunited the two parts of Numidia. An eastern strip of the civil province of Numidia — the area including Hippo Regius, Thagaste, and Calama — was reincorporated into Africa Proconsularis. The ecclesiastical provinces tended to follow the boundaries of the imperial provinces, except that the eastern strip of Numidia remained part of the ecclesiastical province of Numidia rather than being joined into Proconsularis.[5] These redistributions supported Romanization and effective collection of taxes. For imperial personnel stationed in the provinces, the administration of the ill-defined frontiers became easier as each portion of the *limes,* separately defended, became shorter.

Civil affairs in Africa Proconsularis were administered by the proconsul,

2. René Cagnat, *L'armée romaine d'Afrique et l'occupation militaire de l'Afrique sous les empereurs* (Paris: Leroux, 1913), 69; Christian Courtois, *Les Vandales et l'Afrique* (Paris: Arts et métiers graphiques, 1955), 66. On the constant renegotiation of frontier politics, see Brent D. Shaw, "Autonomy and Tribute: Mountain and Plain in Mauretania Tingitana," *Revue de l'Occident musulman et de la Méditeranée* 41-42 (1987): 66-89.

3. Courtois, *Les Vandales et l'Afrique,* 67.

4. For an overview of the various divisions of the Mauretanias and their gradual reconquest from the Vandals and others by the Byzantine Empire, see R. Bruce Hirchner, "Mauritania," *Oxford Dictionary of Byzantium* (New York: Oxford University Press, 1991), 1318-1319.

5. Jean-Louis Maier, *Le dossier du donatisme,* 2 vols. (Berlin: Akademie Verlag, 1987), 1:26.

who reported directly to the emperor. Each of the other provinces in Africa was administered by a governor who was responsible to the vicar, who reported to the emperor through the praetorian prefect for Italy. Occasionally a praetorian prefect was assigned to Africa and resided at Carthage.[6]

Military affairs were under the jurisdiction of different officers: the *magister pedium* and the *magister equitum,* respectively commanders of foot soldiers and cavalry. At the end of the fourth century, these offices were regularly united in one person who exercised decisive influence in the government as well as commanding the military. In Africa a *comes* or count was responsible for military units that were not assigned to the frontier. These officers regularly revolted against the emperor and attempted to establish independent control over the whole of Africa.[7]

In addition to the regular civil and military officials, emperors occasionally appointed special emissaries for particular duties. The office of notary began in the early fourth century as court stenographer. Notaries kept the rolls of civil officials and might have been appointed for special tasks involved with the dispersal of government funds.[8] By the middle of the century, the office had evolved into a much more significant appointment. The imperial notaries Paul and Macarius, for example, were sent by the emperors Constans and Constantius in 346-48 to determine which of the competing Christian groups would receive imperial subsidies. An *executor* was another special emissary, sent to enforce legal judgments. Flavius Marcellinus, tribune and notary, was assigned this position when he presided at the Conference of Carthage in 411, where Caecilianist and Donatist bishops debated which party represented the true church in Africa. He ruled against the Donatists and enforced the legislation which had been held in abeyance during the attempt at reconciliation. Dulcitius, a tribune, was sent by Honorius and Arcadius to Africa in about 420 as an *executor,* charged with forcing the Donatists to turn over the property that had been remanded to the Caecilianists.[9]

The third area of reform for Diocletian was religion. He required participation in traditional Roman religions and the cult of the emperor to establish and strengthen provincial loyalty to the central government. Manichees, practitioners of a dualistic religion that originated in Persia, were considered political subversives — traitors, even — because the Persian court was favoring that religion during the waning days of the fourth century. Because of their religious

6. Maier, *Le dossier du donatisme,* 1:24-29. The province of Asia was also administered by a proconsul.

7. See A. H. M. Jones, *The Later Roman Empire, 284-602: A Social, Economic, and Administrative Survey* (Baltimore: Johns Hopkins University Press, 1986), 97, 124-25, 175-78, 183-85, 341-42, 366-75.

8. Jones, *The Later Roman Empire,* 203, 372-76.

9. Aug. *Ep.* 204.

exclusivism and growing numbers, Christians were also targets of this program, which used traditional religious practice to demonstrate loyalty to the emperor.

Diocletian's division of the empire and redistribution of provinces facilitated the implementation of his religious program. Provincial governors had smaller territories to police. They were able to tour their territories more systematically and thus came to know their populace, its problems, and its deviants better. The names of governors appear in numerous martyr stories, indicating direct involvement by this senior officer. Easier access by governors often made for swifter justice than had been the case in the Decian and Valerian persecutions; cases rarely needed to be prorogued awaiting trial.[10] With the necessity of committing troops to maintain the borders, military personnel were not evenly distributed within provinces. In Africa, they were generally concentrated in the coastal areas, where the population was large, and in the farthest reaches of the empire along its southern borders. Large portions of the interior agricultural area, particularly in the Numidian provinces, would have been without a significant military presence; thus, imperial edicts prosecuting Christians and later laws against the Donatists were unevenly enforced.[11]

## The Persecution of Christians

The single most important aspect of the political background of Christianity in the early part of the fourth century was the persecutions. The Roman Empire allowed a variety of religious traditions, most of which were mutually tolerant. Religious activities with a long history in North Africa continued to function under local control in the cities, but most were assimilated to the worship of Roman divinities. Temples dedicated to the Capitoline Triad — Jupiter, Juno, and Minerva — were at the center of cities large enough to have a forum.[12] The Punic gods Baal and Tanit survived in subordinated cults of Saturn and Caelestis; the African divinity of grain was assimilated to the Roman pantheon under the name Pluto Frugifer.[13]

10. For a trial extended from place to place as a governor toured, see *Pas. Max.* 3.

11. This is the thesis of Emin Tengström, *Donatisten und Katholiken; soziale, wirtschaftliche, und politische Aspekte einer nordafrikanischen Kirchenspaltung* (Göteborg: Elanders Boktr, 1964). It is an alternative to the explanations offered during the immediate post–World War II period when, influenced by the dismantling of colonial empires, some scholars postulated that the Donatist movement was primarily a nationalist movement. For a summary with bibliography, see André Mandouze, "Le Donatisme représente-t-il le résistance à Rome de l'Afrique tardive?," in *Assimilation et résistance à la culture greco-romaine dans le monde ancien: Travaux de VIe Congrès international d'études classiques,* ed. D. M. Pippidi (Paris: Société d'Edition "Les Belles Lettres," 1976), 359-60.

12. See below, pp. 147-55 for the temples at Sufetula.

13. There was a temple dedicated to him at Roman Thugga (modern Dougga), and a plaque with an inscription to him may be found reused in the Byzantine fort at Musti in Tunisia.

In addition to these forms of civic religion, Roman provincial administration promoted the cult of the emperor. Active participation in the worship of the genius or guardian spirit of a living emperor provided a convenient way for members of provincial elites to demonstrate their loyalty, to ingratiate themselves with imperial administrators, and to enter or advance in the imperial service. Mystery religions, such as the cults of Isis and Mithras, provided additional outlets for African religiosity.[14]

Roman respect for ancestral religions provided Jews with an exemption from all requirements to participate in imperial or other cult activities and from conscription into the military, which had its own religious practices. During its early years, Christianity was seen as a sect of Judaism and shared its protection from demands of the civic and imperial cults. By the end of the second century, however, North African Christians had formed a distinct group and were no longer shielded.

Christians in Africa had been persecuted intermittently from 180 C.E. until the reign of Diocletian.[15] In assessing the strength and effects of persecution, one must recognize that not all Christians in every area of the empire were persecuted at the same time in the same way. Even imperial edicts designed to promote empire-wide uniformity depended upon local enforcement, which may have been sporadic or non-existent in one locale while sustained and severe elsewhere. The ambient ideal of human sacrifice, whether in war or at the altar, supported the Christian notion of the acceptability of offering one's life in fidelity, but it should be noted that no motifs of human sacrifice directly color martyrdom narratives.[16]

As long as military authority was unchallenged and the society seemed stable, adherence to Christianity and non-participation in civic and imperial cult could be ignored as minor deviance. However, by the end of the third century, as has been seen, participation in Roman religious life began to be required. Factors contributing to this change included military challenges on the eastern borders of the empire and on the *limes* of Africa as well as the internecine quarrels among members of the Tetrarchy. All of these conspired to make participation in civic ceremonies, and especially the imperial cult, a mark of political loyalty. The emperors did not leave this participation at the voluntary level but

14. For an overview of mystery religions, see Robert Turcan, *The Cults of the Roman Empire* (Oxford, U.K.: Blackwell, 1996).

15. The earliest surviving account of martyrdom in Africa, that of a group of Christians from the town of Scilli, dates from the 180s. See above, pp. 3-4, 7-8.

16. In *Pas. Perp.* 18.4, Christians were forced to wear the garb of Ceres's priestesses whereby executed criminals were dedicated to the goddess. See the commentary by Jacqueline Amat, *Passion de Perpétue et de Félicité: Suivi des actes,* SC 417:164-66. See James Rives, "Human Sacrifice among Pagans and Christians," *The Journal of Roman Studies* 85 (1995): 65-85. Tertullian defended Christian martyrdom by a parallel to Roman practices of human sacrifice: *Scorp.* 7.6.

promulgated several pieces of legislation in the early fourth century to insure the full engagement of all citizens in the state cult.

By far the most influential of the persecutions was that of the waning years of Diocletian's reign. Four edicts were promulgated. The first was issued on February 23, 303, by Diocletian for the East and shortly thereafter by Maximian for the West. It provided for the confiscation of Christian books and the destruction of churches. The upper classes *(honestiores)* were to lose the privileges attached to their rank. In addition, Christians would be prevented from bringing suits in cases of theft, adultery, or personal injury. Slaves who were Christian could never be freed.[17] According to Lactantius, the edict contained no provision for capital punishment;[18] however, by mid-June this edict was used to justify the execution of those who refused to turn over sacred books and vessels, such as Bishop Felix of Thibuca.[19] Diocletian's second edict licensed the arrest and imprisonment of the clergy, while the third called for clergy to be released if they offered sacrifice.[20] Neither the second nor the third edict seems to have been promulgated in Africa. The fourth was issued in the East by Galerius in the spring of 304, during a time when Diocletian was ill. It was ratified in the West by the Senate on April 22, 304. It called for all, not just clergy, to offer sacrifice. While no direct evidence of its promulgation in Africa survives, it must have arrived there over the summer of 304, because its provisions were swiftly used to justify the execution of several lay Christians.[21]

The first edict was enforced in different ways in Africa. In Cirta, the capital of what was then the northern province of Numidia (Cirtensis), the municipal magistrates went to the Christian place of worship to confiscate the property they found there, including the sacred vessels, in the presence of the clergy. They then made the rounds of the homes of the lectors and collected the sacred books.[22] They are not reported to have demolished the building itself.[23] In Abthugni, the magistrate was represented as warning his friend, Bishop Felix, that the imperial order required him to destroy any building in which Christian scriptures were found.[24] In both cities, Christians were depicted as meeting during the persecution in a building located near the cemetery, and therefore

17. Eus. Caes. *Hist. eccl.* 8.2.4.

18. Lact. *Mort.* 13, Eus. Caes. *Hist. eccl.* 8.2.4.

19. See *Act. Zeno.* and *Pas. Fel.*

20. Eus. Caes. *Hist. eccl.* 2.6.8-10.

21. W. H. C. Frend, *Martyrdom and Persecution in the Early Church: A Study of a Conflict from the Maccabees to Donatus* (Garden City, N.Y.: Anchor Books, 1967), 366, 375; Paul Monceaux, *Histoire littéraire de l'Afrique chrétienne depuis les origines jusqu'à l'invasion arabe* (Brussels: Culture et civilisation, 1963), 3:28; corroborated by *Pas. Max.* 1, and *Pas. Crisp.* 1.

22. *Act. Zeno.* 3-5.

23. According to the records of an episcopal meeting in the city a few years later, Felix's basilica still had not been restored to the Christians. See Aug. *Cresc.* 3.27.30.

24. The letter was a forgery but was constructed to represent the actual situation at the time. See *Act. pur. Fel.* 5.

outside the city proper.[25] Another bishop, Felix of Thibuca, was executed in Carthage for refusing to turn over the scriptures that he acknowledged were in his possession. Bishop Secundus of Tigisis, the Primate of Numidia Cirtensis, claimed that many of his colleagues had refused to cooperate with Roman authorities and had suffered for their fidelity.[26] Mensurius of Carthage, however, was able to deceive the agents of the proconsul by substituting irrelevant books for the sacred ones. When his enemies reported the deception, the proconsul apparently declined to pursue the matter.[27] Some Numidian bishops successfully took the same approach.[28] In other instances, both in Proconsular Africa and Numidia, bishops resisted by hiding the scriptures and substituting other books.[29]

The persecution had multiple effects on the church. First, there was the winnowing of leadership. Local and imperial officials would have found it convenient to use turncoat leaders to weaken the loyalty of members of their congregations. The arrest and execution of prominent clergy and laity might have left a community without leadership. Decapitating the movement had been an imperial strategy in the third century that was repeated in the two edicts that seem not to have reached Africa. When clergy were arrested and even executed, however, the strategy was not entirely successful. Some bishops, like Felix, were intransigent; the stories of their deaths provided examples of courage for all Christians.[30] Losing prominent members of a community might have caused some small churches to falter, but it caused others to withdraw socially and hide.[31]

Not all Christians, clergy or laity, held their ground. There is much evidence of collusion with the Roman authorities. Several bishops gathered at Cirta (later called Constantina) either in the waning days of the persecution or at its end, a meeting variously dated from 303 to 305.[32] They quarreled over who

25. *Act. Zeno.* 16, 19 places the episcopal election in a cemetery building. *Act. pur. Fel.* 5 likewise indicates that Christians gathered to pray in a cemetery. The forger Ingentius had been in Abthugni at the time and knew the practice.

26. *Pas. Fel.* Secundus was later shown to have been lying about his own confession (Aug. *Cresc.* 3.27.30).

27. See the notice of a letter of Secundus to Mensurius, evidence read into the records of the Conference of Carthage in 411, according to Aug. *Coll.* 3.13.25. This portion of the record is part of the missing ending of the transcript of the conference. Mensurius discouraged Christians from provoking the authorities into action.

28. For the evidence regarding Marinus of Aqua Tibilitana and Donatus of Calama, see Aug. *Cresc.* 3.27.30.

29. Mensurius was described as claiming to have allowed heretical books to be confiscated in a letter produced by the Donatists; Numidian bishops gave medical texts or martyrs' acts. See Aug. *Coll.* 3.13.25; *Cresc.* 3.27.30.

30. *Pas. Fel.*

31. *Act. Abit.* 3.

32. See the discussion of the date in Albertus Cornelius De Veer, "Le 'Concile' de Cirta," in

was qualified to elect and consecrate a new bishop. Charges of *traditio* — of turning over the scriptures — and even of murder were traded. Once the accusations began, however, it became clear that it would be difficult to establish the integrity of any bishop who had survived a visitation by imperial or municipal officials. The holiness of the church was at stake in the persons of its bishops. So too was the unity of the church, especially when a bishop whose credentials had been impugned threatened to bolt from the meeting. In the end, the ideal of the unity of the church won out over that of the purity of the electors. The primate, Secundus of Tigisis, accepted the suggestion that each one's worthiness should be left to God's judgment. All of the bishops gathered, even those accused of or admitting to *traditio,* were allowed to vote in the selection of a new bishop.[33] The stormy dispute was a portent of a gale that would erupt in 311 over another election in the city of Carthage, when a more rigorous standard would be applied by these same Numidian bishops.

By the end of 304, the worst of the persecutions were over. While Galerius continued to persecute Christians in the East until 311, there is no evidence for the enforcement of anti-Christian legislation in the West between 304 and the accession of Constantine.

## CONSTANTINE AND HIS SONS

### The Liberation of Christianity

The reign of Constantine, beginning in 311, had a profound impact on the status of Christianity in the empire. Constantine did not immediately introduce any radical changes in North Africa when he became western emperor. Local elites continued to be co-opted in the governance of the African provinces.[34] However, he broadened his constituency by courting Christians specifically for their Christian status. Whether this was out of genuine religious devotion, political astuteness, or some combination of the two is irrelevant. He did, however, issue a series of laws favorable to the Christians.

The granting of full legal status to Christianity in North Africa was marked, as elsewhere, by provisions of property and financial subsidies for the clergy. Like Christians in other parts of the Roman Empire, African Christians had begun by gathering in house churches. They soon secured larger assembly spaces and purchased some property even before legalization. Whether the churches mentioned by Cyprian were owned by the community or personally by bishops

---

*Oeuvres de saint Augustin,* 31: *Traités anti-donatistes,* Bibliothèque augustinienne (Paris: Desclée de Brouwer, 1968), 796-98.

33. The record of this meeting is preserved in Aug. *Cresc.* 3.27.30.

34. See, e.g., Victor the grammarian, who testifies that his father was a decurion and that the family with pride traced their lineage to the Mauri, in *Act. Zeno.* 1.

or other Christians is unknown. References to buildings dedicated exclusively to Christian worship begin in the fourth century, and even then, especially during persecutions, Christians still worshiped in houses.[35] Galerius's edict of 311 restored previously confiscated churches to Christian communities in the eastern provinces of the empire.[36] Constantine's parallel legislation required the return of goods confiscated from Christian communities, both those individually and corporately possessed. The edict included provision for the restoration of buildings for assembly.[37]

The oldest evidence of a Christian building specifically set aside for worship comes from the fourth century. Because Christians were relative latecomers to the religious scene, when they did erect churches, they were usually found at the outskirts of towns where property was available, as at Bulla Regia and Thugga. When Christian churches were at or near the centers of towns, they were usually on the sites of reused buildings. At Sufetula, for example, the basilica of Servus was a converted temple, and the basilica of Bellator had replaced another building.[38]

In spite of the paucity of physical evidence for buildings dedicated solely to worship in the early fourth century, Christian communities did amass some collective wealth to which imperial documents give witness. When Roman authorities raided "the house where the Christians gathered" in Cirta, they inventoried and seized not only a considerable amount of plate but also a large store of clothing as well as oil and grain, indicative of large-scale support for the poor.[39] A wealthy woman named Lucilla was accused of using a donation of four hundred *folles* to try to influence the episcopal election at Carthage in the first decade of the fourth century. She was not alone in using bribes to direct decisions.[40] How much this sum would be in modern terms is unknown; however, contemporary sources considered it a substantial sum for a single person to wield.[41]

35. *Act. Zeno.* 3, written in 320, mentions "the house in which Christians gathered" in 303. *Act. Abit.* 2, recorded in the fourth century, tells of a *basilica dominica,* a shrine commemorating a martyr. The assembly of the bishops at Cirta was held in a private home "since the basilicas had not yet been restored" (Optat. *Parm.* 1.14; CSEL 26:16.9-11). See Paul-Albert Février, "Africa — Archeology," in *Encyclopedia of the Early Church,* ed. Angelo Di Berardino (New York: Oxford University Press, 1992), 1:16.

36. Eus. Caes. *Hist. eccl.* 7.12.1. The same edict restored cemeteries, but whether the catacombs of Hadrumetum are old enough to have been included or were used exclusively by Christians are open questions. See Augustin-Ferdinand Leynaud, *Les catacombes africaines: Sousse-Hadrumète* (Alger: Jules Carbonel, 1922).

37. Lact. *Mort.* 48.7; see Eus. Caes. *Hist. eccl.* 10.5.9-11, 15-17.

38. See below, pp. 152-53, 149.

39. *Act. Zeno.* 3. The account makes the bishop and clergy, rather than a resident, responsible for the contents of the building, which seems to have been converted from private to communal use.

40. *Act. Zeno.* 17, 18, 20.

41. The *follis* was first issued under Diocletian. The Constantinian *follis,* a ten-gram, silver-

Like their counterparts elsewhere in the empire, African clergy profited from the legislation of Constantine and his sons. Profits included tax exemptions and freedom from the burdens of municipal service as decurions.[42] This release from duties as decurions indicates that many of the clergy of the period might have come from upper-class households. The exemptions were welcomed, and by the end of the fourth century these privileges were even abused. Legislation was necessary to control the abuse and to determine who were and were not Christian clergy.[43] A person might be ordained in order to gain exemptions, serve as a member of the clergy, and then relinquish or be removed from his post by a church court. Ordination to membership in the clergy did not change a person's status permanently; later emperors required that those who had been expelled from or had abandoned the service of the church must resume their municipal service.[44] These provisions and privileges did not come at the expense of the traditional cults; they did not make Christianity the official religion of the Roman Empire. Instead, it had become one of a number of recognized, protected, and supported religious cults.

By the time of its legalization, in 313, the Christian church counted many more than the nearly ninety dioceses in Roman Africa represented at Cyprian's largest council in 256.[45] In larger cities and even in smaller towns and villages, bishops were in charge and assisted by deacons. Before the fifth century, little evidence can be found for presbyters leading churches in villages.[46] Legal toleration does seem to have occasioned an upsurge in conversions, which meant larger congregations and increased financial resources. These, in turn, increased the demands placed on the time and managerial skills of the bishops. The family names of the bishops as well as their extant correspondence indicate that in general they came from families that could afford to attend to the education of their children, though not all were wealthy.[47]

The story of Melania the Younger and her husband, Pinian, illustrates the situation of clergy from wealthy families. Melania was the daughter of an extraordinarily wealthy Roman family. Her husband also came from the Roman aristocracy. In the aftermath of the Gothic capture of Rome, they retreated temporarily to their properties in North Africa. African congregations were swift to

---

washed bronze coin, contained about 0.2 grams silver. *Act. Zeno.* 16 records a bribe of 20 *folles* from a fuller to be made presbyter.

42. *C.Th.* 16.2.8 (in 343), 16.2.9 (349), and 16.2.10 (320).

43. *C.Th.* 16.2.36 (401).

44. *Sirm.* 9 (408). An instance of such abuse is reflected in Aug. *Ep.* 96.

45. See *Sent.* Augustine reported that seventy bishops gathered in Carthage to depose Caecilian (*Cresc.* 3.3.3; 4.7.9; *Ep. ad Cath.* 18.46). These might have been mostly Numidians, under the control of Secundus of Tigisis, the primate of the province.

46. One such example from a small town is the presbyter Saturninus from Abitina, who appears in *Act. Abit.* 3.

47. *Bru. Hipp.* 11-15, for example, restricts the private financial dealings of bishops and their sons, including a provision that the latter were not to sponsor public games.

notice talented and/or wealthy persons as suitable candidates for the clergy and quickly pressed them into clerical office. Not only did they look for the capabilities of these men, but they also sought the wealth that such clergy would be able to expend on the local church.[48] Augustine was ordained to Hippo under some pressure because of his oratorical abilities. Pinian was subject to intense pressure to be ordained to the same church because of his — and his wife's even greater — wealth. Through the intervention of his wife, he was able to escape ordination, but only by promising that if he ever did become a member of the clergy, it would be in Hippo.[49]

## Religious Non-Conformists

During the fourth and fifth centuries the term "Christianity" is something of a misnomer, as there were various sorts of Christian groups, most of which recognized each other as better or — more commonly — worse Christians. Some groups, however, identified themselves as the only true Christians. This would be especially significant after the legalization of Christianity, when imperial officials had to decide to whom recognition and subsidies ought to be granted. African Christian groups enumerated in imperial and ecclesiastical legislation of the fourth and fifth centuries included not only the recognized Catholics but Manichees, Donatists, and, explicitly or by implication, Arians.[50]

### MANICHEES

Manichees were followers of the Persian prophet Mani (216-277). His adherents often participated in activities of Christians but also formed their own churches composed of adepts and aspirants. Their radical dualism held that two principles — one light and good, the other dark and evil — were locked in everlasting combat for the light-bearing sparks of good within select individuals. Because the evil

48. Augustine (*Serm.* 356.1-2) reported that some of his clergy had spent their resources on church projects. His clergy were unusual, however, because they were required to give away their personal property and live in the bishop's house. Because many of the clergy had families, they retained their property, but they could not will it to non-relatives or non-Catholics. For the relevant canonical legislation, see *Reg. Carth.* 81 (June 401).

49. The incident is explained in some detail in Aug. *Ep.* 124-26. See Maureen A. Tilley, "No Friendly Letters: Augustine's Correspondence with Women," in *The Cultural Turn in Late Ancient Studies: Gender, Asceticism, and Historiography*, ed. Dale B. Martin and Patricia Cox Miller (Durham: Duke University Press, 2005), 40-62.

50. Imperial legislation: *C.Th.* 16.5.5 (in 379), 16.5.9 (382), 16.5.34 (398), 16.5.37-39 (405), 16.5.41 (407), 16.5.54-55 (414); *Sirm.* 14 (409); *Nou. Val.* 18 (445); cf. *C.Th.* 16.5.43 (407). The canons of the North African councils contained legislation against Donatists, Montenses, Novatianists, Pelagians, and schismatics and heretics generally.

principle of the cosmos was responsible for the production of the material realm, members of the religion reputedly disdained that world in which good and evil were mixed together; they participated in a variety of ascetic practices designed to separate the two forces. Most Christians, with the support of the imperial law, rejected their dualism and their soteriology, which had no room for the redemptive death of a truly human Jesus with a real fleshly body.

After a brief period of toleration in Persia, his homeland, Mani became the object of a power struggle in the royal household and was crucified. Officials of the Roman Empire considered his followers Persians or at least allies of Persians; hence, they were subject to suspicion as traitors and religious deviants. The earliest Roman legislation specifically directed against Manichees dates to 372, when they were forbidden to assemble or to bequeath property.[51] When condemned with other heretical groups, they were counted as the lowest among wicked heretics. They were supposed to be deprived of civil service posts, except at the discretion of provincial governors.[52] Manichees continued to be persecuted as late as the reign of the Vandal king Huneric (477-84).[53]

### NOVATIANISTS

Novatianists, a remnant from the third-century rigorist group, rejected baptism and other rituals performed by clergy who had defected during persecutions. They persisted into the fourth century and beyond. Constantine tolerated and even protected them, granting them the legal right to hold their churches.[54] By the time of Theodosius, they were being grouped with heretics in various pieces of legislation, because they rebaptized already baptized Christians who converted to their group.[55]

Often legislation simply mentions heretics with no specific description of their deviations.[56] This more general legislation does not always make clear whether imperial laws were directed against actual, living practitioners in Africa or whether the lists of proscribed sects were as inclusive as possible — that is, naming every group ever recorded in an attempt to cover all deviants from the imperially supported form of Christianity.[57] However, Manichees and Novatianists did continue to exist into the fifth century, both within Christian communities and as separate congregations.

51. *C.Th.* 16.5.3 (372).
52. *C.Th.* 16.6.2 (435).
53. Vict.-Vit. *Hist. pers.* 2.1.
54. *C.Th.* 16.5.2 (326).
55. E.g., *C.Th.* 16.2.59 (423); Angelo Di Berardino, "Novatianists," in *Encyclopedia of the Early Church,* ed. Di Berardino, 2:604-5.
56. *C.Th.* 16.2.7 (330), 16.2.34 (399), 16.4.4 (376/378), 16.5.51 (410), and 16.5.56 (410).
57. *C.Th.* 16.5.12 (383), 16.5.4 (407), and *Sirm.* 12 (408).

## TERTULLIANISTS

There is some evidence for a group of Christians following the rigorist teachings of Tertullian at Carthage, at least until the latter part of the fourth century. As their number diminished, they joined the Caecilianist communion and turned over their basilica to its bishop.[58]

## DONATISTS

The support that Constantine and his successors occasionally granted to African Christians was administered through imperial officials called notaries who distributed the funds. Ordinarily this was simple. Money went through local bishops to the Christian communities to support the clergy (who were already becoming a professional class) and to assist in the erection and maintenance of church buildings. However, very early in Constantine's reign, Christians at Carthage and in other cities divided over the legitimacy of specific bishops. The resulting schism was later named for one of those bishops, Donatus.

The Donatist schism is one founded not so much on belief as on religious practice. The specific practices involved the hallmarks of African Christianity: reverence for the martyrs, the treatment of sin as impurity or physical contagion, and a conception of the tangible indwelling of the Holy Spirit. Many Christians rejected the ministry of those clergy who returned to the ministry of the church after having lapsed during persecution either by sacrificing, handing over copies of the scriptures, or providing assistance to the Roman authorities. Accusations of such failures were brought forward after the persecution, not all of them legitimate.[59] The Donatists worshiped separately from the opposing group, initially named for their leader Caecilian but often called Catholics after their recognition by the Council of Arles in 314.

Some Christians refused to accept Caecilian as Bishop of Carthage because of accusations that when he was archdeacon he had refused to lend aid to rural confessors from Abitina who were imprisoned at Carthage and had prevented their supporters from bringing them food in jail.[60] His accusers may also have contended that he had been ordained without the participation of the bishops

58. Aug. *Haer.* 85. There is no evidence that this group had personal connections to Tertullian when he was alive.

59. The false accusation of Felix of Abthugni was in retaliation for his exposing a colleague, Maurus of Utica (*Act. pur. Fel.* 8). Others, such as Silvanus of Cirta, were clearly guilty (*Act. Zeno.* 13).

60. For documentation and analysis of this episode, see Maureen A. Tilley, *Donatist Martyr Stories: The Church in Conflict in Roman North Africa* (Liverpool: Liverpool University Press, 1996), xxiii-xxv, 25-26. The surviving text itself is briefly discussed as a piece of later propaganda in Maier, *Le dossier du donatisme,* 1:57-58.

normally involved.[61] The most serious accusation was that one of his conse-crators was accused of having handed over the scriptures to imperial author-ities during the persecution by Diocletian.[62] Whatever the truth or falsity of the charges, Caecilian and his supporters represented a wing of the church that supported a rapprochement with the imperial rulers. They accepted imperial subsidies and followed the practice of the Roman church by refusing to rebap-tize those who entered their communion after having been baptized by either *traditores,* schismatics, or most heretics.[63] Although they too refused to allow known apostates to continue in clerical office, they were required to accept into communion any bishops who had been consecrated by an apostate,[64] who had joined the Donatist schism as a bishop, or had been consecrated in it.[65]

Appeals and counter-appeals for the recognition of the overseas churches and the empire were filed. Caecilian was vindicated by imperially appointed commissions of bishops at Rome in 312 and Arles in 314.[66] Nevertheless, the Donatists maintained their own churches across Africa, in southern Spain, and even one in Rome. They became a particular religious group claiming to be faithfully Christian but were not recognized as such by emperors or Christian leaders outside Africa. Instead, the emperors and the overseas bishops sup-ported the Caecilianists, who thereby came to be known as Catholics.

Between 317 and 321, Constantine tried to force the Donatists into union

61. Augustine reported that at the Conference of Carthage in 411, the Donatists asserted that the Bishop of Carthage, as primate, should have been ordained by another primate, specifically that of Numidia. Thus, Caecilian had been rushed into office without awaiting the approval of the Primate of Numidia. Augustine responded that no evidence could be found of such a charge at the time of the ordination itself: the only record (Optat. *Parm.* 1.19) indicated that the objection had been that the ordaining bishops were *traditores.* Augustine then argued that ordination of a primate by a primate was not the ancient or actual practice of the church. The Bishop of Rome was, he observed, ordained not by a metropolitan bishop but by the bishop of nearby Ostia. Rome was the relevant parallel because its bishop became primate upon his ordination. In Africa, the primates of Numidia and other provinces were the longest-serving bishops of the province and thus were already ordained when they assumed the office. *Coll.* 3.16.29.

62. One of the consecrators, Felix of Apthungi, was from Byzacena; the Primate of Numidia, Secundus of Tigisis, was not involved. Felix was charged with *traditio* but cleared by an imperial inquiry (*Act. pur. Fel.*).

63. This change from the third-century African practice was mandated by bishops from the western half of the empire at the *Con. Arel.* a. 314, 9.

64. *Con. Arel.* a. 314, 14.

65. By decision of the Roman bishop, Miltiades. See Aug. *Ep.* 43.5.16. The *Con. Arel.* a. 314, 14 mandated the removal of bishops who had been guilty of apostasy or turning over the scriptures, but not those whom they ordained, as long as they were themselves innocent.

66. Paul R. Coleman-Norton, *Roman State and Christian Church: A Collection of Legal Doc-uments to A.D. 535* (London: SPCK, 1966), 1:49, n. 6, lists five separate investigations into the le-gitimacy of the Donatist case against Caecilian, but the investigations in 312 and 314 were the only ones in which Constantine empaneled Christian bishops as judges. The list of subscriptions to the decrees of *Con. Arel.* shows that they were broadly representative of the western part of the empire. See Maier, *Le dossier du donatisme,* 1:153-71.

with the Caecilianists. A large gathering in the Donatist basilica in Carthage, which included clergy from the outlying towns, refused to give up the building. Although the imperial forces used batons rather than swords to overcome the resistance, a number of people were killed, including a bishop. They were buried in the basilica and commemorated as martyrs.[67]

In 321, Constantine abandoned the attempt to force unity on the African church in order to focus his resources on the upcoming conflict with Licinius for the control of the eastern half of the empire.[68] Between 321 and 346, then, Donatism continued to grow.

Upon the death of Caecilian in 336, Donatus may have attempted to unify the church in Carthage under his own leadership, though no record of such a claim has survived. He may have appealed to Emperor Constans to implement a decision, reached at Rome by Bishop Miltiades in 312, that when a bishop died in a city where there were two bishops in communion, the next senior bishop, whether Donatist or Caecilianist, would head both congregations. Donatus may have appealed to Miltiades' directive; the surviving evidence would explain the failure of such a plan.[69]

Constans later sent two notaries, Paul and Macarius, to attempt a reunion by means of financial enticements, threats, or exercise of force.[70] These efforts provoked Donatist resistance and martyrdoms in Carthage and Numidia. In Numidia, a delegation of bishops was beaten and their leader, Marculus,

67. *Pas. Don.* 6-8, 11-13. Maier, *Le dossier du donatisme*, 1:198-211.

68. Maier, *Le dossier du donatisme*, 1:239-43. Constantine justified this volte-face to the Caecilianists in a letter preserved in an appendix to Optat. *Parm.* See CSEL 26:212-13.

69. W. H. C. Frend's explanation (*The Donatist Church* [Oxford: Clarendon, 2000], 177) that Donatus claimed the position vacated by Caecilian's death according to the provisions of the Council of Arles relies on an extension of the surviving evidence. A sentence in Optat. *Parm.* is an imputation of responsibility to the Donatist leaders for the troubles that followed the death of Caecilian: "illis primo, qui dei populum diuiserunt et basilicas fecerunt non necessarias, deinde Donato Carthaginis, qui prouocauit, ut unitas promimo tempore fieri temptaretur, tertio Donato Bagaiensis, qui insanam conlegerat multitudinem, a qua ne Macarius uiolentiam pateretur, ad se et ad ea quae ferebat, tutanda armati militis postulauit auxilium" (Optat. *Parm.* 3.1; CSEL 26:67.10–68.6). The ruling to which Frend appeals would have to be that of Miltiades, as reported in Aug. *Ep.* 43.5.16, rather than that of Arles. That text, however, does not bear the suggested interpretation, since it assigned the junior bishop to a different congregation as soon as one could be found; Donatus had already completed more than thirty years as a schismatic bishop refusing to submit to that ruling. Could he have expected the emperor to enforce it then to prevent the election of a Catholic bishop? Moreover, Augustine's archival work enabled him to make regular references to the appeals that the Donatists had made to Constantine at the beginning of the controversy; yet he never cited a later appeal by Donatus to Constans. Caecilian, it should be noted, had died no later than 337, when his successor, Rufus, represented the church of Carthage at a synod in Rome. Jean-Louis Maier, *L'épiscopat de l'Afrique romaine, vandale, et byzantine* (Rome: Institut suisse de Rome, 1973), 29, 271.

70. Optat. *Parm.* 3.3 Donatus's response to the mission was reported to be, "What has the emperor to do with the church?" (CSEL 26:73.20).

died in imperial custody.[71] The armed resistance of Donatus of Bagai provoked a military response that resulted in his death and that of many of his supporters.[72] The proconsul in Carthage issued a decree of unification of the churches, which was promptly torn down by a Donatist layman, Maximian, whose action was then supported during his trial by another, Isaac. Both died in prison awaiting exile.[73] Many of the recalcitrant Donatist bishops were sent into exile and some honored as martyrs.[74] Some Donatist bishops and their congregations entered into communion with the Caecilianists.[75] In 348, imperial efforts were discontinued in the face of both their ineffectiveness and the necessity to shift resources to counter incursions into the empire on the eastern borders.

In 362, as part of a general action, Julian allowed the Donatist exiles to return to Africa and reclaim the basilicas that had been turned over to the Caecilianist party in the enforcement of the decree of unification under Constans.[76] A good deal of conflict and some violence accompanied the transfer of buildings back to the Donatists. In Mauretania Sitifensis, Caecilianist deacons were killed in two places, and a number of laity were injured at Tipasa. The Caecilianist party, however, did not honor these persons as martyrs.[77]

During most of the fourth century, however, the imperial government was not actively involved in the controversy; in many places, Donatists and Caecilianists reached a sort of *modus vivendi*. Each side built and maintained its own churches, ordained its own bishops, and propagated its own practices. Caecilianists could count on imperial support, while Donatists scorned it.[78] Donatists usually, but not always, demanded a new baptism and, therefore, a new ordination of Caecilianists seeking to join their group. In periods of clergy shortage, both Donatists and Caecilianists were flexible about how

---

71. *Pas. Marc.* Maier, *Le dossier du donatisme,* 1:287, n. 44, endorses the hypothesis of Ernst Ludwig Grasmück, *Coercitio; Staat und Kirche im Donatistenstreit,* Bonner historische Forschungen, Bd. 22 (Bonn: L. Röhrscheid, 1964), 125-26, that Marculus was being taken to Carthage for deportation when he died a natural death; Macarius attempted to dispose of his body in a way which would have prevented its veneration.

72. Optat. *Parm.* 3.4.

73. *Pas. Isa. Max.* The proconsul attempted to dispose of their bodies in the sea to prevent their veneration.

74. Maier, *Le dossier du donatisme,* 1:256-91. The martyrdom accounts of Maximian and Isaac, and of Marculus, belong to this period. Donatus of Carthage was also honored as a martyr. See Aug. *Don.* 16.20.

75. This is implied by the conflict between bishops recorded in *Con. Carth.* a. 345, 12.

76. Optat. *Parm.* 2.16; *C.Th.* 16.5.37.

77. Optat. *Parm.* 2.16, 18; 6.5-6.

78. An example of government support was Constantine's funding of a Caecilianist church in Cirta/Constantina in 330 because the Donatists had refused to cede the only church building in the city to the Caecilianists. See Coleman-Norton, *Roman State and Christian Church,* 1:159-63, and Constantine's letter to the Catholic bishops of Numidia, CSEL 26:213-16.

clergy and laity crossed the boundaries as long as they wound up on the right side.[79]

Elsewhere in the empire, legislation prohibited the practice of other forms of Christianity, such as Montanism and Novatianism. Their fortunes waxed and waned like that of the Donatists, but surviving legislation for Africa does not indicate that either group claimed numerous adherents. Perhaps imperial authorities simply did not recognize them as separate groups, or their numbers did not warrant significant attention.

## JULIAN TO THE VANDALS

The progress of Christianity through the decades after Constantine's accession seemed unstoppable — that is, until the reign of Julian (361-63). Julian's experience of Christianity was largely colored by Constantius's annihilation of several members of his family. Constantius had been purging the family of relatives of his father who might have threatened his claim to the throne. The young Julian survived, but only on the margins of the court. In addition, he came under the influence of the Neoplatonist Maximus of Ephesus. Beginning in the winter of 361/362, after becoming sole emperor, Julian reversed his predecessors' support for Roman-style Christianity. He began by supporting Donatist and Arian bishops who had been exiled. He granted the petition of the exiled Donatists to return in 362.[80] The Donatists took over many of the congregations they had been forced to leave, cleansed the basilicas, and restored the vigor of their church.[81] In effect, this meant that Donatist bishops were put on equal footing with Caecilianists. It was in Julian's interest to appease as many parties as possible, because he needed stability within the empire while he fought the Persians. Overall, he preferred non-Christians, those who worshiped in the traditional Roman manner. In Byzacena, he packed the municipal senates with those who held the old religion.[82] Caecilianists were on the defensive until Julian's death in 363. At that point, Caecilianists and Donatists seem to have returned to the *modus vivendi* of the pre-Julian years.

79. See Maureen A. Tilley, "Theologies of Penance during the Donatist Controversy," in *Studia Patristica* (Louvain: Peeters, 2001), 35:330-37.

80. Maier, *Le dossier du donatisme*, 2:42-43.

81. An outraged Optatus recounts the sacrilege and violence of the repossession and re-baptism. See *Parm.* 2.16-26; 3.11; 6.1-8; see also Aug. *Petil.* 2.97.244.

82. Julian, *Ep.* 39.

After Julian's death, many Christians on every side tried to regain their favored status. Especially important to them was exemption from taxes and curial duty.[83] The emperors recognized the loss of revenues as a problem and insisted, at least in Byzacena, that wealthy men entering the clerical state not be allowed to take property out of the tax base. In 364, Valentinian I and Valens decreed that the property had to be transferred to a relative or to the municipal assembly to prevent the loss of revenue.[84] The emperors did take care to return to bishops the church buildings that had been seized by Julian and converted into temples.[85] They rescinded Julian's toleration of rebaptism.[86] Finally, their promotion of Christianity and its moral code led the emperors Valentinian II and Theodosius I to provide that female slaves who were used as theatrical performers might leave their profession if they became Christians.[87]

From the death of Julian to the Vandal invasion, bishops became more and more influential in civic society. This was a natural progression as upper classes became Christian and supplied talented men to the episcopate. Influential families expected to remain influential, perhaps even to gain more influence, as they embraced the religion of the emperors. As in other parts of the empire, bishops became arbiters of religious disputes and exercised their prerogative to judge civil suits between Christians. Arcadius and Honorius tried to limit these to cases dealing with religious matters.[88]

In the period immediately after the death of Julian, all sectors of the church flourished. Part of the reason for the success of the *modus vivendi* between Caecilianists and Donatists was the ecclesiastical leadership on both sides. On the Caecilianist side, a succession of lackluster bishops in Carthage from 363 to 393 did their best to bring order and stability to Caecilianists in a post-Julian world. Given that their party was in the minority in many areas, and that the imperial proconsul and vicar may have had Donatist leanings, Caecilianist bishops did not insist on imperial preferences for their community. On the Donatist side, from 362 to 392 (an entire generation), there was only one bishop of Carthage, the gifted Parmenian, who spent his episcopate writing learned treatises and tending to his growing flock.[89]

The political situation was not quite so peaceful in the western part of Af-

---

83. *C.Th.* 16.2.36 (401). Upper-class families who supplied members to a civic council or curia were required to make up the balance of tax assessments that a city was otherwise unable to pay.

84. *C.Th.* 12.1.59 (364).

85. *C.Th.* 16.2.18 (370).

86. *C.Th.* 16.6.1 (373).

87. *C.Th.* 15.7.9 (381).

88. *C.Th.* 61.11.1 (399). For similar legislation in 376 in Gaul, see *C.Th.* 16.2.23.

89. Maureen A. Tilley, *The Bible in Christian North Africa: The Donatist World* (Minneapolis: Fortress Press, 1997), 130-31.

rica. In Mauretania, the increasing burden of taxation fueled anti-Roman sentiment. In 372, leading families rallied around Firmus, the scion of an old native ruling family, in a revolt against Rome. During the uprising, Firmus enjoyed Mauri support and attracted to his side some Donatists. In the course of an intra-familial quarrel, he was invested with the imperial purple. Desperate attempts to back down from the revolt, including sending ecclesiastical envoys to Theodosius, came to nothing, and he was killed by his own brother.[90] In what would dimly foreshadow events of the 390s, Donatists suffered a short period of persecution during this period.[91]

## Destabilization and Suppression

In the final decade of the fourth century, Roman Africa was destabilized on both civil and ecclesiastical fronts. Theodosius and his son Honorius, who succeeded him in the West, had consolidated power and no longer needed to appease minor constituencies. Honorius appointed Catholics to major offices, promoting their dominance in Africa. The reigns of cooperative Bishops on both sides came to an end. On the Donatist side, Parmenian, Bishop of Carthage from 362 until 391/392, was succeeded by a hard-liner, Primian; a convert from the Caecilianist side, Petilian, provided able leadership at Constantina in Numidia.[92] On the Caecilianist side, the irenic Genethlius died in 391/392. Augustine's friend Aurelius became Bishop of Carthage in 393, and these two adopted a more aggressive promotion of the Caecilianist cause. This changing of the guard included a group of Augustine's friends trained in asceticism and the defense of the Caecilianist party. Prime among them were his former companions and now protégé bishops: Alypius — a former imperial operative — in Thagaste, and Evodius in Uzalis. Augustine's former monk and eventually his biographer, Possidius, became Bishop of Calama and one of the most aggressive actors in the judicial struggle against the Donatist party.[93]

On the military front, too, the last decade of the fourth century was one of tumult. In 397 Count Gildo, one of Firmus's brothers, revolted against Rome and attempted to set up his own kingdom. Local partisans joined him, most

90. Ammianus Marcellinus, *Res Gestae* 29.5.2-54. See Frend, *The Donatist Church,* 72-73, 197-98.

91. *C.Th.* 16.5.4 (376) and 16.6.1 (373); Aug. *Ep.* 105.2.9.

92. See Pamela Bright, "Donatist Bishops," in *Augustine through the Ages: An Encyclopedia,* ed. Allan D. Fitzgerald (Grand Rapids: Wm. B. Eerdmans, 1999), 281-84, and Tilley, *The Bible in Christian North Africa,* 93-112.

93. Entries on all of these men may be found in *Augustine through the Ages,* ed. Fitzgerald. On Possidius and his program, see Erika T. Hermanowicz, *Possidius of Calama: A Study of the North African Episcopate at the Time of Augustine* (Oxford: Oxford University Press, 2008).

notably Optatus, the Donatist bishop of Thamugadi. By 398, he had been killed and the rebellion put down by his brother Mascazel, an ally of Rome.[94]

In response to the revolt, imperial authorities began a campaign to unify the empire and once again promoted the conformity of citizens both religiously and politically. A century that had begun with the persecution of Christians closed with imperial decrees against pagans. In 391, the Bishop of Alexandria in Egypt used official neglect of temples and a decree against blood sacrifices as a license to dismantle Alexandria's glory, the Serapeum. The next year Theodosius I forbade all traditional public cults. In 394 and 396 Theodosius's sons, Honorius and Arcadius, revoked any and all privileges accorded to pagan priests. In 408, government funding for building and maintaining temples was withdrawn, and enemies of the Christians were forbidden to work in the imperial service. Eight years later they were excluded from the army as well.[95] Throughout the empire, laws were promulgated against heretics of all sorts. The drive toward unity and uniformity in the first decade of the fifth century was more especially focused on Africa.

## Renewed Conflict between Caecilianists and Donatists

A division in the Donatist church in Africa provided an opportunity that the Caecilianists would exploit in order to apply the full force of imperial law to their opponents. In 393, a group of Donatist clergy and laity in Carthage secured the assistance of the bishops of neighboring provinces in replacing their bishop, Primian, with his deacon, Maximian.[96] With the support of some Numidians, especially Optatus of Thamugadi, Primian brought about the condemnation of the rebels and their supporters by a large council of Donatist bishops.[97] Most of the dissenters submitted to his authority; the few holdouts were hauled before imperial authorities, charged with heresy, and forced to return all their ecclesiastical property to Primian's control. Nearly all these holdouts were forced back into communion, but the Primianists recognized as valid all of the sacramental acts the Maximianist bishops had performed while they were

94. Frank M. Clover, "Carthage in the Age of Augustine," in *The Late Roman West and the Vandals* (Aldershot, Hampshire, Great Britain; Brookfield, Vt.: Variorum, 1993).

95. For the suppression of traditional cults, see Pierre Chuvin, *A Chronicle of the Last Pagans* (Cambridge, Mass.: Harvard University Press, 1990).

96. Acts of the Council of Cebarsussi in Aug. *Psal.* 36.2.20. On this and other facets of the conflict within the Donatist communion and with the opposing Caecilianists, much new evidence and interpretation are offered by Brent D. Shaw, *Sacred Violence: African Christians and Sectarian Hatred in the Age of Augustine* (Cambridge; New York: Cambridge University Press, 2011). It appeared too late to be taken fully into consideration in this study.

97. See the fragments of the Council of Bagai preserved in various writings of Augustine, assembled in CSEL 53:276-78 and Maier, *Le dossier du donatisme*, 2:85-91.

in schism.[98] The Caecilianists attacked this provision as a violation of Cyprian's insistence on the equivalence of schism and apostasy.

In 403, the Caecilianist bishops enlisted the assistance of the proconsul in Carthage to arrange public debates with the Donatists, during which they intended to use the Donatist inconsistency to undercut the legitimacy of their remaining in schism from the larger church.[99] The Donatists' refusal to participate was entered into the public record, thereby providing an opportunity for ridicule. The Caecilianists also sued for the return of Donatist church properties, using the tactics Primian had employed against the supporters of Maximian.[100] In retaliation, Donatists attacked several Caecilianist bishops and other clergy, beating some severely.[101] In self-defense, the Caecilianists then petitioned Emperor Honorius to apply the existing laws against religious deviants to all the Donatists.[102] Faced with the evidence of Donatist violence, Honorius issued legislation requiring the submission of Donatists to the Caecilianists under threat of financial, legal, and physical punishments.[103]

The emperors Arcadius, Honorius, and Theodosius II attempted to enforce Roman practices by outlawing rebaptism, which was a practice of many groups, although only Donatists and Montanists were named in the laws of 405.[104] Manichees were also caught up in the push toward uniformity.[105] By 408, both non-Christians and Christian heretics were banned from the court.[106] The emperors also forbade the traditional pagan religious celebrations.[107] This, however, eventuated in riots during which Caecilianist clergy were killed and a basilica was destroyed.[108]

In 408, the Byzantine general Stilicho, whom Theodosius I had deputized to oversee the government of his young son Honorius, was overthrown and executed. The removal of Stilicho raised hopes among Donatists and traditional religious practitioners, who anticipated that Olympius, Stilicho's successful op-

98. Salvius of Membressa held out, but Felician of Musti and Praetextatus of Assuras eventually submitted. See Aug. *Psal.* 21.2.31; 36.2.20 for a citation of the record.

99. *Reg. Carth.* 91 (in 403) and 92 (in 403/404).

100. *Con. Carth.* (August 25, 403). See Aug. *Ep.* 88.7; *Cresc.* 3.45.49; *Coll.* 3.4.4, 5.6, 8.11.

101. Aug. *Cresc.* 3.42.46–43.47.

102. *Reg. Carth.* 93 (404).

103. The texts of the decrees have not survived in full. See *C.Th.* 16.5.38, 6.3-5 (405); and Aug. *Ep.* 88.7. Aug. *Ep.* 185, written a decade later, reviewed the events. For a careful analysis of the entire sequence, see Hermanowicz, *Possidius of Calama*, chaps. 3-4.

104. *C.Th.* 16.6.3-5 (405); cf. 16.5.39 and 16.11.2 (405).

105. *C.Th.* 16.5.35. The fact that they are mentioned explicitly and without being grouped with other heretics lends credence to the survival of identifiable Manichaean communities as late as 300, when the law was promulgated.

106. *C.Th.* 16.5.42.

107. *Sirm.* 12, issued in November 407, was promulgated in Carthage in June 408.

108. The events took place at Calama in early June, before the actual promulgation of the law. They resulted in the mission of the Catholic bishop Possidius to the imperial court. See Aug. *Ep.* 90-91; 97; 103-4.

ponent, would withdraw the legislation against them in order to secure his position. In January 409, however, Honorius reaffirmed the previous legislation and made physical attack on a Caecilianist bishop a capital offense.[109]

Local officials in Africa did not always enforce the imperial push toward uniformity. Honorius and Theodosius II upbraided them for their laxity and threatened them with loss of office for failure to enforce laws against heretics, Jews, and a new class of religious dissidents, "pagans."[110]

In October 410, Honorius responded to yet another Caecilianist episcopal delegation by calling for a meeting of the African bishops at Carthage under the presidency of the tribune and notary Flavius Marcellinus. After months of preparation, the conference began on June 1, 411, with 267 Caecilianist and 289 Donatist bishops signing the procedural mandate.[111] The bishops met in three sessions spanning nine days. Seven representatives chosen from each side presented their party's historical and theological arguments for being the true church. The minutes of the first two-and-a-half sessions survive and include the full text of many documents read into evidence. In the end, Marcellinus vindicated the cause of the Caecilianists; Honorius then denied the appeal of the Donatists; he issued a series of laws designed to force the Donatists into the Caecilianist communion. Their church property was forfeit; their laity were subject to fines and their clergy to exile. Imperial agents were sent to Africa to enforce these edicts.[112]

The push toward increased imperial control and religious conformity bore down especially hard on Donatists. Conventional wisdom dates the end of Donatism to about 411 because of subsequent imperial enforcement of Marcellinus's decree that year.[113] However, accepting this scenario would be an oversimplification of the situation in the early decades of the fifth century. Imperial attempts to standardize Christianity from Ravenna had to be reinforced and supplemented by changing the situation on the ground in Africa. The repeated legislation attests the difficulty of extirpating the movement.[114] The last records of Caecilianist action come from the year 418. A council made provision for episcopal supervision of Donatist congregations coming into unity and for the discipline of Caecilianist bishops who neglected to petition for imperial action

---

109. A legation was sent from the council of Carthage in October 408 (*Reg. Carth.* 106). The mission of Possidius was reported in Augustine to Paulinus of Nola (*Ep.* 95); the response is in *Sirm.* 14 (409).

110. *Sirm.* 14 (409).

111. *Col. Carth.* 1.98-223. CCSL 149A and SC nos. 193, 194, 224, 373. Aug. *Coll.* 1.14 claimed that once the rolls were checked, the Caecilianists' count rose to 286 and the Donatists' count fell to 279.

112. *C.Th.* 16.5.52, 54, 55.

113. *Edictum Cognitoris, Col. Carth.* (CCSL 149A:177-79).

114. *C.Th.* 16.5.53 (412), 16.6.6 (413), 16.5.54-55 (414), 16.5.56 (415).

to effect these reunions.[115] The last recorded meeting of Donatist bishops, thirty in number, was held about the same time.[116] Shortly thereafter, the tribune and imperial *executor,* Dulcitius, was sent to effect the transfer of property from Donatist to Caecilianist hands. His attempt to confiscate the basilica still held by Donatists at Thamugadi provoked a violent conflict.[117]

Imperial attempts at uniformity had to weather yet another rebellion when in 413 another *comes Africae,* Heraclian, rebelled and nearly became emperor in the West. He too was killed in Africa, not by his family but by Roman agents.[118]

## The Pelagian Controversy

As the Donatist conflict within Africa was working itself out, a second controversy erupted which set the African bishops against their colleagues elsewhere in the empire. Among the refugees from Rome after its sack by the Goths in 410 were Pelagius, a British ascetic, and one of his followers, Caelestius. When Caelestius applied for ordination into the clergy of Carthage, he was accused and found guilty of heresy.[119] Interested Christians in Carthage, including Flavius Marcellinus, questioned Augustine about the issues.[120] Pelagius himself moved on to Palestine, where Latin bishops in exile likewise accused him, but he managed to explain the statements attributed to him and thus to avoid condemnation. His accusers then appealed to Innocent, the Bishop of Rome, and enlisted the assistance of Augustine and his African episcopal colleagues. After reviewing the transcripts of the trial of Pelagius in Palestine, Augustine became convinced that Pelagius was a dangerous prevaricator.[121] In 416, councils of bishops in Numidia and Africa Proconsularis condemned his teachings and forwarded their judgments to the Bishop of Rome.[122] Innocent accepted most of their points, but his successor, Zosimus, failed to discern a problem in the confession of faith submitted by Pelagius, so no action was taken in Rome.[123]

---

115. *Reg. Carth.* 117-123.

116. Aug. *Gaud.* 1.37.47.

117. Aug. *Ep.* 204.

118. Clover, "Carthage in the Age of Augustine," 8.

119. The accuser was Paulinus, one of Ambrose's deacons. The issues were primarily the state of the first human beings before the Fall and the consequences of their sin. On the Pelagian controversy and the relations between Africa and Rome, see B. R. Rees, *Pelagius: A Reluctant Heretic* (Suffolk: Boydell Press, 1988) and Otto Wermelinger, *Rom und Pelagius: die theologische Position der Römischen Bischöfe im pelagianischen Streit in den Jahren 411-432* (Stuttgart: Hiersemann, 1975).

120. Aug. *Pecc. merit.* and *Spir. et litt.* were both addressed to Marcellinus in 411/412; *Ep.* 156-57 were sent to Hilary in Syracuse in 414/415.

121. *Gest. Pel.* 1.1, 34.61, 65. See J. Patout Burns, "Augustine's Role in the Imperial Action against Pelagius," *Journal of Theological Studies,* n.s., 30 (1979): 67-83.

122. Aug. *Ep.* 175-77.

123. Aug. *Ep.* 181-83.

The African bishops responded with a technique they had learned in their conflict with the Donatists. After condemning Pelagius's teachings once again, in May 418, they secured an imperial condemnation, lobbied prominent Roman Christians, and thus achieved Zosimus's cooperation.[124] Eighteen Italian bishops refused to condemn Pelagius; they were forced from their offices and exiled to eastern parts of the empire where their leader, Julian of Eclanum, continued a pamphlet war with Augustine until the latter's death in 430.[125]

## Arians and Vandals

Once the Vandals invaded Africa in 429, the issue was not whether one was a Caecilianist, a Donatist, or a follower of Pelagius, or even a Novatianist or a Manichee, but whether one was an Arian.

The Arian heresy is usually seen as an eastern controversy with little impact on Africa. Caecilian of Carthage's participation in the Council of Nicaea in 325 indicates African acquaintance with Arianism at an early stage; however, African Catholics seem to have paid the issue little heed. Though they were invited to the Council of Ephesus in 431, their attendance was prevented by the Vandal invasion, although Capreolus of Carthage was able to send a letter. Only four Africans were at the Council of Chalcedon in 451.[126] No evidence survives that the continuing rejection of Arian teaching by these councils made much impression in Africa; the Greek concerns over the constitution of the Savior were not high on the bishops' agenda. In the late fourth century, Donatists were accused of being in league with Arians because some had attended the Council of Sardica in 343 that supported Arian dogma. Some Donatists may have corresponded with bishops later known as Arians, though it was not so clear at the time that they would become identified as heretics.[127] Augustine became acquainted with Ambrose's anti-Arian polemics — and politics — during his time

---

124. Aug. *Ep.* 186 to Bishop Paulinus of Nola; *Ep.* 188 to Juliana, a Roman noble protector of Pelagius; *Ep.* 191, 194 to Sixtus, a prominent deacon of the Roman church; *Ep.* 193 to Marius Mercator, involved on Augustine's side; and *Ep.* 201, the reply of Honorius. Zosimus's condemnation was the *Ep. Tract.* (PL 48:90).

125. Most notable of Augustine's responses is his *Nupt.* and *Iul. op. imp.* See Serge Lancel, *St. Augustine*, trans. Antonia Neville (London: SCM, 2002), 325-46, 413-38.

126. On the attendance of Africans at the councils, see Maier, *L'épiscopat de l'Afrique romaine, vandale, et byzantine*, 25, 71-72.

127. Germain Morin, "Une lettre apocryphe inédite de st Jérôme au Pape Damas," *Revue Bénédictine* 35 (1923): 121-25; Alberto Pincerle, "L'arianesimo e la Chiesa africana nel IV secolo," *Bilchnis* 25, no. 3 (1925): 97-106; Donatien de Bruyne, "Une lettre apocryphe de Jérôme fabriquée par un donatiste," *Zeitschrift für die neutestamentliche Wissenschaft* 30 (1931): 70-76. J. Zeillet, "L'arianisme en Afrique avant l'invasion vandal," *Revue historique* 173 (1934): 535-41, concludes that there was no real Arian presence and that the so-called evidence for such was a Catholic slur against the Donatists, having no foundation.

in Milan. Little evidence of Arians in Africa can be found until Augustine's debate with the Arian bishop Maximinus, who came to Africa with a Gothic army officer in 427 or 428.[128] Their doctrines were so little known that Augustine had to explain to Count Boniface the difference between the Arians and Donatists. While Augustine believed that Donatists had an orthodox Trinitarian theology, he did think that they often soft-pedaled it to make common cause with Arians for political reasons.[129] The effective presence of Arians commenced with the invasion by the Vandals in 429. Roman imperial legislation against Arians would have no further force in Africa.

Vandals moved westward across Europe, being driven by the Huns. In 406, they crossed the Rhine, and three years later they were in Spain. Honorius accorded them rights to residency but not necessarily to property.[130] In 410, the Gothic sack of Rome distracted the government from provincial affairs. Later, the Roman *comes Africae* and *magister militum* Boniface revolted against Rome and invited the Vandals to come to Africa in his support.[131] By 429, Vandals had moved southward and crossed over the Straits of Gibralter. As they advanced across Africa, the chroniclers of Carthage saw their own era as the end time and characterized the Vandal king Geiseric as the Antichrist.[132] The history of the Vandal activity in Africa was written largely by the African Catholic Victor of Vita and by the Byzantine historian Procopius of Caesarea.[133] This is the subject of the following chapter.

128. See Michel Barnes, "Maximino Arianorum episcopum, Conlatio con," in *Augustine through the Ages,* ed. Fitzgerald, 549.

129. Aug. *Ep.* 185.1.1.

130. Iord. *Get.* 30.153; Proc. Caes. *Hist. bel.* 3.3.

131. Iord. *Get.* 33.169; cf. Walter Pohl, "The Vandals: Fragments of a Narrative," in *Vandals, Romans, and Berbers,* ed. A. H. Merrills (Burlington, Vt.: Ashgate, 2004), 31-47, and Andreas Schwarcz, "The Settlement of the Vandals in North Africa," in *Vandals, Romans, and Berbers,* ed. Merrills, 49-57.

132. *Lib. Gen.* 618F (the Florentini version) *MGH* AA 9:195. But once Geiseric arrived in town, this reference was expunged from later editions.

133. The two prime histories are Vict.-Vit. *Hist. pers.* and Proc. Caes. *Hist. bel.* Victor was bishop in Africa in 488, and Procopius accompanied Belisaurius in the Byzantine reconquest in 543.

# CHAPTER 3

# Fifth-Century Conflicts:
# Vandal Arians and African Nicenes

..........................................................................................................................

## THE VANDAL CONQUEST OF ROMAN AFRICA

As Augustine lay dying in the summer of 430, Vandal armies surrounded Hippo.[1] Five or so years later, his biographer, Possidius of Calama, wrote that a vast army had poured into Africa from Spain. Led by the Vandal king Geiseric (428-477), this host combined Vandal Hasdingi-Silingi clans and Alans (an assortment reflected in the royal title *Rex Vandalorum et Alanorum*), with Goths and other ethnic groups, including some Hispano-Romans and Suevi. Possidius, who probably witnessed some of what he recounted, claimed that the invaders violently overran the countryside, from Mauretania to Africa Proconsularis, inflicting atrocities, looting and burning cities, destroying churches, and torturing or killing the priests who tried to protect them.[2]

According to Possidius, Augustine was less concerned about loss of property — or even life — than loss of souls. He grieved as he witnessed African churches being emptied of their clergy and destroyed, and ceasing to offer the Holy Sacrament. He also judged the trials to be a form of divine judgment. In a letter to his brother bishop Honoratus, he urged ministers to stay in their posts

---

1. Augustine's date of death, August 28, 430, is recorded in Prosp. *Chron.* 1304 (*MGH* AA 9:473) and Marcellinus *Chron.* 429 (*MGH* AA 11:77).

2. Possid. *Vita Aug.* 28. The *Vita* probably was composed between 432 and 435 — on the dating, see Holmes V. M. Dennis, "Another Note on the Vandal Occupation of Hippo Regius," *The Journal of Roman Studies* 15 (1925): 263-68. On the history of the Vandals' migration into Spain and then Africa, see Andreas Schwarcz, "The Settlement of the Vandals in North Africa," in *Vandals, Romans, and Berbers,* ed. A. H. Merrills (Burlington, Vt.: Ashgate, 2004), 49-57, and Walter Pohl, "The Vandals: Fragments of a Narrative," in *Vandals, Romans, and Berbers,* ed. Merrills, 31-47. On the Vandal period in general, see Frank M. Clover, "Carthage and the Vandals," in *The Late Roman West and the Vandals* (Aldershot, Hampshire, Great Britain: Variorum, 1993).

as long as possible and not to desert the communities that needed spiritual succor.[3] Although exaggerating, Possidius maintained that at the end of Augustine's life only three African churches remained — Carthage, Hippo, and Cirta[4] — and that shortly after Augustine's death, Hippo itself was taken, abandoned by its inhabitants and burned to the ground.[5] The Vandal invasion certainly prevented Capreolus of Carthage (Aurelius's successor as bishop) from attending the Council of Ephesus in 431. In a letter excusing his absence, he explained that the devastation of Africa prevented its bishops from even holding a synod themselves, much less sending representatives abroad.[6]

The invaders were a poly-ethnic multitude (numbering at least 80,000 persons, including children and slaves according to the roughly contemporary chronicler, Victor of Vita). Having been pushed first across the Rhine by the Huns, and then out of Spain (where the Romans and their later-arriving Visigoth allies accorded them residency but not property),[7] they clearly desired both territory and the material resources of the African provinces.[8] According

---

3. Possid. *Vita Aug.* 30; *Ep.* 228.

4. Cirta (Constantina), the capital of Numidia, was taken by the Vandals in 432; Proconsular Africa and Carthage were not taken until 439. Possidius's reference to Cirta by its former name (instead of Constantina) probably indicates only that the old name was still in general use.

5. Possid. *Vita Aug.* 28. The line *ab hostibus fuerit concremata* is difficult to reconcile with the archeological evidence as well as with Hippo's continued survival as an important city and even, for a short time, the Vandal capital. E. C. Howard suggested that Possidius meant Hippo Diarrhythus rather than Regius in "A Note on the Vandal Occupation of Hippo Regius," *The Journal of Roman Studies* 14 (1924): 257-58. This argument was critiqued by Dennis, "Another Note on the Vandal Occupation of Hippo Regius," in which Dennis argued that Possidius is essentially reliable, and that *concremata* does not necessarily indicate that the city was totally destroyed. More likely it was only partially burned and temporarily abandoned, to be reoccupied by the local population, along with the Vandal court, some time after 435.

6. See Karl Joseph von Hefele, *Histoire des conciles d'après les documents originaux,* trans. Henri Leclercq, Nouvelle traduction française faite sur la 2 éd. allemande, cor. et augm. de notes critiques et bibliographiques, par un religieux bénédictin de l'abbaye Saint-Michel de Farnborough (Paris: Letouzey, 1907), 2:287-312; Philippe Labbe and Gabriel Cossart, *Sacrosancta concilia,* 18 vols. (Lutetiae Parisiorum: impensis Societatis Typographicae, 1671), 3:534. Capreolus's letter to the council is found in PL 53:843-49. Emperor Theodosius II had wanted to have Augustine present, and sent him a special invitation, not realizing (because of the troubles in Africa) that Augustine had already died the preceding summer.

7. Iord. *Get.* 30.153. See also Pohl, "The Vandals: Fragments of a Narrative."

8. Vict.-Vit. *Hist. pers.* 1.2; Proc. Caes. *Hist. bel.* 3.5.18-20; *Anec.* 18.6. Both Victor and Procopius give the same number, but while Victor specifies that it included women, children, and slaves, Procopius bases it on the division of Vandals and Alands into eighty companies of a thousand men, and then goes on to question the number, saying that Geiseric only called the companies "chiliarchs" to make it seem that they were so large, adding that it was probably no more than 50,000 men. Nevertheless, if women and children were added to this, the number could be closer to Victor's suggested count. See Walter A. Goffart, *Barbarians and Romans, A.D. 418-584: The Techniques of Accommodation* (Princeton, N.J.: Princeton University Press, 1980), 84-86, who differs on this point from Christian Courtois, *Les Vandales et l'Afrique* (Paris: Arts et métiers graphiques, 1955), 215-17.

---

to Victor, their army laid waste to the land as they invaded, burning orchards and ravaging cities and towns, treating churches and saints' shrines with special ferocity.[9]

The Byzantine historian Procopius of Caesarea blamed the invasion of Africa on Count Boniface, Augustine's friend and collaborator. Having fallen out of favor with the regent Augusta, Galla Placidia (mother of Valentinian III), Boniface decided to establish a defensive alliance with the two sons of King Godigisclus (Geiseric and Gontharis), agreeing that, if successful, each of them should hold one third of Roman Africa and offer mutual defense to the others. Procopius surmised that Boniface's Vandal second wife, Pelagia, had persuaded him to do this, for through her he had formed close ties to the Vandal king. Once back in favor (and cleared of the charge of treason), Boniface regretted this stratagem and tried to persuade the Vandals to withdraw, but it was too late. Thus, in 429, Boniface found himself opposing an incursion of the tribes assembled under the leadership of Geiseric (Gontharis's successor) that he had invited into the region. After unsuccessfully trying to fend off the invaders, Boniface fell back on Hippo Regius with his army of allied Goths.[10]

During what became a fourteen-month siege, Augustine and refugee bishops who had fled from neighboring regions prayed for divine assistance.[11] The enemy briefly retreated to re-supply themselves, but not before Augustine was stricken with a fever and died. Although Boniface received reinforcements from Rome and Constantinople, which were delivered by the Arian and Alan Aspar, the *magister militum* of the Eastern Empire, he was badly defeated after a fierce battle.[12] Recalled to Italy, he died at the battle of Rimini in 432.[13]

In 435, Trigetius, the Praetorian Prefect of Italy, concluded a peace treaty at Ravenna with Geiseric that ceded a portion of Africa (including all of Numidia) to the Vandals, gave them the status of *foederati,* and established Hippo Regius as the Vandal capital of Africa.[14] The treaty was sealed with the handing over of Geiseric's son Huneric as hostage to the Ravenna court as an assurance of good faith.[15] The friendship was not to last. In 439, Geiseric broke his oath, declared his dominion independent of the Roman state, and pushed on to take Carthage,

9. Vict.-Vit. *Hist. pers.* 1.3-4; compare Possid. *Vita Aug.* 28, and the sermon (often attributed to Quodvultdeus, but possibly by Capreolus) *Temp.* 2.

10. Proc. Caes. *Hist. bel.* 3.3.22-25, 30-35. The story of Boniface's treachery is also cited by Iord. *Get.* 33.167-69. Since the more contemporary Prosper Tiro, however, does not note it (*Chron.* 1294-5, s.a. 427), some scholars question the tale. According to some sources, Boniface's wife was a Gothic princess (cf. Sid. *Carm.* 5.203ff.), which may have assisted his rallying Gothic forces to his assistance. This is the argument of Schwarcz, "The Settlement of the Vandals in North Africa." On Procopius's reliability, see Goffart, *Barbarians and Romans, A.D. 418-584,* 61-70.

11. Possid. *Vita Aug.* 28.

12. Proc. Caes. *Hist. bel.* 3.3.34-36. On Aspar as an Arian, see *Hist. bel.* 3.6.3.

13. *Chron. Gall.* 111 (*MGH AA* 9:658).

14. On this treaty, see Proc. *Hist. bel.* 3.4.13-15; Prosp. *Chron.* 1347 (*MGH AA* 9:497).

15. Proc. Caes. *Hist. bel.* 3.4.15.

which became his new capital.[16] He then turned his attention to raiding along the northern coast of the Mediterranean.[17] He attacked Sicily, pillaged and laid siege to Palermo, and (according to contemporary chronicles) initiated a persecution of its Nicene Christians which included attempts to convert them by force to the Vandal form of Arian Christianity.[18]

The threat of these Vandal raids prompted the Roman emperors to attempt pushing the Vandals back. In 441, Theodosius II sent a fleet of ships from the East, and Valentinian III provided reinforcements from Rome. The expedition proved futile, just reaching Sicily before the fleet was recalled to defend the East from the Huns and the Persians. Valentinian then negotiated another peace treaty in 442 that ceded Byzacena, Proconsularis, eastern Numidia, and Tripolitana to the Vandals. In return, western Numidia and the Mauretanias were retroceded to the empire. Valentinian also recognized the Vandal state as an independent kingdom in former Roman territory instead of *foederati*. Africa was thus divided into two distinct sovereign territories.[19]

........................................................................................

## THE VANDAL KINGDOM IN AFRICA

The peace agreement of 442 had not only divided Africa into two distinct parts but also betrothed Valentinian's infant daughter, Eudocia, to Geiseric's eldest son and presumed heir, Huneric.[20] Huneric had been allowed to return to Carthage from Ravenna in 445 or 446.[21] Given the princess's age, the marriage had to be put off. In 455, Petronius Maximus staged an assault on Valentinian III, accomplished his assassination, and proclaimed himself successor to the western throne. He forced Valentinian's widow, Licinia Eudoxia, to marry him and betrothed the princess Eudocia to his own son Palladius.[22]

Licinia Eudoxia then turned to Geiseric to rescue her and her daughters, Eudocia and Placidia. The resulting Vandal expedition overran and sacked Rome (455); Maximus and Palladius were turned on and killed by their own people.[23] The three imperial women were brought to Carthage along with an enormous amount of looted treasure. Eudocia was finally married to Huneric,

---

16. Idat. *Chron.* 107.

17. Proc. Caes. *Hist. bel.* 3.5.

18. Idat. *Chron.* 112.

19. Prosp. *Chron.* 1347 (a. 442). See also Isid. *Hist.* 76.

20. His first wife, the daughter of Theodorid, King of the Visigoths, was cruelly mutilated upon suspicion that she was trying to poison Geiseric or his son, and sent back to her father. This prompted Geiseric to ally himself with Attila in fear that Theodorid would seek revenge. See Iord. *Get.* 36.184-87.

21. Proc. Caes. *Hist. bel.* 3.4.15.

22. Idat. *Chron.* 155; see also Proc. Caes. *Hist. bel.* 3.4.36-39.

23. Proc. Caes. *Hist. bel.* 3.4.36-39, 5.1-3; Idat. *Chron.* 160; Iord. *Get.* 44.235.

a royal marriage that gave the prestige of the Theodosian dynasty to the Vandal royal house.[24] At the request of the eastern emperor Leo (457-474), Licinia Eudoxia and Placidia were transported safely to Constantinople, and Placidia was eventually married to Olybrius, a Roman senator and future consul of Constantinople, who had fled from the Vandal sack of Rome.[25] Unfortunately for her, the princess Eudocia, no longer the daughter of a living Roman emperor, was not the prize that Geiseric had originally sought for his son. Although their only son, Hilderic, was born in the early 460s, the religious differences between the couple were insurmountable, and Eudocia eventually left Africa for the East, probably retiring to a convent near Jerusalem, where she died around 472.[26]

After the Vandal sack of Rome in 455, the emperors tried on at least two occasions to retake Africa; both attempts were disastrous. The western emperor Majorian (457-61) lost most of a significant army to the Vandals and his own life to dysentery.[27] Around 468, after the western general Marcellinus had driven the Vandals out of Sardinia, the eastern emperor Leo I (457-474) gathered a force of more than 400,000 soldiers and sailors under the leadership of Basiliscus.[28] Basiliscus hesitated, accepted a bribe, or fell victim to treason; the Vandals easily destroyed the Roman fleet by setting it on fire. In the meantime, since the Vandals had begun to threaten the coast of Illyricum, the eastern emperor Zeno (474-491) negotiated another peace settlement in 475 that at least secured the safety of Byzantium and remained in effect until Justinian's recapture of Africa in 534.[29]

When Geiseric died in 477, Huneric succeeded him but ruled for only seven years. Unlike his father, he focused primarily on internal policy and remained at peace with the empire. Huneric was succeeded by his nephew Gunthamund (484-96) rather than by his son, Hilderic, who would have been in his early twenties at the time of his father's death.[30] Gunthamund's younger brother, Thrasamund, then came to power (496-523). In Ravenna, he entered an alliance with the Ostrogothic king Theodoric and married his sister, Amalfrida, though he did not share Theodoric's toleration for Nicene Christians. By the end of the fifth century, the borders of the Vandal Kingdom were threatened by the Mauri tribes from the south who had sacked Thamugadi (Timgad) and were raiding

24. Proc. Caes. *Hist. bel.* 3.5.1-7. See also Pohl, "The Vandals: Fragments of a Narrative," 40.

25. Proc. Caes. *Hist. bel.* 3.5.6. The connections established between Geiseric and Olybrius led to Geiseric's two attempts to get Olybrius made Emperor of the West in 461 and 465. Olybrius did claim the title briefly for four or five months in 472.

26. Evag. Sch. *Hist. eccl.* 2.7; Marcellinus, *Chron.* 455; Theophanes, *Chron.* a.m. 5947 and 5964. She may have been buried in the same tomb as her grandmother, Eudoxia. See also Vict.-Ton. *Chron.* 28 (464); Isid. *Hist.* 78.

27. Proc. Caes. *Hist. bel.* 3.7.3-15. See also Isid. *Hist.* 76. An interesting episode describes Majorian's secret visit to Geiseric, disguised as an imperial envoy.

28. Proc. Caes. *Hist. bel.* 3.6 tells the story of the defeat of this combined force by the Vandals.

29. Proc. Caes. *Hist. bel.* 3.7.26.

30. Huneric's death is described by Vict.-Ton. *Chron.* 51 (a. 479), and repeated by Isid. *Hist.* 79 — who says that he ended his life like his "father Arius," with all his intestines pouring out.

other cities in eastern Numidia. Thrasamund was succeeded by Huneric's son Hilderic (523-530), who adhered to the Nicene orthodoxy of his mother, the western princess Eudocia, rather than the Arian creed of his father. Probably because of this, Hilderic broke with the Ostrogoths and allied himself with the Byzantines. Hilderic's being half-Roman, his religious affiliation, his alliances with Emperor Justin and the future emperor Justinian, and his allowances to the African Nicenes made him extremely unpopular among his Vandal subjects. Although he was tolerant of the Vandals and their faith, he was elderly (more than sixty years old at the time of his accession) and perceived as a weakling who was too cozy with the Byzantine rulers and unable to wage war against other enemies of the kingdom.

In 530, Gelimer, Hilderic's cousin and next in line for the throne, deposed and imprisoned Hilderic. Gelimer may have used Hilderic's religion and close alliances with the eastern emperor as pretexts for accusing him of plotting to turn the kingdom over to the Byzantines. In response, Justinian sent envoys to Africa, demanding that Gelimer return the throne to Hilderic, but promising to support him as Hilderic's rightful successor. Gelimer, citing the peace treaty negotiated by Zeno and Geiseric in 475, condemned Justinian for meddling in the affairs of an independent kingdom. Justinian's outrage led to the Byzantine invasion of Africa three years later.[31]

Thus the Vandal era was one of continuity as well as change, and, despite the religious conflicts between the native Nicenes and the Arian newcomers, a time of relative stability: the Carthaginian harbor sustained a lively commercial trade;[32] the baths, circus, and amphitheater were continuing centers of public entertainment;[33] luxurious villas for the wealthy were built and decorated.[34] The Vandals appear to have been determined to establish a kingdom in which their Arian faith would have been the sanctioned state religion, but that would be as civilized, prosperous, and powerful as that of their Roman competitors.

From an archeological standpoint, the Vandal era was not a period of significant or innovative building, but adaptation of late Roman structures and styles. Geiseric reportedly tore down the walls of all the cities except Carthage in order to prevent their becoming strongholds of resistance. He also allowed the walls of Carthage to fall into disrepair, according to Procopius, adding to the ease of the Byzantine reconquest.[35]

31. Proc. Caes. *Hist. bel.* 3.9.6-26.
32. Clover, "Carthage and the Vandals," 8-13.
33. Some of this is depicted by the sixth-century Carthaginian poet Luxorius, who both lauds and derides certain celebrity-status athletes and charioteers. See *Luxorius: A Latin Poet among the Vandals,* with translations and commentary by Morris Rosenblum (New York: Columbia University Press, 1961), Nos. 26, 34, 38, 41-42, pp. 128-37.
34. For example, the fifth- or sixth-century mosaic of the Circus (chariot races) from Capsa, and now in the Bardo Museum, Tunis.
35. Proc. Caes. *Hist. bel.* 3.5.8-9; 3.21.11-12; 3.23.19-20.

## VANDAL ARIANISM

The majority of the Vandal people adhered to a type of Arian Christianity, probably having been converted by followers of the fourth-century Goth and missionary bishop Ulfilas and given support during the reign of the Arian emperor Valens (364-78). Although little is known about their actual theological position, Victor of Vita asserted that they claimed the legitimacy and orthodoxy of the decrees of the Councils of Ariminum and Selucia, presided over by an earlier Arian emperor, Constantius.[36] If Victor's report is accurate, Vandal Trinitarian theology was probably in line with the Homoean doctrine of the later fourth century that affirmed that the Son was "like" but lesser than the Father. This was different from the earlier and continuing "Arian" teaching that the Son was radically different from the Father.[37] Vandal Arianism was probably not unlike that brought to Africa by Gothic mercenaries and allies of the western emperor early in the fifth century.

Augustine had come into contact with Arians while living in Milan before his baptism. However, his first direct contact with Arianism as a competing theology was likely in Africa, around 410, when certain Arian refugees arrived, having fled the Visigothic sack of Rome. Around 418 or 419 he wrote a response to an anonymous Arian sermon, possibly sent to him by a certain Dionysius, who lived about twenty-five miles from Hippo.[38] About a decade later, he agreed to debate the Arian Gothic bishop Maximinus, who came to Africa with Count Sigisvult.[39] Generally, the Arianism that Augustine refuted was the Homoean form, taught by Ulfilas. However, along with his theological objections, Augustine had another grievance. He alleged that Donatists had tried to win the Gothic Arians over to their cause by purporting to hold similar beliefs. Augustine hastened to point out that Donatists confessed that the Trinity is of one substance, while the Arians held differently. Nevertheless, he noted, the two

36. Vict.-Vit. *Hist. pers.* 3.5. Isidore of Seville claimed that Geiseric had converted from the orthodox faith — and was the first of his people to become Arian, although this is a late source (*Hist.* 74).

37. See Andy Merrills and Richard Miles, *The Vandals* (Oxford: Wiley Blackwell, 2010), 177-203.

38. See Roland J. Teske, ed., "Introduction: The Arian Sermon and Answer to the Arian Sermon," in *Arianism and Other Heresies* (Brooklyn, N.Y.: New City Press, 1990), 119-32, which points also to *Ep.* 22A and *Ep. Divj.* 23A* for more evidence about the context of both the sermon and Augustine's response.

39. Aug. *Serm. Arian.; Maxim.* See William A. Sumruld, *Augustine and the Arians: The Bishop of Hippo's Encounters with Ulfilan Arianism* (Selinsgrove, Pa.: Susquehanna University Press, 1994). Maximinus may have authored the *Scolia,* edited by Roger Gryson, CCSL 87; see Michel Barnes, "Maximino Arianorum episcopum, Conlatio con," in *Augustine through the Ages: An Encyclopedia,* ed. Allan D. Fitzgerald (Grand Rapids: Wm. B. Eerdmans, 1999), 549.

shared a similar conviction that rebaptism of converts to either communion was required.[40]

The future Bishop of Carthage, Quodvultdeus, may have been even more attuned to the specific tenets of Vandal Arianism. Even as a deacon, he had exacted a book on Christian heresies from the aging Augustine.[41] His creedal homilies, written in the mid-430s (during the reign of his predecessor, Capreolus) refuted certain Arian teachings on the relationship of the Son to the Father, without specifying those opponents' identity or ethnicity. Quodvultdeus asserted that these heretics denied that the Son and Holy Spirit were omnipotent, and that they insisted the Father was greater than the Son.[42] Since neither liturgical nor doctrinal works from actual Vandal sources exist, knowledge of their particular beliefs (as distinct from Gothic Arianism) comes only from the side of the Nicene defenders.

The Gallican historian and monk Salvian of Marseilles (ca. 400-480) was one of the first to describe the religious practice of the Vandals. His writings are somewhat untrustworthy, however, as he may not actually have visited Carthage. Expressing a strikingly different perspective from Possidius of Calama or Victor of Vita, his treatise *The Governance of God* (written ca. 439-451) characterizes the Vandals as morally superior to the Roman Africans, and he interprets the incursions of barbarian tribes as God's punishment for Christian moral laxity and misbehavior.[43] Although Salvian was probably as biased as any source and less informed than either Possidius or Victor, his assessment provides useful contrast. He asserted that although early Christian Carthage had been home to apostles and martyrs, in later years it had become a city filled with all kinds of iniquities, from effeminate men to unchaste women. While Vandal besiegers encircled the walls, he alleged, Christians in Carthage were reveling in the theaters and going crazy in the circuses.[44] Furthermore, he added, some Christians continued to worship the Roman goddess Caelestis.[45]

Salvian describes Vandals rehabilitating prostitutes by compelling them to marry and enforcing chastity within marriage. All in all, he concluded, the Vandals merely took possession of a corrupt population's property — a punishment

40. Aug. *Ep.* 185.1.1. Apparently, both Gothic and Vandal Arians insisted on rebaptism of Nicene Christians. See discussion below.

41. Aug. *Haer. praef.*

42. Quodu. *Symb.* 1.3.9–4.38 in particular. For discussion of authorship as well as general introduction to the Creedal Homilies (which are not universally attributed to Quodvultdeus), see Quodvultdeus, *Quodvultdeus of Carthage: The Creedal Homilies: Conversion in Fifth-Century North Africa,* trans. Thomas M. Finn, Ancient Christian Writers 60 (New York: Newman Press, 2004).

43. Salu. *Gub.* 7.13; D. J. Cleland, "Salvian and the Vandals," in *Studia Patristica,* ed. Frank Leslie Cross, Texte und Untersuchungen zur Geschichte der altchristlichen Literatur, Bd. 107-8 (Berlin: Akademie Verlag, 1970), 10:270-74.

44. Salu. *Gub.* 6.12.

45. Salu. *Gub.* 8.2.

they richly deserved.[46] He also contended that some of the populace welcomed the newcomers, finding among them an element of ancient Roman dignity despite their oppression, differences in worship, and culture. They preferred to live as free while in captivity, rather than as slaves with only the appearance of liberty.[47]

### REPRESSION OF NICENE CHRISTIANITY

Salvian's characterization of the Vandals as enforcers of traditional moral standards accords with their alleged intent to convert the local population to their own faith or theological position. Unlike other Arian groups (e.g., the Visigoths and Ostrogoths), the Vandals seem to have been intolerant of Christians who confessed the Nicene faith. While other Arian nations often welcomed integration into the political and social life of the Roman Empire, even attaining high military or political rank (e.g., Stilicho or Sigisvult), the Vandals tended to resist assimilation and to seek autonomy.[48] Although certain forms of violent oppression and seizure of property may have been nothing more than territorial conquest, the Vandals seem to have pursued a program of displacing Roman Christianity in Africa. According to contemporary sources, they not only took over church buildings for their own use but confiscated liturgical books and vessels, prohibited house liturgies, and tortured or killed clergy and consecrated virgins.[49] These acts might demonstrate a Vandal determination to replace the Nicene faith and its leaders.[50]

The recorded violence against African Nicene Christians prompts comparison with the programs of earlier Roman emperors, pagan and Christian alike, who deemed religious conformity a civic value, to be achieved by force if necessary. Like the pre-Constantinian persecutions of Christians, Vandal violence against Nicenes produced martyrs who refused to recant their professed faith. When Geiseric took Carthage in 439, he is reported to have driven the Catholic clergy out of the city and handed their churches over to the Arians.[51] He loaded Bishop Quodvultdeus, along with a number of other clerics, onto ships and set

46. Salu. *Gub.* 7.22.
47. Salu. *Gub.* 5.5.
48. See E. A. Thompson, *Romans and Barbarians: The Decline of the Western Empire* (Madison: University of Wisconsin Press, 1982), 230-48; and Heather, "Christianity and the Vandals in the Reign of Geiseric," in *Wolf Liebeschuetz Reflected: Essays Presented by Colleagues, Friends, and Pupils,* ed. John Drinkwater and Benet Salaway (London: Institute of Classical Studies, School of Advanced Study, University of London, 2007), 137-46.
49. Vict.-Vit. *Hist. pers.* 1.4-16, 39, 41-42, 51; Possid. *Vita Aug.* 28 (torture of virgins); and Idat. *Chron.* 110 (the banishment of bishops and clergy, and handing over churches to Arians).
50. See Yves Modéran, "Une guerre de religion: Les deux églises d'Afrique à l'époque vandale," *Antiquité Tardive* 11, no. 1 (2004): 21-44.
51. Idat. *Chron.* 110.

them out to sea.[52] Conversions to Arianism were sought — often coerced — and included rebaptism, a practice particularly abhorrent to both Catholic and Donatist Africans.[53] Contemporary sources also indicate that the Arians sometimes also offered bribes to achieve conversions — and that this approach often worked.[54]

Victor of Vita describes attempts at forcible conversion of Nicene Christians. Sebastian, Boniface's son-in-law and a counsel to King Geiseric, refused to convert to the religion of the Vandals, especially because this would have required that he undergo rebaptism. He argued that, like a pure loaf, made from flour ground in the mill of the Catholic mother, he would not be improved by being moistened and baked a second time. Geiseric, temporarily thwarted, found another reason to execute Sebastian.[55] Victor also reported the martyrdoms of Martinianus and Maxima, both Nicene Christian servants of a Vandal governor *(millenarius),* who resisted his demand that they marry, even though Maxima was a dedicated virgin. They refused to consummate the marriage and fled to monasteries near Thabraca. When their Vandal master discovered their flight, he had them arrested, forcibly rebaptized, and tortured. All of this was to no avail, since the martyrs never surrendered to his demands to consummate their marriage or to commit apostasy by becoming Arians.[56]

Modern scholars have attended to Victor's ideological bias in reporting Vandal persecution of African Nicene Christians.[57] Critical evaluation of Victor's rhetorical strategies reveals colorful exaggerations echoing those of earlier martyrdom accounts. One example of his tendency towards overstatement is Victor's assertion that Quodvultdeus and his fellow bishops were loaded "na-

---

52. Vict.-Vit. *Hist. pers.* 1.15; Quodu. *Temp.* 11, 12. Quodvultdeus arrived in Naples safely and died in exile. See Daniel Van Slyke, *Quodvultdeus of Carthage: The Apocalyptic Theology of a Roman African in Exile* (Strathfield, Australia: St. Pauls, 2003).

53. See also Prosp. *Chron.* 1329; Quodu. *Symb.* 1.13.6 attacks Arian rebaptism (possibly by Goths in this instance) — but it appears that these Arians (like Donatists) generally required rebaptism of their converts.

54. Vict.-Vit. *Hist. pers.* 1.48; 2.28; 3.29 (bribes combined with threats); Quodu. *Prom.* 5.7; *Temp.* 1.8.7; Fulg.-R. *Psal. Ab.,* PLS 3, 1359-1361. These texts are quoted — and somewhat misinterpreted — in Danuta Shanzer, "Intentions and Audiences: History, Hagiography, Martyrdom, and Confession in Victor of Vita's *Historia Persecutionis*," in *Vandals, Romans, and Berbers,* ed. Merrills, 271-90. Shanzer suggests that the bribes might be alms or "social guest gifts." Fulgentius's language clearly suggests threats, terror, and deprivation (along with bribes).

55. Vict.-Vit. *Hist. pers.* 1.19-21.

56. Vict.-Vit. *Hist. pers.* 1.30-34.

57. Christian Courtois, in *Victor de Vita et son oeuvre, Étude critique* (Alger: Impr. officielle du Gouvernement général de l'Algérie, 1954), raised these issues, arguing that Victor's writing should be classified more as hagiography than history. The recent work of Éric Fournier, *Victor of Vita and the Vandal "Persecution": Interpreting Exile in Late Antiquity* (Ann Arbor, Mich.: University Microfilms International, 2008), is an excellent study of this problem. See also S. Costanza, "Vittore di Vita e la Historia persecutionis Africanae provinciae," *Vetera Christianorum* 17 (1980): 229-68, and Shanzer, "Intentions and Audiences."

ked and despoiled onto dangerous ships." He later clarified that they were probably not actually nude but only stripped of most of their personal property.[58] Similarly, his account of Vandals torturing Nicene bishops and priests for their gold and silver was likely modeled on Augustine's account of the barbarians sacking Nola in order to steal Paulinus's personal wealth.[59]

The later Donatist editors of the *Liber Genealogus,* a fifth-century chronicle of the history of the world, were no less hostile in witnessing to the events surrounding the Vandal invasion, which they saw as signs of the end time. In an early version, the *Liber* characterized Geiseric as the Antichrist, a characterization that probably dated to just before the fall of Carthage and was prudently removed from a subsequent edition, perhaps even at the king's insistence.[60] Not surprisingly, this chronicle presents the African Donatist Christians as the persecuted — but true — faithful. Thus the Donatist opposition to Catholic Christianity and their parallel practice of rebaptizing converts do not seem to have won them any allies among the Vandals, who were apparently more intent upon bringing both communities over to Arian faith and practice.

Contemporary sources, in particular the undoubtedly biased chronicle of Victor of Vita, characterize the Vandal religious policy not as evangelization but as violent repression of Nicene Christianity.[61] After he took Carthage, Geiseric exiled Catholic bishops and subsequently refused to allow replacement for those who died in exile. Confiscation of churches and their endowments seems to have been more extensive in Africa Proconsularis than in Byzacena or Numidia, since the treaty made with Valentinian III in 442 made this the center of Vandal holdings.[62] Victor of Vita reported that the Vandals occupied Carthage's Basilica Maiorum, Basilica Celerina and the Scillitanorum (perhaps two different basilicas), Mensa Cypriani, Memoria Cypriani, and Basilica Restituta (the Catholic cathedral).[63] Despite the loss of these churches and the exile of their bishops, however, Victor's chronicle implies that Nicenes were allowed to hold services in basilicas outside the city walls (the basilicas Fausti and Novarum).[64]

An imperial intervention by Valentinian III in 454 led to the consecration of Deogratias (454-457) as Quodvultdeus's successor after a fourteen-year hi-

---

58. See Fournier, *Victor of Vita and the Vandal "Persecution,"* where he notes the parallels between *Hist. pers.* 1.15 and 3.15.

59. Cf. Vict.-Vit. *Hist. pers.* 1.5 and Augustine, *Ciu.* 1.10, noted by Fournier, *Victor of Vita and the Vandal "Persecution,"* 192-93.

60. *Lib. Gen.* 616F (the Florentini version) *MGH* AA 9:194-95.

61. On Victor of Vita as both a historian and a hagiographer, see Shanzer, "Intentions and Audiences."

62. Victor of Vita, Salvian, and Possidius mostly refer to Proconsularis. Archeological evidence for conversion of buildings also seems concentrated around Carthage.

63. Vict.-Vit. *Hist. pers.* 1.9, 15, 16; Proc. Caes. *Hist. bel.* 1.21.18-19. For further information on these buildings, see pp. 134-47.

64. Vict.-Vit. *Hist. pers.* 1.25.

atus.[65] After Valentinian's assassination and the Vandal sack of Rome in 455, Deogratias fell afoul of Vandal authorities, perhaps because he provided a refuge for Roman exiles in the suburban basilicas of Faustus and Novarum.[66] When Deogratias died in 457, the office remained empty for almost twenty-five years. Geiseric further forbade the ordination of any additional bishops for the region around Carthage. He also required anyone serving the Vandal royal household to adopt Arian Christianity and be rebaptized; he prohibited Nicene religious assemblies, forcing them to worship in secret.[67] According to Victor of Vita, the number of Nicene bishops in Africa Proconsularis consequently dwindled to three from an original number of 164.[68] These repressions may have provoked and responded to the attempts of the emperors Majorian, Marcellinus, and Leo I to destroy the Vandal Kingdom in Africa. They set the religious context for Eudocia's decision to abandon her husband, Huneric, and her son, Hilderic, for exile in the East.

Geiseric was succeeded by his eldest son, Huneric (477-484), who initially continued his father's policies. Beginning in 480 or 481, however, he adopted a more moderate stance in negotiations with Emperor Zeno (474-491) and under the influence of Placidia (sister to his departed wife Eudocia). He allowed the Nicenes to elect Eugenius as Bishop of Carthage (481-484). In return for this concession, the Arians were to be allowed to practice their own religion elsewhere in the empire and to preach in the local language.[69] Huneric began to seek out and persecute Manichaeans, perhaps to demonstrate his attachment to orthodoxy as he saw it. Unfortunately, according to Victor, he discovered that many of the Manichaeans he rounded up were actually also adherents of Arianism.[70]

Jealousy soon shattered the peace. Vandals seen going into Nicene churches raised questions about loyalty, and Huneric once again required all court officials to follow the Arian faith, forbade any conversions of Arians, and reinstituted persecutions.[71] When a Nicene bishop died, the property of his church might be seized or a payment required before a successor could be installed.[72]

---

65. Vict.-Vit. *Hist. pers.* 1.24. The significance of this is unclear — it may not indicate suspension of the ban on Nicene services or restoration of churches.

66. Vict.-Vit. *Hist. pers.* 1.26-29. The exiles were fleeing Vandal incursions into the Italian peninsula and the sack of Rome in 455.

67. See, for instance, the case of Saturus, the superintendent of the household of Huneric: Vict.-Vit. *Hist. pers.* 1.48-50. See also Vict.-Vit. *Hist. pers.* 2.1; 1.41; 2.39; 3.4.

68. Vict.-Vit. *Hist. pers.* 1.24-29; Heather, "Christianity and the Vandals in the Reign of Geiseric." The number of bishops (54) at the 484 conference suggests that not all were exiled and that some remained in their sees.

69. Vict.-Vit. *Hist. pers.* 2.1-6. Victor also mentioned Eugenius as bishop from about 480-84 (*Hist. pers.* 2.18, 47-51) and as exiled in 484 (*Hist. pers.* 3.34).

70. Vict.-Vit. *Hist. pers.* 2.1.

71. Vict.-Vit. *Hist. pers.* 2.8-9, 23.

72. Vict.-Vit. *Hist. pers.* 2.23.

Victor reports that the king tortured consecrated virgins, and sent nearly five thousand Nicene deacons, priests, and bishops into exile in the desert.[73]

Intending to show himself as theologically motivated, Huneric ultimately ordered the beleaguered Nicene bishops to a conference (484) to argue their case.[74] The Nicenes asked who would serve as judge. They were told that the Arian patriarch Cyrila had personally selected the jury. The Nicenes then protested Cyrila's claiming the title of patriarch, which only stirred up the Arian side to anger at the perceived insult. Then, led by their bishop, Eugenius, the Nicenes presented a book containing their confession of faith. The Vandals refused to accept it, maintaining that they were unable to read Latin. The Nicenes delivered the document anyway, insisting that the excuse was merely invented for the occasion. Ultimately the Nicenes were denied an actual hearing, in part because the Arians objected to the Nicenes calling themselves "catholics," a term they reserved for themselves. The Nicenes countered by charging that the Vandals were unwilling to accept their "book of faith" because their blind eyes were unable to tolerate the light of truth.[75]

The uproar at this exchange of insults moved the king once again to grant all African churches and property to Arian bishops and to threaten to exile any Nicene cleric who persisted in holding services.[76] Finally, by means of a subterfuge, Huneric rounded up the destitute clergy and demanded that they swear to uphold a document naming his son, Hilderic, as his successor. Whether they succumbed to this demand or not, all were sent into exile — either for disloyalty or for swearing an oath contrary to the commands of the gospel (Matt. 5:33).[77]

Huneric's successor, Gunthamund (484-96), returned to a policy of appeasement and granted the shrine of St. Agileus to Eugenius, the Nicene Bishop of Carthage, when he returned from exile.[78] The expanded shrine served as the Catholic cathedral for most of the rest of the Vandal era in Africa.[79] Gunthamund also allowed some clergy to return. This peaceful interlude served as an opportunity for those Nicenes who had fallen into apostasy, having been rebaptized as Arians, to return to the fold. This concession was resisted by a group of rigorists and required an appeal to the Bishop of Rome, Felix I, who convened a synod in 487 in Rome, and sent a letter to the African bishops with instructions for the readmission of the lapsed.[80]

73. Vict.-Vit. *Hist. pers.* 2.26-32.

74. Vict.-Vit. *Hist. pers.* 2.23-37.

75. Vict.-Vit. *Hist. pers.* 2.53-55; 3.1. The book of the faith begins at 2.56 with a definition of the word *homoousion*.

76. Vict.-Vit. *Hist. pers.* 3.7-14, the Decree of Huneric.

77. Vict.-Vit. *Hist. pers.* 3.17-21.

78. Vict.-Ton. *Chron.* 52 (480); *Later. Wand.* 7-8. See below, p. 139.

79. Identified with Bir el Knissia. See Liliane Ennabli, *Carthage, une métropole chrétienne du IVe à la fin du VIIe siècle,* Études d'antiquités africaines (Paris: CNRS éd., 1997), 38-39, 113-20.

80. 13 March 487, von Hefele, *Histoire des conciles d'après les documents originaux,* 2:934-

When Gunthamund's younger brother, Thrasamund, came to power (496-523), the tide turned again. Thrasamund exiled the Catholic clerics. Initially, he tried to convert Nicenes by offering them financial inducements, prestigious offices, and even pardon for crimes.[81] Around 504, he prohibited episcopal elections that would have filled vacancies in Nicene sees in a simple attempt to have the church die out from lack of leadership. The bishops, however, resisted his order and proceeded with the ordination of new bishops. Their disobedience provoked the king to order exile again.[82] Vacillating between incentives and threats, Thrasamund finally tried theological argument and persuasion to convert the Nicenes. Seeking a worthy opponent who could expound the Nicene position, he recalled Fulgentius, Bishop of Ruspe. Too late realizing the eloquence and learning of his adversary, the threatened Thrasamund sent Fulgentius back into exile,[83] where he wrote the major polemical tracts detailing the objections of the African Nicenes to Arian Vandal theology.[84] As hard as he had tried to compel conversions, at the end of his life Thrasamund allowed the establishment of parallel churches.[85]

Thrasamund was succeeded by Huneric's son, Hilderic (523-530), who adhered to the Nicene orthodoxy of his mother, the western princess Eudocia, rather than the Arian creed of his father. Hilderic broke with the Ostrogoths, allied himself with the Byzantines, recalled any living Nicene clergy from exile, and reopened the churches. The return of the exiled clerics was a triumphant moment for the African church. They were greeted as their generation's heroes and martyrs. Bonifatius was installed as Bishop of Carthage and presided over a council in 525 at the Basilica of St. Agileus. In nearly a century of Vandal rule in Carthage, only three other bishops had held the post, and all had died in exile (Quodvultdeus, Deogratias, and Eugenius). Among the sixty or so bishops present for the council was the twice-exiled Fulgentius.[86] These men had to deal with the reorganization of the African church, which included the calcula-

35; Gian Domenico Mansi, *Sacrorum Conciliorum Nova et Amplissima Collectio,* ed. Jean-Baptiste Martin et al. (Paris: expensis H. Welter, 1901), 7:1171-1174; Jean-Louis Maier, *L'épiscopat de l'Afrique romaine, vandale, et byzantine* (Rome: Institut suisse de Rome, 1973), 73. Four African bishops were in attendance.

81. Proc. Caes. *Hist. bel.* 3.8.8-12.

82. Ferrand. *Vita Fulg.* 13-14.

83. Ferrand. *Vita Fulg.* 20-21, which describes the debate itself.

84. These tracts are *Responsiones ad objectiones Regis Thrasamundi, Ad Thrasamundum libri III* (see mention below), and *Adversus Pintam* (now lost), CCSL 91 and 91A. For an introduction to his life and English translation of other works, see *Fulgentius: Selected Works,* trans. Robert B. Eno, Fathers of the Church, vol. 95 (Washington, D.C.: Catholic University of America Press, 1997). See Susan T. Stevens, "The Circle of Bishop Fulgentius," *Traditio* 38 (1982): 327-40, with a good introductory bibliography up to that publication date.

85. Courtois, *Les Vandales et l'Afrique,* 304.

86. Vict.-Ton. *Chron.* 106 (523); *Later. Wand.* 16; Ferrand. *Vita Fulg.* 26-27.

tions of the seniority of bishops and the regulation of relations between diocesan bishops and monasteries.[87]

Hilderic, however, ultimately was overthrown in 530 by the last Vandal king, Gelimer, who ruled for a scant four years (530-33) before Emperor Justinian I demanded that Hilderic be returned to the throne. When Gelimer refused and had Hilderic imprisoned instead, Justinian mobilized to retake Africa, in part to avenge the overthrow of that Nicene Christian, son of the house of Theodosius.

## The Vandal Imprint

Only a few Vandal-built churches (or significant renovations) have been identified. This suggests not only that the invaders appropriated available buildings for their religious services (as reported by Victor of Vita), but also that the Vandal liturgy required little architectural adaption.[88] Vandal occupation of a formerly Catholic or Donatist church is evidenced by inscriptions, especially Germanic names on funerary plaques. One such inscription, found in what has been tentatively identified as Augustine's basilica in Hippo, names a certain Guilia Runa as a *presbyterissa,* a title that has led some scholars to think that she attained a kind of clerical standing (fig. 125).[89]

The assimilation of the Vandals into late Roman culture may have contributed to the loss of a distinctly Vandal identity. Along with this, they may also have lost the conviction that they were following and spreading the true Christian faith by both word and sword. The time was thus ripe for another attempt at Byzantine reconquest and the reclaiming of Africa for the orthodox faith.

# BYZANTINE AFRICA

## Justinian's Conquest

After Gelimer refused to submit to Justinian's demand that he reinstate Hilderic as king, Justinian decided that it was time (and God's will) that he attempt to retake Africa. Despite being reminded of the disasters suffered in the previous expeditions,[90] General Belisarius led a Byzantine force of 15,000 infantry and cavalry in the spring of 533 from Constantinople to the outskirts of Carthage

87. *Con. Carth.* 5-6 Feb. 525; Maier, *L'épiscopat de l'Afrique romaine, vandale, et byzantine,* 74-76.
88. See discussion below, pp. 95-96.
89. *Ordained Women in the Early Church: A Documentary History,* ed. Carolyn Osiek and Kevin Madigan (Baltimore: Johns Hopkins University Press, 2005), 197-98.
90. Proc. Caes. *Hist. bel.* 3.10.1-24.

(Decimum), arriving the day before the Feast of St. Cyprian (September 14). Being out of the city when Belisarius landed his troops, Gelimer was taken by surprise, executed Hilderic, and attempted to surround the Byzantine forces. But he miscalculated, and the Vandal forces were destroyed.[91] When Belisarius and his infantry reached Carthage itself on the next day, the residents threw open the gates and surrendered the city.[92]

The conquest of Carthage was providential in the eyes of many of its citizens. Procopius's chronicle reports that some recalled an enigmatic and ancient childhood riddle: that gamma should pursue beta and then beta pursue gamma. This was interpreted as an oracle that Geiseric would replace Boniface, and then Belisarius would replace Gelimer. Other Africans testified that St. Cyprian had appeared to them in dreams, assuring them that he would be his own avenger. It was no coincidence, therefore, that the Byzantine entrance into the city took place on that saint's feast day, in time for the African Catholic priests to preside over the celebrations instead of the fleeing Arians.[93]

In another of his chronicles, Procopius described Justinian's rebuilding program for Carthage, which included restoring the wall and constructing new churches (one dedicated to the Theotokos), a monastery, a new forum, and a public bath.[94] Other African cities benefited from this era of reconstruction and elaboration. Byzantine forts were planted, using large blocks of dressed stone in place of the older style of building known as *opus Africanum,* which used stone uprights and horizontal courses filled with mortared loose rubble. New churches were built in nearly every important center. In a later chronicle, Procopius described the harsher realities of the reconquest and imposition of Byzantine rule: the deaths of countless Vandals and the violent repression of Arianism.[95]

A series of Mauri uprisings in the late 530s and early 540s, followed by a mutiny within the imperial army itself, caused the Byzantine general Solomon (Belisarius's replacement) to flee to Syracuse. Some of the Byzantine troops had married Vandal women or, as Goths, were Arians themselves. Apparently, Vandal clergy prompted the rebellion when they were not allowed to baptize their children or celebrate Easter in their own churches.[96] Meanwhile, Romanized, Latin-speaking Africans found themselves caught between a government of Greek-speaking foreigners and a suddenly energized coalition of native tribes, mutinous troops, revenge-seeking Vandals, and rebel slaves. Eventually

91. Proc. Caes. *Hist. bel.* 3.19. See also Isid. *Hist.* 83-84.

92. Proc. Caes. *Hist. bel.* 3.20.

93. Proc. Caes. *Hist. bel.* 3.21.11-25. On the Vandal taking of the shrine, see Vict.-Vit. *Hist. pers.* 1.16 (discussed above). Procopius dates this seizure to the reign of Huneric, Victor to the time of Geiseric.

94. Proc. Caes. *Hist. bel.* 3.23.19-20 (walls), 4.26.17 (monastery); *Aed.* 6.5.8-11 (walls, shrines, forum, bath, and monastery).

95. Proc. Caes. *Anec.* 18.5-13.

96. Proc. Caes. *Hist. bel.* 4.14.25.

Belisarius returned with Solomon and restored relative, but temporary, order.[97] Trouble broke out again, however, in 543, and the whole of Roman Africa was thrown into chaos. Carthage fell again to a Vandal leader, Gontharis.[98] Finally, in 546 a new *magister militum,* John Troglita, defeated the rebellion and reasserted imperial authority.

Corippus authored an eight-volume panegyric on John, the *Iohannis.* Although an African himself, he had no sympathy with the rebels — especially with the natives, whom he described as uncouth and violent worshipers of a bull-god called Gurzil. His writings supply invaluable but undoubtedly biased evidence on contemporary Mauri tribes and customs but also offer perspective on how some Africans viewed the Byzantine army. He describes them as bringing stability and order in the midst of untenable social and civil strife.[99]

## Byzantine Orthodoxy

The Byzantines — no more tolerant of Arian Christians than the Vandals had been of Nicenes — re-established their own faith, restored the native Catholic hierarchy to their former churches, and prohibited Arian sacraments. Nearly a century of Vandal rule and culture was swiftly repudiated. In 535, an edict restored all the rights of the orthodox Nicene church and initiated persecution of Donatists, Jews, Arians, other heretics, and pagans.[100] Despite their reinstatement, the African Catholic bishops soon learned that their Byzantine liberators were actually a new set of elite colonial rulers who kept largely to themselves and controlled both military and civil affairs. Thus, their joy at the defeat of the Vandals soon turned toward dismay, especially since the last of the Vandal kings, Gelimer, may have been more tolerant than their new ruler in Constantinople proved to be.

In matters of religion, moreover, the Greek administrators expected the Africans to conform to orthodoxy as it was defined in the distant, eastern capital.[101] Although the churches retained Latin, their liturgies were inevitably influenced by Byzantine customs, and new buildings were often dedicated to Greek saints. At the same time, certain African architectural traditions were

97. Proc. Caes. *Hist. bel.* 4.8-28 covers this period of disruption.

98. Proc. Caes. *Hist. bel.* 4.35-37.

99. On this treatise and Corippus's coverage of this period in general, see Averil Cameron, "Byzantine Africa — The Literary Evidence," in *Excavations at Carthage,* ed. John H. Humphrey (Ann Arbor: Kelsey Museum, University of Michigan, 1982), 7:29-62, with excellent bibliographical footnotes. Corippus's writings give some precious but problematic evidence on Berber tribes and customs at this time.

100. *Nou. Afr. Ecc.* 37.5-8.

101. Cameron, "Byzantine Africa — The Literary Evidence," 45, notes that the seals are mostly Greek, while only a minority of the Christian epitaphs are Greek.

maintained, including the construction of counter-apses for the burial of clergy, saints, or relics, and the use of mosaic tomb covers.[102] If the rarity of Greek names on bishops' lists for councils in the 540s and 550s is a reliable indicator, African clerics also managed local ecclesiastical politics. Meanwhile, the Byzantine ruler expected them to adopt the hierarchal model practiced in the East — a model in which the provincial primates of sees no longer acted through regular meetings with their fellow bishops but reported directly to the emperor and were obedient to his rulings on ecclesiastical matters.[103]

The Africans continued to act according to many of their own practices and regarded Rome (rather than Constantinople) as their closest ecclesiastical ally, just as they had more than a century earlier during the Donatist and Pelagian controversies. During Vandal rule, moreover, many of the bishops had spent years as exiles in Sicily and elsewhere in Italy, thus strengthening their ties to that church. In 535, under the leadership of Bishop Reparatus (Bonifatius's successor in Carthage), the bishops convoked a council to decide what to do with Arian converts to Nicene orthodoxy. They called upon the Bishop of Rome, John II (and ultimately his successor, Agapetus I), for advice on and support of their decrees. This council refused to recognize Arian orders and reduced clergy who converted to the Nicene faith to lay status. This reversed their earlier practice of allowing readmitted Donatists to retain their offices. In so doing they followed the Roman church's policy for reconciled schismatics at the beginning of the fifth century.[104]

### African Resistance to Justinian

Having survived more than a century in resistance to Vandal repression of their Nicene Christianity, the African clergy resented efforts from the imperial court in Constantinople to impose doctrinal conformity, especially when they judged that compliance would draw them into heresy. A religious crisis erupted in 543-44 when Justinian ordered the African bishops to accept the condemnation of the *Three Chapters*. This anathematized the writings of theologians associated with Nestorius during the Christological debates a century earlier, culminating in the decree of the Council of Chalcedon in 451.[105] Justinian's edict was yet another attempt to reconcile eastern Monophysites by undermining the compromises made at Chalcedon, which the African Catholics (along with the rest of the western church) had staunchly defended. The African bishops were

102. See the discussion of architecture in the Byzantine period, pp. 96-97, 100.

103. On this point, see Cameron, "Byzantine Africa — The Literary Evidence," 45.

104. The first council was in the Basilica of Faustus in 535. See von Hefele, *Histoire des conciles d'après les documents originaux*, 2:1136-39; Mansi, *Sacrorum conciliorum nova et amplissima collectio*, 8:808-9; *Col. Avel.* 85-87; Maier, *L'épiscopat de l'Afrique romaine, vandale, et byzantine*, 77.

105. Theodore of Mopsuestia, Theodoret of Cyrrhus, and Ibas of Edessa.

not especially sympathetic to Justinian's desire to overcome religious conflict within the eastern part of the empire. They joined the other western primates, including the Bishop of Rome, in withholding their consent.[106]

A series of dogmatic treatises produced from the late 540s to the early 560s summarized the Africans' reasons for dissent. These works — produced by Ferrandus, the secretary to Fulgentius of Respue, Facundus, the Bishop of Hermiane, and Liberatus, the Archdeacon of Carthage — show that African clerics presumed the right to judge independently on matters of dogma and discipline. Liberatus composed a *Breuiarium,* summarizing the teachings of Nestorius and the position of the Monophysites in order to educate his fellow Africans on the essentials of the two heresies.[107] Facundus's treatise, *The Defense of the Three Chapters,* came to the attention of Justinian himself and merited specific denunciation in his second edict of 551.[108] The production of such documents showed that the Africans were unconvinced that Theodore's views (in particular) were in any way heretical, although their knowledge of his theology was largely third-hand, from a textbook written by a certain Junillus that was based on the teachings of Theodore's student, Paul of Nisibis.[109]

In Rome, Bishop Vigilius (537-555) succumbed to Justinian's pressure to conform. A council at Carthage (550) excommunicated him[110] and provoked Justinian to summon its leaders — including Reparatus of Carthage, Primasius of Hadrumetum, Firmus of Tipasa, and Verecundus of Iunci — to justify themselves in Constantinople.[111] Reparatus steadfastly opposed the emperor and was sent into exile, where he eventually died.[112] The deacon Primosus, after providing his assent to the condemnation, was installed as Bishop of Carthage, reportedly against the opposition of clergy and people. Firmus also conceded and was allowed to return home but died on the return voyage. Although at first resistant, Primasius ultimately relented, reportedly when the office of primate in Byzacena became available and was offered to him. He was subsequently condemned by his fellow bishops and died in disgrace. Verecundus held fast and died in exile.[113] After the Second Council of Constantinople (553) approved

---

106. See Yves Modéran, "L'Afrique reconquise et les Trois Chapitres," in *The Crisis of the Oikoumene: The Three Chapters and the Failed Quest for Unity in the Sixth-Century Mediterranean,* ed. Celia Martin Chazelle and Catherine Cubitt (Turnhout: Brepols, 2007), 39-82.

107. PL 68:969-1052.

108. CCSL 90A:1-398. See Cameron, "Byzantine Africa — The Literary Evidence," 47.

109. Junillus's treatise is titled *Instituta regularia divinae legis,* PL 68:15-42. Vict.-Ton. *Chron.* 142 (a. 550). See Cameron, "Byzantine Africa — The Literary Evidence," 46, and Tony Honoré, *Tribonian* (Ithaca, N.Y.: Cornell University Press, 1978), 237-42.

110. Vict.-Ton. *Chron.* 141 (550); Cameron, "Byzantine Africa — The Literary Evidence," 47-49.

111. Vict.-Ton. *Chron.* 143 (551).

112. Vict.-Ton. *Chron.* 145 (552), 165 (563).

113. Vict.-Ton. *Chron.* 145 (552); Reparatus died in exile in 563 on the island of Euchaita. Vict.-Ton. *Chron.* 165.

the condemnation of the *Three Chapters*,[114] Reparatus's opponents garnered support for Primosus as Bishop of Carthage.[115]

Victor of Tunnuna, a loyal supporter of Reparatus, chronicled these turns of fortune. His resistance led Primosus to seek his imprisonment as well, along with another African colleague, Theodore of Cebarsussi. First exiled to the monastery that Justinian had earlier established in Carthage (the Mandracium), both were finally shipped off to Egypt. Joining other exiled African bishops, they stood fast against the wishes of the emperor and patriarch in Constantinople.[116] Although African resistance to imperial government interference wavered under pressure, these exiles maintained their opposition until Justinian's death in 565. In the next decades, the theological controversy was overwhelmed by more pressing security matters: the Lombard incursion in Italy and the Persian threat in the east.[117]

## Donatism

Throughout this time, the African church continued to deal with a Donatist presence. The only full list of African bishops, from the Conference of Carthage in 411, indicates that the Donatist church was relatively stronger in Numidia and Mauretania.[118] These were the areas, it will be recalled, that suffered least from Vandal repression, reverting as they did to Roman control in the treaty of 442.[119] Moreover, the Donatist ideology and that church's experience of repression in the early fifth century would have prepared it for the Vandal persecution. The Donatist church seems to have survived in Africa, even under Byzantine rule.

In the 590s, Gregory I wrote to Gennadius, the Exarch of Africa, requesting that he suppress the Donatists and that he support Gregory's efforts to pre-

---

114. Vict.-Ton. *Chron.* 147 (553). The transcript of this council may be read in English in *A Select Library of the Nicene and Post-Nicene Fathers of the Christian Church,* ed. Philip Schaff (Edinburgh: T&T Clark, 1989), 2/14:299-323. The Africans were not alone in their dissent, although Pope Vigilius conformed to the anathema of the *Three Chapters.* The council's decisions were opposed by bishops in the north of Italy (esp. Milan), Gaul, Spain, and Britain as well as in areas of Asia Minor.

115. von Hefele, *Histoire des conciles d'après les documents originaux,* 3:145. Vict.-Ton. *Chron.* 145 (552), 152 (555).

116. Vict.-Ton. *Chron.* 153, 156, 169.

117. Vict.-Ton. *Chron.* 170 (565). The controversy, of course, continued, mainly in Italy, through the seventh century, ending when the Lombards embraced Orthodoxy in 698 at the Synod of Aquileia.

118. See especially the analysis provided by Serge Lancel, "La représentation des différentes provinces à la conférence," in *Actes de la conférence de Carthage en 411,* SC (Paris: Éditions du Cerf, 1972), 194:143-67. The Donatists had half their bishops in those areas, while the Catholics had only a third. The two churches had roughly the same number of bishops.

119. See above, pp. 64-65.

vent former Donatists who had been allowed to serve as Catholic bishops from advancing, through seniority, to the office of provincial primate.[120] This effort seems to have failed, however, since several subsequent letters refer to bishops handing churches over to Donatist clerics and permitting the establishment of Donatist bishops.[121] Gregory insisted that Donatism was spreading and that many Catholics had received rebaptism.[122] Some Catholics, he had heard, were allowing their children and dependents to be baptized by the Donatists.[123] In a separate letter to Pantaleo, Prefect of Africa, Gregory contended that Donatists were even driving Catholic bishops out of their churches.[124] Gregory's letters protest the actions of Catholic clergy and laity in dealing with Donatists primarily, if not exclusively, in Numidia. They indicate, moreover, that Gregory was responding to deacons complaining to an overseas authority about their bishops[125] and that he worked through a few Numidian bishops especially loyal to the Roman church, whom he asked the imperial representative, Gennadius, to support.[126] In one instance, he not only explained his episcopal responsibilities to the primate of Numidia — the most senior bishop in the province — but admonished him to seek and follow the advice of Gregory's favorite, Bishop Columbus.[127] Gregory's interventions may have been viewed in Numidia as those of yet another meddling external authority.[128] The bishops of Proconsular Africa, in contrast, were only too ready to purge the church of all those tainted by "heresy" as well as all who tolerated them.[129]

Gregory's correspondence indicates that Donatism, at least in name, had not disappeared despite centuries of effort at its suppression by both church and state. The tenacity of this ethnically African movement perhaps demon-

120. Greg. Mag. *Ep.* 1.72, 75. In the early fifth century, the African Catholic bishops — contrary to the advice of the bishops of Rome and Milan — had allowed Donatists to gain or retain clerical office when they entered Catholic unity. *Reg. Carth.* 57, 68.

121. Greg. Mag. *Ep.* 1.82; 2.39. In both cases, the Catholic bishops were accused of accepting bribes.

122. Greg. Mag. *Ep.* 2.39; 4.35.

123. Greg. Mag. *Ep.* 6.36.

124. Greg. Mag. *Ep.* 4.32, 35; 6.36.

125. Greg. Mag. *Ep.* 1.82; 2.39. Such action had been forbidden (*Cau. Apiar.* 28).

126. Columbus, Victor, and Paulus, Greg. Mag. *Ep.* 2.39; 3.47; 6.36 (to Columbus), 4.7; 6.62 (to Gennadius), 4.35 (to Victor and Columbus). Columbus himself finally complained that Gregory's frequent communication with him had resulted in his alienation from his episcopal colleagues (Greg. Mag. *Ep.* 7.2).

127. Greg. Mag. *Ep.* 3.48 (to Adeodatus).

128. R. A. Markus, "The Imperial Administration and the Church in Byzantine Africa," *Church History* 36, no. 1 (1967): 18-23; "Donatism: The Last Phase," *Studies in Church History* 1 (1964): 118-26; "Country Bishops in Byzantine Africa," *Studies in Church History* 16 (1979): 1-14; "Reflections on Religious Dissent in North Africa in the Byzantine Period," *Studies in Church History* 3 (1966): 140-49. See also the discussion in Cameron, "Byzantine Africa — The Literary Evidence," 49-51, who does not see evidence for a Donatist revival in Africa.

129. Greg. Mag. *Ep.* 5.3 (to Dominicus of Carthage).

strates a continued disaffection of the native population from a Catholic, Romanized hierarchy as well as from foreign secular authorities.[130] Editions of the Donatist chronicle, the *Liber Genealogus,* were published between 427 and 453. The Bishop of Rome, Leo I, wrote a letter to the bishops of Gaul about possible Donatist refugees in the 450s, and Victor of Vita may have mentioned Donatists as late as the 480s.[131] Archeological evidence of Donatism in the Vandal and Byzantine eras includes certain church inscriptions that mention characteristically Donatist themes (e.g., purity and sanctity), record so-called Donatist watchwords (e.g., *Deo laus*), or employ the term *unitas* (perhaps indicating anti-Donatist sympathies).[132] Apart from these slim indications, however, no literary or archeological records of Donatists in Africa exist for the century before Gregory's writings.

## The Final Debate

A controversy over the nature of the divine will (Monothelitism) that erupted during the first half of the seventh century led to the last significant theological action of the North African church and, once again, demonstrated its doctrinal independence. The surviving documentary evidence indicates that some of the debate was carried on in Greek among Byzantine exiles. Because Greek had not been a language of North African Christianity since the end of the second century, its reappearance shows either the influence of a century of governance from Constantinople or, more likely, an influx of refugees from the Persian and Arab incursions in the East. The debate itself continued a conflict over the interpretation of Chalcedon long considered settled in the west, and the African bishops were only too willing to add their voices to those of the resident Greeks.[133]

Following Justinian's model in the earlier Monophysite controversy, the emperors Heraclius (610-14) and Constans II (641-68) attempted to impose the dogma that the human and divine natures of Christ shared a single, combined activity or will (Monothelitism). As before, the African church resisted.

---

130. W. H. C. Frend, *The Donatist Church: A Movement of Protest in Roman North Africa* (Oxford: Clarendon Press, 2000), chap. 19.

131. Leo I, *Ep.* 168.18; Victor of Vita's passing mention and possible interpolation, *Hist. pers.* 3.71.

132. Frend, *The Donatist Church*, 306-8; Noël Duval and Jean Cintas, "L'église du prêtre Felix (region de Kélibia)," *Karthago. Revue d'archéologie africaine* 9 (1958): 157-265.

133. Cameron, "Byzantine Africa — The Literary Evidence," 52-53, points out that other aspects of eastern religious practice, including the cult of the Virgin, are not strongly evident in Africa — and that the bishops in the mid-seventh century are still Latin-speaking. The Latin bishops cited their own sources — Ambrose and Augustine — in support of their refusal to agree to the innovation.

Opposition was supported by Gregory, the Exarch of Africa, and Maximus the Confessor (580-662), a Byzantine monk who had fled to a Carthaginian monastery from the Persian advance into Anatolia around 630. This same monastery was also home to another refugee and major orthodox figure from the seventh century, Sophronius, later the patriarch of Jerusalem (634-39), who had fled from the invading Muslims. Both Maximus and Sophronius declared Monothelitism a heresy, because it denied the human will of Christ. The African church maintained that this, like the condemnation of the *Three Chapters,* bordered on repudiating the Chalcedonian definition of the faith.

The exarch Gregory sponsored a debate in 645 between Maximus and Pyrrhus. The latter was abbot of Maximus's former monastery and deposed patriarch of Constantinople, who also found his way to Carthage.[134] Pyrrhus was a defender of the Monothelite doctrine; he had been deposed and exiled for political rather than theological reasons. Pyrrhus was no match for Maximus, and the confrontation ended in his recantation.[135] Since the African bishops looked to Rome as an ally in doctrinal questions, both Maximus and Pyrrhus sailed there to seek the assistance of Pope Theodore. Seeing, however, an opportunity to reclaim his status by cooperation with the emperor, Pyrrhus reverted to his former theological position and returned to Constantinople, where he was eventually reinstated as patriarch after the death of his replacement, Paul II (641-653). This betrayal led Pope Theodore to excommunicate him. Emperor Constans II then tried to cut off further argument by issuing an imperial decree that forbade any further discussion of Christ's one or two wills or energies.[136]

In 646, episcopal synods were held in each of the African provinces to condemn the Monothelite doctrine. These synods directed a letter to the Bishop of Rome, seeking his support in resistance to the doctrine and the correction of Paul, the Bishop of Constantinople.[137] The bishops of Byzacena also addressed a letter to the emperor, asking him to suppress the heresy.[138] Finally, the bishops of Proconsular Africa addressed a letter to Paul of Constantinople, disputing the Monothelite teaching as contrary to the decree of the Council of Chalcedon on the integrity of the divine and human natures in Christ. In support of their remonstrance, they cited passages from the exposition *On the Faith,* which

---

134. Pyrrhus was Bishop of Constantinople from 638-641, and again in 654.

135. Maximus, *Disputatio cum Pyrrho,* PG 91:288-353.

136. See the introduction in Andrew Louth, *Maximus the Confessor,* The Early Church Fathers (London: Routledge, 1996), 3-18, and G. Berthold, *Maximus the Confessor: Selected Writings* (New York: Paulist Press, 1985).

137. The common letter of Columbus of Numidia, Stephen of Byzacena, and Reparatus of Mauretania was considered by Bishop Martin at the Roman synod of 649; Mansi, *Sacrorum conciliorum nova et amplissima collectio,* 10:919-23.

138. Read out at the same synod of Rome in 649, Mansi, *Sacrorum conciliorum nova et amplissima collectio,* 10:926-28, with the signatures of the bishops.

Ambrose of Milan had addressed to Emperor Gratian, and two selections from their own Augustine of Hippo.[139]

Meanwhile, in Carthage, the exarch Gregory attempted to set himself up as independent ruler of Africa. His revolt may have been instigated by Maximus's success in the debate against Pyrrhus, and he went so far as to threaten excommunication of the patriarch of Constantinople. Within a year, however, he was dead — killed in one of the first battles with invading Arabs, possibly at Sufetula, where he had established his capital (648). Gregory's death was the beginning of the end of Christian Africa and — more immediately — the collapse of political support for the theologians opposing the Monothelite teaching.[140]

At Rome during these events, the African bishops, not aware of Constans's order of silence, joined forces with Maximus and Pope Martin I (Theodore's successor) to continue the battle at a Lateran synod (649) where they anathematized Monothelitism. A gathering of more than a hundred bishops, most of them from Italy and Africa, reaffirmed Chalcedonian orthodoxy and asserted that its doctrine of Christ's two natures necessitated his also having two wills.[141] The letters of the African synods were read out and affirmed during this synod. After having forbidden any such action, Emperor Constans deemed the synod an act of clear rebellion and ordered the arrest and extradition of Pope Martin to Constantinople, where he was accused of treason (collaboration with Gregory was among other charges), deposed, and sent into exile (he died en route in 655). Maximus was similarly arrested, charged, and sent to be tried in Constantinople (655), where he was also sent into exile. From exile he continued his opposition to Monothelitism, engaging in debates and writing letters to supporters. His obstinacy led to his torture and mutilation. He died an old man in 662.[142]

........................................................................................................................

## ARAB AFRICA

Little is known about the African bishops who returned from the Lateran synod or how they coped with the next fifty years of off-and-on Arab invasions. From the middle of the seventh century, the written record of Christianity in Africa dies out entirely; the only sources are Arabic histories that concentrate on the

139. Ambr. *Fid.* 2.8.70-71, 5.43-45, 6.50–7.57. Aug. *Serm. Arian.* 16.9; *Ep.* 140.4.11.
140. Theophanes, *Chron.* 352, 370 (638, 639).
141. Mansi, *Sacrorum Conciliorum Nova et Amplissima Collectio*, 10:863-1183; von Hefele, *Histoire des conciles d'après les documents originaux*, 3:434-51.
142. See the documents of this period in *Scripta Saeculi VII Vitam Maximi Confessoris Illustrantia* (CCG 39); and the *Acta* of Maximus's trial in PG 90.109-205, 205-21 (recorded by his disciple Anastasius). Maximus died in Georgia on August 13 after having had his tongue and right hand cut off. The Sixth Ecumenical Council at Constantinople in 680 affirmed the two wills of Christ, vindicating Maximus's work against Monothelitism.

conversion of the region to Islam and its transformation from a set of Roman provinces into the Maghreb. Carthage held out longer than many other places, finally falling to the Arabs in 698 after a siege of some months and help from Constantinople sent too late.

Although Christianity may have survived for another century or two, and possibly even longer in rural areas among native tribes who never fully converted to the new religion, the story of one of the most influential and robust of early Christian churches seems to end here.[143] The reasons for its ultimate extinction may not be so puzzling, however, in light of those previous centuries of struggle to maintain identity in the context of successive internal divisions, colonial occupations, and doctrinal controversies. Each new ruler required some level of religious conformity, and perhaps in the great scheme of things, this last arrival was no more "foreign" than any of the others. In fact, it may have seemed more like traditional African Christianity than any of the others in certain respects — including its emphasis on rigorous individual and communal purity; the importance of heroic martyrs and saints; and the perception that only one true community guarded and guaranteed authentic religious faith. Perhaps at least the character (if not the theology) of African Christianity survived in some respect, after all, by being absorbed into the Islam of the Maghreb.

143. On the survival of Christianity in Africa well past the eighth century, see Virginie Prevost, "Les dernières communautés chrétiennes autochtones d'Afrique du Nord," *Revue de l'histoire des religions* 224 (2007): 461-83.

# CHAPTER 4

# Survey of the Archeological Evidence for Christian Practice

........................................................................................................................

## HISTORY AND OVERVIEW OF THE EVIDENCE

A small, rectangular mosaic in Tunis's Bardo Museum offers the only existing contemporary depiction of an African basilica. It also illustrates the way that African Christians thought about the structures that housed their weekly assemblies and ceremonies (fig. 132). Found at the site of ancient Thabraca (modern Tabarka), it most likely dates to the early fifth century. The image depicts a traditional basilica, showing interior and exterior simultaneously. The apse, columned nave, entrance door, patterned mosaic floor, clerestory windows, and tiled roof can be reconstructed fairly easily (fig. 133). Designed as a covering for the tomb of a woman named Valentia, the mosaic's inscription asserts that the church is mother *(ecclesia mater)*. Then, as now, the word "church" (or *ecclesia*) can mean several things: an idealized abstraction, a living community, or a building. In a sense, one always implies the others, giving meaning, identity, purpose, and support in turn. The living congregation is a visual representation of the ideal church; the building is a symbol of both.

African church buildings did not always look like the one depicted on this mosaic. The earliest African Christians most likely gathered for worship in private homes with dining rooms *(triclinia)* for the celebration of their sacred evening banquets.[1] Yet, as their congregations grew in membership, and their primary assemblies transitioned from evening meals to morning eucharistic liturgies as described by Tertullian and Cyprian, these house church communities would have been consolidated and their buildings renovated to allow larger and more varied gatherings. As elsewhere in the Roman world, this initial modification of existing structures (e.g., removal of walls to create halls) eventually

---

1. Cf. discussion of evening banquets below, pp. 234-35, 239-45.

led to the construction of new buildings, but the process was gradual and sometimes had to be repeated when buildings were confiscated or destroyed in times of persecution.[2] In particular, the Diocletian Persecution (in Africa, 303-305) saw at least some of these Christian buildings seized or destroyed. In such circumstances, congregations probably moved their assemblies back into private houses or met in martyrs' shrines within cemeteries outside of the city walls.[3]

Although documentary evidence indicates that many Christian buildings in Africa survived the persecution, almost no archeological evidence survives from this first era of church-building. The lack of remains may be due to the razing of buildings by troops, but also to the destruction caused by later rebuilding projects or even natural disasters, such as earthquakes that ravaged the area in the early 360s.[4] Rebuilding on original foundations might follow the former building's footprint or reuse materials, but reconstructed buildings were more often enlarged and elaborated. New church buildings sometimes were established, as before, on the periphery of a town, but gradually they came into the center, along main streets or near a city's forum, which transformed urban planning.[5]

In addition to paying for new construction, imperial grants after the Diocletian Persecution restored confiscated property to the church, but rival groups claimed rightful ownership to those properties. Throughout the fourth century, alternating periods of suppression and toleration of Donatist congregations caused buildings to change hands and losing parties to rebuild as needed.[6] In 330,

2. For the use of both smaller gatherings in homes and full assemblies in the early third century, see Tert. *Cor.* 3 and *Fug.* 3, as well as the discussion below, pp. 240-42, 251-52. *Act. Zeno.* 3-4 (CSEL 26:186.18–188.32) refers to a house church in Cirta (at the time of the Diocletian persecution) that had a library and a dining room. Interestingly, Optat. *Parm.* 1.14 describes a council at Cirta in 303 that had to take place in the house of Urban Carisus because the basilicas had not yet been restored. Evidence for a basilica in Carthage in the mid-third century includes the charge that Mensurius allowed Roman authorities to confiscate certain books from the Basilica Novarum; cf. Aug. *Coll.* 3.13.25. Compare the report of the looting and leveling of a large Christian church *(editissimum)* in Nicomedia under orders from Diocletian in Lact. *Mort.* 12. See also the account of the proceedings in *Act. pur. Fel.* 9 (CSEL 26:202.19-28) for a description of a house with a cathedra.

3. Tertullian gives evidence of Christian cemeteries *(Scap.* 3.1). The *Act. Zeno.* 16 (CSEL 26:194.11-27) also refers to the *casa maior,* a funerary chapel in the cemetery *(area martyrum),* where the Christians were gathered to elect a bishop two days after the peace, probably because the basilica was not yet restored to them. That the Christians gathered for prayers in a cemetery is also attested in the above account of the proceedings against Felix: *Act. pur. Fel.* 9 (CSEL 26:202.24-28).

4. Liban. *Or.* 11.264; *Ep.* 1359. See Claude Lepelley, "L'Afrique du Nord et le prétendu séisme universel du 21 juillet 365," *Mélanges de l'Ecole française de Rome, Antiquité* 96 (1984): 489-91; and Emanuela Guidoboni, ed., *Catalogue of Ancient Earthquakes in the Mediterranean Area up to the 10th Century,* trans. Brian Phillips (Rome: Istituto nazionale di geofisica, 1994), 259-60.

5. See Anna Leone, *Changing Townscapes in North Africa from Late Antiquity to the Arab Conquest,* Munera 28 (Bari: Edipuglia, 2007), 89-94.

6. Churches changed ownership during the original division, during the mission of Macarius and Paul (345-350), with the return of exiles under Julian (360-363), during the reaction to Julian, and finally after the Conference of Carthage in 411.

for example, Donatists seized the Caecilianist basilica in Constantina (built with funds from Constantine himself); and, although appeals were made, the emperor simply supplied the Caecilianists with funds to build another.[7] In the latter part of the century, the Donatists may have become the majority sect throughout Africa. Unquestionably they were dominant in Numidia.[8] Nevertheless, from 345 to 360, while Constans attempted to force a reunion of the two sects, Caecilianists would have taken control of some Donatist churches.[9] Julian chose to restore Donatist rights and property when, during his brief reign (361-63), he promulgated a re-script of toleration for the sect.[10] At this same time, Donatists began constructing enormous and impressive churches in several Numidian cities, most notably in their center at Thamugadi (Timgad).[11]

The promulgation of legislation suppressing the Donatists, under Emperors Arcadius and Honorius, ostensibly inhibited their building projects. From 408 onwards, Emperor Honorius ordered the transfer of all buildings used by Do-natists to the Caecilianist churches.[12] The bishops' list from the Conference of Carthage in 411 shows that nearly 60 percent of the towns in North Africa had both Donatist and Caecilianist bishops, and, presumably, different church build-ings served the separate congregations.[13] Carthage, for example, had a Caecilian-ist cathedral (called the Basilica Restituta)[14] and a Donatist cathedral, called by a Greek name, Theoprepia (Divine Majesty).[15] Thamugadi, the center of Numidian Donatist power, also had both a Donatist cathedral (possibly built by its notori-ous bishop, Optatus) and a Caecilianist one.[16] In addition, despite their official suppression following the conference of 411,[17] Donatist communities continued to build churches, especially in areas where their influence was still strong.[18]

7. Constantine *Ep. Const. Zeu.*

8. That Catholics were "few in number," see Possid. *Vita Aug.* 7 and Optat. *Parm.* 7.1.

9. For more details on this time, see above, pp. 49-50.

10. The rescript is no longer extant. Evidence for it exists in Optat. *Parm.* 2.16 and *C.Th.* 16.5.37. See above, p. 51.

11. Remains of eleven churches have been excavated in Thamugadi, of which four are possibly from the pre-Vandal period. Almost certainly one of these was the Donatist cathedral founded by Optatus. See Isabelle Gui, Noël Duval, and Jean-Pierre, eds., *Basiliques chrétiennes d'Afrique du Nord, I: Inventaire de l'Algérie, 1* (Paris: Institut d'études augustiniennes, 1992), 263-86; also see the discussion below, pp. 160-62.

12. *C.Th.* 16.5.43.

13. Calculated on the basis of the lists in Jean-Louis Maier, *L'épiscopat de l'Afrique romaine, vandale, et byzantine* (Rome: Institut suisse de Rome, 1973), 44-63.

14. This was where Augustine preached when he visited Carthage (*Serm.* 19; 29; 90; 112; 277). See the discussion below, p. 135.

15. Aug. *Ep.* 139.1; *Psal.* 80; *Col. Carth.* 3.5. See Liliane Ennabli, *Carthage, une métropole chré-tienne du IVe à la fin du VIIe siècle*, Études d'antiquités africaines (Paris: CNRS, 1997), 31-32.

16. See the discussion of Thamugadi below, pp. 160-62.

17. See above, p. 56.

18. *Reg. Carth.* 123, 124. For the discussion of Gregory the Great reporting Donatism as still active in the early seventh century, see above, pp. 80-82.

Meanwhile, the first decades of the fifth century also appear to have been a time of building for the Caecilianist congregations. Many larger cities apparently required several churches as much to serve their growing Christian population as their competing sects. Carthage had as many as a dozen basilicas by the early fifth century. In addition to a cathedral, "parish" churches, located in six ecclesiastical regions, served Carthage's Caecilianist community. Each apparently operated under the supervision of a presbyter, and many had annexed baptisteries for the initiation of converts and, eventually, for the regular baptism of infants.[19]

Other cities do not seem to have been so organized. Rather, some appear to have had multiple churches under the jurisdiction of a single bishop. When Augustine arrived in Hippo Regius in 391, the city had two churches for its Caecilianist community: the Basilica Pacis (or Basilica Maior) — probably the cathedral church — and the older Basilica of Leontius, dedicated to the city's patron saint and former bishop.[20] Another basilica was built (or perhaps expanded from a shrine) during Augustine's tenure as bishop, the Basilica of the Eight Martyrs.[21] In addition, Hippo Regius had at least one Donatist church building. Sometime before 395, a Donatist basilica had been constructed close enough to the Leontian basilica that the Donatists' singing was audible to their Caecilianist rivals.[22]

This church-building boom was offset by the gradual disappearance of pagan temples. Theodosius promulgated laws against pagan sacrifices in 381 and again in 385 and 391. Following on those actions, Honorius handed down edicts abolishing sacrifices, divination, and images of the gods that led to the destruction or the confiscation of temples for public use between 399 and 435.[23] Temples also were transformed into churches. Quodvultdeus, Bishop of Carthage, recorded witnessing his predecessor, Aurelius, seizing Carthage's Temple of Caelestis on Easter, probably sometime after 407.[24] Aurelius and his entourage

19. For the six regions, see Liliane Ennabli, "Topographie chrétienne de Carthage: Les régions ecclésiastiques," *Collection de l'École française de Rome,* 123, no. 2 (1989): 1087-1101; see also the discussion below (on Carthage), pp. 134-47.

20. See the discussion of the Basilica Pacis (Maior) below, pp. 155-58.

21. Aug. *Serm.* 356.10.

22. Aug. *Ep.* 29.11, dated to April/May 395.

23. *C.Th.* 16.10.7-25. Also see Aug. *Ciu.* 18.54.

24. Quodu. *Prom.* 3.38.44. Regarding the date (407), see *C.Th.* 16.10.12.1-2 — the law of Honorius and Theodosius that turned temples over to the church, especially in Africa, by an imperial grant. Prior to that time, temples were meant to be emptied, but left standing and turned over to public use (*C.Th.* 16.10.18-19, dated to November 407 or 408). Citing the earlier legislation, other authors have dated this event to the year 399. See, for example, Serge Lancel, *Saint Augustine* (London: SCM Press, 2002), 221, based on *C.Th.* 16.10.15. For more discussion, see Ennabli, *Carthage, une métropole chrétienne,* p. 35, n. 181. From Quodvultdeus's text, it seems clear that the building was completely destroyed just prior to the Vandal period under the authority of the tribune Ursus (*Prom.* 3.38.44). This would date the church's existence to the years 408-421, more or less.

entered the temple and placed the bishop's throne in the exact place where the goddess's statue had stood. A fragment of a dedicatory inscription reading "Aurelius the Pontiff dedicated" was taken as a miraculous sign, although it probably referred to the emperor Marcus Aurelius in his role as Pontifex Maximus.[25] Augustine also mentioned the transformation of a temple in a sermon he preached in Carthage during 417. He identified the new church as the Basilica Honoriana, a name that suggests that Honorius himself funded the conversion from temple to church, or at least that his legislation made it available.[26]

Similar temple transformations were less dramatic but no less permanent indications that the Christian faith gradually was replacing the older Roman cult. For example, at least one and perhaps two churches in Sufetula, one at Thuburbo Maius and one at the modern town of Djebel Oust, were installed within former temples, the last dedicated to Asclepius (see figs. 75, 103, and 46).[27] In all such cases, the orientation of the building was turned ninety degrees. The formerly open peristyle was transformed into the nave, its columns serving as interior supports for a roof and delineation of aisles. The *cellae* (inner sanctuaries) of these temples, once chambers for the deity's image, became small baptismal chambers attached to a side aisle or narthex. Other transformed temples include the Capitoline temple at Thugga (Dougga), where a church may have been built into the crypt,[28] and the temples of Saturn at Simitthu and Mactaris.[29]

25. *Aurelius pontifex dedicauit.* Quodu. *Prom.* 3.38.44; CCSL 60:185.94-95; SC 102:576.21-22. See Ennabli, *Carthage, une métropole chrétienne,* nos. 13, 21, pp. 31, 35-36. Caelestis was the Romanized name of the Punic goddess Tanit, also identified with Magna Mater — and the tutelary deity of Carthage.

26. Aug. *Serm.* 163.2.2. Augustine does not name the former temple, so its identification with that of Caelestis is uncertain. Ennabli, in fact, is careful not to equate these two churches since the evidence is only circumstantial (Ennabli, *Carthage, une métropole chrétienne,* 31).

27. The original uses of the other two are less certain. The Thuburbo Maius church may have been installed in a temple to Ceres, but this is only a conjecture. Another possibility is that it was formerly a Caelestis temple, like that in Carthage. Temples dedicated to Caelestis tended to be away from the main part of the city. The church of Servus in Sufetula was a converted temple; the basilica of Bellator may also have been one. On Sufetula, see Noël Duval and François Baratte, *Les ruines de Sufetula: Sbeitla* (Tunis: Société tunisienne de diffusion, 1973), 75-78. On Thuburbo Maius, see Aïcha Ben Abed Ben Khader et al., *Thuburbo Majus: Les mosaïques de la région des Grands Thermes* (Tunis: Institut national d'archéologie et d'arts, 1985), 55-60; Noël Duval, "Église et temple en Afrique du Nord," *Bulletin archéologique du Comité des travaux historiques et scientifiques* 7 (1971): 277-90. On Djebel Oust, see Duval, "Église et temple en Afrique du Nord," 292.

28. See Claude Poinssot, *Les ruines de Dougga* (Tunis: Institut national d'archéologie et d'art, 1958), 44. Maier reports a bishop Saturninus there in 256 and a Donatist bishop Pascacius in 411 (Maier, *L'épiscopat de l'Afrique romaine, vandale, et byzantine,* 412, 376).

29. See Fathi Bejaoui, "Découvertes d'archéologie chrétienne en Tunisie," in *Atti del IX Congresso internazionale di Archeologia Cristiana: Roma, 21-27 settembre 1975* (Città del Vaticano: Pontificio Istituto di Archeologia Cristiana, 1978), 1934-37 (re Simitthu); and Françoise Prévot, *Recherches archéologiques franco-tunisiennes à Mactar, 5: Les inscriptions chrétiennes* (Rome: École française de Rome, 1984), 11-18.

In addition to transforming temples and constructing new church buildings for the general assembly of the faithful, Christians undertook other kinds of construction projects. Additional structures of various shapes and sizes are evident in the archeological remains, often spread across a vast area surrounding a basilica. Documents attest to the existence of living quarters for the clergy, small chapels, and scriptoria. Excavations have identified special rooms associated with the rite of initiation and equipped with fonts. Monasteries were built as well, although these were more rare in Africa than in other areas of the early Christian world, and did not appear before the late fourth century. Saints' shrines sprang up in extra-urban cemeteries to honor martyrs buried there, and these martyria quickly became large pilgrimage churches. Initially, at least, these pilgrimage or cemetery churches were sites reserved primarily for communal celebrations of particular saints, but as the Christian population expanded, these suburban buildings became part of a larger parish system.[30] The original cemeteries that were linked with these shrines became sought-after loci for tombs of the ordinary faithful who desired to be buried *ad sanctos* ("near the saints"). These tombs often displayed images and inscriptions that identified their owners by name, gave their age at death, indicated their social or ecclesial roles, and attested to their piety.

Thus, buildings constructed for the community's ritual use usually included more than the main assembly hall and amounted to full-blown ecclesial complexes. Small rooms attached to church apses may have served as sacristies, cabinets for liturgical vessels, or places to store clothing and food for the needy.[31] Housing for the bishop and monastic clergy (as at Hippo) included dining rooms, reception areas, libraries, and even bathing facilities to serve their daily needs.[32] When Augustine felt he needed to increase the size of the bishop's quarters at Hippo Regius, he entered into negotiations to acquire a private house that was next to the Basilica Pacis.[33] There and elsewhere, adjacent small-apsed spaces may have had special liturgical functions, such as *consignatoria* for anointing the newly baptized or classrooms for catechumens. Some

---

30. On this subject, see below, p. 115.

31. See *Act. Zeno.* 3; CSEL 26:187.4-10, for example.

32. The ecclesiastical complex at Sufetula included a bath structure. See Duval and Baratte, *Les ruines de Sufetula,* 57-59. Augustine described the communal life among the clergy in Hippo Regius and made an argument for guest facilities (*Serm.* 355.2). Oil presses were discovered adjoining Byzantine-era churches in Sufetula and Belalis Maior. The proximity of oil presses and episcopal complexes or churches suggests supervision of the industry by church officials, or perhaps a means of financial support for clergy. See Leone, *Changing Townscapes in North Africa from Late Antiquity to the Arab Conquest,* 236.

33. Aug. *Ep.* 99.3. In *Serm.* 355.4 he finally seems to have received the gift — from the owner's estate because the owner left no heirs.

pilgrimage churches had dormitories or housing for guests and even stables for their horses.[34] Double churches also existed, perhaps due to the subsequent construction of an adjacent larger assembly space in order to serve a growing congregation, or to welcome penitent Donatist schismatics back into the fold (e.g., at Bulla Regia, Cuicul, and Sufetula; cf. figs. 10-11, 40, 42, and 68). The twinned churches at Cuicul may have been built simultaneously, with one just slightly larger than the other. Crypts extending below the apses of both of these churches served as a subterranean connection between them. These additions frequently contributed to creating a "Christian quarter" within many cities and towns.

Baptisteries usually were annexed to the cathedral basilica of the city, although more than one font often survived in a single town or village.[35] Unlike the common freestanding baptistery structures to the north (in Italy and Gaul), African baptisteries tended to be small rooms adjoining the main hall or narthex of the church or communicating with it via a series of interconnected rooms. Fonts had a wide variety of shapes, sizes, and depths. They might be polygonal, round, square, poly-lobed, or cruciform. Stone canopies, supported by columns (ciboria), covered most of these fonts in order to protect the consecrated water and perhaps held curtains for privacy. Several of these baptisteries were built into pre-existing bath structures. Many were elaborately decorated with polychrome pavement mosaics and inscriptions that included symbols associated with the rite, mentioned patrons, or alluded to baptism's theological significance.

Compared to monastic communities in other parts of the early Christian world, African monastic communities were slow to appear. The first documented monasteries are associated with Augustine's return from Italy, when he was intent upon establishing a community of men, first on his family estate in Thagaste, and then at Hippo Regius. As a presbyter in Hippo, Augustine finally established a monastery on land granted him by Bishop Valerius, whom he would succeed.[36] He also persuaded one of his own presbyters, Leporius, a man from a distinguished and wealthy family who had given up all his possessions, to found a monastery in a different locale (as well as to establish a hostel for pilgrims that provided some rent to the church).[37] Toward the end of his life, Augustine recorded the existence of monasteries in Carthage as a

---

34. This seems to have been the situation at Theveste. See below, p. 114.

35. See the discussion of baptisteries and fonts below, pp. 103-13.

36. Aug. *Serm.* 355.2. In his *Retract.* 2.21 Augustine described the early fifth century as a time when Carthage began to have monasteries. Victor of Vita refers to a monastery in Thabraca in the Vandal period (*Hist. pers.* 1.32). They seem to have flourished in the Byzantine period. See, for example, Proc. Caes. *Hist. bel.* 4.26.17.

37. Aug. *Serm.* 356.10. This same Leporius was charged by Augustine to build a hostel as well as the Basilica of the Eight Martyrs.

new development; he corresponded with the superior of a monastery near Hadrumetum.[38]

By the time of the Vandal conquest, monasteries were well established. Victor of Vita mentioned convents near Thabraca for both men and women.[39] An anonymous passion story identified the monastery, called Bigua, and attached to the Basilica of Celerina, as the place where seven martyred monks from Capsa (modern Gafsa) were buried.[40] Quodvultdeus also referred to a women's convent attached to a shrine built in Carthage to house St. Stephen's relics.[41] Finally, according to Procopius, Solomon, the praetorian prefect under Justinian, built a fortified monastery, the Mandracium, in Carthage somewhere close to the harbor.[42]

Saints' shrines typically were in cemeteries outside the city walls, and in contrast to monasteries, these were established early. Because the bodies of African martyrs were usually buried in cemeteries rather than being destroyed to prevent veneration, their tombs became pilgrimage destinations. The cemeteries, called *areae*,[43] eventually became the loci for basilicas, initially constructed as shelters for the tables on which visitors could share meals with both the ordinary and the special dead (the saint or martyr buried there). The tables for these funeral meals were permanent structures and are still visible *in situ* in Tipasa, 40 kilometers west of modern Algiers (cf. fig. 112). Such buildings were thus combinations of funerary picnic shelters, pilgrimage churches, and suburban basilicas that might, on occasion, allow for the celebration of the eucharist and perhaps the administration of baptism.[44]

Carthage had at least two major shrines dedicated to Cyprian by the end of the fourth century. The Mensa Cypriani was constructed at the site of his execution, and the Mappalia, now known as the basilica of St. Monica, was the place of his burial.[45] The Basilica Maiorum (fig. 20), the probable site of the shrine to Perpetua, Felicity, and their companions, was well outside the Theodosian city

---

38. *Retract.* 2.21 (where Augustine explains that *On the Works of Monks* was composed for a monastery in Carthage); *Ep.* 214; 215 (directed to the superior of the monastery of Hadrumetum). Augustine's sister was the head of a women's monastery (*Ep.* 211.4).

39. Vict.-Vit. *Hist. pers.* 1.35.

40. See *Pas. sept. mon.* 16. See also Liliane Ennabli, *La basilique de Carthagenna et le locus des septs moines de Gafsa: Nouveaux édifices chrétiens de Carthage,* Études d'antiquités africaines (Paris: CNRS, 2000), and Ennabli, *Carthage, une métropole chrétienne,* no. 26, p. 38.

41. Quodu. *Prom.* 6.9. See Ennabli, *Carthage, une métropole chrétienne,* no. 24, pp. 37-38. See also the evidence there for a monastery of men at Bigua. On this monastery see also Ennabli, *La basilique de Carthagenna et le locus des septs moines de Gafsa,* 81-128.

42. Proc. Caes. *Aed.* 6.5.12 and *Hist. bel.* 4.26.17.

43. See Tert. *Scap.* 3.

44. It is not clear that these churches had resident presbyters, although they did have altars, and some of them also had baptismal fonts. See the discussion below on baptism at pilgrimage churches, p. 105.

45. See the discussion below, pp. 145-47.

walls, as was the Basilica of St. Monica, the presumed locus of Cyprian's tomb (fig. 22).[46] Hippo Regius likewise had a number of shrines. Along with basilicas dedicated to Leontius and the Eight Martyrs, Augustine mentions a chapel for St. Theogenes (the city's bishop during the Decian persecution) outside the city walls[47] and a shrine to the Twenty Martyrs.[48] In contrast, relics of martyrs brought to a city could be housed within its walls. Sometime in the 420s, Augustine's then-deacon and eventual successor, Heraclius, founded a memorial chapel, somewhere near Hippo Regius's Basilica Pacis, to house the relics of St. Stephen that Orosius had brought to Africa.[49]

## Dating the Remains

A number of Christian churches were built toward the end of the fourth or the beginning of the fifth century, possibly in response to the Conference of Carthage in 411. Nevertheless, the earliest evidence is still only tentatively dated to the late fourth or early fifth century. Physical remains of basilicas that might have been built in the pre-Vandal period include five in Carthage: Damous el Karita, Dermech I (the first church), the basilica at Carthagenna, the Basilica Maiorum, and the Basilica of St. Monica. Outside of Carthage, evidence can be found for pre–Vandal-era churches — one at the site of Sufetula (Basilica of Bellator), and two at Belalis Maior (initial phases of basilicas I and II, shown in figs. 5-7). Vestiges of several fourth- or early-fifth-century churches were excavated in Numidia, including basilicas at Tipasa, Theveste (Tebessa), Castellum Tingitanum, Hippo Regius, and Thamugadi (Timgad).[50]

The evidence for new building is somewhat less clear for the early Vandal era. Older scholarship tended to describe the period as one of destruction and decay — an assumption that has been challenged more recently. Nevertheless, examples of Vandal-era churches are limited and ambiguous, especially as it is not possible to distinguish between Nicene and Arian churches on the basis of their architecture. Historians sometimes cite a Vandal-era basilica, the Basilica of Hildegun at Mactaris (fig. 58), as an example of a church built specifically

46. See the discussion below, pp. 145-46.

47. Aug. *Serm.* 273.7; *Serm. Mai* 158(272B).2.

48. Aug. *Serm.* 148; 257; 325.1; 326; *Ciu.* 22.8.

49. Aug. *Ciu.* 22.8 (miracles at the shrine); *Serm.* 318.1; 319.6.7 (where he refers to four lines of a verse he wrote for the shrine), 322, 323 (more miracles at the shrine). Erwan Marec identified this shrine as the trefoil room to the southeast of the basilica; see his *Monuments chrétiens d'Hippone, ville épiscopale de saint Augustin* (Paris: Arts et métiers graphiques, 1958), 163-68, 231-34. This has been challenged. See Serge Lancel, *Saint Augustine*, 236-37, for discussion of the relative nearness of this shrine to the Basilica Pacis (or Major), based on the text of *Serm.* 323.3.4.

50. This list is not exhaustive. Other examples occur at Thabraca, Uppenna, Cuicul, Bennafa, Horrea Caelia, and Ammaedara. Most of those listed here are discussed in more detail below.

for Arian worship, although the recognizably Vandal name likely belongs to a funerary inscription that was simply inserted into an older building.[51] Another Vandal-era basilica found at Carthage's site of Bir el Knissia has been dated to the second half of the fifth century (or early sixth century), and some tomb mosaics inscribed with Germanic names were found in the excavations (along with Punic and traditional Roman pagan inscriptions). This may have been the Basilica of St. Agileus, a church built for the Nicene congregation during a period of Vandal tolerance.[52]

If one guardedly follows textual sources, the Vandal Arians seem mostly to have occupied available churches and would have made few obvious structural modifications.[53] Augustine's Basilica Pacis, for example, probably was seized by Arians after the Vandal invasion of 431 and held until the early sixth century, when it was restored to the Nicene Christians of Hippo Regius.[54] When the cathedral church in Carthage (Basilica Restituta) was taken over by the Arians in 439, the Nicene congregation appears to have moved its *cathedra* first to the Basilica of Faustus and later to the Basilica of St. Agileus (outside the city walls).[55] Other potential Nicene foundations in Carthage during the Vandal era include the underground baptistery in the Sayda quarter and the Monastery of Bigua.[56] Outside of Carthage there may have been more tolerance for Nicene building or renovation. For example, Sufetula's Basilica of Bellator was enlarged,[57] although it probably housed a Nicene congregation.

Whatever the reasons for the dearth of evidence of Vandal-era church construction, the majority of the physical remains of African churches are dated to the Byzantine era (the sixth and seventh centuries). In some cases these were buildings originally constructed in the fourth or early fifth century and significantly renovated or rebuilt during the later period, perhaps after a century of neglect (e.g., the churches at Clipea, Belalis Maior, and Bulla Regia). These rebuilding phases are complicated, difficult to reconstruct, and quite varied;

---

51. The name is derived from an inscription found in the ruins of the basilica. See Prévot, *Recherches archéologiques franco-tunisiennes à Mactar,* 5:45-58.

52. On this basilica, see below, p. 139. See Susan T. Stevens, *Bir el Knissia at Carthage: A Rediscovered Cemetery Church: Report,* Journal of Roman Archaeology 7 (Ann Arbor, Mich.: Kelsey Museum, 1993).

53. The most obvious of these is the account of Vict.-Vit. *Hist. pers.* 1.9, which describes Vandal seizure of churches, especially in Carthage (e.g., Basilica Maiorum, and the Basilica of Celerina and the Scillitani).

54. One piece of evidence for Vandal occupation of this basilica is an inscription dedicated to Guilia Runa, Presbyterissa (her name apparently of Vandal origin); see below, p. 159; p. 431, n. 499; and fig. 125.

55. Possibly the site of Bir el Knissia. See the discussion below, p. 139. In 525 (after the toleration extended by Hilderic in 523), the Catholics were meeting in the church of St. Agileus. There Bonifatius was consecrated and convened the council of 525. *Con. Carth.* a. 525 (CCSL 149:255).

56. See the discussion above, pp. 94, 106.

57. See the discussion below, p. 149.

---

however, certain modifications seem to characterize Byzantine-era churches. Altars tended to be placed closer to (and eventually into) the apse and were typically covered by canopies (ciboria); raised walkways *(soleae)* extended into the main nave (for scripture reading and processions of the gospel book or eucharistic elements); counter-apses were added to house relics or the burial of clergy; second-story galleries became more common; domes were set over naves; and vaults were constructed over aisles. Existing floors of churches, baptisteries, and fonts were replaced with even more elaborately designed mosaic pavements.[58]

Although these adaptations may have accommodated Byzantine liturgical practices, they do not closely imitate churches in Constantinople (e.g., a centralized design with a completely segregated sanctuary). Instead, they maintain a level of continuity with the older African provincial style while modifying it in order to introduce the martyr cult into the urban churches. Rare dedications were made to non-African martyrs or even the occasional eastern saint (e.g., the Basilica of Gervasius, Protasius, and Tryphon in Sufetula).[59] Significantly, few known dedications to the Theotokos (Mary as Mother of God) occur in the Byzantine period; perhaps the only known basilica built in her honor was inside the palace on the Byrsa at Carthage.[60]

Given this tendency towards maintaining older traditions, building materials and construction methods are the most obvious ways to distinguish between earlier and later construction phases. Prior to the Byzantine era, most public buildings in Africa employed a style known as *opus Africanum,* which consisted of stone uprights and horizontal courses filled in with rubble and mortar. Cut or dressed stone walls are more characteristic of churches built during the Byzantine era.

Difficulties discerning such evolutionary changes are exacerbated by the state of the existing evidence, much of it gathered by excavations in the late nineteenth and early twentieth centuries. At the time, these sites were not excavated stratigraphically and were poorly recorded; thus, precisely evaluating the archeological remains is nearly impossible. Given this situation, the dating, identification, and specific regional character of individual buildings must be somewhat speculative and general, even though recent scientific studies and excavations have helped to establish more certain chronologies of building phases, modifications, and renovations.[61] Despite these uncertainties, arche-

58. For example, see H. Maguire, "Mosaics," in *Bir Ftouha: A Pilgrimage Church Complex at Carthage,* ed. Susan T. Stevens, Journal of Roman Archaeology Supplementary Series 59 (Portsmouth, R.I.: Journal of Roman Archaeology, 2005), 303-34.

59. See the discussion below, pp. 153-54.

60. Mentioned in Proc. Caes. *Aed.* 6.5.9, where Solomon literally took sanctuary. Also *Hist. bel.* 4.14.37; see below, p. 141.

61. For a survey of archeology in Roman Africa, see David J. Mattingly and R. Bruce Hitchner, "Roman Africa: An Archaeological Review," *The Journal of Roman Studies* 85 (1995): 165-213.

ologists and architectural historians have long identified certain distinctive features of Christian architecture in Roman Africa.[62]

## Characteristics of African Basilicas

Not surprisingly, given the African church's relationship with Rome, most early African churches were built on the traditional (Constantinian) basilica model — a secular building type adapted for its amenability to Christian assemblies. Unlike a pagan temple, a basilica had a large, interior gathering space, with a door on one side and an apse opposite, giving it longitudinal focus and easily divided sections. Typically weight-supporting, sometimes doubled colonnades created two or more aisles that flanked a high, central nave. A clerestory above filled the interior with light. The quarter-dome that covered the apse's raised platform served as an acoustical device, amplifying and projecting the voice of a speaker seated at the center of the semicircular space. Ambo and altar were placed forward, toward the center of the nave. Roofs were covered with terra-cotta tiles and floors with geometric patterns of colored stone.[63]

These features are all apparent in the Thabraca mosaic (fig. 132). Opposite the entrance, the nave ended in an elevated apse, accessed by a short flight of steps. A high, arched opening, balanced by two smaller and lower arches, led into the elevated apse area (presbyterium) and echoed the architectural shape of a triumphal arch. The vault over the apse appears to have a circular window or, perhaps, a round design in mosaic. Six columns lead from the door to the front and appear to support an architrave just below a clerestory. The roof is tiled, and the floor is decorated with mosaics depicting birds and flowers. The altar seems to stand about a third of the way into the nave.

Many African churches had distinctive modifications of these standard features. Some basilicas were significantly larger than others. One had nine aisles — four on each side of the central nave (Tipasa; fig. 106). A few apparently had galleries (e.g., Carthage's Bir el Knissia, the shrine of St. Crispina at Theveste, and the basilica at Castellum Tingitanum). Exterior walls sometimes boxed in apses and incorporated the flanking side chambers that probably served as sacristies or storage rooms. Many had narthexes; several had large, open atria (e.g., at Theveste and Thamugadi). African basilicas frequently had both a main apse and a counter-apse, requiring that entrances be on the side rather than at the front. These side entrances, aisles, or galleries might have facilitated the separation of men from women in the churches.[64] As noted above, doubled churches occur in a

62. Some of the most important work of this sort in the later twentieth century was done by N. Duval, J. Lassus, P.-A. Février, and F. Bejaoui. See the bibliography at the end of this volume for listings of many of their works.

63. Windows no longer exist, but terra-cotta roof tiles are commonly found in excavations.

64. See *Ciu.* 2.28, where Augustine approved this segregation.

few places (e.g., at Bulla Regia, Cuicul, and Sufetula). Attached mausolea are rare but seem to have existed (e.g., at Thabraca and Carthage's basilica at Bir Ftouha).

Churches often were constructed with the apse toward the east, but orientation is inconsistent. Exceptions are common, especially for churches that appear to have been renovations of existing temples or domestic spaces. Many were otherwise constrained by the presence of existing structures, proximity to main streets, or other site restrictions. This is apparent in Hippo Regius's main basilica, which was directed to the northwest in order to open on to the main road (cf. figs. 48, 50). Some basilicas originally were directed toward the west and then redirected in a later building phase (e.g., the Church of Bellator at Sufetula, which was changed from a southwesterly to a northeasterly orientation). A few were constructed with a broken axis (e.g., Castellum Tingitanum: fig. 33), which indicates that they were probably built or rebuilt into existing buildings or available land.[65]

Roofs were timbered and supported by columns that were cut mostly from local stone with minimal decoration. A few, however, had a variety of more finely carved columns, capitals, and bases, indicating that they were, most likely, *spolia* taken from older temples. Archeological finds also indicate that walls and ceilings were decorated with small, painted terra-cotta tiles that were made from molds and that displayed biblical scenes, figures of saints, or various Christian symbols (see figs. 150, 151).[66] The richly patterned mosaics that decorated floors were heirs to a significant African tradition of elaborate pavement mosaics, but in these churches they often incorporated mosaic tomb covers, placed over the burial sites of privileged members of the community.[67]

As noted above, churches also tended to be built within a complex that included such ancillary rooms as chapels, living quarters for clergy, classrooms for catechumens, and baptismal installations. Few of them were simply freestanding. Large episcopal complexes might even have included bathing facilities, libraries, and scriptoria (e.g., Hippo Regius and Sufetula). Pilgrimage churches could include dormitories for visitors and stables for their horses. In some instances these complexes were walled as if they were fortresses (e.g., Theveste and Thamugadi), perhaps to repel raids from local tribes or even gangs or armies mustered by a competing faction.

One of the most distinctively African features of these basilicas was the existence of double apses, or a primary apse with a subsequently added counter-apse.[68]

65. See the discussion below, pp. 131-34.

66. These tiles have been found on many archeological sites in Tunisia, in particular, and date mostly from the Byzantine era. Only traces of their paint still remain in most instances. See J. Ferron and M. Pinard, "Plaques de terre cuite d'époque byzantine découvertes á Carthage," *Cahiers de Byrsa* 2 (1952): 97-184.

67. See the discussion of these mosaics below, pp. 128-31.

68. See Noël Duval, *Les églises africaines à deux absides, recherches archéologiques sur la liturgie chrétienne en Afrique du Nord,* 2 vols. (Paris: E. de Boccard, 1971).

These counter-apses, often added as late as the fifth or sixth century, served various purposes. Some show evidence of altars and ciboria most likely set over reliquaries. In rare cases they housed the remains of particularly honored clergy (as at Castellum Tingitanum: figs. 33-34). In at least one instance (Bulla Regia), the counter-apse sheltered a baptismal font (figs. 11-12). Occasionally the added counter-apse became the primary apse, redirecting the plan of the church. At least one of Carthage's Byzantine-era basilicas originally was built with two apses (fig. 18). Counter-apses and, in at least one case, a counter-chancel thus served as secondary chapels or shrines within the main church (e.g., Sufetula's basilica near the Forum: fig. 84).[69]

None of these design features can be clearly associated with any particular Christian faction or sect. Just as the various political transitions and dissenting groups within African Christianity seem to have lacked unique liturgical practices, their church buildings required no identifying architectural features. Donatists, for example, do not appear to have built distinctive facilities for baptism, nor do their rivals, the Caecilianists, appear to have made major renovations when formerly Donatist churches passed back into their hands. Yet, Donatists reportedly leveled the altars used by Caecilianists as part of their effort to purify the building for their own liturgical use,[70] and rare inscriptions with certain phrases (e.g., *deo laudes*) or certain martyrs' dedications might indicate Donatist sympathies.[71]

Similarly, Vandal Arians seem to have taken over both Donatist and Caecilianist churches, apparently without needing to renovate them in any significant way apart from removing the tombs of the Nicene dead and reburying them.[72] Here, too, the survival of identifying inscriptions is one way to associate any building with one of these groups. As discussed above, the Byzantine era brought much renovation, enlargement, and beautification of older buildings, as well as the building of new churches, partly as a way to signal Africa's return to Nicene orthodoxy, and partly out of need after a century of neglect. Although some innovative features reflected the style of churches in the East (e.g., central domes, galleries), the general plan appears to reflect the older, provincial style of African architecture.

---

69. Noël Duval argued that the basilica at Theveste also had a counter-chancel, but this has been disputed. See Gui, Duval, and Caillet, eds., *Basiliques chrétiennes d'Afrique du Nord,* I.1:314.

70. Optat. *Parm.* 6.1.

71. For example, a capital from Ras el Oued with the inscription "Deo Laudes," in the Algiers National Antiquities Museum, is identified as "Donatist." W. H. C. Frend believes certain types of phrases (e.g., "deo laudes") or reference to special martyrs may be used as evidence to identify Donatist churches, especially in southern Numidia. See W. H. C. Frend, *The Donatist Church: A Movement of Protest in Roman North Africa* (Oxford: Clarendon Press, 1952, 2000), 307-8.

72. Vict.-Vit. *Hist. pers.* 1.15-16.

In the Thabraca mosaic (fig. 132), the church's altar seems to be positioned in the nave at approximately the third set of columns (out of six). One of the most consistent features of the earliest phase of church-building (i.e., in the fourth and early fifth century) was this original placement of the altar well into the nave, sometimes nearly at the center of the space. In some cases, the altar stood at the end of a chancel extension (e.g., in Hippo's later phase), or it stood within an elevated walkway leading from the raised apse into the center of the nave.[73] The second arrangement tended to be a later development. The altar area usually was segregated from the rest of the center aisle by low walls or partitions (e.g., figs. 26, 60, and 82).[74] Those partitions indicate that the altar was presumably restricted for clergy (including lectors). An exception was made for the newly baptized during the first week of their lives as Christians.[75] This central placement would have allowed the congregation to gather around the altar and come from several directions to receive communion. Over time, and especially during the Byzantine era, renovations to existing spaces tended to reposition altars closer to the apse, an evolution demonstrated by the varying placement of altar footings in the nave floor.[76] An inscribed fragment of at least one chancel screen also suggests that there were segregated areas for consecrated virgins within the congregation.[77]

The altar in the Thabraca mosaic appears to be covered by a linen cloth or surrounded by decorative lattice, and seemingly is set with three tall candles. Augustine and Victor of Vita also mentioned candles or lamps.[78] Victor and Optatus both witness to the use of altar coverings.[79] Given its box-like design, such an altar could have housed a martyr's relics. Documents indicate that altars were often made of wood, possibly to distinguish them from pagan altars,

---

73. These steps are mentioned by Augustine in *Ciu.* 22.8 (CCSL 47:826.454–827.468), where he referred to steps that led to the "raised place" from which he spoke. See also *Serm.* 323.3.4. and *Ep.* 126.1 on the steps separating the apse from the nave. See the description of altar placement relative to the apse and choir and the existence of chancel barriers in N. Duval, *Les églises africaines à deux absides*, 2:340-51.

74. See Aug. *Serm.* 392.5 and *Serm. Dolb.* 2(359B).3, where he describes people leaning on the altar railings to have a better view and hearing of his sermon.

75. See Aug. *Ep.* 34.2 (which indicates that this was also the practice in Donatist churches); *Serm. Mai* 94(260C).7.

76. See the discussion of the Basilica of Vitalis at Sufetula below — p. 151, for example.

77. This conclusion is based upon an extant inscription on a chancel screen. See Joan Branham, "Women as Objects of Sacrifice," in *La cuisine et l'autel: Les sacrifices en questions dans les sociétés de la Méditerranée ancienne,* ed. Stella Georgoudi, Renée Koch, and Francis Schmidt (Turnhout: Brepols, 2005), 371-86.

78. See Vict.-Vit. *Hist. pers.* 2.18 for the lighting of lamps. See Aug. *Serm.* 338.2.2 for the dedication of a church with blessing of candelabra.

79. See Optat. *Parm.* 6.1 and Vict.-Vit. *Hist. pers.* 1.39, 2.18 for linen altar coverings.

although the altar depicted in a mosaic from a church built at the site of Castellum Tingitanum appears to have details that suggest the legs were made of sculpted stone (fig. 35).[80] In order to distinguish its Christian sacrificial function, Cyprian had been particularly careful to use the term *altare* rather than the pagan term *ara*.[81]

In addition to the altar, other liturgical furniture would have included the bishop's chair *(cathedra)* and a pulpit or reader's desk for the lector, also likely made of wood.[82] The bishop's chair was placed at the back of the apse and flanked by a semicircular bench *(synthronon)* for the presbyters (cf. fig. 52).[83] Cyprian's letters testify to the existence of a pulpit in African churches. He described it as elevated so that the entire congregation might easily see and hear the reader.[84] The bishop normally would deliver his sermon seated in his chair, unless he was a guest in another bishop's church, in which case he would preach from the pulpit.[85] Augustine referred to a pulpit accessed by a flight of steps[86] and to another one (in Carthage) that could be moved from the center of the nave (within the chancel) to a place within the apse.[87] The congregation nor-

80. For documentary evidence that early altars were made of wood, see Aug. *Cresc.* 3.43.47; *Ep.* 185.7.27; Optat. *Parm.* 6.1. Sigma-shaped stone tables, found in churches (especially in Provence and Africa) and often referred to as "*agape* tables," may have been used as offering tables rather than as eucharistic altars. See W. Eugene Kleinbauer, "Table Top with Lobed Border," in *Age of Spirituality: Late Antique and Early Christian Art, Third to Seventh Century,* ed. Kurt Weitzmann (New York: Metropolitan Museum of Art, 1979), 637-38. On the transformation of altars, see Catherine Metzger, "Le mobilier liturgique," in *Naissance des arts chrétiens, atlas des monuments paléochrétiens de la France,* Atlas archéologiques de la France (Paris: Imprimerie nationale ed., 1991), 256-67; Xavier Barral i Altet, "Mensae et repas funeraire dans les necropoles d'époque chrétienne de la peninsule Iberique: Vestiges archéologiques," in *Atti del IV Congresso internazionale di Archeologia Cristiana, Citta del Vaticano, 16-22 ottobre 1938* (Roma: Pontificio Istituto di Archeologia Cristiana, 1940), 2:67-68; Henri Leclercq, "Autel," in *DACL,* ed. Fernand Cabrol, Henri Leclercq, and Henri-Irenee Marrou (Paris: Letouzey et Ané, 1924); and Johann P. Kirsch and Theodor Klause, "Altar," in *Reallexikon für Antike und Christentum: Sachwörterbuch zur Auseinandersetzung des Christentums mit der antiken Welt,* ed. Ernst Dassmann and Christian Josef Kremer (Stuttgart: Hiersemann, 2000), 1:343-50.

81. Cypr. *Ep.* 59.18.1. See also *Ep.* 43.5.2; 65.3.3; 70.2.2. Tertullian used the term *ara,* by contrast, in *Or.* 19.3. Neither Arnobius nor Lactantius made Cyprian's careful distinction of the terms for traditional polytheist and either Israelite or Christian instruments of sacrifice.

82. *Cathedrae* were mentioned in Tert. *Praescr.* 36.1; Cyprian used the term frequently — in *Ep.* 3.1.1; 17.2.1; 43.5.2, for example. Augustine used the term as a symbol of the bishop's office: *Parm.* 1.2.3, 3.5; *Bapt.* 2.1.2; *Petil.* 2.51.118, 138; *Cresc.* 3.36.40; 4.7.8; *Coll.* 1.11-14. *Emer.* 7 speaks of a canopied *cathedra,* possibly referring to Optatus's episcopal chair at Thamugadi (*Ep.* 23.3).

83. Clergy benches are mentioned in Cypr. *Ep.* 59.18.1.

84. Cypr. *Ep.* 38.2.1; 39.4.1.

85. Augustine refers to preaching seated (*Serm.* 355.2), and to preaching from a "raised place," perhaps referring to the raised level of the presbyterium, but in other instances he may have meant the pulpit when he was not in his own church. See *Serm.* 134.1.1 (at Carthage); *Serm. Denis* 17(301A).2 (at Bulla Regia); and *Serm. Dolb.* 2(359B).3 (at Carthage).

86. Aug. *Ep.* 23.3, possibly referring to the Donatist cathedral at Thamugadi.

87. Aug. *Serm. Dolb.* 2(359B).3.

mally would stand; seats or pews were virtually absent, except (perhaps) for the elderly or infirm, and then probably only in the side aisles.[88]

## BAPTISMAL ARCHITECTURE

Baptism was the ritual means of becoming a full member of the African Christian community. The unbaptized were believed to be barred from salvation. African theologians frequently spoke of the church as mother and, like other early Christian writers, elaborated this metaphor to speak of the font as the mother's womb, the place where new Christians were conceived and born.[89] Candidates for baptism entered the font naked and were immersed in water to symbolize their death to an old life and rebirth to a new one. They emerged from the watery womb like newborn children, were redressed (in white robes), anointed, and confirmed by the bishop's imposition of hands, and entered the church to join their new Christian brothers and sisters. The spaces in which their stripping, immersion, anointing, and confirmation all took place formed an architectural icon that reflected the symbolism of this sacrament as well as providing simple shelter and appropriate facilities for the ritual actions themselves.

No purpose-built spaces that housed the African baptismal ritual in the third and early fourth centuries have survived. The Dura-Europos house church excavated in modern Syria is a unique example of an early baptismal chamber (ca. 240s); without any comparable evidence, it is impossible to surmise how representative such a space was in general, or how like it a contemporary African baptismal chamber might have been. Despite the dearth of physical remains for baptism prior to the late fourth century, however, the African provinces are rich in evidence from the late fourth through the sixth century. More than fifty early Christian baptisteries have been identified in the modern country of Tunisia, and at least twenty-five survive in Algeria, many of them constructed in more than one phase.[90]

88. See Aug. *Serm.* 274; 355.2; *Catech.* 13.19; *Psal.* 90.1.12; 147.21; Optat. *Parm.* 4.5.

89. See, for example, Cypr. *Ep.* 73; Optat. *Parm.* 2.10; 4.2; Aug. *Bapt.* 1.10.4; *Serm.* 56.10.14; 119.4; 213.8; 216.7; 228.1. See Robin Margaret Jensen, "Mater Ecclesia and the Fons Aeterna: The Church and Her Womb in Ancient Christian Traditions," in *A Feminist Companion to Patristic Literature,* ed. Amy-Jill Levine with Maria Mayo Robbins (London and New York: T&T Clark, 2008), 137-55.

90. Ancient baptisteries have also been discovered in Libya, which would include the Roman province of Tripolitana. The following discussion will not consider these in any detail, however. On ancient baptisteries in general, see the catalogue of S. Ristow, with a general bibliography as well as bibliographies for individual entries: Sebastian Ristow, *Frühchristliche Baptisterien,* Jahrbuch für Antike und Christentum 27 (Münster, Westfalen: Aschendorff Verlag, 1998). Also see Armen Khatchatrian, *Origine et typologie des baptistères paleochrétiens* (Mulhouse: Centre de Culture Chrétienne, 1982), which refers to his earlier work: *Les baptistères paléochrétiens, plans, notices et bibliographie* (Paris: École pratique des hautes études, 1962), and J. G. Davies, *The Architectural*

Because most of the archeological evidence associated with baptism in Roman Africa dates to the fifth through the seventh centuries, it is not easily coordinated with the greatest proportion of theological writings on the ritual. A singular case in which both literary evidence and physical remains potentially overlap in both time and space is the baptistery excavated at the site of Hippo Regius (fig. 54), annexed to what has been identified as Augustine's Basilica Pacis (cf. figs. 48, 50, 51).[91] Other examples of baptismal fonts dated to the pre-Vandal period include those found in Thamugadi (fig. 94), Tipasa (fig. 107), Cuicul (figs. 41-42), as well as the earliest fonts at Belalis Maior (figs. 5, 7) and Sidi Jdidi (Asadi) (fig. 63).

Although documentary material pertaining to baptism is scarce after the mid-fifth century, the rite was unchanged in any major way that would have been reflected in the architecture or design of fonts or baptisteries. In fact, no literary evidence indicates that baptismal rituals differed between Donatists and Caecilianists or included features that would distinguish Vandal practice. Nothing indicates that groups who practiced rebaptism would have had more elaborate fonts or additional rooms. Nor is there reason to believe that Vandals required the repetition of the ritual as Donatists did.[92] Tertullian and the unknown author of *The Treatise on Rebaptism* were the only authors to comment upon varying baptismal rituals that they considered heretical and that might have required distinctive equipment or spaces.[93]

After the Byzantine reconquest, Nicene Christians re-appropriated, restored, renovated, and even reoriented many churches, and with them their baptisteries. The remodeling simply may have been a response to a century of neglect, but it might have been motivated by a desire to assert the presence, power, and piety of the new elite. Fresh pavements were installed in elaborate geometric, floral, and figurative patterns; ciboria were raised over fonts as well as altars. In Sufetula, for example, a new basilica was built next to the older one. In this instance, the font was placed in a chamber behind the main apse rather than in a separate small chapel (fig. 71). The older baptistery may have been

---

*Setting of Baptism* (London: Barrie & Rockliff, 1962). On African fonts in particular, see Walter Berry, "The Early Christian Baptisteries of Africa Proconsularis" (Columbia, Mo.: University of Missouri, 1976), and Jean Lassus, "Les baptistères africains," *Corso di cultura sull'arte ravennate e bizantina* 17 (1970): 235-52. Articles on individual baptisteries mentioned in the following pages will not be extensively cited, since almost all pertinent secondary bibliography is included in Ristow's catalogue.

91. On the baptistery at Hippo Regius, see below, p. 159.

92. The reference to an attempted rebaptism of a Christian virgin by her Vandal master reported by Victor of Vita is difficult to credit as historical; see *Hist. pers.* 1.33.

93. Tert. *Bapt.* 2. The anonymous author of *On Rebaptism* mentions a ritual of fire that might have required some special equipment, but probably not any special furniture or distinct architectural feature. Virtually no information about Arian Vandal rituals is available; it can be argued that the Vandals' appropriation of Nicene churches in the fifth century required very little modification of space, since these were returned to Catholic bishops in the sixth century.

transformed into a shrine dedicated to a former bishop (Jucundus) who had died during the early Vandal period (fig. 66).[94]

## Multiple Baptisteries in a Single Urban Area

The existence of a baptistery in an ecclesial space is often taken to indicate that the building served at some time as the bishop's cathedral. This supposition is based on the assumption that the bishop's imposition of hands was a necessary completion of the baptismal ritual, which would have been conducted in the bishop's own church. A single, unified Christian community, therefore, would have a single cathedral and an attached baptistery. However, archeologists have discovered more than one font in the sites of several larger towns or urban areas (e.g., Belalis Maior, Sufetula, and Thamugadi), and some of these fonts were contemporaneous with one another. This is particularly striking in Carthage, which had at least two — possibly three — baptisteries inside its walls in the Byzantine period, and as many as three just outside or nearby.[95]

More than one baptistery in a single town may be explained in a variety of ways. Some spaces may have been abandoned when newer or larger facilities were built as the community grew or became materially more secure. This seems to have happened at Sufetula. Carthage, however, was divided into distinct regions, perhaps to accommodate different linguistic groups, or as the practice of allowing presbyters to administer the water bath began to be more common, especially for the emergency baptism of infants. In this case the imposition of hands could be offered in a different space and at a later time, where and when the bishop would preside. Additionally, the inclusion of large baptismal fonts in pilgrimage churches (e.g., the two sixth-century baptisteries at Bir Messaouda and Bir Ftouha; fig. 28) suggests the possibility that visitors came to the shrine of a martyr for baptism rather than availing themselves of the urban cathedral for their initiatory ritual.[96]

The existence of multiple baptisteries in a single urban area may also indicate the presence of competing Christian communities and rival bishops. Donatists, for example, had their own cathedrals and used their fonts to baptize those who came over to them from their Caecilianist rivals. Thamuga-

94. See Duval and Baratte, *Les ruines de Sufetula*, 44-47. See also N. Duval, *Les églises africaines à deux absides*, 1:99-144.

95. Byzantine-era baptisteries inside the walls of Carthage include those at Dermech I, Carthagenna, and Bir Messaouda. Outside the walls are those at Damous el Karita, Bir Ftouha, and the possible subterranean font near the basilica called Ste. Monique in the Sayda district.

96. See Robin Margaret Jensen, "Baptismal Practices at North African Martyrs' Shrines," in *Ablution, Initiation, and Baptism: Late Antiquity, Early Judaism, and Early Christianity = Waschungen, Initiation und Taufe: Spätantike, Frühes Judentum und Frühes Christentum*, ed. David Hellholm, 3 vols. (Berlin and New York: De Gruyter, 2010), 1673-1695.

di's several baptisteries are an example. One clearly belonged to the Donatist compound associated with Optatus. At least one other would have served the Caecilianist community in the city. Similarly, a subterranean baptistery at Carthage's Chapel of Redemptus discovered in the Sayda quarter may have been a place for discreet Nicene baptism during the period of Vandal persecution.[97]

## Baptistery Placement and Construction

In contrast to many examples of freestanding baptistery buildings in Italy and Gaul, African baptismal spaces were typically rooms attached to the main church hall or directly connected by doorways to rooms that adjoined the nave.[98] A small number of fonts were located directly behind the apse, a placement that seems particular to North African baptisteries (e.g., at Bir Ftouha, fig. 28; Mactaris, fig. 59; and Sufetula's Vitalis, fig. 71), or to one side of the apse (usually north — e.g., Musti, fig. 61; and Iomnium, fig. 56). Other baptistery chambers were constructed on the left or right side of the entrance of the church with egress into the atrium or rear of the nave (e.g., Bulla Regia, fig. 11, and Thuburbo Maius, figs. 102-104). A few baptistery rooms were separated from the main church building in enclosures that resembled open-air courtyards — for example, the detached fourth-century baptistery of Jucundus, assigned to the Church of Bellator in Sufetula (Basilica III), contained a font installed into what probably was a pre-existing peristyle court (fig. 66). Carthage's sixth-century baptistery at Dermech I (figs. 25-27) is another possible instance. Although the baptistery itself was enclosed, a square colonnade consisting of twelve columns (in addition to a four-columned ciborium) surrounded its font. The baptistery at Tipasa was connected to the main church by a series of communicating rooms (figs. 106-107).[99] One of the two structures often identified as baptismal fonts at Castellum Tidditanorum (Tiddis — fig. 31) has been particularly questioned, primarily because it, like the other (fig. 32), is evidently disconnected from any adjacent church building. Although both of the Castellum Tidditanorum baptisteries look like typical fonts, with ciboria and steps, they could have had different functions (e.g., a fountain or a private bath).[100]

97. Alexandre Lézine, *Architecture romaine d'Afrique,* recherches et mises au point (Paris: Presses universitaires de France, 1962), 145-46; see Ennabli, *Carthage, une métropole chrétienne,* 108-10. See also Vict.-Vit. *Hist. pers.* 3.8.

98. The baptisteries of Jucundus in Sufetula (fig. 66) and Oued Ramel are two known exceptions. Some scholars have suggested that the round monument adjacent to Carthage's Damous el Karita was originally a baptistery, although more recent scholars have disputed that identification. See below, p. 139, n. 218.

99. This is also apparent at Belalis Maior, Thibilis (Announa), Bennafa, El Kantara, Isle of Djerba (Meninx), Cuicul (Djémila), and Sidi Jdidi (Asadi) (phase 2).

100. See Gui, Duval, and Caillet, eds., *Basiliques chrétiennes d'Afrique du Nord,* I.1:203, citing a discussion by P.-A. Février with N. Duval.

Baptisteries occasionally were built into the *cellae* of former pagan temples that had been transformed into Christian churches in the fifth and sixth centuries. In most of these cases, what had been porticoed forecourts of the temples were incorporated into the main halls of the churches. Three examples of this arrangement are the basilica of Servus in Sufetula, inserted into a temple whose original deity is not known (fig. 75), the baptistery and church constructed on the site of the temple of Tanit (Caelestis) at Thuburbo Maius (figs. 102-104), and the basilica and baptistery built into the temple of Asclepius in Djebel Oust (fig. 46). The last was constructed over a sacred spring and inside a still-surviving nymphaeum. The surrounding baths designed to offer cures to pilgrims are still found next to a modern Tunisian health spa.

African baptistery structures were generally quadrilateral, as opposed to the octagonal or circular buildings more characteristic of Italy and Gaul.[101] Although an octagonal plan for a baptismal structure was deemed particularly fitting by Ambrose of Milan,[102] it was rare for North African baptistery construction.[103] Some were exceptional, however, such as the baptistery connected to the twin basilicas at Cuicul (Djémila — fig. 40). While much restored with modern masonry dome and ciborium, this baptistery is unparalleled for its still-standing walls and largely intact floor mosaics (figs. 43-44). In the center, a round font is covered by a ciborium that was supported by four fluted columns (figs. 41-42). The interior of the baptistery as a whole was defined by a double barrel-vaulted ambulatory broken by niches and pilasters (fig. 43). Its design has many features in common with Roman public bath structures; indeed, a tub is still visible in front of the entrance.[104]

Ancillary rooms are often found adjoining the baptismal chamber. The function of these rooms is unclear: they may have been used as places for candidates to wait their turn (the font area was seldom large enough to hold even

101. For example, the baptisteries at the Lateran Basilica in Rome, beneath the cathedral in Milan, in Ravenna, at Forum Iulii (Frejus) and Aquae Sextiae (Aix) (Gaul), and at Albenga and Novara (Italy).

102. A poem (uncertainly) attributed to Ambrose which extols the octagonal shape of Milan's baptistery has been published in several epigraphical collections, including the *CIL* 5:617.2 and the *ICUR* 2.1, p. 161, n. 2; and — most recently — in Ambroise, *Opere poetiche e frammenti, inni, iscrizioni, frammenti,* ed. Gabriele Banterle, vol. 22, Sancti Ambrosii Episcopi Mediolanensis 22 (Milan: Biblioteca Ambrosiana, 1994), 145-66.

103. An exception is the baptistery at Siagu (Bir Bou Rekba), listed as Ksar ez-Zit in Ristow, *Frühchristliche Baptisterien,* no. 729, p. 260. The baptistery at Carthagenna from the Byzantine era has a square exterior and an octagonal interior. Thabraca's urban basilica had an octagonal rotunda, which was long thought to be a baptistery. However, with little evidence of an actual font, it was more likely a martyrium or mausoleum. See Ristow, *Frühchristliche Baptisterien,* no. 750, p. 265.

104. On the architectural parallels between Roman baths and Christian baptisteries, see Robin Margaret Jensen, *Living Water: Images, Symbols, and Settings of Early Christian Baptism,* Supplements to Vigiliae Christianae 105 (Leiden and Boston: Brill, 2011), 234-37.

a dozen people at a time), to disrobe and store clothing, or to receive the final anointing and laying on of hands (a *consignatorium*). These latter rooms, usually identified by an apse at one end and large enough to have aisles divided by columns, occur at Carthage's Dermech Basilica I (figs. 26-27), Sufetula's Basilica of Servus (figs. 75, 78), the Basilica Pacis in Hippo Regius (fig. 51), and the major basilica at Tipasa (fig. 106). The ways in which candidates moved through different rooms for distinct parts in the rite might reflect the emphasis placed on those portions of the ritual itself. In other words, if the imposition of hands was seen as the most important — the most public and inclusive — stage of the rite, it might have been performed in the congregational gathering space, separate from the smaller, private place of the water bath.

## Font Shapes, Sizes, and Depths

Similar to the diversity of placement is the variety of shapes of African fonts. Builders of baptisteries in the provinces of Mauretania and Numidia appear to have used simpler font designs (mostly circular but with some exceptions), while those in Byzacena and Africa Proconsularis generally tended to display more variety. Cruciform fonts occur more frequently in Africa Proconsularis and Tripolitana than elsewhere. Many fonts were constructed from (or revetted with) marble or other fine stone, while some were cut directly into bedrock. Quite a few were covered with polychrome stone mosaic.

These various shapes range from rectangular to octagonal to poly-lobed. A long-standing assumption that shapes developed chronologically, from the simple to complex (e.g., from rectangular to poly-lobed and multiform), has been challenged by the discovery of significant exceptions to that rule.[105] Nevertheless, a square or rectangular shape generally indicates an early font, and this shape is least represented, perhaps because many of these disappeared during the Byzantine era. The font at the site of the first phase of the basilica in Clipea (Kélibia) was a simple rectangle, later replaced by a richly decorated quatrefoil shape in the sixth century (fig. 38).[106] The early-fifth-century font at Cuicul (Djémila — figs. 41-42) was basically a square set into a poly-lobed surround. Poly-lobed fonts built in the Byzantine period also include Horrea Caelia and Naro (fig. 62), but the poly-lobed baptistery at Sidi Jdidi (fig. 63)

---

105. The older idea is exemplified by Davies, *The Architectural Setting of Baptism*, 2-5; but also see Noël Duval, "Church Buildings IV: The Baptistery," ed. Angelo Di Berardino, *Encyclopedia of the Early Church* (New York: Oxford University Press, 1992), 1:173; and Richard Krautheimer, "Introduction to an 'Iconography of Mediaeval Architecture,'" *Journal of the Warburg and Courtauld Institutes* 5 (1942): 22-30.

106. See Christian Courtois, "Sur un baptistère découvert dans la région de Kélibia," *Karthago. Revue d'archéologie africaine* 6 (1955): 97-127; Noël Duval and Jean Cintas, "L'eglise du prêtre Felix (region de Kélibia)," *Karthago. Revue d'archéologie africaine* 9 (1958): 157-265.

can be dated to the end of the fourth century.[107] Thus, establishing a clear and consistent chronological pattern of shape development is not possible.

Round fonts are also among the earliest but often are combined with another shape in intermediate sections. The late-fourth-century font at Tipasa (fig. 107) is constructed of three round sections with a fairly deep well at the center (1 meter). An almost identical font was found at Musti (fig. 61) with a similarly deep central basin, as was one at Iomnium (Tigzirt — fig. 56). The baptistery installed into the former *cella* of a pagan temple in the Church of Servus at Sufetula (fig. 77) progresses from a round well through a four-lobed intermediate section, to a rounded hexagon at the top. Hexagonal and octagonal fonts — or combinations of round shapes with hexagons or octagons — are also fairly common. Examples include the Donatist baptistery at Thamugadi (fig. 94) and Dermech I in Carthage (fig. 27).

Cruciform or modified cruciform plans are well represented in Africa. The sixth-century font at Bulla Regia (in its second phase) has nearly equal horizontal and vertical arms (fig. 12). The central section, however, was blocked off, providing a deep well for the candidate (1.46 m) at the bottom of five steps on either side (fig. 13). The two blocked arms were kept dry for the use of officiating clergy or baptismal assistants.[108] A slightly different cruciform font, now in Tunis's Bardo Museum but originally from Meninx (El Kantara, Isle of Djerba), has equilateral arms and rounded ends (see fig. 47), much like the font at Oued Ramel. A circular central section modified other cruciform varieties, as at Thuburbo Maius (fig. 104). The cross-shaped font at the Byzantine basilica at Carthagenna is set into an octagonal surround and has an octagonal basin (figs. 18-19). The late-fourth-century font at Hippo Regius has a modified cruciform design featuring a rectangle with shallow interior side niches (fig. 55). The fonts at Sabratha and Lepcis Magna in Tripolitana also were constructed as cruciform.

The origins of poly-lobed fonts are hard to determine. The earliest poly-lobed shapes probably were quatrefoil variants on cruciform shapes, but they may also have been influenced by multilobed *caldaria* in local bath structures.[109] These include the original two-lobed font at Sidi Jdidi, and the four-lobed fonts at Clipea (Kélibia — fig. 38), Belalis Maior (figs. 5, 6), Thelepte, Chott Menzell Yahia, and Oumcetren.[110] A six-lobed font was found at Thibilis and Sidi Jdidi (in its second phase — fig. 63). Eight-lobed examples occur at Uppenna (fig.

107. Aïcha Ben Abed-Ben Khader, Michel Fixot, Michel Bonifay, and Sylvestre Roucole, *Sidi Jdidi, I: La basilique sud,* Recherches d'archéologie africaine (Rome: École française de Rome, 2004).

108. A similar structure appears in the font at Oued Ramel.

109. See the lobed examples at Sabratha, Banasa, Lambaesis, and Djebel Oust; the first three are discussed and illustrated in Fikret K. Yegül, *Baths and Bathing in Classical Antiquity* (New York: Architectural History Foundation, 1992), esp. chapter 6, "Baths of North Africa," 184-249.

110. On Thelpte and Chott Menzell Yahia, see Fathi Bejaoui, "Recherche archéologique à Thelepte et ses environs. Note sur les récentes découvertes," in *Histoire des hautes steppes: an-*

116), Horrea Caelia, and Thapsus (fig. 97). These fonts are usually dated to the sixth century and the Byzantine occupation, but some of them may have been built earlier. What was probably a fourth-century, twelve-lobed font at Theveste was replaced in the fifth century by one made up of concentric circles covered by a hexagonal ciborium (the slots for the six supports are still visible; fig. 101). The well of this font contained what appears to have been the top of a round, marble offering table carved with twelve alveoli.[111]

Although the theological symbolism or liturgical significance of these different shapes is difficult to determine without contemporary documentary witness, some scholars have speculated that round fonts might have been intended to symbolize the womb of the mother church, while the cruciform and modified cruciform fonts link the idea of baptism as participation in Christ's death and resurrection with the new birth (cf. Rom. 6).[112] The octagonal font symbolized the eighth day, the day of the new creation.[113] The lip-shaped fonts found at Sufetula are among the most unusual (although not unique) poly-lobed designs. The design of the older, fourth-century Chapel of Jucundus, and its copy in the newer Basilica of Vitalis (figs. 66, 71-72), may have been meant to evoke a woman's vulva and birth canal, underscoring the idea that the church is mother and her font is the womb of newborn Christians.

Font sizes and depths also show great differences from place to place. Some fonts were more or less at floor level, while low walls surrounded others. The baptistery at Carthage's Dermech I (fig. 27) is about one and one-half meters across its hexagonal opening and just over one meter deep. The two arms of the cruciform-shaped font at Bulla Regia (figs. 12-13) are more than two meters in length, and the depth of the font is nearly one and one-half meters. The Clipea font (fig. 38) is about one and three-quarters meters across and slightly more than one meter deep, while the four-lobed font of phase 2 of Belalis Maior's Basilica I (fig. 5) is only one meter across and one-half meter deep. Only a few of these fonts would have allowed full immersion by dunking, so one must assume that assistants poured water over the recipients' heads (perhaps while they knelt) if they were to be drenched fully. Some of the smaller and shallower fonts could have been used for infant baptism.

---

tiquité — moyen age: actes du colloque de Sbeïtla (Tunis: Institut national du patrimoine, 2001), 147-61.

111. Pedro de Palol, "El baptisterio de la basílica de Tebessa y los altares paleocristianos circulares," *Ampurias* 17-18 (n.d.): 282-86.

112. For example, see Davies, *The Architectural Setting of Baptism*, 20-26; Jensen, *Living Water*, 247-51.

113. On the symbolism of the octagon for a baptismal font, see Jensen, *Living Water*, 244-47; on the octagon in general, see Reinhart Staats, "Ogdoas als ein Symbol für die Auferstehung," *Vigiliae Christianae* 26 (1972): 29-53. Other scholars hesitate to assign too much symbolic significance to the shapes of fonts. See Sible de Blaauw, "Kultgebäude," in *Reallexikon für Antike und Christentum; Sachwörterbuch zur Auseinandersetzung des Christentums mit der antiken Welt* (Stuttgart: Hiersemann, 2008), 20:340.

Many of these African fonts were covered with polychrome stone mosaic and set into mosaic pavements, similar to those found in many North African church buildings. Some of these mosaics were exceptionally beautiful and elaborate, enhancing the beauty as well as the symbolic significance of the font and baptistery designs.

Decorative mosaics probably originally covered the pavements of most of the African baptisteries as well as some of the fonts themselves. These can be seen *in situ* at Carthage's Dermech I (fig. 27), Sufetula (Jucundus and Vitalis; figs. 66, 71-72) and Cuicul (figs. 41, 43, 44). In some cases the mosaics have been preserved by removal to museums (e.g., Clipea; figs. 38-39). While most of the decorations of these fonts consisted of stylized geometric and floral patterns as well as birds, fruit trees, fish, shells, candles, and vases of flowers (fig. 121), some exceptional designs included deer coming to streams of water (cf. Ps. 42:1) in the Byzantine-era baptisteries of Bir Ftouha at Carthage (fig. 28), Lepti Minus, Bennafa (fig. 8), and Oued Ramel. A lamb appears as part of the mosaic decoration in the Sidi Jdidi (Asadi) font (phase two), and the motif of lambs on either side of a cross occurs also at Lepti Minus (fig. 57).

Crosses, chalices, an ark, and a descending dove appear in the font at Clipea (Kélibia — figs. 38-39). In many instances, the wells of the fonts are decorated with Christograms, often flanked by an alpha and omega (e.g., at Sufetula-Vitalis, fig. 72; Clipea, fig. 39; and Naro, fig. 62). The recipient would stand or kneel on the sign of Christ as a symbol of participation in Christ's Passion and triumph (i.e., the Resurrection). The imagery of fruit-bearing trees, fountains, birds, and flowers may have been meant to have particular allusions to Paradise and the idea that the rite promises that reward as well as renewal through its water of eternal life. Walls and even ceilings could have been decorated as well as the fonts, although no remains have survived to indicate this.[114]

Mosaic inscriptions also appear on African baptismal fonts. A few were merely dedicatory; others also alluded to the religious meaning or theological significance of the rite. The font of Vitalis at Sufetula simply reads "Vitalis and Cardela fulfilled their vow" (fig. 72).[115] The lobed edges of Oumcetren's font read "Victoricus, subdeacon, returns the gift to God."[116] By contrast, Cuicul's font bore an inspirational prompt: "Come to God and be enlightened."[117] The font at Thapsis (Bekalta; fig. 97) bears the legend "Glory to God in the highest

---

114. For example, the still-standing, highly decorated baptisteries at Ravenna and Naples.

115. See below, p. 152, n. 274.

116. *Victoricus* [in blue]/sudiaconus [in blue and yellow]/donum *domino* [in yellow and red]/ redar [in red]. See Claude Poinssot and Louis Poinssot, "Baptistère découvert dans la région de Sidi Daoud (Cap Bon)," *Karthago. Revue d'archéologie africaine* 6 (1955): 124-25.

117. *[Accedi]te ad D[e]u[m] et illuminamini;* cf. Henri Grégoire, "Les baptistères de Cuicul et de Doura," *Byzantion* 13 (1938): 589-93.

and on earth peace to those of good will we praise you."[118] The entrance to Clipea's font (fig. 38) bears the legend "Peace Faith Love."[119] The word "peace" apparently replaced "hope" in the list of Christian virtues and moved from the second position to the first (cf. 1 Cor. 13:13). Such a substitution may have referred to the congregation being at "peace" with the true church, an essential qualification for salvation in North African theology. The Clipea font also has a longer, dedicatory inscription in mosaic in four lines (one for each side):

> Dedicated to most blessed holy Cyprian, Bishop and High Priest
> along with the holy Adelphius, a presbyter in unity with him.
> Aquinius and Juliana, his (wife), along with their household and
> (thanks be to God!) their children
> built these mosaics for the placid waters of eternity.[120]

The combination of a dedication to Cyprian with the emphasis on the virtue "peace" might refer to the long-standing idea that baptism received outside the "peace of the Catholic church" could not be salvific.[121]

## Additional Structures and Apparatus

Ciboria, or canopies, were commonly set over African fonts. In most cases, these were made of stone, supported by four columns, and placed immediately over the font itself. Similar canopies, raised over church altars and martyria, suggest that a font was regarded as a kind of shrine (cf. fig. 41). Architecturally, this would associate the ritual of baptism both with the cult of martyrs and the celebration of the eucharist. In addition to ciboria, some fonts had slots that could have supported stone or wooden screens that emphasized the separation of the sacrality of the activity and its ritual elements (cf. fig. 101).

Steps often provided access into and out of fonts (cf. fig. 13).[122] Although

118. [Gloria in excelsis Deo]/et in terra pax [h]ominibus bonae/volun[tatis l]audamus t[e]; see N. ben Lazreg and Noël Duval, "Le baptistère de Békalta," in *Carthage: L'histoire, sa trace et son echo* (Paris: Paris-Musées, 1995), 306.

119. *Pax fides caritas*. See Yvette Duval, *Loca sanctorum Africae: Le culte des martyrs en Afrique du IVe au VIIe siècle*, 2 vols. (Rome: École française de Rome, 1982): 1:54-58, no. 25.

120. Sco beatissimo Cypriano episcopo antiste/cum sco Adelfio presbitero huiusce unitatis/ Aquinius et Iuliana eius cum Villa et Deogratias prolibus/tesellu[m] aequori perenni posurunt. An alternative translation of the third line might be "Aquinius and Juliana (his wife), and Villa and Deogratias, their children." Y. Duval, *Loca sanctorum Africae*, 1:54-58, no. 25.

121. "Pax" seems to have had special meaning in the conflict between Donatists and Caecilianists and was invoked frequently by Augustine in his polemical writings.

122. These can be seen clearly at Bulla Regia, Hippo Regius, Sufetula (Vitalis), Meninx (El Kantara, Isle of Djerba), and Bennafa, as well as in the fonts now in Libya (Sabratha and Lepcis Magna).

steps allowed easy access down into the central well and out again, they also may have had a symbolic function. Three steps could indicate the three days Christ spent in the tomb or even the Persons of the Trinity. Some steps were continuous within the font, as at Thamugadi (fig. 94), while others were on opposite ends of the font, as at Sufetula (cf. fig. 71) and Bulla Regia (figs. 12-13). The latter type directed the candidates down (in) and up (out). If the steps were also oriented from west to east, they could also have symbolized movement from darkness to dawn (sunset to sunrise) and thus from death to resurrection.

Some baptisteries were equipped with systems to fill and drain the fonts. The font at Carthage's Dermech I, for example, has a clearly visible drain in the west side of the well. It also had a pipe in the northeast side of its hexagon that probably was fed by a cistern located in the north aisle of the ambulatory (figs. 26-27). Water presumably was collected in an underground reservoir and perhaps evacuated to the street drain. Musti's font (fig. 61) appears to have been filled from a large rainwater receptacle containing a hole for water to run into a channel set into the floor and leading to the font. The font at Carthage's Bir Ftouha was constructed over or near an existing bath complex, as were the fonts at Djebel Oust, Thamugadi, Cuicul (Djémila), and Carthage's Damous el Karita. These structures could have made use of existing systems to supply and to drain water, either into the town sewer or into a soak-away tank.[123] The presumed subterranean font at the Redemptus chapel was built directly over a well. Other fonts may have been filled and drained by bucket-carrying attendants. Cuicul's baptistery still has a bath structure and a latrine directly outside its main entrance (fig. 45), possibly for the use of candidates prior to their undergoing the ritual.

...........................................................................

## ARCHEOLOGICAL EVIDENCE PERTAINING TO THE CULT OF SAINTS

Veneration of the martyrs was incorporated into and accommodated by many African churches in a variety of ways. Often, churches were built directly into cemeteries, presumably over the site of a special tomb (e.g., the Basilica Maiorum in Carthage, which may have been the burial site of Perpetua and her companions). Elsewhere, relics might be transferred to an inaccessible casket beneath a church's pre-existing altar or placed in a crypt that allowed pilgrims some visual or physical access. Square or tri-conch rooms and counter-apses were sometimes annexed to churches to house particular relics (e.g., Castellum Tingitanum, Damous el Karita, and Uppenna). Occasionally, structures were built, originally, as shrines and then extended by the addition of a later church building (e.g., Theveste).

Extant freestanding martyria were rare, although both documentary evi-

123. See Stevens, ed., *Bir Ftouha*, 92-94.

dence and archeological remains suggest that the shrine of Stephen at Hippo Regius may have been a prominent exception.[124] Large circular monuments at some sites (e.g., Damous el Karita, fig. 17; and Tipasa, fig. 108) may also have been shrines dedicated to one or more saints. Many other examples were likely destroyed in response to a decree assigned to the plenary Council of Carthage in 401 that urged bishops to eradicate the ubiquitous memorials that were set up along country roads and in fields, and which could not be authenticated as possessing the remains of a recognized martyr.[125]

One of the largest and most impressive martyria is the site of the shrine of St. Crispina in Theveste (figs. 98-100).[126] The matron Crispina, a native of Thagura, was beheaded in Theveste during the Diocletian Persecution. An enormously popular saint throughout Africa, her story was recounted by Augustine, among others.[127] Crispina's shrine was established shortly after her death (ca. 304) and was an important pilgrimage destination. A complex of basilica, martyrium, monastery, and hostel, it was surrounded by a high wall punctuated by towers and three gates. Several phases of building and modifications, from the late fourth century through the Byzantine era, gave it a monumental shape.

A visitor entered the complex through a large arch that led into a broad forecourt. This forecourt appears to have featured a means of channeling visitors through a system of balustrades. At the end of this, a broad flight of steps led up to a platform and into an open-air atrium that contained a four-lobed fountain surrounded by columns. On either side of this atrium — and at ground level — were a series of rooms, one of which included a baptismal font. From the atrium one entered the basilica through one of three doors. Paired columns supported an architrave and, above it, a gallery. The choir came well into the nave and had footings for an altar at about the middle of the second bay from the apse. The floors of the nave and aisles were paved with mosaics.

The south aisle opened to another staircase that led down into a trefoil martyrium (fig. 100). This structure likely dates to an earlier phase of the building and was erected over an earlier shrine of St. Crispina, although the whole ensemble might have been constructed simultaneously. At the center of the trefoil, square paving stones indicate the place where excavators found the

124. This judgment is disputed; see below, p. 156, n. 289.

125. *Reg. Carth.* 83.

126. On Theveste, see Gui, Duval, and Caillet, eds., *Basiliques chrétiennes d'Afrique du Nord,* I.1:311-17; Noël Duval, Isabelle Gui, and Jean-Pierre Caillet, eds., *Basiliques chrétiennes d'Afrique du Nord, I. Inventaire de l'Algérie, 2* (Paris: Institut d'études augustiniennes, 1992), pp. CL-CLVIII. Also, see Jürgen Christern, *Das frühchristliche Pilgerheiligtum von Tebessa: Architektur und Ornamentik einer spätantiken Bauhütte in Nordafrika* (Wiesbaden: Steiner, 1976), N. Duval, *Les églises africaines à deux absides,* 2:35-40; Paul-Albert Février, "Le culte des martyrs en Afrique et ses plus anciens monuments," *Corso di cultura sull'arte ravennate e bizantina* 17 (1970): 204-7.

127. See Aug. *Serm.* 286.2.2; 354.5.5; *Serm. Morin* 2(313G).3; *Psal.* 120.13, 15; 137.3, 14, 17. Crispina also was honored in Carthage along with a group of other martyrs on December 5. See below, p. 525, n. 32; p. 534, n. 85.

foundations either for an altar and its canopy (ciborium), or perhaps only for a tomb, reliquary, or memorial inscription. In the central niche, a mosaic dated to ca. 350 (at the earliest) reproduced the names of several persons, along with the date (the 11th before the Kalends of January, December 22), which is close to that of Crispina's martyrdom (December 5), and which could refer to the day of the shrine's dedication. Beneath this, excavators discovered a vase containing a few bone fragments. Surrounding this were other mosaics, indicating subsequent burials, most of them clergy.[128]

Carthage had at least three major shrines dedicated to Cyprian by the end of the fourth century; one of these, the Mappalia Basilica, is now known as the Church of St. Monica (the likely site of Cyprian's tomb; fig. 22). Another was built at the site of Cyprian's execution, and known as the Mensa of Cyprian.[129] Carthage also boasted the Basilica Maiorum (to which tradition assigns a shrine of Perpetua and her companions; fig. 20), and in which an inscription was discovered that seemed to confirm the site's connection to these revered third-century martyrs (fig. 21). This shrine initially was set within a large necropolis and, in time, was converted into an elaborate crypt (3.6 × 3.7 m) at the center of the basilica's nave.[130]

Since these structures necessarily were at a distance from the urban center (Roman cemeteries were always outside the city walls), their liturgical function is somewhat ambiguous. Eucharistic services were held on feast days and perhaps as part of a funeral, but it seems unlikely that most of these buildings were used for regular Sunday or weekday services. They were more apt to shelter a changing population of pilgrims and visiting relatives. During the Vandal occupation, they may have served the Nicene congregations. Eventually, as the population grew and suburban churches were needed, these cemetery basilicas must have assumed some of the functions of an ordinary parish church while yet remaining pilgrimage destinations.[131]

Carthage had other enormous suburban basilica-shrines, including those at Damous el Karita (fig. 15) and at Bir Ftouha (fig. 28).[132] The basilica at Damous el Karita had an impressive semicircular atrium with an annexed trefoil chapel that probably functioned as a martyrium. Nearby, a large round monument that was partially subterranean may also have been a martyr's shrine (fig. 17).[133] The basilica at Bir Ftouha had a large polygonal building opposite its apse that included a number of burials. This large structure probably was a

128. In addition to Gui, Duval, and Caillet noted above, see P.-A. Février, "Nouvelles recherches dans la salle tréflée de la basilique de Tébessa," *Bulletin d'archéologie algérienne* 3 (1968): 177-78.

129. See the discussion below, p. 140.

130. See the discussion of this basilica below, pp. 144-45.

131. On the use of cemetery churches during the Vandal occupation, see below, pp. 138-39.

132. Vict.-Vit. *Hist. pers.* 1.3.

133. See the discussion below, p. 139.

martyrium, at least initially.[134] Unlike other pilgrimage churches, Bir Ftouha's shows little evidence of having been built in a pre-existing cemetery; it began attracting burials only after it had become a popular shrine. Thus, a basilica might become a cemetery, rather than be built into one, and a saint's remains might be translated to the site, rather than preceding the building.

A short distance down the coast is the basilica of Uppenna, another instance of a memorial basilica (fig. 115). Here the church appears to have been built in several stages, at least initially to honor a group of local martyrs. In its earliest phase (possibly in the mid-fourth century), the shrine had been in the original apse and dedicated to thirteen saints (Saturninus, Bindemius, Saturninus, Donatus, Saturninus, Gududa, Paula, Clara, Lucilla, Fortunatus, Iader, Cecilius, and Emilius).[135] In its second phase, the basilica's counter-apse was transformed into a small square room and paved with a figurative mosaic that depicted two sheep facing a jeweled cross. Here, the same martyrs were honored in a new mosaic, but the names of Peter, Paul, and another Saturninus (a presbyter) were added at the beginning of the inscription, and set off from the others (figs. 117-118).[136] The addition of Rome's Holy Apostles indicates the arrival of their cult, especially in the Byzantine era. Presumably the cavity beneath this new pavement included imported relics from their tombs. Throughout the stages of the church's building and renovation, burials of local dignitaries continued. These included bishops and other clergy as well as especially honored laypersons (figs. 148-149). Excavators uncovered approximately sixty such tomb mosaics in the early twentieth century. Today they are housed in a small museum in the neighboring town of Enfidha.

Thus, in addition to monumental structures, other archeological evidence testifies to the cult of the saints, including inscriptions and mosaics placed above relics, like the martyrs' dedication at Uppenna. The fragmentary inscription found in the ruins of Carthage's Basilica Maiorum claimed "Here are" (*Hic sunt*) the martyrs Saturus, Saturninus, Revocatus, Secundulus, Felicitas, and Perpetua (fig. 21). Scholars have argued about whether this or other inscriptions taken from the Basilica Maiorum were simply commemorative or covered actual remains or graves of Perpetua or her companions.[137] Other inscriptions could have been only honorific, like the mosaic panel found at Carthage's Monastery of St. Stephen that displayed the names of seven martyrs, probably of

134. See the discussion below, pp. 139-40.

135. See Y. Duval, *Loca sanctorum Africae*, 1:59-67, no. 28-29. The plan and phases of this basilica are very controversial. For a comprehensive study of the site, see Dominique Raynal, *Uppenna: Archéologie et histoire de l'église d'Afrique*, 2 vols., Tempus 32 (Toulouse: Presses universitaires du Mirail, 2006).

136. Half of the older mosaic still exists and is in the museum at Enfidaville.

137. William Tabbernee, *Montanist Inscriptions and Testimonia: Epigraphic Sources Illustrating the History of Montanism* (Macon, Ga.: Mercer University Press, 1997), 105-17. See also Y. Duval, *Loca sanctorum Africae*, 1:13-16.

Perpetua and her companions (Felicity, Saturus, and Saturninus), along with Stephen himself within jeweled wreaths (fig. 30).[138]

Other architectural features marked the placement of martyrs' remains in shrines, basilicas, or pilgrimage churches. The translation of saints' relics seems to have been a fairly common practice in the post-Vandal era, perhaps as a way of re-establishing the Nicene church's authority in Africa. Many relics were placed in special boxes inserted into cavities beneath altars, which themselves would have been covered by canopies (ciboria). For example, the sixth-century Basilica of Melleus at Ammaedara (Haidra), dated to 568/9 (during the reign of Emperor Justin II), appears to have acquired a relic of Cyprian, which was installed under the main altar, covered by a ciborium, and set off by a stone balustrade (figs. 1-2, 4).[139] An inscription that covered the spot at which the relic was inserted reads, "Here have been deposited relics of the holy martyr and bishop, Cyprian, installed here by blessed Bishop Melleus in the fourth year of the Lord Justin, Emperor."[140] These holy remains attracted those who wished to be buried nearby. In time, burials covered most of the church's floor space and were marked by identifying epitaphs (cf. fig. 3).

If relics were installed elsewhere in the space, low walls or other barriers (e.g., screens) would have been installed to keep the faithful at a distance and to provide a kind of sacred enclosure (as at Castellum Tingitanum).[141] Ambulatories were constructed to direct such traffic around the back of the apse (as at Siagu and Bir Ftouha; fig. 28). A pair of candles may have been a standard feature of martyria. The Miracles of St. Stephen recounts the vision of a certain Vitula, who visited the shrine in Hippo Regius and received assurance of her husband's conversion when the two candles near the saint's relics flared up.[142] Two candles often appear in depictions of saints, as on the sixth-century silver Capsella Africana, originally from a sixth-century church in Numidia (Aïn Zirara) and now in the Vatican Museum.[143]

138. See Y. Duval, *Loca sanctorum Africae*, 1:7-10 for a collection of these inscriptions related to saints' shrines.

139. On this basilica (and its shrine), see Noël Duval, *Recherches archéologiques à Haïdra, 2: La Basilique I dite de Melléus ou de Saint-Cyprien* (Rome: École française de Rome, 1981).

140. See Y. Duval, *Loca sanctorum Africae*, 1:117-19, no. 54. The relic disappeared, but the inscription was retrieved, and a fragment is still in the Bardo Museum.

141. See Aug. *Ciu.* 22.8 and *Serm.* 322.

142. See *Mirc. Steph.* 2.2.4.

143. See recent discussion in Galit Noga-Banai, *The Trophies of the Martyrs: An Art Historical Study of Early Christian Silver Reliquaries* (Oxford: Oxford University Press, 2008), 70-80. Note also the appearance of a pair of candles in many of the funerary mosaics discussed below, p. 130.

The attraction of saints' shrines as places for the burial of the rank-and-file faithful was based, at least partly, on the belief that proximity to saints' remains gave some access to their intercessory powers or special assistance on Judgment Day. This belief was as important a feature of African Christianity as it was elsewhere in the Roman world and contributed to the practice of burial at or near martyrs' shrines *(depositio ad sanctos)*.[144] This popular belief and its resulting practice, however, were tenacious, despite certain bishops' admonitions against misunderstanding their value. Augustine's response to a query from his friend Paulinus of Nola on the subject asserted that physical proximity to a martyr's remains (in this case, Felix's) was of no particular religious benefit or help toward salvation. However, burial near a saint's remains could be regarded as a petition for the saint's intercession on the departed's behalf. Thus, the grave's location might have the salutary function of reminding visiting mourners to seek the saint's intervention for divine mercy upon their dead loved one.[145] As Augustine might have expected, his argument had little, if any, influence on such an established custom.

Archeological evidence from Christian cemeteries before and after Augustine (e.g., Carthage's Basilica Maiorum, the basilica at Bir Ftouha, the Basilica of Melleus in Ammaedara, and the cemetery church of St. Salsa in Tipasa) indicates the continued clustering of graves near the tomb or memorial of a martyr. St. Salsa was a fourteen-year-old girl who was executed for tossing the local idols into the sea. Her body, also tossed off a cliff into the waves, was found and buried outside the city, possibly in a family enclosure. The site of her tomb became a magnet for continued burials and eventually covered a huge area to the east of the city (fig. 111). In the fifth century, a small basilica was constructed in this necropolis and dedicated to Saints Peter and Paul. The round mausoleum in the necropolis on the other side of the city might also have been a martyrium (fig. 108).

Thus, people clearly believed there was some benefit to spending the time before the general Resurrection and final Judgment in the vicinity of a saint. The *Acta* of the late-third-century martyr Maximilian at Theveste gives one of the first recorded instances of this. Soon after Maximilian was executed by the sword for refusing military service, a woman named Pompeiana obtained his body from the magistrate and, at her own expense, brought it to Carthage, where she buried it near the body of Cyprian. Thirteen days later, she died and

144. See Yvette Duval, *Auprès des saints corps et âme: L'inhumation "ad sanctos" dans la chrétienté d'Orient et d'Occident du IIIe au VIIe siècle* (Paris: Études augustiniennes, 1988). See also Ann Marie Yasin, *Saints and Church Spaces in the Late Antique Mediterranean: Architecture, Cult, and Community* (Cambridge and New York: Cambridge University Press, 2009), 69-76.

145. See the discussion below, pp. 530, 543-45. Augustine's record of the correspondence with Paulinus is found at *Cur.* 4.6, 5.7, 18.22.

was buried in the same spot.[146] Those who had the means even went further and incorporated relics into their tombs. The chapel of Asterius (fig. 24), also at Carthage, is an example of an elite hypogeum into which relics were placed, somewhat transforming the process of burial *ad sanctos*.[147]

The site of Thabraca (Tabarka) included an urban basilica (with an octagonal rotunda that may have been a martyrium), as well as the so-called Chapel of the Martyrs. The urban basilica had a few burials within its walls, but it was also surrounded by a large necropolis that included a chapel. The buildings and the cemetery all yielded a wealth of funerary mosaics, including the *Ecclesia Mater* mosaic (fig. 132), which was found in front and slightly to the left of the apse of the martyrs' chapel. Although no records of particular saints are recorded for this site, an inscription, found in the excavations of the late nineteenth century, mentions the martyr Anastasia and her companions.[148] Most of the mosaics appear to commemorate fairly ordinary dead members of the community. Yet, several of the mosaics, particularly in the martyrs' chapel, seem to indicate that the deceased had achieved some measure of sanctity, which could be the justification for naming this a "martyrs' chapel." One of these is a dedication to two women, Privata and Victoria, who are described as "celebrating the triumph of consecrated virginity and victorious confession, bearing trophies and wearing angelic robes" (fig. 144). Below, within a wreath, is the legend "A worthy crown for worthy victors."[149]

Another mosaic found in the chapel, and also directly in front of the apse, was dedicated to a certain Crescentinus. A complex composition, it is divided into three horizontal panels inside a decorative border. In the upper panel, three horsemen gallop in a ring. Roses are scattered, and birds peck on the ground. From the top of the frame, a hand offers a wreath, presumably meant for the victor. The lowest panel shows a dolphin swimming towards a ship on the left and a Christogram on the right (fig. 143). Dolphins are symbols of resurrection; the ship is a figure for the church. The large, central panel contains this legend:

> Companion of martyrs and host of angels,
> Breathing a placid life.
> He has gone up to you in safety.
> May he be mindful of us with the grace and piety that is usual for him.
> Crescentinus, deacon, in peace.
> Returned his soul on July 30.[150]

146. *Act. Max.* 3.4.

147. See the discussion below, p. 122.

148. *CIL* 8.173-82. On the tomb mosaics at Thabraca, see Joan Marguerite Downs, "The Christian Tomb Mosaics from Tabarka: Status and Identity in a North African Roman Town" (Ph.D. diss., University of Michigan, 2007).

149. Latin inscription: Privata cum Victoria gaude triumfa consecratae virginitatis et confessionis victricia portantes tropea veste indutae angelica in pace.

150. Latin inscription: Angelorum ospes/martyrum.comes/vitamque.spirans/placidam.ad

In this example, both epitaph and iconography express the hope and beliefs of a donor, along with a prayer directed to the pious deacon Crescentinus. As a "companion of martyrs," he has "gone up to" heaven rather than remaining in a state of rest *(refrigerium)*. As he is now a citizen of that abode, he may make intercession for those who continue to live on earth. His race is won, and his crown has been presented, as in the words of II Timothy: "I have fought the good fight, I have finished the race, I have kept the faith. Henceforth there is laid up for me the crown of righteousness" (4:7-8).

Augustine frequently quoted these lines. In one of his answers to Simplician, he used them as evidence that Paul had first received grace before doing works of righteousness.[151] In a number of sermons and other treatises, moreover, he directly quotes this passage to describe the merits and rewards of the just:

> Where are these saints, do you suppose? Where all is well with them. Why inquire any further? You don't know the place, but think of what earned it for them. Wherever they are, they are with God. . . . Time, he says, presses for me to cast off. I have fought the good fight, I have completed the course, I have kept the faith; for the rest there remains for me a crown of justice. You are right to be in such a hurry, right to rejoice at the prospect of being set apart as a victim; after all, there is awaiting for you a crown of justice.[152]

## ARCHITECTURAL EVIDENCE FOR CHRISTIAN BURIAL

A large body of physical and epigraphic evidence attests to Christian funerary practices in Roman Africa. This includes tombs in surface (open-air) cemetery areas, communal catacombs, and hypogea, as well as burials within shrines, basilicas, and cemetery churches. In addition to sarcophagi (both carved and plain) and dedicatory inscriptions, excavations have uncovered polychrome mosaic tomb covers and tables for funerary meals *(mensae)*, a few decorated with polychrome mosaic designs that are characteristic features of North African burials. Although some late-third-century artifacts have been recorded, most of the physical remains date from the fourth through the sixth centu-

---

te sane/profectus. Sit nost/ri memor. Gratia. Pie/tate qua solet/Crescentinus.diac/in pace. Red. III kal. Aug., now in the Bardo Museum, Tunis. *ILCV* 1:2034; Y. Duval, *Loca sanctorum Africae,* 1:431.

151. Aug. *Simpl.* 1.2.3.

152. Aug. *Serm.* 297.4.5; 299.3. ubi sunt sancti isti, putamus? ibi ubi bene est. quid quaeris amplius? non nosti locum, sed cogita meritum. Ubicumque sunt, cum deo sunt . . . tempus, inquit, resolutionis meae instat. bonum certamen certaui, cursum consummaui, fidem seruaui; de cetero superest mihi corona iustitiae. merito festinas, merito te immolandum esse laetaris: superest enim tibi corona iustitiae. Aug. *Serm.* 298.3.3; SPM 1:97.15-17, 21-24. See also *Serm.* 298.4.4.

ries, thus reflecting funerary customs among Christians from the late Roman through the Vandal and Byzantine eras.[153]

Most Christian surface tombs, like their non-Christian counterparts, were dug into the earth or cut into floors, lined with unmortared stone slabs, covered with ceramic roofing tiles, and, at the surface, sealed with simple, anonymous markers to prevent their being accidentally opened and desecrated. Some markers were inscribed stone slabs or polychrome mosaics that recorded the names and ages of the deceased, occasionally adding details about their character or clerical status. More elaborate markers were rounded or rectangular boxes ("caissons") placed directly over the grave, and many of these boxes were covered with mosaics (see figs. 137, 146). Other economically well-off individuals were buried in stone sarcophagi, adorned with reliefs and left above ground (see fig. 128).[154] The wealthy honored their dead in ways that appear to have ignored the promptings of certain bishops to avoid ostentatious burials.[155]

In addition to surface tombs, Africans buried their dead in catacombs. Among the earliest specifically Christian cemeteries were three of the four catacombs at Hadrumetum (Sousse) — Bon Pasteur, Hermes, and Severus — along with a recently discovered catacomb and underground basilica near the site of Lepti Minus (Lamta). These appear to have been used predominantly (if not exclusively or originally) for Christian burials and accommodated thousands of graves.[156] Dated to the late third or early fourth century, these catacombs were much like their counterparts in Rome. Tunnels dug into soft tufa, they were comprised of long galleries and occasional cubicula. Both floors and walls of these galleries were used for burial. The walls were cut to create stacked loculus graves that were sealed by terra-cotta tiles or marble slabs. These coverings were inscribed with the names of the deceased and sometimes included a simple symbol or image (see figs. 119, 144, 148). Occasionally the galleries opened into cubicula which apparently were constructed for families, like that of Hermes, that also had the means to decorate them with polychrome mosaics (fig. 122).

---

153. Among other helpful works, see the collection of essays edited by David L. Stone and Lea M. Stirling, *Mortuary Landscapes of North Africa* (Toronto: University of Toronto Press, 2007). Of particular interest is the essay by Anna Leone, "Changing Urban Landscapes: Burials in North African Cities from the Late Antique to the Byzantine Periods," 164-203.

154. There were relatively few early Christian decorated sarcophagi found in North Africa, compared to Rome or Gaul, for example, and a large percentage of these would have been imported from Roman workshops. See Brigitte Christern-Briesenick, Friedrich Wilhelm Deichmann, and Jutta Dresken-Weiland, *Repertorium der christlich-antiken Sarkophage 3. Frankreich, Algerien, Tunesien* (Wiesbaden: Steiner, 2003).

155. For Augustine criticizing elaborate or ostentatious tombs, see *Serm. Dolb.* 7(142*).3; *Psal.* 33.2.14; 48.1.13, 15; 48.2.1-8; *Ciu.* 1.12.

156. Augustin-Ferdinand Leynaud, *Les catacombes africaines: Sousse-Hadrumète* (Alger: Jules Carbonel, 1922); Nejib ben Lazreg et al., "Roman and Early Christian Burial Complex at Leptiminus (Lamta): Second Notice," *Journal of Roman Archaeology* 19 (2006): 347-68.

A subterranean Christian burial complex, built adjacent to an existing Roman necropolis, exists at the site of Lepti Minus (Lamta). A vestibule at the foot of the stairs contains tombs and leads to another large, vaulted room containing more tombs (fig. 127). This hypogeum was, in turn, connected to a system of catacombs.[157] Only the wealthiest Christians could afford such hypogea or funerary chapels for their exclusive use. Among these are two Byzantine-era hypogea, the chapels of Asterius and Redemptus found in Carthage, and the hypogeum of the Blossus family in Furnos Minus (fig. 120). Both of these were small rooms designed to look like miniature basilicas, and each included a reliquary. The relics were deposited beneath the raised apse area and, based on the existence of footings, covered by an altar. The pavement of Asterius's subterranean chapel-tomb was covered with mosaics of fish (in the vestibule), medallions with non-figurative designs and birds, and — toward the apse — peacocks flanking a vase (fig. 24). On the step leading into the apse, an inscription named Asterius as one of the faithful and gave his age and the date of his burial.[158]

Specific symbols or phrases — rather than modes of burial — distinguish Christian tombs from pagan ones. Most Christian tomb inscriptions and mosaics were simple, but some could be quite elaborate. An inscription from Hadrumetum shows a Good Shepherd figure — hence the modern name of the catacomb in which it was found (fig. 123). Along with floral or geometric designs were included Christograms, crosses, fish, lambs, anchors, dolphins, birds, vases, and flowers (fig. 121). The more elaborate included portraits of the deceased, usually in the prayer *(orans)* position and flanked by candles, roses, and birds. Epitaphs usually gave the name and age of the deceased, sometimes the title or ecclesiastical rank, and described the departed as "a faithful one," an "innocent one," or "a servant of God." A rare few, like Honorata's (noted below, p. 130), were elaborate and even poetic. Almost always the formula *in pace* ("at peace") was added. Abbreviations were common. Mosaics were often divided into sections that included an epitaph and a Christogram (directly over the head of the deceased — see fig. 148).

Another identifying characteristic of African Christian tombs is that, while well-to-do Romans customarily buried their dead with the extended family in an ancestral mausoleum, most African Christians were inclined to share designated areas of cemeteries with their co-religionists.[159] Consequently, ex-

---

157. See Lazreg et al., "Roman and Early Christian Burial Complex at Leptiminus (Lamta): Second Notice," 347-68.

158. See Ennabli, *Carthage, une métropole chrétienne,* 104-6. Noël Duval, "La chapelle funéraire souterraine dit d'Asterius, à Carthage," *Mélanges d'archéologie et d'histoire,* 71 (1959): 339-57.

159. Cyprian, in *Ep.* 67.6.2, denounced the Spanish bishop Martialis for burying his sons among pagans. His own burial, however, was in a cemetery identified for its (presumably non-Christian) founder — *Act. Procon.* 5. Cyprian's death may have occurred at a time when Christians were forbidden the use of their cemetery, however, under the persecution of Valerian. See

isting inscriptions tended to focus on ecclesial status or church membership rather than familial relationships.[160] An exception is the tomb of the deacon Crescentius, who was buried with his son, Bruttanicus (fig. 148). A comparison of non-Christian and Christian epitaphs from the third century through the sixth century demonstrates a distinction between the two groups. Christians rarely noted filial, parental, or spousal relationships on their tombs. The fourth-century mosaic made for the tomb of Hermes, dear to his wife and children (fig. 122), is one of an exceptional minority.[161] Even here, however, the iconography, with its Christian symbolism (a dolphin wrapped around an anchor), markedly differs from a typical pagan example such as the paired tomb covers of Gaius Julius Serenus and his wife, Numitoria, in which husband (on one) and wife (on the other) are shown reclining on couches, enjoying their funeral banquets, being attended by erotes bearing baskets of flowers and figures of Psyche playing musical instruments (fig. 145). Another shows the deceased upon his couch above a scene of his departure, riding a horse led by the god Hermes into the underworld (fig. 147).

Thus, although traditional Roman burial rites (e.g., funeral processions and banquets) were normally occasions for honoring the extended family (including ancestors), Christian practice downplayed the importance of kinship ties and emphasized identification with the community of faith. While families might still engage in the traditional rituals of mourning, remembrance, and decoration of the grave, they were reticent about displaying their familial and marital relationships. The double tomb of Stercorius and Crescentina, for example, omits any reference to their being married (but does seem to refer to them as *pater* and *mater,* which makes it likely that they were). Instead, it stresses their having received crowns in perpetuity, and thus emphasizes their sanctity.[162]

The church, similarly, could serve the function of a burial society for the poor and unattached, since it forbade membership in a non-Christian burial

---

Eus. Caes. *Hist. eccl.* 7.11.10. The Hadrumetum catacombs produced important exceptions to this, however, as they had a number of cubicula that apparently were meant for families, including the family of Hermes (see fig. 122 and comments below).

160. See the comparative evidence for Rome, collected by Richard P. Saller and Brent D. Shaw in "Tombstones and Roman Family Relations in the Principate: Civilians, Soldiers, and Slaves," *The Journal of Roman Studies* 74 (1984): 124-56.

161. The epitaph reads "Hermes coniugi et fil(iis) dulcissimus." Note the study of Brent D. Shaw, "Seasons of Death: Aspects of Mortality in Imperial Rome," *The Journal of Roman Studies* 86 (1996): 108-11, which draws a similar conclusion for the evidence from Rome. See also the discussion below, pp. 462-63.

162. The tomb was found to hold two skeletons. Based on Downs's reconstruction, the mosaic's inscription reads ". . . ⟨r⟩ed(diderunt) animam pat(er) XVI (die) kal(endas) Nov(embres) mat(er) XV (diebus) kal(endas) M⟨ai⟩as. H(anc) ⟨p⟩erpetuitatis c⟨or⟩ona(m) ac/ce[perunt] quod/d⟨eo⟩ . . . crea/ti St⟨e⟩[rcor]⟨i⟩us et/Cres[centia] in pace/vi⟨xce(runt) an(nis) CLXXX /⟨VI⟩II. For discussion, see Downs, "The Christian Tomb Mosaics from Tabarka," 442-43, no. 90.

club.[163] A related feature of African Christian burials was their tendency to entomb certain honored individuals, especially clergy, within churches and shrines (instead of in communal cemeteries). Pavements were breached to accommodate burial of privileged individuals (clergy, virgins, or donors), whose tombs were covered with similar polychrome mosaic markers that recorded names and ages of the deceased and featured floral or other decorative designs.[164]

Little evidence exists to distinguish Donatist from Caecilianist cemeteries, or even Vandal from Nicene ones. The legend *vixit in pace* ("lived in peace" — fig. 126) could allude to sectarian identity with one or the other side of a schism or controversy, or particular attraction to one of the local saints' shrines for burial *ad sanctos,* but it would be hard to determine which side was being claimed in such cases. Although Optatus reported that Donatists prohibited church burials, a number of mosaic inscriptions were, in fact, found in the site assumed to be the Donatist cathedral in Thamugadi (Timgad).[165] Optatus himself apparently was buried within his cathedral (see fig. 92). Sometimes, however, an inscription suggests identity, as in Hildegun's funerary inscription at Mactaris, Guilia Runa's at Hippo Regius (fig. 125), or that of the fifth-century bishop Victorinus of Ammaedara, whose epitaph appears to have been amended — in the post-Vandal, Byzantine period — to proclaim him "Vandalorum."[166] Yet, Vandal identity is not confirmed by such Germanic-type names, since there was some social and religious migration among the communities. Nor — as in the case of Victorinus — is a Roman name evidence to the contrary.

### Cemeteries and Cemetery Churches

From the mid- or late-fourth century onwards, burials inside of church buildings became more and more common, especially (but not exclusively) in those churches located within cemeteries or outside the city walls. In such places, the remains of privileged Christians (clergy and consecrated virgins, for example) were interred beneath the floors of naves, aisles, and apses. Clergy (bishops in particular) sometimes were buried below the presbyterium, even of churches within the city walls (in the apse, as at Sufetula's Basilica of Servus; fig. 76).

163. Cypr. *Ep.* 67.6.2.

164. Such as the Valentia named in the Thabraca mosaic. See Aug. *Serm. Dolb.* 7(142*).1; *Serm.* 302.6-10, and the discussion below (on funeral mosaics), pp. 128-31.

165. On the prohibition, see Optat. *Parm.* 3.4; see also James H. Terry, "Christian Tomb Mosaics of Late Roman, Vandalic, and Byzantine Byzacena" (Ph.D. diss., University of Missouri–Columbia, 1998), 216.

166. On Hildegun's inscription, see above, pp. 95-96. See Noël Duval, "L'église de l'évêque Melleus à Haidra (Tunisie): La campagne franco-tunisienne de 1967," *Comptes-rendus des séances de l'Académie des Belles-Lettres,* 112, no. 2 (1968): 221-44, esp. 243.

Often the primary apse was used for this purpose, but clergy might also be entombed within a specially constructed enclosure in the main hall or a side aisle. Even when not built as such, churches with martyrs' tombs or relics would subsequently attract burials *(ad sanctos)* both inside and around their perimeters, thus becoming cemetery churches after the fact. Like many of the burials in surface cemeteries, these church tombs were covered with polychrome stone mosaics or simple stone slabs, inscribed with the name of the deceased (fig. 3; Ammaedara). These mosaics created a kind of patchwork-quilt effect across the length of a nave, often with inscriptions running in different directions (cf. fig. 149). Occasionally, when building renovations destroyed existing tomb mosaics, they would be replaced but not exactly replicated, often being incorporated almost seamlessly into the new pavement (fig. 149).[167]

The particular prominence of certain clerical tombs parallels aspects of the saints' cult. As elsewhere in the early Christian world, bishops were especially honored in death. For example, according to his biographer, Ferrandus, the body of Bishop Fulgentius of Ruspe (died ca. 530) was entombed into the cathedral, the church in which he had been consecrated and where he had, at one time, deposited some relics of the Apostles. Ferrandus noted that he was the first person (clergy or lay) to have been buried in this church, but that the esteem of his congregation overcame any reticence. They judged it particularly fitting that Fulgentius's tomb should be installed there, near the remains of the saints, and thus benefited by such proximity and becoming a permanent witness to the church's continuing liturgy.[168] Earlier parallels to this include Optatus's apparent burial in the nave of his cathedral in Thamugadi. The site still retains the tomb's gabled roof, with a hole at the top for pouring libations (fig. 92). Similarly, Uppenna's bishops Honorius (5th cen.) and Baleriolus (6th cen.) were buried in a prime location, in a special enclosure within the apse and directly in front of the martyrs' memorial (cf. the mosaics' current placement, intended to approximate this; fig. 117). A sixth-century bishop, Paulus, noted as the Primate of Mauretania, was interred a long way from home, at Sidi Abiche. Possibly because he was not buried in his own cathedral, his remains were interred in a room south of the baptistery (fig. 129).[169]

Occasionally, whole churches were constructed specifically for the purpose of honoring clergy, as in the case of the cemetery basilica of Alexander in Tipasa (fig. 109).[170] This funerary chapel established by Alexander, the late-

167. Terry, "Christian Tomb Mosaics of Late Roman, Vandalic, and Byzantine Byzacena," 44.
168. Ferrand. *Vita Fulg.* 29.65.
169. Terry judges that Paulus may have sought refuge in Byzacena during the reign of Justinian, when the political situation in Mauretania was unstable. See Terry, "Christian Tomb Mosaics of Late Roman, Vandalic, and Byzantine Byzacena," p. 208, no. 121. Honorius and Baleriolus are both cited by Maier as bishops of Uppenna, although Baleriolus may be given on the strength of this tomb inscription. See Maier, *L'épiscopat de l'Afrique romaine, vandale, et byzantine,* 232.
170. See discussion below, pp. 430-31.

fourth-century Bishop of Tipasa, had a somewhat exclusive purpose. According to a mosaic inscription found on the site, Alexander commissioned the construction of a building within an ancient cemetery to the west of the city that would contain his own tomb (in the apse) as well as the bodies of his nine predecessors.[171] The mosaic inscription named those earlier bishops as Alexander's "righteous predecessors" *(iusti priores)*.[172] A raised rectangular platform at the eastern end of the main hall held the sarcophagi of those predecessors, whose bodies Alexander had transferred from an older, adjacent crypt. The inscription's text declares that whereas these worthies had before been hidden, now they were honored by a new, beautiful, and visible resting place. The rest of the small structure, roughly twenty-three by fourteen meters, was furnished with several semicircular stone couches designed for the celebration of funeral meals (fig. 112). A number of other tombs also filled an attached structure, which was similarly equipped with funerary tables.[173]

### Funerary Banquet or Offering Tables *(Mensae)*

As in the Alexander Chapel, cemeteries and cemetery churches alike contained stone tables and couches that were used for the funeral banquets held at the time of burial and on subsequent occasions, including the birthday of the deceased *(natalicium)* and the old Roman festival known as the *Parentalia*.[174] Despite the objections of church authorities, Christians continued to practice the Roman custom of dining with their dead, which involved preparing and sharing simple food items and pouring out libations on or into the tomb itself. Tertullian associated these meals *(refrigeria* or *convivia)* with pagan idolatry. In his turn, Augustine encouraged families to turn their banquets into alms and bring their commemorations inside the church. Neither one succeeded in rooting out this ancient practice.[175] Tomb epitaphs continued to note the date of death, presumably to mark the anniversary commemorations. Physical evidence shows that cemetery banquets continued through the sixth century, and even well into the late Byzantine era. Burial areas featured communal banqueting tables, as well as facilities for drawing water and washing up, that might have been used by visitors to collective grave areas.

One famous example, an epitaph of a certain Aelia Secundula, dates to 299 C.E. and was found in the region of Mauretania Sitifensis. Also an acrostic, the

171. The inscription for Alexander himself is recorded in *ILCV* 1:1103.

172. *ILCV* 1:1825.

173. On the site of Tipasa and these cemeteries, see Février, "Le culte des martyrs en Afrique et ses plus anciens monuments"; and the critically important survey of Y. Duval, *Loca sanctorum Africae*, 1:357-80, no. 178-79. See also N. Duval, *Les églises africaines à deux absides*, 2:10-20.

174. See the discussion of Augustine preaching on the *Parentalia*, p. 505.

175. See the discussion on pp. 505-6, 512.

first and last letters of each line form the phrase "the children to their sweet mother." Although not unambiguously Christian, the text gives a good description of the way most funeral meals would have been conducted, whether Christian or pagan. In addition to praising the woman, the participants prepared a stone table, laid with food and drink, and told stories about her long into the night:

> To the memory of Aelia Secundula.
> We all sent many worthy things for her funeral.
> Further near the altar dedicated to Mother Secundula,
> It pleases us to place a stone table
> On which we, placing food and covered cups,
> Remember her many great deeds.
> In order to heal the savage wound gnawing at our breast,
> We freely recount stories at a late hour,
> And give praises to the good and chaste mother, who sleeps in her old age.
> She, who nourished us, lies soberly forever.
> She lived to be seventy-five years of age, and died in the 260th year
>      of the province.
> Made by Statulenia Julia.[176]

In addition to Alexander's cemetery basilica, the cemeteries of Tipasa contained a number of *mensae,* both in the necropolis on the west and around the shrine of St. Salsa on the east side of the city. These areas were equipped with tables for memorial feasts, many of them still visible and some with intact mosaic decoration (cf. fig. 113), along with cisterns and systems for drawing water and channeling it onto the tombs.[177] One such mosaic *mensa* from the late fourth century, recovered from a nearby area known as the necropolis of Matares, contains a legend embodying the optimistic spirit of such banquets. In addition to images of fish is a legend that reads "In God (Christ), may peace and concord be on our banquet" (fig. 114).[178]

Other African *mensae* types (both Christian and non-Christian) include simple masonry offering-table attachments added to a tomb marker, such as those found at Sullecthum (Salakta — fig. 86), or added to stone grave mark-

---

176. Memoria Aeliae Secundulae./Funeri mu[l]ta quid[e]m condigna iam misimus omneS,/ Insuper ar[a]equ[e] deposte Secundulae matrI/Lapideam placuit nobis atponere mensaM,/In qua magna eius memorantes plurima factA,/Dum cibi ponuntur calicesq[ue]. E[i] copertaE,/Vulnus ut sanetur nos rod[ens] pectore saeuuM/Libentur fabul[as] dum sera redimus horA/Castae matri bonae laudesq[ue], vetula dormiT/Ipas, q[uae] nutri[i]t, iaces et sobriae semper./V[ixit] a[nnis] LXXV a[nno] p[rovinciae] CCLX,/Statulenia Iulia fecit. *ILCV* 1:1570; *CIL* 8:20.277.

177. See Février, "Le culte des martyrs en Afrique et ses plus anciens monuments."

178. In Deo, pax et concordia sit convivio nostro. The *mensa* from the Mactaris necropolis is now in the Musée de Tipasa. A Christogram between "in" and "Deo" may mean "In Christo Deo."

ers. Some examples include depressions designed to look like dishware that could have accommodated specific kinds of offerings (e.g., grain, pine nuts, olives, figs), while others were permanent representations of traditional funerary foods, such as fish (fig. 95). Libation tubes also appear on many tombs for pouring wine or oil directly into the tomb.[179]

## Mosaic Tomb Covers

Many African tombs were covered with polychrome mosaics. Although this practice is distinctly African, it has parallels in other areas of the early Christian world, most notably Spain and southern Italy.[180] These mosaics also show parallels with earlier Punic grave *stelae* from the region (cf. fig. 153). Most of these were rectangular, corresponding to the size and shape of the simple slab grave beneath, and about one by two meters in size. Though some of them bore a portrait of the deceased, the majority had simple designs: a Christogram within a wreath with an inscription inside a simple geometric border. More elaborate mosaics included birds, animals, fish, or fruit- and flower-filled vases (fig. 121). Rare examples of caisson-type tomb markers covered on five sides with mosaic have also been found (cf. figs. 137, 146). Occasionally, biblical characters (e.g., Daniel, Jonah, or Abraham and Isaac) appear (cf. figs. 120, 138). Some designs were unparalleled, such as the Hermes mosaic that displays a dolphin-entwined anchor (fig. 122), or the *Ecclesia Mater* mosaic that depicts a basilica (fig. 132).

Although some examples of pagan mosaic tomb markers have also been discovered (cf. figs. 145, 147), the majority belong to Christian burials. They date from the late fourth century to the early sixth century; they were less common in the Vandal period, but apparently experienced a resurgence of popularity in the Byzantine era. Some regions appear to have more surviving examples (e.g., Thabraca and Uppenna), and show distinct stylistic and formal differences in motif, design, and lettering that allow art historians to distinguish workshops.[181] Most of the *tesserae* of these mosaics were made from imported marble or limestone, although the yellow marble came from the quarries of

179. See Lea Stirling, "Archeological Evidence for Food Offerings in the Graves of Roman North Africa," in *Daimonopylai: Essays in Classics and the Classical Tradition Presented to Edmund G. Berry,* ed. Rory B. Egan and Mark Joyal (Winnipeg: University of Manitoba Centre for Hellenic Civilization, 2004), 427-51.

180. See James Breckenridge, "Christian Funerary Portraits in Mosaic," *Gesta* 13, no. 2 (1974): 29-43.

181. See the unpublished dissertation of James H. Terry, "Christian Tomb Mosaics of Late Roman, Vandalic, and Byzantine Byzacena." On workshops, see Margaret Alexander, "Mosaic Ateliers at Tabarka," *Dumbarton Oaks Papers* 41 (1987): 1-11; Downs, "The Christian Tomb Mosaics from Tabarka," 535-47.

Simitthu. Occasionally mosaics included glass *tesserae,* but these would not have been as durable for use on floors as those made from stone.[182]

Many of these mosaics covered the tombs that were placed in the aisles or naves of African churches and so became part of the overall decorative mosaic pavement of many such basilicas. Other tomb mosaics were set over tombs in open-air cemeteries, mausolea, or catacombs. The position of the body beneath the mosaic would have corresponded to its shape and decoration. Where it existed, the Christogram or portrait head probably indicated the placement of the corpse's head. Occasionally, new floors were laid over old tombs, and the mosaics were replaced with similar inscriptions (see fig. 149).

Most of these funerary mosaics and epitaphs recorded the person's name, age at death, and the state of the soul (e.g., "at peace"). Ages were given in years, months, days, and even (rarely) hours (cf. fig. 130). Sometimes the deceased's office (e.g., bishop, deacon, or reader; cf. figs. 126, 129, 141, 143, 148), the date of death, or the date of burial was included (cf. figs. 129, 130, 131, 141). A few mention the name of the dedicator and his or her relationship with the deceased (e.g., fig. 122), even adding descriptive characteristics, using such terms as "sweet" *(dulcis),* "faithful" *(fidelis),* and "innocent" *(innocens).* More complex examples provide lists of bishops or martyrs (perhaps buried in one common area) with memorial acclamations. A few were quite poetic. Some also showed the late and continuing influence of ancient, pagan customs or names for the deity. For example, a seventh-century mosaic for an eight-year-old girl, found directly in front of one of the basilicas at Mactaris, reads as follows:

> Earth! You will crush a tender spirit with your unjust weight! How much good you will take from the upper world down to the depths! Honorata leaves her body here but her spirit is with you, Thunderer. Before saying farewell, (your) daughter (pledged) these words to you: "I will leave after completing twice four years." At the end of her life she repaid her debt. Laid to rest the eighth day before the Ides of April, in the fourteenth indication.[183]

Although the inscriptions were ordinarily in Latin, spelling varied, along with syntax and phrasing, from region to region. Even though phrases were similar to inscriptional formulae on Christian epitaphs elsewhere in the Roman world, one common phrase, "lived in peace" *(vixit in pace*; cf. fig. 126), might

---

182. On paleography, materials, and colors as well as workshops, styles, and techniques of mosaic production, see Terry, "Christian Tomb Mosaics of Late Roman, Vandalic, and Byzantine Byzacena," 44-60; Downs, "The Christian Tomb Mosaics from Tabarka," 523-56.

183. See Terry, "Christian Tomb Mosaics of Late Roman, Vandalic, and Byzantine Byzacena," p. 443, no. 90; the English translation is from Terry. Terra! Premes teneros iniusto pondere manes! Quanta tecum bona de summis duces ad ima! Hic Honorata tibi membra ponit animamque Tonati. ⟨H⟩os tibi apices filia baledictura: "Discedam bis quaternos functa annos." Debitum vit(a)e finem reddidit. Sub die deposita (est) octabu id(us) Aprilis, ind(ictione) XIIII.

have alluded to the deceased's membership in the church while still living rather than to the state of his or her soul after death. No known inclusions of evident Donatist expressions occur, however (e.g., *Deo laudes*). One scholar suggested that a characteristically Donatist phrase appears on the mosaic tomb cover of the architect Zarzio, from Uppenna: "May those who are worthy receive similarly" *(Hic qui digni sunt sic accipiant),* but this could as easily be applied to an adherent to the Caecilianist cause, or simply be a laudatory phrase.[184] As noted above, Vandal tombs might be identified by the inclusion of Germanic names, but they are not otherwise distinguishable from Nicene burials (cf. fig. 125).

Portrait types on these tomb mosaics included adult men and women, as well as children. Most of the figures are shown frontally in the standing prayer *(orans)* position (e.g., figs. 130, 131, 134), but sometimes only a bust portrait was presented (e.g., fig. 136). This last example also indicates the individual's profession: he was a measurer of grain. A man seated at a desk with a pen poised in his hand might have been a scribe or a banker (fig. 139), a rare instance of a tomb mosaic showing more than one figure. The other figure — a woman — may have been his daughter and a consecrated virgin, if the inscription is interpreted to be read as *Victoria (F)ilia S(acra) in Pace.*[185]

Birds (guinea hens or other fowl) often appear on the shoulders or near the feet of the person. They might have been meant to represent the soul in Paradise, but may have been merely traditional decorative details. Flowers, especially roses (the traditional gift to the deceased, especially at the festival called the Rosalia), are scattered or gathered into vases. The two lit candles that almost always flank standing figures (cf. figs. 134, 135) possibly alluded to the torches or lights that accompanied the deceased to the tomb during the funeral procession or might have indicated the enlightened soul.[186] Similar candles appear on either side of the saint in the Capsella Africana.[187]

The garb of the deceased may have indicated his/her social status or religious office. Some of the women are shown wearing jewelry (cf. fig. 135), and in some instances wearing stoles that cover the upper body as well as the head, perhaps indicating that the deceased was a consecrated virgin (cf. figs. 139, 142, and cf. fig. 131). Although they are more commonly seen on males, both sexes are depicted as wearing white stoles *(oraria;* cf. figs. 134, 137) whose significance is uncertain.[188] Dalmatics are quite often decorated with *segmenti* (patches; cf.

184. See Terry, "Christian Tomb Mosaics of Late Roman, Vandalic, and Byzantine Byzacena," p. 217, no. 17.

185. For discussion of this inscription and different possible constructions, see Downs, "The Christian Tomb Mosaics from Tabarka," pp. 432-34, no. 86.

186. An exception is fig. 130.

187. See the discussion of candles in churches and shrines above, p. 101.

188. A tomb portrait in the Bardo Museum of a woman named Abundantia appears to feature such a fringed stole, and the individual (Dardanius) depicted in fig. 137 is not identified as holding any specific clerical office. Terry, "Christian Tomb Mosaics of Late Roman, Vandalic, and

figs. 130, 139) and *clavi* (vertical, parallel stripes). Men are often shown with cloaks (*paenulae;* cf. figs. 134, 140) that might simply be secular garments, but also could indicate liturgical or clerical roles. Generally, it seems that members of clerical orders are identified by ecclesial titles (e.g., *episcopus, presbyter, deaconus,* or *matrona vidua*) rather than by any particular garment.[189]

## ECCLESIAL STRUCTURES IN SELECTED CITIES

The second part of this chapter provides more detailed discussion of African ecclesial architecture in particular places: Castellum Tingitanum (Chlef), Carthage, Sufetula, Hippo Regius, and Thamugadi. These sites were chosen in part for their particularly interesting features, but also because they either represent a large site with many churches or are in cities that were especially important to the history and practice of Christianity in Roman Africa. They include single churches as well as larger urban spaces that serve as witnesses to architectural evolution from the fourth through the seventh centuries and from Roman to Vandal to Byzantine occupation. Three of these sites (Carthage, Hippo Regius, and Thamugadi) were home to key theologians and leaders of Christian communities and were places where they presided, preached, defended their practices, and developed their understanding of Christian doctrine.

### Basilica of Castellum Tingitanum (Chlef or Orléansville)

Long considered the oldest surviving evidence of church-building in North Africa, this basilica was discovered in 1843 at the ancient Roman site of Castellum Tingitanum; its remains were studied in depth first by Stéphane Gsell at the beginning of the twentieth century. Unfortunately, most of its traces have been hidden, scattered, or lost. At the end of their excavations, archeologists covered the site and removed some of the mosaics to a nearby (modern) church in the mid-1930s; these too were lost during two earthquakes (1954 and 1980) and then during the French-Algerian War. The plans, published when the site was first excavated and then modified by Gsell, are far from scientific (containing neither dimensions nor orientation marking). Subsequently, other studies and plans have been published with variations or modifications.[190] Considering

---

Byzantine Byzacena," p. 388, no. 63, suggests that the tomb mosaic for Bishop Honorius (fig. 117) includes an *orarium*. See Margaret Alexander, "Early Christian Tomb Mosaics in North Africa" (Ph.D. diss., New York University, 1958), 2:187, n. 297.

189. On the possible significance of the different garments worn by the figures in tomb mosaics, see Downs, "The Christian Tomb Mosaics from Tabarka," 192-221.

190. See Stéphane Gsell, *Les monuments antiques de l'Algérie,* 2 vols. (Paris: A. Fontemoing, 1901), 2:236-41. See also more recent work by Jean-Pierre Caillet, "Le dossier de la basilique chré-

all the different plans, the building seems to have been a relatively small (16 × 26m) double-apsed basilica, whose nave was flanked by two aisles on each side, created by double colonnades (fig. 33).

A dedicatory mosaic in the pavement toward the western end of the nave initially was taken as a basis for dating the building. Its text asserts that the church was founded around 324 C.E. or, according to the inscription, "The 285th year of the Province and on the twelfth day before the Kalends of December."[191] However, the dedication is problematic; the mosaic shows evidence of having being retouched at some point, possibly well after that supposed inaugural year. In addition, art historians have noted the similarity of its decorative style to pavement mosaics in neighboring basilicas of a fifth-century date, including the mosaic in its own, newer counter-apse. Thus, a recent study speculates that the actual structure is best dated to the later period, although it might have been built on an early-fourth-century foundation.[192]

Aside from the problem of date, the basilica's two apses have presented a series of puzzles. Noting evidence of stairs at the western end of the church, early excavators proposed the existence of upper galleries, which may have been added later. The eastern apse, usually assumed to be the original because of its orientation, is slightly out of line with and somewhat narrower than the main nave. It was elevated more than one meter from the floor so that it could cover a crypt that was accessible by a set of steps. Two empty sarcophagi were discovered in this crypt.

The subsequently constructed western apse, by contrast, is the same width as the central nave and on the same axis. Apparently, it was built to house the tomb of the fifth-century bishop Reparatus (d. 475; his presumed remains were found in a lead-and-wood casket during the original excavation in 1844). This addition seems to have closed off the western entry to the church, thus moving the entrances to the sides. The apse's mosaic floor illustrates the triple-arched opening that originally must have separated it from the nave; its center panel holds the Bishop's epitaph: "Here rests our father of holy memory, Repara-

tienne de Chlef (anciennement El Asnam, ou Orléansville)," *Karthago. Revue d'archéologie afric-aine* 21 (1986): 135-61; and Robin M. Jensen, "The Basilica of Chlef and Its Mosaics," *Acta ad archeologiam et atrium historiam pertinentia* (forthcoming, 2014). See also the entry and bibliography in Gui, Duval, and Caillet, eds., *Basiliques chrétiennes d'Afrique du Nord,* I.1:11-14.

191. See Caillet, "Le dossier de la basilique chrétienne de Chlef," 146-50; Pro(uinciae anno)/ CCLXXX et V XII kal(endas)/dec(embres) eius basilicae/fundamenta posita/sunt et . . ./prou(inciae anno) CC et . . . [in?]/mente habea[s] . . . seruum Dei . . . [et in?]/Deo uiuas: *CIL* 8:9708 and *ILCV* 1:1821. See the argument of Noël Duval and Paul-Albert Février, "Le décor des monuments chrétiens d'Afrique du Nord," in *Actas del VIII Congreso internacional de Arqueología Cristiana, Barcelona, 5-11 Octubre 1969* (Barcelona: Consejo Superior de Investigaciones Científicas, 1972), 8, 24, regarding the dating of this mosaic and comparison with mosaics in Cuicul and Theveste. On Castellum Tingitanum, see also N. Duval, *Les églises africaines à deux absides, recherches archéologiques sur la liturgie chrétienne en Afrique du Nord.*

192. Caillet, "Le dossier de la basilique chrétienne de Chlef," 150.

tus the Bishop, who served as priest for eight years and eleven months and went ahead of us in peace on the eleventh day before the Kalends of August in the 436th year of the province" (fig. 34).[193] The upper galleries may have been constructed at the time that the shrine was added, in order to accommodate more pilgrims. Some investigators have proposed that the counter-apse and its mosaic were placed over a previously existing monument, baptistery, or memorial (perhaps to Peter and Paul); others have suggested that this was the original apse of the church, given its size and spatial correspondence to the main nave.[194]

Whatever the original plan, the mosaic floor of the basilica indicates that the raised eastern apse was the main apse in at least the last phase of the building if not throughout the building's use. This three-sectioned pavement has, in the midst of its easternmost panel, a depiction of a table amid vines, indicating the altar's placement in the center of a platform that projected from the apse into the nave (fig. 35). The table, however, is upright only if viewed while facing east — presumably the congregants' viewing angle, but arguably also the celebrant's. In addition, the table's supports appear to be two small columns with bases and capitals, suggesting that the supports, if not also the horizontal surface, were made of stone.

It is unlikely that the counter-apse was original, as it appears to have been added to accommodate a typically African placement of a martyr's shrine in a western (or liturgically western) counter-apse. It seems more likely that the counter-apse was added in the late fifth century to accommodate a saintly bishop's tomb, a transformation that required the addition of doors in the north and south aisles.[195]

The other pavement mosaics (wreathed floral designs within stars made up of interlacing squares) are similar to panels found in the fourth- and fifth-century churches at Hippo Regius, Cuicul (Djémila), and Theveste. One of these wreathed mosaics contains the invocation *Pax, Semper* ("Peace, always"). This inscription has a parallel in a similar round mosaic, found in the remains of another ancient basilica in the neighboring village of Beni Rached. In this instance, the message adds another detail: *Pax Aeclesiae Catolice Semper* (fig. 37).[196]

A rather famous feature of this basilica is a square mosaic labyrinth at the end of the left aisle. Rather than a Minotaur, this maze has a palindrome in its center consisting of variations of the words *Ecclesia Sancta* ("holy church")

193. Hic requiescit sanctae memoriae pater noster Reparatus e.p.s. qui fecit in sacerdotium annos VIII, men. XI et precessit nos in pace die undecimu. kal. Aug prounc. CCCCXXX et sexta. *CIL* 8:9709; *ILCV* 1:1105.
194. See arguments summarized in Caillet, "Le dossier de la basilique chrétienne de Chlef," 135-61.
195. Note the case of the Basilica of Bellator in Sufetula, below, p. 149, fig. 67.
196. *ILCV* 1:1579A.

read in all directions (fig. 36).[197] The labyrinth (or, more correctly, maze) thus symbolizes a circuitous path that inevitably leads to a basic — or central — Christian proclamation. A second palindrome, adjacent to the presbyterium, contained a similar play on the name and title of the bishop Marinus (Marinus Sacerdos), possibly the fourth-century episcopal founder of the church.[198]

Thus, like the Thabraca mosaic (fig. 132), this no-longer-existing church contains some of the most characteristic features of African churches, here even including the doubled apse. Moreover, like the Thabraca mosaic, with its legend *Ecclesia Mater,* the two aisle mosaics in the church of Castellum Tingitanum remind viewers of the centrality and sanctity of the church itself.

## The Churches of Carthage

Currently, the known basilicas of Carthage mostly were constructed in one of two historical periods: the first group dates from the mid-fourth century to the middle of the fifth, and the second was built during the Byzantine period, beginning in the sixth century and continuing until the late seventh. The Vandal era, from the conquest of Carthage (439 C.E.) to the Byzantine reconquest (533 C.E.), was not a time of significant building. It seems to have been, rather, a time when buildings were simply transferred from Nicene to Arian use.[199] One significant exception was the basilica shrine of the martyred St. Agileus, which the Vandal king Gunthamund built (or allowed to be built) for Nicene use late in the Vandal era.[200]

As elsewhere in Africa, almost no third- or early-fourth-century ecclesial architecture remains, possibly due to destruction and rebuilding, or to natural (e.g., earthquake) devastation. Nevertheless, documents refer to at least twenty Carthaginian basilicas in use during the fifth and sixth centuries and serving Caecilianist, Donatist, and Arian communities. In general, coordinating the textual and physical evidence is quite difficult. With certain exceptions, sites witnessed in the literary evidence are only hypothetically identified with excavated ones (e.g., the Basilica Maiorum, the Basilica Restituta, Bir el Knissia, and the Memoria Cypriani).

According to both epigraphic and textual evidence, Carthage was divided

197. *ILCV* 1:1580. Now at the Cathedral of the Sacred Heart, Algiers. This pattern is very similar to that of other Roman mosaic mazes — e.g., a third- or fourth-century pavement now in Tunis's Bardo Museum and originally from Thuburbo Maius.

198. *ILCV* 1:1119. The term *sacerdos* indicates a bishop.

199. According to Victor of Vita, the Arians took over the Basilica Maiorum, the Basilica Celerinae and the Scillitanorum, the Mensa Cypriani and the Memoria Cypriani (*Hist. pers.* 1.9, 16).

200. See the discussion below (Bir el Knissia, p. 139). It's not clear that one can call this a Vandal building, since it was built for Catholics, and perhaps by Catholics themselves on land (a cemetery) allowed them by the Vandal ruler.

into ecclesiastical regions, possibly established during the reign of Bishop Aurelius in the late fourth or early fifth century and revised during the Byzantine era. Efforts to identify these regions have coordinated them with known ecclesial remains.[201] A presbyter under the supervision of Carthage's bishop would have served each region. African episcopal councils were held in the basilica of the second region at least six times between 403 and 419. Augustine seems to have preached at least twice in the basilica identified as being in the third region (the Basilica of Peter), and perhaps once in the basilica in the sixth region (the Basilica of Paul).[202] Epigraphic evidence also mentions these regions (e.g., an epitaph for a deacon from a certain region), and it appears that each had its own cemetery.

Extra-mural churches dating from the pre-Vandal period included the Basilica Maiorum (associated with the burials of Perpetua and Felicity and their companions; fig. 20),[203] the Basilica of Faustus,[204] the Basilica Novarum (perhaps, more accurately, the Basilica of the New Cemeteries),[205] the Basilica of Celerina,[206] and the Basilica of the Scillitan Martyrs (or, more likely, a single basilica dedicated to both Celerina and the Scillitan martyrs).[207] All are attested in the documentary evidence. Augustine also preached in three basilicas that were identified by the emperors who apparently granted the funds for their building: the basilicas of Gratian, Theodosius, and Honorius.[208]

201. See Ennabli, "Carthage: Les régions ecclésiastiques," and Ennabli, *Carthage, une métropole chrétienne,* 142-46. Note that pre-Byzantine-era churches have not been found that correspond obviously to regions 2 and 3. The church for region 1 probably was the cathedral (perhaps the Basilica Restituta). The Circular Monument may have been the basilica of region 4. The Byzantine churches of Dermech may have been constructed near or over the Basilica of Paul in region 6. Some scholars have raised doubts about Ennabli's proposals for the six ecclesiastical regions at Carthage, including Leone, *Changing Townscapes in North Africa from Late Antiquity to the Arab Conquest,* 97-109.

202. African Councils of 403, 404, 405, 407, 409, 410; Aug. *Serm.* 15; 119.

203. See the discussion below, pp. 144-45.

204. Aug. *Serm.* 23; 101; 134; 261 and Councils of 418, 419, 421. See Ennabli, *Carthage, une métropole chrétienne,* no. 10, p. 27, and Vict.-Vit. *Hist pers.* 1.25; 2.18, 48; 3.34. It seems to have become the Cathedral during the Vandal era (see the discussion below).

205. Aug. *Serm.* 14; 37; *Serm. Wilm.* 9(299D); *Serm. Guelf.* 9(299E); Vict.-Vit. *Hist. pers.* 1.25. Ennabli, *Carthage, une métropole chrétienne,* no. 7, pp. 20-21, prefers the name "New Cemeteries." Edmund Hill supposes that this should be constructed "New Market Basilica," by taking "cellarum" as omitted and understood; see Augustine, *Sermons,* ed. John E. Rotelle, trans. Edmund Hill, The Works of Saint Augustine: A Translation for the 21st Century, 3/1-11 (Brooklyn, N.Y.: New City Press, 1990), 1:321-22, n. 1.

206. Aug. *Serm.* 48; 17; *Psal.* 99. Celerina was mentioned in Cypr. *Ep.* 39.3.1, the grandmother of the confessor Celerinus, and the mother of a martyred son who had been in the military. Celerina, therefore, could have been martyred in the early third century, about the same time as Perpetua, Felicity, and their companions.

207. Aug. *Serm.* 155. Victor of Vita speaks of only one basilica dedicated to both Celerina and the Scillitan martyrs (*Hist. pers.* 1.9).

208. Basilica Theodosiana (Aug. *Serm.* 26); Basilica Gratiani (Aug. *Serm.* 156); and Basilica

Augustine's mention of churches dedicated to Peter and Paul, the founding apostles of the Roman see, demonstrate the close ties between the African and Roman churches. On the other hand, that a number of these basilicas were associated with second- and third-century African martyrs (Perpetua and Felicity, Celerina, and the Scillitan martyrs) suggests that earlier churches had been built and dedicated to these regional saints, perhaps on the same sites.

In addition to these, important shrines dedicated to Cyprian frequently are mentioned in the documents: the Mensa Cypriani, the Memoria Cypriani (probably the basilica later named for St. Monica; figs. 22, 23), and a third, somewhere near the port, which could be the place that Augustine identified as the Basilica Tricliarum.[209] The Donatist Basilica (the Theoprepia, or Divine Majesty, known only from textual sources) is also noted, as well as a basilica that Augustine referred to as once belonging to the Tertullianists but handed over to the Caecilianists after the Tertullianists had been converted.[210]

According to Victor of Vita, the Vandals built no churches for themselves but took over most of the churches in the city. Victor's chronicle claims that the Vandals took over all the churches inside the walls (those they did not destroy) as well as two ex-urban shrines: the Memoria and the Mensa of Cyprian. He specifically identified the Basilica Restituta (the cathedral), the Basilica Maio-

---

Honoriana (Aug. *Serm.* 163). See Ennabli, *Carthage, une métropole chrétienne,* nos. 13, 19, 20, pp. 31, 35. The basilica of Honorius seems to have been installed in a former pagan temple, or at least seems to have reused the materials from one. See Aug. *Serm.* 163.2.2: "Notice, dear brothers, how these earthly places are changed for the better. Some of them are demolished and broken up; others are renovated for better purposes. We, ourselves, are not so different." Videte, fratres mei, quemadmodum cum loca ipsa terrena in melius convertuntur, alia diruuntur atque franguntur, alia in meliores usus communtantur; sic et nos sumus (PL 38:890).

209. A shrine of Cyprian near the port is mentioned in Aug. *Conf.* 5.8.15 (where Monica wept and prayed the night that Augustine left for Rome). See also Aug. *Psal.* 32.2.2, which Augustine is said to have preached at the *Domus Sancti Cypriani* or the *Mensa Sancti Cypriani* (which *Psal.* 32.2.2.9 clearly identified as the place of execution); then he says that he is planning to preach at the Basilica Tricliarum (variants: Tricil[l]arum) the next day: *Psal.* 32.2.2.29 (CSEL 93.1B:313.48-50). Both *Serm.* 30 and 53 were preached at the Basilica Triciliarum. It is not clear that the Basilica Triciliarum/Triclarum (Dining Rooms/Garden Pavilions = Triciliarum) was a Cyprianic shrine or the same shrine mentioned in *Conf.* 5.8.15. Further evidence is provided by Victor of Vita, who refers to two unusual and spacious churches dedicated to Cyprian outside the city walls (*Hist. pers.* 1.16). Proc. Caes. *Hist. bel.* 3.21.17 recounts the arrival of the Byzantine troops in Carthage on the feast day of Cyprian and describes a large basilica near the sea, at which the festival for Cyprian took place. This might have been the same one to which Augustine referred in *Conf.* 5.8.15 — and it has been identified with both the basilica of St. Monica and a third shrine inside the city walls. See the discussion of these three different places in Frederik van der Meer, *Augustine the Bishop: The Life and Work of a Father of the Church,* trans. Brian Battershaw and G. R. Lamb (London: Sheed & Ward, 1962), 477; Johannes Quasten, "'Vetus Superstitio et Nova Religio': The Problem of Refrigerium in the Ancient Church of North Africa," *The Harvard Theological Review* 33, no. 4 (1940): 254; and Othmar Perler and Jean-Louis Maier, *Les voyages de saint Augustin* (Paris: Études augustiniennes, 1969), 420-21.

210. Aug. *Haer.* 86. See also Ennabli, *Carthage, une métropole chrétienne,* no. 22, p. 36.

---

rum, and the Basilica of Celerina and the Scillitan martyrs as having been converted to Arian use.[211] Thus, the Basilica Tricliarum, the churches named for Theodosius and Gratian, and the former Donatist cathedral might have been among "the others" that were not destroyed. The Basilica Honoriana may have been at least partially destroyed by 439, as Quodvultdeus insists that the Vandals leveled it to the ground.[212] The Basilica of Faustus and the Basilica Novarum appear to have been in Caecilianist hands at various points in the Vandal period (at other times the Basilica of Faustus was used as a barn), so it seems likely that these were both outside the walls.[213]

Archeological excavations have added additional data for churches and shrines in Carthage. What is often referred to as the Circular Monument (sited northwest of the theater inside the walls) may have been a memorial constructed first in the fourth century, abandoned in the Vandal era, reoccupied briefly in the late fifth century, and then restored in the Byzantine era. This remarkable domed building (approx. 38.60 × 31.20 m) was originally designed as two concentric dodeconal structures, each having twelve arched openings, within a larger rectangle that was completed by a basilica to the west. It has been variously identified as an ancient pagan temple, a private house, and a Christian shrine, but what god or saint(s) it honored is a matter of debate.[214] Some scholars have also speculated that this may have been the Temple of Memory mentioned by Victor of Vita as a place destroyed by the Vandals and where Huneric ordered the Catholic bishops to assemble in 484 (just after the colloquy between the Catholics and the Vandals). It does share certain architectural parallels with a church-shrine and might be compared to the basilica-memoria combination at Damous el Karita.[215]

211. Vict.-Vit. *Hist. pers.* 1.9, 16.

212. . . . sub Constantio et Augusta Placidia quorum nunc filius Valentinianus pius et Christianus imperat, Urso insistente tribuno, omnia illa templa ad solum usque perducta agrum reliquit, in sepulturam scilicet mortuorum; ipsamque viam sine memoria sui nunc vandalica manus euertit (*Quodu Prom.* 3.38.44; CCSL 60:185.100–186.105; SC 102:576.28–578.33).

213. Victor of Vita mentions both (*Hist. pers.* 1.25; 2.18, 48; 3.34).

214. The identifications include a temple of Saturn or Ceres, as well as a shrine to Cyprian. It was not necessarily founded as a Christian cult center. The most significant archeological work on this site was done by Senay and Beauregard. See Pierre Senay and Marc Beauregard, "Monument circulaire de Carthage: Rapport préliminaire des fouilles 1982," *Cahiers des études anciennes* 15 (1983): 187-236, and Ennabli, *Carthage, une métropole chrétienne,* 100-102.

215. Vict.-Vit. *Hist. pers.* 1.8; 3.17. This gathering place was most likely outside the walls, however (unlike the Circular Monument), although this is not explicit in Victor of Vita. The Aedes Memoriae was also the place where Heraclian was caught and executed, strengthening the probability that it was outside the walls (cf. Idat. *Chron.* a. 413, noted in Ennabli, *Carthage, une métropole chrétienne,* p. 102, n. 461). That this could be associated with the church installed in the Temple of Caelestis is unlikely, since the textual evidence implies that that temple was destroyed before 421 (see above, pp. 90-91). See, however, Pierre Senay and Marc Beauregard, " 'L'Aedes memoriae': Un témoignage antique sur le monument circulaire de Carthage," *Cahiers des études anciennes* 19 (1986): 79-85.

In addition to the Basilica Maiorum and Memoria Cypriani (St. Monica), the remains of three large cemetery basilicas have been found outside the city walls. These other ex-urban basilicas, now called Damous el Karita (figs. 15, 16), Bir el Knissia, and Bir Ftouha (fig. 28), have, very speculatively, been identified with churches mentioned in the literary evidence.

Damous el Karita (figs. 15, 16) was built and renovated in several stages, making it difficult to interpret. It was constructed just outside the Theodosian Wall and originally in a cemetery. Poor reporting and archeological procedures of the nineteenth-century excavators compound the interpretive problems. The latest analysis has suggested that it was built in three stages. Its first phase probably dates to the late fourth century, but it may have been founded a bit later.[216] Built over a Roman villa, this was a nine-aisled structure with an apse to the southeast and four aisles on each side of a central nave with a transept at the seventh of eleven bays. The entrances apparently led into this crossing aisle. A small porch structure at the north end may indicate the main entry. Because of its early date and location just outside the Theodosian Wall, scholars have speculated that this basilica may have been either the Basilica of Celerina or the Scillitan Martyrs, or the Basilica of Faustus — a place where the Catholic bishop Deogratias housed Roman refugees fleeing from Vandal attacks in 455.[217]

In its second (early Byzantine) phase, the church was considerably expanded in size and reoriented. The transept became the main aisle, and a new apse was added to the southwest. The northeastern end of the basilica consisted of a semicircular atrium with a central fountain and a small, annexed three-apsed chapel. The altar appears to have been placed at the point of the original crossing and was enhanced with a ciborium. In this phase, a baptistery was annexed to the southwest of the main church in a small, enclosed building. The hexagonal font in its center was covered by a ciborium supported by four columns. Excavations also show that the baptistery was built into an existing bath structure. In a final phase, the building was moved back into its original configuration and, while considerably reduced in size, oriented again as it was originally, with the apse on the north. Annexed to the south was a group of buildings that has been tentatively identified as a monastery.

216. See Heimo Dolenz and Hans Baldus, *Damous-el-Karita: Die österreichisch-tunesischen Ausgrabungen der Jahre 1996 und 1997 im Saalbau und der Memoria des pilgerheiligtumes Damous-el-Karita in Karthago* (Vienna: Österreichish Archäologische Institut, 2001).

217. Vict.-Vit. *Hist. pers.* 1.9, 16 does not list Faustus and Novarum as basilicas that Vandals took over, so they would appear to have been outside the walls. Furthermore, in *Hist. pers.* 1.25; 2.18, 48; 3.34, Victor of Vita refers to them as being in Catholic control, including Deogratias's use of them — and so strengthens the case that they were outside the walls. Of the two, only Faustus is noted to have had a baptistery (cf. *Hist. pers.* 2.47-9; 3.34). Frend, on the other hand, suggests that this could have been the Basilica of Celerina, which would make at least some of the adjoining buildings the monastery of Bigua (see above, p. 94). See W. H. C. Frend, *The Early Church: From the Beginnings to 461* (London: SCM, 1992), 27. Victor's claim that the Vandals took over the Basilica Celerina, however, suggests that it, like the Basilica Maiorum, was inside the walls.

An adjacent underground rotunda, probably built simultaneously with the basilica's latest phase, has been interpreted as a baptistery, a funerary monument, or a saint's shrine.[218] The interior walls of this circular building feature alternating niches and piers set off by columns (fig. 17). Paired stairways down into and up from the rotunda suggest the need for management of candidates seeking baptism or visitors to a shrine. A circle of stones in the center suggests the placement of a font, but only in its shape. At some point an upper monument was added to the original subterranean room, on top of the earlier structure. This upper rotunda was set within a square building and appears to have been joined to a semicircular atrium.

Constructed in an ancient cemetery, Bir el Knissia's first phase may date to the late Vandal period. Oriented to the southeast, it has the classic form of a central nave with two side aisles created by two colonnades of ten columns each. Rebuilt at least three more times from the early Byzantine era to the mid-seventh century, its original foundations appear to date to the end of the fifth century. This corresponds to the time when the Vandal king Gunthamund (484-96) gave the cemetery and, more importantly, its tomb of St. Agileus to Eugenius, the Bishop of Carthage. This happened during one of the periods of toleration after Eugenius had returned from exile (under Hilderic, in 484). Thus, this site may have been the Basilica of St. Agileus.[219] If so, it would have served as the Catholic cathedral for the remainder of the Vandal period, and the site of the council over which Bonifatius presided in 525.[220]

The Christian basilica complex at Bir Ftouha (fig. 28) is more tentatively associated with a documented Carthaginian church.[221] Because of the lack of evidence for pre-Christian burials, it appears that it was not built into an existing cemetery. Excavations in the late nineteenth and early twentieth centuries uncovered a triconch funerary chapel that contained ten sarcophagi and two

218. P. Delattre, who excavated it, argued that it was a baptistery. Other (somewhat more contemporary) views include those of Lézine, *Architecture romaine d'Afrique,* 80-86, and S. Boyadjiev, "La rotonde souterraine de Damous-el-Karita à Carthage à la lumière de nouvelles données," in *Atti del IX Congresso di Archeologia Cristiana: Roma, 21-27 settembre 1975* (Roma: Pontificio Istituto di Archeologia Cristiana, 1978), 117-31, who both consider it a baptistery. N. Duval, however, describes it as a funerary monument: Noël Duval, "Études d'architecture chrétienne nord-africaine," *Mélanges de l'Ecole française de Rome, Antiquité* 84 (1972): 1113-15. More recently, Dolenz and Baldus, *Damous-el-Karita,* 103-4, propose that it was the shrine to a Byzantine saint, perhaps Julian of Antioch. See also Ennabli, *Carthage, une métropole chrétienne,* 127-29.

219. This gift (dated 487) is recorded in the annals of the Vandal kings (*Later. Wand.* 8-9); see Stevens, *Bir el Knissia at Carthage,* and Ennabli, *Carthage, une métropole chrétienne,* 38-39 (esp. n. 204), 113-20.

220. On Bonifatius, see Vict.-Ton. *Chron.* 106(523), 119(535); *Later. Wand.* 16; Ferrand. *Vita Fulg.* 26-27.

221. Susan T. Stevens, "A New Christian Structure on the Outskirts of Carthage: A Preliminary Report on the 1994 Excavations at Bir Ftouha," *Dumbarton Oaks Papers* 50 (1996): 375-78, and Ennabli, *Carthage, une métropole chrétienne,* 135-41.

small basins that may have been baptismal fonts. Later, a fortuitous find produced evidence of a large Byzantine basilica on the site. In the 1990s, more work was done, and the Byzantine basilica was excavated enough to show that this had been an important pilgrimage site from at least the late fourth through the seventh centuries. This large basilica (37 × 18 meters from main entrance to apse) was oriented to the east and had various entrances, the most significant of which opened into a nine-sided martyrium on the western end. It contained at least eleven tombs beneath a mosaic floor patterned with vines and a laurel medallion surrounding lilies.[222]

Behind the apse stood a large and elaborate baptismal chamber, originally covered by a dome and having nearly the same physical area as the basilica itself. The font was about three meters in diameter, set into a cruciform surround, and accessed by three interior steps into a well. A drain channeled the water to a soak-away tank. Attached courtyards, semicircular ambulatories, and aisles provided areas where pilgrims (or candidates) might have waited, changed their clothes, or received exorcisms and preparatory anointings. Decorative mosaics, portraying a doe and a stag drinking from the four rivers of Paradise, were also found in this space (fig. 29).

Some historians wished to identify this large pilgrimage church at Bir Ftouha with the Mensa of Cyprian, since its geographical setting relates well with contemporary descriptions of the place where Cyprian was martyred in the mid-third century.[223] The shrine marking the place where Cyprian was executed rather than buried (i.e., the Basilica Mappalia or Memoria Cypriani) quickly became a place of pilgrimage. By the late fourth century, it was the site of a prominent celebration on the saint's feast day (the 14th of September).[224] The fact that this site was not originally a cemetery adds some credibility to its tentative association with the Mensa of Cyprian. Even if it was not the site of this Cyprian shrine, it seems likely that the building was associated with an important martyr cult and was a pilgrimage destination of some significance. Furthermore, the existence of an enormous baptismal pool in a cemetery church suggests that baptism (or some other ritual) may have been administered at this place as well as in the urban cathedral church.[225]

222. Aug. *Serm.* 304.2.2 names the lily as the flower representing a virgin.

223. The place of Cyprian's execution was located in the Field of Sextus, outside the city walls: *Act. Procon.* 2.5; Pont. *Vita Cypr.* 18; Ennabli, *Carthage, une métropole chrétienne*, 135. Delattre may have been the first to suggest the site of Bir Ftouha as the original setting for this shrine. Stevens, ed., *Bir Ftouha*, 35-36, disagrees, noting the absence of Christian remains prior to the fifth century or any evidence of a villa suitable for a Roman proconsul of the mid-third century.

224. See the discussion below, pp. 536-37. Aug. *Serm.* 311 (preached on the occasion of Cyprian's feast day) describes the rowdiness of the festival, which he denounced. See also *Serm.* 309; 310; 312; *Serm. Morin* 15(306C); *Serm. Denis* 14(313A); 15(313B); 22(313F); and *Serm. Guelf.* 26(313C); 27(313D); 28(313F).

225. Although built as a baptistery, it is significantly different from other African baptisteries,

Once the Byzantines retook Carthage, a new building program began. Byzantine-era Carthaginian churches include the Byzantine rebuilding of Dermech I (in the present archeological park near the Antonine Baths; figs. 25-27), two additional basilicas known as Dermech II and III, a basilica dedicated to the Theotokos inserted into the governor's palace on the Byrsa Hill,[226] another chapel dedicated to St. Prime,[227] and two small funerary chapels (of Redemptus and Asterius; fig. 24).[228] Given the Vandal occupation of the former Catholic cathedral (Basilica Restituta), one might suppose that the Byzantines desired to build a new cathedral and would have hastened to erect a monument that affirmed their re-establishment of the Nicene faith in Carthage. Scholars have speculated that this cathedral might be the one excavated near the Antonine baths, known as either the Basilica of Douïmes or Dermech I, making it the site of the Council of 535, presided over by Reparatus, successor to Bonifatius.[229] A three-aisled building in a different region of the city (Carthagenna; fig. 18), abandoned in the Vandal period and rebuilt in the Byzantine era, also has been identified as a candidate for the fourth-century cathedral (Basilica Restituta). A third possibility is a basilica complex built in the center of Carthage during the early Byzantine era in an area called Bir Messaouda. This large building had a central dome set over the crossing of an imposing transept of three aisles oriented north-south (69 × 17 m). The flanking east-west nave seems relatively shallow (34.5 × 22.5 m). A large baptistery room, with a hexagonal font and colonnaded ambulatories, is found on the south corner of the complex.[230]

in both its size and its openness. The space might have been designed for some ritual of which no literary witness has survived. See the discussion above, p. 105, n. 96.

226. Proc. Caes. *Aed.* (Peri Ktismaton) 6.5.9 — built (he says) by Justinian, and probably the place where rebels attempted an assassination of the Magister Militum (or Praetorian Prefect), the eunuch Solomon (*Hist. bel.* 4.14, 22, 24, 27). It is worth noting that this is the only evident dedication to the Theotokos, perhaps especially for the Byzantine administration of the city of Carthage.

227. Proc. Caes. *Aed.* 6.5.9. (Procopius claimed that this was a local saint.)

228. Named for the inscriptions found there; see Ennabli, *Carthage, une métropole chrétienne*, 103-5.

229. Proc. Caes. *Hist. bel.* 4.26. See Ennabli, *Carthage, une métropole chrétienne*, 77-82, and Duval, "Études d'architecture chrétienne nord-africaine," 1077-78, 1081-92.

230. See Richard Miles, "British Excavations at Bir Messaouda, Carthage 2000-2004, The Byzantine Basilica," *Babesch: Annual Papers on Mediterranean Archaeology* 81 (2006): 199-226; earlier studies of the baptistery found at this place (the "Supermarché" baptistery) include W. H. C. Frend, "A Two-Period Baptistery in Carthage," *Bulletin du centre de documentation archéologique de la conservation de Carthage* 6 (1985): 42-43; and Noël Duval, "Études d'archéologie chrétienne nord-africaine: XVII — une nouvelle cuve baptismale dans le centre de Carthage," *Revue des études augustiniennes* 34 (1988): 86-92.

According to documentary evidence, including several of the headings of Augustine's sermons, the Caecilianist cathedral of Carthage in the fourth and early fifth centuries was the Basilica Restituta (which was just discussed in the previous section).[231] This also was the site of African councils between 397 and 419. Its name might refer either to the Carthaginian bishop Restitutus in the mid-fourth century or perhaps to St. Restituta, who reportedly was martyred in Carthage in the mid-third century. However, because the name lacks the possessive form, it suggests that the building was simply "restored," either after the Diocletian persecution or Donatist damage in 347, or during repair of damage from an earthquake in 365.[232]

A few details about the interior may be gleaned from a sermon of Augustine, preached there in 404.[233] The prior day's service, on the Feast of St. Vincent, had ended with Augustine refusing to speak from a pulpit that had been moved further into the nave to allow the crowd to get closer to him. He complained of the people pushing against the chancel barriers and causing an indecorous disturbance. Apparently, he had preached from that place, inside the chancel and in the midst of the nave, on an earlier occasion, and the people were calling for him to repeat that gesture. From this we know that some pulpits could be moved and, on some special occasions, were set up in the center of the hall.

The Catholic cathedral had to be re-sited after the Vandal seizure of the Restituta in 439. For a while, the Catholics seem to have used the Basilica of Faustus (outside the walls) as their cathedral, a conclusion based on Victor of Vita's claim that it was the site of baptisms in the episcopate of Eugenius.[234] In the late Vandal period, during a time of toleration, St. Agileus became the Catholic cathedral, and hosted the Council of 525. It is possible that a new cathedral (possibly Dermech I) was built within a year or two of the Byzantine reconquest of Carthage.

Whether or not the Byzantine authorities erected a new cathedral soon after 534, the ruin of a Byzantine church inside the ancient city walls (in region 1) and in the area of the ancient forum of Carthage has been identified speculatively as a rebuilt Basilica Restituta (fig. 18).[235] Often referred to as the Basil-

---

231. See, for example, Aug. *Serm.* 19; 90; 112; 277; 341; 369; *Serm. Denis* 13(305A).

232. Discussion of the name can be found in Ennabli, *Carthage, une métropole chrétienne*, 16, 30, and Y. Duval, *Loca sanctorum Africae*, 2:685.

233. Aug. *Serm. Dolb.* 2(359B). The theory that this was preached in the Basilica Restituta is Dolbeau's in *Augustin d'Hippone. Vingt-six sermons au peuple d'Afrique*, ed. François Dolbeau (Paris: Institut d'études augustiniennes, 2009), 320.

234. Vict.-Vit. *Hist. pers.* 1.15; 2.47-48 (the story of a miracle in 484 that involved Bishop Eugenius at the Basilica of Faustus), and 3.34 (the mention of a baptistery). See also *Hist. pers.* 2.18.

235. This is perhaps the oldest surviving structure inside the walls; evidence of a bishop's residence and the central placement are two reasons for identifying this as the cathedral church.

ica Carthagenna (for the area in which it was discovered), the Byzantine-era building was erected upon the foundations of what appears to have been a late-fourth-century, three-aisled basilica that was decorated with mosaic pavements and included a rectangular exedra. The Byzantine basilica, set along the same axis as this earlier building, was significantly larger (approximately 25 × 36 m), having a central nave with two aisles to each side (defined by two colonnades of eight pillars) and two opposing apses. A large baptistery (also Byzantine-era) was located to the southwest, opening into the basilica hall (fig. 19). The baptistery was square on the outside with an octagonal interior; the four "corner" walls were enhanced with apses. It housed a cruciform font surmounted by an octagonal ciborium. A small, apsed room was attached to the northeastern apse sometime later (perhaps in the seventh century), possibly as a relic chapel.[236]

Evidence of earlier ecclesiastical occupation (a bishop's residence), its location, the baptismal font, and Byzantine rebuilding argue for identifying this as the original Caecilianist cathedral (the Basilica Restituta) that was occupied by the Vandals in 439. However, the discovery of another basilica and baptistery at the site of Bir Messaouda about 200 meters to the north has complicated the question.[237] Given its location near the center of the city and the presence of the baptistery, this may have been the site of the old Donatist cathedral, the Theoprepia. It might also have been the sanctuary near the forum mentioned by Procopius. However, the design of this second basilica — with its large transept, many aisles, and ambulatory — suggests an important pilgrimage church rather than a cathedral.[238] A Byzantine-era inscription recovered from a cistern located roughly halfway between these two sites (Carthagenna and Bir Messaouda) refers to the foundation of the Temple of Jerusalem (1 Kings 8:29). The allusion seems to imply that it was made for a cathedral.[239] A Greek cross is inscribed in its center, around which are these words: "Lord, may your eyes be open day and night over this house. By this sign we conquer."[240]

---

See Ennabli, *Carthage, une métropole chrétienne*, 29-31. Against this identification, see Noël Duval, "Compte rendu: L. Ennabli, La basilique de Carthagenna et le locus des sept moines de Gafsa: Nouveaux édifices chrétiens de Carthage," *Antiquité Tardive* 8 (2000): 388, who argues that the design is unusual for a Christian church.

236. See Ennabli, *Carthage, une métropole chrétienne*, 61-70; Ennabli, *La basilique de Carthagenna et le locus des septs moines de Gafsa: Nouveaux édifices chrétiens de Carthage.*

237. See the description above, p. 141, and Miles, "British Excavation at Bir Messaouda, Carthage 2000-2004, the Byzantine Basilica."

238. Ennabli, *Carthage, une métropole chrétienne*, no. 28, pp. 39-40. Proc. Caes. *Hist. bel.* 4.14, 22, 24, 27.

239. See Ennabli, *Carthage, une métropole chrétienne*, fig. 64, p. 69, for a photograph of this inscription.

240. D(omi)ne sint ocu/li tui aperti/super dom(um)/ista(m) die ad no/cte in hoc signum vincimu(s). Liliane Ennabli, *Les inscriptions funéraires chrétiennes de Carthage, 3: Carthage intra et extra muros*, Recherches d'archéologie africaine publiées par l'Institut national d'archéologie et d'art de Tunis (Rome: École française de Rome, 1991), 3:164.

The Basilica Maiorum was the site of several of Augustine's sermons.[241] Victor of Vita describes the Vandal seizure of this church along with the Basilica of Celerina and the Scillitan Martyrs. According to Victor, the bodies of Saints Perpetua and Felicity were buried in the Basilica Maiorum.[242] Although the name "Maiorum" is often translated "Ancestors" (a term which sometimes baffles scholars),[243] the association of the place with the relics of saints would justify that title, although it might also refer to a cemetery (an *Area Maiorum*).

A large Byzantine-era basilica at Mcidfa, excavated by Delattre in 1906-8, is commonly identified as the rebuilt ancient Basilica Maiorum (fig. 20). Situated outside the Theodosian city wall, it is an excellent example of a cemetery church. It was a huge building (61 × 45 meters, excluding the apse), with a nave and eight flanking aisles. In the center of its main hall, a small, nearly square apsed chapel (3.6 × 3.7 meters) may have been built to house relics of a saint or saints. Delattre presumed that this was the martyrium of Perpetua and her companions, martyred in Carthage (traditionally March 7, 203), probably in the nearby amphitheater (fig. 14). Some inscriptional evidence supports Delattre's conjecture.

The basilica was constructed within an ancient cemetery that contained pagan as well as Christian burials. The basilica floor subsequently served as an interior cemetery.[244] Containing a vast number of funerary inscriptions, the site was a treasure trove of epitaphs from the first through the sixth century. Delattre noted one inscription marked *Vibia* (Perpetua's *praenomen*), which suggested to him that this might have been the private, family burial ground of the Vibii.[245] Another, taken from a pit inside the church, was a small stone inscribed with third-century lettering, *Perpetue filie dulcissimae* ("Perpetua, Sweetest Daughter").[246] This, Delattre speculated, may have been Perpetua's actual tombstone, although modern scholars generally discount this possi-

---

241. Aug. *Serm.* 165; 258; 294; *Serm. Denis* 20(16A); *Serm. Morin* 12(25A). In *Serm.* 258, it is identified as Major — but this is usually taken to be this basilica; see notes in Hill, *Sermons, The Works of Saint Augustine*, 3/7:176, n. 1, for an explanation. It may also have been the site of the Council of 390, but only if the name Basilica Perpetua Restituta is taken to mean this basilica on the strength of the association with St. Perpetua. See Ennabli, *Carthage, une métropole chrétienne*, 20.

242. Vict.-Vit. *Hist. pers.* 1.9.

243. See Hill, *Sermons, The Works of Saint Augustine*, 3/5:207, n. 1, for example. He proposes that it refers to an earlier building on the site (a pagan temple?).

244. See Liliane Ennabli, *Les inscriptions funéraires chrétiennes de Carthage, 2: La basilique de Mcidfa*, Recherches d'archéologie africaine (Tunis: Institut national d'archéologie et d'art; Rome: École française de Rome, 1982), 7; Y. Duval, *Loca sanctorum Africae*, 1:13-16, no. 6.

245. See Leclercq, "Carthage," *DACL*, ed. Cabrol et al., 2.2:2247-48. However, if Perpetua and her family were from Thuburbo Minus, it seems unlikely to have been her family's burial plot.

246. See Ennabli, *Les inscriptions funéraires chrétiennes de Carthage*, 2:69; *CIL* 8:25272; and

bility.[247] The fragment of another was decorated with a dove holding an olive branch and a legend that could refer to Perpetua as a martyr, and even another named a certain "faithful" Perpetua.[248] These latter two inscriptions almost certainly refer to other children named Perpetua (perhaps in honor of the martyr) and might simply demonstrate the name's (or saint's) popularity.

While the identification of these objects with the famed third-century martyrs is highly uncertain, Delattre and others took them as indicators that this was the original tomb of Perpetua, since her family would not have referred to her with the title of "saint" or "martyr."[249] That this area was a pilgrimage site shortly after Perpetua's death seems possible, with a martyrium added in the later fourth century. Scholars have dated Delattre's building to the Byzantine era, deeming it an example of rebuilding after the Vandals were driven out. They also have found evidence of an earlier building that would correspond to the one Victor described.

The continuing importance of the basilica as a shrine to Perpetua and her companions (as well as a place for burial at the tomb of a saint) is demonstrated by the discovery of thirty-four fragments of a marble plaque in the crypt of the basilica (and now in the Musée national de Carthage). Reassembled by Delattre, this plaque bears a five-line inscription usually dated to the Byzantine era (fig. 21). According to Delattre's reconstruction, the legend reads, "Here are the martyrs Saturus, Saturninus, Revocatus, Secundulus, Felicitas, Perpetua, who suffered on March 7 (and) Maiulus."[250] The inclusion of Maiulus, not a part of the original group, suggests that the plaque might be simply a recording of martyrs' feast days and not a *mensa* or marker for the actual remains of Perpetua and her companions.[251]

## MEMORIA CYPRIANI (BASILICA OF THE MAPPALIA)

On at least six occasions, Augustine preached at the Memoria Cypriani, also known as the Basilica of the Mappalia, which is one of three possible shrines

reproduction in Leclercq, "Carthage," *DACL*, 2.2:2247-48. It is now in the Musée national de Carthage (inv. no. 1711).

247. See the discussion in William Tabbernee, *Montanist Inscriptions and Testimonia*, pp. 110-11, no. 14.

248. Reconstructed, this may read as follows: [Perp]etua.M. VII/[. . . fid]elis.AN.M.VII/ [. . . mart]yr. pat. *CIL* 8:25273; Leclercq, "Carthage," *DACL*, 2.2:2247-48.

249. This is Leclercq's explanation: Leclercq, "Carthage," *DACL*, 2.2:2248-50.

250. +[Hic] sunt Marty[res]/+Saturus Satu[r]n[inus]/+Rebocatus S[e]cu[ndulus]/+Felicit (as) Per[pe]t (ua) Pas(si) n[on(as) mart(ias)]/+[M]aiulu[s]. Now in the Musée national de Carthage (inv. no. 1715). See Y. Duval, *Loca sanctorum Africae*, 1:13-16, no. 6 — with bibliography.

251. Maiulus was not originally associated with the group but seems to be included here. He seems to have died in 212 and been noted on the calendar of Carthage for May 11 (not March 7). See Tabbernee, *Montanist Inscriptions and Testimonia*, 112.

to Cyprian in Carthage.[252] The Memoria was the site of Cyprian's tomb, originally in a cemetery to which a throng of his devotees carried his body for burial the night after his martyrdom by beheading.[253] By Augustine's time, it was the site of an important and somewhat rowdy celebration on the vigil of the saint's feast day (Sept. 14). This all-night festival of drinking, eating, and dancing (which Augustine decried and tried to abolish) was followed by a more solemn commemoration the next day at the site of Cyprian's martyrdom, the Mensa Cypriani.[254]

This shrine may have been a pilgrimage site for a century and a half by the time Augustine preached there. Despite their being well known in their own time, neither of the Cyprian *memoriae* is clearly and definitively associated with an excavated archeological site. Nevertheless, a certain consensus has emerged to identify the Memoria Cypriani (the Mappalia) with the remains of a basilica known as St. Monica (figs. 22-23).

The church of St. Monica fits the description fairly well, since it was built into a cemetery at the end of the fourth century. Graves were found under the wall foundations as well as within the building. Several thousand inscriptions were found there, dating from the late fourth through the late sixth century.[255] A large space, it was seemingly designed for pilgrimage, and could accommodate a large annual festival. Preceded by a large atrium, it has three aisles on each side of a central nave, set off by thirteen sets of columns. The altar was placed well into the center, between the fifth and sixth columns from the apse. Since the two small sacristies and apse are not in direct line with the main hall, it seems likely that they were earlier constructions that were retained as the building was enlarged, and they might have enclosed the tomb of the saint.[256] In effect, the presiding bishop would be seated over the tomb of Cyprian so that, in a sense, Cyprian himself continued to preside as bishop.

252. Probably Aug. *Serm.* 311; 312; *Serm. Denis* 11(308A); *Serm. Guelf.* 26(313C); 28(313F); *Psal.* 32.2.2. The other two shrines were the Mensa Cypriani and the Basilica Triciliarum (see above discussion, p. 136; p. 136, n. 209).

253. The Cemetery of Macrobius Candidianus on the Mappalian Way. See *Act. Procon.* 5 (CSEL 3.3:113-14); also see Ennabli, *Carthage, une métropole chrétienne*, no. 4, p. 18. Ennabli also identifies the Mappalia as the place where Monica spent the night praying while her son fled to Rome. This seems unlikely, since it is so far from the port (cf. Aug. *Conf.* 5.8.15).

254. The Mensa Cypriani was also a place where Augustine preached, and the site of Cyprian's execution — in the Ager Sexti, on the grounds of the Roman governor's country estate. See Aug. *Serm.* 8; 13; 131; 313; *Serm. Morin* 15(306C); *Serm. Denis* 14(313A); 15(313B); *Serm. Guelf.* 27(313D); *Psal.* 32.2.2. It has not been identified with any archeological site, although Bir Ftouha has been suspected by some scholars.

255. See Liliane Ennabli, *Les inscriptions funéraires chrétiennes de Carthage, 1: La basilique dite de Sainte-Monique, à Carthage*, Recherches d'archéologie africaine (Tunis: Institut national d'archéologie et d'art; Rome: École française de Rome, 1975).

256. L. Ennabli identifies this as Cyprian's burial site (*Les inscriptions funéraires chrétiennes de Carthage*, 1:1075).

A small necropolis, two small oratories (for Redemptus the Archdeacon and Asterius; fig. 24), and an underground baptistery also appear to have been installed nearby (about halfway between St. Monica — the shrine of St. Cyprian — and the area of Dermech) during the Vandal period.[257] Carthage's Nicene community may have constructed the subterranean baptistery shortly after their churches were taken over by Arians.[258] Victor of Vita reported that the Vandals seized the Mappalia early in their occupation of Carthage, and Procopius describes a famous shrine before the city and by the sea that was the venue for a festival called the "Cypriana"; the Vandals occupied the shrine during Huneric's reign. Usurping it for their own worship, the Arians likewise observed the feast, claiming that it (and, by extension, the cult of Cyprian) now belonged to them.[259]

At the end of the Vandal era, the Cyprian shrine at the Mappalia may have played a role in the Byzantine reconquest. According to Procopius, the locals told a story in which St. Cyprian appeared in dreams to reassure the African Catholics that he would be his own avenger.[260] The promised vengeance actually came on the eve of Cyprian's feast (September 14). The Arian clergy were preparing the sanctuary, hanging up votive offerings, arranging the lamps, and preparing church vessels just as Belisarius's forces defeated Gelimir's Vandals at Decimum, a town just on the south, around the Bay of Carthage.[261] When the clergy heard word of the Byzantine victory and approach, they fled from Cyprian's basilica. Meanwhile, the Nicene Christians, learning of the landing, arrived at the church, lit the lamps, and attended to the festival in their customary manner. They believed their dreams had been fulfilled.

## The Churches of Sufetula

The Roman city of Sufetula (modern Sbeitla) in central Tunisia has been extensively excavated. Temples to the three Capitoline gods still stand in its forum (fig. 64) and provide a sense of a small provincial city's pride in its connections to Rome. Located in the province of Byzacena, it was situated in the central highlands of Tunisia and primarily noted for production of wheat and olives. Historians of Christianity have studied its many churches and several

257. Noël Duval and Alexandre Lézine, "Nécropole chrétienne et baptistère souterrain à Carthage," *Cahiers archéologiques; fin de l'antiquité et moyen âge* 10 (1959): 71-147.

258. Vict.-Vit. *Hist. pers.* 1.16.

259. Proc. Caes. *Hist. bel.* 3.21.18-21. This would have been later than Victor of Vita's dating of this event during the reign of Geiseric (d. 477). Huneric was his successor and reigned from 477 to 484.

260. Ironically, in *Laps.* 17, Cyprian had pointed out that the martyrs under the altar in heaven had not succeeded in their petition to be avenged (Rev. 6:10-11).

261. Proc. Caes. *Hist. bel.* 3.21.23-26.

baptisteries, dating from the fourth through the seventh century, in order to gain a more fulsome view of the transitions from Late Antiquity through the Vandal and Byzantine eras. Documentary records list Christian bishops of the town, including Privatianus, present at the Council of Carthage in 256.[262] Two others were noted as attending the Conference of Carthage in 411: a Catholic bishop (Jucundus) and a Donatist bishop (Titianus).[263] Bishop Jucundus was also present at the Council of Carthage in 419. A successor Catholic bishop, Amacius, dedicated an inscription to him, found in the ambulatory of the baptistery of what was, presumably, his basilica. In all, the site of Sufetula contains the ruins of at least six and possibly seven churches, dating from the fourth through the seventh century.

The Vandal occupation of Sufetula began in the late 420s, and one of their bishops, Praesidius, whom Victor of Vita called a "clear-sighted man," was exiled by Huneric prior to the colloquy in 484.[264] In addition to this documentary record are inscriptions of Sufetula's Christian era. One refers to Bishop Jucundus, present at the Conference of Carthage in 411, and another, a mosaic tomb cover dated to the end of the Byzantine era, names the bishop Honorius.[265] According to some scholars, Sufetula's most significant historical event took place in 646, when the imperial exarch, Gregory, proclaimed himself emperor in defiance of the government in Constantinople and moved his seat of power from Carthage to Sufetula. Gregory attempted to repel Arab armies in 647, but the city was sacked and looted; its residents (including Gregory) were massacred.[266]

262. Cypr. *Sent.* 19.

263. *Col. Carth.* 1.126, 207. Maier, *L'épiscopat de l'Afrique romaine, vandale, et byzantine*, 23, 46, 60.

264. Vict.-Vit. *Hist. pers.* 2.39, 45; Maier, *L'épiscopat de l'Afrique romaine, vandale, et byzantine*, 88. Praesidius is listed as an exile in *Not. Africae.*

265. The following summaries of Sufetula's churches are largely derived from the fundamental studies of Noël Duval, *Les églises africaines à deux absides*, vol. 1 *(Les basiliques de Sbeitla)*, and the brief guide that he wrote with François Baratte, *Les ruines de Sufetula*. In addition to these is Noël Duval, "Sufetula: L'histoire d'une ville romaine de la haute-steppe à la lumière des recherches récents," in *L'Afrique dans l'Occident romain: Ier siècle av. J.-C.–IVe siècle ap. J.-C.* (Rome: École française de Rome, 1990). Also see (more recently), Fathi Bejaoui, *Sbeïtla, l'antique Sufetula* (Tunis, 1994); and Noël Duval and Henri Broise, "L'urbanisme de Sufetula — Sbeïtla en Tunisie," in *Politische Geschichte (Provinzen und Randvölker: Afrika mit Ägypten)*, ed. Hildegard Temporini and Wolfgang Haase, Aufstieg und Niedergang der römischen Welt, Teil 2, Bd. 10.2 (Berlin: Walter de Gruyter, 1982), 596-632.

266. See the discussion above, p. 84; Theophanes *Chron.* a.c. 638-39; PG 108:700-702.

The Basilica of Bellator, probably the oldest of Sufetula's surviving churches (figs. 65, 67), likely dates to the late fourth century. This basilica, named for a certain Bishop Bellator, was excavated in the early twentieth century and assumed to be a pagan temple, in part because it incorporated architectural materials from an earlier civic or religious building on the site. This reuse of both materials and land suggests that the church was built after legislation condoning the transfer of such property to Christian use in the early fifth century.[267] A burial inscription in the adjacent baptistery chapel (fig. 66)[268] names that earlier Bishop Jucundus, who was at both the Councils of Carthage in 411 and 419 and who may have overseen the basilica's construction. Its association with Bishop Bellator, possibly one of Jucundus's successors, is based on an inscription fragment discovered among wall remains and identified as part of a sarcophagus lid from the Byzantine era: "Bellator, the Bishop, lived in peace (or in the peace of the church)."[269]

The Church of Bellator was relatively modest in size (about 35 × 15.5 m). Two doors gave entrance to the aisles on either side of the central nave. The aisles were separated from the nave by eight pairs of columns. The most interesting feature of this building is its shifting orientation through different phases of its use. It was originally constructed with a single apse toward the southwest (or toward the decumanus). A counter-apse was added at a later date. In its first phase of construction, the altar stood near the center of the nave (roughly parallel to the fifth pair of columns) and was not connected to the raised chancel area that projected from the apse. After the counter-apse was added, the altar enclosure was enlarged and connected by a walkway *(solea)* to the chancel.

In a third phase, the church was reoriented so that the northeastern counter-apse became the presbyterium, and the altar was moved even closer to it and onto a new chancel platform. The original apse then became a site for burial; sarcophagi are still visible *in situ*. A last stage of construction enclosed both apses on the exterior and pushed the altar even closer to the apse entry.

267. *C.Th.* 16.10.20.1-2 (407).

268. See below, p. 150, n. 270.

269. *ILCV* 1:1112, Bellator, ep(is)c(opu)s, vixi(t) in p(ace). The inscription has been lost. See Henri Leclercq, "Sbeitla," *DACL,* ed. Cabrol et al., 15.1: 960, illus. 10816. On the inscriptions found at Sufetula in general, see Noël Duval, "L'épigraphie funéraire chrétienne d'Afrique: Traditions et ruptures, constantes et diversités," in *La terza età dell'epigrafia,* ed. Angela Donati (Faenza: Lega, 1988), 265-314.

Next to the Basilica of Bellator, a small, apsed structure set into an enclosed peristyle appears to have served as the cathedral baptistery (fig. 66). The font basin is still visible, as are the standing columns that belonged to both the peristyle and the small interior building. The floor of the room was covered in fairly simple geometric mosaics, but the apse contained a more elaborate design of a vase of flowers. In the gallery, a small burial inscription identifies the tomb of Bishop Jucundus, indicating that his remains were interred there by a successor bishop named Amacius: "Here were found the remains of blessed Bishop Jucundus, through the searching of Bishop Amacius."[270]

The baptismal font has an elongated shape, with interior undulating lobes, perhaps intended to resemble a woman's vulva and to refer to baptismal rebirth.[271] It was covered by a ciborium supported by four columns. At some point, it seems to have been covered over, probably after the newer and larger basilica with its annexed baptistery was built nearby. A small column standing inside the font has a small, square recess at its top, possibly meant to hold relics.[272] If this were its purpose, the freestanding baptistery could have been converted into a shrine. Because Jucundus likely died during the Vandal era, he might have been honored as a Nicene confessor, although not necessarily one who suffered for the faith (Amacius's inscription does not specifically call him a martyr).

## THE BASILICA OF VITALIS

Immediately adjacent to the Chapel of Jucundus and the Basilica of Bellator are the ruins of this later church, dated to the late fifth or early sixth century (fig. 69). This structure was built on the site of a large private house that was demolished to build the new church. It probably was built because the congregation needed more space, since this structure was considerably larger (50 × 25 m) than the Basilica of Bellator (35 × 15.5 m). Archeologists discovered a four-lobed basin below the church's nave. This basin was decorated with an aquatic-themed mosaic, suggesting that it originally belonged to the villa's garden (fig. 70). The addition of this building, along with housing and amenities for the bishop and his clergy, created a large ecclesiastical complex (fig. 68).

270. Hic inventa est d(e)p(ositio) s(an)c(t)i Jucundi ep(i)sc(opi) per inquisition(em) Amaci ep(i)sc(o)pi (*ILCV* 1:1112). See Noël Duval, "L'épigraphie chrétienne de Sbeitla (Sufetula) et son apport historique," in *L'Africa Romana: Atti del IV Convegno di studio, Sassari, 12-14 dicembre 1986*, ed. Attilio Mastino, Pubblicazioni del Dipartimento di storia dell'Università di Sassari 7 (Sassari: Gallizzi, 1986), 389, 394-96.

271. See Jensen, "Mater Ecclesia and the Fons Aeterna," 137-55.

272. See Duval and Baratte, *Les ruines de Sufetula*, 47.

Unlike the earlier structures, this church was sited in conformity to the Roman street grid. Also, unlike the last phase of the Basilica of Bellator, the main apse was directed toward the southwest. The faithful entered through one of four lateral doors into a five-aisled basilica; the aisles were set off by eleven rows of double columns, some of them still *in situ*. This church also had a counter-apse to the northeast that held at least one tomb. At a later stage of use, it was enclosed by a chancel screen and held a ciborium-covered altar. The church's primary altar stood at first in the midst of the nave and slightly toward the rear, as in the first phase of the Basilica of Bellator. It was enclosed by a low stone wall and likely accessed by a *solea* connecting it to a colored mosaic-covered platform extending from the presbyterium. The mosaics could be dated to the last phase of construction. About the time that the counter-apse was enclosed and elaborated into what was probably a saint's shrine, the altar was moved closer to the presbyterium and transformed into a small, enclosed island, possibly to allow easier movement between the two apses.

In the central nave, excavators discovered a limestone tile referring to the tomb of the presbyter Vitalis (long considered to have been the founder of the church and, thus, buried close to the altar). This tile was engraved with a small Christogram and the following inscription, which offers some important evidence regarding the dating of the church:

> "In the name of the Father and the Son and the Holy Spirit, Amen. The Presbyter Vitalis lived in the peace of God thirty-eight years. Today I rest, buried here in quiet peace; in dust, I am preserved for the future. A great hope remains for me. For I hope that you, Lord, are coming — you who created all things for yourself — to raise these ashes. He is capable of this. He is more beautiful than the sun, and his light surpasses the whole array of stars. While remaining one, he is capable of all things, remaining in himself and holding all things together. Born [again] in the twenty-eighth year of King Geiseric, on the day before the Ides of September."[273]

The date of Vitalis's death (or, possibly, his baptism) would be September 14, 466, if the year is counted from Geiseric's taking of Carthage in 439.

The name "Vitalis" turns up again on the mosaic decoration of the baptismal font that was built directly behind the presbytery apse of this second

---

273. In nomine Patris et Fi/li(i) et Sp(iritu)s S(an)c(ti), amen/Vitalis Pr(e)sb(yter) ui(xit in pace)/d(e)i annis XXXVIII re(q)ui(esco ho?)/die hic positus pla(cidia in)/pace reserbor pulberi/spes mic(h)i multa manet na(m te)/uenturum spero d(omi)n(u)m qui cuncta/creasti tibi ut cinere(s) istos/suscites ipse potens h(a)ec est/speciorsor sole et super omnem/s(t)ellarum dispositionem/luci conparata invenitur prior/dum sit una omnium potens et/in se permanens omnia inno/dans natus anno XXVIII/Regis Gerisic pridie idus/Septembres (*ILCV* 2:3477). For a photograph of this inscription, see Duval, "L'épigraphie chrétienne de Sbeitla (Sufetula) et son apport historique," tav. III.

cathedral church (figs. 71, 72). With dimensions of 7.5 × 5 meters, the central baptistery room was set between two small, intersecting rooms, each leading into chambers that allowed access to the basilica's side aisles. Both adjoining rooms had cupolas supported by four columns. The central font-room had a small, projecting apse in its southwest wall. The font's design was modeled on its predecessor in the Chapel of Jucundus (fig. 66). Foundations for columns indicate that a small stone canopy rose above the font's well, and three steps on each short side allowed candidates to descend into the pool on one end and then to ascend out of the water on the other.

The font has been restored *in situ* by archeologists. Roses and floral garlands decorate its surround, crosses are visible on the inside walls, and a wreathed Christogram with an alpha and omega appears in the bottom of the well. The font's surround also bears this inscription: "Vitalis and Cardela have fulfilled their vow" (fig. 72).[274] The linking of these two names raises the intriguing possibility that the presbyter Vitalis, who was buried in the nave, had a wife named Cardela, and that they donated the baptistery out of their personal funds to fulfill a vow.

### THE CHURCH OF SERVUS

In 1883, archeologists discovered what they took to be a door lintel in an area near the city's central forum. The stone is inscribed *Hic domus oration(is)* ("This is a House of Prayer"; fig. 73).[275] Although the inscription might have referred to a pagan temple, the team decided that the find indicated the site of a church, and, in the early years of the twentieth century, they excavated a Christian basilica.

Usually dated to the mid-to-late-fifth century, this basilica appears to have been built into the courtyard of a former temple. Its columns were reused to support the roof and delineate the aisles, and an apse was added to the southwest side (figs. 74, 75). The main hall was approximately 33 × 28 meters in size. Some structural evidence indicates that the altar stood in the center of the main nave, slightly toward the rear, and probably was surrounded by a stone chancel screen.

The apse was elevated above the nave and accessed by a short flight of steps. Four large sarcophagi were discovered in the space below the apse, suggesting that it served as a crypt. Among these remains was a fragment from one of the sarcophagus lids with this inscription (following a Christogram within a wreath): "Presbyter Servus, of blessed memory, lived in peace fifty-eight years and was buried on the eleventh of October."[276]

274. Vitalis et carde/la votum s(olveru)n(t).

275. On new discoveries at this site, see Fathi Bejaoui, "Nouvelles données archéologiques à Sbeïtla," *Africa* 14 (1996): 40.

276. "Presbiter Serbus b(eatae) m(emoriae) vixit in pace ann(is) LVIII d(e)p(o)s(i)t(us) V id(es) Octob(re)s" (*ILCV* 1:1185).

The temple's former *cella,* a room about eight meters square, became a baptistery (fig. 77) that opened onto a vaulted corridor separating it from the main
nave. Two columns supported its entrance. The still-visible font is about one
meter deep. Its opening is hexagonal at floor level, quatrefoil-shaped at the next
level down, and round at its bottom. Four extant column bases indicate that it
was covered by a ciborium. A small, apsed room to the east may have been a
*consignatorium* (a place for post-immersion anointing) or a classroom for catechumens (fig. 78).

Although no surviving inscriptional, material, or documentary evidence
supports the identification of this basilica as the Donatist church of Sufetula,
interpreters have suggested this by process of elimination. Jucundus was listed
as the Caecilianist bishop at the Conference of Carthage in 411, and Titianus
as his Donatist counterpart. Presumably, Titianus had a large cathedral of his
own, and this one fits that description.[277] One problem with this identification
is its late date — well after the Conference of Carthage in 411, which would have
made the new construction of a Donatist church unlikely, even in Byzacena.

### THE BASILICA (OR MARTYRIUM) OF SAINTS SYLVANIUS AND FORTUNATUS

This church was discovered some distance from Sufetula's center, in an ancient
cemetery to the southwest of the town, about 600 meters from the forum. Its
situation, the evidence of an earlier building, along with a number of sixth-
century epitaphs and one mosaic inscription indicate that it was originally built
as a shrine for the burial of certain local martyrs and was expanded in the sixth
century (fig. 79).

A relatively small and nearly square building (20 × 25 m), the sixth-century
plan consists of a central nave with two aisles on either side. The apse is enclosed and communicates with two flanking chambers (one of them containing
tombs). Four sets of four column bases in the middle of the main nave indicate
an open area, likely covered by a central dome or cupola. The column capitals
were carved with a basket-weave motif. The basilica's cruciform plan is overtly
Byzantine in style and helps to date the final building phase to the Justinianic
era.

A certain Bonifatius dedicated a small mosaic inscription, possibly belonging to the original basilica, to the saints Sylvanius and Fortunatus. Bonifatius, in
fulfillment of a vow, asked those two saints and their companions to remember
him in prayer (fig. 80).[278] The mosaic was set into the center of the nave, just a
little toward the back of the church, suggesting that it did not cover the tomb of

277. *Col. Carth.* 1.126, 207. See Maier, *L'épiscopat de l'Afrique romaine, vandale, et byzantine,*
343, 426; Duval and Baratte, *Les ruines de Sufetula,* 78.
278. See Y. Duval, *Loca sanctorum Africae,* 1:76-79, no. 34.

the martyrs themselves, but that it was appropriate to place such votive inscriptions directly into the main floor of a shrine.

### THE BASILICA OF SAINTS GERVASIUS, PROTASIUS, AND TRYPHON

This relatively small, three-aisled basilica (approximately 24 × 12.5 m) was located a long distance from the town's forum. Its remains indicate two phases of building, probably at the end of the Byzantine era in the seventh century. The most significant modification in the second phase appears to be the elevation of the apse and its chancel extension in which the altar stood, and the transformation of the semicircular apse into a rectangular shape after the apparent collapse of its vault (figs. 81, 82). The altar contained a cavity for the insertion of relics. An inscription recovered from this cavity indicates that the church was consecrated to the Milanese martyrs Gervasius and Protasius, along with an eastern Christian saint, Tryphon.

### OTHER BASILICAS

Another basilica, discovered on the north side of the forum, has been dated to the sixth century (figs. 83, 84). Although very little of the plan is still visible for this three-aisled basilica, one of its most interesting features is a small counter-choir, placed at its entrance. Enclosed by low stone walls and surmounted by a ciborium, the small platform was probably intended to hold a martyr shrine. As elsewhere in Sufetula, columns — in this case, ten sets of doubled columns — separate the main nave from the aisles. Here, too, a choir or chancel area extended well into the center of the nave, accommodating an altar, which stood approximately in line with the fourth set of columns from the apse. The presbyterium is approached by an extant set of semicircular steps (fig. 84).

Another Byzantine-era church was excavated on the southwest corner of the forum.[279] Here only six sets of doubled columns define the space of the central nave. Two other rows of columns create smaller side aisles that communicate with small annexes (which could have been sacristies) that enclose the apse. A single choir area extends from the raised presbyterium to approximately the center of the nave.

279. Fathi Bejaoui, "Une novelle église d'époque byzantine à Sbeïtla," in *L'Africa Romana: Atti dell'XII Convegno di studio, Olbia, 12-15 dicembre 1996,* ed. Mustapha Khanoussi, Paola Ruggeri, and Cinzia Vismara, 3 vols., Pubblicazioni del Dipartimento di storia dell'Università degli Studi di Sassari 31 (Sassari: Ed. Democratica Sarda, 1998), 3:1173-83.

Discovered in the early 1930s, about three kilometers southeast of Sufetula, this small chapel was only partially excavated. It is often included in the discussion of Sufetula's archeological remains because it may have been a suburban martyr shrine. It was a small building (probably no more than about 15 × 12 m). It contained mosaic pavements, mostly destroyed except for two that are now in the Bardo Museum in Tunis. One remembers the bishop Honorius, whose episcopacy is unrecorded, although he is associated with the siege of Sufetula in the mid-seventh century; the other was found in the pavement beneath the altar and shows a gemmed Christogram with an alpha and omega surrounded by flowers (fig. 85).

## The Ecclesial Complex at Hippo Regius

Hippo Regius (modern Annaba) is best known as the see of Augustine. It is located on the Mediterranean coast, on the western edge of the imperial province of Africa Proconsularis, but was in the ecclesiastical province of Numidia. When Augustine arrived in 391, Hippo Regius had at least four basilicas, and at least one of them belonged to the Donatist congregation.[280]

One of the Caecilianist-held churches was dedicated to the city's patron and one-time bishop, Leontius, and, like the Memoria Cypriani, was the locus of an annual festival, a place where Augustine frequently preached, and the site of the Council of Hippo in 427.[281] The Leontian Basilica likely was near enough to the Donatist church to overhear the rival congregation's singing on a certain feast day, probably the celebration of their patron saint and founding bishop.[282] The Leontian Basilica probably was not the Caecilianist cathedral, but the one Augustine identified as the "old church."[283] The "new" cathedral church is often identified as the Basilica Pacis, although the evidence for this name is slim.[284] The building of a new church, however, may have been a symbol of the resto-

280. Aug. *Ep.* 29.11.

281. Aug. *Serm.* 260; 262.2.2 — preached in the Basilica of Leontius — and *Con. Hipp.* a. 427 (CCSL 149:250.2).

282. Aug. *Ep.* 29.6-11. This document never actually identifies the place as the Basilica of Leontius, however. The identification is merely extrapolated from the fact that Augustine was preaching against a rowdy feast — one celebrated also by the Donatists nearby (*Ep.* 29.11). The feast of Leontius was in the late spring; one year it coincided with the celebration of the Ascension of Jesus (*Serm.* 262.2.2).

283. The best evidence for this is in Augustine's *Ep.* 99.3, noted by Lancel, *Saint Augustine,* 239, in regard to the identification of two houses, one adjoining the "old church" (presumably the Basilica of Leontius) and the other adjoining the other church — a house that Augustine desired to acquire, probably for clergy living quarters.

284. In two places, Aug. *Fel.* 2.1 and *Ep.* 213.1, the term "ecclesia pacis" is found, but this does

ration of the "peace of the church," possibly after its return to the Caecilianists upon Gratian's reversal of Julian's policy of toleration.[285] In addition, Augustine supervised the building of a new basilica dedicated to the Eight Martyrs.[286]

Although the site of Hippo Regius had been known for centuries, scientific excavations began only in the first half of the twentieth century, notably under a French naval officer turned archeologist named Erwan Marec. During the 1920s and 1930s, excavators discovered an impressive city with public baths and a large civic forum, along with an episcopal complex in what Marec termed "the Christian quarter." That complex included a large, three-aisled basilica with a baptistery (figs. 48, 50, 51). It also had adjoining buildings that might have served as a bishop's residence, a monastery, and a scriptorium, and a trefoil structure that has been identified as a possible martyr's shrine (fig. 53).[287] Based on examination of the mosaics, the earliest phase of the basilica is generally dated to the second half of the fourth century.[288] Although it is not certain that this large basilica was Augustine's church, its date, location, physical design, and proximity to both residence and possible shrine strongly suggest that it was the Caecilianist cathedral — the so-called Basilica Pacis or, alternatively, the Basilica Maior.[289]

Apparently the first church was built originally on the site of a block of private dwellings and shops, since it incorporated some of their original features, including some mosaic pavements. The subsequently constructed basil-

---

not necessarily imply a formal name. The name Basilica Pacis appears as the location of the council in Hippo Regius in 393: *Reg. Carth.* I (CCSL 149:182.9).

285. Macarius and Paul were supposed to bring funds for the renewal and decoration of African churches — and they took this to mean Caecilianist churches specifically, so it may be possible to imagine the building of a church at Hippo Regius at this time. See Optat. *Parm.* 3.3.

286. Aug. *Serm.* 356.10.

287. Marec, *Monuments chrétiens d'Hippone*, 23-136; Henri-Irénée Marrou, "La basilique chrétienne d'Hippone d'après le résultat des dernières fouilles," *Revue des études augustiniennes* 6 (1960): 111, 122-23; Gui, Duval, and Caillet, eds., *Basiliques chrétiennes d'Afrique du Nord*, I:1:346-49; and, more recently, George Radan, "The Basilica Pacis of Hippo," in *Augustine in Iconography: History and Legend*, ed. Joseph C. Schnaubelt and Frederick Van Fleteren, Collectanea Augustiniana (New York: P. Lang, 1999), 147-88; Xavier Delestre et al., *Hippone* (Aix-en-Provence: Édisud; [Alger]: INAS, 2005). Serge Lancel evaluated the evidence for the identification in *Saint Augustine*, 241-44.

288. See Jean Lassus, "Les édifices du culte. Autour de la basilique," in *Atti del VI Congresso internazionale di Archeologia Cristiana, Ravenna, 23-30 settembre 1962* (Città del Vaticano: Pontificio Istituto di Archeologia Cristiana, 1965), 587-91.

289. Both names are sparingly witnessed. Basilica Pacis: *Reg. Carth.* I (CCSL 149:182.9); Basilica Maior: the title of Aug. *Serm.* 258 and the text of *Serm.* 325.2. Lancel discusses doubts about this site as Augustine's cathedral (although he accepts it as such on the basis of a sermon in which Augustine suggests that the congregation "turn toward the Lord" in prayer — so that they may face east (*Serm. Dolb.* 28(20B).11), and does not believe the trefoil building to the southwest was the shrine of Stephen; see Lancel, *Saint Augustine*, 242-44). For another argument against the trefoil structure at Hippo Regius being the Stephen shrine, see also Stevens, ed., *Bir Ftouha*, 25. Stevens identifies this as a *triclinium* of an aristocratic house.

---

ica probably underwent its last major renovation just before Augustine arrived in Hippo Regius. Although the earlier building on the site was oriented on an east-west axis, the reconstruction turned and enlarged the edifice so that it was directed toward the northwest, with its entrance door on the southeast side. This new building opened directly off the main street *(cardo)* of the quarter without an entrance porch or narthex. The orientation of the building and its apparent lack of a narthex suggest that it was built into a space made available by the razing of older (probably domestic) structures on the site.

The interior was divided into a nave and two side aisles, and measured 37.5 meters by 18.5 meters, a proportion to which Augustine referred in one of his sermons as the relative dimensions of his "large" church.[290] The aisles were separated from the nave by two ranks of ten piers. Three doors opposite the apse constituted the principal entrance to the building and could have divided the men from the women as they entered and took their places on opposite sides of the hall.[291] The apse was elevated and accessed by a short flight of steps, corresponding to Augustine's reference to steps leading up into the presbyterium.[292] The central door may have been reserved for clergy and the entrance procession.

Like other African basilicas, the altar was most likely moveable and wooden. Marec surmised that the altar would have been placed on a raised platform that served as an extension of the presbyterium into the nave.[293] This platform was likely closed off by a screen and accessed by an open gate and a short flight of steps.[294] However, archeologists also found evidence of a mosaic-covered pavement further into the nave. Marec thought this could have been where the ambo stood, but both Noël Duval and Henri-Irénée Marrou argued that this delineated the altar area. No evidence of a raised walkway was identified between the presbyterium and this area.[295] A small hexagonal opening below the raised presbyterium extension provided access to water in a cistern (fig. 49), possibly for cleaning the floor.

At the back of the apse area, a semicircular bench *(synthronon)* provided

290. Aug. *Ep. Io.* 4.9.

291. Aug. *Ciu.* 2.28.

292. On the existence of steps up into the presbyterium in Augustine's basilica, see Aug. *Ep.* 126.1; *Ciu.* 22.8 (CCSL 47:826.454–827.468).

293. Aug. *Ep.* 185.7.27.

294. The platform was supported by two colonettes, still *in situ.* The steps, however, are not apparent in the excavation. They may have been made of wood. See Gui, Duval, and Caillet, eds., *Basiliques chrétiennes d'Afrique du Nord,* I.1:346-49.

295. The archeological evidence is ambiguous here. Marec, *Monuments chrétiens d'Hippone,* 28-29, placed the ambo in the center of the nave, a placement corrected by Marrou, "La basilique chrétienne d'Hippone d'après le résultat des dernières fouilles," 127-28. The pulpit might also have been placed between the altar in the midst of the nave and the presbyterium, but elevation would enhance both hearing and seeing of lectors and visiting preachers. Augustine mentions a pulpit in *Ep.* 23.3; 29.8 — as does Cyprian (*Ep.* 38.2.1), who speaks of the importance of visibility.

seating for presbyters. In the center of this bench was a space cut out for the bishop's throne (*cathedra;* figs. 49, 52), which probably was made of wood. The curved wall and ceiling of the apse would have amplified the voice of the speaker seated there. The bishop, who was the normal presider at the ritual,[296] preached from his raised throne, slightly elevated above the people so that he could see and be seen.[297]

The worshipers may have been assigned specific places within the building. The newly baptized, for example, were allowed to join the clergy in the chancel area for Easter week.[298] Consecrated virgins and widows might have stood toward the front (outside but gathered around the altar area), while penitents and catechumens would have been grouped toward the back or in the side aisles.[299] The physical remains provide no evidence of galleries. The church was not equipped with benches or chairs for the people. The congregation would have stood for the liturgy; if provision was made for seating the elderly or infirm, evidence of it has not survived. The church would have had a nave and aisle area of about 564 square meters (6,070 square feet). With everyone standing, as was the custom, this church could have accommodated more than 2,000 people for festivals.[300]

The floor of the basilica was covered with polychrome stone mosaics, some of the mosaics from the pre-existing building. Various funeral mosaics were inserted into the pavement of both the nave and the aisles covering tombs of privileged persons who were allowed burial under the church floor. Their different styles suggest different periods of construction. The center of the nave was covered by a rectangular mosaic that marked the burial of two bishops, probably from the period preceding the last renovation of the building.

A large cistern, possibly pre-dating the original building, was located beneath the main nave just above the altar and was used as a crypt (fig. 49). More than a dozen bodies (eleven of them infants) were interred in this vault, possibly after the building ceased to be used as a church. However, one apparently more significant tomb was found among these burials. Although the idea is very speculative, this tomb might have held Augustine's remains — buried quickly in the face of advancing Vandal troops.[301]

296. Aug. *Serm.* 227.

297. Aug. *Ep.* 23.3; *Serm.* 91.5.5, 6.7; 355.2; *Serm. Denis* 17(301A).2.

298. Aug. *Serm. Mai* 94 (260C).7; *Serm.* 353.1.1.

299. This surmise is based on the honor that was accorded to each class and the dismissal of the catechumens and penitents.

300. Aug. *Serm.* 274; *Catech.* 13.19; and Optat. *Parm.* 4.5 indicate that only the clergy had the right to sit in the assembly. Modern safety codes specify three square feet per standing person.

301. Marec, *Monuments chrétiens d'Hippone,* 52-53. Augustine died as the Vandals were besieging Hippo. Bishops were ordinarily buried in their churches by this date, making it quite possible that he was buried within the church and that his remains were relocated later.

The small baptistery (4.8 × 4 m) lay in an area to the northeast side of the entrance to what has been identified as Augustine's cathedral church, the Basilica Pacis (fig. 54). A small vestibule separated it from the church and a larger apsidal room (16 × 4 m) to the north, which might have been a place specifically designated for the ritual anointing following the water bath *(consignatorium)*. The baptistery room itself was vaulted on the eastern side and rectangular on the western side. Like the adjoining rooms, it was paved with polychrome and geometrically patterned mosaics (intersecting cruciform medallions), although the marble-revetted font (2.5 × 1.5 m; fig. 50) took up most of the floor space.[302] Raised nearly a meter off the floor and accessed by a step from the outside, the font contained three steps on the inside down into a well that was about one meter deep (fig. 55).[303] Two interior niches cut into the stone on the inside gave the font interior a cruciform appearance. As elsewhere in Africa, the font was covered by a ciborium, which was supported by four columns.

The small size of the room indicates that only the candidate, bishop, assisting deacon (or deaconess), and perhaps one or two sponsors could have been present at the ritual immersion. Presumably the candidates were kept waiting in the outer room and brought in one by one. Once they had been immersed, they exited into the other room, perhaps waiting as a group for their post-baptismal anointing. After they were all baptized, robed, and anointed, they joined the community for the first time in their prayers and sacred meal. To do this, they would have been escorted through the door at the opposite end of the chapel in which they had been anointed, and the waiting congregation would have immediately welcomed them.

The Vandals most likely occupied Augustine's church complex in 431 when they seized the city of Hippo Regius and made it their base of operation until they took Carthage eight years later. During the Vandal period, the church probably underwent only minor changes (perhaps the insertion of tombs of its Arian occupants, including that of the presbyterissa Guilia Runa; fig. 125).[304]

302. For more details and bibliography, see Gui, Duval, and Caillet, eds., *Basiliques chrétiennes d'Afrique du Nord*, I.1:346-49, and Ristow, *Frühchristliche Baptisterien*, 115, no. 70.

303. The current floor level is that of the basilica.

304. That this could be some evidence of a female presbyter — even an Arian one — has been suggested. See Carolyn Osiek and Kevin Madigan, eds., *Ordained Women in the Early Church: A Documentary History* (Baltimore: Johns Hopkins University Press, 2005), 197-98. Other tombs include one for Ermengon the Suevi, who was the spouse of Ingomar (Marec, *Monuments chrétiens d'Hippone*, 59-64).

Thamugadi (Timgad), in central Numidia, was a center of the Donatist church. It was more important than Carthage (which also had its own Donatist bishop) because of the sect's Numidian origins and strength. Optatus, bishop of the city in the late fourth century, was an older contemporary of Augustine. In addition to being the strongest of the Donatists in Africa and the supporter of groups of marauding Circumcellions, Optatus entered into an unfortunate political alliance with the Moorish revolutionary Gildo against the Romans and was executed as an enemy of the state in 398. Optatus's successor, Gaudentius, continued the resistance to Roman authority, which occasioned one of the most controversial of Augustine's writings on the role of coercion in religious matters.[305]

Although other Donatist strongholds in Numidia, like Bagai, had large churches, and although Theveste held the shrine of the martyr-bishop Marculus along with that of St. Crispina, Thamugadi was the principal city.[306] Archeologists, working from the late nineteenth century until the present, have uncovered as many as eleven church structures dated between the fourth and the seventh century.[307] At least three had attached baptisteries and thus conceivably could have served as cathedrals. One of these must have been for the Caecilianist Bishop of Thamugadi (Faustinianus in the late fourth and early fifth century). This fairly large building (approximately 26 × 13.5 m) apparently had two phases, but it follows the traditional plan of a central nave and two side aisles, a raised apse floor, and a projecting chancel surrounded by a low railing (fig. 87). Two side chambers flank the apse, both communicating with the main nave. One likely served as a small storage room or sacristy; the other, larger and terminating in an apse to the north, might have been a small chapel or a room for catechumens. The baptistery is at the southeast entrance to the church (fig. 88).

A second, smaller basilica (17.5 × 11.7 m) with a detached baptistery is difficult to date. It appears to date to the Byzantine era. Situated in the center of the town and partially built into the home of a certain Januarius, it also may have served as the Donatist cathedral after the imperial *executor,* Dulcitius, confiscated the prior one in 420. Alternatively, it could have been constructed later in the fifth century to serve the Catholics after the Arian seizure of churches in the city. One of its most impressive features is a high, raised apse, which is

305. Augustine wrote *Ep.* 185 to Boniface, the military officer responsible for enforcing the decrees following the Conference of Carthage in 411. Gaudentius would later provoke a major treatise, *Contra Gaudentium Donatistarum episcopum,* by his own threat of mass suicide.

306. Aug. *Psal.* 21.2.26. Marculus was important as the supposed victim of fourth-century persecution, in which the Caecilianists were accused of collaboration. Augustine implies that he was actually a suicide and a model for suicides: *Petil.* 2.14.32, 20.46, 88.195; *Cresc.* 3.49.54; *Eu. Io.* 11.15.

307. Gui, Duval, and Caillet, eds., *Basiliques chrétiennes d'Afrique du Nord,* I.1:263-86.

most easily seen from the back (fig. 90). From this angle, one can make out evidence of the original home: the remains of a bath structure, which included a small, private latrine. A small distance away, built into the courtyard of a former house, is a baptistery with a round font set into a square pavement supporting eight columns. The font was covered by a ciborium held up by an additional four columns (fig. 89).

Although its identity is not absolutely certain (it was often referred to as a monastery), most scholars presume that the enormous walled compound that lies just to the southwest of the main part of the city was Optatus's ecclesial complex, which included his cathedral, a chapel or shrine, the bishop's house, a baptistery, and a series of contiguous chambers of various shapes and sizes (figs. 91, 93). The basilica that lies in the midst of this maze of rooms is enormous. Its dimensions (63 × 22 m), not including its impressive atrium (23 meters square), attest to its significance as much as to the size of its congregation. The atrium in front of the main entrance had six columns on each side, adorned with Corinthian capitals.[308] In the center of the open courtyard was a small basin or fountain. Three entrances led from the atrium into the central nave of the church.

The length of the interior space must have been impressive, especially as it was visually accented by two long rows of columns that separated the two side aisles from the center. These colonnades consisted of sixteen sets of doubled columns. The apse was not elevated but was especially deep. In front of the apse in the main nave were two areas that were apparently set off by barriers. One of these, almost at the middle of the nave, contained a sarcophagus whose gabled lid projected above the floor and was equipped with a tube for receiving libations (fig. 92). This may have been Optatus's tomb. However, because it lacks inscriptions, this identification is speculative. At the very least, this was the tomb of an important saint.

The baptistery, annexed to the western side of the atrium, contained a hexagonal font (fig. 94). Three shallow steps around the interior were covered with mosaics in a chevron pattern; the surround was bordered with a band of leaves that met at the front with a small Christogram. The surrounding floor of the baptistery was covered with mosaic designs that included vases and flowers. A slightly larger room provided access from the baptistery to the atrium. In this room, two small hexagonal basins may have served for the rite of footwashing.[309] Today the baptistery is enclosed in a roofed (and locked) building erected (for its protection) by archeologists in the mid-twentieth century.

In addition to the baptistery, the other annexed rooms could have served pilgrims or gatherings of Donatist bishops from the area. Two inscriptions

308. These may have been *spolia*. See Gui, Duval, and Caillet, eds., *Basiliques chrétiennes d'Afrique du Nord,* I.1:277.

309. Gui, Duval, and Caillet, eds., *Basiliques chrétiennes d'Afrique du Nord,* I.2:CXXXII, fig. 2.

found at the site have been assumed to demonstrate its associations with Optatus, including a mosaic found in what was likely the bishop's house that read "I completed this work under the orders of Optatus, the priest of God" (fig. 96).[310] However, the reconstructions of the inscriptions have been challenged and so are not entirely reliable.[311] Nevertheless, the very size of this basilica and its collection of additional rooms indicate that the church was wealthy and perhaps that its bishop was powerful. Thus it is reasonable to posit that this was Optatus's great cathedral and the very building in which the Donatist bishop Gaudentius and his congregation barricaded themselves, threatening to burn themselves and their church rather than turn it and themselves over to Caecilianist unity.[312]

## CONCLUSION

The archeological remains of North African churches raise several issues. First, although we have evidence for multiple ecclesiastical regions in Carthage, other cities often had more churches than were needed to serve the two (and sometimes three) distinct congregations that emerged out of schism even when the cathedral (as appears at Hippo Regius and Thamugadi) was more than large enough to accommodate a significant population. Some of these structures were cemetery churches or shrines and thus places for pilgrimage or festivals more than for ordinary congregational liturgies. During the Vandal occupation, the Nicenes likely retained many of the extra-mural churches, while others within the urban area — especially cathedrals — were given over to Arian communities. In the Byzantine era, these churches were retaken and renovated, while new basilicas were built (e.g., Carthage's basilicas of Dermech I and Bir Ftouha).

Second, African churches show distinctions that were partially preserved, even in the Byzantine era, including the characteristically North African counter-apse for the burial of clergy or local saints. As the liturgy became more Byzantine in character, however, the altar was moved gradually from the center of the nave towards the apse, arguably emphasizing the separation of the clergy from the laity during the eucharistic liturgy. Nevertheless, even towards the end of the Byzantine era, altars were sometimes still placed in front of the apse

---

310. Haec iubente sacerdote Dei Optato perfeci. See Henri-Irénée Marrou, "Sur une inscription concernant Opat de Timgad," in *Christiana tempora: Mélanges d'histoire, d'archéologie, d'épigraphie et de patristique* (Rome: École française de Rome, 1978), 145-48.

311. See the discussion of E. Albertini and Marrou's different interpretations in Gui, Duval, and Caillet, eds., *Basiliques chrétiennes d'Afrique du Nord*, I.1:274. Frend, *The Donatist Church*, p. 209, n. 3, accepts Albertini's conclusion without noting the difficulties of the reconstruction.

312. Aug. *Ep.* 204 to Dulcitius, and the two books of *Contra Gaudentium Donatistarum episcopum*. This took place in 420.

area, on a platform that would have allowed congregants to surround it on three sides (cf. Sufetula's basilica of saints Gervasius, Protasius, and Tryphon).

Finally, the cult of local martyrs continued to be important well into the Byzantine era. Although Carthage had churches dedicated to Peter and Paul in Augustine's time, and although the Milanese saints Gervasius and Protasius were venerated into the Byzantine era,[313] the popularity of local saints seems to have survived well past the Vandal era. This is clear from the churches in Sufetula (e.g., the martyrium of saints Sylvanius and Fortunatus) as well as in Carthage (e.g., the pilgrimage church at Bir Ftouha).

Thus, the African church was the physical site of salvation. It was the locus of identity and the basis for Christian formation. Made up of many parts, it housed the font that washed away sins and introduced new members into the community of the saints. Its narthex sheltered the penitents, and its hall housed the altar that held the sacrificial food that was the spiritual nourishment of the gathered people, both saints and sinners. That hall also held the reader's desk where the scriptures were read out, and the bishop's chair from which sermons would be delivered. The church building shaped the life and liturgy of the faithful and, when they died, it often opened its floor to receive their bodies.

313. Aug. *Ciu.* 22.8 recounts a miracle performed at their shrine in a town just outside Hippo. Sufetula also had a basilica dedicated to them.

# CHAPTER 5

# Becoming a Christian: The Ritual of Baptism

....................................................................................................................................

## INTRODUCTION

Generally regarded as necessary for salvation, receiving baptism in a Christian community in Roman Africa during the third, fourth, and fifth centuries signified the crossing of a social boundary that separated not only nonbelievers from the faithful and catechumens from communicants, but also members of one Christian party from those of another.[1] Each of these distinctions marked opposed cosmic realms — the kingdoms of Satan and of God, the communities of the damned and the saved. During these centuries, the location as well as the definition of this boundary (and the means of its crossing) changed with shifts of the relation of the Christian communities to their surrounding culture, to imperial governance, and even among competing parties within the church. Consequently, adjustments in the claims made for baptism's cosmic and religious significance were required. For example, the social boundary defined by the distinction between communicants and catechumens became increasingly different from that cosmic division separating the communities of the saved and the damned, defined by anticipation of admission to heaven or dismissal into hell. The status and eternal destination of adherents of certain marginal groups, either outside or inside the borders of the "true church," became more ambiguous and troublesome. The possibility of salvation for the catechumen, the penitent, the schismatic, and even the sinful or half-hearted communicant was questioned. The answers to these questions varied over time and with social context. The practice, meaning, and justification of Christian baptism in North Africa was thus developed and changed by the need to control perceived deviance, in order to forge and preserve communal identity.

1. Tert. *Bapt.* 12.

This chapter begins by considering the practice at the beginning of the third century, primarily as it is reflected in the writings of Tertullian of Carthage. It then examines the practice in the middle of the third century, in the letters, treatises, and decrees of Cyprian and his episcopal colleagues. The discussion next turns to the issues and conflicts that arose around the practice of baptism in the fourth and fifth centuries, using the surviving documents of the Donatist controversy, the writings of Augustine of Hippo, and the legislation of the successive councils of the African episcopate, most of them under Aurelius of Carthage. In each instance, the exposition focuses on the advances in theological understanding that were required by the evolving social context and developing practice.

## BAPTISMAL PRACTICE IN TERTULLIAN'S TIME

### The Rejection of Idolatry

In the early third century, the boundary between the church and non-church was defined primarily in terms of believers and nonbelievers, by distinguishing adherents from idolaters. It separated those who made an exclusive commitment to the cult of the Christian God from those who continued to practice Greco-Roman polytheism or cultivated contemporary philosophical monotheism. Although those inside the Christian community were expected to maintain high standards of conduct (or face expulsion), the division between faithful and lax or saint and sinner was not as fundamental as the distinction between Christian and idolater. Repudiation of the traditional gods of Rome and Africa was central to several aspects of the baptismal rite as outlined in Tertullian's treatise *On Baptism*. This treatise, the only full description of the ritual of the African church, is dated to the beginning of the third century and provides information about baptism in that time and place.

First, Tertullian interpreted the baptismal oath as a verbal denunciation of idolatry and a commitment to Christ, which was subsequently demonstrated through specific practices of daily living.[2] In this pledge, sometimes called "the seal of faith," the Christian initiant forswore the works of the devil as the author and beneficiary of wickedness.[3] Although the devil was credited with instigating all forms of immorality, Tertullian and his fellow Christians identified the demons primarily as the originators of the cult of the traditional gods and thus associated the devil with any activity that brought an individual into contact with those gods, their images, or their celebrations. Since Christians did not establish economically segregated and self-sustaining settlements, they lived and

2. Tert. *Spec.* 4, 24.
3. Tert. *Cor.* 3.

worked in Roman towns and cities, an environment permeated by traditional religious practices that they had committed to shun. For example, they were required to avoid the games and spectacles presented in honor of the Roman state gods, to refrain from occupations that involved the manufacture or worship of idols, and to renounce any office or profession that required participation in the state's religious rituals or the swearing of oaths.[4] They were discouraged from marrying non-Christians because of the danger of contact with idolatry that this would entail.[5] The evil spirits tried to contaminate souls through the superstitious practices surrounding childbirth, although those children born to Christian parents were holy (1 Cor. 7:14).[6] Once baptized, Christians were expected to resist all the aspects of culture that would pollute them. Those who lapsed into idolatry after baptism — even under coercion — were permanently excluded from the communion of the church.[7]

Tertullian's complaints and exhortations indicate that Christians took the rejection of idolatry seriously, although they did not always resist it aggressively. Some women married non-Christians. Owners of properties and businesses found subterfuges that allowed them to formalize contracts despite the idolatrous oaths and formulae that such procedures entailed.[8] Some fled to avoid persecution rather than openly denounce idolatry and pay with their blood for their Christian commitment.[9] Christians continued to live and work, somewhat uneasily, in the imperial economy.[10]

Distinguishing between sinners and non-sinners was, in Tertullian's practice, roughly equivalent to separating idolaters from the faithful. In his castigation of a bishop who allowed repentant adulterers to be reconciled and readmitted to communion, Tertullian invoked the biblical parallel between religious infidelity and sexual infidelity, which demanded that perpetrators of grave sexual offenses be permanently excluded from the church.[11] The baptismal denunciation of pagan idolatry[12] was understood as a renunciation of the other types of sin that had characterized the candidate's former life. Thus, the immediate preparation for the baptismal cleansing involved the penitential practices of fasting and all-night prayer vigils.[13] Yet, Tertullian indicated that this general confession of sins served as an acceptance of a new moral code rather than a revelation of moral failings. It was not to be compared to the specific acknowl-

4. Tert. *Idol.* 7-8. Cf. *Trad. apos.* 16.4-24.
5. Tert. *Spec.* 4, 24; *Idol.* 7-8, 11, 17, 21, 23.
6. Tert. *An.* 39.
7. Tert. *Nat.* 1.5.9; *Pud.* 22.
8. Tert. *Idol.* 11, 17, 21, 23.
9. Tertullian objected to this practice as apostasy in *Fug.* 12.
10. Tert. *Apol.* 37.
11. Tert. *Pud.* 5, 12.
12. Tert. *Cor.* 3; *Spec.* 24.
13. Tert. *Bapt.* 20.

edgment of serious post-baptismal sins, which later might be made before the whole community.[14]

This understanding of baptism as a radical shift in commitment that required active resistance to idolatry and its related transgressions led Tertullian to urge that parents refrain from baptizing children before they were old enough to make a sufficient profession of faith and the vows to live the rest of their lives without committing grave sin. He also discouraged sponsors from making those oaths on a child's behalf, since they could not responsibly guarantee fulfillment of the promises being made, which would put them into peril — especially if they should die before the child could be safely led to virtuous maturity.[15] Tertullian rejected the argument that baptism should be given on demand, a judgment based on the injunction in Matthew 5:42 to "give to everyone that asks," and on the special case of Philip's baptism of the Ethiopian eunuch in Acts 8, and even Paul's own baptism in Acts 9. Instead, he pointed to the admonition in 1 Timothy 5:22: "Do not be hasty in the laying on of hands."[16]

Correspondingly, Tertullian argued that infants had no sins to be forgiven[17] and that adolescents could rely on the integrity of their faith in Christ for salvation so long as they did not use the delay of baptism as an opportunity for sinful living.[18] In contending that baptism should be reserved for adults who had already been instructed in the teaching of Christ and exhibited a willingness to follow the Christian mode of life, Tertullian's arguments gave indirect evidence of the actual practice of baptizing infants and young children who were not in immediate danger of death. His fellow Christians were more anxious than he to secure baptism for their children and may have regarded it as necessary for salvation.

## The Catechumenate

In Tertullian's descriptions, the process of becoming a Christian in the early third century was designed for adults and began with an extended period of preparation. Baptism was not to be granted spontaneously and immediately upon conversion.[19] Candidates not only had to be well established in a life

14. Tert. *Paen.* 9-10.
15. Tert. *Bapt.* 18.4.
16. Tert. *Bapt.* 18.1.
17. Quid festinat innocens aetas ad remissionem peccatorum? *Bapt.* 18.5; CCSL 1:293.31-32. This would indicate that the reference to the "delictis pristinae caecitatis" intends the sins committed by acting on the spiritual blindness in which humans are born, not that the blindness is itself sinful. Tert. *Bapt.* 1.1; CCSL 1:277.1-2.
18. Tert. *Bapt.* 18.6.
19. The instances of Paul and the Ethiopian eunuch (Acts 8, 9) clearly were exceptions; Tert. *Bapt.* 18.1-3.

that eschewed the idolatry of the surrounding Roman culture but also had to demonstrate their ability to maintain the moral standards enjoined upon each member of the Christian community. This period of preparation, the catechumenate, was thus aimed as much at a moral and spiritual transition as at doctrinal instruction and training in scripture.

That the catechumenate could be a somewhat extended period is indicated in the contemporary account of the martyrdom of Perpetua, Felicity, and their companions, most of whom were catechumens identified as Christians. At least in this instance, the individual charged with their instruction (their catechist) belonged to the laity rather than holding clerical rank. Although they were not baptized until just prior to their execution, these martyrs understood themselves (and were regarded by others) as fully committed Christians throughout their imprisonment and trial.[20] That their martyrdom would itself constitute an efficacious baptism (in blood) was also well accepted.[21]

## The Ritual

The early third-century preparation of candidates for baptism included practices that effected the aspirant's separation from idolatry and other forms of sin: prayer, fasting, reverential kneeling, acknowledgment of sin, and oaths binding oneself to the new faith and to God.[22] Although Tertullian was acutely concerned about demonic presences that threatened candidates, his description of the ritual does not mention explicitly a pre-baptismal exorcistic anointing or other kinds of cleansing from Satanic contagion.[23] He urged vigilance about the influence of Satan, especially demonic uses of water that attempted to mimic baptism's power. The treatise was meant to reassure his audience that even if water could be the element of perdition in idolatrous practice, scriptural precedent showed clearly that it could also serve God as the instrument of both cleansing of the flesh and sanctification of the spirit in Christian baptism.[24]

Water, however, was not sanctifying of itself but must receive the power to make holy from the Holy One. Once God was invoked, Tertullian explained, the Holy Spirit would come down to rest upon the water and sanctify it from within.[25] Tertullian associated this invocation with the descent of the Spirit on the primal water (Gen. 1:2) as well as intervention by the holy angel, who again stirred up the waters in the pool of Bethsaida (John 5:4).[26] Guided by his Stoic

20. *Pas. Perp.* 2.
21. Tert. *Bapt.* 16; see also Cypr. *Ep.* 57.4.1; 73.21.1-2, 22.2; *Rebapt.* 11, 14; and *Trad. apos.* 19.
22. Tert. *Cor.* 3.2; *Spec.* 4.1.
23. Tert. *Bapt.* 5.
24. Tert. *Bapt.* 5.4-5.
25. Tert. *Bapt.* 4.4.
26. Tert. *Bapt.* 3, 5.

materialism, Tertullian seems to have thought that the divine being actually mixed with the water; yet, he explained that the Holy Spirit was not conferred in the water itself. The one being baptized was first cleansed from sins by the action of this angel, preparing the way for the Spirit, who would come after the washing.[27] The profession of faith was sealed by the Father, Son, and Holy Spirit. To that divine Triad was added the confession of the church itself, which was characterized as the body in which the Trinity dwelt. Tertullian noted that this pledge of faith was more ample than that enjoined by Jesus in the gospel (Matt. 28:19).[28] The form of the baptism was, then, a triple immersion in which this faith in the Trinity and the church was confessed.[29]

After the baptized came up from the washing, they were anointed, a practice Tertullian compared with the priestly anointing of Aaron by Moses, and they received an imposition of hands to invite the Holy Spirit, which he associated with Joseph's blessing of Ephraim and Manasseh. As human action summoned spirit into the water and empowered it to cleanse the body from sin, Tertullian explained, oil conferred a priestly anointing on the purified flesh and the application of human hands shared the spirit animating Christians.[30] At this moment, according to Tertullian, the Holy Spirit willingly descended to bestow peace upon bodies that had been cleansed and blessed.[31] Tertullian did not recognize any special qualifications of church officers as necessary to perform these tasks; rather, he seems to have insisted on the combined efficacy of material elements and the particular human actions as mediating divine power and sanctification — as opposed to the minister's spiritual endowment or authority. Any baptized person could confer baptism when necessary.[32]

After the rites of baptism were concluded, the neophytes joined the faithful for prayers in their "mother's house," the church.[33] Here they received their first eucharist, which was preceded by a mixed cup of milk and honey, the food of newly born infants.[34] During the following week, the neophytes refrained from the common baths.[35]

27. Tert. *Bapt.* 4-6.
28. Tert. *Cor.* 3.3; *Bapt.* 6.2.
29. Tert. *Cor.* 3.3.
30. Tert. *Bapt.* 7.1–8.2.
31. Tert. *Bapt.* 8.3.
32. Tert. *Bapt.* 17.2.
33. Igitur benedicti quos gratia dei expectat, cum de illo sanctissimo lauacro noui natalis ascenditis et primas manus apud matrem cum fratribus aperitis, petite de patre, petite de domino peculia gratiae distributionis charismatum subiacere. Tert. *Bapt.* 20.5; CCSL 1:295.28-32. The phrase *apud matrem* may refer to a building dedicated to the assembly. It might also refer to the actual assembly of the church members, though the following *cum fratribus* would then seem to be repetitive, and count against this interpretation.
34. Tert. *Cor.* 3; *Marc.* 1.14.
35. Tert. *Cor.* 3.3.

## Age of Candidates for Baptism

In his writings, Tertullian offered some information about other details of the baptismal ritual and urged that the rite be celebrated according to certain rules designed to protect its dignity and sanctity. As noted above, he recommended that candidates be of an age and character to make and keep their baptismal promises, and he exhorted their sponsors to be mindful of the gravity of their role as guarantors. Sponsors apparently made promises that made them responsible for guiding and ensuring the good behavior of their candidates after baptism.[36]

## Ministers of the Sacrament

Tertullian indicated that the privilege of baptizing belonged primarily to the bishop, who might commission presbyters and deacons to serve in his stead.[37] When a catechumen was in danger of death, however, Tertullian asserted that even laypeople had not only the power but the duty to baptize: anyone could give what had been received,[38] and one who refused would be responsible for the damnation of the person dying without being cleansed of sin.[39] This teaching did not betray anti-clerical sensibilities in Tertullian; he insisted that the laity should not usurp the role of the bishop but must baptize only when necessary.[40] Moreover, in his attack on a female heretic, Tertullian objected to women serving even as emergency administrators of baptism and discounted the precedent of Thecla (who baptized herself) as justifying any female prerogative.[41]

## Baptism in Extraordinary Circumstances

As has just been noted, Tertullian insisted that emergency baptism of the dying was the responsibility of the laity when members of the clergy were not available.[42] The account of the martyrdom of Perpetua and Felicity indicates an-

---

36. Tert. *Bapt.* 18.4.

37. *Pas. Perp.* 1.2.

38. Tert. *Bapt.* 17.2.

39. Tert. *Bapt.* 17.3.

40. Tert. *Bapt.* 17.2. Tertullian's understanding of the role of the clergy will be more fully considered in Chapter Eight on orders.

41. Tert. *Bapt.* 17.4-5. This rejection may have been influenced by the polemical objective of the treatise, directed as it was against a woman who was leading candidates away from water baptism. See below, pp. 173-74. *Act. Thec.* 34. Tertullian discounted the document itself as a forgery. See also *Praescr.* 41.5 and *Virg.* 9.1.

42. *Bapt.* 17.2-3.

other context of baptism. Those arrested were catechumens and were baptized while in prison. Perpetua mentioned the presence of the Spirit in the water, but did not indicate the anointing, which may have been omitted because the bishop was not present to perform the ritual.[43] From the Spirit, she prayed for bodily endurance, an indication that the ritual might have been given to identify these confessors fully with the church and to prepare them for the ordeal they faced.[44] Thus, emergency baptism may have included only the washing and the profession of faith. The full efficacy of this abbreviated ritual would be both questioned and affirmed in Cyprian's time.[45]

## Baptismal Space, Time, and Elements

No specific information about the spaces used for baptism has survived, although Tertullian seems to have assumed an outdoor setting and full immersion in water. He made no distinction regarding the source of the water used for baptism. All kinds of water — from sea, pool, river, fountain, cistern, or even tub — were equally acceptable: the Tiber was as holy as the Jordan for the purpose.[46] Any season, day, or even hour was judged suitable for baptism, but Easter and the period of Pentecost were more solemn occasions. An all-night vigil for the celebration of Easter is not yet clearly attested in Africa. The difference in solemnity did not affect the grace imparted.[47]

## Images of Baptism: Biblical Typologies

In the introduction to his treatise *On Baptism,* Tertullian referred to Christians as "little fishes" who should follow the example of their *Ichthys,* Jesus.[48] This famous acrostic, which uses the letters of the Greek word for fish as the first letters of the words "Jesus Christ, Son of God, Savior,"[49] is particularly apt in this treatise to signal the importance of baptism in water. Tertullian went on to insist that, like fish, Christians are born in water and — in order to be safe — must continue to abide in the water. When he spoke of the water itself, he reminded his audience of the places in the sacred text where water appears, beginning from the time before creation when the Holy Spirit hovered over the water be-

---

43. *Pas. Perp.* 2.1, 3.5.
44. Cyprian would use these arguments for extending communion to penitents in anticipation of persecution. *Ep.* 57.2.2, 4.2.
45. Cypr. *Ep.* 69.12.1–14.2.
46. Tert. *Bapt.* 4.
47. Tert. *Bapt.* 19. On the Easter vigil, see *Ux.* 2.4.2.
48. Tert. *Bapt.* 1.3.
49. *Orac. Sibyl.* 8.217-50; see also Optat. *Parm.* 5.4-5.

fore heaven and earth were formed (Gen. 1:2). All water shares in the unoriginate nature of that primordial fluid; thus, water is more pleasing to God than all other elements. It alone, Tertullian insisted, was a perfect material and a vehicle for the divine. Water was the source of life: living creatures were brought forth from it, and humanity itself was created by mixing water with earth.[50] Water's nature allowed it to be penetrated by the Holy Spirit and thus empowered to sanctify. It had the ability to cleanse and wash, and it could be adapted by an angel to this purpose. Such angelic presence in water was exhibited in the story of the healing of the paralytic at Bethsaida (John 5:1-9).[51]

Other types or foreshadowings of baptism that Tertullian found in the Old Testament were the narratives of the Israelites' crossing the Red Sea, Moses' turning Marah's bitter water sweet by throwing a tree (a figure of the cross) into it, and Moses' bringing forth water from the rock in the wilderness. Continuing into the New Testament, he insisted that, from the time of his baptism, Christ was never without the sign of water: changing water to wine at Cana; offering living water at the Feast of Tabernacles; speaking to the Samaritan woman at the well; walking on water; crossing the sea; washing the disciples' feet; witnessing Pilate's hand-washing; and finally, having water gush forth from his wound at the Crucifixion.[52]

## Disputed Issues

### IRREGULAR OR HERETICAL BAPTISM

Tertullian's synopsis of the rite was written not as a set of instructions for performing baptism but as a polemical defense against certain practices that he viewed as deviant and threatening.[53] He cautioned his audience against these and explained the fundamental errors they embodied. In his opening chapter, in fact, he identified a certain female viper of the gnostic Cainite sect who taught an exceedingly poisonous doctrine that would destroy baptism and with it the souls of the already large number of people who had been taken in by her message. Her dangerous teaching, according to Tertullian, used the baptismal elements to attack the faith. Like all vipers, she avoided water; she apparently offered an alternative (and costly) initiatory ritual, which was much more pretentious than the church's simple rites of baptism in water.[54] This woman, whose gender disqualified her from teaching (1 Tim. 2:12), understood very

50. Tert. *Bapt.* 3-4.
51. Tert. *Bapt.* 5.
52. Tert. *Bapt.* 9.
53. See Robin Margaret Jensen, "With Pomp, Novelty, Avarice, and Apparatus: Alternative Baptismal Practices in Roman Africa," in *Studia Patristica* (Leuven: Peeters, 2010), 44:77-83.
54. Tert. *Bapt.* 2.

well how to kill the little Christians by taking them out of the water. Tertullian explained that the "little fishes" knew that they were safe only when they were born in water and abided in it, following their big fish, Jesus Christ.[55]

The counterfeit rituals offered by this woman and others like her were not the only competition for Christian baptism as Tertullian understood it. He noted that initiatory washings also took place in the mystery cults of Mithras and Isis, and he recalled that everyone at the Apollinarian and Pelusian games had themselves baptized in order to be reborn and receive impunity from divine retribution for broken oaths. Water was ritually sprinkled around temples, houses, and even cities to purify them. Statues of the gods were given ritual washings.[56] Tertullian then charged that such baptisms were works of the devil that were outwardly similar to the Christian washing but utterly different in their effects on participants. Like a widow's womb, the water of the pagan cults was barren.[57]

### THE BAPTISM OF JOHN

In addition to the problem of competing — and therefore false — rituals, Tertullian also commented on related issues that seem to have been contested by certain unnamed individuals or groups that were known to him personally. The first was whether John the Baptist's baptism of repentance was from heaven or earth (Matt. 21:25) and whether it was complete in itself or needed supplementing by the gift of the Holy Spirit (Acts 18:25; 19:2). Perhaps in order to undermine the validity of the earthly element of water used in baptism, those who argued that this baptism was incomplete pointed to the Baptist's own statement that another would follow him, baptizing in the Spirit and fire, and they noted that Jesus himself never baptized (John 4:2). Tertullian agreed that baptism administered before Jesus' Passion, Resurrection, and Ascension could not be effective. Although John's baptism was not itself heavenly, it prepared for heavenly things: the coming of Christ and his baptism that would confer the Holy Spirit along with remission of sins.[58]

### REPEATING BAPTISM

Tertullian also affirmed the unrepeatable nature of baptism, which may have been a contested issue in his time. Claiming a scriptural foundation for the

---

55. Tert. *Bapt.* 1-2.
56. Tert. *Bapt.* 5.
57. Tert. *Bapt.* 5.2.
58. Tert. *Bapt.* 10-11.

church's practice of conferring baptism only once, he cited John 13:10 ("one who has bathed does not need to wash") and Ephesians 4:5 ("one Lord, one faith, one baptism"). This position did not, however, imply the recognition of the baptism of heretics: since they claimed neither the same God nor the same Christ, they could neither receive nor give the same baptism.[59] Similarly, he contrasted the single Christian washing to the repeated ablutions practiced by Jews. Because it was defiled, Israel was commanded to wash every day, he explained. By contrast, Christians were to regard the application of baptismal water as permanently cleansing, not as an amusement for sinners.[60]

### BAPTISM AND MARTYRDOM

Immediately after insisting that baptism conferred inside the church was unrepeatable, Tertullian acknowledged a second washing: that of the martyrs in their own blood. Jesus referred to such baptism in the prophecy of his future passion (Luke 12:50), and the evangelist John implied it in writing that Jesus came by both water and blood (1 John 5:6). Tertullian explained that this double understanding of baptism was also prefigured in the water and blood coming from Christ's side in the passion narrative of the Gospel of John (19:34). Such a baptism did not invalidate an earlier washing; it could substitute for it, however, or even restore a water baptism ruined through subsequent grave sin.[61] Thus, Tertullian understood that martyrdom obtained salvation even for catechumens who were not yet admitted or penitents not yet restored to communion within the church. In fact, these exceptional individuals were privileged to go directly into Paradise, while the ordinary faithful had to wait for the Judgment.[62]

## Conclusion

Tertullian understood and presented baptism primarily as a means of separating oneself from the culture of demonic idolatry and adhering to the one true God through the following of Christ. He tended to identify the post-baptismal failures of Christians as a sliding back toward the ever-present lure of idolatry. Although many in the community were apparently satisfied with avoiding specific practices — such as traditional sacrifices and oaths — Tertullian urged a militant resistance to idolatry in all its forms.

59. Tert. *Bapt.* 12.3, 15; *Pud.* 19.5.
60. Tert. *Bapt.* 15.3.
61. Tert. *Bapt.* 16.
62. *Pas. Perp.* 4, 11.

The efficacy of baptism in cleansing from sin and sanctifying the recipient was based upon both the divine power, which was operative in the work of the angel and the coming of the Holy Spirit, and the human response, which was manifest in repentance of sin and profession of faith. Tertullian specified indirectly the integral role of the church in the ritual by asserting that heretical baptism could not be effective and that the minister should be a leader of the congregation or, in an emergency, someone among the (male) faithful. Though the ritual could not be repeated, baptism could be restored, or even replaced, through public confession of Christ under persecution. Tertullian did not reflect a community belief in any inherited sin that would have made the baptism of infants or children necessary for their salvation. Indeed, he asserted that sincere faith and a morally good life could secure the salvation of children and believing adolescents, whose baptism was delayed until they could make a responsible, personal commitment.

The frame of the African practice and understanding of baptism was already articulated in Tertullian's writings. As the situation of the church changed, new challenges would arise and force the clarification of certain issues. Tertullian's specification of the proper minister of baptism, for example, was a function only of good order within the church rather than of divine empowerment or authorization of the clergy through ordination. Still, these writings indicate points of disagreement among Christians, such as baptizing infants and repeating the ritual for converts from Christian heresy. At this time the church in Africa actually accepted a baptism performed in a heretical communion, although Tertullian's position requiring that a convert from a deviant form of Christianity be given a true baptism was affirmed and enforced by a council of bishops meeting under Agrippinus of Carthage shortly after Tertullian's death.[63]

## BAPTISM IN CYPRIAN'S TIME

Cyprian did not write a treatise on the ritual of baptism as Tertullian had. His letters do occasionally address issues related to baptism, such as the procedure followed in the baptism of infants and of catechumens who were dying. Toward the end of his episcopate, however, he engaged in a series of discussions with episcopal colleagues in Africa and an acrimonious debate with the Bishop of Rome over the status of persons who had been baptized outside the unity of their shared communion. The issues raised in this controversy would be the source of conflict and division in the African church in the fourth and fifth centuries.

Tertullian's discussion of baptism was shaped by the conflict with the Cainite minister who offered a radically different ritual. Cyprian's treatment of the

---

63. Cypr. *Ep.* 71.4.1; 73.3.1.

sacrament was influenced by the challenges of the Decian persecution and the competition with schismatic Christians following it. To the baptismal rejection of idolatry was added the adherence to the one church, which alone possessed and exercised the power to sanctify.

## The Ritual

Cyprian left no description of the baptismal ritual in Carthage, but enough references to the rite appear in his letters and treatises to reconstruct its shape in the middle of the third century. He insisted both that baptism was effective only in the unity of the true church, and that the bishops serving in that unity guaranteed the ritual's validity. In addition, Cyprian clearly regarded the rite of baptism as indivisible and insisted that immersion in water with the invocation of the Trinity could not be separated from the giving of the Holy Spirit, which normally was associated with the bishop's imposing hands on the newly baptized.[64]

The first stage of the ritual was the exorcism; the casting out of demons was intended to break their power over the candidate.[65] As has been seen in the writings of Tertullian, the presence and power of the demons were clearly evident to Christians living in the cities and towns of Africa. They were surrounded by statues and temples, by rituals and entertainments that not only challenged their exclusive cult of Christ and their rejection of idolatry but threatened to contaminate their persons. Touching the demonic altars, eating food sacrificed on them, inhaling the smoke of sacrificial victims or incense, or even looking at the statues of the Roman gods were all regarded as dangerous actions for Christians.[66] While Tertullian had mentioned a rite of exorcism,[67] documentary evidence for prescribed rituals of exorcism prior to baptism begins to appear in the middle of the third century.

The ritual of exorcism was thus an essential part of the cleansing of the catechumen. It prevented the power of Satan from penetrating and soiling the community that was set apart for the worship of the one true God revealed by Christ. That ceremony was carried out by a cleric assisting the bishop; it was performed repeatedly in the weeks leading up to baptism.[68] The greatest efficacy in breaking the power of the demons over a candidate, however, was located in the ritual of baptism itself. Just prior to the baptismal washing and

---

64. He insisted that the baptism by pouring water alone when performed by a presbyter for the dying was effective and that the baptismal washing performed in schism could not be counted as partially effective (*Ep.* 69.12.1–14.2).

65. Cypr. *Ep.* 69.15.2.

66. Cypr. *Laps.* 15-16, 23-26; *Ep.* 31.6.2-3. See also Minuc. *Oct.* 27.

67. See Tert. *Spec.* 26 and *An.* 39.

68. Cypr. *Ep.* 69.15.2.

profession of faith, the candidate made a formal, sworn renunciation of Satan and of idolatry in all its forms.[69] A Christian would have violated this oath by any subsequent participation in the Roman state cult.

The ritual of baptism proper began with the consecration of the water in the font. Like Tertullian, Cyprian emphasized the importance of the water bath as a cleansing prior to the reception of the Holy Spirit; unlike Tertullian, he insisted that the water must be purified specifically by a bishop. He argued that only a bishop who had received the Holy Spirit through proper ordination in succession from the Apostles and was serving within the unity of the church had the power to call down the Spirit to sanctify the water.[70] Here, as elsewhere, Cyprian seems to have thought of the Holy Spirit as a physical force that could be passed from one person to either another person or to a ritual element, such as water or oil, in sacramental actions.

Although Cyprian's writings provide no details on the procedure for washing, his polemic in favor of rebaptizing heretics and schismatics involved an appeal to the baptismal creed. During the ritual, the bishop asked the candidates individually for their assent to each portion of that formula. Thus the aspirant made a profession of Christian faith that followed set wording and included not only the Father, Son, and Holy Spirit, but the church itself as both the dwelling place of the Trinity and the means for receiving the forgiveness of sins and attaining everlasting life. The specific wording of one question was cited in the controversy: "Do you [singular] believe in the forgiveness of sins and eternal life through the holy church?"[71] This confession seems to have been part of the washing ritual. The creed professed by those initiated in schismatic sects made the same appeal to the church.[72]

Anointing with oil followed the washing and was essential to making a Christian. Cyprian explained that the one who received the chrism then acquired the grace of God, but he made no explicit connection between the anointing and the gift of the Spirit. Though Cyprian did not specify that the bishop himself performed the anointing, he did specify that the oil itself had been blessed earlier by the bishop in the celebration of the eucharist.[73] The next ritual, the imposition of hands, was assigned to the bishop and was clearly associated with the giving of the Holy Spirit to one already purified and anointed.[74] Some of the participants in the rebaptism controversy could compare this imposition of hands to the formal readmission of penitents into communion after their own period of cleansing.[75] This may indicate that the

---

69. Cypr. *Ep.* 13.5.3; *Laps.* 8; *Dom. orat.* 19; *Pat.* 12; *Fort.* 7; cf. Tert. *Spec.* 4, 24.
70. Cypr. *Ep.* 70.3.1; *Sent.* 18.
71. Cypr. *Ep.* 69.7.1-2; 70.2.1.
72. Cypr. *Ep.* 69.7.1-2; 70.2.1; 73.4.2.
73. Cypr. *Ep.* 70.2.2.
74. Cypr. *Ep.* 73.6.2, 9.1-2; 69.11.3; 72.1.2; 74.5.1.
75. Cyprian rejected this view: *Ep.* 71.2.2; 74.1.2.

newly baptized were brought before the congregation as a group for the imposition of hands.[76] The bishop then traced the sign of the cross of Christ on the forehead of the neophytes, marking them as elect of God, destined for eternal life.[77]

Having been purified through washing and sanctified by the giving of the Holy Spirit, the neophytes could join the community of the faithful for prayer and worship. They were welcomed by sharing of the kiss of peace.[78] The newly baptized immediately participated for the first time in the community's celebration of the eucharist. Unlike Tertullian, Cyprian did not mention their drinking milk and honey. He indicated that they received the bread and wine from the hands of the presiding bishop.[79]

One curious and unique ceremonial act associated with Cyprian and the church at Carthage was the kissing of the soles of the feet of the newly baptized. Cyprian discussed this rite in his letter to Bishop Fidus, who had asked whether he might baptize a baby younger than eight days old (the age of circumcision), and, if so, whether he also should kiss that baby's feet. The bishop may have regarded a child so recently born as still ritually impure.[80] Cyprian insisted not only that the bishop baptize the child, but also that he should kiss its feet. A child fresh from the creative hand of God could not be impure.[81] This exchange does not provide a clear indication that the ritual was performed in baptizing adults. Although evidence for this practice is unknown apart from Cyprian's letter of response, it may have been related or comparable to the ritual of foot washing, later evidenced elsewhere in Africa as well as in Milan, Gaul, and Spain.[82]

## Infant Baptism

Cyprian recounts a story of a baby still in the arms of her nurse who had been fed some food sacrificed to idols and then later vomited up the eucharistic bread and wine. He used it as a warning of the dangers of idolatry; for modern readers, it also provides evidence that infants received both baptism and eucharistic communion.[83] Such a practice contradicted Tertullian's recommendation

---

76. Cypr. *Ep.* 15.1.2; 16.2.3; 17.2.1; 69.11.3; 71.2.2; 73.6.2; 74.1.2. See below, p. 341, for a parallel ritual of reconciliation.

77. Cypr. *Ep.* 73.9.2; *Demet.* 22.

78. Cypr. *Ep.* 64.4.1-2.

79. Cypr. *Ep.* 63.8.3.

80. Cypr. *Ep.* 64.4.1. See G. W. Clarke, "Cyprian's Epistle 64 and the Kissing of Feet in Baptism," *The Harvard Theological Review* 66.1 (1973): 147-52.

81. Cypr. *Ep.* 64.4.2.

82. Aug. *Ep.* 55.18.33.

83. Cypr. *Laps.* 25.

that baptism should be postponed until a candidate was mature, able to confess the faith personally, and well established in a life of continence or marital chastity. Moreover, the conciliar letter from Cyprian and his episcopal colleagues, which was mentioned earlier in connection with the kissing of feet, responded to a question of just how early an infant might be baptized. It suggests that infant baptism was a fairly widespread practice. The question of timing also may indicate a concern with children who were in danger of death. The assembled bishops responded to Bishop Fidus's question that the church need not wait the full eight days prescribed in Jewish law for circumcision. They noted that the seven-day delay for circumcision was symbolic of the Resurrection of Christ on the eighth day, the basis for the spiritual circumcision of Christians. Since Jewish law had been superseded by the Christian gospel, a child could be baptized immediately after birth. Furthermore, they argued, baptism confers the same degree of grace, regardless of the age of the recipient.[84]

These two instances not only provide good evidence that the baptism of infants was perhaps more widely practiced in the middle of the third century than might have been the case a few decades earlier, but they also indicate that the precedent of circumcision was employed to justify the practice. Of course, the high rate of infant mortality in the ancient world could have made baptism of dying infants a fairly common practice among Christian families. A change in belief about the religious status of infants might also have been at work, adding a sense of urgency, even for the baptism of newborn children. In elaborating on his colleague's response to the question, Cyprian observed that, although infants could not have any sin of their own, another's sin was remitted in their baptism: they were born with that "ancient contagion of death" that came from Adam.[85]

## The Worthy Minister

Cyprian's understanding of the ritual of baptism performed inside and outside the unity of the church focused on the power of the minister to sanctify. Christ had founded the episcopal college upon the Apostles and granted to it the gift of the Holy Spirit. Only bishops who were members of that college shared its power to forgive sins. Thus, he asserted that bishops who separated themselves from the church were deprived of sanctifying power and could neither baptize nor celebrate the eucharist.[86] Cyprian also noticed that this problem of spiritual impotence could affect bishops within his own communion: some bishops

---

84. Cypr. *Ep.* 64.4.1–6.2.

85. Cypr. *Ep.* 64.5.2. Although the text of Romans 5:12 is not cited here or elsewhere in Cyprian's work, its influence is evident in linking the transmission of death and some sort of sin.

86. E.g., in the conciliar letter, Cypr. *Ep.* 70.

had failed during and after the Decian persecution; others proved to be partisans of the schismatics.[87]

Cyprian directly addressed the problem of ministers within the Catholic communion who were known to be unworthy: a sinful bishop lost the gift of the Holy Spirit. Consequently, a local community that knowingly supported an apostate or unworthy bishop shared his sin and was deprived of access to the sanctifying power of the church.[88] Moreover, other bishops who knowingly remained in communion with such a colleague were in danger of sharing his sin and losing their own standing within the episcopal college.[89] Bishops known to be sinful had to be removed from office by their colleagues or abandoned by their congregations if they refused to step down once excluded by their fellow bishops.[90]

More complex, and indeed unaddressed, was the question of Catholic bishops whose sin was secret and unknown. Although he insisted that a schismatic bishop's sin of rebellion against the unity of the church would harm his community and pollute even an unwitting convert,[91] Cyprian refused to extend this conclusion to a bishop secretly guilty of other sins within the Catholic communion. He believed that the rituals of the Catholic church would communicate sin only by informed support of the failed minister or communicant. Cyprian developed no explanation, however, for the efficacy of the ministry of a Catholic bishop who had lost the Holy Spirit through a secret sin, one that remained unknown to his colleagues and congregation. He may have trusted that God would not allow such a failure to persist. Indeed, he argued that one of the reasons God had allowed the Decian persecution was to expose and remove such unworthy ministers.[92] Similarly, when he himself was charged with being unworthy, he retorted that God would not have abandoned his congregation and allowed it to lose, unwittingly, access to the church's sanctifying power.[93] He did, however, explain that when baptism was erroneously withheld from a person converting from schism (a failure whose occurrence he acknowledged), the eucharistic communion itself (presided over by a holy bishop) would substitute by providing the purification and sanctification normally received in baptism.[94] A secretly unworthy bishop, however, would be an ongoing danger to the eucharistic communion he served, just as he might be to the convert he baptized.

Cyprian seems to have believed that the problem of unworthy ministers

87. Cypr. *Laps.* 6; *Ep.* 65; 67; 55.11.1-3; 59.10.1–11.3.
88. Cypr. *Ep.* 65.4.1-2; 67.3.1-2.
89. Cypr. *Ep.* 67.5.4, 9.1-3.
90. Cypr. *Ep.* 65.4.2; 68.
91. Cypr. *Ep.* 70.2.3; 72.1.1, 2.3.
92. Cypr. *Ep.* 65.3.2.
93. Cypr. *Ep.* 66.1.2, 7.1–8.3.
94. Cypr. *Ep.* 73.23.1-2.

hidden within the unity of the Catholic church could be addressed only when God had exposed them. Later writers agreed but recognized this problem as a flaw in Cyprian's sacramental theology and tried to discover just how God had solved the problem.

## Baptism and Martyrdom

Like Tertullian, Cyprian recognized that martyrdom or public confession under threat would substitute when baptism had not been received and would restore the efficacy of a baptism that had been soiled by subsequent sin. He explained that a catechumen who died in the confession of Christ would not be hindered by having failed to receive water baptism. In this way, he explained the salvation of the — presumably unbaptized — thief who confessed Christ on his cross.[95] During the Decian persecution — and even immediately after — he urged that those who had fallen into apostasy should redeem their situation by accepting any opportunity to reverse their sin through a public confession of Christ.[96] A schismatic, however, could not gain the reward of the Kingdom by confessing Christ while continuing to oppose the unity of the church.[97]

## Emergency Baptism

Adult catechumens threatened by a death other than by martyrdom, as well as dying infants, needed to be provided with baptism without delay. Although Cyprian insisted that the bishop was the proper administrator of baptism, he recognized that presbyters and deacons should reconcile penitents or baptize catechumens when a bishop could not be present. While he was himself in exile during the Decian persecution and many of his presbyters were no longer available, he specifically instructed the clergy still in Carthage to confer baptism when death threatened.[98] Yet, he unambiguously reserved to the bishop the right to impose hands on the newly baptized,[99] underscoring his claim that only the properly elected and ordained bishop had the power to bestow the Holy Spirit. He offered no theoretical explanation for the power of presbyters and deacons to perform the sacramental actions he required of them. Similarly,

---

95. Cypr. *Ep.* 73.22.1-2. This was not universal belief; see Firmilian of Casesarea in Cypr. *Ep.* 75.21.1.

96. Cypr. *Ep.* 19.2.3; *Laps.* 13, 36.

97. Cypr. *Ep.* 55.29.3.

98. Cypr. *Ep.* 18.2.1.

99. Cypr. *Ep.* 73.9.2.

---

unlike Tertullian and later Augustine, he made no explicit provision for baptism by lay Christians.[100]

The practice of granting emergency baptism to catechumens in danger of death raised the question of how the rite should be administered for a person unable to reach a baptismal font or not healthy enough to be immersed in water. In a letter to a fellow bishop, Cyprian addressed the efficacy of baptizing by sprinkling or pouring a presumably small amount of water on the gravely ill.[101] He asserted that God's blessings could not be weakened or diminished so long as both giver and receiver had total faith. Although the ritual was not at its "fullest" in the sprinkling, it still conferred God's benefits on those who believed. Cyprian further disapproved of the term *clinicus* to characterize as a "second-class Christian" someone who had received baptism in this way. He noted that the paralytic in the gospel (John 5) could have been so described.[102] He did, though somewhat disapprovingly, allow that those who were unconvinced that baptism by sprinkling was fully effective might be ritually immersed later, as long as this did not appear to denigrate the efficacy of the prior ritual.[103]

Cyprian seems to have assumed that an individual who received emergency baptism but survived would seek out the bishop for the imposition of hands and the other rituals to complete the shortened ceremony. If the person died, however, the baptism alone could be trusted to bring the fullness of saving grace.[104]

In like manner, the instructions that Cyprian issued for the care of the catechumens during persecution and plague indicate that the period of preparation should have been shortened if an unbaptized person was in imminent danger of death. This exception was already routine in the cases of the sick and imprisoned. The account of the martyrdom of Perpetua and Felicity indicates that these catechumens were baptized while awaiting martyrdom and that they were served in prison by deacons.[105] As has been noted, Cyprian made the same provision during the Decian persecution.[106]

---

100. Cypr. *Ep.* 18.1.2, 2.2.

101. Cypr. *Ep.* 69.12.1–14.2. The same issue was raised about the schismatic Novatian's own baptism; see Eus. Caes. *Hist. eccl.* 6.43.15.

102. Cypr. *Ep.* 69.12.1, 13.1-2.

103. Cypr. *Ep.* 69.13.3.

104. Cypr. *Ep.* 69.14.1-2. *Rebapt.* 5 assigns the supplemental gift of the Holy Spirit to the direct action of God in such a case.

105. *Pas. Perp.* 2.

106. Cypr. *Ep.* 18.2.1.

Like Tertullian, Cyprian interpreted certain scripture narratives as foreshadowings or figurative references to baptism. In his correspondence with his fellow bishop Caecilian of Biltha, he made the sweeping claim that every reference to water in the sacred text was a prophetic allusion to baptism. This included Moses' bringing water from the rock (Exod. 17:1-7), Christ's proclaiming himself the source of living water to the Samaritan woman (John 4:10), and his promise during the Feast of Tabernacles of water flowing from himself (John 7:37-38); all were fulfilled in the water gushing from Christ's side at his death (John 19:34).[107]

In a letter rejecting the value of the baptism performed by schismatics and heretics, Cyprian compared the church to Paradise — an enclosed garden with fruit-bearing trees watered by the four rivers that provided the salvific water of baptism. Only persons who were inside this garden, he claimed, could drink from those springs. The ground outside was dry and parched; the wretched petitioner would die of thirst.[108] Cyprian reminded his reader that the Lord welcomed the thirsty to receive the living water that flowed from his wound. The heretics, because they separated themselves from the church, had no access to this stream and its saving grace.[109]

## Baptismal Spaces

At the beginning of the third century, Tertullian had indicated that the baptismal water was often found outside an enclosed ritual space; by mid-century, Cyprian clearly supposed that normally it would be in an artificial enclosure within the building used for the assembly rather than in an open, natural site. The image of a sealed fountain to which heretics and schismatics had no access and descriptions of the rivers as not running outside of Paradise both imply that the baptismal pool was in an indoor space controlled by the church, probably one built especially for that ritual purpose.[110]

## The Maternal Church

Tertullian had described the water of baptism as absorbing the power of sanctifying when penetrated by the Holy Spirit.[111] He also referred to baptism as

107. Cypr. *Ep.* 63.8.1–9.1.
108. Cypr. *Ep.* 73.10.3.
109. Cypr. *Ep.* 73.11.1–12.1.
110. Cypr. *Ep.* 69.2.1; 73.10.3.
111. Tert. *Bapt.* 4.1. For a fuller discussion of this theme, see Robin Jensen, "Mater Ecclesia

rebirth and to the church as the mother's house.[112] In Cyprian's work, these maternal images were expanded and developed in support of his insistence that only the church could baptize. "You cannot have God for your Father unless you have the church as your Mother," he proclaimed.[113] Thence he argued that the fidelity of Christ to his bride meant that she alone bore God's children.[114] Using the imagery that the Song of Songs (4:12) applied to the beloved, he described the church as a walled garden whose sealed fountain was accessible only to the faithful, not to heretics and schismatics.[115]

The image of the church as mother was central to Cyprian's thinking about baptism, as it validated his idea of the church as a family whose unity was essential to its identity. The baptized were all children born from the same two parents (God and the church). To separate oneself from this family was thereby to effect one's own disinheritance. Schismatics not only abandoned the protection and promise of salvation offered within the church; by tearing the sacred fabric or familial bond, they literally became her enemies. They were condemned to death for "cursing their mother" (Matt. 15:4).[116] In his treatise on the unity of the church, however, Cyprian borrowed a more benevolent analogy of the earth as a mother whose fertility, abundance, and nurture were beyond measure.[117] The church had a prolific womb and life-giving breasts; she was also inviolate, chaste, and modest, with only one home and one bedchamber. Schismatic and heretical communities were, by comparison, adulterous mothers of bastard children.[118]

The maternal nature of the church seems to have run deeply in African Christian piety. Not only did Tertullian and Cyprian appeal to it when establishing controversial doctrines, but it is found in art as well. From the late fourth-century basilica at Thabraca, the tomb mosaic of a woman named Valentia shows a schematic image of a church building with the legend *Ecclesia Mater* (fig. 132).

and the Fons Aeterna: The Church and Her Womb in Ancient Christian Traditions," in *A Feminist Companion to Patristic Literature,* ed. Amy-Jill Levine with Maria Mayo Robbins (London and New York: T&T Clark, 2008), 137-55.

112. Tert. *Bapt.* 20; *Or.* 2.6.
113. Cypr. *Unit. eccl.* 6; see also *Ep.* 74.7.2.
114. Cypr. *Ep.* 74.6.2, 7.2.
115. Cypr. *Ep.* 73.11.1-2; 74.11.2.
116. Cypr. *Ep.* 73.19.2.
117. Cypr. *Unit. eccl.* 5, 19.3; *Laps.* 2.
118. Cypr. *Unit. eccl.* 6.

### THE POWER TO BAPTIZE

During the Decian persecution, conflict arose over the power to forgive sins and grant readmission to penitents who had been excluded from the communion of the church. Some of the clergy in Carthage honored the letters of recommendation provided by the confessors and martyrs to Christians who had failed to confess Christ when challenged by the imperial authorities. Cyprian insisted that only Christ could forgive this sin and might do so in the Judgment. In anticipation of that event, Christ had authorized the bishops to judge the adequacy of repentance and to allow the penitent to be reconciled to the church.[119] The dissidents formed a distinct communion that relied on the intercession of the martyrs. They eventually established their own bishops and challenged the authority of Cyprian and his colleagues. Cyprian then extended his argument from the local bishop, based on the figure of Peter in Matthew (16:18-19), to the unity of the episcopal college. Christ had first given to Peter alone the power to bind and loose, thereby demonstrating that it was a single power; it could not be divided among competing bishops. Immediately after the Resurrection, Christ then conferred the same power on all the Apostles at once, showing that it could be shared among cooperating bishops. Furthermore, Christ identified the power to forgive as the gift of the Holy Spirit (John 20:22-23). Cyprian explained that the Apostles were established as the episcopal college. This union of all bishops held the power to sanctify in common and exercised it individually for their local churches. Acting together, they transmitted it to their successors in the college.[120]

When the schismatic bishops began to baptize catechumens into their communions, Cyprian and his colleagues denied them the power of forgiveness necessary for that ritual. Because the schismatic ministers were in rebellion against the unity of the episcopal college, they could not share its gift of the Holy Spirit. They could not forgive sins; they could not sanctify water for washing or oil for anointing; they could not confer the Holy Spirit.[121]

The influence of these arguments was evident in Cyprian's consideration of the status of the baptism conferred by John the Baptist. In one instance, he used John as an example of the baptizer's need for the gift of the Holy Spirit: John had received it while still in his mother's womb so that he would be prepared

---

119. Cypr. *Ep.* 33.1.1-2; *Laps.* 29; *Ep.* 59.5.1; 66.3.1-3.

120. Cypr. *Unit. eccl.* 4-6. The critical chapters were written in at least two stages, as Maurice Bévenot's *The Tradition of MSS: A Study in the Transmission of St. Cyprian's Treatises* (Oxford: Oxford University Press, 1961) and his introduction to the text in CCSL 3:244-47 have demonstrated from the manuscript evidence.

121. Cypr. *Ep.* 70.1.3–2.3; 71.3.2; 69.11.1-3; 73.6.2–7.2; 74.7.3.

to baptize Christ when the time came.[122] Later, however, he contested John's status, remarking on the contrast between his baptism and that of a Christian deacon. Peter and John had only laid hands on the Samaritans who were baptized by Philip within the unity of the church (Acts 8:14-17),[123] but Paul had rebaptized those originally baptized by John (Acts 19:1-7). John's baptism, he contended, could not substitute for that given within the unity of the church. If the baptism of Christ's precursor could not be accepted, he then argued, how much less that of his heretical and schismatic enemies?[124] The saving power of the Spirit, he concluded, could be exercised only in the unity of the one church.

Thus Cyprian located the power to sanctify in the communion of the bishops spread throughout the world, which had itself been established by Christ with the Apostles as its original members. Each bishop received this power by being inducted into the college by some of its current members; each made its power available in his local church. Anyone outside such a church community and separated from the episcopal college, therefore, had no access to the power and could neither confer nor receive sanctity. Although Cyprian may be presumed to have extended this power to the presbyters and deacons whom he directed to care for the sick and dying during the persecution, he never spoke of the laity as sharing or exercising the gift of sanctifying.[125]

THE REBAPTISM CONTROVERSY

In the wake of the Decian persecution, the Christian community at Carthage broke into three competing groups. The split occurred over the question of admitting to communion those who had denied Christ. The consequences of this schism became painfully apparent when a member of one community transferred to another. For each of the three bishops in Carthage, this raised the problem of recognizing a baptism performed by a rival bishop outside his own communion and thus apart from "the one true church." The communion in Africa to which Tertullian and Cyprian adhered had earlier recognized such baptism but reversed itself in the 220s by deciding to submit such converts to the efficacious baptism of the true church.[126] The aftermath of the Decian

---

122. Cypr. *Ep.* 69.11.2.

123. Cypr. *Ep.* 73.9.1-2.

124. Cypr. *Ep.* 73.24.3–25.1. Firmilian of Caesarea repeated this point (Cypr. *Ep.* 75.8).

125. Cypr. *Ep.* 18.1.2; 19.2.1.

126. Reference was made to this council in the writings associated with the subsequent controversy: see Cypr. *Ep.* 71.2.1; 43.3.1. In *Ep.* 75.19.3, Firmilian of Caesarea specified that the Africans had changed their earlier practice of accepting heretical baptism. This change was made in the council under Agrippinus. Maier estimates that Agrippinus's council was in the 220s: Jean-Louis Maier, *L'épiscopat de l'Afrique romaine, vandale, et byzantine* (Rome: Institut suisse de Rome, 1973), 18.

---

persecution required the bishops to reassess the implications of this position on baptismal exclusivity and efficacy. When some of the laxists who had broken away from Cyprian's communion repented their rebellion and returned, they were accepted into his church's care as penitents. They had originally been baptized in the true church, and their baptism was not lost by their sin of schism, just as it had not been lost by apostasy. These deserters were received back into Catholic communion through the imposition of hands in penance, as the apostate idolaters eventually had been after the persecution.[127] When some who had joined the laxist communion as catechumens and had subsequently been baptized in it converted to Cyprian's church, however, they were treated not as penitent Christians but as pagans who had never been baptized.

This latter policy ran counter to the practice of the church in Rome, which received into its communion converts baptized in schismatic communities by the imposition of hands alone, rather than by a full baptismal ritual. Its bishop admitted converts from competing communities into fellowship by the ritual for reconciling Christian penitents rather than by the ritual of baptism. The Roman bishops, it should be noted, were dealing primarily with converts who had been rigorist schismatics, who had denied that the church and its bishops had power and authority to forgive the sin of apostasy. Placing their trust in the church's power to forgive post-baptismal sin by the imposition of hands could, then, be accepted as an appropriate demonstration of the sincerity of their rejection of the rigorist belief from which they were turning.[128]

Cyprian, in contrast, was facing a rebellion primarily by laxists who did not restrict sanctifying power to the bishop. Against such opponents, he consistently argued that schismatic bishops did not share the church's gift of holiness and were thus incapable of sanctifying converts in baptism. Instead of cleansing, the rebel leaders actually soiled those whom they washed with the water polluted by their rituals; their contagious touch infected recipients with idolatry; their oil marked people as sinners.[129] Anyone bearing the contagion of such a sacrilegious ritual could pass from the realm of idolatry into that of faithful worship only by being purified in the baptism of the true church founded by Christ upon the Apostles.

The African bishops' adamancy in rejecting the validity of baptism performed in heresy or schism can be understood as a function of their horror of both idolatry and schism. The one rejected Christ and the other the church. Salvation, they judged, was possible only for those who accepted these two as

---

127. Cypr. *Ep.* 71.2.1-2. Cyprian regarded schism as a kind of apostasy (*Ep.* 43.3.1-2).

128. The ancient record provides no Roman explanation of the practice other than a reliance on the efficacy of the name of Christ. For a fuller discussion, see J. Patout Burns, *Cyprian the Bishop* (London: Routledge, 2002), 128-30; and "On Rebaptism: Social Organization in the Third-Century Church," *Journal of Early Christian Studies* 1 (1993): 399.

129. Cypr. *Ep.* 65.4.1-2; 67.9.1-3; 70.2.2-3; 72.1.1.

inseparable. The admission of such persons to communion could be accomplished only by a ritual that could effect the transition from pollution to purity: they required a full bath in sanctified water before hands could be imposed to confer the Holy Spirit.

Cyprian and his colleagues recognized that their practice was an innovation and not universally approved; their predecessors in Africa had received heretics by the imposition of hands alone, and some overseas bishops continued to do so. In the face of widespread apostasy and the challenge of schism, however, the African rejection of alien rituals some thirty years earlier proved its worth and was firmly upheld by Cyprian and his colleagues. Like Tertullian, they found scriptural support for their position in the Acts of the Apostles, especially in the rebaptism of the Ephesians who had received only the baptism of John (Acts 19:1-7).[130] They also argued that receiving converts from schism with the imposition of hands alone would imply that their idolatry and other sins had been forgiven earlier through water cleansed and sanctified outside their church. This in turn implied that their rivals must be true bishops who shared the gift of the Holy Spirit.[131] Because they believed that the church could not be divided into competing parties, they could not recognize the sanctifying power of bishops in a competing communion without thereby abandoning their own claims to be the true church and to mediate salvation.[132] The African position, in contrast to the Roman one, recognized baptism as valid only when administered by a duly consecrated bishop (or his clerical delegate) in good standing within the unity of the true church.

This question of the validity of baptism could not be settled by each local church, since bishops recognized one another and entered into a network of congregations that shared communion, throughout Africa and beyond the sea.[133] Thus, a Christian who had been baptized and participated in the eucharist in a church in any place would expect to be admitted to communion (upon presentation of proper credentials) in any other Christian church.[134] Because of their responsibility to this universal communion, the bishops of Roman Africa determined and implemented common policies on the recognition of baptism and the reconciliation of sinners. Each could be assured that anyone admitted to one local communion by its bishop would have met the purity standards of all.[135] Lists of recognized bishops were even distributed so that a visitor's bap-

130. Cypr. *Ep.* 73.9.1; *Rebapt.* 4; cf. Tert. *Bapt.* 10.

131. Cypr. *Ep.* 70.3.1; 71.1.2; 73.11.3, 25.2; 74.4.2, 7.3.

132. Cypr. *Ep.* 33.1.2; 69.3.1; 70.3.1; 73.25.2; 74.4.2; *Unit. eccl.* 6-8.

133. Local bishops were allowed to proceed as they saw fit in both reconciling apostates and accepting schismatics (Cypr. *Ep.* 55.21.1-2; 72.3.2). Still, those who did not agree with the majority were warned not to act rashly (Cypr. *Ep.* 64.1.1-2).

134. Cypr. *Ep.* 48.3.1, on the assumption that the bishops leading the communities were in communion.

135. Cypr. *Ep.* 64.

tismal credentials could be verified and bishops could evaluate the correspondence they received.[136]

The prohibition of the repetition of true baptism was so generally established in the church by the middle of the third century that it served as a major premise for both sides in the subsequent controversy over rebaptism between the bishops of Africa and Italy. The Roman bishop would rely on the power of Christ himself to authorize his position: baptizing a second time would dishonor the name of Christ that had been invoked when the ritual was originally performed in heresy or schism. For their part, the African bishops focused on the unity and holiness of the church. They believed the baptismal ritual had to be repeated because it could not be effectively performed outside the unity of the true church and, thus, without the Holy Spirit.[137]

## Conclusion

Through his polemical writings on the function of the church and the bishops in securing the efficacy of baptism, Cyprian provided information about the role of the bishop in sanctifying water and oil. Although he clearly distinguished parts of the ritual and allowed different ministers for each, he insisted on the integrity of the rite as a whole. The washing could not be separated and performed outside the church; even in the attenuated form of sprinkling over the sick, it alone would supply the salvific grace of the full ritual. Cyprian did not exclude baptism performed by the laity explicitly; his focus on the role of the bishop may have led him to neglect that resource, however, even in emergencies.

The conciliar letter to Bishop Fidus on infant baptism contradicted Tertullian's assertion that this was unnecessary and inappropriate for sinless infants by assigning to the newborn the contagion of mortality resulting from Adam's sin. The developed theory of inherited guilt, however, did not appear before Augustine's work in the fifth century.

Finally, Cyprian's use of the image of the church as bride and mother began its long career in the African practice of baptism. His maternal analogies, with their emphasis on the importance of familial bonds, reappeared in the writings of Optatus and Augustine against the schismatic communities of their own times. They understood the church's maternal role in a more complex way, which allowed for a broader sense of God's family — one that included even those born to different or surrogate "mothers."

136. This African list was provided to the Bishop of Rome for the same purpose (Cypr. *Ep.* 59.9.3).

137. Cypr. *Ep.* 73.20-25.

This treatise has not been assigned to any known author; this may have been the author's intent because its thesis would have been controversial at the time of composition. The writer defended the acceptance of baptism performed outside the unity of the church as though its rejection were a recent innovation and addressed some of the arguments that were used by Cyprian. Thus, it has been assigned to a North African writer, and usually dated after the outbreak of the controversy between the African bishops and their Roman colleague. However, the shift in North African practice to which the author objects was already decades old by the time that conflict broke out. Hence, the treatise could have been composed before Cyprian's letters on the topic, which then would have been responding to its arguments. The *Treatise on Rebaptism,* then, might have been one of the documents circulating in advance of the council on September 1, 256, at which the African bishops supporting Cyprian's position rejected any baptism performed outside the church.[138]

## The Ritual

As in the writings of Cyprian, remarks about the ritual of baptism itself are incidental to the argument of the *Treatise on Rebaptism.* It does indicate that the profession of faith was made in response to questions posed by the bishop during the water baptism. Apparently not every bishop had mastered the creed, so the interrogation was sometimes muddled. The imposition of the bishop's hands for the giving of the Holy Spirit normally followed the washing immediately.[139]

The author recognized that the Trinitarian formula for baptizing was — and indeed ought to be — used in the church.[140] The invocation of the name of Jesus alone, however, could be legitimated by Acts (4:12) and Philippians (2:9-11), as well as by appeal to the text of Matthew (7:22), in which even those who were not true Christians called upon that name effectively.[141]

Additionally, according to the author of the treatise, some heretics de-

---

138. For a discussion of the dating, see Graeme W. Clarke, *The Letters of St. Cyprian of Carthage* (New York: Newman Press, 1984), 4:223, n. 12. Geoffrey Dunn has argued that the treatise might be identified with the letter which Bishop Iubianus sent to Cyprian (*Ep.* 73.4.1); see Geoffrey D. Dunn, *Cyprian and the Bishops of Rome: Questions of Papal Primacy in the Early Church,* Early Christian Studies 11 (Strathfield, NSW, Australia: St. Pauls, 2007), 167-68. It does deal with the problem of schismatic — as distinguished from heretical — baptism, which was the issue in Cyprian's time but which was not addressed by Tertullian.

139. *Rebapt.* 10.

140. *Rebapt.* 7.

141. *Rebapt.* 6-7.

ceived themselves and the faithful by requiring another form of baptism, in fire. Using the false text *The Preaching of Paul,* they arranged a baptism in which, by some human subterfuge or demonic action, fire seemed to flash from the water when the candidate entered it. The author explained that the proponents of such baptism failed to recognize that in speaking of Jesus baptizing with fire, the Gospels (Matt. 3:11; Luke 3:16) referred to the gift of the Holy Spirit.[142]

The treatise contends that baptism in the name of Jesus cannot be lost. In one instance, however, the author seems to have questioned this point. In dealing with Christians who leave the church to receive the "perfect" baptism by fire that the heretics offered, he warned that they would thereby lose what they had already received. Comparing baptism to a military oath, he argued that a soldier who left the camp in which he had first sworn his oath and then swore another oath in the enemy's camp lost his status in the first.[143] If the analogy is read too closely, it would imply the destruction of the water baptism, during which such an oath was sworn. Since, however, this interpretation runs against the grain of the treatise, the point may have been that the standing in the church conferred by spirit baptism would be lost by the apostasy.

### Contribution to the Controversy

The *Treatise on Rebaptism* laments the arrogance of certain leaders of the church who had challenged the apostolic tradition of accepting water baptism performed outside the unity of the church.[144] In other words, its author challenged the position taken by Tertullian, Agrippinus, and Cyprian that any baptism performed outside the "true church" would be invalid. To counter the arguments brought forth for this perceived change in what it considers apostolic tradition, the treatise distinguishes baptism in the name of Jesus Christ — by water through the invocation of Jesus and by blood through the confession of Christ unto death — from the baptism of the Holy Spirit, which was usually linked to the imposition of the bishop's hands.[145] It argues that the baptism of the Spirit may be given apart from water or blood baptism, either directly by God or through the mediation of the bishop.

No one disputed the efficacy of emergency baptism in water performed by a lower cleric to secure salvation for a dying catechumen, as long as that recipient had true faith and repentance, even if the bishop was not available to impose hands.[146] A scriptural precedent for this salvation by water baptism alone

---

142. *Rebapt.* 16-17.
143. *Rebapt.* 16.
144. *Rebapt.* 1. The reference could be to either Agrippinus or Cyprian.
145. *Rebapt.* 3. *Rebapt.* 7 does not distinguish the efficacy of the name of Jesus from that of the Trinity, which Matt. 28:19 specified as the formula.
146. *Rebapt.* 4-5. Otherwise, the unavailable bishop would be guilty of the loss of the soul.

could be found in Philip's baptism of the Ethiopian eunuch, who went his way apparently without the gift of the Holy Spirit, unlike the Samaritans baptized earlier by the same Philip upon whom the apostles imposed their hands (Acts 8).[147] Assuming that no one could be saved without the Holy Spirit, the treatise then argues that God must give the Spirit directly in such cases.[148] Similarly, the blood baptism realized when a martyr died for the confession of Christ was effective because God gave the Spirit directly and without the imposition of a bishop's hands.[149] The recipient of such baptism must have true faith and repentance: a heretic could not be saved — by either water or blood — through calling upon Jesus in name only and not in truth.[150] Cyprian, it will be recalled, agreed on that point: the martyrs and the sick who were baptized by sprinkling could be saved without the ministration of the bishop, so long as they confessed the true faith within the unity of the church.

The treatise approaches the problem of baptism performed outside the church through the analysis of a water baptism with invocation of the name of Christ in which the recipient did not have true faith or repentance. Such a case was identified in scripture by noting the response of the apostles and disciples of Christ to his passion and death. Their rejection of his predictions of the Passion, their abandonment and even denial of Christ at his arrest clearly indicated, the treatise argues, that they did not yet have true faith — although they were themselves already baptized and were baptizing others. According to the scripture, however, they did not require a new baptism in water; instead God corrected their faith and forgave their sins by baptizing them in the Holy Spirit at Pentecost. This precedent was then applied to those schismatics baptized in water outside the church. Upon their repentance within the church or their coming to it from a heretical communion, the water baptism should be supplemented only by spirit baptism through the imposition of the bishop's hands.[151]

Christ's warning that some who worked miracles in his name would not be saved by calling on him (Matt. 7:22-23) demonstrated that his name could be effectively invoked by those who were not true Christians.[152] By implication, water baptism could be conferred in the name of Jesus, even when it was not salvific.

To meet the objection that the faith of those giving and receiving water baptism outside the church was false, the treatise advanced two arguments about baptism within the unity of the church. It recalled that the disciples of Jesus themselves lacked proper faith during his earthly ministry, even though

147. *Rebapt.* 4. Both narratives are in Acts 8.
148. *Rebapt.* 3.
149. *Rebapt.* 11-12.
150. *Rebapt.* 12-13.
151. *Rebapt.* 6, 8-9.
152. *Rebapt.* 7.

they both received and conferred baptism.[153] Closer to home, it observed that bishops within the unity of the church were sometimes no more worthy to minister the sacraments than heretics and schismatics. Some were sinful, though not yet exposed and deposed or excommunicated. Others were so incompetent that they did not get the wording of the prayers and interrogations right, and the recipients had no idea what creed they were affirming. Yet, none of these baptisms were repeated if and when their inadequacies were discovered.[154] Cyprian, as has been noted above, overlooked the problem of incompetence and seems to have judged that only God could solve that of hidden wickedness.

Therefore, the treatise concludes, baptism in the name of Jesus by water or blood became salvific when it was supplemented by spirit baptism. That spirit baptism was normally conferred by the bishop's hands immediately after water baptism in the church, but it could also be given directly by God either before or after baptism in water or blood.[155] The same must be recognized for those who received water baptism in heresy or schism: they were to be welcomed into the unity and truth of the church by the imposition of the bishop's hands, not a repetition of water baptism.[156]

The general argument of the *Treatise on Rebaptism* is that the saving baptism of the Spirit can be given before or after — and thus independently of — water or blood baptism.[157] Therefore, it argues, the church should either confer the complete rite of baptism at once or should supplement an earlier invocation of the name of Jesus by the imposition of hands to confer the Holy Spirit.[158]

## Conclusion

The theology of the *Treatise on Rebaptism* placed all the power of baptism in the gift of the Holy Spirit and assigned little efficacy to the water baptism in the name of Jesus or the Trinity. It affirmed the belief of Cyprian that true faith and the gift of the Holy Spirit could not be realized outside the unity of the church. It also accepted Tertullian's view that true faith wins the forgiveness of sins.[159] It insisted, against them both, that even those outside the church and not sharing its faith could effectively call upon the name of Jesus to perform baptism in water or receive baptism in blood. Nevertheless, it conceded that such baptisms became salvific only when supplemented by the spirit baptism given either through the church's ministry or directly by God. The analysis of

153. *Rebapt.* 9.
154. *Rebapt.* 10.
155. *Rebapt.* 10.
156. *Rebapt.* 4, 6, 10.
157. *Rebapt.* 5.
158. *Rebapt.* 15.
159. *Rebapt.* 18.

emergency water baptism performed in the absence of a bishop's imposition of hands was foundational to this argument.

Somewhat contrary to Cyprian but in anticipation of Augustine, the treatise argued that baptism could be, and even during apostolic times had been, both conferred and received by persons within the unity of the church who lacked true faith and repentance. Still, the *Treatise on Rebaptism* never compared directly those who received baptism within the church to those who received it outside, as Augustine would in the fifth century.

## THE CONTROVERSY OVER BAPTISM IN THE FOURTH CENTURY

### The Donatist Schism

In the fourth century, the earlier conflict within the church in Africa and the church in Rome over the practice of rebaptizing persons originally baptized in schism and heresy occasioned a major division within the African church. This schism occurred at the end of the Diocletian persecution and divided the African church into a party headed by Caecilian and its rival under the leadership first of Majorinus and then of Donatus. The competing claims to the episcopal see of Carthage required the overseas churches to decide which of the claimants should be recognized. The Donatist party asserted that Caecilian had been tainted by association with a consecrator who was guilty of the crime of *traditio,* turning over the scriptures or sacred vessels to be destroyed.[160] Eventually, they also charged that he had himself committed apostasy through his own collaboration with the persecutors.[161]

Ecclesiastical authorities in Rome were first asked to decide the controversy, and then a council of bishops in Gaul served as a court of appeal. Both decided that Caecilian was the duly elected Bishop of Carthage and declared him free of the crime of apostasy. The latter court condemned the practice of rebaptizing converts from heresy and schism, which had been followed and defended by the African church for nearly a century.[162] Caecilian and his col-

---

160. Felix of Aptungi. The imperial documents collected in the appendix to the text of Optatus of Milevis show that this was also a falsification. See *Parm.* appendix 2 (CSEL 26:197-204).

161. The Donatist version of *Act. Abit.* 20 claims that Caecilian was responsible for their deaths by starvation because he prevented Christians from supplying them with food during their incarceration in Carthage. The Roman authorities jailed but did not execute them. An English translation of this version is provided by Maureen Tilley in *Donatist Martyr Stories: The Church in Conflict in Roman North Africa* (Liverpool: Liverpool University Press, 1996), 25-50. J.-L. Maier argues that this version of the *acta* is a piece of Donatist propaganda composed nearly a century after the alleged events. See Jean-Louis Maier, *Le dossier du donatisme,* 2 vols. (Berlin: Akademie Verlag, 1987), 1:57-92.

162. The specification concludes the letter of the bishops' meeting at Arles to the Roman bishop, Sylvester. It was preserved in Optat. *Parm.* appendix 4 (CSEL 26:206-8).

---

leagues accepted the judgment of their overseas colleagues and desisted from the practice of rebaptism. They thereby gained the approval of the whole Catholic communion outside Africa, as well as the financial and administrative support of the imperial government.[163]

The Donatist party not only refused to accept the verdict of the ecclesial courts in Italy and Gaul but applied the traditional baptismal practice of the African church to the resulting schism. They characterized those baptized by Caecilian, his supporters, or any of their successors as no different from unbaptized pagans. Thus, anyone who deserted the Caecilianist communion to join the Donatists had to agree that the Catholic ritual had not made them Christian because it had been performed by a bishop who was tainted by apostasy and did not share the gift of the Holy Spirit. The Donatists also followed Cyprian's theology in claiming that the Caecilianist baptism and communion actually contaminated its recipients with the sins of apostasy or idolatry. The Christians throughout the world, who had maintained communion with Caecilian despite being warned of his sin, shared his guilt and were likewise deprived of the power to baptize. The Donatist party in Africa claimed that it alone remained the true and faithful church.

The Donatist leaders did not, however, universally apply and enforce the requirement of rebaptism. Donatus of Carthage maintained communion with bishops in Mauretania even though they received Catholic converts who refused to be rebaptized. That practice was subsequently approved by a council of 270 Donatist bishops after Deuterius of Macriana admitted a whole Catholic congregation in this way.[164]

In about 347, the western emperor Constans sent the imperial notaries Macarius and Paul to Africa on a mission of unifying the Donatist and Caecilianist communions. Their project ended in an armed conflict with the forces mustered by the Donatist bishop of Bagai in Numidia, and an attempted suppression of that communion.[165] The emperor Julian reversed this program: he allowed the Donatist leaders exiled under Constans to return and reclaim the basilicas they had lost.[166] The returning Donatist bishops not only purified the churches and their former congregants but rebaptized those who had been baptized by Caecilianists during the intervening fifteen years.[167] Rebaptism of

---

163. The surviving documents, with explanatory notes, are collected in Maier, *Le dossier du donatisme,* vol. 1.

164. Augustine cited Tyconius as his source for this information (*Ep.* 93.10.43). The council is dated in 336 by Paul Monceaux, *Histoire littéraire de l'Afrique chrétienne depuis les origines jusqu'à l'invasion arabe* (Brussels: Culture et civilisation, 1963), 4:333-34.

165. A reference to the mission and its purpose is found in the speech of Gratus, Catholic Bishop of Carthage, which opened the council held after this action (*Con. Carth.* a. 345-48; CCSL 149:3.9-14).

166. A citation of the text of the rescript and an explanation of its consequences were reported by Augustine in *Petil.* 2.97.224. See also Optat. *Parm.* 2.16.

167. Optat. *Parm.* 1.2; 4.4; 6.1, 6, 8.

Caecilianist converts continued to be the characteristic practice[168] of Donatist bishops thereafter.

Donatus of Carthage had died in the exile imposed by Constans. When Julian allowed the bishops to return, Parmenian became Bishop of Carthage and leader of the Donatist party even though he was not a native African. In a letter to which both Optatus of Milevis and Augustine later replied, he may have attempted to address a problem inherent in Cyprian's sacramental theology: a secretly unworthy bishop within the true church did not have the Holy Spirit and thus lacked the power to sanctify. Optatus noted that Parmenian appealed to five endowments of the true church — chair, bishop, font, seal, and altar — as guarantees of the holiness of the church and the efficacy of its rituals.[169] Petilian, the Donatist Bishop of Constantina, first in writing to his own clergy and then in responding to Augustine's criticism of that letter, seems to have remained closer to Cyprian's own view that rituals were sanctifying when performed within the true church and that, as a consequence, sin was transmitted there only by informed consent.[170]

These Donatist theologians followed Cyprian's explanation that Christ had given the power to baptize to his Apostles (excepting only Judas, the apostate and betrayer) and that it had been continued in the church by the bishops who were faithful to Christ.[171] Bishops preserved their fidelity not by maintaining ethical or moral purity[172] but by avoiding apostasy, betrayal, and communion with those who had failed.[173] Those who had not betrayed their faith in Christ had the power to communicate the faith and holiness of Christ in their sacramental ministry.[174] The holiness that the Donatists attributed to their bishops was adhesion to the proper church body and maintaining complete fidelity to Christ. Ethical lapses could be tolerated as long as they did

168. A decree of Valentinian I in February 373 so characterized them (*C.Th.* 16.6.1); similarly, in a letter of a Roman synod, dealing with the opponents of Damasus, reproduced in Maier, *Le dossier du donatisme,* 2:53-54; the full text is in Gian Domenico Mansi, *Sacrorum Conciliorum Nova et Amplissima Collectio,* ed. Jean-Baptiste Martin et al. (Paris: expensis H. Welter, 1901), 3:624-27. The practice might not have been universal even in the second half of the fourth century. A proposal of the Catholic bishops to accept in their offices Donatist bishops who had not rebaptized Catholics indicates that there were some. These, however, may not have received any converts at all and been saved by that circumstance. *Bru. Hipp.* 37.

169. Optat. *Parm.* 2.9-10; 5.3. Augustine's own analysis of Parmenian's letter does not mention this interpretation. He cites texts of Parmenian requiring the fidelity and holiness of the bishop administering baptism (*Parm.* 2.4.8, 6.11, 7.12-13).

170. Augustine pointed out in *Petil.* 1.4.5–5.6 that while this might protect the recipient from sin, it did not provide an explanation of the efficacy of the sacrament.

171. Aug. *Parm.* 2.4.8; *Petil.* 2.22.49, 32.72.

172. Aug. *Parm.* 2.7.13; *Cresc.* 2.28.36.

173. These were the sins that the Donatists insisted had disqualified the Caecilianist bishops: Aug. *Petil.* 2.8.17, 7.14, 32.72, 33.77. They also added the sin of persecuting the true church: Aug. *Petil.* 2.53.121, 77.171, 78.173, 92.202, 103.236.

174. Aug. *Parm.* 2.8.15; *Petil.* 1.4.5; 3.52.64–54.66; *Ep. ad cath.* 24.68; *Cresc.* 3.7.7.

not touch directly on faith.[175] Once the emperors began suppressing idolatry in the last decades of the fourth century, the only real danger for a Donatist bishop was joining the communion of the Caecilianists, whom they considered apostates.[176] Such an act of apostasy itself conveniently removed the offending bishop from office in the Donatist communion. Thus the Donatist church was effectively immune from contamination by apostasy and securely maintained its power to sanctify.

The literature of the controversy does not indicate differences in the baptismal rituals of the two parties but focuses instead on the way the ritual was used.[177] The Caecilianist bishops received converts from the Donatist communion as baptized Christians, through the ritual of the imposition of hands.[178] Such converts were usually forbidden the exercise of clerical office, as penitents would have been.[179] The Donatists, however, usually treated a convert as a pagan and required baptism for initiation into their own communion. Thus they could allow such new Christians to be ordained for clerical office, regardless of their prior status in the Caecilianist communion.[180]

## Optatus of Milevis

In the last decades of the fourth century, Optatus of Milevis wrote a history of the controversy and refutation of the theology of Parmenian.[181] In his attack on the Donatist baptismal theory and practice, Optatus anticipated some of the arguments Augustine would soon elaborate into a fuller understanding of the church and its ministry. Distinguishing three elements in baptism — the Trinity, the faith of the recipient, and the person of the minister — he insisted

175. Aug. *Petil.* 2.27.32; 3.22.26, 27.32; *Cresc.* 2.17.21.

176. Even schism was not considered a disqualifying sin. The Maximianist schismatics were invited and some forced back into the exercise of their offices in the communion of Primian of Carthage. See the *acta* of the Council of Cebarsussi in Aug. *Psal.* 36.2.20 and *Cresc.* 4.9.11 for the unification of Claudianist schismatics that precipitated the conflict; see Aug. *Parm.* 1.4.9; 2.3.7; *Petil.* 1.10.11, 13.14; 2.83.184; and *Cresc.* 3.60.66; 4.25.32 for the way it was ended.

177. Optatus of Milevis asserted that the churches did not differ in sacraments or mysteries (*Parm.* 5.1).

178. This was the decision made by the Council of Arles, 9. The same provision was made for the reception of Donatist clergy by the Council of Nicaea, according to the Latin version which Caecilian brought back from the council and placed in the archives of the Catholic church of Carthage. See C. H. Turner, *Ecclesiae Occidentalis Monumenta Iuris Antiquissima* (Oxonii: E Typographeo Clarendoniano, 1899), 1.1:122-24.

179. In order to encourage the unification of the churches, at the outset of the schism, immediately after Caecilian's death, and in the early fifth century, the Caecilianists offered to accept Donatists in their offices. See pp. 398-401, 424-28.

180. These practices and Caecilianist attempts to change them are discussed below, p. 401, n. 290.

181. Optat. *Parm.* 2.16.

that the first two were unchanging and essential while the third was not significant for the efficacy of the rite.[182] He assigned the principal role to the Trinity, to whom prayer for cleansing was always directed and to whom Paul gave all credit for his work.[183] The role of the faith of the recipient, rather than the holiness of the minister, was established by reference to the efficacy that Christ himself assigned to the faith in those he healed.[184] Optatus further observed that Christ had never performed the ritual of baptism himself but always acted through his disciples, both before and after his death and resurrection.[185] He concluded that the ministers of the sacrament were like the waiters at a banquet who dispensed the host's food and like dyers of wool who only applied a color derived from the bodies of fish.[186] Thus he accused Parmenian of ignoring the faith of the convert and usurping the divine role of providing the gifts conferred in baptism.[187]

Optatus employed the symbolism of the maternal church in the same way. Christians were conceived through the mingling of heavenly and spiritual seeds, having God as their father and the church as their mother. An unworthy minister of the sacrament could not harm the church's power to generate; that power belonged to the womb of the bride rather than to her dowry or ornaments, as Parmenian may have claimed.[188] While such family bonds could be strained by discord, they could never be severed; estranged siblings were still kin to one another since they were all born of the same sacramental womb.[189] The one church claimed all the baptized as members, however unwilling they might be to acknowledge their siblings.

The treatise of Optatus against Parmenian provides an indication of the Caecilianist attempts to answer the Donatist appeals to the theology of Cyprian and thereby to explain the practice of acknowledging the ritual even when it was performed in schism. Optatus's emphasis on the instrumental role of the minister and the importance of the dispositions of the recipient would be elaborated by Augustine.

---

182. Optat. *Parm.* 5.4.
183. Optat. *Parm.* 5.4, 6-7.
184. Optat. *Parm.* 5.8.
185. Optat. *Parm.* 5.5.
186. Optat. *Parm.* 5.7.
187. Optat. *Parm.* 2.10.
188. Optat. *Parm.* 2.9-10. Parmenian claimed the *dotes* of the true church for his communion alone.
189. Optat. *Parm.* 4.2.

In the final decade of the fifth century, a conflict between the successor of Parmenian as Donatist Bishop of Carthage and one of his deacons forced that party into what the Caecilianists regarded as a compromise in the rejection of schismatic baptism. In 392, the deacon Maximian revolted against Bishop Primian. His supporters assembled at Cebarsussi in the neighboring province of Byzacena in June 393 to condemn and depose Primian for the excesses of his rule. Maximian was subsequently elected and consecrated bishop in Carthage. Primian struck back in April of the following year, gathering more than three hundred bishops at Bagai in Numidia, under the protection of the powerful Donatist bishop Optatus of Thamugadi. That council condemned Maximian and his twelve consecrators in the strongest terms but offered the bishops who had condemned Primian at Cebarsussi the opportunity to return to the unity of the Donatist communion without forfeiting their offices. The baptisms and other actions they had performed in schism were recognized as valid; they were not to be repeated when the congregations returned to Primian's communion.[190]

The Caecilianists then charged that the Donatists had violated their own Cyprianic principles by accepting the schismatic bishops back into communion and recognizing the sacramental actions they had performed while separated.[191] In their condemnation of the Maximianists at Bagai, the Donatist supporters of Primian had used some of the same scriptural texts that Cyprian himself had cited to denounce his rivals for the crime of schism. Moreover, the African councils meeting under Cyprian's leadership in the spring and fall of 256 had clearly asserted that schismatic bishops could not perform effective rituals or be allowed to return to clerical office in the unity of the church.[192] The Caecilianists were on firm ground in accusing the Donatists of infidelity to Cyprian, who had judged schism equivalent to the crime of apostasy. The Donatists, however, might have replied that the schismatics had not joined the Caecilianists and been tainted by the apostasy of their founder. The Donatists had charged the Caecilianists with tolerating apostasy and abandoning Cyprian; the Caecilianists retorted that the Donatists had tolerated schism and, thereby, abandoned Cyprian. Thus was the stage set for Augustine's own attack on the Donatist practice of rebaptizing Caecilianist converts, his revision of Cyprian's theology, and his development of a sacramental theory that would serve the African church.

---

190. See Gerald Bonner, *St. Augustine of Hippo: Life and Controveries* (Norwich: Canterbury Press, 1996), 246-49, for summary and references.

191. *Reg. Carth.* 69.

192. Cypr. *Ep.* 72; *Sent.*

## Conclusion

The division of the African church in the aftermath of the Diocletian persecution focused on the practice of baptism and the role of the minister in the ritual action of the church. The Donatists followed Cyprian's theology, requiring that individual bishops and the full episcopal college be free from all taint of apostasy and schism in order to guarantee the operation of the Holy Spirit in their sacramental ministry. While denying that their own communion was polluted, the Catholic bishops who gathered at Arles insisted that baptism was never to be repeated, implying that its efficacy was independent of the status of the minister and the community by whom it was conferred. The Caecilianists in Africa adopted this Catholic practice and were faced with developing a theology that would justify it. Optatus of Milevis focused on the invocation of the Trinity to justify refusing to repeat the ritual and added an appeal to the faith of the recipient to account for its sanctifying effect.

Faced with the presence of unworthy bishops and divisions in their own ranks, the Donatists also had to adjust Cyprian's theology. Parmenian may have appealed to the endowments of the true church, which were independent of the holiness of the individual bishop. The Council of Bagai accepted the validity of baptism performed in schism while breaking its link to the crime of apostasy, which would ruin sacramental ministry.

## BAPTISM IN AUGUSTINE'S TIME

Augustine's writings against the Donatists developed the baptismal theology the Caecilianists had inherited from Cyprian to enable them to recognize the baptism performed by an unworthy minister inside or outside the unity of their church. His sermons to the newly baptized also provide a more detailed description of the ritual than has been gleaned from the earlier writers. Archeological remains, moreover, facilitate the location of the ritual in its space. The foundations and even some walls of baptisteries attached to African church buildings have survived. Moreover, in many instances the actual fonts have been preserved: they were constructed of stone and masonry, usually at and below ground level. Thus, the ritual of baptism in the late fourth and early fifth century can be studied in its physical context.

### The Ritual

Although the surviving literature of North African Christianity never repeats the systematic account of the process provided in Tertullian's treatise *On Baptism,* Augustine's extensive writings permit a fuller and more detailed description of the ritual as practiced in the fifth century than is possible for the third century.

## ENROLLMENT OF CATECHUMENS

By the fifth century, children born to Christians were regularly enrolled as catechumens shortly after birth, including Augustine himself. Their foreheads were marked with the sign of the cross, and they were given a taste of blessed salt.[193] Baptism was often delayed until later in life, though it would be performed immediately if the child were in danger of death. Augustine spoke regularly and movingly of the haste in which parents brought their ill infants to the church for emergency baptism.[194] Yet some healthy children were also presented for baptism, at least in the Donatist church.[195]

The initiation of adult converts began with an inquiry and instruction preliminary to admission to the status of catechumen. The process was carried on by a lay catechist who asked the candidates to explain their current forms of livelihood and their motives for seeking incorporation into the Christian church. Those whose professions involved idolatry or immorality were required to renounce them before being allowed to proceed.[196] Inadequate motives, however, did not disqualify candidates, as long as they confessed a basic fear of God and desire for salvation; the church's catechetical program helped them purify their desire to follow Christ.[197] In a brief instruction, the catechist explained the unity of the Old and New Testaments, the ideal of love of God and neighbor, and the necessity of living according to Christian morality. The candidates who accepted the Christian message and declared themselves willing to follow its form of life were admitted as catechumens by a signing with the cross, the imposition of hands, and a tasting of salt.[198] Some of these rituals might have been

193. So Augustine reported of himself (*Conf.* 1.11.17). For a full discussion of the preparation and ritual, see William Harmless, *Augustine and the Catechumenate* (Collegeville, Minn.: Liturgical Press, 1995).

194. In his own case, *Conf.* 1.11.17, he explained the motivation for the delay: fear that he would soil himself again once cleansed from sin. In *Conf.* 4.4.8, he recounted the emergency baptism of an adult friend. The reference to the parents hurrying to the church is a standard of the Pelagian controversy. The most moving such story involves the resuscitation of an infant through the intercession of St. Stephen (*Serm.* 324). None of these parents seem to have considered baptizing the children themselves, as Tertullian would have presumed they would.

195. A decision of the Catholic bishops at the Council of Carthage on August 13, 397, made special provision to remove disabilities from Donatists who had been baptized as children in that church (*Reg. Carth.* 47).

196. *Reg. Carth.* 63. A person involved in the theater who became a Christian must not return or be forced to return to that work.

197. Aug. *Catech.* 5.9, 9.13, 17.26.

198. Aug. *Conf.* 1.11.17; *Catech.* 26.50; *Pecc. merit.* 2.26.42. See Matt. 5:13.

regularly repeated for the individual catechumens; the giving of salt was compared to the eucharist received by the faithful and was continued even during the Easter season when the other rites were suspended.[199]

The catechumenate itself was an apprenticeship in Christian living rather than a schooling in doctrine.[200] Long-term catechumens were instructed along with the faithful by the sermons of the bishop. Augustine himself, it will be recalled, had attended the sermons of Ambrose in Milan while still a catechumen; and he often addressed the unbaptized present in his own church at Hippo.[201] With the toleration and support of the church by the imperial government during the fourth century, the rigor of the moral code that may have distinguished the Christian community from the general culture had gradually relaxed.[202] In his sermons, Augustine extended the requirements of Christian morality to catechumens by referring to the cross of Christ they bore on their foreheads: they were urged to act in a way worthy of it.[203] He also exhorted them to imitate the penitents in repenting the sins that would be washed away in baptism.[204]

The surviving evidence does not specify the ordinary or minimum length of the catechumenate for adult converts. Many who were born into Christian families, of course, were dedicated to Christ as infants and lived much of their lives as catechumens.[205] Augustine himself, many of his friends, and perhaps his father as well were examples of this practice. Those who committed to Christianity for the first time as adults, however, might have proceeded to baptism more expeditiously.

While the catechumens regarded themselves as Christians and may have attended sermons regularly, they were not allowed to be present for the eucharistic prayer and communion.[206] Such a firm distinction between the baptized and the catechumens might have been difficult to enforce in large cities, where visitors were frequently present; it was perhaps more rigorously observed in

---

199. *Bru. Hipp.* 3; Aug. *Pecc. merit.* 2.25.42.

200. Aug. *Catech.* 25.48, 27.55; *Fid.* 6.9.

201. The sequence of sermons (*Eu. Io.* 1-12 and *Psal.* 119-133), which were intertwined over a four-month period, contain twenty-two references to the catechumens. They indicate the range of themes that the catechumens would have heard. See Marie-François Berrouard, *Introduction aux homélies de Saint Augustin sur l'Évangile de saint Jean* (Paris: Institut d'études augustiniennes, 2004), 22-27.

202. As the neophytes joined the community of the faithful, Augustine warned them against the models of bad behavior they would encounter. See *Serm. Mai* 94(260C).

203. Aug. *Serm.* 302.3.

204. Aug. *Serm. Dolb.* 14(352A).4.

205. Augustine invited the catechumens to put in their names for baptism; see *Serm. Lamb.* 26(335H).3. The death of an unbaptized catechumen was a particular occasion for warning against delay. *Serm. Dolb.* 7(142*).4.

206. Aug. *Psal.* 103.1.14; *Serm.* 49.8; *Eu. Io.* 96.3. *Serm.* 234.2; 235.3; 307.2.3 and *Eu. Io.* 11.3 all make clear that the catechumens did not understand references to the eucharistic celebration.

---

the towns and villages whose populations were more stable. By remaining at the margin of the community, the catechumens exempted themselves from the moral demands of the church and disciplinary authority of the bishop.[207] Yet by having been dedicated to Christ and by declaring an intention to enter the church, they qualified for immediate baptism — and thus salvation — should they be overtaken by deadly illness or accident.[208]

## LENTEN PREPARATION

Though baptism could be celebrated at any time, Augustine explained that the joy of the Easter season made it a particularly appropriate time.[209] Each year at the beginning of the Lenten preparation for Easter, the catechumens were invited to submit their names for baptism.[210] Those who responded were classed as *competentes*[211] (co-petitioners), and began the arduous process of purification and prayer that would culminate in their formal reception into the community at the Easter vigil. Like the devout among the faithful, they fasted by eating only once each day, in the middle of the afternoon,[212] and they abstained from eating meat, drinking wine, and engaging in sexual relations.[213] In addition, the petitioners were forbidden to attend the theater and the public baths.[214] They enacted a Christian segregation from the common life of the Roman town; few of them had been so observant as catechumens, and only the more devout would continue so after baptism.[215] To these exercises of separation from the Roman culture were added those of adhesion to the Christian community: practicing

207. Aug. *Serm.* 132.1; *Eu. Io.* 11.1; *Serm. Casin.* 2.114(97A).3-4; *Serm. Mai* 94(260C).1.

208. Augustine recounted the baptism of a friend through the agency of his family. The man had lost consciousness in his illness and had earlier joined Augustine in mocking Christian practice. Yet he was baptized because he had been enrolled as a catechumen. See *Conf.* 4.4.8. *Bru. Hipp.* 32 specified that such persons should be baptized.

209. Aug. *Serm.* 210.1.2. No canonical legislation excluded other times for the preparation and administration of baptism, but the surviving literature does not witness an alternative practice.

210. Aug. *Serm.* 132; *Serm. Lamb.* 26(335H).3; *Eu. Io.* 10.10, 11.1-6.

211. Augustine does not mention a ritual used for this procedure but does indicate that some of the candidates were judged unworthy (*Fid.* 6.8, 17.31, 18.33). The term is explained in *Serm.* 216.1; 228.1; 392.1; *Fid.* 6.9.

212. Aug. *Ep.* 54.7.9; *Mor. eccl.* 2.13.39. Christ fasted after his baptism, but Christians fasted before baptism; *Serm.* 210.2.3, 4.5.

213. *Serm.* 207.2.

214. On bathing, see Aug. *Ep.* 54.7.9-10. As was indicated in the discussion of the kiss of peace in Tertullian, fasting placed a person in a position apart from normal social interaction. Augustine asserted that a Christian boycott would have ruined the theaters financially (*Serm. Dolb.* 26(198*).10; *Serm. Denis* 14(313A).3-4).

215. Aug. *Psal.* 25.2.9; 30.3.2; 147.7. On days when games were presented, the congregation was small (*Serm.* 51.1.1).

almsgiving,[216] attending homilies on the scriptures, and receiving instruction in the Christian mode of life. Catechists taught the candidates separately, and the bishops addressed them in homilies preached to the whole community.[217] The subject matter seems to have been primarily moral; the doctrinal portion was concentrated in the final stage of the preparation and associated with the explanation of the creed, which was to be memorized and recited.[218] Because of the intensity of the program, some candidates from outlying districts moved into the towns and cities to be near the bishop for the whole of Lent.[219] Augustine noted the differences in the educational backgrounds and abilities that existed in a cohort of petitioners. He was particularly concerned that none of the less advantaged should become discouraged and abandon the process.[220]

Progress toward baptism was marked by four ceremonies: the scrutiny, the renunciation of the devil, the giving and reciting of the creed, and the giving of the Lord's Prayer. These normally would have been held in the final weeks of Lent, perhaps in the presence of the congregation as a whole.

The first ceremony, the scrutiny or examination, was preceded by an all-night vigil of prayer.[221] The candidates were stripped of their outer garments and head coverings, and individually were brought to stand on the *cilicium,* a mat made from a goatskin or of sackcloth woven from the hair of goats.[222] It recalled the garments given to Adam and Eve after their fall and symbolized the sinners who would be condemned in the Judgment.[223] The candidates were sharply questioned about their lifestyle and behaviors in preparation for baptism; as they answered, they stamped on the goat-hair symbol of human sinfulness. An exorcist then approached the candidates individually, hissing and cursing at the devil, blowing on the candidates as a symbolic invocation of the Holy Spirit's power to expel the forces of evil.[224] Hands were then imposed

---

216. Augustine recommended that the results of fasting should be given in alms: *Serm.* 205.2; 206.2; 208.2; 209.2; 210.10.12.

217. Aug. *Serm.* 5; 352; 392. See Suzanne Poque, ed., *Sermons pour la Pâque,* SC (Paris: Éditions du Cerf, 1966), 116:25; Harmless, *Augustine and the Catechumenate,* 259.

218. Aug. *Serm.* 212-214.

219. Aug. *Cur.* 12.15.

220. Aug. *Catech.* 8.12, 9.13, 13.18, 16.24.

221. For evidence on the (disputed) timing of the scrutiny, see Poque, *Sermons pour la Pâque,* SC 116:26-27; Harmless, *Augustine and the Catechumenate,* 262; Thomas M. Finn, *Early Christian Baptism and the Catechumenate: Italy, North Africa, and Egypt,* Message of the Fathers of the Church 6 (Collegeville, Minn.: Liturgical Press, 1992), 6-7. *Serm.* 216 is the only record of Augustine preaching at the scrutiny and seems to date before his episcopate. Quodvultdeus described the ritual itself in *Symb.* 1.1.5.

222. Aug. *Serm. Dolb.* 26(198*).5; *Serm.* 216.11.

223. Aug. *Serm.* 216.10-11. Poque, *Sermons pour la Pâque,* SC 116:28, argues that it was not a skin but a garment made from the hair.

224. Augustine referred to this part of the ritual in *Symb.* 2; *Serm.* 398.2. See also *Ep.* 194.46. For further interpretation of the significance of the ritual, see Tert. *Idol.* 11.7; Poque, *Sermons pour la Pâque,* SC 116:27-28; Harmless, *Augustine and the Catechumenate,* 264.

---

upon the candidates, with the invocation of the Holy Spirit to protect them from all further assaults by the demons.[225] Finally, their bodies were examined for signs of disease that might indicate the power of Satan over them.[226] In the fifth century, this exorcism seems to have been directed at the candidates' voluntary association with the works of evil and the remnants of demonic worship such as fortune-telling, charms, and magical cures,[227] rather than the ritual contamination by contact with idolatrous rites or involuntary possession that had been the primary focus of this ritual in the third century. Many of the candidates had been catechumens since their earliest years and may never have been involved in or associated with the traditional cultic rituals that earlier had been practiced widely and publicly in the Roman Empire. After being outlawed by Theodosius I and his son Honorius at the end of the fourth century, these rituals were seldom staged in public.[228]

The formal renunciation of Satan followed the scrutiny and preceded the reception of the creed in this later period.[229] As with the exorcism, the object of this renunciation was not the direct service of the demons through idolatrous worship but the "love of the world," as manifest in the attractions that Roman culture continued to present to the Christian.[230] Augustine specifically attacked its characteristic desire for public recognition and glory in the initial books of *The City of God*.[231]

Two weeks prior to Easter, the creed was presented to the candidates. Like the baptismal and eucharistic rituals themselves, the creed was subject to the discipline of secrecy. It was committed to memory rather than written out, and it was not regularly recited in the church.[232] The catechumens heard the creed for the first time when the bishop explained each of its affirmations to them.

225. Poque, *Sermons pour la Pâque,* SC 116:28.

226. *Serm.* 216.11. For interpretation, see Benedictus Busch, "De Initiatione Christiana secundum Sanctum Augustinum," *Ephemerides Liturgicae, pars prior, analecta historico-ascetica* 52 (1938): 159-78, 385-483; Albert Dondeyne, "La discipline des scrutins dans l'église latine avant Charlemagne," *Revue d'histoire ecclésiastique* 28 (1932): 5-33, 751-87; Harmless, *Augustine and the Catechumenate,* 263; Finn, *Early Christian Baptism and the Catechumenate,* 155; Frederik van der Meer, *Augustine the Bishop: The Life and Work of a Father of the Church,* trans. Brian Battershaw and G. R. Lamb (London: Sheed & Ward, 1962), 358.

227. Aug. *Serm. Guelf.* 18(260D).2; *Serm.* 286.8.7; 328.9.6 (*Serm. Lamb.* 13); *Serm. Lamb.* 6(335D).3, 5; *Serm. Dolb.* 26(198*).58.

228. *C.Th.* 16.10.12, 15. Pierre Chuvin, *A Chronicle of the Last Pagans* (Cambridge, Mass.: Harvard University Press, 1990), and others make the point that, although traditional Roman religious rituals were outlawed and public cult was indeed rare, some ritual did continue.

229. The difficulty in dating this action would seem to indicate that it was performed more than once. See Aug. *Serm.* 215.1; Quodu. *Symb.* 1; van der Meer, *Augustine the Bishop,* 364; Poque, *Sermons pour la Pâque,* SC 116:29-30; Finn, *Early Christian Baptism and the Catechumenate,* 7.

230. Aug. *Serm.* 144.5.6; *Serm. Lamb.* 6(335D).4; *Psal.* 34.1.4; 79.13; 141.14; *Eu. Io.* 28.9; 52.7-10.

231. Aug. *Ciu.* 5.12-15.

232. Aug. *Serm.* 213.2; 214.1.

The text used in Augustine's church can be reconstructed through quotations preserved in his sermons:

> We believe in God the Father almighty, the Creator of all things,
>   king of the ages, immortal and invisible;
> We believe in his Son Jesus Christ, our Lord,
> born of the Holy Spirit and the virgin Mary;
> crucified under Pontius Pilate and buried;
> on the third day he rose again from the dead;
> he ascended into heaven;
> he is seated at the right hand of the Father,
> [and] thence he will come to judge the living and the dead;
> We believe in the Holy Spirit;
> In the forgiveness of sins,
> In the resurrection of the flesh,
> and in eternal life through the holy church.[233]

This formula corresponds to the references made to the baptismal profession of faith by Tertullian and Cyprian. Slightly different wording is attested by Quodvultdeus of Carthage later in the fifth century and Fulgentius of Ruspe in the sixth.[234] In all cases, the African creed was closer to the Roman version than to the Greek conciliar creeds of the fourth century.

The candidates were required to commit the creed to memory during the following week in preparation for its public recitation.[235] Some might have found this task challenging: they had heard it only once, and many, especially those who came in from the countryside, might have had a limited facility in Latin. Augustine assured them that they should not worry overmuch about the exact wording and recommended that they seek help from friends among the faithful in securing the formula. This strategy would have engaged other members of the community in the initiation process and brought them eagerly to witness and support the recitations at the end of the week.[236]

Once the creed had been successfully mastered, the bishop gave the Lord's Prayer to the candidates.[237] He took the occasion to explain each of the peti-

---

233. Aug. *Serm.* 215; *Symb.*, reconstructed in J. N. D. Kelly, *Early Christian Creeds,* 3rd ed. (London: Continuum, 2006), 175-76.

234. See Kelly, *Early Christian Creeds,* 172-81, for these creeds and several hypotheses on the relation of the African and the Roman creeds.

235. Children seven years and older were required to perform (Aug. *Anim.* 1.10.12).

236. Aug. *Serm.* 213.11; 215.1; 58.1.1, 11.13. For the effect of the rituals on the faithful, see *Fid.* 6.9, which provides indirect evidence that the faithful recited the creed regularly in private and could thereby help others with it.

237. Aug. *Serm.* 59.1.1 correlates the return of the creed and the giving of the prayer.

tions and recommended that the prayer be committed to memory by regular recitation.[238]

## HOLY WEEK AND BAPTISM AT THE EASTER VIGIL

By the Thursday before Easter, the preparation for baptism had been completed. The candidates broke their fast and enjoyed a much-needed bath.[239] Their assistance and participation in the celebration of the Lord's Supper on Thursday and of the Passion on Friday was still limited by their status as catechumens. During the day on Saturday, Augustine seems to have delivered an instruction to them, in the presence of the congregation, in which he described the baptismal ritual itself, explaining the significance of each of its stages.[240] The initiation of the candidates would serve as a renewal for the faithful as well.

## THE BAPTISMAL WASHING

The baptismal ritual itself was part of the celebration of the Easter vigil service that began once the sun had set on Saturday and would last through the major portion of the night.[241] The design of the church building in Hippo, like that of many other churches in Africa, was such that the candidates might have entered the baptistery from the street rather than through the interior of the church (fig. 50).[242] Thus they would have been making a symbolic journey from the darkness outside the church, through the baptistery, and thence into the main body of the lighted basilica. Once inside the church compound, they stood in a small vestibule. There, having left the town and about to enter the church, they pronounced a final renunciation of Satan and commitment to Christ. First, each candidate turned toward the west, toward the darkness into which the sun had set; each then repeated the renunciation of Satan and all the ways of evil.[243]

238. Aug. *Serm.* 56-59. See Harmless, *Augustine and the Catechumenate,* 286-89, for an attempt to specify the sequence of actions. The notes to the edition of *Serm.* 56 by L. DeConinck, B. Coppieters, and R. Demeulenaere, in CCSL 41Aa:150-51, provide a summary of the recent scholarship on the matter.

239. Aug. *Ep.* 54.7.10; they were joined by many of the faithful who had accompanied them in their fasting. They had not bathed during the Lenten fast. See above, p. 204.

240. Aug. *Serm. Guelf.* 7(229A).1; *Serm.* 228.3 specifies that sermons have already been given on the creed, the Lord's Prayer, and baptism, and that one was owed now on the eucharist. The eucharistic sermon was generally on Easter day.

241. Aug. *Serm.* 221.2; *Serm. Wilm.* 7(223G).1.

242. The following discussion is based on the assumption that the baptistery excavated in Hippo was the facility used for the ritual in Augustine's time. See above, p. 158.

243. Aug. *Psal.* 102.19. *Psal.* 80.19 refers to a renunciation of sin that might have been part of the baptismal ritual. The location of the basilica and its baptistery within a town did not always

Immediately turning toward the east, toward the anticipated rising of the sun, the direction from which Christ was expected to return in glory, each swore allegiance to Christ, an oath Augustine compared to that taken by a military recruit.[244]

With the chanting of Psalm 42 — "As the hart longs for the springs of water, so does my soul long for you, O God" — the candidates were led into the room adjoining the baptistery for the first time. The text was particularly apt, Augustine noted, because the deer's thirst was a consequence of killing and eating snakes, which represented human sins and vices.[245] As the candidates waited, they might have heard the bishop praying over the water and invoking the name of Christ; he also traced the sign of the cross over it.[246] This prayer did not follow a set formula but could be improvised by the bishop, who might have followed the model of a more learned colleague.[247]

Still waiting in the anteroom, the candidates would have been called forward one at a time by the deacons or presbyters assisting the bishop. Inside the baptistery, the font at its center left room for only a few persons: the bishop, a deacon or presbyter, and the candidate, who might have been joined by sponsors (fig. 54). At some point in these proceedings, the candidate removed all clothing in anticipation of entering the font to be reborn.[248]

The candidate stepped over the lip, went down three steps into the cruciform font, and stood in the water.[249] In many fonts, the candidate stood on a mosaic of the Christogram, symbolizing faith in Christ. This act contrasted with the earlier act of standing on the goat-hair *cilicium* symbolizing sin, during the scrutiny at the beginning of the baptismal preparation. Overhead was a decorated ciborium, supported by four columns. The bishop posed the three creedal questions, to which the candidate responded affirmatively in profession of faith. Then the bishop pronounced the formula of baptism in the name of the Father, Son, and Holy Spirit,[250] as the candidate was either submerged in the water or had it poured over head and body by an attendant — perhaps a deacon.

---

permit a clear east-west orientation. Nevertheless, the two directions were associated with the powers of good and evil (*Serm. Dolb.* 22(341*).9).

244. For Augustine's comparison of baptism to a military induction, see, for example, *Parm.* 2.13.29; *Psal.* 39.1.

245. Aug. *Psal.* 41.1-3. In this sense, the psalm was appropriate for the whole period of baptismal preparation.

246. Aug. *Eu. Io.* 118.5; *Serm.* 352.1.3.

247. Aug. *Bapt.* 6.25.47 remarks on the limitations of the doctrinal knowledge and grammatical skill of the bishops, which did not hamper the effectiveness of this prayer of consecration.

248. New ceremonial clothing would be received immediately after baptism. The practice of nude baptism is fully attested elsewhere in the contemporary Christian world: *Trad. apos.* 21.3, 5, 11; *Didasc. ap.* 16; Cyr. Jer. *Cat. myst.* 2; Theo. Mp. *Lib. bapt.* 4; In. Chry. *Cat.* 2.24.

249. Aug. *Serm.* 125.6. Some baptisteries allowed the west-to-east movement. In Hippo, the font was on a north-west to south-east axis.

250. Aug. *Bapt.* 3.14.19; 6.25.46; *Ep.* 23.4; *Petil.* 2.80.178.

After walking up the steps on the opposite end, over the lip of the font and onto the floor, the neophyte was toweled dry and clothed in a white linen tunic, which symbolized the new and pure life into which the Christian had just been born.[251] The head then might have been veiled.[252] Special sandals were placed on the feet to protect them during the following week.[253] These symbolized the purity effected by baptism, as well as freedom from mortality, its earthly concerns, and the minor failings of day-to-day Christian living.[254] The neophyte was then led into an adjoining chapel, the *consignatorium,* which itself opened onto the nave of the basilica (cf. fig. 48).[255] (In Hippo, as elsewhere, this room had an apse at one end where the oils could have rested on an altar.) The bishop then turned to greet the next candidate entering the baptistery.

## ANOINTING AND IMPOSITION OF HANDS

Once all of the candidates had been baptized, the bishop and his assistants moved into the adjoining chapel, where the neophytes were assembled.[256] Each of the newly baptized came forward. As the bishop invoked the name of Christ,[257] a deacon or presbyter anointed them with oil that the bishop had consecrated earlier.[258] Imposing his hands on the head of each, the bishop prayed that the Holy Spirit would descend upon and work within the new Christian.[259] Like Tertullian (but unlike Cyprian), Augustine understood this anointing as priestly, conferring a share in Christ's priesthood on all the baptized.[260]

251. Aug. *Serm.* 223.1; *Serm. Mai* 94(260C).7.

252. Aug. *Serm. Denis* 4(376A).2.

253. Aug. *Ep.* 55.19.35.

254. Aug. *Eu. Io.* 56.3-5.

255. This may also have been the space used for training the catechumens in some basilicas. See examples of other likely *consignatoria* (cf. fig. 78), and discussion above, pp. 92, 153, 159.

256. See the above description of the existing archeological remains in Hippo, p. 159.

257. Aug. *Petil.* 3.35.40.

258. Aug. *Petil.* 2.103.237. The grammatical construction of the sentence implies that the bishop did not himself apply the oil: "quorum capita oleo tuo perierunt" (CSEL 52:151.24-25). This anointing may have covered only the forehead rather than the whole body, as was the Roman bathing custom. However, the specification of the head in this text may have come from the verses of the psalms that were being used by Petilian and Augustine (*Psal.* 133.2; 141.5). *Con. Carth.* a. 390, 3 and *Bru. Hipp.* 34 restrict the making of chrism to the bishop.

259. Aug. *Serm. Guelf.* 15(229M).2. *Serm.* 324, which describes the baptism of an infant resuscitated through the intercession of St. Stephen, sets out the sequences of actions: continuo tulit illum ad presbyteros, baptizatus est, sanctificatus est, unctus est, imposita est ei manus, completis omnibus sacramentis, assumptus est (PL 38:1446-447). Note that this entire ritual was performed by the presbyters, presumably in the absence of the bishop. Neither of these texts, however, allows a determination of whether the imposition of hands was normally performed in the segregated space or in the presence of the entire congregation.

260. Tert. *Bapt.* 7.1, 8.2; Cypr. *Ep.* 70.2.2; Aug. *Serm. Dolb.* 26(198*).53; *Qu. eu.* 2.40.3. The

Baptized, dressed, and anointed, the neophytes joined the community for the first time in prayer and the eucharist.[261] They were escorted directly into the aisle of the basilica through a doorway at the opposite end of the chapel in which they had been anointed. When the bishop moved to the altar to lead the community in prayer, the neophytes followed him into the chancel, the area containing the altar and separated by a low railing from the surrounding space in which the congregation stood.[262] After the formal eucharistic prayer, they received the bread and cup for the first time.

## SUBSEQUENT INSTRUCTION

On Easter morning, the neophytes returned to the church for a second eucharistic celebration, at which they received instruction on the sacrament of the Lord's Supper, in which they had participated for the first time during the night vigil.[263]

During the remainder of the week following their baptism, the neophytes wore their baptismal robes and the sandals that prevented them from touching the earth. They participated in the daily eucharist within the chancel, like newborns in their cradle, standing with the clergy rather than the congregation.[264] The sermons they heard concentrated on the Resurrection and on the sacraments of baptism and eucharist that they had received.[265]

On the Sunday following Easter, the neophytes completed the initiation ritual.[266] They put aside their special garments and shoes, returned to their habitual dress, left the chancel, and joined the congregation.[267] This symbolized the transition to the routine of Christian living — with its daily failings. Augustine exhorted them to diligence. He warned that they would find both good and bad models in the congregation; he urged them to emulate the good and tolerate the evil.[268] Even their Christian friends, he warned, would try to drag

---

African ritual of ordination did not contain an anointing that would distinguish the priesthood of the clergy from that of the faithful.

261. Aug. *Serm. Guelf.* 7(229A).3; *Serm.* 227.

262. Aug. *Serm. Mai* 94(260C).7.

263. Aug. *Serm.* 227; 229; 272; *Serm. Guelf.* 7 (229A).

264. Aug. *Serm. Dolb.* 27(360C).7. See also *Ep.* 34.2, in which Augustine described a similar Donatist ceremony.

265. Gregory Dix, *The Shape of the Liturgy* (London: Dacre Press, 1945), 331. Aug. *Serm.* 260; 224-29; *Serm. Denis* 8(260A).

266. Aug. *Serm. Denis* 8(260A).4.

267. Aug. *Serm.* 353.1.1; 260; *Serm. Mai* 94(260C).7; *Serm. Denis* 4(376A).1.

268. Aug. *Serm.* 224.1; 228.1; *Serm. Denis* 8(260A).4; *Serm. Mai* 94(260C).7; *Serm. Guelf.* 18(260D).2.

them back to the public entertainments they had abandoned at the beginning of the baptismal preparation.[269]

## FOOT WASHING

In some churches in Roman Africa, though perhaps not in Hippo, a ritual washing of the feet of the newly baptized was performed, during or at the end of the week following the baptism so that it would not be confused with the baptismal washing.[270] Augustine explained the symbolism of the foot washing as the removal of those sins that occurred in daily Christian living. In the future, these sins would normally be forgiven through private penance: the recitation of the Lord's Prayer, the forgiving of others, and acts of kindness towards the poor.[271] In this sense, the foot washing was appropriately celebrated on the day the neophytes took off their special garments and shoes, resumed wearing their normal clothing, and joined the congregation in Christian living.

## Infant Baptism

The church in the fifth century continued the custom of baptizing infants, at least those in danger of death.[272] On the basis of the practice, Augustine argued for both the necessity and the efficacy of baptism. Though the children as yet had no sin of their own, they were bound by the guilt of Adam's sin, which could be loosed only through the grace of Christ.[273] As the sacrament of faith, baptism itself supplied for the conversion and assent of the infant, whose personal choice posed no obstacle to the divine operation.[274] The Holy Spirit united the sponsors to the child they presented and thus allowed their profession of faith to stand for its own.[275] Augustine also implied that the normal practice was to give the eucharist to infants at the time of their baptism, as necessary for their salvation.[276] In later years, the salvation of infants through baptism would become Augustine's preferred example of the efficacy of divine grace.[277]

269. Aug. *Psal.* 80.11.
270. Aug. *Ep.* 55.18.33.
271. Aug. *Eu. Io.* 56.3-5; 58.4-5.
272. *Reg. Carth.* 110.
273. Aug. *Ep.* 98.8.
274. Aug. *Ep.* 98.9-10.
275. Aug. *Ep.* 98.6-7.
276. Aug. *Ep.* 186.8.30.
277. Aug. *Iul.* 4.8.42-44.

Augustine provided clear evidence for the practice of emergency baptism of those in danger of death, both infants and adults. During the Pelagian controversy, the practice of bringing infants for emergency baptism was regularly used not only as evidence for Christian belief in their sharing of Adamic sin[278] but as an indication of the operation of God's election and predestination of those infants who lived long enough to be baptized and then died shortly afterwards.[279] In his preaching, Augustine occasionally referred to the danger of delaying baptism until late in life or in anticipation of death.[280] In one instance, he had to face a congregation overcome with grief by the unanticipated death of a young man who had delayed baptism too long.[281] The legislation of the African bishops made explicit provision for the baptism of even the unconscious dying, as long as the person had given prior indication of the desire for the sacrament.[282]

Although the account in *Confessions* of the emergency baptism of his friend implies that the ritual was performed at the sick person's home,[283] Augustine spoke elsewhere of the dying person, most often an infant, being carried to the church for baptism.[284] The ritual seems to have involved the full service when this was possible: baptism, anointing, and imposition of hands. Augustine told the story of just such a case, which involved a miracle at the shrine of St. Stephen in Uzalis. An infant child suddenly became ill, and, even though his mother hurried to the church, her son died unbaptized in her arms. Fearing his eternal condemnation, the mother then ran to the shrine and prayed there that her son be restored to life, at least to receive baptism. The saint responded to her prayer and raised her son from the dead long enough for the presbyters to baptize, anoint, and lay hands upon him. Thus was his salvation assured.[285]

## Ministers of the Sacrament

Augustine recognized that the normal minister of the sacrament of baptism was the bishop or another cleric he authorized. In the case of emergency baptism, especially in rural parishes, a presbyter would be more regularly available

---

278. Aug. *Ep.* 98.1; *Nat. et grat.* 4.4.
279. Aug. *Pecc. merit.* 1.21.29–22.32; *Ep.* 186.4.11–5.14.
280. Aug. *Serm. Dolb.* 7(142*).4.
281. Aug. *Serm. Dolb.* 7(142*).
282. *Bru. Hipp.* 32.
283. Aug. *Conf.* 4.4.8.
284. Aug. *Serm.* 393.1.
285. Aug. *Serm.* 323; 324.

for the task.[286] The bishop's ministry was engaged by the use of anointing oil, which he alone could bless.[287] At the end of his treatise *On Baptism,* Augustine tentatively explained that the ritual could be performed by anyone, even an unbeliever who had no connection with the church, as long as the proper form was used.[288] This does not, however, seem to have been the practice: parents preferred to bring their sick infants to the church, even though this placed them in danger of dying before they arrived.[289] Augustine and his colleagues do not seem to have instructed parents that the ministry of the clergy was not essential to the efficacy of the rite.[290]

## A Theology of Baptism

Like his predecessors in the third century, Augustine was faced with the task of developing a theology that would explain and justify his church's practice of baptism. Because the theory had to address the conflict within Africa between Caecilianists and their Donatist opponents on the policy of rebaptizing, it had to engage Cyprian's assumptions and conclusions, most of which remained common to all African Christians. Thus, Augustine had to maintain that salvation could not be found outside the visible unity of the church but that the one baptism of Christ could be conferred outside that unity. He also had to explain how grace and salvation were communicated only through the ministry of the church, although the efficacy of that ministry was independent of the religious and moral status of the clergy. The Caecilianist party had gathered the evidence from imperial court records to establish that their bishops had been innocent and some leading Donatist bishops guilty of the crime of apostasy by handing over the scriptures during the Diocletian persecution. Still, a theological explanation had to deal with ministers whose innocence could not be established. Thus, Augustine had to defend his own party's ministry in fact, but in principle he had to show that clerical fidelity and holiness were irrelevant to the efficacy of Christian ministry. He also had to justify the practice of accepting the baptism performed by Donatist bishops, despite their

---

286. Aug. *Serm.* 324.

287. *Con. Carth.* a. 390, 3 and *Bru. Hipp.* 34 restricted the making of chrism to the bishop. The restriction implies that presbyters sometimes used the chrism and might have been blessing it themselves.

288. Aug. *Bapt.* 7.53.101-102.

289. Aug. *Gen. litt.* 10.11.19; *Petil.* 2.101.232; *Ep. Io.* 4.11; *Ep.* 166.7.21, 8.23-24; *Anim.* 2.9.13; 3.11.15; *Nupt.* 2.2.4; *Iul.* 1.7.31; 6.7.17; *Ciu.* 13.4; *Iul. op. imp.* 1.52; *Serm.* 56.9.13; 174.7.8; 183.8.12; 246.5; 293.10.

290. The surviving sermons of Augustine contain no such instruction or exhortation. These represent a small, and possibly select, fraction of his preaching.

acting in schism and their remaining in historical communion with confessed and proven apostates.[291]

Augustine's theology of baptism was developed in response to the beliefs and practices of the Christians of Africa. He built on the Catholic acceptance of schismatic baptism and explained the rightness of what the Caecilianists did and what they refused to do. He also had to make a plausible appeal to the Donatists: offering a different interpretation of their foundational texts, safeguarding the purity of the one true church, and explaining the efficacy of the rituals, even when performed by the unworthy and the rebellious. He had, for example, to show the Caecilianists why they should trust Donatist baptism even when the Donatists rejected theirs.

In developing his theory, Augustine distinguished between the ritual and the two realities that it signified and conferred: dedication to Christ and sanctification of the baptized. The baptismal theology itself was then built on four propositions Augustine adapted from his predecessors in the third and fourth centuries.

First, he asserted that Christ himself gave baptism through the minister as his agent, so that the properly performed ritual was always effective. To repeat the ritual would be either to deny Christ's power or to attribute its efficacy to the minister who enacted the ritual.[292] The author of the *Treatise on Rebaptism* had pointed out that the apostles, rather than Christ himself, conferred baptism during his earthly ministry, though they did not yet have true faith and the gift of the Holy Spirit.[293] Augustine had also observed that the minister of baptism within the true church was sometimes sinful or incompetent, a point that Cyprian himself acknowledged, at least indirectly.[294] The *Treatise* cited the military oath to show that the promises made in baptism were binding and never needed to be repeated. Augustine elaborated this analogy by noting that the legionary tattoo was permanent and bound its bearer to service even if it had been fraudulently obtained.[295] In the same way, the baptism of Christ was independent of the person who performed it and the context in which it had been received.

Second, Augustine taught that the church was the necessary mediator of the sanctifying effect of the sacrament because the Holy Spirit conferred upon it the power to forgive sins. Using the empowering of the disciples in John

---

291. *Act. Zeno.* This is part of a dossier of documents now attached to Optatus of Milevis's response to the Donatist leader Parmenian. It indicated that some of the founding generation of Donatist bishops were keenly aware of failures within their own ranks. For the innocence of Caecilian's consecrator, see the *Act. pur. Fel.* in the same dossier.

292. Aug. *Eu. Io.* 5.6-11, 18.

293. *Rebap.* 6, 9. Augustine used the example of Judas in *Petil.* 2.44.104; 3.35.41, 55.67; *Cresc.* 2.19.24.

294. Aug. *Bapt.* 3.17.22, 18.23; 4.2.2-3; 5.10.12–14.16, 20.27; 6.12.19, 24.43, 26.50.

295. *Rebap.* 16-17; Aug. *Eu. Io.* 6.15; *Psal.* 39.1; *Serm. Dolb.* 3(293A).16; *Serm. Denis* 8(260A).2.

---

(20:22-23), Cyprian had shown that the power to forgive sins was the gift of the Holy Spirit. He had also identified the recipients of this gift as the Apostles, functioning in unity as the original episcopal college, in which the power had been transmitted to later bishops. He then interpreted the commissioning of Peter in Matthew (16:19) as a demonstration of the unity of that power by its being conferred first upon Peter as representative of all bishops. A single power and authority was shared by the united college of bishops. Augustine modified Cyprian's theory by using the charge to the whole community in Matthew (18:18) to extend the power of sanctification beyond the clergy to the whole body of the faithful.[296] He then used the statement of 1 Peter (4:8) to identify the power of forgiveness with the Spirit's gift of charity, which joined the faithful together in the unity of the church and covered or forgave their sins.[297]

Third, Augustine asserted that although the ritual of baptism was always effective in conferring forgiveness and grace, only those who repented of sin and believed in Christ actually retained these baptismal gifts. Those who acted insincerely in their profession of faith or rejection of sin thereby alienated themselves from the unity of the church, which was built on faith and love. Though the baptismal dedication to Christ endured in them, they immediately lost its saving effects.[298] In the third century, the *Treatise on Rebaptism* had called attention to the inadequacies of the minister within the church and relied on the presumed good faith of the recipient. In the fourth, Optatus had excluded the holiness of the minister and stressed the power of the Trinity, which the candidate professed. In the fifth, Augustine called attention to the inadequacies of both the minister and the candidate: he could point to the deceptions of those who sought baptism under pressure of the Theodosian laws privileging Catholic Christianity. In examining their intentions, he found a parallel between the person baptized in heresy or schism and the person who sought baptism in the Catholic church in order to secure some civil or economic advantage. After some uncertainty, he decided that through the divine power, all the baptized actually received the forgiving grace of the Holy Spirit; the unfaithful and deceiving, whether inside or outside the visible church, immediately lost that gift.[299] In this way, he could also explain the salvation of infants through baptism: they placed no obstacle to the divine bestowal of grace in the ritual.[300]

Fourth, Augustine taught that the enduring efficacy of baptism could restore an originally insincere recipient who later converted and repented: a

296. Thus, for example, in Aug. *Eu. Io.* 22.7; 50.12; 118.4; 124.5; the same interpretation of John 20:23 was offered in *Bapt.* 3.18.23; *Eu. Io.* 121.4; *Serm.* 99.9; 295.2.2.

297. That text is cited some 23 times, primarily in the writings against the Donatists. See, for example, Aug. *Bapt.* 6.24.45; *Gaud.* 1.12.13; *Cresc.* 2.12.15.

298. Aug. *Bapt.* 1.11.16–12.20; 3.13.18, 16.21–17.22.

299. Aug. *Bapt.* 1.11.15–1.12.20.

300. The baptism of infants was initially discussed in Aug. *Ep.* 98 and *Bapt.* 4.24.32. It later became an example of the gratuity of salvation: *Ep.* 186.4.11; *Perseu.* 11.25.

Donatist might later come into union with the church; an insincere or weak Catholic might believe and repent. Through the enduring baptismal dedication was restored the saving grace that had been lost by infidelity. Cyprian and his colleagues had specified that a baptized Christian who deserted the church and joined a schismatic communion but later returned was to be received by the ritual of repentance rather than a new baptism.[301] Augustine extended this concession both to Donatists baptized in schism when they joined the Catholic communion and to repenting Catholics who rejected the lying confession or erroneous faith in which they earlier had been baptized in the unity of the church.[302] Those among the baptized who never converted, repented, and became joined into the charity of the saints would, however, be rejected by Christ in the Judgment. Although Augustine recognized that no one could be certain of the salvation of any particular person who died within the communion of the visible unity of the church, he denied any hope for those who died in the open rebellion of heresy or schism.[303]

In developing this fourth point, Augustine had to explain the status of the baptism of John, since Paul had required that those who had received it be baptized a second time (Acts 19:1-7). In preparation for the work of Christ, Augustine proposed, John had been assigned a baptism peculiarly his own; it was prophetic, like the baptism of Israel in the cloud and the sea (1 Cor 10:2). The baptism that Christ himself brought was given through his disciples; it actually conferred the forgiveness that the baptism of John gave only in hope. Thus the disciples of Christ neither repeated the baptism of John nor offered a baptism of their own; they gave only the baptism of Christ. Further, Augustine objected to any attempt to draw a parallel between the ministry of John the Baptist and that of unworthy bishops, either inside or outside the unity of the church. John was joined to Christ in faith and love; the failed bishops were not. In ordering the rebaptism of John's disciples, moreover, Paul did not reject John's ministry but completed it by providing that new baptism of Christ for which John had prepared.[304]

In developing his theology, Augustine disagreed with Cyprian and with his Donatist followers in four significant ways. First, he insisted that the efficacy of the sacrament did not depend on the status of the minister, either as a legitimate bishop in the episcopal college or as one of the faithful endowed with the Holy Spirit. Anyone could baptize, even someone who was not a Christian.[305]

Second, he identified the power of forgiveness as charity — love of God and neighbor — and the gift of the Holy Spirit (Rom. 5:5). Christ had conferred this gift upon his disciples and taught its power in John 20:22-23. The Spirit

301. Cypr. *Ep.* 71.2.1-2.
302. Aug. *Bapt.* 2.13.18–14.19; 3.13.18, 16.21; 6.4.6–5.7.
303. Aug. *Ciu.* 22.24.
304. Aug. *Bapt.* 5.9.10–12.14; *Petil.* 2.37.86-87; *Unic. bapt.* 7.9-11.
305. Aug. *Eu. Io.* 5.15; *Bapt.* 7.53.101-2.

dwelt in the saints within the church, who exercised forgiveness by prayer and mutual love.[306] A minister of the sacrament acted as the agent of Christ and of the saints as his ecclesial body, which was joined to him in love.

Third, Augustine realigned the cosmic boundary between the divine and demonic realms so that it ran through the visible communion of the church rather than coinciding with its social limit. The saints hidden within the visible church were the true city of God on earth, on pilgrimage toward heaven. The Holy Spirit joined them in mutual love, even if they could not securely identify one another as being the true faithful among the unrepentant sinners in the assembly. The love of these saints was extended to converts and penitents; it won the forgiveness of both their sins and those of the saints as well, according to the petition of the Lord's Prayer and the promise made in Matthew (18:18).[307]

Fourth, that baptism proper to Christ and the unity of the church could be found outside the visible unity, though it would confer salvation only upon those intentionally joined into that unity existing among the saints. Thus, baptism could be given and received by the unworthy either inside or outside the visible communion; holiness could be received and maintained only by those intentionally joined into the loving union of the saints. Augustine illustrated the implications of this theory: in an emergency, Catholic catechumens might properly receive baptism from even a Donatist cleric; they would gain the salutary effects of the ritual through their intention to join in loving unity to the Catholic saints rather than the schismatic rebels, though death might prevent them from actually sharing the eucharistic fellowship of the true church.[308]

Addressing Cyprian's assertion that only those who have the church for mother can have God for Father, Augustine appealed to the Genesis narrative of the family of Jacob. As the patriarch claimed the children born to him not only by his wives but also by their servants, so did God acknowledge the Christians baptized in schismatic or heretical communions as well as those born in the faithful church.[309]

Augustine's baptismal theology was developed in close dialogue with his church's pastoral practice and designed to respond to the challenges posed by the inadequacies of both clergy and laity. It was presented most fully in controversial treatises directed at Donatist writers. In his congregational preaching, however, it was fully integrated into his broader understanding of the church as the body of Christ and the temple of the Holy Spirit, which was symbolized by the eucharist.

---

306. Aug. *Ep.* 98.5; *Bapt.* 3.17.22–18.23; 6.3.5–4.6.
307. Aug. *Bapt.* 3.17.22–18.23, 19.26; 5.21.29; 6.4.6–5.7; *Eu. Io.* 121.4; *Serm.* 99.9.
308. Aug. *Bapt.* 1.1.2–2.3; 7.52.100.
309. Aug. *Serm. Caes. eccl.* 5.

# Conclusion

The ritual of baptism and the space in which it was performed can be correlated for the first time in the fifth century. No major changes emerge in the description of the rite, though new elements can be perceived from the remains of fonts and the fuller literary evidence of this period. The elaborate preparations for baptism during the season of Lent brought an extended catechumenate to its fulfillment. The scrutiny, the exorcism, the giving and returning of the creed, and the explanation of the Lord's Prayer all built to the climax of the vigil service at Easter. The celebration then continued for another week, as the neophytes wore their baptismal garments and joined the clergy in the chancel for the daily celebration of the eucharist. For adults, the ritual marked a change in their commitment to the church, a readiness to undertake the Christian life with a fullness that most had hitherto avoided.

Some elements of the ritual itself can be further specified by observing the arrangement of the space. The baptismal washing was private rather than public: most Christians witnessed only their own. That ritual seems to have involved full nudity of the body either submerged or immersed with water poured over it. The anointing and the imposition of hands were performed in a separate chapel, in the presence of other initiants rather than in the midst of the community assembled in the nave of the basilica. Only once fully initiated did the candidates join the faithful for prayer and eucharist.

Augustine's baptismal theology interpreted the ritual itself, but its shape was dictated by the conflicts over the independence of the efficacy of the sacrament from the qualifications of its minister and even its recipient. Without compromising the necessity of submitting to the ritual, Augustine distinguished two separable realities that it signified: the dedication of the baptized person to Christ and the sanctification conferred by the gift of the Holy Spirit.

The dedication was identified as being reborn, becoming a child of God, entering the visible society of the Christian church even in heresy or schism. The oaths rejecting Satan and affirming Christ, along with the profession of Trinitarian faith, established a permanent and unbreakable relationship to God, Christ, and the church. It affected all the baptized: converted and unconverted, in truth or in heresy, in unity or in schism, in the fullness of life or the face of death.

The sanctification was the gift of charity, through the indwelling of the Holy Spirit, which worked the forgiveness of sins, and empowered the recipient to love God and neighbor and to live the Christian life. Although this sanctification might have been received by every person, it would be lost immediately by the unrepentant who clung to their sins, the unfaithful who affirmed Christ for earthly gain, and any who refused the loving unity of the church.

The initial efficacy of the ritual depended on the power of Christ alone; the minister need only have intended to perform and the recipient not to reject baptism. The dispositions of the recipient determined whether the sanctification was retained and became fruitful in Christian living. In virtue of baptism's permanent dedication of a person to Christ, however, the sanctifying gifts would be granted again when the baptized rejected sin and turned to Christ in true faith and loving unity. The baptismal dedication was never to be repeated, though its sanctification might be revived by the imposition of hands in penance or reception into the unity of the visible church.

Augustine did not neglect the role of the church in the sacramental action. He believed that only those actually endowed with holiness could confer it on others. The hard experience of the Donatist controversy had demonstrated, however, that the clergy were not reliable ministers of the gift of the Spirit. To solve this problem, Augustine identified the gift of the Spirit as the love of God in the hearts of the faithful, and argued that this was inseparable from the love of neighbor, which actually forgave sins. The society of saints joined together in this love constituted the intentional unity of the church, which was recognized as, at once, the place of the Spirit's indwelling, the minister of the Spirit's forgiveness, and the communicator of the gift of charity. Those intentionally joined to the saints shared these blessings; those separated in heart lost them.

Augustine then identified the loving union of the faithful in the visible unity of the church as the body of Christ, which shared his holiness and exercised his power in the sacramental actions of the clergy. Thus, he justified the African practice of including the confession of the church as the medium of salvation in the baptismal creed. In his reflections on the eucharistic ministry, Augustine would further identify the society of saints as the body of Christ, whose priestly power it exercised.[310]

## GENERAL OBSERVATIONS

### Correlation of Archeological and Literary Evidence

For the most part, the archeological remains related to baptism — and other practices — have not survived from the period prior to the fourth century. In some instances, however, the literary evidence indicates the existence of buildings, furnishings, and decorations during this earlier period. For example, Tertullian's reference to the "mother's house"[311] in which the neophytes prayed for the first time following their baptism would indicate some sort of building in which the community assembled to celebrate the eucharist together.

310. See below, pp. 282-83, 428-29, 617.
311. Apud matrem, Tert. *Bapt.* 20.5. For the ambiguity of the phrase, see above, n. 33.

Several decorative motifs are prominent in the decoration of African baptismal fonts. Among these are representations of various fish and aquatic creatures that were common in the decoration of fountains and pools in secular settings. The baptistery from Clipea (fig. 38) provides an extraordinary example of this iconography.[312] In baptisteries these images may have had greater symbolic significance, perhaps recalling Tertullian's imagery of Christ as the big fish and Christians as the little fish who follow him, abiding in the water for safety.[313] Optatus's references to the fish acrostic and to the baptismal pool as an "ancient fishpond" suggest that aquatic images had a long history in African baptisteries.[314]

The Clipea font was also decorated with mosaic designs of fruit trees, flowers, birds, and lit candles (figs. 38, 39). The Thapsus font was similarly covered with lavish images of birds, vines, and flowers (fig. 97). Date palm trees are pictured in the font at Oued Ramel and Naro (fig. 62). This décor seems to reflect the idea that the newly baptized are returned at least briefly to Eden, and it evokes Cyprian's description of the church as a walled garden that enclosed fruit trees and a sealed font.[315]

The pavements of several African fonts depict deer coming to drink at streams of water or from a cantharus that is brimming or bubbling (figs. 8, 29). Such images suggest the opening words of Psalm 42, perhaps chanted by the candidates as they processed to the font.[316] The imagery of Psalm 23 is suggested by the inclusion of sheep (e.g., fig. 57, but also in the baptistery of Sidi Jdidi). Augustine also drew a parallel between the washing of the ewes (Song 4:2; 6:6) and the descent into the font.[317] In preaching at Cyprian's shrine on the saint's feast day, Augustine referred to the ritual, saying that the congregation had received the fleeces of shorn ewes — the flock that just had been baptized.[318]

Other fonts contain images of lit tapers or suspended lamps (e.g., fig. 9) and suggest the liturgical use of candles or other lights at baptism. Sometimes crosses or Christograms appear on the floors of the wells of baptismal fonts (cf. figs. 39, 72, 97). The candidates' standing or kneeling on such a symbol while affirming faith in Christ and the Trinity may have been an intentional contrast

312. Other examples are at Lepti Minus and Naro (figs 44, 62).
313. Tert. *Bapt.* 1.3.
314. Optat. *Parm.* 3.2.1-12.
315. Cypr. *Ep.* 73.10.3.
316. On this, see Aug. *Psal.* 41.1.
317. Aug. *Doct. Chr.* 2.6.7.
318. Aug. *Serm. Denis* 15(313B).3. This sermon was preached at the Mensa Cypriani, which some scholars have tentatively identified with the basilica of Bir Ftouha and which had a monumental baptistery. See above, pp. 139-40.

to standing on the goatskin or *cilicium* when they renounced Satan during the scrutiny.[319]

The font at Clipea has four additional images that belong to the general iconography of baptism: a dove descending, a brimming chalice, a cross under a ciborium, and a box-like ark (figs. 38, 39). This last image may have been intended to represent the Ark of the Covenant or, more likely, Noah's Ark because of the presence of a dove holding an olive branch in its beak immediately next to it. The inclusion of this ark may reflect the long-popular typological interpretation of Noah's story as a baptism of the faithful within the safe "ship/ark" of the church (1 Pet. 3:18-21).[320]

## SHAPES, SIZES, AND DEPTHS OF FONTS

African baptismal fonts were especially varied in size, depth, and shape, in contrast to fonts in Italy or Gaul, which tended to be uniformly octagonal or hexagonal. These differences among the African fonts cannot be correlated with differences in belief; they may be due to local styles or workshops. Font shapes included rectangular, circular, polygonal, polylobed, cruciform, and labial.[321]

Font shapes may have been selected to symbolize certain aspects of the rite. The church's maternity may have been symbolized by fonts designed to replicate the shape of the birth canal (e.g., fig. 71). Cross-shaped fonts would have expressed the connections between Christ's crucifixion and the death of the candidate's old self (e.g., figs. 12, 47). Octagonal fonts could point to Christ's Resurrection on the eighth day, the beginning of the new age (cf. figs. 18, 27). Augustine, for example, equated the number eight with both the day of Resurrection (Easter) and rebirth.[322] In this respect, he may have followed Ambrose's allusion to the number eight as being particularly fitting for a baptistery.[323]

Fonts generally had steps to allow the candidates to descend into the water and ascend from the font (cf. figs. 12, 71), proceeding from symbolic or actual west (dark) to east (light). Some fonts with a longer axis clearly indicated a directional pathway, a transitional movement from sin and subjection to the devil to membership in the body of Christ. The width and depths of some baptistery

319. Aug. *Serm. Dolb.* 26(198*).5; *Serm.* 216.11.

320. See Tert. *Bapt.* 8.3-5; Cypr. *Unit. eccl.* 6; *Ep.* 69.2.2; 74.11.3; Aug. *Serm.* 264.5; *Catech.* 20.32, 34.

321. See discussion above, pp. 108-10.

322. Aug. *Ep.* 55.13.23; *Ciu.* 22.30.

323. A poem (uncertainly) attributed to Ambrose which extols the octagonal shape of Milan's baptistery has been published in several epigraphical collections, including the *CIL* 5:617.2 and the *ICUR* 2.1, 161 n. 2; Most recently, it has been published in Ambroise, *Opere poetiche e frammenti, inni, iscrizioni, frammenti,* ed. Gabriele Banterle, Sancti Ambrosii Episcopi Mediolanensis 22 (Milan: Biblioteca Ambrosiana, 1994), 145-66.

wells would have allowed full immersion (e.g., fig. 12), but in other cases a candidate would have stood or knelt in water and been washed by the water poured from overhead, possibly from a special vessel held by a deacon (e.g., figs. 5, 7). In these instances, the "immersion" may have been achieved simply by getting the candidate fully wet.[324]

Based on the evidence of footings for columns on font surrounds, most were also covered with a stone and concrete canopy or ciborium, which might have held draperies (cf. figs. 41, 54). Whatever their purpose, their appearance would have enhanced the idea that the font was a kind of shrine, akin to an altar or a martyr's reliquary, where the same arrangement of columns is often found.

## PLACEMENT OF BAPTISTERIES

Few free-standing baptisteries were built in Africa; most of the baptismal chambers were attached to churches and had direct access into the main nave, sometimes through additional communicating rooms (e.g., figs. 50, 106). Their placement was varied, however, possibly owing to the size and shape of the site available. Baptisteries were found behind the apse (e.g., Sufetula, Vitalis, fig. 71; and Mactaris, fig. 59), to the left of the apse (e.g., fig. 61), or in a chamber near the entrance to the church (e.g., figs. 26, 103). Baptisteries were also placed in the converted *cellae* of pagan temples taken over for Christian use (e.g., figs. 74, 75, 103).

Many of the baptismal chambers had adjoining rooms (e.g., figs. 26, 50, 78), some with apses that might have served as places for pre-baptismal rites (renunciation of Satan, disrobing, and — possibly — exorcistic anointing) and for post-bath ceremonies (robing, chrismation, and the imposition of hands). This allowed the ritual to be presented in progressive stages, leaving behind the old, being reborn in Christ, receiving the Holy Spirit, and only then entering into the community of the saved. In some instances, access to the baptismal chambers was possible from outside the church, and many chambers (or their connecting rooms) had communicating doors that would have allowed neophytes to transition through the baptismal area directly into the church. The spiritual journey from outside to inside the Christian community was realized in the path of the ritual.

## MULTIPLE FONTS

The presence of multiple fonts in urban centers, such as Carthage and Sufetula, may indicate the functioning of competing Christian communities, such as the

324. Pouring water would have been a bathing technique familiar to Africans.

Caecilianists, the Donatists, and even the Arians. In other instances, they raise the possibility of baptism being conferred by the same communion in multiple locations within a city. This arrangement could also have made baptism more easily available for the sick in emergency circumstances.

These multiple fonts sometimes indicate the displacement of communities from their cathedral settings, such as the exclusion of the Nicenes by the Vandal Arians, which resulted in the need for a baptistery in a less prominent church or even one outside the limits of the city.[325]

Some of these fonts were in cemetery churches that were primarily pilgrimage sites. In some instances, these might have been used by Nicenes during the period of Arian domination. In the case of Carthage's basilica of Bir Ftouha (fig. 28), however, the basilica and baptistery are dated to the Byzantine era. These pools may indicate a loosening of ties to the local cathedral church, the conferral of baptism under the patronage of a saint whose relics were venerated on the site, or some other ritual of which no literary evidence has survived.

### PRIVACY OF THE RITUAL

The size of the baptismal spaces suggests that Christians usually were not baptized in the presence of either the community or one another. This might have helped the African Catholics to think about baptism as an interaction between God and the individual, without full involvement of the community, and thus to distinguish baptism from eucharist and penance as something that could be celebrated outside the unity of the church. The anointing and gift of the Holy Spirit were performed in the presence of the other neophytes, though apparently not before the whole assembly.

## Correlation of Theology and Practice

### REBAPTISM

The practice of accepting or rejecting baptism performed outside the unity of the church was a much-debated one, on which African practice changed at least twice. Tertullian rejected heretical baptism, but the African church seems to have accepted it until a council of bishops held sometime in the 220s required a new baptism for converts entering their communion. Cyprian extended this position to converts from schism and defended it against the Roman bishop, though he recognized that individual bishops might not follow it. Another Afri-

---

325. During the Vandal period, the shrine of St. Agileus served as the Catholic cathedral. See above, p. 139.

can, however, defended the earlier practice in the *Treatise on Rebaptism*. Thus, when the African church split at the beginning of the fourth century and the followers of Caecilian agreed to accept baptism performed in heresy or schism, they were departing from Cyprian but not from all earlier — and perhaps even continuing — African practice. Moreover, during the fourth century, Donatus and his colleagues allowed exceptions to the general policy of rebaptism practiced by their party.

Baptism had two closely related but different roles and meanings in Christian practice: it could signify a rejection of and purification from idolatry and a commitment to Christ; it could also effect an initiation into the Christian community, with the conferral of the sanctity proper to that community. Accepting and rejecting baptism performed in heresy or schism can be correlated with an emphasis on one or the other of these two functions.

When baptism was understood primarily as a rejection of idolatry and commitment to Christ, it could be recognized even when performed in a heretical or schismatic communion. Tertullian's writings reflect his church's emphasis on the baptismal oaths that separated a convert from the traditional Roman religious practices. Yet Tertullian's identification of the church with Christ and as the body of the Trinity provided a basis for the rejection of baptism performed outside it, a rejection later realized in Agrippinus's council. Cyprian not only accepted this identification of baptism as the means of entering the community that exercised the power of sanctification, but also characterized schism as a form of idolatry. Baptism performed outside the holy communion of the true church not only failed to purify but actually polluted its recipient, just as did the rituals of idolatry. Although the Donatists did not follow Cyprian in regarding all schism as demonic and, thus, the equivalent of idolatry and apostasy, they rejected the baptism performed by the Caecilianists because they claimed that it transmitted the apostasy of its minister (which that community did not regard as vitiating the sacramental action). The Donatists credited their own ritual with communicating the pure faith of its minister. In arguing for the limited efficacy of schismatic baptism, Augustine explained that it did cleanse the recipients from the sin of idolatry even as it burdened them with that of schism. Unlike his predecessors, he was willing to extend the presence of the church and even the efficacy of its sanctifying power beyond the boundaries of the visible communion. Moreover, he focused the rejection of Satan on the moral life rather than on the avoidance of all forms of contact with idolatry. The gradual Christianization of Roman society during the fourth century had made that form of apostasy less of a challenge to Christian fidelity. Thus, he compared receiving baptism in schism not to idolatry or apostasy — as Cyprian and the Donatists did — but to a false profession of faith or a failure to repent of other sins within the true church.

The second function of baptism, as initiation into the community of salvation, gradually became the primary understanding of the ritual in Africa, displacing separation from idolatry. In the second century, even heretical baptism could be accepted as a rejection of the idolatry that was pervasive in the culture. Under the weight of systematic persecution in the third century, schism was interpreted as a form of idolatry and rebaptism became a requirement. In the early fourth century, a perceived danger of pollution by contact with apostates drove the Donatists to focus on the fidelity of the church. As the empire became increasingly supportive of Christianity, however, immorality replaced idolatry as the greater threat. Augustine then interpreted schism as a form of immorality — a violation of mutual love. By acknowledging that his own communion could not claim purity on this broader and more exacting standard, he recognized that the Donatists could not be excluded from sharing the gifts and endowments of the earthly church on the grounds of schism alone. As a failure in charity, schism could be recognized as a particularly flagrant form of that sin common to both Donatists and Caecilianists. It brought damnation only when a Christian refused to repent — by returning to unity — prior to death. Thus, as the religious character of Roman society changed, the church's identifying marks and the meaning of maintaining its boundary also changed. The condition of schismatics could be understood as like that of unfaithful Catholics within the unity of the church rather than as demonic apostates.

### THE POWER TO SANCTIFY

Closely related to the efficacy of baptism was the church's power to sanctify and the qualifications of the minister of its rituals. Two different approaches were used. The first, most clearly identified with Cyprian, identified the power to sanctify with a certain presence of the Holy Spirit and had to specify the manner in which this was received, maintained, and exercised. The second, developed by Augustine, regarded this power as a delegation, an authority to act for another, and had to specify the person by whose power the minister acted and the manner of authorization.

In the African church at the end of the second century, the power to sanctify, at least by forgiving sins, was associated with the gift of the Holy Spirit. This was evident in the claims being made (and rejected by Tertullian) for the confessors and martyrs on the basis of their Spirit-inspired witness to Christ. The Bishop of Carthage at the time also claimed that the church had the power to forgive sins by the ritual of penance as well as baptism. Tertullian himself recognized the validity of the assertion but located the power not in the office holders but, initially, in the whole community and, later, in those who followed the directives of the Spirit in the New Prophecy. Cyprian explicitly identified the gift of the Holy Spirit as the power to sanctify: he assigned it exclusively to the episcopal college and to the individual bishops who were its members. To maintain access to this power, bishops were required to adhere to the unity of the college and to avoid disqualifying sins, particularly apostasy and schism. Cyprian's theory proved impossible to implement because neither the congregations nor their episcopal colleagues could assure themselves of the purity of individual bishops.

Both the author of the *Treatise on Rebaptism* and Optatus of Milevis refused to assign the power of sanctifying to the church itself; it belonged to and was exercised by God. The Donatists followed Cyprian in assigning the power to the bishop but narrowed the criteria for his maintaining it so that disqualifying apostasy was easily recognized in a bishop's abandoning the pure communion to join the apostate Caecilianists. Augustine refused to accept the solution of Cyprian, Optatus, or the Donatists. He identified the power to sanctify as the gift of charity, recognized its operation in the mutual forgiveness of Christians, and assigned it to the saints within the church, among whom the clergy might (or might not) be counted.

Some form of delegation was, however, integral to the functioning of the church's power of sanctification. Cyprian, for example, seems to have assumed that he could delegate to — or withhold from — his clergy the power to forgive and sanctify. The confessors in prison anticipating martyrdom delegated their intercessory power to other confessors, empowering them as agents after their own deaths. The *Treatise on Rebaptism* restricted sanctifying power to Christ but explained that the clergy could act as his agents, independently of their personal holiness. Optatus of Milevis proposed this same solution, insisting that the efficacy of the ritual depended on the Trinity, whose benefit was dispensed by the church's minister. Parmenian of Carthage may have used a theory of church endowments that guaranteed the power of its ministry, even when the ministers themselves were unfaithful. Even Augustine had to rely on the notion of delegation to explain why the baptismal consecration need never be repeated: the minister acted as the agent of Christ, whose power could not fail. His more developed theory of baptismal sanctification identified the ministers as agents of the saints within the church who actually held the Spirit's gift of forgiving charity and were identified with Christ as his body.

These variations in the explanations of the power of sanctifying and its exercise were a function of two factors: the need to justify the church's claim to possess the power and the need to determine or regulate its use. Christians seem to have believed that only a holy person could hold and exercise the power to sanctify. The challenge arose in specifying the necessary kind of holiness and the methods or criteria for judging its presence and operation, so that the unqualified ministers could be identified, removed, and replaced. Tertullian affirmed that all Christians shared the power, but he finally disqualified anyone who would actually exercise it by forgiving serious post-baptismal sin. Cyprian limited the power to bishops in the unity of the episcopal college who were not (or were not known to be) apostates or seriously immoral. The Donatists restricted this power to bishops free of apostasy, both personally and through association with their colleagues. Augustine, however, specified that only those endowed with charity, the principle of moral goodness, could hold and exercise the power to sanctify. As a consequence, however, he explained that the saints within the church as a group rather than as identifiable individuals held the power and exercised it through the clergy as their agents. Augustine's theory was a creative response to the practical problem of identifying the holy persons who held sanctifying power. By refusing to identify the individuals forming the society of saints or body of Christ, his theory avoided the difficulties of enforcement.

The second problem was regulating the use of the power: for this, specific individuals had to be authorized to act. Because baptism gave its recipient access to the eucharistic communion, it had to be dispensed under the control of the community and its officers. The common practice was to place the ritual under the supervision of the bishop, sometimes even in case of emergency. Tertullian justified the restriction by appeal to the need for good order in the church, although he specified that all Christians were empowered to baptize. Cyprian restricted the power of baptizing to the bishops in the unity of the episcopal college; in practice, he allowed clerics to act as delegates of the bishops, but without explaining the authorization. Augustine argued that the authority to act for the church by conferring baptism was given to the clergy through the ritual of ordination and, like baptism itself, that delegation could be maintained and transmitted outside the unity of the church. Yet, he allowed that in emergency anyone could confer Christian baptism.

Although African Catholics recognized that baptism was necessary for salvation, even of infants, they seem to have been reluctant to take advantage of the right of anyone other than the clergy to exercise the church's power to purify and sanctify. Even in emergencies, they preferred to seek a clerical minister rather than securing salvation by having someone immediately available administer the sacrament. This may have been a continuing influence of Cyprian's insistence — kept alive by the Donatists — on the exclusive power of the faithful clergy to act for Christ.

Like the understanding of the ritual itself, the explanation of its power to sanctify and of the qualifications of its minister changed over time. The dual practical needs of identifying a group qualified to hold the gift of the Holy Spirit and finding a means of controlling its exercise persisted. The bishops were in the best position to control access to the eucharistic communion through baptismal purification, but they — like any identifiable individual or group — proved incapable of maintaining the level of fidelity necessary to guarantee the presence of sanctifying power. The African Christians provided competing solutions, each of which would make its contribution to the western church.

In grappling with the problems of baptism performed outside the normal setting, which was by the bishop in the cathedral church, some writers assigned different effects to the individual parts of the ritual. In his discussion of its parts, Tertullian distinguished the preparatory washing from the conferral of the Spirit by the bishop's imposition of hands. He did not, however, restrict the efficacy of the washing ritual when it was performed in emergency, even by a layperson. The *Treatise on Rebaptism,* for example, distinguished water and spirit baptism. It then argued that in the absence of a bishop, anyone could confer water baptism, and God would supply the sanctifying spirit baptism. A parallel argument seems to have been used to justify the validity of baptism performed in schism, which would then be supplemented by the conferral of the Holy Spirit through a legitimate bishop. Cyprian, however, insisted that the efficacy of the ritual could not be so divided: water baptism performed in emergency in the absence of a bishop carried the full efficacy of the sacrament. Outside the church, he argued, the ritual had only a polluting effect. Augustine distinguished two effects of the ritual: dedication of the recipient to Christ and sanctification by the Holy Spirit. He judged that the first was given whenever the ritual was properly performed, even outside the unity of the church. He argued that the sanctification might also be conferred in this circumstance, but he believed that it could be retained only by those who were intentionally united to the church by conversion and love. He provided some evidence that presbyters were authorized to perform the full ritual, including the imposition of hands for conferring the Spirit, in the absence of the bishop.

The indivisibility of the sanctifying power of the ritual seems to have been a practical necessity. When the ritual was recognized as necessary for salvation, its power had to be available even in the absence of a bishop, when the full rite could not be performed. Attempts to separate the parts of the ritual in order to assign a partial efficacy to baptism given in heresy or schism were unsuccessful.

### BAPTISM OF INFANTS

The practice of infant baptism was attested from the time of Tertullian. It seems to have been justified as a means of incorporation into the church, thus giving access to the salvation provided by Christ. Tertullian, who understood baptism primarily as a rejection of idolatry and an act of allegiance to Christ, argued that infants and even adolescents were incapable of such self-disposition. He asserted that adolescents could be saved through their growing faith but offered only their freedom from sin as an explanation of the salvation of infants. He was, however, arguing against an established practice in the church. Most Christians seem to have regarded baptism as necessary for salvation and therefore to have provided it to infants. Cyprian offered both direct and indirect evidence of the practice. He argued that, unlike circumcision, baptism could be given immediately after birth. In specifying its effect, he focused on the mortality inherited from Adam and its contagion rather than on personal sinfulness. He also indicated that small children participated in the community eucharist, for which baptism was required. By Augustine's time, the practice and even necessity of infant baptism was well established and could be used as an argument for the inheritance of and participation in the guilt of the Adamic sin.

The practice of baptizing infants seems to have arisen from the understanding of baptism as the ceremony of incorporation into the church, which was the community and means of salvation. Tertullian argued against the practice on the grounds that the children had no sin and were incapable of making a meaningful rejection of idolatry and commitment to Christ. When Cyprian approved the practice because it gave the children access to the grace of Christ, he attempted to identify some form of sin from which the infants were being freed. He specified the contagion of death arising from Adam's sin, rather than any guilt of the child. Augustine constructed a more elaborate argument to complete the transition to the necessity of forgiveness achieved by incorporation. Since only those who were joined to Christ through the church could be saved, infants would be denied salvation unless they were baptized. God, however, could not justly condemn these children unless they were carrying some guilt of sin. Since they had not yet had the opportunity to sin in their individual lives, they must be sharing in the guilt of Adam's sin.[326] Thus, Augustine constructed his theory of inherited guilt on the basis of the church's baptismal practice, which was itself grounded in the belief that incorporation into the church was necessary for salvation.

## Transition

The twin issues of church purity and the efficacy of baptism were at the heart of African Christian practice and controversy from the third through the fifth centuries. By purifying converts to the faith, the ritual of baptism established the holiness of the church, and its very power to purify. The holiness of the community was considered essential to the meaning and efficacy of common prayer and the eucharistic ritual. Maintaining that purity became the pressing issue facing the church. Thus penitential rituals of exclusion and reconciliation

---

326. The argument developed in Aug. *Gen. litt.* 10.4.7; 14.23-16.29; *Pecc. merit.* 1.23.33, 28.55, 30.58; 3.3.6. It was a commonplace by *Iul. op. imp.* 3.3.9.

were intimately connected to the church's power to sanctify, as will reappear in the consideration of the practices of penance and orders. The role and qualifications of the minister of each of these rituals were involved in the discussion and debate from the outset. Attention now turns to the rituals of eucharist, penance, and ordination. The elements that have been uncovered in the study of baptism will reappear in related forms and roles.

# CHAPTER 6

# Living in Peace:
# The Celebration of Word and Eucharist

## INTRODUCTION

The eucharistic celebration was the central ritual of the Christian church of North Africa. The community gathered in different configurations, in the morning or in the evening, to share the bread and cup that joined them to the supper Christ celebrated with his disciples on the night before his death. Sharing the eucharistic communion was believed to be an essential preparation and qualification for attaining the salvation promised by Christ. Baptism purified converts for participation in this ritual; penance permitted serious sinners to return to its fellowship after being excluded. Orders designated the persons authorized to lead it.

Christian eucharistic practice and theology developed as the community grew and its relationship to the imperial culture changed. The focus shifted from the evening meal celebration, which was modeled on the Lord's dining with his disciples before his death, to the morning prayer service at which the food was only a token of that full meal. Under the pressure of Roman demands to participate in the sacrifices of the state cult, Christians emphasized the sacrificial character of their eucharistic ritual. Once the empire became Christian, this ritual would replace the traditional religious ceremonies as the celebration of major imperial events.

The controversies following the Decian and Diocletian persecutions were focused on baptism and penance; they resulted in schisms — divisions in the communion — because these rituals controlled access to the eucharist. The understanding of the eucharist itself as the sacrament of unity was affirmed indirectly. Cyprian and Augustine developed a distinctively African explanation of the presence of Christ in the bread and wine centered on the community that shared the sacrament.

The eucharistic rituals have left less archeological evidence than those of baptism. Unlike the stone or masonry baptismal pools that were imbedded in the ground, the furniture for eucharist was wooden and moveable; its implements were small and made of easily reused metal.[1] The foundations of church buildings from the period after the Diocletian persecution show the placement of altars, the elevated space and benches for the clergy, and the footings of chancel screens separating the altar area from the nave of the church. On these outlines, the ritual actions can still be traced, using such words and descriptions as the literary record has preserved.

## WORD AND EUCHARIST IN TERTULLIAN'S TIME

Tertullian did not provide a detailed explanation and defense of the eucharistic ritual similar to the one he did for baptism. His writings do, however, provide information about the celebration in Carthage at the end of the second century and the beginning of the third century.

### The Ritual

Tertullian referred to communal gatherings for religious rituals *(sollemnia)* that ran a definite course but with certain variations. The order of the service is set out most fully in his *Apology* (a document purporting to be written for outsiders). He described a program consisting of prayers for the safety of the state and the world, readings of the sacred texts, and exhortations or rebukes based on the scriptures.[2] Slightly later in the same text, he also outlined a meal in the evening that began and ended with prayer, which he called a love feast *(dilectio).*[3] Tertullian implied that the participants in this meal were drawn from all social classes and that an unusual respect was shown for the poor.[4] In other places, he called this evening meal the Lord's — or God's — Banquet or dinner.[5] He rarely used the term *eucharistia,* but he applied it both to the food itself and to the ritual action of its offering, placing it under the general category

---

1. Optat. *Parm.* 6.1-2 charged that the Donatists scraped down or broke up wooden altars and melted metal chalices. See also Aug. *Ep.* 185.7.27, which describes Maximianus, the Caecilianist Bishop of Bagai, being beaten by Donatists with pieces of wood that had been broken off the altar.

2. Tert. *Apol.* 39.2-4.

3. Tert. *Apol.* 39.16-18. In *Bapt.* 9.2, he used the Greek term, *agapē.*

4. Tert. *Apol.* 39.16.

5. *Conuiuium dominicum* (Tert. *Ux.* 2.4.2). This was contrasted with other evening celebrations, including non-Christian dinner parties and the nighttime paschal celebration. He also used *conuiuio dei* (*Ux.* 2.8.8) and *cena dei* (as contrasted with *cena daemoniorum*): *Spec.* 13.4. The term *cena* especially denotes an evening meal. He used the term *agapē* (*Ieiun.* 17.2-3), but not in clear reference to a meal. An *agapē* meal is mentioned in *Pas. Perp.* 17.1, and contrasted with a *cena libera* as celebrated by gladiators on the night before the games (*Apol.* 42.5).

---

of a sacrament.[6] In a doctrinal treatise, he again described a religious service that included readings, the chanting of psalms, the delivery of a sermon, and prayers; but there he did not mention any sharing of food.[7] In one of his disciplinary writings, he spoke of "the Banquet of God" and the church's sacrifices, but he added nothing about these rituals.[8] In his treatise *On Prayer,* however, he considered the reception of the Lord's body in a morning service of sacrificial prayers, with the faithful standing at God's altar. He suggested that those who did not want to stop their fasting on that day by receiving the Lord's body should reserve it to eat later, presumably at the mid-afternoon end of the fast.[9] He noted that this morning service — outside the normal meal times — was an innovation of the church rather than the fulfillment of a command received from the Lord.[10]

## READINGS

The reading of the scriptures in the Christian assembly is well attested in Tertullian's works. In defending the church's right to interpret the Bible, he asserted that the true and proper texts were those read aloud in the gatherings of the communities that had been founded by the apostles themselves.[11] Thus, the church at Carthage used not only the Gospels and apostolic letters but the Old Testament, referred to as the Law and the Prophets.[12] Tertullian placed a high value on the communal hearing of the word of God, counting it among the legitimate reasons for Christian women to leave the shelter of their homes and appear in public.[13]

According to Tertullian's witness, the preaching was focused on establishing and maintaining the discipline of Christian life.[14] He asserted that the scrip-

6. Tertullian used this term only seven times in his extant writings. For the food: *Or.* 19.1-2; *Cor.* 3.3; *Praescr.* 36.5; *Pud.* 9.16, 18.8. For the ritual: *Or.* 24; *Marc.* 4.34.5.

7. Tert. *An.* 9.4. The context seems to be a large gathering. It might have been in the morning.

8. Tert. *Ux.* 2.8.8, *conuiuium Dei.*

9. Tert. *Or.* 19.1-4. This interpretation differs from that in Andrew McGowan, "Rethinking Agape and Eucharist in Early North African Christianity," *Studia Liturgica* 34 (2004): 165-76. Our reading understands *accepto* and *reservato* as two different, mutually exclusive actions, both of which are salutary. McGowan interprets them as two parts of the same action: that the eucharistic food was received and reserved for later use by all present, not only by those observing a fast. The failure to mention the reservation of wine might indicate either that it was not taken away or that the liquid did not break the fast.

10. Eucharistiae sacramentum, et in tempore uictus et omnibus mandatum a domino, etiam antelucanis coetibus nec de aliorum manu quam praesidentium sumimus. *Cor.* 3.3 (CCSL 2:1043.19-22).

11. Tert. *Praescr.* 36.1.

12. Tert. *Praescr.* 36.5.

13. Tert. *Cult. fem.* 2.11.1-2.

14. Tert. *Apol.* 39.3-4; *Pud.* 1.5.

ture not only nourished faith and hope but inculcated good habits, reinforced moral precepts, and strengthened resolve during times of danger or loss.[15]

<br>

## PRAYER

In his *Apology,* Tertullian spoke of the prayers of the community for the good of the empire and its leaders.[16] Earlier in this same treatise, he had described prayer as the offering Christians made to God in place of the sacrifices of the imperial religion.[17] In his treatise *On Prayer,* he discussed prayer both in the assembly and in private. He considered the Lord's Prayer both innovative and foundational; it was a synthesis of the gospel.[18] When the Lord's Prayer was recited in the assembly, petitions that addressed particular personal or communal circumstances might be added to those of the gospel text.[19]

Tertullian considered the proper preparation for prayer. This included resolving conflicts among members of the community and setting aside mental turmoil or distraction.[20] He did not grant, however, the necessity of washing hands before prayer, unless some specific defilement had made them particularly unclean.[21] Specifically, he made provision for cleansing in preparation for the service of praise that followed the communal meal.[22]

The performance of prayer also received full consideration. During prayer, Christians stood,[23] with hands raised and extended. They modeled their prayer posture on that of Christ crucified.[24] Tertullian warned that one should not extend the hands so far or raise them so high as to attract attention (cf. figs. 120, 130).[25] Both fasting and kneeling for worship were forbidden on the Lord's Day and even on weekdays between Easter and Pentecost.[26] Prayers were not to be spoken too loudly, since this could appear immodest and vain; the volume of

---

15. Tert. *Apol.* 39.3.

16. Tert. *Apol.* 39.2.

17. Tert. *Apol.* 30.5.

18. Tert. *Or.* 1.

19. Tert. *Or.* 10; *Apol.* 30-32, 39.

20. Tert. *Or.* 11, 12.

21. Tert. *Or.* 13 was written as a kind of polemic against those who washed hands as part of commemorating "the surrender of the Lord." Tertullian insisted that a pure spirit was more important than clean hands. Baptism was a sufficient cleansing for prayer.

22. Tert. *Apol.* 39.18.

23. Tert. *Or.* 16. Sitting was irreverent. The congregation stood to receive the eucharist; see *Or.* 19.

24. Tert. *Or.* 14, 28, 29.

25. Tert. *Or.* 14. It cannot be determined whether this Christian posture differed significantly from the Roman position of prayer.

26. Tert. *Cor.* 3.4.

the voice brought no advantage in communicating with God.[27] Tertullian argued that removing cloaks, like washing hands, was an empty gesture. Women, however, were to dress modestly and have their heads veiled.[28] Finally, Tertullian considered prayer the sacrifice that the Christian offered to God, in place of the abolished sacrifices at the Jerusalem temple — a sacrifice with full efficacy and operative only for good.

## KISS OF PEACE

Tertullian referred to a kiss of peace that seems to have been a mouth-to-mouth sharing of the Spirit. He praised it as the "seal of prayer."[29] He cautioned that nonbelieving husbands might be suspicious of their wives' exchanging this kiss with their Christian brothers, which confirmed that it involved bodily contact.[30] Because some felt that sharing the kiss of peace was inappropriate while fasting, Tertullian recommended that it be omitted during common worship on the fast days observed by the whole community. When individuals were fasting as a private devotion, however, he suggested that they share the communal kiss of peace, in obedience to the Lord's mandate of concealing their pious work (Matt. 6:16-18). In private devotions within the home, of course, the kiss of peace could be omitted because the fast would have been known to all participants in the worship.[31] Tertullian did not explain the hesitation to share the kiss of peace while fasting. As a penitential action, fasting might have precluded full participation in community life. Alternatively, all oral contact might have been avoided by fasters. Those who were fasting refrained not only from the kiss of peace and the pleasure of bathing but apparently from eating the eucharist as well, as has been noted.[32]

## OFFERING

The part of the community's liturgy that encompassed the offering, blessing, and sharing of bread and wine seems to have been included, in Tertullian's explanations, under the general heading of the prayer to which he referred as

---

27. Tert. *Or.* 17.

28. Tert. *Or.* 20, 21, 22 (citing 1 Cor. 11:1-16; 1 Tim. 2:9). In *Virg.* 17.4, he noted that some who otherwise refused to wear veils used a head covering for prayer.

29. Tert. *Or.* 18.1. See also below, p. 267, n. 278.

30. Tert. *Ux.* 2.4.

31. Tert. *Or.* 18.1-7.

32. On not bathing during fasting, see Tert. *Ieiun.* 1.4 and *Ux.* 2.4; also, Aug. *Ep.* 54.7.9-10. On the eucharist, see Tert. *Or.* 19.1-4. The newly baptized also avoided the common baths during the week following that ritual (Tert. *Cor.* 3.3).

sacrifice.[33] Attending this sacrifice, like hearing the scripture read out, was a legitimate reason for Christian women to go out in public.[34] Though he provided no version of the formula of offering,[35] Tertullian clearly marked the connection between the Christian eucharist and the action of Jesus at the supper.[36] In contesting the anti-materialist tendencies among some Christians of his day, he regularly referred to Christ's use of bread and wine as a means of indicating his body and blood in the eucharistic offering. He used the term *figura* to signify the typological or representative relationship of these earthly elements to the flesh and blood in which the Savior accomplished the salvation of humanity.[37] This, he argued, showed that Christ's body and blood were of the same order of reality as the bread and wine, disputing the belief of some Christians that the divine Savior had not taken earthly realities to himself.[38] Indeed, in his treatise *On the Resurrection of the Dead*, Tertullian asserted that the eucharistic reception of Christ nourished and prepared the body to share the soul's reward.[39] Finally, he noted that Christians held the bread and wine in reverence; they were upset when any of it accidentally fell to the ground.[40]

Christians not only received the blessed food in the assembly but also took bread home with them for consumption at other times. Such a practice is evidenced in different contexts. Because some Christians apparently absented themselves from the morning eucharist to preserve their observance of a fast, Tertullian recommended that they attend the community sacrifice but take the bread home with them to eat at the time they broke their fast later in the day.[41] Eating the reserved bread at home also seems to have substituted in some cases for participating in the communal celebration. A Christian matron married to a non-Christian husband would have to be most discreet, Tertullian observed, in taking the eucharistic bread at home before any other food. Her spouse might regard it with some suspicion and would not understand the true nature of this food.[42]

---

33. Tert. *Or.* 19.1.

34. Tert. *Cult. fem.* 2.11.1-2.

35. A discipline of secrecy with regard to the eucharist was clearly attested later — e.g., Aug. *Serm.* 131.1; 132.1; 307.2.3; *Psal.* 103.1.14. Christians were willing to be misunderstood rather than to reveal the details of their eucharistic practice. See, for example, Minuc. *Oct.* 9.6–10.3.

36. Tert. *Marc.* 3.19.4; 4.40.3, 4.

37. Tert. *Marc.* 1.14.3, 23.9; 3.19.4; 4.40.3-6; 5.8.3. For a discussion of the significance of the term *figura* in this context, see the analysis of Victor Saxer, "Figura Corporis et Sanguinis Domini," *Rivista di archeologia cristiana* 47 (1971): 65-89.

38. Some Christians insisted that Christ had not assumed human flesh because it would have involved the divine in contact with matter, which was considered incapable of redemption. See Tert. *Carn. Chr.* for a discussion.

39. Tert. *Res.* 8.3; *Or.* 6.2.

40. Tert. *Cor.* 3.4.

41. Tert. *Or.* 19.1. Tertullian made liberal use of the term *sacrificium* and here even used the term *ara* (19.3), the term applied to the traditional Roman altars of sacrifice.

42. Tert. *Ux.* 2.5.2.

---

The Christian assembly seems to have been held on more than one day during the week, and to have included stational days on Wednesday and Friday, when many of the faithful fasted.[43] Tertullian's recommendation that a surviving spouse make the offering on the anniversary of death for a deceased partner might indicate that a eucharistic celebration of some type was or could be held on all days of the week.[44] He provided evidence for both the full-meal celebration in the evening and the distribution in the morning before daybreak.[45] A preference for taking the eucharistic bread before any other food may have influenced the institution of this morning distribution.[46] Tertullian tended to use the terms *cena* and *conuiuium* for the evening celebration and *sacrificium* for the morning one — which might have indicated its being a prayer service.[47]

The eucharistic ritual was also used in contexts that did not include the full assembly of the congregation. Tertullian explained that the Lord had commanded that the sacrament also be taken at meal times and by all alike.[48] Private celebrations in households, where any Christian could serve as leader and priest, are evidenced in his writings.[49] Some of these might have been in the form of an evening dinner limited to the household. Not all the family rituals would have been eucharistic, however. In his advice on sharing the kiss of peace, Tertullian supposed that some Christians would continue fasting through a household ritual that included the kiss of peace, thus indicating a prayer service during the daytime.[50] Such private celebrations could have marked the mid-afternoon ending of

43. In *Or.* 18-19, Tertullian distinguished the liturgy held on the Sabbath, which was a fast day, from that held on other days when the church as a whole did not fast. In *Ieiun.* 2.3, 14.2, he specified the stational days; in *Ieiun.* 2.2, he indicated that fasting on stational days was not mandatory. The fast was broken at the ninth hour and not extended beyond the time of Christ's death on the cross (*Ieiun.* 2.3, 10.5-6, 14.2). The fasts followed by adherents of the New Prophecy, however, were extended to the evening (*Ieiun.* 1.4, 10.1-12).

44. Tert. *Mon.* 10.4; see also *Cor.* 3.3. In *Cast.* 11.2, it is clear that the offering was made by a priest *(sacerdos)* in the presence of the enrolled widows. Tertullian argued that the Christian who had remarried would be ashamed to appear before such once-married persons to make the annual offering.

45. See Tert. *Apol.* 39.16-18 for the evening; Tert. *Or.* 19.1 and *Cor.* 3.3 for the morning. See McGowan, "Rethinking Agape and Eucharist in Early North African Christianity."

46. Tert. *Ux.* 2.5.2 specifies that the reserved eucharistic bread was eaten before other food. The first meal of the Roman day was about noon.

47. Tert. *Apol.* 39.16, 17; *Or.* 18.8; 19.1, 6. *Cult. fem.* 2.11.6 uses *sacrificium* but does not indicate the time.

48. Tert. *Cor.* 3.3.

49. Christian spouses would share the *conuiuium dei* (Tert. *Ux.* 2.8.6), which may be the one described in *Apol.* 39.16-18. *Cast.* 7.3 asserted that when the clergy were not present, lay Christians made the offering.

50. Tert. *Or.* 18.6. The advice on the kiss of peace might have been intended for prayer services which did not have a eucharistic element.

the normal fast; there the withholding of the peace would indicate the practice of the devotees of the New Prophecy, who extended the fast until evening.[51]

## The Evening *Agapē*

One form of Christian celebration seems to have been what Tertullian described as a community meal, named explicitly as a love feast. Such meals were not limited to household or friendship groups; they provided food for the needy. This, indeed, may have been the source of the meal's name.[52] The Christian poor were guests at the dinner and were treated with a respect clearly distinguished from the humiliation that dependents often suffered in exchange for their being fed by wealthy patrons.[53] Tertullian also asserted that the community did not waste its common funds on elaborate banquets: it devoted them to care of the poor, needy, and oppressed of the community.[54] Reference to an *agapē* meal, named as such, can also be found in the contemporary martyrdom account of Perpetua and Felicity; it was celebrated on the evening before their execution.[55]

The participants first offered prayer to God, and then they reclined at table to eat a modest banquet. After the meal, the diners washed their hands, lights were brought in, and individuals were called forward to lead the community in praising God, either from the scriptures or with a song newly composed by the singer. This sobriety, Tertullian believed, clearly distinguished the celebrations from the traditional *symposia* and gatherings of the *collegia*.[56] The feast closed with communal prayer.

Tertullian did not refer specifically to the commemoration of Christ and the sharing of the eucharistic food at this banquet, perhaps because this explanation was in an apologetic work. If it was included, however, the sharing of the eucharistic elements would have begun the feast, since in all other contexts he implied that the eucharist would precede other food.[57] The relation between these meal

---

51. That the fast ended at the ninth hour is indicated by the practice of Peter (Acts 3:1), but it also ended then because of the Lord's death at the ninth hour. The followers of the New Prophecy continued their fast until the end of the day (Tert. *Ieiun.* 10.6-12). For other prayer times, see *Or.* 25.

52. *Dilectio.* Tert. *Apol.* 39.16, following the intention of 1 Cor. 11:17-23.

53. Tert. *Apol.* 39.16-18.

54. Tert. *Apol.* 39.5-6.

55. *Pas. Perp.* 17.1. It replaced the permitted *cena libera.* No reference to clerical leadership was made.

56. For a consideration of Christian communities in such a context, see Robert Louis Wilken, *The Christians as the Romans Saw Them,* 2nd ed. (New Haven: Yale University Press, 1984), 31-47, and Dennis Edwin Smith, *From Symposium to Eucharist: The Banquet in the Early Christian World* (Minneapolis: Fortress Press, 2003).

57. Tert. *Ux.* 2.5.2; *Or.* 19.1. The reference to prayer before reclining to begin the meal might also refer to the eucharistic celebration (*Apol.* 39.17). Fasting before receiving the elements was

celebrations and the private eating of blessed bread brought home from the communal service remains uncertain. The latter may have been used by those who did not celebrate domestically because their household was not Christian.[58]

The description that Tertullian provided of the banquet indicates that it involved reclining and a full meal.[59] These meetings would, then, have been in private homes or public facilities appropriately equipped with the Roman *triclinium,* a set of couches surrounding a small table. A modified form of this arrangement, the semicircular *stibadium* associated with outdoor meals, is often pictured in funerary art.[60] Because surviving examples of couch arrangement and images of the *stibadium* indicate that neither would accommodate a large group, this evening banquet in a private home would not have included the whole Christian community.[61] The presentation of such meals nightly, or even regularly, for a significant portion of the community would have required the expenditure of resources which Tertullian claimed were directed to the poor rather than to community feasts.[62] Thus, although the evening love feast may have been considered the preferred form of eucharistic ritual because it was patterned on the New Testament models, it was not necessarily the one most regularly practiced and experienced by African Christians at the end of the second century.[63]

## The Morning Ritual

The morning service is well attested in Tertullian's works as the church's innovation for which scripture provided no precedent.[64] Unlike the evening banquet, this service did not involve a full meal and dining furniture; it might have accommodated the entire assembly.[65] The clergy would have presided, led the

---

certainly the common practice in Augustine's time. Andrew McGowan argues that this evening meal was indeed a eucharistic celebration (McGowan, "Rethinking Agape and Eucharist in Early North African Christianity"). As has already been noted, eucharist may have been a regular part of household meals.

58. Tertullian referred to the practice in such a context: *Ux.* 2.5.2.

59. *Conuiuium.* Prayer preceded the reclining to eat. Tert. *Apol.* 39.17.

60. Examples of the *triclinia* and *stibadium* are common in the Roman catacombs (both Christian and pagan).

61. In certain facilities, such as the Carpenter's Guild in Ostia, multiple couches were set up in adjoining rooms; see Smith, *From Symposium to Eucharist,* 102-4. The largest dining facility of which evidence survives in Africa is in a fourth-century mosaic; it used benches and tables; it accommodated twenty-four persons. See the image, with the text of Mohamed Yacoub, in *Splendeurs des mosaïques de Tunisie* (Tunis: Ministère de la culture, Agence nationale du patrimoine, 1995), 243-48.

62. Tert. *Apol.* 39.5-6.

63. Tertullian noted that the morning assembly, outside of mealtimes, was an innovation (*Cor.* 3.3).

64. Tert. *Or.* 19.1-4; *Cor.* 3.3.

65. Tert. *Fug.* 3.2, 14.1 refer to a full assembly.

---

prayers and the readings, delivered the exhortations and rebukes,[66] and distributed the eucharistic food.[67] They had the privilege of sitting while the laity stood.[68] This full assembly — whether in the morning or at some other time — might also have been the context for those rituals requiring the presence of the full community: baptism of converts, reconciling of penitents, and the declaration of marriages.[69] These full assemblies, rather than the smaller gatherings for the dinner or banquet, made Christians vulnerable in time of persecution.[70] By the end of the second century, morning assemblies were apparently a normal and even essential Christian practice.

## Presiders

Although Tertullian argued that, in case of necessity, any Christian, or at least any male Christian, could perform the priestly function of leading the community in prayer or offering the sacrifice,[71] he recognized the clergy or office holders as the normal ministers or leaders of the communal eucharist and other rituals.[72] These clergy were distinguished from other members of the community by their following some of the Levitical purity regulations.[73] Unlike the Roman civic officers who served as priests, Tertullian remarked, the Christian leaders were chosen for their piety and exemplary lives.[74]

According to Tertullian, any Christian could preside at a eucharist where clergy were not present.[75] Presumably the head of a household functioned as leader at prayer and eucharistic rituals associated with domestic meals. Though Tertullian himself would probably have objected, a widow who managed her own home might have functioned in some leadership capacity in or for her household.[76] Tertullian used the term *sacerdos* for the presider at these meals,

66. The ritual is described in Tert. *Apol.* 39.1-5.

67. Tert. *Cor.* 3.3.

68. Tert. *Cast.* 7.3-4; *Or.* 19.3.

69. Tert. *Bapt.* 17.2; *Paen.* 7, 9, 10; *Pud.* 5, 7, 18; *Mon.* 11.1.

70. The smaller evening gatherings were still possible; they could be moved to a different time and place to avoid drawing attention (Tert. *Fug.* 14.1).

71. Tert. *Bapt.* 7.1.

72. Tert. *Cor.* 3.3; *Bapt.* 17.2-3.

73. Thus in *Cast.* 7.2-5, he argued that the discipline of having a single spouse applied properly to all Christians.

74. Tert. *Apol.* 39.5.

75. Tert. *Cor.* 3.3. Christian spouses would share the *conuiuium dei* (*Ux.* 2.8.6), which may have been the community meal described in *Apol.* 39.16-18. But those who were fasting could assist without offense at what must have been a simpler ritual described in *Or.* 18.6. *Cast.* 7.4-5 makes clear that this offering was not made by the laity in the presence of the clergy.

76. This suggestion is advanced by Carolyn Osiek and Margaret Y. MacDonald, *A Woman's Place: House Churches in Earliest Christianity* (Minneapolis: Fortress Press, 2006), 157-62. Tertullian himself objected to the woman serving as minister of emergency baptism (*Bapt.* 17.4-5). As

indicating a sacrifice broadly conceived, since he used the term generically for communal prayer.[77] He also interpreted the baptismal anointing as a priestly one.[78] Moreover, his argument in support of the New Prophecy's program of extending the clergy's single-marriage discipline to the laity, on the grounds that they could exercise the clerical roles, required a meaningful similarity — if not an exact parallel — between eucharistic services led by the laity and the rituals at which the clergy presided.[79]

## Food Elements

In his *Apology,* Tertullian discussed the use of wine at the evening love feast, stressing that the gathering partook abstemiously, since they were participating in an act of religious service and carrying on conversation that God might hear. They remained sober enough to stand and sing psalms or praise God in their own words.[80] Later, however, when he had come under the influence of the New Prophecy, Tertullian seems to have been more ambivalent about the ritual use of wine. In his polemic against the "Psychics" (who refused the New Prophecy) in *On Fasting,* he defended the practice of dry fasts or *xerophagies,* in which one ate only dry food and abstained from any drink flavored with wine, as well as avoiding other worldly pleasures, such as eating meat and bathing.[81] He did not, however, speak directly against the use of wine at the banquet. Meanwhile, documentary evidence demonstrates that some sectarian Christians — Montanists, Marcionites, Manichaeans, certain Encratites, and a group

has been noted above, however, that treatise was directed against a heretical minister who offered an alternate form of baptism. In *Ux.* 1.7.5, however, he applied the priestly discipline of single marriage — which was required for Christian clergy — to women as well as men among the laity.

77. Differentiam inter ordinem et plebem constituit ecclesiae auctoritas et honor per ordinis consessus sanctificatos deo. Vbi ecclesiastici ordinis non est consessus, et offers et tinguis et sacerdos es tibi solus; scilicet ubi tres, ecclesia est, licet laici. Tert. *Cast.* 7.3 (CCSL 2:1024.17-1025.22). Claudio Moreschini construed the text somewhat differently in the *Sources chrétiennes* edition: Differentiam inter ordinem et plebem constitutit ecclesiae auctoritas et honor per ordinis consessum sanctificatus. See Tertullien, *Exhortation à la chasteté,* ed. Claudio Moreschini, trans. Jean-Claude Fredouille, SC 319 (Paris: Éditions du Cerf, 1985), and commentary, 162-63. Although the latter part of the sentence is ambivalent (the manuscript tradition shows that scribes had trouble deciding its meaning), Tertullian's essential point is clear: the difference between clergy and laity derived from the church, not from God.

78. Tert. *Bapt.* 7.1.

79. Tert. *Cast.* 7.3. In this section, he argued that the householder was therefore subject to the priestly discipline of single marriage; the language seems to limit the discussion to males.

80. Tert. *Apol.* 39.

81. Tert. *Ieiun.* 1.4 specifies that meat and broth, juicy fruits, and anything tasting of wine were avoided. Tertullian cited the avoiding of wine and meat by Daniel, Elijah, the repentant David, Samson, and even Timothy as precedents for the xerophagy (*Ieiun.* 9.2-9). The avoidance of bathing is also attested in *Ux.* 2.4.

known as the Aquarians (Waterers) — substituted water for wine in their religious meals.[82] Since Tertullian's criticism of Marcion, for example, lacked any mention of his refusal to use wine, it seems reasonable to suspect that at least on some occasions he too preferred to use water in place of wine, because of his own devotion to the New Prophecy.[83]

Tertullian did not explicitly mention the use of wine at the morning ritual, perhaps because his discussion focused on the bread that could be taken away for later use so as not to break the fast.[84] Later, under the influence of the New Prophecy, he would most certainly have insisted that wine also broke the fast.[85] Nor could he have defended its use in the morning as inoffensive in the imperial culture, as he did for the evening banquet.[86] In his attack on those who used water in the morning and wine in the evening, Cyprian would later concede that this practice was not without precedent or defenders.[87]

The only other type of food used with the eucharist is in a particular context. The newly baptized were given a cup of mixed milk and honey at their first eucharist, as a symbol of their status as "new born children."[88]

The evidence of Tertullian's writings does not allow the specification of the eucharistic component of the morning ritual: whether bread and wine (if used) may have been newly consecrated and distributed, or a new and wider distribution was made of bread consecrated in the preceding evening's Banquet of God. However, the practical problems with the regular presentation of the evening meal that were noted above indicate that eucharistic elements may have been newly sanctified for the morning ritual. Thus, both bread and wine (or water) may have been used.

## Additional Issues

### PURITY

Tertullian insisted that any contact with either the demonic rituals of idolatry or the immorality of public entertainments made a Christian unfit for participation in the eucharist. Following Paul, he asserted that a Christian could not

---

82. See Andrew McGowan, *Ascetic Eucharists: Food and Drink in Early Christian Ritual Meals* (Oxford: Clarendon Press, 1999), 143-74.

83. Tert. *Marc.* 1.14.3; 4.40.3-4. See McGowan, *Ascetic Eucharists,* 164-65. Presumbly, Tertullian could have inhibited the use of wine only in private assemblies of like-minded Christians.

84. Tert. *Or.* 19.1, 4. The Christian wife of a traditionalist husband had only bread to eat at home (*Ux.* 2.5.2).

85. Tert. *Ieiun.* 1.4.

86. Tert. *Apol.* 39.17.

87. Cypr. *Ep.* 63.14.1, 16.1-2.

88. Tert. *Cor.* 3.3. See also *Marc.* 1.14.3. Its use in *Pas. Perp.* 4.9 seems more closely related to baptism than to eucharist.

share the table of God and that of the demons; hands that had served idols must not handle the eucharistic body of Christ (1 Cor. 10:21). Although his concern seems to have been one of ritual purity arising from physical contact, it was not exclusively so: he objected as well to Christians bestowing on actors and gladiators the praise they should have reserved for Christ.[89] Renunciation of any profession or occupation that supported idolatry, it will be recalled, had been required as a condition for baptism.[90]

### EXCOMMUNICATION

In one of his earliest writings, Tertullian indicated that Christians guilty of grave sin were excluded from sharing the community eucharist.[91] In one of the latest, he argued for the rigorist position that serious sinners must never be allowed to return to the eucharistic fellowship once they had been excluded. This later treatise offers extensive evidence for the practice of temporary excommunication during a time of repentance, which was then followed by reinstatement.[92] It also indicates that certain sins — idolatry, adultery, and murder — had entailed a permanent exclusion.[93] Tertullian objected to the bishop's proposal to allow adulterers to return to communion after penance.[94] The practice of denying reconciliation to these sinners implied that the community trusted that a penitent who died outside its eucharistic fellowship could win pardon and salvation directly from Christ. This suggests that they believed that access to the Heavenly Banquet did not require sharing in the earthly one.[95]

## Conclusion

Tertullian provided clear evidence for ordered, solemn services: an assembly of the community in the morning, a *conuiuium* for smaller groups in the evening, and household gatherings. Thus, he seems to have known a differentiated eucharistic practice, with one commemoration as part of an evening meal where many of the customary dining practices were followed, including reclining at table and a program after the meal (the singing of psalms or proclaiming praise

89. Tert. *Spec.* 13.4, 25.5; *Idol.* 7.
90. Tert. *Spec.* 4, 24; *Idol.* 7-8, 11, 17, 21, 23.
91. Tert. *Mart.* 1.6.
92. Tert. *Pud.* 13.10-12; 14.17; 15.3, 9-11; 18.2, 8, 12-18; 14.16 refer to the role of the presider of the church in excommunicating.
93. Tert. *Pud.* 5.
94. Tert. *Pud.* 1.6.
95. Tert. *Pud.* 18.18, 19.6. It will be recalled that Tertullian did not consider baptism essential for the salvation of children (pp. 167-69).

spontaneously). These assemblies seem to have included a cross-section of the community, in which social class distinctions were not maintained. The whole community also gathered for a ritual that was incorporated into a morning service of prayers and readings, in which the eucharistic bread and perhaps wine were consumed, and presumably with the congregation standing throughout the prayers and distribution. The nature of the household celebrations remains unclear: these might have been in the evening *agapē* form and included eucharistic bread and wine. They could also have been simpler rituals, even ones in which blessed bread brought from a community ritual was consumed; prayer services without any food may have been held at other times during the day, such as the mid-afternoon ending of a fast. The leaders of the community presided over the general assemblies, but any Christian could conduct the household gatherings. At least some Christians took the eucharistic bread home with them and received it in private, either early in the morning or later to break a fast.

All these celebrations commemorated the last meal that Christ shared with his disciples. This form of prayer was also understood as a sacrifice that displaced the idolatrous rituals of the imperial culture. Although Tertullian used the language of symbol and representation, he taught that the bread and wine of the eucharist carried the power of the resurrected flesh and blood of Christ to nourish the bodies of its recipients and prepare them for an eternal reward.

Participation in the eucharist was restricted to baptized members of the community who were in good standing. Participants either were not guilty of serious sin or had been reinstated after publicly and sufficiently repenting of it.

## WORD AND EUCHARIST IN CYPRIAN'S TIME

Cyprian's writings provide evidence for the evening meal ritual but demonstrate a continuation of the shift towards the morning assembly as the preferred form of eucharistic celebration. The events of the Decian persecution and the subsequent divisions within the church at Carthage moved Cyprian to emphasize the eucharist as a sacrament of the unity of the local church, at which all the members should be present. This, however, could be accomplished only in the morning assembly. Participation in this communion was understood by the congregation, and then by Cyprian himself, as necessary for salvation.[96] The persecution also provoked Cyprian to reflect on the sacrificial character of the eucharist and its relation to the offering made in Christian martyrdom. These developments came together when Cyprian faced a controversy about the use of wine rather than water in the ritual.

96. For a fuller discussion of this conflict, see J. Patout Burns, *Cyprian the Bishop* (London: Routledge, 2002), 44-48.

Cyprian clearly recognized the evening banquet[97] but distinguished it from what had become the community's primary eucharistic ritual, celebrated in the morning[98] on a daily basis.[99] Christians may have continued to gather in multiple places within the city for the evening celebration, but the full morning assembly over which the bishop presided had grown in importance.[100] At this gathering, the faithful stood;[101] when the penitents were present, they knelt or prostrated themselves[102] with other gestures of humility and supplication.[103] The presbyters and bishop sat together for at least part of the ceremony.[104]

## The Ritual

### READINGS

The lector read standing at a pulpit,[105] where he could be visible and audible to all. These ministers apparently proclaimed the Gospel passage as well as the texts chosen from the Old Testament and apostolic letters.[106] Accounts of the passions of the martyrs may also have been read out on the anniversaries of their deaths.[107] The *Acts of the Scillitan Martyrs* and the *Passion of Perpetua, Felicity, and Companions* would have been traditional by this time. The account

97. Cypr. *Don.* 16. The celebration was styled a *conuiuium sobrium* and included the singing of psalms. *Ep.* 63.16.1-2 also refers to an evening *conuiuium* at which a mixed chalice was offered. This seems to have been a domestic ritual at which the full community was not present.

98. Also, in *Ep.* 63.16.1-2, Cyprian insisted that the reality of the sacrament of the Lord was celebrated in the morning ritual, with the whole community, rather than in the evening. Although Christ had celebrated in the evening to indicate the ending of the world, the Christians celebrated the Resurrection of the Lord in the morning. *Ep.* 63.15.1 also indicates that it was a morning sacrifice.

99. *Cotidie;* Cypr. *Ep.* 57.3.2; 58.1.2. The group that celebrated the eucharist with water alone seems to have made the same distinction, using water in the morning and the mixed cup in the evening (*Ep.* 63.16.1).

100. Cypr. *Ep.* 63.16.1. The continued use of multiple locations, some of which might have been house churches, seems necessary to explain the ease with which schismatic communions broke off from Cyprian's leadership.

101. The contrast between the *stantes* and the *lapsi* would thus seem to reflect the postures of the different groups in the assembly (Cypr. *Laps.* 3, 4, and *Ep.* 15.1.2, 2.1).

102. Thus in *Laps.* 33, Cyprian spoke of the impenitent apostates as falling down when they should have stood and then standing when they should have been prostrate. The penitents were clearly present on occasion, since they were addressed directly in *Laps.* 32-36.

103. In *Dom. orat.* 6, Cyprian described the publican with neither eyes nor hands lifted up.

104. In *Ep.* 40.1, 3 Cyprian described Numidicus as sitting with him among the clergy. See also *Ep.* 39.5.2 for the clergy sitting together.

105. Cyprian provides the first evidence of this liturgical furniture in *Ep.* 38.2.1; 39.4.1.

106. Thus the confessors Aurelius and Celerinus were described as reading the gospel at the elevated pulpit (Cypr. *Ep.* 38.2.1; 39.4.1).

107. Cypr. *Ep.* 39.3.1.

of Cyprian's own confession, the *Proconsular Acts,* was written shortly after his death, presumably for such use. The bishop's exposition of the scripture followed,[108] based on the readings themselves,[109] and perhaps drew upon a collection of scripture texts dealing with particular topics such as those found in Cyprian's *To Quirinus.* Two surviving orations, *On the Lapsed* and *On Unity,* also demonstrate his practice of collecting texts relevant to his themes from different parts of scripture,[110] particularly ones that provide vivid images and types, such as the seamless garment of Christ, the ark of Noah, and the house of Rahab.[111]

### PRAYER AND KISS OF PEACE

A prayer for the penitents and catechumens may have preceded their dismissal prior to the petitionary prayer of the community.[112] The closing exhortation of a letter that Cyprian wrote during an early stage of the Decian persecution may parallel the introduction to this part of the ritual:

> What we must do is to beg the Lord with united and undivided hearts, without pause in our entreaty, with confidence that we shall receive, seeking to appease him with cries and tears as befits those who find themselves amidst the lamentations of the fallen and the trembling of the remnant still left, amidst the host of those who lie faint and savaged, and the tiny band of those who stand firm. We must petition that peace be promptly restored, that help be quickly brought to our places of concealment and peril, so that those things may be fulfilled which the Lord decides to reveal to his servants — the restoration of his church, the certitude of our salvation, bright skies after rain, light after darkness, a gentle calm after wild storms. We must beg that the Father send his loving aid to his children, that God in his majesty perform as so often, his wondrous works, whereby the blaspheming of the persecutors may be confounded, the repentance of the fallen may be restored, and the courageous and unwavering faith of the persevering may be glorified.[113]

108. Cypr. *Ep.* 58.4.1.

109. Cyprian claimed to have been encouraged by the gospel text in beginning *De mortalitate* (*Mort.* 1).

110. Thus Cypr. *Laps.* 19, for example, refers to the ineffective intercessions of Moses, Jeremiah, Noah, Daniel, and Job.

111. Cypr. *Unit. eccl.* 6-8.

112. No direct evidence of the presence of the catechumens during the readings and their dismissal after the sermon has survived for this period. The penitents were addressed in Cypr. *Laps.* and hence may be presumed to have been present for the sermon, if the occasion was a eucharistic assembly.

113. Cypr. *Ep.* 11.8, translation adapted from Graeme W. Clarke, *The Letters of St. Cyprian of Carthage* (New York: Newman Press, 1984), 2:80-81. Nos tantum sine cessatione poscendi et

The prayers of petition may have followed immediately upon such an invitation. Petitions were made for the dead,[114] for the faithful,[115] for benefactors,[116] and for enemies.[117] Cyprian included prayer for the martyrs on the anniversaries of their deaths, perhaps in order to rank them with the ordinary faithful.[118] In addition, a specific commemoration of any penitent being reconciled and readmitted to communion was made during the offering.[119]

All the faithful were to pray in unanimity in this communal prayer of the church. The refusal of some to join in praying for others was, Cyprian charged, one of the many faults God was correcting by allowing the imperial government to persecute the church.[120] These petitions were probably concluded with the recitation of the Lord's Prayer, which only the baptized shared.[121] The pledge of mutual forgiveness in this prayer may have been followed by the kiss of peace, in preparation for the offering.[122]

### OFFERING

The members of the community, even the poor, presented their gifts of bread and wine.[123] Such an offering accepted from a reconciled sinner indicated re-

---

cum fide accipiendi simplices et unanimes dominum deprecemur, cum gemitu pariter et fletu deprecantes, sicut deprecari oportet eos qui sint positi inter plagentium ruinas et timentium reliquias, inter numerosam languentium stragem et exiguam stantium paucitatem. Rogemus pacem maturius reddi, cito latebris nostris et periculis subueniri, impleri quae famulis suis dominus dignatur ostendere, redintegrationem ecclesiae suae, securitatem salutis nostrae, post pluuias serenitatem, post tenebras lucem, post procellas et turbines placidam lenitatem, pia paternae dilectionis auxilia, diuinae maiestatis solita magnalia, quibus et persequentium blasphemia retundatur et lapsorum paenitentia reformetur et fortis et stabilis perseuerantium fiducia glorietur (CCSL 3B:65.146–66.158). A shorter parallel is to be found at *Ep.* 59.18.3, and another parallel can be identified in a letter of the Roman clergy to Cyprian, *Ep.* 30.6.2.

114. As Cypr. *Ep.* 1.2.1 indicates, these prayers might be withheld in the case of a person who had violated the laws of the community.

115. Cypr. *Ep.* 37.1.2; 61.4.2; 62.4.2; *Demet.* 20.

116. Cypr. *Ep.* 62.4.2.

117. Cypr. *Dom. orat.* 17.

118. Cypr. *Ep.* 39.3.1; see also *Ep.* 12.2.1. Because of his struggle with the laxist clients of the martyrs, Cyprian was reluctant to recognize their intercessory power; the church prayed for rather than to them.

119. Cypr. *Ep.* 15.1.2.

120. Cypr. *Dom. orat.* 17; Cypr. *Ep.* 11.3.1. He claimed that the church had been admonished through a vision to pray for certain individuals and that some of the faithful had refused.

121. Cypr. *Dom. orat.* 9 indicates that only those reborn as children of God might utter the address.

122. Cypr. *Dom. orat.* 23-24. See also *Unit. eccl.* 13.

123. Cypr. *Ep.* 34.1; *Eleem.* 15. Cyprian chided the wealthy for receiving from the gifts of the poor but not making their own contributions.

turn to fellowship in the communion.[124] In keeping with his emphasis on the eucharist as the sacrament of unity, Cyprian observed that the bread, made by the fusion of many grains, symbolized the joining of the individual members of the community into the body of Christ. The wine represented the blood of Christ, and the water mixed into it symbolized the inseparable unity of the people with Christ.[125]

The prayer of thanksgiving, *eucharistia,* was then pronounced by the presider over the gifts placed upon the altar.[126] He began with a call to attentive prayer, "Lift up your hearts," to which the congregation replied, "We have them up with the Lord."[127] The offering was performed in commemoration of the Passion of Christ and contained some narrative of that event.[128] Cyprian appealed to the institution narratives in Matthew (26:26-29) and 1 Corinthians (11:23-26) to confirm the precedent and pattern that Christ had specified to be followed in the celebration.[129] The Old Testament events to which Cyprian elsewhere referred as prefiguring the sacrifice of Christ — and thus the Christian eucharist — might also have been commemorated in the thanksgiving prayer itself: the drunk and naked Noah, the bread and wine offered by Melchizedek, the banquet of wisdom.[130] Finally, the prayer may have contained a reference to the Heavenly Banquet, itself prefigured in the church's eucharist, where the Christian anticipated and desired drinking new wine in the Kingdom of the Father.[131] Unlike Tertullian, Cyprian focused on the sacrifice of Christ's death more than the shared meal.

The consecrated elements, both bread and wine, were then distributed by the clergy to all the baptized, including infants.[132] The faithful received the bread in their hands.[133] They could take home and preserve part of it for private reception on days when they did not attend the community service.[134] The cup was apparently distributed only at the celebration itself.[135]

124. Cypr. *Ep.* 34.1.
125. Cypr. *Ep.* 63.13.1, 5; 69.5.2. A parallel for the bread is found in the *Didache* (9.4), but there the union is eschatological rather than realized, as it is in Cyprian.
126. Cypr. *Sent.* 1, *eucharistiam facere.* Firmilian of Caesarea in Cappadocia used similar language (*Ep.* 75.10.5). In both cases, the descriptions applied to people acting in opposition to the church.
127. Cypr. *Dom. orat.* 31. This is the earliest evidence of the preface dialogue.
128. Cypr. *Ep.* 63.17.1.
129. Cypr. *Ep.* 63.9-10.
130. Cypr. *Ep.* 63.3-7.
131. Cypr. *Ep.* 63.9.3.
132. Cypr. *Laps.* 25.
133. Cypr. *Laps.* 15, 26.
134. Cypr. *Laps.* 26.
135. Cypr. *Ep.* 58.1.2.

Although the evening banquet was apparently the preferred celebration in Tertullian's time, the morning service had already begun to emerge as the more frequent or regular gathering of the whole community. The evening meal certainly included both bread and wine, along with other food. During Cyprian's time the evening service continued, but the morning assembly became the central celebration primarily because it included the whole community. This transition is evident in Cyprian's response to an inquiry from his colleague Caecilian of Biltha. In it, Cyprian discussed the use of wine in the morning ritual (a subject on which Tertullian had been silent). The communities represented by Bishop Caecilian's letter followed the earlier practice of having the main celebration in an evening supper at which Christians gathered in smaller groups and at which wine mixed with water was used.[136] Cyprian, however, indicated that in Carthage the preferred service had become the assembly of the whole community in the morning, and included the reception of mixed wine (rather than water alone), since it properly signified the blood of Christ.[137] This shift — which was recognized as contrary to the otherwise normative practice of Christ — was explained by Cyprian as a consequence of the increased size of the community.[138] The full assembly was necessary for realizing the meaning of the sacrament, but all could not be accommodated in the evening banquet setting.[139] In the morning, though, they could participate while standing and share the more symbolic eating.

Although Cyprian provided evidence of private reception of the reserved eucharistic bread in homes, his writings offer no evidence of private or household celebrations; the eucharist was apparently celebrated by the whole community. The evening love feast, *conuiuium sobrium,* was used elsewhere in Africa and seems to have been the only alternative to the morning ritual. Association of the eucharist with regular household meals — as described by Tertullian — is not evidenced in Cyprian's writings.

Cyprian's insistence on the priority of the morning service at which the entire community assembled was influenced by the separate celebrations in the two schismatic communities in Carthage, which may have been household banquets.[140] These congregations were organized in protest over the bishops' policy

---

136. Cypr. *Ep.* 63.16.1.

137. Cypr. *Ep.* 63.2.1. In *Ep.* 63.9.3, Cyprian insisted that if there was no wine in the cup, the Lord's sacrifice was not duly consecrated and celebrated. Caecilian's community appears to have been concerned about having the smell of wine (Christ's blood) on the breath in the morning, perhaps exposing them to persecution. Cf. *Ep.* 63.15.

138. Cypr. *Ep.* 63.16.2–17.1.

139. Cypr. *Ep.* 63.16.1.

140. These celebrations may also have been the foci of the New Prophecy movement earlier in the century. They may have continued to be represented by the Tertullianists, whose community survived until the late fourth century. See Aug. *Haer.* 86.

on the exclusion from communion of Christians who failed during the Decian persecution. These were led by dissident clergy and met at one or more locations in the city, apart from the assembly presided over by Cyprian and his clergy.[141] Cyprian charged the dissidents with violating the eucharist by casting the flesh of Christ outside the one house in which Passover was to be eaten and by setting up a rival altar.[142] As a result of this conflict, the morning service became a symbol of the unity of the church and the authority of the presiding bishop; the household meal services became instruments of division and rebellion.

## Presiders

The bishop presided at the common eucharist when he was present; presbyters were authorized to lead the community worship in his absence.[143] They managed to celebrate the offering with confessors in prison during the persecution.[144] Certain of these presbyters held services at which they admitted apostate Christians to communion, under the patronage of the martyrs but contrary to episcopal instructions.[145] Cyprian claimed the authority to suspend from this ministry of leading the eucharist any presbyters who acted contrary to his directives.[146]

## Food Elements

Cyprian's writings indicate that his community's celebration of the eucharist was focused on the symbolic significance of the bread and wine. He explicitly linked the wine to the blood of Christ[147] and assigned to it the power of strengthening the martyrs for their sacrifice.[148] He warned that the eucharistic elements could harm those who received them unworthily.[149] The community sharing the eucharist itself was symbolized by the water mixed into the wine and as the body of Christ by the bread made of many grains. The *Didache,* written more than a century earlier, uses similar images but in expectation of es-

141. On the development of the laxist schism, see Cypr. *Ep.* 34.2.1, 3.2; 41.1.1-2; 43.1.2–3.2.

142. Cypr. *Unit. eccl.* 9, 17.

143. Cypr. *Ep.* 41.1.2, 2.1 indicates that the schismatic presbyters had easily established alternate celebrations in the city, and a variant of the text may name one of these as being on the hill which was at the center of the city. See the text in CCSL 3B:197.23, 34. See also the evaluation of this evidence in Clarke, *The Letters of St. Cyprian of Carthage,* 2:207, n. 8.

144. Cypr. *Ep.* 5.2.1.

145. Cypr. *Ep.* 34.1–3.2; 43.2.1–2.

146. Cypr. *Ep.* 16.4.2; 34.1. The worst offenders were excommunicated (*Ep.* 42).

147. Cypr. *Ep.* 63.13.1, 5.

148. Cypr. *Ep.* 57.2.2, 3.2; 58.1.2.

149. Cypr. *Laps.* 25-26.

chatological fulfillment; Cyprian affirmed that the union was achieved in the church on earth.[150]

A preference for understanding the eucharist as a sacrifice is also evident in the discussion of celebrating with water rather than wine. Certain sectarian groups — such as Montanists, Marcionites, and Encratites — were known for using water rather than wine, either as a form of ascetic practice or as a repudiation of the material creation.[151] The case for the use of water, at least for the morning service, was presented by Bishop Caecilian of Biltha, who was a senior member of the African episcopate.[152] Cyprian's letter of response allows a reconstruction of his colleague's arguments for the use of water. Since many regarded the evening meal as the appropriate time for drinking wine, they were confident that they celebrated the "truth" of the sacrament at least at those celebrations, even if the whole community was not present. Others used wine at the evening celebration but not at the morning ritual, reasoning that because the Lord had served wine at the evening meal, it would be inappropriate to take wine in the morning.[153] Cyprian charged that the water drinkers feared public identification as Christians by the smell of eucharistic wine on their breath in the morning.[154]

Cyprian responded to his senior colleague with deferential firmness. He acknowledged that the water practice was not a recent innovation and could claim some precedent.[155] His first and principal objection, therefore, was its deviation from the true standard, found in the clear practice and instructions of Christ, the founder of the cult.[156] He held that the presider at the Christian eucharist must offer the sacrifice as Christ did, since he served in Christ's place.[157] The prefigurations of the eucharist in the Old Testament — Noah, Melchizedek, the table set by Wisdom — also indicated the necessity of wine.[158] Other foreshadowings that might favor water, such as the water flowing from the rock struck by Moses (Num. 20:11) and the water Christ promised would flow from himself (John 7:37-38), were properly understood as prophecies of baptism.[159] The New Testament texts not only required wine, but by doing so, linked the eucharist to both the Passion and the Heavenly Banquet.[160] The cup of wine mixed with water, moreover, symbolized the union of Christ and the church.[161]

---

150. *Didache* 9.4 and Cypr. *Ep.* 63.13.4.

151. See McGowan, *Ascetic Eucharists*, 143-74.

152. He is listed immediately after Cyprian among the bishops sending *Ep.* 67 and voted first in the council of 1 September 256.

153. Cypr. *Ep.* 63.16.1-2.

154. Cypr. *Ep.* 63.15.2.

155. Cypr. *Ep.* 63.14.1.

156. Cypr. *Ep.* 63.1.1-2, 9.2–11.1, 14.1-3.

157. Cypr. *Ep.* 57.14.4.

158. Cypr. *Ep.* 63.3.1–7.2, 11.2-3.

159. Cypr. *Ep.* 63.8.1-4.

160. Cypr. *Ep.* 63.9.2-3.

161. Cypr. *Ep.* 63.13.1-3.

The objection to wine in the eucharist may have arisen also from its role as a sacrificial food in Roman private and public practice.[162] Yet, this very connection between the eucharistic wine and the sacrifice of Christ was important to Cyprian's own understanding of the ritual. He interpreted the Last Supper as a sacrificial meal because of its link to the death of Christ. The Christian eucharist, as its repetition and continuation, shared its sacrificial character and efficacy.[163]

## Additional Issues

### PRIESTHOOD AND SACRIFICE

Cyprian demonstrated an understanding of the eucharist as a sacrifice prefigured in the practices specified by the ritual law in the Old Testament.[164] The specific sacrifice performed in the Christian eucharist, however, had been established by Christ at the Last Supper with his disciples and intended for the commemoration of his death, burial, and resurrection.[165]

Unlike Tertullian, Cyprian asserted a clear distinction between the roles of clergy and laity in the eucharistic celebrations. He affirmed that a specifically Christian priesthood had been established by Christ and that the presider at the eucharist functioned as Christ's representative.[166] He did not hesitate to restrict this role to the clergy, whose episcopal leaders God had chosen in succession to the Apostles.[167] He insisted, moreover, on both the ritual and the moral purity of the Christian priest: any cleric who had proven himself unworthy had to be removed from his office.[168] Unlike Tertullian, he did not attempt to extend the priestly code of holiness to all the faithful. Because unsullied purity was demanded of the clergy and not of the laity, Cyprian could allow those who had repented of failure in persecution to rejoin the communion in the ranks of the laity without endangering the efficacy of the rituals performed by the bishop and his assistants.[169]

162. The pouring of libations was one of the ways of participating in the sacrifice required during the Decian persecution; it was a ritual regularly practiced in using wine. See McGowan, *Ascetic Eucharists*, 64.

163. Cypr. *Ep.* 63.

164. Cypr. *Ep.* 63.3-7.

165. Cypr. *Ep.* 63.9-10, 17.

166. Cypr. *Ep.* 63.18.3.

167. Cypr. *Ep.* 70.2.2. The assertion that those outside the church could not sanctify through baptism applied to the celebration of the eucharist as well.

168. See, for example, Cypr. *Ep.* 65 on the necessity of preventing an apostate bishop from returning to his ministry. Even presbyters who had fled during the persecution without authorization could not return to their offices before they had been exonerated of any wrongdoing (*Ep.* 34.4.1-2).

169. The African bishops decided that the penitent lapsed might be admitted to communion so that they could be presented to Christ for judgment with the prayers of the church for his mercy

The challenge of the Decian edict, which required that all Romans actually sacrifice to the imperial deities, disposed Cyprian to use the language of priesthood and sacrifice more specifically than Tertullian had.[170] Tertullian had applied the term to various forms of Christian prayer.[171] Cyprian drew a firm line between the holy sacrifice of Christ and the idolatrous sacrifices of the Roman state cult.[172] Each had its own power: Christ's to sanctify the worthy and harm the unworthy, even physically; that of the idols to pollute and kill.[173] Unlike Tertullian, Cyprian avoided the term *ara*,[174] which was used for the Roman altar of sacrifice; he substituted the term *altare* to refer to the Christian offering table.[175] He extended this contrast to the ritual action of schismatic Christians, which he also regarded as demonic and contaminating.[176]

### EUCHARIST AND MARTYRDOM

In insisting that wine mixed with water (rather than water alone) must be used in the eucharistic celebration, Cyprian suggested that persecution had made participation in the community eucharist itself a form of public witness. He charged, it will be recalled, that some might prefer water because wine could be detected on their breath after the morning service and would mark them as Christians.[177] Thus, the imperial decree that all inhabitants of the empire sacrifice to its gods was mirrored by the episcopal insistence that all Christians identify themselves by sharing in the celebration of the sacrifice of Christ.

With the threat of renewed persecution under Emperor Gallus, the African bishops acted on a different connection between martyrdom and sharing the eucharist. When informants in Rome warned of an impending imperial decree, the bishops decided to allow the lapsed who had submitted to penance to return immediately to communion. The letter in which they informed Cornelius, the Bishop of Rome, of their decision focuses on the connection between the

---

upon them. They were not, however, allowed to exercise leadership roles. See Cypr. *Ep.* 55.6.1-2; 59.1.1–2.2.

170. This change was particularly evident in his appeals to the privileges of Aaron as a precedent for the status of the Christian bishop in the controversy over the power of schismatics to baptize. See Cypr. *Ep.* 69.8.1-2; 67.3.2; 73.8.1-2.

171. For example, Tert. *Or.* 18.4-5; 19.1, 4; 28.3-4.

172. Cypr. *Ep.* 55.11.2-3; 65.2.1–3.3; 67.1.1–3.2.

173. Cypr. *Laps.* 15-16, 23-26; *Ep.* 57.2.2. In *Ep.* 24, he considered the case of a woman whose arms had been physically manipulated into performing the act of offering incense, even as she screamed in protest. He considered her polluted by the coerced contact with idolatry.

174. Tert. *Or.* 19.3.

175. Thus in Cypr. *Ep.* 43.5.2; 65.3.3; 70.2.2. See especially *Ep.* 65.1.2, where he contrasted the two terms.

176. Cypr. *Ep.* 70.2.3; 72.1.1.

177. Cypr. *Ep.* 63.15.2.

eucharistic sacrifice and martyrdom. During the Decian persecution, Cyprian had suggested that public confession of Christ was the appropriate means for the fallen to regain access to the eucharistic fellowship.[178] Facing the new threat, however, Cyprian joined his colleagues in reasoning that those who were already penitents would be strengthened and protected by the body and blood of Christ. Sharing Christ's blood would encourage the shedding of their own blood; the cup of the Lord would prepare them for the cup of martyrdom;[179] the church's eucharistic sacrifices would prepare victims for God's sacrifice.[180] Thus, the bishops linked together the death of Jesus, the eucharistic offering, and the sacrificial death of the Christian martyr.

In this, the bishops faced an objection: martyrdom was itself a baptism in blood; thus, it was more powerful than the church's penitential ritual through which they proposed to admit the lapsed to the eucharist. Reconciling the future martyrs was unnecessary.[181] The bishops responded that the ritual of reconciliation restored the Holy Spirit, who would then speak through the confessor, and the reception of the eucharist would itself strengthen the heart for martyrdom.[182] As Tertullian had credited the eucharist with preparing the body to share the soul's reward of immortal life, Cyprian affirmed that the presence of Christ in the bread and wine would prepare the martyr to witness to Christ. By implication, sharing of the eucharist would prepare the whole community to make public confession of Christ.

## EXCOMMUNICATION

The challenge of the Decian persecution, in which all citizens of the empire were required to offer sacrifice to the state gods, focused the attention of Cyprian and his community on the eucharist as necessary for salvation. Those who had failed and were excluded from communion became most anxious to be received back into communion before they died and faced the Judgment of Christ.[183] When the bishops originally required that the rest of the sinner's life be spent in penance, they promised the penitents readmission to communion as their deaths approached. They anticipated that denying the sinners any hope of restoration to communion before death would move them to despair of salvation outside the

---

178. Cypr. *Ep.* 19.2.3; 55.4.1-2.
179. Cypr. *Ep.* 57.2.2; 58.1.2.
180. Cypr. *Ep.* 57.3.2.
181. This was not unlike the argument that Cyprian himself had made during the Decian persecution (*Ep.* 19.2.3).
182. Cypr. *Ep.* 57.4.1-2.
183. Cyprian asserted that those who died outside the communion would not be accepted by Christ (*Ep.* 55.29.2; 57.1.1). Tertullian witnessed to the earlier practice of permanent exclusion from communion and lifelong penance in hope of receiving forgiveness directly from God (*Pud.* 3.3-4).

church and result in their abandoning repentance and the Christian commitment itself.[184] Despite this promise, many of the lapsed accepted the opportunity for immediate entrance into a schismatic communion established by rebel presbyters in Carthage.[185] Some of the faithful objected to the admission of the fallen, however, apparently fearing that their idolatry would contaminate or bring down the wrath of Christ on the entire communion, thereby cutting off all from salvation.[186] These conflicts demonstrate that the eucharist was being understood as the necessary means of adhesion to the unity of the church and a condition of being accepted by Christ into his Kingdom.

The value that Cyprian, his colleagues, and their congregations placed on the communion of the church was evident in two contrasting assertions: even martyrdom could not win salvation if Christ was confessed in schism and opposition to the unity of the church,[187] yet eucharistic participation could substitute for a proper baptism that had been erroneously or unintentionally omitted.[188] The first explained why schismatics could not be saved outside unity; the second accounted for the salvation of converts from schism whose bishops erroneously refused to perform a new baptism for them. Participation in the communion of the church was the common factor that either enabled or prevented salvation.

## PURITY

Cyprian asserted that the attempt to divide the communion by establishing a rival altar and offering the eucharist in rebellion was a sacrilege no less outrageous to God than the sacrifices of idolatry.[189] Clergy who had presided at schismatic services, for example, were to be treated exactly as those who had offered sacrifice to the Roman gods: they might be admitted to the church's communion only among the laity.[190] Though Christians who had been contaminated by idolatry or schism could not be accepted as clergy, they posed no threat to the purity and holiness of the eucharistic communion when they were admitted among the people. The baptismal and eucharistic rituals of the Catholic church — unlike those of the schismatics — were holy in themselves and would transfer neither sin nor impu-

184. Cypr. *Ep.* 55.28.1–29.1; a similar argument is reported in Tertullian's *Pud.* 3.2.

185. In *Ep.* 43.4.3; 55.15.1, Cyprian observed that if the lapsed were refused the opportunity for repentance, they would join the schismatics.

186. They apparently believed, however, that penitents dying outside the communion could appeal to the mercy of Christ and be forgiven when they appeared before his tribunal. Cyprian seems to have been representing and rejecting the Novatianist position in his report of the episcopal decision (*Ep.* 55.28.1–29.2).

187. Cypr. *Ep.* 55.29.3.

188. Cypr. *Ep.* 73.23.1.

189. Cypr. *Ep.* 69.8.1–9.2; see also *Ep.* 73.21.1-3; 74.11.1-3.

190. Cypr. *Ep.* 72.2.1-3. This included both those who had left the church after being ordained and those ordained in schism.

rity from one communicant to another. Cyprian insisted that, within the unity of the church, one person could participate in the sin of another only by actually approving of it.[191] Further, he demonstrated by examples that sinners were themselves endangered by the power and holiness of the Christian eucharist; the unworthy had suffered bodily harm when they approached it. In his exhortation to penance at the end of the Decian persecution, for example, he recalled instances familiar to his congregation. A child who had been taken to an idolatrous ritual by her nurse vomited out the eucharistic wine the deacon had gave her. An older man who had hidden his failure watched the eucharistic bread he had accepted turn to ashes in his hand. A sinful woman was prevented from secretly receiving in private by fire flashing out from a domestic *arca* where the eucharistic bread was reserved.[192] The eucharist had become a powerful sign of divine presence, countering the demonic power in the Roman world.

### IMAGES OF THE EUCHARIST

Cyprian's theological ideas were often encapsulated in powerful images: the united communion of the church was the seamless tunic of Christ, or the ark of Noah riding the Flood; its exclusive holiness was the walled garden planted with fruit trees; its sanctifying baptism was a sealed well.[193] He also exploited the symbolism of the eucharistic bread and wine. The mixture of wine and water in the cup figured not only the sacrificial blood of Christ but the inseparable union of Christians with him. Similarly, the bread made by grinding many grains of wheat into flour and then mixing it with water to form a loaf represented the unity of Christians as the body of Christ. The bread and wine not only symbolized the unity of the ecclesial body of Christ but also effected the incorporation of those who shared it.[194] Yet, these images did not exhaust the meaning of the eucharist for Cyprian. He referred to it as the Christian sacrifice, the paschal meal at which the Lamb was eaten, the anticipation of the messianic banquet in the Kingdom of Christ, the wedding of Christ and church, the inebriating drink that empowered Christians to witness to Christ even by shedding their own blood.[195] Within the practice of the community, the celebration and sharing of the eucharist was the primary ritual through which the Christian community defined, affirmed, and realized its distinct reality as a pure and holy people set apart by its expectation of the Kingdom of Christ.

191. Cypr. *Ep.* 55.27.3. This was one of the problems with accepting bishops who were known to have been apostates (*Ep.* 65.4.2).

192. Cypr. *Laps.* 25-26. The child resisted receiving from the cup, but the deacon forced it upon her.

193. Cypr. *Unit. eccl.* 7; *Ep.* 73.10.2–11.2; 74.11.1-3.

194. Cypr. *Ep.* 63.13.1-4.

195. Cypr. *Ep.* 63.9.3, 14.3-4, 15.2; *Unit. eccl.* 8.

## Conclusion

The different accounts of the eucharistic celebration provided by Tertullian and Cyprian indicate another of the significant changes in North African Christianity during the first half of the third century.[196] The focus of eucharistic practice shifted from the evening *convivia,* presumably in private homes, to a centralized morning service in which only bread and wine were shared by the full assembly. This change was already underway when Cyprian became the Bishop of Carthage, but it was confirmed by the impact of the Decian persecution and the schisms provoked by Cyprian's policy on dealing with the lapsed.

Cyprian and his colleagues refused to honor the letters of peace provided by the martyrs and confessors to those who had failed to confess Christ during the persecution; instead, they insisted that the apostates engage in lifelong penance and be readmitted to communion at the time of death. In defiance of this episcopal decision, some of the clergy welcomed the apostates into communion at separate eucharistic celebrations. Cyprian, in response, insisted on the unity of the church, the one altar, and the single priesthood. By attempting to set up a second altar, he argued, the schismatics had deprived themselves completely.[197] His focus was on the one celebration at which the entire community gathered, under the presidency of its bishop.

The implications of this continuing conflict for the eucharistic celebration are evident in the correspondence between Cyprian and Caecilian of Biltha. After advancing and clarifying the precedents in the Old Testament for the use of wine, Cyprian turned to the unity of the church with Christ symbolized by the bread and cup. The mixing of wine and water in the eucharistic cup symbolized the uniting of the faithful to one another in Christ. Many grains were ground to make flour and then moistened with water to make the bread symbolizing the one body of Christ in which all the faithful were joined together. The priest could no more celebrate with water alone than with dry and unbaked flour.[198] The symbolism of unity of the faithful in Christ was, he judged, essential to the reality of the eucharist.

The discussion then moved to a tension between the morning and evening celebrations of the eucharist. The morning ritual itself violated the precedent of Christ's foundational evening meal, to which Cyprian had appealed for the use of wine. The true reality of the eucharist, which required both wine and the full assembly of the faithful, could not be celebrated only in the smaller gather-

---

196. As discussed above in the consideration of baptism, Tertullian condemned the existing policy of receiving converts from heretical communions without requiring the church's own baptism; a council under the leadership of Agrippinus reversed the objectionable practice; Cyprian and his colleagues insisted on their own baptism for all converts, despite the threat of a break with the Roman church.

197. Cypr. *Ep.* 43.4.3; 70.2.2; *Unit. eccl.* 17.

198. Cypr. *Ep.* 63.13.1-4.

ings.[199] Similarly, because the bread symbolized the union of all the members in Christ, the eucharist was most properly celebrated with the whole assembly present.[200] Christ offered it in the evening in order to indicate the sacrificial character of the meal; by offering it in the morning, the church celebrated his morning Resurrection.[201] By the use of wine at this ritual, Cyprian observed, the sacrificial death of Christ was also remembered.[202]

The existing tension between the morning assembly of the entire community and the gatherings by household, friendship, or religious preference is evident in Cyprian's response to Caecilian. The devotees of the New Prophecy in Tertullian's day might have gathered as such a subgroup within the church of Carthage.[203] The laxist clergy used a similar structure to reintegrate the apostates into eucharistic communion at a gathering that they controlled. Cyprian insisted on the primacy of the morning celebration that engaged the entire fellowship of the church. The private offering and the evening banquet were deficient precisely because they could not realize the truth of unity in Christ that the eucharistic bread and wine themselves symbolized.

The bishops' response to the challenge of schism following the Decian persecution also required that they emphasize the primacy of the morning ritual, which was under their direct control. Tertullian had argued that any male Christian could preside at a household ritual, but good order required that the bishop preside at the celebration in which the whole church gathered.[204] In focusing on the morning ritual at which all assembled, Cyprian gained episcopal control over the eucharist. Not only would the bishop be able to enforce the requirement of public penance by himself, excluding serious sinners from communion, but he could insist that only those clergy he delegated could lead eucharistic celebrations. When clerics did not follow his directives, Cyprian threatened and then forbade them to celebrate.[205] Cyprian extended this development by preferring the sacrificial character of the eucharist to its function as a community meal. He referred regularly to the priestly character of the bishop[206] and the holiness essential to the one who offered the community's sacrifice to God.[207] All these

199. Cypr. *Ep.* 63.16.1.

200. Cypr. *Ep.* 63.13.5.

201. Cypr. *Ep.* 63.16.2.

202. Cypr. *Ep.* 63.17.1.

203. See the discussion of the context of prophecy in William Tabbernee, "To Pardon or Not to Pardon? North African Montanism and the Forgiveness of Sins," in *Studia Patristica*, ed. Maurice Frank Wiles, Edward Yarnold, and Paul M. Parvis (Leuven: Peeters, 2001), 36:382-83.

204. Tert. *Cast.* 7.3. In *Ep.* 58.4.1, written in anticipation of a renewal of persecution, Cyprian counted the inability to gather the entire community as one of the distressing results of imperial action.

205. Cypr. *Ep.* 16.4.2; 34.3.2.

206. Cypr. *Ep.* 43.3.2, 5.2, 7.1; 59.5.1; 63.14.4.

207. Cypr. *Ep.* 65.2.1; 67.2.1-2.

developments were congruent with the primacy of the morning ritual and the discounted significance of the evening banquet.

Cyprian's emphasis on the morning eucharist (at which the whole congregation assembled) as the sacrament of the unity of the church was recognized and accepted by his people. They believed that salvation depended upon their participating in this ritual. Private celebrations, especially under lay leadership, must have been suppressed because they were associated with the crime of schism. The evening banquet seems to have lost its eucharistic character. It might have been replaced by celebrations of the festivals of the martyrs, of which Cyprian's own became the most elaborate and ostentatious model.

The response of Cyprian and his episcopal colleagues to the challenge of the Decian persecution and the schisms that followed in its aftermath completed the transformation of the African eucharistic celebration from being a meal shared by small groups, following the pattern of the Lord's Supper, to a ritual sacrifice performed in the full assembly by a designated priest, focused on the death of Christ and enacting the unity of the church.

## WORD AND EUCHARIST IN AUGUSTINE'S TIME

Augustine's surviving sermons provide more information about the actual celebration of the eucharist in the African church during the fourth and fifth centuries than can be gleaned from the combined writings of Tertullian and Cyprian in the second and third centuries. Moreover, Christian basilicas dating from this period have been excavated not only at Carthage and at Hippo but elsewhere in Tunisia and Algeria. Although the wooden altars and bishop's chairs did not survive, evidence of their placement has. The remains of these churches permit a reconstruction of the ritual and an understanding of the spatial relation of its components, which is not possible for the earlier periods. For the purpose of the following discussion, the basilica excavated at the site of Hippo will be presumed to be Augustine's cathedral and to follow the basic plan of the church of his time, with adjustments for changes that can be assigned to the Byzantine period.[208] Finally, the influence of Cyprian's writings, which was mediated through the continuing problem of schism, on Augustine's eucharistic theology was no less decisive than on his understanding of baptism. He affirmed Cyprian's emphasis on the eucharist as the ritual of Christian unity and the food elements as symbolic of the church as the body of Christ.

208. See discussion of this building above, pp. 156-58.

### ENTRANCE PROCESSION

In Augustine's church, the congregation arrived through the main doors (to the left or right of the center rear door) and segregated themselves by sex on opposite sides of the central nave.[209] Those in special ecclesial ranks — widows, consecrated virgins, monks, and clergy below the order of presbyter — may have stood closer to the front; the faithful, the penitents, and the catechumens may have been ranked behind them. The altar and lectern occupied the center of the nave. To preserve sight lines, the people may have stood in and along the aisles, turned somewhat toward the center. Since benches or chairs were provided only for the bishop and presbyters, the other clergy and the laity stood throughout the service. People left the church if they required rest or refreshment.[210]

A procession of the clergy may have passed through the center entrance door and down the center of the nave toward the apse,[211] perhaps through a gate in the wooden screen that marked off the chancel area around the altar, and finally to the places reserved for the presbyters and bishop along the apse wall.[212] Somewhat less ceremoniously, the clergy might have entered through the doors of rooms adjoining the nave.[213] The bishop took his place on the raised *cathedra* (chair) at the center of the apse wall,[214] while the presbyters sat on the curved stone benches that were built against that apse wall, on either side of the *cathedra*. The deacons and other clergy apparently stood like the faithful. No indication of singing during the entrance has survived.

The bishop greeted the people: "The Lord be with you." To this the community responded, "And with your spirit."[215] He then may have introduced the liturgy with remarks about the feast day and season. No indication of an opening penitential rite or an introductory prayer has survived. The first communal prayer seems to have been delayed until after the dismissal of the catechumens and other non-baptized persons.[216]

209. Aug. *Ciu.* 2.28. Aurelius of Carthage had separated the sexes in the church during vigils; see *Serm. Dolb.* 2(359B).5. The preacher's remark that a large number of the women left at one point during the sermon would provide further evidence for division of the sexes (*Serm.* 32.23).

210. *Catech.* 13.19; *Serm.* 274; 355.2; *Psal.* 90.1.12; 147.21.

211. In *Serm.* 61.12.13, Augustine indicated that the beggars pled with him to urge the congregation to generosity whenever he entered or left the building. This suggests that he entered and left through the doors the congregation itself used, which opened directly onto the public street.

212. Aug. *Ciu.* 22.8.

213. The central door opened almost immediately onto the street, so that the procession would have had to form in a public space, and unprotected from the winter rains.

214. Aug. *Ep.* 23.3. The term was used in secular culture for a teacher's chair; it was used in Africa in Cyprian's time for the chair from which the bishop presided.

215. Aug. *Serm. Guelf.* 7(229A).3.

216. The sequence is given in Aug. *Serm.* 49.8.

As the reader ascended the lectern on a platform, the people greeted him with "Peace be with you," but he did not respond.[217] One or two readings from the Prophets and Apostles, depending on the day and the discretion of the presider, were proclaimed.[218] A chanted or recited psalm followed, to which the congregation responded, using all or part of one of the verses.[219] The "alleluia" was said or sung on Sundays[220] and throughout the fifty days of Eastertide.[221] A selection of the Gospel followed,[222] apparently read by a deacon.[223] The continuous reading of one Gospel book seems to have been employed, at least in some instances, with interruptions for the feasts of martyrs.[224] The *acta* of the martyrs were also read on their feast days; these were the only noncanonical books used in the service.[225] No evidence survives of a procession of the books, of the number of readers, or the disposition of the readers during the remainder of the service. The book (or books) may have resided on the lectern.

The bishop preached while seated on his elevated chair and would have been required to project his voice for the people standing in the aisles and nave to hear.[226] He may have held a book of scripture and referred to passages that were appropriate to his message.[227] The sermon would have lasted between a quarter hour and a full hour. Normally, the bishop presided and preached, but presbyters also were allowed to preach.[228] When the preacher was not the presiding bishop, the sermon was given standing, from the lectern. Augustine would have preached in this way while serving as a presbyter in Hippo and later

217. *Bru. Hipp.* 1a. The people's greeting of the lector is known only by Augustine's report of the Donatist liturgy: *Ep.* 43.8.21; 53.1.3.

218. Aug. *Serm.* 176.1; 65.1.1; 180.1.1; 315.1.1; 45.1; 48.1-2; 289.3; 302.1; 362.1.1; *Psal.* 138.1; *Ep.* 29.4-5.

219. Aug. *Psal.* 119.1; 44.1; 138.1; *Serm.* 176.1; 165.1.1. *Psal.* 40.7 provides an instance of the responsory.

220. Aug. *Ep.* 55.15.28.

221. Aug. *Serm.* 252.9; *Psal.* 106.1; 110.1; *Ep.* 55.28.

222. Aug. *Serm* 49.1; 176.1; 165.1.1; Augustine exhorted the people to hear the words as though they were coming from Christ himself (*Eu. Io.* 30.1).

223. Aug. *Serm.* 382.3.

224. See below, in the discussion of the lectionary, pp. 269-70.

225. On the reading of the *acta,* see Aug. *Serm.* 259.2, 6; 274.1; 275.1; 280.1-4; 301.1.2; 309; 325.1. This was formally approved by the Council of Hippo of 393, 5, and the Council of Carthage a. 397, 36d. For the list and restriction to canonical scriptures, see *Bru. Hipp.* 36; Augustine rebuked a reader who did otherwise (*Ep.* 64.3).

226. Aug. *Serm. Denis* 17(301A).2; *Serm.* 134.1.1; 355.2.

227. Aug. *Serm.* 37.1 indicates that he had a book in his hand; it would hardly have been the entire Bible. *Ep.* 29.4-5 shows Augustine moving back and forth between different passages dealing with the abuse of food and drink.

228. Augustine himself was so commissioned (Possid. *Vita Aug.* 5). See also Aug. *Ep.* 41.1; *Serm.* 20.5.

whenever he spoke in another bishop's church.[229] The people listened while standing.[230] Some would go out during a long sermon to refresh themselves; not all would return.[231] On one occasion, for example, a large number of the women seem to have walked out during the sermon.[232] The sermon usually ended with a prayer, which is preserved in two different versions:[233]

> Turning to the Lord, let us pray. May he look upon us and perfect us by his saving word and grant us to rejoice in accord with him and live in accord with him. May he put away from us the prudence of the flesh; may he throw down the enemy under our feet, not by our efforts, but by his holy name, in which we have been cleansed through Jesus Christ our Lord.[234]

> Turning to the Lord, let us bless his name. May he grant us to persevere in his commandments, to walk in the right way of his instruction, to please him with every good work, and so forth.[235]

This prayer brought to an end the part of the service at which the nonbaptized might be present.

The sermon was normally given by the bishop himself, but there were exceptions. Augustine had preached from the time of his ordination to the presbyterate because of the limitations of his bishop's facility in Latin.[236] Aurelius of Carthage instituted the practice of having his presbyters preach even when he was present.[237] Presbyters would also have presided and preached in rural

---

229. Aug. *Serm.* 23.1; *Serm. Dolb.* 2(359B).3, 23; 25(360B).5. He would have continued to preach in this way even as assistant bishop, until Valerius's death.

230. Aug. *Serm.* 274; 355.2; *Catech.* 13.19; *Psal.* 90.1.12; 147.21; Optat. *Parm.* 4.5.

231. Aug. *Catech.* 13.19.

232. Aug. *Serm.* 32.23.

233. Serge Lancel has argued from *Serm. Dolb.* 19(130A).12 that this prayer was said facing the east, which would have required a half-turn in Augustine's own church. See Serge Lancel, *Saint Augustine,* trans. Antonia Neville (London: SCM Press, 2002), 240-42. It would have meant that Augustine and his clergy stood and turned.

234. Aug. *Serm. Dolb.* 28(20B).11: conuersi ad dominum petamus: respiciet nos atque perficiet in uerbo saluatore suo, et det nobis secundum se gaudere et secundum se uiuere. auertat a nobis carnalem prudentiam; subiectum faciat sub nostris pedibus inimicum, non uiribus nostris, sed nomine sancto suo, in quo mundati sumus per Iesum Christum dominum nostrum. François Dolbeau, "Un sermon inédit de saint Augustin sur la santé corporelle, partiellement cité chez Barthélemy d'Urbino," *Revue des études augustiniennes et patristiques* 40 (1994): 298, ll. 170-74.

235. Aug. *Serm. Dolb.* 30(348A).13: conuersi ad dominum benedicamus nomen eius. det nobis perseuerare in mandatis suis, ambulare in uia recta eruditionis suae, placere illi in omni opere bono, et cetera talia. François Dolbeau, "Le sermon 348A de saint Augustin contre Pélage. Éditions du texte intégral," *Recherches augustiniennes et patristiques* 28 (1995): 61.

236. Aug. *Ep.* 21.3. *Ep.* 29.7 recounts a sermon preached for Valerius.

237. Aug. *Ep.* 41.1.

parishes that were not served by a bishop[238] and in episcopal sees when the bishop was away.[239]

## DISMISSAL

At the conclusion of the sermon, the catechumens were dismissed with a blessing.[240] The porters then would have shut and guarded the doors, preserving the secrecy of the eucharistic ritual, which could be witnessed only by the baptized.[241] The penitents seemed to have been dismissed for separate prayer.[242]

## PRAYERS

The bishop introduced the petitionary prayers.[243] During Lent, the community knelt but remained standing in other seasons.[244] The deacon then would announce each of the intercessions;[245] after the community had prayed in silence, the bishop gathered and offered the prayer to the Father.[246] These prayers regularly included petitions for the enemies of the church,[247] the conversion of the heathen, the inspiration of the catechumens to accept baptism, and the preservation of the faithful.[248] To these might have been added intentions particular to the season and circumstances of the church and society.

## PRESENTATION AND PREPARATION OF GIFTS

The wooden altar was covered with a linen cloth and perhaps set with candles, as depicted in a mosaic from Thabraca (fig. 132).[249] The wine in one or more

238. Augustine inferred that presbyters did preach (*Serm.* 20.5).

239. Aug. *Serm.* 196.4.

240. Aug. *Serm.* 49.8. The catechumens had no idea what sort of ritual followed the sermon (*Psal.* 109.17).

241. Aug. *Psal.* 103.1.14; *Serm.* 131.1; 132.1; 307.2.3.

242. They were regularly addressed in the sermon. Aug. *Serm.* 232.8 also seems to indicate that they were dismissed.

243. Aug. *Ep.* 149.2.16. The sequence of events is provided in *Serm.* 49.8.

244. Aug. *Ep.* 55.15.28.

245. Aug. *Ep.* 55.18.34.

246. Aug. *Serm.* 49.8; *Ep.* 217.7.26. The endings to *Serm.* 361.21.20; 362.30.31 might give some indication of the ending to this prayer.

247. Aug. *Ciu.* 21.24.

248. Aug. *Ep.* 149.2.17; 217.1.2, 7.26; *Haer.* 88.4; *Perseu.* 7.15, 23.26; *Serm.* 110.1.

249. Optat. *Parm.* 6.1. See fig. 132 and the discussion of this mosaic on p. 87.

metal chalices or containers,[250] perhaps already mixed with water, and several loaves of bread needed for the offering and distribution[251] were placed on the altar.[252] Augustine acknowledged that vessels made of silver and gold were used in the ritual but that no religious significance was assigned to the material; they were holy only by dedication to God.[253] He noted that incense had no role in the rite.[254] The faithful brought gifts of various kinds to present to God; most of these were directed to the poor who were dependents of the church.[255] A period of preparing the altar, between the community prayers and the beginning of the eucharistic prayer, may have been filled with the singing of psalms.[256]

### EUCHARISTIC PRAYER AND DISTRIBUTION

The presiding bishop or presbyter, assisted by one or more deacons, stood in the center of the main body of the church at the altar separated by a low chancel screen. The community gathered around, standing.[257] The presider began the prayer with an introductory dialogue and response following what was already a traditional pattern:

Bishop:  The Lord be with you.
People:  And with your spirit.
Bishop:  Lift up your heart (singular).
People:  We have it up to the Lord.
Bishop:  Let us give thanks to the Lord our God.
People:  It is right and just.[258]

The eucharistic prayer was spoken in a clearly audible voice,[259] perhaps following a set formula.[260] No wording has survived, even in a partial quotation in

250. Optat. *Parm.* 6.2, 5.

251. Aug. *Serm. Guelf.* 7(229A).1.

252. No textual evidence of a "great entrance" or an offering procession has survived, but the discipline of secrecy may have required that the gifts not be visible until the unbaptized had departed. The bread and wine were distinguished from the other gifts (*Ep.* 149.2.16). Limitation to bread and wine mixed with water was affirmed in *Bru. Hipp.* 23; Aug. *Serm. Guelf.* 7(229A).1.

253. Aug. *Psal.* 133.2.6.

254. Aug. *Serm. Dolb.* 23(374*).17-19.

255. Aug. *Psal.* 129.7; *Serm.* 82.2.3. In *Conf.* 5.9.17, Augustine remarked on Monica's habit of making daily offerings. *Ep.* 111.8 speaks of Christian women who had been taken captive by barbarians.

256. Aug. *Retract.* 2.11.

257. Aug. *Serm. Dolb.* 26(198*).53.

258. Aug. *Serm.* 19.4; 25.7; 53.13.14; 227; 237.3; *Psal.* 31.2.21; 124.10; 148.5; *Serm. Denis* 6(229).3; *Serm. Guelf.* 7(229A).3.

259. Aug. *Petil.* 2.30.68.

260. Aug. *Petil.* 2.30.68-69; *Reg. Carth.* 103. For an analysis of this canon, see Edward Kilmar-

a sermon or other text; it may not have been written at all — in keeping with the discipline of secrecy. Various commemorations preceded or followed the calling down of the Holy Spirit and the institution narrative.[261] The church itself was commended to the martyrs by name.[262] The faithful departed were recalled,[263] with the consecrated virgins first,[264] then the bishops,[265] then other members of the local church, ending with a general commemoration of all the faithful departed of the universal church.[266] The clergy of the local church and bishops in the communion were also commemorated.[267] To these may have been added the names of particular benefactors of the church.[268] The bread and wine were offered to the Father,[269] with the sign of the cross traced over the elements[270] and the narrative of institution taken from the New Testament.[271] The people responded at the end with "Amen."[272] The breaking of the bread in preparation for its distribution followed the eucharistic prayer.[273] The Lord's Prayer was recited,[274] led by the presider;[275] the people and sometimes the presider beat their breasts audibly at the petition for the forgiveness of sins.[276]

The presider introduced the kiss of peace by saying "Peace be with you," to which the community responded, "And with your spirit."[277] The kiss exchanged by the members of the congregation seems to have been on the lips.[278] The

---

tin, "Early African Legislation concerning Liturgical Prayer," *Ephemerides Liturgicae* 9 (1985): 105-27.

261. Edward Kilmartin suggested this order based on the parallels in Ambr. *Sac.* 4.5.21-22; 6.26-27 and the old Roman Canon. See Kilmartin, "Early African Legislation concerning Liturgical Prayer," 116-18. He argued that the commendations did follow a set formula.

262. Aug. *Serm.* 159.1.1; 273.7; 284.5; 285.5; 297.2.3; 325.1; *Eu. Io.* 84.1; *Ciu.* 22.10.

263. Aug. *Ciu.* 20.9; *Cur.* 1.3; *Nat. et or.* 2.15.21; *Serm.* 172.2.2-3; 284.5; 285.5.

264. Aug. *Virg.* 45.46.

265. Aug. *Serm.* 359.6; *Col. Carth.* 3.230.

266. Aug. *Cur.* 4.6.

267. Aug. *Ep.* 78.4; *Parm.* 3.6.29.

268. Cypr. *Ep.* 62.5.

269. *Bru. Hipp.* 21. The text is slightly different in Council of Carthage in 525, *concilio tertio* (L) and in *Bru. Ferr.* 219; see CCSL 149:265.124-26, 264.412-14, 305. Augustine pointed out that offerings were never made to the martyrs but to God: *Ciu.* 8.27; *Faust.* 20.21.

270. Aug. *Eu. Io.* 118.5.

271. Aug. *Serm.* 227; *Serm. Denis* 6(229).3.

272. Aug. *Serm. Denis* 6(229).3.

273. Aug. *Ep.* 149.2.16; 36.12.28.

274. This prayer followed the eucharistic prayer rather than being recited immediately after the bidding prayers which preceded it. Aug. *Serm.* 227; *Ep.* 149.2.16.

275. Aug. *Serm.* 58.10.12.

276. Aug. *Serm.* 17.5; 351.3.6; *Psal.* 140.18; *Ep.* 265.8.

277. Aug. *Serm.* 227; *Psal.* 124.10; *Ep.* 43.8.21. In the third century, the kiss might have been exchanged immediately after the prayers, before the offering. The evidence for that period, however, is ambiguous.

278. labia tua ad labia fratris tui accedunt. Aug. *Serm.* 227; SC 116:240.68.

---

presider then pronounced a blessing with hands outstretched over the people, who were about to receive the eucharist.[279]

Distribution of the bread and wine took place at the chancel rail,[280] where the people stood and received from the hands of the presider and the deacons. Bread was placed into the joined hands[281] with the words "the Body of Christ," to which the recipient responded, "Amen."[282] The cup was offered to each by a deacon, with a similar exchange.[283] Not every member of the congregation approached the rail to receive. Some refrained out of personal devotion and reverence for the sacrament.[284] Those formally enrolled as penitents were already dismissed. Others, engaged in a private repentance under the direction of the bishop, also abstained from receiving the eucharist during their time of purification.[285] Those known to be guilty of unconfessed sin were warned to refrain.[286] During the distribution of the bread and cup, the community chanted psalms, including Psalm 33, with the refrain "Come and be enlightened."[287] The eucharist was received as the first food of the day.[288]

The eucharistic bread was reserved in the church but not in private homes, as it had been in the third century.[289] This provision may have been made for communication of the dying, especially for catechumens baptized or penitents reconciled in anticipation of death. Placing the eucharist in the mouth of a deceased person was forbidden.[290] The laity may have taken the eucharistic bread, however, on their journeys.[291]

### ENDING

The service ended with thanksgiving, though a particular prayer was not specified.[292] The presider and clergy then processed out of the basilica.[293]

279. Aug. *Ep.* 149.2.16 seems to place this blessing or prayer prior to the participation in the sacrament. See also Aug. *Ep.* 175.5; 179.4; *Reg. Carth.* 103.

280. Aug. *Serm.* 392.5.

281. Aug. *Parm.* 2.7.13; *Petil.* 2.23.53.

282. Aug. *Serm.* 272; 181.5.7; *Psal.* 32.2.1.4.

283. Aug. *Serm.* 181.5.7; 304.1.1; 382.3; *Serm. Denis* 3(228B).3; *Psal.* 32.2.1.4; *Faust.* 12.10.

284. Aug. *Ep.* 54.3.4.

285. Aug. *Ep.* 54.3.4.

286. Aug. *Serm.* 392.5.

287. Aug. *Retract.* 2.11; *Psal.* 33.2.10; *Serm.* 225.4.4.

288. Aug. *Ep.* 54.6.8.

289. Optat. *Parm.* 6.2, 5.

290. Bru. *Hipp.* 4a.

291. Ambr. *Exc.* 1.43; The brother of Ambrose, Satyrus, was given a portion of the eucharistic bread and saved by it during a shipwreck on a trip to Africa; one cannot be sure that an African practice was being followed by the traveler.

292. Aug. *Ep.* 149.2.16.

293. Aug. *Ep.* 29.11 describes the end of an evening service.

## Daily Eucharist

The eucharist was celebrated in the morning, before eating the first meal at midday.[294] In some places, such as Hippo, it was offered daily;[295] in others it was offered at intervals during the week.[296] Some of the faithful attended the eucharist every day,[297] and usually received the bread and cup.[298] Clearly not all of the congregation attended every day, or even weekly.[299] Other services were held in the church, such as morning and evening prayers, which the pious would also attend.[300] The evening *agapē* meal, however, was no longer a practice.[301] During the reform of the African church under Aurelius of Carthage, banqueting in the church building was discouraged except when necessary to provide hospitality to travelers.[302] No mention was made of household meal celebrations.

## The Lectionary

Efforts to reconstruct Augustine's lectionary have met with limited success. They are dependent upon both explicit reference to a text as having been read before a particular sermon and the dating of the sermon itself within the liturgical year.[303] The maximum number of texts normally used seems to have been four: an Old Testament passage, a psalm, a New Testament text other than a Gospel, and a Gospel selection.[304] The exception was, of course, the Easter vigil, at which a greater number of Old Testament texts and psalms were read and sung.[305] Only

294. Aug. *Ep.* 54.7.9 speaks of an exception on Holy Thursday, when provision was made for both morning and evening services. *Serm.* 128.4.6 indicates that on Saturday the faithful assembled early for hearing the word of God.

295. Aug. *Ep.* 54.2.2, 3.4; 228.6; *Serm.* 56.6.9; 58.4.5, 10.12; *Serm. Wilm.* 9.2 (229D); *Eu. Io.* 26.15; *Ciu.* 10.20.

296. Aug. *Eu. Io.* 26.15.

297. Aug. *Conf.* 5.9.17, referring to Monica.

298. Aug. *Ep.* 54.3.4.

299. Aug. *Serm.* 51.1.1; 303.1.

300. Aug. *Eu. Io.* 3.21; *Psal.* 33.2.4; 49.23; 66.3.

301. Aug. *Ep.* 54.5.6-7. Christians were confused about the relationship of the supper to the eucharist. Some thought that the apostles had eaten another meal before the "eucharistic" one.

302. *Bru. Hipp.* 29.

303. The most successful is that of Geoffrey Grimshaw Willis, *St. Augustine's Lectionary* (London: SPCK, 1962). Suzanne Poque, ed., *Sermons pour la Pâque*, SC 116 (Paris: Éditions du Cerf, 1966), 69-115, discusses the readings for the Easter season, and the same author discusses the Gospels of Easter week in "Les lectures liturgiques de l'octave pascale à Hippone d'après les Traités de S. Augustin sur la 1re épître de S. Jean," *Revue Bénédictine* 74 (1964): 217-41.

304. Evidence for the order of the readings has not survived.

305. Willis, *St. Augustine's Lectionary*, finds evidence for Gen. 1:1-5; Exod. 15:1-21; Rom. 6:4-11; Ps. 117; Ps. 12; Ps. 17; Matt. 28.

accepted or canonical scripture texts could be used for reading during the eucharist. The bishops had approved a list of these,[306] and Augustine objected to the inclusion of texts not on that list.[307] The only exceptions were the *acta* of martyrs read at the celebration of their feasts.[308]

Augustine's sermons do provide some information about the texts used for specific feasts. The narrative of the Passion was read from Matthew. Augustine attempted to use all four accounts in successive years, but the people objected, and he returned to the customary use.[309] The Resurrection narrative from Matthew was read during the Easter vigil; the narratives from the other Gospels were read in order during the following week:[310] Mark, with the longer ending;[311] Luke, in at least two parts;[312] and John, in three parts.[313] The order for Mark and Luke may have varied.[314] The reading of Acts was begun after the celebration of the Passion and the Resurrection; it continued through the entire book.[315] Occasionally, Augustine chose a text for continuous exposition, such as the Gospel and the First Letter of John.[316] These programs were interrupted, however, by the texts set for particular feast days,[317] though not apparently for (presumably scheduled) Sunday readings.[318] Specific texts were used for feasts of Christ and the martyrs.[319] On occasion, Augustine coordinated the psalm and the Gospel text, adapting one to the theme of the other.[320] The Gospel readings could be quite short: a single parable or the Gospel's explanation of a parable.[321]

306. *Con. Hipp.* a. 393, 5; *Bru. Hipp.* 36.

307. Aug. *Ep.* 64.3.

308. Aug. *Serm.* 37.23; 51.1.2; 273.2; 280.1. *Con. Hipp.* a. 393, 5; *Bru. Hipp.* 36d. The *acta* of the colloquy with the Donatists in 411 were read out during the following Lent but before the eucharistic liturgy rather than during it (*Ep. Divj.* 28*.3).

309. Aug. *Serm.* 232.1.

310. Aug. *Serm.* 231.1; 232.1; 234.1; 247.1; *Serm. Mai* 86(229I).1.

311. Aug. *Serm.* 233.1; 234.1; 235.1; 239.1.1.

312. Aug. *Serm.* 247.1.

313. Aug. *Serm.* 243.1.1; 247.1.

314. Different orders in Aug. *Serm.* 232.1 and 247.1.

315. Reading of Acts began at Easter; see Aug. *Serm.* 315.1.1; 227; *Eu. Io.* 6.18.

316. Aug. *Serm.* 25.7-8 also seems to indicate a continuous reading of the Gospel of Luke.

317. Aug. *Ep. Io.* Prol., 9.1 indicate the interruption of the *lectio continua* for certain feasts that came annually. The same is evident in the preaching on the Gospel of John (e.g., *Eu. Io.* 8-10, 19-23, 34-37).

318. Aug. *Eu. Io.* 12.1.

319. For the selection of certain readings for the feasts of Christ and the martyrs, see Wunibald Roetzer, *Die Heiligen Augustinus Schriften als liturgie-geschichtliche Quelle: eine liturgie-geschichtliche Studie* (Munich: M. Hueber, 1930), 104-8.

320. Aug. *Psal.* 90.2.1.

321. Aug. *Serm.* 73.1; *Serm. Cail.* 2.5(73A); *Eu. Io.* 7.3.

Outside of the daily preaching during Lent and Eastertide, Augustine delivered sermons on Saturday, Sunday, and feast days of Christ and the martyrs.[322] When he was engaged in continuous exposition of a biblical book, however, Augustine might preach every day.[323] When a scheduled sermon was omitted for some reason, he felt obliged to make it up on another day.[324] The Saturday congregation was more interested in the scripture and its interpretation, so that these sermons were generally longer and more detailed than those delivered on Sunday, when the congregation was larger.[325] Similarly, when games or shows kept many from the service, Augustine felt free to provide a fuller exposition for the devout who had come.[326] On major feast days, such as Christmas, the church was filled with occasional and uninterested listeners who were impatient with the length of the sermon.[327] Augustine tended to focus on those who were interested and hope to do some good for the others,[328] though he was more leisurely in his exposition when the devout composed the majority of the congregation. On one occasion, he noted but made no concession to the impatience of those who wanted to get to their dinners.[329] On what probably became a well-remembered New Year's Day, he preached for almost three hours, thereby keeping his congregation from joining in the traditional — non-Christian — celebrations and enforcing his exhortation to fast for the salvation of the revelers.[330]

Though Augustine's preaching tended to follow the text of scripture and to give the impression of spontaneity, the sermons were well prepared.[331] One day the reader erred in following the bishop's instruction of which psalm to read. Augustine took this error as an indication of God's intention that he preach on that text. The resulting exposition, however, lacked the focus and coherence that characterize most of his surviving sermons.[332]

Augustine's style must not be taken as representative of the preaching of his colleagues in the African episcopate, since he was among the most talented rhetoricians of his time. However, much of what happened in the basilica at Hippo could hardly have been unique. The bishop frequently found his congregation tiring and their attention wandering.[333] He encouraged the hearers to take a more

322. Aug. *Serm.* 139.1.1; *Psal.* 33.1.11; 38.7; 63.1.
323. Aug. *Eu. Io.* 2.1-2.
324. Aug. *Serm.* 149.1.1.
325. Aug. *Serm.* 128.4.6; *Eu. Io.* 47.9.
326. Aug. *Serm.* 51.1.1.
327. Aug. *Serm.* 51.1.1.
328. Aug. *Psal.* 128.1.
329. Aug. *Serm.* 264.1.
330. Aug. *Serm. Dolb.* 26(198*); *Eu. Io.* 7.24.
331. Aug. *Serm.* 149.14.15.
332. Aug. *Psal.* 138.1.
333. Aug. *Serm.* 37.27; 45.8; 101.2.

active role. Augustine posed questions for their response.[334] He used particularly ingenious interpretations of texts that occasionally provoked cheering.[335] He allowed the people to anticipate where an exposition was headed,[336] and delayed after beginning a scriptural quotation so that they would finish it.[337] Some were quicker to understand than others[338] and had to be urged to patience;[339] they occasionally helped their fellows along by explaining an unfamiliar reference.[340] The people appreciated praise and the preacher's understanding of the difficulties of their lives.[341] They groaned when he referred to ill fortune that might befall them,[342] or when their failings were addressed.[343] On one occasion, they even interrupted the preaching with cheering over a miracle just performed at the shrine of Stephen.[344] Augustine acknowledged that some of his sermons were too long but claimed that the congregation's eagerness urged him on.[345] He praised their devotion: the zeal and stamina of the crowds in the amphitheater could not, he exclaimed, match those of his congregation.[346]

## The Congregation

The practice of standing for the readings, sermon, and eucharistic offering was a sign of respect but a burden for some members of the community.[347] Augustine remarked that some simply could not remain standing for the time required by the service. They left the church and did not partake of the sacrament but were embarrassed to explain their action. Acknowledging the difficulty, he praised the arrangements made in overseas churches for the weak to be able to sit, but he did not introduce the practice into Africa.[348]

The congregation varied in size and composition. On Sunday, the group was larger and preferred a shorter sermon and service.[349] On major feast days, the church was full of people who rarely attended and who wanted to get on to

334. Aug. *Serm.* 81.2, 4-5.
335. Aug. *Serm.* 37.17; *Psal.* 136.10.
336. Aug. *Serm.* 131.4-5; 151.8.8; *Psal.* 88.1.10; *Serm. Guelf.* 15(229M).3; *Serm. Lamb.* 7(335E).2.
337. Aug. *Serm.* 52.12.13; 131.5.
338. Aug. *Serm.* 117.8.11.
339. Aug. *Serm.* 169.7.7; *Psal.* 90.2.1.
340. Aug. *Serm.* 23.8.
341. Aug. *Serm.* 132.4; 164.4.6; *Psal.* 147.15.
342. Aug. *Serm.* 86.10.11, 12.14; *Psal.* 38.12.
343. Aug. *Serm.* 86.12.14; 332.4.
344. Aug. *Serm.* 323, recounted in *Ciu.* 22.8.
345. Aug. *Psal.* 35.18; 38.23; 41.13; 93.30; 120.12; *Serm.* 99.4, 6; 179.6.
346. Aug. *Psal.* 147.21.
347. Aug. *Ep. Divj.* 28*.3.
348. Aug. *Catech.* 13.19.
349. Aug. *Serm.* 128.4.6.

their celebratory dinners.[350] A promise made in advance to treat a difficult and interesting problem in the scripture could also swell the congregation.[351] The sequential reading and preaching of a text — such as the Gospel or the First Letter of John — may have had the same result. On days when games or spectacles were being presented in the city, the congregation was significantly reduced.[352]

## Fasting before Eucharist

In his responses to Bishop Januarius about proper practice, Augustine indicated that reception of the eucharist while fasting was the general custom of the church.[353] At least up to Augustine's time, the first meal of the day *(prandium)* appears to have been near midday, about eleven A.M. On a fast day, the first meal was taken at mid-afternoon, approximately three P.M.[354] If the eucharist were always celebrated in the morning, a particular fast would not have been necessary. A question did arise with funerals, since burial tended to follow as soon as possible after death, and that ritual normally included a eucharistic commendation. In 393, the council of bishops held at Hippo adopted a general policy requiring that presider and people celebrate the eucharist fasting. If they had already eaten, presumably at midday, the commendation of the deceased was to be made by prayers but not the eucharist.[355] In the codification of this legislation in 401, an exception to the general rule of fasting was noted: the annual celebration of the Lord's Supper just before Easter, which was the only remaining evening celebration of the eucharist.[356] The review of prior legislation at the Council of Carthage in 525 omitted the burial context in which the question had originally arisen but retained the reference to the Lord's Supper.[357]

As the conciliar legislation indicated, the annual celebration of the Lord's Supper on the fifth day of the last week of Lent constituted a special problem because evening was the preferred time for the celebration.[358] Augustine discussed this matter more fully in his letter to Januarius. He observed that Christ had offered the sacrament to the Twelve after the meal but that Paul's letter to the Corinthians identified the eucharist itself as the meal, and the entire church

---

350. Aug. *Serm.* 51.1.1; 264.1.
351. Aug. *Eu. Io.* 6.1.
352. Aug. *Serm.* 51.1.1.
353. Aug. *Ep.* 54.6.8.
354. Aug. *Ep.* 54.5.6–7.9; 65.2. Augustine preached through the first mealtime on New Year's Day (*Serm. Dolb.* 26(198*).6), thus forcing a fast.
355. *Con. Hipp.* a. 393, 4. See below, pp. 503-4.
356. *Bru. Hipp.* 28.
357. *Con. Carth.* a. 525.
358. Aug. *Ep.* 54.5.6. Augustine preferred to number the days of the week than to use their "pagan" names; see *Psal.* 93.3.

had adopted the practice of taking the eucharist while fasting. This, Augustine decided, was a matter that Christ had left to the discretion of the apostles; the Holy Spirit then had guided them into the practice of taking the eucharist fasting, out of reverence.[359]

The annual celebration of the dinner before the death of Jesus was in the evening. Augustine allowed that some followed this practice because this particular service commemorated the institution of the eucharist after the evening meal. Even those who were continuing the Lenten fast that day would receive the eucharist after the mid-afternoon meal that broke their fast. A morning celebration actually had been added to accommodate the faithful who joined the petitioners preparing for baptism in bathing on that day: they could not bathe without having eaten.[360] Augustine also indicated that the practice of receiving the eucharistic bread and wine before any other food was otherwise universal, thus ruling out any evening meal that would have concluded with the eucharistic celebration.[361] By this time, the eucharistic bread and wine had been disassociated from other food; their morning reception was not considered to break a fast, as had been the case in Tertullian's time.

## Eucharistic Theology

Augustine's theology of the eucharist, and particularly of the reality which was symbolized and made present in the bread and wine of the ritual, can be considered from different perspectives.[362] Which approach best represents the actual genesis of Augustine's eucharistic theology would be impossible to determine because the major issues are dealt with primarily in sermons that are difficult to date, even relative to one another. The influence of Cyprian and the problems that arose in the Donatist controversy were certainly important, if not decisive. If the sacramental theology that Augustine developed for baptism were applied to eucharistic practice, this would have validated schismatic celebrations and consequently communions in an inappropriate way. His innovative explanation of the presence of Christ in the bread and wine appears to have adapted Cyprian's emphasis on the eucharist as a sign of unity, and thus found a solution for those problems. Unlike baptism, eucharist was the sacrament of the church's unity as the body of Christ; it could not be celebrated in opposition to the reality it symbolized.

359. Aug. *Ep.* 54.5.6–6.8. Augustine seems to have been unaware that the practice had been different, even as late as Tertullian's time.

360. Aug. *Ep.* 54.7.9-10. This interpretation follows the punctuation introduced by Klaus D. Daur's edition (CCSL 31:233.177-79) of the key sentence rather than that of the Maurists and Alois Goldbacher (CSEL 34:168.4-6).

361. Aug. *Ep.* 54.6.8.

362. See J. Patout Burns, "The Eucharist as the Foundation of Christian Unity in North African Theology," *Augustinian Studies* 32 (2001): 1-24.

As has already been noted, the Catholics in North Africa accepted the Roman and Gallic belief that certain sacraments — specifically, baptism and ordination — could be performed in a schismatic or heretical communion, even when the rituals did not sanctify those recipients. The specific issues raised by the Council of Arles were the repetition of baptism and failing to respect the ordination of clerics by requiring that they perform public penance for serious sin;[363] the Roman bishop added a recognition of schismatic ordination.[364] The rituals of baptism and ordination were properly performed only once for an individual, whose status they permanently changed. The single access to penance was not discussed; it may have been a disciplinary rather than a doctrinal issue. The question of the validity of schismatic eucharist was not raised, perhaps because that sacrament was so frequently celebrated.

To develop a coherent explanation of the practice of accepting baptism performed outside the unity of the church, Augustine, as has been discussed, distinguished between the sacramental ritual, the reality effected — a permanent dedication to Christ — and the sanctification communicated. He explained that because the divine power of Christ was operative in the conferring of baptism, it could be performed inside or outside the church, and its effect must never be defaced by repetition of the ritual. He identified the dedication signified and effected by the sacrament as the marking and claiming for Christ of its recipient, which he compared to a military tattoo. This marking was always accomplished by the ritual and could be neither destroyed nor lost. The sanctification that baptism communicated was identified as the Holy Spirit's gift of charity that both moved the recipient to love of God and neighbor and granted the forgiveness of all prior sins. Unlike the sacrament and dedication, the retention of this sanctification depended upon the dispositions of the recipient of the sacrament. A person filled with faith and repentance for sins was cleansed and transformed. A person who rejected faith or refused to repent of sin either did not receive this sanctification or lost it immediately after reception. Self-love drove out love of God, and an evil intention held to its sins. The sanctification that baptism conferred was regularly rejected, Augustine explained, both outside and inside the unity of the church. Because of the permanent dedication of the baptized to Christ, the lost sanctification could be restored at any time by faith and conversion, which were ritualized — both for the schismatics and for Catholic penitents — through the imposition of the bishop's hands to give the Holy Spirit.[365]

In elaborating this baptismal theology, Augustine explained the saving effect of the sacrament in the same way that Cyprian had: it conferred forgiveness of sins and sanctification by the action of the Holy Spirit. He added a mediating

363. *Con. Arel.* a. 314, 9, 14.
364. Miltiades, as cited in Aug. *Ep.* 43.5.16.
365. *Bru. Hipp.* 30c; Aug. *Bapt.* 2.7.11; 5.23.33; *Serm.* 296.15.

element: the permanent dedication and mark that made the person forever a Christian. He also exploited an element that Cyprian had neglected: the dispositions of the recipient both inside and outside the church. Finally, he rejected an element that had been central for Cyprian: the status and holiness of the minister.

In approaching the eucharist, Augustine used a parallel three-part structure — the sacrament performed, the reality effected, and the sanctification conferred — that he had developed to deal with Cyprian's baptismal theology and the affirmation of sacramental efficacy that the church courts in Rome and Gaul had asserted against Donatist claims and then required the Caecilianists to accept. In the eucharist, Augustine distinguished the sacrament of bread and wine blessed and shared, the reality of the body and blood of Christ both signified and effected by the bread and wine, and the sanctification of a worthy recipient. The first element could be understood as it had been in baptism. The divine power operating through the prayer of offering made the bread and wine into the sacrament of the body and blood of Christ, independently of the holiness of the minister performing the ritual.[366] Similarly, the parallel worked for the third element. The dispositions of the communicant determined whether sharing the loaf and cup signifying the body and blood of Christ would sanctify.[367] As in baptism, such an explanation would have accounted for the efficacy of the ritual performed by a sinful bishop in the Catholic communion or a schismatic bishop in Donatist communion. Similarly, a worthy Catholic recipient would be sanctified by sharing the sacrament, while an unworthy Catholic or a schismatic Donatist would be spiritually harmed.

The second element in the explanation presented a problem. The baptismal dedication to Christ signified by the ritual corresponded to the eucharistic reality of the body and blood of Christ, which was signified by the bread and wine. Cyprian had understood this representation in a realistic way: to receive the eucharistic bread and wine in the true church was to come into direct contact with the body and blood of Jesus. These would strengthen the faithful even for martyrdom; they could harm and even destroy the polluted. Outside the true church, in Cyprian's judgment, the schismatic rituals were as polluting as a sacrifice offered to idols; there the eucharist could not be celebrated, and Christ's body and blood could not be presented. Augustine could not affirm that the body and blood of Jesus were realized in schismatic celebrations and orally received by those who rejected the unity of the church. He had to treat the second element in the eucharistic theology differently than he treated the second element in his baptismal theology.

Augustine, then, took a different approach than he had used in considering baptism. He conceded to the schismatics and other unworthy Christians the

366. Aug. *Serm.* 227.12; 229.1, 3; *Serm. Guelf.* 7(229A).1.
367. Aug. *Eu. Io.* 26.18.

sacramental sign — the offering of bread and wine in imitation of Christ in an attempt to represent his body and blood. To such persons and communities, however, he would grant neither the reality signified nor the sanctification it conferred. Unlike baptism, the eucharistic ritual could be empty, meaningless, and ineffective. To justify this eucharistic theology, Augustine developed Cyprian's understanding of the link between the eucharistic elements and the church as the body of Christ in a way that meant it could not be realized outside the unity of the church.

In his letter to Caecilian of Biltha, it will be recalled, Cyprian had urged that the full reality of the eucharist should be realized not in the evening banquet that gathered small numbers of the faithful, but properly at the morning celebration where the whole fellowship assembled. The bread and wine, he urged, represented the one Christ and included the whole people as his members.[368] Augustine retained Cyprian's reference to the flesh and blood of Jesus but emphasized the full reality of Christ, specifically the social body through which Christ continued to be present on earth. The bread and wine pointed to a reality that — unlike the name and baptismal mark of Christ — could be found only in the unity of the church, and there only among the faithful who were joined in love to Christ and one another — the society of saints. This social body, he insisted, could be found only within the Catholic communion. Because the Christian eucharist was the sacrament or sign of the unity of the body of Christ, the schismatic ritual and its elements were a void and empty sign — a word that was contradicted, negated, and deprived of meaning because its very speaking in separation denied the united reality it attempted to signify.[369]

Augustine's understanding of the church as the body of Christ was based on his reading and interpretation of 1 Corinthians 11–12, but it was elaborated by the use of many scriptural resources.[370] In his sermons and commentaries on the Psalms, for example, Augustine explained that in the scriptures Christ speaks and is spoken about in three ways: as eternal God equal to the Father; as simultaneously divine and human, and thus head of the church; and as the Whole Christ in the fullness of the church, both head and body. The nature of a particular statement indicated how it should be applied to Christ.[371] This

---

368. Cypr. *Ep.* 63.13.1-5, 16.1.

369. This was an application of the assertion that the sanctification of baptism, identified as the Holy Spirit and the uniting gift of charity, could not be retained in the schismatic communion. Cyprian regarded schism as a kind of apostasy (*Ep.* 43.3.1-2; 71.2.1-2).

370. 1 Cor. 12:12 in Aug. *Pecc. merit.* 1.31.60; *Psal.* 30.2.1.4; 142.3; *Serm.* 294.10.10; *Serm. Mai* 98(263A).2. 1 Cor. 11:27 in Aug. *Cresc.* 1.25.30; *Eu. Io.* 62.1; *Serm.* 227.1.

371. Aug. *Serm.* 341.1.1–3.3, 9.11; *Psal.* 39.5; 40.1; 56.1; 58.1.2. Some statements, such as those in which he claimed to perform the Father's works, belong to him only in his divinity (*Eu. Io.* 18-20). Others, such as his expression of fear before his Passion, do refer to his own humanity but as head of the church, because he freely takes on and experiences the feelings of his members (*Psal.* 40.6; 42.7). In some instances, such as the confession of sins and the complaint of Paul's persecution (Acts 9:4-5), Christ speaks as identified with his members (*Serm.* 345.4; *Psal.* 90.2.5; 123.1).

---

exegetical practice was based on Augustine's understanding of the relation of divine and human in Christ. When the Word was united to flesh in the womb of the Virgin Mary, he became both an individual human being and the head of the church as a social body in which others were joined to him through faith and love.[372] All the righteous, from Abel onward, were members of this one body of the Whole Christ, which Augustine also called the City of God.[373]

When Augustine dealt with the presence of Christ in the eucharist, he employed this rich understanding of Christ, as both an individual and a society. Speaking of Christ as an individual human, he could describe him as presenting himself to his disciples with his own hands at the Last Supper,[374] as offering his body and blood on the cross as food and drink,[375] as shedding the blood in which his repentant slayers would later be washed,[376] and that they would then drink.[377] Yet, Augustine was very careful to explain that this eating and this drinking were not to be understood in a way that separated Christ as an individual from his identity as head joined to his ecclesial body. In the sixth chapter of the Gospel of John, the disciples had misunderstood eucharistic eating, just as Nicodemus had earlier taken rebirth too literally (John 3:1-4).[378] Jesus had tried to overcome their resistance by indicating that he would ascend to heaven in his flesh, whole and entire: his followers would not be required (or allowed) to feast on his cadaver.[379] At the supper, Christ had then presented the disciples with his eucharistic body and blood while he was still alive and with them, so that they would think of his presence in the eucharist in a symbolic rather than a literal and carnal way.[380] Although Augustine definitely affirmed the bodily presence of Christ in the eucharistic elements, he protected this belief from too materialistic an interpretation by reminding his congregation that the flesh born from Mary was resurrected and had ascended; it was in heaven and no longer on earth.[381] In the eucharist, then, the faithful received Christ not as an isolated individual but as the head joined to his body, the church, of which they were themselves mem-

---

This procedure was developed by Augustine's appropriation of Tyconius's *Rules*. See *Doct. Chr.* 3.30.42–37.56.

372. Aug. *Psal.* 44.3; 56.1; 74.4; 90.2.1; 123.1; 118.29.9. In *Psal.* 36.3.4, he included the angels as well, though in *Ep. Io.* 1.2, 2.2 he made a definite link between the flesh of Christ and his role as head of the church.

373. Aug. *Psal.* 36.3.4; 56.1; 90.2.1; 118.29.9.

374. Aug. *Psal.* 33.1.10.

375. Aug. *Serm.* 366.6.

376. Aug. *Serm. Guelf.* 10(229F).1.

377. Aug. *Serm.* 77.2.4; 80.5; 87.11.14; 352.1.2; *Serm. Denis* 15(313B).4; *Serm. Guelf.* 9(229E).2; 28(313E).4; *Serm. Mai* 26(60A).2; 86(229I).3; *Serm. Casin.* 2.114-15(97A).2; *Serm. Wilm.* 9(229D).2; *Psal.* 45.4; 66.9; 93.8; 134.22; *Eu. Io.* 31.9; 40.2; *Ep. Io.* 1.9; *Symb.* 7.5.

378. Aug. *Eu. Io.* 11.5.

379. Aug. *Eu. Io.* 27.2-3, 5; *Serm.* 131.1.

380. Aug. *Psal.* 98.9; 54.23.

381. Aug. *Eu. Io.* 50.13; *Serm.* 242.3.5, 6.8–7.10.

bers. Augustine elaborated this interpretation of the eucharist as the sacrament of the Whole Christ in two sermon settings: the lectures on the sixth chapter of the Gospel of John and the sermons to the neophytes on Easter day, the morning following their baptism and first reception of the eucharist.

In Augustine's explanation of the Gospel of John, the issue was the true meaning of eating the life-giving body of Christ. As each person's body lived by its spirit, he explained, so the body of Christ lived by the Spirit of Christ. Thus, those who were converted and incorporated into the church received the Holy Spirit and lived in the body of Christ. The eucharistic bread, as exemplified by Paul's reference in 1 Corinthians (10:17), was the sacrament or sign of the unity of charity that formed the local and universal community of the church.[382] When Christ spoke of himself as true food and drink that gave eternal life to all who partook of it, he was indicating the unity of his body and its members, the holy church as it existed in those who were being saved.[383] Augustine's point may be grasped by using the terminology reviewed earlier: the eucharistic bread and wine was the sacrament; the Whole Christ (head and ecclesial body) was the reality that it signified; eternal life was its sanctifying effect for the faithful communicant.[384] Augustine concluded his exposition with an exhortation that Christians eat and drink the body and blood of Christ not only by taking its sacrament but by sharing in his Spirit, that they live by his Spirit and thus persevere as members of the body of Christ.[385] In this exposition of the Gospel of John, Augustine taught that the community of the saints — the true church which lived by the gift of the Holy Spirit — was integral to the life-giving reality signified by the bread and wine.[386] The faithful received this reality and attained eternal life; the unfaithful refused this reality, received only the sacramental elements, and would perish in eternal death.

The second exposition of this understanding of the eucharist is preserved in a series of sermons for Easter day, when Augustine explained to the newly baptized the meaning of the ritual that they had witnessed and shared for the first time during the service on the night before.[387] In these sermons, he used the text of 1 Corinthians 12:27, "you are the body of Christ and his members," to identify the reality symbolized by the bread and wine as the Whole Christ. The neophytes themselves were the mystery that was placed on the Lord's Table, which they then received.[388] He elaborated an analogy between the process of

---

382. Aug. *Eu. Io.* 26.13.
383. Aug. *Eu. Io.* 26.15.
384. Aug. *Eu. Io.* 26.15.
385. Aug. *Eu. Io.* 27.11.
386. Reference to this explanation can be found in Aug. *Ep.* 149.2.16.
387. They apparently had no prior preparation for the ritual. These sermons might have been preached in the afternoon service at which only the baptized were allowed to be present, in order to preserve the secrecy protecting this ritual. Aug. *Serm.* 225.3.3.
388. Aug. *Serm.* 272; *Serm. Guelf.* 7(229A).1.

their initiation and the making of the eucharistic bread. They had been ground and pounded by fasting and exorcism, moistened by the water of baptism, and baked by the heat of the oil of anointing.[389] As the juice of many grapes was poured into one vessel, so Christ wanted all the faithful to be joined in unity and peace.[390]

Yet, Augustine insisted that the eucharistic elements referred to Christ not only in his social reality but also in his individuality as Jesus, the son of Mary. The neophytes should recognize in the bread the body that hung on the cross and in the cup the blood that poured from Christ's side.[391] This eucharistic bread and wine, the sacramental symbols, were food that would be assimilated into their bodies; by receiving these symbols in faith, the neophytes had been sanctified; by living well, they would be assimilated into the reality symbolized, the ecclesial body of Christ.[392]

In his identification of the church as a reality signified by the eucharistic bread and wine, Augustine was careful to distinguish the union of the saints from those unrepentant sinners whom they tolerated in the congregations. The sharing of the love given by the Holy Spirit, moreover, joined and united the saints not only within a local church but with all the faithful throughout the earth, and indeed with all the saved awaiting the Resurrection. Thus, the visible company of the baptized communicants was the determinate group allowed to remain in a given church (after the dismissal of catechumens) to pray together, and to eat and drink the sacrament. The full society of the saints was at once smaller and larger than this clearly identifiable congregation. Augustine did not presume that it included all the communicants in his local congregation: some of them were present only for temporal advantage, exercising little love for God or neighbor. The full society of saints reached beyond this congregation; it could not be counted, listed, or set apart by any human agency. God had predestined these saints, called and justified them, and would glorify them; God knew them as members of Christ.[393] Most of the saints living on earth would have been found within the unity of the visible congregations, but some were actually outside: some clung to unity despite having been unjustly excommunicated by an erroneous or abusive exercise of episcopal power;[394] others were penitents excluded from communion during their purification, but anticipated being readmitted before death; still others were permanently excommunicate because they had sinned a second time after once submitting to public penance and being reconciled — they hoped to be received by Christ himself in the

389. Aug. *Serm.* 227.1; 272.
390. Aug. *Serm.* 272; *Serm. Guelf.* 7(229A).2. This reverses Cyprian's explanation in *Ep.* 63.13.1-3, where the wine represents Christ and the water the people.
391. Aug. *Serm. Denis* 3(228B).2.
392. Aug. *Serm. Denis* 3(228B).3.
393. Aug. *Eu. Io.* 26.15.
394. Aug. *Bapt.* 1.17.26; *Ep.* 250.1.

Judgment.[395] This entire invisible communion was made symbolically visible in the eucharistic bread and wine presented on the altar, as the ecclesial body of the Whole Christ. In eating and drinking it, the saints were joined not only to Christ as their head but to all their fellow members who were vivified by his Spirit.

In contrast to the full participation of the saints, unworthy communicants within the unity of the church shared only the sacramental bread and wine, and that to their judgment and condemnation.[396] Because they rejected the Spirit of Christ, because they remained outside the intentional unity of Christ's body, because they refused to love and forgive his members, they could not receive the reality signified, the Whole Christ.[397] Nor would they share the sanctification, the eternal life God had bestowed on the head and prepared for the body of Christ.[398]

As he had in developing his baptismal theology, Augustine then compared schismatic Donatists to unworthy Caecilianists receiving the eucharist. The one loaf was a sign of unity of the body formed of all true Christians. Because schismatics rejected that unity, they could have only the sacramental sign and not the reality of the Whole Christ it represented. Similarly, these enemies of unity rejected the Holy Spirit that animated the body of Christ and thus excluded themselves from becoming its living members.[399] They received only the sacrament of unity, neither the body of Christ it signified nor the sanctification it conferred.[400]

Augustine did not, then, allow an exact parallel between his baptismal and eucharistic theologies. In each instance, he asserted that the unworthy, both inside and outside the unity of the church, received the sacrament: washing, anointing, and imposition of hands in baptism; eating and drinking the blessed bread and wine of the eucharist. He argued that, in baptism, the unworthy received the dedication that made them Christians; consequently, he allowed that they might receive but not retain the sanctification of this sacrament — the love and forgiveness of the Holy Spirit. In dealing with the eucharist, however, he insisted that the unworthy did not receive the Whole Christ signified by the sacrament; consequently, they did not receive its sanctification — the Holy Spirit and everlasting life. Precisely because the reality signified by the loaf and cup was at once both the individual and the ecclesial body of Christ, it could be received only by those willingly joined into the society of saints, the true church, which was that social body. Christ's individual and ecclesial bodies were inseparable; the head could not be separated from his members.

395. Aug. *Ep.* 153.3.6-8.
396. Aug. *Serm.* 272; *Psal.* 39.12; *Eu. Io.* 26.11-12, 15, 18; *Ep. Io.* 7.6.
397. Aug. *Eu. Io.* 26.18; *Ep.* 185.11.50.
398. Aug. *Eu. Io.* 16.11.
399. Aug. *Ep.* 185.11.50.
400. Aug. *Serm.* 229.2.

Thus, Augustine developed Cyprian's understanding of the reality symbolized by the eucharistic bread and wine as the body and blood of the Whole Christ. During Christ's earthly life, the individual body born of Mary was itself the visible symbol of the social body of all the faithful. The eucharist celebrated in the Lord's Supper and later in the church symbolized the same Whole Christ: head and members. The Christian faithful received what they were becoming; sinners within the communion and schismatics outside it received an empty sign.

The ecclesial focus of Augustine's understanding of the eucharist is indirectly evidenced in the absence of miracles he attributed to the sacramental bread and wine. A single healing — the opening of the eyelids of a child — was attributed to contact with the eucharistic bread.[401] Augustine did report that the celebration of the eucharistic ritual had freed a plantation from demonic possession; it was subsequently protected not by the reserved sacrament but by earth brought from Jerusalem.[402] This paucity of bodily wonders associated with the eucharist stands in startling contrast to the multitude worked by the remains of the individual body of Stephen, when a small portion of the dust from his tomb was brought from Palestine.[403] The eucharistic bread and wine did not exercise the power to heal that had been manifest in the individual body of Christ during his pre-resurrection life. Their symbolism was focused instead on the body of Christ, the church, whose holiness was not displayed by such wonders.

## Theology of Priesthood

As has already been seen in the discussion of the baptismal ritual, Augustine insisted that the efficacy of the sacramental rituals depended not on the holiness of the clergy but on the operation of Christ, acting through and with the saints within the communion of the church. He extended to the eucharistic ritual this understanding of the relation of Christ, the church as his body, and the clergy who served as its leaders.

Parmenian, the Donatist primate who rebuilt his church after the emperor Julian released the schismatic bishops from exile, had insisted in a letter of rebuke to the lay exegete Tyconius that the bishop serves as mediator between God and the Christian people.[404] Augustine attacked this teaching by pointing out that Christ shares his priestly and royal anointing not only with good bishops but with the whole of his body, which the First Letter of Peter addresses as

401. Aug. *Iul. op. imp.* 3.162.
402. Aug. *Ciu.* 22.8.
403. Aug. *Ciu.* 22.8; *Serm.* 319-22. See below, p. 546.
404. Aug. *Parm.* 2.8.15-16; *Serm. Dolb.* 26(198*).28.

a holy people, a royal priesthood (1 Pet. 2:9). Augustine observed that bishops were indeed called priests, but only because they served as leaders and spokesmen of this priestly community. The priesthood of the clergy, he declared, was derived from that of the whole church, the one shared by all the faithful who make up the body of Christ, himself the only true priest.[405]

Augustine elaborated this theme dramatically in a sermon he preached on New Year's Day, probably in 404. Turning to the Letter to the Hebrews, he noted that the Israelite ritual had specified that the priest must enter alone into the Holy of Holies, leaving the assembly of the people to stand outside. In fulfillment of this precedent, Christ had entered into the heavenly sanctuary while the Christian people still waited outside it. How, he asked, was this relationship enacted in the Christian eucharistic ritual? The bishop and clergy were not inside, separated from the people standing outside the building. Rather, both clergy and congregation were gathered inside the basilica: seeing and hearing, offering and receiving. He concluded that this people assembled around the earthly altar symbolized and prefigured its future standing with Christ inside the heavenly sanctuary, when it would be the resurrected body of the one priest. The Whole Christ was priest, he concluded, offering one sacrifice in heaven and on earth. Thus Augustine united the priesthood of the church with that of Christ and the priesthood of the clergy with that of the laity. The bishop was priest as one of the faithful; he was called priest because he was leader of the church, itself the body of the Whole Christ, the only priest.[406]

Augustine thus distinguished two roles of the clergy: they acted as priests along with the other members of Christ's body, and they acted as supervisors set over the church to govern and guide it. These roles were dramatically enacted by the architecture of the basilicas of North Africa. The bishop preached while seated on his elevated chair at the center of the rounded apse, which formed one end of the building; the people stood facing him in the center and along the aisles of the building. The arrangement was adapted from the civic basilica, a king's hall, which enabled the one speaker to use the apse as a voice amplifier and thus address a large assembly. From his elevated position, the bishop taught, exhorted, and admonished; he guided and ruled the church. At the time of prayer and offering, however, the bishop descended from his chair to the altar set at floor level in the central part of the building. The people then gathered around the altar, separated from it only by the low railing of the chancel screen (cf. figs. 26, 82). Surrounded by the faithful and the clergy, the bishop led the offering as a member of and spokesman for the community, participating in the one priesthood that Christ shared with his body.[407]

405. Aug. *Serm. Dolb.* 26.49.

406. Aug. *Serm. Dolb.* 26(198*).53-54, 57. See also *Parm.* 2.7.12–8.16; *Petil.* 2.105.241; *Psal.* 64.6; 67.23; 109.18; 130.4; 132; *Serm.* 351.4.7.

407. For the configuration of the church in Hippo, see pp. 156-58.

Augustine was called to the ministry by the congregation of Hippo, because he was needed as a preacher in the church and a spokesman against its local opponents, both Manichees and Donatists. He preached in Hippo for more than thirty-five years. When traveling, he seldom stopped overnight in an African city without being required by its bishop to address the local congregation. Through the years, his understanding of the preacher's task and craft developed. Those portions of his treatise on preaching, *On Christian Teaching,* that were composed early in his ministry focus on the resources needed for interpretation of scripture. When he came to complete the work late in his life, he was interested in the different objectives of preaching and the techniques proper for each purpose. The sermons he delivered between his writing of the two parts of the work contain many reflections on the ministry of preaching and the divine grace that makes it effective. The results are, not surprisingly, parallel to those he reached in his thinking about the efficacy of the rituals of baptism and eucharist.

The scriptures themselves were filled with divine truth, which was to be presented and explained to the faithful. God and Christ spoke, then, in the readings, the singing, and the preaching.[408] The bishop, he explained, was God's attorney: he could neither neglect a warning given by God nor offer a promise God had not made.[409] Using Christ's own advice on the teaching of the Pharisees from the chair of Moses (Matt. 23:2), Augustine explained that the congregation could tolerate the preaching ministry of unworthy and incompetent bishops because they delivered God's own truth, even if they did not live by it.[410] Because God acted in and through both good and bad clergy,[411] the Christian's trust should be in God rather than in the holiness, learning, or example of the bishop.[412] Finally, Augustine affirmed that this ministry of speaking God's word was not limited to the clergy; the urging of the laity brought many to seek baptism.[413]

Even though he was far better trained for reading and explaining the scripture than his congregants, Augustine insisted that he was not their teacher but their fellow student.[414] The truth they were all seeking was a gift of God to be received in faith rather than attained by human ingenuity and evaluated by human judgment. He spoke from an elevated chair not because he was a master giving instructions and orders but only so that he could be heard.[415] He charac-

408. Aug. *Serm.* 2.5-6; 17.1, 3.
409. Aug. *Serm.* 339.8-9.
410. Aug. *Serm.* 46.20-22; 74.3-4; 101.10.
411. Aug. *Serm.* 46.23-27.
412. Aug. *Serm. Guelf.* 32(340A).9-10.
413. Aug. *Psal.* 96.10.
414. Aug. *Serm.* 298.5.5.
415. Aug. *Serm. Denis* 17(301A).2.

terized himself as a servant in the household, dispensing the Master's food by which he and the congregation would live.[416]

Augustine's understanding of the interaction of the human ministry of preaching and the divine operation of sanctification was more fully developed in his attempts to understand the process of conversion. In his earliest consideration of the activities of teaching and learning, in a dialogue with his son Adeodatus, he reached the conclusion that divine illumination brings a person to understand what a human teacher tries to explain.[417] Very early in his clerical career, he noted that preaching and exhortation were necessary elements in repentance and faith: a person had to be called in order to believe and convert.[418] Shortly after he was made bishop, he argued that divine mercy would effect the faith of the elect by adapting the preacher's call to the existing dispositions of a chosen individual.[419] This insight was amply illustrated in the narrative of the *Confessions:* as a child, Monica had been turned from the path of drunkenness by a servant's taunt; Antony of Egypt's vocation, as well as the conversions of both Augustine and his friend Alypius, were provoked by biblical verses apparently selected at random.[420] Even the most persuasive preacher, he argued, could not draw upon that exhaustive knowledge of interior dispositions and desires that would enable him to present just the right appeal and motive to even one of his listeners. God, however, did have such knowledge and could guide the preacher onto the particular track that would move many chosen hearts. As he preached, therefore, Augustine prayed that God would stir up joy in his own heart and adapt his discourse to inspire his congregation to good action.[421]

Later, in the midst of the Pelagian controversy, Augustine's careful reading of scripture brought him to the realization that God not only adapted the preacher's message to the hearer but moved the heart of the hearer to heed the sermon.[422] Thereafter, Augustine repeated again and again that God's interior working made the preacher's teaching, correcting, and exhorting take root and bear fruit in the lives of the faithful.[423] When the congregation applauded in delight at a truth well expressed, Augustine praised Christ for opening their hearts to know and love that truth.[424] His sacramental theology, which required direct

416. Aug. *Serm.* 261.2; *Serm. frg. Verbr.* 40(319A).
417. Aug. *Mag.* 40.
418. Aug. *Quaest.* 68.5; *Rom. prop.* 54.3; *Psal.* 84.8.
419. Aug. *Simpl.* 1.2.13-15, 22.
420. Aug. *Conf.* 8.12.29-30; 9.8.18.
421. Aug. *Psal.* 96.3.
422. For a full discussion of this change, see J. Patout Burns, *The Development of Augustine's Doctrine of Operative Grace* (Paris: Études augustiniennes, 1980) and "From Persuasion to Predestination: Augustine on Freedom in Rational Creatures," in *In Dominico Eloquio = In Lordly Eloquence: Essays on Patristic Exegesis in Honor of Robert Louis Wilken,* ed. Paul M. Blowers, Angela Christman, David Hunter, and Robin D. Young (Grand Rapids: Wm. B. Eerdmans, 2002), 249-316.
423. Aug. *Serm.* 264.4; 152.1; 153.1.1; 224.3; *Psal.* 70.2.6; 109.12; 146.10; *Eu. Io.* 26.7; 40.5.
424. Aug. *Serm.* 179.7.

divine operation for the rituals enacted by the clergy to sanctify the recipients, became the model by which he understood the efficacy of preaching.

Augustine's own conversion, as well as his experience in exhorting and admonishing his congregation in Hippo, certainly convinced him of the weakness that afflicted humanity. In dealing with the Donatist bishops, however, he ran up against what he took to be a refusal to hear and respond to the plain truth; he found this sort of hardness of heart amply documented in both scripture and the imperial court records. He remarked on this determined deafness occasionally in his preaching,[425] but his encounter with Emeritus, the Donatist Bishop of Caesarea in Mauretania, displayed its manifest form. Though he had come to Caesarea on a different mission, Augustine sought out Emeritus, who had been one of the seven spokesmen of the Donatist party at the imperial Conference of Carthage in June 411. Augustine convinced him to come to the church and to engage in a discussion of the issues still separating them. Emeritus agreed to accompany Augustine but then refused to speak; he sat in silence through Augustine's exhortation to join the unity of the church and left as he had arrived, persistent in his refusal.[426] Augustine never ceased trying to persuade the Donatists, but such experiences made him increasingly certain that only God's grace could move the human heart, and this grace was not always given.[427]

Augustine's theology of divine election and the operation of salvation was developed by his innovative reading of Paul's letters and John's Gospel, but it was inspired and guided by his practice of preaching. In its turn, it can be interpreted accurately only in that context.

## Conclusion

Augustine's writings and the legislation of his episcopal colleagues provide clear evidence for the final shift to the morning celebration of the eucharist, with its offering and distribution of bread and wine. The evening celebration was reduced to the fifth day of Holy Week and did not include any other food. Except for that one celebration, the eucharist was always received as the first food of the day. The possible exception for the communication of the dying was never discussed, nor was the reception of privately reserved eucharistic bread mentioned in contemporary African sources.

Augustine developed and integrated both the interpretations of the eucharistic presence of Christ that Cyprian had used. He affirmed that the bread and wine signified the flesh and blood of Christ in its full reality, which included

---

425. Aug. *Serm.* 164.10.14; 359.8; *Psal.* 30.3.8.

426. Aug. *Emer.* and *Serm. Caes. eccl.* For an exposition of the event, see Lancel, *Saint Augustine,* 351-53.

427. The interaction of the human ministry and divine grace is clearly articulated in Augustine's discussion of the abbot's correction of monks, in *De correptione et gratia.*

the social body in which the saints were joined to Christ. Thus, the eucharist could achieve its essential meaning only when celebrated within the unity of the church.

Augustine applied to the church's preaching the same understanding of divine initiative and human collaboration that had been developed in his sacramental theology. The efforts of the preacher and the prayers of the congregation, as well as the careful attention of both to the words of scripture, were necessary for the divine communication of truth and its understanding. Through the reform effort led by Aurelius of Carthage, presbyters were authorized and urged to extend preaching beyond the episcopal celebrations, both in the cities and the villages.

The eucharistic celebration had become a congregational rather than a household ritual, under the control of the clergy. The *agapē* and the domestic offering over which a householder might preside, as well as the private consumption at home, were actually replaced by the morning ritual at which the assembly was led by the clergy.

## GENERAL OBSERVATIONS

### Correlation of Archeological and Literary Evidence

#### CHURCH FURNISHINGS

The literature of each period provides evidence of the Christian church furnishings. Although Tertullian used the common Roman term *ara,* Cyprian avoided this one and used *altare,* apparently to distinguish the Christian from the Roman sacrifice.[428] Optatus and Augustine confirmed, at the end of the fourth century, what might have been anticipated: that the altar table was made of wood rather than the stone of the Roman sacrificial altar.[429] Optatus and Victor of Vita mentioned the use of a linen cloth to cover the wooden table; Victor added a reference to the use of candles.[430] The mosaic from Thabraca entitled *Ecclesia Mater* (fig. 132) includes an image of the altar that is consonant with these witnesses.[431]

Cyprian introduced the term *pulpitum* for the elevated lectern from which the scriptures were read out to the people. Augustine later referred to it as the place from which he preached when visiting in Carthage.[432]

428. In *Ep.* 59.18.1, Cyprian sharply contrasted the idolatrous *ara* with the Christian *altare.*
429. Optat. *Parm.* 6.1, 5; Aug. *Cresc.* 3.43.47; *Ep.* 185.7.27.
430. Optat. *Parm.* 6.1; Vict.-Vit. *Hist. pers.* 1.39, 2.18.
431. See above, p. 87. Another depiction of an altar occurs in the mosaics from Castellum Tingitanum, which shows neither cloth nor candles (fig. 35).
432. Cypr. *Ep.* 38.2.1; 39.4.1; Aug. *Serm. Dolb.* 2(359B).23.

Tertullian referred to the *cathedrae* that the apostles established in the churches they founded. Cyprian identified this bishop's *cathedra* as one of the signs of the unity of the local church. It was a symbol of the teaching and governing authority of the bishop in Cyprian's attacks on the schismatics. The Donatist leader Parmenian used the term in the same sense, as one of the endowments of the church.[433] In his preaching, Augustine also referred to his own position, seated in the apse of the basilica. Although none of the episcopal chairs have survived, the slot into which they were placed is clearly evident in Hippo, for example (fig. 52).[434]

Cyprian referred to the seating of the clergy[435] and, indirectly, to what was to become a stone or masonry bench built into the apse on which the presbyters (and any visiting bishops) were seated (cf. fig. 52). Augustine indicated that, in Africa, the congregation stood through the whole service. The people were free to move about, and he occasionally had to ask for quiet so that he could be heard. All this is compatible with the material remains of the basilicas in which the services were held.

The placement of the altar within the basilica was subject to some variation. In the fourth and fifth centuries, it was in the nave, usually surrounded by a stone screen and slightly raised above floor level (cf. figs. 1-2, 33). This, as has been noted, can be correlated with Augustine's observation that the community was gathered with its bishop at the altar in anticipation of being with Christ in the heavenly sanctuary. The arrangement makes intelligible his sharp distinction between the roles of the bishop in preaching and in making the offering. It also fits his characterization of the separated area around the altar as the "cradle" in which the neophytes participated in the eucharist during their first week after baptism. In a change usually assigned to the Byzantine period, the altar in Hippo and some other African churches was moved toward the apse and linked to the area reserved for clergy, thus effectively separating the clergy from the community in both preaching and leading the eucharistic celebration.[436] This change clearly reflected a different understanding of the status and role of the clergy in the church as separated from and even superior to the congregation. Augustine might not have offered his interpretation of the eucharist in such a church building.[437]

During the third century, in response to the growth of the communities and the need to engage all members in decisions such as the reconciliation of penitents, the ritual shifted from household gatherings for meals in the evening to full assemblies for symbolic eating in the morning. The choice of the basilica

433. Optat. *Parm.* 2.10.
434. Tert. *Praescr.* 36.1; Cypr. *Unit. eccl.* 4-6; *Ep.* 43.5.2; Aug. *Serm.* 23.1.
435. Cypr. *Ep.* 59.18.1.
436. See above, p. 97.
437. See above, nn. 401-404. He certainly might not have preached *Serm. Dolb.* 26(198*) in such a building.

style for the Christian church building accommodated these needs. While allowing participation in the community's business, it permitted the exclusion of those who were not yet full members and the discipline of secrecy for the rites of baptism and eucharist.

## Correlation of Theology and Practice

### FROM EVENING *AGAPE* TO MORNING EUCHARIST

Tertullian considered the evening love feast the primary form of Christian eucharist. This ritual followed the model of the supper that Jesus celebrated with his disciples. It seems to have been used both in community and in household settings, though even the community feasts could not have included the full congregation of Carthage. He also provided evidence for the morning ritual at which some sacred food was distributed. This ritual was recognized as an innovation, one for which a scriptural precedent could not be cited. It was, however, necessary for business that engaged the full community, such as the reconciliation of penitents and the declaration of marriages.

In Cyprian's time, the evening love feast continued but was no longer the principal eucharistic celebration, at least in Carthage. Cyprian justified the shift from the evening to the morning service on the grounds that it alone realized the full meaning of the eucharist by gathering the entire community. A number of developments may have made full assembly more significant at this time. Decius, for example, had required that the whole Roman people participate in his sacrifice for the good of the empire. In the aftermath of the persecution, the church in Carthage was divided among factions, which would have been celebrating the eucharist separately from one another. By insisting on the primacy of the morning eucharist, over which the bishop or the clergy he authorized could preside, Cyprian realized the unity he considered essential to the church in its eucharistic celebration.

This transition from the full evening meal to the more symbolic sharing of bread and wine at the morning eucharist opened the way for further elaboration of the ritual itself. Even in Tertullian's time, the evening feast had been less structured than the morning gathering, which included readings and preaching in addition to prayer and praise. The morning ritual also allowed the focus of the celebration to shift from the meal to the remembrance of the death of Christ and thereby the preparation for martyrdom. The food itself became more symbolic: the bread and the cup of wine mixed with water signified the union of Christians with one another and with Christ. The systematic persecutions of the 250s brought the eucharistic offering into direct competition with the Roman rituals of sacrifice and thereby facilitated the understanding of the eucharist as a sacrifice.

This transition from the many love feasts to the common eucharist accompanied and supported the growing belief that a person had to be sharing in the eucharistic communion in order to be accepted by Christ. The celebration became a medium of the eschatological fulfillment it signified.

By Augustine's time, the only remaining evening eucharist was on the Thursday before Easter, an explicit commemoration of the Last Supper. Augustine seems unaware that the practice had ever been different. As a consequence of the division between the Caecilianists and the Donatists, the emphasis on unity that Cyprian had introduced had become the eucharist's primary meaning. Although Augustine would recognize baptism and orders celebrated in schism, he argued that the eucharist was an empty and meaningless sign when celebrated in opposition to the unity of the universal communion. While affirming that the eucharistic bread and wine symbolized the human flesh and blood of Christ, Augustine preferred to treat the elements as signs of the Whole Christ, who joined the faithful together in himself. The eucharist became the ritual in which the true and pure church became symbolically visible. The shift in the practice and understanding of the eucharist was, then, in response to the schisms which plagued the African church from the middle of the third century.

### EUCHARIST AS SACRIFICE

Tertullian did not distinguish sacrifice from other forms of Christian prayer. Every Christian, in virtue of baptismal anointing, shared Christ's priesthood and exercised it daily. He did not insist on the use of wine in the eucharist. Tertullian may have preferred to emphasize that the Christian celebration was a banquet or symposium and thus avoid parallels to idolatrous rituals.

Cyprian, in contrast, taught that Christ had founded a new sacrificial system, which had been prefigured in the practice of Israel. The presider at the eucharist functioned as the representative of Christ and had to perform the ritual — using wine rather than water — as he had specified. He then clearly distinguished the idolatrous *ara* from the Christian *altare*. The renewal of persecution presented the opportunity to interpret the eucharist as the means for preparing Christians to follow Christ in sacrificing themselves as offerings to God.

Augustine used the typology of the Letter to the Hebrews to understand the Christian celebration as an anticipation of and a participation in the offering that Christ was already making in heaven. Unlike Cyprian and in opposition to the Donatists, he insisted that Christ shared his priesthood with all the faithful. The presider led the full community in making the offering in which all, as members of Christ, were presented to God. This interpretation gave particular meaning to the already traditional introduction of the eucharistic prayer. The Christians responded to the presider's invitation by affirming that their hearts were already "lifted up to the Lord," whose continual offering in the heavenly sanctuary they were about to join on earth.

Although the assimilation of the precedents in the religion of Israel was the primary influence in the emergence of a sacrificial understanding of the eucharist, the competition with Roman religion that was forced by the Decian and Diocletian persecutions contributed to the development.

## PREACHING AND PREDESTINATION

Augustine's doctrine of effective grace, along with its corollaries of gratuitous election and predestination, was developed in his struggle to understand Paul's teaching in the letter to the Romans. That theology was, however, both confirmed and illustrated by his practice of preaching to congregations throughout Africa. After some years of preaching as a presbyter in Hippo, he explained that God moves the hearts of the elect by guiding the preacher to offer the gospel in a way adapted to the disposition of the hearer who had been chosen for conversion. Later in his career, particularly after decades of failure in his attempts to move the Donatists to unity, he recognized that God must change the dispositions of the hearer and adapt them to the message as it was being preached. The primacy of divine grace in converting and sustaining the Christian was recognized in the prayer that Augustine prayed with his congregation at the conclusion of every sermon in Hippo: "May he throw down the enemy under our feet, not by our efforts, but by his holy name."[438]

## THE ROLE OF THE CLERGY

In the third century, Tertullian protested against an identification of the clergy as the holders of the sanctifying power of the church; he insisted that every Christian shared and could exercise the priestly power. In order to maintain good order, the clergy alone played the priestly and governing roles when the community assembled. Faced with schism, Cyprian argued that the bishop, as a member of the college founded upon the Apostles, maintained and exercised sanctifying power within the church. This theology was developed by the Donatist party in the fourth century; the sacramental efficacy of the church was secured by the fidelity of each member of the episcopal college. Within each local church, the role of Christ was both symbolized and exercised by the bishop.

The Donatist schism demonstrated that Cyprian's understanding of the role of the clergy was impractical: the purity of individual bishops could be established only by so narrowing the criteria of holiness that it became mean-

438. Aug. *Serm. Dolb.* 28(20B).11.

ingless as a guarantee of sanctifying power. Augustine worked out his own understanding of the church and its relationship to the divine power by weaving together a number of different strands. In response to the Donatist baptismal practice, he identified the power to sanctify with the Holy Spirit's gift of charity, thereby locating the power in the society of saints within the unity of the church. In rejecting Parmenian's assertion of the role of the bishop as mediator between God and congregation, Augustine once again turned to the society of saints, this time identified as the ecclesial body of Christ, which shared his priestly power. In the Pelagian controversy, Augustine insisted that the efficacy of preaching depended primarily, though not exclusively, on the preparation of the hearers' hearts by the Spirit, acting in accord with the prayers of the saints. In each case, Augustine focused not on the episcopal office but on the whole church, understood as an intentional union of the saints, as the mediator of sanctifying power.

Augustine's explanation of the relation between the bishop and the saints within the assembly of the church was most effectively symbolized in the eucharistic celebration. At baptism, the washing, anointing, and perhaps even the imposition of hands were performed in segregated and even secret spaces. In preaching, the bishop spoke from the elevated *cathedra* in the apse or, occasionally, the elevated *ambo* or *pulpitum.* Only in making the offering did the bishop stand in the center of the nave, surrounded by the people standing at the same level. As has been noted, Augustine explicitly identified the clergy as members of the one body, acting on earth in unity with its head, whose perpetual offering all hoped to join in the heavenly sanctuary. The bread and wine on the altar, moreover, symbolically realized not only the heavenly Christ but his ecclesial body: here alone was the society of saints made visible. The eucharistic celebration was, for Augustine, the central sacrament of the church and its power to sanctify.

The relation between bishop and people, as members of Christ, which was symbolized in the fifth-century African ritual, became normative for Augustine's understanding of the bishop's functioning within the church. Despite his elevated position in the *cathedra* and well-appreciated rhetorical gifts, Augustine regularly reminded his congregation that he was like them, a listener and a learner, their fellow pupil of Christ, the one teacher who acted through his ministry. He baptized and reconciled as the agent of the Whole Christ, not of the heavenly head alone but of the ecclesial body through whom the cleansing and sanctifying gift of charity was communicated, and apart from which it could not be retained.

Augustine's peculiar understanding of the nature of the church's relationship to Christ and the role of its clergy was shaped by many forces, particularly the Pauline eucharistic theology mediated by Cyprian, the Donatist controversy, and the Christic interpretation of the psalms. The plausibility of that ecclesiology was symbolized by and grounded in the spatial arrangement of the basilica, with its altar at floor level in the center of the nave, in the midst of the congregation. Once the Byzantines moved the altar back and up, to connect it to the clerical space in the apse, Augustine's ecclesiology was no longer practiced and could be understood only with difficulty, on the basis of his texts.

## Transition

Like baptism, the eucharistic celebration was a foundational and defining practice of Christians. As a weekly and even daily community ritual, the eucharist became the principal practice by which Christians enacted their relationships to Christ and to one another. It presupposed baptism and required penance to maintain its holiness and sanctifying power. The theories which were developed for understanding the purifying rituals had to be adapted in their application to the eucharistic celebration.

Under the pressure of congregational growth, persecution, and schism, eucharistic practice and theology changed radically in the third and fourth centuries. These developments would then require new understandings of the practice of penance and orders.

CHAPTER 7

# Keeping the Church Pure:
# Excluding and Readmitting Sinners

## INTRODUCTION

The rituals of penance and reconciliation were developed to deal with sins that
Christians committed after baptism. For the most part, the sins that Christians
acknowledged and repented were those of daily living — sins of negligence,
which neither violated their baptismal rejection of the idolatrous forms of life
nor caused serious injury to another human being. These minor sins were forgiven through the sinner's asking forgiveness of God, undertaking fasting and
almsgiving, and seeking pardon from the one harmed — along with granting
pardon to any who had harmed the sinner. The church had no formal ritual of
repentance and forgiveness for them. The major sins, by contrast, did challenge
the Christian's adherence to Christ, and thus the holiness of any community
that might tolerate members guilty of them. Instances of these sins were initially identified by an adaptation of the portions of Jewish law imposed on the
Gentile Christians (Acts 15:20) to indicate idolatry, adultery, and murder. Many
other types of action — such as theft, lying, and fraud — were also judged incompatible with participation in the eucharistic communion. The sinners were
excluded, were given the opportunity to repent of their failing and change their
behavior, and — with some exceptions — were eventually readmitted to church
membership.

Among the consistently debated questions in the African church were the
source and the agent of the power to forgive sins and the relation of that power to
the practices of exclusion and readmission to communion. God was recognized
as the ultimate grantor of forgiveness: the Christian and the church pleaded before God through prayer and penitential works for that gift of divine mercy. The
contested issues in the practice of penance and reconciliation included the relation between the forgiveness of God and the peace of the church, which was fo-

cused on God's authorization of church leaders to exclude sinners and readmit penitents. At the beginning of the third century, most Christians believed that the three extreme sins — adultery, idolatry, and murder — entailed permanent exclusion from the church. Those who sinned in a major but lesser way were allowed to repent and return to communion but were refused a second readmission if they then failed once again. During the first half of the third century, many came to believe that only those actually sharing the church's communion at the time of death could gain access to God's mercy in the final Judgment. The practice of permanent exclusion for an extreme sin or for a second major sin after readmission, therefore, implied not only that the church could not tolerate such a sinner as a communicant but that God would not grant forgiveness and thereby salvation. These developments forced a reconsideration of the church's authority to reconcile and God's willingness to forgive. Might readmission be allowed even after extreme sin? If so, who was empowered or authorized to act for God in forgiving the sin?

During the centuries considered in this chapter, the Christian community in the Roman Empire passed from being a despised and even persecuted minority to become a privileged and protected majority. The moral standards necessary to maintain the identity and promote the cohesion of the community, standards enforced by the rituals of penance, changed with the social status of the Christians. Theological understanding, as shall be seen, not only kept pace with the shifts but required some of the changes in practice.

## THE PRACTICE OF PENANCE IN TERTULLIAN'S TIME

Tertullian set the ritual of penance within the general context of the forgiveness of sins that was accomplished primarily through baptism. His early treatise, *On Repentance,* begins with a discussion of rejecting sin and making satisfaction, both of which were required before baptism. Only then does it turn to the second form of repentance, which could be used if the Christian sinned significantly after baptismal cleansing. Later, under the influence of the New Prophecy movement, Tertullian changed his views on the forgiveness of sins committed after baptism and argued for a more restrictive policy in his treatise *On Modesty.* His earlier essay may be presumed to reflect the practice of the Carthaginian church at the end of the second century; the later one records his opposition towards two attempts to change that practice. The bishop adopted a more lenient policy, and the reforming movement of the New Prophecy insisted on a more rigorist one. Tertullian's later work also suggests that the role of public penance was expanding in the church and being applied to sins that had earlier been left to private repentance. He provided information on the classification of sins, the structure of the rite of repentance, and the practices by which the church dealt with failures among its members.

The ritual of repentance for significant sins was called by the Greek term *exomologesis*,[1] which named a confessing of sins to God in the presence of the congregation. The proclamation of sinfulness was not intended as a means of informing God or, in many cases, even the community. Instead, it was intended to arouse regret in the sinner, to appease God, and to enlist the community's prayer for God's forgiveness.[2] The penitent would normally initiate the process of repentance by acknowledging a sin that was known to the community and its leaders or by disclosing one that was hidden from them.[3] If necessary, the church leaders might take the first step toward reconciliation by accusing the sinner and threatening a permanent exclusion from the communion.[4] Tertullian's writings do not describe the specificity with which the sinner declared the sin, though he did recognize that it entailed a shame comparable to revealing a sexual disease to a physician.[5] This confession was an integral part of the penitential process.

If the sin fell within the authority of the church to forgive, the sinner was then allowed to begin the process of repentance, which would lead to reconciliation and reintegration. The penitents were suspended from participation in the community's prayers and eucharist; their penitential actions were closely supervised. They engaged in activities of repentance that continued the work of the initial acknowledgment: rejection of sin, satisfaction of God, prayer for forgiveness, and appeal for community support. Some activities would have been carried on in private; others were performed at the entryway of the church; still others were obvious even to non-Christians.[6] Fasting encouraged and demonstrated the sinner's sense of loss and regret: only one meal was eaten each day; fine and festive foods were replaced by a cheap and simple diet.[7] Suffering hunger and thirst not only symbolized the loss of holiness but supported the petition for God's forgiveness.[8] The soul was cast down in sorrow as the penitent groaned, wept, and mourned to God day and night.[9] Penitents prayed kneeling with weeping and lamentation,[10] or might disfigure themselves with the biblically sanctioned sackcloth and ashes.[11] They gave up the comfort of the baths,[12] allowing the natu-

1. Tert. *Paen.* 9, 10, 12; *Or.* 7.1.
2. Tert. *Paen.* 9.1-2, 12.8; *Or.* 7.1, 10.2.
3. Tert. *Paen.* 3.9-10, 7.10, 10.7.
4. Tert. *Pud.* 7.16.
5. Tert. *Paen.* 10.1.
6. Tert. *Paen.* 7.10.
7. Tert. *Paen.* 9.4, 11.2-3; *Pat.* 13.2; *Pud.* 1.21, 13.14.
8. Tert. *Paen.* 9.4, 11.1; *Pat.* 13.3.
9. Tert. *Paen.* 9.4.
10. Tert. *Pud..* 1.21, 5.14.
11. Tert. *Paen.* 9.4, 11.1; *Pud.* 5.14, 18.13; *Pat.* 13.2.
12. Tert. *Paen.* 11.1-3.

ral accumulation of dirt to disfigure their bodies;[13] they stopped styling their hair, polishing their teeth, and trimming their nails.[14] Penitents might grasp and kiss the knees of the faithful as they entered and exited the assembly, begging for their intercessory prayers.[15] Though not all of these actions were manifest outside the community of the faithful, the suspension of normal grooming would have drawn the attention of the general public. Such practices of dress, food, and prayer not only humbled the penitents before the church and before God, but disrupted the social patterns and contacts that may have led them into sin.[16]

The penitents were not isolated from the church during the period of penance. They gathered at the threshold of the church and knocked on its door, asking to be allowed back into the community.[17] As the process developed, any members of the community who had been injured declared their forgiveness of the sin; the whole body of believers wept and grieved with its wounded member, begging God to grant pardon.[18] In his early exhortation to repentance, Tertullian assured the penitents of the efficacy of the congregation's intercession by identifying the church with Christ: when the church prayed to God for forgiveness, Christ himself interceded, and his petition could be trusted to prevail.[19]

These exhortations and explanations were based upon the community's general practice of extending personal forgiveness for injury, praying for divine forgiveness of guilt, and supporting the sinner who acknowledged and repented a sin. Though the process of repentance involved separation from the eucharist and even humiliation of the sinner, the ritual actually repaired and strengthened the bonds of affection between the penitent and the congregation that had been disrupted; it was an essential preparation for the subsequent reconciliation and reintegration of the penitent. It also reminded and warned all the faithful of the danger of sin that all faced.[20]

The duration of the periods of public penance are not specified in Tertullian's writings, though these may be presumed to have varied with the nature and circumstances of the sin and the status of the sinner within the local church. When the leaders judged that the process had attained its objective, the penitent was brought before the assembly. Here, the ritual reached its culmination: the penitent made a final confession of sin, kissing the feet of the faithful, grasping their knees and begging for their prayers, and bowing to the presbyters,

13. Tert. *Paen.* 9.4, 11.1; *Pud.* 13.14; *Pat.* 13.2.
14. Tert. *Paen.* 11.1, 12.7; *Pud.* 13.14.
15. Tert. *Paen.* 9.4, 10.5; *Pud.* 18.13.
16. Tert. *Paen.* 9.3, 11.6.
17. Tert. *Paen.* 7.10.
18. Tert. *Paen.* 2.10, 10.5-6; *Pud.* 13.10-12. To refuse to forgive another was to demonstrate ingratitude toward God *(Paen.* 2.10).
19. Tert. *Paen.* 10.6. The parallel persisted in *Pud.* 19.25-26 but without the guarantee of Christ's acting with the church.
20. Tert. *Pud.* 3.4.

1. Ammaedara (Haidra), Melleus basilica

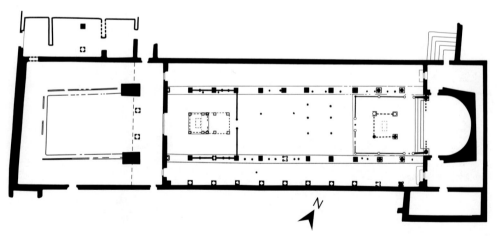

2. Ammaedara (Haidra), Melleus basilica
(Plan after Baratte and Duval [1974], p. 51, fig. 19. Drawn by E. Brown)

3. Ammaedara (Haidra), tomb inscription of Cresconia, from nave, Melleus basilica

4. Ammaedara (Haidra), detail of reliquary emplacement in nave, Melleus basilica

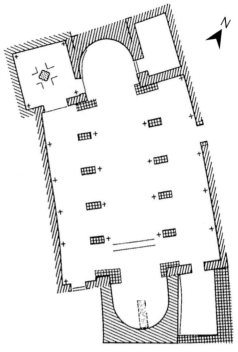

5. Belalis Maior, basilica I, phase II, baptismal font

6. Belalis Maior, basilica I, phase II (Plan after Lassus [1970a], p. 222, fig. 2. Drawn by E. Brown)

7. Belalis Maior, basilica II (cathedral?), phase II, baptismal font

8. Bennafa (La Skhira), mosaic pavement from baptistery, near Gabès, Tunisia,
now in the Sfax Archaeological Museum

9. Bennafa (La Skhira), mosaic pavement from baptistery, near Gabès, Tunisia,
now in the Sfax Archaeological Museum

10. Bulla Regia double church (basilica I) — looking toward apse

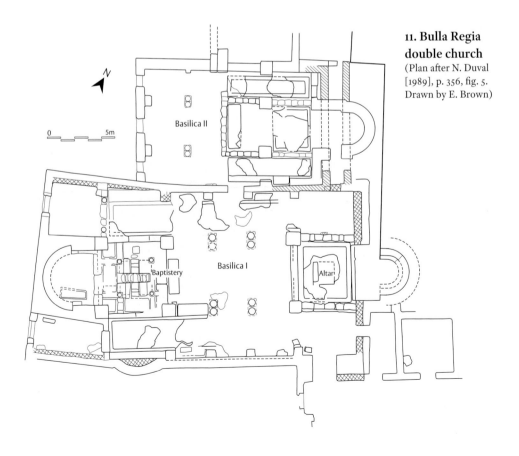

**11. Bulla Regia double church**
(Plan after N. Duval [1989], p. 356, fig. 5. Drawn by E. Brown)

N

0    5m

Basilica II

Baptistery

Basilica I

Altar

12. Bulla Regia double church, baptismal font

13. Bulla Regia,
baptismal font steps

14. Carthage, Roman amphitheater

15. Carthage, site of Damous el Karita

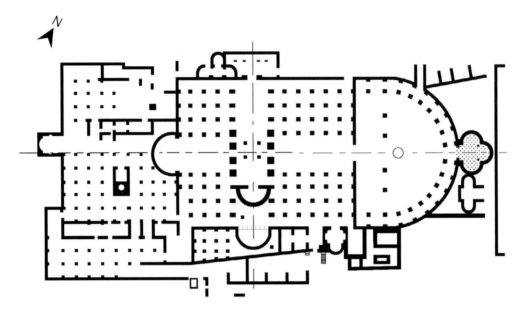

**16. Carthage, Damous el Karita** (Plan developed from N. Duval [1972], p. 1112, fig. 17. Drawn by E. Brown)

**17. Carthage,
Damous el Karita,
round monument**

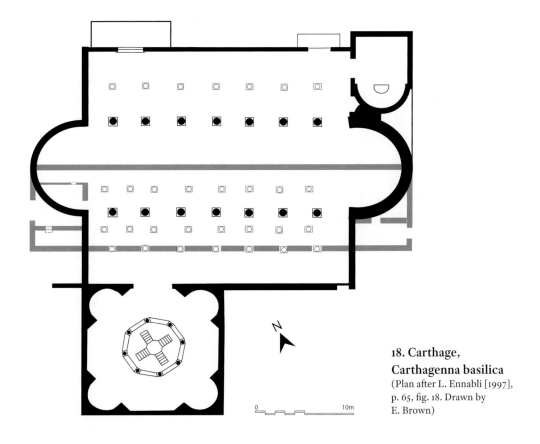

**18. Carthage,
Carthagenna basilica**
(Plan after L. Ennabli [1997],
p. 65, fig. 18. Drawn by
E. Brown)

0      10m

19. Carthage, site of Carthagenna basilica, showing baptistery wall

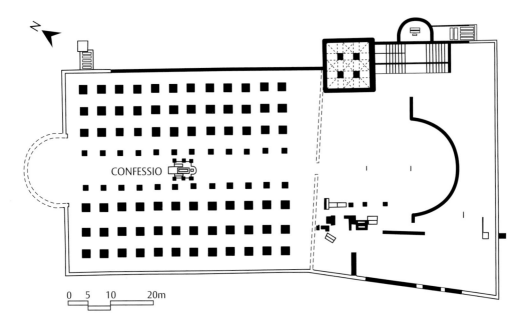

CONFESSIO

0 5 10 20m

**20. Carthage, Basilica Maiorum** (Plan after L. Ennabli [1997], p. 133, fig. 82. Drawn by E. Brown)

21. Carthage, inscription from Basilica Maiorum, now in the Carthage Museum

22. Carthage, site of
St. Monica basilica

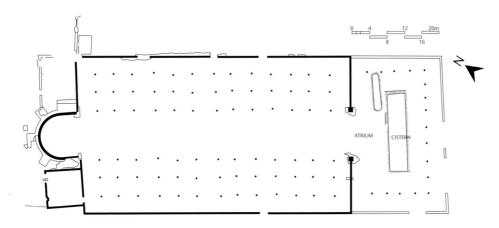

23. Carthage, St. Monica basilica (Plan after L. Ennabli [1997], p. 130, fig. 80. Drawn by E. Brown)

24. Carthage,
chapel of Asterius,
floor mosaic

25. Carthage, overview of
Dermech I basilica

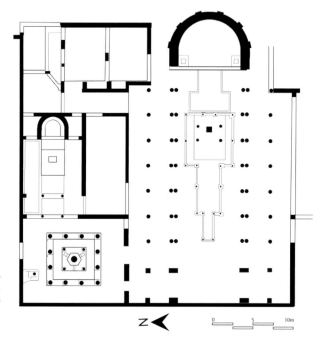

26. Carthage, Dermech I basilica
(Plan after Gauckler [1892-1904], pl. 5.
Drawn by E. Brown)

Z◀        0    5    10m

27. Carthage, baptistery at
Dermech I basilica

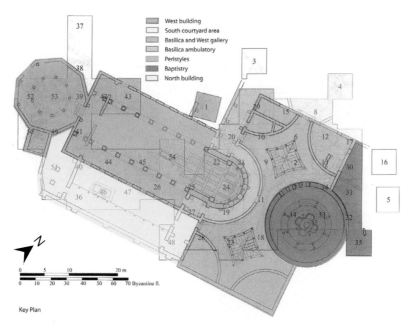

**28. Carthage, Bir Ftouha basilica**
(Plan drawn by B. Dayhoff and reproduced with permission from S. T. Stevens, A. V. Kalinowski, and H. vanderLeest, *Bir Ftouha: A Pilgrimage Church Complex at Carthage* [2005], p. 38, fig. 2.2)

**29. Carthage, mosaic from Bir Ftouha basilica, now in the Bardo Museum, Tunis**

**30. Carthage, mosaic for Perpetua, Stephen, and Companions (from the chapel of the monastery of St. Stephen), now in the Bardo Museum, Tunis**

31. Castellum Tidditanorum (Tiddis), baptistery I

32. Castellum Tidditanorum (Tiddis), baptistery II

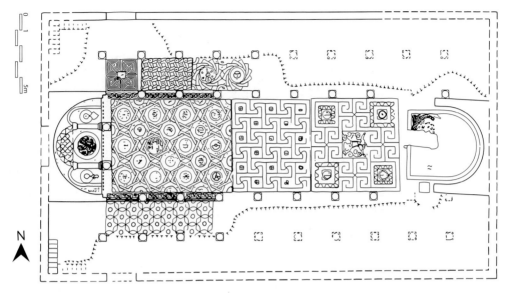

**33. Castellum Tingitanum (Chlef, Orléansville), approximate plan of basilica**
(Plan after N. Duval and Fevrier, 1972], p. 24, fig. 6. Drawn by E. Brown)

**34. Castellum Tingitanum, Reparatus epitaph in counter-apse**
(After drawing reproduced in Gui et al. [1992], pl. 16.2. Drawn by E. Brown)

**35. Castellum Tingitanum, altar mosaic**
(After drawing reproduced in Gui et al. [1992], pl. 15.2. Drawn by E. Brown)

36. Castellum Tingitanum, labyrinth mosaic, now in the Cathedral of the Sacred Heart, Algiers
(Photo: Annewies van den Hoek. Used with permission)

37. Beni Rached (near Castellum Tingitanum) mosaic, "Pax Aeclesia Catolice Semper"

38. Clipea (Kélibia), baptismal font, now in the Bardo Museum, Tunis

39. Clipea (Kélibia), baptismal font, detail of base with Christogram

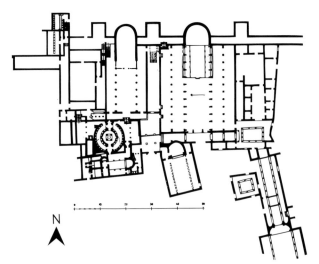

**40. Cuicul (Djémila), double churches, episcopal complex** (Plan after Lassus [1970a], p. 226, fig. 4. Drawn by R. Bockmann)

N

41. Cuicul (Djémila), baptismal font

42. Cuicul (Djémila), double churches with baptistery in background

44. Cuicul (Djémila), detail, pavement mosaic in baptistery

43. Cuicul (Djémila), ambulatory, baptistery

45. Cuicul (Djémila), bath next to baptistery

46. Djebel Oust, baptismal font

47. El-Kantara, Isle of Djerba (Meninx), baptismal font, now in the Bardo Museum, Tunis

48. Hippo Regius, basilica overview

49. Hippo Regius, basilica detail with cistern in foreground

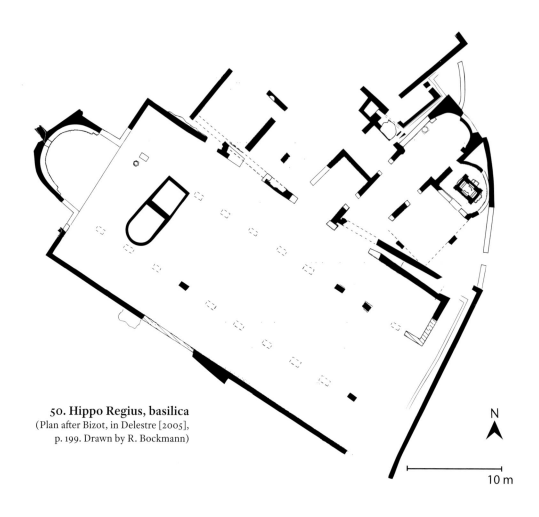

**50. Hippo Regius, basilica**
(Plan after Bizot, in Delestre [2005],
p. 199. Drawn by R. Bockmann)

N

10 m

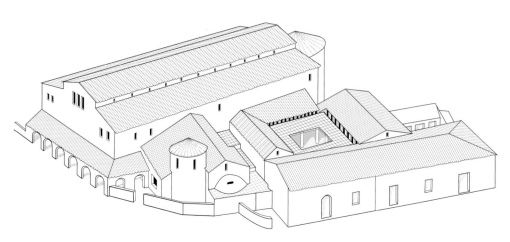

**51. Hippo Regius basilica, axonometric drawing of Hippo basilica complex**
(After Marec [1958], p. 131, fig. 19, with modifications suggested by authors. Drawn by E. Brown)

52. Hippo Regius, detail, area of cathedra

53. Hippo Regius, trefoil building

54. Hippo Regius, detail, baptistery

55. Hippo Regius, detail, baptismal font

**56. Iomnium (Tigzirt), baptismal font** (Photo: Michael Flecky, S.J. Used with permission)

**57. Lepti Minus (Lamta), mosaic pavement from baptistery, now in the Lamta Museum**

58. Mactaris (Maktar), Hildegun basilica

59. Mactaris (Maktar), baptismal font, Hildegun basilica

60. Mactaris (Maktar), Thermes basilica

**61. Musti, baptistery and font (with church apse)**

**62. Naro (Hammam Lif),
baptismal font**
(After drawing by Gsell, fol. xxi, no. 5, in
Berry [1976], p. 47. Drawn by E. Brown)

**63. Sidi Jdidi (Asadi), baptistery** (Photo: Nathan Dennis. Used with permission)

64. Sufetula (Sbeitla) Forum at site of Sufetula (Sbeitla), Tunisia

65. Sufetula (Sbeitla), Bellator basilica

66. Sufetula (Sbeitla), Jucundus chapel, adjacent Bellator basilica

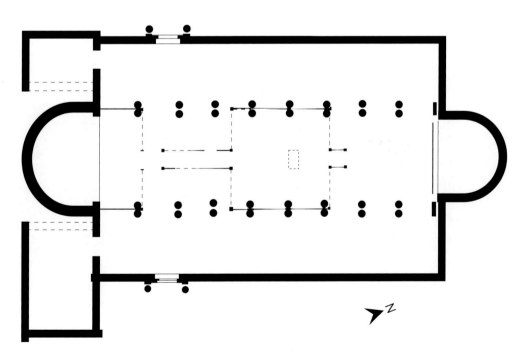

**67. Sufetula (Sbeitla), Bellator basilica, phase II**
(Plan after Duval and Baratte [1973], p. 38, fig. 22b. Drawn by E. Brown)

**68. Sufetula (Sbeitla), ecclesial complex**
(After Duval and Baratte [1973], p. 34, fig. 18. Drawn by E. Brown)

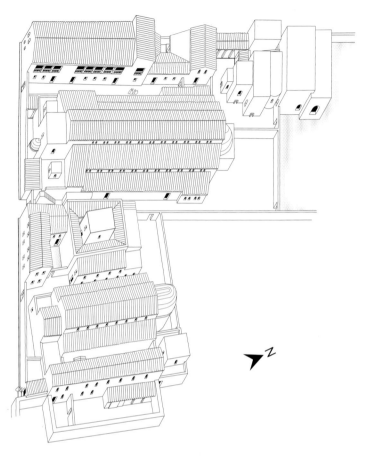

69. Sufetula (Sbeitla), Vitalis basilica, looking toward apse

70. Sufetula (Sbeitla), ancient piscina, found in the center aisle of Vitalis basilica

71. Sufetula (Sbeitla), baptismal font, Vitalis basilica

72. Sufetula (Sbeitla), details, baptismal font,
Vitalis basilica

73. Sufetula (Sbeitla), inscription from Servus basilica

74. Sufetula (Sbeitla), site of Servus basilica

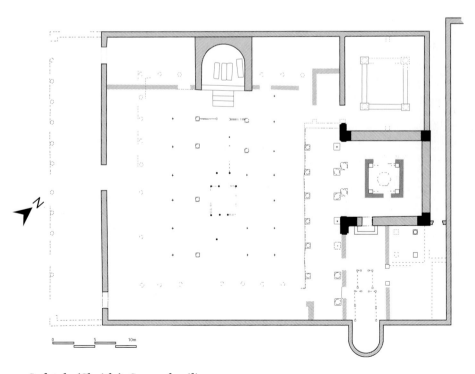

75. Sufetula (Sbeitla), Servus basilica
(Plan after Duval and Baratte [1973], p. 76, fig. 48. Drawn by E. Brown)

76. Sufetula (Sbeitla), Servus basilica, apse with sarcophagi

77. Sufetula (Sbeitla), Servus basilica, baptistery

78. Sufetula (Sbeitla), Servus basilica, apsed chapel or *consignatorium*

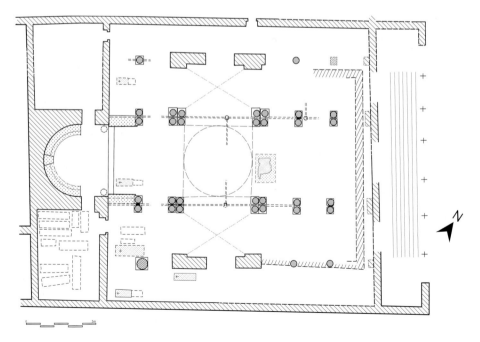

**79. Sufetula (Sbeitla), Sylvanius and Fortunatus basilica**
(Plan after Duval and Baratte [1973], p. 105, fig. 61. Drawn by E. Brown)

80. Sufetula (Sbeitla), from nave of Sylvanius and Fortunatus basilica, martyrs' mosaic inscription, now in the Sbeitla Museum

81. Sufetula (Sbeitla), Gervasius and Protasius basilica, showing altar base with cuttings for legs and a cavity for a reliquary

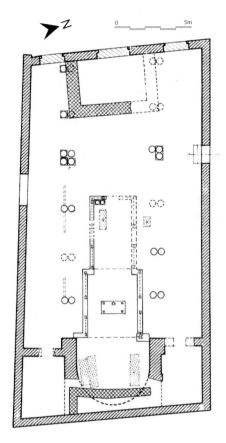

**82. Sufetula (Sbeitla), Gervasius and Protasius basilica** (Plan after Duval and Baratte [1973], p. 100, fig. 59. Drawn by E. Brown)

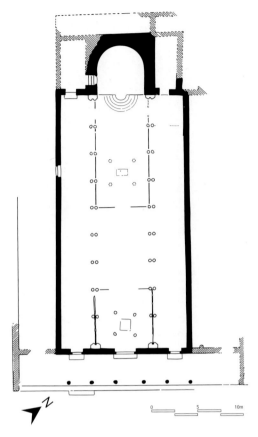

**83. Sufetula (Sbeitla), Forum basilica**
(Plan after Duval and Baratte [1973], p. 32, fig. 16. Drawn by E. Brown)

**84. Sufetula (Sbeitla), Forum basilica**

85. Sufetula (Sbeitla), mosaic from Honorius basilica, now in the Bardo Museum, Tunis

86. Sullecthum (Salakta),
tomb with attached *mensa*

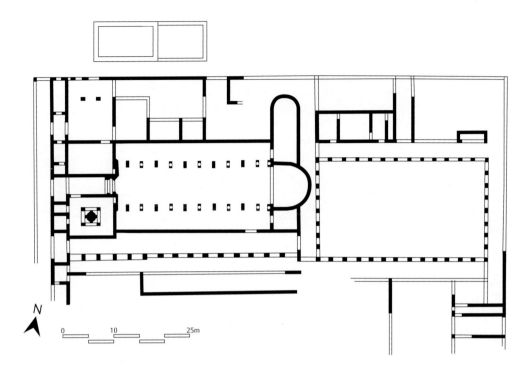

**87. Thamugadi (Timgad), Caecilianist church** (Plan after Christofle [1935], p. 365. Drawn by E. Brown)

88. Thamugadi (Timgad), baptismal font, Caecilianist church

89. Thamugadi (Timgad), font near the House of Januarius

90. Thamugadi (Timgad), back of basilica near the House of Januarius

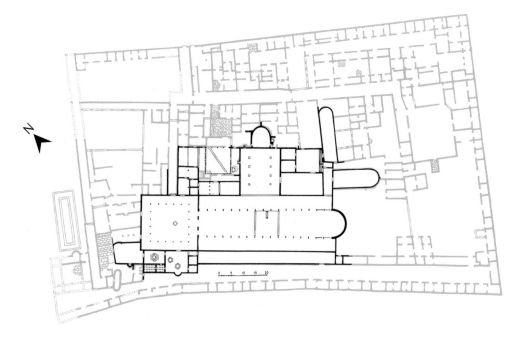

**91. Thamugadi (Timgad), Donatist Cathedral**
(Plan after Ballu [1911], pp. 38-39, and Christern [1976], p. 221, fig. 34. Drawn by E. Brown)

**92. Thamugadi (Timgad), possible tomb of Optatus**

93. Thamugadi (Timgad), chapel of the Donatist Cathedral
(with Capitolium in the background)

94. Thamugadi (Timgad), Donatist baptistery

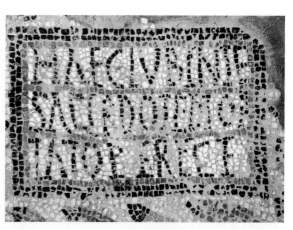

96. Thamugadi (Timgad), Optatus inscription from basilica, now in the Timgad Museum

95. Thamugadi (Timgad), funerary *mensa* outside the Timgad Museum

97. Thapsus, baptismal font found near Bekalta, now in the Sousse **Archaeological Museum** (Photo: Nathan Dennis. Used with permission)

98. Theveste (Tebessa), basilica of St. Crispina

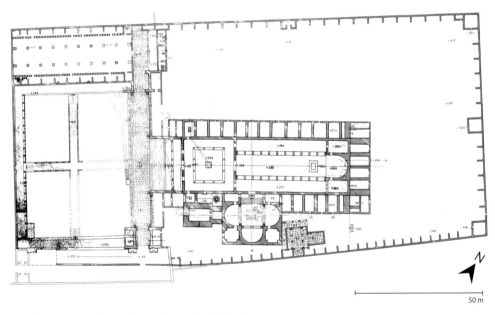

50 m

99. Theveste (Tebessa), basilica of St. Crispina
(Plan after Lassus [1970a], p. 229, fig. 6. Drawn by E. Brown)

100. Theveste (Tebessa), trefoil shrine

101. Theveste (Tebessa), baptismal font

102. Thuburbo Maius, basilica

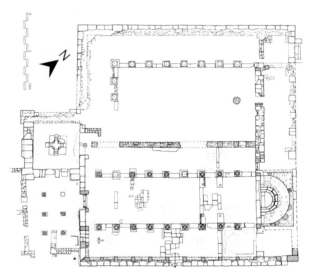

103. Thuburbo Maius, basilica
(Plan after Lézine [1968],
p. 25, fig. 6. Drawn by E. Brown)

104. Thuburbo Maius, baptismal font

105. Tipasa,
cathedral

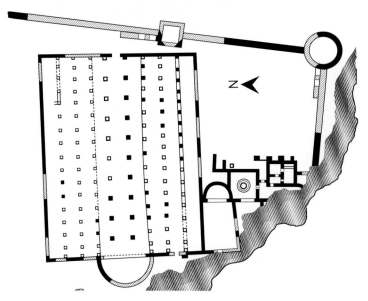

106. Tipasa, cathedral
(Plan after Gsell and Lassus
as in N. Duval [1989], pp.
352-53, figs. 2a-3.
Drawn by E. Brown)

107. Tipasa,
baptismal font

108. Tipasa, round monument/mausoleum

109. Tipasa, cemetery chapel of Bishop Alexander

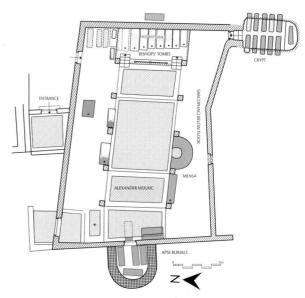

110. Tipasa, cemetery chapel of Bishop Alexander
(Plan after N. Duval in Gui [1992], vol. 2, p. xxxvi, fig. 1. Drawn by E. Brown)

111. Tipasa, St. Salsa basilica

112. Tipasa, *mensa* from cemetery basilica of Alexander

113. Tipasa, *mensa* mosaic, now in the Museum of Tipasa

114. Tipasa, *mensa* mosaic, now in the Museum of Tipasa

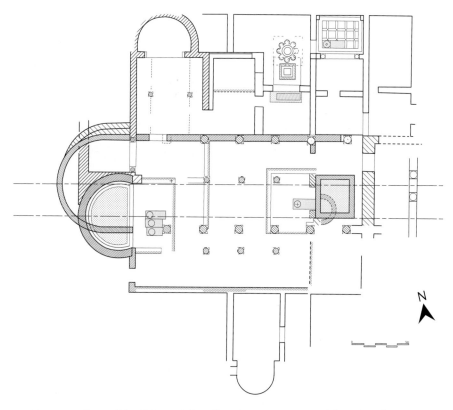

**115. Uppenna (Henchir Chigarnia), reflecting two stages of the church**
(Plan after N. Duval [1971-73], vol. 2, p. 150, fig. 2. Drawn by E. Brown)

**116. Uppenna (Henchir Chigarnia), baptismal font**

117. Uppenna (Henchir Chigarnia), martyrs' funerary mosaic and inscription from chancel area, Uppenna (basilica II). Left and right of the martyrs' mosaic, tomb mosaics of Honorius and Baleriolus. Now in the Enfidha Museum

118. Uppenna (Henchir Chigarnia), martyrs' mosaic detail

119. Bennafa (La Skhira), tomb mosaic for Matrona Vidua,
now in the Enfidha Museum

120. Furnos Minus
(Borj el Youdi), tomb
mosaic from the
mausoleum of Blossus,
now in the Bardo
Museum, Tunis

121. Furnos Minus (Borj el
Youdi), tomb mosaic of Bishop
Vitalis, now in the Bardo
Museum, Tunis

122. Hadrumetum (Sousse), tomb mosaic for Hermes from cubiculum of Hermes, now in the Sousse Archaeological Museum

123. Hadrumetum (Sousse), tomb inscription from the Good Shepherd cubiculum, funerary mosaic pavement

124. Hadrumetum (Sousse), dedicatory funeral plaque to Varia Victoria, now in the Sousse Archaeological Museum

125. Hippo Regius, tomb mosaic for Guilia Runa
(Photo: Michael Flecky, S.J. Used with permission)

126. Lepti Minus (Lamta), tomb mosaic for Pascasius, now in the Lamta Museum

127. **Lepti Minus (Lamta), catacomb** (Photo from Ben Lazreg et al. [2006], p. 361, color fig. 3. Reproduced with permission)

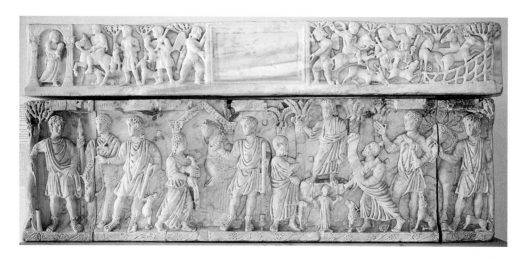

128. Lepti Minus (Lamta), sarcophagus of Secundinus, now in the Lamta Museum

129. Sidi Abich, tomb mosaic for Bishop Paulus, Primate of Mauretania, now in the Enfidha Museum

130. Taparura (Sfax), tomb mosaic of Quiriacus, now in the Sfax Archaeological Museum

131. Taparura (Sfax), tomb mosaic of veiled woman, now in the Sfax Archaeological Museum

132. Thabraca, Ecclesia Mater tomb mosaic (chapel of the martyrs), now in the Bardo Museum, Tunis

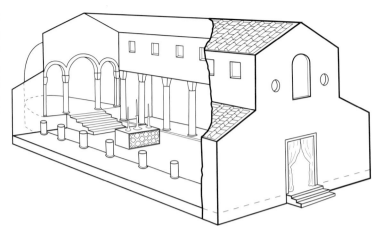

**133.** Axonometric
projection of the
Ecclesia Mater
mosaic (Thabraca)
(After Ward-Perkins and
Goodchild [1953], pp. 57-58,
fig. 28. Drawn by E. Brown)

**134.** Thabraca, tomb portrait mosaic
of Iovinus (Urban basilica cemetery
enclosure), now in the Bardo
Museum, Tunis

**135.** Thabraca, tomb portrait mosaic of
Crescentia (Urban basilica cemetery), now
in the Bardo Museum, Tunis

136. Thabraca, tomb portrait mosaic of grain measurer (Urban basilica cemetery), now in the Bardo Museum, Tunis

137. Thabraca, mosaic caisson-style sarcophagus of Dardanius (Urban basilica cemetery enclosure), now in the Bardo Museum, Tunis

138. Thabraca, tomb mosaic showing Jonah (Urban basilica cemetery), now in the Bardo Museum, Tunis

139. Thabraca, double tomb portrait mosaic (martyrs' chapel), now in the Bardo Museum, Tunis

140. Thabraca, tomb mosaic for Victor (south auxiliary chapel on left of martyrs' chapel), now in the Bardo Museum, Tunis

142. Thabraca, tomb mosaic for Pompeia Maxima, *famula dei* (left side auxiliary chapel to martyrs' chapel), now in the Bardo Museum, Tunis

141. Thabraca, tomb mosaic for the presbyter Privatus (northwest chapel/cemetery), now in the Bardo Museum, Tunis

144. Thabraca, tomb mosaic for Privata and Victoria (martyrs' chapel), now in the Bardo Museum, Tunis

143. Thabraca, tomb mosaic for the deacon Crescentinus (martyrs' chapel), now in the Bardo Museum, Tunis

145. Thaenae (Henchir Thina), double tomb mosaic for a couple, C. Julius Serenus and Numitoria Saturnina, now in the Sfax Archaeological Museum

146. Thaenae, caisson tomb and detail of tomb, now in the Sfax Archaeological Museum

147. Thaenae, tomb mosaic, now in the Sfax Archaeological Museum

148. Uppenna (Henchir Chigarnia), funerary mosaic of Deacon Crescentius and his son, now in the Enfidha Museum

149. Uppenna (Henchir Chigarnia), secondary funerary mosaics of Faustina and Spendeu, now in the Enfidha Museum

150. Abraham and Isaac on terra-cotta tile, from area of Kasserine, now in the Bardo Museum, Tunis

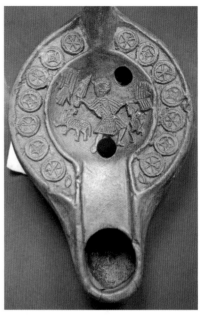

151. Adam and Eve on terra-cotta tile from Hadrumetum (Sousse), now in the Sousse Archaeological Museum

152. Terra-cotta lamp with Abraham offering Isaac, now in the Timgad Museum

153. Punic *stelae* from Thamugadi, outside the Timgad Museum

with tears and lamentation.[21] The bishop preached on the mercy and kindness of God, recalling the parables of forgiveness in the Gospel of Luke (15).[22] After the petitions and intercession, the bishop spoke a declarative absolution, dismissing the sin and loosening the bonds of the penitent.[23] The purified sinner was then admitted to share the prayer and communion of the faithful. This ritual would have been performed at an assembly of the whole community, which gathered for the morning prayer service. It required a fuller participation, and thus a larger space, than the evening love feast in private homes could provide.

## Using the Ritual of Repentance

Tertullian's understanding of the proper use of the ritual of repentance may have been somewhat more demanding than was the norm for his fellow Christians. He argued that penance must be undertaken for sins of intention as well as overt actions, since the mind's intention made an action good or evil.[24] God held a person guilty for an evil intention even when it did not issue in action.[25] Conversely, true repentance could not be achieved by interior dispositions alone but must be acted out before the congregation. Thus, sins of both intention and performance must be repented in action. Nor should the ritual of penance be reserved for publicly committed or notorious sins. In order to attain forgiveness, a Christian could be required to reveal a private sin, one otherwise hidden from the community. Tertullian urged that despite the shame and embarrassment this might entail, public confession was better than private damnation.[26]

Tertullian offered a number of arguments for these positions. Public action was required by the close unity of mind and body in human beings.[27] Although the inward faith of Abraham had earlier been adequate and acceptable to God, the sacrament had been expanded so that outward performance was required after the death and resurrection of Christ.[28] Just as Christ himself worked in the flesh, so must the Christian, by submitting to penitential suffering for

---

21. Tert. *Paen.* 9.4, 10.5; *Pud.* 5.14, 18.13. The ritual itself seems to be summarized in *Pud.* 13.6-7.

22. Tert. *Pud.* 13.7. These parables are reviewed in *Pud.* 7, where Tertullian noted that the image of the good shepherd carrying the lost sheep was depicted on Christians' drinking cups (*Pud.* 7.1).

23. Tert. *Paen.* 10.8. See *Pud.* 1.6, 18.18 for the role of the bishop, *Pud.* 21.17 for the spiritual prophet.

24. Tert. *Bapt.* 4.5.

25. Tert. *Paen.* 1.11-16, 4.1.

26. Tert. *Paen.* 10.1, 8.

27. Tert. *Paen.* 10.1, 8.

28. Tert. *Bapt.* 13.1-2; *Paen.* 10.1, 8.

sin.[29] To repent only within one's heart and not in open practice, Tertullian argued, would be to separate body and spirit. Could a person preserve interior holiness while sinning in action, or have one's body in hell and spirit in heaven?[30] Confession and public satisfaction should be required, therefore, both in preparation for baptism and for the forgiveness of post-baptismal sins through reconciliation.

Tertullian's writing of the exhortation *On Repentance* may indicate that a significant number of his fellow Christians in Carthage avoided the public rituals of penance for sins that were only intentional or that were not already generally known in the community. The treatise itself offers arguments and incentives for a voluntary type of practice that many may have judged unnecessary and that the leaders of the community could not enforce — because the sins in question were not manifest.

### Access to the Ritual

Penance, Tertullian warned in his early treatise, should be undertaken only once, prior to baptism, and for sins that might be excused because of the ignorance in which they were committed before a person became Christian. A return to sin — after a believer had ostensibly repented of evil and learned to fear God — would indicate that the original conversion had not been sincere. In this case, God had not been deceived by the false repentance: the promised cleansing from sin in the baptismal washing had been granted, but God had then allowed the sinner to return openly to evil.[31] Divine mercy thus provided the Christian a second opportunity for the full and effective repentance that should have preceded baptism. Second penance might then be undertaken only once; it was the final offer of forgiveness.[32] To return to sinning yet again, Tertullian inferred, would be a clear sign of insincerity and abuse of the divine mercy.[33] Tertullian rationalized this limitation by interpreting penance as an extension of baptism, a second opportunity for the only true repentance, which effected a permanent rejection of sin. Other Christians might have recognized this limit to the church's authority to grant reconciliation and readmission but could have insisted that God might still forgive a recidivist at the Judgment following the Resurrection.[34]

The post-baptismal ritual of repentance mediated the church's forgiveness

29. Tert. *Pat.* 13.1.
30. Tert. *Paen.* 5.10, 9.1.
31. Tert. *Paen.* 5.1-6, 6.11-13.
32. Tert. *Paen.* 7.2-3, 10-11; 9.1.
33. Tert. *Paen.* 7.2.
34. The evidence for this restriction in Africa prior to the late fourth century is actually quite sparse. In *Paen.* 7.10-11, Tertullian seems to have advanced his own argument, which precluded

of a broad range of sins, excluding a very few which were committed against —
and therefore reserved to — God. These were generally identified as idolatry,
adultery, and murder.[35] In the more restricted penitential practice inspired by
the New Prophecy, which will be considered below, nearly all major sins were
excluded from the church's power of forgiveness and reserved to God's judgment.

## Withholding the Ritual

The sins committed against God as well as a fellow human — primarily idolatry, but extended to adultery and murder — were judged to lie outside the
church's power of forgiveness and reconciliation. Such sinners were urged to
undertake repentance, but they were not allowed to participate in the rituals
of repentance and to share the place set aside for others preparing for readmission. The door of penance was shut to them; forever outsiders, they were not at
the threshold waiting to enter.[36] The immediate fruit of the ritual of penance,
the pardon and peace of the church, was not available to them.[37]

These sinners were not, however, abandoned by the church as lost. Instead,
they were urged to repent by putting an end to sinning and to seek forgiveness
directly from God in the Judgment.[38] They were supported by the care and the
intercessory prayers of the community,[39] but they were not allowed to petition
in the midst of the assembly in anticipation of readmission.[40] The compassion
and tears of the community would be more effective in winning the forgiveness of God for the excluded penitent, Tertullian explained, than the gesture of
granting communion.[41]

## The Penitential Works

Many other sins could be forgiven through the church's rituals of repentance
and engagement in activities leading to reconciliation. Tertullian characterized the objective and effect of the penitential works by a set of contrasts: the

---

another divine forgiveness of sin on the grounds of the insincerity of the baptismal repentance. He
might not have reflected a generally accepted view.

35. In the contemporary Tert. *Spec.* 3.2, but without the reference to Acts 15. In the later
*Marc.* 4.9.6 and *Idol.* 1.1-5, these sins are parts of longer lists. These three sins are the focus of
attention and linked to Acts 15 in, e.g., *Pud.* 12.4, 21.13.

36. Tert. *Paen.* 7.10; *Pud.* 3.5, 6.1, 13.7.

37. Tert. *Pud.* 3.3, 9.20.

38. Tert. *Pud.* 18.18, 19.6.

39. Tert. *Pud.* 13.12.

40. Tert. *Pud.* 13.7.

41. Tert. *Pud.* 3.5.

penitent's self-denunciation replaced God's wrath, temporal affliction removed eternal punishment, abasement raised up, squalor cleansed, self-accusation excused, condemning absolved, suffering cured, satisfaction elicited clemency, fearing punishment honored God, not sparing oneself moved God to spare.[42] Tertullian offered two different explanations of the efficacy of the penitential works. The reference to sin as debt *(debitum)* in the Lord's Prayer suggested that penitential works could serve as the payment or satisfaction of an obligation owed to God.[43] The more immediate objective was actually to put an end to sinning, which then served as a basis for God's granting of pardon. Thus Tertullian argued that repentance would never be undertaken in vain, even if the church could or would not offer reconciliation for the major sins. God's pardon and, by implication, granting of salvation could be won even outside the church's peace and communion.[44]

## Forgiveness through Martyrdom

Tertullian provided an early witness to the belief that public witness to Christ had the effect of cleansing from all sin;[45] when it resulted in death, it brought an immediate heavenly reward.[46] Baptism was the proper standard for understanding the power of martyrdom: the two were symbolized as equivalent by the water and blood flowing together from the side of the crucified Christ.[47] On various occasions, Tertullian explained the efficacy of laying down one's life in imitation of Christ: the martyr paid God for sins with blood[48] and exercised a fullness of charity which itself won forgiveness.[49] In his later writings, Tertullian suggested that the parables of forgiveness in the Gospel of Luke (15) — the lost sheep, the lost coin, and the prodigal son — actually referred to martyrdom rather than the rituals of second repentance. They showed that martyrdom, like baptism, forgave even those sins committed against God, sins that were judged to be beyond the authority of the church and the power of its ritual of repentance. This violent form of baptism, moreover, prevented any further sinning and secured salvation by removing the Christian from earthly life.[50] A confes-

42. Tert. *Paen.* 9.5-6, 10.8, 11.3; *Pat.* 13.3.

43. Tert. *Or.* 7.1. The term *debitum* occurs regularly in his writings: *Paen.* 7.12; *Or.* 23.4; *Bapt.* 20.1; *Pat.* 13.4; *Cult. fem.* 1.1.1; *Pud.* 13.14; *Ieiun.* 3.3-4 (where fasting makes up for the sin of forbidden eating).

44. Tert. *Pud.* 10.14, 18.18; in contrast, *Paen.* 9 deals only with the efficacy of the works forming part of the ritual.

45. Tert. *Pud.* 22.2-4, 9-10.

46. Tert. *An.* 55.5; *Res.* 43.4.

47. Tert. *Bapt.* 16.1-2.

48. Tert. *Apol.* 50.15.

49. Tert. *Scorp.* 6.10-11.

50. Tert. *Pud.* 9.21; *Scorp.* 6.9.

sor — someone who survived a trial for professing Christ — gained forgiveness and readmission to the communion of the church but remained subject to the uncertainties and temptations of earthly life. Such a Christian could still fail and require yet another opportunity for public witness.[51]

Tertullian also noted the belief current among his contemporaries that martyrs — and even confessors — could secure the forgiveness of the sins of other Christians. The practice of appealing to those who had been imprisoned or sent to be worked to death in imperial mines was especially important for sinners guilty of the major sins of adultery, idolatry, and murder. These sinners were required to engage in penance throughout their lifetimes in order to gain God's pardon.[52] Through the intervention of the confessor or martyr, however, these penitents hoped to regain the communion of the church before they died. Tertullian explained that this extraordinary practice was based upon the belief that Christ himself suffered and triumphed in the confessors and martyrs, thus giving them access to his own power of forgiveness.[53] The foundation of this belief might in turn have been the presence of the Spirit, which empowered the confessor to witness for Christ (Matt. 10:20).[54] This divine indwelling and operation would have given the martyrs an intercessory power greater than that of the congregation and an authority to grant reconciliation broader than that of the bishop.

Once he had become a devotee of the New Prophecy, however, Tertullian rejected this practice of allowing confessors and martyrs to intervene in the church's reconciliation of sinners.[55] He attacked the power of those undergoing public trial on the grounds that they were still beset by temptation and struggling to secure their own salvation until the very moment of death. How could they promise salvation to another when they could not presume it for themselves?[56] This dispute over the proper role of the confessors and martyrs in the forgiveness of sinners and their restoration to the communion of the church would recur during Cyprian's episcopate.

## The Development of Penitential Discipline

In his earlier exhortation *On Repentance,* Tertullian did not define or illustrate the distinction between sins that were to be addressed by the ritual of public penance and those sins that might be forgiven without the formal ritual. His explanation of

51. Tert. *Pud.* 22.1-2.

52. Tert. *Pud.* 22.1-2; *Mart.* 1.6. A variant at *Paen.* 10.4 may refer to confessors by *et caris dei adgeniculari.* The better attested reading for *caris* is *aris,* but its plural form presents problems. See CCSL 1:336.16-17 and CSEL 76:163.17.

53. Tert. *Pud.* 22.6.

54. Tert. *Fug.* 14.3.

55. Tert. *Pud.* 22.7, 17.

56. Tert. *Pud.* 22.3-5.

the church's practice of allowing formal penance and reconciliation only a single time after baptism, moreover, implied that the rituals were primarily intended for such sins as would constitute a violation of the baptismal repudiation of Satan and demonic works.[57] Sins that arose from human weakness were apparently to be forgiven through regular, even daily, appeal for Christ's intercession.[58] Neither did Tertullian explicitly distinguish those extreme sins that were beyond the capacity of the penitential ritual to provide readmission to communion, though the contemporary reference to sinners' seeking the peace of the church through the martyrs might imply such a limitation.[59] In writing this exhortation to undertake public repentance, he addressed neither the lesser nor the extraordinary sins, both of which he considered outside the scope of this ritual.

In the later treatise *On Modesty,* Tertullian indicated that he had become convinced of the teaching of the New Prophecy, which demanded a higher disciplinary standard and a more restricted practice of reconciling penitents. The treatise itself was provoked by an innovation of the Bishop of Carthage, who would allow those guilty of adultery to be admitted to public penance and through it to gain pardon and readmission to communion.[60] Tertullian's arguments against this decision provide a clearer picture of the established practice of the church in Carthage and the way in which it was being challenged by both its laxist bishop and the rigorist New Prophecy movement.

### THE NEW PROPHECY

In representing the teaching of the New Prophecy, Tertullian distinguished four types of sin on the basis of their consequences when committed after baptism. Some sins would not be forgiven even by God; those who committed them had to be permanently expelled from the church.[61] Other sins might be forgiven only by God; the congregation could urge repentance and support the penitents but could not allow them to return to its communion.[62] A third type

57. Tert. *Paen.* 7.10-11.

58. The explanation of the church's intercession offered in Tert. *Paen.* 10.6 was applied to private penance in *Pud.* 19.23.

59. Tert. *Mart.* 1.6. The sinners might have been attempting to avoid the burdens of the ritual of penance, which was available to them.

60. Tert. *Pud.* 1.6. On the identification of the bishop as that of Carthage rather than Rome, see Timothy David Barnes, *Tertullian: A Historical and Literary Study,* 2nd ed. (Oxford: Clarendon Press, 1985), 30-31, 141, 247, whose judgment is here followed. For the contrary opinion, see Allan Brent, *Hippolytus and the Roman Church in the Third Century* (Leiden: Brill, 1995), 503-35; Jane E. Merdinger, *Rome and the African Church in the Time of Augustine* (New Haven: Yale University Press, 1997), 32-33; Eric Francis Osborn, *Tertullian, First Theologian of the West* (Cambridge, U.K.: Cambridge University Press, 1997), 175, n. 3.

61. Tert. *Pud.* 4.5, 13.12.

62. Tert. *Pud.* 5.13-14; 9.9, 20; 12.5; 13.2; 19.25, 26, 28; 21.2.

of sin would be forgiven by God through the ritual of penance so that the congregation could grant readmission.[63] The fourth type of sin would be forgiven by God through the private repentance of the sinner; this required neither exclusion from the communion nor the ritual of penance.[64] Because the treatise in which Tertullian explained the teaching of the New Prophecy was primarily directed against the innovative policy of the Bishop of Carthage on adulterers — thus, it concerned sins that had been categorized in the second type but were being moved to the third — he did not carefully delineate the distinction between sins of the third and fourth types and the proper means of dealing with each. The scope and purpose of the ritual of repentance might have changed significantly in the communities following the discipline of the New Prophecy. Tertullian, however, explained this change only to the extent necessary to attack the expansion of penitential discipline for those other Christians who were under the guidance of the Bishop of Carthage. No other African author provided so careful and detailed a distinction of the categories of sin.

In the first set of sins, Tertullian placed the monstrosities in which the law of nature itself was violated, citing incest (1 Cor. 5:5) and blasphemy (1 Tim. 1:19).[65] Paul turned such persons over to Satan for their own destruction, which would lead to the warning and correction of others.[66] God would forgive such sins in baptism but not when they were committed after baptism. In support of this position, Tertullian cited John's advice that Christians not pray for sinners guilty of deadly sins (1 John 5:16).[67] Thus, members of the church were required to expel such persons not only from their communion but from their minds and hearts as well.[68] Apparently, they were judged to be among the damned.

A second set of sins was specified as committed directly against God or as violating the temple of God, though in a way that God was prepared to forgive.[69] Such sins were separated from the outrageous crimes of the first category by statements in scripture distinguishing them. For example, incest was differentiated from fornication as an unnatural sexual deviance. These sins were separated from the third and fourth categories by reference to the command given to Peter that he must forgive sins committed against himself (Matt. 18:21-22). By linking this command to the power of keys also given to Peter, Tertullian reasoned that in being commanded to loose all sins committed against himself as a fellow human, by implication Peter was required to bind the sins commit-

---

63. Tert. *Pud.* 7.15, 18.18.

64. Tert. *Pud.* 7.20, 19.23-25.

65. Tert. *Pud.* 4.5; 13.12, 19. The denial of Christ during time of persecution might also have been in this category, on the basis of the threat in Matt. 10:33.

66. Tert. *Pud.* 13.16-25.

67. Tert. *Pud.* 2.14.

68. Tert. *Pud.* 13.12.

69. Tert. *Pud.* 18.13, 21.2.

ted against God.[70] The primary subjects of debate in the treatise *On Modesty* were two sins in this second category, adultery and fornication, jointly defined as sexual relations with someone who was not a marriage partner.[71] Tertullian argued that such sins had always been recognized as beyond the authority of the church to forgive.[72] In Acts (15:20), for example, when the other points of the Mosaic Law were all made remissible for the sake of the nations, the three sins of murder, adultery, and idolatry were held as irremissible for everyone.[73] Tertullian then extended this prohibition by elaborating the different forms that these three sins could take. Blasphemy and apostasy were specifications of idolatry.[74] Heresy was a form of adultery against the faith itself.[75] By using the Decalogue, false testimony[76] and fraud[77] were added to the sins listed in Acts. Tertullian also linked idolatry to lasciviousness, drunkenness, and vanity, as well as other sins.[78]

If any sin in this second category was committed by a Christian after baptism, Tertullian argued, the church must not presume to accept the sinner as a penitent, to whom it would subsequently grant peace and readmission to communion.[79] The community should exhort the sinner to undertake the works of repentance and should support that prayer with its own intercession. The penitent could still hope to receive the forgiveness of God at the Judgment.[80]

Sins of the third type were committed against a fellow human being or oneself but not specifically as a temple of God. These were the object of the formal ritual of repentance. Some of the sins in this category involved vices such as immodesty, anger, or cruelty, which were indulged principally by attending the circus, the amphitheater, or the theater.[81] Other sins occurred through indirect contact with idolatry or magic in some official or social capacity rather than by full participation or direct performance. Such sins might occur in the attendance of a banquet or festival, in the exercise of public office, or by coopera-

70. Tert. *Pud.* 21.14.

71. Tert. *Pud.* 19.25-26, 28. Adultery added the violation of the marriage of at least one of the parties. Theodore Mackin, *Divorce and Remarriage* (New York: Paulist Press, 1984), 166-72, suggests that persons who remarried after dismissing an adulterous spouse, according to the provisions of Roman law, were also considered guilty of adultery but were not usually required to return to the original spouse.

72. Tert. *Pud.* 5.13-14, 7.15, 19.25-26; *Spec.* 3.2; *Marc.* 4.9.6.

73. Tert. *Pud.* 12.5-6.

74. Tert. *Pud.* 9.9, 13.20, 19.25-26; *Marc.* 4.9.6.

75. Tert. *Pud.* 19.6.

76. Idolatry, blasphemy, homicide, adultery, illicit sexual intercourse, false testimony, fraud: these were his seven capital sins. Tert. *Marc.* 4.9.6.

77. Tert. *Spec.* 3.2; *Marc.* 4.9.6; *Pud.* 18.7-8.

78. Tert. *Idol.* 1.1-5.

79. Tert. *Pud.* 9.20, 13.7.

80. Tert. *Pud.* 3.1-6.

81. Tert. *Pud.* 7.15; *Spec.* 16.1, 17.1, 18.1, 19.1.

tion in another's idolatry.[82] The use of an equivocal expression that could imply apostasy or blasphemy without actually committing it — and thus concealing one's Christian identity or evading a law requiring the forbidden acts — would also fit in this category.[83] Still other sins would lead to damnation only if left unrepented, such as leaving the community in anger, pride, or jealousy.[84] All the sins of this third type could be forgiven by the church's rituals of exclusion and reconciliation. In singling them out, moreover, Tertullian did not repeat his earlier explanation that this ritual could be used only once after baptism. Indeed, the sins he listed in this later treatise do not seem to provide the evidence of a failure to repent at baptism that had justified this restriction in his earlier *On Repentance.*[85] In his treatise *On Modesty,* however, Tertullian was primarily concerned with the binding and loosening of the second category, sins against God. For these, not even a single penance was to be allowed, lest this encourage further sinning. Thus, he had no reason to repeat the earlier assertion and explanation that the ritual of penance could be used only once after baptism. The omission of this argument does not indicate of itself that the repetition of the ritual was allowed in the practice of the New Prophecy movement.[86]

Finally, a fourth category encompassed sins resulting from daily temptation or negligence; these might be forgiven without the public ritual of penance. Tertullian suggested, for example, that the parable of the drachma lost in a house might be appropriately applied to minor sins that were removed and forgotten as soon as they were discovered and repented.[87] In talking about sins that could be forgiven thus, he listed many that seem to have fallen below the threshold of the church's formal discipline: unrighteous anger allowed to continue beyond sundown, striking or cursing another, swearing out of habit rather than with deliberation, violating one's word, lying through shame or under compulsion.[88] To these might also be added others, which have been listed in the third category above: failing to reject and avoid idolatry in the management of business, public office, or commercial transactions. All of these might have involved casual contact with the traditional Roman religion through presence in a government building, the forum, or because of a reference to these gods in the wording of a contract.[89] Finally, he listed casual failures in eating,

82. Tert. *Pud.* 7.15.

83. Tert. *Pud.* 7.15.

84. Tert. *Pud.* 7.15.

85. Tert. *Paen.* 7.10-11. Note in particular the final group — leaving the community in anger, pride, or jealousy — which would bring condemnation if left unrepented.

86. Tert. *Paen.* 7.7-10. Instead, he wanted to distinguish the sins that the church and bishop could forgive from those that could not be so forgiven: *Pud.* 7.15, 18.18, 21.7. The limitations of this evidence are parallel to those of *Paen.:* the objectives of the two treatises might account for what is overlooked and what is emphasized.

87. Tert. *Pud.* 7.20.

88. Tert. *Pud.* 19.23-25.

89. Tert. *Pud.* 19.23-25. For instances of such practices, see *Idol.* 23 and *Fug.* 5.3, 12-14.

drinking, watching, or listening.[90] Such sins might have been forgiven through the profession of regret and the regular practices of fasting and almsgiving.[91] In warning against refusal to submit to correction within the church, Tertullian implied that some of the sins in this fourth category might engage the disciplinary authority of the church, particularly if the offender refused to be privately reconciled.[92]

Although Tertullian did not provide a full description of the penitential practice of the Christians following the guidance of the New Prophecy, much can be discerned from his arguments. Some sinners simply were excluded or excluded themselves by refusing to repent; they were judged no longer worthy of the church's prayer and exhortation. Others were excluded from communion but remained in the care of the church. They might hope to regain access to the eucharist by suffering for public confession of Christ or to be forgiven by the judgment of God. Those who had sinned in some significant way against their fellows were temporarily excluded from communion and required to perform public penance. This ritual may have been used more than once in a person's lifetime and thus may have engaged a greater proportion of the community than the traditional practice.[93] The most regular practice, however, was certainly the daily, private repentance for sins of inadvertence and negligence in self-control.

## EPISCOPAL INNOVATION

Both the established practice of the church and the discipline of the New Prophecy recognized that the church had no authority to readmit to communion those guilty of certain sins committed against God or in violation of the temple of God.[94] The continuing practice, however, was to urge all guilty of such sin to undertake penance in the hope of receiving forgiveness directly from God at the Judgment. Early in the third century, the Bishop of Carthage judged that sinners guilty of certain types of sexual offenses might be allowed to return to communion, though he continued to refuse reconciliation after idolatry and murder.[95] These sinners, however, might have benefited from the intercession of the confessors suffering for Christ in their attempt to regain the communion of the church.[96] In his objection to the granting of reconciliation, Tertullian indicated the reason for the bishop's decision to readmit adulterers

90. Tert. *Pud.* 19.24.
91. Tert. *Ieiun.* 3.3-4.
92. Tert. *Pud.* 7.15.
93. It may have found regular use in the gatherings of adherents of the New Prophecy.
94. Tert. *Pud.* 21.2. This formula links the transgression of a moral code to the violation of a purity rule.
95. Tert. *Pud.* 22.11-15.
96. Tert. *Pud.* 22.1-10.

to communion after public penance. He recounted his opponents' argument for the innovation:

> If some form of penance does not receive forgiveness, you will not perform it at all. Nothing is done in vain. Penance, however, would be performed in vain if it did not attain forgiveness. All forms of penance ought to be performed. Therefore, every penance should lead to forgiveness, so that it is not performed in vain — since it ought not actually be performed if it is in vain. It will be performed in vain, however, unless it receives forgiveness.[97]

This argument extended beyond the sin of adultery to which the laxists were applying it, as Tertullian would retort. The point at issue, moreover, was not God's forgiving the sin but the bishop's allowing the sinner to return to the communion of the church after publicly repenting it. Tertullian responded that by giving up the solace and security of the church's peace, the penitent focused directly on satisfying God, thereby making the penitential acts and prayers more effective.[98] The sympathy and prayers of the faithful interceding with Christ for the sinner could be more helpful than their communion.[99] Thus, Tertullian argued not that these sinners must be sent away — as those guilty of monstrosities and unnatural acts were — but that the church should retain them in its care, exhort them to repentance, and intercede for their forgiveness and salvation. They were, apparently, to be granted the same status and perhaps allowed to follow the same regimen of penitential activities as those who could regain the church's peace and communion, which would not be available to them.

As will be discussed below, Cyprian later reported that the innovation in granting peace after repentance for adultery had been adopted by most bishops in Africa. He would himself use the argument Tertullian rejected in support of the bishops' decision to extend reconciliation to repentant idolaters.[100]

## The Power to Forgive Sins

Even in his earlier treatise *On Repentance,* Tertullian was concerned that forgiving sin might encourage its repetition. He urged that baptism be preceded by a sustained penance and a full turning away from sin. If baptism was delayed

---

97. Tert. *Pud.* 3.1-2. Si enim, inquiunt, aliqua paenitentia caret uenia, iam nec in totum agenda tibi est. Nihil enim agendum est frustra. Porro frustra agetur paenitentia, si caret uenia. Omnis autem paenitentia agenda est. Ergo omnis ueniam consequatur, ne frustra agatur, quia non erit agenda, si frustra agatur. Porro frustra agitur, si venia carebit. CCSL 2:1286.3-8.

98. Augustine would later use a similar argument to explain the church's practice of removing from office the clergy guilty of serious sin: it promoted their repentance. Aug. *Ep.* 185.10.44.

99. Tert. *Pud.* 3.4-5.

100. Cypr. *Ep.* 55.20.2, 28.1–29.1.

---

in order to create the opportunity for continued sinning even after the truth of God's commands and authority was recognized, he argued, then the eventual baptism itself would not prove an end but only a temporary interruption of sinning.[101] God's granting a second opportunity for repentance after baptism must not be treated as a license for deliberate sinning but must be recognized as a concession to human frailty.[102] Thus one reconciliation after penance was to be allowed for Christians.

When Tertullian later wrote the treatise *On Modesty,* he defended the New Prophecy's objective of preventing further sinning by requiring permanent exclusion of some sinners from the church's communion. He attacked the bishop's claim that the church had the power to forgive sins by appealing to a contemporary prophecy: the Spirit refused to exercise that power lest further sinning ensue.[103]

To rationalize this restrictive program, Tertullian argued not simply that granting reconciliation was an imprudent pastoral practice but that the church lacked the necessary power to forgive or that its exercise had been recently forbidden by God. The arguments presented by the defenders of traditional church practice are evident in Tertullian's responses to them. The defenders claimed that when Christ conferred on Peter the power of the keys, of binding and loosening on earth and in heaven, he had thereby authorized every bishop to forgive sins. Tertullian responded that this divine power had been granted to Peter personally rather than being attached to his episcopal office. This was demonstrated by his later receiving similar powers to raise the dead and heal the sick (Acts 9:36-43; 3:1-10) — deeds subsequent bishops had not been able to perform. Peter himself, moreover, had exercised that power of binding and loosening with a considerable degree of severity, at least in the case of Ananias and Sapphira (Acts 5:1-11). Similarly, Paul struck Elymas blind (Acts 13:8-12). Tertullian conceded that the Old Testament prophets had forgiven even the major sins of adultery and murder. He responded that they had practiced a restraint in exercising this power of which the bishops were now proving incapable.[104]

Tertullian readily agreed that the church had been given the power to for-

---

101. In *Paen.* 5.2, Tertullian explained that ignorance might mitigate the evil of pre-baptismal sin. That would not apply to catechumens who delayed baptism. Similarly, in *Pud.* 1.20 and 9.9-11, he argued that the church could not warn Christians to avoid major sins as great evils and then forgive those sins once committed.

102. Tert. *Paen.* 7.2.

103. Tert. *Pud.* 21.7: "The church can forgive offenses, but I will not do it, lest others then sin." Potest ecclesia donare delictum, sed non faciam, ne et alia delinquant (CCSL 2:1326.30-31). For a discussion of such oracles, see William Tabbernee, "To Pardon or Not to Pardon? North African Montanism and the Forgiveness of Sins," in *Studia Patristica,* ed. Maurice Frank Wiles, Edward Yarnold, and Paul M. Parvis (Leuven: Peeters, 2001), 36:375-86.

104. Tert. *Pud.* 21.1-5.

give, but he denied that this authority was attached to the office of bishop. Unlike the Prophets and the Apostles, the bishops were not authorized to act on their own authority, but could only carry out God's directives. They were ministers rather than rulers, endowed not with *uirtus* or *imperium* but entrusted with *ministerium*.[105] In contrast, Tertullian identified the truly spiritual persons who followed the severe discipline advocated by the New Prophecy as those who held the power of forgiveness given to the church. The authority to forgive sins was actually granted only to those who would follow the directives of the Paraclete and thus refuse to exercise it.[106] This rigorist program did not restrict the practice of mutual forgiveness among Christians for the offenses they committed against one another, as long as these remained minor and did not injure the other as a temple of God. Similarly, the daily failures continued to be forgiven through prayer, fasting, and almsgiving.

Tertullian's approval of the message of the New Prophecy may have been facilitated by his prior concern to prevent the moral decline of the Christian movement through its allowing repeated forgiveness for those sins that undermined the commitment made in baptism. The particular oracle to which Tertullian appealed may have arisen within the Carthaginian church itself. It could indicate a significant conflict within the membership of the church over the bishop's decision and a broad concern over moral decline within the community.[107] The attempt to prevent sin by restricting access to the ritual of reconciliation would recur in the North African church.[108] The conflict over the holding and exercising of the church's authority to forgive sins would also continue, though it would be transformed by Cyprian.

## Conclusion

Tertullian's writings clearly indicate a period of turmoil and conflict in the practice of penance for sins committed after baptism and the granting of readmission to the communion of the church. The received distinction between sins committed against God and sins against a fellow human was proving difficult to apply and enforce. The three sins against God — adultery, idolatry, and murder — had to be elaborated into various forms and types, not all of them equally serious. The Bishop of Carthage proposed that reconciliation should be allowed in some instances; the New Prophets responded by extending the prohibition to cover all serious sin. This conflict would continue in various forms.

105. Tert. *Pud.* 21.6.
106. Tert. *Pud.* 21.17. In context, these spiritual persons would seem to be identified as those following the discipline of the New Prophecy.
107. William Tabbernee developed this interpretation in "To Pardon or Not to Pardon?"
108. The Novatianist movement began in Rome and attempted to spread to Africa in the aftermath of the Decian persecution.

Another question focused on the nature of the power to forgive sins. In some discussions, the church's power was considered intercessory. The sinners made a private or public renunciation of sin and a plea for God's forgiveness; they strengthened their repentance and appeal by fasting, almsgiving, and other good works. Their prayers were joined by the congregation, the martyrs and confessors, and by Christ himself, all of whose intercessory power was based on their own rejection of sin and their fidelity to God. In some instances, this penitential pleading might continue until the time of death without ever gaining the peace of the church. In most cases, however, it seems to have reached its fulfillment in the penitent's being readmitted to eucharistic communion, which implied that God had forgiven the sin. The bishop's role would have been to declare that forgiveness, or at least to make the prudential judgment that the penitent had been forgiven by God and no longer constituted a danger to the holiness of the communion.

The Bishop of Carthage against whom Tertullian argued seems to have claimed not an intercessory role but a divinely delegated authority to declare forgiveness and admit to communion, even when this involved going beyond the traditional limits regarding adultery. Tertullian challenged that assertion by denying that such power was attached to the episcopal office. He conceded that it had been given to the Prophets, the Apostles, and even the church. Nor did he assign it to all (male) Christians, as he had the power to baptize and celebrate eucharist. Instead, he claimed it for the devotees of the New Prophecy on the grounds that they followed the disciplinary directives of the Spirit and would obey the injunction against abusing that power to allow serious sinners back into communion. Thus, the conflict over the source and holders of the power to forgive was driven by the question of its nature and proper exercise.

Finally, Tertullian's writings show two different contexts of the church's dealing with post-baptismal sin. He noted a great variety of sins — mostly related to human weakness and the difficulties of Christian life in a culture firmly committed to demonic idolatry — that were not subject to the formal ritual of excommunication, public satisfaction, and reconciliation. Although he did not specify the means through which these lesser sins might be forgiven, he did indicate that these could be repented (and, by implication, committed) over and over. In general, they were classified as lesser sins against human beings. In some cases, they would have been forgiven through direct interaction with the fellow Christians who had been harmed. In other cases, such as negligence in repudiating idolatry, one's ordinary congregation might have been engaged. This type of penance could have been practiced in daily household gatherings for prayer and celebration of the love feast, because it did not require the approval of the whole community and intervention of the clergy. In contrast, the more serious sins committed against humans, and all those directly against God or against human temples of God, required exclusion from the communion of the church; they engaged the full assembly under the direction of its officers.

Some could be addressed through the formal ritual of excommunication and reconciliation, under the supervision of its clerical leadership. Others engaged the intercessory prayer of the church but were beyond its authority to pardon. Under the influence of the New Prophecy, Tertullian preferred the kind of penitential practice conducted between offender and offended, in the context of household prayer or a love feast. Citing the Gospel of Matthew (18:20), Tertullian specifically privileged the gathering of two or three spiritual persons — those following the discipline of the New Prophecy — as constituting the forgiving church.[109] He insisted that the clergy must excommunicate those who sinned against God but could not reconcile and readmit them to communion.[110] Even as the New Prophecy was limiting the use of the ritual of public penance practiced in the full assembly, it seems to have encouraged the repeated use of a less formal confession and forgiveness within the smaller gatherings by calling attention to the numerous sins for which some communal action was appropriate. In this sense, it celebrated the power to forgive that all Christians shared and were commanded to exercise.

## THE PRACTICE OF PENANCE IN CYPRIAN'S TIME

During the period separating the end of Tertullian's writing career from the election of Cyprian as bishop, penitential practice in North Africa continued to evolve. The New Prophecy's rigorist program did not prevail. A council of African bishops formally adopted the policy of reconciling Christians who had confessed and repented of the forms of sexual irregularity classified under the general title of adultery. Individual bishops were allowed to implement the new policy or retain the prior restrictions at their own discretion. The change won wide acceptance, and Cyprian subsequently claimed that it had no negative impact on the practice of sexual morality, continence, and virginity among Christians.[111] Under the impact of the Decian persecution, the bishops had to reassess their permanent exclusion of Christians who were guilty of public sins of idolatry: penitents who persevered in submission to the authority of the bishop and the discipline of the penitential ritual were reconciled and granted the church's peace as their lives ended. Threatened with a renewal of systematic persecution, the bishops decided to admit all the penitent lapsed to communion.

Cyprian, however, clarified the distinction between the reconciliation offered by the church under the judicial authority of its bishop and the actual forgiveness of the sin, which was the divine prerogative. The bishop could readmit

---

109. Tert. *Pud.* 21.16-17.

110. For a fuller discussion of this contextual issue, see Allan D. Fitzgerald, "Innocent I: Insight into the History of Penance," *Revue des études augustiniennes* 54 (2008): 95-110.

111. Cypr. *Ep.* 55.20.2, 21.1.

a penitent to communion on the basis of a public demonstration of repentance; only God, however, could read the dispositions of the heart, judge its sincerity, and forgive the sin. Thus the bishop could grant the peace of the church; God would forgive or punish the sin.[112]

Because of the conflict over the necessity and efficacy of the ritual of reconciliation for the cleansing of the apostates who had failed during the Decian persecution, Cyprian's correspondence and treatises provide extensive information about the penitential procedures that were used to deal with the major sin of idolatry. Fewer details are provided about the full range of penitential practices.

## The Ritual of Penance

The process to which Cyprian referred as "full penance"[113] would restore to the fellowship of the congregation, and perhaps the favor of God, those Christians who had violated their baptismal commitment and thereby lost the sanctification it had conferred. This procedure began with the acknowledgment (or accusation) of a violation of the Christian law, formal suspension from participation in the eucharist, and admission to the status of penitent. The sinner then engaged in public acts of repentance, through which the sin was rejected and commitment to Christ renewed. These exercises culminated in a confession of sin before the community as a whole and the judgment of the adequacy of the satisfaction that had been performed. The bishop and clergy then imposed hands to restore the penitent to membership in the communion. Finally, the reconciled sinner made an offering and shared the eucharist.[114]

Cyprian did not specify a ritual through which a baptized Christian was suspended from communion,[115] though this exclusion was clearly a formal status recognized by the church rather than one undertaken by the individual's decision alone.[116] The sinner had then to petition and be accepted as a penitent. In dealing with the sinners who sought to return after abandoning his communion for a rival one, Cyprian noted the presence of the entire community at the hearing and a full debate over these petitioners prior to their being granted the status of penitents. Cyprian had to work to convince his congregation that certain of these rebels — who had earlier rejected the bishop's demand for public penance — should even be given the opportunity to prove their repentance and

---

112. Cypr. *Ep.* 55.20.3.

113. Cypr. *Laps.* 16, 32; *Ep.* 4.4.1; 19.2.1; 55.18.1; 57.1.1; 64.1.1.

114. Cypr. *Ep.* 15.1.2; 16.2.3; 17.2.1; *Laps.* 16.

115. Cypr. *Dom. orat.* 18. In *Ep.* 34.1, 3.2; 41.2.2; 42. Cyprian orders excommunications and praises his clergy and other delegates for executing them.

116. Cypr. *Ep.* 55.6.1. Good standing was also recognized (*Ep.* 12.2.2; 41.1.2).

commitment.[117] If accepted, the penitents were then supervised by the bishop and supported by the prayer and encouragement of the congregation.

Under the influence of the Roman bishop and under pressure from the penitents and their supporters, Cyprian and his episcopal colleagues also agreed that any penitent who was in danger of immediate death would be granted peace, admitted to communion, and assured the intercession of the church for a favorable judgment by Christ.[118] He later judged that any bishop who refused reconciliation to a dying penitent should be removed from office.[119]

As a penitent, the sinner was allowed to advance, both literally and symbolically, to the threshold of the church[120] to engage in satisfactory prayer and works.[121] The prayer was directed to winning the forgiveness of God for the sin that had been committed, and it was characterized by Cyprian most often as *deprecatio,* a begging for mercy.[122] This begging included weeping,[123] lamentation,[124] sorrow,[125] fasting,[126] and other manifestations of loss and grief,[127] which fell under the scripturally derived heading of sackcloth and ashes.[128] Friends and relatives, the bishop, and the whole congregation joined in these prayers and in fasting to support the penitent's petition to God for forgiveness.[129] The bodily wounds or scars resulting from an unsuccessful attempt to defend the faith under torture, Cyprian observed, served as a particularly effective plea to God.[130] The satisfactory works of repentance were, like the prayers and fasting, intended to manifest the changed disposition of the penitent to the congregation and to win the favor of God.[131] Principal among these were almsgiving,[132] care for exiles and refugees from the persecution,[133] and

---

117. Cypr. *Ep.* 59.15.1-4, 16.3.

118. Cypr. *Ep.* 55.13.1. In *Ep.* 18.1.2, Cyprian allowed this reconciliation for only those penitents who had letters of peace from the martyrs. The Roman clergy asserted that the proper practice was to reconcile all dying penitents (*Ep.* 8.3.1), to which Cyprian then agreed (*Ep.* 20.3.2). After the persecution, all the bishops ratified this judgment (*Ep.* 55.13.1).

119. Cypr. *Ep.* 68.1.1–2.2.

120. Cypr. *Ep.* 55.6.1; 57.3.1.

121. Cypr. *Unit. eccl.* 19; *Laps.* 14, 17; *Ep.* 17.2.2; 43.2.2, 5.3; 59.13.2-4, 17.1, 20.2.

122. Cypr. *Ep.* 17.2.2; 56.2.1; 57.1.1-2; 59.13.4; *Laps.* 16. Other terms used were *preces* in *Ep.* 16.2.3; 59.17.1, and *obsequium* in *Ep.* 19.1.

123. Cypr. *Ep.* 34.2.1; *Laps.* 29, 32, 35; *Ep.* 55.28.1; 57.2.1.

124. Cypr. *Laps.* 16, 35; *Ep.* 57.1.2; 59.17.1.

125. Cypr. *Ep.* 57.1.1.

126. Cypr. *Laps.* 29, 35; *Dom. orat.* 32-33.

127. Cypr. *Laps.* 30.

128. Cypr. *Laps.* 35.

129. Cypr. *Ep.* 21.2.1, 3.2; 59.18.3; *Laps.* 22, 32.

130. Cypr. *Laps.* 13.

131. Cypr. *Ep.* 16.2.3; 18.2.1; 19.1; 55.22.1, 28.1; *Laps.* 35, 36.

132. Cypr. *Ep.* 55.22.1.

133. Cypr. *Ep.* 21.2.2, 4.1; 55.13.2.

other assistance offered to the poor.[134] Christians who had complied with the emperor's decree in order to protect their property from confiscation by the imperial treasury, for example, were advised that giving away a portion of that treasure would be a particularly effective form of repentance.[135] Like weeping and prayer, these charitable works were regarded as an acknowledgment and a repudiation of sin.[136] The entire process of prayer and works was described as both a cleansing from sin and a satisfaction of God.[137] It also demonstrated to the congregation the intensity of the penitent's regret and intention to remain loyal in the future. Thus, the penitential acts served as the basis for the people's advice and the bishop's decision to allow the penitent to return to their communion.

During this period of public repentance, the sinners seem to have been excluded from the eucharistic assembly itself. They stood or prostrated themselves at the doorway, pleading to be admitted.[138] Although they were not allowed to join the congregation, they had not been abandoned. Because they were recognized as penitents, the community encouraged their confession and joined their prayer for forgiveness; and the bishop promised immediate reconciliation in the face of death.[139]

In the middle of the third century, a standard length of time for repentance for particular sins does not seem to have been specified. Usually, Cyprian referred to the length of penance in general terms, as fitting or appropriate.[140] About six months after the onset of the Decian persecution, for example, he directed that the confessors in prison should recommend for reconciliation only those penitents whose satisfaction they judged to be nearly complete.[141] Later he judged that two years' penance was quite adequate for apostates who had fallen under torture inflicted in a second process under the proconsul, after first standing firm in a hearing before local magistrates.[142] In anticipation of a renewal of persecution, the African bishops decided to reconcile all those who had been doing penance for the sin of idolatrous sacrifice, although the crime

134. Cypr. *Laps.* 30.

135. Cypr. *Laps.* 35.

136. Cypr. *Ep.* 59.16.3.

137. Cypr. *Laps.* 35; *Ep.* 55.20.3, 28.1; 66.9.1.

138. Cypr. *Ep.* 57.3.1. Similar information about the place occupied by the penitents in Rome is given in *Ep.* 30.6.3, where they are described as knocking at the door but not entering. The term *lapsi* (*Laps.* 33), by which the sinners were contrasted with the faithful or *stantes,* may have indicated their prone posture at prayer.

139. Cypr. *Ep.* 16.3.2; 55.6.1; 57.1.1; 59.13.6. Abandonment of those who had engaged in outrages against nature, which Tertullian reported or recommended (*Pud.* 4.5; 13.12, 19), was apparently not practiced.

140. Cypr. *Ep.* 4.1; 16.2.3.

141. Cypr. *Ep.* 15.3.1-4.

142. Cypr. *Ep.* 56.2.1. The first would have been before a local commission and the second before the proconsul or provincial governor.

had taken place less than three years earlier.[143] In practice, then, the duration of the period of repentance seems to have been at the discretion of the bishop, who would have considered the sin and its circumstances, the situation of the community, and perhaps the persistence of individual penitents in their satisfactory works.

This process of repentance culminated in a ritual of public confession — for which the Greek term *exomologesis* continued to be used — before the bishop, the clergy, and the entire community.[144] The sinner completed the cleansing of body and spirit by this public display of humility and repentance.[145] The bishop then reviewed the individual cases, the sin and the subsequent conduct of the penitent. The community offered advice to the bishop in a process that might have brought forward differing judgments. This would have been the point at which a letter of peace given by a martyr before death or the intercession of a surviving confessor might have been appropriately taken into consideration.[146] This general consultation was an essential part of the ritual, since the sinner was being welcomed back into the community, rather than foisted upon it by the bishop. During the persecution, Cyprian insisted that a policy for reconciling apostates required the advice of the community as well as the deliberation of his episcopal colleagues, and thus had to await the restoration of peace.[147] Later, he and his colleagues reprimanded a bishop who had admitted a penitent without this consultation of the faithful.[148]

Many different considerations were relevant to the judgment that the satisfaction had been adequate and the penitent should be readmitted to communion. The nature of the sin was most important: the person may have failed during the persecution by actually sacrificing to idols or only by claiming to have done so in order to escape torture or punishment.[149] The nature of the intent was considered: Had the person acted voluntarily or under coercion,[150] at the first threat or after active resistance and suffering,[151] by deceit or in ignorance that a particular legal subterfuge was forbidden?[152] Circumstances were also relevant: Had a head of household forced his clients and dependents to join in the sin, or had he shielded them through his own compliance?[153] The satisfactory actions were also judged. The penitent should have manifested disposi-

---

143. Cypr. *Ep.* 57.1.2.
144. Cypr. *Ep.* 15.1.2; 16.2.3; 17.2.1; 18.1.2; 19.2.1; 20.3.1; 55.17.1, 29.2; 59.13.6, 14.1; *Laps.* 16, 28.
145. Cypr. *Laps.* 16.
146. On the status of the martyrs and confessors, see Graeme W. Clarke, *The Letters of St. Cyprian of Carthage* (New York: Newman Press, 1984), 1: 272, n. 1; 274, n. 8; 298, n. 5.
147. Cypr. *Ep.* 19.2.2.
148. Cypr. *Ep.* 64.1.1.
149. Cypr. *Ep.* 55.13.2; *Laps.* 28.
150. Cypr. *Laps.* 13, 14; *Ep.* 55.13.2; 56.1–2.1.
151. Cypr. *Ep.* 56.1–2.1; *Laps.* 13.
152. Cypr. *Ep.* 55.14.1.
153. Cypr. *Ep.* 55.13.2.

tions of meekness, humility, patience, and obedience before the congregation and the bishop appointed by God.[154] The current situation of the local church and the individual might also be considered. Withholding reconciliation might have led the penitents to despair and revert to the imperial cults, or to seek admission to the eucharist in a schismatic Christian community and take their dependents along with them.[155] Yet, admitting one sinner during persecution could undermine the perseverance of others and thus infect the whole flock.[156] A new persecution might be threatening, so that the penitents required the encouragement afforded by the solidarity of the community and sharing in the eucharistic ritual.[157] The objective was to judge whether the penitent had indeed rejected the sinful action, had satisfied both the justice and the corrective purpose of God, and had demonstrated a renewed commitment to the standards of the church.[158] Yet, all recognized that humans could discern interior dispositions only on the basis of external behavior and that God alone could read the heart itself and forgive the sin. The judgment of the congregation and its bishop was necessarily provisional; it would be affirmed or reversed by Christ at the time of the Judgment.[159]

The ritual culminated in the imposition of hands by the bishop and clergy, conferring the right to communion and thus restoring the individual to participation in the prayer and eucharist of the assembly.[160] The penitent then presented gifts, apparently of bread and wine, which were offered by the bishop and shared by the community in the eucharistic celebration welcoming the sinner back into communion.[161]

## Using the Ritual of Penance

This ritual of penance and reconciliation was used for crimes the church considered so grave that the sinner had to be formally purified before being allowed to participate in the common prayer and eucharistic celebration. Among the sins Cyprian specified in various contexts were apostasy and idolatry, schism, adultery, fraud through violation of a trust, breaking a vow of consecrated virginity,

---

154. Cypr. *Ep.* 15.3.1; 18.2.1.

155. Cypr. *Ep.* 55.6.1, 7.2, 15.1.

156. Cypr. *Ep.* 19.2.3; 59.15.2. Cyprian pointed out that admitting adulterers in the past had not had a deleterious effect on the Christian practice of chastity (*Ep.* 55.20.2).

157. Cypr. *Ep.* 57.1.2, 2.1.

158. Cyprian interpreted the persecution as a divine correction and call to repentance; the danger in admitting sinners to communion without adequate repentance was flouting that divine intention and incurring God's wrath. *Ep.* 11.5.3–6.1; *Laps.* 5-7.

159. Cypr. *Ep.* 57.1.1, 3.3.

160. Cypr. *Ep.* 16.2.3.

161. Cypr. *Ep.* 16.2.3–3.2; 34.1.

---

and persistent disobedience of the bishop.[162] These sins were all of action or performance, rather than of intention alone. Although sins of intention that had not issued in action required repentance, Cyprian and his colleagues did not employ the public ritual of penance for these.[163]

As has been seen, the appropriateness of reconciling certain types of sinners had been disputed in Tertullian's time; that debate continued during Cyprian's episcopate. Earlier North African practice had judged that sins committed against God (or a human being as a temple of God) were beyond the capacity of the church to forgive. Cyprian reported that a council of bishops under one of his predecessors had agreed to admit repentant adulterers but that some bishops had subsequently refused to do so.[164] Initially, Cyprian himself argued that the sin of denying Christ could not be forgiven by the church because Christ himself had threatened to deny those who denied him (Matt. 10:32-33).[165] Further consultation with his fellow bishops — and pressure from his congregation — moved him to change that judgment. Among the most important considerations was the widespread belief of Christians at this time that only those who died as participants in the communion of the church would have the opportunity to be saved by Christ. One's status was determined at the end of earthly life: the rituals of *exomologesis* and reconciliation could not be performed in the afterlife between death and resurrection.[166] Cyprian himself came to share the belief that sinners who had remained bound on earth would be bound before Christ; sins had first to be loosened by the church on earth so that they might then be loosened by Christ in heaven.[167] In a development of the argument advanced by Tertullian's episcopal opponent, he also observed that a sinner could be convinced to undertake penance only if the church promised to grant reconciliation before the time of death. If the church refused to promise its peace, the sinner would either seek the help of the martyrs by joining the communion of the laxist schism or give up all hope of salvation by abandoning the Christian life.[168]

Thus, Cyprian, his colleagues, and their congregations recognized an essential but limited role for the church's rituals of penance and reconciliation. The bishop and the church could not effectively declare the sin forgiven because they could not judge unerringly the interior dispositions of repentance. They could, however, readmit to communion those who gave appropriate signs of repentance, and, in so doing, they would grant access to the forgiveness that Christ could bestow.

---

162. Cypr. *Ep.* 3.4; 43.1.2; 41.2.1; 50.1.2; 55.21.2, 26.1–27.2; 67.5.3; 69.7.1.

163. Cypr. *Laps.* 28-29; *Ep.* 55.13.2–15.1.

164. Cypr. *Ep.* 55.20.2, 21.1.

165. Cypr. *Laps.* 17.

166. Cypr. *Ep.* 55.17.3, 29.2: apud inferos, CCSL 3B:276.287, 294.539.

167. Cypr. *Ep.* 57.1.1, 3.3, 4.3-5.2. For a fuller discussion of this disputed point, see J. Patout Burns, *Cyprian the Bishop* (London: Routledge, 2002), 40, 70-71.

168. Cypr. *Ep.* 55.28.1–29.3.

On the basis of this belief in the necessity of sharing the communion of the church as a condition for winning the forgiveness of Christ, the practice of a private reconciliation of dying penitents developed, serving a function similar to the emergency baptism of catechumens. During the persecution, Cyprian extended this privilege first to those who had letters of recommendation from the martyrs and then — under pressure from the Roman clergy — to all the penitents.[169] After the persecution, he adopted a general policy of reconciling dying penitents.[170] A presbyter, or even a deacon, would be called to the dying person to receive the final confession of sinfulness, presumably before such witnesses as may have been present. Reconciliation and readmission to communion would then be conferred upon the dying penitent through the imposition of the cleric's hands.[171] The surviving evidence does not clearly indicate that the dying person received the eucharist, though the bread could have been provided from a domestic or church reservation.[172] If the reconciled sinner recovered from the illness, as apparently many did, no further penance was required, and apparently no public rituals of *exomologesis* and imposition of hands were performed.[173] The person enjoyed full communion and could attribute to the mercy of God both the forgiveness of sins and the healing from illness.

This privilege of repentance upon one's deathbed was extended only to those sinners who already had made confession of sin before the community and were following the process of repentance under the supervision of the clergy. A sinner who had given no forethought to death and had not been enrolled as a penitent prior to the illness was to be refused the peace of the church on the grounds that the plea for reconciliation was motivated by fear of judgment rather than repentance.[174]

This change in penitential practice was made for penitents who had already confessed the sin of idolatry and undertaken satisfactory works. No evidence has survived that a death-bed reconciliation was offered to those who had been reconciled once and subsequently were excluded for sinning a second time. The difficulty that Cyprian experienced in effecting this concession for first-time idolaters, moreover, suggests that a second reconciliation would not have been offered to those who fell again.[175]

---

169. Cypr. *Ep.* 18.2.1; 8.3.1; 20.3.2.

170. Cypr. *Ep.* 55.13.1.

171. Cypr. *Ep.* 18.2.1; 19.2.1; 20.3.1.

172. The continued use of a domestic *arca* is witnessed in Cypr. *Laps.* 26.

173. Cypr. *Ep.* 55.13.1.

174. Cypr. *Ep.* 55.23.4. In later centuries, the sinner might enroll as a penitent by confessing the sin, neglect the satisfactory works, and then appeal for deathbed reconciliation (Aug. *Serm.* 232.8; 392.6; 393.1).

175. As has been previously noted, the evidence for the limitation of public penance to a

In some instances, Cyprian seems to have recommended a procedure that involved a voluntary suspension from communion and performance of satisfaction but was less elaborate than the process of full penance.

After the Decian persecution, some of the faithful admitted to the bishop that they had intended to perform the sacrifice should imperial commissioners actually have required it of them. Fortunately, they had escaped attention; thereby they avoided an act of apostasy and remained in good standing in the church. Cyprian commended those who had admitted their secret sin and warned them that Christ would certainly judge them according to their intention rather than only on their having escaped its performance.[176] He then urged everyone guilty of such an intentional failure to confess the sin to the bishop and undertake penance. In the meeting of the bishops of Africa about a month later, however, apparently no provision was made for the disposition of such cases. Moreover, the bishops ruled that even those who had avoided the sacrifice by seeking or accepting a false certificate of compliance should be readmitted to communion after only a brief period of public penance.[177] Thus the African bishops may have corrected Cyprian's judgment and ruled that public repentance was to be used only for sins of actual performance of a clearly forbidden action. They may have judged that they could not require such public penance of those who had failed only in the steadfastness of their intention.

A second instance involved consecrated virgins sharing sleeping quarters with men, one of whom was a deacon. The judgment of Cyprian and the colleagues whom he consulted was that all involved were to be suspended from communion for an action that was clearly improper and offensive to Christ. If the virgins were willing to submit to penance for the unlawful contact, they were then to undergo physical examinations to verify their assertions that they had preserved their bodily integrity. If their claims were established, they were to be readmitted to communion with the understanding that they would avoid such conduct in the future. If the examination showed that they had been corrupted, they and their accomplices were to undergo *exomologesis* and full pen-

---

single use is quite limited in the second through the fourth centuries. See above, p. 300, n. 34; p. 307, n. 86.

176. Cypr. *Laps.* 28. The motivation of this confession cannot be easily discerned. These people may have been interceding for the fallen, pointing out the unfairness of the sharp difference between their own standing in the church's communion and the exclusion of the fallen, particularly of those who had received certificates. In response, Cyprian warned them that their status in the church should not lead them to presume the approval by Christ.

177. Cypr. *Ep.* 55.14.2. In seeking such a certificate, they had at least indirectly confessed to the commissioners their status as Christians who were forbidden to perform the sacrifice itself. Tertullian had distinguished the great guilt of apostasy from the lesser sin of using an equivocation to escape a clear confession of Christ (*Pud.* 7.15); the latter, he allowed, could be forgiven by the church's penitential process. See above, p. 307.

ance before being readmitted to communion. The bishops observed that the men and the virgins had sinned by the very fact of bodily contact; moreover, they might have polluted themselves in a way that could not be detected by a midwife's examination. Yet the bishops declined to require full public penance when the accused denied the major sin and no evidence suggested otherwise.[178]

In these cases, the admitted offenses fell short of the standard set for excommunication and full penance but went beyond the sins to which a committed Christian might fall victim daily or by inadvertence. Both the intention to sacrifice and the violation of consecrated bodies were serious sins that might be expected to outrage Christ and incur his condemnation. Some sort of penance under episcopal supervision was judged necessary, but a full process of public repentance was inappropriate. A precedent for this penance might have been that used for the third category of sins specified by Tertullian under the influence of the New Prophecy.[179] This type of acknowledgment of sin, temporary abstinence from the eucharist, and repentance under the supervision of the bishop or some group within the congregation may have been widely used in the second and third century. It would be well attested later, even for serious sins, in the period after the imperial establishment of the church.

### Repentance by the Clergy

Cyprian's correspondence evinces several instances of the application of penitential discipline to the clergy. He insisted that any bishop who had failed must be permanently removed from office. The Italian bishop, Trofimus, was allowed by Cornelius, the Bishop of Rome, to return to communion as a layman when he brought back the congregation he had led into apostasy.[180] Bishops who sacrificed were excluded from communion.[181] Two bishops in Spain had been allowed by their colleagues to undertake penance, but they were removed from office.[182]

The African bishops showed greater flexibility in dealing with presbyters and deacons. Cyprian advised a colleague who had a rebellious deacon that he might either remove him from office or excommunicate him.[183] Another deacon, who had been sharing the bed of a consecrated virgin, was suspended but apparently allowed to return to office after undergoing a penitential process.[184] Two subdeacons and an acolyte who abandoned their positions during

178. Cypr. *Ep.* 4.1.
179. See above, p. 307.
180. Cypr. *Ep.* 55.11.1-3.
181. Cypr. *Ep.* 59.10.2-3; 65.2.1-2.
182. Cypr. *Ep.* 67.1.1-2, 6.1-3.
183. Cypr. *Ep.* 3.3.3-4.
184. Cypr. *Ep.* 4.4.1.

the persecution were suspended from office and salaries until their cases could be judged by the whole congregation.[185] Any presbyter or deacon who refused to follow the bishop's directive to withhold communion from those who lapsed during the persecution was to be excommunicated and allowed to return only with the approval of the entire congregation.[186] A presbyter who sacrificed was subject to the same discipline as the laity.[187] Schismatic presbyters and deacons were allowed to return to the church but only among the laity.[188]

The clergy, then, were subject to the same penitential discipline as the laity. When they were reconciled, however, the bishops were excluded from their leadership positions, but presbyters and deacons may have been allowed to return to their offices, depending on the nature of their offenses.[189]

## Forgiveness through Martyrdom

The fullest and most complete form of repentance for sin committed after baptism was martyrdom, which entailed a complete forgiveness of all sin and immediate reward of glory.[190] Public confession of Christ under imperial interrogation, even without torture or death, would also reverse and win forgiveness for the sin of a prior denial. Thus, during the persecution, Cyprian urged the fallen who were impatient with the penitential process to make a public confession of Christ and thereby regain the right to communion.[191] Immediately afterward, he judged that such a confession and the ensuing punishment of exile should be the basis for readmission.[192] Confession of the name of Christ, even if it resulted in execution, would be ineffective, however, for schismatics opposing the unity and love of the church.[193]

In urging the fallen to undertake the process of repentance, Cyprian asserted that the clear sign of an effective penance, one which had won divine forgiveness, was the granting of the opportunity and strength to win the crown of martyrdom.[194] Such a penitent would approach the judgment seat of Christ in full confidence of being rewarded. Those who had received reconciliation by

185. Cypr. *Ep.* 34.4.1-2.

186. Cypr. *Ep.* 34.3.2; 31.6.1-3; 42. In Rome, Cornelius accepted schismatic clergy back into office because they had the full support of the people.

187. Cypr. *Ep.* 64.1.1.

188. Cypr. *Ep.* 72.2.1-3.

189. In a celebrated case in Rome, clerical confessors who had supported Novatian's rebellion against Cornelius were allowed to return to their offices; they enjoyed the full support of the community (Cypr. *Ep.* 49.2.1-5).

190. Cypr. *Ep.* 55.20.3.

191. Cypr. *Ep.* 19.2.3; 55.4.2.

192. Cypr. *Ep.* 24.1.1; 25.1.1; *Laps.* 13.

193. Cypr. *Ep.* 60.4; 73.21.1.

194. Cypr. Ep. 24.1.1; 25.1.1; *Laps.* 36.

the bishop and congregation, in contrast, still had to fear Christ's scrutiny of their intentions.[195]

## The Forgiveness of Daily Sins

In his treatise on the Lord's Prayer, Cyprian clearly indicated that Christians asked daily for the forgiveness of their minor failures.[196] They prayed by using the very words that Christ, himself their advocate before the Father, had specified, and they prayed in the confidence inspired by his assurance that forgiveness would be given to those who confessed their sin.[197] Cyprian noted that in praying for the sanctification of God's name in the Lord's Prayer, Christians asked that the holiness God had worked in them by cleansing them from all sin in baptism would be preserved.[198] Thus, minor sins were confessed daily to God in the private or communal recitation of the Lord's Prayer; these were believed to be forgiven without the employment of any formal ritual or the intervention of the clergy.

## The Power of the Church to Forgive Sins

Some Christians who failed during the Decian persecution shared the traditional uncertainty about the power invested in the church to forgive their sin of apostasy or idolatry, since it had been committed directly against God. Others were unwilling to undergo an indefinite period of public repentance in which reconciliation was promised only at the time of death. These followed a traditional but contested alternative: they sought the assistance of martyrs as a way of winning forgiveness directly from Christ and thus gaining admittance to the communion of the church.[199]

According to Christ's promise, the martyrs were to reign, to sit with him at the Judgment, to advise him in much the way the assessors of a Roman official did, and even to enjoy the prerogative of the first, guiding opinion. By inference, they might exercise a similar function on earth by providing letters of peace testifying to the sincerity of certain penitents and urging the bishop to readmit them to communion.[200] Cyprian admonished the confessors still facing trial in Carthage, who might still become martyrs by dying in prison, to follow the standards of judgment proper to Christ's gospel and the precedents

195. Cypr. *Ep.* 55.20.3.
196. Cypr. *Dom. orat.* 12.
197. Cypr. *Dom. orat.* 3, 22.
198. Cypr. *Dom. orat.* 12.
199. Tertullian witnessed this practice and rejected it: *Mart.* 1.6; *Pud.* 22.
200. Cypr. *Ep.* 16.3.2; 18.1.2; 21.3.2; 22.2.1.

established for their role in the penitential process. They should recommend to the bishop only individuals of whose repentance they had personal knowledge and whose satisfaction they judged nearly adequate. Their letters were to specify individuals rather than households or groups.[201] Thus, the confessors and martyrs were to act like other members of the church, as advisers in the process of discerning the repentance that qualified penitents for reconciliation; they were not to set themselves up as agents of divine forgiveness, independent of the bishop and the congregation.

The letters of peace sought by the lapsed were actually written by the confessors still in prison, in anticipation of their deaths under torture. These letters were validated by their dying for Christ.[202] Some confessors abused their privilege by handing out letters wholesale, recommending indefinitely large groups of sinners.[203] One surviving confessor claimed that a martyr, before his death, had authorized the issuing of letters of peace in his name to anyone who asked.[204] On this basis, a group of confessors finally proclaimed a general forgiveness for all the apostates.[205] They explained that they were coming to the rescue of the church, which itself had no power or authority to forgive this sin.[206] Through their witness and suffering, martyrs had been credited with the privilege of interceding for the forgiving of the sins that was otherwise reserved to the discretion of Christ at the final Judgment. Most of the confessors in the Decian persecution did recognize the right and responsibility of the bishop, clergy, and people in the ritual of reconciliation to judge the conduct of the fallen — to inquire into their repentance and their mode of life after the sin. The confessor's own role was to authorize the reconciliation of those apostates who were then found worthy.[207] However, the martyrs and confessors omitted requiring explicitly that the sinners perform the prayers and works of penitence that were otherwise prerequisite for such reconciliation. Many of the fallen who had obtained letters of peace then demanded immediate admission to communion, on the basis of the martyr's privileged access to Christ himself. Some of the clergy gave in to the pressure — even assaults — of these apostates. Others were only too ready to place their trust in the martyrs' power: they refused to enforce the bishops' demand that public repentance be performed for a public repudiation of Christ and the church.[208]

Cyprian responded to the claims being made for the power of the martyrs in two stages. First, he asserted that the martyrs' privilege of intercession was based

201. Cypr. *Ep.* 15.3.1-4.
202. Cypr. *Ep.* 16.3.2; 21.3.2; 22.2.1.
203. Cypr. *Ep.* 15.4.
204. Cypr. *Ep.* 22.2.1.
205. Cypr. *Ep.* 23.
206. Cypr. *Laps.* 20.
207. Cypr. *Ep.* 22.2.2; 23.
208. Cypr. *Ep.* 27.2.2–3.1.

upon Christ's promise to recognize them in heaven for their confession of him on earth. They could not, therefore, simply disregard Christ's parallel threat to disown all who had denied him on earth (Matt. 10:32-33), nor could they trample on the gospel precepts that required sincere repentance for sin. They had to accept the limits imposed by the same gospel texts that were used to establish their authority.[209] Second, the efficacy of the martyrs' intercession could not be presumed. The scripture itself clearly witnessed that other friends of God had not been granted their every petition.[210] In particular, the martyrs were pictured in Revelation calling for immediate vindication upon their enemies but were told to wait patiently (Rev. 6:10-11). How could martyrs be presumed to win a special favor for anyone else when their own plea for vindication clearly had not yet been granted?[211] Thus, Cyprian asserted that the martyrs' privilege of advising could apply only to the final Judgment, once they had themselves been vindicated and Christ was ready to sentence sinners and reward saints. The martyrs, therefore, had no role in the deliberations of the bishop and people on earth, prior to the return of Christ. Cyprian cautioned the sinners to place more trust in what the intercession of the bishops and the just works of the faithful could achieve on their behalf.[212] Though he clearly recognized the limits of the church's authority to forgive sins, Cyprian resolutely insisted on the integrity of the earthly process of repentance as a precondition for the efficacy of the heavenly one.[213]

### The Authority and Power of the Bishop

Like the unnamed bishop whom Tertullian opposed in *On Modesty,* Cyprian insisted that the power of sanctification had been conferred upon Peter in his capacity as bishop and thus belonged to all the bishops in the church. Through his three conflicts — with proponents of the martyrs' power, with schismatic bishops in Africa, and with the Bishop of Rome — Cyprian developed a complex theory of the church's power to forgive sins. During the persecution he insisted that the power of sanctification had been entrusted to the bishops rather than to the martyrs or any other group in the church.[214] In direct contradiction of the claims for the martyrs, he later insisted that their power to confess was itself given by God through the ministry of the church and its bishop.[215] When

209. Cypr. *Ep.* 28.2.3; *Lap.* 20.
210. Cypr. *Laps.* 19. He cited Exodus 32:31-33; 33:11 for Moses; Jeremiah 11:14; 7:16 for Jeremiah; and Ezekiel 14:13-16 for Noah, Daniel, and Job.
211. Cypr. *Laps.* 18.
212. Cypr. *Laps.* 36.
213. See above, p. 319.
214. Cypr. *Ep.* 33.1.1-2. Tertullian had granted this power only to the spiritual persons in the church, denying it to both martyrs and bishops (*Pud.* 21-22).
215. Cypr. *Ep.* 57.4.1-2.

he returned to Carthage from exile to face the schismatics, he asserted that the power to forgive had been given to Peter as representative of each of the local bishops and thus could be held and exercised only by the one church.[216]

In the midst of his later conflict with the Roman bishop over the question of rebaptizing converts originally baptized in schism, Cyprian had to defend the independent authority of the individual bishops against the assertion of supervisory power by the Roman bishop, as the representative of Peter. He then argued that the power to forgive had actually been given twice, first to Peter alone (Matt. 16:19) to show that it was a single power, and then to the assembled disciples after the Resurrection ( John 20:21-23), to demonstrate that it was shared by the whole college of bishops. The second conferral clearly associated the power to forgive sins with the gift of the Holy Spirit.[217] On this basis, Cyprian insisted that only bishops who served within the unity of the church, and not those who rebelled against it by attempting to divide the flock of Christ, could hold and exercise this power to bind and loose. His evidence and argument would also have disqualified and invalidated the ministry of any bishops, even within the unity of the church, who had lost the gift of the Holy Spirit by a sin that made them unworthy of their office. Cyprian himself never drew this conclusion, though he did insist that sinful bishops be removed from office whenever their unworthiness was manifest.[218]

Cyprian remained convinced that the church had an essential but limited role in the forgiveness of sins. He recognized, as has been noted, that the clergy and people, as human judges, could be misled about the sincerity of repentance because they had to rely on the satisfactory works as indicators of the penitent's internal dispositions. Christ would read and judge the intentions themselves and would either ratify or reverse the decision to grant reconciliation that the bishop had made with the advice of his congregation.[219] Secondly, Cyprian was not certain that the church had been given the authority to loosen the sin of the apostates, whom Christ himself threatened with rejection. How, he asked, could the bishop presume to forgive a sinner whom Christ himself had threatened with damnation?[220] In explaining the power of binding and loosening, therefore, he made a distinction. In bestowing the power to forgive on Peter

216. Cypr. *Unit. eccl.* 4 (PT). On the two versions of this text, the Primacy Text and the Received Text, see Maurice Bevenot, *The Tradition of MSS: A Study in the Transmission of St. Cyprian's Treatises* (Oxford: Oxford University Press, 1961), and his introduction to the text in CCSL 3:244-47 and the bibliography provided at pp. xvii-xxi. This was a development of the argument made by his predecessor in Tertullian's day (*Pud.* 21.9).

217. Cypr. *Unit. eccl.* 4-5, *textus receptus.* This idea is developed in texts which may be contemporary to the revision: *Ep.* 69.11.1-2; 73.7.2. On the two versions of this text, see M. Bévenot's introduction in CCSL 3:244-47 and the bibliography provided at pp. xvii-xxi.

218. Cypr. *Ep.* 59.10.2; 65.1.1–5.2; 67.2.1–3.2.

219. Cypr. *Ep.* 55.18.1; 57.3.3.

220. Cypr. *Laps.* 17. Here he judged that a second opportunity for martyrdom might be the fruit of repentance (*Laps.* 36).

and on all the Apostles, Christ had asserted that sinners whom they held bound on earth would be bound in heaven. Cyprian concluded that the binding power of the church was effective: those whom the bishop held bound on earth would not be forgiven by Christ when he came to judge.[221] Any bishop who refused reconciliation, therefore, might be responsible for the loss of penitent sinners who died outside the communion. The bishop's loosening power was provisional, however, and subject to review by Christ at the final Judgment.[222] The proper role of the bishop, therefore, was to grant readmission to communion for all whom he judged worthy and, in anticipation of death, for all who had undertaken penance. Thus, the penitent sinners could be presented to Christ, with the support and prayers of the church, for his penetrating judgment. The congregation need not protect itself either from involuntary contamination by the sinful intentions of its false penitents or from the impurity that clung to those who had been in contact with the rituals of idolatry; it must only avoid condoning, approving, or encouraging their sinful behavior. It accomplished this by requiring public manifestations of repentance in *exomologesis* and sustained works of satisfaction. By demanding submission to these public rituals, the congregation could readmit the sinner to communion while still dissociating and protecting itself from complicity in the sin.[223]

## Integration into the Community

Cyprian provided fuller evidence than Tertullian had on the role of the community in the process of reconciliation. The sin of apostasy or denial of Christ through voluntary participation in the idolatry of the imperial cult struck at the very identity of the Christian community. At baptism, each of its members had rejected Satan and all the idolatrous practices that were associated with the power of evil in the world. Those guilty of major sins after baptism had, therefore, denied the community's realization and mediation of holiness. Such sinners had to be excluded. For their readmission, the Christian community had to require a sustained demonstration of repentance for the violation of its norms of behavior, a manifestation of renewed commitment to its way of life, and a recognition of the efficacy of its rituals.

During the persecution, Cyprian insisted that the decision to admit the apostates to communion would require a consultation that involved not only the bishops and clergy of Africa but also the laity. In particular, as long as any

221. Cypr. *Ep.* 57.4.3–5.2. This conclusion was clearly articulated in the justification of the decision to grant forgiveness in anticipation of the renewal of persecution.

222. Cypr. *Ep.* 57.1.1. The interpretation of this text offered here is elaborated in Burns, *Cyprian the Bishop*, 40, 71-72, with the accompanying notes.

223. Tertullian did not consider participation in the communion of the church essential to attaining forgiveness from God; Cyprian did.

members of the community were at risk of arrest or were suffering in prison or exile for their confession of Christ, he refused to allow back into communion anyone who had denied Christian commitment in order to make peace with the empire.[224]

Some of the sinners attempted to circumvent this process of full penance by joining a schismatic community that granted immediate reconciliation by appealing to the martyr's intercession. Cyprian and his colleagues steadfastly resisted the pressure of these rebels to be accepted back into communion as a group, under the terms of the pardon put forward by the martyrs during the persecution.[225] When some of these schismatic apostates attempted to return individually, their petitions to be admitted as penitents were subjected to extended scrutiny and even sustained objections by the faithful. Cyprian described raucous proceedings in which he attempted to move his congregation to pity and acceptance, and bemoaned the discouragement in which some of the petitioners withdrew.[226]

By requiring a public repudiation of the sin of apostasy, demonstrated through sustained works of repentance, the Christian community made clear its own rejection of that failure. Had it admitted the apostates to its communion without requiring penance, the congregation would have appeared to condone their failures and thus alienated itself from Christ.[227] By demanding a penance as public and even more sustained than the failure, the community demonstrated its own rejection of the sin even as it extended compassion to the sinner, whom it eventually would admit to communion and recommend to Christ in the Judgment.[228]

For two years and in the face of renewed persecution, sinners demonstrated loyalty to the congregation by submitting to its ritual of penance; this became an effective appeal for reconciliation. The penitents persevered in the works of satisfaction even though the schismatic community offered them immediate admission to its communion. Cyprian interpreted that temptation to schism as a continuation of the original persecution and the penitents' steadfast rejection of it as a witness to Christ and the unity of his church.[229] When a new imperial persecution threatened, he and his colleagues admitted all these penitents into communion.[230]

---

224. Cypr. *Ep.* 19.2.2-3; 26.1.1-2; 55.3.2-4.3.

225. Cypr. *Ep.* 23.

226. Cypr. *Ep.* 59.15.1-4.

227. Cypr. *Ep.* 11.3.1-6.2; 16.4.1; *Laps.* 7.

228. This is the thesis of Cypr. *Ep.* 55, which defends the bishops' decision to readmit penitents at the time of death.

229. Cypr. *Ep.* 43.3.1-2; *Laps.* 16; *Unit. eccl.* 3-8.

230. Cypr. *Ep.* 57.1.1-3.3.

During the episcopate of Cyprian, the North African church changed its penitential practice significantly. The bishops claimed for the church the power to grant at least a provisional forgiveness for all sins, those committed against God and against human beings. The ritual of repentance continued to focus on appeals to and satisfaction of God for the sin that had been committed. In practice, however, the works of repentance also functioned as a means of achieving an understanding and a reconciliation with the congregation. The sinner had broken faith not only with God but with the community and thus had to demonstrate a new commitment before being accepted back. In requiring this sustained repentance, the community showed God its own rejection of the sin. In extending its peace and support to the penitents, it affirmed its own mediatorial role in the process of salvation: only those who shared the love and unity of the church could enter into the Kingdom of God. The initial success of the laxist schism in Carthage forced Cyprian, his colleagues, and the congregations they served to reconsider the unity of the church and its relationship to Christ. Having grasped the essential role of the church's communion in the process of salvation, they then had to extend its peace to all whom they urged to repent and seek salvation. In their creed, they confessed that forgiveness of sins was given only through the church.[231] In this program, African Christians definitively rejected Tertullian's program of exclusion from the communion and insistence on the sinner's direct appeal to Christ for pardon.[232] Moreover, these Christians recognized the essential role of the bishop in mediating God's sanctifying power; they repudiated Tertullian's appeal to a spiritual church set over against the "church of the number of bishops."[233]

## The Purity of the Church

Tertullian had been concerned to preserve the purity of the whole church against the inroads of sin. Each Christian shared the priesthood of Christ; all had to follow priestly discipline in order to present the sacrifice of pure prayer to God. In order to integrate the repentant sinners, Cyprian had to distinguish the roles and responsibilities of the clergy from those of the laity. The sanctifying power of the Holy Spirit, which had been given to the church by Christ, was held by the episcopal college and exercised by individual bishops for their congregations. These bishops had to be faithful and free of all serious sin, both

231. Cypr. *Ep.* 69.7.1-2.
232. This program was continued by the rigorist schismatics, led by Novatian in Rome, which failed to win significant support in Africa.
233. Tert. *Pud.* 22.17.

individually and as a group, in order to preserve this sanctifying power. The congregations themselves might include repentant sinners, as long as the rituals of reconciliation enacted a clear and public repudiation of the sin on the part of both the penitents and the accepting communities.

The holiness of the church was a gift of God rather than the achievement of its members. Cyprian used wonderfully graphic images for the church and the holiness it bore. It was the bride of Christ washed clean, the walled garden in whose midst stood the sealed fountain of holiness, the Paradise watered by four rivers. Its baptismal waters flowed from Christ, pure and undefiled. It was the ark of Noah and the house of Rahab, into which the saved were gathered.[234]

## Conclusion

Cyprian was faced with a massive failing that involved a sin against God and that challenged the bishop's authority to deal with that sin by a schismatic subgroup within the church at Carthage. As a result, his analysis of penitential practice was diametrically opposed to that of Tertullian. His focus on the sins of apostasy and schism required him to engage the role of the bishop as leader of the united community and to draw the faithful into accepting and supporting his decisions. Although he limited the church's power to forgive sins — committed against either God or a fellow human — on the grounds that no human being could securely judge the penitent's dispositions, he insisted that the bishop had been authorized by Christ to make a decision based on penitential works and to reconcile and readmit to communion those who appeared to repent of such sins.

Like Tertullian, Cyprian continued to understand the process of forgiveness as intercessory: the penitent, the bishop, and the congregation all pleaded with God for the forgiveness of sins. Unlike Tertullian, however, he and his community considered inclusion in the eucharistic communion of the church a necessary condition for the success of that appeal: only those whom the church accepted and recommended would be forgiven by Christ. The bishop's power to forgive was, therefore, his authority to reconcile excommunicated sinners to the communion of the church and thus to guarantee them the opportunity to present their plea to Christ. As a member of the episcopal college founded on the Apostles and endowed with the power of binding and loosening, the bishop held and exercised the church's sanctifying power. Like Peter, each bishop was Christ's chosen and empowered delegate.

Because sharing the church's communion was a necessary condition for receiving Christ's forgiveness, every penitent had to be granted the peace of the church prior to death. At the Judgment, the faithful church — bishops, martyrs, confessors, and faithful — could then intercede for its repentant members.

234. Cypr. *Ep.* 69.2.1-2, 4.1; 73.10.3, 11.1-2; 74.11.1-3.

---

The Donatist use of the rituals of penance and reconciliation after the Diocletian persecution both followed and differed from that of Cyprian. At the meeting to choose a bishop to succeed Paulus in Cirta in March 307,[235] the Primate of Numidia, Secundus of Tigisis, questioned the suitability of some of his fellow bishops to participate in the consecration of the new bishop because they had been guilty of handing over sacred books and vessels to the government during the persecution. When challenged by Purpurius of Limata about his own record, however, Secundus allowed the suitability of each to be deferred to the divine Judgment.[236] The bishops then proceeded to choose and consecrate as bishop a deacon who was guilty of the same sin, over the strenuous objections of members of his congregation.[237]

This practice of referring serious sin to the divine Judgment was not, however, continued once the schism against Caecilian had been established at Carthage. Donatus was subsequently condemned for following Cyprian's practice of imposing hands in repentance upon bishops who had been guilty of sin.[238] The Council of Arles in 314 specified that bishops who had committed apostasy must be removed from office, but it did not require that they be subjected to public penance.[239]

When the Donatist bishops were permitted by the emperor Julian to return from their exile in 362, they took over — in some cases forcibly — the basilicas and congregations that had passed to the control of the Caecilianists during the mission of Macarius and Paul some fifteen years earlier.[240] They subjected to penance the bishops, presbyters, and deacons serving those churches, thereby disqualifying them from the clergy.[241] Many of these originally would have been Donatists and then joined the Caecilianists when other Donatist leaders were sent into exile.[242] By ministering in the Caecilianist communion, they had become guilty of the sin of apostasy, which the Donatists believed infected all who had accepted Caecilian as Bishop of Carthage. Since they had originally been baptized in the Donatist church, however, these clerics could not be purified by rebaptism. Hence, they had to use penance and were excluded from office. The Donatist leaders also washed down basilicas, scraped or replaced the wooden

---

235. See Jean-Louis Maier, *Le dossier du donatisme,* 2 vols. (Berlin: Akademie Verlag, 1987), 1:112-14, for date and details.

236. Aug. *Cresc.* 3.27.30.

237. *Act. Zeno.* 16; Aug. *Cresc.* 3.29.33.

238. Optat. *Parm.* 1.24.

239. *Con. Arel.* a. 314, 14.

240. Optat. *Parm.* 2.17-19.

241. Optat. *Parm.* 2.21-25; 3.4.

242. Optat. *Parm.* 3.12. In the Council under Bishop Gratus (a. 345-48), 12, what may have been a complaint against such a former Donatist was discussed.

---

altar tables, and subjected the people to penance. That penance also prevented any of the laity from serving as clergy: only those who had kept free of the alleged apostasy of the Caecilianists were eligible for office.[243] In addition, any who had been baptized in the Caecilianist communion during the exile were subjected to rebaptism.[244]

Some thirty years later, the Donatist Council of Bagai in 393 resolved the conflict between Maximian and Primian over the bishopric of Carthage by deciding that the dissenting bishops who had consecrated Maximian, along with the clergy of the church of Carthage who witnessed the rite, must be subjected to penance and removed from office. Those bishops who had deposed Primian at the separatist council of Cebarsussi were given eight months to return to Primian's communion, after which they would be subjected to the same penalty.[245] In fact, however, even the consecrators of Maximian were (forcibly) readmitted into communion and allowed to retain their offices.[246] Although they had been guilty of schism, they could not be charged with apostasy, because they had not joined the Caecilianists.

Thus, the Donatists modified the procedures of Cyprian: they followed his practice by requiring penance of apostates, both clerical and lay, who had left their communion for that of Caecilian and prohibited them from exercising clerical office; they did not, however, follow him in requiring penance and excluding from office those who had been guilty of schism alone. The Caecilianists, in contrast, recognized both the baptism and the ordination of schismatics; they imposed penance on laity who had deserted their communion and reduced clergy to the lay state without requiring formal penance.[247] They were willing to allow those baptized and ordained in schism to exercise clerical office in their communion.

. . . . . . . . . . . . . . . . . . . . . . . . . . . . . . . . . . . . . . . . . . . . . . . . . . . . . . . . . . . . . . . . . . . . . . . . . . . . . . . . . . . . . . . . . . . . .

## THE PRACTICE OF PENANCE IN AUGUSTINE'S TIME

In the late fourth and early fifth centuries, idolatry was no longer the major challenge to the Christians of Africa. Emperor Theodosius and his successors withdrew imperial support from the traditional cults and began to remove them from the center of urban life. Nor were Caecilianist Christians attracted to the Donatist communion, which also came under state sanctions and disabili-

---

243. Optat. *Parm.* 2.21-26; 6.1, 6, 8. Optatus noted that in areas where wood was scarce, the returning Donatists scraped the altars rather than destroying them.

244. Optat. *Parm.* 4.4, 6.

245. Aug. *Cresc.* 3.22.35; 4.4.5. The reconstructed text of that decree is reprinted in Maier, *Le dossier du donatisme,* 2:84-92.

246. Aug. *Parm.* 1.4.9; 2.3.7; *Petil.* 1.10.11, 13.14; 2.83.184.

247. Aug. *Unic. bapt.* 12.20; *Cresc.* 2.16.19; *Serm.* 296.15.

ties.[248] In dealing with the sins committed by Christians who had been baptized and lived their religious lives within the unity of the Caecilianist communion, Augustine focused on a different set of crimes, such as perjury and fraud in the imperial courts, and the sexual abuse of servants. In his preaching, he urged the private practices through which the sins of daily living were repented and forgiven. His writings and the legislation of the African bishops also provide evidence of the development of a private penance for serious sins, some of which would have required the public ritual in an earlier age.

A general theory of the church's power to forgive sins through sacramental action was developed in the controversy over the practice of rebaptism. This theory structured Augustine's understanding of penance and the ritual of imposing hands, which the Caecilianists used to receive converts from schism.[249] He recognized a tension between the interior dispositions of the penitent and the church's power of the keys. The penitent was required not only to repent and desist from sinning but also to submit to the rituals of binding and loosening. The identification of the charity given by the Holy Spirit as the power through which the church could forgive sins enabled him to locate the holiness from which that power derived within the communion of the faithful rather than in the bishop alone. Sacramental efficacy no longer depended upon the fidelity and purity of the clergy. His understanding of the importance of the intentional union of the faithful in love as the medium of forgiveness also guided Augustine to emphasize the role of those penitential activities that promoted unity within the church through mutual care and forgiveness, rather than ascetical exercises that might satisfy divine wrath or justice.

This section will proceed by considering Augustine's treatment of the different kinds of sin; then the rituals through which they were forgiven; and finally the operation and efficacy of the church's power to forgive.

## Types of Sin

In the narrative of his conversion and the reflections on his life as a bishop in books eight and ten of *Confessions,* Augustine shone a bright light on the conflicting loves which divided the intentions and desires of the offspring of Adam and Eve. In his later conflict with the Pelagians, he insisted that the failure to love God with one's whole heart was itself sinful and must be repented. A person might hold back from carrying out or even consenting to an evil deed, but the disordered desire that was made evident in the emergence and persistence of the many forms of pride and lust was itself a violation of

---

248. Serge Lancel, *Saint Augustine,* trans. Antonia Neville (London: SCM Press, 2002), 221, 290-304.

249. The Donatists rebaptized Catholic converts to their communion. See above, pp. 196-97.

the Great Commandment of wholehearted love of God.[250] A regularly cited sin of daily living was the enjoyment of sexual intercourse by married couples who did not intend thereby the procreation of children. Augustine insisted that this sinful act did not jeopardize salvation as long as it was restrained by fidelity to the marriage bond.[251] In his sermons, he identified other such sins: the immoderate use of such bodily necessities as food and drink, failures in the conversation and action of social life, lapses of attention in prayer, and the general wandering of the mind and imagination. These almost inevitable sins, he explained, were each negligible, like drops of water seeping through the seams of a ship; yet, if they were not repented, as bilges were regularly pumped, they could overwhelm a person's love for God.[252] He insisted that even faithful Christians were sinners throughout their earthly lives and therefore urged that they be penitents as well.

Following the established tradition, Augustine identified some major sins as requiring exclusion or withdrawal from the eucharist, confession in public or private, a significant period of penitential works, and formal release from the guilt that would entail condemnation. The Decalogue provided a basic list of such sins: murder, adultery and fornication, theft and robbery, and false witness.[253] To these Augustine added sins from the list provided by Paul in Galatians (5:19-21) — sorcery, enmity, strife, jealousy, anger, dissension, party spirit, envy, drunkenness — which ends with the warning "those who do such things shall not gain possession of the Kingdom of God."[254] On occasion, he was able to specify ways in which idolatry was still practiced, such as consulting astrologers, having spells cast, or trying to cure illness by incantations and charms.[255] Augustine also identified the sexual abuse of slaves as the most common form of adultery.[256] Increased access to imperial courts made false witness and fraud great dangers for Christians.[257] Certain other sins and attitudes appeared occasionally in his preaching: blasphemy, usury, and dealing in slaves.[258] Finally, he noted that some sins, such as hatred and following the calendar observances of

---

250. Aug. *Psal.* 118.3.1; 50.3. See also *Spir. et litt.* 36.65; *Nat. et grat.* 62.72; *Ep.* 196.2.6; *Perf.* 5.11, 11.28; *Nupt.* 1.23.25, 27.30, 29.32; *Iul.* 4.2.7; 5.7.29; 6.16.50.

251. Aug. *Nupt.* 1.14.16, 24.27; *Bon. coniug.* 6.6.

252. Aug. *Serm.* 56.8.12; 57.11.11–12.12; *Serm. Dolb.* 12(354A).12; *Enchir.* 21.78.

253. Aug. *Serm.* 56.8.12. For individual sins: murder: *Eu. Io.* 41.10; adultery: *Serm.* 261.9; *Serm. Guelf.* 33(77A).4; *Eu. Io.* 41.10; *Ep. Io.* 3.9; fornication: *Serm.* 261.9; *Eu. Io.* 41.10; theft: *Serm.* 261.9; *Serm. Guelf.* 33(77A).4; *Eu. Io.* 41.10; robbery: *Serm.* 261.9; false witness: *Serm.* 261.9; *Serm. Guelf.* 33(77A).4; *Ep. Io.* 3.9.

254. Aug. *Serm.* 261.9; *Serm. Guelf.* 33(77A).4.

255. Aug. *Serm. Dolb.* 18(306E).7; *Serm. Guelf.* 33(77A).4; *Ep. Io.* 3.9.

256. Aug. *Serm.* 9.3-4, 11; 392.3-5.

257. False witness: Aug. *Serm.* 97.4; 107.9.10; 159.4.5; *Serm. Cail.* 2.6(94A).2; *Serm. Denis* 17(301A).5; *Serm. Dolb.* 18(306E).10. Fraud: Aug. *Serm.* 137.11.14; *Psal.* 96.15; 103.4.6.

258. Blasphemy: Aug. *Serm. Guelf.* 33(77A).4; usury and extortionate interest: Aug. *Serm.* 86.3.3; *Serm. Guelf.* 33(77A).4; *Ep. Io.* 3.9; slave-dealing: Aug. *Ep. Io.* 3.9.

false religions, might be considered trivial were they not specified as serious by the teaching of the Gospels and the Apostolic Letters.[259]

Augustine asserted that all of these sins could be forgiven through the ritual of reconciliation.[260] In commenting on the incestuous man at Corinth (1 Cor. 5:3-6), for example, he argued that the exclusion Paul commanded was intended to promote the sinner's conversion and that the community had been required to continue interceding for him.[261] Tertullian, it will be recalled, had insisted that monstrous crimes of this type committed after baptism could win forgiveness neither through the church nor directly from God.[262] Augustine's only attempt at a complete commentary on Paul's letter to the Romans failed to solve the question of the unforgivable sin.[263] As his appreciation of the church and its power of forgiveness developed, he identified this sin as rejecting the unity of the church and the divine gifts of faith and charity, since these were essential to the forgiveness of sin.[264] Only impenitence, then, was an unforgivable sin.

A middle category of sins, more serious than the negligence and failure accompanying daily life, did not require formal penance, even if the sinner was prepared to perform it.[265] Such sins might need the medicine of rebuke and correction but were not of such seriousness that they could be repented only once, as was specified for those subject to the full ritual of penance.[266] A particularly striking example of such a sin was continuing in a schism that one had not initiated or personally chosen. Donatist laity who had been born into that community, even if they had been baptized there as adults, were admitted to Caecilianist communion by the imposition of hands alone, without an extended penance.[267] Sins such as avarice and hatred, as well as sins of intention that were not manifest in action, also may have been in this category. In response to the questions posed by the monks at Hadrumetum, Augustine explained the salutary practice of rebuke by an abbot, through which God corrects and saves the elect.[268] In all these instances, some form of penitential action was required, but the full public penance of the church was judged inappropriate.

---

259. Aug. *Enchir.* 21.79.

260. Aug. *Enchir.* 17.65.

261. Aug. *Parm.* 3.1.3.

262. Tert. *Pud.* 13-16.

263. *Epistulae ad Romanos inchoata expositio* did not continue beyond Rom. 1:7.

264. Aug. *Serm.* 71.3.5–14.24. In practice, this meant rejecting the unity of the church — whether inside or outside the visible church (*Serm.* 71.17.28, 21.34–23.37). Augustine also explained that because sins are retained by unbelief and forgiven by faith, not to believe in Christ was an unforgivable sin (*Serm.* 143.2; 144.1.1; *Eu. Io.* 95.2).

265. Aug. *Quaest.* 83, 26.

266. Aug. *Fid. et op.* 26.48.

267. *Reg. Carth.* 57. The proposal to allow such persons to be ordained to Catholic ministry clearly indicated that they had not been subjected to formal penance, which was an obstacle to ordination. *Con. Carth.* June 401.

268. Aug. *Corrept.* 5.7; *Parm.* 3.1.2.

Essential to the process of forgiveness was the rebuke and correction of sinners by those whom they had harmed, or by others responsible for their well-being and that of the community. Augustine regarded this as one of the most important of his episcopal responsibilities: correction of the congregation is clearly evident in his preaching;[269] he criticized bishops who deferred to the wealthy and powerful rather than warning them of danger.[270] This ministry was not limited to the clergy: anyone who had responsibility for others within a family or household should undertake their correction.[271] Any Christian with knowledge of a significant sin should act,[272] or at least resist by refusing to cooperate in or approve the evil.[273] Those without the social power necessary to intervene might appeal to the bishop for his action.[274]

Augustine recognized that sinners often rejected the rebuke and even attacked the clergy who confronted them.[275] They might assert their own righteousness,[276] blame God for making them the way they were,[277] or dismiss their failings as common ones that God would certainly overlook.[278] Sinners who acknowledged their failure often delayed repentance,[279] assuming that God would allow them plenty of time and warning before death.[280]

## The Rituals: Daily Private Penance

The standard means of gaining forgiveness for sins of daily living was through their acknowledgment in the Lord's Prayer and by fulfilling its commitment to forgive others. When the prayer was recited during the celebration of the eucharist, all the participants struck their breasts at the petition for forgiveness.[281] Augustine regularly warned that God would hold Christians to the bargain: they would be forgiven only if they in turn forgave whenever their pardon

269. Aug. *Serm.* 113.3.3; 132.4; 137.11.14; 343.3.
270. Aug. *Serm.* 137.10.12; *Serm. frg. Verbr.* 7(77C); *Eu. Io.* 46.8.
271. Aug. *Serm.* 343.3; *Psal.* 102.14.
272. Aug. *Serm.* 164.2.3, 6.8, 7.10-11.
273. Aug. *Serm.* 88.18.19.
274. Aug. *Serm.* 392.4.
275. Aug. *Psal.* 128.4; *Ep. Io.* 3.9.
276. Aug. *Psal.* 50.15.
277. Aug. *Ep. Io.* 3.9.
278. Aug. *Psal.* 42.3; 35.3; 52.2, 4.
279. *Psal.* 32.2.10; 55.6; 102.16; *Serm.* 339.7-8.
280. Aug. *Serm.* 20.3-4; 40.1-5; 82.11.14; 87.9.11; *Serm. Cail.* 2.5(73A).1-2.
281. Aug. *Serm. Dolb.* 8(29B).2.

was asked[282] and without limit.[283] It was, he pointed out, the only part of the prayer on which Christ commented after delivering it to his disciples.[284] Thus, he observed that the desire to exercise the right to vengeance was particularly dangerous precisely because it blocked access to the gift of forgiveness of one's own sins.[285]

To the private and communal recitation of the Lord's Prayer were added the works of mercy. Aside from forgiving others, almsgiving was the most important and effective of the penitential works.[286] Fasting was a traditional penitential practice, but Augustine required that it both discipline the individual and help the community: what one refrained from eating must be given to the poor.[287] Some Christians also abstained from the eucharist at times when they judged that they had not lived purely enough, though others insisted that this medicine was needed precisely when Christians were falling short. Augustine honored both practices.[288]

This emphasis on the sins of daily living made confession of sinfulness, repentance, and forgiveness a regular part of the ritual life of Christians. When the Pelagians insisted that God gave every Christian the power to live without sin, Augustine responded by citing the petition for forgiveness in the Lord's Prayer, which Christ had enjoined upon all.[289] In Africa, this argument seems to have ended the debate.

Augustine also urged mutual confrontation, correction, forgiveness, and reconciliation among the members of the community. First, Christians should seek the pardon of those whom they had harmed, either by a direct apology or — in dealing with servants — by unmistakable acts of kindness.[290] Christians must always forgive those who sought their pardon;[291] indeed, they should follow Christ by granting forgiveness even when it was not asked.[292] Second, correction must always be undertaken in a spirit of love and gentleness, so that the offender was moved to repent.[293] Patient tolerance of evil must not result in neglect of the welfare of the sinner.[294] Indeed, punishment should be applied

---

282. Aug. *Serm.* 58.6.7; 206.2; 210.10.12; 211.5; 259.4; 278.6.6, 10.10–11.11; *Psal.* 131.2; 147.13.

283. Aug. *Serm.* 83.3.3–6.7; 114.1-5.

284. Aug. *Serm.* 56.7.11–9.13; 58.9.10; *Serm. Dolb.* 12(354A).12; *Enchir.* 19.71, 73-74; *Fid. et op.* 26.48.

285. Aug. *Serm.* 57.11.11; 59.4.7; *Serm. Wilm.* 2(179A).1. One had a right to vengeance but not to forgiveness.

286. Aug. *Serm.* 9.17-18, 21; 56.7.11–8.12; 58.9.10; 83.2.2.

287. Aug. *Psal.* 42.8; *Serm.* 205.2; 206.2; 208.2; 209.2; 210.10.12.

288. Aug. *Ep.* 54.3.4.

289. E.g., Aug. *Gest. Pel.* 31.56; *Pelag.* 1.14.28; 3.5.14–7.17.

290. Aug. *Serm.* 211.4.

291. Aug. *Serm.* 56.9.13–13.17; 83.3.3–7.8; *Serm. Wilm.* 2(179A).1, 6, 7.

292. Aug. *Serm.* 382.2; 386.1-2.

293. Aug. *Serm.* 82.3.4, 8.11–9.12; 88.18.19; *Serm. Frang.* 9(114A).5-6.

294. Aug. *Serm.* 4.20; 5.2-3, 8; 164.2.3, 6.8, 7.10-11; *Serm. Frang.* 9(114A).5-6.

to those for whom a Christian had responsibility,[295] though alms must not be withheld from the sinful poor.[296] Third, when Christians forgave one another on earth, they loosened the sin in heaven as well; no one, however, could bind another by refusing pardon when it was sought.[297] Instead, refusing forgiveness to another undid the forgiveness of one's own sins.[298]

## The Rituals: Formal Public Penance

The process of formal public penance for deadly sins stood at the opposite end of the ritual spectrum, far removed from daily private penance. As it had in Tertullian's description, the process began with a confession or accusation of sin before the bishop. The legislation of African councils and Augustine's own witness indicate that the bishop had the power and even the responsibility to excommunicate notorious sinners.[299] When a particular sin was widely known in the community or had been established through the imperial or ecclesiastical courts, the bishop was required to exclude the sinner from communion and to exact a public manifestation of repentance before allowing a return.[300] Augustine declared that in certain instances, he had indeed forced sinners to accept public penance.[301] Even when the sin was not secret, however, the bishop had to exercise prudence in making accusations and in excommunicating. If he forced the issue, the sinner might refuse to undertake penance, withdraw from the church, and be lost.[302] If he allowed someone widely believed to be guilty to remain in the communion, however, he might damage the morale and weaken the moral standards of the community.[303] Recognizing the limits of his ability to act, he exhorted the community to tolerate the unrepentant sinners in their midst in the hope that they would be converted eventually.[304] The bishop's public silence should not, he asserted, be interpreted as approval of the sin or even a failure to confront the sinner in private.[305]

Once excommunication was formally pronounced by a bishop on a member of his church, it could be lifted only by him or his delegate. Any other bishop

295. Aug. *Serm.* 13.7-8; 56.13.17; 83.7.8; *Serm. Dolb.* 21(159B).4; *Psal.* 50.24; 102.11, 14.

296. Aug. *Serm. Lamb.* 28(164A).1-4.

297. Aug. *Serm.* 82.4.7. The same held for the binding power of the church: refusal to loose a sin could not harm the truly repentant (*Ep.* 153.3.7; *Serm.* 20.2).

298. Aug. *Serm.* 57.11.11–12.12; 59.4.7; 211.5.

299. *Con. Carth.* a. 390, 7; *Aug. Serm.* 232.8. In *Ciu.* 20.9, Augustine interpreted the setting up of a judgment seat as belonging to the time of the church.

300. *Bru. Hipp.* 30c.

301. Aug. *Serm.* 232.8; *Ep.* 153.3.6.

302. Aug. *Serm.* 17.3.

303. Aug. *Ep.* 95.3.

304. Aug. *Serm.* 4.20; 5.3, 8. Such people harm only themselves (*Serm.* 164.7.11).

305. Aug. *Serm.* 82.8.11–9.12.

or presbyter who did not honor the excommunication and sided with the sinner would incur the same penalty.[306] Responding to the appeal of a Christian who had been rashly excommunicated by another bishop, Augustine advised the accused to submit, apologize, and perform some penance.[307] He did, however, write to the bishop suggesting that he reconsider the penalty.[308] Only in emergency might a presbyter act without the prior approval of the bishop to reconcile privately even someone who had submitted to penance.[309]

The length of the formal penance was established by the bishop as appropriate for the particular sin.[310] Augustine observed that the efficacy of the penitential process depended more on the dispositions of sorrow and reform of the penitent than upon the actual works performed. Because these dispositions were difficult for human beings to judge, however, the bishop usually set a definite length of time for the penance, based on the nature and circumstances of the sin itself.[311] No evidence of common guidelines for the appropriate lengths of penance has survived in the legislation of the African councils.

Some of the Christians who sought or accepted the status of penitent made little or no effort to reform their lives and regain access to communion.[312] They may have come to church regularly and have hands imposed on them during the eucharistic ritual but did not engage in penitential works.[313] The practice of granting reconciliation to all penitents at the time of death, however, had been established in Cyprian's time, just as baptism was granted under similar circumstances to those who had enrolled as catechumens.[314] These dilatory penitents, therefore, seem to have used their status as a form of long-term affiliation with the church, which would then grant its peace and communion during the final stage of their lives.[315] Augustine warned that the insincerity of such penitents was evident and that they could not presume that a death-bed reconciliation had the same efficacy as a death-bed baptism, which would guarantee salvation. He did not, however, threaten to withhold that reconciliation.[316]

Another reason for delay in seeking reconciliation was the continuing restriction of formal, public penance to once in a lifetime. Anyone who had completed the penitential process, was readmitted to the peace of the church, and fell again into another serious sin would be banished from communion, even

306. *Con. Carth.* a. 390, 7.

307. Aug. *Ep. Divj.* 1*.2, 5.

308. Aug. *Ep.* 250.1-2.

309. *Con. Carth.* a. 390, 4. In emergency, the presbyter could act without consulting the bishop (*Bru. Hipp.* 30b).

310. *Bru. Hipp.* 30a.

311. Aug. *Enchir.* 17.65.

312. Aug. *Serm.* 232.8; 392.6; *Serm. Lamb.* 26(335H).3.

313. Aug. *Serm.* 232.8.

314. Aug. *Adult.* 1.28.35; *Con. Carth.* a. 390, 4; *Bru. Hipp.* 30b. Cypr. *Ep.* 55.13.1.

315. Aug. *Serm.* 232.8; 392.6.

316. Aug. *Serm.* 393.1.

at the time of death. Ironically, this restriction of penance had the effect of delaying the first repentance and perhaps actually increasing sin. Yet, some persons did find themselves permanently excluded for sinning after once having been reconciled. Augustine judged that they should be exhorted to undertake penance and then appeal to the mercy of Christ at the Judgment. Their repentance and charity would not be in vain, he believed, even if the bishop had to refuse them communion.[317] Unlike Cyprian, Augustine did not believe that the church's failure or refusal to loosen would bind a repentant sinner and prevent an appeal to the mercy of Christ at the Judgment.[318]

The ritual of reconciliation by the bishop's imposing hands upon the penitent in the nave of the church brought the process of repentance to completion.[319] A similar ritual was apparently used for the acceptance of schismatics into communion and was interpreted as the conferral of the Holy Spirit and the gift of charity, through which sins were forgiven.[320] The African conciliar legislation specified that this ritual was always to be performed by the bishop rather than a delegated presbyter.[321] In the case of a dying penitent, however, a presbyter who was present should grant reconciliation, even if he could not consult the bishop.[322] Augustine himself drew the parallel to the emergency baptism of a catechumen: the reconciliation was to be given even if the penitent was unconscious, the penance incomplete, and the manner of life itself unreformed.[323] African Christians continued to set a high value on the peace of the church, at least when they were being summoned to the Judgment of Christ.

## The Rituals: Penance Performed in Secret

A less formal type of penance came into broader use sometime during the fourth century and is well evidenced at the beginning of the fifth century. The procedure was apparently designed to protect Christian sinners who were guilty of crimes that could be punished through imperial courts and who therefore were reluctant to admit their guilt before a congregation. A sinner who had been denounced to the bishop or who voluntarily revealed a crime that was not

317. Aug. *Ep.* 153.3.7; *Serm.* 20.2.
318. This attitude may have been a consequence of his use of mutual forgiveness in the congregation as the model for public penance: a victim's refusal to grant pardon when asked could not bind the offender.
319. *Bru. Hipp.* 30c required this procedure in the case of generally known crimes.
320. Aug. *Bapt.* 2.7.11; 5.23.33; *Serm.* 296.15. In this instance, however, it may not have ruled out a subsequent formal penance.
321. *Con. Carth.* a. 390, 3.
322. *Con. Carth.* a. 390, 4. When the presbyter acts in emergency, he should consult the bishop, but the subsequent *Bru. Hipp.* 30b does not include this provision.
323. Aug. *Adult.* 1.28.35.

publicly known could undergo penance without being publicly exposed. When the crime was not general knowledge but had been reported by a member of the community, the bishop could confront and exhort the accused person to repent.[324] If the sinner denied the charge or even acknowledged the sin but refused to withdraw from communion and undertake penance, the bishop could not reveal the crime or take any public action. If the bishop attempted to force the issue and the sinner denied making the private confession, the bishop had to allow the individual to remain in communion. A bishop who publicly refused communion and thereby exposed a person he privately knew was guilty would himself be faced with excommunication by his colleagues.[325]

The objective in most private correction and in anonymous public rebukes was to find a way for the sinner to perform penance without attracting the public attention that would alert personal enemies to a crime, such as adultery, murder, false testimony, theft, or fraud, and thereby provide evidence that could be used in court.[326] When the serious sin was not a crime subject to imperial courts, such as the sexual abuse of one's own servants, the bishop had more freedom. Augustine urged wives who could not themselves curb their husbands' infidelities to report them to him privately so that he might attempt to correct and save them.[327] Though much of this correction was effected in private, he occasionally warned the guilty in public without singling them out. They should voluntarily refrain from coming to the chancel rail to receive the eucharist unworthily and provoke a confrontation with the bishop that would expose the sin they both knew.[328] In other instances, Augustine may have sought to provide a means of avoiding the familial or social disruption that public penance would have entailed. In these circumstances, some Christians argued that their repentance was best done in the privacy of the heart, without admitting their crime to the church or the bishop. Augustine responded that some form of ecclesial penance was necessary in order to gain access to the power of the keys, the authority to loosen on earth and in heaven, which had been conferred upon the church. A person must not despise the church's proper role in the process of forgiveness.[329]

On the basis of this evidence, the structure of private penance for serious sins may be inferred. The penitent would have acknowledged the sin voluntarily or in response to the bishop's rebuke, thereby replacing the ritual of con-

324. Aug. *Serm.* 82.8.11–9.12; 232.8.
325. *Con. Carth.* 30 May 419, 132-33. Reaffirmed: *Con. Hipp.* a. 427, 8, and in the *Bru. Fer.* 73.
326. Aug. *Serm.* 82.8.11–9.12; 113.3.3.
327. Aug. *Serm.* 392.4; 82.9.12.
328. Aug. *Serm.* 392.5; 132.4. The reception of the eucharist while in sin was an empty action which brought condemnation: *Serm.* 272; *Psal.* 39.12; *Eu. Io.* 26.11-12, 15, 18; *Ep. Io.* 7.6. This confrontation may be presumed to have occurred prior to the legislation of 419 forbidding such public rebuke.
329. Aug. *Serm.* 392.3; *Eu. Io.* 50.12.

fession or *exomologesis* before the congregation. The penitent would then have withdrawn from sharing in the eucharist.[330] The public display of penitential works also might have been omitted. Prayer, fasting, and especially almsgiving almost certainly would have been performed, since these were used regularly for less serious sins and thus would not have revealed the existence of a secret serious sin. The penance would have been completed with the ritual of reconciliation, almost certainly in private, in which the church's power to forgive and to loosen the bonds of guilt was engaged.

This private penance under episcopal supervision should not be confused with the less formal correction and repentance for sins that were not deadly. This form of rebuke had been used already in the times of Tertullian and Cyprian, as has been seen, and continued in Augustine's day. In contrast to the earlier practice, however, the new private ritual was used for deadly sins; it required the authoritative action of the bishop and was thus an alternate form of full public penance. The examples of sins handled in this manner included fornication, adultery, and murder, all of which had required public penance in the third century.[331] This shift in practice, however, also allowed for an expansion of the sins for which episcopally supervised penance could be required.[332] Augustine's list of deadly sins that required full penance was comparable to the third category in Tertullian's later writings and significantly longer than that mentioned by Cyprian. Augustine could also impose this form of private penance for sins that might earlier have been tolerated without episcopal intervention.[333] This procedure, moreover, might have been repeated during a person's lifetime.[334] Still, this private form of penance did not fully displace the traditional public ritual: Augustine testified that his congregation had many public penitents.[335]

### The Rituals: Reception of Those Baptized without True Conversion

Yet another form of penance seems to have been employed when the efficacy of baptism had been compromised by a failure of repentance and conversion. Those who were born into the Donatist schism and had never been Caeci-

330. Private withdrawal from the eucharist need not have implied a serious sin (*Ep.* 54.3.4).

331. Aug. *Serm.* 82.8.11.

332. This may well have been the practice which Augustine was defending in *Ep.* 54.3.4, against those who insisted on either full communion or full public penance.

333. Thus avarice, drunkenness, adultery, theft, lying, false witness, blasphemy, heathen charms, spells and superstition, usury and extortionate interest in Aug. *Serm. Guelf.* 33(77A).4. *Serm.* 261.9 adds fornication to adultery, robbery to theft, and sacrilege, while repeating false witness.

334. The performance of the ritual of repentance would have been known only to the penitent and the bishop. Tertullian did not specify that the sins on his longer list were subject to the rule of a single penance. See above, p. 307.

335. Aug. *Serm.* 232.8.

lianist communicants were received into unity by the public imposition of hands. This ritual was interpreted as a form of penitential reconciliation, so that they would recognize that they had sinned by adhering to the schism.[336] The procedure did not, however, have the requirements or effects of formal penance.[337] The only satisfactory work required was the acknowledgment of the sin of schism accomplished by publicly moving from the Donatist to the Caecilianist communion. For those born into the sect and baptized there as children, submission to the ritual of the imposition of hands did not necessarily prevent their being ordained to clerical office.[338] Nor did the ritual seem to have prevented a subsequent penance and reconciliation for a serious sin.[339] For Caecilianists who had deserted to the Donatist schism, however, the ritual of return was formal public penance, which prevented their attaining clerical office.[340] Caecilianist deserters who brought native Donatists with them into unity when they returned were, however, received like their companions, without penalty.[341]

A similar practice may have been employed when an adult received baptism in the Caecilianist communion without a true conversion of heart. Augustine compared such a person to a convert from the Donatist schism, arguing that baptism was not to be repeated but that reconciliation and peace revived the efficacy of the baptism.[342] The sins being forgiven were those that had not been effectively removed by the baptism. A person also might have been baptized within the true church while holding an erroneous or heretical understanding of the creed; when the person discovered and embraced true faith, the error alone was to be corrected, apparently without any formal ritual.[343]

## Penance for the Clergy

The ritual of public confession, penitential works, and reconciliation by the imposition of hands was not used for members of the clergy. Instead, they were removed from office and communicated among the laity. This had not been Cyprian's practice: the change in Caecilianist practice may have been a result of the judgment of the Council of Arles, which is reported to have

336. Aug. *Bapt.* 5.23.33.

337. Aug. *Serm.* 296.15 contrasted it with the formal penance required of Caecilianist deserters.

338. *Reg. Carth.* 47, 57. If the Donatist convert was subject to penance in that church, the same regimen would be required by the Caecilianists: *Ep.* 35.3.

339. Aug. *Bapt.* 5.23.33 shows Augustine working to minimize the effects of this ritual.

340. Aug. *Serm.* 296.15; *Cresc.* 2.16.19.

341. Aug. *Serm. Denis* 8(260A).2.

342. Aug. *Bapt.* 1.12.18–13.21.

343. Aug. *Bapt.* 3.14.19.

condemned Donatus himself for the practice of imposing hands on penitent clergy.[344]

Exceptions were made for the Donatist bishops and clergy, whom the Caecilianists invited to join their communion. For the good of unity, a converting Donatist cleric might be allowed to retain and exercise his office without being subjected to any imposition of hands, as either reconciliation or ordination.[345] The forgiveness of the sins of these clerics was achieved by the union of charity, which they effected by coming into the universal communion.[346] The newly Caecilianist bishop could even supervise the full penance of a Caecilianist apostate whom he had himself drawn into the Donatist schism and then brought back into union.[347] A person who had been guilty of a crime (other than schism and rebaptizing) that normally required public penance, however, was forbidden to become or remain a cleric.[348]

## Penitential Works

Augustine provided far less information on the actual practices in which the penitents engaged than had Tertullian and Cyprian. In the fifth century, penitents seem to have been segregated within the nave of the basilica during services rather than required to remain outside the area of the assembly. They were occasionally addressed in sermons.[349] After the sermon, hands were sometimes imposed on them, and they were dismissed with the catechumens: Augustine once remarked on the great number who had lined up for that ceremony.[350] According to Augustine, this ritual of imposing hands was a prayer said over a person; unlike baptism, it could be repeated.[351]

The first objective of penitential works, according to Augustine, was to repudiate and distance oneself from the sinful attitude and action, and thus to align one's own intention with God's will.[352] Citing the response of the citizens of Nineveh to the preaching of Jonah, Augustine explained that God did not have to destroy the sinful city because its citizens themselves destroyed it by turning away from their shared evil intention and becoming a good city.[353]

344. See Optat. *Parm.* 1.24.
345. Aug. *Parm.* 2.13.28; *Bapt.* 1.1.2.
346. *Bru. Hipp.* 37.
347. Aug. *Cresc.* 2.16.19.
348. Aug. *Ep.* 184.10.45.
349. Aug. *Serm.* 392.2, 6.
350. Aug. *Serm.* 232.8.
351. Aug. *Bapt.* 3.16.21.
352. Aug. *Psal.* 58.1.13; 140.14; *Serm.* 20.2; 29.6; *Serm. Dolb.* 8(29B).1-4, 6. God did not have to punish those who punished themselves: *Psal.* 44.18; *Ep.* 153.3.6.
353. Aug. *Serm.* 361.21.20; *Psal.* 50.11.

Penitents simultaneously could be guilty because of the evil they had done and righteous by accepting God's just condemnation of their sin.[354] This repentance and rejection of sin was the spiritual resurrection symbolized by Lazarus's coming forth from the tomb.[355]

A second objective, to which Augustine referred less regularly, was the satisfaction of divine justice through self-inflicted punishment. Many of the sufferings of human life were identified as divine punishments for the sin of Adam and Eve, in which all their children shared.[356] Additional punishments were imposed in retribution for individual sins, not all of which were intended to correct and purify.[357] Unrepentant sinners would be punished finally by alienation from God and by bodily pain in hell.[358] He suggested that the hardships of penitential practices could serve to replace and thus turn aside the punishments which would otherwise be imposed by divine justice.[359]

Because of his understanding of the operation of the power of forgiveness, Augustine stressed those manifestations of repentance that reunited the sinner to the church community and strengthened the bonds of union within the congregation. As has already been noted in describing daily repentance, the most important means of petitioning God for forgiveness was to forgive others; God would not forgive those who were themselves unforgiving.[360] Indeed, Christians were not only to forgive when asked but to seek reconciliation through rebuke of those who harmed them and prayer for their conversion.[361] Weeping and groaning were also mentioned, though not with the frequency and detail found in the writings of Tertullian and Cyprian.[362] Instead, Augustine stressed almsgiving, broadly interpreted to include all the works of charity: feeding the hungry, giving drink to the thirsty, clothing the naked, extending hospitality to the stranger and shelter to the fugitive, visiting the sick and imprisoned, ransoming captives, guiding the wanderer, advising the perplexed, and comforting the sorrowful. "Charity," he was fond of quoting from 1 Peter 4:8, "covers a multitude of sins," by removing rather than hiding them.[363] The practice of love of neighbor, through forgiveness and care, was the most effective means of eradicating sin and winning the forgiveness of God.

The community was also called upon to support the penitents. The teach-

354. Aug. *Psal.* 140.15.

355. Aug. *Serm.* 352.3.8; *Psal.* 101.2.3; *Eu. Io.* 22.7.

356. Aug. *Psal.* 37.26; 50.10; *Serm. Dolb.* 21(159B).7-8.

357. Aug. *Ciu.* 21.13.

358. Aug. *Ciu.* 21.9-11; *Serm.* 75.8.9; 148.2; 171.5; *Psal.* 52.4; 57.17; 88.2.1.

359. Aug. *Serm. Dolb.* 8(29B).1-4; *Psal.* 42.8.

360. Aug. *Serm.* 56.9.13–13.17; 57.12.12; 59.4.7; *Enchir.* 19.71, 74. This did not, however, provide a license to continue sinning (*Ciu.* 21.21-22, 27).

361. Aug. *Serm.* 56.9.13–13.17; 83.7.8; 90.9-10; 386.1-2.

362. Aug. *Ep.* 153.3.7.

363. Aug. *Ep. Io.* 5.1-3; *Psal.* 31.2.9; *Bapt.* 1.18.27; 6.24.45; *Gaud.* 1.12.13; 1.39.54; *Cresc.* 2.12.15; 4.11.13; *Ep.* 108.2.5, 3.9, 5.15; 185.10.43, 45.

ing of Christ and the practice of Paul both indicated that the faithful should be concerned for the salvation of their sinful fellows, praying for their conversion and forgiveness.[364] On one occasion, Augustine called his congregation's attention to the conversion of an astrologer who had renounced his profession and presented his books for burning. He was to be welcomed, congratulated, and supported in his good purpose.[365] On a less happy occasion, he remonstrated with the people for refusing to accept a Donatist whom they suspected of converting only to protect his property from imperial sanctions.[366] Whatever his unworthy motives, Augustine insisted, the man might eventually have been brought round. As a consequence of their rejection, he complained, the word spread throughout the city and region that Caecilianists were unwilling to welcome schismatic converts.[367]

## The Necessity of the Ritual of Reconciliation

Once a Christian had acknowledged and repented sin, the bishop was sought for the process of loosening the bonds of guilt through the ritual of reconciliation.[368] The necessity of submitting to this ritual was not a disputed question for Augustine; he treated it much like the ritual of baptism, which was necessary to forgive sins and give access to the eucharistic communion. The church's power of binding and loosening both on earth and in heaven meant that excommunicated sinners should be reconciled before death.[369] Ordinarily, then, Christians were not allowed to die outside the church's unity of peace, and reconciliation was extended to dying penitents even if they had not completed their satisfactory works.[370] Augustine urged that the clergy must not take flight in time of distress and warfare because this would thereby deprive their people of the opportunity for being admitted to penance and being reconciled.[371]

Augustine did not, however, regard the completion of the ritual of reconciliation and readmission to eucharistic communion as essential to salvation, as Cyprian and other third-century Christians seem to have done. He recognized exceptions. He explored the pastoral implications of the church's rule that public penance and reconciliation could be granted only once after baptism. What

364. Aug. *Parm.* 3.1.3; *Ep.* 153.3.6; *Fid. et op.* 3.3; *Serm. Dom.* 1.20.65.

365. Aug. *Psal.* 61.23.

366. *C.Th.* 16.5.17 (a. 389) prevented the passing of property by inheritance. *C.Th.* 16.5.21 (a. 392) and 16.2.29 (a. 395) threatened the confiscation of any property on which a cleric had been ordained for a deviant form of Christianity.

367. Aug. *Serm.* 296.15.

368. Aug. *Serm.* 352.3.8; *Psal.* 101.2.3; *Eu. Io.* 22.7.

369. Aug. *Eu. Io.* 50.12.

370. *Adult.* 1.28.35.

371. Aug. *Ep.* 228.8.

was the bishop to say to a person who fell a second time, into the same or a different sin? That the sinner continued to enjoy earthly life and its blessings could be interpreted as a sign that God was patient and allowing time for repentance. Recognizing that he could not fail to urge the sinner to repent and that perseverance in penance required the expectation of winning forgiveness, Augustine suggested that God might forgive even when the church could or would not reconcile. He recognized that the sinner could not be formally enrolled as a public penitent, though he did not exclude the support and guidance of the bishop for a regimen of private penance. Since reconciliation would not be given at the time of death, as it would be to one enrolled as a penitent in the church, the sinner would have to appeal to the mercy of God, with the prayers of the church but not its communion.[372] The mercy of Christ towards sinners gave these penitents reason to hope that their prayers and works would be successful.

Augustine made a similar argument for the salvation of Christians who were unjustly excommunicated by their bishops. As long as their intention joined them to the unity of the church in love, they would not be lost.[373] A correspondent complained that one of Augustine's colleagues had unjustly excommunicated him, his family, and his entire household. Explaining that only the local bishop had the authority to lift the excommunication, Augustine advised the man to submit to penance and thereby regain the communion. At the same time, Augustine wrote to the bishop, urging that he had acted rashly against the man, and beyond any scriptural warrant in excommunicating the entire household.[374]

Donatist bishops who entered Caecilianist communion were allowed to retain their offices and thus were not subjected to the penitential ritual, which would have disqualified them from serving as clergy. In these instances, Augustine explained, the greater good of the church's unity took precedence over the good that the individual might attain by accepting the public humiliation.[375] The prayers of the two congregations, now united in charity, would certainly win the forgiveness of their bishop's sin of schism.[376] Thus, these clerics could be saved without having submitted to the ritual of reconciliation.

In his interpretation of Christ's raising of Lazarus as a figure of the repentance and forgiveness of a person guilty of grave or sustained sin, Augustine indicated the reasoning that supported these judgments. Lazarus had been called back to life by Christ and actually left the tomb; only then were the disciples commanded to unwrap the grave clothes that bound him so he could move freely. Augustine thereby distinguished Christ's gracious gift, which moved a

372. Aug. *Ep.* 153.3.7.
373. Aug. *Bapt.* 1.17.26.
374. Aug. *Ep.* 250.1-2; *Ep. Divj.* 1*.
375. Aug. *Ep.* 185.10.44-47.
376. *Bru. Hipp.* 37.

sinner to recognize, confess, and repent a sin, from the following action of the ministers of the church, which then allowed the penitent to rejoin the congregation. In the case of grave sin, a person must submit to the church for the loosening of the bonds of guilt. Augustine did not attribute to the ritual of penance, however, the conversion and renewal symbolized by the resurrection of Lazarus and his coming forth from the tomb by the grace of Christ.[377]

Thus, while Augustine believed that the ritual of reconciliation was necessary for loosening the bonds of sin and ecclesiastical excommunication, he recognized that God's grace could not be restricted in individual cases by church practices adopted for the good of the majority or restrained by clerical ineptitude. Forgiveness and salvation depended upon the gift of charity that joined a penitent into the unity of the church; a person who rejected that unity by refusing to undergo penance thereby abandoned its saving love; one who was involuntarily or even unjustly excluded from eucharistic participation might actually remain a member of the communion of love and share the true church's salvation. One will here recognize a parallel to the relation between the grace and ritual of baptism.

### The Power to Forgive and the Efficacy of Penance

Tertullian and Cyprian both began their consideration of the efficacy of the church's power to forgive sins in conflicts over the rituals of penance and reconciliation. Cyprian was then required by a second controversy over the efficacy of baptism to extend his explanation of the origin, transmission, and exercise of that power in the rituals of public penance. In contrast, Augustine began by dealing with the sacrament of baptism in the context of the Donatist controversy over the theology inherited from Cyprian. His explanation of the process of the forgiveness of post-baptismal sins is found in his sermons to the people more than in his controversial works. As a consequence, he tended to understand the mutual forgiveness of Christians as the regular and standard method of forgiveness. The church's public ritual of reconciliation was understood as a special form of this private and informal process, an extraordinary instance in which the entire congregation had to call the sinner to account for an offense that questioned the nature of the church itself. Rebuke, forgiveness, and reconciliation could not be left to the discretion of the individuals directly harmed.

In contrast to both Tertullian (in his late works) and to Cyprian, Augustine understood that the power of the keys had been given to Peter neither for a role peculiar to him as an individual nor as a representative of the entire episcopal college. For Augustine, Peter was a symbol of the whole church, or rather of

377. Aug. *Eu. Io.* 49.24; *Psal.* 101.2.3; *Serm.* 98.6; 295.2.2; 352.3.8.

the true Christians gathered within it.[378] The power of forgiveness he received was actually conferred upon the unified communion of the church. Because he identified the power to forgive with the gift of charity, he agreed with Cyprian, who insisted that it belonged only to the unity of the church and could not be exercised in schism.[379] Augustine refused to read Matthew 16:19 in the isolation that characterized Tertullian's treatment of Peter's role. Like Cyprian, he linked that text to John 20:22-23.[380] Unlike Cyprian, who applied that text narrowly to the Twelve as establishing the college of bishops, Augustine more carefully followed the wording of the Gospel of John in explaining that the power had been given to all the disciples of Jesus.[381] In a move that may have been guided by Tertullian's work, Augustine observed that Matthew 18:18 conferred that same power of binding and loosening on all Christians in their seeking and offering pardon.[382] By identifying the power of forgiving received from the Holy Spirit with the gift of love or charity, he was able to specify it as the common possession of all the faithful within the visible unity of the church, collectively referred to as the society of saints.[383]

By interpreting charity as the presence and effect of the Holy Spirit in the saints, Augustine was able to establish a crucial link between the intentional unity of the holy church and the power of sanctifying. When Christians sought and offered forgiveness among themselves, they were joined together in a love that won God's forgiveness of both the pardoner and the pardoned. Those who forgave others were themselves forgiven by God. This sanctifying power of love was exercised regularly in the mutual forgiveness of daily offenses. Charity was no less effective, Augustine insisted, in the actions that the bishop and other clergy performed as the leaders of the community, the rituals of baptism and reconciliation. When Christians repented a major post-baptismal sin within the unity of the universal communion, the prayers of the holy persons — the saints — won the forgiveness of that sin. Penitents received the Holy Spirit through the ritual, but by virtue of their intentional union with the society of saints.[384] This process was most dramatically illustrated in the acceptance of Donatist bishops as leaders of united congregations without using the formal ritual of reconciliation. Although these leaders had been guilty of the grave sin

378. Aug. *Eu. Io.* 50.12; *Serm.* 149.6.7; 232.3-4; 295.2.2; *Serm. Guelf.* 16(229N).2; *Serm. Lamb.* 3(229P).1, 4. Tertullian had taken the opposite position in *Pud.* 21.9-15. Augustine said the same of Peter's confessing for the whole church (*Serm.* 270.2; 295.3.3).

379. Aug. *Enchir.* 17.65.

380. Aug. *Serm.* 295.2.2.

381. Aug. *Bapt.* 5.21.29; *Eu. Io.* 121.4.

382. Aug. *Serm.* 99.9. For the parallels in Tertullian's *Paen.* 10.6 and *Pud.* 21.16-17, see above, pp. 298, 313.

383. Aug. *Serm.* 295.2.2; *Serm. Guelf.* 16(229N).2; *Eu. Io.* 121.4; *Bapt.* 1.11.15; 3.18.23; 5.21.29; 6.1.1, 3.5, 14.23.

384. Aug. *Bapt.* 5.21.29.

of schism and in some cases the crime of rebaptizing Caecilianist Christians, the prayers of the united congregations would win forgiveness and sanctification for their bishops.[385]

Augustine's identification of the Holy Spirit as the author of both the unity and the holiness of the church resulted in a coherent theory of repentance and reconciliation. All the forms of penance and forgiveness were focused on the practice of charity that overcame division and promoted unity within the church community. This thesis found a variety of applications. Forgiving others was the essential condition, even the necessary means, of receiving forgiveness.[386] The penitential works were focused on the care and service of neighbor.[387] The same process and power were operative in encounters among individuals and in the rituals of the community. Accusation of sin by the victim or the bishop, apology to an individual and confession to the assembly, pardon and reconciliation were worked out both among the members and before the congregation.[388] In all cases, the effect was achieved by the divine power of forgiveness through the charity that had been granted to the saints.[389] Whether it was realized between two individuals, between a public sinner and the assembled congregation, or even between a private sinner and the bishop, the process was essentially the same. The grace of repentance prepared the penitent to receive the Holy Spirit communicated through the saints by appropriate signs of reconciliation and reunion.

The distinction between the scope of the efficacy of the rituals of baptism and reconciliation, which had prevailed in the third and fourth centuries, could not be sustained in the light of this explanation. Unlike Tertullian, Augustine listed no crimes against nature which would not be forgiven by God. Unlike Cyprian, he and his colleagues did not hesitate to offer reconciliation even to apostates and others who sinned against God.[390] He identified the unforgivable sin against the Holy Spirit as a despising of the power of the church to forgive sins, resulting in a failure to seek and thus receive that forgiveness.[391] This change in penitential practice may have accompanied a gradual lowering of the moral expectations of the church, particularly after it was established as the religion of the empire. It was, however, fully justified and even required by Augustine's solution to the problem of the location and exercise of the power

---

385. *Bru. Hipp.* 37. The overseas bishops refused to sanction this procedure; the Africans acted on their own judgment.

386. Aug. *Serm.* 56.9.13–13.17; 59.4.7; 82.2.3; 114.1-5; 278.6.6, 10.10–14.14; *Serm. Wilm.* 2(179A).6-7.

387. Aug. *Serm.* 259.4.

388. Aug. *Serm.* 83.33–7.8; 114.1-5; 211.4; 386.1-2.

389. Aug. *Serm.* 295.5.5; 351.5.12; *Serm. Guelf.* 16(229N).2.

390. *Bru. Hipp.* 33. The same privilege was accorded to those who were connected with the theater.

391. Aug. *Serm.* 71.23.37; *Enchir.* 22.83.

of forgiveness within the church. That theory, moreover, set a higher standard of mutual care and forgiveness than had been acknowledged in the prior centuries, when sinners could be expelled rather than being corrected with patience and in hope.

Augustine's theory explained, moreover, why forgiveness could be extended to the repentant even when the ritual was omitted. As the victim who refused pardon could not bind the repentant offender,[392] so an outraged bishop could not effect the condemnation of a penitent whose excommunication he refused to lift,[393] nor did the church's withholding a second reconciliation for a post-baptismal sin prevent the salvation of a penitent.[394] Even when the ritual was withheld, the church, as the society of saints united in love, could mediate forgiveness and salvation. The penitent was saved by refusing to abandon the loving unity of the saints, even though its institutional structures or officers failed or refused to acknowledge that intentional bond by offering communion.

## Intercession of the Martyrs

Augustine acknowledged the privileged role of the martyrs in the final Judgment by Christ, as Cyprian had. The martyrs would serve as the advisors to Christ in the Judgment,[395] where they would judge both the humans who persecuted them and the demons who had instigated those attacks.[396] To the martyrs, Augustine added the apostles, including Paul,[397] and those servants of God who had sold their goods and given them to the poor (using Matt. 19:27-28).[398] Many more Christians would be gathered and approved at the right hand of Christ.[399]

Because the Caecilianist communion to which he belonged was not actively prosecuted by the Roman state during Augustine's ministry, he did not have to deal with the intercessory power of confessors in the way that Tertullian and Cyprian had. All the martyrs were safely dead and presumed to be in heaven; they could not write letters urging the bishop to readmit individual sinners to communion.[400]

392. Aug. *Serm.* 82.4.7.
393. Aug. *Bapt.* 1.17.26.
394. Aug. *Ep.* 153.3.7.
395. Aug. *Serm.* 303.2.
396. Aug. *Psal.* 110.8.
397. Aug. *Psal.* 90.1.9, using Matt. 19:27-28.
398. Aug. *Psal.* 49.8-10; 90.1.9; 112.9.
399. Aug. *Psal.* 112.9, 121.12.
400. A number of Catholic clergy were attacked and even killed by Donatists (Aug. *Ep.* 105.2.3; 134.2; *Cresc.* 3.42.46–43.47, 3.48.53). Augustine rarely referred to them as martyrs. *Ep.* 139.2, an appeal to commute the death sentence for the murderers, is an exception to that rule.

# Conclusion

Two important changes separate Cyprian's third-century penitential practice from that of the early fifth century, when Augustine served. First, the Donatist controversy required a reconsideration of Cyprian's thesis that the church's power of sanctification must be located in the office and person of the local bishop. Cyprian's explanation of sanctifying power had required that bishops be holy. When the African church could not settle the practical problems that arose from charges of episcopal failure during the Diocletian persecution, Cyprian's theology became a source of division rather than a basis for unity. The bishops whom Constantine gathered at Arles to judge the conflict between Donatus and Caecilian imposed practices which were incompatible with Cyprian's theology. Optatus and then Augustine eventually provided a new theological foundation to justify the Caecilianist communion's recognizing the ministry of unworthy bishops. Second, the Theodosian suppression of traditional religious practices and its imperial establishment of Catholic Christianity meant that the Caecilianists in Africa faced new challenges in defining the church's relationship to the institutions of imperial culture. The identity and the moral standards through which the church's holiness had been expressed and the disciplinary processes of maintaining it had to be reconsidered and adapted.

The challenges of the Donatist controversy are reflected in Augustine's practice and theory of penance for post-baptismal sins. Cyprian's distinction between the church's granting reconciliation and God's granting forgiveness was maintained, along with the limitation of full penance to once in a lifetime. Augustine agreed that God could withhold forgiveness even when the church reconciled a penitent, but he insisted that God might forgive — through the union of the saints — even a sinner whom the bishop declined to readmit to communion. He offered the same explanation for the efficacy of baptism and penance: the intercessory prayer of the saints was inspired by the Holy Spirit's gift of charity and mediated divine forgiveness. Those Christians intentionally joined into the union of love manifest in the church's universal communion were forgiven; those who rejected that love, outside or even inside the communion, thereby bound themselves in sin. Augustine's development not only explained why the rituals of baptism and reconciliation could address the same range of sins but demonstrated the fundamental unity between all the practices of penance, from the mutual forgiveness practiced daily by Christians through the full penance exercised only once in a lifetime before the assembled congregation. His emphasis on the sharing of charity also explained why sins could be loosened for those unwillingly outside and held bound for those only apparently inside the communion. It shifted the meaning of penitential practices, focusing them on integration into the community, without neglecting their role of satisfying God's justice. The bishop could reconcile sinners subject to full penance, but his more important role was to exhort sinners to repent of their sins and to forgive their fellows within the unity of the church.

The Theodosian establishment of Catholic Christianity brought the disciplinary procedures of the church into conflict with the judicial processes of the state. No longer could Christians be required to make public confession of sins that were also crimes. Only sinners whose crimes were already public and notorious could be involuntarily excommunicated by the bishops. Moreover, Christians had new and complex responsibilities for the institutions of the state, with consequent engagement in the judicial torture and executions, which many found so troubling. The immediate consequence was not only the delaying of baptism and penance until the end of life, but the restriction of public confession to sins already commonly known. The development of a system of private penance — confessing to the bishop in secret, undertaking penitential actions that did not reveal the particular sin involved, and receiving private reconciliation — not only protected the sinner from state action but allowed an expansion of the penitential practice itself. A greater range of serious sins could be confronted directly and privately by the bishop and the penitent; the private ritual might even have been repeated as needed. The loss came in the public identity of the church: congregants would not always know that sinners had been rebuked, had confessed, and were repenting. They could not identify themselves as a community of the pure and faithful — a title the Donatists may have claimed, albeit in a very restricted sense. Instead, they had to acknowledge that they formed a mixed body, just as individuals recognized themselves as sinners, in need of the forgiveness they offered. To be devout and holy, communally and individually, was not to be sinless and righteous, but both repentant and forgiving.

## GENERAL OBSERVATIONS

### Correlation of Archeological and Literary Evidence

#### PLACEMENT OF THE PENITENTS

The literary evidence for the ritual of penance indicates that the penitents were segregated from the community in the eucharistic celebration. The archeological remains, however, do not allow a further specification of their location.

Tertullian and Cyprian both indicated that sinners were introduced into the midst of the assembly to confess their sin and be enrolled as penitents. Tertullian described them afterwards as kneeling at the entrance of the assembly space, begging the faithful to intercede for their forgiveness. Cyprian addressed them in his preaching, at least to exhort those who had failed during the persecution to undertake and persevere in public repentance. Thus, the penitents seem to have been at the threshold or in the vestibule rather than outside the building and exposed to the curiosity of passersby in the street. At the end of their penance, they would again appear before the assembly to be readmitted to communion. Since no remains of third-century African churches (or Christian assembly spaces) survive, none of these locations can be determined. This evidence would seem to indicate, however, that the interior space was differentiated to segregate penitents during the assemblies. If the buildings used by Christians in the late second and early third centuries had been adapted from designs originally intended for domestic use, a series of rooms or spaces can be conceived that would have allowed the types of ritual action described by Tertullian and Cyprian.

The surviving footprints of church structures evincing fourth- and fifth-century practice — rather than later Byzantine revisions — do not seem to permit the rituals and location of penitents described in the third century. Some but not all of these basilica-style buildings have the necessary narthex or vestibule separated from both the public street and the interior assembly room in which the eucharist was celebrated (cf. fig. 103). These changes in architecture can be correlated with a shift in the status of penitents and the ritual itself. Augustine spoke of the penitents as present for the readings and sermons but leaving after a regular ritual of imposing hands in prayer. Many of the baptized seem to have spent much of their lives in this liminal state: enrolled as penitents but not actively seeking readmission to the eucharist. Others would have been permanently excluded for having sinned yet again after penance and reconciliation. The first type of penitents might have been treated somewhat like those enrolled indefinitely as catechumens. They would have considered themselves Christian and associated with a particular congregation, with the right to immediate reconciliation when threatened by death. The second retained an association with the congregation that assured them of its intercessory prayer for their forgiveness.

## Correlation of Theology and Practice

The holiness and purity necessary for the identity of the church was often at issue in conflicts over the forgiveness of post-baptismal sin and the readmission of sinners to the communion of the church. Shifts in the practice of penance, however, were also driven by changes in Christians' belief about the role of the church's communion in the process of salvation. Tertullian, Cyprian (at least initially), and Augustine judged that a person could be saved even if not allowed to participate in the eucharistic communion at the time of death. Many of their contemporaries did not trust this understanding and insisted that Christians undertaking penance eventually must be offered reconciliation, at least at the time of death. Although this view generally prevailed, Augustine modified it by insisting that once baptized, a sinner would be lost only through a failure to repent or a refusal to accept the ministry of the church. Even those permanently excluded from communion might remain attached to and under the care of the church.

### THE POWER TO FORGIVE SINS

The church's authority to forgive sins through the ritual of baptism was discussed in an earlier chapter. That power was not fully identified with the forgiveness of post-baptismal sins, however, until the time of Augustine. Until that time, bishops remained somewhat uncertain about the range of their authority to forgive serious sins committed after baptism, while being generally secure in the belief that all prior sins, no matter how heinous, were fully forgiven in the ritual of baptism. Because of this uncertainty about post-baptismal sins, conflicts arose early about the nature and limits of the power to forgive them.

Tertullian disputed an already established belief that martyrs and confessors had the power to win the forgiveness not only of their own post-baptismal sins but of the serious sins of other Christians. He criticized imprisoned confessors for promising liberation from guilt to penitents who had been excluded from the communion of the church even as these confessors were themselves struggling against trial and torture to secure their own salvation.

The Bishop of Carthage at the beginning of the second century claimed that in the power of binding and loosening, which Christ had conferred upon Peter, all bishops had been authorized to declare sins forgiven by God. Tertullian countered by distinguishing the divine power *(uirtus* or *imperium)* that had been delegated to the Prophets and Apostles from the agency *(ministerium)* that had been given to the bishops. The former had not only demonstrated their power by signs and wonders but had judged with both mercy and severity. The latter had a more limited authority that had been further restricted by the dictates of the Holy Spirit given through the New Prophecy. Concretely, Tertullian insisted that the church could no longer exercise the power or authority to forgive sins that had been committed against God or against a human being as the temple of God. Such sins could be repented, but only God could forgive them.

After the Decian persecution, Cyprian was faced with a claim that the martyrs could provide forgiveness for the sin of apostasy over which the bishop had no authority. He responded by asserting that the bishops had a limited but necessary role in the process of winning God's forgiveness for any post-baptismal sin. The bishop could not presume to loosen what Christ had threatened to hold bound; nor could he inspect the dispositions of the sinners' hearts. Judging the sinners' repentance on the basis of their works of satisfaction, however, the bishop could allow the penitents to return to the communion of the church. They would then be presented, with the intercessory prayers of the church, to

Christ for judgment. Anyone who refused to submit to the bishop's judgment would be excluded from the communion that delimited the church and would be rejected by Christ. Those who had placed their full trust in the intercession of the martyrs surely would be disappointed.

Cyprian also argued, in much the way that Tertullian's bishop had, that Christ had indeed empowered the bishops as a body to forgive sins. He cited not only the commissioning of Peter but the giving of the Holy Spirit to the disciples on the evening of the Resurrection. At the same time, the shift in the laity's appreciation of the role of the church's communion as providing the only access to the salvation of Christ was a crucial element in the development of an understanding of the power of the church and its officers to play a limited but necessary role in the process of forgiving post-baptismal sin.

Augustine's conflict with the Donatists was primarily over the qualifications of the bishop to exercise the church's power to forgive sins through the ritual of baptism. Unlike his predecessors, he focused on the daily repentance and pardoning that Christians practiced among themselves. This practice, which was itself essential for salvation but involved neither ritual nor clerical intervention, became the foundation of a unified theory of forgiveness that could be applied to the rituals of both baptism and penance, even when the clergy were not available.

What Tertullian had called the *uirtus* or *imperium,* and what Cyprian had claimed as the power of the Holy Spirit upon the Apostles, Augustine identified as the gift of charity poured out in the hearts of all the faithful. The saints within the church interceded for the forgiveness of sins; the sincere penitents were joined into their unity and through them received the gift of charity. Charity itself purified the heart and won divine forgiveness. The exercise of this power could be symbolized by the informal forgiveness of personal injuries among members of the congregation, by the baptismal washing, and by the bishop's imposition of hands that returned the penitent to communion. The power could work, moreover, even when the bishop and congregation failed or refused to symbolize its efficacy. This occurred with schismatic clergy who could not be subjected to formal penance, with the penitents who had sinned a second time after baptism and were thus refused admission to penance and reconciliation, with the faithful unjustly excommunicated by their bishop, and with repentant Christians who were refused the forgiveness sought from a fellow Christian.

Thus the forgiveness of sins depended upon the power given to the church as a whole and the connection of the sinner to the unity of the saints through the gift of charity. The power of binding and loosening exercised by the bishop in baptism and penance was not of itself adequate to forgive sins in the absence of repentance. The penitent could not, however, gain access to forgiveness while refusing to submit to and seek union with the church through these rituals.

Augustine's explanation of the power to forgive and its exercise depended not so much upon a change in practice or ecclesial context as upon a new appropriation of the intercessory role that Tertullian assigned to the congregation and upon attention to the perennial process of mutual forgiveness among Christians.

## SINS THE CHURCH COULD NOT FORGIVE

The rule of permanent exclusion for sins committed against God — idolatry, adultery, and murder — was already under challenge at the beginning of the third century. The Bishop of Carthage proposed to readmit adulterers to communion after appropriate penance, though not apostates and murderers.

The argument offered for the change — that penance could be sustained only if the peace of the church was promised — showed the growing belief that a person had to be participating in the eucharistic communion in order to attain the salvation of Christ. Opponents of the change argued that the sincerely repentant could indeed win forgiveness directly from God through a lifetime of satisfactory works. The church, however, had no jurisdiction over sins against God.

The confusion about acceptable forms of evasion and the massive defections during the Decian persecution required the reconsideration of the sin of apostasy. After first insisting that forgiveness could be received only from God, Cyprian promised to allow penitents to be reconciled just before death. The difficulties of administering this policy and the desire to strengthen the penitents in anticipation of renewed persecution moved the bishops to allow immediate reconciliation of those who had persevered in penitential works. They recognized that unless penitents were given hope of returning to communion before death, they would not sustain extended penance. Those who had fallen were, however, excluded from serving in clerical office, even after being reconciled.

After the Diocletian persecution, no restrictions were placed on the types of sins that might be forgiven through the ritual of penance. Although reconciliation was promised at the time of death to all formally enrolled penitents, they were warned that the effect of the ritual depended on the sincerity of their repentance. Formal repentance and reconciliation continued to disqualify a person from exercising clerical office.

The attempt to prevent certain types of sin by threatening permanent exclusion from the church's communion had proven impossible to implement. When the church refused to offer reconciliation, penitents tended to despair of salvation. The bishops prudently decided to promise reconciliation, at least at death, and let Christ himself judge the sinner. The only remaining restriction was imposed on those who sinned seriously after once having been reconciled. They could not be enrolled as penitents again and were not promised a second reconciliation. This seems to have been a disciplinary decision: no argument was presented that purported to explain that penance, like baptism, could be received only once. Thus, Augustine urged the permanently excommunicated sinners to continue in private penance in hope of receiving from God the forgiveness that the church would not ritualize.

## RITUALIZING REPENTANCE

In the surviving writings on repentance for post-baptismal sin, most attention is devoted to determining the sins that could and could not be addressed through the rituals of excommunication, *exomologesis,* and reconciliation. In two instances, however, these rituals were seldom used. The New Prophecy movement insisted that the Paraclete had forbidden their use lest they encourage sin. Once the empire had become functionally Christian toward the end of the fourth century, crimes that were subject to the imperial judiciary were not publicly confessed unless their perpetrators' guilt was already notorious. These two developments allowed the church to develop different forms of penitential practice that did not engage the full assembly of the congregation. Because the public ritual of reconciliation could be performed only once in the lifetime of a Christian, it was reserved for the most serious and unusual sins; all other significant sins were left to private repentance. When alternate forms of supervised penance were developed, they may not have been restricted to a single use. This change may have allowed the bishop to engage a broader range of sins which were more serious than the inevitable failings of daily life.

Tertullian listed a wide range of sins as subject to practices of penance employed by the devotees of the New Prophecy. Many of these sins can be recognized as among the failings of human weakness rather than significant violations of the baptismal commitment. The extension of a presumably less formal ritual to such sins implies that the community could intervene many times to accuse and forgive a member.

At the end of the Decian persecution, Cyprian noted that some had confessed to having sinned in intention though not in action: they had determined to perform the idolatrous rituals if they had been required to do so. He urged them to repent of that sin but did not require that they submit to the regimen of excommunication and satisfaction. His colleagues made a somewhat similar decision for those who had evaded the challenge by deception. They seem to have judged that the one ritual of penance at their disposal was too harsh for this sin.

By Augustine's time, the bishops of Africa had decided that a sin should not be publicly confessed if it was also an imperial crime. An alternate ritual was developed in which the sinner confessed privately to the bishop, undertook penitential works under his supervision, was eventually reconciled, and was returned to communion. Augustine seems to have used this process in other instances, when penitents were unwilling to make public acknowledgment of their sins but would repent in private. He advised his congregation that he was able to confront and correct in private many who would have abandoned the church in response to a public rebuke. The very rigor of public penance made it, in the judgment of the bishops, an inappropriate and ineffective instrument for addressing certain sins and sinners. Although he was prepared to make such adaptations, Augustine insisted that the sinner's submission to the church, as represented by the bishop, was essential to receiving God's forgiveness.

The African church apparently recognized that it required some flexibility in the rituals of penance and eventually developed an understanding of its power and authority to forgive that justified its actions. Augustine and his colleagues realized that repentance, like conversion, was a gratuitous divine gift. It was mediated by the church and, like the sanctification of baptism, could not be received and retained in opposition to the unity of the church. Its efficacy, however, could not be frustrated by the clergy's refusal to lift an excommunication and grant reconciliation, any more than it could by the refusal of an offended party to forgive a repentant offender.

### THE RITUALS OF RECONCILIATION

Although the rituals of public acknowledgment of sin, display of repentance by satisfactory works, and reintegration of the penitent into the eucharistic fellowship seem to have been structurally similar in the third through the fifth century, the symbolism of the ritual had changed. In his account of the rite, which antedated his commitment to the New Prophecy, Tertullian described the penitent seeking the intercession of the faithful for the forgiveness of sins. Because the community was identified with Christ, its prayers could be effective. Later he would reject explicitly the bishop's claim to exercise a power of forgiveness by virtue of his office. Cyprian, in contrast, described the ritual as a judicial procedure in which the bishop, serving as a magistrate chosen by Christ to act until his return, sought the advice of the congregation before issuing a judgment that would bind or loosen the restrictions on the penitent. Cyprian believed that the bishop's decision to loosen the bonds of sin was necessary, although Christ would review and either affirm or reverse it in the Judgment.

Augustine seems to have considered the mutual apology and forgiveness practiced by the members of the congregation — as specified in Matthew 18:15-20 — the model for the more formal ritual, which was necessary when the sin attacked the holiness of the church itself and thus engaged the whole community. Although the ritual specified the imposition of the bishop's hands as the decisive prayer for forgiveness, Augustine applied the same theory to penance as he did to baptism. The prayers of the faithful saints within the church made the ritual effective and won the forgiveness by welcoming the penitent into the union of love that formed the Body of Christ within the visible community.

## Transition

The three rituals that have been treated to this point are shown to be closely connected. Changes in the practices of one of them tended to require a new understanding and even a change in practice of the other two. Penance, like baptism, was focused on the danger of sin, which might destroy the holiness and efficacy of the eucharistic celebration. A fourth practice, the choice and ordination of leaders, was also modified by changes in these three. Community leaders were charged with performing the three rituals. Debates over the rituals eventually required the further specification of the status and qualifications of those clergy who would perform them. From this a fourth sacramental ritual was identified, which was assigned a permanent effect on its recipient's relation to God and the church: ordination.

CHAPTER 8

# Leadership: The Clergy and the Sacrament of Orders

························································································································

## INTRODUCTION

The understanding of the status of leadership of the Christian church evolved significantly in Africa. Tertullian asserted that all baptized male Christians shared the religious power necessary to govern the congregation and lead its worship. Individuals were chosen for office on the basis of their character and talents; roles were distinguished among Christians to maintain good order within the church.

Cyprian developed a significantly different understanding of the role of the clergy in the church. Through their selection and ordination, the bishops were authorized to act in the place of Christ, endowed with powers of sanctification not generally shared in the community. The bishops received these powers through their induction — by ordination — into the worldwide communion of bishops and then used them for sanctifying their people. Their standing before God and among their fellow bishops was essential to their ministry. The local bishop delegated the exercise of this authority and power to his presbyters and deacons.

At the beginning of the fourth century, attempts to enforce Cyprian's understanding of the bishop's status led to a major division within the African church, the Donatist schism. Both parties to the dispute had modified the third-century theory, but the Caecilianist bishops were required by their overseas colleagues to accept some of the very practices that Cyprian and his colleagues had rejected. Only late in the fourth century and early in the fifth century did the Donatist Parmenian of Carthage and the Caecilianists Optatus of Milevis and Augustine of Hippo attempt to develop the theoretical foundations that would enable their competing communions to respond more creatively, if not successfully, to the schism. Augustine, in particular, recovered much of Tertullian's perspective in his modifications of Cyprian.

At the beginning of the fifth century, the Catholic bishops also developed a system of deliberative meetings, which produced a coherent body of legislation to guide the life of their congregations and the ministry of their clergy.

## THE CLERGY IN TERTULLIAN'S TIME

Tertullian did not claim to be among the clergy of the church of Carthage, and his writings do not assert any essential difference between the clergy and the laity. Unlike later writers, and even some of his contemporaries, he rejected the bishop's claims for special powers and understood the distinction of clergy from laity as functional and necessary primarily for maintaining order and unity within the community.

### Clerical Ranks

On a number of occasions, Tertullian listed the three ranks of the clerical order of the church: bishop, presbyter, and deacon. In most cases, the three were named together,[1] though the bishop and the deacon were mentioned in one case without reference to the office of presbyter.[2]

The bishop was clearly the leader of the community with the responsibility of admitting members through baptism,[3] leading them in communal prayer and eucharistic offering,[4] excluding[5] and readmitting through reconciliation[6] those who sinned. The bishop also guided the common life of the congregation in such matters as fasting.[7] His may have been the primary teaching office as well, since Tertullian appealed to the succession of bishops in the churches deriving from the Apostles as a guarantee of the preservation of true doctrine and right interpretation of scripture.[8]

The presbyter and the deacon were in subordinate ranks; they owed deference and obedience to the bishop. They could baptize by delegation of the bishop; otherwise they could do so only in emergency, a time when any Christian was obligated to act.[9] The presbyters *(seniores)* were among the leaders of

---

1. Tert. *Praescr.* 41.8; *Bapt.* 17.1; *Fug.* 11.1; *Mon.* 11.1.
2. Tert. *Praescr.* 3.5.
3. Tert. *Bapt.* 17.1.
4. Tert. *Cor.* 3.3; *Bapt.* 17.2-3.
5. Tert. *Pud.* 14.16.
6. Tert. *Pud.* 18.18; see also *Paen.* 10.8 and *Pud.* 1.6; 13.7; 21.16-17.
7. Tert. *Ieiun.* 13.3.
8. Tert. *Praescr.* 32.1; *Marc.* 4.5.1-2.
9. Tert. *Bapt.* 17.1.

the community, chosen for their worthy character.[10] They were singled out as persons to whom the petitions of the penitents for intercessory prayer were addressed, but they do not seem to have been directly engaged in supervising the penitential process and performing the reconciliation ritual.[11] Tertullian also mentioned their ministry in offering prayers for the dead prior to burial.[12] The role of the presbyters in the congregation's celebration of the eucharist is not explicit in Tertullian's writings. They may have been the leaders from whom the bread and wine were received in the common worship.[13] Their role in the evening love feasts,[14] which are presumed to have served subgroups of the community in multiple locations simultaneously, was mentioned only indirectly: the leaders were given double portions at those meals.[15]

## Clerical Life

In contrast to the practice of the heretics, Tertullian asserted, the orders of the true church were stable and regular. A person assigned to one rank did not take over the office of another.[16] Clerics were not to be converts from heresy and should be communicants of long standing.[17] They were held in honor and, as noted, given double portions at community banquets.[18] Bishops, presbyters, and deacons all were required to submit to the discipline of monogamy: they could be married only once after baptism. Upon the death of a spouse, they were required to remain widowers. If they married again, they were to be removed from office, though Tertullian implied that this rule was not always obeyed or enforced. (He argued that it should be applied to all Christians.)[19] Neither were those in clerical orders to be engaged in business that would compromise their suitability for leadership in the church.[20] Although Tertullian did not specify this second restriction with the same care as he did that of monogamy, the con-

---

10. Tert. *Apol.* 39.5 (CCSL 1:150.19-20). In this section the general assembly of the congregation is being described, so that the term *senior* seems to refer to the clerical officer rather than, as often later, a lay leader, as might be expected when he comes to discuss the *cena* at *Apol.* 39.16.

11. Tert. *Paen.* 10.8.

12. Tert. *An.* 51.6 recounts the marvel of a holy widow's dead hands moving from her sides up into the gesture of petition as soon as the presbyter began to pray.

13. Tertullian used a form of the same word, "praesidere," for those who administered the eucharist as he did for the leaders of the community: *Apol.* 39.5; *Cor.* 3.3. In both cases, plural forms of the nouns and verbs are used, indicating that the roles were not restricted to the bishop.

14. Tert. *Apol.* 39.16-19.

15. Tert. *Ieiun.* 17.4.

16. In contrast to the heretics: Tert. *Praescr.* 41.8.

17. Tert. *Praescr.* 41.6.

18. Tert. *Ieiun.* 17.4, reported with disapproval.

19. Tert. *Cast.* 7.2-6; *Mon.* 11.1, 4; 12.1-2.

20. Tert. *Praescr.* 41.6, again by contrast to the heretics.

cern seems to have been with occupations that might require or risk indirect contact with idolatry. Holding public office, for example, might involve cooperating, even if only indirectly, in idolatrous practices.[21] Trading — as distinguished from farming — not only gave free rein to covetousness, but it often required contact with the materials used in the sacrifices and other rituals of the polytheist idolaters. Such, he contended, was forbidden to all Christians.[22]

## Clergy as Governing Officers

Even in the apostolic age, Tertullian asserted, the congregations were organized by the distinction of clergy and people, and by the three ranks of the clerical order. He did not, however, identify the Twelve as bishops.[23] The difference between the *ordo* and the *plebs* was for the good order and administration of the church; it did not reflect special powers belonging only to the clergy. Instead, Tertullian insisted that all Christians were fundamentally equal in being made priests by God, and all were to follow the same priestly discipline. For peace and good order, the laity were not to infringe on the sacramental ministry of the clergy in meetings of the congregation. When the faithful were alone or in a small group, however, any (male) Christian could perform the functions of the priesthood. Tertullian based this assertion on two principles: (1) a person could give whatever had been received; and (2) the sacraments belonged to God, who intended that they be available at all times. Thus every member of the community had the right of priesthood. Each might offer prayer or the eucharist in private and must be prepared to confer baptism in an emergency.[24] He explicitly restricted the application of these principles to male Christians. Women could not baptize, offer the eucharist, teach, lead the community in prayer, or exercise any priestly office.[25] Although Tertullian used this principle of universal male priesthood as an argument for the extension of the discipline of monogamy to the entire community, the position could not have been developed for that purpose alone: it had to have been independently accepted — at least by some portion of the congregation — to offer support for his contention that all were subject to the rule of one marriage.[26] When he challenged a bishop who claimed the

21. Tert. *Pud.* 7.15.
22. Tert. *Idol.* 11.8.
23. Tert. *Praescr.* 32.1; *Marc.* 4.5.1-2.
24. Tert. *Bapt.* 17.1-3. The text of *Bapt.* 17.3 is somewhat obscure. This interpretation follows Evans's construal: see *Tertullian: de Baptismo Liber, Homily on Baptism,* ed. and trans. Ernest Evans (London: SPCK, 1964), 34-36. *Cast.* 7.3-6 is much clearer: the laity must follow priestly discipline because they must perform priestly functions when necessary. For the restriction of communal performance, see also *Praescr.* 41.8.
25. Tert. *Virg.* 9.1.
26. Tert. *Mon.* 12.2.

power to forgive the sins of adultery and fornication, he conceded that the church itself held the power to forgive sins but asserted that this was to be exercised through the spiritual persons rather than being the prerogative of a particular office or role, such as bishop, confessor, or even martyr.[27] Tertullian seems to have believed that the sacramental powers were conferred upon the church itself and thus belonged to all the faithful, though they should be exercised in general assemblies only by properly designated males. In practice, therefore, this would have restricted nonclerical Christians to performing baptism in emergency and presiding at prayer or eucharist only in household gatherings.

Tertullian's views may not have been shared by the majority of his fellow Christians in Carthage. His argument that all the baptized were subject to the discipline of monogamy because they all shared the priesthood had to be qualified to meet an anticipated objection. Someone might respond that the laity could perform priestly functions only in emergency and the discipline of monogamy was not required of them. Tertullian then added a second argument for lay monogamy: if the laity were not monogamous, where would candidates for the clerical order be found?[28] This may indicate that his audience regarded the clergy as subject to this discipline of single marriage specifically because they were sanctified for the sacramental ministry.[29] Similarly, the bishop with whom Tertullian disagreed on the forgiveness of deadly sins seems to have claimed that the power given to Peter had been attached to the episcopal office rather than bestowed on the church as a whole.[30] Thus, his community may have attributed a special power and status to the clergy that was not shared by the laity.

In other areas, however, Tertullian reflected the general practice of the congregation in assigning sacred functions to the laity. Male Christians performed exorcisms[31] and cures;[32] they taught and defended the faith.[33] The office of reader may not yet have been among the clerical roles at this time.[34] The only function that Tertullian seemed to allow to women was seeking revelations.[35] The virgins and widows were mentioned as occupying a special place of honor among the laity but were not assigned sacral functions.[36] As long as the Christian communities in Africa were still meeting in homes for the evening love

27. Tert. *Pud.* 21.16-17; 22.
28. Tert. *Cast.* 7.6; *Mon.* 11.4, 12.1.
29. Tert. *Cast.* 7.5-6.
30. Tert. *Pud.* 21.9.
31. Tert. *Spec.* 29.3; *Idol.* 11.8; *Praescr.* 41.5.
32. Tert. *Spec.* 29.3; *Praescr.* 41.5.
33. Tert. *Praescr.* 41.5 — as he did himself. He also mentioned the *doctores* in *Praescr.* 3.5.
34. Tert. *Praescr.* 41.8 contrasts the presbyter and the reader in a series in which at least one if not both of the other members express a contrast between clergy and laity.
35. Tert. *Spec.* 29.3, by contrast with *Praescr.* 41.5, where he failed to object to women in heretical communions seeking revelations. As an adherent of the New Prophecy, he did recognize the revelations given to female prophets in his own community: *An.* 9.4; *Virg.* 17.3.
36. Tert. *Praescr.* 3.2; *Mon.* 11.1; *Pud.* 13.7.

feast, a significant minority of the membership might have exercised some office, at least in these small assemblies.

## Status of Martyrs and Confessors

The martyrs constituted a special class within the Christian church even in Tertullian's time. The term was used for all who suffered for public witness to Christ, even if they did not lose their lives in the process.[37] Thus, martyrs could be found living within the community after winning their victories. While confessing the faith might have been regarded as a particular qualification for selection as a cleric, it did not itself confer that rank in Africa.[38] The exercise of powers assigned to the martyrs — particularly in giving the peace of the church to sinners — could infringe on the responsibilities of the clergy and upset the good order of the local church. In his early exhortation to the martyrs incarcerated in Carthage, Tertullian observed that they were acting under the influence of the Holy Spirit, without whose power they would not have gained the status of public witnesses. They should be careful, therefore, to follow the guidance of the Spirit and, in particular, to preserve peace and harmony among themselves. Sinners who had lost the peace of the church would seek to recover it from these confessors.[39] Toward the end of his career, however, Tertullian contradicted both points. He did not allow that the martyrs were filled with the Spirit in the way that Israelite prophets and Christian apostles had been; they could not therefore claim the power to forgive sins. Nor could anyone still surrounded by the temptations of earthly life enjoy such security in their own fidelity as to promise the Spirit's forgiveness to someone else. The martyrs would be fortunate to win their own salvation by giving their lives for Christ; they should not burden themselves with the sins of others.[40] If Tertullian's descriptions of the claims made for the martyrs reflected actual practice, they would have constituted a serious challenge to the authority of the bishop. The surviving evidence does not indicate the severity of the problem. Such a conflict would, however, erupt into open schism in the middle of the century, as has been seen in the discussion of penance.[41]

37. The term is used broadly in *Ad martyras,* and especially in *Pud.* 22.1-2.

38. Tert. *Val.* 4.1. *Trad. apos.* 10 would assert that all who confessed Christ thereby attained clerical status and need not even be ordained; see *The Treatise on the Apostolic Tradition of St. Hippolytus of Rome, Bishop and Martyr [Apostolikē Paradosis],* trans. Gregory Dix (London: SPCK, 1937), 39-40. Alistair Steward-Sykes interprets this presbyterate as an honor rather than an office in his translation and commentary: *Hippolytus: On the Apostolic Tradition,* trans. Alistair Stewart-Sykes (Crestwood, N.Y.: St. Vladimir's Seminary Press, 2001), 92-93.

39. Tert. *Mart.* 1.3, 6.

40. Tert. *Pud.* 22.

41. See the discussion of the conflict between bishops and martyrs in the time of Cyprian, pp. 324-26.

## Spiritual Prophets

Tertullian also named the prophets as a special group within the church who were not among the clergy. Careful study of the oracles that are reported by Tertullian and in the surviving Montanist writings indicate that these prophets often worked by developing and expanding verses of scripture to make them applicable to the questions currently faced by the church.[42] The oracle to which Tertullian appealed — "The church can indeed forgive sins, but I will not do it, lest others sin" — seems to be an elaboration of the texts conferring this power on Peter, the church, and the disciples in Matthew (16:18-19; 18:15-20) and John (20:22-23). Other oracles came in the form of visions experienced during the liturgy; these were recounted, written down, and tested by a group within the congregation. Tertullian himself had a significant role in this process, to which he only alludes.[43] In defending these revelations, he proposed rules by which their authenticity could be judged: they should be doctrinally orthodox; they should tighten rather than relax discipline; and they should be concordant with the scriptures.[44]

## Lay Elders

Finally, Tertullian may be read as indicating a role for lay elders, distinct from the clerical order. The single statement referring to leadership in the general assemblies of the community is, however, ambiguous at best.[45] Tertullian also alluded to a special role for those in the community who had the literary skills to record and catalog visions and prophecies.[46] In *The Passion of Perpetua and Felicity,* however, the *seniores* exercise a role in the heavenly liturgy that might parallel that in the earthly one. They are, moreover, distinguished from the *presbyteri*.[47] The distinction between clergy and laity was still being developed,

---

42. Dennis Groh, "Utterance and Exegesis: Biblical Interpretation in the Montanist Crisis," in *The Living Text: Essays in Honor of Ernest W. Saunders,* ed. Robert Jewett and Dennis Groh (Lanham, Md.: University Press of America, 1985), 73-95.

43. Thus Tert. *An.* 9.4 and *Virg.* 17.3. See William Tabbernee, "To Pardon or Not to Pardon? North African Montanism and the Forgiveness of Sins," in *Studia Patristica,* ed. Maurice Frank Wiles, Edward Yarnold, and Paul M. Parvis (Leuven: Peeters, 2001), 36:379-81.

44. Thus in the defense of the rule of monogamy, Tert. *Mon.* 2.2-4.

45. The statement in Tert. *Apol.* 39.5 may simply refer to the clergy: Praesident probati quique seniores, honorem istum non pretio, sed testimonio adepti, neque enim pretio ulla res Dei constat (CCSL 1:150.19-21). See the discussion of Brent D. Shaw, "'Elders' in Christian Africa," in *Mélanges offerts en hommage au Révérend Père Étienne Gareau, Cahiers des études anciennes* 14 (1982):207-26 (Ottawa: Éditions de l'Université d'Ottawa, 1982), 209, and in n. 10 above.

46. Tert. *An.* 9.4; *Virg.* 17.3. See the discussion in Tabbernee, "To Pardon or Not to Pardon?," 380-81.

47. *Pas. Perp.* 12.4. The parallel to Rev. 4:8 is not exact. See the analysis in Shaw, "'Elders' in Christian Africa," 209-10.

---

particularly in the context of the smaller assemblies. Thus, some "leaders" of these communities may have been informally recognized rather than ritually authorized to act on their behalf.

## Conclusion

In Tertullian's view, the clergy were authorized by the congregation to act for it: they were assigned jurisdiction over the life of the church. They were not, however, the holders and conveyers of special powers that did not belong to every Christian. He did accord such a role to the spiritual persons within the church, particularly the devotees and practitioners of the New Prophecy. In both these judgments, however, he may have differed sharply from others — even the majority — of the Christians of Carthage. The general view may have regarded the bishops, presbyters, and deacons as endowed by God with distinctive powers and therefore subject to a corresponding discipline of separation or purity.

## THE CLERGY IN CYPRIAN'S TIME

Because he was himself a bishop and involved in conflicts between bishops in Africa, Spain, Gaul, and Rome, Cyprian's writings provide significant information on this office and its functioning in the third-century church. His letters provide incidental evidence for the roles of other members of the clergy.

## Clerical Offices

### SUBDEACONS, ACOLYTES, READERS, AND EXORCISTS

Cyprian employed the Greek term *hypodiaconus,* in contrast to the Latinized *subdeaconus* used by the Roman clergy in their correspondence.[48] The only responsibility specified for the six Carthaginians who held this office was carrying letters.[49] They, along with other clergy, were salaried by the church and must have had additional roles.[50]

---

48. Cypr. *Ep.* 8.1.1; 9.1.1 both refer to the same Crementius, who may have been a member of the Roman clergy.

49. Thus Optatus (*Ep.* 29.1.2; 35.1.1); Fortunatus (*Ep.* 36.1.1); Mettius (*Ep.* 45.4.3; 47.1.2); and Herennianus, who headed the mission to the confessors in the mines (*Ep.* 77.3.2; 78.1.1; 79.1.1). Philumenus and a second Fortunatus fled during the Decian persecution (*Ep.* 34.4.1).

50. Cypr. *Ep.* 34.4.2, referring to two subdeacons. The payment may have been in kind rather than in coin.

Acolytes shared the responsibility for episcopal correspondence,[51] but more regularly were charged by Cyprian during the Decian persecution with delivering funds or material assistance. One of the acolytes brought funds from Cyprian's place of refuge into Carthage for the support of the refugees and the poor.[52] During the Valerian persecution, Cyprian entrusted a subdeacon and three acolytes with letters and supplies for the confessors who had been condemned to the mines.[53] A total of six acolytes were named in Cyprian's writings, but no reference was made to their liturgical functions.[54] The acolytes also received a monthly stipend from the community.[55]

Readers *(lectores)* were charged with sounding out the texts of scripture (including the gospel) from the raised pulpit in the assembly[56] and with assisting the presbyters in the instruction of the catechumens.[57] Later evidence indicates that they may have been responsible for preserving the books themselves.[58] Readers were also used as carriers of episcopal correspondence, Saturus being ordained specifically for this responsibility.[59] In ordaining two confessors to the order of reader, Cyprian directed that they receive the stipend fixed for the presbyters.[60] Thus, readers themselves might not have received a regular salary. Clerical careers might often have begun with the reader's office, in which a person received basic training in literacy, which qualified the candidate for the higher offices of subdeacon, deacon, or presbyter.[61]

The office of exorcist is not well attested. An unnamed exorcist is cited as witness to the general decree of forgiveness issued by the confessors in prison

---

51. Neciphorus carried a letter to Rome and brought Cornelius's response (Cypr. *Ep.* 45.4.3; 47.1.2; 49.3.1; 52.1.1).

52. Cypr. *Ep.* 7.2.

53. Cypr. *Ep.* 77.3.2; 78.1.1; 79.1.1.

54. Narcius (*Ep.* 7.2); Neciphorus (*Ep.* 45.4.3; 49.3.1; 52.1.1); Lucanus, Maximus, and Amantius (*Ep.* 77.3.2; 78.1.1; 79.1.1; Amantius is omitted). The acolyte Favorinus fled during the persecution and was suspended from office (*Ep.* 34.4.1).

55. Cypr. *Ep.* 34.4.1.

56. Cypr. *Ep.* 39.4.1-2, 5.2.

57. This had been the role of Optatus, who was subsequently made a subdeacon (Cypr. *Ep.* 29.1.2).

58. *Acta apud Zenophilum* as Appendix 1 of Optat. *Parm.* (CSEL 26:186.21-31).

59. Cypr. *Ep.* 29.1.2. His discharging this responsibility is attested in *Ep.* 35.1.1. He may be identical with the Satyrus who was named as a lector and letter carrier in *Ep.* 32.1.2.

60. Cypr. *Ep.* 39.5.2. These two were not old enough to be made presbyters, though they were honored with the stipend appropriate for presbyters rather than of lectors (if lectors were salaried).

61. Optatus had been a lector before being made a subdeacon (Cypr. *Ep.* 29.1.2). The deacon Victor had been a lector (*Ep.* 13.7). The two confessors, Aurelius and Celerinus, were ordained lectors and destined to be presbyters (*Ep.* 38; 39). Reading and writing (by taking dictation) were valuable professional skills distinct from the literary education that only the wealthy received.

---

during the persecution.[62] Exorcism itself seems to have been performed, even repeatedly, in preparation for baptism.[63]

The Roman clergy also referred to church officers responsible for collecting and burying the bodies of the martyrs.[64] The one individual credited with performing this role in Carthage, Tertullus, seems to have acted out of personal devotion rather than as a designated officer of the church.[65]

## DEACONS

The deacons had a more significant role in the church than any of the lower clergy. When Cyprian was in exile from Carthage and Rome's martyred bishop had not been replaced, his letters to the two churches were regularly addressed to the presbyters and deacons, without mention of the other clergy.[66] He included the deacons among the officers responsible for governing the community.

The deacon ministered the cup at the eucharist.[67] When the presbyter went to celebrate the eucharist in prison, he was accompanied by a deacon; the personnel were changed so that attention would not be drawn to any individual.[68] One of the deacons accompanied Cyprian into exile.[69] In Carthage, deacons may have served with a specific presbyter.[70] The deacons were not the ordinary ministers of the rituals, though they were authorized by Cyprian to baptize catechumens and to grant the peace of the church to dying penitents in case of emergency.[71] The deacons may have been responsible for the material resources of the church. They were specifically assigned primary responsibility for the material care of the confessors who were in prison.[72] Perhaps as a result of this work, two of the deacons in Carthage were subsequently accused of misusing church funds.[73] Cyprian also used deacons to carry and interpret important correspondence.[74]

62. Cypr. *Ep.* 23.
63. Cypr. *Ep.* 69.15.2.
64. Cypr. *Ep.* 8.3.2.
65. Cypr. *Ep.* 12.2.1; he advised Cyprian to remain in exile (*Ep.* 14.1.2).
66. Cypr. *Ep.* 5; 7; 11; 12; 14; 15; 16; 18; 19; 26; 29; to Rome: *Ep.* 9; 20; 27; 25; 35.
67. Cypr. *Laps.* 25.
68. Cypr. *Ep.* 5.2.2.
69. Victor (Cypr. *Ep.* 5.2.2; 13.7). He sent 175 sesterces to supplement the 250 sesterces sent by Cyprian himself for the support of the confessors. He had been a lector.
70. Thus Gaius Didensis and his deacon are excommunicated (Cypr. *Ep.* 34.1). One of the offenses of Novatus was in taking Felicissimus to be his deacon — or perhaps in making Felicissimus a deacon — but in any case the two were closely associated (*Ep.* 52.2.3).
71. Cypr. *Ep.* 18.1.2, 2.2.
72. Cypr. *Ep.* 15.1.2.
73. Cypr. *Ep.* 41.2.1; 42.
74. Rogatianus was charged with a long journey to win the support of Firmilian of Caesarea during the controversy over the rebaptism of schismatics (Cypr. *Ep.* 75.1.1).

The deacon Felicissimus, perhaps by force of personality rather than authority of office, played a major role in opposing Cyprian's penitential policy and in organizing the schismatic community in Carthage.[75] He served as that group's emissary to Rome, attempting to discredit Cyprian and to shift the recognition of the Roman church to Fortunatus, the bishop established by the laxist schismatics.[76] This mission would indicate that his diaconal office made him a member of the governing council of the church, both in Carthage and in Rome.

## PRESBYTERS

The presbyters were men of maturer years, subject to an age requirement, which is not specified in the surviving evidence.[77] In support of their ministry, they received what must have been a higher stipend than the lower clergy.[78] They could have been married and already have raised children.[79] In the assembly, they were seated with the bishop in a place of honor.[80] The presbyters do not appear to have participated in offering the eucharist in the presence of the bishop.[81] They were, however, normally authorized to celebrate the eucharist in his absence (as during Cyprian's two exiles),[82] and may have been responsible for regional communities in various parts of Carthage.[83] They offered the

75. Augendus was also a leader in the schism (Cypr. *Ep.* 41.2.1-3; 42).

76. Cypr. *Ep.* 59.1.1.

77. Cypr. *Ep.* 39.5.2.

78. The presbyteral stipend was assigned to the readers who had been confessors (Cypr. *Ep.* 39.5.2). Cyprian himself, it may be presumed, was supported by his own funds, which he dispensed generously for the support of the community during the persecution.

79. Novatus was charged with causing his wife's miscarriage (Cypr. *Ep.* 52.2.5). Numidicus was rescued by his adult daughter after his wife had been burned to death and he left for dead (*Ep.* 40.1). Cyprian himself was unmarried and had served as a presbyter (Pontius, *Vita Cypr.* 2-3); so also did Cornelius of Rome, who had gone through every grade of the clergy before being made bishop (*Ep.* 55.8.2-3).

80. Cyprian referred to the *consessus* (*Ep.* 39.5.2; 40.1; 45.2.5) and to the *congestus* of the clergy (*Ep.* 59.18.1).

81. Albano Vilela pointed out that the term *celebrare,* which would indicate the solemn ritual of the whole community, was used only for the bishop: Cypr. *Laps.* 26; *Ep.* 39.3.1; 57.3.2; 63.16.1-2. *Offerre* was used for the bishop as well (*Ep.* 39.3.1; 63.17.1-2; 73.9.2). The term *offerre* was used for presbyters serving the confessors in prison (*Ep.* 5.2.1), but thereafter only in the context of their unauthorized serving of the lapsed (*Ep.* 15.1.2; 16.2.3, 4.2; 17.2.1, 4.2; 34.1; 68.2.1). It was used for bishops and presbyters acting in schism: *Ep.* 67.6.3; 68.2.1; 69.8.3; 72.2.1; 73.2.3. See Albano Vilela, *La condition collégiale des prêtres au IIIe siècle* (Paris: Beauchesne, 1971), 321-22.

82. In *Ep.* 16.4.2, Cyprian threatened to prohibit the presbyters who were communicating with the lapsed from offering the eucharist.

83. The reading of "in monte" in *Ep.* 41.2.1 (CCSL 3B:197.34) may indicate a separate community on the Byrsa. In any case, the facility with which the laxists set up a separate communion

sacrifice for the confessors in prison.[84] They were charged with emergency care for the dying: baptizing catechumens and reconciling penitents.[85] Some of the presbyters also were designated as teachers and charged with preparing the catechumens for baptism.[86]

The presbyters took full responsibility for the administration of the church in Carthage while Cyprian was in exile during the Decian and Valerian persecutions, each more than a year in length.[87] The presbyters in Rome also undertook this role after the death of Fabian; they acted as a council in governing that church throughout the Decian persecution.[88] Although Cyprian stressed the essential role of the bishop in the constitution of the church, he dealt with the Roman council of presbyters as equals rather than subordinates.[89] Presbyters were charged with carrying particularly important letters; they not only could deliver written messages but could expand on the circumstances to which the letters referred.[90]

Determination of the number of presbyters in Carthage at any given time has proven quite difficult. Four of them opposed the election of Cyprian as bishop and later formed the core of the schismatic communion.[91] An equal number may have supported him.[92] Other presbyters lapsed during the persecution, though none of them is named in the surviving correspondence.[93] In the desperate shortage caused when five presbyters went into schism, Cyprian received a confessor who had been serving as presbyter for another bishop.[94]

---

in the city indicates that the church used multiple locations for some of its worship. *Ep.* 63.16.1 implies that the evening meal celebrations were held with portions of the community.

84. Cypr. *Ep.* 5.2.1.

85. Cypr. *Ep.* 18.1.2, 2.2; 19.2.1.

86. Cypr. *Ep.* 29.1.2; 73.3.2.

87. While Cyprian sent them explicit instructions, he was dependent upon their discretion in carrying them out. Eventually he decided to place a commission of exiled bishops and local presbyters in charge of the church (*Ep.* 41).

88. Some of their correspondence with the church in Carthage and with Cyprian survives (*Ep.* 8; 30; 36).

89. The relationship began badly (Cypr. *Ep.* 8-9) but was soon functioning smoothly (*Ep.* 20; 27; 35).

90. Thus Primitivus in Cypr. *Ep.* 44.2.2.

91. During the persecution, Donatus, Fortunatus, Novatus, and Gordius were already admitting the lapsed back into communion. The four wrote to Cyprian about the matter (*Ep.* 14.4); but it is clear that they were already giving communion to the fallen (*Ep.* 15.1.2; 16.1.2; 17.2.1). Gaius Didensis, who may have been a refugee from elsewhere, was later excommunicated (*Ep.* 34.1).

92. Sergius and Rogatianus were confessors early in the persecution and addressed in Cypr. *Ep.* 6. Rogatianus was subsequently entrusted with funds for support of the refugees and the poor (*Ep.* 7.2). Virtius was steadfast in his loyalty (*Ep.* 43.1.1). Primitivus was entrusted with a delicate mission to Cornelius in Rome immediately after Cyprian's return from exile, though his name did not appear earlier in the surviving documents (*Ep.* 44.2.2).

93. Cypr. *Ep.* 14.1.1; 40.2.

94. Numidicus seems to have been serving in another church and was added to the presbyterate of Carthage after he survived a mob attack during the persecution itself (Cypr. *Ep.* 40).

---

At one point in the conflict over his penitential policy, Cyprian could apparently count on the support of only three presbyters in the city.[95] An additional presbyter was later mentioned by name for the first time six years later.[96] A full complement of presbyters in Carthage before the persecution began would have been less than ten.

### BISHOPS

In the assembly, the bishop presided from his raised chair, *cathedra*, the symbol of his authority in the community.[97] He represented Christ as priest, pastor, and judge.[98] He was the ordinary minister of the rituals of baptism, the eucharist, and the reconciliation of sinners; presbyters could perform these services as his delegates.[99] He supervised the clergy of the community, who were chosen by him with the advice of the people.[100] He was responsible for preaching the gospel and interpreting the standards of Christian life for the people.[101] Finally, he had general responsibility for the property and finances of the community.[102]

## Electing and Rejecting a Bishop

The establishment of a new bishop required the collaboration of the bishops of other church communities. Each local church had a single bishop whose office was symbolized by the commissioning of Peter as the foundation of the church.[103] A bishop was elected only upon the death or deposition of his predecessor; thus, individual bishops were not responsible for the selection and installation of their own successors.[104] The candidate was chosen through the

95. Rogatianus, Virtius, and Numidicus (Cypr. *Ep.* 43.1.1).

96. Julianus, *Act. Procon.* 5.5.

97. Cypr. *Ep.* 73.2.3.

98. The term "priest," *sacerdos,* was used only for the bishop, and the bishop represented Christ in the offering of the sacrifice (Cypr. *Ep.* 63.14.4). He had been assigned a portion of Christ's flock to shepherd (*Ep.* 46.1.2). He served as judge within the church until the return of Christ (*Ep.* 59.5.1; 66.4.2). See Vilela, *La condition collégiale des prêtres au IIIe siècle,* 281-85.

99. Cypr. *Ep.* 16.2.3; 63.14.1; 69.11.1; 76.3.1. Deacons functioned in emergencies during the persecution.

100. Cypr. *Ep.* 29.1.2; 38.1.1; 39.5.2.

101. Cypr. *Ep.* 58.4.1.

102. According to Cyprian, some bishops neglected all other aspects of their office to pursue this one (*Laps.* 6).

103. Cypr. *Ep.* 43.5.2; 46.1.2.

104. The basic objection to Novatian's election in Rome was that Cornelius was already bishop and thus the second "bishop" was successor to no one (Cypr. *Ep.* 11.3.2; 46.1.2; 55.8.4).

collaboration of the people and clergy of the church in question and the bishops of the neighboring churches, following — without casting lots — the precedent used by the Apostles for the replacement of Judas by Matthias.[105] The clergy offered witness to the suitability of the candidate; the people accepted or rejected the proposal; and the neighboring bishops gave consent.[106] The clergy might disagree with the people, as the majority of the presbyters did in the selection of Cyprian to be Bishop of Carthage, but the voice of the people could override the recommendation of the clergy.[107] Cyprian explained that the people knew the candidates intimately and were fully acquainted with their way of life. A congregation that chose a bishop who was unworthy of the office thereby participated in his sin.[108] Once the people had approved a candidate, he was installed in office by the bishops of the neighboring churches. Thereby he became not only the leader of the local church but a member of the episcopal college, which bore responsibility for the worldwide church.

Cyprian never reported the procedure of his own ordination but did provide information on others. Cornelius was made Bishop of Rome by sixteen bishops.[109] When the presbyter Fortunatus was set up as a rival bishop of Carthage by the schismatic community, he claimed twenty-five consecrators.[110] Each new bishop wrote to more distant colleagues, announcing his election and installation; they responded with letters of recognition and communion.[111] When a succession was disputed, as happened when Novatian contested the selection of Cornelius at Rome, the successful candidate would be the one recognized by bishops outside the immediate dispute, who could thereby link his church to congregations in other regions. Both candidates in the Roman schism appealed to the African bishops, as well as those of other areas, for recognition. The Africans then sent a delegation to investigate the dispute (which recommended the recognition of that candidate whom they determined had been properly elected and installed). Only then did they begin to correspond with Cornelius.[112] The African bishops maintained and distributed a list of their own members in good standing, so that usurpers and schismatics could not claim recognition by soliciting correspondence from overseas bishops.[113] Thus, Cyprian upbraided Cornelius of Rome for giving a hearing to the envoys of the schismatic Bishop of Carthage, Fortunatus, whose name did not appear on

105. Cypr. *Ep.* 67.4.2, 5.1.

106. The role of the people and the other bishops is underlined in Cypr. *Ep.* 59.5.2; 67.5.1. In *Ep.* 55.8.4, dealing with the election of Cornelius, the role of the clergy is also mentioned.

107. Pontius, *Vita Cypr.* 5 and *Ep.* 43.1.2.

108. Cypr. *Ep.* 43.1.2-3; 55.8.4; 59.6.1; 67.4.1-2, 4, 5.1-2.

109. Cypr. *Ep.* 55.24.2.

110. Cypr. *Ep.* 59.11.1. Cyprian corrected the claim: only five had been present (*Ep.* 59.10.2-3).

111. Cypr. *Ep.* 45.3.1.

112. Cypr. *Ep.* 45.1.2, 2.1; 48.3.2; 55.1.1.

113. Cypr. *Ep.* 59.9.3.

the list he had been sent.[114] This elaborate process of election and recognition identified the candidate whom God had selected to head a particular church. Those who continued to oppose a bishop once he was legitimately installed and recognized were, therefore, rebelling against the divine will.[115]

A bishop normally served for the remainder of his life. If he proved unworthy, however, he could be removed from office by a process similar to his selection and installation: by the judgment of a council of his colleagues, rejection by the people, and withdrawal of recognition by other bishops. A council of ninety bishops expelled Privatus from his office in Lambaesis for an unspecified crime.[116] Other bishops were removed because they were guilty of sacrifice during the persecution.[117] By general practice, a bishop who confessed his failure and relinquished his office would be accepted as a penitent and subsequently returned to communion among the laity through the ritual of reconciliation; he could not hold office again.[118] Nor could anyone who had rebelled against the church ever hold office within it, since the crime of schism was judged equivalent to idolatry.[119] The Roman church made some concessions to apostate bishops who were able to return their entire congregations to unity, allowing them to avoid public penance, though not to retain their office.[120] The Africans made no such concessions themselves, to either apostates or schismatics: all were required to submit to public penance before being allowed to enter the church (among the laity).[121] When the lapsed and schismatic bishops gathered by Privatus of Lambaesis sought reinstatement in their offices, they were consistently refused, even though they may have promised to bring congregations with them into unity.[122]

Within the unity of the church, unworthy bishops posed an immediate danger only to themselves: if they approached the altar with the impurity contracted by idolatrous rituals, they could suffer the punishment threatened against the Israelite priests who were impure.[123] Once their sin was known, however, they had to be removed from office not only for their own protection but because they were incapable of representing the congregation before God. Having lost the Holy Spirit, Cyprian explained, such a priest could not

114. Cypr. *Ep.* 59.9.1-3.
115. Cypr. *Ep.* 43.1.3; 59.5.2; 66.1.1-2; 68.2.1.
116. Cypr. *Ep.* 59.10.1. He seems to have retained a following, however.
117. Cypr. *Ep.* 59.10.2-3. Iovinus, Maximus, and Repostus were sacrificers. The crime of Felix was not specified. These formed the nucleus of the schismatic episcopate.
118. Cypr. *Ep.* 67.6.3. Cyprian asserted that this had been agreed with Cornelius, the Bishop of Rome. Fortunatus of Assuras was allowed to do this (*Ep.* 65.1.2, 5.1).
119. Cypr. *Ep.* 72.2.1-3.
120. The Africans accepted this concession which had been made by Cornelius to Trofimus, perhaps to prevent him from joining the Novatianist schism (Cypr. *Ep.* 55.11.1-3).
121. See Cypr. *Ep.* 64.1.1; 67 for apostates and *Ep.* 72.2.1-3 for schismatics.
122. Cypr. *Ep.* 59.10.1-3.
123. Cypr. *Ep.* 65.2.1; 67.1.2.

sanctify the eucharistic offering or the waters of baptism;[124] nor would God attend to the prayer a sinful bishop offered for his people.[125] Although these principles should have invalidated the ministry of bishops whose sins were not yet manifest, Cyprian could apply them only when the crime was made known. He contended that God had allowed the persecution in order to unmask unworthy bishops through their public apostasy. Once God had made a bishop's sin clear, a congregation that allowed him to remain in office would thereby share his sin and incur God's condemnation.[126] By implication, this applied to his fellow bishops who failed to break communion with a colleague known to be sinful.[127]

## Authority of the Bishop

Cyprian claimed that, within each local church, the bishop exercised the authority of Christ between his Ascension and his return. At the Judgment to follow the Resurrection of all, the bishop's decisions would be subjected to review: Christ would condemn anyone who had deceived the bishop and would hold the bishop responsible for anyone lost through his harshness or injustice.[128] In practice, the bishop consulted with his colleagues in setting policy for the readmission and exclusion of sinners, and then with the local clergy and people in judging individual cases. During the Decian persecution, Cyprian had insisted that he would not consent to admitting the lapsed to communion under the patronage of the martyrs because this required a broad consultation of the whole church.[129] The deliberations of the bishops on the appropriate penance for those who had failed included a review of the relevant teaching of scripture, the different forms of sin, and the circumstances of the failures. The bishops also considered such pastoral factors as the danger of sinners despairing of forgiveness from the church; they might then return to the idolatry of the imperial culture or accept the reconciliation and communion offered by the schismatics. The bishops also had to face the appeals made by some of the sinners' dependents, whose apostasy had shielded and enabled them to remain in communion.[130] When schismatics sought to return to the communion of the church, however, Cyprian had to labor to convince his people to accept and

---

124. Cypr. *Ep.* 65.2.2, 4.1; 66.5.1-2.

125. Cypr. *Ep.* 67.2.2.

126. Cypr. *Laps.* 6-7; *Ep.* 65.3.1-3; 67.3.1-2. In these cases, the conflict was over allowing a return to office by bishops who had failed.

127. Cypr. *Ep.* 67.5.4, 6.3, 9.1-3.

128. Cypr. *Ep.* 59.4.1-3, 5.1; 66.4.2; 69.9.1-2.

129. Cypr. *Ep.* 14.4; 19.2.2. He repeated this point in *Ep.* 43.7.2.

130. Cypr. *Ep.* 55.6.1, 15.1, 17.2, 26.1; 57.4.1-4. Many of the dependents pointed out that they had been protected as a consequence of the head of their household complying with imperial law.

support them as penitents.[131] Though a bishop might claim to speak for God, the exercise of his authority was clearly guided and even limited by his clergy and people. Cyprian and his episcopal colleagues changed their policies on extending reconciliation to the lapsed during the persecution, immediately after it, and in anticipation of a renewal of state action. The letters explaining these decisions clearly indicate the influence of the laity and clergy.[132]

Finally, Cyprian did not hesitate to claim that the bishop's authority was equivalent to that of the Israelite priest or judge. God had amply demonstrated the punishments that awaited those who tried to usurp the position of Aaron: fire from heaven had consumed them; the earth had opened to swallow them up; their incense burners were beaten into plates and set up as warnings against future rebellions.[133] He asserted that a similar condemnation awaited all who rejected episcopal authority.

Although the bishop might appear to be an officer appointed by the congregation and serving at its pleasure, Cyprian insisted that the people's vote was itself the instrument for manifesting divine choice.[134] The bishop had been selected to represent and act for Christ; he was, therefore, the true successor to the Israelite priest and the heir to Christ's authority, even if only until his return to judge. The bishop represented the community before God and God to the community.

## Appointment and Discipline of Other Clergy

The ranks of the laity were regularly reviewed to identify appropriate candidates for promotion to the clergy. Saturus, whom Cyprian raised to the office of lector during his exile, had been placed in this rank, which was identified as "near to the clergy." The term may have designated a special location where this group stood during the Christian assembly.[135] The committee of bishops and presbyters that represented Cyprian in Carthage during the early months of 251 was charged with identifying suitable candidates for office to replace those who had failed during the persecution or gone into schism. These were to be selected by their age, situation, and merits. In the context, these qualifications certainly would have included their witness to the faith — at least by declining to act on the imperial command to sacrifice that began the Decian persecution — as well as their support of the bishops' policy that those who had fallen were to be reconciled only through extended penance rather than by the patron-

---

131. Cypr. *Ep.* 59.15.2-3.
132. Cypr. *Ep.* 20.3.2; 55.13.1–15.1; 57.2.1–3.1.
133. Cypr. *Ep.* 43.7.1; 69.8.1; 73.8.1-2.
134. Cypr. *Ep.* 43.1.2; 55.8.1; 59.5.2-3; 66.1.2.
135. Thus Saturus was described as *clero proximus* before being made a reader (Cypr. *Ep.* 29.1.2).

age of the martyrs.[136] While still in exile, Cyprian appointed two confessors to serve as readers with the proposal that they should be advanced to the presbyterate once they reached the required age for that office.[137] Public confession of Christ did not of itself qualify a person for clerical status.[138] Though Cyprian did appoint four confessors during his exile,[139] he publicly rebuked others who refused to respect the moral standards of the community or the authority of its bishop.[140]

Clerical appointments were made by the bishop upon the advice and consent of the laity. During the Decian persecution, Cyprian had to dispense with the formal consultation of the laity because of his exile but explained to them his reasons for doing so.[141] The term *ordinare* was used for placing individuals in office.[142]

Clergy who had failed in their duties were removed from office by an episcopal decision, usually after consultation of the faithful. The bishop, Cyprian explained, could remove any person he had placed in office.[143] At the outbreak of the persecution, the presbyter Novatus was facing a formal hearing that was expected to result in his removal from office and excommunication.[144] Cyprian warned that clerics who had taken flight during time of persecution without his approval[145] or had allowed the unrepentant lapsed into their communion[146] would be disciplined by the judgment of the congregation as a whole.[147] Cornelius, the Bishop of Rome, received the approval of his congregation to reinstate a presbyter who was a confessor but had been guilty of schism by supporting the attempt to establish Novatian as bishop.[148]

The growing distinction of the clergy from the laity is evident in the restriction of their nonreligious activities and their receiving regular financial support

136. Cypr. *Ep.* 41.1.2: aetas, condicio et merita. CCSL 3B:196.16.

137. Cypr. *Ep.* 39.5.2. The required age was not specified in his correspondence.

138. Nor did it do so in Rome, where the confessors who had supported Novatian were readmitted to communion with an amnesty. One of them, Maximus, returned to his presbyteral rank, but the others were welcomed among the laity (Cypr. *Ep.* 49). This evidence explicitly contradicts the apparent specification in *Trad. apos.* 10, and would count against its third-century dating in Rome. See above, n. 38, for Alistair Stewart-Sykes's resolution to the problem.

139. Optatus the subdeacon, Aurelius and Celerinus the lectors, and Numidicus the presbyter (Cypr. *Ep.* 29; 38; 39; 40).

140. Cypr. *Ep.* 14 for the first set of exiles; *Ep.* 27 for the problems with Lucianus.

141. Thus in the appointments of Saturus and Optatus (Cypr. *Ep.* 29.1.2); Aurelius and Celerinus (*Ep.* 38, 39); and Numidicus (*Ep.* 40). See also *Ep.* 3.3.1.

142. Cypr. *Ep.* 38.2.2 (CCSL 3B:185.37).

143. Cypr. *Ep.* 3.3.1-3.

144. Cypr. *Ep.* 52.3.

145. Cypr. *Ep.* 34.3.2, 4.1.

146. Cypr. *Ep.* 16.4.2; 34.1.

147. Cyprian was himself in voluntary exile, which he claimed was for the good of the community as a whole (*Ep.* 20.1.1-2; 43.4.1-2).

148. Cypr. *Ep.* 49.2.1-5.

from the community. All the clergy were expected to dedicate themselves to the work of the altar, to prayer, and to supplication for the community. Clergy were forbidden even from acting as trustees or taking responsibility for the finances of children.[149] Instead, they were supported by both a monthly salary and a portion of the food gifts made by the faithful.[150] They did, however, retain their own property and funds;[151] they lived with their families;[152] they adopted no distinctive garb.[153]

## The Martyrs

The authority of the local bishop was challenged, as it had been in Tertullian's day, by the privilege assigned to the martyrs of gaining for other Christians the forgiveness of serious sins committed after baptism. Because of the large number of failures during the Decian persecution and doubts about the efficacy of the church's ritual of reconciliation for dealing with idolatry, lapsed Christians besieged the martyrs with requests to intercede in heaven once they died for confession of Christ and immediately received their promised crowns from him.[154] Their letters of peace authorized, and finally even instructed, the bishops to admit the sinners to the communion of the church. Some martyrs recognized the authority of the bishop — in consultation with the congregation — to examine the conduct and judge the sincerity of the penitents, and then to admit those they approved by the imposition of hands.[155] The fallen themselves asserted, however, that the clergy had no right to delay or withhold the peace that had already been granted to them by Christ in heaven through the intercession of the martyrs.[156]

Initially, Cyprian recognized the right of the confessors and martyrs to advise the bishop and, thus, to recommend penitents for reconciliation — a right that he extended in some form to all the faithful communicants. He advised the

149. Cypr. *Ep.* 1.1.1, 2.1; fraud in such responsibilities was one of the charges against the deacon Novatus (*Ep.* 52.2.5).

150. Referred to as *sportuli* and *divisiones mensurnae* (Cypr. *Ep.* 1.1.2; 34.4.2; 39.5.2). The growing wealth of the African church is evident in this development.

151. Not only Cyprian but the deacon Victor made personal contributions to the support of the confessors during the persecution (Cypr. *Ep.* 13.7).

152. Novatus was clearly living with his family, since he was charged with kicking his wife's belly and causing the death of their child (Cypr. *Ep.* 52.2.5). Numidicus and his wife were attacked by the mob, after which he was rescued by his daughter (*Ep.* 40.1).

153. The *byrrum* and *dalmatica* which Cyprian removed in preparation for his execution were normal pieces of clothing (*Act. Procon.* 5).

154. Cyprian attempted to address the problem diplomatically in *Ep.* 15. For a fuller treatment, see the earlier discussion, pp. 324-26.

155. Cypr. *Ep.* 23.

156. Cypr. *Ep.* 27.2.1–3.2.

imprisoned confessors to consider the gravity of the sin, the sincerity of the penitents' remorse, and the satisfactory works the penitents had performed. Their letters, he explained, should always specify the recommended individuals by name, rather than refer to indefinitely large groups, such as a household.[157] When the confessors issued a blanket grant of forgiveness, however, Cyprian broke off attempts to cooperate and opposed their claims.[158]

In the treatise *On the Lapsed,* which he addressed to the community upon his return from exile in spring 251, Cyprian moved to limit the authority of the confessors who had been brought before the imperial authorities and imprisoned. He praised those who had made public witness to Christ, but he extended the title of confessor to everyone who had declined to fulfill the requirements of the imperial decree by the specified deadline. Those who remained in the city had indicated thereby a readiness to confess Christ publicly. They were due the same status as those who had been brought before the authorities and those who had abandoned their possessions by taking flight into voluntary exile.[159] His action increased the religious authority of those who had remained faithful and were supporting the bishops' position against the demands of the lapsed and the claims they made for the martyrs.

Cyprian then insisted that the martyrs, who were represented by the letters they had given before their deaths and by the confessors claiming to have been commissioned as their agents, could exercise an intercessory function, but only in person at the Judgment, when they would sit as advisors to Christ. In the meantime, he observed, the bishop had been charged and authorized to exercise the function of judgment, with the advice of the faithful people who were alive in the church on earth. He pointed out, moreover, that the friends of Christ did not always receive the favors they requested. Without denying the authority of the martyrs, Cyprian effectively disenfranchised them within the church and warned the lapsed not to trust them as advocates in the final judgment.[160] He asserted, moreover, that only those whom the bishops had first freed from the bondage of their sins would be able to plead their case before Christ and thereby benefit from the assistance of the martyrs.[161]

## Prophets and Visionaries

Cyprian provided no evidence of challenges from prophets who claimed to guide the church by oracles. Instead, he claimed divine guidance through dreams and visions for himself and his colleagues. In explaining the causes of

157. Cypr. *Ep.* 15.
158. Cypr. *Ep.* 23; 26.
159. Cypr. *Laps.* 2-3.
160. Cypr. *Laps.* 17-20.
161. Cypr. *Ep.* 57.1.1, 3.3–4.4.

the Decian persecution — why God had allowed these troubles to come upon the church — Cyprian recounted no less than three visions he had received in which the church had been warned and threatened.[162] A bit later, he recounted two additional revelations: one was his own and the other a waking vision by young boys in his company.[163] The confessor Celerinus also received a vision in which the personified church herself instructed him to accept the clerical appointment that Cyprian was urging upon him.[164]

When the bishops decided to change their program of demanding lifelong penance from those who failed by actually sacrificing to the idols and, instead, to grant them immediate reconciliation, Cyprian justified the decision by appealing to the signs and warnings received by the bishops. These indicated that persecution was about to be renewed. The Holy Spirit, he claimed, had guided and authorized the change in penitential policy.[165] In rebuttal to a critic who disparaged his appeal to dreams and visions, Cyprian asserted that he had been granted an oracular warning to pass along: "Whosoever does not believe in Christ appointing a bishop shall begin to believe hereafter in Christ avenging that bishop."[166]

This trust in divine inspiration may have been peculiar to Cyprian rather than characteristic of his church. Yet, in his *Life of Cyprian,* Pontius the Deacon continued this program of attributing prophetic dreams and oracles to Cyprian. He reported that on the second day of his final exile and one year before his death, Cyprian recounted a dream in which he had foreseen in detail his future trial and sentencing.[167]

Thus Cyprian claimed for his person, if not his episcopal office, the gifts of the spiritual prophet and confessor. His own confession as an episcopal martyr in Africa not only enhanced his stature but confirmed his teaching that the bishop, rather than the martyr or prophet, serves as Christ's agent on earth.

## Lay Elders

Cyprian did not refer to elders *(seniores)* who were not ordained members of the clergy. Because his episcopate engaged the authority and roles of the clergy and laity, and because the records are relatively full, this omission is significant. One might have expected, for example, that during the persecution, when he was experiencing such difficulty in controlling the situation in Carthage, his

---

162. Cypr. *Ep.* 11.3.1, 4.1, 5.1.
163. Cypr. *Ep.* 15.3.2; 16.4.1.
164. Cypr. *Ep.* 39.1.2.
165. Cypr. *Ep.* 57.1.2, 2.1, 5.1-2.
166. Cypr. *Ep.* 66.10.1. itaque qui Christo non credit sacerdotem facienti postea credere incipiet sacerdotem uincidanti (CCSL 3C:444.177-78).
167. Pont. *Vita Cypr.* 12.

letters addressed to the laity might have contained an appeal to any elders who were recognized as leaders.[168] Similarly, in *On the Lapsed,* he made no reference to elders or their role in helping the church bear up under the persecution. Cyprian's failure — or refusal — to acknowledge lay elders might, of course, have been part of his program of focusing leadership in the clergy.

## Apostolic Succession and the Episcopal College

The Apostle Peter held a central place in the emerging African understanding of the episcopate and the unity of the church it served. Peter was primarily the exemplar of the local bishop, who served as the foundation for each Christian community. Peter was also the symbol of the unity of the episcopate as a whole.

In commissioning Peter as the rock upon which he would build the church, Cyprian contended, Christ established the office of bishop. The successors of Peter in each and every church governed its actions and maintained its unity.[169] Thus, Cyprian was outraged when the laxist rebels appealed to the church of Rome, which had been the see of Peter, in an attempt to break the unity of the church in Carthage.[170] The local church, then, consisted of the people who remained united with their bishop, himself symbolizing Peter, upon whom the church was built.[171]

Peter was not the only bishop, nor was the church found in only one locality; rather, the church spread throughout the world, and the episcopate had expanded to serve it. Again, Peter served as an indicator of unity. Christ had charged Peter to feed his sheep, underscoring the one flock served by many pastors in unity.[172] Christ had given the authority to bind and loosen, Cyprian explained, on two occasions: first to Peter alone, to show that it was a single power; and afterward to all the Apostles together, to show that they held and exercised it as a shared endowment.[173] The Apostles were, then, the first bishops; their group of Twelve was the founding episcopal college. The episcopate itself was a unified body through which each of the bishops shared responsibility for the universal church.[174]

Yet, individual bishops were assigned different parts of the flock of Christ,

168. Cypr. *Ep.* 17 was addressed to the laity. The omissions in *Ep.* 38-40 might also be significant because they address the presbyters, the deacons, and all the people, without signaling out any lay leaders. The same might be said of *Ep.* 43, dealing with episcopal leadership.

169. Combining the twin assertions in Cypr. *Ep.* 33.1.1 and *Ep.* 43.5.2.

170. Cypr. *Ep.* 59.14.1.

171. Cypr. *Ep.* 66.8.3; 70.3.1.

172. Cypr. *Unit. eccl.* 4 (PT). On the two versions of this text, see above, p. 327, n. 216.

173. Cypr. *Unit. eccl.* 4 (RT), and *Ep.* 73.7.1-2, where the point is to show that the power itself is the gift of the Holy Spirit.

174. Cypr. *Unit. eccl.* 5 (RT).

and each was to govern his portion to the best of his ability, being answerable to the Lord for his decisions and actions.[175] Thus, each bishop had a particular responsibility for his own local church and a shared responsibility for the whole church. Because of the unity of both the flock and the episcopate that served it, the bishops were required to collaborate with one another — and even intervene together — to assist any local church if its bishop failed or went wrong.[176] The concord of the many bishops joined their individual churches together to realize the unity of the church and the episcopate that was grounded in the unity of God and Christ.[177]

This understanding of the episcopate and the unity of the church was manifest not only in councils that set common policy but also in the consultations among bishops in different parts of the world. Many of Cyprian's letters respond to questions and problems of bishops in Africa, either in his own name or as presider at a council.[178] He carried out extensive correspondence with the Roman bishops Cornelius,[179] Lucius,[180] and Stephen[181] to coordinate the practices and even to urge joint efforts to solve problems in Spain and Gaul. He successfully intervened to resolve a dispute between Cornelius and a group of schismatic confessors in Rome.[182]

Cyprian also warned that the intentional union of the episcopal college could serve as a conduit for participation in the sin of another. A bishop who knowingly supported a sinful colleague would thereby share his sin, become equally unworthy of the gift of the Holy Spirit, and deprive himself and his community of the power of sanctification.[183] Moreover, anyone who had been guilty of the sin of apostasy or schism could never serve as a bishop: the sincerity and efficacy of their repentance, their winning God's forgiveness, and their consequent possession of the gift of the Holy Spirit could not be trusted.[184] The local congregation could tolerate communicants of doubtful sanctity, helping them prepare for the Judgment of Christ; the episcopal college could not tolerate sinners because each of its members was a necessary instrument in the sanctification and salvation of others.

---

175. Cypr. *Ep.* 55.24.2; 59.14.2.
176. Cypr. *Ep.* 68.3.2, 4.2. The argument was developed to justify his intervention in Arles, where a Novatianist bishop was refusing reconciliation to dying penitents.
177. Cypr. *Ep.* 66.8.3.
178. Cypr. *Ep.* 56.3; 64; 67; 70.
179. Cypr. *Ep.* 44; 45; 47-52; 59; 60.
180. Cypr. *Ep.* 61.
181. Cypr. *Ep.* 68; 72.
182. Cypr. *Ep.* 37; 46; 53; 54.
183. Cypr. *Ep.* 67.9.1-3.
184. Cypr. *Ep.* 65.4.1; 72.2.1-2.

The cooperation of neighboring bishops, which was necessary for the selection and installation of a local bishop, formed a practical basis for more extensive episcopal collaboration in the governance of their regional church. This system of mutual consultation was functioning before the outbreak of the Decian persecution and the challenges it posed to episcopal leadership. Episcopal meetings already had decided to allow the reconciliation of adulterers,[185] had reversed the policy of accepting baptism performed in heresy,[186] and had removed unworthy bishops.[187]

During the Decian persecution, Cyprian was following such precedents when he insisted that a policy for the cleansing and reconciliation of the lapsed would have to be developed and approved by episcopal deliberations.[188] In his correspondence, he began to build the foundation for cooperation, which was realized in the decisions that were made in the series of councils of the African bishops meeting in Carthage each year after Easter.[189] In the council of 251, the bishops considered both the biblical teaching and the pastoral problems that faced them. They realized that scriptural arguments could be made for both permanent exclusion and immediate inclusion of the lapsed. They recognized that they were adapting to new circumstances when they set out the provisions for reconciling the fallen.[190] In anticipation of a new persecution, the bishops later decided to offer immediate readmission to all the fallen who had submitted to the church's penitential discipline.[191] In other councils, the bishops of Africa worked out common policies regarding the engagement of the clergy in secular work, the status of schismatic clergy who returned to their communion, and the proper method of receiving converts who had been baptized in schismatic communions.[192] In some instances, the councils allowed that any individual bishop could follow a more restrictive practice.[193] However, they

185. Cypr. *Ep.* 55.20.1, 21.1.

186. Cyprian recognized this in *Ep.* 71.2.1, 4.1 and *Ep.* 73.3.1. He named his predecessor, Agrippinus, as leading the council that made the decision. Firmilian of Caesarea noted it in *Ep.* 75.19.3.

187. Privatus of Lambaesis seems to have been removed from office before the persecution (Cypr. *Ep.* 59.10.1).

188. Cypr. *Ep.* 17.3.2.

189. Thus in Cypr. *Ep.* 24; 25; 26.1.2; 43.3.2, 7.2.

190. Cypr. *Ep.* 55.6.1.

191. Cypr. *Ep.* 57.1.2. Forty-two bishops are named in the heading of the letter to Cornelius reporting their action.

192. Cypr. *Ep.* 1.1.1 for the restrictions on clerical occupations; *Ep.* 55.20.2 for the decision to allow reconciliation of adulterers; *Ep.* 70.1.2 (50 bishops) and *Ep.* 71.4.1 for the earlier decision about schismatic baptism; and *Ep.* 72 for schismatic baptism and clergy.

193. Cypr. *Ep.* 55.21.1-2 for the freedom to be more restrictive; *Ep.* 64.1.1 for the threat against a bishop who had been more liberal. See also *Ep.* 57.21.1; 72.3.1 for the issues of reconciling the penitents and rebaptizing schismatics.

seem to have trusted that their decisions were guided by the Holy Spirit, which they shared. They questioned whether one who dissented was truly within the episcopal college.[194]

The numbers of bishops involved in these meetings can sometimes be determined from the letters that reported their decisions. Cyprian claimed that ninety bishops had met to condemn Privatus of Lambaesis.[195] Sixty-six bishops met, probably in Spring 252, and responded to questions about baptizing infants.[196] Forty-two bishops met in Spring 253 and decided to allow all the penitents to be reconciled.[197] In Spring 254 or 255, thirty-two bishops of Proconsular Africa responded to a letter from eighteen Numidian bishops.[198] A meeting of thirty-eight bishops was held somewhat later in this time frame in order to respond to an appeal from Spanish churches for help in excluding unworthy bishops.[199] Seventy-one bishops met in Spring 256 to address the baptismal controversy.[200] Finally, eighty-seven episcopal judgments were pronounced at the culminating meeting in September 256, which rejected Stephen of Rome's directive that they cease rebaptizing schismatics.[201] Thus, it appears that the bishops of Africa expected to travel to meetings, usually after the celebration of Easter, and to make common decisions. Sometimes they met in provincial groups; but for particularly important issues they assembled from throughout Africa, usually in Carthage.

### PRIMATE BISHOPS

In Africa, the Bishop of Carthage had a particular role in maintaining this collaboration among his colleagues. He was in closest contact with the Roman bishop and could control communication. Thus he informed his colleagues of the decision of the episcopal commission that they had sent to investigate the disputed election in Rome, and he collected their letters of communion for forwarding to Cornelius.[202] Individual bishops and provincial councils referred questions to him that he placed before meetings of his colleagues or an-

194. Cypr. *Ep.* 68.3.2. The particular case was the refusal of a bishop to allow even the death-bed reconciliation of penitents.

195. Cypr. *Ep.* 59.10.1.

196. Cypr. *Ep.* 64. See Graeme W. Clarke, *The Letters of St. Cyprian of Carthage,* 4 vols. (New York: Newman Press, 1984), 3:302-3.

197. Cypr. *Ep.* 57. All the bishops were from places within 200 kilometers of Carthage. See Clarke, *The Letters of St. Cyprian of Carthage,* 3:213-14.

198. Cypr. *Ep.* 70; Clarke, *The Letters of St. Cyprian of Carthage,* 4:192-93.

199. Cypr. *Ep.* 67; Clarke, *The Letters of St. Cyprian of Carthage,* 4:21-27.

200. Cypr. *Ep.* 73.1.2. Clarke, in *The Letters of St. Cyprian of Carthage,* 4:219-21, judges that this letter is itself the report from that meeting.

201. Cypr. *Sententiae episcoporum.* Only eighty-five bishops were actually present.

202. Cypr. *Ep.* 45.1.3; 55.1.1.

swered himself when necessary.[203] During the Decian persecution, his church supported refugees from the smaller cities of Africa. Later, he organized a collection to provide ransom for Christian captives; during the Valerian persecution, he sent assistance to the confessors in the imperial mines.[204] The Bishop of Lambaesis played a similar but more restricted role for the bishops of the province of Numidia.[205] Thus, the system of first or metropolitan bishops was emerging.[206]

A system of seniority among bishops was also developing; bishops voted and were listed in communications according to the length of their service. The Bishops of Carthage and Lambaesis stood outside these rankings, as leaders whose position was based upon the prominence of their cities.[207]

Because his see was the largest city and the capital of Roman Africa, as well as by force of his own personality, Cyprian functioned as the leader of the African episcopate. His position was not yet formalized in the specific office of primate, which would emerge later in African ecclesial practice. It was regularized, however, in that his name always appeared first or alone in the heading of common letters.[208]

## Conclusion

Cyprian's writings provide a fully elaborated theory to justify the claims that his predecessor in Tertullian's time had made for holding the powers that had been conferred upon Peter. He understood Peter not only as a figure of the local bishop but as a member of the college of bishops, which Christ had established in choosing the Twelve and endowing them with the gift of the Holy Spirit. Individual bishops shared a common power to govern and sanctify; they shared responsibility for the entire church, though each had his own portion to govern. This, in turn, provided a scriptural foundation for the authority of regional councils of bishops, which could limit the discretion of individual bishops and churches.

Thus, Cyprian was able to reject the claims of religious authority and

203. Thus he advised Caldonius on the reconciliation of those who had first fallen and then recovered by confessing Christ (Cypr. *Ep.* 25.1.1); he referred a related question to a council (*Ep.* 56); he defended the decisions of councils (*Ep.* 55; 73).

204. Cypr. *Ep.* 76-79.

205. Januarius is addressed first in Cypr. *Ep.* 62 and 70 as leader of the Numidian bishops who consulted their colleagues in Proconsular Africa. He was, apparently, sixth in seniority among the bishops assembled in September 256 (Cypr. *Sent.* 6).

206. A similar role for Firmilian of Caesarea in Cappadocia is evinced by Cypr. *Ep.* 75.

207. Lambaesis was the headquarters of the Legio III Augusta. See Jerome H. Farnum, *The Positioning of the Roman Imperial Legions* (Oxford, Eng.: Archaeopress, 2005), 28.

208. Thus Cypr. *Ep.* 57; 61; 62; 64; 67; 70; 72.

power being made for the martyrs. He insisted that the clergy not only had been authorized to act for Christ but actually had been given the power necessary to do so. He based his jurisdictional claims, his right to act for Christ and to control access to the eucharist, on the power that had been communicated to him from Christ through apostolic succession within the episcopal college. The bishop had this power and made it available within the local church; it was not shared by all Christians by virtue of their baptismal initiation and eucharistic participation. The bishops, he contended, were chosen for their offices individually by God, who guided the election by the congregation and clergy, and they were inspired by the kinds of divine assistance that had earlier been the prerogative of the Spirit-filled prophets. The other clergy served as assistants to the bishop, exercising authority he delegated to them.

Thus, Cyprian witnessed to (and promoted) a growing differentiation between clergy and laity, in which the clergy were credited with powers peculiar to their offices and were required to follow disciplines of separation and holiness that were not required of all Christians. This focus on the clergy as the guarantors of the holiness of the church and the efficacy of its ministry, however, would not succeed. The failure of members of the African episcopate during the Diocletian persecution, their subsequent refusal to repent and give up their offices, and the consequent division of the church would force the development of a new theology that blended the viewpoints of Tertullian and Cyprian.

## THE CLERGY DURING THE FOURTH CENTURY

### The Donatist Schism

At the close of the Diocletian persecution, a group of bishops from Numidia, under the leadership of the primate, Secundus of Tigisis, brought charges of apostasy against one of the consecrators of the deacon Caecilian, who was elected to replace Mensurius as Bishop of Carthage. The Numidians, some of whom were themselves guilty of the very crime they alleged, then elected and consecrated a rival bishop; a competing episcopal college was formed.[209]

The conflict eventually came to judgment under the supervision of the emperor and the Roman bishop. In the process of judgment and appeal, a number of issues were decided. Apostate bishops were not to be subjected to the penitential regimen, but they were to be removed from office and allowed to

---

209. Optat. *Parm.* 1.18-19. A review of the surviving evidence can be found in Jean-Louis Maier, *Le dossier du donatisme*, 2 vols. (Berlin: Akademie Verlag, 1987), 1:128-35.

communicate among the laity.[210] The validity of an ordination was not affected by the prior apostasy of the consecrators.[211] The crime of schism was addressed differently. Those bishops responsible for the original schism against Caecilian, as well as those they subsequently ordained in their competing communion, were to be allowed to return to the unity of the church and retain their status as bishops without being subjected to either penance or penalty.[212] If this provision resulted in two bishops having a claim to the same congregation, the more recently consecrated one was to cede the position and be given a different congregation.[213]

A decade later, the disciplinary decrees of the Council of Nicaea dealt with similar issues. As Catholic Bishop of Carthage, Caecilian attended the council and brought home a copy of its decrees, disciplinary as well as dogmatic. Any Christian guilty of apostasy during persecution could never be a cleric; if such a person were ordained in error or by deception, he was to be removed from office as soon as the crime was discovered.[214] Schismatic clergy were allowed to remain in their offices when they joined the unity of the Catholic church.[215] The imposition of hands by which they were to be received was understood in different ways: the African Latin version of the canon specified it as reconciliation;[216] other Latin and Greek versions identified it as ordination.[217] Only one bishop was to govern a congregation: the converted schismatics were to be assigned as presbyters for an urban congregation or as bishops in a rural

210. *Con. Arel.* a. 314, 14; the failed bishops who performed the consecrations were to be removed from office. The decision from Arles is not generally referred to in the African councils; Augustine mentions it for the first time in *Ep.* 43.6.20, but without any details of the decision and its canons. Optat. *Parm.* 1.24 reported that Donatus had been condemned for imposing penance on bishops.

211. The Council of Arles in 314 asserted that ordinations by lapsed bishops were valid as long as the person ordained had been faithful: 14(13).

212. Augustine cited this provision of Miltiades (*Ep.* 43.5.16; 185.10.47).

213. Aug. *Ep.* 43.5.16. This provision would have regularly resulted in the schismatic returning to his original congregation and the Catholic replacement being assigned to another city.

214. Council of Nicaea, 10. In Caecilian's version it reads thus: Quicumque ordinati sunt per ignorantiam aut dissumlationem ordinantium de his qui in persecutione sunt lapsi, nullum ecclesiastico canoni preiudicium faciunt; cogniti enim cum fuerint deponuntur. See C. H. Turner, *Ecclesiae Occidentalis Monumenta Iuris Antiquissima*, vols. 2 in 7 (Oxonii: E Typographeo Clarendoniano, 1899), 1.2:122-24.

215. Council of Nicaea, 8. In Caecilian's version: De his qui se dicunt Catharos si ueniant ad ecclesiam catholicam, placuit sanctae et magnae synodo ut manus eis inpositio fiat et in clero maneant. Turner, *Ecclesiae Occidentalis Monumenta Iuris Antiquissima,* 1.2:122.

216. unde omnes siue in uicis siue in ciuitatibus si inueniantur, inpositis manibus reconciliationis in schemate maneant clericorum. Turner, *Ecclesiae Occidentalis Monumenta Iuris Antiquissima,* 1.2:124.13-17.

217. Rufinus (Turner, *Ecclesiae Occidentalis Monumenta Iuris Antiquissima,* 1.2:203-7) and Socrates, *Hist. eccl.* 1.9. Cyprian and his colleagues had regarded schism as a form of apostasy and explicitly refused to allow schismatic clergy to retain their offices in the Catholic communion (*Ep.* 72.2.1-3).

church;[218] they had to remain subordinated permanently to an originally Catholic bishop.[219]

Numerous conflicts among these decisions and with traditional African practice are immediately evident. Cyprian and his colleagues had regarded schism as equivalent to apostasy, and they refused to allow anyone guilty of either to serve in the Catholic clergy. They subjected apostate and schismatic bishops to public penance, including the imposition of hands. Schismatic and known apostate bishops were judged incapable of sanctifying by either baptism or ordination: any ritual they performed had to be repeated by a Catholic bishop in good standing.[220] The practice of the Roman church had been similar: following the Decian persecution, Cornelius had required penance of both apostate and schismatic bishops, accepting them into communion only as laity.[221]

The stipulations of the judges in Rome and Arles generally were accepted by the Catholics in Africa as the price of the recognition of Caecilian and their standing in the universal communion. They followed the Roman practice, rather than the later decree of the Council of Nicaea, by receiving schismatic clergy without the imposition of hands, and they did not subordinate a returning schismatic bishop to his Caecilianist counterpart. Evidence of Donatist bishops joining the Caecilianist communion under these provisions begins in the middle of the fourth century.[222]

Though it maintained an outpost in Rome, the Donatist church was otherwise found only in Africa. The Caecilianists enjoyed the communion of the universal church and the support of the imperial government. Within Africa, the two churches or parties maintained parallel governing structures, though they differed in their understanding of the sacraments of baptism and orders, and of the efficacy of the episcopal ministry.

## Clerical Office

Little evidence has survived of clerical office and the numbers of persons serving congregations during the fourth century. The records of imperial actions at Cirta in Numidia provide the names of the clergy of that church on two occasions, in 303 and 320. At the beginning of the century, Bishop Paulus was assisted by four presbyters, two deacons, four subdeacons, seven readers, and

218. Council of Nicaea, 8. Caecilian's version is in Turner, *Ecclesiae Occidentalis Monumenta Iuris Antiquissima*, 1.2:122-24.

219. Socrates specified that they could neither nominate nor ordain clerics.

220. Cypr. *Ep.* 70.1.3, 2.2-3; 72; 74.5.4.

221. Eusebius, *Hist. eccl.* 6.43.10; Cyprian, *Ep.* 55.11.1-3; 67.6.3. He had made a singular exception of a schismatic confessor whom he accepted back as a presbyter (*Ep.* 49.2.1-5).

222. The first evidence of a negotiated return is in *Con. Carth.* a. 345-48, 12.

five gravediggers. The readers turned over to the imperial authorities thirty-four volumes of sacred books that were being kept in their houses. Two of these readers were identified as having other occupations: one was a grammarian and the other a tailor. In 320, Bishop Silvanus was assisted by five presbyters (one of whom had received the office by bribing Silvanus), three deacons, two subdeacons, and two gravediggers.[223]

Silvanus himself was accepted by a divided congregation as a replacement for Paulus in a tumultuous meeting over objections that as a subdeacon he had been guilty of apostasy by personally handing over one of the sacred vessels to Roman authorities.[224] He was then consecrated by neighboring bishops — many of whom admitted the same crime — under the direction of the Primate of Numidia, Secundus of Tigisis.[225]

A good number of the clergy compromised with the imperial officials and became guilty of the crime of *traditio,* which was then understood as a form of apostasy.[226] By Cyprian's theology, which the church was nominally following, such bishops should have been removed from office, subjected to public penance, and, after reconciliation, allowed to communicate among the laity. The actions of the African bishops, as has been noted, did not follow exactly the requirements of Cyprian's theory and practice.

In 313, Constantine exempted the Christian clergy from all civic responsibilities.[227] In 326, he renewed the exemption but restricted it to the Catholics; heretics and schismatics were to be bound to the public service.[228] A few years later, however, the Catholics had to appeal for imperial intervention to secure these privileges against Donatist aggression. Constantine affirmed the privileges, extending them to subdeacons and readers, and requiring the governor of Numidia to enforce the decree.[229] Valentinian I excluded any bishop who engaged in rebaptism as unworthy of these immunities.[230]

## Lay Elders

At the beginning of the fourth century, a series of judicial procedures associated with the Diocletian persecution and the consequences of episcopal failure

223. *Act. Zeno.* 5; the data is summarized in Maier, *Le dossier du donatisme,* 1:213-14.
224. *Act. Zeno.* 13, 16.
225. Aug. *Cresc.* 3.27.30 quoted the records of the meeting. See also Optat. *Parm.* 1.14-15.
226. *Act. Zeno.* 3-5 contains the official record of a demand for and turning over of sacred books and vessels in Cirta.
227. The response of the proconsul, Anullinus, is preserved in Aug. *Ep.* 88.
228. *C.Th.* 16.5.1.
229. Constantine's response is preserved in the documents appended to Optat. *Parm.* no. 10; the letter to Valentinus, the governor of Numidia, is in *C.Th.* 16.2.7.
230. *C.Th.* 16.6.1.

during the persecution provide clear indicators of the functioning of elders (*seniores*), within the Christian congregations in Africa. At the end of the century, the conflict within the Donatist church between Primian and Maximian also involved these elders.

The *Passion of St. Felix* (Felix was the Bishop of Thibiuca in Proconsular Africa) recounts that the local official first asked the elders to secure the turning over of the sacred books; he then turned to the presbyter and readers.[231] It may be presumed that the elders themselves did not have access to the books, though they might have provided the names of the clergy who then were questioned. The elders may have been targeted because they were prominent persons, well known to the authorities.

The *Gesta apud Zenophilum* are the records of a hearing held in 320, during which the report of an imperial visitation at the church of Cirta in Numidia in 303 was read into evidence. The bishop at the time, Paulus, may have been executed for his refusal to cooperate. One of his subdeacons, Silvanus, was recorded as turning over a sacred vessel to the Roman authorities. This same Silvanus subsequently was a candidate for bishop of the church in a conflicted election. The elders and people strongly objected to Silvanus because he was generally known to have committed apostasy. They were, however, overcome by pressure from his supporters, including (it was alleged) prostitutes and a gladiator.[232] One of the elders later admitted that he knew of Silvanus's crime but claimed that the elders and people were unable to stop the election.[233] A synod of bishops under the presidency of Secundus of Tigisis (discussed above) reviewed the situation and accepted the election.[234] An episcopal report — which might have been a protest by some who had opposed the election and confirmation of Silvanus — served notice to the bishops who had supported him, as well as the clergy and elders of the church of Cirta, that they were fully aware that their bishop was both an apostate and a thief.[235]

A dozen years later, Silvanus got into a violent conflict with one of his deacons, Nundinarius. This deacon sought the assistance of neighboring bishops to resolve the dispute. Purpurius of Limata, a long-time associate of Silvanus, advised him to employ the clergy and elders to resolve the conflict.[236]

---

231. *Passio Sancti Felicis Episcopi;* Herbert Musurillo, *The Acts of the Christian Martyrs* (Oxford: Clarendon Press, 1972), 266.

232. The congregation was locked up in an assembly space in the cemetery (*Act. Zeno.;* CSEL 26:194.11-29). Maier, in *Le dossier du donatisme,* 1:233, n. 121, dates the election in 307 or 308.

233. The deacon Nundinarius introduced the evidence in the *Act. Zeno.* (CSEL 26:188.34–189.8, 192.18–193.2).

234. This hearing discovered that a number of bishops had been guilty of the same crime (Aug. *Cresc.* 3.27.30).

235. *Act. Zeno.;* CSEL 26:188.34–189.8. The report of Bishop Fortis is also found in Aug. *Cresc.* 3.29.33. For an explanation of these events, see Shaw, "'Elders' in Christian Africa," 207-26.

236. *Act. Zeno.;* CSEL 26:189.21-24.

Purpurius himself then wrote directly to them, citing Exodus 12:21 on the consultation of the elders of Israel as a precedent for their intervention.[237] The language of his letter clearly indicates that he expected the elders to exercise a judicial role, though perhaps an informal one.[238] A second bishop, contacted by Nundinarius, also wrote to the clergy and elders, urging on them the responsibility for resolving disputes without recourse to secular courts, as the Apostle Paul had admonished the church in Corinth (1 Cor. 6:5-6).[239] The record of these proceedings clearly indicates that the elders were distinct from the clergy. Their status among the people gave them a certain independence from the bishop, which empowered them to intervene in conflicts within the church.[240]

As these events were transpiring in Numidia, a division was developing within the church in Carthage, to which its elders contributed. Bishop Mensurius was arrested and sent to Rome for trial. Before leaving, he committed the treasures of the church to the elders for safekeeping. He took the precaution of entrusting an inventory to an old woman in the congregation, who was to deliver it to his successor in case he did not survive and return.[241] Once Caecilian was elected bishop and received the inventory, he found that the elders were unable to account for the treasure. They then broke off communion with him and supported the action of the Numidian bishops against him.[242]

In the investigation of the charge of apostasy against Felix of Abthugni, the Donatist elders, rather than the clergy of the church, were the actors in the imperial judicial procedure.[243] Donatist elders had been involved in the ecclesiastical charges as well. Felix was originally accused of apostasy by Ingentius, who had been a secretary to one of the city officials in Abthugni during the persecution. This charge was in retaliation for Felix's own accusation against Maurus, the Bishop of Utica and a friend of the accuser. Ingentius proceeded to fabricate evidence against Felix. Taking three elders from Utica with him, he attempted to trick his former employers in Abthugni into implicating Felix in apostasy.[244] The scheme was uncovered when the city officials testified before the proconsul in Carthage.[245]

237. *Act. Zeno.;* CSEL 26:189.27-33.

238. *Act. Zeno.;* CSEL 26:190.4-9.

239. *Act. Zeno.;* CSEL 26:191.5-8.

240. Shaw provides a full analysis of the evidence (Shaw, "'Elders' in Christian Africa," 211-17), though this interpretation does not follow his emendation of the text to read *seniores* for *fossores.*

241. Optat. *Parm.* 1.17. She was not identified as a widow; Mensurius's objective may have been to find someone who would not be suspected as his agent. Even if the story is a fabrication, it shows that the elders might have exercised such a role.

242. Optat. *Parm.* 1.18.

243. *Act. pur. Fel.;* CSEL 26:198.21-22.

244. *Act. pur. Fel.;* CSEL 26:201.15-23.

245. *Act. pur. Fel.;* CSEL 26:203.3-204.4. This incident shows that during and after the per-

At the end of the fourth century, the elders of the Donatist church in Carthage played a major role in the conflict between Bishop Primian and one of his deacons, Maximian. The elders sought the intervention of neighboring bishops in response to the aggressive actions of this new bishop, the successor of Parmenian. Primian refused to cooperate with the episcopal synod meeting in early 393, but he used agents to disrupt its proceeding and harass the participants. The elders themselves were attacked in the basilica, and some of them were killed.[246] Primian was deposed by a council meeting at Cebarsussi in Byzacena, and Maximian was elected and consecrated bishop in Carthage. The Donatist council at Bagai subsequently overruled the actions taken against Primian and condemned the consecrators of Maximian. The elders of the Donatist churches at Musti and Assuras then instigated legal procedures for recovering their basilicas from the bishops who refused to submit to Primian.[247]

Because most of this fourth-century evidence is imbedded in imperial court records, it presents what may be too narrow a view of the role of the elders in the Christian congregations. The elders were part of the people rather than the clergy. Only Victor at Cirta was in both groups, identified as a reader during the imperial visitation in 303 and as an elder, both during the election of the bishop a few years later and at the trial in 320. Unlike the clergy who are identified by name and office in the official reports, the elders remain anonymous — even Victor's dual role has to be inferred from Nundinarius's questioning. The elders functioned somewhat independently of the clerical structure and thus were expected to help resolve conflicts, even within the clergy. They led the opposition to Silvanus's election and later were asked by neighboring bishops to help rein in his abuse of power. Ingentius planned to use elders from Utica as witnesses against Felix of Abthugni. The Donatist elders of Carthage, rather than the clergy, attempted to resolve the conflict between Primian and the rest of that church. Elders also seem to have had some responsibility for the goods of the church. Mensurius entrusted the treasures of the Carthaginian church to them during the persecution; Donatist elders initiated the judicial action for recovery of the basilicas from their Maximianist bishops.

As nonclerical leaders within the congregation, the elders were peculiar to the African church; their presence and actions are evidenced nowhere else in the ancient church. Their functioning may have developed from the parallel role of elders in the towns and villages that did not use the Roman structures of municipal governance.[248]

---

secution, locally based officials, like the *duouiri,* protected Christian bishops because of ties of friendship.

246. Aug. *Psal.* 36.2.20 provides details of the conflict.

247. The records are found in Aug. *Cresc.* 3.56.62.

248. This is the argument of Brent Shaw's analysis in his "'Elders' in Christian Africa." He further develops this in Brent D. Shaw, "The Structure of Local Society in the Early Maghreb: The

The practice of holding synods of bishops continued in the fourth century, though the records of those meetings are quite limited. The African church divided into competing communions early in the century because of a conflict over the election and consecration of Caecilian as Bishop of Carthage in late 311 or early 312, as has been seen. Bishops from Numidia met in Carthage, probably shortly after Easter in 312, to reject Caecilian. They then elected and consecrated Mensurius as his replacement.[249]

A council of about 270 bishops met in 336, under the presidency of Donatus.[250] He had been elected bishop of the anti-Caecilianist party upon the death of Mensurius sometime before October 313, the time when Donatus represented his party before the ecclesiastical tribunal convoked in Rome by Constantine.[251] After the return from exile allowed by the emperor Julian, a council of Donatist bishops was held at Theveste in Numidia, where a Caecilianist bishop appeared to protest the killing of two of his deacons in the assault on his basilica.[252]

At the end of 392, the lay elders of the Donatist church of Carthage called for a council of bishops to deal with the conflict between the new bishop, Primian, and his clergy. Forty-three bishops, mostly from Proconsular Africa and Byzacena, gathered in Carthage early in 393. Primian refused to deal with this council and blocked its work.[253] A second council met on 24 June 393 at Cebarsussi in Byzacena; its *acta* give the names of sixty supporters of the action against Primian.[254] The following April, Primian and Optatus of Thamugadi gathered a council of about 310 bishops at Bagai in Numidia to put down the rebellion.[255]

After the imperial suppression of Donatism at the Conference of Carthage in 411, thirty bishops who clung to that communion held a council in 418 or 419; they offered to receive back into their communion any bishop or presbyter who had been forced to join the Caecilianists. If these clerics had not exercised their ministry as Caecilianists — by preaching or celebrating the eucharist — they would have been allowed to reclaim their office in the Donatist church.[256]

The Caecilianists met under their bishop of Carthage, Gratus, in 348, af-

---

Elders," *Maghreb Review* 16 (1991): 18-55. It would require the transfer of the function to churches in municipalities, such as Cirta and Carthage, where the elders had no civic role.

249. See Maier, *Le dossier du donatisme*, 1:128-35.

250. Aug. *Ep.* 93.10.43.

251. Optat. *Parm.* 1.23; see Maier, *Le dossier du donatisme*, 1:151-52.

252. Optat. *Parm.* 1.18.

253. Aug. *Cresc.* 4.6.7–7.9; see Maier, *Le dossier du donatisme*, 2:73.

254. See Aug. *Psal.* 36.2.20; Maier, *Le dossier du donatisme*, 2:73-82.

255. Aug. *Cresc.* 3.53.59; 4.10.12, 28.35; *Petil.* 1.10.11.; Maier, *Le dossier du donatisme,* 2:84-91.

256. Aug. *Gaud.* 1.37.47-48.

ter the mission of Macarius and Paul, which attempted unification of the two churches. Seventeen bishops are indicated as present, and reference is made to one other bishop.[257] The next Caecilianist meeting whose *acta* survive was in 390, under Geneclius in Carthage.[258]

In 393, the Caecilianists began a series of councils, which were held regularly until 427, under the direction of Aurelius of Carthage. The bishops deliberately collected and organized their legislative work. The decisions were edited as the *Breuarium Hipponensis* in 397, a collection was made in 419, the *Canones in Causa Apiarii,* and subsequently as the *Registri Ecclesiae Carthaginensis Excerpta.*[259] These councils produced a comprehensive body of law, dealing primarily with the clergy.

## Orders as a Sacrament

By the fourth century, the ritual of orders was being understood in much the same way as baptism. Independent of the holiness of the minister, it effected a permanent change in a person's standing before God and within the church. The influence of this way of thinking is evident in the decisions made regarding the Donatist charges against Caecilian. The Roman bishop Miltiades allowed the bishops opposing Caecilian and any whom they had ordained to rejoin the Catholic communion and exercise their ministry in it without being reordained.[260] The Council of Arles in 314 insisted that an apostate bishop could ordain another bishop, who could then function in the Catholic communion, though the apostate himself had to be removed from office.[261] Those who had been ordained, moreover, were not to be subjected to the rituals of penance, though they were to be removed from office if guilty of a major sin.[262]

The actions of the Donatist exiles returning in 362 demonstrated a similar concern with the long-lasting effects of the ritual of ordination. They scraped not only the wooden altars to purify them from the Caecilianist sacrifices but also shaved the heads of the priests who had served the communities.[263]

Optatus himself argued that the custom of the church was to respect the ordination and, thus, not to impose hands on the clergy in penance.[264] To con-

257. *Con. Carth.* a. 345-48 (CCSL 149:3-10).
258. *Con. Carth.* a. 390 (CCSL 149:12-19).
259. CCSL 149:30-53, 173-247, 94-149.
260. Aug. *Ep.* 43.5.16.
261. *Con. Arel.* a. 314, 14.
262. Donatus was condemned for both rebaptizing and imposing hands in penance on apostate bishops (Optat. *Parm.* 1.24).
263. Optat. *Parm.* 6.1; 2.23-25. These clergy would have been ordained and perhaps even baptized by Catholics.
264. Optat. *Parm.* 1.24.

demn the Donatist purifying of the priests, he appealed to the respect that God had commanded and that David had shown toward those whom God had chosen and anointed.[265] Stephen, the Roman bishop, had made a similar argument against Cyprian's practice of rebaptizing those upon whom Christ's name had been invoked, albeit in schism.[266] Augustine, in his own response to Parmenian, would formalize the argument, equating the efficacy and persistence of ordination with that of baptism, and noting that neither sacrament was to be repeated.[267]

This understanding of the sacramental nature of ordination was itself the foundation of a renewed practice of allowing Donatist clergy to exercise their offices when they joined Catholic communion.

## Assimilating Schismatic Clergy

Under the leadership of Aurelius of Carthage and the prodding of Augustine of Hippo, the Caecilianists took a new approach to the assimilation of Donatist clergy. The first of a series of councils over which Aurelius presided was held in Hippo Regius in 393. A proposal was made that Donatist bishops be welcomed to assume the episcopal office in the Caecilianist communion if either they had not practiced rebaptism of converts or they could bring their congregations with them into union.[268] A second proposal was advanced in 397: to allow the ordination of converts who had been baptized as children in the Donatist communion.[269] The proposals were aimed at meeting the needs of Donatist congregations coming into Catholic unity: they might retain their existing clergy and make new appointments from among their own membership. Some of these clergy, however, would have been guilty not only of participating in an established schism but also of repeating the baptism of a convert to their communion. The Caecilianist bishops noted that preceding councils had forbidden the acceptance of Donatist clerical converts in their orders, though no such evidence has survived for Africa. In 386, a Roman council, whose decisions

265. Optat. *Parm.* 2.23. Optatus used the text of Ps. 105:15: "Touch not my anointed ones, do my prophets no harm." He identified the "anointed ones" as kings and priests by means of Ps. 133:2 and 1 Sam. 15:1. The use of this text does not of itself establish what is not otherwise witnessed: that anointing was part of the ritual of clerical ordination. The imposition of hands in the ordination ritual would have paralleled the placing of the eucharistic elements on the altar and justified the Donatist action. See below, pp. 414-15.

266. Cypr. *Ep.* 73.20-25.

267. Aug. *Parm.* 2.13.28. The imposition of hands in penance might have given the impression to the faithful that the sacrament of orders could be removed, since the cleric was no longer allowed to exercise the office.

268. *Bru. Hipp.* 37. It might have been a proposal of the council of 397 that edited the canons of the prior council of Hippo.

269. *Reg. Carth.* 47.

were communicated to the Africans by Bishop Siricius, specified that Donatist converts were to be received by the imposition of hands "because they violated the baptisms of their converts."[270] This phrase probably referred to Catholics who had been rebaptized by Claudianus, the Donatist Bishop of Rome, and who had then returned to Catholic communion after his expulsion from the city.[271] In Africa itself, the Roman decision might have been read as aimed specifically at Donatist clergy who had performed the ritual of rebaptism.[272] The African bishops justified their proposal by observing that the Donatist laity and clergy had been following an allegiance and a practice handed down to them rather than acting on their own initiative.[273] Moreover, the sins of such clergy — particularly that of rebaptism — could be forgiven through the prayers of the united congregations.[274] They decided, however, to consult with Siricius in Rome and Simplician in Milan before proceeding.[275]

During the summer of 401, the Caecilianist bishops returned to the question of accepting Donatist clergy. In a meeting of the bishops of Proconsular Africa in June, Aurelius of Carthage proposed to send a new delegation to press for the advice of the overseas bishops on ordaining Donatist laymen and accepting clerics.[276] When the general council of African bishops met in September of that year, the bishops decided to move ahead with their program, despite the apparently negative response their delegates had received in Italy.[277] They decreed that any cleric who wished to come to the Catholic church from that of the Donatists might

270. "Because they rebaptize." Ut uenientes a Nouatianis uel Montensibus per manus impositionem suscipiantur, (ex eo quod rebaptizant). The entire text of Siricius's letter to the Africans is in the *acta* of the *Concilium Thelense*, CCSL 149:59.19–63.113; the cited text is at 61.69-70. Some of the decrees of this council are paralleled in those of African councils; see Charles Munier's analysis in CCSL 149:54-55.

271. See the discussion in Maier, *Le dossier du donatisme*, 2:73. The texts of the synodal letter setting his expulsion are in Gian Domenico Mansi, *Sacrorum Conciliorum Nova et Amplissima Collectio*, ed. Jean-Baptiste Martin et al., 58 vols. (Paris: expensis H. Welter, 1901), 3:625-26. Emperor Gratian's act of expulsion is preserved in the *Col. Auel.* 13.8-10 (CSEL 35:56-57).

272. See Maier, *Le dossier du donatisme*, 2:73. A. C. De Veer works from this interpretation in "L'admission aux fonctions ecclésiastiques des clercs donatiste convertis," in *Oeuvres de saint Augustin*, 31: *Traités anti-donatistes* (Paris: Desclée de Brouwer, 1968), 766-71. The surviving text from Siricius actually addressed the reception of schismatic clerics in their honors only by implication: the imposition of hands interpreted as penitential would have disqualified them for clerical office. The evidence is inadequate to establish either interpretation of the Roman decision.

273. The parallel was the Catholic insistence that the bishops of the universal church could not be guilty of the reputed apostasy of Caecilian's consecrator, Felix, since they trusted the judgment of the bishops who judged the matter in Rome in 312 and Arles in 314.

274. *Bru. Hipp.* 37.

275. *Bru. Hipp.* 37; *Reg. Carth.* 47.

276. *Reg. Carth.* 57.

277. The prefatory notation in the *Reg. Carth.* reads: In hoc concilio litterae leguntur Anastasii Romani pontifici de Donatistis catholicos episcopos admonentis. CCSL 149:198.561-62. The contents of the letter were not recorded.

be accepted in his rank if the Caecilianist bishop of the place judged that the act would promote the peace of the church. The bishops knew that this had been the directive of the earlier Roman bishop, Miltiades, and the policy of the African church during the early days of the schism.[278] The Africans promised to respect the authority of the overseas councils and to follow their judgments wherever and whenever that did not impede the peace and unity of their church.[279]

This initiative seems to have met with some success. In 402, the Caecilianist Bishop of Bagai resigned his office and was replaced by his brother; both were converts from the Donatists.[280] The former may have been the same Maximianus who was seriously injured by a Donatist mob and whose subsequent appeal for redress sparked the imperial program that culminated in the Conference of Carthage in 411.[281]

On February 15, 405, Emperor Honorius issued a set of laws whose objective was an end to the schism.[282] Legislation adopted by a plenary council of African bishops who met in Carthage in June 407 indicates that the program of accepting Donatist clergy with their congregations had met with further success. The bishops allowed Donatist congregations that entered Catholic unity with their own bishops the right to continue choosing a bishop of their own rather than submitting to the local Caecilianist bishop.[283] The converted congregations might elect one of their own: a presbyter, a deacon, or a layman ordained or baptized in schism.

In anticipation of the imperial Conference of Carthage in 411, the Caecilianist bishops proposed a plan for transitional shared governance, gradually leading to a single bishop of a unified congregation in each place.[284] This pro-

---

278. *Reg. Carth.* 68. Augustine had established that this policy had been ordered by the Roman bishop, Miltiades (*Ep.* 43.5.16).

279. *Reg. Carth.* 68.

280. *Reg. Carth.* 88; Aug. *Ep.* 69.1.

281. The wording of Aug. *Ep.* 69.1 is compatible with this interpretation. The identification of this bishop with the one attested in the canon of the Council of Milevis in 402 is discussed in Albertus Cornelius De Veer, "Maximianus évêque catholique de Bagaï," in *Oeuvres de saint Augustin,* 31: *Traités anti-donatistes* (Paris: Desclée de Brouwer, 1968), 815-17. The further identification of this individual with the Maximianus of Bagai who suffered at the hands of the Donatists and provoked the imperial decree of unity in 405 (Aug. *Cresc.* 3.43.47) is judged uncertain by De Veer, though Serge Lancel affirmed it in his *Saint Augustine,* trans. Antonia Neville (London: SCM Press, 2002), 289-90.

282. Parts of the legislation are recorded in *C.Th.* 16.5.38, 6.3-5, 11.2, but the provision to which subsequent episcopal legislation appealed, such as for the Catholic acquisition of the resources of the Donatist churches, has not been preserved.

283. *Reg. Carth.* 99.

284. Augustine proposed this scheme in *Ep.* 128.2-3 before the conference and reported it in his summary of the proceedings (*Coll.* 1.5). Years later, he recalled it in trying to win over Emeritus, who had been his counterpart as representative of the Donatist bishops at Carthage (*Emer.* 5). Augustine also made public reference to the proposal in *Serm.* 358.4 and *Serm.* 359.5, which are dated immediately before and after the conference.

posal was affirmed in the decision of the imperial commissioner at the end of the conference. The conference itself had been so acrimonious, however, that few of the Donatist bishops accepted the opportunity at that time.[285] Some of these arrangements for transitional governance were modified at the general council of African bishops in 418.[286] The general principle of accepting Donatist bishops into Catholic communion, however, remained firmly in place.

An exception to this generous practice was made by the Caecilianists, as it had been by the Donatists, for any who left their communion to join the rival church and then sought to return. Because such persons were deserters and subject to full public penance, they were forbidden to function as clergy, even if they had been ordained in the other church.[287] Innocent, who was Bishop of Rome during much of the implementation of Aurelius's program, also insisted that Caecilianist deserters must be subjected to lengthy penance and could not serve as clerics in that church.[288]

Augustine also specified, as his own practice, that if a Donatist cleric had been disciplined and removed from office, he should not escape that penalty by entering the Caecilianist church; he was not allowed to function as a cleric.[289] He remonstrated with his Donatist counterparts for taking a very different approach to the problem of accepting Caecilianist clerics, even those who had been degraded for violations of the moral law. The Caecilianist deserter was treated as a pagan who had never been baptized. All prior sinfulness was removed by the administration of baptism; the convert could be ordained into the clergy without obstacle.[290]

## Conclusion

Cyprian's explanation of the status of the clergy provided the theological foundation for the Donatist objection to the leadership of Caecilian and their division from his communion at the beginning of the fourth century. The Donatists affirmed that the clergy had to be free of the crime of apostasy, both in their own conduct and in the conduct of the bishops with whom they entered into communion. In practice, the standard proved difficult to realize. Secundus of Tigisis and other initiators of the schism had ignored among themselves the

285. *Edictum Cognitoris*, CCSL 149A:178.65–179.79.

286. *Reg. Carth.* 117, 118.

287. Aug. *Unic. bapt.* 12.20. Augustine noted, however, that not all of his Catholic colleagues abided by this rule.

288. Innoc. *Ep.* 2.8.11; 17.5.11; 39. He cited a ruling of Nicaea that no one who had been subjected to penance could serve in the clergy. The only relevant canon is 10, which prevented apostates.

289. Aug. *Ep.* 35.3, which was written in the first year of his episcopate.

290. Augustine refers to this case in *Ep.* 35.2-3 and again, with another case, in *Ep.* 108.6.19. Both occurred in Hippo. See also *Petil.* 3.38.44.

very crime of which they charged Caecilian's consecrators. Optatus of Thamugadi finally resolved the Maximianist schism by forcing back into Primian's communion two of the bishops who had been condemned as instigators, without formal penance or penalty.

The Caecilianists had been able to establish, at least to the satisfaction of their overseas Catholic colleagues and that of the Roman government, that the bishops of their communion were not guilty of the crimes the Donatists alleged. Yet the decisions of the episcopal tribunals at Rome and Arles had made their corporate innocence theologically irrelevant: apostate bishops could consecrate validly; only those personally guilty need be removed from clerical office once discovered; schismatic clergy might be allowed to exercise their offices in the Catholic communion. The Caecilianists had no difficulty in meeting their standard for holiness; their challenge was to justify it. Their bishops were moving toward an understanding of orders that paralleled the validity of baptism. They had not, however, succeeded in clearly articulating and justifying either practice. That would be the work of Augustine.

## THE CLERGY IN AUGUSTINE'S TIME

The writings of Augustine, particularly his sermons, provide details not available for earlier periods about the clergy and their living arrangements. The severe clergy shortage that the Caecilianist church in Africa suffered at the end of the fourth century — caused in part by the efforts to assimilate Donatist congregations — moved the bishops to offer ordination to converting Donatists and then to invite Donatist bishops to exercise their offices within the Caecilianist communion. These innovative moves required historical and theological justification, which Augustine provided.

### Clerical Offices

The writings and sermons of Augustine, along with the legislation of the councils of the African bishops in the first third of the fifth century, witness to the different clerical offices, their privileges and responsibilities. As is usual, more evidence is available for the office of bishop than for the other types of clergy.

#### DOORKEEPERS

The doorkeeper was a particularly important functionary in a time of competing communions and is witnessed for both Donatist and Caecilianist congregations. Augustine reported that this officer questioned strangers on their affiliations and turned away those who should not have been allowed to enter the church. He also would have been responsible for assuring that only the baptized remained for the prayers and eucharistic celebration that followed the sermon. The Donatist church might have been especially careful about nonmembers during periods of imperial suppression, when their assemblies were illegal.[291]

### ACOLYTES

Albinus, the only acolyte named during the fifth century in Africa, appeared in the role of a letter carrier. He seems to have been a Roman serving as courier between Augustine and Sixtus.[292] This office is otherwise unattested in the African church during the fifth century.[293]

### READERS

The reader or lector was responsible for proclaiming the scriptures in the liturgy.[294] The office is well documented as an entry-level position; those mentioned were often quite young. In one instance, however, the lector was an adult who was entering upon a clerical career.[295] Augustine referred to the reader twice during his surviving sermons, in each case because he mistakenly had sung a psalm other than the one assigned.[296] Readers may not have been formally ordained: under canonical legislation, anyone who had served even once in a church was considered a cleric belonging to that church and could not be moved to office in another without his bishop's permission.[297] The synodal laws indicated that not all the readers would continue in the service of the

291. In Aug. *Serm.* 46.31, the function is specified, but the officer is not named. In *Psal.* 103.4.10, Augustine described the function of this person in a large private house.

292. Aug. *Ep.* 191.1; 192.1. For the Catholic, see *Ep. Divj.* 26*.1.

293. The description of the ordination rituals of an acolyte in canon 6 of the Fourth Council of Carthage in the *Collectio Hispana* cannot be credited as genuine. The following specification of the ordination of a lector in canon 8, for example, is contradicted by what is otherwise known about the way this person was placed in office in Africa. See CCSL 149:344.68-73, 81-85.

294. Antoninus, later Bishop of Fussala, had begun his career as a lector in Hippo (Aug. *Ep.* 209.3). The case of another young person was in dispute because it was not clear that he had been a lector, since he seems to have read noncanonical scriptures. Privatianus wanted to enter the monastery in Hippo, and Augustine had accepted him there, but not into the clergy. Aug. *Ep.* 64.3; see also *Cons.* 1.10.15.

295. Timothy had committed himself to one church as a lector and then moved to another church as subdeacon (Aug. *Ep.* 63.1-4).

296. Aug. *Serm.* 352.1.1; *Psal.* 138.1.

297. Aug. *Ep.* 63.1, 2; *Bru. Hipp.* 19b; *Reg. Carth.* 54 (*Con. Carth.* a. 397, 90; *Con. Mil.* a. 402). The latter case may be in response to the problem addressed in *Ep.* 63. In one instance, Augustine expressed doubt that reading noncanonical scripture might qualify a lector (*Ep.* 64.3).

church: when they reached puberty, the boys were suspended from the exercise of their office until they either married or professed continence.[298] Thereafter, they were not restricted in their marriage rights, except in being required to give up the office if they married a second time, after a spouse's death.[299] As boys being prepared for a clerical career, readers were precious to the bishops, who might have provided their training in literacy.

### SUBDEACONS

Subdeacons were counted among the professional clergy; theirs was the next step to which readers advanced.[300] They were often assigned as assistants to the presbyters who served rural parishes.[301] In Hippo, Augustine named only one among his clergy, Valens, who was living in the bishop's house according to the discipline of common life. His brother was serving the church of Milevis in the same office.[302] Subdeacons also appear in Augustine's writings as letter carriers.[303] The subdeacons may have been required to abstain from sexual relations with their wives, but the record is ambiguous.[304]

### DEACONS

Most of the deacons to whom Augustine referred served in the bishop's church.[305] Only one is named as serving a rural congregation, and he may have

---

298. *Con. Hipp.* a. 393, 2; *Bru. Hipp.* 18.

299. *Con. Hipp.* a. 393, 3.

300. Timothy was a lector and was ordained a subdeacon (Aug. *Ep.* 63.2).

301. Thus the subdeacon Timothy was serving in Subsana, having been ordained by Severus of Milevis (Aug. *Ep.* 63.1). The subdeacon Primus, who went over to the Donatists after being removed from the Catholic clergy for irregular relationships with dedicated virgins, is described as a *colonus,* living on a rural estate (Aug. *Ep.* 35.2). Another Catholic subdeacon, Rusticus, had gone over to the Donatists after being excommunicated by his supervising presbyter (*Ep.* 108.16.19). When the Donatist presbyter Marcianus, serving in Urgensis, became Catholic, he had to flee the town; his subdeacon was killed (*Ep.* 105.2.3).

302. Aug. *Serm.* 356.3. There was a problem in his disposing of his property, which he shared with his brother, who might not have been required to give it up by the practice of the church of Milevis.

303. Asterius carried a letter from Jerome to Augustine (*Ep.* 39.1). An unnamed subdeacon carried the correspondence to Quodvultdeus, and was titled an ecclesiastic in *Ep.* 223.1, 3.

304. This is specified in canon 25 of the collection made for dealing with the case of Apiarius but is not otherwise attested. *Reg. Carth.* 70 says that although only bishops, presbyters, and deacons were required to abstain, other clerics must observe the custom of their local church.

305. In addition to his own clergy, Augustine's correspondence names Quodvultdeus, the deacon and subsequent bishop of Carthage (*Ep.* 191; 192).

been relegated to that role after some failure.[306] In his sermon dealing with the possessions of the clergy living in his house, Augustine named four deacons who had property and indicated that the others, whose number he did not specify, did not own anything. The church might have had seven deacons, following the apostolic precedent.[307] Faustinus and Severus were not natives of Hippo but had come to the service of its church. Another deacon, a native of Hippo, owned slaves whom he was preparing to emancipate.[308] Heraclius (a deacon who would later become a presbyter and then be named Augustine's successor as bishop) used his patrimony to make an investment in the name of the church.[309] Another deacon, Lazarus, had read the section from the Acts of the Apostles that introduced the sermon.[310] In the liturgical action, the deacons may have read the gospel texts; they also introduced the prayers and distributed the cup to the communicants.[311] Heraclius clearly had responsibilities for managing property, an office that Augustine recognized as belonging to the Roman deacon and martyr Lawrence.[312] Augustine also referred to two deacons of the Donatist church in Hippo who had lost their offices through sin.[313] The deacons were required to abstain permanently from sexual relations with their wives and could not marry a second time after being widowed.[314]

## PRESBYTERS

The presbyters were the most important of Augustine's clergy in Hippo. The sermon just discussed that accounted for the finances of the clergy of Hippo was occasioned by the death of the presbyter Januarius. Not only had he retained property he claimed to have given up, but he had made a will in which he assigned to the church funds that should already have passed to his son and

306. Aug. *Ep. Divj.* 18* was written to the church at Membliba, which had asked Augustine that the deacon Gitta, then serving in Unapompei, should be made their presbyter. Augustine replied that he had to be removed from office altogether.

307. The deacon Lazarus had been assigned to read the lesson from Acts (4:32-35) on the sharing of goods in the Jerusalem community, which was Augustine's text for the day (*Serm.* 356.1).

308. Aug. *Serm.* 356.6.

309. Aug. *Serm.* 356.7. Severus and Heraclius were said to have made housing arrangements for their mothers, indicating that they would have moved them to Hippo after they entered the church's service there.

310. Aug. *Serm.* 356.1; the occasion was an unusual one, however, and this might have been the ordinary role of the lector.

311. Augustine attributed the office of administering the chalice and reading the gospel to the martyr-deacons Stephen and Lawrence (*Serm.* 304.1.1; 319.2.3; 382.3).

312. Aug. *Serm.* 303.1; his responsibility for the church treasury is recognized in the story of his witness.

313. Aug. *Ep.* 78.8. The crime itself was not specified, though the Donatists boasted that their discipline was stricter and the clerics would not have been punished in the Catholic communion.

314. *Con. Carth.* a. 390, 2; *Reg. Carth.* 70.

daughter.[315] In his report to the congregation, Augustine mentioned only two other presbyters in Hippo at the time, Leporius and Barnabas. The former was quite a wealthy man whose gifts had enlarged and elaborated the church complex. Barnabas was responsible for founding and supervising a monastery, apparently after he was already among the clergy.[316] Augustine later nominated Heraclius, who had subsequently become a presbyter, to succeed him as bishop. The record of that nomination and the congregation's approval repeats the names of Leporius, Barnabas, and Heraclius; it then adds four additional presbyters: Saturninus, Fortunatianus, Rusticus, and Lazarus. Lazarus, like Heraclius, had been named as a deacon in the earlier sermon accounting for clerical finances. An additional presbyter, Boniface, was mentioned in a letter written as much as twenty years earlier and does not appear in these sermons.[317]

The responsibilities of the presbyters were manifold. Augustine's own preaching and engaging in controversy while still a presbyter were unusual at the time.[318] He did this not only because of his personal ability but because the bishop, Valerius, was not fluent in Latin.[319] Subsequently, however, presbyters were authorized and even encouraged to preach.[320] Once Heraclius had been accepted by the congregation as Augustine's successor, he took over many responsibilities of the church so that Augustine could devote his energies to finishing his writing projects.[321] Barnabas and Boniface each were engaged with supervising a monastery.[322] During Augustine's many absences from Hippo, the presbyters would have been responsible for the liturgy and for discipline.[323] When traveling, presbyters carried letters from their bishops certifying their status, which may have entitled them to privileges, such as hospitality, in churches they visited.[324]

315. Aug. *Serm.* 355.3. He was presumably a widower, since he was living in the bishop's house and made no provision for his wife in his will. Both children were living in monasteries at the time of his death. The requirement that the clergy give up their property was peculiar to Augustine's own practice; it was not a general practice in the African church.

316. Aug. *Serm.* 356.15. It was rumored that Barnabas had purchased for himself the property upon which the monastery was situated. Augustine clarified the situation and removed him from its supervision in order to stop the gossip.

317. Aug. *Ep.* 78 reports to the congregation and clergy that Boniface had been accused of some moral failing and was being sent to the shrine of St. Felix at Nola with his accuser, in the hope that the saint could manifest the truth.

318. Aug. *Ep.* 29 recounts his preaching to force a change in the way the martyrs' feasts were celebrated. He even preached to the bishops of Africa at the Council of Hippo in 393; the text survives as *De fide et symbolo*, *Retract.* 1.17; *Ep.* 23 challenged the Donatist Bishop of Hippo.

319. Possid. *Vita Aug.* 5.3; Aug. *Ep.* 29.7; *Serm.* 355.2.

320. Aug. *Ep.* 41.1.

321. Aug. *Ep.* 213.5.

322. Aug. *Ep.* 78.1; *Serm.* 356.15.

323. Aug. *Serm.* 196.4. The presbyters were unable to dissuade the people from participating in a pagan festival.

324. The presbyter Boniface, who was sent to the shrine of Felix of Nola for a test of his verac-

Rural parishes were under the direction of presbyters, and ecclesial legislation regulated their actions.[325] Thus, the presbyters were forbidden to sell or give away the property of the church without permission of the bishop.[326] They had to secure the bishop's permission for celebrating the eucharist outside a church and reconciling penitents, except in emergency.[327]

## BISHOPS

A local church had a single bishop who served that congregation from election to death. Only the bishop carried the Latin title of priest, *sacerdos,* though Augustine preferred the Latinized Greek title, *episcopus,* because it designated the function of oversight and guidance rather than the mediatorial role that the Donatists claimed for their leaders.[328] This officer bore primary responsibility for the life of the community: Augustine understood their succession to the Apostles in this sense.[329] In the basilica, the bishop sat on a raised throne in the center of the apse, with the presbyters seated on benches to his sides.[330] The bishop was the primary minister of baptism, the eucharist, the reconciliation of sinners, the ordination of clergy, and preaching.

The bishop was responsible for the property of his church. He had to receive or purchase property and sell it when necessary. Augustine estimated that he managed property worth more than twenty times his own meager inheritance, which he had donated to the church at Thagaste upon his ordination for the church in Hippo.[331] Augustine refused some gifts because of their implications. Thus, he judged that the shipping company offered by one of the faithful would expose the church to risks and conflicts that were inappropriate; he also refused to accept the gift of the presbyter Januarius that would have deprived his children of their rightful inheritance.[332] The bishops had to raise money for building projects and the other needs of the

---

ity in the conflict with the monk Spes, voluntarily dispensed with such a letter in order to maintain his accuser's equal standing (Aug. *Ep.* 78.4).

325. The independence of such clerics is clear in Aug. *Ep.* 65.

326. *Con. Hipp.* a. 427, 4, 9; *Cau. Apiar.* 33.

327. *Con. Carth.* a. 390, 3-4, 9. *Bru. Hipp.* 30b made the restrictions on reconciling dying penitents more realistic.

328. Aug. *Psal.* 126.3.

329. Aug. *Psal.* 44.32.

330. Aug. *Serm.* 359.5.

331. Aug. *Ep.* 126.7.

332. Aug. *Serm.* 355.4-5. In case of shipwreck, the survivors of the crew might have been required to testify under torture in an inquiry into responsibility; to protect them, the church would have had to maintain a reserve fund to repay shippers for their loss. This would have required withholding available funds from the needy, which Augustine was unwilling to do.

churches.[333] Before selling or giving away the property of his church, a bishop was required to obtain the permission of the primate of the province or at least the advice of neighboring bishops; he could be required to justify his actions to a council.[334]

In addition to his sacral and administrative functions, the bishop was authorized to hear and decide civil cases when both parties agreed to submit their dispute to him.[335] Though he often tried to find a compromise, his judgment was final.[336] He was also required to represent the church's interests to the governing officials, most often by seeking enforcement of imperial decrees in favor of the church or by interceding to mitigate the punishment of the condemned.[337] Bishops were regularly sent by councils to represent the interests of the African church at the imperial court.[338] Individual bishops also could plead the interests of their own churches, though only with the permission of their provincial primate.[339]

The bishops bore a shared responsibility for the governance of the church at the provincial and regional levels. In all meetings, bishops spoke according to rank, based on the date of their ordination.[340] The senior bishop in each of the ecclesial provinces was responsible for the affairs of the church and organizing his colleagues.[341] The Bishop of Carthage served this function for Proconsular Africa — independently of his length of service — and bore general responsibility for the whole of Roman Africa.[342] In other provinces, the primate seems to have been the bishop with the greatest seniority in office.[343] A local bishop

333. In *Psal.* 103.3.12, Augustine appealed for a colleague while visiting his church, so that the bishop would not have to do it himself.

334. *Cau. Apiar.* 26, 33; *Con. Hipp.* a. 427, 4, 9.

335. Aug. *Psal.* 118.24.3. This was based on Paul's admonition that Christians should not have recourse to secular judges. The role had first been authorized by Constantine (*C.Th.* 1.27.1); Arcadius and Honorius restricted it to civil cases and specified that both parties had to agree (*C.Th.* 1.27.2). It functioned as a kind of binding arbitration.

336. Aug. *Psal.* 25.2.13. He sometimes urged the honest party to make a concession to the swindler just to get peace (*Serm.* 167.3.4).

337. Thus bishops were required to follow up on the imperial action against the Donatists (*Reg. Carth.* 123). On the reduction of sentence, see, for example, Aug. *Ep.* 133.

338. Alypius did this regularly. The councils of Carthage on 27 April 399 and 16 June 404 both sent delegations. Individual bishops could also represent the interests of their churches, as did Maximianus of Bagai (Aug. *Cresc.* 3.43.47).

339. Permission was required according to the collection (*Cau. Apiar.* 23).

340. When a bishop was ordained, he was to be given a letter by his consecrators specifying the date and year, so that there would be no disputes about seniority (*Reg. Carth.* 89).

341. *Bru. Hipp.* 5 specified that they were to hold provincial synods and send legates to the general synod.

342. Aurelius presided not only at synods of the bishops of Proconsular Africa but also at general councils of the bishops of Africa.

343. Augustine, *Ep.* 59, objected to the efforts of a colleague to circumvent the authority of the Primate of Numidia, Xanthippus of Tagonensis.

could be called upon to help supervise the election of a new bishop and partic-ipate in his ordination. Bishops also served as judges in the trials of their own clergy and those of other churches.[344]

## Lay Elders

The record of the work of elders in congregations during the fifth century is much more limited than it is for the fourth. They are mentioned explicitly in only a single case, but their intervention can be glimpsed in a second instance and inferred in others.

At the plenary council of Caecilianist bishops in June 407, Maurentius of Thubursicu complained that, for the third time, the elders of the village of Nova Germania had failed to appear and present their complaint against him, as they had been ordered by the primate of Numidia. Maurentius asked that his name be cleared. The bishop of a neighboring city, Placentinus of Madaura, inter-vened in support of the elders. The council then approved an alternative plan. The case was to be transferred back to Numidia and heard in Thubursicu by twelve judges, six chosen by each side. Maurentius named his six judges on the spot, and they were approved by the council. The primate was directed to ar-range for the elders to select six more judges to fill out the panel.[345] The elders of this small village in Numidia had succeeded in moving their hearing to the diocesan seat, instead of being required to travel to Carthage and argue their complaint before a council of bishops. By this concession, they could choose judges they considered sympathetic and could bring local witnesses to support their complaint against their bishop. This incident shows episcopal deference to these leaders of the laity, but it does not establish that these were *seniores* of the church.

That Augustine's congregation in Hippo had its own elders is clear from three incidents. One letter is addressed to the "clergy, elders, and whole people of the church of Hippo whom I serve in the love of Christ."[346] Earlier, while still a presbyter, Augustine encountered significant opposition in reforming the festivals of the saints and martyrs, specifically of Leontius, who had built the principal basilica early in the fourth century. The final stage in overcoming opposition was an early morning meeting with a small group of congregants who were holding out for the traditional banquet. Once he had won them over,

344. When a presbyter or deacon was accused, the bishop added five colleagues (for a pres-byter) or two colleagues (for a deacon) to hear the case. A bishop could hear cases of others alone. *Bru. Hipp.* 8a-b.

345. *Reg. Carth.* 100.

346. Dilectissimis fratribus, clero, senioribus et uniuersae plebi ecclesiae Hipponiensis, cui seruio, in dilectione Christi Augustinus in domino salutem. Aug. *Ep.* 78 (CCSL 31A:83.1-3). Aug. *Ep.* 50 is addressed to elders of the place, not the church.

the matter was settled.[347] Even if these were not formal elders, they certainly served the same purpose. A third instance is provided in Augustine's account of the attempt of the congregation in Hippo Regius to draft Pinian into their clergy on the occasion of his visit to the church with his wife, Melania the Younger. Augustine provided a detailed account of the event, including his negotiations with members of the congregation who can be recognized in the role of elders. As the people were shouting for Pinian's ordination, Augustine gathered a small group of respected and worthy men in the apse. He explained to them that he had promised Pinian that he would not participate in a forced ordination. They proposed bringing in another bishop to ordain Pinian for their church. Augustine responded that another bishop could act for their church only with his permission, which he could not give without breaking his promise to Pinian. He then explained that, if they forced Pinian to be ordained, he would flee from Hippo at the first opportunity, and they would have gained nothing. They refused to believe that Pinian would abandon his office, even if it were forced upon him. The renewed uproar of the people, down a few steps in the nave of the church, broke off the conversation.[348] Pinian himself broke the impasse by swearing a carefully worded oath and then breaking it by leaving town the next morning.[349] The role of these elders as mediators between the people and their bishop can be perceived in this incident. Apparently, they were not elected officials but respected men who could be trusted to deal fairly.

Augustine's accounts of the extended conflict between Antony of Fusalla and his congregation do not mention any role for elders, though they do recognize the intervention of a property holder and her manager.[350] On an estate, these persons might have assumed the responsibility for representing the interests of a congregation that its own elders would exercise in a village.

Some of the judicial interventions undertaken by the elders in the previous century were assigned to a new imperial officer, the *defensor ecclesiae.* The bishops of Africa petitioned for this assistance, and Emperor Honorius granted it in 407.[351]

347. Aug. *Ep.* 29.8.

348. Aug. *Ep.* 126.1. Augustine referred to them as *honoratiores et grauiores,* perhaps realizing that Albina — a Roman matron — would not understand the peculiarly African institution of *seniores.*

349. Aug. *Ep.* 126.5, 11-13. Augustine's account implies that Pinian and Melania planned the deception that allowed them to extricate themselves.

350. Aug. *Ep. Divj.* 20*.10, 14, 17-19. The reference to Celerinus's exercise of power against Antony in Aug. *Ep.* 209.5 is unclear but does not seem to identify him as one of the locals.

351. *Reg. Carth.* 97 and *C.Th.* 16.2.38. Antony of Fusalla appointed his own, who then narrowily escaped imperial punishment for abuse of power; see Aug. *Ep. Divj.* 20*.6, 29.

The process of the selection of clergy is attested five times in Augustine's writings. Each of these, however, was extraordinary. Augustine recounted his own selection for the presbyterate and then the episcopate.[352] He had been trying to avoid clerical office but was drafted into the clergy of Hippo during a visit there. Later, he was made bishop while his predecessor, Valerius, was still alive, but limited in his ability to function. Through Augustine's work on the assimilation of Donatist clergy, he came to realize that having two bishops in a city had been forbidden by the Council of Nicaea.[353] Decades later, the Hippo congregation attempted to force the ordination of Pinian. Augustine blocked the popular will — which was viewed by Pinian's family as a bold attempt to make his extreme wealth available for their church — by asserting that he would not ordain anyone to the clergy who was unwilling to take up its burden.[354]

Some of the bishops made provision for the selection of their successors, perhaps so that their church would not be hampered by a long delay while a suitable candidate was identified.[355] Severus of Milevis decided upon his successor and secured the agreement of the clergy, but he did not present it to the laity. Upon his death, then, a controversy erupted when the people objected to the candidate. When Severus's own intention was revealed, the candidate was finally approved and ordained. Augustine reported that the people certainly would have acceded to Severus's recommendation had he made it to them himself.[356] Forewarned, Augustine proposed to his own congregation that Heraclius, who had been a deacon and presbyter in the church, should succeed him as bishop after his death. The congregation approved. Heraclius then took over much of the day-to-day administration of the church so that Augustine could attend to his writing. He remained a presbyter, however, until after Augustine had died.[357]

Augustine also nominated one of his own clergy to be Bishop of Fussala, a rural parish belonging to the diocese of Hippo, in which a minority Catholic population was served by presbyters. When the Donatist congregation entered into Catholic unity, the enlarged church merited a bishop of its own. Augustine,

352. Aug. *Serm.* 355.2.

353. Aug. *Ep.* 213.4. Augustine explained that the Council of Nicaea had forbidden the ordination of two bishops in the same city. This was one of the proposals for dealing with returning Donatists, and the problem may have been discovered at that time.

354. Aug. *Ep.* 126.

355. The shortage of clergy meant that capable bishops were in short supply. In the plenary council of September 401, bishops who were given administration of vacant sees were warned to supply a bishop within a year; there was apparently some danger of the supervisor absorbing the other diocese into his own (*Reg. Carth.* 74).

356. Aug, *Ep.* 213.2.

357. Aug. *Ep.* 213 records the exchange and agreement between Augustine and his congregation. A full record of the proceedings was written down.

whose responsibility it was to initiate the process, identified a presbyter who had the necessary qualifications, including facility in the Punic language. He invited the senior bishop of Numidia to come for the ordination. The selected candidate withdrew, however, and Augustine settled on Antony, who had the necessary language skills but whose clerical experience was limited to having served as a reader in the church of Hippo. Augustine proposed the candidate to the faithful, and they accepted the young man on his recommendation.[358] He turned out to be a very troublesome bishop.

On another occasion, the people of Membliba apparently made a request for the services of Gitta, the deacon of another parish, to be their presbyter. Upon examination, Augustine found that the candidate had been guilty of an illicit sexual relationship; he had to remove the man from office altogether. He encouraged the people to continue looking for a presbyter and promised to provide a candidate himself if they did not identify one.[359]

The conciliar legislation set some guidelines for the appointment of clergy. Those who were subject to the rule of sexual continence — subdeacon, deacon, and presbyter — had to be at least twenty-five years old.[360] They also had to be approved by the bishop and the people.[361] All the members of their households, including the spouses of their children, had to be Catholic Christians.[362] They had to put aside all secular occupations that would distract them from their duties, such as administering property, serving as bailiff of an estate, or serving as guardian of minors. All were forbidden to assign them such responsibilities after their ordination.[363] Yet Augustine's account of the financial affairs of his own clergy clearly indicated that some of them had these responsibilities for church property.[364] Bishops, in addition, were often entrusted with the legacies of orphans and served as their protectors.[365]

One of the major problems facing the Caecilianist bishops was a shortage of clergy.[366] This need resulted in attempts to recruit candidates from other dioceses. Augustine's correspondence, for example, contains details of a disagreement with his friend Severus of Milevis over a reader recruited from one of his rural parishes[367] and a complaint to Aurelius of Carthage over the ordination

---

358. Aug. *Ep.* 209.
359. Aug. *Ep. Divj.* 18*.1-2.
360. The age limit was set for both clerics and consecrated virgins: *Bru. Hipp.* 1b; *Cau. Apiar.* 16.
361. *Bru. Hipp.* 20; Aug. *Serm.* 355.6.
362. *Bru. Hipp.* 17.
363. *Con. Carth.* a. 345-348, 8-9; *Bru. Hipp.* 15. Constantine had freed them from municipal responsibilities. See above, p. 392.
364. Heraclius, Leporius, and Barnabas (Aug. *Ep.* 356.7, 10, 15).
365. Aug. *Ep.* 176.2.
366. This is attested for the first time in *Bru. Hipp.* 37.
367. Aug. *Ep.* 62; 63.

412    LEADERSHIP: THE CLERGY AND THE SACRAMENT OF ORDERS

of a monk who had left the Hippo monastery without approval.[368] Such problems resulted in legislation forbidding raids on the clergy of other dioceses.[369] Bishops were also forbidden to recruit from monasteries outside their dioceses without the permission of the local bishop.[370] One of the monks in Hippo wanted to enter the clergy, but Augustine withheld the required approval.[371] Bishops could also request that a cleric be released for the needs of another church. The Bishop of Carthage was authorized by his colleagues to require the release when a presbyter was chosen to be bishop of another church.[372]

Augustine recognized that a person might decline the call to become a bishop because he considered himself unworthy or unqualified.[373] A council specified, however, that any cleric who refused a promotion within his own diocese was to be removed from the clergy altogether.[374] The transfer of a bishop from one church to another was forbidden, and the prohibition seems to have been enforced.[375]

The selection and ordination of bishops was different from that of other clergy in that it required the collaboration of other bishops; it was not only a local matter. The candidate had to be approved both by the congregation he was to serve and by his fellow bishops.[376] The Donatists seem to have used twelve bishops as consecrators.[377] Perhaps in response, the bishops of Numidia proposed that the Caecilianists also require twelve consecrators of a new bishop; the general council refused because of the lack of bishops in some provinces. Aurelius of Carthage observed that Tripolitana, for example, had only five bishoprics and could hardly muster more than three of the four surviving bishops for the ordination of a new colleague. The traditional minimum of three continued to be required.[378] If the qualifications of the candidate were challenged, however, two

368. Aug. *Ep.* 60.

369. Such a law is found in *Con. Carth.* a. 345-48, 5, and again in *Bru. Hipp.* 19; *Reg. Carth.* 54, 90.

370. *Reg. Carth.* 54, 80.

371. The monk, Spes, was in a conflict with the presbyter, Barnabas, and attempted to extort clerical promotion (Aug. *Ep.* 78.3).

372. *Reg. Carth.* 55.

373. Aug. *Cresc.* 2.11.13.

374. *Con. Hipp.* a. 427, 3. Earlier, Augustine had allowed the presbyter he proposed from Fussala to withdraw at the last minute (Aug. *Ep.* 209.3).

375. *Reg. Carth.* 48; Aug. *Ep.* 209.7.

376. *Bru. Hipp.* 38a-c.

377. Aug. *Cresc.* 3.52.58; 4.4.4-5; *Ep.* 185.4.17.

378. *Reg. Carth.* 49. The five episcopal cities in Tripolitana were all represented at the Conference of Carthage in 411; Girba and Tacapae each had both a Donatist and a Catholic bishop; Lepcis Magna and Oea had only a Donatist present; Sabratha had only a Catholic in Carthage but a Donatist at Cebarsussi in 393. When Aurelius pointed out the small number of bishops in Tripolitana in August 397, he may have neglected to recognize that not all five episcopal cities had an incumbent in his communion. See Jean-Louis Maier, *L'épiscopat de l'Afrique romaine, vandale, et byzantine* (Rome: Institut suisse de Rome, 1973), pp. 147, 161, 183, 194, 207.

additional bishops had to be summoned to decide whether the ordination should proceed.[379] The senior bishop of the province had to approve of the ordination; he was often present to supervise the choice and lead the ritual of installation.[380] When a new bishopric was being created, usually to provide for a Donatist congregation coming into unity, the bishop who had responsibility for the area (and thus from whose care the congregation was to be taken) also had to approve the new bishop.[381] In some instances, bishops experienced great difficulty in finding a suitable candidate.[382] The Donatists claimed that a primate had to be ordained by another primate, as their first bishop of Carthage had been by the Primate of Numidia.[383] The Caecilianists did not follow this practice for their bishop of Carthage.[384] Only the Bishop of Carthage became a primate upon his election and ordination; in other African provinces, the primate was the longest-serving bishop, and the Donatist "rule" was inapplicable.

Little information about the ordination ritual itself has survived. The imposition of hands by at least three other bishops was specified as essential.[385] Optatus compared its effect to the anointing of an Israelite king or priest and to the commissioning of a prophet, which brought these individuals under divine protection. The reference in his text to anointing seems to have derived from the Psalm (105:15) that warned against attacking those whom God had chosen rather than a ritual, which would not have applied to a prophet.[386] In his own discussion of priestly anointing, Augustine referred only to the baptismal rit-

---

379. *Reg. Carth.* 50. They were to consider the person of the objector and then the issue raised.

380. This is clear from Aurelius's intervention in the discussion in August 397, when he reported that he participated in an episcopal ordination nearly every Sunday (*Reg. Carth.* 49). Either he was exaggerating or the ordinations must have been performed in Carthage, since travel to various cities would have kept him always on the road. In *Ep.* 209.3, Augustine indicated that the primate of Numidia traveled to the ordination, at least when a new bishopric was established.

381. *Reg. Carth.* 56. This was the reason that Augustine was responsible for the selection of Antony for Fusalla.

382. See Aurelius's introduction to deliberations at the council of Proconsular bishops in June 401 (*Reg. Carth.* VI preceding canon 57). Augustine's problems in finding a bishop for Fusalla might not have been only because of the fluency in Punic language required but also because of the danger of going to serve a formerly Donatist congregation.

383. This rule was followed for the ordination of the schismatic Majorinus and perhaps for Donatus as well. His successor, Parmenian, was apparently ordained during the exile (347-362). No record of Primian's ordination has survived. His rival, Maximinian, was not ordained by a Numidian, but this does not appear as an objection to his legitimacy in the available records, all of which are in the writings of Caecilianists. For a discussion of this question at the Conference of Carthage in 411, see Aug. *Coll.* 3.16.29 and above, p. 48, n. 61.

384. Aug. *Coll.* 3.16.29. This is sometimes cited as one of the means used to challenge the legitimacy of the ordination of Caecilian, but the earliest record of this objection dates to a century after the event.

385. *Reg. Carth.* 49.

386. Optat. *Parm.* 2.23. See above, p. 398, n. 265.

---

ual, which conferred Christ's priesthood on all Christians; he never mentioned a second anointing as part of the ordination ritual.[387]

## Clerical Life

Augustine would have preferred to continue living in a monastic community after he was made bishop, but he found that the responsibilities for providing hospitality to visitors were impossible to fulfill in that context. Hence, he organized the clergy of the church in Hippo into a community, whose guiding rule of shared property was laid out in Acts 4:32-35.[388] None of the subdeacons, deacons, or presbyters were married or retained private property. All lived by a common fund;[389] all were required to eat at the common table.[390]

When Augustine discovered upon the death of the presbyter Januarius that some of his clergy had not divested themselves of their property, he provided to the congregation a full accounting of the financial status of each. In many instances, the claims of other members of the family upon the property meant that the cleric had not been able to liberate himself completely. Even in these cases, Augustine assured the people, the property met the cleric's obligations to his parents or siblings, or it was used for the benefit of the church itself.[391] At that point, early in 426, Augustine offered to relax the rule that required that all clergy of the cathedral live in the bishop's house. He preferred that his colleagues have the option of retaining both their property and their offices rather than live in deceit.[392] Apparently, none of them chose that option; all remained in the common life.[393]

In the bishop's house, the clergy shared a common fund and received their other necessities in the same way. As bishop, Augustine was prepared to receive gifts of food and clothing, provided that they could be shared by all.[394] The

387. Aug. *Serm. Dolb.* 26(198*).53.

388. Aug. *Serm.* 355.2. The rural clergy lived differently, since they were generally isolated.

389. Aug. *Serm.* 355.2; 356.1-2. Augustine's general rule that the goods of the cleric became the property of the church in which he was ordained was articulated in *Ep.* 83.4. Augustine also refused to allow clerics to disinherit their children in favor of the church (*Serm.* 355.4-5). Augustine's review of his own clergy indicates that none of them were currently married.

390. Aug. *Serm.* 356.13.

391. Aug. *Serm.* 355; 356.3-10. Augustine did not allow clerics to completely alienate their property until they had proven stable in their calling — thus the cases of the subdeacon Valens and the deacon Heraclius.

392. Aug. *Serm.* 355.6.

393. In *Serm.* 356, Augustine reviewed the financial arrangements of all his clergy and showed that none of them had retained personal property.

394. Aug. *Serm.* 365.13. He sold any garment that was too fine or costly to be suitable for a cleric. Only those who were sick might eat apart from the common table, and he welcomed special gifts intended to speed their recovery.

clergy of the church had a general right, he claimed, to be supported by the faithful. They were not to be treated as beggars.[395]

The presbyters who served the village churches outside Hippo, under Augustine's supervision, were subject to the same requirement of disposing of their property.[396] Because they were alone or assisted only by a subdeacon, however, they lived more independently. In certain instances, this freedom provided ample opportunities for transgression of their Christian commitments, and they had to be disciplined.[397]

Augustine's arrangements were unusual. The conciliar legislation assumed that clerics would have families and children for whom they were responsible. It set strict limits on the women who could live in their homes: mothers, grandmothers, aunts, sisters, and nieces, as well as other relatives to whom they had offered shelter before they were ordained. They could also accept into their homes the wives of their children and slaves.[398] They could make gifts only to Christians[399] and bequests only to relatives who were Christian.[400] They could eat or drink in inns or shops only when they were traveling[401] and could visit in another city or town only with the approval of the local bishop or presbyter.[402]

The councils showed particular concern in protecting the property of the church from being appropriated by the clergy.[403] Any property that a cleric acquired after ordination was to be dedicated to the church he was serving or to some other religious purpose.[404] Four instances of misuse of property are recorded in Augustine's correspondence. The presbyter Abundantius had embezzled a gift made to his church.[405] Bishop Paulus had disposed of his property at his ordination; he later purchased property for himself when a loan was repaid to him, and he used the church's tax exemption to defraud the government. His successor had to straighten out the resulting mess.[406] Antony of Fussala, though acquitted on charges of sexual misconduct, was found guilty of defrauding and abusing his congregation by stealing property, confiscating harvests, and even tearing down houses to use the stone in his own building projects.[407] Finally,

395. Aug. *Serm.* 46.3-4; *Psal.* 103.3.9-10.

396. Aug. *Ep.* 83.4 applies the rule to all clergy subject to Augustine.

397. Aug. *Ep.* 65.1. Another cleric of the diocese of Hippo had earlier been removed from office for the same type of infraction.

398. *Bru. Hipp.* 16.

399. *Bru. Hipp.* 14.

400. *Reg. Carth.* 81.

401. *Bru. Hipp.* 26.

402. *Bru. Hipp.* 35.

403. *Cau. Apiar.* 33; *Con. Hipp.* a. 427, 10.

404. *Cau. Apiar.* 32; *Con. Hipp.* a. 427, 5a-c.

405. Aug. *Ep.* 65.1.

406. Augustine admonished him about his lifestyle in *Ep.* 85 and wrote *Ep.* 96 to support his successor's appeal for a pardon.

407. Aug. *Ep.* 209.4; *Ep. Divj.* 20*.5-6.

Augustine and Alypius had to settle the affairs of a presbyter who became a monk but failed to provide for the disposition of his property. The congregation he had been serving claimed his estate, as did his legal heirs. The bishops agreed that the civil law had to prevail, and they agreed to compensate the congregation.[408]

## The Organization of the Episcopate

### PROVINCIAL ORGANIZATION

The church in Roman Africa was divided into a set of provinces that did not exactly correspond to the divisions of the provinces of the empire.[409] Proconsular Africa was central because it was the seat of Roman administration at Carthage; it bordered Byzacena on the south and Numidia on the west. South and east of Byzacena was the small province of Tripolitana, which had only five bishops at the end of the fourth century. At the Council of Hippo in 393, the church in Mauretania — to the west — was separated from that in Numidia, though at that point no distinction was made between the two Roman provinces, Mauretania Sitifensis and Mauretania Caesariensis.[410] At the Council of Carthage in May 419, however, the two Mauretanias were represented by distinct sets of three legates each, implying that they had been established as distinct ecclesiastical provinces.[411] At the Council of Carthage in 418, legates from Hispania were also present.[412]

Each of these provinces had its own primate or "bishop of the first chair," who was to be referred to as such and not as "Chief of the Priests" or "High Priest."[413] His was an administrative office, not one of higher rank above that of his fellow bishops. Only the Bishop of Carthage held his primacy on the basis of his city; all others apparently were determined on the basis of seniority of service. The Bishop of Carthage presided over the whole of the African church. He served as convener of the plenary councils of bishops, even when they were held in another province. In its name, he communicated the decisions of its councils to overseas bishops and issued the letters of instruction to episcopal legates who were sent on missions by their colleagues.[414] His church

---

408. Aug. *Ep.* 83.

409. See Map of Roman Africa, pp. xlii-xliii.

410. *Bru. Hipp.* D; *Cau. Apiar.* 17; that Mauretania had recently received its own primate is implied in the error which Victorinus made in inviting some of those bishops to a provincial council for Numidia (Aug. *Ep.* 59.1).

411. Subscriptions, CCSL 149:152-55.

412. This was for the condemnation of Pelagius and his supporters (CCSL 149:69.7).

413. princeps sacerdotum aut summus sacerdos (*Bru. Hipp.* 25). The Donatists apparently used such terminology (Aug. *Coll.* 3.16.29).

414. *Bru. Hipp.* 27b; *Reg. Carth.* 85.

maintained the list of recognized bishops of the Catholic communion in Africa.[415] He communicated to the provinces the date on which Easter was to be observed and the plenary council held (if one was scheduled for that year).[416] He was recognized as bearing responsibility for the whole African church and was empowered, as has been seen, to call presbyters from one church to be bishops of another. Between the councils at Hippo in 393 and 427, Bishop Aurelius of Carthage presided over nearly twenty plenary and provincial synods, most of them in Carthage. Nearly all the legislation of the African church that survives in the various collections was enacted under his leadership.

In each of the provinces, the senior bishop or primate was responsible for maintaining good order. He called and presided over any council of the bishops of his province and usually took part in any plenary council of Africa. He wrote the letters of his councils to overseas bishops.[417] His approval was necessary for the ordination of a bishop, for establishing a new bishopric, and for selling church property. He normally oversaw the election and ordination of each new bishop, maintained the list of approved bishops of his province, and communicated changes to the Bishop of Carthage.[418] Once he had received the date for the celebration of Easter from the Bishop of Carthage, the primate informed the bishops of his province. The primate had ultimate responsibility for appointing judges to hear charges against bishops, presbyters, and deacons, and he served as a manager of appeals of their decisions. If a bishop wished to travel overseas, to the court or the city of another bishop, he required the primate's letter of approval for the mission.[419]

The provincial synod was to be held annually at a time and place specified by the primate. All the bishops of a province who were well enough to travel were expected to attend.[420] This council ruled on issues that faced the church in the province. Its approval eventually was required for the establishment of new bishoprics;[421] it could review and approve the sale of church property;[422] it could act as a court of appeal for decisions of episcopal courts; and it could enforce depositions of bishops.[423] It was also to elect and instruct three legates to the plenary council of Africa if one was to be held later in the year.[424] In 416, provincial councils at Milevis in Numidia and at Carthage in Proconsular Africa

415. Reported in *Bru. Fer.* 84, and *Con. Carth.* a. 525 (CCSL 149:267.515-17).
416. *Reg. Carth.* 51. At the council in September 401, the bishops insisted that the date of Easter had to be set by mid-August so that meetings could be scheduled without conflict (*Reg. Carth.* 73).
417. *Bru. Hipp.* 27b.
418. Reported in *Bru. Fer.* 84, and *Con. Carth.* a. 525 (CCSL 149:267.515-17).
419. *Bru. Hipp.* 27a; *Con. Carth.* a. 397; *Cau. Apiar.* 23; *Reg. Carth.* 106.
420. *Concilium Thusdritanum* a. 417, a provincial council of Byzacena; *Bru. Fer.* 76.
421. *Reg. Carth.* 98.
422. *Cau. Apiar.* 26; *Con. Hipp.* a. 427, 4.
423. *Reg. Carth.* 125.
424. *Reg. Carth.* 76; *Cau. Apiar.* 14.

took the lead in the condemnation of Pelagius and Caelestius. For the most part, however, the work of the provincial council was disciplinary rather than doctrinal.

## STRUCTURE OF THE AFRICAN CHURCH

The first of the plenary councils held under Aurelius, at Hippo in 393, ambitiously decided that a plenary council of the African church was to be held every year. Each province was to send three episcopal legates, excepting Tripolitana, which was to send only one.[425] The plan was for the annual council to circulate among the provinces, but the three held in Numidia — at Hippo Regius in 393 and 427, and at Milevis in 402 — were the only ones recorded outside of Carthage. When the bishops of Mauretania objected in 397 that the council had not yet been held in their province, Aurelius explained that the distance of travel was simply too great and the journey too dangerous because of the number of barbarians in that part of the empire.[426] A large number of Proconsular bishops sometimes attended the plenary councils rather than being represented only by the province's three legates.[427] By 401, special efforts were necessary to secure the participation of the delegates from other provinces.[428] In 407, the council passed a resolution declaring the annual plenary councils onerous; it decided that, in the future, these would be called only when necessary and that provincial councils would be held annually to deal with ordinary business.[429] But violent conflict with the Donatists required councils in the following years. After 411, however, the records of general councils show that they did not meet regularly, and greater reliance seems to have been placed on the provincial meetings. At the last general council of their episcopates, at Hippo in 427, Aurelius thanked Augustine for his efforts in bringing the bishops together.[430]

The African bishops were very conscious of their legislative role. Their meetings regularly repeated and approved the decisions of earlier councils. Moreover, Aurelius oversaw the preparation and approval of three significant collections of rulings. In August 397, the bishops of Byzacena arrived in Carthage on 13 August, more than two weeks before the scheduled opening of the council. Aurelius asked them to draw up a list of the decisions that had been

---

425. *Bru. Hipp.* 5b; *Cau. Apiar.* 14.
426. *Reg. Carth.* 52.
427. No bishops signed the *acta* of the council of 25 May 419 precisely as legates of Proconsular Africa, though eight bishops identified by sees in that province signed between the delegates of Numidia and Byzacena. Some 217 bishops were present in addition to the legates. CCSL 149:150-55.
428. *Reg. Carth.* 76.
429. *Reg. Carth.* 95; *Bru. Fer.* 77.
430. CCSL 149:250.6-15.

made at the council of Hippo in 393. The resulting *Breuarium Hipponensis,* containing some 37 canons, was approved by the plenary council meeting on 28 August 397.[431] When the bishop of Rome challenged the authority of the African bishops to make the final judgment on the charges against the priest Apiarius and to forbid any appeal outside Africa, the council meeting on 25 May 419 approved a new collection of the legislation of the African church. This was sent to Rome for the purpose of demonstrating to its bishop that the African church was quite capable of governing itself.[432] The circumstances of the editing of the *Registri Ecclesiae Carthaginensis Excerpta* are unclear. It is limited to the councils under Aurelius but includes decrees beginning at the end of the *Breuarium Hipponensis.* It was probably the basis for the collection *Canones in Causa Apiarii,* and it was cited extensively in the council held under Bonifatius for the reconstitution of the Catholic hierarchy of Africa in 525.

## DISCIPLINING CLERICS

In their meetings, the African bishops were most occupied with the judicial procedures necessary for handling accusations against themselves and their clergy. The sustained conflict with the Donatists had been provoked by charges of apostasy against a bishop at the end of the Diocletian persecution. The ecclesial and imperial processes by which Caecilian and his consecrators were judged failed to bring an acceptable solution to the conflict. In the years following, the bishops in his communion never tired of defending Caecilian and of pointing out the failings of the founding bishops of the Donatist church and their successors. This made the bishops particularly sensitive to the good reputation of their own clergy and anxious to demonstrate that they dealt fully and fairly with all accusations brought against them.

The African church claimed the right to discipline its own officers and members through its own courts. Any cleric who transferred the hearing of a criminal accusation against himself from church to imperial court was immediately deposed from his office. If he filed a claim for civil damages in an imperial court, he could retain his office only if he forfeited anything that was gained through the process. Clerics, the legislation insisted, must be satisfied with the judges that the church provided.[433] If a cleric did make an appeal to the emperor, he was to petition for episcopal rather than imperial judges.[434]

Church courts, like the imperial judiciary, were not served by public prosecutors. A bishop or presbyter responsible for a church could initiate action

431. *Reg. Carth.* 34.
432. *Cau. Apiar.,* CCSL 149:133-45.
433. *Bru. Hipp.* 9; *Cau. Apiar.* 15.
434. *Reg. Carth.* 104. This may have been intended to contrast with the Donatist appeal directly to Constantine; see the letter of Anullinus to Constantine in Aug. *Ep.* 88.2.

against a cleric when a serious infraction came to his attention. Otherwise, an accuser had to bring and prove a charge. The church courts, like the imperial ones, disqualified some persons from making charges. Only those currently in good standing in the Caecilianist communion could accuse someone; those convicted of crimes and not yet returned to communion were barred.[435] Anyone whom the imperial law disqualified in its court was also disqualified in ecclesiastical court: slaves, freed persons in cases against their patrons, persons who had lost civil rights after being convicted of certain crimes, and outsiders such as heretics, pagans, and Jews.[436] These disqualified persons could not bring charges for violation of church law, though they could apply to church courts for redress of injuries afflicted upon them personally by a cleric.[437] Those who were barred from accusing were also excluded as witnesses, as were members of an accuser's household and persons less than fourteen years of age.[438] Finally, if a person brought multiple charges, the failure to prove any one of them would result in the dismissal of the others.[439]

In certain instances, the local bishop could punish his clergy. In cases involving clerics who were below the rank of deacon, the bishop was authorized to make and enforce a judgment, whether he initiated the action or responded to an accusation.[440] A presbyter charged with responsibility for a rural church could also take action against a subordinate, as one of Augustine's presbyters did against a subdeacon named Rusticus, who then fled to the Donatist bishop, was received, rebaptized, and ordained deacon.[441] Augustine also considered himself empowered to remove from office even presbyters subject to him for offenses that were reported to him by other members of the clergy.[442] He threatened such action, for example, against any who concealed personal property while claiming to have disposed of it.[443] In one instance, a monk of Augustine's monastery and a presbyter of the church accused one another. Augustine strongly suspected that the monk was lying, but he could not be certain. He decided to send both to the shrine of Felix at Nola, where he hoped that God would reveal the truth of the matter — as a perjured thief had been forced to confess his crime at a shrine in Milan while Augustine was living there.[444]

435. *Con. Carth.* a. 390, 6; *Cau. Apiar.* 8; *Reg. Carth.* 128; *Con. Hipp.* a. 427, 6; Aug. *Ep.* 251.

436. *Reg. Carth.* 129; *Con. Hipp.* a. 427, 6. Infamy was attached to certain crimes. It was imposed on Manichees by Theodosius (*C.Th.* 16.5.3, 7) and upon Donatists by Honorius in 405 and again in 414 after the Conference of Carthage (*C.Th.* 16.6.4, 16.5.54).

437. *Cau. Apiar.* 19; *Reg. Carth.* 129; *Con. Hipp.* a. 427, 6.

438. *Reg. Carth.* 131.

439. *Reg. Carth.* 130; *Con. Hipp.* a. 427, 7.

440. *Bru. Hipp.* 8b; *Cau. Apiar.* 20b.

441. Aug. *Ep.* 108.16.19.

442. Aug. *Ep.* 65.2.

443. Aug. *Serm.* 355-56.

444. Aug. *Ep.* 78. The presbyter was Boniface, whose name does not appear again in Augustine's writings.

When charges were brought against a bishop, presbyter, or deacon by someone other than the bishop, however, the canonical legislation required a more formal process. The bishop had to establish a court of episcopal judges to hear the accusation: six bishops for a presbyter or three for a deacon.[445] The local bishop might sit on a panel judging his own presbyter or deacon.[446] When the panel was hearing an appeal against the bishop's own judgment, however, he would leave the case to neighboring bishops.[447] When either the accuser or the accused had reason to fear violence, a change of venue for the hearing could be requested and granted.[448]

When a bishop was accused of wrongdoing, the matter was referred to the primate of the province, who established a panel of twelve episcopal judges. A letter was issued to the accused by the primate requiring him to appear before the court one month after the receipt of the summons. If necessary, he could be granted an additional month's delay. If he failed to appear within this two-month period, however, the accused was suspended from communion until he had cleared his name. The accuser also was required to appear at the specified time. Failure to do so would result in the accuser's suspension from communion and the restoration of the bishop, if he had been suspended. If, however, the accuser could show that some legitimate cause had prevented appearance, the case could still go forward.[449] The same times and conditions were to be observed in the hearing of charges brought against presbyters and deacons.

A bishop might refuse to appear before a provincial tribunal and present himself directly before the next plenary council of Africa. If he failed to appear even there, however, he would remain suspended from communion with his fellow bishops and restricted to his own church.[450] Thus, the Council of Carthage in September 401 asked the Primate of Numidia to warn Bishop Cresconius that he would be summarily condemned if he failed to appear at the next council.[451] If the accusers then refused to appear before the general council, the bishops had to find some other means of settling the case. In one such case, the accuser first petitioned to appear before the general council but then changed his mind and withdrew. The council suspended the accused bishop, Quodvultdeus, from episcopal communion but refused to remove him from office until the case was actually determined.[452] Five years later, another bishop, Maurentius, complained that his accusers had refused to appear, as ordered by the Pri-

---

445. *Con. Carth.* a. 345-48, 11; *Con. Carth.* a. 390, 10; *Cau. Apiar.* 12, 20.
446. *Bru. Hipp.* 8a.
447. Aug. *Ep.* 65.2; Augustine allowed that other bishops might reverse his judgment on Abundantius but that they could not force him to take the offender back into his clergy.
448. *Cau. Apiar.* 30; *Con. Hipp.* a. 427, 2.
449. *Bru. Hipp.* 6a-c, 7b; *Cau. Apiar.* 19.
450. *Bru. Hipp.* 7a.
451. *Reg. Carth.* 77.
452. *Reg. Carth.* 87.

mate of Numidia. Instead of condemning the accusers for obstinacy, the council directed the primate to set up a tribunal to hear the case. Maurentius chose his six judges on the spot, who were then appointed by the council itself; the primate was to insure that the accusers named their episcopal judges and that the matter was quickly settled.[453]

Appeals from the decisions of bishops were allowed but limited. A deacon or presbyter who had been disciplined by his bishop could appeal to a panel of three or six neighboring bishops, who might then effect a reconciliation. Augustine noted in the case of the presbyter Abundantius, whom he had dismissed, that this appeal had to be made within one year, thus reflecting the legislation of the Council of Carthage in 401.[454] Any cleric might appeal to the primate or as a last resort to the plenary council of Africa.[455] When the primate or council reversed the judgment of a panel of bishops, the action had no negative consequence for the bishops who were overruled.[456] When the parties to the conflict had agreed upon the composition of the panel of judges, either for the trial or the appeal hearing, no further appeal was allowed: the parties had to be satisfied with the ruling.[457]

In two instances of which records survive, individuals made appeals beyond Africa to the Bishop of Rome. When the presbyter Apiarius appealed in 418, the African bishops challenged the authority of the Roman bishop to intervene in cases that fell within their jurisdiction. In response, the Roman bishop claimed that the canons of Nicaea had made him an appellate judge for the entire church. The African bishops asserted that no such canon could be found in the copies of the decrees of Nicaea that Caecilian had brought back to Carthage and suggested that Greek versions of the records be sought from Constantinople. In the meantime, however, they agreed to abide by the claim put forward by the Romans.[458] A local court that Augustine had set up condemned Antony of Fussala for abuse of his office before the jurisdictional dispute was settled. Instead of appealing to the next council of Numidian bishops or the plenary council of Africa, Antony took his case directly to Rome. At the urging of Pope Boniface, the Africans accorded him a new trial in which his rights were protected scrupulously. When even this court, half of whose twelve judges had been selected by him, condemned Antony, he made a second appeal to Rome.[459] Then the presbyter Apiarius got into

453. *Reg. Carth.* 100.
454. Aug. *Ep.* 65.2; *Reg. Carth.* 79.
455. *Reg. Carth.* 125.
456. *Bru. Hipp.* 10a.
457. *Bru. Hipp.* 10b; *Reg. Carth.* 96, 122; *Cau. Apiar.* 15.
458. The *acta* are in CCSL 149:89-94. See Lancel, *Saint Augustine,* 357-59. Apiarius's crimes are not specified in the surviving record.
459. The details of Antony's case are to be found in Aug. *Ep.* 209 and *Ep. Divj.* 20*. He was guilty of enriching himself by stealing from his congregants and diverting the assets of the church to his own use.

trouble again, and the African bishops insisted that no appeals could be made to Rome. They demonstrated that the canons that the Roman bishops had cited to establish their jurisdiction were not in the Greek record of the Council of Nicaea and, thus, were not to be observed. With politeness barely cloaking their outrage, they admonished the Bishop of Rome to cease interfering in the workings of the African church.[460] The bishops also decreed that, in the future, they would refuse communion throughout the whole of Africa to anyone who appealed beyond their plenary council.[461]

The normal penalty imposed on clerics was removal from office rather than excommunication. This was the action Augustine took against Abundantius.[462] Excommunication or suspension from communion was often used, however, as a step in the judicial process.[463] Thus, presbyters who had been excommunicated by their bishops were advised not to celebrate the eucharist in schism; they were to appeal instead to neighboring bishops and be reconciled to their own bishop.[464] Other clerics who were awaiting a hearing after having been disciplined by their bishops were warned that they would pronounce sentence on themselves by communicating.[465] Thus Augustine refused to accept a presbyter who had been suspended from communion by Aurelius; he required that the man await the disposition of his case in Carthage.[466] Years before the problems with Apiarius's appeal to Rome, a council at Carthage ruled that accepting communion overseas while being excommunicate in Africa would be punished by loss of clerical status.[467] Bishops, presbyters, and deacons who were finally convicted of crimes were removed from office. They were not to have hands imposed on them in penitence but could communicate among the laity.[468]

## The Sacrament of Orders and the Status of the Clergy

As has been noted in the discussion of the clergy in the fourth century, the Donatist controversy forced a consideration of the clergy and the efficacy of their ministry. Augustine's understanding of the ritual of ordination and the relation between Christ, the clergy, and the people was coordinated with his theory of the efficacy of baptism and the church's power to forgive sins. He made a

460. The proceedings of the second case are in CCSL 149:169-72.
461. *Cau. Apiar.* 28.
462. Aug. *Ep.* 65.2.
463. The subdeacon Rusticus had been so treated by his presbyter (Aug. *Ep.* 108.6.19).
464. *Cau. Apiar.* 10-11.
465. *Cau. Apiar.* 29; *Con. Hipp.* a. 427, 1.
466. Aug. *Ep.* 64.2.
467. *Reg. Carth.* 104.
468. *Cau. Apiar.* 27; this was the disposition of the case of Abundantius (Aug. *Ep.* 65).

clear distinction between the church's power to sanctify and the authority of the clergy to exercise that power. In particular, he clearly distanced himself from Cyprian's teaching on the power of the bishop and recovered aspects of Tertullian's emphasis on the faithful's sharing in the gifts of the church, if not their exercise. This theology was developed in response to specific historical circumstances: the breakdown of Cyprian's theory and the imperial attempts to re-unite the divided African church. These events and the Catholic response to them will be recalled briefly to clarify the problem to which Augustine was responding.

## THE SACRAMENT OF ORDERS

As has been noted in the discussion of the relation between the Donatist and the Caecilianist communions in the fourth century, attempts were made to bring the dissident clergy back into unity, beginning with the offer of the Roman bishop Miltiades and continuing through the restoration of freedom and property to the Donatists under the emperor Julian. The acrimony and conflict associated with the Donatist leaders' repossession of the basilicas and congregations they had lost fifteen years earlier brought the attempts at reconciliation to an end. Thirty years later, when Donatists reintegrated their own Maximianist schismatics without depriving the clergy of their offices, the Caecilianists seized this precedent as a justification for renewing their own program of accepting Donatist clergy into communion in their offices. This program was supported — in a halting and inconsistent manner — by the imperial government, and it culminated in the Conference of Carthage in 411.

The acceptance of schismatic clergy into communion in their offices, by both Donatists and Caecilianists, violated the principles of Cyprian's theology. The practice was required of the Caecilianists as a condition of their communion with the Roman and other overseas churches; the Donatists adopted it as a means of healing an embarrassing conflict within their church. Justifications of this practice have been preserved in the writings of Optatus, Augustine, and the records of the councils of Caecilianist bishops. Donatist defenses of the acceptance of the Maximianist schismatics have not survived independently.[469]

In his response to Parmenian of Carthage, Optatus of Milevis had compared a cleric to a king, priest, or prophet; each was set apart under God's protection. As a result, he argued, clerics must not be subjected to public penance; the attack on their sin would defile the ordination as well.[470] Anyone who had already submitted to public penance was barred from being ordained.[471] Clergy

---

469. Augustine charged that Petilian was unable to respond (*Petil.* 3.39.45).
470. Optat. *Parm.* 2.25.
471. Optat. *Parm.* 2.26.

were like waiters at the banquet of Christ, dispensing a feast that they had not prepared.[472]

Augustine developed Optatus's argument in his own response to the letter of Parmenian and subsequent works. Like baptism, ordination — the power to confer baptism and to celebrate the eucharist — was an enduring sacramental reality that a schismatic retained upon leaving and brought upon returning to the unity of the church.[473] A schismatic cleric might be allowed or forbidden to exercise his office in unity, but in no case was the sacrament itself to be dishonored either by a new ordination or by the ritual of penance.[474] Augustine then compared baptism and orders. Both derived their efficacy from the invocation of the divine name rather than the holiness of the minister. They differed in that orders were given for the salvation of others, while baptism was for the good of the individual. Thus, an ordained minister was to be allowed and required to exercise his office when that would contribute to the good of the faithful in the unity of the church; he was to refrain or to be suspended when it would not.[475] To drive this point home, Augustine constructed an ironic illustration. A Donatist bishop might persuade a layperson to desert Catholic unity and join his schism. Later, this same bishop might lead his whole congregation into Catholic unity. After having been confirmed in his episcopal office by a Caecilianist bishop, the formerly Donatist bishop would then supervise the extended penance required for the readmission of the lay deserter and finally impose hands in forgiveness for the very sin he had provoked. The bishop originally baptized and ordained in schism could hold an office in Catholic unity in which the fallen layperson was barred from communion because of the desertion and until the penance was completed.[476]

Once the Caecilianist program of accepting Donatists had been in place for some years, Augustine responded to an objection that it was inconsistent. The practice of the church, at least since Cyprian's time, had been to bar from the exercise of clerical office anyone who had been guilty of serious sin and was therefore subjected to the ritual of penance. The Caecilianists insisted that the Donatists were sinning seriously by maintaining their schism and rebaptizing converts. Yet the Caecilianists were willing to receive Donatist clerics into communion without the ritual of penance and then allow them to exercise their offices. The objector concluded that either the Donatists were not wrong to be in schism or the Caecilianists had no concern for the holiness of their clergy. In response, Augustine contended that the church's power to forgive sins and, thus, to restore fallen clerics to their ministry never had been in doubt. The

---

472. Optat. *Parm.* 5.7. He also compared the clergy to dyers, who did not produce the purple color they applied to cloth.

473. Aug. *Parm.* 2.13.28.

474. Aug. *Parm.* 2.13.28. See also *Bapt.* 1.1.2.

475. Aug. *Cresc.* 2.11.13–12.14.

476. Aug. *Cresc.* 2.16.19.

practice of removing clerics from office had been adopted to promote the humility of the sinner and prevent a false repentance motivated only by the desire to retain a position of honor. When the good of the church outweighed that of the individual penitent, however, this prohibition could and should be lifted. Thus, the Caecilianist bishops' willingness to accept Donatist clergy showed the high value they were placing on the unity of the church and the salvation of the Donatist faithful through their reunion.[477] A canon attributed to the Council of Hippo in 393 made much the same argument: hearing the prayers of the community united in peace and love, God would be merciful to the sins of clerics who had come to unity from schism.[478]

The Caecilianist program responded to the acute shortage of clergy to staff the Donatist churches coming into Catholic communion. Aurelius of Carthage gave this explanation when he urged his colleagues to disregard the reservations of the overseas bishops, who would not approve the African plan to accept Donatist clerics in their offices: "We can ignore no longer the daily groans of the congregations that are dying out. Unless we provide some aid to them soon, the grave and inexcusable complaint of these innumerable perishing souls will stand against us before God."[479] Aurelius unwittingly echoed the words of his predecessor, Cyprian. Acting as spokesman for the Council of Carthage in 253, he urged his colleagues to grant reconciliation to all penitents in anticipation of renewed persecution: the bishop who refused "would have to render on the day of judgment an account to the Lord for his unseasonable severity and his inhuman harshness."[480] As Cyprian developed a new theory of the purity of the church to meet the pastoral crisis of his day, Aurelius called for a new understanding of the efficacy and holiness of its ministers.

Augustine's explanation of the sacrament of orders did not base the minister's authority to perform the rituals on his holding a power of sanctification granted only to the clergy, as Cyprian's explanation had done. Instead, he drew on Tertullian's theory that the clergy were authorized to exercise a power that all faithful Christians shared. Unlike Tertullian, however, he and his colleagues affirmed the legitimacy and efficacy of the hierarchal structures that Cyprian's theology had attempted to justify. Though bishops and other clergy might be chosen by the congregations they were to serve, they were

477. Aug. *Ep.* 185.10.44-45.

478. *Bru. Hipp.* 37.

479. Et quotidianos planctus diuersarum paene emortuarum plebium iam non sustinemus, quibus nisi fuerit aliquando subuentum, grauis nobis et inexcusabilis innumerabilium animarum pereuntium causa apud Deum mansura est. This was the Primate of Africa's introductory statement to the council of Proconsular Africa, 16 June 401 (CCSL 149:195.427-30).

480. Cypr. *Ep.* 57.5.2. Clarke, *The Letters of St. Cyprian of Carthage*, 3:59. Quod si de collegis aliquis extiterit qui urgente certamine pacem fratribus et sororibus non putat dandam, reddet ille rationem in die iudicii domino uel inportunae censurae uel inhumanae duritia suae (CCSL 3B:309.126-30).

installed in office by the other bishops who ordained a new bishop and then by the bishop who ordained the presbyters, deacons, and other clergy of the local church. Bishops placed the chosen candidate in his office, and only bishops could suspend or remove one of their number who subsequently proved unworthy. The authority of the bishop and his clergy to govern and sanctify was not, however, dependent upon their individual participation in the gifts that Christ had bestowed upon the Apostles in their role as the episcopal college. Instead, Augustine developed Optatus's judgment that the bishops and their clergy acted as agents of Christ and his ecclesial body, dispensing goods that were not their own.

Augustine did recognize that Tertullian and Cyprian were right in insisting that Christ had conferred the power of sanctifying upon the church. In his theology of baptism, he specified that this power, identified with the Holy Spirit's gift of charity, was held by the faithful within the unity of the church and exercised through their prayers. His theology of the episcopate generalized this explanation and applied it to the ministry of the clergy.

## THEOLOGY OF THE EPISCOPATE

Augustine's explanation of the sacrament of orders was constructed largely in response to the challenge of admitting Donatist clergy into the clergy of Caecilianist communion without re-ordaining them. It followed the general lines of his parallel explanation of the admission of Donatist laity into the Caecilianist congregations without their rebaptism. His theology of priesthood also was structured by the Donatist controversy and his explanation of the efficacy of the sacraments in conferring holiness.[481]

The successor to Donatus as Bishop of Carthage, Parmenian, had asserted that the bishop functions as a mediator between God and the Christian people.[482] He faithfully followed the theology of Cyprian. Augustine responded that assigning the bishop this role would not only multiply mediators, but would displace Christ, contradicting the Pauline assertion in 1 Timothy (2:5) that Christ was the one mediator between God and humanity, between God and his own body, the church.[483] All the members of Christ's body were anointed at baptism to share in the priesthood of Christ, their head. The bishops might be called priests, but that title properly belonged to the whole body. The bishops bore it only as members among the faithful and presiders at their offering.[484] Christ was the only priest; the church was priestly as the body of Christ; the

481. These have been reviewed in the preceding chapters on baptism, eucharist, and penance.

482. The assertion is reported and discussed in Aug. *Parm.* 2.8.15-16 but without the elaboration found in the sermon.

483. Aug. *Serm. Dolb.* 26(198*).52.

484. Aug. *Serm. Dolb.* 26(198*).53.

ministers were priestly as members of that body; so bishops were called priests because they presided over the church.[485]

Augustine next observed that nowhere in the Old Testament did one find prayer offered for the priest; rather, the priest interceded for the people. This foreshadowing was fulfilled in Christ alone: he prayed for himself, but no one else prayed for Christ. Rather, Christ prayed and interceded for his people.[486] The Christian people prayed for one another and for their clergy but not for Christ.[487] The bishops of a church, it will be recalled, were specifically included in the prayers for the faithful departed during the eucharistic prayer.[488] The anniversaries of their death were also listed in the calendar of the church of Carthage.[489]

This explanation of the priesthood of Christ and the church paralleled the explanation of the power of sanctification that Augustine had developed in his reflections on baptism. The sanctifying power belonged to Christ as God, and Christ exercised it.[490] It was, however, shared with the saints who formed Christ's true body on earth. Those clergy who were counted among the good shared this priesthood; they exercised it as members of the body, no differently than the laity.

Although Augustine carefully rejected Cyprian's explanation of the sanctifying power of the bishop, he seems to have accepted his assertion of the role of the bishops in governing the church. As has been seen, Augustine was an instigator and close collaborator with Aurelius of Carthage in the reform of the African church through extensive disciplinary legislation, all of it enacted and enforced by episcopal councils. Like those of the third century, councils of African bishops in this period never doubted their own authority: they adopted a policy of admitting Donatist clergy to office in Catholic unity that the bishops of Rome and Milan refused to endorse. They challenged the rulings of the bishops of Palestine and Rome on the orthodoxy of Pelagius and his disciples, and they insisted on their right to discipline their clergy and colleagues — Apiarius and Antony — without the interference of bishops outside Africa.

Yet Augustine never attempted to justify the authority of these synods of bishops, as Cyprian did, by appealing to an episcopal college founded by Christ, from which the universal church derived and upon which it depended. Against the Manichees, Augustine did cite the continuous succession of bishops as effective witnesses to the text of scripture and its interpretation.[491] Against

485. Aug. *Serm. Dolb.* 26(198*).49-50.
486. Aug. *Serm. Dolb.* 26(198*).54.
487. Aug. *Psal.* 36.2.20.
488. Aug. *Serm.* 359.6; *Col. Carth.* 3.230 (for Caecilian of Carthage).
489. *Kal. Carth.*
490. Aug. *Psal.* 145.9, 17.
491. Aug. *Faust.* 11.2, 5; 13.5; 28.4; 33.9.

the Donatists, he pointed to the churches founded and addressed by apostles, from whom the schismatics had broken and refused to recognize, even as they continued to read the letters addressed to them by the apostles.[492] Yet he never even referred to a college of apostles or bishops.

Almost as an aside, in explicating Psalm 45:16 ("sons are born to you in place of your fathers"), Augustine commented on the status of the bishops. The Apostles who were originally sent by Christ as fathers to the churches were now gone. The church, as mother, had brought forth sons and established them as fathers — i.e., as bishops — to whom she had assigned the places the Apostles had occupied.[493] Elsewhere, he noted that all these bishops were pastors in the same way that they were priests, as bodily members of the one pastor who is Christ.[494] Augustine seems to have believed that the bishops, individually and corporately, derived their governing authority in the same way as their sanctifying power. In both baptizing and ordaining, the bishops exercised the power the church shared with Christ as his bride and body.

Augustine still had to reckon with the clergy's success and failure in teaching and in preaching the gospel. There he applied the guidance of Jesus regarding the teaching role of the Scribes and Pharisees, who spoke the truth given to Moses (Matt. 23:2-3). God could use evil bishops to speak the truth of the gospel, even though they might fail to act upon it. Their teaching for earthly profit made them hirelings, but it did not vitiate the truth they spoke.[495] Those who chose to follow their examples rather than their teachings were responsible for their own failure.[496] Augustine occasionally recognized the limits of this explanation: some bishops did not preach the gospel but promised earthly rewards rather than warning of persecution.[497] They claimed a divine authority for themselves, appropriating to themselves what belonged to Christ and his church.[498]

## THE STATUS OF THE CLERGY

Despite Augustine's attempts to limit the role of the clergy to governance rather than sanctification, and to teach both his congregation and his colleagues that the holiness of the church depended upon the whole body of the faithful, African Christians continued to treat their bishops as the bearers of a sacred power. Clerical titles (*episcopus, diaconus, lector,* etc.) were among the few regularly

492. Aug. *Cresc.* 3.18.21; *Ep.* 53.1.3.
493. Aug. *Psal.* 44.32.
494. Aug. *Serm. Guelf.* 16(229N).3.
495. Aug. *Serm.* 46.20-22; 74.3-4; *Eu. Io.* 46.5-6.
496. Aug. *Serm.* 137.7.7–8.8.
497. Aug. *Serm.* 46.11-12.
498. Aug. *Serm.* 137.7.7–8.8.

included in Christian burial inscriptions (cf. figs. 126, 129, 141, 143, 148).[499] The apse (or counter-apse) of a basilica was not only the site of the bishop's throne but possibly of his tomb as well (cf. fig. 76). Bishops and clergy were more likely than other faithful to be buried in the interior of an urban or cemetery church (e.g., fig. 117). The fifth-century bishop Reparatus was buried in the counter-apse of the basilica in which he served at Castellum Tingitanum. The mosaic covering his tomb depicts a triple arch and includes this epitaph: "Here rests our father of holy memory, Reparatus the bishop, who served as priest for eight years and eleven months and went ahead of us in peace on the eleventh day before the Kalends of August in the 436th year of the province" (fig. 34).[500] That same church also had an inscription near the *presbyterium,* in the form of an acrostic naming a Bishop Marinus.[501]

In Tipasa, the remains of several bishops were placed beneath an elevated area within a funerary chapel and marked with a mosaic attesting to their "righteousness."[502] The late-fourth-century founder of the chapel, Bishop Alexander, was buried there also (figs. 109, 110). Although the fourth century produced some Donatist martyrs, and although the Vandal occupation in the fifth gave many Nicene Christians the opportunity to suffer for their faith, African Christians tended to look upon at least some of their bishops and clergy as unusually endowed with the gifts of the Spirit, which guaranteed the holiness of the church. In this sense, at least, Augustine's understanding of the status and role of the clergy failed to influence the practice of the African church.

## Conclusion

Augustine's theology of priesthood and ministry employed a distinction between sanctifying power and governing authority. He identified the first as the Holy Spirit's gift of charity, which was shared by all the faithful within Catholic unity. Similarly, the governing authority exercised by the bishops, both individually and corporately, was conferred upon them by the church in its identification with Christ. The clergy would share this power and authority if they were among the faithful and holy. Their authority to minister, the efficacy of their

499. One enigmatic instance of a *presbyterissa,* Guilia Runa (fig. 125), occurs at Hippo and appears to date to the Vandal era. On the question of women in office, see *Ordained Women in the Early Church: A Documentary History,* ed. Carolyn Osiek and Kevin Madigan (Baltimore: Johns Hopkins University Press, 2005), 174-83, 197-98.

500. Hic requiescit sanctae memoriae pater noster Reparatus e.p.s. qui fecit in sacerdotium annos VIII, men. XI et precessit nos in pace die undecimu kal. Aug prounc. CCCCXXX et sexta (*CIL* 8.9709; *ILCV* 1.1105). The death year was 435. See the discussion above, pp. 132-33.

501. *ILCV* 1.1119. See above, p. 134.

502. See discussion of this above, pp. 125-26. The inscription is found in *ILCV* 1.1825: iustos in pulchram sedem gaudent locasse priores.

rituals, the power of their teaching, and the legitimacy of their governing did not depend upon their personal holiness. It was a delegation, by ordination, to act for the church in its identity with Christ; it was given and withdrawn, exercised and restricted for the good of the church itself rather than the individual minister.

## GENERAL OBSERVATIONS

### Correlation of Archeological and Literary Evidence

The relative status of the bishop and presbyters is apparent in the placement of the *synthronon,* a semicircular bench attached to the main apse, with a place for the episcopal *cathedra* in its center (cf. fig. 52). The bishop's elevated and central seat was, thus, one focus of the congregation during the liturgy, since he would ordinarily have sat there to deliver his homily, while the people stood in the nave of the basilica.

Their burials also indicate the high status of the clergy, as has been noted above. Such burial not only indicated their status within the congregation but also suggests that they were regarded as officers endowed with a certain sanctity. They were perhaps not entirely different from martyrs, whose remains might be interred in a repository under the altar or in a counter-apse. The evidence for honorific burial of bishops and other clergy is particularly rich. The burial of Reparatus in the basilica at Castellum Tingitanum and of the bishops of Tipasa in the cemetery church constructed by Alexander already have been noted. The cemetery church of Lepti Minus included an apse mosaic identifying two priests, Pascasius (fig. 126) and Januarius.[503]

The remains of the fifth-century bishop Jucundus, found after some searching by a successor bishop, Amacius, seem to have been buried in the baptistery annexed to the church of Bellator in Sufetula.[504] Similarly, the tombs inserted throughout the church at Uppenna included bishops (Honorius and Baleriolus, fig. 117) as well as a presbyter and a deacon (Emeritus and Crescentius, fig. 148). In this place (a shrine basilica), Bishop Baleriolus's tomb was given an honored position near the martyrs' tomb; Honorius's tomb mosaic may depict an episcopal stole in its upper band.[505] Another Bishop Honorius appears to have been

503. See Fathi Bejaoui, "À propos des mosaïques funéraires d'Henchir Sokrine (environs de Lepti Minus, en Byzacène)," in *L'Africa Romana: Atti del IX Convegno di studio, Nuoro, 13-15 dicembre 1991,* ed. Attilio Mastino, Pubblicazioni del Dipartimento di Storia dell'Università di Sassari 20 (Sassari: Gallizzi, 1992), 229-36. See also Ann Marie Yasin, *Saints and Church Spaces in the Late Antique Mediterranean: Architecture, Cult, and Community* (Cambridge and New York: Cambridge University Press, 2009), 91-97.

504. See the discussion above, p. 150. This inscription is found in *ILCV* 1.1112.

505. James H. Terry, "Christian Tomb Mosaics of Late Roman, Vandalic, and Byzantine Byz-

buried in the main nave of the Byzantine church just outside of Sufetula.[506] The deacon Crescentinus was honored by burial just in front of the apse in the funerary chapel in Thabraca. His tomb mosaic indicates that he may have been deemed a saint (fig. 143).[507] The early-sixth-century tomb of a certain Paulus, identified as the Primate of Mauretania, was inserted into the baptistery of the basilica at Sidi Abiche, near the coast in Byzacena (fig. 129).[508] His honorific burial at such a great distance from his episcopal city clearly indicates his honored status.[509]

Some of the figures depicted on portrait-type tomb mosaics wear garb that may reflect clerical status. One such item is a white stole *(orarium)* with fringed ends (fig. 137). Such an item might have been worn by a bishop, or perhaps even a deacon.[510] Others are wearing a cloak *(paenula* — perhaps the precursor of a chasuble) that could have alluded to some special status (figs. 134, 140), although in no instance are these items worn by individuals who are specially identified as clergy. One of Augustine's sermons offers some evidence for special dress for clergy, and even distinctive garb for bishops, although he disapproved of the practice. He said that he wished to receive as gifts only clothing that he could share in common with his fellow monks and clergy (those who lived with him).[511]

Clergy were also honored by inscriptions on baptismal fonts. Vitalis and Cardela, a presbyter and his wife, are named in the "new cathedral" of Sufetula; they appear to have provided the font as a votive gift (fig. 72). Cyprian, "Bishop and High Priest," is honored along with Adelphius, a priest in "unity with him," in the inscription found on the Clipea baptistery (fig. 38). Victoricus, a subdeacon, seems the likely donor of the font at Oumcetren bearing his name.[512]

The title "senior" or "elder" appears rarely in these contexts. The name "Nardus Senior" occurs on a tomb mosaic from Pupput (Hammamet), but this is followed by two other names (Turassus and Restitutus), each identified by

---

acena" (Ph.D. diss., University of Missouri–Columbia, 1998), no. 63, pp. 388-89, describes this stole, although no literary evidence supports this as a particular episcopal vestment.

506. See above, p. 155.

507. See the discussion above, pp. 119-20.

508. The mosaic cover is now in the Enfida Museum.

509. Terry, "Christian Tomb Mosaics of Late Roman, Vandalic, and Byzantine Byzacena," 208, has speculated that he may have sought to be closer to the center of power during the turbulent early years of Justinian's reign.

510. See Ferrand. *Vita Fulg.* 15. The individual depicted in fig. 137 is not identified as holding any specific clerical office, however. Terry, "Christian Tomb Mosaics of Late Roman, Vandalic, and Byzantine Byzacena," no. 63, p. 388, suggests that the tomb mosaic for Bishop Honorius (fig. 117) includes an *orarium*. Against this, in a tomb portrait in the Bardo Museum, a woman named Abundantia also appears to wear such a stole. See Margaret Alexander, "Early Christian Tomb Mosaics in North Africa" (Ph.D. diss., New York University, 1958), 2:187, n. 297.

511. Aug. *Serm.* 356.10.

512. See above, p. 111.

the contrasting "iunior."[513] One indication of a senior identified with the church at Carthage also attests not only his status but his membership in a designated group of elders.[514]

These tomb memorials provide an independent witness to the ranks of clergy and to the high status they enjoyed in the community.


## Correlation of Theology and Practice

The clergy were generally assigned two roles: governance and sanctification. Under the pressure of events, the understanding of the relationship between the authority to govern and the power to sanctify changed radically during the centuries this study considers. These changes resulted in the recognition that ordination, like baptism, effected a permanent change in the religious or ecclesial status of the clergy. Ordination began to be understood as a sacrament not unlike baptism.

This understanding of orders derived from and helped explain the acceptance of baptism performed outside the unity of the church. Later, it allowed clergy from schismatic communions to exercise their ministry in unity when this would promote the good of the church as a whole.

A third development, again under the pressure of events, was the use of episcopal synods to decide questions that were not clearly addressed in the scriptures and that affected more than an individual congregation. In the third century, councils changed the penitential discipline and shifted the principal eucharistic celebration from evening to morning.[515] In the fifth, Augustine argued that Christ had left certain matters — the eucharistic fast — to be determined by the apostles and bishops.[516] This involved an understanding of the episcopal college as having been established by Christ to govern the church as a whole. In developing this theory, Cyprian explained that individual bishops were responsible not only for their local congregations but, in cooperation with their colleagues, for the universal church.


513. Terry, "Christian Tomb Mosaics of Late Roman, Vandalic, and Byzantine Byzacena," no. 71, pp. 404-5.

514. *ILCV*, 384: Flavius Valens senior sodalici memoria hac fecit sic semper (with alpha, omega, and Christogram). Flavius Valens, elder, made this for the memory of his fraternity, may it be always so. See Shaw, "'Elders' in Christian Africa," 225.

515. Cypr. *Ep.* 55.6.1; 63.16.2–17.1.

516. Aug. *Ep.* 54.7.9-10.

The relationship between the governing authority of the bishop and his exercise of the church's power to sanctify proved difficult to manage for African Christians. Tertullian explicitly separated them by insisting that all Christians participated in the holiness of the church and the power to communicate that holiness through the rituals of baptism and eucharist. He based the clergy's supervision of the common life of the congregation and privilege of presiding at community rituals on the need for harmony and good order. Other Christians in Carthage at the beginning of the third century vigorously disputed Tertullian's understanding of the status of the clergy. The bishop claimed to have received with his office the powers that Christ had conferred specifically upon Peter. The confessors and martyrs were credited by some Christians with the power of winning forgiveness for sins, and the devotees of the New Prophecy claimed that power for themselves, under condition that they not exercise it.

Cyprian was caught between two schisms, each of which denied the bishop's exclusive access to the power of forgiving and sanctifying, as well as his right to govern the congregation. The laxist clergy relied on the power of the martyrs to forgive sins and maintain the church's relationship with God, while the rigorists recognized only the power of Christ to deal with sins committed against God. In response, Cyprian assigned the two powers of sanctifying and governing to the bishops both as individuals and as a unified group. Their power was not dependent upon the consent of the laity, though it could be maintained only on the condition of their fidelity to Christ and adherence to the unity of the church. Thus, Cyprian argued that the authority of the bishop arose not from the need for good order in the congregation but from the power to sanctify, which had been conferred upon the Apostles as a body, and which was held and exercised by the members of the episcopal college. He thereby justified the hierarchical organization of local churches, the authority of the regional synods, and the consultation that had already begun to function among primate bishops throughout the world.

Cyprian's theory failed, however, because it could not be put into practice in the crisis following the Diocletian persecution. Charges were brought that certain bishops had lost the power to sanctify and the authority to govern their congregations. Bishops who refused to repudiate and to break communion with them would share the sin they tolerated. These charges implied that the whole episcopate could be rendered sinful and impotent by an error in judging the guilt of some of its members. In reality, many of the charges of apostasy could not be judged with any certitude, at least not to the satisfaction of the opposing parties in the African church.

The overseas churches that were called upon to judge the African conflict asserted that the authority to act for Christ depended neither upon possessing the power to sanctify nor upon adherence to the unity of the church. Instead, it derived from the ritual of ordination itself, which authorized its recipient to act as Christ's delegate and empowered him to authorize others to do the same. A bishop who had been ordained could ordain another, even if both minister and recipient were apostates or in schism against the unity of the church. If convicted on firm evidence of apostasy or some other sin, a bishop should be removed from office, but a schismatic could be invited to continue his ministry in the unity of the church. Ordination, then, began to be treated like baptism — as a ritual that established a lasting relationship to Christ and was never to be repeated or dishonored.

During the fourth century, the Caecilianists labored to defend and justify the decisions of the overseas churches, which had undercut Cyprian's justification of clerical authority and sanctifying power. The Donatists, for their part, upheld Cyprian's theology; but they found themselves forced to restrict the list of crimes that would deprive a bishop of the power to sanctify and thereby disqualify him for office. At the beginning of the fifth century, Augustine demonstrated that Cyprian's theory was completely unworkable.

Augustine finally proposed a theology that would rationalize the practice of recognizing the efficacy of the ministry of bishops who were not endowed personally with the power to sanctify, as this was identified with the indwelling of the Holy Spirit. The power that Cyprian had assigned to the bishops was recognized as the endowment of the church as a whole or, more specifically, of the saints united by charity within it. This priestly power belonged to Christ and was shared by his body. The authority to govern the church and to exercise sanctifying power as agents of Christ and his church was shared by all bishops by virtue of the sacrament of orders. Outside the unity of the church, the clergy might receive and give the sacrament of orders, just as they did that of baptism. As separated from the body of Christ, however, they could exercise the power to sanctify only as agents of the faithful living in the unity of the church.

## ACCEPTANCE OF SCHISMATIC CLERGY

Cyprian and his colleagues had insisted that anyone who had attempted to exercise clerical office in opposition to the unity of the church could be allowed into their communion as a layperson, but only after sustained penance. Not only had they engaged in sacrilegious rites, but they were responsible for the damnation of all those whom they had led astray.[517]

In an attempt to heal the division in the African church after the Diocletian persecution, however, the Roman church offered to accept in his office any schismatic bishop who returned to unity. The African church continued this policy during the first half of the fourth century and revived it at the beginning

---

517. Cypr. *Ep.* 72.2.1-3.

of the fifth century, even against the advice of the Bishops of Rome and Milan. The unity of the church was so precious and the need for clergy so dire that former Donatists would be allowed and encouraged to continue their ministry in Catholic unity. They explained that the united prayers of the formerly divided Caecilianist and Donatist congregations would certainly win God's forgiveness of their bishop's sins, even of the crime of rebaptizing.

Here one finds an application of Augustine's theory that the power of sanctification and authority to govern resided in the unity of the saints within the church rather than in the clerical office.

### EPISCOPAL COLLEGE

The system of episcopal governance in individual congregations required collaboration among the bishops. A congregation could choose — or assent to the choice of — a bishop only after his predecessor's death; the candidate had to be approved and ordained by the bishops of neighboring congregations. The newly ordained leader then had to be recognized by the bishops of other churches, particularly those of the larger cities in the region.

The need for coordinated action by the bishops to solve disciplinary problems and to establish shared norms for governance is also evident, even in the first part of the third century. Bishops in Africa met to decide at least two disputed questions: they rejected baptisms performed by heretics outside their own communion, and they allowed the reconciliation of adulterers after sustained penance.

By the time the Decian persecution threw the church into turmoil, the bishops had developed systems of collaboration that they then employed to deal with the laxist schism, to establish policy for the penance and reconciliation of the lapsed, and to respond to the rigorist schism in Rome. As Bishop of Carthage, Cyprian regularly received questions about practice, so he could present them to his colleagues for judgment at their meetings. Some of these, such as the reconciliation of penitent apostates and the rebaptism of converts from heretical or schismatic communities, were not clearly settled by the scriptures. The bishops had to seek the guidance of the Spirit in deciding how to proceed.[518]

The actual practice of episcopal collaboration, along with the challenge of the establishment of a laxist episcopate, moved Cyprian to develop a formal theory of the episcopal college. As he explained it, Christ had selected the Apostles and endowed them with an indivisible power of sanctifying, which authorized them to govern the church as his agents. Individual bishops were responsible for their congregations, but they shared a responsibility for the church

---

518. Cypr. *Ep.* 55.6-7.

as a whole. Cyprian refused to recognize the authority of any one bishop over another, but he judged that an individual who rebelled against the consensus of his colleagues might alienate himself from their unity and lose participation in their power and authority. He believed that the Holy Spirit guided the deliberations of bishops and brought them to agreement on the right course of action.

During the third century, the bishops met in provincial and regional councils; they consulted with the churches in Rome and other major cities. A more general consultation became possible when Constantine employed the resources of the imperial government to deal first with the schism in Africa, at a council of western bishops in Arles, and then a universal council at Nicaea once he had become sole ruler of the empire. By the time Augustine considered the deliberative process of bishops in his treatise *On Baptism* in the early fifth century, the church had extensive experience in reaching — and failing to reach — agreement on doctrinal and disciplinary matters. Augustine explained that the church learns the truth of the gospel by experience. The scripture stands as the norm, but it is not always clear and evident. The judgments of individual bishops were confirmed or corrected by their colleagues, particularly by councils of bishops. Regional councils were reviewed by plenary ones; earlier councils were corrected by subsequent ones.[519] The Donatists, for example, were wrong to hold to Cyprian's teaching once it had been shown inadequate, once it had been reviewed and corrected by larger and later meetings of bishops. Cyprian, Augustine insisted, always had been prepared to be corrected by others.

Under the leadership of Aurelius, the Caecilianist bishops of Africa had organized themselves into provincial and regional groups that met regularly to deal with routine questions and could respond quickly and effectively to emergencies and opportunities. They developed an organized body of legislation to govern their churches. Their disciplinary procedures were specified in detail, along with provision for appeals. When one of their presbyters attempted to evade their courts by appealing directly to the Bishop of Rome, they politely but firmly declined outside intervention, demonstrated the inaccuracy of the Roman church's copy of the decrees of the Council of Nicaea, and sent over a copy of their procedures, the likes of which have not survived for the Roman church.

### Conclusion

The African church developed a theology that addressed the clergy in its twin roles of governance and sanctification, as Augustine indicated, through experience. Theories were proposed to justify practices already in place; these were modified when experience demonstrated them to be inoperable. Unlike

---

519. Aug. *Bapt.* 2.3.4.

the Donatists, the Caecilianists were able to adapt in the transition from being a church only tolerated to one supported by the imperial government. They could govern their own church without resort to imperial force and could exploit the opportunities that imperial protection provided them to re-establish unity.

# CHAPTER 9

# Forms of Christian Life:
# Marriage, Virginity, and Widowhood

........................................................................................................

## INTRODUCTION

In the second and third centuries, African Christians completely rejected Roman religious practices and many other forms of civic life. Individual families, however, continued to be divided in religious commitments, so marriage and the life of the extended family were shared by Christians and non-Christians. As a result, Christians had to negotiate points of difference and separation. Because of its role in producing and educating succeeding generations of citizens, in transmitting property, and in building cooperative alliances among groups, the family was a social institution regulated by the imperial government. Christians were not only sympathetic to these imperial objectives but found religious foundations for many of them in the Old Testament legislation, which was itself designed to maintain and protect an ethnic community through marriage, the generation and education of children, and the protection of land ownership.

Still, Christians introduced changes into Jewish and Roman family practices for two principal reasons. First, the church was a voluntary rather than a genetic community: membership was initiated and maintained by commitment to a set of beliefs and standards of conduct. From its beginnings and into the fifth century, a congregation could still expect to maintain itself and grow by recruiting converts from traditional religions rather than by generation and education of children within Christian families. Second, at various times during this period, many Christians anticipated that a divine intervention would soon end the entire earthly order of life: a next generation might become superfluous at any point. Christians, therefore, encouraged the renunciation of marriage and either common ownership of property or sharing of income. Imperial legislation, in contrast, penalized refusal or failure to produce children and used family relationships to maintain economic stability.[1]

In the fourth century, however, Christianity became the favored religion of the empire: Christians went from being outsiders to sharing responsibility for maintaining the government and economy, and then to assuming it entirely. Anticipation of the end time was transformed into a concern for Christ's judgment of individuals after their deaths. Christian teachers began to question the superiority of sexual continence and virginity over marriage as a Christian form of life.[2] Christianity struggled to maintain a balance between hope for the heavenly future and concern for the earthly present. Augustine, in particular, exploited the complex metaphors describing the relationship between Christ and his spouse — the church — that was at once virgin, mother, and widow to explain and evaluate the roles of the married and the single within the Christian community.

## MARITAL PRACTICE IN TERTULLIAN'S TIME

Tertullian understood sexual relations and marriage as instituted by God to serve the increase of the human race and, thus, as good. Although idolatrous practices had been added to the marriage ritual, these vitiated neither its goodness nor God's protection of it.[3] Marriage was a blessing given at the creation and fostered to serve the expansion of the race during the patriarchal period.[4] More regularly, however, Tertullian understood marriage and generation as necessary to maintain the human race in the face of death. He specified that Adam and Eve actually began their married life only after they were exiled from Paradise[5] and that marriage would not continue in the resurrected condition, when death would be put aside[6] and humans would enjoy an angelic condition.[7]

---

1. On the development of Roman marriage practice and law, the following studies have proven useful: Susan Treggiari, *Roman Marriage: Iusti Coniuges from the Time of Cicero to the Time of Ulpian* (Oxford: Clarendon Press, 1991); Judith Evans Grubbs, *Law and Family in Late Antiquity: The Emperor Constantine's Marriage Legislation* (Oxford: Clarendon Press, 1995); Judith Evans Grubbs, *Women and the Law in the Roman Empire: A Sourcebook on Marriage, Divorce, and Widowhood* (London and New York: Routledge, 2002).

2. Jovinian, for example, explained the Pauline teaching in 1 Cor. 7:25-40 as advice for living in the present, not as a promise of greater reward in the future. For a full treatment of the ensuing controversy, see David G. Hunter, *Marriage, Celibacy, and Heresy in Ancient Christianity: The Jovinianist Controversy* (Oxford: Oxford University Press, 2007).

3. Thus, in *Idol.* 16.1-3, Tertullian argued that a Christian could attend a pagan marriage ritual because the idolatrous practices were incidental. This did not mean, however, that he thought a Christian could participate in a sacrifice as part of a marriage celebration, as *Cor.* 13.4 makes clear.

4. Tert. *Marc.* 1.29.2-4; *Ux.* 1.2.1-2.

5. Tert. *Mon.* 5.5, 17.5.

6. Tert. *Res.* 61.4; parallel in *Res.* 36.5-6.

7. Tert. *Ux.* 1.1.5.

Later in his life, however, Tertullian interpreted marriage against the horizon of the end of the age and the return of Jesus. He followed Paul in insisting that the time remaining was short and that those who were married should live as though they were not.[8] Responsibility for a spouse and children could be a hindrance to the practice of Christian virtue: it made a person less ready and willing to face persecution and give up earthly life when fidelity to Christ required it.[9] In troubled times, he argued, the truly faithful should be more concerned to send their wives and children ahead to God than to leave them as a legacy on earth.[10]

Tertullian also distinguished different forms of marriage practice that God had instituted and allowed during the successive phases of human history. Originally, God had established marriage as absolutely monogamous: a single man and a single woman were to be joined into one flesh; neither was to have a second partner.[11] This dispensation continued through Noah and ended with Abraham's circumcision.[12] A descendant of Cain named Lamech[13] introduced polygamy, which was subsequently allowed during the patriarchal period, until Moses introduced divorce for the time of the Law.[14] Christ began the restoration of the primitive discipline[15] and established the church as his virgin-bride.[16] He allowed marriage and even remarriage after the death of a spouse, however, because of the initial weakness of Christians. After more than a century, when his teaching had taken root, Christ sent the Holy Spirit, as the initiator of the New Prophecy, to complete the restoration of the original discipline by forbidding a second marriage, even after the death of a spouse.[17] Thereafter, a Christian was to have only one spouse.

The devotees of the New Prophecy encouraged virginity and continence, considered marriage a concession, and made continued widowhood obligatory for those whose spouses had died. They objected, however, to the doctrine of the Marcionites, who rejected the Hebrew Bible and Israelite religion as irrelevant for Christians and required that marriage and sexual practice be renounced as a condition for baptism.[18]

The majority of Christians — to whom Tertullian referred as sensualists or psychics rather than spirituals — rejected the New Prophecy and agreed on

8. Tert. *Ux.* 1.5.4; *Cast.* 6.1-2; *Mon.* 7.4.
9. Tert. *Ux.* 1.5.2; *Cast.* 12.3.
10. Tert. *Ux.* 1.5.1.
11. Tert. *Cast.* 2.1-2; *Mon.* 4.2.
12. Tert. *Mon.* 4.5; Tertullian argued for this interpretation of Abraham in *Mon.* 6.2.
13. Tert. *Cast.* 5.4; *Mon.* 4.4.
14. Tert. *Ux.* 1.2.2; *Mon.* 14.
15. Tert. *Ux.* 2.2.8, 7.1; *Mon.* 5.1, 14.
16. Tert. *Cast.* 5.1-4; *Mon.* 5.7.
17. Tert. *Mon.* 3.1–4.1.
18. Tert. *Marc.* 1.29.1; 5.7.6.

a discipline that allowed virginity, continence, marriage, widowhood, and re-marriage after the death of a spouse. Christians who were not yet married or had already been widowed at the time of their baptism had the right to marry, at least once, after coming to the faith.[19] Some dedicated themselves to virginity or continence from the time of their conversion.[20] Those who were divorced, however, were forbidden to marry again, presumably as long as their former spouses were alive.[21]

Christians who were married at the time of their conversion were to remain in these marriages, even if their spouses did not become Christians. Paul had recognized that the grace of conversion sanctified the spouse to whom a Christian was united at the time.[22] Those who were married at or after baptism were allowed to continue sexual relations,[23] though the devotees of the New Prophecy considered this a concession to weakness.[24] When both partners were Christian, however, they might voluntarily practice continence within marriage.[25] Divorce was allowed only for the cause of adultery, but even then a new marriage was excluded.[26]

Christians also disagreed on the acceptability of marriage to a non-Christian. Some regarded it — whether a first or a second marriage — as a sin that could be forgiven.[27] Even before his commitment to the discipline of the New Prophecy, however, Tertullian strongly objected to a Christian's beginning a union with a non-Christian, insisting that Paul had forbidden it. Not only did he impugn the motives of the Christians — primarily women — who sought such marriages, but he argued that these were the religious equivalent of marrying a slave in imperial law and would result in the loss of Christian freedom.[28] He argued that the grace of God would sanctify only that non-Christian partner to whom a Christian was already joined at the time of conversion.[29] Many of Tertullian's arguments were practical and arose from the control that a Roman husband exercised over his wife. Would he approve of her going out to take care

---

19. Tertullian, however, regarded this as a concession which should not be exploited (*Mon.* 11.9-13).

20. Tert. *Ux.* 1.6.2.

21. Tert. *Mon.* 11.9-10.

22. Tert. *Ux.* 2.2.9.

23. Tert. *Mon.* 3.2.

24. Tert. *Mon.* 3.8, 10.

25. Tert. *Ux.* 1.6.2; *Cast.* 1.4.

26. Tert. *Ux.* 2.2.8, 7.1; *Mon.* 9.1, 7-8.

27. Tert. *Ux.* 2.3.1; *Mon.* 11.10.

28. Christian widows wanted high lifestyles and could not find rich men in the Christian community who were unmarried and would give them this lifestyle (Tert. *Ux.* 2.8.3). Tertullian adapted the argument from the contemporary law regulating the marriage of a free woman to a slave, by which she could become subject to his master (*Ux.* 2.8.1). For the development of the law, see Grubbs, *Women and the Law in the Roman Empire*, 143-44.

29. Tert. *Ux.* 2.2.9.

of the poor, to attend services at night, especially the Easter vigil? What would he think of her kissing the brethren, washing the feet of the saints, or offering hospitality to a Christian traveler? Would he tolerate her making the sign of the cross over their bed and her body, getting up to pray during the night, rising early to eat the eucharistic bread she brought home? Would he tolerate her refusal to explain her practices, as was required by the Christian discipline of secrecy?[30] Thus Tertullian's consideration was focused on a Christian woman marrying a husband who followed traditional Roman religious practices. Although taking a non-Christian wife may not have given rise to these conflicts, Tertullian gave no indication that it was acceptable.[31]

## The Rituals

Tertullian referred to the rituals of betrothal and marriage at use in imperial culture.[32] The promise that began the marriage involved a greeting, a joining of right hands, a kiss, and the giving of a ring. These steps, he argued, initiated the union of male and female; thenceforth the virgin should be regarded as a married woman.[33] In describing the marriage of two Christians, Tertullian adapted five elements of the traditional family ritual to the Christian practice: the church arranges, the offering strengthens, the blessing signs, the angels witness, and the Father affirms.[34] At least some of these elements, specifically the arranging and the blessing, may have reflected actual practice.[35] In the absence of additional corroborating evidence, however, such an interpretation can be only hypothetical.[36]

Tertullian did witness clearly to two aspects of Christian marriage practice: the use of a contract, or *tabulae nuptiales,* and a declaration before the congregation. Both served the church's interest in making the marriage definite and public. Marriage and fornication were distinguished, as Tertullian observed, primarily by that formal contract.[37] He did not imply that the *tabulae* were issued or approved by the church rather than the families involved in the marriage, but only that the *tabulae* distinguished legitimate sexual relations from

---

30. Tert. *Ux.* 2.5.2.

31. Tert. *Marc.* 5.7.8; *Mon.* 11.10-11.

32. See Treggiari, *Roman Marriage,* 125-60; Grubbs, *Law and Family in Late Antiquity,* 140-202.

33. Tert. *Virg.* 11.3, 5; *Or.* 22.10; *Apol.* 6.4.

34. Tert. *Ux.* 2.8.6.

35. See Kenneth Stevenson, *Nuptial Blessing: A Study of Christian Marriage Rites* (New York: Oxford University Press, 1983), 18-19.

36. Following David G. Hunter, "Augustine and the Making of Marriage in Roman North Africa," *Journal of Early Christian Studies* 11 (2003): 66-71.

37. Tert. *Cast.* 9.3-4.

---

those which were forbidden to Christians. Tertullian indicated that the *tabulae* might be used by Christians to defend against charges of adultery, which could have resulted in excommunication. He pictured a Christian trying to escape condemnation by presenting to the tribunal of Christ *tabulae* for a marriage to a non-Christian[38] or for a second marriage to a Christian.[39]

Christians also may have declared their marriages in the presence of the community. Those who attempted a union without first professing it before the church were in danger of being judged guilty of adultery or fornication.[40] Tertullian challenged the audacity of the Christian who appeared in the assembly to seek recognition of a second marriage in the presence of the clergy and widows, who were explicitly forbidden to remarry.[41] These instances provide evidence not for a church ritual of marriage but only for acknowledgment or approval of a marriage structured by imperial law.

## Virginity

Dedicated virginity from birth was understood as a gift of grace and an especially holy form of life open to both men and women.[42] Men who followed this way of life did not distinguish themselves in the assembly,[43] but women indicated their special status by remaining unveiled in the Christian assembly, like girls.[44] Tertullian objected to this practice. Representing the viewpoint of the New Prophecy, he specified that all females should be veiled in the assembly from the time of puberty, just as they would be when they appeared in public.[45]

## Widowhood

Christians whose spouses died were encouraged to remain continent and not marry again.[46] Although Paul had discouraged it, remarriage was allowed because of the difficulty of practicing continence.[47] The devotees of the New Prophecy, as has been noted, asserted that the Holy Spirit had removed this

38. Tert. *Ux.* 2.3.1.
39. Tert. *Pud.* 1.20.
40. Tert. *Pud.* 4.4.
41. Tert. *Mon.* 11.1.
42. Tert. *Apol.* 9; *Cast.* 1.4; *Ux.* 1.8.2.
43. Tert. *Virg.* 10.1-2, 4, 14-16.
44. Tert. *Virg.* 2-8, 9.1, 16.4.
45. Tert. *Virg.* 13.1.
46. Tert. *Ux.* 1.7.2.
47. Tert. *Ux.* 2.1.3.

concession.[48] Tertullian recommended that a widower who was lonely or had difficulty managing his household should offer hospitality to one or more widows rather than remarrying.[49] The refusal of second marriages was made more complex by the imperial laws that encouraged remarriage and the generation of children by specifying civil and financial disabilities for those who did not meet the standard.[50] Tertullian recognized the problem but insisted that Christians should not be concerned with such matters.[51]

Widows (but apparently not widowers) were accorded a privileged status within the Christian community, providing that they met the requirements of 1 Timothy (5:9): that they had been married only once, had attained sixty years of age, and had borne and raised children.[52] In one instance, which Tertullian regarded as clearly inappropriate, a bishop enrolled a consecrated virgin who was not yet twenty years old among the widows in order to provide recognition of her status.[53] Like the clergy, the widows were seated in places of honor rather than being required to stand in the assembly.[54] They also provided a presence of and a witness to holiness in the assembly. The faithful appeared before them on special occasions, such as a penitential reconciliation[55] and a declaration of a marriage.[56] They were, however, subject to the same constraints as other women: they should not teach, speak in church, baptize, or celebrate the eucharist even outside the assembly.[57] Tertullian suggested that they provided advice and support to matrons who were raising children[58] and were available to manage households for widowers.[59]

---

48. Tert. *Mon.* 14.

49. Tert. *Cast.* 12.2; *Mon.* 16.3.

50. By the legislation of Augustus, inheritance was restricted for those who did not produce three children or who failed to remarry within three years after the death of a spouse. See Grubbs, *Women and the Law in the Roman Empire*, 83-87.

51. Tert. *Mon.* 16.4; *Cast.* 12.3.

52. Tert. *Virg.* 9.3; *Ux.* 1.7.4.

53. Tert. *Virg.* 9.2. The advantage of being recognized as a widow or the obstacle to enrollment as a virgin was not explained. Later legislation would allow enrollment as a virgin before the prescribed age in order to help a person resist pressure to marry. *Reg. Carth.* 126; see below, p. 464.

54. Tert. *Cast.* 11.2; *Virg.* 9.3.

55. Tert. *Pud.* 13.7.

56. Tert. *Mon.* 11.1.

57. Tert. *Virg.* 9.1.

58. Tert. *Virg.* 9.3.

59. Tert. *Cast.* 12.2; *Mon.* 16.3.

Marriage was immediately related to procreation for Romans and for most Christians. Tertullian followed literally and seriously the Pauline marriage teaching, which had been enunciated for what was anticipated would be the short period of time before the return of Jesus. As a result, he discounted the generation and education of children, offering instead a different foundation for the value of marriage. His attitude was modified by his engagement with the New Prophecy movement, but it did not change radically.

The contemporary treatises *On the Dress of Women* and *To His Wife* indicate Tertullian's thinking on marriage that may have been shared by other serious Christians. In each of these, he took a negative stance toward sexual desire even within marriage. Christ, he asserted, taught that sexual desire was morally equivalent to illicit intercourse (Matt. 5:27-28). Hence a Christian woman should not only strive to maintain herself free of lust but should refrain from arousing it toward her own person by provocative dress and cosmetics.[60] Even within marriage, a wife should cultivate chastity rather than beauty as a means of pleasing a Christian husband or of assuring a non-Christian one of her fidelity.[61]

The reflections and advice that Tertullian addressed to his wife clearly were intended for people who were already married at the time of their conversion to Christianity. Because divorce was forbidden, the partners were to continue in marriage, even if only one was Christian. Once the marriage ended in death, a second marriage was conceded only because of the difficulty of living in continence.[62] Tertullian also presented a description of the joys of marriage between two Christians. The partners shared one hope, desire, discipline, and service. They were one in flesh and spirit: sharing and encouraging one another in private and communal religious observance and prayer, as well as service to others. They were joined together in Christ, whose peace and presence they enjoyed.[63] A family built upon such a marriage would itself have been a church community.[64]

In the *Exhortation to Chastity,* written a few years later, Tertullian no longer affirmed that God was conceding sexual relations to married Christians because of human weakness. The divine command to increase and multiply, he explained, had been replaced by one of continence. Hence Christians should abstain from sexual union within an existing marriage and refrain from marrying

---

60. Tert. *Cult. fem.* 2.2.

61. Tert. *Cult. fem.* 4.2.

62. Tert. *Ux.* 2.1.3; the alternative motives, such as greed and ambition, were clearly to be rejected (*Ux.* 1.4.2; 2.8.3-4).

63. Tert. *Ux.* 2.8.6-9.

64. Tert. *Ux.* 2.8.9.

again after the death of a spouse.[65] Marriage was tainted by sexual desire in its origin and practice; sexual relations between spouses were distinguished from illicit intercourse legally but not morally.[66] Carnal practice hindered prayer, he asserted, and blocked the gifts of the Holy Spirit.[67]

The treatises *Monogamy* and *Modesty* represent the full flowering of Tertullian's commitment to the rigorism of the New Prophecy. The teachings of these treatises do not represent contemporary Christian thought or practice, yet they might have developed and exploited attitudes that were broadly shared. Tertullian once again recognized that the Paraclete continued to allow Christians to have one marriage and sexual relations within it, but only as a concession to their weakness.[68] With monogamy thus established as the commanded practice, he defined matrimony as God's joining two into one flesh or blessing the union of two already joined in one flesh. Whether a marriage union had been broken by divorce or death, the joining of either partner to alien flesh was then adultery.[69] To justify this assertion that the marriage continued through death, he exploited the role of mutual consent in Roman marriage law. He observed that the intentional union joining two souls actually preceded their bodily union and served as a sacrament or symbol of the spiritual union of Christ and the church.[70] The spiritual union of Christian marriage, which was in the soul, not only survived the death of the body but became fuller and deeper in the resurrection of the flesh.[71]

Thus Tertullian would address the widow: Could you repudiate the husband taken from you by the death that all humans must undergo; who had lived with you in peace; who had never repudiated you? In the Resurrection, he warned, a widow would have to give her spouse an account of her life after his death. How would she justify admitting another person into the soul which she had joined to his?[72] Because marriage was primarily an intentional joining of two souls and only consequently the sharing of one flesh, moreover, that spiritual union became more noble as it became more pure and free of fleshly desire.[73] Tertullian used the later Pauline teaching on marriage as the symbol of the union of Christ and the church to support the New Prophecy's demand that Christians not remarry after the death of a spouse. Thus, he extended the marriage into the Resurrection and eternal life, there freeing it from all association with sexual union.

65. Tert. *Cast.* 6.1-2.
66. Tert. *Cast.* 9.1-4.
67. Tert. *Cast.* 10.2, 11.1.
68. Tert. *Mon.* 3.8, 10.
69. Tert. *Mon.* 9.4.
70. Tert. *Mon.* 5.1, 7.
71. Tert. *Mon.* 10.4, 8.
72. Tert. *Mon.* 10.1-5.
73. Tert. *Mon.* 10.8.

## Conclusion

In Tertullian's view, marriage originally belonged to the natural realm, which Christians shared with everyone else. Thus, God forbade breaking marriage commitments by adultery or divorce, and God confirmed the existing marriages of converts to Christianity. Because the imperial marriage rituals were only incidentally idolatrous and the marriage itself was good, a Christian could participate in its celebration, even when the union was between non-Christians. The grace of conversion sanctified both the Christian and a non-Christian spouse because of their union.

Monogamy was the original form of marriage that God instituted in Adam and Eve, and then restored in Christ. The intentional union of Christian spouses represented the spiritual union of Christ and the church; consequently, it could be broken by neither divorce nor death. Neither was ever to be joined, in flesh or spirit, to another spouse. Marriage between non-Christians could not be ended by divorce or the conversion of one party to Christianity. Such a union, however, was permanently ended by death prior to the conversion of either spouse, and a single remarriage was then allowed to the survivor who became Christian. No such concession was made for a convert who had a living non-Christian spouse at the time of baptism. Neither did Tertullian indicate that converts who had been divorced before baptism were allowed to marry again as Christians. In his view, the marriage bond could be broken by death, but only when neither party was Christian. This understanding of the permanence of marriage contributed to Tertullian's argument that any violation of the marriage bond of a Christian — by adultery or remarriage — must entail permanent exclusion from the church's communion.

Marriage originally was blessed with fecundity for the increase and — after sin introduced death — for the preservation of the race. The blessing of fecundity was no longer appropriate for Christian life, however, because of the approach of the end time. Sexual relations were permitted within marriage not for procreation but only as a concession to human weakness. The preferred state was continence before marriage, within marriage, or after the death of a spouse.

Tertullian's restrictive view of marriage was not generally shared by his fellow Christians. They allowed remarriage after the death of one's spouse and tolerated marriage to non-Christians. They had even begun to allow those who violated the marriage bond to repent and be readmitted to the communion of the church, thus implying that breaking marriage was a matter between humans, not involving a direct attack on God or on the temple of God, such as was found in idolatry or murder.

Cyprian used analogies and images of marriage and family to explain and justify his understanding of the role of the church in the process of salvation. The church was the mother of all those who have God for father.[74] The church, as figured in the Song of Songs (4:12-15), was the bride of Christ, set apart and entrusted with the gifts through which baptism and eucharist were effective.[75] Cyprian did not, however, apply these images to the marriage of Christians; he never argued that the monogamy of Christ was normative for his followers, as Tertullian had.[76]

## The Rituals

Cyprian referred on a single occasion to what may be interpreted as the celebration of marriage by Christians. He advised that Christian virgins should not be present for the celebration of weddings because the festivities focused on arousing lust in the groom and encouraging the bride to endure it. Persons who had renounced such behavior should not be present where it was so openly the focus of attention.[77] The objection did not refer to idolatry, so the celebration may have been between Christians, though it hardly could have been a church celebration.[78]

## Family Life

Like Tertullian, Cyprian was concerned that Christians should not marry outside the faith.[79] The Decian persecution, however, showed that this was not an adequate safeguard against idolatry. Some Christian households did stand together against the demands of the imperial government, either by suffering imprisonment[80] or taking flight.[81] In other instances, the heads of households acted to protect their wives, children, and dependents by securing a certificate

74. Cypr. *Ep.* 74.7.2.
75. Cypr. *Ep.* 74.11.2.
76. Tert. *Cast.* 5.1-4; *Mon.* 5.7.
77. Cypr. *Hab. uirg.* 18.
78. For this argument, see Hunter, "Augustine and the Making of Marriage in Roman North Africa," pp. 69-70 and n. 28, who credits the interpretation to Victor Saxer, *Vie liturgique et quotidienne à Carthage vers le milieu du 3ème siècle, le témoignage de saint Cyprien et de ses contemporains d'Afrique* (Città del Vaticano: Pontificio Istituto di Archeologia Cristiana, 1969), 325-26.
79. Cypr. *Test.* 3.62.
80. Cypr. *Ep.* 6.3.1 notes the presence of women in the prison among the confessors.
81. Thus the parents of the infant who had been contaminated by her nurse (Cypr. *Laps.* 25).

of compliance with the edict or even performing the required sacrifice. The imperial government apparently allowed them to act as representative of the entire group, while the church regarded them as having acted alone.[82] Later, their entire households would support their repentance, intercede for the forgiveness of their sin, and threaten to follow them into schism if reconciliation was refused them.[83] Other heads of households, however, not only failed but forced both their families and their retainers to follow them in sacrificing individually.[84] Some of these then sought letters of peace from the martyrs for the whole group; they attempted to force the bishops to allow twenty or thirty people to return to communion on the strength of a martyr's recommendation.[85] Cyprian imaginatively described for his congregation the reproaches that infants appearing before the Judgment of Christ would heap upon their parents for having deprived them of salvation by leading them through the ritual of sacrifice to the gods and thereby denying Christ.[86] In one dramatic event, a wife refused to accompany her husband in offering the sacrifice. He forced her to appear before the magistrates, whose assistants then held her firmly and dragged her hand through the performance of the required action. Because she persisted in shouting out her refusal and protest, she was punished by exile.[87]

The response to persecution demonstrated that family ties did pose the challenges to Christian commitment that Tertullian had predicted. Christian husbands compromised to protect their wives, children, servants, and property. Family structures also limited or eliminated the freedom of wives, children, and servants to contradict the decisions of the heads of households.

## Virginity

Cyprian's writings indicate the growth and development of the practice of consecrated virginity in the Christian community. Virgins were noted among those faithful who withstood the Decian persecution.[88] Cyprian was able to defend the episcopal decision to allow penance and reconciliation for the sin of idolatry by pointing out that having granted forgiveness earlier for fornication and adultery had not dulled the ardor of Christians for virginity and continence.[89] Virgins were also mentioned among the captives taken by raiders in Numidia; the virgins were then ransomed with funds provided in large part by Christians

82. Cypr. *Ep.* 55.13.2.
83. Cypr. *Ep.* 55.15.1.
84. Cypr. *Ep.* 55.13.2.
85. Cypr. *Ep.* 15.4.
86. Cypr. *Laps.* 7.
87. Cypr. *Ep.* 24.1.1.
88. Cypr. *Laps.* 2.
89. Cypr. *Ep.* 55.20.2.

in Carthage.[90] At the outset of the Valerian persecution, consecrated virgins were also among the confessors sentenced to the mines in Numidia.[91]

In his early treatise *On the Dress of Virgins*, Cyprian explained the vocation of virgins differently than Tertullian had. He did not appeal to the shortness of time before the return of Jesus as a basis for a command to practice continence, with permission for marriage granted only as a concession to weakness. Instead, he explained that because the earth had been adequately populated, Christians had the freedom to embrace continence as a fulfillment of the renewing grace of baptism. Undertaking such celibacy was not fulfilling a divine command but exercising free choice.[92] Consecrated virginity was understood as a commitment to an exemplary Christian life, one which rivaled martyrdom in its renunciation and endurance.[93] Cyprian praised his Roman colleague Cornelius's dedication to virginal chastity in defending him against charges of disciplinary laxity and offered that continence as a qualification for his being elected bishop.[94]

The problems that Cyprian faced were involved in the development of a discipline appropriate for this form of life, so that it encompassed not only sexual renunciation but a fuller Christian commitment. Some of the virgins continued a privileged and even luxurious lifestyle, one that did not separate them from the activities and entertainments customary for their status in imperial society. They enjoyed their wealth by maintaining their usual dress and grooming, attending traditional celebrations of marriage and displaying themselves in the public baths.[95] Cyprian urged that their commitment ought to include not only a withdrawal from sexual engagement, marriage, and childbearing but a separation from the honors and enjoyments that were offered them by imperial culture. He believed that dedicated virgins should not only suppress their own sexual desire but should also take care not to arouse such desire in others.[96] Thus, they should not dress and deport themselves in the same way as married or marriageable women.[97] Virginity, moreover, should be particularly manifest in generosity toward the poor.[98]

Cyprian also had to deal with the problem of the living arrangements for consecrated virgins, since separate houses or monasteries had not yet been developed. Some of the virgins, it was discovered, had been sharing housing, and

90. Cypr. *Ep.* 62.2.3.

91. Cypr. *Ep.* 76.6.1.

92. Cypr. *Hab. uirg.* 23.

93. Cypr. *Hab. uirg.* 21. The martyrs earned a hundred-fold reward and the virgins a sixty-fold reward (*Ep.* 76.6.1).

94. Cypr. *Ep.* 55.8.3.

95. Cypr. *Hab. uirg.* 5, 7, 9, 10, 18-20.

96. Cypr. *Hab. uirg.* 9, 18, 19, 21.

97. Cypr. *Hab. uirg.* 5, 7, 10.

98. Cypr. *Hab. uirg.* 11.

even beds, with clerics and other Christian men. Though the women claimed to be physically inviolate, Cyprian and his colleagues retorted that bodily integrity was not the sole standard of virtue. Their conduct had endangered both themselves and their accomplices; they also had set a bad example for other Christians.[99] The bishops laid down the principle that since the virgins were espoused to Christ, they must meet at least the standard of conduct that was expected of a married woman.[100] Henceforth, they decided, virgins should be subject to the supervision of the bishops.[101] At the same time, the bishops reminded the virgins that if they were unwilling to sustain the commitment they had made, they could and should marry.[102]

A similar problem of irregular contact seems to have arisen with the initial set of confessors in the Decian persecution who were released or exiled after refusing to perform the required sacrifice. Cyprian insisted that they maintain the high standards of conduct appropriate to their status in the community.[103]

Unlike the widows and orphans, the virgins may not have been formally enrolled in an order of the church, since they did not require financial support.[104] They were, nevertheless, a recognizable group within the community.

## Widowhood

The church at Carthage had a formal order of widows who, like the orphans, were supported by the offerings of the faithful.[105] Not all the widows in the community, however, required such assistance. This can be inferred from Cyprian's including the widows, along with the virgins and matrons, in his prohibition of the use of cosmetics, which were a luxury in the ancient world.[106] While the special status must have required that the widow promised not to remarry, it is not evident that the age and single-marriage requirements specified in 1 Timothy (5:9) were being enforced. The most important qualification would seem to have been economic.[107]

99. Cypr. *Ep.* 4.2.3–3.1.

100. Cypr. *Ep.* 4.3.2. In *Hab. uirg.* 20, he accused those who displayed their bodies in the public baths of being adulterous toward Christ.

101. Cypr. *Ep.* 4.2.1.

102. Cypr. *Ep.* 4.2.3.

103. Cypr. *Ep.* 13.5.1; 14.3.2; and 11.1.3 may refer to the same incidents. Later, in *Unit. eccl.* 20, Cyprian was more explicit in accusing the confessors of fornication and adultery.

104. They are not listed with the groups requiring care in Cypr. *Ep.* 7.2; 52.1.2, 2.5; this may only have meant that they were not supported by the church, as orphans and widows were.

105. Cypr. *Ep.* 7.2; 52.1.2, 2.5; *Eleem.* 15.

106. Cypr. *Hab. uirg.* 15.

107. Cyprian cited the text of 1 Tim. 5:3, 6, 8, 11-12 in *Test.* but without the specification of age and having had only one husband in 1 Tim. 5:9, which he never cited.

## Conclusion

Cyprian's writings provide far less information about Christian marriage practices than Tertullian's did. The decade of intermittent persecution during which Cyprian served as Bishop of Carthage amply demonstrated the dangers to which Christians were subject through their commitment to marriage, child-rearing, and the management of a household. His efforts seem to have been focused on achieving a greater degree of separation from the imperial culture, especially for the dedicated virgins. The order of widows continued to function, though it seems to have been a means of assisting the poor rather than a form of asceticism. Cyprian also indicated that the church was caring for orphans.

## MARITAL PRACTICE IN AUGUSTINE'S TIME

By the time Augustine became Bishop of Hippo, Christian emperors had long ago removed the financial penalties earlier imposed on those who refused to marry or to remarry after the death of their spouses. Constantine also lifted the restriction on inheritance for those who did not produce children.[108] At the end of the century, Theodosius even imposed restrictions on widows who married too quickly after the death of their husbands and granted benefits to mothers who did not remarry at all.[109]

Augustine was also drawn into a conflict outside of Africa over the value of dedicated virginity, which engaged Jovinian and Jerome. The former believed that avoiding marriage fostered the Christian life and prevented many troubles but brought no particular heavenly reward. The latter followed an earlier tradition, retorting that marriage was a concession to weakness and valuable only in being a lesser evil than fornication.[110] Augustine rejected both positions but insisted that marriage and its renunciation found their value only through participation in the church's relation to Christ.

### Forms of Marriage

Christian marital practice in the late fourth and early fifth century continued to be defined largely by the imperial legislation and culture. It deviated on some points, such as exposing unwanted children and remarriage after divorce,

---

108. *C.Th.* 8.16.1, 17.2. See Grubbs, *Women and the Law in the Roman Empire,* 102-4.

109. *C.Th.* 3.8.1, 2; 5.1.8; 8.13.1; *C. Just.* 5.10.1. See Grubbs, *Women and the Law in the Roman Empire,* 223-24, 229-32.

110. Hieron. *Iou.* 1.5, 7-13. See Hunter, *Marriage, Celibacy, and Heresy in Ancient Christianity,* 30-35.

which the Christian emperors did not attempt to suppress.[111] It also challenged the cultural standards that allowed the sexual exploitation of servants, and it demanded the same fidelity of husbands that traditionally had been required of wives.[112]

Augustine's surviving writings provide evidence of Christian marriage practices. The wedding was celebrated by Christians in the home rather than the church.[113] The marriage contract, which specified the property involved and its disposition at the end of the marriage, was read out in the presence of witnesses and signed by them.[114] If invited, the bishop was among the witnesses to this agreement.[115] The church's particular interest in the marriage contract was its provision that the conjugal union was entered for the purpose of generating children.[116] Fathers gave daughters in marriage so that they might become mothers, Augustine observed, rather than for gratifying their husbands' lust.[117] A father, he remarked, usually had a deeper appreciation for the chastity of his daughter than for his own chastity, or even that of her mother, whose body he enjoyed.[118]

Despite the terms of the marriage contract regarding children, Augustine assumed that most Christians entered into marriage to satisfy their sexual lust or their desire for luxury. Anyone capable of practicing continence, he believed, would avoid the trials of married life.[119] He noted that even if children had not been sought, their parents were moved to love them once they were born.[120] The standard of Christian practice within marriage — the limitation of sexual relations to the purpose of generating children — was not achieved normally. Indeed, on the basis of his conversations with married men, Augustine judged that complete continence within marriage was easier to sustain than engaging in sexual intercourse on such a restricted basis.[121] Sexual relations for the satisfaction of lust were judged sinful even within marriage, though fidelity to the bond of marriage made this disorder a minor sin. Unlike adultery and fornication, married Christians could be forgiven this sin of lust through the almsgiving and prayer that won pardon for all the failings of daily living.[122] Augustine explained that this freer exercise of sexual

---

111. Augustine indicated that the practice of exposing children continued (*Psal.* 137.8).
112. Aug. *Serm.* 9 is largely dedicated to this problem.
113. With music and songs (Aug. *Psal.* 41.9).
114. Aug. *Serm.* 51.13.22.
115. Aug. *Serm.* 332.4; *Psal.* 149.15; Possid. *Vita Aug.* 27.5.
116. Aug. *Serm.* 51.13.22; *Mor. eccl.* 2.18.65; *Faust.* 15.7; *Pecc. or.* 38.43; *Ciu.* 14.18; *Iul.* 3.21.43.
117. Aug. *Serm.* 51.13.22.
118. Aug. *Serm.* 343.7.
119. Aug. *Bon. coniug.* 13.15; *Serm. Dolb.* 12(354A).10-12.
120. Aug. *Conf.* 4.2.2.
121. Aug. *Serm.* 278.9.9.
122. Aug. *Serm.* 9.18; 51.13.22; 278.10.10; *Iul.* 3.21.43; *Bon. coniug.* 4.4–6.6. Interestingly, Au-

relations — rather than marriage itself — was the concession to Christians that Paul had recognized.[123]

Ordinary Christian practice did include temporary suspension of sexual relations within marriage for the purpose of prayer. Augustine particularly recommended this abstinence as part of the Lenten preparation for Easter.[124] During this season, it was required of those engaged in immediate preparation for baptism.[125]

Complete renunciation of sexual relations and commitment to continence within marriage are well evidenced for Christians in the early fifth century.[126] After they had lived together for some years, a couple might dedicate themselves together to serving God and undertake the practice of continence.[127] The couple's objective was to focus their marriage partnership, and not just their individual intentions, on pleasing the Lord in the way that those who remained unmarried did not accomplish.[128] Augustine insisted that this decision had to be mutual; it could not be imposed on one spouse by the other.[129] The Christian whose spouse was unable or unwilling to practice continence must continue to engage in sexual relations for the sake of that partner. Such a person might choose a more limited form of continence by conceding but not demanding the marriage right.[130] Augustine provided no indication of how widespread or satisfactory such a practice might have been.

Augustine insisted that Christians should not break their marriages, either for the sake of continence or because of barrenness.[131] No Christian who had a living spouse was allowed to marry again, even if that other party had broken the marriage.[132]

Concubinage was practiced commonly prior to marriage. Male catechumens in particular regularly took a concubine whom they later dismissed in anticipation of marriage or baptism (something that Augustine himself had done).[133] When Augustine argued against the practice, his attention was directed primarily at the men; he recognized that the social status of the women involved often allowed them little control over their bodies. He judged that these women might not be sinning in any way, as long as they were faithful to

gustine always interpreted the shame and secrecy associated with sexual practice as an indicator of its moral ambiguity rather than of any ritual impurity it entailed.

123. Aug. *Serm. Dolb.* 12(354A).7-9.

124. Aug. *Serm.* 205.2; 206.3; 208.1; 209.3; 210.6.9.

125. See above, p. 204.

126. Aug. *Serm.* 51.13.21.

127. Aug. *Bon. coniug.* 12.14.

128. Aug. *Bon. coniug.* 3.3.

129. Aug. *Serm. Dolb.* 12(354A).3-6.

130. Aug. *Serm. Dolb.* 12(354A).12; *Psal.* 147.4; 149.15.

131. Aug. *Psal.* 149.15: *Bon. coniug.* 7.7, 24.32.

132. Aug. *Serm.* 260; 392.2.

133. Aug. *Serm.* 392.2.

their partners, sought children in the union, and remained continent after they had been dismissed.[134]

Concubinage during marriage was regularly denounced in Augustine's preaching. Usually the offender was a husband who had established a sexual relationship with one of his female slaves, though Augustine suggested that wives might also be guilty of abusing male slaves.[135] He refused to accept the excuse that this behavior was permissible because it substituted for the violation of another's spouse.[136] Nor was it punishable in imperial law. Augustine actively fought this abuse of servants.

Augustine recognized that wives had limited resources for restraining their husbands from adultery and that the culture praised wives who were tolerant of their husbands' escapades. He argued that as Christians they must be more concerned for their spouses' salvation. If they failed to effect a change of behavior, he suggested that they report the offenders to the bishop so that he could confront them.[137] Although he never named individuals before the congregation, he warned adulterers not to come forward at the distribution of the eucharist lest they be humiliated by his refusal of communion.[138] Legislation adopted by the African church late in Augustine's episcopate forbade the exposure of a person guilty of any punishable crime; such episcopal threats against adulterers may have provided one reason for the restriction.[139]

The evidence for the Christian practice of marriage addresses primarily, if not exclusively, the union of free persons in what the imperial legislation called *coniugium*. A slave was incapable of entering into this form of marriage. Roman law recognized the union of a slave to either another slave or a free person under the title of *contubernium*. It specified the rights of the master of the slave over the union and its offspring, and the conditions under which a free partner in such a union might avoid enslavement.[140] It did not grant to slaves the rights over their bodies that free persons enjoyed.

Slaves were baptized members of the church. The celebrated third-century martyr, Felicity, was a mother and may have been a slave.[141] The legislation of the African church specified that no one could be ordained bishop, presbyter,

---

134. Aug. *Bon. coniug.* 5.5; *Serm.* 224.3. See *Conf.* 6.15.25 for this decision by Augustine's own concubine. Such women may have been recognized as widows, though clear evidence of such a status is not available.

135. Aug. *Serm.* 9.4.

136. Aug. *Serm.* 9.11; he never addressed the question of the violation of a marriage between Christian servants by a master's abuse of one of the servants.

137. Aug. *Serm.* 392.4.

138. Aug. *Serm.* 392.5.

139. *Con. Hipp.* a. 427, 8.

140. See Grubbs, *Women and the Law in the Roman Empire*, 102-4.

141. *Pas. Perp.* 2, 15. Revocatus was also described as *servus* (*Pas. Perp.* 2). Unlike Perpetua, the other mother in this account, Felicity's marital status is not described.

or deacon unless his entire household was already Christian.[142] In the same context, restrictions were set on the women who could be allowed to live in the household of a married cleric. In addition to his blood relatives, allowance was made for the introduction of the wives of his sons and servants.[143] Augustine assumed that Christians would have their slaves baptized.[144] Some provision must have been made for their marriage. Yet in his attacks on the sexual abuse of slaves, Augustine never denounced this sin as adultery, a violation of what may be inferred to be the marriage rights of their Christian partners.[145]

In one instance, Augustine considered a situation parallel to that of slaves. He described a relationship of a man and a woman, neither married to anyone else, who agreed to limit their sexual relations to one another and to continue so until the death of one party, with the further proviso that they were open to the generation of children, though this was not the reason for their union.[146] He judged that if these conditions were realized, the agreement might be called a marriage.[147] This he clearly distinguished from the temporary concubinage in which a woman of a lower station was taken as a sexual partner until a suitable marriage for the ambitious male was arranged. The bishop seems not to have concerned himself more directly and explicitly, however, with the marriages of Christian slaves, even in Christian households.

Some evidence of Christian marriage between slaves in this period may be provided by the inscription on a marble plaque (fig. 124), dated to the second half of the fourth century and found in the Christian catacomb of Severus at Hadrumetum. It was prepared by Urbanus for the tomb of his wife, Varia Victoria, and it commemorates their forty-five-year relationship. The inscription describes their union: "Urbanus, husband *(maritus)*, made this for the sake of his dear wife *(coniunx)*, Varia Victoria, in memory of their forty-five-year *contubernium*."[148] Neither Urbanus (nor Varia Victoria) can be identified with cer-

142. *Bru. Hipp.* 17.

143. *Bru. Hipp.* 16. The term *ducere* was not restricted to a *coniunx*, though it was the term used for marriage.

144. In dismissing the argument that virgins did not bear children for the church, Augustine pointed out that they could purchase slaves and have them made Christian (*Virg.* 9.9).

145. Aug. *Serm.* 9.11 and *Serm.* 224.3 certainly provided the occasion for such an argument. Masters may have avoided slaves who had a partner within the household, but the silence might also indicate a lack of concern for the Christian rights of the slaves.

146. The explicit provision of procreation in imperial marriage practice was related to the transmission of property. Slaves' right to property and its disposition were subject to the discretion of their masters. Thus the case Augustine described would have fit a marriage agreement between slaves.

147. Aug. *Bon. coniug.* 5.5.

148. Varie+Victoriae+Coniugi+Karissimi+Urbanus+Maritus+Memoriae+Causa+Obcontu-bernio+Anni+XLV+Fecit. The translation (above) is hypothetical, since the grammar is slightly irregular. For example, "Varie" might not be part of the woman's name (from the gens Varius), but rather a modifier of "conuigi," just as "karissimi" appears to be a misspelled dative form.

tainty as Christian, though the location of this epitaph in a Christian catacomb suggests that as probable.[149] The union is characterized as a *contubernium,* in which at least one party would have been a slave. The partners, however, are titled *maritus* and *coniunx,* terms proper to the free-born or freed partners in a *coniugium.*[150] Since the dedication was for a person buried in a Christian catacomb, it might indicate that the church recognized the married status of the couple, at least one of whom was or had been a slave.

## Family Relationships

Augustine indicated that most of the households in Hippo were headed by Christians and that all of them included at least some Christians.[151] Most of what he had to say about family life, however, was focused on the relationship of the spouses. In this, his sermons do not mirror the remarkable observations about childhood and childrearing that are found in the initial books of the *Confessions.*

Most of Augustine's observations about parenting in the sermons were intended to help the congregation understand the ways that God dealt with them. The attention that parents lavished on their children could help them appreciate God's generosity and care for them. Though some parents turned their children over to nurses and pursued their own pleasures,[152] most cared for their children's needs themselves. He remarked, for example, on the way mothers rubbed their children vigorously in the bath to make them healthy.[153] Some parents also tried to limit the number of their children, so that they would be able not only to provide for their care but to leave each with sufficient resources for independent living.[154] Augustine recognized providing an inheritance for children as a legitimate parental responsibility.[155]

149. The small crosses that separate the words may be only decorative details, and the inscription does not include any of the expected Christian assertions (e.g., "fidelis in pace"; cf. fig. 124). But it does omit the traditional pagan evocation of the *Dis Manibus Sacrum* ("sacred to the shades of the dead") and any specific indicators of the partners being free, freed, or slaves, which is characteristic of Christian inscriptions.

150. It is extremely unlikely that Victoria was a freedwoman in relationship with her slave Urbanus, since for a woman to enter such a relationship would have been a crime in most parts of the empire, unless Urbanus was an imperial slave (cf. *C.Th.* 4.12.1-4). That Victoria was someone else's slave seems equally unlikely. The social status of the partners may have changed during their long union, thus accounting for the conflict in terminology.

151. Aug. *Serm.* 302.19.

152. Aug. *Serm. frg. Verbr.* 2-3(4A).2.

153. Aug. *Psal.* 33.2.20.

154. Aug. *Serm.* 57.2.2.

155. Thus he rebuked a mother who had given away the property her son could have expected to inherit, refused to accept gifts which would disinherit children, and limited his appeals for almsgiving and gifts to the church. See Aug. *Ep.* 262.8; *Serm.* 355.4-5; 356.7, and *Serm.* 9.20; 86.9.11–11.12; *Psal.* 48.1.14; 131.19.

The heads of households in particular were called to imitate the divine care by training their children and servants in true religion and proper conduct. They were to exercise their authority to make sure that they were Christian, Catholic, and free of heresy.[156] A man had to have accomplished this in order to qualify for the office of bishop, presbyter, or deacon.[157] The head should then ensure that the behavior of the members of the household was proper for Christians, requiring them to fulfill the baptismal promises that had been made for them as infants or urged upon them when they were older.[158] Forgiving offenses did not mitigate the responsibility of householders to administer the punishments that would promote the good conduct and salvation of their dependents. To refrain from correcting was cruelty, not mercy; to discipline was right, provided that it was prompted and guided by love and concern for salvation.[159] A father should expect to be feared as well as loved.[160] The master in turn should be prepared to listen to others and adapt to them in order to maintain the unity of the family.[161]

In some instances, however, Augustine warned parents against opposing the proper and legitimate aspirations of their children. The demands of family relationships, even those sanctioned by the Decalogue, must be subordinated to the love and service of God.[162] Love of spouse and children must never, for example, hold a person back from witness to Christ.[163] A son who wanted to become a monk or a daughter who wanted to become a consecrated virgin might have had to oppose the preferences of a father who wanted an heir and a mother desiring grandchildren.[164]

Augustine occasionally acknowledged the most complex set of relationships within Christian families and households: those centered on the slaves. He knew that slavery was bitter and that slaves were often justified in grumbling about their work.[165] Masters had control of the slaves and all of their possessions, which masters could confiscate to satisfy for negligence and loss.[166] He knew that masters regularly neglected the spiritual welfare of their servants and

156. Aug. *Serm.* 94.

157. *Bru. Hipp.* 17. In *Virg.* 9.9, Augustine noted that a wealthy virgin could buy slaves and make them Christians, thus contributing more members to the church than she could by marrying and raising children.

158. Aug. *Serm.* 50.24.

159. This point is made repeatedly in Augustine's writings: *Serm.* 5.2; 13.9; 83.7.8; *Serm. Dolb.* 21(159B).1, 5, 7; *Serm. Frang.* 5(163B).3; 9(114A).6; *Psal.* 62.10; 88.2.2; 102.14; 140.18; *Eu. Io.* 51.13; *Ciu.* 19.12.

160. Aug. *Psal.* 118.31.3.

161. Aug. *Serm. Dolb.* 13(159A).13.

162. Aug. *Serm.* 344.2; *Serm. Etaix* 1(65A).5-7; *Serm. Dolb.* 13(159A).6-13.

163. Aug. *Serm. Etaix* 1(65A).9-11; *Serm. Lamb.* 15(335G).1.

164. Aug. *Serm.* 161.12.12; *Serm. Denis* 20(16A).12; *Psal.* 44.11.

165. Aug. *Psal.* 99.7.

166. Aug. *Psal.* 49.17; *Serm. Dolb.* 21(159B).5, 7; *Serm.* 296.4.

did not seek their improvement.[167] Yet, Augustine followed the scriptural standard in affirming the institution itself: slaves were not to expect manumission from Christian masters. They were to submit to their masters, even when these were not good persons. In this way, servants could contribute to the unity of the household.[168] Masters for their part were required to seek forgiveness, at least from God, for harsh treatment and abuse of servants. Though they did not have to humble themselves by seeking the servant's pardon, Augustine taught, they should convey their remorse and apology by acting with special gentleness toward those they had offended or harmed.[169]

The clergy also owned slaves. Before being ordained, bishops, presbyters, and deacons had to have made all their slaves Christians; they could retain them in their households after being ordained and even acquire partners for their slaves if none were available in the household.[170] Members of the clergy of the church of Hippo continued to own slaves. They freed the slaves when Augustine required it after an audit of their personal possessions.[171]

Masters and estate owners apparently dictated the religious affiliation of their slaves and agricultural workers *(coloni)*. Augustine used this power against the Donatists by appealing to landlords to secure the adherence of their workers to the Catholic communion.[172] He protested when a Donatist bishop leased an imperially owned estate and rebaptized its staff.[173]

In many ways, slaves seem to have been invisible to church leaders. Augustine, as has been noted, never protested against the violation of the marital relationship of the servants who were sexually abused. During the Pelagian controversy, he neither cited the absence of autonomous free choice in slaves' conversion and baptism, nor did he use it as an example of the way in which God worked for their salvation.

Family and other social relationships seem to have been considered significant only during earthly life. Christian tomb epitaphs typically recorded the name of the deceased, the age at death, and often the person's ecclesial status (e.g., "faithful, innocent, lived in peace"). Only rarely were family relationships mentioned, and the ancestral family name *(nomen)* was often omitted. This conformed to the growing use of a single name in the Late Empire, but it might reflect also a Christian practice of eschewing social class distinctions.[174] Ordinarily, only the first name *(praenomen)* appears, such as Crescentia or Darda-

---

167. Aug. *Serm. Dolb.* 21(159B).4.
168. Aug. *Psal.* 124.7.
169. Aug. *Serm.* 211.4.
170. *Bru. Hipp.* 16-17.
171. Aug. *Serm.* 356.6-7.
172. Aug. *Ep.* 58.1.
173. Aug. *Ep.* 66.1.
174. See Benet Salway, "What's in a Name? A Survey of Roman Onomastic Practice from c. 700 B.C. to A.D. 700," *Journal of Roman Studies* 84 (1994): 124-45.

nius (figs. 135, 137), and exceptions are rare: the memorial of Blossus (fig. 120), whose nomen may indicate aristocratic status. Additionally, while clerical or ecclesial role might be included (e.g., *episcopus* or *diaconus*), and the deceased might be identified as being a servant of God (*famulus/a dei,* fig. 141), indicators of social status such as slave or freed (*libertus/a* or *servus/a)* are virtually never included. Moreover, Christians tended to be interred within dedicated areas of cemeteries or in funerary churches that were not organized to encourage burials according to familial groups.[175] In fourth- and fifth- century practice, marriage and family ties were for earthly life alone, contrary to Tertullian's insistence that Christian marriage lasted into the resurrection of the dead.

A possible exception to the practice of ignoring family relations is the rare double-portrait mosaic from Thabraca dated to the late fourth or early fifth century. It shows a male seated at a desk and a female standing in the prayer position (fig. 139), and it covered a single sarcophagus that contained two bodies of persons who almost certainly died at the same time. These two individuals appear to have been father and daughter rather than a married couple, and the daughter a consecrated virgin. This interpretation is based on a reconstruction of the epitaph as identifying her as *Victoria filia Sacra* (Victoria, sacred daughter).[176] She wears a veil that covers her head and upper body.[177] Over the man's head are the remains of the formula, *In Pace.* He holds a stylus in his right hand and appears to be writing on a tablet or scroll. The letters MAR (or MAI) are visible, and they suggest that he may be producing a list (or calendar) of martyrs.

## Virginity

Augustine's writings and the contemporary legislation of the African councils indicate that consecrated virginity was widespread and flourishing. Though some Christian parents resisted the desires of their children to dedicate themselves to this practice, the church as a whole held these women in high honor.[178] In the celebration of the eucharist, for example, the deceased virgins were commemorated immediately after the martyrs.[179]

175. See the above discussion of funerary inscriptions and mosaics, pp. 120-24. On this question, generally, see Ann Marie Yasin, "Funerary Monuments and Collective Identity: From Roman Family to Christian Community," *The Art Bulletin* 87 (September 2005): 433.

176. This reading is based on rendering what appears on the mosaic as "Iilia" to be "Filia" and taking the final "S" (before "in pace") to be an abbreviation for "Sacra." An alternative rendering, "Puella," has been suggested, which seems implausible, although this is the suggestion of Yvette Duval, *Loca sanctorum Africae: Le culte des martyrs en Afrique du IVe au VIIe siècle,* 2 vols. (Rome: École française de Rome, 1982), 1:431.

177. See below, pp. 465, 479, for a discussion of this as a possible *mitra.*

178. Aug. *Serm.* 161.10.10, 12.12.

179. Aug. *Virg.* 45.46.

Though virginity was an individual decision and a woman could follow this way of life in her family home, her status was formalized by her making a vow and receiving a head covering, called a *mitra,* which indicated her bridal relationship to Christ.[180] Councils in the 390s restricted the ritual of dedication to the bishop and only later allowed a presbyter to preside with the bishop's permission, presumably in a rural congregation.[181] Formal consecration of a virgin was to be delayed until her twenty-fifth year, the same age specified for ordination to the first of the clerical grades for which sexual continence was required.[182] A later council decided that the ritual might be performed earlier for a virgin, if she was being pressured by a marriage proposal, was in danger of being abducted and ravished, or was in danger of death. The protection of the church might have been helpful in preserving from harm a girl whose family lacked the standing to do so. Even in these cases, however, the virgin had to be at least twenty years old, well past the initial age of betrothal and marriage.[183] Augustine himself had responsibility for an orphaned girl who expressed a desire to become a consecrated virgin. He considered her much too young to be taken seriously in this regard, though she was already being pressed by a suitor for marriage.[184]

The living arrangements for virgins were still developing even in the fifth century. Some lived with their families and continued to be subject to their parents.[185] A council recommended that upon the death of their parents, they should be placed in the homes of serious Christian women, who might be understood as widows, though this was not specified. In any case, they were to be supervised and not allowed to wander.[186] If the Victoria described above (fig. 139) was, indeed, a consecrated virgin and was buried with her father, then she may have continued to live with her birth family at home, even after her consecration. Other virgins seem to have lived independently, retaining their property and using it at their discretion.[187] As in Cyprian's time, some of these were accused of living in luxury, contrary to their high calling.[188]

---

180. Aug. *Serm.* 148.2; *Reg. Carth.* 126; on the head covering, see Optat. *Parm.* 2.19. In *Parm.* 6.4 the head covering is used as a sign of the vow. The term used in *Parm.* 2.19, *mitra,* was derived from Isaiah 61:10 in the African Latin version of the text. It was used by Tertullian in *Virg.* 17 in this sense, and in *Marc.* 4.11.7 for Christ. The text was applied to Christ and the church in Aug. *Ep.* 140.6.18; *Ep. Io.* 1.2; *Psal.* 30.2.1.4; 74.4; 101.1.2; *Serm.* 91.7.8; *Serm. Dolb.* 22(341*).19.

181. *Con. Carth.* a. 390, 3; *Bru. Hipp.* 24, 34; *Reg. Carth.* 38.

182. *Bru. Hipp.* 1b; *Cau. Apiar.* 16.

183. *Con. Carth.* a. 418; *Reg. Carth.* 126.

184. Aug. *Ep.* 253-55. Augustine judged that she was also too young to choose a husband, though he considered the suitor himself unworthy because he was not a Christian.

185. *Bru. Hipp.* 31; Aug. *Ep. Divj.* 13*.2; *Con. Carth.* a. 345-48, 3-4.

186. *Bru. Hipp.* 31. The woman identified by her honorific tomb cover as a "matrona uidua" might have been such a supervisor of virgins (fig. 119).

187. Aug. *Serm.* 355.6.

188. Aug. *Virg.* 34.34.

---

Finally, monasteries for women were beginning to develop. They included virgins who sold their property and lived by the common fund. Such seems to have been the status of the minor daughter of the presbyter Januarius, whose failure to dispose of his property caused such problems.[189] Augustine's own sister, presumably a widow rather than a virgin, was head of one such community for which he later wrote a rule of life. The ideals he set for the monastery were those he attempted to realize in the common life of his clergy: living from a common fund and in the sharing of goods, providing mutual support in the dedicated life, and caring for one another by correction and punishment when necessary. Augustine was particularly concerned that these women guard not only their bodies but their intentions by opposing the first movements of sexual attraction and taking care not to desire to be attractive to others.[190] Another Victoria (who was buried in the same martyrs' chapel as the Victoria called "daughter" in fig. 139) is addressed both as "mother" *(mater)* and as "servant of God" *(famula dei)*. Another woman, Glyceria, appears to have commissioned the tomb mosaic. While Glyceria may have been Victoria's daughter by birth, Victoria's identity as "mother" as well as "servant of God" might indicate that she was the head of a community of women.[191] Another instance is found in the portrait-type tomb mosaic made for Pompeia Maxima, servant of God (fig. 142). Like the Victoria in the double-portrait mosaic from Thabraca (fig. 139), Pompeia is depicted wearing a veil, which might be a *mitra,* the covering specified for a consecrated virgin.

When a consecrated virgin violated her vow, even by marrying, she was considered an adulteress against Christ. Her offense was not in the marrying itself, however, but in having turned away from the high station to which she had committed herself.[192] Augustine did not make a judgment on the status of the marriage, as he did recognize that of a dedicated widow who had violated her promise and married.[193]

The canonical legislation and Augustine's own correspondence indicate that the bishops had reason to worry about the safety and the good reputation of women whom they had consecrated as virgins. A mid-fourth-century council of Carthage specified that virgins were neither to live with men nor permit men to have access to them.[194] This, it will be recalled, had been a problem a century earlier, in Cyprian's time. Some problems continued to arise from relationships with clerics. Continent clerics — which would have included deacons

---

189. Aug. *Serm.* 355.3.

190. Aug. *Ep.* 211, esp. 211.10.

191. If not, this is another example of the rare appearance of a family relationship in a Christian tomb mosaic.

192. Aug. *Psal.* 83.4. Augustine refused to apply the same term to widows who married (*Vid.* 9.12–10.13).

193. See below, pp. 467-68.

194. *Con. Carth.* a. 345-48, 3.

and presbyters — were forbidden to visit widows or virgins except with the permission of or at the command of a bishop or presbyter (presumably the pastor in a rural church). Moreover, that superior was to specify a suitable clerical or lay companion to accompany them on the visit. Even bishops and presbyters were to have a companion, another cleric or a serious lay Christian, when they undertook such a visit.[195] The concern was not without foundation. A Donatist bishop was accused of raping a virgin whom he had himself dedicated.[196] Augustine reported that both a rural subdeacon and a monk had to be punished for inappropriate contact with consecrated virgins. The former bolted to the Donatist communion and took two virgins *(sanctimoniales)* with him, where they led dissolute lives.[197]

The greatest danger, however, came not from wayward clerics seeking the company of nuns but from men abusing their positions of power. Augustine had to deal with two instances in which an official had violated a consecrated virgin. The bailiff on a country estate had violently assaulted a virgin who came from another estate to work wool. He was forced to undergo public penance and was removed from his office by the proprietor. Augustine urged that no further action be taken in imperial court, where the rape would have brought a severe penalty.[198] In another instance, he responded in outrage to the intervention of the Roman bishop demanding the disciplining of clerics of the diocese of Hippo who had attacked a man of standing in the imperial service. The petitioner had neglected to inform the Roman bishop that he had abducted and raped a nun. The clerics in question had tracked him down, rescued the nun, and administered a sound beating to the man. Augustine pointedly demanded whether the Roman bishop was suggesting that a person who considered himself beyond the reach of imperial prosecution and cared nothing for the sanctions of the church should have been treated with greater respect by the clerics — not to mention being defended by the Roman bishop.[199]

The virgins themselves were not always well-behaved. While visiting an estate on church business, one of Augustine's clerics had been approached by a virgin during the night. The deacon contended under questioning that he had maintained his distance as best he could and had found a way to extricate himself from the situation without betraying the indiscretion of the virgin. She apparently came to grief some years later, when the cleric was already serving as a presbyter; she then accused him of causing her downfall.

195. *Bru. Hipp.* 24.
196. Optat. *Parm.* 2.19. The incident occurred during the repossession of the basilica at Tipasa and may have been intended to degrade her for having gone into Catholic communion during his exile.
197. Aug. *Ep.* 35.2; *Ep. Divj.* 20*.5.
198. Aug. *Ep. Divj.* 15*.3; *C.Th.* 9.25.1, 3.
199. Aug. *Ep. Divj.* 9*.

Augustine trusted the cleric, and his rural congregation affirmed his good character.[200]

## Widowhood

Dedicated widows were distinguished by a vow not to marry again.[201] Unlike the provision made for the dedication of virgins, the canonical legislation did not specify that only a bishop or delegated presbyter could confirm such a vow.[202] The widows followed a discipline that was not significantly different from that of consecrated virgins: only males who were blood relatives could live in their households,[203] and they could be visited by clerics accompanied by suitable companions only as permitted or directed by the bishop.[204] Augustine indicated that the requirements of widows to have been married only once and to be sixty years of age were not being enforced.[205] He did not specify that these women dressed differently than other widows.[206]

Widows were exhorted not simply to combat sexual temptations but to beware lest their suppression of sensuality leave them open to other vices, particularly to a love of money.[207] They should, then, dedicate themselves to prayer, fasting, reading psalms, studying the scripture, and assisting the poor.[208] The tomb of a certain widow (*vidua*) named Matrona describes her as "living in the faith" and now resting in peace (fig. 119). Matrona may or may not have been enrolled in a class of dedicated widows.[209]

In some instances, widows broke their vow and married again. Some teachers judged that these persons were guilty of adultery against Christ: their marriages should be broken, and they should be required to return to their celibate state. Augustine disagreed strongly with this position. He judged, on the basis of a careful analysis of 1 Timothy (5:11-12), that the failed widow's sin was not in

200. Aug. *Ep. Divj.* 13*.1-3.

201. Aug. *Vid.* 8.11, 19.23; *Ep. Divj.* 3*.3; *Serm.* 208.1.

202. For the virgin, *Con. Carth.* a. 390, 3; *Bru. Hipp.* 24, 34; *Reg. Carth.* 38.

203. *Con. Carth.* a. 345-48, 4. The same rule applied to both men and women who were dedicated.

204. *Bru. Hipp.* 24; *Reg. Carth.* 38.

205. The example is given in Aug. *Vid.* 13.16 that a young woman who has been married twice for short periods of time and then dedicated herself to widowhood might be better than one who had been married only once for a long time.

206. Aug. *Ep.* 262.9 deals with a married woman who dressed like a widow.

207. Aug. *Ep.* 130.3.7-8; *Vid.* 21.26.

208. Aug. *Vid.* 14.17, 21.26.

209. The inscription here reads "Matrona vidua vixit in fide et requievit in pace die non(o) kal(endas) Febr(u)arias." See James H. Terry, "Christian Tomb Mosaics of Late Roman, Vandalic, and Byzantine Byzacena" (Ph.D. diss., University of Missouri–Columbia, 1998), no. 133, pp. 528-29.

the marriage itself, which was a good. The sin was the prior desire to marry she had nurtured after making a commitment to living as a widow. She had set out on a higher path and then turned back. Thus, she was guilty of infidelity to God but not of adultery against Christ. The marriage itself was not to be disturbed, lest the partner from whom the widow would be separated become an adulterer by marrying again.[210] This judgment indicates that the vow of widowhood — unlike the marriage that broke it — was not considered an impediment to the woman's marriage. The analysis of this widow's failure was not unlike that of a dedicated virgin who decided to marry; in both cases, Augustine seems to have condemned their turning back from a higher calling rather than the marriage itself.[211]

In one instance, Augustine also reported the abduction of a widow, presumably a younger woman, by a youth who wanted to take her as his wife. The young man, a catechumen, was warned in a dream not to harm her; he repented, returned her to the bishop, and was apparently so shaken by the experience that he sought baptism.[212]

Another form of widowhood appears only indirectly in the literature on marriage. Ambitious men — such as Augustine himself — regularly took concubines from a lower social class and dismissed them before entering into an advantageous marriage. To these women, Augustine recommended the life of continence that his own partner had embraced.[213] Since the regulations on age and childrearing were no longer being applied, such women may have been regarded or even enrolled as widows.[214]

Dedicated widowhood appears to have functioned as a recognized and approved form of asceticism. The order of widows to which 1 Timothy referred was a means of specifying the destitute who needed the church's support; this aspect of the practice is not evidenced in Augustine's writings.

### Theology of Marriage

Augustine's doctrine on marriage was subject to many different influences. He found himself an early victim of his sexual urges. Through his stable relationship with the mother of his son and the experience of childrearing, he seems to have found something of a remedy for that sense of disintegration. Reaction

---

210. Aug. *Vid.* 9.12–11.14.

211. Aug. *Psal.* 83.4; *Agon.* 31.33.

212. Aug. *Dulc.* 7.3. The events occurred in Mauretania Sitifensis, and Augustine claimed that all the parties were still alive at the time of his writing.

213. Aug. *Bon. coniug.* 5.5; *Serm.* 224.3. *Conf.* 6.15.25 narrates the decision of the mother of his son.

214. Augustine's concubine may have undertaken such a life in Thagaste; see Garry Wills, *Saint Augustine* (New York: Viking Press, 1999), 65.

---

against the extreme Manichean doctrine must have played a part in his coming to the judgment that sexual differentiation and generation were integral to the original divine plan for the creation and humanity's role in it. The controversy over the relative values of marriage and continence, which pitted Jerome against Jovinian, may have exercised literate Christians, especially in Carthage, and may be reflected in Augustine's insistence on the primacy of the marital bond as a form of Christian charity.[215] In the end, in *On the City of God,* he asserted that human sexual differentiation transcended its temporary function of generation; the sexual organs endured as ornaments decorating the resurrected body, inspiring praise of the wisdom and mercy of the Creator, who did not sacrifice beauty to utility in forming the human body.[216]

Sexual differentiation and marriage were assigned different roles in the successive stages of the building of the city of God. As with most other things Augustine puzzled over, his understanding changed over his career of writing. His explanation of Christian marriage reflected both the practice of his congregation and the growing attraction of the monastic life.

## THE UNITY OF HUMAN SOCIETY

The primary function of sexual differentiation and generation in the divine plan was the uniting of human society through bonds of affection, a role assigned to marriage in Paradise and retained in the fallen world. Sexual differentiation established a natural hierarchy that contributed to the stability of the marital union, a hierarchy that was not to be confused with the mastery imposed as a punishment for the Fall or the servitude that resulted from the sinful drive to dominate.[217] Had God given Adam a male rather than a female companion, then the ordering of their society might have been based upon age or some other difference; sexual differentiation served this purpose admirably.[218] Generation also promoted an affective bond. The formation of Eve from Adam himself and the derivation of all human beings from that one couple added the link of kinship to that of participation in a common nature.[219] Augustine recognized a unitive value in parent-child relationships but not in sexual intercourse itself. In Paradise, where sexual activity would have been free of the violence and irrationality that characterized it after the Fall, it would express — but not itself

---

215. On this, see David Hunter's treatment in "Augustine and the Making of Marriage in Roman North Africa."

216. Aug. *Ciu.* 22.15, 17, 24.

217. Aug. *Bon. coniug.* 3.3; *Gen. litt.* 11.37.50. The original hierarchal relation of male and female was based on love. The one which resulted from sin and extended to the domination of one male by another was not based on love.

218. Aug. *Gen. litt.* 9.5.9.

219. Aug. *Bon. coniug.* 1.1; *Gen. litt.* 9.9.14-15; *Ciu.* 12.21, 27; 14.1; 22.17.

contribute to building — a tender love between the spouses.[220] Among Christians, he claimed, a mutually agreed continence built a stronger marriage union than sexual practice.[221]

The blessings of affective unity promoted by marriage became even more important in the fallen state of humanity. Augustine explained that the prohibition of marriage between siblings and the avoidance of marriage between cousins was aimed at joining together more individuals and families by adding a second form of kinship to the blood bond. The prohibition of marriage within families extended these marital relations to new individuals and groups: through marriage, people gained new relatives rather than strengthening their links to those received through birth. Moreover, societies tended to restrict marriage groups somewhat, to prevent the dissipation of the binding power of such relationships.[222] During the patriarchal period in Israel, the natural hierarchal ordering of the sexes permitted a single man to take many wives and thus establish even wider family unions.[223]

For all their value, the affective bonds of marital companionship and kinship were still viewed by Augustine as ambivalent forces. Following 1 Timothy (2:14), he insisted that Adam had disobeyed God's command not because he was deceived by Satan but through affection and concern for his wife.[224] A similar analysis of the deleterious effects of human fellowship had been advanced earlier in the recounting of the stealing of pears in *Confessions*.[225] Augustine did not blame sexual attraction for all disorder: Adam was drawn into his sin by affection, not lust, which he did not experience until after the Fall.[226] Solomon did not fare so well.[227]

Yet marriage remained a significant means of achieving human unity even in the fallen world. In the Christian era, its unitive function actually took precedence over childbearing: no spouse could be put aside because of sterility; even among the elderly, marriage retained its full value.[228] In Augustine's view, however, continence within marriage fostered a deeper and more lasting bond than sexual relations; not only was the voluntary union of souls bet-

220. Even the reference to leaving father and mother to become one flesh with a wife (Gen. 2:24) was said not to apply to Adam and Eve but to be prophetic of Christ or descriptive of marriage in the fallen state (Aug. *Gen. litt.* 2.13.19).

221. Aug. *Bon. coniug.* 3.3.

222. Aug. *Ciu.* 15.16.

223. Aug. *Bon. coniug.* 17.20; *Nupt.* 1.9.10. A union of many men to one woman would have violated the hierarchical order of nature, while offering no increase in fertility.

224. 1 Tim. 2:13-14; Aug. *Gen. litt.* 11.42.59; *Ciu.* 14.12-14.

225. Aug. *Conf.* 2.8.16.

226. Aug. *Gen. litt.* 11.42.59; *Ciu.* 14.12. In *Gen. litt.* 11.41.57, Augustine rejected the interpretation that Adam and Eve sinned by having sexual intercourse prior to the time allowed by God.

227. Aug. *Ciu.* 14.11.

228. Aug. *Bon. coniug.* 1.1, 3.3, 24.32.

ter and stronger than the pleasurable joining of bodies, but it would endure eternally.[229]

Thus, Augustine gave the bonds of marriage and kinship an instrumental or secondary role in building the unity of the Christian church and the heavenly city of God. That wider union of souls, he never tired of explaining, was established by the gift of charity, the living presence of the Holy Spirit that joined together in love persons who did not even know each other in the flesh. As shall be seen below, the power of concupiscence and the demands of living as a family in the fallen state hampered even the faithful and loving union of man and wife; these made consecrated virginity or continence within marriage more effective than sexual relations in building the Kingdom of God.

### PROCREATION

The second necessary role of sexual differentiation and marriage in the divine plan for creation was the multiplication and spread of the human race over the earth. Sexual generation was chosen by God originally to complete the blessing and decoration of the earth by filling it with humans. After the fall of Adam and Eve, procreation assumed the added burden of checking the effects of mortality by replacing the dying with the living. Further, the promise God made to Abraham was fulfilled through marriage and procreation; these were necessary to develop and sustain the people God had assigned the role of preparing for the coming of Jesus. Genetic relationships retained no such role in the Christian period, however, when the divine gifts reached beyond the confines of a single ethnic group to embrace the whole of humanity. Once the destined number of the saints had finally been regenerated in the church through baptism, both marriage and procreation would cease. They would have no place in the final perfection of the city of God. These variations in the procreative function of marriage in the stages of the divine plan of creation, redemption, and fulfillment require more attention.

During the first decade and a half of his writing career, Augustine avoided all discussion of the role of marriage and procreation in Paradise. He offered figurative, spiritualized interpretations of the formation of male and female, and of the divine command to increase, multiply, and fill the earth. Sexual generation seemed to have belonged only to the fallen world. In the paradise narrative, Adam and Eve served as allegorical figures for the intellectual and emotive faculties of the soul, which were commanded to cooperate in producing the offspring of good works.[230] Such spiritualizing interpretation continued through *Confessions,* where the command to generate was interpreted as an order to ex-

---

229. Aug. *Bon. coniug.* 3.3, 8.8, 9.9; *Nupt.* 1.11.12. This was the position taken by Tertullian.
230. Aug. *Gen. Man.* 1.19.30; 2.11.15, 13.21.

ercise the mind's creativity by multiplying linguistic expressions of a single idea and uncovering the multitude of meanings carried by a single expression.[231] This figurative meaning of sexual generation was also used in *On the Good of Marriage,* but there Augustine finally considered the literal sense: the multiplication of the race. He assumed that only mortal bodies could engage in sexual intercourse and generation. Sexual generation would have been possible in Paradise, he explained, if Adam and Eve had mortal bodies that were somehow preserved from actual death.[232] In the third book of *The Literal Commentary on Genesis,* Augustine briefly considered the possibility of sexual intercourse and birth in bodies that were immortal by nature. But for the Fall, he speculated, Adam and Eve might have parented a holy and just society.[233] Soon enough, however, Augustine turned away from exploring generation and multiplication in spiritual or immortal bodies.[234] In the ninth book of *The Literal Commentary on Genesis* and consistently thereafter, he maintained that only naturally mortal bodies could engage in sexual intercourse and generation, though such naturally mortal bodies would have been preserved from actually undergoing death. Through Adam and Eve, the destined number of humans would have been sexually generated in mortal bodies, he explained, which would then have been transformed — a generation at a time or all at once — into an immortal condition, without ever passing through death.[235]

By the final books of this commentary, Augustine had severed any necessary link between carnal concupiscence and copulation, which had prevented his acknowledging sexual generation in Paradise.[236] Had they only been faithful to God, Adam and Eve would have enjoyed sexual relations free from the violence, irrationality, and domination that characterized the fallen condition. In Paradise, neither sexual relations nor even birth would have caused any harm to the female body.[237] In *On the City of God,* the tree of life was assigned the function of preventing the actual death of Adam and Eve's naturally mortal bodies, whose corruptible nature was required for the completion of the creation by the sexual generation of humans in Paradise.[238] Thus Augustine explained that sexual generation had been integral to the divine plan for humanity and required bodies that were naturally mortal. In Paradise, these bodies had been protected from corruption and death; their sexual activities were

231. Aug. *Catech.* 18.29 and *Conf.* 13.24.37.

232. Aug. *Bon. coniug.* 2.2.

233. Aug. *Gen. litt.* 3.21.33.

234. For Robert J. O'Connell's interpretation of this passage, see *The Origin of the Soul in St. Augustine's Later Works* (New York: Fordham University Press, 1987), 207-8.

235. Aug. *Gen. litt.* 9.3.5-6, 5.9–6.10, 9.14-15.

236. For example, Aug. *Gen. Man.* 1.19.30 and *Gen. litt.* 3.21.33.

237. The problem itself was asserted in Aug. *Gen. Man.* 1.19.30 and *Catech.* 18.29. The solution was proposed in *Gen. litt.* 9.9.14–13.23. It was repeated in *Pecc. or.* 35.40 and *Nupt.* 2.13.26.

238. Aug. *Ciu.* 13.20, 23.

free of the lust that Augustine found so pervasive and disruptive of relations among fallen humans.

Through the fall into sin, humanity lost the paradisial protections against actual mortality. Sexual generation became the necessary — but now painful — means not only of filling the earth and completing the destined number of saints, but also of replacing the dying. By God's subsequent intervention, the descendants of Abraham, Isaac, and Jacob became a genetic community that was to foreshadow and prepare for the coming of Christ. The patriarchs, therefore, accepted procreation as a divinely imposed duty, to which they dedicated themselves despite what Augustine believed was their virtuous preference for sexual continence.[239] They even accepted multiple wives and the servants provided by their spouses in holy obedience to the divine command to be fruitful.[240] Within these complex marriages, he claimed, they used sexual relations only for the procreation of children.[241]

In the Christian period, the link between generation and the economy of salvation was finally loosened. The church, which replaced Israel as the sign of the invisible city of the saints on earth, was no longer established and maintained by the generation of a race or an ethnic community. Instead, the church acquired its members by conversion from among the nations and spiritual regeneration in baptism. The rate of carnal generation among the non-Christian nations, Augustine contended, was quite adequate to supply the number of saints determined by God for the heavenly city. Hence, Christians had no duty to raise up children for the Kingdom of God: they were free to practice either virginity or continence within marriage.[242] Among Christians, therefore, procreation no longer made a necessary contribution to building the city of God, which was better served by continence and efforts to convert pagans. Unlike the patriarchs, Augustine observed, Christians generally sought children for carnal rather than spiritual motives.[243]

Augustine did not follow his African predecessors in focusing on Paul's assumption that marriage and procreation were superfluous because the time before the return of Christ was short. Instead, he argued that the coming of the end depended on completing the number of the saints.[244] Indeed, if all Christians were to accept the divine call to continence, the predestined number of saints would be achieved in them, and the Lord would return.[245]

In the heavenly city of God, which would be brought to fullness in the

239. Aug. *Bon. coniug.* 9.9, 16.18; *Nupt.* 1.13.14. They would have preferred continence: *Bon. coniug.* 15.17, 17.19.

240. Aug. *Bon. coniug.* 13.15, 15.17, 16.18; *Nupt.* 1.9.10.

241. Aug. *Bon. coniug.* 13.15, 17.19.

242. Aug. *Serm. Dolb.* 12(354A).10-12.

243. Aug. *Bon. coniug.* 17.19.

244. Augustine firmly rejected all attempts to calculate the end of time. Instead, he focused on the end of individual lives. *Serm.* 93.7.8; 97.1; 109.1, 4; *Psal.* 88.2.5.

245. Aug. *Bon. coniug.* 10.10.

Resurrection, neither marriage nor procreation would have any role.[246] Sexual differentiation, however, would remain, since it was the original constitution of humanity and thus integral to its perfection. In the formation of the human body, Augustine observed, God seems never to have sacrificed beauty to utility. Thus the sexual organs would remain as ornaments of the resurrected body once their generative function had passed. They would be contemplated by the saints without any admixture of desire for intercourse, as indeed they were in Paradise at the beginning. God would be praised in this way for sexual bodies.[247]

### THE COMPETITION OF THE AGES

Augustine considered Paul's reflections in 1 Corinthians (7:25-40) on the ways in which marriage distracted Christians from the service of Christ in *On the Good of Marriage*. He decided that Paul was referring to the demands that the present sinful age placed upon those who married, raised children, and thus engaged in civil affairs.[248] Augustine also noticed Paul's exhortation to those already married to live as though they were not (1 Cor. 7:29). It was possible, he argued, for married Christians to turn away from the pursuit of the status prized in imperial culture and to dedicate themselves to the Lord. Such a conversion could be accomplished, however, only among spouses who esteemed and appreciated one another's fidelity to Christ, modesty, and other virtues rather than honorable social position, wealth, and beauty.[249] Though Christian spouses might rise to such a way of life, he cautioned, no one originally intended marriage as a means to attain such virtue.[250] Once again, Augustine concluded that marriage, of itself, made no contribution to the Christian life.

Augustine might have been expected to incorporate into the building of the church and the heavenly city the loving care extended by parents to their children. On more than one occasion, he demonstrated his sensitivity to the efficacy of his mother's love for him and the way he was moved by the intelligence and goodness of his son.[251] His analysis in *On the City of God* acknowledged that

---

246. Aug. *Serm. Lamb.* 22(335L).2.

247. Aug. *Ciu.* 22.15, 17, 24; *Serm.* 243.3.3–8.7. Augustine explained that Adam and Eve did not procreate in Paradise because God had not yet commanded it before the Fall, and they had no lust to move them to sexual activity (*Gen. litt.* 9.4.8; *Ciu.* 14.21).

248. Aug. *Bon. coniug.* 10.10.

249. Aug. *Nupt.* 1.13.15.

250. Aug. *Bon. coniug.* 12.14.

251. Aug. *Conf.* 9.6.14; 9.8.17–11.28. Not least among these is his observation that the dead must be unaware of the plight of the living because he could not imagine that his mother could have known his cares and sufferings since her death without ever visiting him in his dreams (*Cur.* 13.16).

the love of God did move Christians to concern for others. The objective of such engagement, however, should be eternal salvation rather than the passing goods of earthly life. The command proper to the Christian age was to multiply spiritually rather than carnally.[252] The loving labor that provided physical and mental nurture for children somehow escaped his attention and appreciation. Moreover, even the emotional turmoil that resulted from Christian love and concern for another's salvation was interpreted as a sign of human weakness in the fallen condition.[253]

## THE BOND OF MARRIAGE

Augustine rejected a role for marriage and procreation in the heavenly city of God, for he believed the New Testament clearly taught this in Christ's response to the question about the woman who buried seven husbands (Matt. 22:30) and in Paul's assertion that a widow is no longer bound to her husband (Rom. 7:2). Yet he did recognize marriage as integral to the city of God on earth: first, in Paradise for completing the beauty of creation, and then, after the Fall, for establishing the Jewish people to carry the promise of salvation. Once the earthly city of God passed into the Christian era, however, the role of marriage became radically restricted: procreation was no longer necessary; the affection that united the church community was to be a universal charity rather than the family ties fostered by marriage and childbearing.

In the bond of marriage, however, Augustine discerned a particular form of charity and mutual service that was particularly well-suited to the weakness of humanity in its fallen condition. He agreed with Tertullian that the union of souls between a man and a woman was essential to marriage. This union could be achieved even in the absence of any sexual relations,[254] but it usually was realized in their fidelity to one another in an exclusive bodily union.[255] Although their sexual relations should have been directed to the generation of children, they actually served in assisting one another to contain the forces of lust that assailed them. The partners exercised mutual charity by submitting to and serving each other's sexual needs, which were inseparable from the fallen condition.[256] The partner seeking the satisfaction of desire was dominated by lust and thereby sinned, though fidelity to the bond of marriage rendered that sin minor and easily forgiven.[257] The partner who only served

252. Aug. *Bon. coniug.* 17.19; *Serm. Guelf.* 32(340A).7.
253. Aug. *Ciu.* 14.9.
254. Aug. *Bon. coniug.* 3.3, 6.6, 23.28.
255. Aug. *Bon. coniug.* 3.3, 4.4.
256. Aug. *Bon. coniug.* 4.4, 6.6.
257. Aug. *Serm.* 51.13.22; *Serm. Dolb.* 12(354A).7-9.

the spouse's sexual need rather than his or her own desire acted not in lust but in virtuous love.[258]

Continence within marriage was a recommended Christian practice. As has been indicated above, Augustine insisted that it should be attempted only when both partners agreed to it, and it must not be imposed by one on the other.[259] If one was unwilling or unable, the spouse seeking a higher form of life might refrain from initiating sexual relations but must not reject the advances of the partner.[260] Although Augustine did not develop the parallel, this form of restrained sexual practice mirrored the virtuous conduct of the patriarchs, who engaged in sexual intercourse only for the purpose of fulfilling the divine command to generate children. The Christian, however, sought the spiritual good of the spouse.[261]

The bond of marriage was constituted not by the exclusivity of bodily relations but by the union of souls. Thus, Augustine insisted that spouses had to love rather than use one another. Chaste love within marriage was gratuitous; it focused on the person of the spouse rather than on one's private good in the gifts that might be bestowed by a spouse. Thus, calamities and adversity, he observed, often proved marriages chaste and faithful.[262] He lamented the failure of many parents to appreciate this Christian love when they sought a wealthy rather than a virtuous partner for their child.[263] To marry for riches, Augustine warned his congregation, was a perversion comparable to preaching the gospel for personal gain.[264]

Augustine's understanding of the faithful bond of marriage was a development of Tertullian's notion that marriage did not end in death, since it belonged primarily to the soul. Augustine, however, understood marriage as a particular and temporary form of Christian love that would be perfected and surpassed when charity reached its fullness and universality in the Resurrection.

### THE SACRAMENT OR SIGN

Augustine recognized different symbolic or sacramental functions of marriage in the successive conditions of humanity. The statement in Genesis

---

258. Aug. *Bon. coniug.* 4.4, 6.6.

259. Aug. *Serm. Dolb.* 12(354A).3-6, 12.

260. Aug. *Serm. Dolb.* 12(354A).12; *Psal.* 147.4; 149.15. In this, the rights of the wife were the same as those of the husband.

261. David Hunter developed this point in "Augustine and the Making of Marriage in Roman North Africa."

262. Aug. *Serm.* 137.8.9; *Psal.* 55.17.

263. Aug. *Psal.* 72.33; Augustine knew whereof he spoke, though he did not criticize this failing in his mother (*Conf.* 6.13.23).

264. Aug. *Serm.* 137.8.9.

(2:24) that a man leaves his father and mother in order to cling to his wife could not have applied literally to Adam and Eve in Paradise, because they had no parents to leave.[265] It referred most fully to Christ, who left the Father to come to the church, his bride, who was formed from his side as he slept on the cross.[266]

The marriages of the patriarchs to their many wives foreshadowed the union of the many nations to Christ in the church. Their families, beset by jealousy and conflict, symbolized the imperfect church of the present age, which is itself divided by the presence of sinners within its communion.[267]

The monogamous marriage of Christians, however, symbolized the eschatological union of Christ and the purified church. There the faithful would be united perfectly in mind and heart, so that they would constitute a single bride for Christ. This union was signified most fully by the discipline the church applied to its clergy: they might have only a single wife during the whole of their lives.[268] The marriages of lay Christians also manifested the union of Christ to the church: the union of the partners took precedence over their generation of children, and it could not be broken even by infidelity.[269] Christian virginity and widowhood, as has been noted, symbolized other aspects of the church's relation to Christ: the integrity of its faith and its total trust.[270]

In his treatise *On the Good of Marriage*, Augustine went further in developing his understanding of the indissolubility of marriage by drawing a parallel to the sacrament of orders. Although Christians entered marriage for the purpose of generating children, the holiness of the sacrament endured even when no children were born; it could be broken only by death. Similarly, a cleric was ordained for the service of a congregation, but the sacrament of the Lord remained upon him even if no congregation was formed or if he was removed from office for misconduct.[271] This undeveloped analogy was intended to link the permanence of Christian marriage to that of orders and, by implication, baptism. In a long and rambling New Year's Day sermon, Augustine gave another hint of a more elaborate parallel between the symbolic meaning of marriage and orders. An Israelite priest, he remarked, had to be without bodily defect because his wholeness symbolized the perfect sinlessness of the soul of Christ, the true priest.[272]

In his later treatise *On Marriage and Concupiscence*, Augustine drew out the parallel between the efficacy of marriage and that of baptism. The ritual

265. Aug. *Gen. litt.* 2.13.19.
266. Aug. *Gen. Man.* 2.24.37; *Ciu.* 22.17; *Psal.* 138.2.
267. Aug. *Bon. coniug.* 18.21.
268. Aug. *Bon. coniug.* 18.21.
269. Aug. *Bon. coniug.* 7.7, 15.17, 18.21.
270. Aug. *Virg.* 2.2; *Serm.* 192.2; 196.2.
271. Aug. *Bon. coniug.* 24.32.
272. Aug. *Serm. Dolb.* 26(198*).49.

of baptism, he recalled, established a permanent relationship between Christ and the Christian, a sign that survived even if the faith it symbolized was lost. Similarly, marriage created a bond between the partners that lasted as long as they were both living; the reality signified was the exclusive bodily union in which they persevered. Even if the bodily union was disrupted, the marriage bond itself endured and made any other bodily union adulterous. This same sign and union was preserved forever in the union of Christ and his church.[273]

Augustine's understanding of marriage engaged the levels of sign and reality found elsewhere in his sacramental theology. The shared promise that constituted marriage was a sign of the bodily union of the spouses, which was itself a sign of the spiritual union of their souls, and both, in turn, were signs of the union of Christ to the church. Both the bodily and the intentional unions of marriage, like that of Christ and the church, were charged with the complex interaction of sin and grace in the fallen world. Each, however, had a positive role in the mystery of salvation. For Augustine, marriage and sexual union were goods rather than tolerated evils; though burdened by mortality and lust, they were yet a realization of charity and a sign of salvation.[274]

## Theology of Virginity

Augustine's discussion of the practice of virginity in his treatise on that subject was dominated by the controversy aroused by Jovinian, who contended that continence was of no more religious value than marital chastity. Augustine indicated that the question was being widely discussed, so he was impelled to respond in the two treatises *On the Good of Marriage* and *On Virginity*.[275] The latter treatise dealt with issues of scriptural interpretation that were peculiar to the theological controversy and were not reflected in Augustine's preaching on the subject of marriage and vowed continence. Chief among these were the veracity of Paul's statements in affirming the goodness of marriage[276] and whether the advantage of virginity was limited to avoiding troubles during earthly life or included a greater heavenly reward as well.[277]

The virginity that Augustine saw as religiously significant was not focused on the physical integrity of the body that would be lost through sexual intercourse. This bodily virginity was a natural condition replicated in all offspring, he observed, and thus without particular religious value. Similarly, the maiden who was anticipating marriage and motherhood was surpassed by the chaste

273. Aug. *Nupt.* 1.10.11, 21.23, 29.32–30.33.
274. Aug. *Bon. coniug.* 8.8.
275. Aug. *Retract.* 2.22-23.
276. Aug. *Virg.* 16.16–18.18.
277. Aug. *Virg.* 13.13, 19.19, 23.23–27.27.

matron who had already attained these goals. Even by the Pauline standard, the latter was superior because her distraction was limited to pleasing only one husband, not many suitors.[278] Physical integrity was, however, essential to the consecrated state recognized in the church. A woman who had been forcibly violated was disqualified, even though she was innocent of any wrongdoing.[279] Moreover, once bodily virginity had been lost, it could not be restored in any way.[280]

In Augustine's view, bodily virginity was valuable as a symbol of the integrity of faith, the fidelity of the church to Christ.[281] To serve as that sign, however, it had to be vowed by the individual and consecrated by the church. The Christian virgin must not only abstain from sexual intercourse but manifest a fidelity to Christ in all her conduct: living in chastity and modesty, avoiding the arousal of lust, shunning luxury, and adorning herself with virtues to please Christ.[282] The consecrated virgin thereby entered into and symbolized the marital relation of the whole church to Christ.[283] Thus, Augustine consistently applied to the church that text of Isaiah (61:10) on the adornment of the bride, which was used to name the *mitra* or head covering given the virgin at her dedication.[284] All the members of the church were called to share this spiritual fidelity to Christ in the exclusivity of their faith; only the consecrated virgins realized that integrity in their bodies.[285] For this reason, consecrated virginity in schism from the church, among the Donatists, was an empty sign, contradicting itself.[286]

Augustine, his congregation, and indeed the church of Africa never seem to have doubted that virginity and sexual continence were of high value for Christians. On the popular scale of holiness, virginity was exceeded only by martyrdom. In the liturgy, the deceased virgins were commemorated immediately after the martyrs; they were followed by those committed to continence, such as the dedicated widows, the monks, and the higher ranks of the clergy. The practice of marital chastity held the next position.[287] Virginity was particularly valued, Augustine explained, because it preserved the body in its original integrity for its creator, undamaged by the violence and lust necessary for

278. Aug. *Virg.* 11.11.

279. Aug. *Bon. coniug.* 18.21.

280. Aug. *Virg.* 29.29.

281. Aug. *Virg.* 2.2; *Serm.* 184.1.1; 188.3.4.

282. Aug. *Virg.* 8.8, 34.34; *Serm.* 132.3; 161.10.10, 12.12.

283. Aug. *Eu. Io.* 9.2.

284. Aug. *Ep.* 140.6.18; *Ep. Io.* 1.2; *Psal.* 30.2.1.4; 74.4; 101.1.2; *Serm.* 91.7.8; *Serm. Dolb.* 22(341*).19. Their Latin version, based on LXX, attributed both parts of the Hebrew parallel to the bride, the *mitra* and *ornamenta*. For the use in the dedication ritual, see Optat. *Parm.* 2.19; CSEL 26:54.19. Tertullian applied the text to the church (*Marc.* 4.2.7).

285. Aug. *Virg.* 2.2; *Psal.* 90.2.9; 147.10; *Eu. Io.* 13.12.

286. Aug. *Psal.* 44.31-32; *Eu. Io.* 13.13.

287. Aug. *Serm.* 343.4; *Vid.* 45.46.

sexual activity after the Fall. Only Mary, the mother of Christ, was granted the privilege of motherhood without suffering bodily injury.[288]

Marriage had been of particular value as it prepared for the coming of Christ, but it did not make the same contribution to the church, which was constituted by spiritual rather than bodily relationships.[289] Marriage brought forth children in Adam, who must then be reborn spiritually through the church.[290] Indeed, a wealthy Christian virgin could purchase and convert more slaves than a mother could bear and raise children.[291] So the blessing of fertility no longer compensated for the loss of bodily integrity.[292] More importantly, the toils and troubles of married life took their toll on the Christian's attention to pleasing Christ: the jealous suspicions of spouses, the danger and concerns of having and raising children, the sorrow and worries of widowhood.[293] The virgin was spared because her spouse was Christ, whom she could trust without fear of being misunderstood. She was not, however, promised a blissful life on earth: her reward was in heaven.[294]

While Augustine recognized and affirmed the superiority of consecrated virginity to marital chastity, he refused to let the perfection of Christian life be measured primarily by a standard of sexual practice. Christ taught and practiced goodness in many forms, as was clear in the Beatitudes (Matt. 5:3-12). The Holy Spirit bestowed many different gifts for the building up of the body of Christ. Most of these virtues and gifts were received and exercised by Christians without any differentiation based on their marital status. Indeed, the ideal of Christian communal life, which was the abandoning of private possessions to share a common fund, was not generally practiced by virgins.[295]

In Augustine's view, Christian virgins in North Africa were subject to a particular failing of self-satisfaction or pride arising from their high standing within the communities.[296] They tended to look down on the married, even their own parents.[297] Augustine suggested a number of different considerations through which this temptation might be overcome. Humility was, he reminded them, the teaching and exemplary practice of Christ.[298] It was better to be married

---

288. Aug. *Virg.* 8.8; *Gen. litt.* 9.3.5-7, 10.18.

289. Aug. *Serm. Dolb.* 12(354A).10-12; *Vid.* 3.3.

290. Aug. *Virg.* 7.7.

291. Aug. *Virg.* 9.9.

292. Aug. *Virg.* 9.9.

293. Aug. *Virg.* 16.16, 55.56.

294. Aug. *Virg.* 22.22, 55.56.

295. Aug. *Virg.* 45.46–46.46. In the Rule, the church's practice of common life, mutual care, fasting, and prayer were added to the renunciation of marriage (*Ep.* 211.2).

296. Augustine began addressing the question in *Virg.* 31.31 and continued with it for the remainder of the treatise.

297. Aug. *Serm.* 354.4.4, 7.8–8.9.

298. Aug. *Virg.* 31.31–33.34; 35.35; 37.38.

and humble than virginal and proud of it.[299] Like all other Christians, virgins should confess and seek pardon for their sins. Indeed, they should count as forgiven all those sins from which they were delivered by their high calling.[300] This calling was itself a gift that God both gave and preserved; indeed, the wisdom to recognize its gratuity was itself a gift.[301] More incisively, Augustine observed that the whole church recognized martyrdom as a greater gift than virginity. This virtue, however, lay hidden in the soul until its presence — or absence — was manifest by some test. Virgins should acknowledge, therefore, that many married women were already martyrs in their hearts, while they themselves might be faithful only because they were protected by God from a challenge to which they were not equal.[302] As the virgins were honored in the church, therefore, so should they in turn honor the married.[303]

## Theology of Widowhood

The life of the dedicated widow was understood in the same way as that of the consecrated virgin: she was free of the distractions of pleasing a husband and could therefore give her attention to the Lord.[304] Like the virgin, the widow had to struggle against sexual temptations, but these were greater in her case because she had added to the lust that all people suffered as a consequence of the Fall a habit of enjoyment that she had acquired during her married life.[305]

Augustine insisted that the widows held a higher place within the body of Christ than the married and a lower place than the virgins. A widow's status was, however, completely dependent upon her membership in that body and, thus, on the other members. The church included all three states of life and was richer for the variety than it would have been with only one.[306] Actually, the church was herself a widow, just as she was a virgin and a mother.[307] She was deprived of the physical presence of her husband and depended on God alone for all her strength.[308] This trust and hope in God seem to have been the value of Christian life symbolized by the dedicated widows. In this sense, every Christian was called to be a widow and to participate in this virtue of the church.[309]

299. Aug. *Serm.* 213.8; *Psal.* 99.13.
300. Aug. *Virg.* 40.41; 48.48–52.53.
301. Aug. *Virg.* 40.41–43.44; 52.53.
302. Aug. *Virg.* 44.45–47.47. In *Eu. Io.* 51.13, he made a similar comparison between bishops and married people; many martyrs were married people rather than clergy.
303. Aug. *Serm.* 354.4.4.
304. Aug. *Vid.* 2.3.
305. Aug. *Iul.* 6.18.55.
306. Aug. *Vid.* 3.4–6.9.
307. Aug. *Serm.* 192.2; 196.2.
308. Aug. *Psal.* 131.23; 145.18; *Qu. eu.* 2.45.2; *Iob* 24.
309. Aug. *Psal.* 131.23.

Augustine indicated that some were teaching that the widow became a bride of Christ by vowing never to marry again. If she went back on that vow and married, she would become an adulteress against Christ, and the marriage must be dissolved. Augustine rejected this position. He insisted that the widow's relationship to Christ was not equivalent to the one she had to an earthly husband; the language of marriage was used in a metaphorical way and indeed was mediated through the church's relationship to Christ. To prove his point, he proposed the case of a married woman who, with the approval of her husband, pledged herself to continence within marriage. Would this mean, he asked, that the woman had committed adultery with Christ, since her earthly husband was still alive and she was still married to him?[310] Thus, he agreed that a failed widow had sinned by breaking her vow, but she was not guilty of adultery. Her new marriage, itself a good, was not to be disturbed.[311]

Augustine affirmed the established pattern of setting the martyrs and virgins at the top of the hierarchy of lifestyles in the Christian church, with widows and celibate clergy following directly, and then the married laity. He confessed no little difficulty in working out the symbolism of the three levels of reward indicated in the parable of the sower (Matt. 13:18-23). All the forms of Christian life, he insisted, were to be honored.[312] Each was a participation in and an enrichment of the life of the church itself, and, therefore, as its members, Christians shared in all of them.

### Conclusion

Augustine witnessed to the development of marriage practice in the imperial culture that supported Christian faith. The church accepted and even approved remarriage after the death of a spouse. The status of the consecrated virgin was formalized, and laws were established for the age of consecration, the cleric presiding at the ritual, and the supervision of her living arrangements. Some of the virgins were organized into religious communities of shared goods. The status of consecrated widows was similar to that of virgins; their earlier qualifications for financial assistance were no longer related to their status in the church, and even the wealthy could be recognized for renouncing another marriage.

Augustine rejected the positions taken by both Jovinian and Jerome, each of which focused on virginity as an individual's relationship to God and Christ. Instead, he insisted that the church itself embraced all three roles; thus, individ-

---

310. Aug. *Vid.* 10.13; *Agon.* 31.33.

311. This language turned up again in the Spanish collection of the legislation of the African church, into which it was interpolated (*Con. Carth.* a. 398, 104). See Charles Munier, CCSL 149:326-28, 353, for the text and the judgment of its inauthenticity.

312. Aug. *Virg.* 45.46–46.46; *Serm.* 304.2.2; *Ciu.* 15.26.

uals participated in the virginal, widowed, or marital state of the church. Each of the three symbolized a different aspect of the church's complex relation to Christ and, as such, shared in the other two. None of the states in itself determined personal holiness or standing before God.

Augustine's understanding of marriage was developed in response not only to the conflict over virginity but to the challenge of Manicheism. He affirmed that sexual differentiation and marriage were integral to the original divine plan for creation. Sexual intercourse and generation were possible, however, only in a mortal body. Thus, Augustine explained that the paradisial bodies of Adam and Eve had been mortal by nature but protected from actual death, and that the resurrected body would be sexually differentiated but would not engage in sexual activity.

Procreation had a religious role in filling the earth by establishing the human race, and then in building and maintaining Israel in preparation for the coming of Christ. The city of God in its Christian form could be established, maintained, and completed by conversion rather than generation. Christian marriage maintained its value, however, by fostering the intentional union of charity and by restraining the lust that was consequent upon the Fall. But this marital love had to transcend the boundaries that were integral to its sexual fidelity and the limits of even an extended family. Virginity and widowhood, along with the practice of continence within marriage, were necessary to symbolize the fullness that Christian love would attain in the heavenly city.

In making the principal good of marriage the intentional union of the spouses in Christian love and insisting that these bonds were built more effectively by shared continence than by sexual practice, Augustine reversed the prior understanding of virginity and widowhood in terms of marriage. The virgin or widow did not substitute a heavenly for an earthly husband; she enjoyed a relationship of marriage to Christ only as a member of the church. Turning back from this vow by marrying was not to be understood as adultery against Christ. Instead, all three states were defined by the standard of charity, the spiritual love of God and neighbor that constituted the church community. Marriage could foster such love primarily by transcending the affection engendered by sexual union and generation. Virginity and widowhood had to cultivate the same spiritual love. The particular value of each of the three states was in symbolizing and enacting the complex relationship of the church to Christ.

## GENERAL OBSERVATIONS

### Correlation of Archeological and Literary Evidence

Bonds of affection between spouses, parents, siblings, and children are well-recorded on funerary epitaphs in Late Antiquity. They provide evidence of the quality and kind of domestic and marital relationships as well as indicating religious affiliation. Studies of such epigraphical remains have demonstrated that Christians were different in certain respects from their traditionalist neighbors by the inclusion of certain phrases and the avoidance of others. Christian burial inscriptions generally used only a single name, omitting the ancestral family name and only rarely mentioning the donors of a monument or other relationships. Additionally, social status is almost always missing (e.g., *libertus* or *servus*). This practice grew in the Late Empire, and exceptions are rare. By contrast, the funerary inscriptions of some upper-class pagans prominently feature their ancestral names (cf. fig. 145, featuring two mosaics which record the full names of Gaius Julius Serenus and Numitoria Saturnina) and include the common Roman evocation of the sacred shades — *Dis Manibus Sacrum*). Moreover, Christians tended to be interred within dedicated areas of cemeteries or within churches, rather than with members of their birth families. Christian cemeteries and funerary churches were not organized to encourage burials according to familial groups.[313] In most instances where epitaphs name two individuals, no familial relationship is mentioned, even if they are assumed to be related. One exception is the tomb mosaic of the deacon Crescentius, aged 65, and his son Bruttanicus, aged 28 (fig. 148). A more typical example is the tomb of the two virgins Privata and Victoria (fig. 144).

One well-preserved exception, a tomb mosaic from the Christian catacombs of Hadrumetum, shows several fish and a dolphin entwined upon an anchor (fig. 122). The epitaph included with the iconography reads "Hermes to his sweet wife and children."[314] Hermes's name suggests that he originally was a pagan, but the iconography itself is typically Christian.

Another exception seems to indicate rather complex family relationships (fig. 124). A marble plaque dated from the mid-fourth to the late fourth century was inscribed from Urbanus of Hadrumetum for the tomb of his wife, Varia Victoria. It has been discussed above as indicating a possible instance of marriage of a Christian slave. Commemorating their forty-five-year relationship, the inscription describes their union: "Urbanus, husband, made this for the sake of his dear wife, Varia Victoria, in memory of their forty-five-year *contubernium*." At some point in their years together, however, that status was changed, as indi-

---

313. For the discussion of funerary inscriptions and mosaics, see above, pp. 120-24. On this question, generally, see Yasin, "Funerary Monuments and Collective Identity."

314. Hermes conuigi et fil(iis) dulcissimis.

---

cated by the use of the words "wife" *(coniunx)* and "husband" *(maritus),* which are titles granted only to legally married free or freed persons.[315] This change of status might be alluded to in the first word of the inscription. Rather than being a part of the woman's name (Varia, for the *gens* Varius), it might modify her spousal status as "changed" over time. Thus, Urbanus and Victoria both may have been slaves who were freed at some point, or Urbanus may have been free-born and entered this semi-sanctioned relationship with his slave concubine.[316]

A third exception is the double-portrait mosaic from Thabraca that shows a male seated at a desk and a female standing in the prayer position (fig. 139). It too has been discussed above.[317] Another tomb mosaic from the same chapel in Thabraca was found to cover a sarcophagus containing two skeletons. Although not a portrait mosaic (the image includes a cantharus, two lambs, doves, and a Christogram), the reconstructed epitaph indicates that this was probably a married couple whose names were Stercorius and Crescentina. In this instance the two seem to have been considered martyrs, as their epitaph speaks of their having crowns in perpetuity.[318]

In some instances, in addition to Victoria, *filia sacra* (fig. 139), and the two virgins Privata and Victoria (fig. 144), the tomb mosaics appear to identify consecrated women as such. For example, the epitaph for a certain Victoria reads *mater dei famula* — she may have been the superior of a convent of nuns. The portrait and inscription for Pompeia Maxima shows her wearing a veil and describes her also as *famula dei* (fig. 142).

Thus, the archeological remains show that Christians distanced themselves from traditional Roman practice by granting a more limited significance to the multi-generational family. They did not regularly include family identifiers and relationships in burial inscriptions. Instead, they seem to have been more interested in representing their religious status (e.g., *fidelis*) or role within the religious community (e.g., *episcopus, vidua, famulus/a dei, presbyterissa*) that might continue to carry weight in the afterlife. Tertullian's thesis that Christian marriage survived death and was revived in the Resurrection did not reflect broader or subsequent attitudes and practices.

315. For the text and its peculiarities, see above, p. 459, n. 148.

316. On their relationship, please see n. 150 above.

317. See above, p. 463.

318. Margaret Alexander reconstructed this epitaph as including the words "perpetuitatis coronam acceperunt quod Deo." See Margaret Alexander, "Early Christian Tomb Mosaics in North Africa" (Ph.D. diss., New York University, 1958), 2:231. Presumably those buried in Thabraca's Chapel of the Martyrs (cf. Crescentinus, fig. 143) would have died during the Vandal era, possibly as faithful Nicenes, persecuted for their faith. See the discussion of Vandal persecution above, pp. 69-75.

### THE BOND OF UNITY AND THE GENERATION OF CHILDREN

The generation of children was a primary purpose of marriage in both Roman and Jewish practice because the good of the society depended upon preparing the next generation to continue the life of the family and the community. Mortality itself was a primary enemy of the society, always threatening its existence. Christianity focused on an eschatological good that was to be attained by each of its adherents beyond the limits of mortal existence. It was, moreover, a voluntary society that could fill its membership by recruiting converts rather than relying on generation and education. Thus, it had a radically different attitude toward marriage and family life. The Christian teachers were more interested in the quality and stability of the affective bond between the married couple and in their sexual fidelity to one another than in the generation of children and the transmission of property through families.

Although they considered generation the primary reason for the sexual differentiation of humanity and the objective that should be used to regulate sexual relations within marriage, none of the teachers considered the generation and education of children a religious responsibility of Christians. Tertullian asserted, without developing a coherent explanation, that procreation was a concession to mortality. He believed that the battle against human extinction would be carried on by others — it was not the responsibility of Christians. Although Augustine taught that sexual generation was the original divine plan for the expansion of the human race and was not initially necessitated by the onset of mortality after the Fall, he argued that God's objectives would be fulfilled without the engagement of Christians in procreation. Since others would produce an adequate number of human beings, Christians should attend to filling up the determined number of the saints by converting others and persevering in holy living. Sexual continence would promote the achievement of that goal more expeditiously. Tertullian and Cyprian both noted, moreover, that responsibility for a family and household placed a Christian in even greater danger of apostasy during time of persecution: many householders failed to confess Christ, because they sought to shield and protect their dependents and the property that supported them. Working as he did in an age when Christianity was not only tolerated but supported by the imperial government, Augustine showed a greater appreciation for the social roles of marriage in procreating and providing for the successive generations. He found a remnant of the conflict between Christian and family responsibilities, however, in parents' opposition to their children's desires to serve as clergy, monks, or nuns. Like his predecessors, he insisted that the primary religious value of marriage was to be found not in procreation but in the affective union between the partners.

Tertullian identified the intentional union of the spouses as the religious value of Christian marriage. Because this union both preceded and survived the bodily union, he concluded that marriage continued through death and reached its fullness in the Resurrection. Thus, a Christian should have only a single marriage partner. The sexual, bodily union was, in his judgment, a concession to human weakness that made no contribution to the intentional union constituting the marriage. The ideal Christian marriage was, then, a partnership in serving God, one that would prove a support rather than a hindrance to piety, even in time of persecution. Such an affective union between spouses functioned as a sign or symbol of the spiritual union between Christ and the church.

Augustine also affirmed the primacy of the affective union of Christian spouses. With charity as its foundation, marriage could be both a realization and a symbol of the love that joined the church to Christ. The universality of the charity that established the intentional union of marriage was, however, in tension with the limits of the relations built on family bonds and the exclusivity of sexual union between the partners. Thus, sexual fidelity, even when limited to a single lifetime spouse, could symbolize only imperfectly the affective union of Christian marriage and that of the church to Christ. Although the sexual union could express the mutual care of the partners — particularly in containing the forces of lust — it could not establish the kind of affective union proper to Christian marriage. The marriage itself could not survive in the Resurrection, where charity reached its fullness and universality. Augustine noted that marriage could grow into a partnership in the service of God, often by the partners' decision to embrace continence, but that it was seldom, if ever, undertaken for this purpose. Those who were capable of doing so would prefer to avoid the troubles of married life and embrace the continence of consecrated life from the beginning.

### INTEGRATING CONSECRATED VIRGINS INTO THE CHURCH

Consecrated virgins, mostly female, were highly honored in the Christian church, surpassed only by the martyrs and confessors. Like the confessors, who survived their witness to Christ, the virgins often proved independent and disruptive members of the community. Because their glory was in their bodily integrity, as the confessors' was in their scars, they sometimes had to be reminded that their achievement did not constitute the fullness of the Christian life; they had to be exhorted to join the community in the practice of Christian virtues. Tertullian had to insist that they wear the veil of mature women rather than parading as perpetual adolescents. Similarly, Cyprian declared that virgins were espoused to Christ and therefore should exercise the modesty and restraint characteristic of matrons. The imperial support for virginity and widowhood beginning in the second half of the fourth century, as well as its cultivation by Ambrose and Jerome, led to new levels of conflict.

Augustine countered the virgin's pride by explaining that every Christian's relationship to Christ was mediated by that of the church itself. The church as a whole was the bride of Christ and mother of Christians. Married couples displayed this relationship in their affective union and fidelity. The integrity of the virgin's body symbolized the church's fidelity to Christ alone. Widows lived the earthly church's longing for the return of her spouse. Though Augustine affirmed a hierarchy in the symbolic value of these ways of life — with virginity highest and marriage lowest — he insisted that this hierarchy did not determine the religious standing of individuals before God. A matron might far surpass a virgin, for example, in the holiness constituted by charity. He insisted, moreover, that the relation of the virgin and widow to Christ was symbolic of the church's status. One who turned back from her good purpose and married did not thereby commit adultery against Christ, just as a matron who dedicated herself to continence with her husband's permission did not thereby commit adultery with Christ.

Thus, Augustine attempted to understand the three bodily states as symbols of an intentional union of faith and love that participated in the church's union with Christ.

### THE CHANGING STATUS OF WIDOWS

At the end of the second century, all married Christians were encouraged to embrace widowhood after the death of their first spouse. Such practice was required of the clergy, and the adherents of the New Prophecy insisted that it be embraced by all. The requirements specified in 1 Timothy (5:9) distinguished those widows who enjoyed special status within the community. In Cyprian's time, the status seems to have been conferred primarily on the basis of economic need, with the stipulation that the widow promise not to remarry.

In the fourth century, the emperors removed the financial disabilities that earlier legislation had imposed on widows who had not yet produced the requisite number of children. By Augustine's time, widows were distinguished only by their vow not to marry again; the economic and childrearing requirements were no longer operative. Neither did the status seem, of itself, to have qualified those who assumed it for financial support from the community. Augustine's innovation was to note the widowed state of the church itself, which these women symbolized.

## Conclusion

Unlike the other rituals that constituted the church — baptism, eucharist, penance and orders — marriage would not be identified as a "sacrament" until the medieval period. Along with virginity and widowhood, however, it already was being treated as a form of life which enacted and symbolized the church's complex relationship to Christ. Marriage was recognized as an integral part of the created order, necessary for the establishment of the human race and for preserving it from extinction after the Fall. In their Christian form, however, marriage, virginity, and widowhood together were understood as means of developing the universal love that transcended the natural order.

# CHAPTER 10

# The Ending of Christian Life: Death and Burial

## INTRODUCTION

Both archeological and literary evidence attest to practices and beliefs associated with death and burial. As in the case of marriage, Christians shared burial practices with the traditional culture but differentiated themselves in subtle ways. In the absence of grave goods or burial markers carrying identifying themes, such as the Christogram, the Christian graves are not distinguishable. Thus, the archeological evidence for Christian practices consists principally in the inscriptions and decorations on the surviving grave markers. The literary evidence, especially from Tertullian, indicates that Christians did reject some practices, particularly those that closely paralleled the traditional cult of the gods. Other practices, such as meals celebrated at the tomb, were adapted to Christian belief.

## THE RITUALS OF DEATH IN TERTULLIAN'S TIME

The earliest evidence for Christian practices surrounding death, burial, and mourning is almost entirely incidental to other concerns. Tertullian's primary objectives were separation from the practices of idolatry, the discipline of refusing a second marriage after the death of a spouse, and defense of the resurrection of the flesh.

## Preparation for Death

The belief that baptism was necessary for salvation is already evident from Tertullian's writings.[1] In case of emergency, it should be administered by any of the (male) faithful.[2] He also indicated that the people who had been excluded from the communion for crimes often sought reconciliation before their deaths. For at least some of these sins, especially apostasy, the church judged itself unauthorized to grant forgiveness: the crimes were reserved for the Judgment of God. The withholding of the church's loosening did not, in Tertullian's judgment, preclude receiving forgiveness directly from Christ and thereby gaining salvation.[3]

## The Rituals of Burial

Christians' practices of burial and mourning were intended to separate them from the customary rituals that Tertullian associated with idolatry. He asserted that the honors which traditional polytheists extended to their gods were parallel to those they accorded to their dead, and that, in fact, one practice had grown out of the other. In his view, the Roman gods were actually dead humans. They were unconscious of the sacred rites given them. Their images were fashioned out of ordinary destructible material, were nesting places for birds and small animals, were commonly bought and sold, and were even melted down to make cooking vessels.[4] These gods, he observed, were accorded gifts and tributes similar to those given to the other dead, including temples, altars, statues, images, feasts, games, and sacrifices.[5] The ancients, he explained, believed that they were doing a service to the dead and appeasing their souls by immolating captives or slaves on the funeral pyre. In time, they made the transition to gladiatorial combats and wild beast shows — both of which involved killing humans — similarly thinking that they honored the dead through these cruel spectacles. The images of the dead were the abode of demons, and propitiatory offerings made to them were a form of idol worship.[6]

Since Christians rejected the cult and the displays through which the gods were honored, Tertullian argued, they also ought to avoid many of the traditional funeral rituals. They were to take no part in funeral oblations, feasts, or

1. Tert. *Bapt.* 12-13. He argued against routinely giving it to children and youths.
2. Tert. *Bapt.* 17. His exclusion of women as emergency baptizers may derive from the treatise having been written against a female minister of an alternate ritual.
3. Tert. *Pud.* 21-22. Tertullian's argument indicated that forgiveness was beginning to be extended to adulterers.
4. Tert. *Apol.* 12-13.
5. Tert. *Apol.* 13; *Spec.* 11.
6. Tert. *Spec.* 12.

games.[7] Tertullian further specified, for example, that the corpse was not to be crowned. However, he did approve the use of incense in funerals and the anointing of the body of the deceased as a solace to the living.[8]

Christian belief in the resurrection of the body provided a foundation for the preference of inhumation to cremation. The continuing use of cremation in the Roman military was one of the objections Tertullian posed to Christians serving in it.[9] He explained that some followed a similar practice by keeping a portion of the body intact in order to maintain a habitation for a part of the soul. However, Christians believed neither that the soul could be so divided nor that it remained in the vicinity of the corpse.[10]

The Christian burial ritual seems to have been quite simple. The body was washed[11] and laid out with the arms at its sides.[12] Prayers were offered before placing it in the grave.[13] The corpse was placed in a grave for what Tertullian believed would be a short wait before it was ordered forth by God.[14] Christians already may have had sectors of the burial areas set aside for their use.[15] Although Tertullian did not elaborate on the procedures involved, he asserted that providing burial for the poor was one of the proper uses of community funds.[16]

Family members did continue to celebrate the funeral feasts of the dead, although Tertullian had compared them to the feasts of devils. He denied that Christians partook of them.[17] In his treatise *On Monogamy,* however, Tertullian remarked on the duties of a wife to her dead husband and made passing reference to traditional funeral customs that he assumed even Christian widows would observe:

> Indeed, she prays for his soul, and requests refreshment in the waiting period[18] for him, and companionship (with him) in the first resurrection; and

7. Tert. *Spec.* 13.

8. Tert. *Cor.* 10; *Idol.* 11.2; *Apol.* 42.4; *Res.* 27. Compare Minuc. *Oct.* 12.6, 38.3-4, which speaks of Christians anointing their dead but refusing to place garlands on their tombs.

9. Tert. *Cor.* 11.3. For comparison, see the criticism of the pagan interlocutor in Minuc. *Oct.* 11.2-4. Inhumation had always been practiced by Romans but became widespread in the second century of the Christian era. See J. M. C. Toynbee, *Death and Burial in the Roman World,* Aspects of Greek and Roman Life (Ithaca, N.Y.: Cornell University Press, 1971), 39-42.

10. Tert. *An.* 51.

11. Tert. *Apol.* 42.4.

12. Tert. *An.* 51.

13. Tert. *An.* 51.6-7. Tertullian recounted the miracle of the body of a young woman assuming the posture of prayer (arms raised) until the presbyter's graveside prayer was concluded. He attributed the action to divine power rather than a remnant of her soul.

14. Tert. *Res.* 27.5. He reported and approved the use of spices to promote the "storage" of the body.

15. Tert. *Scap.* 3.1 records an objection to separate burial grounds for Christians; *An.* 51 implies that Christians were buried in proximity to one another.

16. Tert. *Apol.* 39.6.

17. Tert. *Apol.* 13; *Spec.* 13.

18. This is the *refrigerium interim.*

she makes offerings on the anniversaries of his falling asleep. For, unless she does these things, it is as if she has truly divorced him.[19]

Tertullian admonished a widower against remarrying, since doing so would require him to offer the annual oblations for his first wife in the presence of his second.[20] The anniversary "offerings" that Tertullian commended might have been gifts brought to the church, but the practice could have been a Christian adaptation of the traditional anniversary meal at the grave, not unlike the *agape* banquet.[21] In another place, Tertullian mocked the offerings brought by traditional pagans to the tombs of their dead as being more for the enjoyment of the living than for the benefit of the departed. Yet, he noted that no one would dare to speak ill of the dead while reclining at a sumptuous funeral banquet at the tomb, since the honored dead were thought to be, in some manner, present at the party.[22]

## The Condition of the Dead

After death, all souls — except those of the martyrs — waited for the resurrection of the flesh and the Judgment in a vast space called Hades in the interior of the earth.[23] Tertullian relied on Revelation (6:9) and Perpetua's vision of the paradise into which she would be introduced after martyrdom for proof of the already popular belief that the souls of the martyrs were introduced immediately into glory.[24] During their residence in the underworld, the souls of the other dead were subject to punishment or consolation; they also might undergo discipline for their improvement. Tertullian reasoned that the soul was the primary instigator of bodily action and might even act independently of the body. Hence, it might begin to reap the fruits of its actions — reward or punishment — before it was reunited with the flesh.[25] Nevertheless, every soul, what-

---

19. Enimuero et pro anima eius orat, et refrigerium interim adpostulat ei, et in prima resurrectione consortium, et offert annuis diebus dormitionis eius. Non haec nisi fecerit, uere repudiauit, quantum in ipsa est; Tert. *Mon.* 10.4; CCSL 2:1243.23-27. The verb here *(offert)* does not make it clear, however, what or where she "offers."

20. Tert. *Cast.* 11.

21. See also Tert. *Cor.* 3, in which he mentions occasions for making offerings for the dead *(oblationes pro defunctis pro nataliciis annua die facimus)*. In *Cast.* 7.3, he used this term for the eucharist offered by the laity in the absence of the clergy. For the traditional meals at the grave, see Toynbee, *Death and Burial in the Roman World*, 61-64.

22. Tert. *Test.* 4. Here he comments on the inconsistency of believing that the dead were beyond feeling, but at the same time making them offerings and worrying about their opinion. See also *Res.* 1.

23. Tert. *An.* 55. It was to this place that Christ's soul went between death and resurrection.

24. Tert. *An.* 55; *Pas. Perp.* 4.

25. Tert. *An.* 58.

---

ever its age at death, remained in that state awaiting reunion with the body and final Judgment. Tertullian speculated that Hades might have two regions: one place of refreshment for virgins, infants, and other pure and innocent souls; and another place where the souls of the wicked resided in exile.[26] In any case, during this time of waiting and preparation, the soul also might have been assisted by the offerings that were made for the departed on the anniversary of death.[27] With God's permission, souls in Hades could be returned to earthly life; this was evidenced in the resuscitations that were performed by the Prophets, Christ, and the Apostles.[28]

Tertullian's treatise *On the Resurrection of the Flesh* clearly defines his position on the bodily resurrection.[29] The work itself defends the essential goodness of the flesh. Inasmuch as the body was created by God (in fact, before the soul was) and was taken on by Christ in the Incarnation, it was worthy of redemption and would rise in the wholeness it had enjoyed in life.[30] The corruptible would become incorrupt, and the mortal be transformed into the immortal, thereby achieving its full potential and becoming whole while yet remaining flesh. It would retain its particular characteristics (e.g., teeth, reproductive organs, intestines), its individuality (age, disposition, tastes), and even its recognizable appearance.[31] The body, in Tertullian's view, was fundamentally associated with the identity of the person.[32]

Like many of the poets and philosophers, Tertullian acknowledged, Christians proclaimed that God would finally judge all souls. Because they believed in the fleshly resurrection, they assumed that reward or punishment would be both bodily and specific. Those found wanting would be consigned to Gehenna, a subterranean repository of secret, everlasting fire. Those found worthy would be welcomed into Paradise, a place of divine delights, the abode of the spirits of the saints, which was separated from knowledge of the earthly realm by a zone of fire.[33]

26. Tert. *An.* 56.

27. This was a particular responsibility of the surviving spouse and one of the reasons Tertullian offered against a second marriage (*Cast.* 11; *Mon.* 10.4). See also *Pas. Perp.* 7-8.

28. Tert. *An.* 57.

29. One may want to compare Tertullian's position on bodily resurrection with that of Minucius Felix, another North African. See *Oct.* 11, 34.

30. Tert. *Res.* 5-6.

31. Tert. *Res.* 57; *An.* 31.

32. Tert. *Res.* 55-56.

33. Tert. *Apol.* 47; *An.* 13; *Res.* 34, 35. Compare Minuc. *Oct.* 35.

## Conclusion

Tertullian's references to the preparation for death and the care of the dead show an interaction between Christian practice and theology. Belief in the resurrection of the flesh strengthened the cultural preference of inhumation over cremation of the corpse. The rejection of practices connected with idolatry was also influential in excluding certain traditional rituals of burial, though not anniversary meals at the tombs. An imaginative construction of the condition of the dead during their wait for Resurrection was developing. Though it was clearly incomplete, it did include a distinction between the martyrs and the other faithful, the reward and disciplining of the soul, and provision for assistance of the dead by the living through prayer and pious works.

## THE RITUALS OF DEATH IN CYPRIAN'S TIME

The only Christian funeral in North Africa described in any detail was a very unusual one: that of the martyr-bishop Cyprian. On the day of his trial and execution, Carthage was filled with animosity toward the Christians. His body was taken by the congregation from the place of execution and sequestered during the remainder of the day. Late in the evening, a torchlight procession of Christians escorted the body to a common cemetery, where it was buried.[34] This triumphal parade certainly reflected some Roman customs, particularly the burial at night. The delay until evening, however, might also be explained by the danger of riot and assault upon his remains during the hours following Cyprian's final defiance of imperial authority and his immediate execution. Thus, the circumstances were so exceptional that the account cannot be used as a basis for determining ordinary Christian practice.

### Mortality

Cyprian understood death as a consequence of the first sin, which affected all of humanity. Christians were not protected from sickness and other sufferings associated with the death they shared with their traditionalist neighbors.[35] Their freedom from fear in the face of death, however, was a sign of faith and trust in the promises of God.[36] Christians, then, were exhorted to accept death as

---

34. *Act. Procon.* 5; CSEL 3.3:cxiii. Christians might have been denied access to their own cemeteries during the persecution (Eus. Caes. *Hist. eccl.* 6.13.3). Cyprian's *Ep.* 80.1.4 specifies that Sixtus was executed in the cemetery in Rome.

35. Cypr. *Mort.* 8.

36. Cypr. *Mort.* 3, 6.

a means of following after Christ and gaining access to him.[37] Thus, Cyprian explained that the martyr's firm faith in the face of death could be realized in the dying of every Christian. God prized not the blood of the martyrs but their faith.[38] By this reasoning, Cyprian could hold up to every Christian the possibility of attaining the immediate access to glory that the church had recognized as the crown of martyrdom.[39]

## Preparation for Death

By Cyprian's time, the practice of granting admission to communion in anticipation of death was well established. During the Decian persecution, for example, Cyprian instructed his clergy to keep a careful watch over the catechumens so that none of them would die without the baptism and eucharist for which they were preparing.[40] The episcopal decision that children could be baptized immediately after birth rather than waiting for the eighth day, on which circumcision (a foreshadowing of Christian baptism) had been performed, may have been approval of an emergency ritual in the face of death.[41] In response to a question, Cyprian also specified that baptism performed by the pouring or sprinkling of water on adults who were seriously ill brought the full salvific effect of the sacrament.[42]

The question of providing reconciliation and eucharistic communion to penitents was debated more seriously. During Tertullian's time, the forgiveness of some crimes was left to the discretion of God; penitents repenting these sins were not granted eucharistic communion before death. Cyprian indicated that this practice had changed in regard to adultery during the intervening period.[43] How to deal with failure during persecution, understood as apostasy or idolatry, was disputed during his episcopate. During the Decian persecution, Cyprian initially restricted deathbed reconciliation to the penitents who had been recommended by the martyrs.[44] Under pressure from the clergy of Rome and his own people, however, he changed his position and ordered that all the penitent apostates should be reconciled in anticipation of death.[45] After the persecution, the Af-

37. Cypr. *Mort.* 14.
38. Cypr. *Mort.* 17.
39. Cypr. *Mort.* 20, 26.
40. Cypr. *Ep.* 18.2.2.
41. Cypr. *Ep.* 64.2.1: the issue was settled on this basis: sed uniuersi potius iudicauimus nulli hominum nato misericordiam dei et gratiam denegandam (CCSL 3C:419.24-25).
42. Cypr. *Ep.* 69.12.1–16.2.
43. Cypr. *Ep.* 55.20.2.
44. Cypr. *Ep.* 18.1.1–2.1; 19.2.1.
45. The Roman recommendation is in Cypr. *Ep.* 8.3.1, and Cyprian's agreement is in his response to the Romans in *Ep.* 20.3.2. The letter conveying this decision to the clergy of Carthage has not survived.

rican bishops determined to continue this practice of offering reconciliation to all penitents at the time of death.[46] Only those who had already undertaken the penitential process of the church would be accorded this privilege: any who had waited until the hour of death to repent and seek the assistance of the church would be rejected as insincere.[47] The earlier practice of commending a dying penitent to the divine mercy without granting the communion of the church seems to have been continued by the partisans of the schismatic Bishop of Rome, Novatian; but it won only a small following in Africa.[48]

## Burial

By the middle of the third century, the church seems to have assumed a more prominent role in providing burial for the dead. Cyprian praised Tertullus, who had the responsibility of caring for the bodies of the martyrs, indicating that his work was more difficult in time of persecution.[49] He can be presumed to have acted as the agent of the church in securing burial for Christians even during peacetime. During the plague of the summer of 252, Cyprian exhorted the community to follow the example of Tobias in caring for the dead and to extend their services even to those who were not Christian.[50] Later, he strongly criticized a Spanish bishop who was a member of a non-Christian burial society and had his own sons buried among pagans through its rituals.[51] This accusation — along with the archaeological excavations of later Christian cemeteries and funerary churches — offers evidence that, at least in Carthage, Christian graves were grouped together.[52]

## Mourning and Commemorating the Dead

Christians engaged in private mourning practices, such as weeping, wearing black clothing, and neglecting personal grooming. Although Cyprian exhorted his congregation not to mourn the death of Christians, he did not seem to consider the sorrow of the bereaved a failure in faith.[53]

---

46. The decision is explained and defended in Cypr. *Ep.* 55.17.3.
47. Cypr. *Ep.* 55.23.4.
48. Cypr. *Ep.* 55.3.1, 24.1–26.1.
49. Cypr. *Ep.* 12.2.1.
50. Cypr. *Mort.* 10; Pont. *Vita Cypr.* 9-10.
51. Cypr. *Ep.* 67.6.2.
52. See discussion of the archeological evidence above, pp. 122-24. No Christian evidence earlier than the fourth century has survived.
53. Cypr. *Laps.* 30; Cyprian criticized the fallen for not expressing their sorrow for sin in the way they would have manifest grief at the death of a friend (*Mort.* 20, 22).

---

The church's intercession for and commemoration of the dead is attested amply. Writing while exiled during the Decian persecution, Cyprian instructed his clergy to keep a careful record of the death dates of all who died as a result of imperial action, so that they could be commemorated as martyrs. He noted that he was celebrating these deaths immediately with "offerings and sacrifices" and looked forward to future celebrations with the community.[54] He referred again to the customary celebrations of the anniversaries of the passions of the martyrs and the sacrifices that were offered. His speaking of the sacrifices being offered "for" the martyrs suggests that these commemorations were performed regularly for all the faithful when they died.[55] The practice of offering the eucharist for the recently deceased is indicated also by a directive to withhold these prayers as punishment for certain violations that would be discovered only after the death of the offender — as a kind of posthumous excommunication.[56]

## The Condition of the Dead

Like Tertullian, Cyprian and his congregation believed that the souls of the dead were in a state of waiting between the time of death and resurrection, upon which Christ would judge all whose souls had been waiting in Hades.[57] He used this delay to explain the reconciliation of the lapsed before death. No one could delay repentance of sin until after death and still gain salvation.[58] The penitents readmitted to the communion of the church in anticipation of death could, however, continue their process of repentance and cleansing until the Resurrection. Cyprian characterized the condition in death of these reconciled sinners as an imprisonment until the last penny of debt was paid. Unlike the martyrs who were crowned and rewarded, these penitents would have to approach the Judgment of Christ in fear and trembling.[59] His exhortations to the faithful during persecution and plague, however, foreshortened the time between death and resurrection: like the martyrs, the faithful could move di-

54. Cypr. *Ep.* 12.1.2–2.1. He regarded anyone who died in prison as a martyr, even if torture had not been applied.

55. Cypr. *Ep.* 39.3.1. This specification may have been intended to assimilate them into the rest of the faithful. This particular letter was written during a period of conflict between Cyprian and the confessors over the power of the martyrs to win the forgiveness of sins for apostates.

56. Cyprian enforced this sanction for a bishop who had appointed one of his clergy executor of his estate and guardian of his family (*Ep.* 1.2.1-2).

57. Thus Cyprian described it in *Ep.* 55.29.2; 58.10.1-2. In the polemic of *De lapsis,* he also placed the intercessory role of the martyrs at the Judgment to accompany the return of Christ in the indefinite future (*Laps.* 17).

58. Cypr. *Ep.* 55.29.2.

59. Cypr. *Ep.* 55.20.3.

rectly through death to an eternal joy.[60] This way of speaking also advanced his program, begun immediately after the Decian persecution, of assimilating the faithful into the martyrs: both could enjoy an immediate entrance into glory.[61] Just on the other side of death, even by sickness, they would not only be reunited with friends and family but be admitted to the company of the patriarchs, prophets, apostles, and martyrs.[62] In his exhortation in anticipation of the Valerian persecution, for example, Cyprian placed the coming of Christ for judgment and reward immediately after the manifestation of the anti-Christ in the persecution.[63] Thus, the Resurrection, with its full and glorious reward, could be anticipated shortly after death.[64]

### Conclusion

The Christian practices surrounding death and burial were substantially the same in the mid-third century as they had been at the end of the second. Cyprian's writings provide greater detail in a number of areas, particularly the sacramental preparation for death and the remembrance of the departed in the community's celebration of the eucharist and other prayers. The questions of the authority of the church to forgive and reconcile apostates also focused attention on the condition of the soul between death and resurrection, and on the intercessory power of the bishops, the martyrs, and the faithful to prepare and support the penitents for their appearance before the judgment seat of Christ.

### THE RITUALS OF DYING IN AUGUSTINE'S TIME

In dealing with other topics, we have seen that Augustine's extensive writings and especially his sermons provide a fuller record of Christian practices; such is also the case with the topic of dying. The Pelagian controversy, moreover, included a debate over the original condition of humanity: had humans been

---

60. Cypr. *Mort.* 2, 3, 7. This is most evident in *Mort.* 17, 26, where he avoids in his exposition any notice of the "sleeping," which is dominant in the quoted text of 1 Thess. 4:13-14; he uses "remaining" in its place. As has been seen above, the deaths of the faithful were being assimilated into those of the martyrs.

61. Cypr. *Laps.* 1-3; *Mort.* 14-15. It also served, of course, to undercut the special authority claimed for the martyrs.

62. Cypr. *Mort.* 26. Some had complained that they would have been ready to redeem their situation by public confession of Christ and regretted dying of illness instead. Cyprian reassured them that God would reward them for their intentions; he had already showed that they might actually suffer more from the plague than the imperial torturers (*Mort.* 17, 14).

63. Cypr. *Ep.* 58.7.1.

64. Cypr. *Ep.* 58.10.1-2.

created mortal or immortal? Augustine also dealt more extensively than his predecessors with the terminal state of the good and the evil.

## Mortality

Through his successive commentaries on the initial chapters of Genesis, Augustine developed a theology of death. Humanity originally was created mortal, but it was protected against corruption and death by a gift that was symbolized by the tree of life (Gen. 2:9). By faithful observance of the divine law, humans would have earned the reward of full immortality, in which they would be incapable of dying. Through the sins of pride and disobedience, however, Adam and Eve lost this protection and incurred the necessity of dying, not only for themselves but for all their offspring. Though humans shared with animals a nature capable of dying, their actual mortality was a consequence of sin.[65] Thus, humans still longed for the original gift: to avoid death and be transformed into eternal life.[66] Death, therefore, ought not be sought as a release from earthly existence but borne in patience and in hope of Resurrection.[67]

Bodily mortality was not only a punishment for the sin of pride but a means of provoking repentance. Humans could be humbled by their weakness and the uncertainty of their lives.[68] The fear of death haunted life, especially in its most prosperous times.[69] The proud, however, were insulted by their mortality; the devil still encouraged them to disbelieve that they would actually die.[70] They were only too ready to expend their entire fortunes in the attempt to live a little longer.[71] In his preaching, Augustine exhorted his hearers to focus their attention on the spiritual death and punishment that they could avoid rather than on vain attempts to evade the inevitable death of the body.[72]

To die a death that would be followed by happiness, one had to live a good life.[73] The connection was perhaps most fully illustrated in Augustine's preaching on almsgiving. He encouraged the faithful to invest their earthly treasure in heaven, so that they might gain eternal life. He used a variety of images and analogies to relate the two realms. One could loan to Christ on earth and

---

65. Aug. *Serm.* 165.6.7–7.9; *Psal.* 34.2.3; 50.1; 51.2. For a fuller explanation, see *Gen. litt.* 9.3.5-6, 5.9–6.10, 9.14-15; *Con. Carth.* a. 418, 1.

66. Aug. *Serm.* 344.4; *Serm. Lamb.* 4(359A).8.

67. Aug. *Serm.* 299.8-11. The martyrs did not seek death. Even Enoch and Elijah would die when they returned to witness.

68. Aug. *Serm. Dolb.* 25(360B).5-6.

69. Aug. *Serm.* 38.7.

70. Aug. *Serm. Guelf.* 31(335B).1-2.

71. Aug. *Eu. Io.* 49.2.

72. Aug. *Eu. Io.* 49.2; *Serm.* 127.5.7; 161.4.4–5.5; 279.9.

73. Aug. *Serm.* 102.1.2–3.4.

collect, at a high interest rate, in heaven.[74] Because Christ identified with the Christian poor, what was given to them was received by him; they could be used as porters to carry wealth from earth to heaven.[75] Rather than leaving all their estate to their children, Augustine urged, the wealthy should count Christ among their heirs and, thus, take goods with them into the next world.[76]

## Preparation for Death

The immediate preparation for Christian death involved both repentance for sins and sharing in the eucharist. The African church affirmed the teaching Augustine enunciated so insistently during the Pelagian controversy: that baptism was necessary for salvation.[77] The first reforming council organized by Aurelius of Carthage affirmed that dying catechumens were to be baptized on the strength of their prior expression of commitment to Christ, even if illness or injury prevented them from professing faith for themselves.[78] A later council insisted that dying infants could be saved only through baptism.[79] Christians trusted, moreover, in the efficacy of the ritual of baptism to bring them to salvation.[80] Augustine, for example, was confident that his father, Patricius, had been saved through his conversion and baptism at the end of his life.[81] Occasionally, however, an adult catechumen died suddenly without baptism and was deeply mourned as among the damned.[82] One result of this teaching seems to have been the practice of allowing presbyters to perform the full ritual of baptism in emergencies. Augustine told the story of a miracle that took place at Uzalis, where his friend Evodius was bishop. A woman's infant son suddenly took ill; even though she hurried to the church, he died in her arms as an unbaptized catechumen. Believing he would be condemned without hope of salvation, the mother then ran to the local shrine of St. Stephen and prayed that her son be restored to life, at least long enough to be validly baptized. The saint heard her prayer, and the son was baptized, sanctified, anointed, and had hands laid upon him — all by the presbyters of the church. Once all the rituals of baptism were

74. Aug. *Serm.* 9.21; 38.9; 39.6; 86.3.3; 345.2-3; 367.3; *Serm. Morin* 11(53A).6; *Serm. Mai* 14(350A).4.

75. Aug. *Serm.* 18.4; 25.8; 36.9; 60.6; 311.18.15; 389.3; *Serm. Morin* 11(53A).6; *Serm. Lamb.* 1(105A).2; *Serm. Frang.* 9(114A).4.

76. Aug. *Serm.* 86.3.3; *Psal.* 48.1.14.

77. Aug. *Ciu.* 20.9.

78. *Bru. Hipp.* 32; see also Aug. *Adult.* 1.26.33.

79. *Con. Carth.* a. 418, 2-3.

80. Aug. *Serm.* 393.2-5 contrasts the certitude of the catechumen who is baptized as death approaches with the insecurity of the penitent who has delayed reconciliation.

81. Aug. *Conf.* 9.9.22, 13.37; *Serm.* 243.5.5.

82. Aug. *Serm. Dolb.* 7(142*).2-3. Augustine found this sermon extremely difficult to deliver.

completed, he died again. His mother was able to bury him with the firm belief that she was laying her son not in Hades, but in the lap of the saint.[83]

The practice, which had been instituted in the third century, of reconciling penitents just prior to death continued to be observed in Augustine's time.[84] He warned, however, that those who continued to sin during their time of penance in anticipation of reconciliation — and a presumed forgiveness — at the time of death could not be assured of salvation.[85] A greater efficacy was attributed to the ritual of baptism at the time of death than to that of penance. Augustine also reminded sinners that though they could trust in God's mercy to forgive when they truly repented, they had not been promised a long life and adequate warning of the approach of death.[86]

The evidence for administration of the eucharist at the time of death is indirect. The Council of Hippo in 393 formally authorized the baptism of unconscious catechumens, but it forbade giving the communion bread to the dead, because they could not "take and eat."[87] This suggests that the communion bread was given to the dying who were able to receive it. The restriction of the eucharist to the living also justified denying baptism to those already dead.[88]

## The Funeral Ritual

Augustine gave a quick summary of the actions leading from death to burial in commenting on Jesus' saying "let the dead bury the dead" (Matt. 8:22). When someone died, the spiritually dead ran to the scene, prepared the grave, wrapped the body, carried it out, and buried it.[89] The Christian ritual was only slightly more complex.

In those cases for which some evidence survives, burial was completed on the day of death.[90] A ruling of the Council of Hippo in 393 specified that the eucharist could be celebrated as part of the burial only if the bishop and peo-

---

83. Aug. *Serm.* 323; 324. The imposition of hands by a presbyter is unusual and may indicate the importance of belonging to the communion of the true church, rather than being a Donatist, where one received baptism but could not retain the Holy Spirit. See above, pp. 210-13.

84. Aug. *Ciu.* 20.9.

85. Aug. *Serm.* 393. Those who repented, were reconciled, and then lived with only minor sins could die in secure hope.

86. Aug. *Serm.* 20.3-4; 40.1-5; 339.7. In particular, they were not to combine an astrologer's promise of a long life with God's promise of forgiveness for repented sin: *Serm. Dolb.* 14(352A).7.

87. Canon 4; CCSL 149:21.37-39. The revision of this canon in the *Bru. Hipp.* 4a specifies that the cadaver can neither take nor eat.

88. *Bru. Hipp.* 4.

89. Aug. *Serm.* 127.5.7.

90. Thus in Aug. *Serm. Lamb.* 21(335K).1, the day of death and the day of burial are the same. Such was Augustine's death and burial (Possid. *Vita Aug.* 31.42). The description of Monica's death and burial in Ostia (Aug. *Conf.* 9.12.32) indicates a different practice.

---

ple had not yet eaten their first meal, which was at midday. If they had eaten, prayers were to be offered, but the divine mysteries were not to be celebrated. No exception was made for the burial of clergy.[91] If the funeral could be delayed until the following day, the eucharist could be celebrated. Moreover, the eucharist was not to be celebrated in the presence of the corpse, nor were the eucharistic elements to be shared with a lifeless cadaver.[92] The African bishops might have been changing their own practice with the first part of this legislation, for Monica's funeral in Ostia (outside Rome) had included the celebration of the eucharist at the burial site in the presence of her body.[93] When Possidius described Augustine's funeral, nearly forty years later, he also reported the offering of the eucharist prior to the burial, though he did not specify the presence of the corpse.[94]

In some instances at least, the funeral ritual included preaching. Augustine's sermon for the burial of Bishop Florentius, at whose death he had been present, has been preserved. Though he touched on the goodness of his friend's life and the blessed condition to which he had passed, Augustine exhorted the congregation of Hippo Diarrhytus to face, in faith and hope, the bitterness of death and their own loss of their bishop.[95]

After the church service, the mourners followed the body to the grave.[96] Unbaptized persons were not buried in the same place as the faithful, especially not within a church where the sacraments were celebrated. This would indicate both separate Christian cemeteries — or sections within common cemeteries — and the practice of burying at least some of the faithful within a church building.[97] The unbaptized catechumen who had not been present for the eucharistic liturgy in life could not be allowed to be present in death.

Augustine recognized that burial rituals varied within the Christian world. He noted that the Gospel of John's specifying that Jesus was buried according to the Jewish custom was intended to legitimate the following of local practices.[98]

91. *Con. Hipp.* a. 393, 4. Slightly different versions are found in *Bru. Hipp.* 28 and *Reg. Carth.* 41.

92. *Con. Hipp.* a. 393, 4.

93. Aug. *Conf.* 9.12.32.

94. Possid. *Vita Aug.* 31.42.

95. Aug. *Serm.* 396.

96. Aug. *Serm.* 302.7.

97. The case is a catechumen who died without baptism, whose family appears to have been seeking burial within the church itself: Aug. *Serm. Dolb.* 7(142*).1; *Serm.* 302.6-10. Burial within both urban and cemetery churches is well attested by archeological remains; see pp. 124-26, 144-45, 149-52.

98. Aug. *Eu. Io.* 120.4.

Augustine was not able to look beyond death to the joys of the afterlife quite so easily as Cyprian had been in his exhortations to fidelity in anticipation of renewed persecution. In the sermon Augustine preached at the funeral of his friend Florentius, just noted, he made little attempt to conceal his own and the congregation's sadness. Even among the tribulations of earthly life, he reflected, we hate to lose good companions; to wish to hold them here, however, would be to envy their happiness and security.[99] As had his narrative of his mother's death in the *Confessions*,[100] so his sermons as bishop articulated the grief that he shared with the congregation.[101] How sad when the body loses all its wonderful movements, when the ruined dwelling lies abandoned by its invisible inhabitant.[102] Even Christ wept, he recalled, not for Lazarus, whom he was soon to revive, but at death itself, which had issued from sin. Far better to mourn with hope so that the heart might be healed rather than to make it inhumanly hard by refusing to face its loss.[103]

Specific practices of mourning in the days immediately following death are not well documented. The death of a promising cleric at Uzalis was mourned at the grave with hymns for three days, and the eucharist was offered on the third day.[104] In another context, Augustine recommended that Christians celebrate the seventh day after death rather than the ninth, which terminated the mourning period in traditional Roman practice.[105] He could find scriptural precedent for the seventh day in the Egyptian mourning of Joseph, but he found none for the ninth day. More importantly, the interval symbolized the Sabbath rest, which the deceased was enjoying.[106]

Augustine recalled the sorrow of death and loss in sermons that may have been preached during the annual Roman observance of deceased ancestors, the *parentalia*.[107] Christians in Africa seem to have observed the custom of banqueting at family tombs on these days, despite their bishops' objections.[108] In

99. Aug. *Serm.* 396.1.

100. Aug. *Conf.* 9.12.31.

101. Aug. *Serm.* 172.2.2-3; 173.2; 361.5.5.

102. Aug. *Serm.* 173.2; 361.5.5, 6.6, 12.12.

103. Aug. *Serm.* 173.1.

104. Aug. *Ep.* 158.2.

105. Toynbee, *Death and Burial in the Roman World*, 51.

106. Aug. *Hept.* 1.172.

107. Aug. *Serm.* 173.1 begins with a reference to the celebration of the days of the departed brethren. *Serm.* 172 uses the same scripture text (1 Thess. 4:13) in the same ways. *Serm.* 361 might also have been preached at this time, since it was preached during a winter festival and on the topic of the Resurrection and the avoidance of feasts at the grave (*Serm.* 361.4.4–7.7). On the *parentalia*, see Toynbee, *Death and Burial in the Roman World*, 63-64.

108. Ambrose had forbidden the Christian observance of this festival by banqueting at the tombs. See Neil B. McLynn, *Ambrose of Milan: Church and Court in a Christian Capital,* The Trans-

a letter written during his service as presbyter, Augustine urged Aurelius, the new Bishop of Carthage, to take the lead in curbing this practice of feasting at the tombs of the martyrs and the faithful.[109] He suggested that scripture be used to demonstrate that food offerings did the dead no good at all, as even the pagans knew.[110] Better indeed that the eucharist should be celebrated piously in the church[111] and that alms should be given to the poor for the benefit of the deceased.[112] Even so, family memorial meals apparently continued, as they were deeply entrenched customs. A significant number of tomb inscriptions noted the date of death (or burial), which suggests that the anniversaries were being celebrated (cf. fig. 129). In *On the City of God,* Augustine praised those "better" families who had abandoned the practice.[113]

Physical evidence of Christians celebrating funeral banquets in the cemeteries is attested extensively from the fifth century onward. This evidence includes fixed masonry tables and couches (fig. 112) as well as facilities for drawing water and washing up in various cemeteries. Some of the tables were elaborately decorated with polychrome mosaic and inscriptions (figs. 113, 114). Other recorded inscriptions also attest to the practice: for example, the epitaph of Aelia Secundula, probably written by her children, which describes the stone table set with food and cups set out at her tomb after her funeral.[114]

## Tombs

The care of the body of the deceased and the preparation of the tomb were clearly affirmed by Augustine as works of Christian piety. He cited Paul's comparison (Eph. 5:29) to a husband's caring for his wife as he would for his own body to approve the honor given to the bodies of loved ones.[115] The benefit of this service, however, was to the living, as acts of faith and love, respecting the bodies through which good works had been done.[116] In view of the Res-

---

formation of the Classical Heritage 22 (Berkeley and Los Angeles: University of California Press, 1994), 236-37. Monica was rebuffed by the gatekeeper as she went to follow the African practice of eating at the tombs of the martyrs (Aug. *Conf.* 6.2.2). For Augustine's objection, see *Serm.* 361.4.4–7.7.

109. Aug. *Ep.* 22.1.6.
110. Aug. *Ep.* 22.1.6; *Serm.* 361.6.6.
111. The reference to an offering in Aug. *Ep.* 22.1.6. In *Serm.* 361.6.6, preached years later, the substitution of the eucharist for the banquet is explicit.
112. Aug. *Ep.* 22.1.6; *Cur.* 18.22; *Serm.* 172.2.3.
113. Aug. *Ciu.* 7.26; much of the following discussion was covered more briefly in Johannes Quasten, "'Vetus Superstitio et Nova Religio': The Problem of Refrigerium in the Ancient Church of North Africa," *Harvard Theological Review* 33, no. 4 (1 October 1940): 253-66.
114. *ILCV* 1.1570. The inscription is cited and translated above, pp. 126-27.
115. Aug. *Cur.* 7.9.
116. Aug. *Cur.* 3.5, 7.9, 9.11; *Serm.* 172.2.3.

---

urrection, God might even count this care of the body as a form of alms given by the faithful.[117] The dead themselves could be neither harmed nor helped by what was done to their bodies.[118] Even the traditionally dreaded denial of burial could do no harm, and those who had been devoured by beasts or left on the field of battle were not in any way hindered from bodily resurrection.[119] Thus, Augustine expatiated on the folly of the wealthy who prepared magnificent funerals and ostentatious tombs in which their bodies would rest undisturbed while their souls burned in hell.[120] Again, he recommended prayer and almsgiving as being of great help to the dead.[121]

African Christians tended to bury their dead in Christian cemeteries but not necessarily in family mausolea. The privileged or special dead (e.g., saints or prominent clergy) might be buried inside the church. The practice does not seem limited to Caecilianists or Nicenes, since some evidence shows that Donatists and Arian Vandals also buried their special dead within church buildings.[122] Characteristically, in Africa, the dead would be placed in lead or unmortared stone-slab coffins. Although the majority were probably simple and unmarked, many of these sarcophagi were covered with polychrome mosaic that included the name of the deceased, the age at death, and some abbreviated information about his or her character. These included terms of affection (e.g., "sweet") or piety (e.g., "innocent," "faithful," "servant of God," "devoted to God"), the state after death ("in peace") or a clerical title (e.g., "bishop," "deacon"). The formula "lived in peace" (cf. fig. 126) might indicate membership in a particular eucharistic communion. In some instances, the sarcophagus itself was covered on all sides (cf. figs. 137, 146); in most cases, the mosaic was placed on the top of the tomb at floor or ground level. Most are about two meters in length by one meter in width. Portrait images might also depict the deceased's secular profession (cf. fig. 136).

These polychrome mosaic tomb covers are particularly representative of African funerary practice. Although they have counterparts elsewhere in the Late Antique Mediterranean world, it is possible that the practice began in Africa and was exported elsewhere, rather than vice versa.[123] The earliest exam-

---

117. Aug. *Cur.* 3.5.
118. Aug. *Cur.* 2.4, 7.9.
119. Aug. *Ciu.* 1.12.
120. Aug. *Serm. Dolb.* 7(142*).3; *Psal.* 33.2.14; 48.1.13, 15; 48.2.1-8; *Ciu.* 1.12.
121. Aug. *Serm.* 172.2.3.
122. Evidence of Donatist and Vandal (Arian) inscriptions and mosaic tomb covers has been identified in various places, including Hippo (e.g., Guilia Runa, fig. 125) and Thamugadi. Optatus recounts Donatist bishops trying to distance themselves from Circumcellions during a military action against them. When a certain presbyter (Clarus) attempted to bury some of those who died during the revolt inside the church, the bishop made him remove the bodies and rebury them elsewhere (Optat. *Parm.* 3.4).
123. See James Breckenridge, "Christian Funerary Portraits in Mosaic," *Gesta* 13, no. 2 (1974): 29-43, for a discussion of the parallels and possible influence.

ples date to the late fourth century, and they continued to be produced until the middle of the Byzantine era, although there seems to have been a falling off of the practice during the Vandal era and a renaissance in the early Byzantine period. Certain regions were more likely to produce these monuments than others, and styles vary widely from place to place. Examples from any one region probably were the products of one or two workshops with limited catalogs of motifs. Scholars have tended to establish their dates by attending to details of iconography, inscriptions, and lettering styles.[124]

Death days are often included, perhaps to establish the anniversary commemoration *(natalicium)*. Family relations (e.g., "mother," "spouse," "son"; cf. figs. 122, 148) were rarely mentioned — an indication that familial connections were less important to Christians than to their non-Christian neighbors.[125] Similarly, Christians avoided noting the social status of their dead. Indications that an individual was a freedman or freedwoman are almost nonexistent in these epitaphs.[126]

In addition to epitaphs, these tomb covers included iconography. Most of the designs included Christograms, flowers, birds, canthari, and even animals. Roses are an extremely popular motif and probably refer to the feast of the Rosalia, when family members brought roses to the cemeteries. Portraits of the deceased were popular in certain regions (e.g., the examples from Thabraca). The portrait-styled tomb covers usually show the deceased standing in prayer (hands outstretched) between two candles. Women often wear veils (cf. figs. 131, 139, 142), which could indicate that they were no longer girls; and men sometimes wear fringed stoles *(oraria;* fig. 137) or cloaks *(paenulae;* figs. 134, 140), which might reflect particular clerical status.[127] A few show biblical scenes (e.g., figs. 120, 138).

Possible antecedents for both the practice and the style of the portrait-type tomb covers are the Punic effigy *stelae* (fig. 153). They also share some common aspects with the sarcophagus portraits made in Egypt (the Fayuum paintings). In both instances, the living opted to portray the figure of the deceased, even if somewhat schematically or merely by inscribing name and age. Such an act linked the dead with their buried remains and perhaps reminded the living to pray for them while they awaited the general resurrection.

---

124. On the dating of these mosaics, see the helpful summary of James H. Terry, "Christian Tomb Mosaics of Late Roman, Vandalic, and Byzantine Byzacena" (Ph.D. diss., University of Missouri–Columbia, 1998), 56-70, 116-73. See Margaret Alexander, "Mosaic Ateliers at Tabarka," *Dumbarton Oaks Papers* 41 (1987): 1-11, for an example of a careful iconographic study of two different workshops operating at about the same time.

125. See the discussion above, pp. 463, 484-85.

126. In traditional Roman inscriptions, the name of the benefactor granting the manumission is often mentioned as well.

127. On the meaning of this garb, see the discussion above, p. 130, n. 188; p. 433.

Augustine continued and developed the explanation of the condition of the dead between death and resurrection that was already in use during the third century. Christ himself provided the primary instance of the transition from earthly to heavenly existence.[128] Between his death and resurrection, he was still identified with his body, though it was dead in the tomb.[129] In his human reality, he went into the underworld to visit and release those who were there at rest.[130] Yet, as divine Word, he was already in Paradise, with the thief whom he had saved on the cross.[131] After his resurrection, he ascended — body and soul — into heaven.[132]

Like the thief who confessed the dying Christ, the souls of the martyrs enjoyed the privilege of entering into the presence of Christ immediately after death.[133] They had not yet received their full reward; that would be given only in the redemption of their bodies in the Resurrection.[134]

The souls of the faithful entered a condition in which they would await the Resurrection. They were safer than they had been during earthly life because they anticipated the Judgment in confidence of salvation: they could suffer no loss during the wait.[135] However, their life was not necessarily more enjoyable than the earthly life they had lost through death.[136] The souls of those who were not to be saved were also in a state of expectation, though they were already being punished for their sins. The distinction between the two conditions was symbolized (or even described) by the parable of the rich man and the beggar: the saved were in the bosom of Abraham; the damned were in fire.[137] Augustine used these bodily images in his preaching; in his writings, however, he attempted to develop an explanation more adequate to both the incorporeality of the soul and the language of scripture.[138] After the resurrection of the body and the Judgment, the saints would enter into glory as equals of the angels.[139]

---

128. Aug. *Serm. Morin* 11(53A).13.

129. Aug. *Eu. Io.* 47.12-13; *Serm. Denis* 5(375B).8.

130. Aug. *Serm.* 67.4.7; 265.1.2; 285.2; *Serm. Mai* 127(70A).2; *Serm. Liver.* 8(265A).1; *Serm. Casin.* 2.76-77(265B).1.

131. Aug. *Serm.* 36.7; *Serm. Morin* 11(53A).13; *Serm. Lamb.* 2(335C).12; *Serm. Denis* 5(375B).8. As divine and human, Christ was simultaneously in heaven and on earth, in Paradise and in the underworld (*Serm.* 67.4.7).

132. Aug. *Serm.* 265.1.2; *Serm. Casin.* 2.76-77(265B).1.

133. Aug. *Serm.* 328.8.6 (*Serm. Lamb.* 13); *Serm. Lamb.* 2(335C).12; *Psal.* 48.1.13.

134. Aug. *Serm.* 312.1; 313.5.

135. Aug. *Serm.* 328.6.5 (*Serm. Lamb.* 13); *Psal.* 36.1.10.

136. Aug. *Psal.* 48.1.13.

137. Aug. *Psal.* 85.17-18.

138. The fullest discussion is in Aug. *Gen. litt.* 12.32.60–34.67.

139. Aug. *Psal.* 36.1.10; *Eu. Io.* 49.10.

The damned would be sent, body and soul, into eternal fire, where their souls would be tormented by the loss of God.[140]

For Augustine — at least in his later writings — humans and angels were different kinds of beings; the perfect condition of humans, then, must be a bodily rather than only a spiritual existence. Bodily resurrection did not mean a return to the original human condition, in which mortality had been suspended so long as Adam and Eve remained faithfully obedient to the divine commandments and were protected by the reality signified by the tree of life. The final state of blessed human beings would be one in which they could not die in either their bodies or their souls. Moreover, in that condition of beatitude, they would know with assurance that they could not fail.[141]

When Augustine dealt with the bodily resurrection of humans, he tackled questions like those Paul had (1 Cor. 15:35): How are the dead raised, and with what kind of body? His answer was similar, if more specific.[142] He insisted that the gender differentiation of human beings was an original good of nature, not a defect, neither an anticipation nor a consequence of sin. The blessed would be raised male and female, though they would be free of engagement in sexual intercourse and childbirth. Without any movement of lust, they would enjoy and appreciate the great loveliness of the human body, whose members were formed for beauty as well as utility. Some organs, such as male beards and nipples, were given by God only as decorations.[143] Deformities, which were defects of nature, would be eliminated; but the wounds that martyrs had suffered in defense of their faith would appear as trophies, though their severed limbs would be restored.[144] In short, each person's body would have the size and dimensions which it had attained, or was to attain, at maturity, according to the design implanted in each individual, so that its appropriate beauty was preserved in the proportions of all its parts. All ugliness, weakness, sluggishness, corruption, and anything else inconsistent with that kingdom of happiness would be eliminated.[145] The blessed would be able to recognize one another, even if they had not been acquainted on earth; they would know the thoughts of each other's hearts, which had been hidden on earth by the mortal flesh. Augustine cited the example of his own father, whom none of his congregation had known but might expect to meet after the Resurrection, since he had been baptized at his death and was thus secure in salvation.[146]

---

140. Aug. *Psal.* 57.17; *Eu. Io.* 49.9-10; *Serm.* 65.7.8.

141. Aug. *Ciu.* 22.30.

142. Aug. *Ciu.* 22.12-24; *Serm.* 242; 243; *Psal.* 146.

143. Aug. *Ciu.* 22.15, 17, 24. Augustine explained that Adam and Eve did not procreate in Paradise because God had not yet commanded it before the Fall and they had no lust to move them to sexual activity (*Gen. litt.* 9.4.8; *Ciu.* 14.21).

144. Aug. *Ciu.* 22.17-19, 24.

145. Aug. Ciu. 22.20.

146. Aug. *Serm.* 243.5.5; 252.7.

Some Christians believed that during the interim between death and resurrection, some of the more significant sinners would be prepared for divine mercy at the Judgment: they would be granted the forgiveness of their sins, which they had not received during earthly life. For these souls, the punishment following death would have been temporary and remedial rather than eternal and penal. To sustain this position, these Christians attempted to specify the minimum qualifications for such divine mercy. Some claimed that God would extend mercy to all, fallen angels and humans alike, perhaps through the intercession of the saints — an extension or revival of the third-century belief in the efficacious advocacy of the martyrs.[147] Others theorized that the fortunate group would include only those who had been baptized and had received the eucharist within the Catholic communion, or perhaps even outside it in heresy or schism.[148] Other theories extended the divine mercy to those who persevered within the unity of the true church, even though they had lived wicked lives, or only to those who had offset their own wickedness by forgiving that of others and performing acts of mercy.[149] Augustine agreed that the scriptures provided a foundation for the hope that some might be saved through punishment and correction during the interim between death and resurrection; they could be granted forgiveness and salvation by Christ at the final Judgment.[150]

In attempting to evaluate the arguments for specifying who might qualify for such mercy, Augustine excluded all who had not at least attempted to live well within the unity of the church, even if they had otherwise given alms and forgiven others.[151] He explained that some of the sinners among the faithful actually held to Christ as the foundation of their lives, because they had put nothing else ahead of him. Though they failed to attain and follow Christ's standard in loving other persons and things, they had been disposed and prepared to give up any and all of these for his sake had this actually been required of them. Paul might have intended such persons in speaking about being saved through fire (1 Cor. 3:13). The sufferings through which their inordinate loves were to be burned out might indeed be found between death and resurrection, but the scope of their purification need not be so limited. Augustine noted that dying itself, the suffering of persecution, and the trials of earthly life could have this same purifying effect on the faithful.[152] In his sermons, he regularly noted the way that God used punishment to correct those for whom salvation was intended.[153]

147. Aug. *Ciu.* 22.17-18.
148. Aug. *Ciu.* 22.19-20.
149. Aug. *Ciu.* 22.21-22. Some speculated that those who forgave others would thereby have all their own sins forgiven and be saved without any further punishment.
150. Aug. *Ciu.* 21.24.
151. Aug. *Ciu.* 22.23-25, 27.
152. Aug. *Ciu.* 22.26.
153. Aug. *Serm. Dolb.* 21(159B).4; *Serm. Mai* 22(341A).2-3; *Psal.* 44.17; 50.15; 138.15.

Augustine taught that during the time of waiting between death and resurrection, the dead were cut off from knowledge of the affairs of the living. The dead were not directly aware of the vicissitudes of the living, just as the living could not know the joy or sorrow of the dead. For this judgment, Augustine could cite scripture, such as the promise to Josiah that he would die before seeing the destruction about to be visited on his people.[154] On a more personal level, he observed that his own mother's regular interventions in his life had not continued after her death; this he judged clear evidence that she must be unaware — he hoped blissfully — of his subsequent troubles and conflicts.[155]

Even without specific knowledge of their status, however, the living were in a position to assist the dead as they awaited the Judgment of Christ. During the eucharistic prayer and after the commemoration of the martyrs, whose intercession the church sought, prayer was offered for the consecrated virgins, the bishops who had served the particular church, and all the dead.[156] Caecilian of Carthage, whom the Donatists had accused of apostasy, was mentioned by name in the Catholic liturgy in that city.[157] This prayer was offered, however, only for the baptized: the unbaptized had not been incorporated into the body of Christ and thus would not be saved.[158] Not all the faithful were named individually, but the universality of the prayer was explicit.[159] To these intercessions were added the private prayers of the faithful, such as the prayer that Augustine offered for Monica in response to her deathbed request.[160]

In addition to prayer, Augustine strongly recommended almsgiving for the dead. He regularly urged that when children died, their portion of the inheritance should be given in alms, so that it might benefit the deceased.[161] The banquets celebrated at the tomb could provide actual consolation for the deceased, he explained, if the food and drink were distributed to the poor who also gathered in the cemeteries at the time of the annual commemoration, rather than being poured into or merely left by the tomb (cf. figs. 86 and 95 for examples of *mensae* or grave markers with depressions for leaving food).[162]

Not everyone could be helped by prayer and almsgiving. The deceased could not begin repentance for their sins and undertake in the afterlife the good works that they had neglected while on earth: the prayers and alms of their

154. Josiah in 2 Kings 22:18-20 (Aug. *Cur.* 13.16).
155. Aug. *Cur.* 13.16.
156. Aug. *Serm.* 159.1.1; 172.2.2; 237.7; 284.5; 297.2.3; *Eu. Io.* 84.1.
157. *Col. Carth.* 3.230; *Serm.* 359.6. His death day was not, however, listed in the *Kal. Carth.*
158. Aug. *Anim.* 2.15.21.
159. Aug. *Cur.* 4.6.
160. Aug. *Conf.* 9.13.35.
161. Aug. *Serm.* 9.20; 86.9.11–11.12.
162. Aug. *Ep.* 22.1.6.

survivors could only be added to the good they had already done.[163] Thus, the faithful sought not to change these dead themselves but to render God more merciful to them than their works and sins deserved.[164]

Augustine's belief that the dead were unaware of the living might not have been shared by African Christians generally. They traditionally had sought the intervention of the martyrs for the forgiveness of sins and other favors. In some instances, however, they seem to have hoped for the continuing intercession of those who had served them during their lives. A mosaic covering the tomb of a deacon not explicitly recognized as a martyr expresses this faith (fig. 143): "May he be mindful of us with the grace and piety that is his custom. Crescentinus, deacon. In peace."[165]

## Conclusion

Augustine's writings provide more evidence of Christian practices of mourning and commemoration than those of his predecessors. The burial ritual could include a eucharistic celebration but not in the presence of the remains of the deceased, lest the bishop share the bread and cup — given only to the living — with the dead. Explaining that bodily death was a punishment for sin, Augustine supported the sorrow of the bereaved and the rituals of mourning. He insisted, however, that when the deceased had been a faithful Christian, the people were addressing their own loss rather than that of the dead. Their care of the corpse was an act of service, but the elaboration of the gravesite and subsequent anniversary remembrances were a comfort for themselves rather than an amelioration of the status of the deceased.

Augustine did, however, explore the services which the living might render to the dead. He accepted the traditional view that most of the dead were in a state of waiting for the Resurrection and Judgment before they could enter into glory. During this time, the process of correction and purification that had characterized the lives of the faithful in the church might be continued, to prepare them to be accepted by Christ in the Judgment. God's mercy might bring remedial punishments on them. The living could intercede for them not only by prayer but by those good works — particularly almsgiving — that the deceased had used during their lifetimes to seek God's mercy. Thus, Augustine attempted to modify the practices of mourning, suggesting that the living could benefit their dead more effectively by feeding the poor than by feasting or leaving food at their graves.

In his explorations of the original condition of humanity and the Fall and its

163. Aug. *Serm.* 172.2.2.
164. Aug. *Serm.* 172.2.2.
165. See above, p. 119, for full text and translation.

consequences, Augustine elaborated an understanding of death. Humans were created mortal in nature — as was necessary for sexual generation — but were protected from dying and could have attained immortality without undergoing death had they remained faithful and obedient to God. The actual experience of death was a consequence, a punishment, and even a corrective for the sin of pride that continued to characterize humanity's relation to God. In the Resurrection given through Christ, all humans would be reconstituted in an immortality that would bring their bodies to perfection. For the saved, this would bring unending happiness; for the damned, suffering without relief.

## GENERAL OBSERVATIONS

### Correlation of Archeological and Literary Evidence

As was demonstrated in Chapter Four, practices of burial, mourning, and the cult of the saints are well evidenced in the archeological record. Christian burials are identifiable primarily through their inscriptions and decoration. Christians, unlike their non-Christian neighbors, buried their dead inside churches and funerary chapels as well as in cemeteries. Like their traditionalist neighbors, they continued feasts at the tomb in observance of the anniversaries of their family members as well as the church's special dead. Particular terms, such as "lived in peace" and "faithful," usually identify a Christian. Symbols on tomb covers or grave markers, such as the Christogram and cross, marked a Christian burial. Other formulae in an individual's epitaph indicated innocence, piety, fidelity, or devotion to God. Church officials or consecrated virgins were also identified. In the same way, the absence of certain traditionalist formulae (e.g., D.M.S.) also characterized Christian tomb inscriptions.

In the absence of these markers, proximity to sacred realities, such as burial near or within the church or the tomb of a martyr, suggests that the grave was prepared for a Christian.[166] Basilicas and other shrines were built in cemeteries, at least some of which provided facilities not only for the celebration of the eucharist but for feasts in honor of the dead.

The Christian practice of feasting at the tomb of family dead is reported by Tertullian and Augustine. It is evidenced also by inscriptions, such as that for Aelia Secundula, and by the presence of facilities for dining in cemeteries. The practice of communicating with the dead through food offerings is not as well evidenced for Christians.

As has already been noted in the studies of orders and the forms of life, the tomb inscriptions are a rich source of information on the differentiation of roles within the congregation and the forms of address and dress that marked these.

166. See pp. 118-20 and 530-31 for the discussion of burial *ad sanctos*.

Christian practices associated with death and dying were subject to significant controversy and dispute only indirectly, in the controversy over the reconciliation of dying penitents following the Decian persecution. Otherwise, the written record indicates remarkable continuity in practice and belief. Martyrs were immediately rewarded by entering into the presence of Christ. The souls of the other dead waited in the underworld for the Resurrection and Judgment. The wicked began to be punished in various ways even during this interim. The saints could rejoice only in the security of their salvation.

### PRAYER FOR THE DEAD

Prayer and offering for the dead are well evidenced in Tertullian's writings, particularly in the responsibility of a widowed partner to keep alive the affective union with the departed spouse in anticipation of their reunion in the Resurrection. The practice of praying and offering for the dead implied that the living could improve or at least alleviate the condition of the dead during a period of waiting between death and resurrection. Perpetua's intercession for her brother clearly improved his condition.[167] Tertullian thought the faithful departed might be subject to further discipline during their time of waiting. He did not indicate a particular concern on the part of Christians in helping the dead to prepare for the Judgment of Christ at the time of the Resurrection. In contrast to the ordinary faithful, martyrs were thought to enter immediately into glory.

Cyprian and his congregation had to deal with the admission of apostate penitents to communion, at least on their deathbeds, even though their standing before God was uncertain. As a consequence, he was more concerned with correction and improvement in the period between death and the Resurrection, after which all would be judged. Only those who already had repented and submitted to the church's rituals of penance while on earth could continue the process of satisfaction after death. They could be assisted, as they had been while on earth, by the intercessory prayers of the faithful. At the Judgment, the martyrs and the whole church could intercede for them.

Unlike Tertullian, Cyprian tended to assimilate the Christian faithful into the martyrs, implying that they too might enter immediately into glory. This change reflected two concerns in his ministry. In order to convince the apostate lapsed to undertake the process of ecclesial penance, he had to moderate the intercessory power of the martyrs by assimilating them into the ordinary faithful. He also sought to distance those who had been faithful and could approach

---

167. See above, p. 495, n. 27.

Christ in security from the reconciled penitents who awaited the Judgment in fear and trembling because they had been guilty of serious (and perhaps unforgivable) sin.

Augustine's discussion of the condition of the dead reflected the Christian practice of prayer and intercession on the part of the living. He taught that the religious status of the dead could not deteriorate during their wait for Resurrection, though it could be improved. Those who had been baptized and attempted to live well in the unity of the church might be purified in love by a remedial punishment, leading to the forgiveness of their sins in the Judgment. After death, they might be purified of their too earthly loves, just as they could have been through tribulation during earthly life. Thus, they might attain a forgiveness and mercy in the Judgment that they had not received — or deserved — during their earthly lives. Though Augustine did not fully elaborate a theology of the state of the faithful departed, his persistent analysis showed the coherence of popular belief and church practice with the teaching of scripture. The living could supply at least some of what the dead had omitted and thus help them attain, through the divine mercy, lasting salvation.

This belief and practice of praying and doing good works for the dead led inevitably to speculation on the ways in which these prayers and deeds were efficacious. Could the dead continue to repent of their sins and improve their chances of being approved by Christ, or were the living trying to change Christ's attitude toward the dead, rendering him more benevolent and merciful? Augustine's understanding of the efficacy of divine grace in transforming the dispositions of the human heart might have been applied to solving this problem. Though this is not clearly evidenced in his surviving works, his descriptions of the prayers and good works offered for the dead are compatible with such an understanding.

Despite the complex problems raised by prayer and works for the dead — particularly setting the minimal standard that qualified a person to benefit from such intercession — the practice seems to have been well grounded in a number of other practices. The delay of baptism and penance until the last possible moment created differentials between persons for whom salvation was expected — such as Augustine's mother and father — which seemed to require some equalization during the period between death and resurrection. Some of these tensions and puzzles were reflected in Augustine's doctrine of the gratuity of divine election and predestination — a doctrine largely accepted in Africa, though it generally was rejected elsewhere.

All three of the authors surveyed discouraged the belief that the Christian dead — even the martyrs — could intercede for and win benefits for the living. That belief, however, continued and spread beyond the martyrs to include at least some of the dead who had exercised intercessory roles during their lifetimes, such as the deacon Crescentinus.

Christian belief in the Resurrection contributed to the practice of caring for the bodies of the dead, including an avoidance of cremation. During the Decian persecution, the church in Carthage worked to recover and bury the bodies of the martyrs who died under torture. This was particularly evidenced in the care shown to protect Cyprian's body after his execution. Augustine would later explain that the practices of honoring the bodies of the dead did not reflect a concern that their future resurrection could be prevented by their being desecrated or going unburied.

## TRANSITION

The rituals of baptism, eucharist, and penance could be administered in immediate preparation for death. The burial ritual involved prayer and could include the eucharist. Subsequent care for the dead included the rituals of mourning and family meals at the grave. Through prayer and almsgiving, the living attempted to improve the status of the deceased in Christ's anticipated judgment of them. Not only martyrs but other privileged members of a congregation were buried in its urban basilica, in a shrine, or in a cemetery church where the eucharist was celebrated. Each of these indicated a continued sharing of life between the living and the dead. Such issues reappear as this study moves to the honoring of the martyrs and practices of prayer.

MEMORIA
BLOSSI HONO
RATVS INCENVS ACTOR
PERFECIT

# CHAPTER 11

# Honoring the Victorious Heroes: The Cult of the Martyrs

........................................................................................................

## INTRODUCTION

The veneration of Christians who had suffered for their faith in Christ was one of the most deeply ingrained characteristics of African Christianity. The earliest surviving evidence of Christianity in Africa is the account of the witness of Christians from Scilli before the proconsul, which is dated about 180. Thereafter, martyrdom accounts were regularly written, from the autobiographical narrative of Perpetua's dreams and visions, to the spare imperial records of the Decian and Diocletian persecutions. Even after imperial persecution of orthodox Christians stopped in the fourth century, Africans continued to read the *acta* of local and overseas saints. They even produced new accounts that were elaborated to make the earlier martyrs endorse later doctrinal and disciplinary judgments. No later than the fourth century, shrines were built to honor the bodies and other relics of the martyrs. These became destinations for pilgrimage, designed to accommodate large crowds coming to honor the special dead and to celebrate the Christian victory over traditional Roman religion. The translation of the relics of St. Stephen from Palestine brought a proliferation of healing miracles as pinches of the dirt into which his body had decomposed were taken from his tomb and distributed across the world, where shrines were built to house them.

This chapter will outline the development of the cult of the martyrs in Africa, using the more limited literary evidence to interpret the abundant archeological remains.

Tertullian had a great deal to say about martyrdom and about those who suffered in the process of confessing Christ. They were under the care of the community and were held in high honor.[1] He objected to the popular belief that they were capable of winning the forgiveness of the serious sins of others who flocked to the prisons and mines to seek their intercession.[2] Yet he recognized that the martyrs alone entered immediately into Paradise, rather than going to the underworld to await their resurrection.[3] Little is to be found in his writings, however, about the honors paid to the martyrs after their deaths. In his defense of Christian martyrdom, he compared the hymns sung in honor of their victories to those in praise of wisdom.[4] Accounts of the martyrdoms of the Christians from Scilli and of Perpetua, Felicity, and their companions were already in circulation and use.[5] The first is a straightforward report of the trial and execution, without any elaboration of the dispositions of either the witnesses or the proconsul judging them. The second, however, is presented as a largely autobiographical account of Perpetua's final days, fully displaying her dispositions, prayers, and visions as she worked out her relationship to her family and her fellow Christians. The narrative of the executions themselves is from another hand, though that report continues to focus on the dispositions of the martyrs. This *passio* indicates contemporary interest both in the interior life of these ideal Christians and in their ordeal as a participation in the ongoing struggle between Christ and the demonic forces.

Although material remains of the cult of the martyrs of this period — Perpetua and her companions, the Scillitans, and Celerina — have been found, these cannot be securely dated to this early phase of African Christianity. That the names and victories of these Christians were remembered and cherished is certain. That veneration of relics was already practiced is suggested by the blood in which the martyr Saturus soaked a ring, which he then gave to a sympathetic soldier immediately before his death.[6] It cannot be established that their bodies were honored shortly after their deaths at tomb shrines or that those monuments became pilgrimage sites.

During this period, imperial prosecution of Christians was not systematic, and the number of martyrs remained small. Though both martyrs and confessors (who suffered but did not die for confessing Christ) were highly honored in the communities, a significant number of Christians preferred to avoid open

---

1. Tert. *Ux.* 2.4.2; *Scorp.* 11.3.
2. Tert. *Mart.* 1.6; *Pud.* 22.1-5. See above, p. 303.
3. Tert. *Res.* 43.4.
4. Tert. *Scorp.* 7.2.
5. Perpetua's visionary tour of paradise is cited in Tert. *An.* 55.4.
6. *Pas. Perp.* 21.5. Saturus took a ring from Pudens, dipped it in his blood, and returned it to him, as a *pignus et memoriam sanguinis.* Pudens was himself commemorated as a martyr at Carthage on April 29.

conflict with the imperial authorities. They objected, for example, to the soldier who, by publicly refusing to wear a wreath during a distribution of imperial gifts, had provoked his own execution and placed other Christians in danger.[7]

## SYSTEMATIC PERSECUTION IN CYPRIAN'S TIME

Although the Decian persecution was not aimed at Christians, it did require their participation in the traditional cult and specified procedures to secure compliance. A large number of Christians were required to defend their faith under pressure, and a respectable number succeeded in doing so. Many of them suffered deprivation of property and temporary exile; others were tortured, and some died under that coercive pressure. Once peace was restored, Cyprian and his colleagues faced the problem of assimilating into their communities both the heroes, to whom extraordinary powers were attributed, and the defeated, who were eager to facilitate their rehabilitation by accessing the intercessory power of the martyrs and confessors.

During the persecution, Cyprian instructed the clergy in Carthage to maintain records of the death dates of martyrs so that the memorials of their victories might be added to the list of those already being celebrated. Indeed, he was already celebrating their witness to Christ with "offerings and sacrifices" and looked forward to memorializing them when peace was restored to the community as a whole.[8] Later, Cyprian cited the ancestors of the confessor Celerinus as being among the martyrs already commemorated annually on the days of their deaths.[9]

Although the church was caring for the burial of the martyrs,[10] Cyprian provided no specific evidence of a cult associated with their bodies. The account of Cyprian's death testifies to a practice like that indicated in the *passio* of Perpetua and Felicity. As he was prepared for beheading, cloths and napkins were spread on the ground before him, presumably to catch his blood.[11] Though his burial is recounted and the cemetery located, nothing is recorded in contemporary documents about further honors paid to his body or those of other martyrs.

The honoring of the martyrs of the Decian and Valerian persecutions in Africa was complicated by the appeals made to the confessors by Christians who had failed to defend their faith against the assault. Exercising the power ascribed to them by the faithful since Tertullian's day, the martyrs and confessors authorized the bishops to confer the peace of the church upon any whom they regarded as

7. Tertullian defended the martyr's action in *De corona*.
8. Cypr. *Ep.* 12.1.2–2.1.
9. Cypr. *Ep.* 39.3.1. These may have been executed during the same persecution as Perpetua and Felicity, since they were the grandmother and uncles — on both sides — of the confessor.
10. Cypr. *Ep.* 12.2.1.
11. Pont. *Vita Cypr.; Act. Procon.* 5.

penitent and prepared to receive it.[12] Some of the failed Christians insisted that the bishops must recognize this patronage and readmit them to communion without their following normal penitential procedures. Although Cyprian allowed the reconciliation of dying penitents even during the persecution,[13] he followed Tertullian in opposing the presumption that the martyrs could win the forgiveness of the sin of denying Christ. As Bishop of Carthage and a leader of the African episcopate, however, he was in a more effective position to resist than Tertullian had been. If the status of the martyrs and confessors depended upon Christ's promise to acknowledge those who had confessed him, Cyprian argued, the confessors and martyrs had to respect his threat to deny those who had refused to do so (Matt. 10:32-33). Neither could it be presumed that their intercession would be effective. The martyrs who begged God to take vengeance on their persecutors were not immediately accommodated (Rev. 6:9-11), nor did the great friends of God — Noah, Moses, Jeremiah, Daniel, and Job — always win the favors they asked.[14]

Cyprian took a second approach to restraining enthusiasm for the martyrs and especially the confessors, who had survived the persecution and became a force within the congregation. In his address to the congregation in Carthage immediately upon the return of peace, he reasoned that every Christian who had not performed the required sacrifice or sought certification of compliance by the established deadline had defied imperial power and confessed Christ.[15] A year later, exhorting his people to courage in the face of plague and to generosity in caring for the sick, he argued that God sought their faith rather than their blood. The martyr's reward of immediate entry into Paradise awaited all who placed their trust in God and risked their lives in serving others.[16]

Thus, Cyprian restrained the community's enthusiasm for the martyrs and their influence upon God and the bishop. Their intercessory power, he insisted, was to be exercised at the Judgment of Christ and never to be confused with or substituted for the divine mercy, upon which the forgiveness of Christians depended.[17] He even preferred to speak of the church as praying for, rather than to, the martyrs.[18]

The schism effected by those laxist clergy and congregations that accepted and relied on the intercessory power of the martyrs moved Cyprian to insist that only confessing Christ within the unity of the true church would win the martyr's reward from Christ and earn the praise of the church.[19] Later he ar-

12. Cypr. *Ep.* 23. See also *Ep.* 21.2.1; 22.2.1.

13. Cypr. *Ep.* 20.3.2.

14. Cypr. *Laps.* 18-20, 36. The observation that the two parts of Matt. 10:32-33 were inseparable may have been suggested to him by the Roman presbyters (*Ep.* 30.4; 36.2.1-2).

15. Cypr. *Laps.* 3.

16. Cypr. *Mort.* 1-3, 16-20.

17. Cypr. *Laps.* 17-18.

18. Cypr. *Ep.* 39.3.1.

19. Cypr. *Unit. eccl.* 14, 19.

gued that only the church could prepare a person for martyrdom by the gift of the Spirit and by sharing in the eucharistic blood of Christ.[20] The argument that not everyone who died in the confession of Christ should be recognized as a true witness and martyr would play a major role in the Donatist controversy during the next century.

The Decian persecution and subsequent Valerian persecution resulted in the veneration of a number of martyrs in Carthage and elsewhere in Africa; these included the bishops Cyprian of Carthage, Theogenis of Hippo, and Quadratus of Uzalis.[21] The *acta* of Cyprian's trial and execution, like the account of his life, heap praise upon the bishop. The actual events, however, are presented in a style closer to that of an official record.

The account of Cyprian's death shares some of the characteristics of the fuller *passio* of Marian and James and that of Montanus and Lucius, all of which were set in the Valerian persecution.[22] All three make use of visions that predict victory, but the latter two dwell on the dispositions of the martyrs, the violence to which they were subjected, and their freedom from any suffering. These two also use the more elaborate style of the *passio* of Perpetua and Felicity, which would subsequently be developed even further in some of the accounts of martyrdom set in the Diocletian persecution. The veneration of Cyprian himself is already evident in the report of his having appeared in the visions of the later martyrs to encourage and strengthen them.[23]

## THE DIOCLETIAN PERSECUTION

The disruptions effected by the Diocletian persecution resulted in a cult of the martyrs in the fourth century, amply reflected in both literary and archeological evidence. The practice of venerating the relics of martyrs is well attested in both. Many of the *acta* and *passiones* written in this period are characterized by a focus on the sufferings of the martyrs that is absent in most earlier narratives. The Donatists directed their own accounts against not only the Roman imperial persecutors but their Caecilianist collaborators. For the first time, archeological remains of burials and shrines clearly attest the honoring of the bodies of the martyrs. This inquiry will proceed by examining first the literary and then the archeological evidence.

20. Cypr. *Ep.* 57.4.1-2.
21. *Kal. Carth.* lists Mappalicus, Castus and Aemilius, the Massa Candida, Quadratus, Marian and James, Lucius, Montanus, and companions. The latter two groups have surviving *acta.* Aug. *Serm.* 273 witnesses to Theogenes and *Serm. Morin* 15 (306C) to Quadratus.
22. *Act. Procon.; Pas. Mar. Iac.; Pas. Mont. Luc.*
23. *Pas. Mar. Iac.* 6; *Pas. Mont. Luc.* 13, 21.

The Diocletian persecution was not so sustained in Africa as in the eastern part of the empire. Yet the enforcement of the requirement that the scriptures be handed over to the imperial officials for destruction did result in some episcopal martyrdoms (Felix of Tibiuca), some evasions (Mensurius of Carthage), and apparently a good number of failures (Silvanus of Cirta). The first resulted in new *acta* and *passiones;* some follow the terse reporting style of imperial court records, but others were greatly elaborated. The Donatists structured some of this second group in a way that supported their claims that Donatists had remained faithful and that Caecilianists had betrayed Christ and aided the persecutors.

The initial actions in the Diocletian persecution were aimed at purifying the army. Christians had been serving — and occasionally running into difficulty — in the Roman legions during the third century. Tertullian dealt with the case of a Christian who brought down punishment upon both himself and others when he refused to wear the crown appropriate to receiving the emperor's gift.[24] When Cyprian identified the confessor Celerinus, who had been punished and expelled from the military during the Decian persecution, he named uncles on both sides of his family as soldiers who had earlier been executed for their Christian witness.[25] No accounts of these martyrdoms — other than Cyprian's brief reference in his letter about Celerinus's own confession — have survived. In contrast, Christians in Africa at the end of the third century were portrayed as actively renouncing military service rather than being expelled by their commanders.

Maximilianus refused to be enlisted at Theveste on the grounds that service of Christ and service of the worldly powers were incompatible. He did not contest the recruiter's claim that other Christians found no such difficulty; some even served in the imperial guard. He was executed for refusing enlistment.[26] Marcellus already was serving as a centurion at Tingis when he decided that the unavoidable contact with idolatry could no longer be tolerated. He made the same judgment that Maximilianus had: service of Christ did not allow participation in the army of an earthly power.[27] The recorder at his trial, Cassian, was inspired to follow his example.[28]

The civilian martyrdoms in Africa were set during the year-long enforcement of decrees that required turning over the scriptures and offering sacrifices. The *passio* of Felix, Bishop of Tibiuca, follows the spare narrative style of the military accounts. The bishop refused to turn over the scriptures that he admitted were in his possession, and he was executed summarily after a trial before the Proconsul Anullinus at Carthage.[29] The interrogation of the matron

24. Tert. *Cor.*
25. Cypr. *Ep.* 39.2.1–3.2.
26. *Act. Max.*
27. *Act. Marcelli.*
28. *Act. Cassiani.*
29. *Passio sancti Felicis.*

Crispina, who refused to offer sacrifice, was conducted by the same proconsul at Theveste. In the style of an official record, the narrative is limited to the words of the two adversaries, without comment on their dispositions or motives. The only exceptions are the final description of Crispina's "making the sign of the cross on her forehead," and the explanation of her death: "she was beheaded for the name of the Lord Jesus Christ, to whom is honor forever, Amen."[30] Neither of these martyrs was subjected to torture, nor did either make any statement referring to events beyond the immediate issues of their trials.

The martyr accounts from the same persecution that are attributed to the Donatist party are radically different in style from those just reviewed.[31] The *passio* of Maxima and Donatilla and of Secunda (who joined them voluntarily after their initial trial) was set on an estate where every other Christian is reported to have capitulated to the imperial demand for sacrifice. The three virgins verbally sparred with the proconsul, Anullinus, calling him a sorcerer and an agent of the devil. He does not follow this procedure in the account of the trials of Felix and Crispina; instead, he is depicted as ordering that the confessors be tortured, and then as being himself worn down by their endurance. Only after a bear refused to harm them did Anullinus finally order their beheading. Two versions of this text have been transmitted, one of which might have been used by the Caecilianists.[32]

The *acta* of the Abitinian martyrs develop this narrative strategy by including a general apostasy, the proconsul's use of torture, and the confessors' victory over Anullinus. The bishop and many of the clergy of the town are reported to have failed; the presbyter who served this small congregation was the only minister to stand fast. The methods of torture, the gruesome injuries to the confessors' bodies, and the sufferings they endured are all detailed. Each of them freely admitted gathering for the Lord's service *(dominicum)*, an action that no surviving imperial decree had forbidden. By steadfast endurance, successive confessors forced the proconsul to call a halt to their interrogation and torture. One of them, Victoria, is credited with earlier having thrown herself off a cliff to escape a forced marriage and miraculously having been preserved from harm. Although the narrative may have been built on an eyewitness report of the interrogation, it freely elaborates the events and comments upon the dispositions and intentions of all the parties.

The Donatist account of the Abitinian martyrs introduces elements that are proper to the later conflict between the partisans of Caecilian and Donatus. The trial was located in Carthage, more than forty miles from the place of arrest; its bishop, Mensurius, and his deacon, Caecilian, were then implicated in the imperial torture of the confessors. These two were accused of violently preventing

30. *Passio sanctae Crispinae.*

31. See Maureen A. Tilley, *Donatist Martyr Stories: The Church in Conflict in Roman North Africa* (Liverpool: Liverpool University Press, 1996).

32. *Pas. Max.* Martyrs from Thuburbo (Maius or Minus cannot be determined) were celebrated at Carthage on July 30, the death date given in the alternate version. See Hippolyte Delehaye, "Contributions récentes à l'hagiographie de Rome et d'Afrique," AnBoll 54 (1936): 296-300.

other Christians from bringing food or drink to the confessors in prison. The proconsul forgot about his prisoners; they died of starvation because Mensurius and Caecilian prevented their receiving food.[33] Mensurius also was charged with handing over the scriptures, in contradiction of his contemporary correspondence with Secundus of Tigisis, in which he admitted using an evasion to avoid such action.[34] A council of clerical confessors from different parts of Africa was convened in the imperial prison at Carthage to denounce its bishop and his deacon.[35] The Abitinian martyrs then condemned to eternal punishment all who had failed by turning over the scriptures to be burned and warned that they would prevent anyone who entered into communion with traitors from sharing the eternal life of which they, as martyrs, were confident.[36]

Although these *acta* were set in the Diocletian persecution, the elements included in the narrative suggest that the text was designed to explain the later schism and support the charges of the Donatist party against Caecilian. At the Conference of Carthage in 411, the Donatist bishops used the *acta* for just this purpose. They introduced them as a counterpoint to the *acta* of the episcopal synod in Cirta, by which the Catholics attempted to demonstrate that the Numidian bishops who supported the Donatist side in Carthage already had either admitted or tolerated the very crime of which they would later accuse Caecilian of tolerating in one of his consecrators.[37] The *acta* of the Abitinians show that the cult of the martyrs could be used to vilify ecclesiastical opponents as well as the Roman government.[38]

Three of these narratives affirm that the civilian martyrs had practiced sexual renunciation. Felix claims to have preserved his chastity; Maxima and Donatilla were consecrated virgins; Secunda and Victoria had taken radical steps to avoid marriage and had thus prepared themselves for martyrdom. Two of the narratives also may have served to promote voluntary martyrdom: Victoria threw herself from a cliff, and Secunda jumped from a balcony. The Donatist

33. This charge does not appear in contemporary accounts of the subsequent proceedings against Caecilian.

34. Mensurius of Carthage and Secundus of Tigisis, the Primate of Numidia, corresponded about 305. Aug. *Coll.* 3.17.32; *Don.* 14.18; *Gaud.* 1.37.47.

35. *Act. Abit.* 19-20.

36. *Act. Abit.* 21.

37. Aug. *Coll.* 3.17.31-32; the issue was the form of dating. The Donatists also claimed that a council of bishops could not have gathered in Cirta during the persecution. They may be presumed to have presented a different version of these *acta,* one which did not include the council of confessors gathered in the prison at Carthage.

38. Although the text survives in six manuscripts, the critical edition of P. Franchi d'Cavalieri shows that none of them is compatible with the Catholic position in the controversy. Biblioteca Apostolica Vaticana and Franchi Pio de' Cavalieri, "La 'Passio' dei Martiri Abitinensi," in *Note agiographiche 8,* vol. 65, Studi e Testi/Biblioteca Apostolica Vaticana (Città del Vaticano: Biblioteca Apostolica Vaticana, 1935), 3-46. See as well Delehaye's review in his "Contributions récentes à l'hagiographie de Rome et d'Afrique," 293-96.

version of the *acta* of Cyprian does not contain the questioning on the first day during which, according to the other versions, Cyprian asserted that Christian discipline forbade voluntary martyrdom.[39]

The last of the Caecilianist martyrdom accounts belong to the Diocletian persecution. The Donatist church, however, continued to produce both martyrs and narratives of their witness during the fourth century, after the overseas churches and the empire rejected its appeals for recognition. A sermon preached in the Donatist basilica at Carthage praised the witness and suffering of those who had been killed while preventing its confiscation by imperial forces. The preacher accused Caecilian, who had become the city's Catholic bishop, of provoking the imperial attempt to clear the building, during which Donatist clergy and laity died — despite the army's use of cudgels rather than edged weapons in order to avoid killing anyone.[40] The preacher closed his narrative with a plea that both the glory of the martyrs and the perfidy of their persecutors never be forgotten.

After the death of Caecilian, Emperor Constans attempted a union of the competing communions in Africa through the mission of Paul and Macarius. In Carthage, a Donatist layman named Maximian tore down the imperial edict of unity and was arrested; a spectator at his trial, Isaac, supported his protest and also was arrested. The tortures of each are described in somewhat less detail than those of the Abitinian martyrs, but the narrative attempts to achieve the same effect of demonizing the imperial officials and demonstrating the superior strength of the martyrs.[41] Elements introduced in this account are an apparition of a crown to Maximian, predicting his victory, and a dream vision of renewed torture and victory given to Isaac.[42] The bodies of these and other confessors destined for exile were dumped into the sea, but then they were delivered back to the shore by an elaborately described series of waves, so that the relics could be venerated by the faithful.[43] Like the *acta* of the Abitinians, this narrative condemns the traitors and exhorts the Donatist confessors. It does not, however, accuse by name either the Caecilianist clergy of Carthage or the Roman proconsul.[44]

The passion of Marculus, a Donatist bishop who led the episcopal opposition to the mission of Paul and Macarius in Numidia, also uses visions to predict the action.[45] Torture plays an important role — the confessor is preserved from both pain and harm — but it is not accompanied by significant dialogue

---

39. The Donatist version is reproduced in Jean-Louis Maier, *Le dossier du donatisme,* 2 vols. (Berlin: Akademie Verlag, 1987), 1:123-26.

40. *Pas. Don.*

41. *Pas. Isa. Max.* 5-7.

42. *Pas. Isa. Max.* 4, 8-9.

43. *Pas. Isa. Max.* 12-16.

44. Both of these may have been unknown to its author.

45. *Pas. Marc.* 8.

between the confessor and the imperial official.[46] After a confrontation, the imperial notary Macarius took Marculus along in his retinue, perhaps having destined him for exile, but the confessor died at Nova Petra. That death is described as a secret execution by beheading, with precipitation from a cliff to prevent the veneration of his remains.[47] A divine intervention similar to the one that prevented harm to the Abitinian virgin Victoria (or to Secunda when she joined Maxima and Donatilla) preserved Marculus's body from further harm. A luminous mist led faithful Christians of the area to the body so that it could be recovered for burial and veneration.[48]

Caecilianist polemicists would later accuse Donatist fanatics of voluntary self-precipitation in order to attain the glory of martyrdom.[49] The narrative of the death of Marculus may have provided an example to be followed, though he there was said to have been pushed by the executioner (after being beheaded). Self-precipitation to avoid marriage was attributed to Secunda and Victoria, both of whom were preserved from harm so that they might later bear public witness to Christ.[50]

The importance of the cult of the martyrs in both Caecilianist and Donatist churches is evidenced also by the production of *acta* that have little historical foundation. The story of St. Salsa was based on a tombstone commemorating a holy matron named Salsa *(matri sanct),* whose inscription was reinterpreted as that of a thirteen-year-old holy martyr *(marturi sanct).* Despite the fabrication, she was venerated in the community, and her story became part of the African lore. Salsa's intercession was credited with saving Tipasa from capture in the rebellion of Firmus.[51] The story of Typasius, an ascetic veteran recalled to military service under Diocletian, is filled with wondrous events. It continues a theme that appeared in the pre-Constantinian military *acta:* the conflict between serving Christ and serving in the army of an earthly state. The specific issue was idolatry, but Typasius's attitude was more broadly stated as a conflict between serving Christ and serving any temporal power. The *passio* of Fabius, a standard bearer, belongs to the same genre and period; it is, however, more fully elaborated and filled with miraculous events.[52] One can only speculate on the religious culture that produced and cherished these.

After the cessation of systematic persecution of Christians by imperial officials, new martyrdom accounts continued to be written. These later narratives are more fully developed into contests between good and evil, with details of

46. *Pas. Marc.* 4-6.
47. *Pas. Marc.* 12.
48. *Pas. Marc.* 12-15. For his memorial, see Yvette Duval, *Loca sanctorum Africae: Le culte des martyrs en Afrique du IVe au VIIe siècle,* 2 vols. (Rome: École française de Rome, 1982), 1:158-60.
49. See Aug. *Petil.* 2.20.46; 2.88.195; *Cresc.* 3.49.54; *Eu. Io.* 11.15.
50. *Pas. Max.* 4; *Act. Abit.* 17.
51. See Henri Grégoire, "Sainte Salsa, roman épigraphique," *Byzantion* 12 (1937): 213-24.
52. *Pas. Typ.; Pas. Fab.*

the tortures used and the attitudes of both the persecutors and the martyrs. These *acta* seem to have become a propaganda tool of the Donatist party in the ongoing conflict against the imperially favored Caecilianists. As such, they may reflect the religious culture that produced them with greater accuracy than the nature of the conflict during which the events are purported to have occurred.[53]

Both the Catholic and the Donatist bishops had to curb excesses in the cult of martyrs, insisting on a distinction between true and false confession of Christ. The Donatist bishops forbade honorific burial to irregular fighters who upset the social order, against whom they had called upon Count Taurinus.[54] A council of Catholic bishops meeting in Carthage after the work of Macarius and Paul forbade giving the honors of a martyr to anyone who had been guilty of the sin of suicide.[55] Half a century later, the Catholic bishops were still trying to control the proliferation of shrines in rural areas dedicated to unattested martyrs.[56] Their legislation might indicate that such persons were being honored by the Donatist faithful.[57]

## Relics

The veneration of a martyr is indicated also by the practice of carrying pieces of the body, usually bone, presumably in small caskets. In a conflict dated before the outbreak of the Diocletian persecution, the matron Lucilla was rebuked by Caecilian, still a deacon, for kissing the bone of a reputed martyr before taking the eucharist. She was apparently carrying this relic with her during the eucharistic service. Caecilian objected, Optatus explained, not to the veneration itself but to her preference of the relic over the eucharistic food. The authenticity of the relic was questioned also.[58] By the middle of the fourth century, however, the Caecilianist bishops were concerned that the title of "martyr" was being applied indiscriminately to suicides and other sinners. They decreed that the mercy of Christian burial might be offered to bodies that were found in the open, but they were not to be venerated as were those of martyrs unless some reliable connection to persecution and confession could be established.[59]

53. For example, the refusal to serve in the imperial army articulated by the military martyr accounts set in the Diocletian persecution may more accurately reflect Donatist opposition to imperial rule after the mission of Macarius and Paul.

54. Optat. *Parm.* 3.4. At least one presbyter had already interred some of them in his church.

55. *Con. Carth.* a. 345-48, 2.

56. *Reg. Carth.* 83, from Carthage in September 401.

57. Might the self-precipitation later reported have been some form of testing or declaring one's own commitment to Christ? Could the actors have been led by the martyrdom accounts to anticipate being rescued by God?

58. Optat. *Parm.* 1.16. In this narrative, the event explained her subsequent opposition to Caecilian as Bishop of Carthage.

59. *Con. Carth.* a. 345-48, 2.

## Burial *ad Sanctos*

The practice of venerating the bodies of martyrs evident in the accounts of Maximian, Isaac, and Marculus is attested elsewhere as well. The *acta* of Maximilian end with provision for his burial. A woman named Pompeiana secured his body and placed it in her own tomb at Theveste. In anticipation of her death, she later had it transferred to Carthage and placed near the body of Cyprian, where she also was to be buried. This account provides indirect evidence that the tomb of Cyprian was regarded as a sacred site. It is also the first evidence of a belief in the advantage of burial near the body of a martyr.[60] The defenders of the Donatist basilica in Carthage were buried in that church, forming a crown around the altar.[61]

## Shrines

The practice of venerating the martyrs at their tombs was probably an extension and an expansion of the honors paid to dead family members that Christians had brought with them from the imperial culture. The development of facilities in the cemeteries on both the eastern and western sides of Tipasa, for example, indicates a practice of open-air dining near ordinary tombs. The cult of the community dead — the martyrs — led to a significant expansion of the facilities at the shrine of St. Salsa as well as the vast cemetery, round mausoleum (fig. 108), and funerary chapel built behind the cathedral (figs. 109, 110). The chapel, built by Bishop Alexander, provided elaborate facilities for feasting within the building itself (fig. 112).[62] No apparent provision seems to have been made in this basilica for the celebration of the eucharist, though some other cemetery basilicas could serve for regular worship.[63] A famous martyrs' *mensa* (table top) from Mauretania Sitifensis includes the names of six martyrs who were "born with Christ."[64]

Variations on the practice of building a basilica for the cult of one or more martyrs can be found throughout Africa. In Carthage, for example, the places of Cyprian's execution and burial were each marked by a church in which elaborate rituals were held on the anniversary of his confession, execution, and

---

60. *Act. Max.* 3.

61. *Pas. Don.* 13.

62. See above, pp. 125-26, and the study of Paul-Albert Février, "Le culte des martyrs en Afrique et ses plus anciens monuments," *Corso di cultura sull'arte ravennate e bizantina* 17 (1970): 191-215.

63. When the Vandals took over the urban basilicas in Carthage, for example, the Catholics used the cemetery basilicas. See above, p. 96; p. 134, n. 199.

64. See Duval, *Loca sanctorum Africae*, 2:331-37, no. 157.

---

burial.[65] The Basilica Maiorum honored Perpetua, Felicity, and their companions (figs. 20, 21).[66] Another basilica was dedicated to Celerina and the Scillitan martyrs.[67] The round, subterranean monument associated with the basilica known as Damous el Karita was almost certainly the shrine of a (now unidentifiable) saint (fig. 17).[68] At Sufetula, the basilica of Sylvanius and Fortunatus was located outside the walls and some distance from the city itself (figs. 79, 80).[69] Augustine referred to the celebrations at the basilicas of the Twenty Martyrs and of Theogenes, bishop of the city at the time of the Valerian persecution, both of which were outside the city walls of Hippo.[70]

Later, basilicas and other shrines within the city walls would be dedicated to the martyrs. The Basilica of the Eight Martyrs, for example, was built in Hippo during Augustine's episcopate.[71] A shrine was prepared to receive the relics of St. Stephen near (or even within) the cathedral in Hippo during the 420s.[72] The addition of counter-apses in African basilicas may have provided places for the deposit of saints' relics as well as accommodating the burial of bishops. For example, the basilicas of both Bellator and Vitalis at Sufetula had such counter-apses (see figs. 67, 68). The basilica at Uppenna was built in stages to honor a group of local martyrs. First, a counter-apse was transformed in the Byzantine era into a small oratory with an elaborate mosaic naming the original thirteen saints; later, the name of another local saint and those of Peter and Paul were added (figs. 117, 118).[73]

Additional evidence for the fourth-century cult of the martyrs is found in Augustine's recounting of his mother's participation in the established practice of eating and drinking at their tombs.[74] The explanation that he offered his congregation for the custom of celebrating the feast of Leontius — a fourth-century Bishop of Hippo — also indicates that the roots of the practices were in the period immediately following Constantine's toleration of Christianity.[75] The difficulty that Bishop Aurelius of Carthage experienced in reforming the celebration of the martyrdom of Cyprian at the end of the fourth century also implies that the custom was a long-standing one.[76]

65. See above, pp. 145-47.

66. See above, pp. 136, 144-45.

67. See above, pp. 71, 94, 135-36.

68. See above, pp. 138-39.

69. See above, pp. 153-54.

70. See above, p. 95.

71. Under the supervision of the presbyter Leporius (Aug. *Serm.* 356.10).

72. See above, pp. 95, 124; p. 156, nn. 287, 288. On the question of the location, see Serge Lancel, *Saint Augustine,* trans. Antonia Neville (London: SCM Press, 2002), 243-44.

73. See references and a longer description of this basilica above, pp. 116-17.

74. Aug. *Conf.* 6.2.2.

75. Aug. *Ep.* 29.9.

76. Aug. *Serm. Denis* 13(305A).4.

## Dedications

Some inscriptions indicate the attitudes of the Christians who prepared and placed them. About two hundred inscriptions connected with the shrines and burials of martyrs in Africa have been collected.[77] Most of these give only the names of the martyrs, though some add the times of their deaths. About a quarter include the names of persons who made the dedication, set up the memorial, or took some other role in honoring the martyrs. Of these, about a third are clergy — most often the bishop, but presbyters and deacons are also named — and these are credited with helping set up the memorial or placing relics in it.

When the patrons are named in the inscription, about a quarter of them proclaim that the dedication was the fulfillment of a vow or promise they had made, or that the martyrs had ordered that the shrine be set up (presumably in a communication between the dead and the living). A single presbyter was responsible for three of these; the other ten were made by lay Christians. Twenty percent of the inscriptions that mention someone other than a martyr include petitions that God or the saint would hear the prayers made by the named dedicators or by persons visiting the shrine. An inscription in the basilica of Alexander in Tipasa advises those who cannot make a similar dedication to give alms to the poor instead.[78] Only six of the total are associated immediately with the burial of someone other than the martyr, whose protection is evoked upon that dead person.

These inscriptions, most of which only name the martyrs themselves, indicate that the faithful were actually more interested in honoring the martyrs than in obtaining favors from or through them. Only a small percentage seek or acknowledge favors. This evidence, then, serves as a corrective to the impression created by the miracle stories, all of which narrate the martyr's response to a request for special blessings.

## Conclusion

The combination of the experience of systematic persecution at the beginning of the fourth century and the subsequent conflict within the church in Africa over the fidelity of its leadership resulted in a flourishing of the cult of the martyrs. The patronage of the emperor made funds available for repair and construction of basilicas. The newly granted right to own property and an increase in membership meant that the church was in a position to undertake a sustained building program. The cult of the saints, first in the cemeteries and then in the urban basilicas as well, was the beneficiary.

---

77. Duval, *Loca sanctorum Africae,* vol. 1.
78. Duval, *Loca sanctorum Africae,* 1:365-66, no. 173.

---

When the Donatist leaders failed to win the support of the emperors, they identified their communion with the church of the martyrs, which suffered persecution. The cult of their special dead offered a new front for regular opposition to the Caecilianists.

## THE FIFTH AND FOLLOWING CENTURIES

The Diocletian persecution and Constantine's support for Christianity brought a new realization of the role of the martyrs in Christian practice. Their resistance had not only won salvation for them and encouraged their companions in faith; it had broken the power that the demons had exercised over the imperial government through idolatrous cults. As the fourth century progressed, the attempted revival of traditional practice under Julian failed, and Theodosius established Christianity as the protected and supported religion of the Roman Empire. Public martyrdom in the face of imperial prosecution passed from living memory and was replaced by the veneration of the heroes of the past.

In Africa, this cult was one of the battlegrounds in the conflict between the Donatist and the Caecilianist parties. The Donatists claimed to maintain the faithful resistance of the martyrs by refusing communion with Christian apostates and by suffering persecution through the restriction of legal rights at the hands of the imperial government in its support of a false and apostate church. They accused their Caecilianist rivals of honoring the betrayers of the gospel and collaborating with the persecutors. They honored their supporters who fell under continuing imperial oppression of the Donatist cause. The Caecilianists, for their part, honored the martyrs who had achieved the triumph of Christianity in the Roman world.[79] Augustine labored to convince his congregation that their celebrations should be appropriate to the religious victory that had been won. To honor martyrs by excessive drinking and wild parties was to continue the devil's persecuting work.[80]

The cult of the martyrs, then, was a popular devotion that required little or no encouragement (but much regulation and guidance) from the clergy. A large number of shrines were built to honor the bodies of these special dead, at which services and celebrations were held on the anniversaries of their glorious deaths. The names of locally important martyrs were recalled daily during the eucharistic prayer. They were expected to receive the greatest reward, surpassing not only the clergy and monks but the virgins and widows as well.[81] Dedicated Christians were greeted by their fellows as disciples of the martyrs.[82]

79. Aug. *Serm.* 280.6; 295.8.8; 318.3; 325.1; *Serm. Dolb.* 25(360B).19, 24; *Psal.* 118.9.2-3.
80. Aug. *Serm.* 273.8; *Serm. Denis* 13(305A).4; *Psal.* 59.15.
81. Aug. *Virg.* 45.46; *Qu. Eu.* 1.9; *Psal.* 67.36.
82. In Numidia by "If you overcome," whereas in Proconsular, Byzacena, and Tripolitana they used "By your crown." See Aug. *Serm. Cail.* 2.6(94A).6.

The days specified for the festivals of martyrs may not have been uniform across Africa. A calendar of the church of Carthage has survived, but it does not correspond exactly to the celebrations evidenced through Augustine's sermons in Hippo Regius.[83] Some of the saints were widely if not universally honored — for example, the martyrs from the town of Scilli, Perpetua and Felicity, and Cyprian.[84] The matron Crispina, like some others, was given especial appreciation in her native Numidia, though she was recognized elsewhere in Africa as well.[85] Crispina's shrine, at Theveste, was one of the largest anywhere in the early Christian world, and in Africa paralleled only by the shrines of Cyprian or Perpetua and her companions in Carthage.[86] Local saints, such as the Eight Martyrs honored at Hippo, were not included in the calendar of Carthage.[87]

Some of the more popular martyrs were not Africans. The Apostles Peter and Paul were usually celebrated together.[88] Lawrence of Rome and Vincent of Saragossa were honored because of their particularly gruesome deaths and apparent protection from all pain.[89] The first of the martyrs for Christ, Stephen, became widely appreciated in Africa — at least among the Caecilianists — after relics from his grave in Palestine were distributed there.[90] The seven brothers commemorated in Maccabees were celebrated, though Razias was rejected, at least by the Caecilianists, because of his self-immolation.[91] Both the nativity and the martyrdom of John the Baptist were celebrated.[92] John and the other prophets were recognized as witnesses to Truth and, thereby, to Christ.[93] The innocent children killed by Herod were deemed martyrs to Christ.[94] The *Calendar of Carthage* also noted the burial dates of the Catholic bishops who served that

83. Carthage celebrated them on July 30, perhaps to avoid the Lenten fast; Hippo (and Rome) observed their death-date, March 7 (*Kal. Carth.*; Aug. *Serm.* 280.1; 345.6).

84. *Kal. Carth.* Perpetua, Felicity, and Cyprian were the African martyrs celebrated in Rome according to the "Feriale Ecclesiae Romanae," *Chron. Min., MGH* AA, 9:71-72.

85. December 5, as one of a group in Carthage; in Hippo, she was celebrated alone and had a shrine. Augustine compared her to the Roman Agnes and the Spanish Eulalia (*Serm.* 286.2.2; 354.5.5; *Serm. Morin* 2(313G).3).

86. See the discussion of Crispina's shrine in Theveste, pp. 114-15.

87. Their shrine was built in Hippo during Augustine's episcopate (*Serm.* 356.10).

88. Aug. *Serm.* 8.15; 279.13, 295-299; 381.1; *Serm. Dolb.* 4(299A); *Serm. Guelf.* 23(299B); 24(299C).

89. Lawrence, Aug. *Eu. Io.* 27.10, 12; *Serm.* 302-305; *Serm. Denis* 13(305A).1. Vincent, Aug. *Serm.* 4.36; 274-77; *Serm. Cail.* 1.47(277A).1.

90. December 26: Aug. *Serm.* 314-24.

91. August 1: Aug. *Serm.* 300; 301; *Serm. Denis* 17(301A). On Razias, see *Gaud.* 1.31.36-38.

92. John's nativity was celebrated on the summer solstice, his beheading on Dec. 27: Aug. *Serm.* 287-93; 307-8; *Serm. Dolb.* 3(293A); *Serm. Frang.* 8(293B); *Serm. Mai* 101(293C); *Serm. Guelf.* 22(293D).

93. Aug. *Psal.* 140.26; *Serm. Cail.* 2.6(94A).1.

94. December 28, in Carthage. See also *Serm.* 373.3; 375 preached for Epiphany in Hippo.

church from the mid-fourth to the mid-fifth centuries; Augustine was so honored as well.[95] Other bishops were commemorated in their own churches, such as Theogenes and Leontius in Hippo Regius[96] and, later, Jucundus in Sufetula.[97]

## Festivals

The annual celebration of the martyr's heavenly birthday always included the eucharistic ritual, which could be held at a shrine containing part of the body.[98] In addition to the regular — and in some cases specially chosen — readings, the account of the martyr's trial and death was read out and commented upon in the sermon.[99] The reading of these nonbiblical texts was approved and recommended by the bishops.[100] In Hippo, Augustine embellished the biblical narrative of the death of Stephen by reading accounts of the healing miracles performed at his shrines and by his relics.[101] Festivals of a martyr always included a sermon.[102]

The most elaborate African festival was that of Cyprian.[103] The Carthaginian community apparently gathered first at the shrine built at the site of his burial, the Mappalia or Memoria Cypriani,[104] for a vigil service. This might have commemorated the community's all-night watch outside the Roman official's house where Cyprian was kept between his initial appearance before the proconsul in the afternoon and his trial the next day. The Christians had taken control of the street, probably to make sure that Cyprian's martyrdom would be completed in Carthage and that they would not lose control of his body.[105] Augustine preached at this service a number of times.[106] The next morning, the community gathered for the eucharist and a sermon at the Mensa Cypriani, the basilica erected over the spot where Cyprian had been executed immediately after his trial, once again surrounded by his congregation. Augustinian sermons are identified as having

95. Gratus, Restitutus, Genethlius, Aurelius, Capreolus, and Quodvultdeus.

96. Aug. *Serm.* 273.7; 262.2.2.

97. See above, p. 150.

98. *Serm.* 273.2; 356.10; *Psal.* 120.13, 15.

99. Aug. *Serm.* 51.3.2; 273.2, 6; 274; 275.1; 276.1; 280.1; 282.2; 310.1; 326.2; *Serm. Denis* 16(299D).7; *Serm. Guelf.* 30(299E).2; *Serm. Lamb.* 9(299F).1; *Serm. Frang.* 6(335A).1.

100. *Con. Hipp.* a. 393, 5, and *Bru. Hipp.* 36d.

101. Aug. *Serm.* 319.7.7; 320-22. The *Mirc. Steph.,* which survived, reflects a later Christian culture; its accounts of the works of Stephen do not correspond to those in *Ciu.* 22.8.

102. Aug. *Serm.* 256.3; 330.1; *Psal.* 63.1.

103. On this festival, see Robin Margaret Jensen, "Dining with the Dead," in *Commemorating the Dead: Texts and Artifacts in Context: Studies of Roman, Jewish, and Christian Burials,* ed. Laurie Brink and Deborah A. Green (Berlin and New York: Walter de Gruyter, 2008), 137-41.

104. The two are clearly identified in Aug. *Serm. Dolb.* 2(359B).5.

105. *Act. Procon.* 2; Pont. *Vita Cypr.* 15. This is also found in the Donatist version of the text. A similar exercise had secured his election as bishop (*Vita Cypr.* 5).

106. Aug. *Serm. Denis* 11(308A); *Psal.* 32.2.1; 85.

been preached at this service as well.[107] These sermons at the place of death refer to the *Acta Proconsularia,* the Catholic account of Cyprian's trial and martyrdom, which was to be read aloud, along with the scriptures. In the afternoon of the same day, yet another service, which included a sermon, was held at the Mappalia, perhaps to commemorate the burial there.[108] On at least one occasion, Augustine preached in both the morning and the afternoon.[109]

These two shrines seem to have remained under the control of the Catholic Bishop of Carthage until the Vandal conquest. It may be presumed that an elaborate celebration was staged by the Donatist bishop either in his cathedral or in another pilgrimage church.[110] In the fourth century, the night vigil for Cyprian had been filled with eating and drinking, singing and dancing. Soon after his election as Bishop of Carthage, Aurelius moved to eliminate these practices in favor of a ceremony more appropriate to the saint's achievement. Opposition and near-riot greeted this reform, but his persistence overcame it.[111]

While still a presbyter, Augustine faced and dealt with a similar situation in Hippo, where Caecilianists and Donatists each held a rowdy festival for the burial day of Leontius, the Bishop of Hippo Regius at the time of the Diocletian persecution, who had built a basilica still in use in the fifth century.[112] In their public debate in Hippo in 392, Faustus the Manichee alerted Augustine to the ambiguity of the Christian practices traditionally involved in celebrating the festivals. The martyrs, he observed, had been substituted for the traditional gods, but the feasting and drinking remained exactly as they had always been in Roman practice.[113] Augustine avoided the question of excesses in the celebrations; he insisted that Christians had never identified the martyrs as gods: they were not offering divine honors to dead humans.[114] He understood the point, however, and he acted upon it. The feast of Leontius had been celebrated not only by the standard eucharist and sermon but by a dinner held in the church itself during the afternoon, with what Augustine described as abundant wine.

---

107. Aug. *Serm.* 309.4.6; *Serm. Denis* 14(313A); 15(313B); *Psal.* 32.2.2.

108. At Mappalia, Augustine preached sermons identified by internal references: *Serm.* 311.5.5; 313.5; *Serm. Guelf.* 26(313C).2. *Psal.* 86 may have been preached at this service, because *Psal.* 86.9 refers back to *Psal.* 85.23.

109. *Serm. Denis* 22(313F).1 indicates that it was preached in the afternoon, after a sermon which Augustine had preached in the morning.

110. A Donatist cathedral, the Theoprepia, is named in Aug. *Ep.* 139.1, in *Col. Carth.* 3.5, and in the title to *Psal.* 80, discovered by Adolf Primmer, "Die Mauriner-Handschriften der Enarrationes in Psalmos," in *Troisième centenaire de l'édition mauriste de saint Augustin: Communications présentées au colloque des 19 et 20 Avril 1990* (Paris: Institut d'études augustiniennes, 1990), 184.

111. Aug. *Ep.* 22; *Serm.* 311.5.5–6.6; *Serm. Dolb.* 2(359B).5; *Serm. Denis* 13(305A).4; *Psal.* 32.2.1.5.

112. Aug. *Serm.* 262.2.2. He provided no direct evidence that Leontius was a martyr, but his festival had been similarly observed by both Donatists and Caecilianists (*Ep.* 29.11).

113. Aug. *Faust.* 20.4.

114. Aug. *Faust.* 20.21.

After a preparatory preaching campaign lasting almost a week and some last-minute negotiations with objectors, Augustine convinced the community to forego the banquet in favor of an extended ceremony of readings and psalms, including a second sermon.

The pious Christians of Hippo objected to the change; they pointed out that their feast was the traditional practice and that similar celebrations continued at the shrine of St. Peter in Rome. Augustine defended his innovation by an explanation that apparently was accepted as true. When Christianity was freed from persecution by Constantine, many people who had delayed their commitment were willing to enter the church. They preferred, however, not to abandon the festivals associated with the traditional Roman worship. The bishops offered a compromise: they allowed certain excesses in food and drink in the celebration of the Christian martyrs in order to put an end to the practices of idolatry. Now, Augustine claimed in language similar to that he would use later to describe his own conversion, it was time for these excesses to stop. To the people's "Why now?" he responded "Why not now?"[115] He explained that because the shrine of Peter in Rome was somewhat distant from the church and residence of the bishop, he could not effectively control what happened there. Ambrose had been more successful in Milan.[116] After some discussion and grumbling, the congregants agreed and followed the new regimen with what Augustine claimed was enthusiasm. The Donatists down the street, he observed, could be heard trying Leontius's patience with their (pagan) revels while the Caecilianists delighted him with their psalms in the settling darkness.[117] Augustine later compared the joy of these celebrations to that expressed by the Israelites as they approached Jerusalem, singing the psalms of ascent.[118]

The changes initiated by Aurelius, Alypius, and Augustine were approved by their colleagues at the council of Carthage in 397: henceforth church buildings were to be used to feed only traveling clerics; the laity were to be prevented from using them for banquets whenever possible.[119]

Augustine returned to these points regularly in his preaching to make sure that his congregation was not confused about the object of its devotion — and would provide no foundation for future accusations of covert idolatry. Though the saints were commemorated by name in the eucharistic prayer and though the body of a particular martyr might be beneath the altar of the shrine, the offering was never made to the saints but only to God.[120] Christians realized,

---

115. Aug. *Ep.* 29.8, cf. *Conf.* 8.12.28. The whole incident is recorded in this letter to Alypius, who was attempting similar reforms in Thagaste, where he was bishop.

116. Aug. *Ep.* 29.9-10.

117. Aug. *Ep.* 29.11.

118. Aug. *Psal.* 121.2.

119. Aug. *Bru. Hipp.* 29.

120. Aug. *Serm.* 273.3, 6, 7; 318.1; *Serm. Dolb.* 26(198*).46-47. He made the same points in *Ciu.* 8.27.

---

he insisted, that all the benefits they received through the intercession of the martyrs were provided by and had to be attributed to God.[121] No one, moreover, would ever confuse a Christian martyr with a pagan deity: among the saints, any old woman was stronger than Juno, and any old man more powerful than Hercules.[122] When Rome was sacked by the Goths, he chided the traditionalists for complaining that the tombs of Peter and Paul had not protected their city. Had Peter given his life, he asked, to preserve the stones of Roman monuments?[123]

The objection raised by Faustus and the success of the explanation Augustine offered to the congregation in Hippo might provide clues that Christians regarded these celebrations of martyrs primarily as markers of cultural and religious identity rather than liturgies of praise and thanksgiving. This would help to explain the primacy of food and drink, the singing and dancing, and the reluctance to set aside these practices. Though Augustine always defended the Christian celebrations of the martyrs against attack, he continued to urge his congregation to avoid the behaviors that he considered an embarrassment to the church and gave, he judged, more joy to the unclean spirits than to the martyrs.[124]

## Purpose of the Cult

The approach that Augustine (and presumably his episcopal colleagues) took to the cult of the martyrs was not tolerance of practices they could not eradicate. He found much that was good and uplifting in the regular memorializing of the struggles and victories of the Christians who had suffered to establish the faith in Africa. He appreciated the reading out of the *passiones* and the *acta*. These accounts exhibited the power of God in human beings, even before the outbreak of the healing miracles that accompanied the arrival of the relics of Stephen.

The great achievements of the martyrs displayed the power of God perhaps even more effectively than the deeds of Christ himself.[125] Their patient endurance of suffering was not to be attributed to human effort; it was the work of Christ[126] and the Holy Spirit in the martyrs.[127] They witnessed not only to the power but also to the justice of God. Theirs was a spectacle more rivet-

---

121. Aug. *Ciu.* 22.10.

122. Aug. *Serm.* 273.6.

123. Aug. *Serm.* 296.6-9, 12.

124. Aug. *Serm.* 273.8; *Serm. Lamb.* 6(335D).1; *Serm. Denis* 13(305A).4; *Psal.* 59.15.

125. Aug. *Psal.* 59.15; *Serm. Denis* 13(305A).4.

126. Aug. *Eu. Io.* 47.11; *Serm.* 4.37; 94.2; 275.1; 276.1, 4; 329.2; 331.1.1; *Serm. Cail.* 1.47(277A).2; *Psal.* 141.5.

127. Aug. *Serm.* 68.13; 328; *Serm. Lamb.* 9(299F).2; *Psal.* 141.5.

ing than the shows and games; Christians could appreciate the beauty of justice amid the gore of torture, and they could discern the skill with which the martyrs' Spirit-inspired patience exasperated and defeated their human judges and demonic adversaries.[128] Indeed, by identifying the devil as the true enemy fomenting and guiding the assault, the Christian martyrs and their devotees could follow the example of Christ in forgiving and in praying for the conversion of their human tormenters.[129] The struggle between Bishop Cyprian and Proconsul Galerius Maximus, for example, had been for the allegiance of the people of Carthage. Augustine surmised that many of the original spectators at the execution had been converted, just like those Jews whose hearts were moved by the death of Christ (Luke 23:48). The martyr had indeed triumphed: descendants of the persons who had stood in that hostile crowd now gathered in the shrine at that same spot to honor Cyprian's witness and to confess the power of Christ.[130]

Christians owed and paid a debt of gratitude to the martyrs who had gone before them. They had symbolically thrown their bodies on the road by which Christ came to the nations; they had smoothed the way for those who came after them.[131] Christ's death had been the falling into the ground of a seed from which much grain would come; the martyrs then sowed that grain as new seed and watered it with their blood.[132] Everyone in the church, then, had the martyrs to thank for the faith having been planted and taken root in them.[133] Augustine found that Stephen amply demonstrated this process in his intercession for the forgiveness of those who were killing him.[134] As Stephen's prayer had won the conversion of Paul and many others, so had the prayers of those who followed him raised Christ among the nations[135] and brought an end to persecution through the conversion of their enemies.[136] The Christian people continued to seek the help and support of the demonstrably effective intercession of the martyrs,[137] already in heaven, where they continued to pray that God would correct and convert the enemies of the church.[138]

The proper celebration of the martyrs, Augustine explained, was to imitate their struggle and share their victory.[139] The most important gift that Christians

128. Aug. *Serm.* 51.1.2; 274; 275.2; *Serm. Denis* 14(313A).3; *Psal.* 64.8.

129. Citing Eph. 6:12; Aug. *Serm. Lamb.* 6(335D).3-4.

130. Aug. *Serm. Denis* 15(313B).2-4.

131. Aug. *Serm.* 280.6; 295.8.8; 318.3; 325.1.

132. Aug. *Serm.* 22.4; 116.7.7; 280.6; 286.5.3; 300.1; *Psal.* 40.1; 88.1.10; 140.20-21.

133. Aug. *Serm.* 280.6.

134. Aug. *Serm.* 317.5.5-6.5.

135. Aug. *Serm. Dolb.* 25(360B).19, 24; *Psal.* 43.22; 118.9.2-3.

136. Aug. *Psal.* 118.9.2-3.

137. Aug. *Serm.* 284.5; 285.5; 297.2.3; *Serm. Lamb.* 9(299F).4; *Serm. Dolb.* 18(306E).1.

138. This was the only interpretation of the prayer in Rev. 6:10 that Augustine could make compatible with Christ's prohibition of vengeance (*Psal.* 78.14).

139. Aug. *Serm.* 273.9; 302.1; 311.1.1; 317.1.1; 325.1; *Serm. Dolb.* 13(159A).1; *Psal.* 69.4.

were to seek when they prayed at the tomb-altars of the saints on earth was the strength to witness to Christ.[140] The crown of martyrdom, though won in secret during a time of peace with the empire, was no less a victory for the contemporary Christian. The conflict with the demonic forces need not always be a public spectacle. Christ had been victorious over the devil in the solitude of the desert. Had God not inspired the prophet Daniel to intervene on her behalf, Susanna would have won a private crown by her public condemnation rather than being praised for refusing to commit adultery to save her life.[141] Thus, Augustine urged, Christians could imitate the martyrs by resisting temptation every day;[142] they were persecuted, as Lot had been in Sodom, by the evil people among whom they lived.[143]

For the most part, Christians would suffer internally and spiritually rather than publicly in their bodies.[144] Even in peace time, however, some of their witness to Christ could be public or could result in bodily suffering and death. They could abandon earthly hope by selling their goods and distributing the proceeds to the poor.[145] They could imitate John the Baptist by speaking the truth, even when a powerful person threatened them with loss of life or property for refusing to lie under oath.[146] They could fight and overcome the demons even on their sickbeds. As their fever mounted and the physician's art failed, a servant or friend might approach them with some demonic charm that was guaranteed to overcome their illness and save their lives. If they refused the idolatry, the disease might bring them a martyr's death and crown just as surely as the executioner's sword would have in an earlier time.[147]

Going a step further, Augustine suggested that Christians could imitate Christ and Stephen by forgiving and praying for reconciliation with their enemies.[148] The bishops themselves provided an example for their people by interceding with the emperor for clemency whenever Donatists were to be punished for killing a Caecilianist cleric.[149] Augustine generally avoided claiming the title of martyr for those who suffered or even lost their lives at the hands of the Donatists. He detailed the attacks suffered and persons killed but did not accuse the Donatists — whom he hoped to bring into Catholic union — of doing Satan's own work.[150] A singular and quite restrained exception may have

140. Aug. *Ciu.* 8.27.
141. Aug. *Psal.* 90.1.2; *Serm.* 343.2.
142. Aug. *Serm.* 4.37; 328.
143. Aug. *Psal.* 69.2.
144. Aug. *Psal.* 69.9.
145. Aug. *Psal.* 49.8-10; 90.1.9.
146. Aug. *Serm. Cail.* 2.6(94A).2, 4; *Serm. Dolb.* 18(306E).11.
147. Aug. *Serm.* 286.8.7; 318.3; 328; *Serm. Dolb.* 18(306E).7-8. Augustine did not question the efficacy of the demons over bodily disease.
148. Aug. *Serm.* 304.4.3; 314.2; 317.1.1–2.2, 6.5.
149. Aug. *Ep.* 139.2.
150. Aug. *Cresc.* 3.42.46–43.47.

been an epitaph for a Donatist deacon who had been killed after he became Caecilianist. In the Latin original, the poem is an acrostic consisting of eight lines of hexameter, which spells out *diaconus*.

> Donatists' cruel attack killed him.
> In pious praise, Nabor's body is buried here.
> After he had been a Donatist for some time,
> Converted, he loved the peace for which he would die.
> Outstanding is the cause for which he is clothed in purple blood.
> Not in error did he perish; he did not kill himself in a fury.
> Unyielding in true piety, he proved himself a true martyr.
> Scan the first letter of each line to name his office.[151]

In his controversial works, Augustine consistently refused to follow the Donatist pattern of glorifying those who died in the sectarian conflict as martyrs, and vilifying thereby those responsible for their deaths. In this funerary setting, however, he was willing to recognize the witness of one who suffered for the unity of the church.

Christ had suffered not only to redeem but to provide an example that Christians follow (1 Pet. 2:21). The martyrs were not exceptional, Augustine insisted, but models for every Christian.[152]

## True and False Martyrs

In addition to guiding his congregation into the right and fruitful way of confessing their faith, Augustine had to face and respond to the claims that only the Donatist church realized the ideal of witness to Christ. The Donatists claimed to be continuing the fidelity of those Christians who had suffered in the third and fourth centuries. Their own resistance to the attempts of the Roman Empire to enforce the decisions of the ecclesiastical courts in Rome and the Council of Arles in 314 witnessed to their identity as the persecuted church.[153] They characterized the Caecilianists as apostates for accepting alleged traitors among their bishops and for collaborating in the persecution of the faithful (Donatist) Christians.[154]

As he had in dealing with the origins of the schism itself, Augustine re-

---

151. Donatistarum crudeli caede peremptum,/Infossum hic corpus pia est cum laude Nabori(s)./Ante aliquot tempus cum donatista fuisset,/Conversus pacem pro q(ua) moreretur amavit./Optima purpureo uestitus sanguine causa,/Non errore perit, non se ipse furore peremit./Verum martyrium uera est pietate probat(um)./Suspice litterulas primas, ibi nomen honoris (PLS 2:356-57).

152. Aug. *Serm.* 325.1.

153. Aug. *Parm.* 3.6.29.

154. Aug. *Coll.* 3.4.4; *Don.* 1.1, 23.39.

sponded by using the historical records of the conflict. He observed that the Donatist party had initiated the appeal for imperial judgment and support. Those who maintained the schism were only suffering the punishments and deprivations their predecessors had attempted to inflict upon Caecilian and his colleagues through the imperial power. Had the decisions of the courts and councils gone otherwise, they would have been rejoicing in the suffering of the Caecilianists.[155] So too of those who had resisted the attempts of Emperor Constans to effect reunion through the mission of Macarius and Paul in the 340s. He questioned the Donatist accounts of their century of suffering. Had the Roman envoys really ordered the execution of Marculus and of Donatus of Bagai by the uncharacteristic punishments of being thrown off a precipice and being thrown down a well?[156] Could the Circumcellions (who were organized by some Donatist bishops to terrorize any who opposed them) plausibly be honored as martyrs when they happened to die while enforcing Donatist discipline?[157]

Gradually, Augustine built an argument that defined true martyrdom by contrasting it with false. First, he insisted that suffering itself did not make a martyr. Evil people, he observed, often suffer far more pain than the good;[158] merchants endure great trials in their trading and pursuit of profit.[159] A standard based on suffering would identify all criminals punished by the magistrates as martyrs[160] and would fail to distinguish the unrepentant thief from his companions in crucifixion.[161] When the Donatist Circumcellions suffered for their criminal acts or brought death upon themselves, reportedly by throwing themselves off cliffs, they were following the devil's advice, as was clear from the temptation of Christ and the destruction of the herd of swine (Luke 4:9-12; 8:30-33). In killing themselves, they imitated not the endurance of the seven brothers and their mother recounted in Maccabees but the rashness of Razias.[162] Having failed to overcome the Christian martyrs, the devil had then attempted to pervert their witness by glorifying their suffering rather than their cause.[163]

Even a religious cause, however, might not make a person a true witness to Christ. The Donatist Circumcellions, Augustine claimed, had provoked the wrath of Roman traditionalists during their festivals not to attack their idols but

155. Aug. *Ep.* 89.3.

156. Aug. *Eu. Io.* 11.15. Augustine implied that he was a suicide: *Petil.* 2.14.32, 20.46, 88.195; *Cresc.* 3.49.54.

157. Aug. *Ep.* 88.8-9; 89.2-3; 105.2.5.

158. Aug. *Psal.* 68.1.9; *Serm.* 335.2; *Serm. Lamb.* 15(335G).

159. Aug. *Serm.* 331.6.5; 332.2.

160. Aug. *Parm.* 1.8.13; *Psal.* 34.2.1, 13.

161. Aug. *Serm.* 325.2; 331.2.2; 335.2; *Serm. Morin* 11(53A).13.

162. Aug. *Parm.* 3.6.29; *Petil.* 2.49.114, 71.160, 87.193; *Gaud.* 1.27.30, 31.36-38; *Serm. Guelf.* 28(313E).6.

163. Aug. *Serm. Dolb.* 2(359B).16-18.

only to bring about their own deaths.[164] The traditionalist idolaters were currently suffering because Christian emperors forbade their sacrifices and closed their temples; some of them had even died defending their statues from destruction. The demons themselves had been persecuted in the closing of those temples.[165] Surely, these could not be honored as martyrs, though the source of conflict was religious.

Indeed, Augustine argued that the bodily suffering itself was not essential to the witness of martyrdom. Perpetua, Lawrence, and Vincent were portrayed as feeling none of the pain their executioners attempted to inflict upon them.[166] Clearly, what God valued in true martyrdom was justice rather than pain.[167] Augustine insisted over and over that the cause gave honor and dignity to an act of witness: the martyr faced opposition for the sake of Christ, for justice, for truth.[168] In the opening line of Psalm 43, the Christians prayed that God would judge and distinguish their cause — not their suffering — from an unholy people.[169] In his preaching, then, he dwelled not on the bodily suffering of the martyrs — even when the *passio* was gory — but on their inspiring display of justice, their calm patience, and the frustration and fury their endurance obviously provoked in their persecutors.[170]

In response to the Donatist claim to be the true church because it bore witness to Christ by suffering at the hands of the Roman state, Augustine showed not only that its founding bishops had admitted betraying the gospel but that its members suffered for their own party spirit, and that its criminal and seditious activities brought down well-deserved punishments from the Roman courts. They should stake their claim to fidelity, he insisted, on the justice of their cause rather than on the sufferings consequent upon pursuing it.

## Burial *ad Sanctos*

In Africa, at least from the fourth century onward, the practice of burial close to the tomb of a martyr is well attested in the use and expansion of cemetery churches at the sites of martyrs' graves or shrines.[171] Among these are the Basil-

164. Aug. *Ep.* 185.3.12; *Serm. Guelf.* 28(313E).7.

165. Aug. *Parm.* 1.9.15–10.16.

166. Aug. *Serm.* 276.2; 280.4; *Serm. Cail.* 1.47(277A).2; *Eu. Io.* 27.12.

167. Aug. *Serm.* 285.2, 5.

168. Aug. *Serm.* 285.2; 306.2.2; 325.2; 327.1-2; 328.4.4; 328.8.6; 335.2; *Serm. Lamb.* 2(335C).5; 15(335G).2; *Serm. Morin* 14(306A); *Serm. Cail.* 2.6(94A).1; *Parm.* 1.9.15–10.16; *Petil.* 2.23.52; *Ep.* 89.2; 189.9.

169. Aug. *Ep.* 185.2.9; *Serm. Lamb.* 15(335G); the text is cited some 59 times in Augustine's writings.

170. Aug. *Serm.* 274; 275.1-2; 276.3; *Serm. Cail.* 1.47(277A).

171. The practice has already been discussed in the chapter on Christian buildings and monuments. See above, pp. 124-26, 113-17.

ica Maiorum in Carthage (the site of the shrine to Saints Perpetua and Felicity and their companions — figs. 20, 21) and the basilica known as St. Monica (figs. 22, 23), which may be the site of Cyprian's grave, known as the Mappalia Cypriani. In the Byzantine era, at least two other large pilgrimage churches were established, one outside the city walls at Bir Ftouha (fig. 28) and the other at Bir Messaouda, in the center of Carthage. Both of these basilicas were equipped with baptisteries and designed to allow crowds to move efficiently through the space. The subterranean rotunda at Damous el Karita also seems to have been a destination for pilgrims. Presumably, all three of these basilicas either had or acquired relics of a prominent saint. Bir Ftouha also became a popular place for the burial of the faithful, although it seems not to have been established in an existing cemetery — a fact that led some scholars to speculate that it might have been the site of Cyprian's martyrdom, the Mensa Cypriani.[172]

At the end of the third century, as was noted above, a matron named Pompeiana arranged to have the body of the martyr Maximilian buried near the tomb of Cyprian and herself buried close to him.[173] Late in the fourth century, Ambrose planned his own burial near the relics of Gervasius and Protasius in the cathedral of Milan.[174] When an African matron's son died while they were in Nola, she petitioned Bishop Paulinus for permission to bury him in the shrine of the martyr-bishop Felix. Paulinus was puzzled by the request and wrote to his friend Augustine for some explanation of the practice.

Paulinus's plea for help provided the opportunity for Augustine to sort out his understanding of the role of the martyrs in the salvation of the faithful.[175] He responded that physical proximity to the remains of a martyr brought no particular religious benefit. The living and the dead could communicate and assist one another only through prayer, to which almsgiving should be added.[176] However, burial near the shrine of a saint could be regarded as a prayer and a plea for the saint's intercession on behalf of the departed. The location of the burial also might remind the surviving relatives, as well as pilgrims to the shrine, to pray for divine mercy upon the deceased who were buried there.[177]

Thus, Augustine assimilated the practice of burial in a shrine to that of burial in or near an urban or cemetery church. The faithful might have been placing great value on physical proximity to the remains of the saint, thereby giving some indication that the African tradition of appealing to the martyrs for support in winning forgiveness for sins continued to guide the actions of the faithful. Augustine's denial of the efficacy of physical proximity shaped but did not deny that belief. He insisted that its real effect would be inspiring prayer

---

172. See the discussion above, pp. 139-40.
173. *Act. Max.* 3.4.
174. Though Augustine seems to have been unaware of this.
175. See the account of the delay in his response in Lancel, *Saint Augustine*, 464.
176. Aug. *Cur.* 4.6, 18.22.
177. Aug. *Cur.* 5.7, 18.22.

to God, which was the medium of communication between the living and the dead.[178]

Such a belief inevitably led to the translation of relics, thus creating new pilgrimage churches that might accommodate burial *ad sanctos*. Perhaps one of the most vivid examples of this is the basilica established by Bishop Melleus at Ammaedara (Haidra) in the late 560s, upon the receipt of relics of Cyprian (figs. 1, 2, 4). Within a brief time, the basilica had become the site of many burials, the tombs marked by simple stone inscriptions (cf. fig. 3).

## Miracles at the Shrines

When the Spanish presbyter Paul Orosius returned from Palestine to Africa in May 416,[179] he carried along a small portion of the relics of St. Stephen, whose tomb had just been found while Orosius was journeying there. He parceled out this precious dust among the bishops whom he visited, and they in turn shared it with their colleagues. Shrines to house these relics were quickly built, and, to everyone's surprise, miracles of healing began to occur.[180]

Augustine was no stranger to healing miracles. He had himself experienced God's relieving a toothache during his stay at Cassiciacum between his conversion and his baptism.[181] Upon his return to Carthage, he had witnessed the sudden cure, in response to prayer, of a friend facing a surgical procedure.[182] He had even associated cures with the relics of martyrs, having been present in Milan when the relics of Gervasius and Protasius, discovered by Ambrose, had publicly cured a blind man and thus identified themselves as belonging to martyrs.[183] The intercession of the same saints had been effective against demonic possession both in Milan and at a villa thirty miles outside of Hippo.[184] Augustine knew that certain saints could uncover false oaths and sent two members of his church community to Nola in the hope that its martyr-bishop Felix would disclose which of them was falsely accusing the other.[185]

The Donatists claimed — perhaps even before the arrival of Stephen's relics — that wondrous works had been performed by their leaders; Donatus's prayer

---

178. Tertullian had acknowledged but disputed the role of the saints: *Mart.* 1.6; *Pud.* 22.1-5. Cyprian limited their influence to the Judgment of Christ but did not dispute its efficacy: *Laps.* 17.

179. On Orosius's role, see Aug. *Ep.* 175.1; *Ep. Divj.* 19*.1.

180. The primary shrine was in Uzalis, presided over by Evodius; the shrine in Hippo was built through the good offices of Heraclius, who would be Augustine's successor (*Serm.* 356.7).

181. Aug. *Solil.* 1.12.21.

182. Aug. *Ciu.* 22.8; CCSL 48:816.

183. Aug. *Conf.* 9.7.16; *Ciu.* 22.8; CCSL 48:416; *Serm.* 286.5.4.

184. Aug. *Cur.* 21; *Ciu.* 22.8; CCSL 48:820.

185. Aug. *Ep.* 78.3.

had been answered by God's voice from heaven.[186] But Augustine warned his congregation to be cautious. Jesus had predicted that false prophets would arise to perform signs and wonders (Mark 13:22), and Simon Magus (Acts 8:11) had done so, just like the magicians of Pharaoh before him. Even the gods worshiped by the idolaters were credited with miracles.[187] Following the warning of Paul (1 Cor. 13:2) and the admonition of Christ (Luke 10:20), Christians should be more concerned to act charitably and to have their names written in heaven than to receive miraculous favors.[188]

When healings and even resuscitations of the dead began to be worked through the relics of Stephen, Augustine's attitude began to change. A brother and sister were cured at the shrine in Hippo — one of them during his sermon on the other — and he was fully won over. He made immediate provision for a full written account of these miracles.[189] He later reported that seventy such records had been collected at Hippo. The list was longer at Calama, and he urged Evodius to record those cures worked in Uzalis.[190] The result must have been a series of accounts similar to those he drew upon in the final book of *On the City of God*.[191]

Augustine's interest in publicizing the miracles of Stephen might have been something more than an expression of gratitude and encouragement of devotion. These wonders may have provided a significant weapon in the final stages of his unending struggle against the Donatists, who had been defeated in the Roman courts and gradually deprived of their churches by imperial agents but had retained the loyalty of many Christians in Africa. Stephen had been the first to shed his blood in confessing Christ; he was a martyr of the universal church whose *acta* were recorded in the canonical scriptures. That this martyr had added his support to the Caecilianist church in Africa could be neither discounted nor duplicated. Each miracle would indicate clearly the divine approbation and superior status of the Caecilianists, who remained in communion with the founding church in Jerusalem to which Stephen had belonged.

The outbreak of miracles in Africa, and particularly in Hippo, led Augustine to reflect further on these phenomena, which he had originally regarded as belonging primarily (if not exclusively) to the time of the church's initial spread beyond its Jewish roots.[192] He insisted that the dead were not directly aware of the vicissitudes of the living, just as the living could not know the joy or sorrow of the dead.[193] Instead, the martyrs interceded constantly for those to whom

---

186. Aug. *Eu. Io.* 13.17.
187. Aug. *Ciu.* 22.10.
188. Aug. *Eu. Io.* 13.17.
189. Aug. *Serm.* 319-22.
190. Aug. *Ciu.* 22.8.
191. Aug. *Ciu.* 22.8; and not to be confused with the fantastic stories of the *Mirc. Steph.*
192. See Lancel, *Saint Augustine*, 464-70.
193. See above, pp. 512-13.

they were joined in the body of Christ.[194] They prayed for all the living without knowing about particular individuals, just as the living prayed for all the dead.[195] The martyrs could intercede for a particular petitioner only when God made them aware of the person's need; they could warn in a dream[196] or heal at a shrine only when God chose them for that mission.

Augustine also considered the possibility that the saints were unaware of their being seen in dreams and visions, just as he could testify that he was unaware of having appeared to others who claimed visions in which he gave them advice.[197] Thus, Augustine worked to reverse the popular understanding of the process of intercession. Instead of the martyr petitioning God to grant a favor for a living person, the living must petition God to honor the martyrs by associating them in these works of mercy.[198]

Augustine's explanation of the indirect communication between the faithful and the martyrs, however, was hardly what the faithful believed and practiced. The accounts of appearances in dreams and visions, with prophecies and cures, as well as the cult of relics, all evince a continuing belief that the martyrs served as intercessors before Christ to win favors for individuals who prayed directly to them.[199] Augustine, however, was no more ready to credit the merits of the dead martyrs than the works of the living saints as the basis for divine gifts. Cures and other favors were the work of God; these were distributed gratuitously, like the spiritual gifts, for the good of the whole church.[200] The gifts of salvation and immortal life, in contrast, were promised to all who imitated the faith and fidelity of the martyrs.[201]

God did work cures, as Augustine knew, which had no connection to the martyrs, their relics, or their shrines. Yet God had revealed the locations of the bodies of some saints and worked miracles to identify them.[202] When further healings were granted at the memorials, they not only encouraged faith in Christ for whose confession these martyrs had suffered but also displayed the honor to which they had been raised, and confirmed that their dead flesh

194. They were symbolized by his bloody sweat in the garden (Aug. *Psal.* 85.1; 93.19; 140.4); he spoke as their voice in the cry of abandonment from the cross (Aug. *Ep.* 140.10.27, 13.35).

195. Aug. *Cur.* 16.20; *Psal.* 85.24.

196. Aug. *Serm.* 286.7.6.

197. Aug. *Cur.* 10.12–12.15. He did not, for example, contradict the story of his appearing to a sick person and directing him to the shrine of Stephen in Hippo (*Serm.* 322).

198. Aug. *Cur.* 5.7; 13.16–16.19; 18.22.

199. In *Serm.* 319.6.6–7.7, Augustine himself repeated a story from the books of miracles of Stephen which portrayed him as struggling to obtain a miracle from God for an unworthy petitioner, and in *Serm.* 324 of a distraught mother addressing the saint directly. On the latter, see above, p. 213. Augustine provided fuller evidence of these beliefs in *Cur.* 10.12; 13.16; 15.18–18.22, and in *Ciu.* 22.8.

200. Aug. *Cur.* 16.20.

201. Aug. *Serm.* 286.5.5.

202. Thus for Gervasius and Protasius, Vincent and Stephen (Aug. *Ciu.* 22.8; *Serm.* 275.3; 318.1).

would be resurrected to join their souls in immortal life.[203] God might even use the martyr as an instrument of that good work — as God sometimes used living humans or angels as agents.[204] The miracles, like the veneration of the faithful these encouraged, added nothing to the blessedness of the martyr, whose glory was already being enjoyed among the angels.[205] They were intended to build the faith of the living.

## Conclusion

In the early fifth century, the martyrs continued to be regarded as privileged dead, enjoying a status higher than that of others but still incomplete as they waited for Resurrection. Augustine's sermons on the feasts of martyrs and his reports of the miracles associated with the relics of St. Stephen give ample evidence that the faithful regarded the martyrs as intercessors who could either perform extraordinary deeds or win them as favors from God. Augustine did not challenge the practice of asking favors from the martyrs, and he celebrated the miracles that were granted at their memorials. He insisted, however, that the living and the dead could communicate only through God's intervention. The divine mercy had first to inform the martyr of the petition, and then God performed the great work being requested — sometimes through the agency of the martyr — for the benefit of the petitioner and the confirmation of the church's faith. This argument seems to have had little influence on the faithful's trust in the intercessory power of the martyrs.

## GENERAL OBSERVATIONS

### Correlation of Archeological and Literary Evidence

The martyrs became the common ancestors of Christians, whose festivals replaced those of the traditional Roman heroes and helped to establish community identity — even in the competition between Caecilianists and Donatists.

The practice of honoring the martyrs and of relying on their continuing good will toward the community of the living is well attested in the mosaic covers of their tombs. The so-called martyrs' chapel at Thabraca had several examples of individuals who may have been honored as martyrs, or at least particularly revered among the dead. Among these are Stercorius and Crescentina, who are described as having earned their crowns. Another, Crescentinus, is not

---

203. Aug. *Cur.* 16.20; *Serm.* 275.3; 277.3.3.
204. Aug. *Cur.* 20-21; *Ciu.* 22.9.
205. Aug. *Serm.* 277.1.1; 325.1.

---

specifically named as a martyr, but he is depicted as winning his race and described as a companion and friend of angels and martyrs (fig. 143). The inscription specifically asks him to pray for "us," as is his custom. Privata and Victoria are identified as consecrated virgins and confessors who carry their trophies of victory as they are inducted into the ranks of angels (fig. 144).

In Carthage and elsewhere in Africa, archeologists have identified basilicas outside the urban areas that seem to have been built in the fourth and following centuries to serve as shrines for the veneration of martyrs. Unlike the buildings used for regular congregational worship, these were designed to facilitate the circulation of large numbers of people. Some of these buildings are also equipped with pools that are significantly larger than the baptismal fonts found in the urban churches (e.g., Bir Messaouda, Siagu, and Bir Ftouha; fig. 28). The surviving literary record has yielded no explanation of the ritual use of these facilities. It may be that people sought to be baptized at the site of a saint's tomb or relics, just as they sought to be buried near them.[206]

The practice of burying the faithful near the tombs of martyrs is attested in the archeological evidence, the *acta* of Maximilian, and in Augustine's treatise *On Care for the Dead*. It grew into the practice of building basilicas in the cemeteries in which the special dead could be placed, both to draw pilgrims and to symbolize the congregation of the dead awaiting Resurrection.

The inscriptions on memorials for the martyrs and the celebrations of their anniversaries indicate that they were primarily honored for their victories rather than sought as benefactors providing favors. These celebrations were essential markers in the formation of a new civilization which refused, even after its emancipation, to identify itself with the glories of the Roman Empire.

## Correlation of Theology and Practice

### ROLE OF THE MARTYRS

The early cult of the martyrs in Africa was characterized by a reliance on their intercessory influence to win favors from God and Christ — particularly the forgiveness of sins. Tertullian strongly objected to practices that relied on the achievements of the martyrs and confessors to win concessions for those who had failed to meet Christian moral standards. In this, he clearly worked against the custom in which penitents used a confessor's letter of peace to regain access to the communion of the church.

206. See Robin Margaret Jensen, "Baptismal Practices at North African Martyrs' Shrines," in *Ablution, Initiation, and Baptism: Late Antiquity, Early Judaism, and Early Christianity = Waschungen, Initiation und Taufe: Spätantike, Frühes Judentum und Frühes Christentum,* ed. David Hellholm, 3 vols. (Berlin and New York: Walter de Gruyter, 2010), 1673-95.

Cyprian recognized the intercessory power of the martyrs for the forgiveness of sin, but he worked to limit their influence in the church on earth. They would serve as advisers to the judging Christ and could then intercede for penitents who had been reconciled and readmitted to the communion of the church. In the face of a schism that relied on the authority of the martyrs to question the governance of bishops, Cyprian discounted their status.

Cyprian seems to have been successful in wresting from the martyrs the authority to determine who should and should not be allowed into the communion of the church. The practice of burial *ad sanctos* indicates, however, that they were still sought as intercessors before the tribunal of Christ.

Christians in Augustine's time believed that the martyrs could intercede to win favors for them. The arrival of the relics of Stephen and the healing miracles that accompanied the spread of his cult firmly established this role for martyrs. Other than the healing miracles, the benefits sought from the martyrs in this period are not well attested. Augustine's writings assign them no role in the penitential process; though the need for forgiveness had expanded during the fourth century, so had the availability of reconciliation after major sins. Yet the practice of calling upon the martyrs clearly continued. Augustine labored to explain that God had to direct the petition to the saint and that God had to use the saint to fulfill it. The dead were otherwise unaware of the triumphs and travails of the living, and they were joined to the living only by the sharing of charity among the members of the body of Christ. Augustine refused to credit the martyrs as mediators, though he recognized it as popular belief.

### TRUE AND FALSE MARTYRDOM

The problem of distinguishing true from false martyrs can be documented in Africa no later than the time of Cyprian, who insisted that only those joined to the unity of the one church were true martyrs. In the fourth and fifth centuries, it was a problem for both Caecilianists and Donatists. The imperial attempts to force unity upon the African church resulted in deaths that one or another party, and sometimes both, refused to recognize as true witnesses to Christ. Voluntary martyrdom, by suicide or by provoking pagans, was denounced by the Caecilianists and apparently ignored by embarrassed Donatists. Martyrdom accounts themselves became propaganda pieces by which the conflict between the parties was pursued. Each party had to develop criteria for which martyrs would be recognized and venerated: unity on the one side and rejection of apostasy on the other became touchstones of fidelity.

Into the fourth century, Christian celebrations for the victory of the martyrs over the demonic powers who inspired and guided the Roman Empire were expressions of faith. Tertullian's defiant "Blood is the seed of Christians" was a classic assertion of the eschatological faith he shared.[207] The *acta* that contrasted the martyrs' calm patience — and sometimes even protection from bodily pain — to the frustration and fury of their oppressors were similarly intended to demonstrate this victory. Once Constantine and Licinius had liberated Christianity and Theodosius and his sons had established its orthodox form, a very different triumph could be attributed to the martyrs. Their blood had not only been the seed sown to spread Christianity over the earth; it had actually broken the power of the demons over the imperial government, which was now in Christian hands. Fifth-century Christians were exhorted to demonstrate their gratitude to the martyrs not only for their faith but for the civil peace and protection they enjoyed. Even in Augustine's day, the ambiguity of that particular victory was becoming evident. His *On the City of God* clearly distinguished the heavenly kingdom from any earthly regime.

## ADAPTATION OF THE MEANING OF WITNESS TO CHRIST

Cyprian initiated an important change when he insisted, after the Decian persecution, that all the faithful who had let the deadline for compliance pass had confessed Christ and stood fast in their faith. He later identified risking one's life in voluntary exile or in care of the dying during plague as a witness to Christ that could bring the same immediate reward.

After the toleration and establishment of Christianity, Augustine continued this reinterpretation of martyrdom by identifying other ways in which Christians could witness to Christ. Refusing a demonic cure or a powerful person's demand for false testimony could cost a faithful Christian's life. Forgiving oppressors and praying for their conversion and salvation could be no less difficult a witness. The best way to venerate the martyrs, Augustine urged, was to follow their example in a new — but no less challenging — world. In the century of Vandal rule that followed, many Christians would have the opportunity to follow that example quite literally.

207. Tert. *Apol.* 50.13.

# CHAPTER 12

# Pious Practices of Christian Living

........................................................................................................................

## INTRODUCTION

Each of the four practices considered in this chapter has been touched upon
in the preceding studies. Prayer, fasting, and almsgiving were forms of piety
which Christians inherited from Jewish piety. They required no justification
but only specification in the new culture and integration with the perspectives
peculiar to Christianity. African Christianity never granted the high status to
rigorous ascetic practices that the churches in Egypt and Syria, for example, accorded them. Augustine's discussion of the role of asceticism in the *Confessions*[1]
was unusual in African Christian literature. Yet these three forms of practice
were integral to Christian life and the celebration of the sacraments. Baptism
was preceded by an extended period of fasting and eucharist by a short one.
Almsgiving was integral to maintaining the unity of the church and winning the
forgiveness of sins. Prayer, both private and communal, was a daily and constitutive practice of Christian life.

The fourth practice, confessing Christ or martyrdom, is here studied because it changed so radically over the centuries under consideration. In the second and third centuries, Christian exclusivism was challenged daily by pervasive idolatry. By the fourth, idolatry was on the wane, but the diabolical enemy
had entered the church, to foment schism and conflict among Christians. In the
fifth century, however, even once the public rituals of idolatry were forbidden
and dying out, Augustine was able to discern the cult of false gods in less con-
spicuous private practices.

1. Aug. *Conf.* 10.

The prayer that is the focus of this section was a private exercise of piety outside the eucharistic liturgy of the community. It might have been practiced in a congregational service, in a small group, or even individually.

## Tertullian

Tertullian understood both communal and private prayer as the Christian form of sacrifice that had replaced the offering rituals of Israelite religion.[2] On this understanding, he was prepared to specify the proper procedures for prayer. The principal Christian prayer, which set the pattern for all other forms, was the prayer given by Jesus himself. Thus the heart of Tertullian's treatise on the subject was an explanation of the text of the Lord's Prayer, followed by prescriptions and recommendations for using it.

Tertullian explained that personal prayer should be offered at least three times each day, though he recommended that it be practiced even more often.[3] The first prayer of the day was offered upon rising at daybreak.[4] It was then repeated during the day, at the third, sixth, and ninth hours, times related to the coming of the Holy Spirit at Pentecost, the prayer of Peter at Joppa, and the prayer of the disciples in the temple.[5] The day was closed with an offering of this prayer before retiring.[6] These prayers might have involved the entire household.[7] The set times were supplemented by prayers that marked the beginning and end of the day's activities. One should pray before eating or going into the bath, when greeting a friend, upon entering or departing a house.[8] In addition to this oral prayer, Christians traced the sign of the cross on their foreheads.[9] They were urged to perform this ritual at every change of activity: when coming and going, when dressing and putting on shoes, when bathing, when at table, when lighting the lamps.[10] Before retiring, they signed both themselves and the bed.[11] Tertullian noted that they used the sign of the cross and an oath to cure the bite of a scorpion.[12]

2. Tert. *Apol.* 30.6; *Marc.* 4.1.

3. Tert. *Or.* 25.

4. *Or.* 23.3, 25.

5. Tert. *Or.* 25; *Ieiun.* 10.

6. Tert. *Or.* 25.5.

7. Tert. *Or.* 18.6, when the kiss of peace could be deferred because the household knew of the fast. Similarly, *Cast.* 7.3 dealt with the offering that was performed in the absence of clergy.

8. Tert. *Or.* 25.6–26.1.

9. Tert. *Apol.* 21.2; *Marc.* 3.22.5-6.

10. Tert. *Cor.* 3.4.

11. Tert. *Ux.* 2.5.14.

12. Tert. *Scorp.* 1.3. They also smeared the insect's body on their heel. Tertullian linked the efficacy to Paul's encounter with the viper in Acts 28:3.

In addition to the prayers and rituals performed every day, Tertullian also referred to the special prayers that characterized fast days.[13] The fast was always ended with prayer, whether at three in the afternoon or later in the day.[14] He also referred to vigils — prayers offered during the night — and to gatherings of the faithful after dark, though he did not specify the practices.[15]

In private, Christians seem to have prayed on their knees rather than standing, or so Tertullian recommended. At least the first prayer of every day and all the prayers on a fast day were to be performed kneeling. On Sundays and during the entire period from Easter to Pentecost, however, Christians always prayed standing. Some had begun to stand on Saturday as well, though Tertullian considered this inadequately supported by scripture and a source of dissension within the church.[16] During prayer, the arms were to be extended and the hands uplifted (see figs. 120, 130, 131, 134, 135, 137, 139, 140).[17] Men were to pray with their heads uncovered.[18] Women ought to follow the apostolic precept of covering their heads, even in private prayer.[19] Tertullian found no reason for Christians to wash their hands before prayer, since their whole bodies had been made ritually and morally pure in the once-for-all washing of baptism.[20] Hands were washed between the meal and the prayer segments of the Lord's Banquet, the *agapē*, probably because they were dirty.[21] Whenever a group of Christians were praying together, he recommended that they should end with the kiss of peace, which sealed their prayer.[22]

Christians practiced prayer differently than the traditional polytheists. They need not remove their cloaks, or sit down after praying. They should not spread their arms ostentatiously to get God's attention or shout out long and elaborate petitions to move God to generosity.[23] By praying in secret, Christians confessed that God saw and heard everything. They prayed to one God alone, who gave all blessings. They were restrained in words because God already knew and would provide everything that they needed.[24] Indeed, the Lord's Prayer itself contained all that a Christian needed to present to God,[25] though they were free to make more specific requests.[26] Such petitions should

13. Tert. *Or.* 23.4, 29.3. These were referred to as "stational" days.
14. Tert. *Ieiun.* 10.13.
15. Tert. *Or.* 29.3; *Ux.* 2.4.2. The *nocturna conuocatio* was distinguished in his text from the *conuiuium dominicum.*
16. Tert. *Or.* 23.1-4.
17. Tert. *Or.* 14; *Apol.* 30.4; *An.* 51.6.
18. Tert. *Apol.* 30.4.
19. Tert. *Or.* 21-22.
20. Tert. *Or.* 13.1.
21. Tert. *Apol.* 39.18.
22. Tert. *Or.* 18.1-5.
23. Tert. *Or.* 15-17.
24. Tert. *Or.* 1.4-6.
25. Tert. *Or.* 1.6.
26. Tert. *Or.* 10.

be made for everyone, even their enemies, persecutors, and calumniators, that they might receive God's mercy and that God's name might be sanctified in them.[27] Christians might pray for the necessities of life — food and clothing — but not for superfluities.[28] In particular, they regularly prayed for a deceased spouse, with whom they could hope to be reunited in the Resurrection.[29]

Tertullian was of two minds about praying for the coming of the end-time. In the *Apology,* he claimed that Christians prayed for a quiet life, the good of the empire, and the delay of the troubles which would accompany the end.[30] In his exposition of the Lord's Prayer, however, he criticized those who prayed for a continuation of the present order and thus a delay in the coming of the Kingdom of God. They should prefer reigning sooner to serving longer.[31]

In guiding prayer, Tertullian advised his fellow Christians to be more concerned with spiritual than temporal benefits. They should seek strength and endurance rather than deliverance from the troubles of this age.[32]

## Cyprian

Cyprian's treatise *On the Lord's Prayer* was inspired and guided by that of Tertullian. He repeated, with some elaboration, the specifications of the times of day at which a Christian should pray. The morning and evening prayer, for example, were linked to the Resurrection and the hope for the coming of Christ, whose light would continue unending. The prayer at the ninth hour was occasioned by the death of Jesus rather than the Apostles' practice of going to the temple at that hour.[33] He recommended prayer in secret, in a low rather than a loud voice.[34] He referred more regularly to the keeping of vigils but provided no more details of the practice than Tertullian had.[35] Christians were to pray not only for one another but for their enemies, that they might receive the grace of God and be converted.[36]

Because of the divisions in the church preceding, during, and after the Decian persecution, Cyprian insisted on unanimity in prayer. The persecution had been brought on by the refusal of some to join in praying for the good of others.[37]

---

27. Tert. *Or.* 3.4; *Apol.* 31.2; *Pat.* 6.5; *Marc.* 4.16.1.
28. Tert. *Or.* 6.1, 4.
29. Tert. *Cast.* 11.1-2; *Mon.* 10.23, 11.8.
30. Tert. *Apol.* 32.1.
31. Tert. *Or.* 5.1.
32. Tert. *Or.* 29.
33. Cypr. *Dom. orat.* 34.
34. Cypr. *Dom. orat.* 4.
35. Cypr. *Dom. orat.* 29; *Ep.* 11.5.1.
36. Cypr. *Dom. orat.* 17; *Zel. et liu.* 15.
37. Cypr. *Ep.* 11.3.1.

God would deliver the community only if all were to pray with one heart for the good of everyone.[38] During the schisms after the persecution, he insisted that only unanimous prayer would be effective.[39] In anticipation of a renewal of persecution, he urged prayer for the whole church.[40] In the Lord's Prayer, he observed, Christ taught his disciples to pray together in the plural rather than the singular, saying not "My Father" and "give me," but "Our Father" and "give us."[41]

Faced with the massive failure of Christians during the Decian persecution, Cyprian insisted that the fallen must beseech Christ for the forgiveness of their sin and the strength to stand fast in the future.[42] Even those who had been preserved from such major failings, however, must pray daily for the forgiveness of their sins of negligence.[43]

Cyprian also urged that fasting and almsgiving would make prayer effective,[44] especially in time of persecution.[45] Fasting, in particular, drew the soul away from the distractions of earthly pleasures so that the person would sustain the pleading for deliverance.[46]

Finally, Cyprian's community had suffered persecution and anticipated its renewal; he did not recommend prayer for the delay of the end-time. Instead, he noted that the Lord's Prayer specified the needs of the present day and not those of the morrow. Christians should not anticipate being long in the world.[47]

The peculiar emphases of Cyprian's recommendations for Christian prayer can be understood as a response to the reality and threat of persecution, the failure to resist it, and the resulting divisions among Christians. Thus he insisted on the unanimity of the community as it stood before God in prayer.

## Augustine

In the *Confessions,* Augustine described a particular type of prayer that proceeded by tracking the intelligibility and beauty found in sensible realities back through the human mind to the intelligible light by which they were understood, and thence to the divine reality that was their source. He demonstrated that this form of prayer could be intermittent at best because of the conflicting loves of fallen humans; he concluded that one had to proceed to God by a more

38. Cypr. *Ep.* 11.2.2, 7.3.
39. Cypr. *Unit. eccl.* 12, 13, 25.
40. Cypr. *Ep.* 60.5.2.
41. Cypr. *Dom. orat.* 8.
42. Cypr. *Laps.* 35.
43. Cypr. *Dom. orat.* 22; adding fasting and almsgiving to their prayer (*Eleem.* 4).
44. Cypr. *Dom. orat.* 32-33; *Mort.* 10.
45. Cypr. *Ep.* 11.1.1; 60.5.1.
46. Cypr. *Ep.* 11.6.2.
47. Cypr. *Dom. orat.* 19-21.

humble route, led by the Incarnate Word.[48] He later recounted a similar ascent in conversation with his mother at Ostia shortly before her death.[49] Then in reflection on his life as a Christian, he described the way in which he continued to practice such prayer.[50] Contemplative prayer, Augustine certainly realized, was unusual among the Christians to whom he ministered. When he wished to intimate to them the experience of heaven, he turned not to this intelligible light but to the spoken Word of God, on which they would be fed. Heaven would be somewhat like their being in church, he suggested, away from their daily work, listening to the scripture read and expounded.[51] Augustine explained prayer to his congregants and warned them against deviations from right practice.

The closest Augustinian parallels to the discussions of the forms of Christian prayer that are to be found in Tertullian's *On Prayer* and Cyprian's *On the Lord's Prayer* are in his *On the Lord's Sermon on the Mount* and the surviving sermons to the catechumens about the Lord's Prayer.[52] He focused on the meaning of the petitions and on the realities that might properly be asked of God rather than on the appropriate times and positions for prayer. These details of fifth-century practice can be discovered only in asides, during other expositions and arguments.

Augustine did specify that Christians prayed in the early morning and said the Lord's Prayer many times during the day.[53] Christians seem to have prayed standing, for the most part, and were urged to face the east.[54] The prayer with which Augustine regularly ended his sermons began with "Turning to the Lord," and the entire congregation may have turned toward the east, with their backs to the preacher, for this.[55] Augustine explained that since God was present everywhere, such turning had a symbolic meaning. As the human body faced the greater heavenly body, the sun, so the mind should be directed to the greater nature, God. If some in the congregation imagined God living in the eastern heavens, that was at least better than thinking that God lived on earth.[56] Praying in secret was not considered particularly important: Augustine interpreted Christ's injunction in Matthew (6:6) figuratively as a warning not to seek praise from human beings by ostentatious forms of prayer.[57]

The sign of the cross had been traced on the forehead of each Christian at the beginning of the catechumenate.[58] Although the sign was never referred to

---

48. Aug. *Conf.* 7.10.16–20.26.
49. Aug. *Conf.* 9.10.23-24.
50. Aug. *Conf.* 10.40.65.
51. Aug. *Serm.* 104.4, 7.
52. Aug. *Serm. Dom.* 2.4.15–11.39; *Serm.* 56-59.
53. Aug. *Psal.* 118.29.4; *Serm. Dom.* 2.7.26.
54. Aug. *Serm.* 333.2.
55. See Serge Lancel, *Saint Augustine,* trans. Antonia Neville (London: SCM Press, 2002), 240, using *Serm. Dolb.* 19(130A).12. This interpretation is highly speculative.
56. Aug. *Serm. Dom.* 2.5.18.
57. Aug. *Serm. Dom.* 2.3.11.
58. Aug. *Serm.* 160.6; 215.5; 302.3; 342.1; *Serm. Casin.* 2.114-15(97A).3; *Serm. Denis* 17(301A).8.

as visible on the face, Christians seem to have been acutely aware of its invisible presence and to have marked it regularly with a finger.[59] When frightened, they quickly traced it to claim divine protection.[60] In certain circumstances, Augustine suggested, that sign would be a confession of faith;[61] but it could not substitute for a more public signal of Christian commitment.[62]

In Augustine's view, the intention of the heart was the essence of prayer. Desire to pray could itself fulfill Paul's exhortation to pray continuously (1 Thess. 5:17).[63] The words and set formulae of prayers could recall to mind the thoughts that the Christian should present to God.[64] They also served to open the heart and prepare a person to receive the spiritual gifts being sought.[65] In *Confessions,* he gave eloquent testimony to the power of the chanting of Psalms to lift his own mind to God,[66] and his sermons taught the congregation how to pray these texts as members of Christ.[67]

All the things a Christian should ask of God were laid out, Augustine taught the catechumens, in the Lord's Prayer.[68] The divine gifts were primarily spiritual, particularly eternal life itself, because these remained and did not fail.[69] In interpreting the petition for daily bread, Augustine observed that it referred not primarily to the eucharist but to spiritual sustenance provided by the Word of God. The eastern church did not communicate every day, he explained, and they could not have ignored or violated a clear and explicit command of the Lord.[70] But when preaching to catechumens in Hippo, he preferred the eucharistic meaning, while acknowledging the alternative.[71] Observing that Christians were not spared the troubles of earthly life, he concluded that the petition for deliverance and escape from temptation must refer to the divine gifts of strength and endurance. Christ had indicated this meaning by praying that the faith of the Apostles be confirmed (John 17). He rejected a Pelagian interpretation that the petition's objective was being spared from the bodily accidents that a person could not prevent by foresight and prudence.[72]

59. Aug. *Psal.* 48.2.2; 59.9; 73.6; 85.13; 91.7; 141.9; *Serm.* 32.13.

60. Aug. *Psal.* 50.1.

61. Aug. *Psal.* 68.1.12.

62. Aug. *Serm. Denis* 17(301A).7. The catechumen excused his attendance at the theater on the grounds that he was not yet baptized; Augustine noted that he took into that place the forehead bearing the sign of Christ.

63. Aug. *Psal.* 37.14.

64. Aug. *Serm. Dom.* 2.3.13.

65. Aug. *Serm. Dom.* 2.3.14; *Serm.* 56.3.4.

66. Aug. *Conf.* 10.33.49-50.

67. For example, Aug. *Psal.* 85.1; 140.3.

68. Aug. *Serm.* 56.3.4.

69. Aug. *Serm. Dom.* 2.3.14, 7.25; *Psal.* 144.21; *Serm.* 80.7; *Serm. Morin* 16(77B).1.

70. Aug. *Serm. Dom.* 2.7.26.

71. Aug. *Serm.* 56.6.9; 57.7.7; 58.4.5; 59.3.6. See *Serm.* 58.4.5 for the word of God meaning eucharist.

72. Aug. *Serm. Dolb.* 30(348A).1-2.

Still, Augustine did not insist that the Lord's Prayer referred only to spiritual benefits; he allowed petitions for the transitory goods of earthly life.[73] Christians prayed for such things as food and drink, clothing and housing, rain for crops, health for themselves and their neighbors.[74] Such prayer recognized that these needs were supplied by God and that they must not be sought from the demons.[75] Earthly goods were to be asked for in moderation, since God knew individual needs and should be trusted to supply what was necessary.[76] Even transitory goods, however, were to be petitioned with the name of Christ and for the sake of the Kingdom of Heaven, as supports for salvation.[77] Riches and superfluities must not be sought from God, therefore, since no one was called to follow Christ for the sake of these pleasures and advantages.[78] In fact, God bestowed them on the most disreputable and base people precisely to show that they were of no real and lasting value.[79]

Christians were forbidden, Augustine insisted, to pray that God take vengeance on sinners and on their own enemies in particular.[80] This prohibition required some careful scriptural interpretation. The prophets might seem to have been calling down divine punishments when they were only foretelling and warning what God was about to do; they were not wishing harm on anyone.[81] Similarly, the martyrs crying out from beneath the heavenly altar (Rev. 6:10) were pleading for an end to the dominion of sin, under which they had suffered, rather than asking for divine retribution on their persecutors.[82] God had avenged neither Christ nor Stephen nor the other martyrs. Instead, time was being allotted for the conversion of sinners.[83] Christians must not, then, ask God to bring harm upon their enemies. The Christian banging his head on the floor of the church as he demanded that God kill a particular evil man had best be careful, he observed, lest God start by slaying the wicked petitioner himself.[84] To praise God for the misfortune that befell another was, in effect, to make God a collaborator in one's own hatred.[85] Christians were to pray for the conversion rather than the punishment of their enemies.[86] If Christ himself seemed beyond imitation, let them take as their model Stephen, who prayed for

---

73. Aug. *Serm. Morin* 16(77B).2-3.
74. Aug. *Serm.* 58.4.5; 57.7.7; *Serm. Morin* 16(77B).2.
75. Aug. *Serm.* 56.2.2.
76. Aug. *Serm.* 80.7; 354.7.7; *Serm. Wilm.* 12(61A).3-6.
77. Aug. *Serm. Dolb.* 28(20B).3.
78. Aug. *Serm.* 302.2-5.
79. Aug. *Serm. Lamb.* 1(105A).1-2.
80. Aug. *Serm.* 211.6.
81. Aug. *Serm. Dom.* 1.21.72; *Serm.* 56.3.3.
82. Aug. *Serm. Dom.* 1.22.77.
83. Aug. *Serm.* 58.7.8.
84. Aug. *Serm.* 382.5.
85. Aug. *Psal.* 39.4.
86. Aug. *Serm.* 56.10.14–11.15.

those who harmed him, or Paul, who had ordered prayers even for persecuting kings (1 Tim. 2:1-4).[87] They might hate the sin, but they must love and seek only good for the sinful person.[88]

Following in the tradition well evidenced in the writings of Tertullian and Cyprian, Augustine insisted that Christians were sinners who must pray daily for forgiveness.[89] Thus he repudiated the statement of the Jewish leaders in John (9:31), to the effect that God does not hear the prayer of sinners — a text that Cyprian had applied to unworthy and schismatic bishops.[90] Scripture testified in multiple places that God does hear the prayer of sinners,[91] most notably the plea of the publican (Luke 18:9-14).[92] Indeed, the very prayer which Christ gave his followers proved that all who prayed it were sinners by including a petition for forgiveness.[93]

Augustine warned that Christians should assign no particular significance to God's answering their specific requests. Paul had been told that he would not be liberated from the trouble he was suffering (2 Cor. 12:7) — which Augustine thought might have been a bad headache.[94] In contrast, Satan was immediately granted permission to test Job,[95] and the demons were allowed to enter the swine.[96] God sometimes delayed answering the saints, as Christ did with the Canaanite woman (Matt. 15:21-28), in order to build their desire for the good they sought and thereby open their hearts to receive it.[97] In contrast, God sometimes granted the petitions of sinners,[98] or turned them over to the desires of their hearts, so that they might eventually grow weary and repent.[99] Augustine's teaching on prayer expanded that of Tertullian and Cyprian primarily by focusing on the spiritual goods which the Christian must seek from God.

Reciting the Psalms was a major form of Christian liturgical and private prayer. Augustine reflected on the way they were to be understood and prayed. The Psalms, like the whole of scripture, referred to Christ in three different ways: as the eternal Son of God, as the human son of Mary and head of the church,[100] and as the whole Christ including both head and members.[101] Ev-

---

87. Aug. *Serm.* 149.16.17.

88. Aug. *Psal.* 138.27-28.

89. Aug. *Serm.* 58.9.10; 59.4.7; 351.1.1–4.7; 352.2.7; *Psal.* 140.18.

90. Cypr. *Ep.* 65.2.2; 67.2.2; 70.2.3.

91. Aug. *Serm.* 135.5.6-7.8; 136.2; *Serm. Mai* 130(136A).2.

92. Aug. *Serm. Lamb.* 10(136B).2; 11(136C).4.

93. Aug. *Serm.* 135.6.7–7.8.

94. Aug. *Serm. Morin* 15(306C).7; *Serm. Dolb.* 28(20B).12.

95. Aug. *Serm. Dolb.* 28(20B).6.

96. Aug. *Serm. Morin* 15(306C).7; 16(77B).4.

97. Aug. *Serm.* 77.1.1; 61.4.5–5.6; 80.2; *Serm. Guelf.* 33(77A).1; *Serm. Morin* 16(77B).1.

98. Aug. *Serm.* 354.7.7.

99. Aug. *Serm. Dolb.* 28(20B).6.

100. The fear he expressed before his Passion did refer to his own humanity, but as head of the church, as he took on the feelings of his members (Aug. *Psal.* 31.2.26; 40.6; 42.7).

101. Aug. *Serm.* 341.1.1–3.3, 9.11; *Psal.* 37.6, 27; 39.5; 40.1; 56.1; 58.1.2.

---

ery statement and petition was either of or about Christ. This was illustrated in the attribution of Psalm 21 (22) to the dying Christ in the Gospels (Mark 15:34; Matt. 27:46).[102] Some of the prayers in the Psalms, such as those asking for forgiveness, could be attributed to Christ only in unity with his body, the church.[103] As Christ prayed the Psalms with the church, so the church prayed them with Christ.[104] Christ himself could speak both as head and as one with the members of his body; the members could speak as a body identified with their head, but not in the person of the head.[105] This principle was extended to the entire psalter, including the statements of Christ as divine and as son of Mary, not just to the prayers Christ could offer only with his body. Augustine's explanation of the praying of the Psalms finds no parallel in the work of Tertullian and Cyprian. It would help shape a long and illustrious practice of communal prayer.

Augustine's writings provide additional information and instruction on community prayer that was not directly associated with the celebration of the eucharist. As has already been seen in detail, the program of the reform of the celebration of the feasts of the saints brought a service of readings, psalms, preaching, and hymns in place of the banquets that had been offered in the churches.[106] While still a presbyter, Augustine introduced the change in Hippo for the feast of St. Leontius, the martyr-bishop of that city. Aurelius of Carthage supported the program,[107] and a late-fourth-century episcopal council forbade all banqueting by the clergy in church buildings, except to feed travelers, and urged that the congregations be restrained from doing so as much as possible.[108] Change in the celebration of the martyrdom of Cyprian in Carthage was even more dramatic. The Basilica Mappalia had been built at the tomb of Cyprian and was the site of a traditional all-night vigil, filled with singing, dancing, and drinking. It was replaced by a service of readings, psalms, and preaching.[109] Augustine preached at this service on a number of occasions, and again the next day at the eucharistic offering in the basilica called the Mensa Cypriani, where the great bishop had been executed.[110]

102. Aug. *Psal.* 34.2.5.
103. In some instances, such as the confession of sins and the complaint of Paul's persecution (Acts 9:4-5), Christ speaks as identified with his members: Aug. *Serm.* 345.4; *Psal.* 37.6; 90.2.5; 101.1.2; 123.1.
104. Aug. *Psal.* 85.1; 140.3; 118.32.1; 122.2; 130.1.
105. Aug. *Psal.* 142.3.
106. Aug. *Ep.* 29.10-11 describes the ritual for the feast of Leontius, the first Bishop of Hippo. See above, pp. 536-38.
107. In *Ep.* 22 to Aurelius, Augustine sought his leadership.
108. *Bru. Hipp.* 29.
109. Aug. *Serm.* 311.5.5–6.6; *Serm. Denis* 14(313A); *Psal.* 32.2.1.5.
110. This corresponds to the identification of the place and time of his preaching of *Serm. Denis* 11(308A), which was clearly preached on the vigil, and *Psal.* 32.2.1. This pattern corresponds to the view of Maria Boulding that *Psal.* 32.2 was preached in the vigil at the Mappalia and then

## Conclusion

The Lord's Prayer was at the center of Christian practices of prayer in the African church. It was recited multiple times each day and guided other forms of prayer: what should be sought from God — both spiritual and bodily blessings — and what must not — harm of one's enemies. Cyprian placed particular emphasis on unanimity in prayer. Although Augustine developed a Christian form of philosophical contemplation, his principal contribution to church practice was an explanation of the Psalms as the prayer of the whole Christ, head and members.

## CONTROLLING BODILY APPETITE BY FASTING

Abstaining from food during a major part of the day was an established penitential practice, used to seek divine forgiveness for the sins of daily living as well as a part of the formal penitential rite by excommunication and reconciliation. The New Prophecy movement adopted and urged a more rigorous form in the late second century. Cyprian recommended it for adding urgency — and efficacy — to petitionary prayer. Augustine set the practice in the broader context of his understanding of the church.

## Tertullian

As has already been seen, Tertullian taught that restricting food and drink was a penitential practice, a means of strengthening one's prayer for the forgiveness of sins in preparation for baptism and in the ritual of reconciliation.[111] Fasting was, however, one of the regular practices of the Christian life that many undertook weekly.

Unlike the community fasts at set times of the year that had been specified in the Mosaic Law, Christians considered their own fasting voluntary. The manner and time of fasts had not been set by Christ; these were determined by individual choice or the decision of the church leaders.[112] Still, Christians did look to scripture for guidance. The text of Matthew 9:14-15, which named the time when "the bridegroom had been taken away from them" as proper for fasting,[113] provided a justification for avoiding fasting during the whole of the Easter season, from the

---

that *Psal.* 32.2.2 was preached the next day at the Mensa. See Augustine, *Expositions of the Psalms,* trans. Maria Boulding, ed. John E. Rotelle (Brooklyn, N.Y.: New City Press, 2000-2004), 3/15-20/15:392, 406. For a contrary view, see Augustine, *Sermons,* trans. Edmund Hill, ed. John E. Rotelle /1-11 (Brooklyn, N.Y.: New City Press, 1990), 3/9:121-22.

111. Tert. *Bapt.* 20; *Paen.* 9.
112. Tert. *Ieiun.* 2.1-2.
113. Tert. *Ieiun.* 2.2, 13.1.

celebration of the Resurrection until Pentecost.[114] The rest of the year, then, was the proper time. The entire community fasted on the Friday when the death of Jesus was commemorated,[115] and some continued the fast on Saturday as well.[116]

Like other Christian practices, fasting was based not on scripture alone but was developed by community traditions. All avoided fasting on Sunday and most on Saturday as well.[117] Wednesday and Friday outside of Eastertide were called stational days, when members of the community might fast until mid-afternoon.[118] The ending time was justified by appeal to scriptural precedents: the time of the death of Jesus or the time when Peter went into the temple to pray.[119] The latter explanation may indicate that the fast was closed with a service of prayer. Bathing was also omitted on fast days.[120] The actual fast was voluntary, and it was not observed by all members of the community. At the morning liturgy, those fasting thought that they should neither take the eucharist nor share the kiss of peace. Yet, these refusals could not but call attention to their pious exercise.[121] It will be recalled that Tertullian suggested that they share the peace and take the eucharistic bread home with them.[122] On days when the entire community was fasting, however, the kiss of peace was omitted at the end of prayer.[123] Those days of fasting were called by the leader of the community in support of its prayer for some particular need or as a means of raising money for the support of the poor.[124]

The devotees of the New Prophecy amplified and extended these practices by committing themselves to all the observances rather than regarding them as optional matters of private devotion. They extended the stational fasts until the end of the day, preferring not to refresh themselves until the hour when Jesus had been laid to rest in the tomb.[125] They followed a regimen of "dry" fasting, a *xerophagia*, which seems to have consisted of bread and water. They avoided meat, succulent fruit, and anything flavored with wine. As part of the dry regimen, they avoided the baths as well.[126] During two weeks of the year, which Tertullian neglected to specify, they practiced the *xerophagia* for five days running, omitting Saturday and Sunday.[127]

114. Tert. *Cor.* 3.4.

115. Tert. *Or.* 18.7; *Ieiun.* 14.2.

116. Tert. *Ieiun.* 14.3.

117. Tert. *Cor.* 3.4; *Ieiun.* 14.3, 15.2.

118. Tert. *Ieiun.* 2.3, 13.1.

119. Tert. *Ieiun.* 2.3, 10.1-6. Acts 3:1. Christians fasted while Jesus suffered and ate once he had died.

120. Tert. *Ux.* 2.4; *Ieiun.* 1.4.

121. Tert. *Or.* 18.1, 6; 19.1.

122. See above, pp. 238-39.

123. Tert. *Or.* 18.7.

124. Tert. *Ieiun.* 13.3-4. The funds which were not spent on food were presumably given to the poor.

125. Tert. *Ieiun.* 1.4, 10.8.

126. Tert. *Ieiun.* 1.4. Tertullian cited scriptural precedents for this form of fasting (*Ieiun.* 9).

127. Tert. *Ieiun.* 15.2.

Tertullian explained the function of fasting in a number of ways. It added to the power of prayer, both in asking forgiveness of sins and in requesting favors from God.[128] As fasting was helpful in driving out demons, so did it open the way for the entrance of the Holy Spirit.[129] Finally, he observed that the dry fasts were particularly helpful in hardening the body to withstand pain in time of persecution and thus to prepare for witness to Christ under torture. He objected to the full meals which other Christians provided to confessors in prison, rendering them unfit for the trials.[130]

## Cyprian

Cyprian exhorted his people to add fasting and almsgiving to their prayers for protection and deliverance during the Decian persecution.[131] Similarly, in anticipation of a renewal of persecution under Valerian, he urged that the congregations commit themselves to prayer, with vigils and fasting, to gain divine protection and support.[132] In more general discussions, such as his treatises *On the Lord's Prayer* and *On Works and Alms,* Cyprian presented almsgiving, along with fasting, as appropriate to make intercessory prayer fruitful.[133]

Repentance for sins was, however, the primary focus of Cyprian's discussion of fasting. In *On the Lapsed,* he insisted that fasting was necessary to reverse the sin of eating the sacrificial meat and the habits of self-indulgence which had contributed to the failure of so many Christians.[134] Almsgiving was also essential to making satisfaction for sin, following the exhortations of Joel (2:12-13) and Isaiah (58:1, 7-9).[135] Thus Cyprian urged fasting as part of a program of repentance in which it was accompanied by prayer and care for the poor.

Cyprian did not provide information, as Tertullian had, on the weekly and annual practices of fasting followed by the Christians in Carthage. One letter, however, gave indirect evidence that Christians did not fast during the period between Easter and Pentecost. The writer indicated that even after Easter he continued the penitential activities he had undertaken on behalf of two friends who had failed to confess Christ in Rome.[136]

---

128. Tert. *Bapt.* 20; *Paen.* 9; *Ieiun.* 7.
129. Tert. *Ieiun.* 8.3.
130. Tert. *Ieiun.* 12.
131. Cypr. *Ep.* 11.1.1.
132. Cypr. *Ep.* 60.5.1.
133. Cypr. *Dom. orat.* 32; *Eleem.* 5; in both cases citing Tob. 12:8-9.
134. Cypr. *Laps.* 29-31, 35.
135. Cypr. *Eleem.* 4; *Ep.* 55.22.2.
136. Cypr. *Ep.* 21.2.1. Celerinus had been in the Roman military. He subsequently returned to Carthage and was ordained into Cyprian's clergy (*Ep.* 39).

Augustine's letters and sermons provide fuller information on the practices and meaning of fasting in his time than do the writings of Tertullian and Cyprian.

### THE PRACTICE OF FASTING

Augustine distinguished between a fasting and an eating day on the basis of the midday meal, *prandium,* which was the first meal of the day. On a fast day, Christians did not take that meal; instead, they ate at the ninth hour of the day. This afternoon meal was apparently the only one eaten, considered the major meal of the day, *cena.*[137] If a person could not follow this regimen, Augustine recommended that eating and drinking be restricted to the meal times; nothing should be taken outside of the *prandium* and *cena.*[138]

By the fifth century, Wednesday and Friday were well established as the Christian fast days during the week.[139] Augustine connected both days to the death of Jesus: the Jewish leaders had plotted his capture on Wednesday, then carried out his arrest and execution on the night and day of Friday.[140] In some parts of Africa, Christians fasted on Saturday as well, a custom which was well established in Rome. There it was related to Peter's fasting in preparation for the confrontation with Simon Magus; Peter continued his fasting in honor of its success.[141] No Christian was to choose Sunday as a day of fast,[142] especially since the Manichees had made it an obligatory day of abstaining from food. If, however, a Christian had committed to a longer period of fasting, a Sunday that happened to fall within the period could be included in the fast.[143] The festivals of the martyrs were also exempt from fasting.[144] Fasting was suspended from Easter to Pentecost,[145] and the weekly fasts began again immediately after Pentecost.[146]

An annual forty-day fast preceded Easter and was called *quadragesima.*[147] Fasting was observed for five days of the week, but not on Saturday and Sun-

137. Aug. *Ep.* 36.2.4.
138. Aug. *Ep.* 211.8; *Reg. Praeceptum* 3.3.1.
139. Aug. *Ep.* 36.4.7-8.
140. Aug. *Ep.* 36.13.30.
141. Aug. *Ep.* 82.14; 36.4.8, 5.9, 8.19.
142. Aug. *Ep.* 36.1.2–2.3, 7.16, 8.19, 12.27.
143. Aug. *Ep.* 36.12.27, 29.
144. Aug. *Ep.* 36.9.21; *Serm. Dolb.* 26(198*).9.
145. Aug. *Ep.* 36.8.19; 55.15.28; *Serm.* 210.1.2, 3.4, 6.8; 252.12.
146. Aug. *Serm.* 357.5.
147. Aug. *Emer.* 4; *Quaest.* 1.169; *Ep.* 55.15.28; *Ep. Divj.* 28*.2; *Eu. Io.* 17.4; *Serm.* 205.1; 206.1; 207.1; 209.3; 210.1.2; 252.10-11.

day.[148] It was performed by all the *competentes* preparing for baptism and by those among the faithful who wished to accompany them on the journey.[149] On Thursday of the final week, the *competentes* and these faithful broke the fast and went to the baths, in preparation for the celebration of baptism. Others continued the normal fast.[150] All fasted again on Friday, to honor the death of Jesus, and on Saturday, in sympathy for the grief of the Apostles.[151] Augustine recognized that the faithful could not sustain the forty days without food and drink that characterized the fasts of Moses, Elijah, and Jesus; he urged, however, that they abstain from sexual relations for the whole time.[152] Some Christians changed rather than curtailed their diets: they substituted exotic fruit juices for wine and elaborately prepared vegetable dishes for meat.[153] Augustine condemned this practice, insisting that *quadragesima* was the time for everyone to eat the kinds of food that the poor ate always.[154] They should then give to the poor whatever savings were realized by their shift to a less expensive diet.[155]

Fasting was practiced on some particular days, such as the vigil of Christmas.[156] Augustine recommended fasting in anticipation of the feast of Cyprian, perhaps as part of the campaign to change the tone of that celebration in Carthage.[157] He also urged that fasts be observed on the major feasts of the traditional Roman religion,[158] particularly the first of January.[159] Although Augustine characterized this abstaining from food as a prayer for the conversion of the pagans and an imitation of Christ, who suffered for the whole world,[160] the practice would also have curtailed Christian participation in the celebrations. On one occasion, he extended the sermon through the time of the midday meal to accomplish this end.[161]

One of the objectives of fasting was to wean the soul away from the pleasure of satisfying the body's need for food and to shift attention from temporal to eternal delights. Augustine suggested that this could be accomplished even during meals by engaging in religious conversation. This would distract attention from the unavoidable pleasure of eating and drinking.[162]

---

148. Aug. *Serm.* 210.6.9; *Ep.* 36.8.19.
149. Aug. *Fid. et op.* 6.8; *Psal.* 80.10; *Serm.* 210.1.2; 229.1-2.
150. Aug. *Ep.* 54.7.9-10.
151. Aug. *Ep.* 82.14; 36.13.31.
152. Aug. *Serm.* 210.6.9.
153. Aug. *Serm.* 207.2; 210.8.10–9.11.
154. Aug. *Serm.* 210.9.11.
155. Aug. *Serm.* 209.3; 210.10.12; 390.1.
156. Aug. *Ep.* 65.1-2.
157. Aug. *Serm. Frang.* 5(163B).6.
158. Aug. *Psal.* 98.5; *Serm. Dolb.* 22(341*).26; 26(198*).6.
159. Aug. *Serm. Dolb.* 26(198*).8.
160. Aug. *Serm. Dolb.* 26(198*).58.
161. Aug. *Serm. Dolb.* 26(198*); the sermon may have lasted more than two hours.
162. Aug. *Iul.* 4.14.71; *Ep.* 211.8.

Because none of these practices of fasting were specified in the New Testament, they varied by region and even between individual churches within the same area. The Saturday fast was observed in Rome but not in Milan and in only some churches in Africa.[163] Augustine regularly recommended the advice that Ambrose had given to his mother when she complained that the church in Milan did not fast on Saturday: follow the local custom or at least the practice of the local bishop. In these matters, the peace and unity of the church were more important;[164] they should not be disturbed by attempts to establish the superiority of one's religious knowledge or culture.[165] Citing the Psalms (45:14-15), Augustine distinguished between the interior beauty of the queen, symbolized by the faith itself, and her multicolored garments, represented by the many ways of living it.[166] A great variety of practices was compatible with the Christian faith, and no one of them was significantly more successful in promoting morality.

### THE MEANING OF FASTING

Augustine considered fasting a regular discipline of living the Christian life. In his reflections on the difficulties of daily life in *Confessions,* he pointed to the challenge presented by eating and drinking. These were necessary for maintaining the mortal body, but the replenishment was pleasurable and easily drew a person beyond what was necessary and profitable.[167] To maintain proper control and avoid crossing over to the superfluous, therefore, a person had to pull back somewhat even from what was allowed.[168]

More generally, Augustine considered fasting a symbolic withdrawal from the pleasures of bodily life[169] and even from the vices of the soul.[170] Christians should always be fasting from the dominant culture, from that demonically influenced way of life.[171] Giving up food was not enough, but it represented a broader attempt to reorient desire from passing to lasting goods.

Desire was appropriately trained by fasting in times of both sorrow and joy. The first was linked to the absence of the Bridegroom but expanded to encompass times of tribulation, conflict, and temptation. Christ set an example in the

163. Aug. *Ep.* 54.2.2; 36.1.2, 9.22–11.25.
164. Aug. *Ep.* 36.1.2, 9.22–11.25, 14.32; 54.2.2-3.
165. Aug. *Ep.* 54.2.3. Augustine was unusually harsh in his condemnation of liturgical absolutists.
166. Aug. *Ep.* 36.9.22, 13.31.
167. Aug. *Conf.* 10.31.43-44.
168. Aug. *Util. iei.* 5-6.
169. Aug. *Perf.* 8.18; *Bon. coniug.* 10.11; *Serm.* 205.2.
170. Aug. *Serm.* 80.3; 206.3; 207.3; 209.3.
171. Aug. *Serm.* 125.7, 9; 252.10-11; 264.5; 270.3; *Serm. Mai* 98(263A).4.

fast following his baptism and in anticipation of the struggles of his ministry. The soul was humbled by the deprivation of the body and thus provided with a powerful weapon for fighting against the demon.[172] One should also fast during times of spiritual joy, in order to keep the goods of the spirit free from adulteration by fleshly pleasures. As a new patch could not be sewn onto an old garment or new wine stored in old skins, so the joys of the spirit must be kept separate from those of the flesh.[173]

Fasting should always be joined to prayer and almsgiving.[174] It purified prayer and thus gave wings to the soul; it strengthened petitions by acting out the prayer.[175] It was never to be separated from help given to the poor.[176] These three also served as the traditional means of seeking forgiveness for sins. Weekly fasts were necessary, Augustine explained, to repent the small sins of daily living, to pump the bilges so that the ship did not slowly sink from small leaks.[177]

While affirming the traditional rituals of fasting, Augustine attempted to integrate the practice into a broader context. He was as interested in struggling against the vices of the spirit as in suppressing the pleasures of the body. He refused to separate the asceticism of the individual from love and care for Christ in the persons of the poor.

### Conclusion

Periodic abstaining from food and drink was a Christian practice that was integral to prayer, repentance, and helping the poor. The specific practices were associated with scriptural precedents — such as the fasts of Christ, Moses, and Elijah — and with events, particularly the death of Christ. Fasting was both effective in separating Christians from bodily satisfactions and symbolic of the purification of their desires; it oriented them toward the gifts of the Spirit and the glories of the world to come. Tolerating the pain of hunger and thirst trained the Christians to suffer for Christ; the self-indulgent would not withstand pressure and maintain the confession of their faith. Augustine also suggested that on the festivals of traditional polytheist idolatry Christians should fast not only as a way to separate themselves from the feasting but as a petition for the conversion and salvation of their neighbors.

172. Aug. *Cons.* 2.4.9, 27.63; *Serm.* 210.2.3–4.5.
173. Aug. *Cons.* 2.27.63; *Qu. eu.* 2.18; *Serm.* 210.3.4.
174. Aug. *Parm.* 2.10.20; *Ep.* 130.24; *Psal.* 42.8; 66.7; *Perf.* 8.18; *Serm.* 9.17, 21; 150.6.7; 206.3; 207.1, 3; 351.3.6; *Serm. Dolb.* 26(198*).56.
175. Aug. *Serm.* 210.6.9; 358.6; *Ep.* 130.13.24; *Psal.* 50.11; *Serm. Dolb.* 26(198*).8.
176. Aug. *Serm.* 150.6.7.
177. Aug. *Parm.* 2.10.20; *Qu. eu.* 2.18; *Eu. Io.* 12.14; *Psal.* 66.7; *Serm.* 351.3.6.

Offering material assistance to the poor was inseparable from prayer and fasting. Like fasting, it was a penitential practice that helped Christians separate themselves from the attachments leading them into sin. The sharing of goods within a congregation realized its unity and symbolized its hope of sharing eternal life.

## Tertullian

Tertullian's writings indicate that almsgiving was a regular practice among the Christians of his day. He noted that giving money to a non-Christian would place the donor in an awkward situation. The grateful beggar would normally call down on the benefactor a blessing from one of the traditionally honored deities. The Christian who did not repudiate that good wish not only failed to confess Christ but allowed the glory of the good deed to be credited to a demon.[178] In another context, he argued that marrying a fellow Christian could forestall conflicts over almsgiving (as well as prayer and fasting) that were certain to arise in a union with a non-Christian.[179] In a treatise on the virtue of patience, he observed that a Christian who could not suffer the loss of earthly goods with equanimity would never be able to give alms voluntarily to feed and clothe the needy.[180] Further evidence of the practice was provided by Christians defending as an alms a bribe paid to escape persecution because it used earthly goods to secure or at least prevent the loss of a heavenly one. Tertullian retorted that the imperial official or soldier who accepted the gratuity certainly did not regard it as an alms and did not invoke a blessing upon the donor, as was customary for beggars. The appropriate payment for a heavenly reward in such a situation, he observed, was in blood rather than money.[181]

Tertullian did not discuss almsgiving as a penitential work; he focused instead on prayer and on fasting with sackcloth and ashes.[182] When Tertullian did discuss Christian wealth and its proper use, his concern was the danger of idolatry associated with the execution of contracts.[183] He never appealed to the precedent of the sharing of goods in the Jerusalem community for the establishment of an alternate economy within the church.

Tertullian indicated that the church had a common fund to which the faithful contributed according to their resources and choice. The funds were

178. Tert. *Idol.* 22.
179. Tert. *Ux.* 2.8.
180. Tert. *Pat.* 7.8, 10, 13.
181. Tert. *Fug.* 12-13.
182. Tert. *Paen.* 9.4; 11.1.
183. Tert. *Idol.* 23.

used not for lavish entertainments but to support the needy: the poor, the orphaned, the elderly, the shipwrecked, and those being punished for confession of Christ.[184] Even the regular community meal was an opportunity for feeding the hungry, presumably among the faithful, without subjecting them to the humiliation they often suffered from patrons.[185]

The absence of a fuller discussion of wealth and almsgiving suggests that the Christian community in Carthage at the end of the second century did not include a significant number of families whose financial status made the sharing of goods a particular challenge to their fidelity to Christ and their following of his teaching. A different situation would be clearly manifest a half-century later in Cyprian's attempts to deal with the devastation wrought by the Decian persecution.

## Cyprian

Contributing to the support of the community and its members was widely practiced and is well evidenced in the middle of the third century in Carthage. The operational costs of the church, including the monthly stipends of the clergy, must have come from voluntary gifts made by some members of the congregation.[186] The episcopal correspondence at the time of the Decian persecution provides no indication that the church in Africa owned lands or other income-producing resources that would have been subject to confiscation.[187] After the persecution, Cyprian charged that bishops had acquired farms by fraud. This accusation came under the category of abandoning pastoral responsibilities and was accompanied by complaints of their searching for trading opportunities and loaning money at interest. These bishops were being accused of enhancing their personal fortunes while their fellow Christians went hungry.[188] Thus the funds used for the support of the church and its ministries seem to have come not from church properties but from the free-will offerings of the faithful.

In ordinary times, the funds of the church were dispersed by the clergy to those in need. In addition to widows, the sick, and the poor,[189] Cyprian indicated that some persons whom the church had required to give up livelihoods tainted by idolatry as a condition for acceptance were then supported by the resources of the church.[190] During the Decian persecution, similar assistance

184. Tert. *Apol.* 39.5-6.
185. Tert. *Apol.* 39.16.
186. These are evidenced in Cypr. *Ep.* 34.4.2; 39.5.1.
187. Cypr. *Ep.* 66.4.1 provides evidence of an attempt to confiscate Cyprian's personal property.
188. Cypr. *Laps.* 6.
189. Cypr. *Ep.* 7.1.
190. Cypr. *Ep.* 2.2.3.

was extended to those imprisoned for confession of Christ, to workers whose tools and goods were confiscated, and to refugees or exiles attempting to evade imperial attention.[191] Such funds were to be given only to those remaining steadfast in their faith and commitment to the community.[192] Some of these funds were provided from Cyprian's own resources.[193] During the subsequent Valerian persecution, the church in Carthage sent funds for the alleviation of the suffering of Christians condemned to working in the imperial mines.[194]

Cyprian and other bishops responded to an appeal from Numidian colleagues for funds to ransom Christians taken captive by raiders.[195] The amount of the funds raised from the clergy and laity of Carthage was quite large, equivalent to the monthly wages of 3,000 day-laborers, and indicated that the church had access to significant resources, probably among wealthy members like its bishop, who contributed in case of emergency.[196]

The financial crisis occasioned by the Decian persecution and the generosity of wealthy Christians made almsgiving a much more significant practice in the middle of the third century than it seems to have been in Tertullian's time. The Decian edict, which required participation in a sacrifice for the good of the empire, resulted in the first systematic persecution of Christians. Persons who refused to comply could be stripped of their property and sent into exile. The wealthy, along with church leaders, were among the first to be prosecuted: they were not only prominent but worthwhile targets for the imperial treasury. Some Christians abandoned their property and went voluntarily into exile. Others, however, found methods of protecting their holdings, jeopardizing their status within the church. Many performed the sacrifice; others paid a bribe or fine to avoid the requirement. During and immediately after the persecution, Cyprian charged that wealth had proved the undoing of these Christians; it was an enemy within their households that had betrayed them.[197]

Almsgiving as an antidote to avarice and individualism would then play a significant role in the process of repentance and the reconstitution of the church after failures during the persecution. Those who had fallen through their attachment to money and property were urged to demonstrate both their change of heart and their commitment to the church by dispersing some of the funds they had protected and retained by sinning. During the persecution, some of these Christians undertook the care of exiled confessors and of the refugees

191. Cypr. *Ep.* 5.1.2.
192. Cypr. *Ep.* 5.1.2; 12.2.2; 41.1.2.
193. Cypr. *Ep.* 7.2.
194. Cypr. *Ep.* 77.3.2; 78.3.1; 79.1.1.
195. Cypr. *Ep.* 62.
196. The figure of 100,000 sesterces is given in Cypr. *Ep.* 62.3.2. The value is calculated in Graeme W. Clarke, *The Letters of St. Cyprian of Carthage* (New York: Newman Press, 1984), 3:284-85, n. 11.
197. Cypr. *Ep.* 11.1.2; *Laps.* 6, 10-12, 35.

who fled to the larger cities where they would escape detection and prosecution. Christians of Carthaginian origin in Rome undertook the support of the exiles there.[198] In Carthage, the wealthy who had complied with the imperial edict in order to protect their own households also provided shelter to these refugees.[199] Cyprian's charge that the confessors in prison were being bribed to intercede for the fallen may have been an interpretation of the practice of supporting the families of those under pressure.[200] When Cyprian finally returned to Carthage and urged those who had failed during the persecution to undertake the penance necessary to win the forgiveness of Christ, he recommended almsgiving as the most appropriate means of purification and repentance.[201] He also cited the sharing of goods practiced by the Jerusalem community as a means to strengthen unity even if the giving of alms was not required as a penitential work to wipe out the crime of apostasy.[202] Clearly, Cyprian viewed almsgiving as a means for both the fallen and the faithful to demonstrate commitment to the church community.

In exhortations delivered in the years following the Decian persecution, Cyprian continued to stress the necessity and efficacy of almsgiving in the Christian life. In his explanation of the Lord's Prayer, he observed that selling goods and distributing the proceeds to the poor set a follower of Christ free from all the connections that could bind to family and imperial culture.[203] He warned Christian virgins that their wealth had been given to them not for personal enjoyment but as a means of helping others. To expend it on costly clothing and ostentatious living was to miss the point of their renunciation of marriage.[204] Such had not been the focus of Tertullian's fulminations on the dress of virgins and married women.[205]

Cyprian's concern with the proper use of wealth was most evident, however, in the collection of scriptural passages on this topic in *To Quirinus*. It contains thirty-four citations, of which only two focus explicitly on the use of alms as a means of gaining the forgiveness of sins.[206] His treatise *On Works and Alms* repeats half the scriptural citations collected in *To Quirinus* and adds another thirty. Although it begins with an appeal to the efficacy of alms in winning the forgiveness of sins committed after baptism, its scope is broader than in the writings composed immediately following the Decian persecution. Cyprian observed that no one could claim a pure heart and that repentance was nec-

198. As reported by the confessor Celerinus (*Ep.* 21.2.2, 3.2).
199. Cypr. *Ep.* 55.13.2.
200. Cypr. *Ep.* 15.3.2.
201. Cypr. *Laps.* 35, repeated in *Unit. eccl.* 26 and in *Ep.* 55.22.1, 28.1.
202. Cypr. *Laps.* 35.
203. Cypr. *Dom. orat.* 20.
204. Cypr. *Hab. uirg.* 11.
205. See, for example, Tert. *Cult. fem.* 1.4-9, 2.1-2 and *Virg.* 14.
206. Cypr. *Test.* 3.1.

essary even for sins which did not require the public ritual of *exomologesis*. He asserted that those who wanted to win forgiveness must supplement fasting and prayer with almsgiving and care of the poor.[207]

Two arguments in *On Works and Alms* indicate that fellow Christians were the primary if not exclusive recipients of alms. First, Cyprian explained that alms made prayer effective by enlisting the prayers of the poor, which were heard by God. He then cited the intercession of the needy who had been helped by Tabitha; these had won restoration of bodily life for her through the miracle worked by Peter (Acts 9:36-41).[208] Second, referring to the warning of eschatological judgment in Matthew (25:31-46), he argued that Christ himself was served in the poor and had promised to reward the least gift made to them.[209]

Cyprian also considered objections that might be advanced against the practice of almsgiving he was recommending. A property owner who followed his advice might soon find himself among the poor, unable to feed himself and his family, much less care for anyone else. In response, Cyprian explained that alienating one's sources of income was an act of faith in God's own care. Christ had named Zacchaeus a son of Abraham precisely because he had followed the patriarch's example of faith in disposing of his wealth. Thus a Christian should trust that the prayers of those who had been helped would make God generous to the newly destitute benefactor.[210] Retaining one's wealth, in contrast, courted becoming enslaved to it again after once having been set free by Christ.[211] Indeed, Cyprian observed, some of the wealthy were already living off the generosity of the poor: they arrived empty-handed at the community celebrations and shared the (food) offerings made by others.[212] A second objection asserted that parents had no right to deprive children of their inheritance by dispersing it to the poor. Cyprian appealed again to almsgiving as an exercise of faith: Christians should love God more than their families.[213] Indeed, they would serve their children better by following the example of the widow who gave Elijah the last of her food and thus preserved both herself and her child from starvation.[214] Christians might instruct their children in almsgiving, as Tobias had,[215] or win the forgiveness of their children's sins by their own alms, as Job did by daily sacrifice.[216]

207. Cypr. *Eleem.* 1-4, 14, using Isa. 58:7-9.

208. Cypr. *Eleem.* 5, 9, 6. A similar point, without this explanation, was made in *Dom. orat.* 32-33.

209. Cypr. *Eleem.* 8, 23. Cyprian had not made the transition to identifying the presence of Christ in the non-Christian; that would be made later.

210. Cypr. *Eleem.* 8-9, 11-12.

211. Cypr. *Eleem.* 10, 13, 14.

212. Cypr. *Eleem.* 15.

213. Cypr. *Eleem.* 16.

214. Cypr. *Eleem.* 17, 19.

215. Cypr. *Eleem.* 20.

216. Cypr. *Eleem.* 18.

In responding to these objections, Cyprian also introduced a scripturally based consideration that would have a long life in African Christian piety: almsgiving was a means of transforming earthly into heavenly treasure. By entrusting their family wealth to God, parents could leave their children an abiding heavenly inheritance rather than a transitory earthly one.[217] By providing food, drink, and clothing to the poor, Christians helped Christ himself and would be amply repaid in heavenly goods.[218] Cyprian then addressed the wealthy members of his congregation by contrasting the ostentatious gifts the Roman nobility made to their cities with those of Christians toward the church. The civic benefactors considered themselves blessed in the opportunity to demonstrate their generosity in the presence of important personages and gloried in dedications made to the imperial deities. In serving the poor, by contrast, Christians sought approval and reward from God.[219] As judge, Cyprian claimed, Christ would bestow not only a purple crown of martyrdom but a white crown for good works.[220]

In Cyprian's community, the possession of wealth constituted a challenge to the Christian life. During the Decian persecution, the faithful who owned and were unprepared to abandon a patrimony — along with the status it conferred — were forced to choose between the Christian and the imperial cultures. In responding to failures during that crisis, Cyprian made almsgiving central to Christian piety. He promoted generosity to the poor as an exercise of faith that prepared Christians for the confession of Christ and even martyrdom by requiring them to cast all their hope upon Christ, to trust that God would care for the families who were willing to offer the parent providing their financial support. Almsgiving became an appropriate and even necessary part of repenting for the apostasy brought on when a person was unwilling to give over property in order to preserve faith. Since attachment to property caused the sin, only giving away property could win its forgiveness.

In Cyprian's explanation of the efficacy of almsgiving, the primary recipients of alms were assumed to be fellow Christians. The prayers of the powerful poor would not only win a hearing for the petitions of the donor but render God generous to those who had impoverished themselves by almsgiving. The identification of the poor with Christ, who was served in them, also evinced an assumption that the primary recipients of alms were Christian. Finally, the financial and political protection that the lapsed provided to faithful Christians during the persecution later became a basis for the church's forgiving, readmitting, and commending them to the divine mercy.

---

217. Cypr. *Eleem.* 19. He cited Ps. 36:25-26 and Prov. 20:7.
218. Cypr. *Eleem.* 24, repeated in *Mort.* 26 and *Hab. uirg.* 11.
219. Cypr. *Eleem.* 21-22.
220. Cypr. *Eleem.* 26.

---

The next substantial witness to the practice of almsgiving and the management of wealth by Christians in North Africa comes at the end of the fourth and the beginning of the fifth century, in the writings and the preaching of Augustine. The Constantinian support and Theodosian establishment of Christianity resulted in greater wealth among Christians — often by the conversion of the aristocracy. In the churches, it brought the ownership of productive property, along with increased responsibilities for the poor. Augustine's exhortations and advice were complex because he addressed both rich and poor simultaneously and often in relationship to one another.

The congregation to which Augustine preached at Hippo seems to have included both rich and poor. He described most of the members of his congregation as poor,[221] though he would use the same term to characterize himself and his family.[222] The public accounting he gave of the finances of his clergy indicates that some of them had owned income-producing property and were skilled in its management.[223] The fate of the rich man in the parable of Luke (16:19-31) would inspire a collective groan of fear in the congregation and require the preacher to explain that this person had been condemned not for his possessions but for his failure to share them.[224] Augustine also warned the poor that the beggar in the parable had been saved by his piety, not his poverty.[225] He admonished the poor in the congregation to avoid the common saying that only the rich really live.[226] In this context, Augustine made extensive use of 1 Timothy (6:6-10, 17-19), which addresses both rich and poor. He explained that Paul had not required the alienation of riches that had been urged by Christ; instead, he warned that possessions must not be permitted to engender pride.[227] The poor, also subject to avarice, should be content with food, shelter, and clothing.[228] The true danger, Augustine argued, was not in the possession of riches and their proper use but in eagerness to acquire and increase them.[229] This view, in its turn, might have been influenced by his supposition that the quantity of riches in the world was unchanging, so that one person's gain came only at another's loss.[230] Thus, to desire gain for oneself was to wish loss for another.

---

221. Aug. *Serm.* 85.2.2–3.3.

222. Aug. *Serm.* 356.13. Augustine's father was a *curialis* of Thagaste, a rank based on wealth (Aug. *Conf.* 2.3.5; Possid. *Vita Aug.* 1.1). See Lancel, *Saint Augustine*, 6-7.

223. Aug. *Serm.* 356.

224. Aug. *Serm.* 367.2-3; *Serm. Mai* 13(113B).4; *Serm. Guelf.* 9(299E).3.

225. Aug. *Psal.* 51.14.

226. Aug. *Serm.* 345.1.

227. Aug. *Serm.* 177.7; 345.1; *Serm. Dolb.* 5(114B).12-13; *Psal.* 48.1.3; 132.4; 136.13.

228. Aug. *Serm.* 61.10.11; 85.5.6; *Serm. Morin* 11(53A).3.

229. Aug. *Serm. Lamb.* 4(359A).6; *Serm. Dolb.* 5(114B).9-10, 12.

230. Aug. *Psal.* 64.9.

Christian almsgiving was not restricted to the church community. Many of the beggars for whom Augustine sought the generosity of the congregation gathered in the street outside the doors of the church rather than standing within it.[231] He clearly asserted that support was to be extended to pagans, Jews, and Christian heretics.[232] The collection at the beginning of the winter was for the support of both the local poor and foreigners stranded in Hippo by the close of maritime shipping.[233] Christian generosity was extended to sinners and enemies as well as the deserving.[234] In a discussion of gifts made to the unjust, however, Augustine specified that the donor must be focused on meeting the needs of the human being created by God and not on encouraging sinful behavior: giving to arena performers and prostitutes was suspect.[235] Thus, while Christians should give of their excess to the needy who approached them, they had a responsibility to seek out the particularly deserving. Because the true servants of God were more likely to suffer in silence, the faithful ought to be solicitous of their needs.[236]

In practice, most Christian almsgiving seems to have been focused on the church and the congregation. Augustine's appeal to the practice of the Jerusalem community described in Acts (4:32) encouraged the wealthy to make most of their gifts within the church.[237] He also insisted that by identifying himself with the faithful (Matt. 25:40), Christ had given his followers the opportunity to serve him as Martha had,[238] and thereby to gain an eternal reward.[239] This gave the Christian poor a special claim on the generosity of their fellows.[240] In an extended analysis of Christ's promise that gifts to the righteous and to disciples would be rewarded in Matthew (10:41-42), and the more general exhortations of Luke (6:30) and Romans (12:20), Augustine was able to show that all Christian almsgiving should promote conversion and salvation, thereby qualifying the donor for a heavenly reward.[241]

Augustine insisted that almsgiving was the responsibility of all Christians, not just the rich.[242] The poor could give alms out of the little they had,[243] as

231. Thus in Aug. *Serm.* 61.12.13; a similar appeal was made in *Serm.* 66.5, at its end.

232. Aug. *Psal.* 32.2.2.29. In *Psal.* 46.5, he remarked that the non-Christians seek alms but not faith from the Christians.

233. Aug. *Serm.* 25.8.

234. Aug. *Serm. Lamb.* 4(359A).11; 28(164A).1-4.

235. Aug. *Psal.* 102.12-13.

236. Aug. *Psal.* 146.17.

237. Aug. *Psal.* 44.28.

238. Aug. *Serm.* 103.1.2; 179.3; 239.3.3. He made the same connection with the widow of Zareptha's service of Elijah: *Serm.* 277.1.1; *Serm. Lamb.* 10(136B).4.

239. Aug. *Serm.* 236.3; 239.4.4, 5.6–6.7; 389.6; 399.7.

240. Aug. *Serm.* 25.8; 38.8; 41.7; 86.3.3, 4.5; 123.4; 206.2; 345.2, 4; *Serm. Mai* 13(113B).4; *Serm. Lamb.* 4(359A).11.

241. Aug. *Serm. Lamb.* 28(164A).4; *Serm.* 359.3; *Psal.* 102.12-13; 103.3.10.

242. Aug. *Psal.* 49.13-17.

243. Aug. *Serm.* 39.6; 85.5.6; *Serm. Lamb.* 4(359A).12.

was made clear by Christ's promise that even the gift of a cup of cold water, by one who had no resources to heat it, would not go unrewarded.[244] He suggested that alms could be given by service as well as money: guiding the blind, carrying the lame, and consoling the perplexed. It would be very difficult to find someone, he concluded, who had no resources for assisting another.[245] The wealthy faced the opposite dilemma: determining how much of their resources should be given in alms. Unlike Cyprian, Augustine did not require or urge that all possessions be dispersed,[246] or even that the wealthy sacrifice their more refined lifestyle.[247] Instead, he suggested that a tithe was the minimum for these Christians, whose justice should exceed that of the Pharisees.[248] Whatever funds they determined they could afford should be set aside, as a sort of tax for the treasury of Christ. Thus, when the time came for giving, they would not feel that they were depriving their own households for the sake of others.[249]

As bishop, Augustine followed the practice of retaining principal and distributing income in the administration of the property belonging to his church. He claimed to manage more than twenty times the inheritance he had himself donated to the church in his hometown of Thagaste upon his ordination.[250] Those responsible for church property — presbyters and bishops — were forbidden to sell any of it without prior consultation and approval of episcopal supervisors.[251] Augustine insisted that the income from church property had to be shared with the poor,[252] following the established practice.[253] Funds given to the church for the support of operations and the care of the poor were clearly distinguished, in Augustine's judgment, from those used to build a basilica for the congregation's use.[254]

Augustine assigned many functions to almsgiving in the Christian life. It was a way to make petitionary prayer effective.[255] The presence and needs of the poor were a test for the rich: to demonstrate and maintain that poverty of

244. Aug. *Serm. Lamb.* 1(105A).1; 5(107A).8; *Psal.* 125.11-12.

245. Aug. *Serm.* 91.7.9; *Psal.* 36.2.13; 125.12-13.

246. Aug. *Serm.* 39.6.

247. Aug. *Serm.* 61.11.12.

248. Aug. *Serm.* 85.4.5; *Psal.* 146.17.

249. Aug. *Psal.* 146.17.

250. Aug. *Ep.* 126.7; see also *Serm.* 355.2; 356.10.

251. *Cau. Apiar.* 33. Presbyters cannot sell the goods of the church without the permission of the bishop, just as bishops cannot do so without the advice of the council or their presbyters.

252. Aug. *Serm.* 355.4-5. He refused to accept the gift of a shipping company because the church would have had to maintain a reserve fund to repay shippers for any losses. This would have required withholding available funds from the needy.

253. In the *Acta apud Zenophilum,* the governor was astonished to learn that the poor had received nothing of the money that Lucilla had given to the bishops Silvanus and Purpurius or that Victor had paid to Silvanus to make him a presbyter: CSEL 26:194.36–195.2, 195.30–196.2, 196.26–197.7.

254. Aug. *Serm. Lamb.* 5(107A).9.

255. Aug. *Serm.* 206.2.

spirit that prevented avarice.[256] Almsgiving was a well-established means of acting out repentance and praying for the forgiveness of sins; Augustine reminded his people regularly that they should seek the divine mercy for their daily sins by the twin acts of almsgiving and forgiving one another.[257] Fasting, also employed as a means of repentance, was ineffective unless joined to almsgiving.[258] Some Christians judged the practices of giving and forgiving so effective that Augustine had to caution that these would not substitute for repentance and reform of life. One could not continue to sin and to refuse canonical penance in the mistaken hope that salvation would be secured by generously dispersing to the poor a portion of ill-gotten gains.[259]

Alms were also given to win mercy for the deceased in the Judgment. Although the dead could not merit for themselves, Augustine asserted that some Christians had lived well enough to be judged worthy of benefiting from the good works of others after their deaths. Praying and working for the salvation of the dead could be understood as similar to seeking the conversion and perseverance of the living: in both, the divine mercy was implored. Since no one could be sure of the status of anyone among the dead, Augustine recommended that alms and prayers be offered for all.[260] He recognized that Christians would make gifts for the benefit of their family and friends, expecting that the same would be done for them eventually.[261] Indeed, he urged this almsgiving as a better way to honor and comfort the dead than observing the traditional feasts at their tombs.[262]

In his sermons, Augustine regularly commended almsgiving as a means of turning earthly into heavenly treasure.[263] Building on Christ's self-identification with the Christian poor, he characterized them as porters who could carry wealth from earth to heaven[264] and their hungry bellies as storehouses where the wealthy could safely store their surplus grain.[265] Any Christian eager for true profit could lend to Christ in this world and collect from him in the next, at an exorbitant rate of interest.[266] In response to the claim that a patrimony had to be maintained and expanded for future generations, Augustine suggested

256. Aug. *Serm.* 177.5, 10.

257. Aug. *Serm.* 9.17-18, 21; 42.1; 56.7.11; 83.2.2; 389.5.

258. Aug. *Serm.* 390.1.

259. The fullest discussion is in Aug. *Ciu.* 21.22-23, 27; see also *Enchir.* 20.75-77; *Serm.* 113.2.2; 178.4.4–5.5; *Serm. Lamb.* 4(359A).13.

260. See the discussion above, p. 512.

261. Aug. *Serm.* 9.20; 86.8.9.

262. Aug. *Ep.* 22.1.6.

263. Aug. *Serm.* 86.1.1; 177.10; 302.8; 357.5; 367.3; 389.3-4; *Serm. Morin* 11(53A).6.

264. Aug. *Serm.* 18.4; 60.6; 114.5; 311.5.5; *Serm. Morin* 11(53A).6; *Serm. Frang.* 9(114A).4-5; *Serm. Lamb.* 2(335C).8-9.

265. Aug. *Serm.* 36.9; 376A.3.

266. Aug. *Serm.* 38.9; 86.9.11–11.12; 123.5. He cited the *fac trajectitium,* a commercial loan that was made in one part of the empire and repaid in another (*Serm.* 390.2).

that parents ought to pay out in alms the patrimony of those children who predeceased them, rather than dividing the inheritance among the survivors.[267] If their children were all still alive, they might count Christ among their heirs, giving him an equal portion of their estates.[268] In practice, Augustine was careful of inheritance rights. He refused to participate in a scheme by which one of his clergy would have disinherited his children in favor of the church, though he did accept bequests which were not so encumbered.[269] He refused to accept the gift of patrimony offered by the deacon Heraclius, who was still a young man.[270] He strongly chastised a mother who had bestowed her property on monks — of questionable virtue — and thereby compromised her son's future.[271]

Augustine's preaching on almsgiving mirrored the changes in the economic profile of the Christian community a century after the Constantinian emancipation of the church. The church continued to include both rich and poor among its members. By the fifth century, however, they were integrated into Roman society, and their property was protected from the confiscation that had been experienced during major persecutions. Augustine did not urge the full alienation of property, though this remained an option for the clergy and the practice of those joining a monastic community.[272] He encouraged the practice of making gifts for the religious benefit of the dead and attempted to provide a rationale for it. In this, he developed the connection that Cyprian had made between Christ and the poor to whom alms were given.

## Conclusion

Although almsgiving is well attested in the writings of Tertullian, the explanation of its role in the Christian life was more fully developed by Cyprian and Augustine. The Decian persecution demonstrated that wealth could be an obstacle to fidelity in time of persecution. Cyprian stressed almsgiving as a means of distancing oneself from possessions and the imperial culture: it was useful to prepare for public confession of Christ and to repent for apostasy. In the face of division and conflict, he also recommended the sharing of resources and prayer

---

267. Aug. *Serm.* 170.2.

268. Aug. *Serm.* 86.11.13; *Psal.* 48.1.14.

269. Aug. *Serm.* 355.3-4.

270. Aug. *Serm.* 356.7. He feared that the family would judge that he had exercised inappropriate influence to deprive the young man.

271. Aug. *Ep.* 262.7-8. The husband had legal control over his wife's property. She should have recognized as well that she had no right to force her son to become a monk or a cleric by depriving him of the resources he needed for a family of his own.

272. It had been a requirement of the clergy of Hippo, but Augustine decided to relax it rather than have it violated in secret (*Serm.* 356.14). The legislation of the plenary council in 401 on the disposition of the property of bishops assumed that they would retain their property: *Reg. Carth.* 81.

between rich and poor as a way to strengthen the unifying bonds of the community and even transform earthly goods into heavenly treasure. This interaction within the community was further developed by Augustine. He identified pride as the temptation of the rich and avarice as that of the poor: both were to be overcome by gifts of money and service to others. When Christians gave alms, they should attend to human need: they must neither punish nor reward sinners; they should be seeking out the poor who suffered patiently and not attend only to the demanding.

Cyprian and Augustine displayed attitudes towards the preservation of wealth that contrasted sharply. Cyprian encouraged the rich to trust in God and dispose of both their income and the property that produced it, leaving their children only a heavenly inheritance. Augustine's advice reflected a different age and social setting: Christians should not seek to increase their property — achieved only by depriving others — but might maintain it as a source of the income that they shared with the needy. He declined to criticize the rich for providing a better style of life for their households and supported their efforts to insure an inheritance for their surviving children. His program reflected the practice of the church itself: it maintained the property that it had received and dispensed its surplus income to the poor.

Cyprian recommended almsgiving as a penitential work to reverse the attachment to riches which had led to sin. For Augustine, however, giving and forgiving were the primary works of repentance: fasting was effective only when it resulted in almsgiving.

## CONFESSING CHRIST

The culture of the Roman Empire presented a challenge to the exclusive monotheism of Christians. Christian theology, following the lead of Paul (1 Cor. 8:4; 10:19-21) identified the traditional religion as an elaboration of the demons, who had set themselves up in opposition to God. The idols were of no significance in themselves, but they served as instruments of the demons in leading humans astray. The symbols and rituals of the traditional religion, as Tertullian observed, were everywhere and unavoidable in a Roman city or town. Christians had to develop techniques for maintaining their baptismal renunciation of all the works and displays of Satan. Prudential adaptations changed with shifts in imperial attitudes toward Christianity; the circumlocutions that were acceptable in peacetime could not be tolerated under persecution. When Theodosius I forbade the traditional rituals, Augustine had to identify other ways in which the demons challenged Christians' commitment to Christ. Witnessing to Christ could range, then, from dying in the arena, to turning aside when sacrifice was offered at a relative's party, to waving off the blessing of a beggar, to refusing the curative amulet offered by a servant.

Tertullian explained that the idols, which usually had a human form, were actually the images of people who had lived in the past and been venerated after their deaths. The traditional ritual was a cult of the dead, and it was continued in funeral practices. The demons had taken over this ancestor cult and used it to lead humans away from God. The observances themselves, therefore, had to be avoided because they were being used as a demonic assault on the sovereignty of God.[273]

### PROHIBITED PRACTICES

Roman public life was permeated with idolatry. A person could not walk around in a town or city without looking at idols, smelling the smoke of sacrifices, or passing through crowds caught up in festivals and observances.[274] To respect their baptismal commitment, Tertullian urged, Christians ought to avoid what they could. They should not attend public shows and spectacles; indeed, they should avoid the places and buildings where these were presented even when they were not in use.[275]

The theater was forbidden because of the lewdness of the shows.[276] When a Christian woman was being exorcised after being possessed in the theater, the demon protested that she had been in its domain and was quite legitimately invaded.[277] After attending a tragic play, another woman was warned in a dream and then died.[278] Christians should avoid not only food offered to idols, Tertullian argued, but the banquets presented to honor the dead, since the whole demonic cult was an elaboration of the funeral rituals.[279]

Christian rejection of idolatry extended to all the commercial and cultural practices that supported it. God had clearly forbidden the making of idols[280] and the practice of astrology.[281] Tertullian urged that Christians should also refrain from trading in the supplies that were used in the cult: they could buy and use incense for their own purposes but must not supply it to others for their idolatrous worship.[282] How could a Christian spit on an incense burner

273. Tert. *Idol.* 15.1-2.
274. Tert. *Mart.* 2.7.
275. Tert. *Spec.* 4.1, 3; 8.10.
276. Tert. *Spec.* 17.5-6.
277. Tert. *Spec.* 26.1-2.
278. Tert. *Spec.* 26.3-4.
279. Tert. *Spec.* 13.4.
280. Tert. *Idol.* 4.1.
281. Tert. *Idol.* 9.1.
282. Tert. *Idol.* 11.2-7. Christians used incense in their funerals.

as he passed by if he had sold the mixture?[283] Tertullian also argued, as the emperor Julian would later decree, that Christians should not teach literature: it necessarily involved the promotion of idolatry through treating the myths. The entire teaching schedule, moreover, was based on a participation in religious festivals. Studying literature was permissible as the only means of education. Pupils could avoid the associated religious practices that their master could not. Still, Christian students must be forearmed with knowledge to combat the catechesis inherent in the literature they read.[284]

### ACCEPTED PRACTICES

Tertullian did recognize some compromises that had been developed among Christians. They could share the necessities and even reasonable comforts of life with their idolatrous neighbors. Thus they could eat the meat of the kinds of animals used for sacrifices, and they could burn incense to cover noxious odors. They could wear the types of clothing that indicated civil but not religious status. They need reject only those items that had been developed specifically for idolatry, but they should avoid ceremonials associated with more common items.[285]

A Christian could attend celebrations of events common to human life, such as a marriage, the giving of a name, or the taking of clothing appropriate to a stage of life. If a sacrifice was offered as part of the festivities, the Christian should avoid taking an active part but could attend as long as the religious ritual was only incidental to the principal purpose of the gathering.[286] When the invitation was for the sacrifice itself, however, the Christian should decline.[287] Slaves and members of the household of a pagan should also refuse or avoid actual participation in the ritual.[288]

Finally, Christians could not really avoid using the names of the traditional deities, since these identified buildings and were used as proper names for people with whom they had to deal. But they could decline to use their titles, except in disparaging ways, such as "so-called gods," or by referring to the usage that others made of them, "the gods of the nations."[289]

---

283. Tert. *Idol.* 11.7.

284. Tert. *Idol.* 10.5-6, 18. See Julian's *Ep.* 61; the decree is witnessed in Augustine, *Conf.* 8.5.10 and *Ciu.* 18.52.

285. Tert. *Cor.* 8.5; 10.4-5. Christians did not have to avoid chicken because Socrates had sacrificed a rooster.

286. Tert. *Idol.* 16.1-5.

287. Tert. *Idol.* 16.14-15.

288. Tert. *Idol.* 17.1. This would have implied that a servant could be a Christian only with the consent of the master or mistress.

289. Tert. *Idol.* 20.

Tertullian approved these concessions to the common life of Christians and Roman traditionalists. Since he took a rigorist stance on these matters, particularly once he became a devotee of the New Prophecy, it may be assumed that these adaptations were commonly accepted by the Christians of the time.

## DISPUTED PRACTICES

Tertullian's writings provide evidence of a number of disputes about proper Christian practice in relation to the traditional religion. Most of these seem to have occurred within the Christian community itself. Some, such as the followers of Valentinus, believed that a Christian need not make public profession of faith and suffer the consequences of avoiding idolatry. Tertullian strongly objected, arguing that in clearly prohibiting idolatry, God willed the martyrdom that could be the consequence of obedience.[290] Most of Tertullian's fellows would certainly have agreed to this, since they venerated the martyrs as heroes.

Tertullian's treatise *On the Crown* focused on a Christian soldier who had provoked his superiors by throwing off the garland worn on a festival day to receive an imperial distribution of gifts. Some objected that this display was unnecessary: the soldier should have passively endured the crown and thus avoided trouble not only for himself but for other Christians serving in the ranks.[291] Tertullian took the opposite stance, disapproving such collaboration in idolatry. He took the opportunity to argue that a Christian should not join the military. A soldier who converted should find a way to leave the service, undertaking the complex task of working out permission to do this, or be prepared to accept martyrdom. Necessity was no excuse.[292] He argued elsewhere that all Christians had been disarmed by Christ in the person of Peter (Matt. 26:51-53) and should avoid military service — even if all compromises with idolatry could be eliminated.[293]

The same problems arose, Tertullian argued, for Christians who attempted to hold civic office. They had to steer clear of arranging and participating in sacrifices, spectacles, and anything else connected with idolatry. As judges, they could deal only with cases involving money; they should not judge, condemn, or execute criminals. Because of these restrictions, they did better to shun the honor of offices altogether.[294] Indeed, the power of the state was arrayed against God; Christians should have no part in it.[295]

In time of persecution, Christians attempted a variety of evasions and jus-

290. Tert. *Scorp.* 4.3-4.
291. Tert. *Cor.* 1.1-5.
292. Tert. *Cor.* 11.4-6.
293. Tert. *Idol.* 19.
294. Tert. *Idol.* 11.7, 17.2-3.
295. Tert. *Idol.* 18.8.

tifications for using them, most of which Tertullian disputed. The faithful could not deny being Christian, explaining that they thereby denied themselves but not Christ.[296] Christians should not flee from the city to avoid prosecution. Christ's directive to flee persecution (Matt. 10:23) applied only to the original apostles sent to evangelize the Jews; it was explicitly limited to the cities of Judea and could not be used by Africans.[297] Flight for fear of failing in the trial was already an apostasy, at least in intention, if not in deed. Christians should trust that God, who sent the trial, would provide the strength to endure it.[298] Christians, either individually or as a community, must not bribe soldiers or imperial officials to ignore them; this was itself a form of flight. They could not claim to have made a confession of Christ by acknowledging their identity in offering the gratuity, nor could they rationalize the bribe as an alms.[299] During times of civil disturbance and persecution, then, Christians ought to be about their normal routines: they should assemble at the normal times and in normal numbers. If absolutely necessary, they might switch to nighttime gatherings or meet in smaller groups.[300]

Normal civic life also gave rise to disagreements about what was compatible with a commitment to Christ. To some Christians, decorating their doors, exchanging gifts in celebration of the new year, and showing up for parties — as long as an active role in idolatry was avoided — seemed appropriate for maintaining good social relations. By totally refusing to share in civic life, Christians would provoke animosity. In response, Tertullian cited the account of a Christian whose servants had decorated the door of the house while he was away. Upon his return, he made them take down the offending signs at once. Yet the poor man was then chastised in a dream for the offense.[301] Tertullian concluded that Christians should completely reject participation in traditional festivals.

Christians could not simply retreat into silence. When someone called upon a traditional god — in curse, oath, or blessing — Tertullian insisted that a Christian must immediately object. Silence would be construed as an affirmation of the majesty and power of the god. The case was worse when a beggar offered a blessing in response to a gift. The honor for the kindness was being credited to some demon. Could the Christian fail to defend the glory of God, who had inspired the good generosity?[302]

The situation became even more complex when an oath was required to execute contracts for money or property. Some Christians argued that as long as they said nothing but only wrote a formula that the other party dictated,

296. Tert. *Scorp.* 9.12.
297. Tert. *Fug.* 4.1; 6.1-7.
298. Tert. *Fug.* 5.1-3.
299. Tert. *Fug.* 12.1-2; 13.1, 5.
300. Tert. *Fug.* 3.4; 14.2.
301. Tert. *Idol.* 13-15.
302. Tert. *Idol.* 21-22.

they had not actually violated the prohibitions against oaths or calling on other gods. In response, Tertullian pointed out that they could not distinguish between speaking and writing; they would be bound by the document in any legal proceeding. Better for Christians to deal only with other Christians, or to avoid such business completely.[303]

As these examples indicate, the Christian community at Carthage was divided in its stance toward the idolatry that permeated the customary practices of civic life. Some tried to work out compromises that allowed them to live and work in a culture that actively opposed their religious beliefs and practices. Tertullian could hardly have been alone in his more separatist position, insisting that Christians must actively resist idolatry, even incurring resentment, animosity, and alienation from their neighbors. In arguing for his position, Tertullian occasionally referred to the teachings of the New Prophecy,[304] but he also called upon dreams and visions that might be more broadly credited by Christians.[305]

## Cyprian

Because he had to deal with the Decian and Valerian persecutions, the first systematic imperial actions that affected all Christians, most of Cyprian's attention was focused on the appropriate response to demands for participation in traditional Roman religious rituals of supplication. The decree of the Roman government in 250 did not require anyone to renounce other practices or beliefs. Still, most Christians understood that compliance with the edict broke their baptismal oath to Christ. Later, the decree authorizing the Valerian persecution seems to have forbidden Christian practice itself. Cyprian himself went into voluntary exile during the Decian persecution to avoid a confrontation; in the Valerian persecution, he was involuntarily exiled and then executed.

### PROHIBITED PRACTICES

Cyprian provided very little information on the interaction of Christians with the traditional religious culture during peacetime. He did indicate that Christians were forbidden to work as actors in the theater and to train others to do so.[306]

Christians who were apprehended by imperial authorities during persecution and required to participate in idolatrous rituals had only one approved

303. Tert. *Idol.* 23.
304. Tert. *Cor.* 1.4; *Fug.* 9.4.
305. Tert. *Spec.* 26.1-3; *Idol.* 15.7.
306. *Ep.* 2.1.1-2.

option: to resist and refuse, even at the cost of their lives. Those who complied — either voluntarily, or under torture, or even by failing to maintain control of their bodies — had to undergo penitential cleansing, whose length and intensity depended upon the degree of their consent and participation in the action.[307] In arguing for his decision to allow those who sacrificed to undertake penance and eventually to be returned to communion, Cyprian observed that some had immediately and voluntarily complied, while others did so only under pressure; some required that their entire household participate, while others made the offering themselves and shielded their dependents; some used the status gained by complying with the edict to provide safe haven to exiles and refugees attempting to evade its enforcement.[308]

Cyprian and his community believed that a ritual pollution resulted from even involuntary contact with idolatry. He referred regularly not only to the conscience soiled by intention[309] but to the hand, mouth, and eyes contaminated by any contact.[310] The Roman clergy took a similar stance in letters to Cyprian.[311] A child's body was polluted by sacrificial meat that had been fed to her by a nurse; she immediately vomited up the eucharistic wine after it was given to her by the deacon.[312] Those who sinned intentionally suffered even greater harm.[313] An idolatrous Christian bishop or presbyter could spread contamination to the community that accepted his ministry.[314] Cyprian and his colleagues later made assertions about the polluting effect of baptism performed in schism: even a person who was ignorant of the wrong was contaminated by the minister's sin of rebellion.[315]

In both Africa and Rome, Christians attempted to avoid imperial punishment by obtaining certificates testifying to their having performed the sacrifice, although they carefully avoided doing so. In some cases, they used agents to obtain the documents, thereby hoping to excuse themselves of any wrongdoing.[316] Others acknowledged that they were Christians and asked for the favor of being spared a forbidden action.[317] The bishops ruled that this procedure was also a denial of Christ, since the certified were willing to have it generally believed that the certificate was true: that they had sacrificed and thus denied Christ. These sinners were required to cleanse their polluted consciences.[318]

---

307. A woman whose hand was held and forced through the action, in *Ep.* 24; others fell under torture, *Ep.* 56; most volunteered to comply, *Laps.* 8-9, 13.

308. Cypr. *Ep.* 55.13.2.

309. Cypr. *Ep.* 55.14.2.

310. Cypr. *Ep.* 20.2.2; 30.3.2; 59.15.3.

311. Cypr. *Ep.* 31.7.1.

312. Cypr. *Laps.* 25.

313. Cypr. *Laps.* 23-26.

314. Cypr. *Ep.* 65.2.1-2, 3.3, 4.1; 67.2.2, 3.1, 9.2.

315. Cypr. *Ep.* 70.3.1; 72.2.2; 73.21.2; *Unit. eccl.* 11.

316. The Roman clergy provided a description of the process in Cypr. *Ep.* 30.3.1.

317. Cypr. *Ep.* 55.14.1.

318. Cypr. *Laps.* 27; *Ep.* 55.14.2.

In defending against the revolt of the laxists in Carthage, Cyprian argued that the division of the church was a second stage in the demonic attack initiated in the Decian edict. As such, it presented an opportunity for the fallen to confess Christ by holding to the unity of the church and submitting to its penitential ritual. Their loyalty would reverse their earlier apostasy, secure its forgiveness, and prepare them for winning the crown of martyrdom.[319] With his episcopal colleagues, he later asserted that the rituals of baptism and eucharist, when celebrated in schism, were as polluting as the sacrifices of traditional polytheism.[320]

## ACCEPTED PRACTICES

Cyprian took a rigorist stance toward the consequences of contact with idolatry, but he was more liberal in approving means of avoiding it. He himself went into exile after the civil disturbances that accompanied the initial enforcement of the Decian edict. He was recognized as a prominent person in Carthage,[321] and he claimed to have withdrawn in order to prevent a focus of imperial and popular attention on the Christian community.[322] Fear of provoking a riot against the Christians kept him away for more than a year.[323] He did not allow the same privilege of voluntary exile to other members of the clergy, whose social station did not attract the same attention.[324]

Cyprian asserted that flight from persecution had been both practiced and urged by Christ. Rather than relying on Christ's directive to missionaries to move on when rejected (Matt. 10:23), which Tertullian had disputed, Cyprian cited the directive to avoid impurity by withdrawing (Isa. 52:11) and the command to abandon Babylon the Great (Rev. 18:4), and alluded to Christ's own withdrawals to avoid confrontation (Luke 4:30; John 8:59).[325] In a direct response to Tertullian's own argument that flight was equivalent to failure, Cyprian asserted that martyrdom was the gift of God, who would find a way to give it to the chosen. Christians might withdraw and await God's initiative.[326] Those who had the option of flight, however, would have risked having the imperial treasury confiscate any property they left behind, as Cyprian himself appar-

---

319. Cypr. *Ep.* 43.3.1-2, 6.1–7.2; *Laps.* 33-36; *Unit. eccl.* 3, 10, 19.

320. Cypr. *Ep.* 72.2.1-2.

321. Cypr. *Ep.* 8.1.1. The Roman clergy recognized him as a *persona insignis*.

322. Cypr. *Ep.* 7.1; 20.1.2; he claimed a divine mandate for his action but did not quote a scriptural text.

323. Cypr. *Ep.* 14.1.2; 43.4.1-2.

324. Cypr. *Ep.* 14.2.1; 34.4.1. The surviving evidence does not indicate whether action was taken against other clergy who left Carthage.

325. Cypr. *Laps.* 10.

326. Cypr. *Laps.* 10.

ently did. That many Christians refused to abandon their wealth demonstrated that for others even flight was a form of confession.[327]

Even more striking than Cyprian's rejection of Tertullian's position on flight from persecution was his attention to a variety of ways to confess Christ. During the persecution, he insisted that all the imprisoned who died for the faith, even if they died from hunger or disease, were to be counted as martyrs. Those who refused to deny Christ had offered themselves to God, even if they did not die under torture.[328] Going further, he exhorted the faithful who had not been apprehended to stand fast. They need not fear the end of persecution and coming of peace before they could confess, suffer for Christ, and thus win the crown. God knew and would crown their resolve and intention.[329] Immediately upon his return to Carthage, he praised all who had taken no initiative to obey the edict: by allowing the deadline for compliance to pass, they had confessed Christ.[330] Both those who had stayed in Carthage and those who had abandoned their property to take flight were confessors in private; in honor they were only one degree below those who had won public victories.[331] Cornelius, the newly elected Bishop of Rome, received similar praise. He had been prepared to follow the footsteps of his predecessor to a martyr's death; in accepting the office, he suffered all that God allowed.[332] As the persecution of Gallus approached, Cyprian advised flight: Christ would be the Christians' companion in exile and would witness to their martyrdom, even if death was incurred by accident, bandit, or wild beast.[333] Christ would honor among the martyrs all who had been willing to leave all and follow him.[334]

In a move that again directly contradicted Tertullian and anticipated Augustine, Cyprian extended the argument to those who might die of fever during the summer plague. They must not regret that they had died in bed of fever and thus failed to gain a martyr's death and crown. Martyrdom had failed their spirits; they had not failed martyrdom. God, he explained, seeks faith, not blood.[335]

Tertullian, particularly when he reflected the spirit of the New Prophecy, urged Christians to an active confrontation of the idolatry of Roman culture. Cyprian, faced with a systematic imperial attack, argued that Christians could and indeed should avoid such confrontations whenever doing so did not involve

---

327. Cypr. *Laps.* 11-12.
328. Cypr. *Ep.* 12.1.2-3.
329. Cypr. *Ep.* 10.5.1-2.
330. Cypr. *Laps.* 3.
331. Cypr. *Laps.* 2-3.
332. Cypr. *Ep.* 55.9.2.
333. Cypr. *Ep.* 58.4.1-2.
334. Cypr. *Fort.* 12.
335. Cypr. *Mort.* 17; see Tert. *Fug.* 9.4; Aug. *Virg.* 44.45–46.47.

a denial of Christ. They could use their lower social status to avoid attention; they could take refuge in another city where they would not be recognized as Christian; they could abandon their patrimony and retreat into exile. His own practice was to avoid provoking a conflict that might put others to the test. If God had chosen a Christian for the crown of martyrdom, then God could be trusted to provide the occasion for trial and public victory. God, moreover, would reward all whose hearts were ready for that call, even if they died of fever in their beds.

Cyprian also recognized that a Christian could fail as secretly as they could confess. After the Decian persecution, some who had escaped detection and apparently been faithful admitted that they had in fact failed. They confessed that they had decided that if they were brought to trial, they would comply with the edict and participate in the sacrifice. These Cyprian urged to engage in penance, as privately as they had sinned, and beg for God's forgiveness.[336]

## Fourth-Century Witnesses

The Christians of Africa experienced a brief period of persecution under Diocletian, which was focused on the confiscation of sacred vessels and books. It resulted in some deaths. After judicial attempts to resolve the schism between Caecilian and Donatus, Constantine ordered the confiscation of Donatist churches. That provoked resistance in Carthage. An extended period of toleration was terminated by a new attempt at reunion of the churches by Constans, which brought more extensive resistance and the exile of Donatist leaders. Under Julian, the Donatist leaders were allowed to return and reclaim their basilicas; that takeover resulted in the deaths of some Caecilianists. Similarly, Honorius's attempts to bring about a settlement of the division again resulted in violent resistance and some deaths.

At the end of the Diocletian persecution, the Council of Arles distinguished three forms of apostasy in Africa: handing over the scriptures to be burned, handing over the sacred vessels to be destroyed, and identifying other Christians to the authorities.[337] Court records show that some bishops and clergy had provided no resistance to the confiscation of sacred vessels but had refused to cooperate by giving the names of the readers who held the sacred books.[338] In other instances, both in Carthage and in Numidia, bishops resisted by sub-

---

336. Cypr. *Laps.* 28.
337. *Con. Arel.* a. 314, 14; CCSL 148:12.42-51.
338. *Act. Zeno.;* CSEL 26:186.31–187.2. Strikingly, two of the subdeacons who had just carried out the church's sacred vessels absolutely refused to betray the readers, preferring to be killed (26:188.1-2).

terfuge: they hid the scriptures and substituted profane or heretical books.[339] At least some bishops stood their ground and paid with their lives.[340]

After the persecution, the bishops had to remove unworthy colleagues from their offices without giving occasion for false accusations and unending conflict. A meeting of Numidian bishops in Cirta agreed to leave all charges of betrayal to the divine Judgment.[341] The council meeting in Arles to deal with the Donatist schism decided that any cleric whom public records proved guilty of betrayal was to be excluded from office. Private accusations were not to be credited. The provisions set forth by the Roman bishop, Miltiades, enforced these decisions.[342]

The Caecilianist or Catholic party in Africa did not claim the title of confessor or martyr for those who suffered at the hands of Donatist schismatics during the ensuing conflict. The Donatists, however, honored their members who continued to resist imperial attempts to enforce the unity of the church. Those who died when the government used force in 317 to confiscate the Donatist basilica in Carthage were buried in that church and proclaimed martyrs.[343] In a sermon commemorating the event, the crown of martyrdom was assigned to all who participated in the resistance, on the grounds that God rewarded the faith and not only the blood of believers.[344] When Constans attempted to achieve unity by financial inducements, the Donatists again honored their resisters. The Numidian bishops Marculus and Donatus of Bagai lost their lives and were treated as martyrs.[345] In Carthage, two Donatist laymen, Maximian and Isaac, died in prison awaiting punishment for tearing down the decree of unification of the churches; they were honored with an account of their suffering.[346] The Donatist bishops who were sent into exile for refusing to join the Catholic communion were also recognized as having confessed Christ.[347]

Optatus, the Donatist Bishop of Thamugadi in southern Numidia, allied himself with Gildo in revolt against the government of Honorius in 397. When the

339. Mensurius was described as claiming to have allowed heretical books to be confiscated in a letter produced by the Donatists; Numidian bishops gave medical texts or martyrs' acts. See Aug. *Coll.* 3.13.25; *Cresc.* 3.27.30.

340. *Pas. Fel.*

341. Aug. *Cresc.* 3.27.30.

342. *Con. Arel.* a. 314, 14; Aug. *Ep.* 43.16.

343. *Pas. Don.* 6-8, 11-13. Jean-Louis Maier, *Le dossier du donatisme,* 2 vols. (Berlin: Akademie Verlag, 1987), 1:198-211.

344. *Pas. Don.* 9.

345. *Pas. Marc.* The *passio* of Donatus has not survived. The events are mentioned in Optat. *Parm.* 3.4. Augustine objected to their being honored as martyrs, among other reasons, because their modes of death — precipitation from a cliff and drowning in a well — were not normal Roman methods of execution but could have been means of suicide (Aug. *Eu. Io.* 11.15).

346. *Pas. Isa. Max.* The proconsul attempted to dispose of their bodies in order to prevent their veneration.

347. Augustine reported that Donatus of Carthage was honored as a martyr (*Don.* 16.20).

uprising was put down in 398, both Gildo and Optatus were executed. Some of the Donatists regarded Optatus as a martyr for his resistance;[348] others found his resort to violence in this and other instances a great embarrassment to their cause.[349]

An irregular force of Donatist fighters, the Circumcellions, made its first appearance in the 340s and played a much-discussed role in the conflict between the Donatists and the Caecilianists that continued through Honorius's attempts to achieve unity in the early fifth century.[350] Augustine reported that these individuals actively sought death in the service of their church and were widely venerated among the Donatists as martyrs.[351]

A number of Caecilianists were attacked and some killed by Donatist forces attempting to prevent the unification of the two churches under Emperor Honorius. Laity were also threatened with the destruction of their property.[352] The imperial commissioner Marcellinus may have paid with his life for his judgment in favor of the Caecilianist party at the Conference of Carthage.[353] A series of presbyters whom Augustine had appointed to serve the formerly Donatist congregation in Fussala were mistreated and killed.[354] Yet, none of these Caecilianists were honored as martyrs, though they had died in the course of service to Christ and the church.

When the government of Honorius outlawed not only idolatrous rituals but the display of statues of the gods, some Caecilianists undertook to enforce the edict themselves.[355] Riots ensued and lives were lost.[356] None of those killed was honored as a martyr, and the bishops discouraged any further confrontations.[357]

The Donatists celebrated the resistance of their bishops and laity to the empire's efforts to bring about a union of the two churches. Those who suffered injury, exile, or death at the hands of either the imperial forces or the polytheists protecting their statues and temples were regarded as martyrs, even if they had provoked the violence. The Caecilianists, however, did not celebrate the sacrifices of their clergy who were victims of Donatist violence. They may have

---

348. Aug. *Ep.* 76.3.

349. Augustine noted that the Donatists were embarrassed by Optatus (*Petil.* 2.23.53, 92.209).

350. First mentioned in Optat. *Parm.* 3.4.

351. He claimed that they not only engaged in criminal activities but threw themselves off cliffs — in imitation of the reported death of Marculus — or forced others to kill them: Aug. *Ep.* 88.8-9; 89.2-3; 105.2.5; *Parm.* 3.6.29; *Petil.* 2.49.114, 71.160, 87.193; *Gaud.* 1.27.30, 31.36-38; *Serm. Guelf.* 28(313E).6. Their shrines may have been the object of the attempt to determine the authenticity of martyrs (*Reg. Carth.* 83).

352. An early summary is provided in Aug. *Cresc.* 3.41.45–48.53.

353. Aug. *Ep.* 151.

354. Aug. *Ep.* 209.2.

355. Quodu. *Prom.* 3.38.44 reports the takeover of the temple of Juno Caelestis in Carthage. See also Aug. *Serm.* 105.9.12.

356. Aug. *Ep.* 50; *Serm.* 24.5.

357. Aug. *Serm.* 62.11.17–12.18.

judged that labeling the Donatists as agents of demonic oppression would undermine their attempts to achieve reconciliation and unity.

## Augustine

The Christian community of the early fifth century faced a very different imperial culture than that of the late second and third centuries. Constantine and Licinius had liberated Christians from persecution and civil disabilities. Apart from a brief period of alienation under Julian, Christians found themselves increasingly at home in the Roman world. At the end of the fourth century, Theodosius I not only privileged Christians but withdrew state support from the traditional rites; his sons completed the process by outlawing public displays and sacrifices in honor of the traditional gods. Augustine observed in his sermons that the cult of the traditional deities had disappeared from Rome and was being driven out of Carthage.[358] Christians, he counseled, should leave this process in the hands of the imperial authorities; they were not to act outside the law by tearing down statues or invading country estates to destroy shrines.[359] He warned that persecution remained even in the new, Christian age; it would be limited and hidden.[360] In his sermons, he pointed out ways in which the demons continued their assault on Christians, attacks to which Christians should respond in faith and thus bear witness to Christ.

### DISPUTED PRACTICES

Although many traditional entertainments and practices presented temptations to Christians, Augustine did not rank participation in these as direct denials of Christ. He did not warn against idolatry when he urged Christians to stay away from the theater, the races, and blood spectacles. Instead, he cited their lewdness, cruelty, and vanity as incompatible with Christian morals.[361] In the initial legislation of the reform program mounted by Aurelius of Carthage, the children of bishops were forbidden to present or attend games.[362] Later, the bishops complained that the churches were sparsely attended on the octave of Easter and attempted to prevent games and spectacles on Sundays and Christian feast days.[363] Augustine also tried to convince his parishioners that Christians should prefer worship to the pagan dramas.[364] The readings of the *acta* of the martyrs

358. Aug. *Serm.* 24.6; 105.9.12.
359. Aug. *Serm.* 62.11.17–12.18.
360. Aug. *Serm.* 62.10.15.
361. Aug. *Ep. Io.* 2.13; *Psal.* 18.2.1; *Serm.* 198.3.
362. *Bru. Hipp.* 11; repeated in *Cau. Apiar.* 15.
363. *Con. Carth.* June, a. 401; *Reg. Carth.* 61.
364. Aug. *Psal.* 30.3.2; 50.1; 147.7.

provided a better spectacle,[365] he claimed, whose actors were fit models for imitation.[366] Parents did not want their children to grow up to be jugglers, tight-rope walkers, or gladiators; why should they encourage and support such people?[367] He urged Christians to boycott the theaters and games. Preaching in Bulla Regia, he berated the congregation for the flourishing condition of their town's entertainments. In many places, he claimed, Christians had refused to attend such presentations and thereby shut them down. In Simitthu, in particular, the population had refused to watch a special show provided by an imperial official.[368] If the Christians stopped attending, the pagans would be embarrassed by the small audiences, and the whole business would soon shut down.[369]

### PROHIBITED PRACTICES

The traditional festivals were a concern for the bishops, particularly the first of January and the midsummer celebration — that coincided with the Christian feast of the birth of John the Baptist. Augustine preached his longest surviving sermon on the January feast, urging his congregation to fast and pray for their neighbors' conversion and salvation, rather than eating, drinking, gambling, and exchanging presents.[370] The midsummer activities included bonfires on the vigil and cavorting in the sea on the feast day. This latter was a mockery, he claimed, of John's baptizing work.[371] The Jews, he proclaimed, were models in rejecting these pagan celebrations.[372]

In the Christian empire, oaths no longer presented the same challenge as they had earlier, when one was required to call upon a demon — in the guise of a traditional god — as witness. The danger was perjury, or committing to perform an evil action. God could swear oaths without danger of perjury, but humans could not be sure that they were telling the truth.[373] Humans could not see one another's hearts, so they required oaths to impede lying. To require an oath knowing that the other person would lie, however, was to force another to sin and even to murder one's own soul.[374] In any case, an oath should be broken to prevent a greater sin in carrying it out.[375]

365. Aug. *Serm.* 51.1.2; 300.1.
366. Aug. *Serm. Denis* 14(313A).3.
367. Aug. *Psal.* 102.13.
368. Aug. *Serm. Denis* 17(301A).7-9.
369. Aug. *Serm. Denis* 14(313A).3-4; *Serm. Dolb.* 26(198*).9.
370. Aug. *Serm. Dolb.* 26(198*); see also *Serm.* 196.4.
371. Aug. *Serm.* 196.4; 279.13; *Serm. Frang.* 8(293B).5.
372. Aug. *Serm.* 196.4.
373. Aug. *Psal.* 109.17; *Serm.* 307.3.4.
374. Aug. *Serm.* 308.3.3–5.5.
375. Aug. *Serm.* 308.2.2.

Astrologers and soothsayers still worked their trades, claiming to provide information about the future course of events. The problem was widespread enough for Augustine to discuss it twice in *Confessions*.[376] He attacked it in his sermons as a temptation but not as a major sin.[377]

### RECOMMENDED PRACTICES

The culture did, however, provide occasions for true apostasy. When faced with these crises, a Christian had to decide for or against Christ. In either case, life itself could be at stake.

Augustine described a situation in which a person might be pressured to lie in court. A powerful person might require a poor person to give false testimony in support of a fraudulent suit. Credible threats against life and property were made if the witness testified truthfully. By refusing the perjury, a Christian witnessed to and might suffer for Christ, who was identified as Truth.[378]

Illness presented a second challenge to the Christian. Healing practices related to traditional religion or magic were still available. A Christian lying on a sickbed might be approached by a friend or a servant with an amulet or an incantation that was said to have worked a cure for others. Hanging the charm around one's neck or even calling upon God and the angels in some special way would guarantee a cure. Augustine did not dispute the efficacy of such practices for healing the body. Instead, he asserted that these cures were the work of the demons and called upon Christians to reject them. Those who did so thereby confessed Christ; if they died as a consequence, they would win the martyr's crown.[379]

Such martyrs as these did not win public victories; their tombs would not be shrines; they would not be commemorated in the liturgy on the anniversaries of their death. Instead, they would be crowned in secret by Christ, as Cyprian had taught about voluntary exiles. Commenting on the trial of Susanna, Augustine pointed out that God did not always deliver the innocent; but for Daniel's inspired intervention, the faithful matron would have been a martyr in secret.[380]

In another context, Augustine expanded this new understanding of witness to Christ. Martyrdom was the highest of God's gifts, but it could remain a virtuous attitude hidden in the soul. On occasion it would be publicly tested and made manifest; more regularly it remained unrecognized. In contrast, the gifts of consecrated virginity and declared widowhood were public ones. Those

376. Aug. *Conf.* 4.3.4-6; 7.6.8-10.
377. Aug. *Serm.* 4.36; 9.3, 17; *Serm. Denis* 21(15A).4; *Serm. Dolb.* 26(198*).58.
378. Aug. *Serm.* 97.4; *Serm. Cail.* 2.6(94A).2-3; *Serm. Denis* 17(301A).5; *Serm. Dolb.* 18(306E).10.
379. Aug. *Serm.* 4.36; 286.8.7; 318.3; 328.9.6 (*Serm. Lamb.* 13); *Serm. Lamb.* 6(335D).3, 5; *Serm. Dolb.* 18(306E).7-8.
380. Aug. *Serm.* 343.2.

who had received them must remember that some of their fellows, among them matrons, might indeed have answered, albeit secretly, the higher calling of martyrdom and would receive a greater honor.[381]

## Conclusion

Tertullian's treatment of Christian witness had been focused on practices that demarcated the boundary separating the holy realm of the church from that of demonic idolatry. He was more insistent in asserting Christian faith and challenging the practices of idolatry than most of his contemporaries and successors. Under the pressure of persecution, Cyprian added considerations of the interior dispositions that could accompany flight from persecution and even death from sickness. Augustine noted more subtle but no less real ways in which the demons continued to challenge Christian faith. He focused on the witness of a moral life, which was more regularly challenged. Still, he found ways in which Christians could still witness to faith in Christ, both publicly and privately, though their victories might be recognized only by their own families and rewarded in secret by Christ.

## GENERAL OBSERVATIONS

### Correlation of Archeological and Literary Evidence

The practices discussed in this chapter — prayer, fasting, almsgiving, and confession of Christ — leave few physical remains with which the literary evidence can be correlated. The cult of the martyrs, as distinguished from the practice of martyrdom itself, has left significant material evidence, particularly in the tomb covers for burials that occasionally express the prayers of the faithful for the assistance of the martyr (cf. fig. 143). A number of these also provide illustrations of the posture that Christians assumed for prayer: standing with arms outstretched (e.g., figs. 120, 130, 131, 134, 135, 137, 139, 140).

Some material remains have no corresponding textual evidence but might be considered indicators of everyday pious practices. These include innumerable examples of the distinctive African red slipware, including bowls, lamps, cups, vases, and platters. Many of these were decorated with biblical figures, saints, or other Christian symbols (e.g., fish, Christograms) applied to the wet clay and fused as low relief in the process of firing (cf. fig. 152).[382] Tertullian

---

381. Aug. *Virg.* 44.45–46.47.

382. See John Herrmann and Annewies van den Hoek, *Light from the Age of Augustine: Late Antique Ceramics from North Africa (Tunisia)* (Cambridge, Mass.: Harvard Divinity School, 2002).

---

commented (negatively) on the use of drinking goblets or glasses that were decorated with figures of the Good Shepherd, possibly because they reminded him of fancy wine cups with the image of Bacchus.[383]

In the fifth and sixth centuries, potteries began producing decorative tiles with Christian designs. These tiles, originally painted with bright colors, were intended for the decoration of walls and ceilings. They have been found in quantities at the sites of Byzantine-era churches but may have also been used in ordinary homes (cf. figs. 150, 151).

Other small items that reflected an owner's religious sentiments in an everyday manner were finger rings and seals that featured incised gems or simple etched designs, including the legend ΙΧΘΥΣ with a fish, or a Good Shepherd figure.[384]

## Correlation of Theology and Practice

### PRAYER

The discussion of prayer in each of the African theologians tended to focus on problems that could be identified in the community. In a congregation that could not hope to secure its position in the imperial culture and economy, Tertullian urged that intercessory prayer should focus on spiritual rather than material benefits. Cyprian was attempting to manage a church divided by conflict even before the crisis of the Decian persecution, when these rivalries broke out into open schism and competing Christian communions were formed within the city. He focused on the unanimity and mutual support that make prayer effective before God.

In Augustine's preaching and writing on prayer, theology and practice influenced one another. At the heart of the Donatist controversy was the church's power to forgive sins; the animosity between the two communions frustrated all attempts to settle the historical issues and to develop a more adequate understanding of the church. Augustine focused on the petition for forgiveness and the promise to forgive others linked together in the Lord's Prayer. He not only exhorted believers to the practice of forgiveness but built a theology of the church in which the mutual forgiveness of the Christian faithful was the exemplary exercise of the power to forgive. He added that Christians must neither pray that God execute vengeance on their enemies nor give thanks to God for the misfortunes that befell them.

The method of interpreting the Psalms that Augustine developed on the

---

383. Tert. *Pud.* 10.

384. For examples, see Jeffrey Spier, *Late Antique and Early Christian Gems,* Spätantike, frühes Christentum, Byzanz., Reihe B (Wiesbaden: Reichert, 2007), nos. 191, 152, 194, 364.

basis of Tyconius's *Rules* transformed these prayers into a means of enacting an understanding of the church as the body of Christ. Praying the Psalms in union with Christ and, thus, with the universal church would become foundational to the work of monks in their daily office.

## FASTING

Tertullian and Cyprian understood fasting primarily as a support for prayer, either interceding for forgiveness or asking for divine assistance. To this, Tertullian added the notion that the control of bodily desires prepared a person to withstand coercion. Augustine's focus was more on fasting as an exercise of control of the appetites and desires associated with bodily living, so that the mind might be freer for seeking God. Using his understanding of the unity of the body of Christ, he argued that fasting should not just deprive one person but should benefit another: either the food or the money saved by fasting should be given to the poor. Fasting became an exercise of affirming the unity of Christians as members of Christ.

## ALMSGIVING

Tertullian remarked on both communal and individual almsgiving, which was extended to both fellow Christians and to traditionalists. After the Decian persecution, Cyprian insisted on almsgiving as a means of overcoming the attachment to wealth that had led so many Christians to compromise their commitment to Christ. Giving their resources to the community and the Christian poor was also a means of transferring uncertain earthly wealth to the security of heavenly treasure. Cyprian did not recognize a need to retain capital assets in order to care for one's own family. Later, in the radically different social situation of an empire in which Christians were protected and could expect a delay of the end-time, Augustine approved the preservation of income-producing principal by churches and by families; he urged that the income must be shared. An appreciation of the church as the body of Christ, moreover, enabled Augustine to explain that care of fellow Christians was a privileged means of caring for Christ and thus transforming earthly into heavenly wealth. This theology required that every Christian should be a donor; the poor had time and physical labor to share, even if they had no money to give away. The sharing of resources was itself a sign of the unity of the church as Christ's body.

African Christianity was characterized by a militant confrontation with idolatry; its practices changed not with the development of theology but with the social location of the church. Though Tertullian allowed that Christians might participate in activities in which direct contact in idolatry was avoidable, he insisted that Christians must do nothing that would support the traditional religions, even by supplying materials for their rituals. In time of persecution, moreover, Christians must neither seek nor avoid confrontations: they should be ready to witness to their faith when God required it of them. Because he was dealing with sustained and systematic persecution, Cyprian approved prudent retreat from confrontation. He was able, moreover, to recognize different forms of demonic assault on the church, and thus to identify schismatic Christian rituals as equivalent to idolatrous ones. In the fourth century, the Donatists identified confessing Christ with resisting the remnants of apostasy within the church, while the Caecilianists — following Cyprian — found the demons at work in the continuing schism. Augustine lived to see the empire prohibit idolatrous rites and to hear reports of Christians attacking the temples and destroying the statues of the traditional gods. He warned, however, that the challenge of witnessing to Christ was still at hand. A Christian might be threatened for refusing to lie in court or might risk death by declining to employ a cure for illness that relied on the power of a demon. The mode of witness might change, but the temptation to demonic idolatry remained. In the following century, African Christians would once again experience the uncertainty of living under a government hostile to their Nicene Christianity.

# CHAPTER 13

# The Church and Its Holiness

## INTRODUCTION

The church, as the medium of sanctification and salvation, was at the center of Christian thought and practice in Roman Africa. The life of the individual Christian was firmly set within the matrix of this community; the holiness of individuals was inseparable from that of the ecclesial communion to which they belonged. The major crises and conflicts — from Montanism in Tertullian's time, through laxism in response to the Decian persecution, to the century-long dispute between the Caecilianists and the Donatists — were all focused on the preservation of the holiness of the church and its identity as the assembly of those being saved. As its relationship to the imperial society changed, so did the challenges its members faced and their understanding of the holiness of the church. Standards of practice that had functioned well in one era became the basis of division and conflict in a later one. Reference points along the trajectory of African theology — Tertullian, Cyprian, Tyconius, Parmenian, and Optatus of Milevis — will be reviewed before considering the fully elaborated ecclesiology of Augustine, which became foundational but neither unchallenged nor unmodified in Latin Christianity.

## TERTULLIAN: REJECTING IDOLATRY AND ADHERING TO CHRIST

At the turn of the third century, Tertullian defined Christianity according to its dual baptismal oaths: first, as the rejection of the traditional practices of Punic and Roman idolatry; and second, as a commitment to Christ that was to be lived by faithful adherence to the church's ritual, moral, and ascetic practices. Although he recognized human weakness, Tertullian required a high ritual and moral standard of all Christians, refusing to assign responsibility for the holiness of the church to a particular class of its members.

Prayer was the central form of sacrifice,[1] and all Christians were priests.[2] All were warned to avoid contact with idolatry in its many forms.[3] All were called to affirm the ideals that may have been realized in the lives of only some: the active confrontation of idolatry achieved by the martyrs,[4] the sexual continence practiced by the widows and virgins,[5] the single marriage required of the clergy,[6] and the rigorous fasts embraced by the devotees of the New Prophecy.[7] Imperfection could be tolerated, but only within narrow limits: anyone who violated the baptismal oaths, by idolatry or any other sin forbidden by the Decalogue, must be excluded from the eucharistic fellowship. Only some of these sinners were allowed readmission after penance.[8] The church as a whole and each of its members had to be holy because it was identified with Christ and shared his intercessory role.[9] Its intercessory prayer could win salvation for its weaker members and for those infants and adolescents not yet capable of the baptismal commitment. Its penitents could be helped only by a church that maintained its purity by excluding them from eucharistic communion.[10]

The church community constituted by these commitments, rituals, and practices was itself the sacrament of the divine presence on earth and the necessary medium for participation in the salvation accomplished in Christ. As the individual Christian was the temple of God, so the community was the body of the Trinity.[11] After the three divine persons, it was the fourth major element in the baptismal confession of faith. The union of Christ and the church was symbolized by the intentional union of marriage partners; it would survive death and would be violated by either adultery or remarriage.[12]

Not everyone in Tertullian's community accepted his stark understanding of the church's nature and role. Its bishop claimed authority to forgive sins by

1. Tert. *Apol.* 30.6; *Marc.* 4.1.

2. Tert. *Bapt.* 17.1-3; the text of *Bapt.* 17.3 is somewhat obscure. This interpretation follows Evans's construal: Tertullian, *De Baptismo Liber, Homily on Baptism,* ed. Ernest Evans (London: SPCK, 1964), p. 34. *Cast.* 7.3-6 is much clearer: the laity must follow priestly discipline because they must perform priestly functions when necessary.

3. Tert. *Idol.* 4.1; 9.1; 11.2–3.7; 17-19; *Cor.* 11.4-6.

4. Tert. *Idol.* 22.

5. Tert. *Ux.* 1.6.2; *Cast.* 1.4.

6. Tert. *Mon.* 11.1; *Pud.* 1.20.

7. Tert. *Ieiun.* 1.4; Tertullian cited scriptural precedents for this form of fasting (*Ieiun.* 9).

8. Tert. *Pud.* 5.13-14, 9.9, 20, 12.5, 13.2, 19.25, 26, 28, 21.2.

9. Tert. *Paen.* 10.6. The parallel persisted in *Pud.* 19.25-26 but without the guarantee of Christ's acting with the church.

10. Tert. *Pud.* 3.5, 13.12; *Bapt.* 18.

11. Tert. *Bapt.* 6.2; *Pud.* 21.2.

12. Tert. *Mon.* 5.1, 7; 10.4, 8.

virtue of the power of office bestowed upon Peter.[13] Though the clergy were charged with maintaining a ritual purity,[14] the married claimed the concession of sexual relations and even a second marriage after the death of a spouse.[15] Many defended taking flight or bribing imperial officials to avoid confessing Christ at the cost of their fortunes and lives.[16] Despite this dissent, Tertullian articulated an ideal of life and community that would mark African Christianity; his standards of conduct seem to have been espoused by a community of devotees in Carthage until the last decades of the fourth century.[17]

## CYPRIAN: REJECTING SCHISM IN A UNITED CHURCH

The shock of the Decian persecution showed the fault lines and fragility of Christian communities. Many Christians failed outright; others compromised; most hid; a few publicly confessed Christ and suffered for their faith; some died as martyrs.[18] The fallen looked to the few — the martyrs and confessors — to exercise the church's intercessory and mediating function for them. Once assured of their patronage, they demanded that the clergy readmit them to communion, in some cases without either demonstration of repentance or rituals of cleansing.[19] The purists — some of them confessors — responded by insisting that the church must uphold the inviolability of its baptismal commitment to Christ. Only by preserving its holiness from pollution by the apostates tainted with idolatrous sacrifices could it exercise its salvific role; it could help the lapsed only by permanently excluding them.[20] As tensions mounted and the church divided into competing congregations, the bishops — led by Cyprian of Carthage — claimed for themselves that sanctifying power that Tertullian had insisted was distributed over the whole church and not associated with an office.

Cyprian shared Tertullian's understanding of the church as the faithful community joined together in and to Christ, as the body in which the Trinity dwelt. Like Tertullian, Cyprian characterized the church by its purity and its rejection of idolatry; in the face of schism, however, unity became the ultimate test of fidelity to Christ. In the face of revolt by both the laxists and the rigorists, however, he asserted that the unity of the church gathered around its bishops

13. Tert. *Pud.* 21.9.
14. Tert. *Mon.* 12.1-2.
15. Tert. *Mon.* 11.9-13.
16. Tert. *Fug.* 4.1; 6.1-7; 12.1-2; 13.1, 5.
17. Aug. *Haer.* 86 reported that the Tertullianists had recently given up their basilica and joined the Catholics.
18. Cypr. *Laps.* 2-4.
19. Cypr. *Ep.* 27.2.2–3.1.
20. Cypr. *Ep.* 46; 55.6.1; 24.1; 68.

derived through Christ from the Trinity and could not fail.[21] Dissenters could desert but not divide the church.[22] Those who split off — even to protect purity — thereby abandoned Christ and lost all access to holiness and salvation.[23] Though the schismatics claimed to share the Christian faith and sacraments, Cyprian insisted that they were enemies of Christ and no better than the idolaters; their rituals were polluted rather than sanctifying.[24] In the final section of the baptismal creed they claimed to share, they acknowledged that the united community alone could mediate holiness, forgiveness, and everlasting life.[25] In Cyprian's theology, then, the unity of the church's communion became constitutive of its holiness.

In asserting that the unity of the church's communion was essential to its holiness, Cyprian built on a momentum that had been growing since Tertullian's day. Many Christians believed that salvation was available only to those actually participating in the eucharistic fellowship of the church.[26] Parents had their infants baptized. Adult converts were quickly baptized if they became ill. Penitents demanded to be reconciled before death so that they would face the Judgment of Christ as members of the communion.[27] Contrary to the rigorist views that were represented by Tertullian and then by Novatian, most Christians had come to believe that the church could help them only by readmitting them to communion. To prevent sinners from losing all hope and to maintain that the church was the necessary mediator of salvation, then, Cyprian had to accept into communion some whose commitment to Christ had once failed and whose freedom from the contamination of idolatry was far from certain.[28]

To maintain the full holiness of the church — in its rejection of idolatry, its adherence to Christ, its moral and ascetic rigor — Cyprian provided for a differentiation of classes or orders within the church, with different responsibilities and powers. The bishops and clergy alone were entrusted with the church's sanctifying power, and they were charged with guarding the fidelity and purity necessary for maintaining it.[29] The laity could then include not only the strong and committed but the weak and even reconciled penitents who would be presented to Christ with the prayers of the church.[30]

Cyprian explained that Christ had conferred upon the church a real, though limited, power of sanctification, through which repentant apostates,

21. Cypr. *Unit. eccl.* 6.
22. Cypr. *Unit. eccl.* 6-9.
23. Cypr. *Unit. eccl.* 18-23.
24. Cypr. *Ep.* 70; 72.1.12.1-3; 73.21.2.
25. Cypr. *Ep.* 69.7.2.
26. Cypr. *Ep.* 55.17.2; 57.4.1-4.
27. Cypr. *Ep.* 63; 18.1.2; 20.3.1-2; 55.28.1–29.2.
28. This is most evident in the case of those anticipating martyrdom (Cypr. *Ep.* 57).
29. Cypr. *Ep.* 33.1.1; *Unit. eccl.* 4-5.
30. Cypr. *Ep.* 55.18.1, 20.3; 57.3.3.

schismatics, and other sinners could be readmitted to its communion. A single, indivisible gift of the Holy Spirit — a power to bind and loosen — had been conferred on the episcopal college formed by the Apostles; then it had been transmitted to their successor bishops who were joined in a unified body.[31] This sacralization of the internal structures of the church was then employed to explain the efficacy of the sacraments. Only the bishop acting in the unity of the church could sanctify the water of baptism, could offer the sacrifice established by Christ, could consecrate the oil of anointing, and could confer the Holy Spirit through the imposition of hands.[32] Acting as Christ's delegate, the bishop could judge the repentance of the sinner[33] and loosen the bonds of sin on earth so that the penitent might be presented with the prayers of the church for the Judgment of Christ.[34] To maintain the power of the Holy Spirit within the church, the bishops had to be individually and collectively free of violations of the baptismal oath and its moral commitments. Any who were discovered to have failed must be excluded from the episcopal college and replaced as leaders of local communities. Tolerating them would imply approval of their failure; it would contaminate the local congregation and the episcopal college; it would deprive not only a single local congregation but the universal church of access to sanctifying power.[35]

The crisis of division within the church provoked a fuller appreciation of the intentional union of its members. Cyprian found many ways of driving this point home. Unanimity in commending the needs of all was essential to the efficacy of a congregation's prayer.[36] The truth of the eucharist was realized by its celebration in the full assembly of the faithful rather than in household meetings; the unity of the faithful was symbolized by the many grains joined to make the bread that became the body of Christ; their union with him was represented by the mixture of water into the eucharistic wine.[37] Christ himself was served by the alms offered to a fellow Christian or the gifts made to the community.[38] The unity of the church extended to the dead, who continued to be purified from sin as they awaited the Resurrection and the Judgment of Christ, at which they would be supported by the intercessory prayers of the bishops, the martyrs, and all the faithful.[39]

This church was thus formed of interlocking communions. A single universal communion of bishops maintained holiness by fulfilling the standards of

31. Cypr. *Unit. eccl.* 4-5; *Ep.* 66.8.3.
32. Cypr. *Ep.* 70.
33. Cypr. *Ep.* 59.5.1; 66.3.1-3.
34. Cypr. *Ep.* 57.1.1.
35. Cypr. *Ep.* 67; 68.
36. Cypr. *Unit. eccl.* 12, 25; *Ep.* 11.3.1.
37. Cypr. *Ep.* 63.13.1-5, 16.1.
38. Cypr. *Eleem.* 8, 23.
39. Cypr. *Laps.* 36.

faith and morals; they shared the Spirit's power to sanctify and Christ's authority to govern. The many local congregations were constituted by the faithful joined to their bishop, and through him to the episcopal college and the other congregations throughout the world. Cyprian explained that sanctifying power had been communicated to and was preserved by the bishops for the good of the whole church; the fidelity and purity of the college of bishops assured the holiness necessary for the church to function as the mediator of salvation.

## THE DONATISTS: REJECTING APOSTASY IN A PURE CHURCH

The Diocletian persecution at the beginning of the fourth century showed the weakness of Cyprian's theology, as the Decian persecution had Tertullian's. When required to turn over the scriptures and sacred vessels to imperial officials for destruction, many of the bishops complied or compromised. In the aftermath, the provincial and regional episcopal colleges proved incapable of judging and purging failed members, and thus of maintaining the holiness of the church. Two parties formed in Africa, led by Caecilian, who was charged with abetting apostasy, and Donatus, who was accused of fomenting schism. In Cyprian's view, either sin would disqualify a bishop. If tolerated, the sinful bishop would contaminate not only his own congregation but any colleagues who accepted him into communion — and thus other (unwitting) congregations — and the whole college of bishops would be corrupted. During the fifty years following the end of the persecution, the bishops of Italy and Gaul, as well as the newly Christian emperors to whom the Donatists appealed, were unable to adjudicate the factual foundations and ecclesial implications of the conflict to the satisfaction of the parties. The African church remained divided. The next theoretical development occurred within the Donatist communion.

In the last third of the fourth century, a Donatist layman named Tyconius developed a set of seven rules to guide the interpretation of the Bible. He noted that the scripture regularly speaks of Christ himself and of the church as his body, as though referring to a single person: the same subject, for example, is called both bridegroom and bride (Isa. 61:10, Rev. 22:16-17). The interpreter must discern which statements could be understood as referring to Christ as an individual and which must be assigned to him as head of the church.[40] The second rule states that scripture refers to the body of Christ, the church, as both good and evil (Song 1:5). Like Israel in Paul's analysis (Rom. 10:21–11:2, 28), Tyconius explained, the church had two parts: one would be saved and the other condemned.[41] The seventh rule elaborated this point by asserting that the bodies of Christ and Satan, which were formed by good and evil persons, were

40. Tyc. *Reg.* regula prima, de Domino et corpore eius.
41. Tyc. *Reg.* regula secunda, de Domini corpore bipertito.

mixed together in the church and would be separated only at the Judgment.[42] Tyconius's insight into the relation between Christ and the church would be exploited by Augustine. His interpretative rules were refused, however, by his own party.

The Donatist bishops, led by Parmenian of Carthage, rejected Tyconius's interpretative principles and condemned his conclusions. In his review of Parmenian's letter of rebuke to Tyconius, Augustine initially reported that the dispute focused on the interpretation of Daniel's prophecy that the stone cut from the mountain itself became a mountain and filled the whole earth (Dan. 2:34-35). Tyconius asserted that the church, as the body of Christ, filled the whole world — rather than being restricted to Africa.[43] Elsewhere in his response, Augustine acknowledged that the affirmation of the presence of both good and evil within the one church was no less an issue.[44] As required by Cyprian's system, the Donatist bishops considered themselves faithful and holy; this made them mediating agents of salvation. Parmenian argued that Christ declared the Apostles pure after excluding the traitor Judas; only then did he give them the Holy Spirit and the power to baptize.[45] The faithful bishops transmitted to their people true faith or fidelity, and with it the holiness of Christ himself.[46] They could function as ministers of Christ and conduits of his holiness, however, only because they and their church were faithful.[47]

Optatus of Milevis and Augustine both disputed Parmenian's condemnation of Tyconius. Optatus provided historical evidence to show that Tyconius was justified in calling the (Donatist) church a mixture of good and evil; its bishops were guilty of both apostasy and crimes. Augustine added to this historical documentation and followed Tyconius in admitting the full range of sins within the communion of the church on earth, even as he maintained the real but imperfect holiness of the true body of Christ contained (and hidden) within the Caecilianist (and Catholic) communion.

In practice, the Donatists did not take account of the moral failures to which Tyconius had found reference in scripture and their Caecilianist opponents tirelessly recounted. Instead, they narrowed their operative definition of the purity of the church to freedom from apostasy and idolatry. The Donatists accused their Caecilianist rivals of the sins that would disqualify a bishop: apostasy, betrayal of Christ through turning over the scriptures, communion with those who did so, and persecution of the true church.[48] If bishops — or layper-

---

42. Tyc. *Reg.* regula septima, de diabolo et corpore eius.

43. Tyc. *Reg.* regula prima. For Augustine's explanation, see *Parm.* 1.1.1.

44. This was at issue in both the second and the seventh rules, where Tyconius insisted that the bodies of Christ and Satan were both within the church: Aug. *Parm.* 2.21.40, 2.22.42, 3.3.17.

45. Aug. *Parm.* 2.4.8; *Petil.* 2.22.49, 32.72.

46. Aug. *Parm.* 2.8.15; *Petil.* 1.4.5.

47. Aug. *Petil.* 3.52.64–54.66; *Cresc.* 3.7.7; *Ep. ad cath.* 24.68.

48. The Catholics communicated with apostates and betrayers: Mensurius (Aug. *Petil.*

sons — were guilty of such sins, they had to be excluded from communion. The sinners could be readmitted after penance, but clerics could not be restored to office.[49]

The toleration of schism and moral failure was also necessary for the Donatists, though Cyprian had considered these disabling crimes. Their church suffered a series of divisions after the return of its leaders from exile in 362: Rogatists in Mauretania, Claudianists in Carthage, and Maximianists in Proconsular Africa and Byzacena. Primian of Carthage provoked the Maximianist schism by admitting the Claudian schismatics into his communion, presumably without rebaptism or penance.[50] He later accepted two of the bishops who had consecrated Maximian back into his communion in their clerical offices, although they had rebuffed the condemnations imposed on them and refused invitations to return until threatened with physical violence. The Donatist communion was also embarrassed by Optatus of Thamugadi's violent suppression of dissent and his support for the rebellion of Gildo against the imperial government. At the beginning of the fifth century, however, many Donatist bishops sponsored or tolerated violence against their Caecilianist opponents.[51]

The type of fidelity that defined the Donatist church and its clergy can be illustrated by the reaction of its defenders to an objection and a proposal. Augustine described a scenario in which a Donatist bishop might be secretly unfaithful and thus, by his church's principles, incapable of transmitting saving faith to the persons he baptized. He even proposed a solution to the problem he described, drawing on the teaching of the *Treatise on Rebaptism*.[52] His Donatist respondents, Petilian and Cresconius, both found this scenario itself unintelligible: the infidelity that would disqualify a bishop in the Donatist communion could never be secret.[53] The Caecilianists then proposed that Donatist bishops bring their congregations into Catholic communion, where they would continue to lead and serve their congregations. In response, the Donatists professed astonishment that the Caecilianists would invite bishops whom they regarded as being outside the true church to join their communion without requiring any form of public purification, such as rebaptism or public

---

2.92.202), Caecilian (because of his alleged role with the Abitinian martyrs), and Felix (*Petil.* 2.8.17, 32.72). They were in communion with those who betrayed Christ: *Petil.* 2.7.14, 33.77. They persecuted the true church: *Petil.* 2.17.38, 32.72, 33.77, 53.121, 77.171, 78.173, 92.202, 103.236.

49. Donatus was condemned for imposing hands on bishops in penance according to Optat. *Parm.* 1.24. Optatus complained that after their return from exile, the Donatist leaders also had forced bishops to undergo penance, presumably for the crime of communion with apostate Caecilianists (*Parm.* 2.24). The Donatists objected that the Catholics did not exclude the impure from their communion (Aug. *Parm.* 3.2.11).

50. From the *acta* of the Council of Cebarsussi (Aug. *Psal.* 36.2.20 and *Cresc.* 4.9.11).

51. A summary was offered by Augustine in *Cresc.* 3.41.45–46.50.

52. *Parm.* 2.11.23; *Petil.* 3.49.59, on the supposition that Augustine was proposing a response to his own question.

53. Aug. *Petil.* 3.36.42, 52.64; *Cresc.* 2.17.21.

---

penance.[54] For their part, the Caecilianists judged that the sin of schism disabled a bishop and that it would be removed by reunion. Donatists believed that communion with apostates and persecutors — i.e., the Caecilianists — was the easily discovered sin that would contaminate and disqualify one of their bishops. Donatists might allow that their church included some who harbored sympathy for the apostates but could sincerely claim that they had not manifested and defiled themselves by entering communion with them.[55]

This restriction of the test for episcopal holiness to the crime of apostasy — or its toleration — was not only necessary to maintain its plausibility but brought a significant advantage to the Donatist cause. Constantine had put an end to imperial requirements that Christians participate in traditional idolatry. His son Constans made a single attempt, in the late 340s, to entice or coerce the Donatists into unity with the (apostate) Caecilianists. Those who submitted — to avoid being sent into exile — were easily stigmatized, forcibly subjected to penance, and permanently excluded from the clergy.[56] In the period between the reprieve granted by Julian in 362 and the decree of unity by Honorius in 405, a Donatist bishop could commit apostasy only by voluntarily leaving his church to join the communion of the Caecilianists, which was contaminated by both old apostasy and more recent collaboration in the imperial persecution of the true — Donatist — church. The defection of such persons, however, purified rather than polluted that church.

The Donatist church would claim to be holy, faithful to Christ, and as pure as it would be in the Resurrection, all because it rejected demonic idolatry and suffered persecution for its fidelity to Christ. Thus, it communicated true faith and provided effective sacraments to its members.

## OPTATUS OF MILEVIS: DIVINE OPERATION SANCTIFIES CHRISTIANS

Optatus, the Caecilianist Bishop of Milevis in Numidia, argued against Parmenian that the efficacy of the church's ministry derived not from the fidelity or holiness of the minister himself, but from the ritual invocation of the Trinity and the faith of the recipient, which were the two constant and unchanging elements in baptism.[57] From Cyprian, he recalled that the unity of the church was more important than its punishing sin and maintaining purity. The church

54. Aug. *Ep.* 185.10.44. The Donatists objected that the Catholics did not exclude the impure from their communion (Aug. *Petil.* 3.36.42–37.43; *Col. Carth.* 3.257, 258, 263).

55. *Col. Carth.* 3.258; Aug. *Cresc.* 2.17.21.

56. The clergy, congregations and even basilicas were ostentatiously purified when the Donatist exiles returned. Optat. *Parm.* 2.21-26; 6.1-8.

57. The person of the minister was not always the same and was therefore irrelevant to the nature and efficacy of the sacrament (Optat. *Parm.* 2.10; 5.1, 4). Optatus compared the church's minister to a waiter at a banquet who dispensed food belonging to the host (*Parm.* 5.7).

could enfold and sustain repentant apostates and schismatics in a motherly embrace rather than protecting itself from their sins.[58] The love evident in church unity would forgive many sins.[59] He reminded his readers that Peter had been guilty of betraying not the words written in the scriptures but Christ who spoke them. Yet, Christ had entrusted the keys to this sinner so that he would open the Kingdom to sinners, rather than giving the power to bind and loosen to some innocent leader who might then lock out the sinners and destroy that unity essential to Christ's Kingdom.[60] In his emphasis on the primacy of unity and the power of love to forgive sin, Optatus appealed to the divine holiness authorizing and working in the church's sacramental actions. He did not, however, clearly address the question raised by Cyprian and pursued by the Donatists: Was the holiness of the church essential to its ministry of sanctifying its members?

## AUGUSTINE: CHRIST SANCTIFIES HIS ECCLESIAL BODY

When Augustine began dealing with the conflict between the Donatists and the Caecilianists, the issues were already well defined. The Donatists followed Cyprian in focusing the holiness of the church on the episcopal college. Unlike Cyprian, they seemed to have judged that neither schism nor moral failure was a sign of diabolical presence in the church and its bishops, sins which would destroy its holiness and disable its sacramental ministry. In response, Optatus appealed to the divine holiness working through the church's ministers but did not locate sanctifying power within the church itself.

Augustine's challenge was to develop a theory which would locate the gift of the Holy Spirit within the church while insuring that the gifts of holiness and sanctifying power were not compromised by the failings — in faith or morals — of either the clergy or the laity. He recognized that the cause of the church was served inadequately by proving, through citation of imperial court records, that Caecilian and his consecrators were innocent while the founders of the Donatist party were guilty of apostasy: he had to show that the issue of episcopal innocence was irrelevant to the efficacy of the church's sanctifying power.[61] The bishops at the Council of Arles in 314 had grasped this point and insisted

58. Nam peccator talis, quales fuerunt uestri maiores, si ad ecclesiam ueniat et necessitatis suae rationem ostendat, primo recipiendus est, deinde sustinendus pio sinu matris ecclesiae (Optat. *Parm.* 7.2; CSEL 26:168.10-13).

59. Bono unitatis sepelienda esse peccata hinc intellegi datur, quod beatissimus Paulus apostolus dicat caritatem posse obstruere multitudinem peccatorum. He then cited Gal. 6:2 and 1 Cor. 13:4, 5. See Optat. *Parm.* 7.3 (CSEL 26:171.9-12).

60. Provisum est, ut peccator aperiret innocentibus, ne innocentes clauderent contra peccatores et, quae necessaria est unitas, esse non posset (Optat. *Parm.* 7.3; CSEL 26:173.18-20).

61. Imperial records demonstrated that the consecrator of Caecilian, Felix of Abtungi, had

that even apostate bishops could perform sanctifying rituals.[62] Augustine's task was to explain and establish what they asserted: that the holiness of the church could not fail.

The Augustinian understanding of the church was developed in two different moments. His controversial writings against Donatist authors — principally Parmenian, Petilian, Cresconius, and Gaudentius — along with a series of letters and the texts produced in connection with the Conference of Carthage in 411 focused on the adaptation of the theories of Cyprian to the radically different social and religious context of the fourth and fifth centuries, when the Roman Empire attempted to support and unify the Christian church. In these works, Augustine argued that the holiness of the church derived from the Spirit's gift of charity that also effected the church's unity and universality. This appeal to charity enabled an expansion of the standard of purity beyond avoidance of idolatry. Augustine's approach reversed the Donatist reading of Cyprian that privileged purity over unity and allowed a limitation of the standard of holiness. Augustine's preaching, in contrast, provided a very different context for reflection on the church, one in which he elaborated this perspective on holiness into a more comprehensive explanation of Christian life. He understood the church as a social body animated by the gift of the Holy Spirit, with Christ identified as its head and faithful Christians as its members. Using this foundational idea, he explored the nature and efficacy of the rituals of baptism and eucharist, the role of the clergy, the sharing of spiritual and material goods, and the mutual care that characterized the life of the community. These two expositions of Augustine's understanding of the church — controversial and pastoral — will be considered sequentially, beginning with that of the controversial works.

## Controversial Writings

Augustine's analysis of the purity necessary to maintain the holiness of the church and the efficacy of its sacraments in his writings against the Donatists is generally known and may be summarized. The holiness and purity of the church were based in charity, the gift of the Holy Spirit, which established an intentional unity among the members of the communion. Charity had three roles in moving a Christian: loving God for God's sake and the neighbor for God; loving, willing, and performing the good works commanded by Christ; and forgiving offenses suffered and thus gaining God's forgiveness for offenses committed.[63] During earthly life, charity remained imperfect and was resisted

---

been falsely accused and that among the consecrators of Majorinus was an apostate (*Act. pur. Fel.* in appendices of Optat. *Parm.* in CSEL 26).

62. They could both baptize and ordain others, though they had to be removed from office as soon as discovered (*Con. Arel.* a. 314, 9, 14).

63. Much of Augustine's understanding of charity is worked out in his early commentaries

by the various forms of inherited and acquired lust. Christians remained sinners.[64] They were constantly being purified by repenting their own sins and pardoning those of others. As long as they persisted in the unity of the church, where there were many who rejected charity and sought only their own advantage, the charity exercised by the faithful won the forgiveness of its own inadequacies.[65] The visible communion, as Tyconius had observed, was a mixture of good and evil, of the divine and the demonic.

Because he considered the holiness of human persons imperfect throughout earthly life, Augustine followed Optatus in attributing the efficacy of the sacraments to the divine power rather than to the purity of the minister. Christ used the clergy as authorized ministers or agents of his own sanctifying action — in baptism, eucharist, and penance — but endowed them with no distinctive power by virtue of their offices. Augustine insisted, however, that a power to sanctify actually had been communicated to and was exercised by the church. He identified that power to forgive sins, relying on John (20:22-23) and 1 Peter (4:8), as the gift of charity that joined the faithful to one another and maintained the unity of the church. His model for the efficacy of the sacramental ministry was the informal mutual asking and granting of pardon practiced daily by the faithful within the congregation. Those who were loving and forgiving — a group Augustine named the society of saints and symbolized by the dove — acted with Christ in the work of sanctifying.[66] By being joined to these saints in love, the sinner received the gift of charity and thus the forgiveness of sins.[67] Sacramental rituals — most regularly eucharist — formalized and symbolized this constant process of sanctification carried on among the members of the congregation.

Augustine developed and applied this explanation to the baptismal ritual in the conflict with the Donatists. The minister of the sacrament, normally a member of the clergy, acted as the agent of Christ himself, whose power and holiness guaranteed the efficacy of the ritual so that it need never be repeated.[68] Indeed, to repeat baptism was to doubt the saving power of Christ.[69] Baptism had two effects: it dedicated the recipient to the worship of God and service of Christ; and it communicated the gift of the Holy Spirit — charity — through which the individual was moved to love and thereby purified of sin. The two effects were radically different: the dedication established a permanent rela-

---

on Paul: *Quaest.* 66; *Rom. prop.* 12.2, 7-12; 52.15; 53.7; 67.1-3; *Gal.* 3.2, 43.3, 44.3-5, 49.5-6; *Simpl.* 1.1.7-10.

64. Aug. *Quaest.* 66.2-3, 5-6; *Rom. prop.* 12.10; 38.1, 7; 42.2; *Gal.* 22.7; 46.7; *Simpl.* 1.1.10, 13.

65. Aug. *Bapt.* 1.9.12, 18.27; 2.14.19, 15.20; 3.16.21.

66. Aug. *Bapt.* 5.21.29; 6.3.5.

67. Aug. *Bapt.* 6.4.6, 14.23.

68. Aug. *Parm.* 2.6.11, 11.23-24; *Bapt.* 2.11.24; 3.14.19–15.20; 4.4.5, 11.17; 5.12.14–15.18; 6.25.47; *Petil.* 2.5.11, 6.13, 37.87-88, 51.118.

69. Aug. *Bapt.* 3.10.15, 15.20; 6.36.70.

tionship to Christ that could not be destroyed; charity remained only so long as the baptized did not neglect it or refuse to act as it prompted. Those who repented their sins, who accepted and practiced the faith and love communicated to them in baptism, were incorporated into the invisible church, what Augustine called the society of saints or the dove.[70] Any who held to their prior sins or resisted the unity of love — deceivers within the communion of the church or schismatics outside it — immediately lost these gifts.[71] In virtue of the permanent dedication of baptism, however, charity could be restored by repentance and conversion.[72]

Augustine explained that the power of forgiving sins, with which Christ had endowed the church, was identified with the Spirit's gift of charity. Relying on the statement in 1 Peter (4:8) that love covers a multitude of sins[73] and on the instruction on mutual forgiveness in Matthew's Gospel (18:15-20),[74] he asserted that all who lived in charity exercised the power of forgiveness toward one another. Sins were loosened when a penitent accepted the gift of love extended through the saints who formed the core of the church's unity; sins were bound when a sinner persisted in rejecting that love.[75] When the clergy performed the rituals of baptism and penance, therefore, they exercised the power of forgiveness rooted in the charity that flourished among the saints, who formed the dove or society of saints within the church.[76] Those clergy who were themselves among the saints actually shared this power; those who were sinners — within visible unity or outside in schism — acted as agents performing an action whose efficacy came from others.[77] The spiritual reality symbolized and effected by the ritual, however, was the uniting of the sinner to the saints that resulted in purification and the forgiveness of sins. Thus the church could tolerate sinful clergy and could even welcome clergy repenting their schism and allow them to exercise their ministry within its unity. The clergy were agents of Christ and of the true Christians joined to form the unity of the church.

Augustine's understanding of the holiness of the church was built on the unity of mutual charity; this was the foundation of such purity as the church on earth enjoyed. This gift of the Holy Spirit also empowered the sacramental ministry carried out by the clergy. That divine principle of unity and sanctity was located in the communion of the saints who formed the inner core of

---

70. Aug. *Bapt.* 1.12.18–13.21; 3.17.22–18.23; 4.4-5; 5.16.21, 18.24, 21.29; 6.4.6, 14.23; 7.47.93; *Cresc.* 2.21.26.

71. Aug. *Bapt.* 1.11.15–12.20; 3.13.18, 16.21–17.22; 4.4.6, 16.23; 5.22.30; 7.22.43.

72. Aug. *Bapt.* 1.13.21; 2.7.11, 15.20; 3.13.18, 16.21; 4.3.4; 6.4.6–5.7.

73. That text is cited some 23 times, primarily in the writings against the Donatists. See, for example, Aug. *Bapt.* 6.24.45; *Gaud.* 1.12.13; *Cresc.* 2.12.15; 4.11.13.

74. Aug. *Bapt.* 6.24.45; *Cresc.* 2.12.15; 4.11.13; *Ep.* 93.10.40; 108.3.10, 5.15; 141.13; 185.10.43-44.

75. Aug. *Bapt.* 3.16.21–18.23, 19.26; 5.21.29, 23.33; 6.4.6–5.7.

76. On the society of saints, see Aug. *Bapt.* 3.17.22–18.23, 19.26; 5.21.29; 6.3.5–5.7; *Ep.* 98.5.

77. Aug. *Parm.* 2.11.24; *Bapt.* 5.21.29; 7.12.22-23.

the church. These true disciples were represented by their predecessors in the church upon whom Christ conferred the Holy Spirit as the power of binding and loosening in John (20:22-23).[78]

This understanding of the church's role as the mediator of salvation challenged the Donatists by exploiting Tertullian's theology of universal priesthood for the purpose of subverting Cyprian's reliance on the episcopate. The standard of holiness was set as both fidelity to Christ and an active love of God and neighbor. To maintain these was the role not of the episcopal college but of a group within the visible church that would be identified only at Christ's separation of wheat from chaff, though its presence and operation could be discerned in the unity, cohesion, and openness of the visible communion. Although the church's holiness was realized only partially, its very persistence won the forgiveness of its limitations. As shall be seen, Christ supplied for its inadequacy.

This was Augustine's response to the Donatists. His pastoral teaching for Caecilianists was a much more elaborate version of the same theory.

### Pastoral Writings

In his preaching and in his commentaries in sermon form, Augustine adapted Tyconius's exegetical methods to develop a new interpretation of the church's relationship to Christ that clarified its holiness and its participation in Christ's mediation of salvation through its rituals. Tyconius's methods and the results Augustine achieved through them were not used in his writings against the Donatists, perhaps because Parmenian and his colleagues had already rejected the principles upon which they were based and the conclusions to which they led.

To bring the rules of interpretation into practice, Augustine had to distinguish three, rather than Tyconius's two, different meanings of Christ as the subject to whom the whole of scripture referred. First, Christ could speak and be spoken of as the Word of God, eternally begotten and equal to the Father. The prologue of the Gospel of John and the hymns in Philippians and Colossians began with reference to Christ in his divine state, prior to and independent of the Incarnation. Second, the scripture referred to Christ as the Word of God incarnate and the head of the church. Each of the texts just noted also included such a reference.[79] Third, the scriptures described "the Whole Christ in the fullness of the church," comprising both head and members.[80] The Colossians hymn included such a reference to the third form, but Augustine found it most strikingly evident in Christ's challenge to Saul in Acts 9:4: "Why are you perse-

78. Aug. *Bapt.* 3.18.23; 5.21.29; 6.1.1, 3.5, 14.23.
79. Aug. *Serm. Dolb.* 22(341*).2-3, 11.
80. Totus Christus in plenitudine ecclesiae (Aug. *Serm. Dolb.* 22(341*).2); Augustin d'Hippone, *Vingt-six sermons au peuple d'Afrique,* ed. François Dolbeau (Paris: Institut d'études augustiniennes, 2009), 554.24-25.

---

cuting me?" As Word, he could not be attacked; as an individual human, he was safely in heaven; clearly he spoke in the third sense, as identified with his body on earth, the object of Saul's attacks.[81] Further distinctions were necessary in this third form of interpretation. Christ spoke in union with different groups of his members: some were at rest, but others were still in labor.[82] Christ sometimes spoke only for his bodily members and not for himself as head: though sinless as an individual, he prayed the penitential psalms as the voice of his members.[83] Augustine provided a summary illustration of the three modes of speaking: Christ is prayed to as God, prays for the faithful as their priest, and prays in them as their head. In this last role, the faithful were exhorted to recognize their own voices in his and his voice in their own.[84] These forms of interpretation that understood Christ speaking with or for the church as his body and members were used almost exclusively in the sermons.[85]

Augustine explained the constitution of the body of Christ in his preaching in the same way that he had understood the "society of saints" within the visible church in his controversial works: all faithful Christians united in Christ through their sharing of the gift of charity and their common intention to adhere to the visible church.[86] In preaching, however, he used somewhat different language: the Word became the head of the church by taking flesh in the womb of the virgin; Christ's own flesh was the firstfruits of the church; the believers were joined into and became the limbs of his body.[87] The Holy Spirit was the soul which gave life to the body of Christ[88] and worked in all its members.[89] Anyone cut off from the union of love within the church — by schism or some other sin against charity — retained the shape but not the life of a member.[90]

Augustine characterized the Whole Christ as a community sharing heavenly and earthly, spiritual and material goods. The chief of the spiritual goods was, of course, the Spirit's gift of charity through which the members were

81. Aug. *Serm.* 345.4.
82. Aug. *Psal.* 30.3.1.
83. Aug. *Psal.* 40.6; 140.6; 101.1.2; 118.22.5.
84. Aug. *Psal.* 85.1.
85. The phrase "the Whole Christ," Christus totus — with or without the qualifiers head and body, or head and members — appears only four times outside the preached works of Augustine. Moreover, in those collections which include both written and preached expositions, such as *Enarrationes in Psalmos* and *In euangelium Ioannis tractatus,* it appears only in the sections that were preached. The search in the database of *CAG 2* (an electronic resource: *Corpus Augustinianum Gissense* [Basel: Schwabe, 2005]) was conducted using combinations of the roots for *Christus, totus, caput, corpus,* and *membrum,* within six words. The uses outside the sermons are in *Ep. ad cath.* 4.7; *Trin.* 3.10.20; and *Perseu.* 7.14. An appearance of the words in *Faust.* 12.32 is not relevant.
86. Aug. *Serm.* 354.1.1; *Psal.* 30.2.1.3; 122.1. See *CAG 2.*
87. Aug. *Psal.* 44.3; 148.8; *Serm.* 161.1.1; *Serm. Dolb.* 26(198*).43; *Ep. Io.* 1.2, 2.2. Had Christ taken only a human soul and not flesh, Christians could not be his members.
88. Aug. *Eu. Io.* 26.13.
89. Aug. *Serm.* 267.4; 268.2.
90. Aug. *Serm.* 267.4; 268.2.

bound together in love, empowered to obey the commands and enact the teachings of Christ, and to forgive one another. This foundational gift of charity was the common possession of all the faithful in the church rather than being received and maintained by a particular group, such as the clergy or the ascetics. The first effect of this gift of charity was the unity of the church itself; it was also operative in the sanctifying rituals of baptism, eucharist, and reconciliation of sinners.

As has been noted already, Augustine interpreted Matthew 18:15-18 as the paradigmatic instance of the forgiveness of sins: when Christians forgive one another, God forgives them both.[91] Other texts were understood in the light of this one. Peter had received the power to forgive sins as representative of the whole community of the faithful,[92] just as he had made the confession of faith that was the basis for Christ's conferral of the power.[93] Similarly, in interpreting the giving of the Holy Spirit as the power to forgive sins to the disciples on the evening of the Resurrection (John 20:22-23), Augustine recognized that the power was conferred upon all who formed the living temple in which the Spirit dwelt.[94] By repenting, a catechumen or penitent was freed from sin and was joined into the body of the faithful. The intentional unity thus realized communicated the gift of charity from the faithful to the petitioner. In Augustine's graphic image, the church sanctified by chewing, swallowing, and digesting sinners, by assimilating them into itself and sharing its life with them.[95]

The close relation between the physical and the social bodies of Christ was also evident in Augustine's expositions of the symbolism and efficacy of the eucharistic celebration. He referred to the individual body of Christ: Christians drank the blood that had once been shed on the cross.[96] More regularly, however, he described the eucharistic bread and wine as symbolizing the body of the Whole Christ, the fellowship of head and members.[97] He exhorted the faithful in Hippo to become the reality they received in the celebration, the church spread throughout the world.[98] The ecclesial body of the Whole Christ was symbolically interchangeable with the flesh that the Word assumed in the womb of Mary, raised from the dead, and carried into heaven. This body of Christ remained hidden among the sinners in the visible communion of the

91. The text is quoted explicitly only in Aug. *Serm.* 17.6; 82.4.7; 83.1.1; 295.2.2.

92. Not as an individual for the work of founding the church (Tertullian) or as representative of the episcopal college (Cyprian): Tert. *Pud.* 21; Cypr. *Unit. eccl.* 4-5. Tertullian's opponent made the same argument (*Pud.* 22).

93. Aug. *Serm.* 67.2.3; 76.1.1; 149.6.7–7.8; 232.3; 295.2.2; *Serm. Mai* 16(23A).2; *Serm. Guelf.* 16(229N).2; *Serm. Lamb.* 3(229P).1; *Psal.* 54.5; 101.2.3; 108.1; *Eu. Io.* 50.12; *Ep. Io.* 10.1, 10.

94. Aug. *Serm.* 99.9; 295.2.2. The parallel explanation can be found in *Bapt.* 1.11.15; 3.18.23; 5.21.29; 6.3.5, 14.23, but not elsewhere in Augustine's writings against the Donatists.

95. Aug. *Serm. Denis* 15(313B).3; *Psal.* 34.2.15; 88.1.24; 94.11; 103.3.2; 123.5.

96. Aug. *Serm.* 229.3; *Serm. Denis* 3(228B).2-3.

97. Aug. *Eu. Io.* 26.15.

98. Aug. *Serm. Guelf.* 7(229A).1.

earthly church, in the underworld awaiting resurrection, and in heaven; only in the eucharistic bread and wine was it symbolically manifested and received.

Augustine insisted that Christ was the only priest and mediator. No other human individual could exercise that function or claim that title: bishops were overseers and pastors but neither mediators nor priests. Christ's priesthood, however, was proper to his incarnate state and was thus shared with his body, the church.[99] Bishops, then, were called priests because they were leaders and — if holy — members of this priestly body.[100] Exploiting the typological interpretation of Israelite sacrifice in the Letter to the Hebrews, Augustine illustrated the relationship of the church to Christ as priest. The Israelite high priest had entered alone into the earthly tabernacle to make the offering, with the people assembled outside. The Christian people — together with their clergy — stood at the altar inside the earthly sanctuary, symbolically anticipating the Resurrection, when they would join Christ their head at the heavenly altar.[101] Because the minister functioned as agent of the Whole Christ, head and members, he could exercise sanctifying power only in union with the church. A faithful minister, one who was a member of the body, deployed a power that he shared. Someone who was an unworthy minister within the communion, or a schismatic or heretic outside it, was united to Christ and the church not in love but only by the intention to perform the sacramental action; he acted as the agent of another's power in which he had no part. In all cases, the sanctifying effect depended upon the recipient's intentional union with and incorporation into the ecclesial body of Christ.

The church as a community of spiritual gifts was also evident in Augustine's adaptation of the Pauline preference (1 Cor. 13–14; Rom. 12:3-13) for the virtues that belonged to the whole body of the faithful over those that differentiated individuals from one another. This was most evident in his consideration of the privileged states of virginity and widowhood. The bodily integrity that dedicated virgins preserved was symbolic of the integrity of faith, without which their bodily virginity was of no religious value. That integrity of faith defined the virginity of the church and was to be maintained by all Christians.[102] Thus the virgin was symbolically Christ's bride by participating in his union in faith to the faithful church.[103] Similarly, the widow who vowed not to marry again symbolized the church's fidelity and hope as she lived in expectation of the return of her bridegroom.[104] Married Christians were joined to these celibates

---

99. The fullest development is in Aug. *Serm. Dolb.* 26(198*).49-53; it is echoed in *Ep. Io.* 1.8. The anointing is affirmed in *Psal.* 26.2.2.

100. Aug. *Serm. Dolb.* 26(198*).49-50.

101. Aug. *Serm. Dolb.* 26(198*).53; see also *Psal.* 25.2.10; 64.6.

102. Aug. *Serm.* 188.3.4; *Serm. Dolb.* 22(341*).12; *Psal.* 90.2.9; 147.10; *Eu. Io.* 13.12. One will recognize here the fidelity which the Donatists required of their clergy.

103. Aug. *Eu. Io.* 9.2.

104. Aug. *Psal.* 145.18.

in faith and charity; they accomplished in them what they were unable do in themselves.[105] For their own part, the fidelity of the married symbolized, however imperfectly, the eschatological union of Christ and the purified church.[106] Augustine also explained that the gift of the Holy Spirit at Pentecost, by which each of the disciples spoke all the languages of humanity, was subsequently extended to the church as a whole: the entire body spoke in all lands, and each Christian could still claim the languages of all.[107]

Thus, all the various powers and gifts distributed by the Spirit among the members belonged to the whole church; each member did whatever good was performed within the body of the Whole Christ. The full church gloried in the fidelity of the martyrs, the bloody sweat of the body of Christ.[108] The ecclesial body of Christ was like one person spread throughout the world, praying for deliverance; Christ himself was the petitioner when the church prayed in unity.[109] Augustine found an illustration of this sharing of gifts in the way the hand moves to protect the eye, guarding the power of one member for the use of the whole body.[110]

The participation of the church as his body in the endowments of Christ its head provided a means for understanding the community of religious powers and spiritual gifts among the members. The holiness of the church was defined as the Holy Spirit's gift of charity; this was indefectible in Christ its head and unfailing among his members, mixed though they were with sinners until the Resurrection and Judgment.[111] The value of this theory was not simply explanatory: it appealed to the Christian imagination and thus moved the faithful to mutual service.

The sharing of material goods was even more effective in illustrating the nature of the church. Augustine defined the true church as that intentional union of the faithful that was within but could not be fully identified with the visible communion. He ran a risk of failing to connect this invisible communion — whose members could be identified only by God — to the functioning social body of actual congregations, whose membership was often evidently unworthy of its calling. He moved toward a solution to this problem by pointing to the actions that identified the ecclesial body of Christ, particularly the sharing of material goods. Some goods were common and meant to be shared by all. By

---

105. Aug. *Psal.* 121.10.

106. Aug. *Bon. coniug.* 7.7, 15.17, 18.21.

107. Aug *Psal.* 18.2.10; 147.19; *Eu. Io.* 32.7.

108. Aug. *Psal.* 140.4; 118.30.5.

109. Aug. *Psal.* 39.28; 60.1-2; 122.1; 130.1.

110. Aug. *Psal.* 130.6; *Eu. Io.* 32.8.

111. Aug. *Serm.* 264.5; 354.1.2–2.2; *Psal.* 25.2.5-6; 85.4; 119.9; 126.8; 127.11; 146.9. Augustine made no explicit connection between the fidelity of the ecclesial body and the grace of perseverance, though he did recognize that gift in the soul of Christ himself as well as in his elect members (*Perseu.* 24.66-67).

maintaining silence and order, a congregation could listen together to the reading of scripture and the sermon explaining it.[112] Similarly, each member could receive the whole benefit of the eucharist rather than only a portion. The use of other goods was necessarily divided: food and clothing, even if drawn from a common store, had to be apportioned and consumed by distinct individuals. Although Augustine recognized this limit, he attempted to promote a certain type of common possession and use of even these consumable goods. Christ became head of the church by taking human flesh; his body was recognizable in its sharing of the goods that sustained bodily life.

The life of the Jerusalem community, as described in the Acts of the Apostles (2:43-47), provided an earthly intimation of the heavenly life of the angels and the blessed.[113] This ideal of shared possession and use continued to be realized in monastic and clerical communities, such as the ones Augustine established in Hippo.[114] Within families, Augustine urged that inheritances should be held in common by siblings rather than parceled out among them.[115] In the local congregation, he promoted not a community of property but a sharing of income and of the supplies necessary for survival.[116] By using their goods to support one another, Christians recognized themselves as members of the one body of Christ; they served Christ himself in one another.[117] In receiving the commission to care for Christ's flock (John 21:15-17), as in receiving the power to bind and loose, Peter represented the whole church; Christ had entrusted his disciples to one another.[118] Thus alms were to be given to fellow Christians not because these poor were particularly righteous or deserving but simply because they were needy.[119] Providing support to the undeserving was even a form of forgiving enemies.[120] Augustine insisted that service be mutual, that the poor must act as benefactors as well as recipients: they could provide the cup of cold — unheated — water; they could offer bodily service to the blind, the lame, and the weak.[121] In like manner, the rich should not only provide funds

112. Aug. *Serm. Dolb.* 27(360C).1.

113. Aug. *Serm.* 355.2; *Serm. Dolb.* 26(198*).48.

114. Aug. *Serm.* 355; 356 report on these arrangements.

115. In commenting on Luke 12:13-15, Augustine explained Christ's refusal to act as arbitrator in the division of an estate as approval of the brother's plan that the whole estate should continue to be held in common: *Serm.* 107.1.2; 265.9.11; *Serm. Lamb.* 5(107A).1.

116. Augustine noted that the Pauline letters did not require giving up all one's property: *Serm.* 14.5; *Serm. Mai* 13(113B).2, 6; *Serm. Dolb.* 5(114B).12-13.

117. Aug. *Serm.* 9.21; 25.8; 38.8; 86.3.3; 239.5.6–6.7; 345.4.

118. Aug. *Serm. Lamb.* 3(229P).4; *Ep. Io.* 5.5.

119. Even the wealthy approach God as beggars, since all humans are needy (Aug. *Serm.* 61.7.8; 259.3).

120. *Serm. Lamb.* 4(359A).11. Christ on the cross accepted a drink from one of his mockers, *Serm,* 41.7. This did not mean, however, that the sinner should go unrebuked, *Serm. Lamb.* 28(164A).1-4.

121. Aug. *Serm.* 39.6; *Serm. Lamb.* 1(105A).1; 4(359A).12; 5(107A).8; *Psal.* 125.11-13.

to feed the poor but actually serve them.[122] Rich and poor Christians should be bound together in mutual sympathy as they faced the uncertainties of earthly life.[123]

Augustine did not limit almsgiving to the Christian community. He exhorted the congregation to be generous to polytheists, Jews, and heretics.[124] He noted in satisfaction that beggars gathered outside the basilica at the time of services because they found Christians open-handed.[125] Giving to persons outside the body of Christ, however, did not carry the same religious significance as sharing with fellow Christians.[126] Also, almsgiving was never to be confused with wasting money on gladiators, charioteers, and other such performers,[127] or even with building a new basilica for the congregation's worship.[128]

In his sermons, Augustine repeatedly reminded his congregation that the Christian life consisted in the two foundational practices of giving and forgiving.[129] He explained each of these as means of salvation for the individual, but their efficacy depended on understanding the church as the body of Christ. Forgiving others was essential to winning forgiveness for one's own sins, according to the petition of the Lord's Prayer.[130] Almsgiving was a mechanism for turning earthly into heavenly treasure; the bellies of the poor were the storehouses of God.[131] In giving and forgiving, Christians were building the body of Christ, establishing and strengthening the union of charity that bound them to one another and to Christ. No less importantly, they were making that body visible in their good works.

........................................................................................................

## CONCLUSION

The challenge for African Christianity was to define the holiness of the church in a way adequate to its role of serving as the mediator for the salvation of humanity. The church had to manifest the saving power of Christ in its communal life and exercise his ministry in its rituals. Tertullian judged that each member of the community must accept responsibility for the fullness of that holiness by actively combatting idolatry and rigorously observing the moral teaching

122. Aug. *Serm.* 259.3-5.
123. Aug. *Serm.* 259.5. The poor must never be despised because of their need (Aug. *Psal.* 103.1.19).
124. Aug. *Serm.* 359.9; *Psal.* 32.2.2.29.
125. Aug. *Psal.* 46.5.
126. Aug. *Psal.* 44.28.
127. Aug. *Psal.* 102.13.
128. Aug. *Serm. Lamb.* 5(107A).9.
129. Aug. *Serm.* 9.17-18, 21; 83.2.2; 259.4; *Serm. Wilm.* 2(179A).6; *Psal.* 111.4.
130. Aug. *Serm.* 114.1-5; 211.5; 278.6.6, 10.10–11.11; 315.7.10; *Psal.* 54.14.
131. Aug. *Serm.* 18.4; 36.9; 60.6; 114.5; 311.18.15; 345.2-3; 389.3-4; 390.1; *Serm. Frang.* 9(114A).4; *Serm. Lamb.* 2(335C).8-9; *Serm. Mai* 14(350A).4; *Serm. Morin* 11(53A).6.

of Christ. Those who fell short in minor ways could be tolerated, but those who failed in their baptismal commitment must be excluded. Every Christian could then exercise the sanctifying power of the church by performing the rituals and prayer. Cyprian followed the same standards but narrowed the group responsible for maintaining holiness and exercising power to the clergy, specifically the college of bishops. Thus he could allow even Christians who had denied Christ to regain a place in the communion and could condemn all who were outside in schism or heresy. The Donatists followed Cyprian's lead but restricted the standards of fidelity to the avoidance of idolatry and rejection of apostasy. Augustine returned to Tertullian's schema, with three significant changes. He laid the theoretical foundations for church identity in the sharing of charity; he specified that charity be operative in mutual forgiving and care; and he restricted the performance of the rituals to the ordained clergy, except for emergency baptism.

North African Christianity faced a great challenge in identifying a social group that held and exercised the sanctifying power of Christ in the church. Tertullian's community could not maintain its purity; Cyprian's bishops proved as fallible and self-serving as the laity; Donatist clerics were not required to be visibly moral, though they were not apostates; Optatus's ministers were agents exercising an absentee leader's power. By focusing on the body of Christ living by the Spirit's gift of charity, Augustine was able to establish a link between fidelity, moral living, and sanctifying power. He was also able to demonstrate that charity was self-correcting and inseparable from Christ's power. The problem was to make the true church visible, to acknowledge that it was fallible and defectible without abandoning its claim to be Christ's living presence. This he accomplished by characterizing it as a community of giving and forgiving, of sharing spiritual and material endowments.

When Augustine addressed a Christian congregation, he often referred to its members as "your holiness," but his preferred term, used five times more often and nearly five hundred times in surviving sermons, was "your charity."[132] It was his proper name for the church, the body of Christ.

---

132. 479 in contrast to 107, according to *CAG 2*.

# Bibliography

*Actas del VIII Congreso internacional de Arqueología Cristiana, Barcelona, 5-11 Octubre 1969.* Studi di antichità cristiana 30. Barcelona: Consejo Superior de Investigaciones Científicas, 1972.

*Actes du Ve Congrès international d'archéologie chrétienne, Aix-en-Provence, 13-19 Septembre 1954.* Studi di antichità cristiana 22. Città del Vaticano: Pontificio Istituto di Archeologia Cristiana, 1957.

*Actes du XIe Congrès international d'archéologie chrétienne: Lyon, Vienne, Grenoble, Genève et Aoste (21-28 Septembre 1986),* edited by Françoise Baritel, Noél Duval, and Philippe Pergola, Collection de l'École française de Rome 123; Studi di antichià cristiana 41. Roma: École française de Rome; Città del Vaticano: Pontificio Istituto di Archeologia Cristiana, 1989.

*L'Africa Romana: Atti del IV Convegno di studio, Sassari, 12-14 dicembre 1986,* edited by Attilio Mastino. Pubblicazioni del Dipartimento di Storia dell'Universià di Sassari 7. Sassari: Gallizzi, 1986.

*L'Africa Romana: Atti del IX Convegno di studio, Nuoro, 13-15 dicembre 1991,* edited by Attilio Mastino. Pubblicazioni del Dipartimento di Storia dell'Universià di Sassari 20. Sassari: Gallizzi, 1992.

*L'Africa Romana: Atti del XII Convegno di studio, Olbia, 12-15 dicembre 1996.* Edited by Mustapha Khanoussi, Paola Ruggeri, and Cinzia Vismara. 3 vols. Pubblicazioni del Dipartimento di Storia dell'Università degli Studi di Sassari 31. Sassari: Editions Democratica Sarda, 1998.

Alexander, Margaret. "Early Christian Tomb Mosaics in North Africa." Ph.D. diss., New York University, 1958.

———. "Mosaic Ateliers at Tabarka." *Dumbarton Oaks Papers* 41 (1987): 1-11.

Amat, Jacqueline. *Passion de Perpétue et de Félicité; Suivi des actes.* SC 417. Paris: Éditions du Cerf, 1996.

Ambroise. *Opere poetiche e frammenti, inni, iscrizioni, frammenti.* Edited by Gabriele Banterle. Sancti Ambrosii Episcopi Mediolanensis 22. Milan: Biblioteca Ambrosiana, 1994.

————. *Sancti Ambrosii Episcopi Mediolanensis Opera.* Milan: Biblioteca Ambrosiana, 1979.

*Atti del IV Congresso internazionale di Archeologia Cristiana, Città del Vaticano, 16-22 Ottobre 1938.* Studi di antichità cristiana. Pubblicati per Cura del Pontificio Istituto di Archeologica Cristiana 16, 19. Rome: Pontificio Istituto di Archeologia Cristiana, 1940.

*Atti del VI Congresso internazionale di Archeologia Cristiana, Ravenna, 23-30 Settembre 1962.* Studi di antichità cristiana 26. Città del Vaticano: Pontificio Istituto di Archeologia Cristiana, 1965.

*Atti del IX Congresso internazionale di Archeologia Cristiana, Roma, 21-27 Settembre 1975.* Studi di antichità cristiana 32. Città del Vaticano; Rome: Pontificio Istituto di Archeologia Cristiana, 1978.

Augustin. *Oeuvres de saint Augustin, 31: Traités anti-donatistes.* Edited by Albertus Cornelius De Veer. Translated by Guy Finaert. Bibliothèque augustinienne. Paris: Desclée de Brouwer, 1968.

Augustin d'Hippone. *Vingt-six sermons au peuple d'Afrique.* Edited by François Dolbeau. Collection des études augustiniennes 147. Paris: Institut d'études augustiniennes, 2009.

Augustine. *Expositions of the Psalms.* Translated by Maria Boulding. The Works of Saint Augustine: A Translation for the 21st Century, 3/15-20. Edited by John E. Rotelle. Brooklyn, N.Y.: New City Press, 2000.

————. *Sermons.* Edited by John E. Rotelle. Translated by Edmund Hill. The Works of Saint Augustine: A Translation for the 21st Century, 3/1-11. Brooklyn, N.Y.: New City Press, 1990.

————. *The Works of Saint Augustine: A Translation for the 21st Century.* Edited by John E. Rotelle. Brooklyn, N.Y.: New City Press, 1990-.

Ayres, Lewis. *Nicaea and Its Legacy.* Oxford: Oxford University Press, 2004.

Ballu, Albert. *Guide illustré de Timgad (antique Thamugadi).* Paris: Neurdein Frères, 1910.

————. *Les ruines de Timgad (antique Thamugadi): Sept années de découvertes (1903-1910).* Paris: Neurdein Frères, 1911.

Barnes, Michel. "Maximino Arianorum episcopum, Conlatio con." In *Augustine through the Ages: An Encyclopedia,* edited by Allan D. Fitzgerald, 549. Grand Rapids: Wm. B. Eerdmans, 1999.

————. "Maximinum Arianum, Contra." In *Augustine through the Ages: An Encyclopedia,* edited by Allan D. Fitzgerald, 550. Grand Rapids: Wm. B. Eerdmans, 1999.

Barnes, Timothy David. *Tertullian: A Historical and Literary Study.* 2nd ed. Oxford: Clarendon Press, 1985.

Barral i Altet, Xavier. "Mensae et repas funéraire dans les nécropoles d'époque chrétienne de la péninsule Ibérique: Vestiges archéologiques." In *Atti del IV*

*Congresso internazionale di Archeologia Cristiana, Città del Vaticano, 16-22 Ottobre 1938,* 2:49-69. Rome: Pontificio Istituto di Archeologia Cristiana, 1940.

Baratte, François, and Noël Duval. *Haidra, les ruines d'Ammaedra.* Tunis: Société tunisienne de diffusion, 1974.

Bejaoui, Fathi. "A propos des mosaïques funéraires d'Henchir Sokrine (environs de Lepti Minus, en Byzacène)." In *L'Africa Romana: Atti del IX Convegno di studio, Nuoro, 13-15 dicembre 1991, 229-36.* Edited by Attilio Mastino. Pubblicazioni del Dipartimento di Storia dell'Università di Sassari 20. Sassari: Gallizzi, 1992.

———. "Découvertes d'Archéologie Chrétienne en Tunisie." In *Atti del IX Congresso internazionale di Archeologia Cristiana: Roma, 21-27 Settembre 1975,* 1927-60. Studi di antichità cristiana 32. Città del Vaticano; Rome: Pontificio Istituto di Archeologia Cristiana, 1978.

———. *Histoire des hautes steppes: Antiquité — moyen age. Actes du colloque de Sbeïtla.* Tunis: Institut national du patrimoine, 2001.

———. "L'architecture et le décor: État des découvertes d'époque chrétienne des dix dernières années en Tunisie." *Antiquité Tardive* 10 (2002): 197-211.

———. "Note préliminaire sur l'église et le baptistère de Henchir Sokrine." *Africa* 10 (1988): 98-104.

———. "Nouvelles données archéologiques à Sbeïtla." *Africa* 14 (1996): 37-63.

———. "Recherche archéologique à Thelepte et ses environs: Note sur les récentes découvertes." In *Histoire des hautes steppes: Antiquité — moyen age: Actes du colloque de Sbeïtla,* 147-61. Tunis: Institut national du patrimoine, 2001.

———. *Sbeïtla, l'antique Sufetula.* Tunis: Institut national du patrimoine, 1994.

———. "Une novelle église d'epoque Byzantine à Sbeïtla." In *L'Africa Romana: Atti dell'XII Convegno di studio, Olbia, 12-15 dicembre 1996,* edited by Mustapha Khanoussi, Paola Ruggeri, and Cinzia Vismara, 3:1173-83. Pubblicazioni del Dipartimento di Storia dell'Università degli Studi di Sassari 31. Sassari: Editions Democratica Sarda, 1998.

Berrouard, Marie-François. *Introduction aux homélies de saint Augustin sur l'Évangile de saint Jean.* Collection des études augustiniennes 170. Paris: Institut d'études augustiniennes, 2004.

Berry, Walter. "The Early Christian Baptisteries of Africa Proconsularis." Master's thesis, University of Missouri, 1976.

Berthold, G., trans. *Maximus the Confessor: Selected Writings.* New York: Paulist Press, 1985.

Bévenot, Maurice. *The Tradition of MSS: A Study in the Transmission of St. Cyprian's Treatises.* Oxford: Oxford University Press, 1961.

Blowers, Paul M., Angela Christman, David Hunter, and Robin D. Young, editors. *In Dominico Eloquio = In Lordly Eloquence: Essays on Patristic Exegesis in Honor of Robert Louis Wilken.* Grand Rapids: Wm. B. Eerdmans, 2002.

Bonner, Gerald. *St. Augustine of Hippo: Life and Controversies.* Norwich: Canterbury Press, 1996.

Bowman, Alan K., Averil Cameron, and Peter Garnsey, editors. *The Cambridge An-*

*cient History,* vol. 12: *The Crisis of Empire, A.D. 193-337.* 2nd ed. Cambridge and New York: Cambridge University Press, 2005.

Boyadjiev, S. "La rotonde souterraine de Damous-el-Karita à Carthage à la lumière de nouvelles données." In *Atti del IX Congresso internazionale di Archeologia Cristiana: Roma, 21-27 settembre 1975,* 117-31. Città del Vaticano; Rome: Pontificio Istituto di Archeologia Cristiana, 1978.

Branham, Joan. "Women as Objects of Sacrifice." In *La cuisine et l'autel: Les sacrifices en questions dans les sociétés de la Méditerranée ancienne,* edited by Stella Georgoudi, Renée Koch, and Francis Schmidt, 371-86. Bibliothèque de l'École des Hautes Études 124. Turnhout: Brepols, 2005.

Breckenridge, James. "Christian Funerary Portraits in Mosaic." *Gesta* 13.2 (1974): 29-43.

Brent, Allan. *Hippolytus and the Roman Church in the Third Century.* Leiden: Brill, 1995.

Bright, Pamela. "Donatist Bishops." In *Augustine through the Ages: An Encyclopedia,* edited by Allan D. Fitzgerald, 281-84. Grand Rapids: Wm. B. Eerdmans, 1999.

Brink, Laurie, and Deborah A. Green, editors. *Commemorating the Dead: Texts and Artifacts in Context: Studies of Roman, Jewish, and Christian Burials.* Berlin: Walter de Gruyter, 2008.

Burns, J. Patout. "The Atmosphere of Election: Augustinianism as Common Sense." *Journal of Early Christian Studies* 2 (1994): 325-39.

———. "Augustine's Role in the Imperial Action against Pelagius." *Journal of Theological Studies* n.s., 30 (1979): 67-83.

———. *Cyprian the Bishop.* Routledge Early Church Monographs. London: Routledge, 2002.

———. *The Development of Augustine's Doctrine of Operative Grace.* Paris: Études Augustiniennes, 1980.

———. "The Eucharist as the Foundation of Christian Unity in North African Theology." *Augustinian Studies* 32 (2001): 1-24.

———. "From Persuasion to Predestination: Augustine on Freedom in Rational Creatures." In *In Dominico Eloquio = In Lordly Eloquence: Essays on Patristic Exegesis in Honor of Robert Louis Wilken,* edited by Paul M. Blowers, Angela Christman, David Hunter, and Robin D. Young, 249-316. Grand Rapids: Wm. B. Eerdmans, 2002.

———. "How Christ Saves." In *Tradition and the Rule of Faith in the Early Church: Essays in Honor of Joseph T. Lienhard, S.J.,* edited by Ronnie J. Rombs and Alexander Hwang, 193-210. Washington, D.C.: Catholic University of America Press, 2010.

———. "On Rebaptism: Social Organization in the Third-Century Church." *Journal of Early Christian Studies* 1 (1993): 367-403.

Busch, Benedictus. "De Initiatione Christiana secundum Sanctum Augustinum." *Ephemerides Liturgicae, pars prior, analecta historico-ascetica* 52 (1938): 159-78, 385-483.

Cabrol, Fernand, Henri Leclercq, and Henri-Irénée Marrou, eds. *Dictionnaire d'archéologie chrétienne et de liturgie.* Paris: Letouzey et Ané, 1905-1948.

Cagnat, René. *L'armée romaine d'Afrique et l'occupation militaire de l'Afrique sous les empereurs.* Paris: Leroux, 1913.

Caillet, Jean-Pierre. "Le dossier de la basilique chrétienne de Chlef (anciennement El Asnam, ou Orléansville)." *Karthago. Revue d'archéologie africaine* 21 (1986): 135-61.

Cameron, Averil. "Byzantine Africa — The Literary Evidence." In *Excavations at Carthage,* edited by John H. Humphrey, 7:29-62. Ann Arbor: Kelsey Museum, University of Michigan, 1982.

*Carthage: L'histoire, sa trace et son écho: Les Musées de la Ville de Paris, Musée du Petit Palais, 9 Mars–2 Juillet 1995.* Paris: Paris-Musées, 1995.

Charles-Picard, Gilbert. *Les religions de l'Afrique antique.* Civilisations d'hier et d'aujourd'hui. Paris: Plon, 1954.

Chazelle, Celia Martin, and Catherine Cubitt. *The Crisis of the Oikoumene: The Three Chapters and the Failed Quest for Unity in the Sixth-Century Mediterranean.* Studies in the Early Middle Ages, vol. 14. Turnhout: Brepols, 2007.

Christern, Jürgen. *Das frühchristliche Pilgerheiligtum von Tebessa: Architektur und Ornamentik einer spätantiken Bauhütte in Nordafrika; mit 64 Tafeln, 5 Faltkarten, 48 Figuren.* Wiesbaden: Steiner, 1976.

Christern-Briesenick, Brigitte, Friedrich Wilhelm Deichmann, and Jutta Dresken-Weiland. *Repertorium der christlich-antiken Sarkophage 3. Frankreich, Algerien, Tunesien.* Wiesbaden: Steiner, 2003.

Christofle, Marcel. *Rapport sur les travaux de fouilles et consolidations effectuées en 1930-1931-1932 par le Service des Monuments historiques de l'Algérie. Gouvernement général de l'Algérie.* Alger: Imp. la Typo-litho et J. Carbonel, 1935.

Chuvin, Pierre. *A Chronicle of the Last Pagans.* Cambridge, Mass.: Harvard University Press, 1990.

Clarke, Graeme W. "Cyprian's Epistle 64 and the Kissing of Feet in Baptism." *Harvard Theological Review* 66.1 (1973): 147-52.

———. *The Letters of St. Cyprian of Carthage.* 4 vols. New York: Newman Press, 1984.

———. "Third-Century Christianity." In *The Cambridge Ancient History,* vol. 12: *The Crisis of Empire, A.D. 193-337,* edited by Alan Bowman, Averil Cameron, and Peter Garnsey, 589-671. 2nd ed. Cambridge and New York: Cambridge University Press, 2005.

Cleland, D. J. "Salvian and the Vandals." In *Studia Patristica,* edited by Frank Leslie Cross, 10:270-74. Texte und Untersuchungen zur Geschichte der altchristlichen Literatur 107-8. Berlin: Akademie Verlag, 1970.

Clover, Frank M. "Carthage and the Vandals." In *The Late Roman West and the Vandals.* Aldershot, Hampshire, Great Britain: Variorum, 1993.

———. "Carthage in the Age of Augustine." In *The Late Roman West and the Vandals.* Aldershot, Hampshire, Great Britain: Variorum, 1993.

Coleman-Norton, Paul R. *Roman State and Christian Church: A Collection of Legal Documents to A.D. 535.* London: SPCK, 1966.

*Corpus Augustinianum Gissense [CAG 2].* Basel: Schwabe, 2005.

*Corpus des mosaïques de Tunisie: Atlas archéologique de la Tunisie, feuille 35, volume 2: Région de Zaghouan.* Tunis: Institut national d'archéologie et d'art, 1980.

*Corpus Inscriptionum Latinarum, Consilio et Auctoritate Academiae Litterarum Regiae Borussicae Editum.* Deutsche Akademie der Wissenschaften zu Berlin. Berolini: Apud G. Reimerum, 1862.

Costanza, S. "Vittore di Vita e la Historia persecutionis Africanae provinciae." *Vetera Christianorum* 17 (1980): 229-68.

Courtois, Christian. *Les Vandales et l'Afrique.* Paris: Arts et métiers graphiques, 1955.

———. "Sur un baptistère découvert dans la région de Kélibia." *Karthago. Revue d'archéologie africaine* 6 (1955): 97-127.

———. *Victor de Vita et son oeuvre, Étude critique.* Alger: Impr. officielle du Gouvernement général de l'Algérie, 1954.

Cross, Frank Leslie, ed. *Studia Patristica, 10-11: Papers Presented to the 5th International Conference on Patristic Studies held in Oxford 1967.* 2 vols. Texte und Untersuchungen zur Geschichte der altchristlichen Literatur 107-8. Berlin: Akademie Verlag, 1970.

Dassmann, Ernst, and Christian Josef Kremer, editors. *Reallexikon für Antike und Christentum; Sachwörterbuch zur Auseinandersetzung des Christentums mit der antiken Welt.* Stuttgart: Hiersemann, 2000.

Davies, J. G. *The Architectural Setting of Baptism.* London: Barrie & Rockliff, 1962.

de Blaauw, Sible. "Kultgebäude." In *Reallexikon für Antike und Christentum; Sachwörterbuch zur Auseinandersetzung des Christentums mit der antiken Welt* 20:340. Stuttgart: Hiersemann, 2008.

de Bruyne, Donatien. "Une lettre apocryphe de Jérôme fabriquée par un donatiste." *Zeitschrift für neutestamentliche Wissenschaft* 30 (1931): 70-76.

de'Cavalieri, Pio Franchi. "La 'Passio' dei Martiri Abitinensi." In *Note agiografiche 8,* 3-46. Studi e Testi/Biblioteca Apostolica Vaticana 65. Città del Vaticano, 1935.

Delehaye, Hippolyte. "Contributions récentes à l'hagiographie de Rome et d'Afrique." AnBoll 54 (1936): 265-315.

Delestre, Xavier, ed. *Hippone.* Aix-en-Provence: Edisud; [Alger]: INAS, 2005.

Dennis, Holmes V. M. "Another Note on the Vandal Occupation of Hippo Regius." *Journal of Roman Studies* 15 (1925): 263-68.

De Veer, Albertus Cornelius. "L'admission aux fonctions ecclésiastiques des clercs donatistes convertis." In *Oeuvres de saint Augustin,* 31: *Traités anti-donatistes,* 766-71. Bibliothèque augustinienne. Paris: Desclée de Brouwer, 1968.

———. "Le 'Concile' de Cirta." In *Oeuvres de saint Augustin,* 31: *Traités anti-donatistes,* 796-98. Bibliothèque augustinienne. Paris: Desclée de Brouwer, 1968.

———. "Maximianus évêque catholique de Bagaï." In *Oeuvres de saint Augustin*, 31: *Traités anti-donatistes,* 815-17. Bibliothèque augustinienne. Paris: Desclée de Brouwer, 1968.

Di Berardino, Angelo. "Novatianists." In *Encyclopedia of the Early Church,* edited by Angelo Di Berardino, 604. New York: Oxford University Press, 1992.

———, editor. *Encyclopedia of the Early Church.* New York: Oxford University Press, 1992.

Diehl, Ernst. *Inscriptiones Latinae Christianae Veteres. Impressio altera lucis ope perfecta et nonnullis locis correcta.* Berolini: Weidmann, 1961.

Dix, Gregory. *The Shape of the Liturgy.* London: Dacre Press, 1945.

———, translator. *The Treatise on the Apostolic Tradition of St. Hippolytus of Rome, Bishop and Martyr.* London: SPCK, 1937.

Dolbeau, François. *Augustin d'Hippone. Vingt-six sermons au peuple d'Afrique.* Edited by François Dolbeau. Collection des études augustiniennes 147. Paris: Institut d'études augustiniennes, 2009.

———. "Le sermon 348A de saint Augustin contre Pélage. Éditions du texte intégral." *Recherches augustiniennes et patristiques* 28 (1995): 37-63.

———. "Un Sermon inédit de saint Augustin sur la santé corporelle, partiellement cité chez Barthélemy d'Urbino." *Revue des études augustiniennes et patristiques* 40 (1994): 279-303.

Dolenz, Heimo, and Hans Baldus. *Damous-el-Karita: Die österreichisch-tunesischen Ausgrabungen der Jahre 1996 und 1997 im Saalbau und der Memoria des pilgerheiligtumes Damous-el-Karita in Karthago.* Wien: Österreichishe Archäologische Institut, 2001.

Dondeyne, Albert. "La discipline des scrutins dans l'église latine avant Charlemagne." *Revue d'histoire ecclésiastique* 28 (1932): 5-33, 751-87.

Dossey, Leslie. *Peasant and Empire in Christian North Africa.* The Transformation of the Classical Heritage 47. Berkeley and Los Angeles: University of California Press, 2010.

Downs, Joan Marguerite. "The Christian Tomb Mosaics from Tabarka: Status and Identity in a North African Roman Town." Ph.D. diss., University of Michigan, 2007.

Dunn, Geoffrey D. *Cyprian and the Bishops of Rome: Questions of Papal Primacy in the Early Church.* Early Christian Studies 11. Strathfield, NSW, Australia: St. Pauls, 2007.

Duval, Noël. "Church Buildings." In *Encyclopedia of the Early Church,* edited by Angelo Di Berardino, 1:168-75. New York: Oxford University Press, 1992.

———. "Compte rendu: L. Ennabli, La basilique de Carthagenna et le locus des sept moines de Gafsa: Nouveaux édifices chrétiens de Carthage." *Antiquité Tardive* 8 (2000): 386-91.

———. "Église et temple en Afrique du Nord." *Bulletin archéologique du Comité des travaux historiques et scientifiques* 7 (1971): 265-96.

———. "Études d'archéologie chrétienne nord-africaine: XVII — une nouvelle cuve baptismale dans le centre de Carthage." *Revue des études augustiniennes* 34 (1988): 86-92.

―――. "Études d'architecture chrétienne nord-africaine." *Mélanges de l'École française de Rome. Antiquité* 84 (1972): 1071-1172.

―――. "La chapelle funéraire souterraine dit d'Asterius, à Carthage." *Mélanges d'archéologie et d'histoire* 71 (1959): 339-57.

―――. "L'église de l'évêque Melleus à Haidra (Tunisie): La campagne franco-tunisienne de 1967." *Comptes-rendus des séances de l'Académie des Belles-Lettres* 112.2 (1968): 221-44.

―――. "L'épigraphie chrétienne de Sbeitla (Sufetula) et son apport historique." In *L'Africa Romana: Atti del IV Convegno di studio, Sassari, 12-14 dicembre 1986,* edited by Attilio Mastino, 385-414. Pubblicazioni del Dipartimento di Storia dell'Università di Sassari 7. Sassari: Gallizzi, 1986.

―――. "L'épigraphie funéraire chrétienne d'Afrique: Traditions et ruptures, constantes et diversités." In *La terza età dell'epigrafia,* edited by Angela Donati, 265-314. Epigrafia e Antichità 9. Faenza: Lega, 1988.

―――. *Les Églises africaines à deux absides, recherches archéologiques sur la liturgie chrétienne en Afrique du Nord.* 2 vols. Paris: E. de Boccard, 1971-73.

―――. "Les Mosaïques funéraires d'Algérie comparées à celles de Tunisie." In *Corso di cultura sull'arte ravennate e bizantina,* 149-59. Ravenna: Edizioni Dante, 1970.

―――. "L'évêque et la cathédrale en Afrique du Nord." In Actes du XIe Congrès International d'archèologie Chrétienne: Lyon, Vienne, Grenoble, Genève, et Aoste (21-28 Septembre 1986), 1:345–403. Collection de l'Ecole française de Rome, 123; Studi di Antichità Cristiana, 41; Roma: École française de Rome; Città del Vaticano: Pontificio Istituto di Archeologia Cristiana, 1989.

―――. *Recherches archéologiques à Haïdra, 1: Les inscriptions chrétiennes.* Collection de l'École française de Rome 18. Rome: École française de Rome, 1975.

―――. *Recherches archéologiques à Haïdra, 2: La Basilique I dite de Melléus ou de Saint-Cyprien.* Collection de l'École française de Rome 18. Rome: École française de Rome, 1981.

―――. "Sufetula: L'histoire d'une ville romaine de la haute-steppe à la lumière des recherches récents." In *L'Afrique dans l'Occident romain: Ier siècle av. J.-C.–IVe siècle ap. J.-C.* Collection de l'École française de Rome 134. Rome: École française de Rome, 1990.

―――, editor. *Les premiers monuments chrétiens de la France.* Atlas archéologiques de la France. Paris: Picard, 1995.

Duval, Noël, and Alexandre Lézine. "Nécropole chrétienne et baptistère souterrain à Carthage." *Cahiers archéologiques, fin de l'antiquité et moyen-âge* 10 (1959): 71-147.

Duval, Noël, and François Baratte. *Les Ruines de Sufetula: Sbeïtla.* Tunis: Société tunisienne de diffusion, 1973.

Duval, Noël, and Henri Broise. "L'urbanisme de Sufetula — Sbeïtla en Tunisie." In *Politische Geschichte (Provinzen und Randvölker: Afrika mit Ägypten,* edited by Hildegard Temporini and Wolfgang Haase, Aufstieg und Niedergang der römischen Welt, Teil 2, Bd. 10.2, pp. 596-632. Berlin: Walter de Gruyter, 1982.

Duval, Noël, and Jean Cintas. "L'eglise du prêtre Felix (region de Kélibia)." *Karthago. Revue d'archéologie africaine* 9 (1958): 157-265.

Duval, Noël, and Paul-Albert Février. "Le décor des monuments chrétiens d'Afrique du Nord." In *Actas del VIII Congreso internacional de Arqueología Cristiana, Barcelona, 5-11 Octubre 1969,* 5-55. Studi di antichità cristiana, 30. Barcelona: Consejo Superior de Investigaciones Científicas, 1972.

Duval, Noël, Isabelle Gui, and Jean-Pierre Caillet, editors. *Basiliques chrétiennes d'Afrique du Nord, 1. Inventaire de l'Algérie, 2. Illustrations.* Collection des études augustiniennes 130. Paris: Institut d'études augustiniennes, 1992.

Duval, Yvette. *Auprès des saints corps et âme: L'inhumation "ad sanctos" dans la chrétienté d'Orient et d'Occident du IIIe au VIIe siècle.* Paris: Études augustiniennes, 1988.

———. *Loca sanctorum Africae: Le culte des martyrs en Afrique du IVe au VIIe siècle.* 2 vols. Collection de l'École française de Rome 58. Rome: École française de Rome, 1982.

Edgar, C. C. *Zenon Papyri in the University of Michigan Collection.* Michigan Papyri, vol. 1. Ann Arbor: University of Michigan Press, 1931.

Ennabli, Liliane. *Carthage, une métropole chrétienne du IVe à la fin du VIIe siècle.* Études d'antiquités africaines. Paris: CNRS, 1997.

———. *La Basilique de Carthagenna et le locus des septs moines de Gafsa: Nouveaux édifices chrétiens de Carthage.* Études d'antiquités africaines. Paris: CNRS, 2000.

———. "Les inscriptions chrétiennes de Carthage et leur apport pour la connaissance de la Carthage chrétienne." In *L'Africa Romana: Atti del IV Convegno di studio, Sassari, 12-14 dicembre 1986,* edited by Attilio Mastino, 189-203. Pubblicazioni del Dipartimento di Storia dell'Universià di Sassari 7. Sassari: Gallizzi, 1986.

———. *Les inscriptions funéraires chrétiennes de Carthage, 1: La basilique dite de Sainte-Monique, à Carthage.* Recherches d'archéologie africaine. Tunis: Institut national d'archéologie et d'art; Rome: École française de Rome, 1975.

———. *Les inscriptions funéraires chrétiennes de Carthage, 2: La basilique de Mcidfa.* Recherches d'archéologie africaine. Tunis: Institut national d'archéologie et d'art; Rome: École française de Rome, 1982.

———. *Les inscriptions funéraires chrétiennes de Carthage, 3: Carthage intra et extra muros.* Recherches d'archéologie africaine publiées par l'Institut national d'archéologie et d'art de Tunis. Rome: École française de Rome, 1991.

———. "Topographie chrétienne de Carthage: Les régions ecclésiastiques." *Collection de l'École française de Rome* 123.2 (1989): 1087-1101.

Eno, Robert B., translator. *Fulgentius: Selected Works.* Fathers of the Church 95. Washington, D.C.: Catholic University of America Press, 1997.

Evans, Ernest, editor and translator. *Tertullian: de Baptismo Liber: Homily on Baptism.* London: SPCK, 1964.

Farnum, Jerome H. *The Positioning of the Roman Imperial Legions*. BAR International Series 1458. Oxford, England: Archaeopress, 2005.

Ferguson, Everett. *Baptism in the Early Church: History, Theology, and Liturgy in the First Five Centuries*. Grand Rapids: Wm. B. Eerdmans, 2009.

"Feriale Ecclesiae Romanae." In *Chronicorum Minorum Saec. IV., V., VI., VII. MGH AA*, 9:71-72. Berlin: Weidmann, 1892.

Ferron, J., and M. Pinard. "Plaques de terre cuite d'époque byzantine découvertes à Carthage." *Cahiers de Byrsa* 2 (1952): 97-184.

Février, Paul-Albert. "Africa — Archeology." In *Encyclopedia of the Early Church*, edited by Angelo Di Berardino, 1:16. New York: Oxford University Press, 1992.

———. "Le culte des martyrs en Afrique et ses plus anciens monuments." *Corso di cultura sull'arte ravennate e bizantina* 17 (1970): 191-215.

———. "Nouvelles recherches dans la salle tréflée de la basilique de Tébessa." *Bulletin d'archéologie algérienne* 3 (1968): 167-92.

Finn, Thomas M. *Early Christian Baptism and the Catechumenate: Italy, North Africa, and Egypt*. Message of the Fathers of the Church 6. Collegeville, Minn.: Liturgical Press, 1992.

———, translator. *Quodvultdeus of Carthage*. Ancient Christian Writers 60. New York: Newman Press, 2004.

Fitzgerald, Allan D. "Innocent I: Insight into the History of Penance." *Revue des études augustiniennes* 54 (2008): 95-110.

———, editor. *Augustine through the Ages: An Encyclopedia*. Grand Rapids: Wm. B. Eerdmans, 1999.

Fournier, Éric. *Victor of Vita and the Vandal "Persecution": Interpreting Exile in Late Antiquity*. Ann Arbor, Mich.: University Microfilms International, 2008.

Frend, W. H. C. *The Donatist Church: A Movement of Protest in Roman North Africa*. Oxford: Clarendon Press, 1952, 2000.

———. *The Early Church: From the Beginnings to 461*. London: SCM, 1992.

———. *Martyrdom and Persecution in the Early Church: A Study of a Conflict from the Maccabees to Donatus*. Garden City, N.Y.: Anchor Books, 1967.

———. "A Two-Period Baptistery in Carthage." *Bulletin du centre de documentation archéologique de la conservation de Carthage* 6 (1985): 42-43.

Fulgentius. *Fulgentius: Selected Works*. Translated by Robert B. Eno. Fathers of the Church 95. Washington, D.C.: Catholic University of America Press, 1997.

Funk, F. X. von, editor. *Didascalia et Constitutiones Apostolorum*. Paderbornae, in libraria Ferdinandi Schoeningh, 1905.

Gamber, Klaus. "Ordo Missae Africanae: Der Nordafrikanische Meßritus zur Zeit des hl. Augustinus." *Römische Quartalschrift für christliche Altertumskunde und Kirchengeschichte* 64 (1969): 139-53.

Gauckler, Paul. *Basiliques chrétiennes de Tunisie (1892-1904)*. Paris: A. Picard et fils, 1913.

Georgoudi, Stella, Renée Koch, and Francis Schmidt, editors. *La cuisine et l'autel: Les sacrifices en questions dans les sociétés de la Méditerranée ancienne*. Bibliothèque de l'École des Hautes Études 124. Turnhout: Brepols, 2005.

Goffart, Walter A. *Barbarians and Romans, A.D. 418-584: The Techniques of Accommodation.* Princeton, N.J.: Princeton University Press, 1980.

Grasmück, Ernst Ludwig. *Coercitio; Staat und Kirche im Donatistenstreit.* Bonner historische Forschungen 22. Bonn: L. Röhrscheid, 1964.

Grégoire, Henri. "Les baptistères de Cuicul et de Doura." *Byzantion* 13 (1938): 589-93.

————. "Sainte Salsa, roman épigraphique." *Byzantion* 12 (1937): 213-24.

Grenfell, Bernard P., and Arthur S. Hunt, eds. *The Oxyrhynchus Papyri,* Pts. 1-13: Memoirs 1-2, 5-6, 8-16 of The Egypt Exploration Fund, Graeco-Roman Branch. London: Egypt Exploration Fund, 1898.

Groh, Dennis. "Utterance and Exegesis: Biblical Interpretation in the Montanist Crisis." In *The Living Text: Essays in Honor of Ernest W. Saunders,* edited by Robert Jewett and Dennis Groh, 73-95. Lanham, Md.: University Press of America, 1985.

Grubbs, Judith Evans. *Law and Family in Late Antiquity: The Emperor Constantine's Marriage Legislation.* Oxford: Clarendon Press, 1995.

————. *Women and the Law in the Roman Empire: A Sourcebook on Marriage, Divorce, and Widowhood.* London and New York: Routledge, 2002.

Gsell, Stéphane. *Les monuments antiques de l'Algérie.* 2 vols. Paris: A. Fontemoing, 1901.

Gui, Isabelle, Noël Duval, and Jean-Pierre Caillet, editors. *Basiliques chrétiennes d'Afrique du Nord, I: Inventaire de l'Algérie, 1. Texte, 2. Illustrations.* Collection des études augustiniennes 129. Paris: Institut des études augustiniennes, 1992.

Guidoboni, Emanuela, editor. *Catalogue of Ancient Earthquakes in the Mediterranean Area up to the Tenth Century.* Rome: Istituto nazionale di geofisica, 1994.

Harmless, William. *Augustine and the Catechumenate.* Collegeville, Minn.: Liturgical Press, 1995.

Haury, Jacobus, editor. *Procopii Caesariensis Opera Omnia.* Lipsiae: B. G. Teubneri, 1962-64.

Heather, Peter J. "Christianity and the Vandals in the Reign of Geiseric." In *Wolf Liebeschuetz Reflected: Essays Presented by Colleagues, Friends, and Pupils,* edited by John Drinkwater and Benet Salaway, 137-46. London: Institute of Classical Studies, School of Advanced Study, University of London, 2007.

Hefele, Karl Joseph von. *Histoire des conciles d'après les documents originaux.* Translated by Henri Leclercq. Nouvelle traduction française faite sur la 2 éd. allemande, corrigée et augmentée de notes critiques et bibliographiques, par un religieux bénédictin de l'abbaye Saint-Michel de Farnborough. Paris: Letouzey, 1907.

————. *A History of the Councils of the Church: From the Original Documents.* Edinburgh: T&T Clark, 1883.

Hermanowicz, Erika T. *Possidius of Calama: A Study of the North African Episcopate at the Time of Augustine.* Oxford and New York: Oxford University Press, 2008.

Herrmann, John, and Annewies Van Den Hoek. *Light from the Age of Augustine:*

*Late Antique Ceramics from North Africa (Tunisia)*. Cambridge, Mass.: Harvard Divinity School, 2002.

Hippolytus. *On the Apostolic Tradition*. Translated by Alistair Stewart-Sykes. Crestwood, N.Y.: St. Vladimir's Seminary Press, 2001.

Hirchner, R. Bruce. "Mauritania." *Oxford Dictionary of Byzantium*. New York: Oxford University Press, 1991.

Honoré, Tony. *Tribonian*. Ithaca, N.Y.: Cornell University Press, 1978.

Howard, E. C. "A Note on the Vandal Occupation of Hippo Regius." *The Journal of Roman Studies* 14 (1924): 257-58.

Humphrey, John H., and Ma'had al-Qawmi lil-Athar wa-al-Funun bi-Tunis. *Excavations at Carthage*. American Schools of Oriental Research. Tunis: Cérès Productions, 1976-.

Hunter, David G. "Augustine and the Making of Marriage in Roman North Africa." *Journal of Early Christian Studies* 11 (2003): 63-85.

———. *Marriage, Celibacy, and Heresy in Ancient Christianity: The Jovinianist Controversy*. Oxford Early Christian Studies. Oxford: Oxford University Press, 2007.

*Inscriptiones Christianae Urbis Romae Septimo Saeculo Antiquiores: Nova Series*. Rome: Pontificale Institutum archaeologiae christianae, 1956.

Jensen, Robin Margaret. "Baptismal Practices at North African Martyrs' Shrines." In *Ablution, Initiation, and Baptism: Late Antiquity, Early Judaism, and Early Christianity = Waschungen, Initiation und Taufe: Spätantike, Frühes Judentum und Frühes Christentum*, edited by David Hellholm, 3 vols., pp. 1673-95. Beihefte zur Zeitschrift für die neutestamentliche Wissenschaft und die Kunde der älteren Kirche 176. Berlin and New York: Walter de Gruyter, 2010.

———. "Dining with the Dead." In *Commemorating the Dead: Texts and Artifacts in Context: Studies of Roman, Jewish, and Christian Burials*, edited by Laurie Brink and Deborah A. Green. Berlin and New York: Walter de Gruyter, 2008.

———. *Living Water: Images, Symbols, and Settings of Early Christian Baptism*. Supplements to Vigiliae Christianae 105. Leiden and Boston: Brill, 2011.

———. "Mater Ecclesia and the Fons Aeterna: The Church and Her Womb in Ancient Christian Traditions." In *A Feminist Companion to Patristic Literature*, edited by Amy-Jill Levine with Maria Mayo Robbins, 137-55. London and New York: T&T Clark, 2008.

———. "With Pomp, Novelty, Avarice, and Apparatus: Alternative Baptismal Practices in Roman Africa." In *Studia Patristica* 44:77-83. Leuven: Peeters, 2010.

Jones, A. H. M. *The Later Roman Empire, 284-602: A Social, Economic, and Administrative Survey*. Baltimore: Johns Hopkins University Press, 1986.

Joyal, Mark, and Rory B. Egan, eds. *Daimonopylai: Essays in Classics and the Classical Tradition Presented to Edmund G. Berry*. Winnipeg: University of Manitoba Centre for Hellenic Civilization, 2004.

Julian, Emperor of Rome, 331-363. *Oeuvres complètes*. Edited by Joseph Bidez, Gabriel Rochefort, and Christian Lacombrade. 4 vols. Collection des universités de France. Paris: Société d'édition "Les Belles Lettres," 1924-1965.

Kelly, J. N. D. *Early Christian Creeds*. 3rd ed. London: Continuum, 2006.

Khader, Aïcha Ben Abed Ben, and Michel Bonifay. "Les deux baptistères de Sidi Jdidi (Tunisie)." *Antiquité Tardive* 11 (2003): 129-49.

Khader, Aïcha Ben Abed Ben, Michel Fixot, Michel Bonifay, and Sylvestre Roucole. *Sidi Jdidi, I: La basilique sud*. Recherches d'archéologie africaine. Rome: École française de Rome, 2004.

Khader, Aïcha Ben Abed Ben, Mongi Ennaifer, Marie Spiro, and Margaret Alexander. *Thuburbo Majus: Les mosaïques de la région des Grands Thermes*. Corpus des mosaïques de Tunisie, feuille 35, fasc. 2. Tunis: Institut national d'archéologie et d'arts, 1985.

Khatchatrian, Armen. *Les baptistères paléochrétiens, plans, notices et bibliographie*. Paris: École pratique des hautes études, 1962.

———. *Origine et typologie des baptistères paleochrétiens*. Mulhouse: Centre de Culture Chrétienne, 1982.

Kilmartin, Edward. "Early African Legislation Concerning Liturgical Prayer." *Ephemerides Liturgicae* 9 (1985): 105-27.

Kirsch, Johann P., and Theodor Klauser. "Altar." In *Reallexikon für Antike und Christentum; Sachwörterbuch zur Auseinandersetzung des Christentums mit der antiken Welt*, edited by Ernst Dassmann and Christian Josef Kremer, 343-50. Stuttgart: Hiersemann, 2000.

Klauser, Theodor. *Reallexikon für Antike und Christentum; Sachwörterbuch zur Auseinandersetzung des Christentums mit der antiken Welt*. Stuttgart: Hiersemann, 1950.

Kleinbauer, W. Eugene. "Table Top with Lobed Border." In *Age of Spirituality: Late Antique and Early Christian Art, Third to Seventh Century*, edited by Kurt Weitzmann, 637-38. New York: Metropolitan Museum of Art, 1979.

Knipfing, John R. "The Libelli of the Decian Persecution." *The Harvard Theological Review* 16.4 (1923): 345-90.

Krautheimer, Richard. "Introduction to an 'Iconography of Mediaeval Architecture.'" *Journal of the Warburg and Courtauld Institutes* 5 (1942): 1-33.

Krueger, Paul, editor. *Corpus Iuris Civilis*. Hildesheim: Weidmann, 1989.

Labbe, Philippe, and Gabriel Cossart. *Sacrosancta Concilia, Ad Regiam Editionem Exacta, Quae Nunc Quarta Parte Prodit*. 18 vols. Lutetiae Parisiorum: impensis Societatis Typographicae, 1671.

Lancel, Serge. *Actes de la conférence de Carthage en 411*. SC 194, 195, 224, 373. Paris: Éditions du Cerf, 1972.

———. "La représentation des différentes provinces à la conférence." In *Actes de la conférence de Carthage en 411*. SC 194:143-47. Paris: Éditions du Cerf, 1972.

———. *Saint Augustine*. Translated by Antonia Neville. London: SCM, 2002.

Lassus, Jean. "La basilique africaine." *Corso di cultura sull'arte ravennate e bizantina* 17 (1970): 217-34.

————. "Les baptistères africains." *Corso di cultura sull'arte ravennate e bizantina* 17 (1970): 235-52.

————. "Les édifices du culte: Autour de la basilique." In *Atti del VI Congresso internazionale di Archeologia Cristiana, Ravenna, 23-30 settembre 1962*, 581-610. Studi di antichità cristiana 26. Città del Vaticano: Pontificio Istituto di Archeologia Cristiana, 1965.

Lawless, George. *Augustine of Hippo and His Monastic Rule.* Oxford and New York: Clarendon Press; Oxford University Press, 1987.

Lazreg, Nejib ben, and Noël Duval. "Le baptistère de Békalta." In *Carthage: L'histoire, sa trace et son echo*, 304-7. Paris: Paris-Musées, 1995.

Lazreg, Nejib ben, Susan T. Stevens, Lea Stirling, and J. P. Moore. "Roman and Early Christian Burial Complex at Leptiminus (Lamta): Second Notice." *Journal of Roman Archaeology* 19 (2006): 347-68.

Leclercq, Henri. "Autel." In *Dictionnaire d'archéologie chrétienne et de liturgie*, edited by Fernand Cabrol, Henri Leclercq, and Henri-Irénée Marrou, 1.2:3155-3190. Paris: Letouzey et Ané, 1924.

————. "Carthage." In *Dictionnaire d'archéologie chrétienne et de liturgie*, edited by Fernand Cabrol, Henri Leclercq, and Henri-Irénée Marrou, 2.2:2190-2330. Paris: Letouzey et Ané, 1924.

————. "Sbeitla." In *Dictionnaire d'archéologie chrétienne et de liturgie*, edited by Fernand Cabrol, Henri Leclercq, and Henri-Irénée Marrou, 15.1:949-80. Paris: Letouzey et Ané, 1924.

Leglay, Marcel. "Note sur quelques baptistères d'Algérie." In *Actes du Ve Congrès international d'archéologie chrétienne, Aix-en-Provence, 13-19 Septembre 1954*, 401-6. Studi di antichità cristiana 22. Città del Vaticano: Pontificio Istituto di Archeologia Cristiana, 1957.

Leone, Anna. *Changing Townscapes in North Africa from Late Antiquity to the Arab Conquest.* Munera 28. Bari: Edipuglia, 2007.

————. "Changing Urban Landscapes: Burials in North African Cities from the Late Antique to the Byzantine Periods." In *Mortuary Landscapes of North Africa*, edited by Lea M. Stirling and David L. Stone, 164-203. Toronto: University of Toronto Press, 2007.

Lepelley, Claude. "L'Afrique du Nord et le prétendu séisme universel du 21 juillet 365." In *Mélanges de l'École française de Rome. Antiquité* 96 (1984): 463-91.

Leynaud, Augustin-Ferdinand. *Les catacombes africaines: Sousse-Hadrumète.* Alger: Jules Carbonel, 1922.

Lézine, Alexandre. *Architecture romaine d'Afrique, recherches et mises au point.* Paris: Presses universitaires de France, 1962.

————. *Thuburbo Majus.* Tunis: Société tunisienne de diffusion, 1968.

Libanius. *Libanii Opera.* Edited by Richard Foerster. Editio stereotypa. Hildesheim: G. Olms, 1963.

Lietzmann, Hans. *Die drei ältesten Martyrologien.* Kleine Texte für Vorlesungen und Übungen 2. Bonn: A. Marcus and E. Weber, 1911.

Louth, Andrew. *Maximus the Confessor.* The Early Church Fathers. London: Routledge, 1996.

Mackin, Theodore. *Divorce and Remarriage.* New York: Paulist Press, 1984.

Maguire, H. "Mosaics." In *Bir Ftouha: A Pilgrimage Church Complex at Carthage,* edited by Susan T. Stevens, 303-34. Journal of Roman Archaeology, Supplementary Series 59. Portsmouth, R.I.: Journal of Roman Archaeology, 2005.

Maier, Jean-Louis. *Le dossier du donatisme.* 2 vols. Texte und Untersuchungen zur Geschichte der altchristlichen Literatur, 134-35. Berlin: Akademie Verlag, 1987.

————. *L'épiscopat de l'Afrique romaine, vandale, et byzantine.* Biblioteca Helvetica Romana 11. Rome: Institut suisse de Rome, 1973.

Mandouze, André. "Le Donatisme représente-t-il le résistance à Rome de l'Afrique tardive?" In *Assimilation et résistance à la culture greco-romaine dans le monde ancien: Travaux de VIe Congrès international d'études classiques,* edited by D. M. Pippidi, 357-66. Paris: Société d'edition "Les Belles Lettres," 1976.

Mansi, Gian Domenico. *Sacrorum Conciliorum Nova et Amplissima Collectio.* Edited by Jean-Baptiste Martin, Louis Petit, Philippe Labbe, and Gabriel Cossart. 58 vols. Parisiis: expensis H. Welter, 1901.

Marec, Erwan. *Monuments chrétiens d'Hippone, ville épiscopale de saint Augustin.* Paris: Arts et métiers graphiques, 1958.

Markus, R. A. "Country Bishops in Byzantine Africa." *Studies in Church History* 16 (1979): 1-14.

————. "Donatism: The Last Phase." *Studies in Church History* 1 (1964): 118-26.

————. "The Imperial Administration and the Church in Byzantine Africa." *Church History* 36.1 (1967): 18-23.

————. "Reflections on Religious Dissent in North Africa in the Byzantine Period." *Studies in Church History* 3 (1966): 140-49.

Marrou, Henri-Irénée. *Christiana tempora: Mélanges d'histoire, d'archéologie, d'épigraphie et de patristique.* Collection de l'École française de Rome 35. Rome: École française de Rome, 1978.

————. "La basilique chrétienne d'Hippone d'après le résultat des dernières fouilles." *Revue des études augustiniennes* 6 (1960): 109-54.

————. "Sur une inscription concernant Opat de Timgad." In *Christiana tempora: Mélanges d'histoire, d'archéologie, d'épigraphie et de patristique,* 145-48. Collection de l'École française de Rome 35. Rome: École française de Rome, 1978.

Martin, Dale B., and Patricia Cox Miller, editors. *The Cultural Turn in Late Ancient Studies: Gender, Asceticism, and Historiography.* Durham: Duke University Press, 2005.

Mattingly, D. J., Lea Stirling, and N. ben Lazreg. "Excavation at Site 10: A Roman Cemetery on the Southeast Edge of Leptiminus." *Journal of Roman Archaeology, Supplementary* 4 (1992): 177.

Mattingly, David J., and R. Bruce Hitchner. "Roman Africa: An Archaeological Review." *The Journal of Roman Studies* 85 (1 January 1995): 165-213.

Maximus. *Maximus the Confessor: Selected Writings.* Translated by George C. Berthold. Classics of Western Spirituality. New York: Paulist Press, 1985.

McGowan, Andrew. *Ascetic Eucharists: Food and Drink in Early Christian Ritual Meals.* Oxford Early Christian Studies. Oxford: Clarendon Press, 1999.

———. "Rethinking Agape and Eucharist in Early North African Christianity." *Studia Liturgica* 34 (2004): 165-76.

McLynn, Neil B. *Ambrose of Milan: Church and Court in a Christian Capital.* The Transformation of the Classical Heritage 22. Berkeley and Los Angeles: University of California Press, 1994.

Merdinger, Jane E. *Rome and the African Church in the Time of Augustine.* New Haven: Yale University Press, 1997.

Metzger, Catherine. "Le mobilier liturgique." In *Naissance des arts chrétiens, atlas des monuments paléochrétiens de la France,* 256-67. Atlas archéologiques de la France. Paris: Imprimerie nationale éd., 1991.

Miles, Richard. "British Excavations at Bir Messaouda, Carthage, 2000-2004, the Byzantine Basilica." *Babesch: Annual Papers on Mediterranean Archaeology* 81 (2006): 199-226.

Mitteis, Ludwig, Ulrich Wilcken, and Ruth Duttenhöfer, editors. *Griechische Urkunden der Papyrussammlung zu Leipzig* 2: Archiv für Papyrusforschung und verwandte Gebiete. Beiheft 10. Leipzig: B. G. Teubner, 1906.

Modéran, Yves. "L'Afrique reconquise et les Trois Chapitres." In *The Crisis of the Oikoumene: The Three Chapters and the Failed Quest for Unity in the Sixth-Century Mediterranean,* edited by Celia Martin Chazelle and Catherine Cubitt, 39-82. Studies in the Early Middle Ages 14. Turnhout: Brepols, 2007.

———. "Une guerre de religion, les deux églises d'Afrique à l'époque vandale." *Antiquité Tardive* 11.1 (2004): 21-44.

Mommsen, Theodor, editor. *Codex Theodosianus.* Hildesheim: Weidmann, 1990.

Monceaux, Paul. *Histoire littéraire de l'Afrique chrétienne depuis les origines jusqu'à l'invasion arabe.* Bruxelles: Culture et civilisation, 1963.

Moreschini, Claudio, editor. *Tertullien: Exhortation à la chasteté.* Translated by Jean-Claude Fredouille. SC 319. Paris: Éditions du Cerf, 1985.

Morin, Germain. "Une lettre apocryphe inédite de s. Jérôme au Pape Damas." *Revue Bénédictine* 35 (1923): 121-25.

Morin, Germain, and Antonio Casamassa, editors. *Miscellanea Agostiniana.* Rome: Typis polyglottis vaticanis, 1930.

Musurillo, Herbert. *The Acts of the Christian Martyrs.* Oxford Early Christian Texts. Oxford: Clarendon Press, 1972.

Noga-Banai, Galit. *The Trophies of the Martyrs: An Art Historical Study of Early Christian Silver Reliquaries.* Oxford Studies in Byzantium. Oxford: Oxford University Press, 2008.

O'Connell, Robert J. *The Origin of the Soul in St. Augustine's Later Works.* New York: Fordham University Press, 1987.

Osborn, Eric Francis. *Tertullian: First Theologian of the West.* Cambridge, U.K.: Cambridge University Press, 1997.

Osiek, Carolyn, and Margaret Y. MacDonald. *A Woman's Place: House Churches in Earliest Christianity.* Minneapolis: Fortress Press, 2006.

Osiek, Carolyn, and Kevin Madigan, editors. *Ordained Women in the Early Church: A Documentary History.* Baltimore: Johns Hopkins University Press, 2005.

Palol, Pedro de. "El baptisterio de la basílica de Tebessa y los altares paleocristianos circulares." *Ampurias* 17-18 (n.d.): 282-86.

*Papiri Greci e Latini.* Pubblicazioni della Società Italiana per la ricerca dei papiri greci e latini in Egitto. Firenze: Felice le Monnier, 1912.

Perler, Othmar, and Jean-Louis Maier. *Les voyages de saint Augustin.* Paris: Études augustiniennes, 1969.

Pincerle, Alberto. "L'arianesimo e la Chiesa africana nel IV secolo." *Bilchnis* 25.3 (1925): 97-106.

Pohl, Walter. "The Vandals: Fragments of a Narrative." In *Vandals, Romans, and Berbers,* edited by A. H. Merrills, 31-47. Burlington, Vt.: Ashgate, 2004.

Poinssot, Claude. *Les ruines de Dougga.* Tunis: Institut national d'archéologie et d'art, 1958.

Poinssot, Claude, and Louis Poinssot. "Baptistère découvert dans la region de Sidi Daoud (Cap Bon)." *Karthago. Revue d'archéologie africaine* 6 (1955): 124-25.

Poque, Suzanne. "Les lectures liturgiques de l'octave pascale à Hippone d'après les Traités de s. Augustin sur la Ire épître de s. Jean." *Revue Bénédictine* 74 (1964): 217-41.

———, editor. *Sermons pour la Pâque.* SC 116. Paris: Éditions du Cerf, 1966.

Preisigke, Friedrich. *Sammelbuch griechischer Urkunden aus Ägypten, herausgegeben im Auftrage der wissenschaftlichen Gesellschaft in Strassburg.* Strassburg: K. J. Trübner, 1915.

Prevost, Virginie. "Les dernières communautés chrétiennes autochtones d'Afrique du Nord." *Revue de l'histoire des religions* 224 (2007): 461-83.

Prévot, Françoise. *Recherches archéologiques franco-tunisiennes à Mactar, 5: Les inscriptions chrétiennes.* Collection de l'École française de Rome 34. Rome: École française de Rome, 1984.

Primmer, Adolf. "Die Mauriner-Handschriften der Enarrationes in Psalmos." In *Troisième centenaire de l'édition mauriste de saint Augustin: Communications présentées au colloque des 19 et 20 Avril 1990,* 169-201. Collection des études augustiniennes 127. Paris: Institut d'études augustiniennes, 1990.

Procopius. *Procopii Caesariensis Opera Omnia.* Edited by Jacobus Haury. Lipsiae: B. G. Teubneri, 1962-64.

Quasten, Johannes. "'Vetus Superstitio et Nova Religio': The Problem of Refrigerium in the Ancient Church of North Africa." *The Harvard Theological Review* 33.4 (1 October 1940): 253-66.

Quodvultdeus. *Quodvultdeus of Carthage: The Creedal Homilies: Conversion in Fifth-*

*Century North Africa.* Translated by Thomas M. Finn. Ancient Christian Writers
60. New York: Newman Press, 2004.

Radan, George. "The Basilica Pacis of Hippo." In *Augustine in Iconography: History
and Legend,* edited by Joseph C. Schnaubelt and Frederick Van Fleteren, 147-
88. Collectanea Augustiniana. New York: P. Lang, 1999.

Raynal, Dominique. *Uppenna: Archéologie et histoire de l'église d'Afrique.* 2 vols.
Tempus 32. Toulouse: Presses universitaires du Mirail, 2006.

Rebillard, Éric. *Christians and Their Many Identities in Late Antiquity, North Africa,
200-450 C.E.* Ithaca: Cornell University Press, 2012.

———. "Sermons." In *Augustine through the Ages: An Encyclopedia,* edited by Allan D. Fitzgerald, 773-92. Grand Rapids: Wm. B. Eerdmans, 1999.

Rees, B. R. *Pelagius: A Reluctant Heretic.* Suffolk: Boydell Press, 1988.

Ristow, Sebastian. *Frühchristliche Baptisterien.* Jahrbuch für Antike und Christentum 27. Münster, Westfalen: Aschendorff Verlag, 1998.

Roetzer, Wunibald. *Die Heiligen Augustinus Schriften als liturgie-geschichtliche
Quelle: Eine liturgie-geschichtliche Studie.* München: M. Hueber, 1930.

Rombs, Ronnie J., and Alexander Hwang, editors. *Tradition and the Rule of Faith in
the Early Church: Essays in Honor of Joseph T. Lienhard, S.J.* Washington, D.C.:
Catholic University of America Press, 2010.

Rosenblum, Morris, translator and commentator. *Luxorius: A Latin Poet among the
Vandals.* Records of Civilization: Sources and Studies 62. New York: Columbia
University Press, 1961.

Ruinart, Theodoricus. *Acta martyrum.* Regensburg: Joseph Manz, 1859.

Rzach, Aloisius, editor. *Oracula Sibyllina.* Vindobonae: F. Tempsky, 1891.

Saller, Richard P., and Brent D. Shaw. "Tombstones and Roman Family Relations
in the Principate: Civilians, Soldiers, and Slaves." *The Journal of Roman Studies*
74 (1984): 124-56.

Salway, Benet. "What's in a Name? A Survey of Roman Onomastic Practice from c.
700 B.C. to A.D. 700." *The Journal of Roman Studies* 84 (1994): 124-45.

Saxer, Victor. "Figura Corporis et Sanguinis Domini." *Rivista di archeologia cristiana* 47 (1971): 65-89.

———. *Vie liturgique et quotidienne à Carthage vers le milieu du 3ème siècle, le témoignage de saint Cyprien et de ses contemporains d'Afrique.* Città del Vaticano:
Pontificio Istituto di Archeologia Cristiana, 1969.

Schaff, Philip, editor. *A Select Library of the Nicene and Post-Nicene Fathers of the
Christian Church.* Edinburgh: T&T Clark, 1989.

Schnaubelt, Joseph C., and Frederick Van Fleteren, eds. *Augustine in Iconography:
History and Legend.* Collectanea Augustiniana. New York: P. Lang, 1999.

Schwarcz, Andreas. "The Settlement of the Vandals in North Africa." In *Vandals, Romans, and Berbers,* edited by A. H. Merrills, 49-57. Burlington, Vt.: Ashgate, 2004.

Senay, Pierre, and Marc Beauregard. "'L'Aedes memoriae': Un témoignage antique sur le monument circulaire de Carthage." *Cahiers des études anciennes* 19
(1986): 79-85.

———. "Monument circulaire de Carthage: Rapport préliminaire des fouilles 1982." *Cahiers des études anciennes* 15 (1983): 187-236.

Shanzer, Danuta. "Intentions and Audiences: History, Hagiography, Martyrdom, and Confession in Victor of Vita's *Historia Persecutionis.*" In *Vandals, Romans, and Berbers,* edited by A. H. Merrills, 271-90. Burlington, Vt.: Ashgate, 2004.

Shaw, Brent D. "Autonomy and Tribute: Mountain and Plain in Mauretania Tingitana." *Revue de l'Occident musulman et de la Méditerranée* 41-42 (1987): 66-89.

———. "'Elders' in Christian Africa." In *Mélanges offerts en hommage au Révérend Père Étienne Gareau, Cahiers des études anciennes* 14 (1982): 207-26. Ottawa: Éditions de l'Université d'Ottawa, 1982.

———. "Seasons of Death: Aspects of Mortality in Imperial Rome." *The Journal of Roman Studies* 86 (1996): 100-138.

———. "The Structure of Local Society in the Early Maghreb: The Elders." *Maghreb Review* 16 (1991): 18-55.

Smith, Dennis Edwin. *From Symposium to Eucharist: The Banquet in the Early Christian World.* Minneapolis: Fortress Press, 2003.

Spier, Jeffrey. *Late Antique and Early Christian Gems.* Spätantike, frühes Christentum, Byzanz. Studien und Perspektiven 20, Reihe B. Wiesbaden: Reichert, 2007.

Staats, Reinhart. "Ogdoas als ein Symbol für die Auferstehung." *Vigiliae Christianae* 26 (1972): 29-53.

Stevens, Susan T. *Bir El Knissia at Carthage: A Rediscovered Cemetery Church: Report.* Journal of Roman Archaeology, Supplementary Series 7. Ann Arbor, Mich.: Kelsey Museum, 1993.

———. *Bir Ftouha: A Pilgrimage Church Complex at Carthage.* Journal of Roman Archaeology, Supplementary Series 59. Portsmouth, R.I.: Journal of Roman Archaeology, 2005.

———. *A Cemetery of Vandalic Date at Carthage.* Journal of Roman Archaeology, Supplementary Series 75. Portsmouth, R.I.: Journal of Roman Archaeology, 2009.

———. "The Circle of Bishop Fulgentius." *Traditio* 38 (1982): 327-40.

———. "A New Christian Structure on the Outskirts of Carthage: A Preliminary Report on the 1994 Excavations at Bir Ftouha." *Dumbarton Oaks Papers* 50 (1996): 375-78.

Stevens, Susan T., Maʿhad al-Waṭanī lil-Turāth, and Kelsey Museum of Archaeology. *A Cemetery of Vandalic Date at Carthage.* Portsmouth, R.I.: Journal of Roman Archaeology, 2009.

Stevenson, Kenneth. *Nuptial Blessing: A Study of Christian Marriage Rites.* New York: Oxford University Press, 1983.

Stewart-Sykes, Alistar, translator. *Hippolytus: On the Apostolic Tradition.* Crestwood, N.Y.: St. Vladimir's Seminary Press, 2001.

Stirling, Lea. "Archeological Evidence for Food Offerings in the Graves of Roman North Africa." In *Daimonopylai: Essays in Classics and the Classical Tradition Presented to Edmund G. Berry,* edited by Rory B. Egan and Mark Joyal, 427-51. Winnipeg: University of Manitoba Centre for Hellenic Civilization, 2004.

Stone, David L., and Lea M. Stirling, editors. *Mortuary Landscapes of North Africa.* Toronto: University of Toronto Press, 2007.

Sumruld, William A. *Augustine and the Arians: The Bishop of Hippo's Encounters with Ulfilan Arianism.* Selinsgrove, Pa.: Susquehanna University Press, 1994.

Tabbernee, William. *Montanist Inscriptions and Testimonia: Epigraphic Sources Illustrating the History of Montanism.* Macon, Ga.: Mercer University Press, 1997.

———. "To Pardon or Not to Pardon? North African Montanism and the Forgiveness of Sins." In *Studia Patristica,* edited by Maurice F. Wiles, Edward Yarnold, and Paul M. Parvis, 36:375-86. Leuven: Peeters, 2001.

Temporini, Hildegard, and Wolfgang Haase, editors. *Politische Geschichte (Provinzen und Randvölker: Afrika mit Ägypten).* Aufstieg und Niedergang der römischen Welt Teil 2, Bd. 10.2. Berlin: Walter de Gruyter, 1982.

Tengström, Emin. *Donatisten und Katholiken; soziale, wirtschaftliche und politische Aspekte einer nordafrikanischen Kirchenspaltung.* Göteborg: Elanders Boktr, 1964.

Terry, James H. *Christian Tomb Mosaics of Late Roman, Vandalic, and Byzantine Byzacena.* Ph.D. diss., University of Missouri-Columbia, 1998.

Teske, Roland J., editor. "Introduction: The Arian Sermon and Answer to the Arian Sermon." In *Arianism and Other Heresies,* The Works of Saint Augustine: A Translation for the 21st Century 1/18:119-32. Brooklyn, N.Y.: New City Press, 1990.

———, translator. *Arianism and Other Heresies.* The Works of Saint Augustine: A Translation for the 21st Century 1/18. Brooklyn, N.Y.: New City Press, 1990.

Thompson, E. A. *Romans and Barbarians: The Decline of the Western Empire.* Wisconsin Studies in Classics. Madison: University of Wisconsin Press, 1982.

Tilley, Maureen A. *The Bible in Christian North Africa: The Donatist World.* Minneapolis: Fortress Press, 1997.

———. *Donatist Martyr Stories: The Church in Conflict in Roman North Africa.* Translated Texts for Historians 24. Liverpool: Liverpool University Press, 1996.

———. "No Friendly Letters: Augustine's Correspondence with Women." In *The Cultural Turn in Late Ancient Studies: Gender, Asceticism, and Historiography,* edited by Dale B. Martin and Patricia Cox Miller, 40-62. Durham: Duke University Press, 2005.

———. "Theologies of Penance during the Donatist Controversy." In *Studia Patristica* 35:330-37. Louvain: Peeters, 2001.

Toynbee, J. M. C. *Death and Burial in the Roman World.* Aspects of Greek and Roman Life. Ithaca, N.Y.: Cornell University Press, 1971.

Treggiari, Susan. *Roman Marriage: Iusti Coniuges from the Time of Cicero to the Time of Ulpian.* Oxford: Clarendon Press, 1991.

Turcan, Robert. *The Cults of the Roman Empire.* Oxford, U.K.: Blackwell, 1996.

Turner, C. H. *Ecclesiae Occidentalis Monumenta Iuris Antiquissima,* 2 vols. in 7. Oxonii: E Typographeo Clarendoniano, 1899.

van der Meer, Frederik. *Augustine the Bishop: The Life and Work of a Father of the*

*Church.* Translated by Brian Battershaw and G. R. Lamb. London: Sheed & Ward, 1962.

Van Slyke, Daniel. *Quodvultdeus of Carthage: The Apocalyptic Theology of a Roman African in Exile.* Early Christian Studies 5. Strathfield: St. Pauls, 2003.

Verheijen, Luc. *La règle de Saint Augustin.* 2 vols. Paris: Études augustiniennes, 1967.

Vilela, Albano. *La condition collégiale des prêtres au IIIe siècle.* Théologie historique 14. Paris: Beauchesne, 1971.

Ward-Perkins, J. B., and R. G. Goodchild. *The Christian Antiquities of Tripolitania.* Oxford: Printed by Charles Batey for the Society of Antiquities of London, 1953.

Weitzmann, Kurt, editor. *Age of Spirituality: Late Antique and Early Christian Art, Third to Seventh Century: Catalogue of the Exhibition at the Metropolitan Museum of Art, 1977-78.* New York: Metropolitan Museum of Art, 1979.

Wermelinger, Otto. *Rom und Pelagius: die theologische Position der römischen Bischöfe im pelagianischen Streit in den Jahren 411-432.* Stuttgart: Hiersemann, 1975.

White, L. Michael. *The Social Origins of Christian Architecture.* Harvard Theological Studies 42. Valley Forge, Pa.: Trinity Press, 1996.

Wilken, Robert Louis. *The Christians as the Romans Saw Them.* 2nd ed. New Haven, Conn.: Yale University Press, 1984.

Williams, Stephen. *Diocletian and the Roman Recovery.* New York: Methuen, 1985.

Willis, Geoffrey Grimshaw. *St. Augustine's Lectionary.* Alcuin Club Collections 44. London: SPCK, 1962.

Wills, Garry. *Saint Augustine.* New York: Viking Press, 1999.

Yacoub, Mohamed. *Splendeurs des mosaïques de Tunisie.* Tunis: Ministère de la culture, Agence nationale du patrimoine, 1995.

Yasin, Ann Marie. "Funerary Monuments and Collective Identity: From Roman Family to Christian Community." *The Art Bulletin* 87.3 (2005): 433.

———. *Saints and Church Spaces in the Late Antique Mediterranean: Architecture, Cult, and Community.* Cambridge and New York: Cambridge University Press, 2009.

Yegül, Fikret Kutlu. *Bathing in the Roman World.* Cambridge: Cambridge University Press, 2009.

———. *Baths and Bathing in Classical Antiquity.* New York: Architectural History Foundation, 1992.

Zeillet, J. "L'arianisme en Afrique avant l'invasion vandal." *Revue historique* 173 (1934): 535-41.

# Index of Persons and Groups

Aaron (Israelite priest), 170, 255n.170, 379

Abitinian martyrs (Donatist), 525-28

Abraham (patriarch), 99, 128, 153, 229, 443, 471, 473, 509, 574, 596-97; fig. 152

Abundantius (presbyter, diocese of Hippo Regius), 416, 423, 424

Adam (first human), 471, 474n.247, 510n.143
  and death, 180, 190, 212-13, 230, 471-72, 483, 501, 510
  marriage of, 442, 450, 469-70, 477
  and original sin, 205, 212-13, 230, 334, 346, 470

Adelphius (presbyter, Clipea), 112, 433

Aelia Secundula (in Mauretania Sitifensis), 126-27, 506, 514

Agapius (martyr, bishop), 23, 24, 25

Agrippinus (bishop, Carthage), 4, 176, 187n.126, 192, 259n.196, 386n.186

Albinus (acolyte, Hippo Regius), 403

Alexander (bishop, Tipasa), 125-26, 431-32, 530, 532

Alypius (bishop, Thagaste), 53, 285, 408n.338, 417, 537

Amacius (bishop, Sufetula), 148, 150, 432

Ambrose (bishop, Milan), 82, 84, 107, 203, 487, 537, 544, 545, 568

Antoninus (bishop, Fussala), 403n.294, 410, 412, 414n.381, 416, 423, 429

Anullinus (proconsul, Africa), 392n.227, 420n.434, 524, 525

Apiarius (presbyter, Sicca Veneria), 420, 423-24, 429

Apostles, 376, 384-85
  as bishops, 428, 435, 437-38
  succession from, 384-85, 407, 430

Arcadius (emperor, 395-408), 37, 52, 54, 55, 89, 408n.335

Arians, 58-59, 67-69, 72-74, 78

Arnobius (Christian writer, Sicca Veneria), 5, 31, 102n.81

Asterius (Christian, Carthage), 119, 122, 141, 147

Augustine (bishop, Hippo Regius), 201-20, 261-87, 333-54, 402-32, 455-83, 500-514, 533-48, 557-63, 566-69, 576-80, 593-96, 610-20, *et passim*

Augustus (emperor 27 B.C.E.-14 C.E.), 36, 447n.50

Aurelius (bishop, Carthage), 53, 62, 135, 412, 414, 424, 502
  anti-pagan, 90-91
  as reformer, 166, 264, 269, 287, 397, 408n.342, 413, 418-20, 427, 429, 438, 506, 531, 536-37, 582, 593
  and Donatists, 398-99, 401, 427, 429
  as Primate, 414, 418

Baal (Punic god), 38

Baleriolus (bishop, Uppenna), 125, 432

Barnabas (presbyter, Hippo Regius), 406, 413n.371

Basiliscus (Byzantine general), 65
Belisarius (Byzantine general), 75-77
Bellator (bishop, Sufetula), 149
Blossus (Christian family, Furnos Minus), 122, 128, 236, 463, 508
Boniface (bishop, Rome), 423
Boniface (count of Africa), 59, 63, 76, 160n.305
Boniface (presbyter, Hippo Regius), 406, 421n.444
Bonifatius (bishop, Carthage), 74, 96n.55, 139, 141, 420
Byzantines, 66, 75-84

Caecilian (bishop, Biltha), 184, 251, 253, 259-60, 277
Caecilian (bishop, Carthage), 47, 49, 195, 394, 396, 512, 529, 590
   and cooperation with the Empire, 48, 527, 542
   at Nicaea, 58, 198n.178, 390, 423
   ordination of, 48, 394, 414
   and receiving schismatics, 225, 391
   as *traditor*, 47, 48, 195-96, 332, 389, 401, 420, 525-26, 606, 608n.48, 610
Caecilianists
   origin of, 47-51
   and reunion with Donatists, 54-57, 398-401
Caelestis (Roman African goddess), 38, 68, 90-91, 107
Caelestius (disciple of Pelagius), 57, 419
Cainites, 173, 176
Capreolus (bishop, Carthage), 58, 62-63, 68, 535n.95
Celerina (martyr, Carthage), 11, 135, 136, 520, 531
Celerinus (confessor and lector, Carthage), 11, 17-19, 135, 383, 521, 524, 565n.136
Circumcellions, 160, 507n.122, 542, 592
Claudianus (Donatist bishop, Rome), 399, 608
Columbus (bishop, Numidia), 81, 83
Constans (emperor, 337-350), 37, 49, 50, 89, 196-97, 527, 542, 590-91, 609
Constans II (emperor, 641-668), 82-84
Constantine (emperor, 312-337), 35, 36, 438, 531
   as liberator of Christianity, 42-44, 46, 51, 392, 408n.335, 533, 537, 551, 593, 609

   and Donatists, 47, 48-49, 50n.78, 89, 353, 396, 590
   and marriage legislation, 441-42, 455
Constantius (emperor, 337-361), 37, 51, 67
Cornelius (bishop, Rome), 276, 385, 387, 453
   as martyr, 21, 589
   and Novatian schism, 29, 375n.104, 385
   and penitential practice, 28-29, 255-56, 322-23, 377n.118, 380, 391
Crescentinus (martyr and deacon, Thabraca), 119-20, 433, 485n.318, 513, 516
Crescentius (deacon, Uppenna), 116, 121-23, 432-33, 484, 507-8, 513, 516, 548-49
Cresconius (Donatist layman, Constantina), 608, 611
Crispina (martyr, Theveste), 114-15, 525, 534
Cyprian (martyr and bishop, Carthage), 176-90, 246-61, 313-33, 370-89, 451-55, 496-500, 521-23, 556-67, 565, 571-75, 586-93, 603-6, *et passim*
Cyrila (Arian bishop, Carthage), 73

Daniel (prophet), 128, 243n.81, 248n.110, 326n.210, 522, 540, 595, 607
Dardanius (Christian, Thabraca), 121, 128, 130, 433, 463, 507-8
Decius (emperor, 249-251), 12-16, 18, 20, 22, 26, 289
Deogratias (bishop, Carthage), 71-72, 74, 138
Deuterius (Donatist bishop, Macriana), 196
Diocletian (emperor, 284-305), 16, 35-40, 48, 88, 528, 590
Dionysius (bishop, Alexandria), 12, 20, 21, 22-23, 33
Donatilla (martyr), 525, 526, 528
Donatists, 47-57, 79-82, 389-92, *et passim*
   origins of, 47-48
   persecution of, 49-50, 89
   and reunion with Caecilianists, 48, 55-57, 89, 398-401, 425-28
Donatus (Donatist bishop, Bagai), 50, 542, 591
Donatus (Donatist bishop, Carthage), 47, 49, 195, 353, 396, 428, 590, 606
   as martyr, 50n.74, 197, 591n.347
   ordination of, 414n.383

and rebaptism, 196, 225, 397n.262
and repentance of clergy, 332, 344-45,
 390n.210, 397n.262, 608
Dulcitius (imperial *executor*), 37, 57, 160

Eight Martyrs (Hippo Regius), 95, 156, 534
Elijah (prophet), 243n.81, 501n.67, 567,
 569, 574, 577n.238
Emeritus (Donatist bishop, Caesarea in
 Mauretania), 286
Eraclius. *See* Heraclius (bishop, Hippo
 Regius)
Eudocia (daughter of Valentinian III), 64-
 66, 72, 74
Eudoxia (wife of Theodosius II), 64, 65
Eugenius (bishop, Carthage), 72-74, 139,
 142
Eusebius (bishop, Caesarea in Palestine),
 7, 10, 25, 26, 31, 33
Eve (spouse of Adam), 471, 474n.247,
 510n.143
 and death, 471-72, 483, 501, 510
 marriage of, 442, 450, 469-70, 477
 and original sin, 205, 334, 346
Evodius (bishop, Uzalis), 53, 502, 546

Fabian (bishop, Rome), 15n.79, 374
Fabius (military martyr), 528
Facundus (bishop, Hermiane), 79
Faustina (Christian, Uppenna), 116, 125, 129
Faustus (Manichean teacher, Milevis), 536,
 538
Felicissimus (schismatic deacon, Car-
 thage), 27, 373
Felicity (martyr, Thuburbo Minus), 8,
 458n.141
 *acta*, 247, 369, 519, 520, 523
 cult, 94, 115-117, 135-36, 144-45, 520, 521,
 531, 534, 544
 martyrdom, 9-10, 169, 171-72, 183, 240,
 521
Felix (bishop and martyr, Thibuca), 40-41,
 393, 524-26
Felix (bishop, Abthugni), 47n.59, 195n.160,
 394-95, 399n.273
Felix (presbyter and martyr, Nola), 118,
 421, 544-45
Felix I (bishop, Rome), 73
Ferrandus (secretary to Fulgentius), 79, 125
Fidus (bishop, Africa), 29, 179, 180, 190

Firmilian (bishop, Caesarea in Cappado-
 cia), 33, 187n.126, 250n.126, 388n.206
Firmus (African usurper), 53, 528
Florentius (bishop, Hippo Diarrhytus),
 504, 505
Fortis (Donatist bishop, Numidia),
 393n.235
Fortunatianus (presbyter, Hippo Regius),
 406
Fortunatus (Donatist bishop, Assuras),
 377n.118
Fortunatus (schismatic bishop, Carthage),
 373, 374n.91, 376
Fulgentius (bishop, Ruspe), 74, 79, 125, 207

Gaius Didensis (presbyter, Carthage),
 372n.70, 374n.91
Gaius Julius Serenus (pagan, Thaenae), 123,
 128, 484
Galerius (emperor, 305-311), 40, 42, 43
Galerius Maximus (proconsul, Africa), 535
Galla Placidia (empress, mother of Val-
 entinian III), 63, 137n.212
Gallienus (emperor, 253-68), 20, 22-26
Gallus (emperor, 251-253), 20-22, 255, 589
Gaudentius (Donatist bishop, Thamugadi),
 160, 162, 611
Geiseric (Vandal king, 428-477), 35, 59,
 61-72, 76, 151
Gelimer (Vandal king, 530-534), 66, 75-77
Genethlius (bishop, Carthage), 53, 535n.95
Gennadius (exarch, Africa), 80, 81
Gervasius (martyr, Milan), 154, 163, 544,
 545, 547n.202
Gildo (count and usurper, Africa), 53, 160,
 591-92, 608
Gitta (deacon, Unapompei), 405n.306, 412
Godigisclus (Vandal king), 63
Gontharis (Vandal king), 63, 77
Gratian (emperor, 367-383), 84, 135, 137,
 156, 399n.271
Gratus (bishop, Carthage), 196n.165, 396,
 535n.95
Gregory (exarch, Africa), 83-84, 148
Gregory I (bishop, Rome), 80-82
Guilia Runa (presbyterissa, Hippo Regius),
 75, 124, 130, 159, 459, 460n.149, 484,
 507n.122
Gunthamund (Vandal king, 488-496), 65,
 73-74, 134, 139

Gurzil (African god), 77

Heraclian (count, Africa), 57, 137n.215
Heraclius (bishop, Hippo Regius), 95, 405, 406, 411, 415n.391, 545n.180, 580
Hercules (Roman divine hero), 538
Hermes (Christian, Hadrumetum), 121-23, 128-29, 484, 508
Hilarianus (proconsul, Africa), 8, 10
Hildegun (Christian, Mactaris), 95, 106, 124, 223
Hilderic (Vandal king, 523-530), 65-66, 72-79, 96n.55, 139
Honorata (Christian, Mactaris), 122, 129
Honorius (bishop, related to Sufetula), 148, 155, 432-33
Honorius (bishop, Uppenna), 125, 131n.188
Honorius (emperor, 393-423), 52, 53, 55, 59, 135, 408n.335, 410
    and Donatists, 37, 55, 56, 89, 400, 421n.436, 590, 591-92, 609
    anti-pagan, 54, 55, 56, 90-91, 206, 592
Huneric (Vandal king, 477-484), 46, 63-65, 72-74, 137, 147-48

Ingentius (Christian, Abthugni), 394-95
Innocent (bishop, Rome), 57, 313n.110, 401
Isaac (Donatist martyr, Carthage), 50, 527, 530, 591
Isaac (patriarch), 99, 128, 473, 596-97

James (deacon and martyr, Lambaesis), 25, 523
Januarius (bishop, Lambaesis), 388n.205
Januarius (bishop, Lepti Minus), 432
Januarius (Christian, Thamugadi), 160
Januarius (presbyter, Hippo Regius), 405, 407, 415, 465
Jeremiah (prophet), 248n.110, 326n.210, 522
Jerome, 455, 469, 482, 487
Job, 248n.110, 326n.210, 522, 561
John (apostle), 187
John (evangelist), 175, 305, 350
John II (bishop, Rome), 78
John the Baptist, 174, 186-87, 189, 217, 534, 540, 594
John Troglita (Byzantine *magister militum*), 77

Jonah (prophet), 121, 128, 130, 345, 433, 507-8
Jovinian (Christian heretic), 442n.2, 455, 469, 478, 482
Jucundus (bishop, Sufetula), 105, 148, 149, 150, 153, 432, 535
Judas (apostle), 197, 376, 607
Julian (bishop, Eclanum), 58
Julian (emperor, 361-363), 51
    and Donatists, 50-52, 88n.6, 89, 156, 196-97, 282, 332, 396, 425, 590, 593, 609
    and pagans, 51, 533, 583
Juno Caelestis (Roman goddess), 13, 38, 538, 592n.355
Jupiter (Roman god), 13, 38
Justin (emperor, 518-527), 66
Justin II (emperor, 565-574), 117
Justinian (emperor, 527-565), 65, 66, 75-80, 82, 94, 141n.226, 153

Lactantius (Christian writer), 5, 14, 22, 31, 40
Lawrence (deacon and martyr, Rome), 405, 534, 543
Lazarus (deacon and presbyter, Hippo Regius), 405, 406
Lazarus (of Bethany), 346, 348, 349, 505
Leo I (bishop, Rome), 82
Leo I (emperor, 457-474), 65, 72
Leontius (bishop, Hippo Regius), 95, 155, 409, 531, 535, 536, 537, 562
Leporius (presbyter, Hippo Regius), 93, 406, 412n.364, 531n.71
Liberatus (deacon, Carthage), 79
Licinia Eudoxia (wife of Valentinian III), 64, 65
Licinius (emperor, 308-324), 49, 551, 593
Lucianus (confessor, Carthage), 19, 380n.140
Lucilla (Christian matron, Cirta/Carthage), 6, 43, 529, 578n.253
Lucius (bishop and martyr, Rome), 21, 385
Lucius (martyr, Carthage), 25, 523

Macarius (imperial notary), 37, 49-50, 156n.285, 196, 332, 397, 527-29, 542
Majorian (emperor, 457-461), 65, 72
Majorinus (Donatist bishop, Carthage), 195, 414n.383, 611n.61
Mani (religious founder), 45, 46

Manichees, 37, 45-46, 55, 58, 72, 243, 284, 421n.436, 429, 469, 485, 536, 566

Marcellinus (Roman general), 65, 72

Marcellinus, Flavius (imperial tribune), 37, 56, 57, 592

Marcion (Christian heretic), 4, 244

Marcionites, 4, 8, 243, 244, 253, 443

Marculus (Donatist bishop and martyr, Numidia), 49, 50n.71, 160, 527-28, 530, 542, 591, 592n.351

Marian (lector and martyr, Lambaesis), 25, 523

Marinus (bishop, Castellum Tingitanum), 134, 431

Martin I (bishop, Rome), 83n.137, 84

Mary (mother of Jesus), 97, 207, 278, 280, 282, 480, 561, 562, 616

Matrona Vidua (Christian, Bennafa), 121, 464n.186, 467

Maurentius (bishop, Thubursicu Numidarum), 409, 422-23

Maurus (bishop, Utica), 47n.59, 394

Maximian (Donatist martyr, Carthage), 50, 527, 530, 591

Maximian (Donatist schismatic bishop, Carthage), 54, 55, 200, 333, 393, 395, 608

Maximianus (bishop, Bagai), 234n.1, 400, 408n.338

Maximilian (martyr, Theveste), 118, 524, 530, 544

Maximinus (Arian bishop), 58, 67

Maximus (presbyter and confessor, Rome), 380n.138

Maximus the Confessor (monk, Carthage), 83, 84

Melania the Younger (Roman aristocrat), 44, 410

Melchizedek (priest), 250, 253

Melleus (bishop, Ammaedara), 117, 545

Mensurius (bishop, Carthage), 41, 88n.2, 389, 394, 396, 524-26, 591n.339

Miltiades (bishop, Rome), 48n.65, 49, 275n.364, 397, 400, 425, 591

Minucius Felix (Christian writer), 5, 31, 495n.29

Monica (mother of Augustine), 136, 146n.253, 266n.255, 269n.297, 285, 504, 506n.108, 512

Montanus (martyr, Carthage), 25, 523

Moses (Israelite lawgiver), 170, 284, 430, 443, 567, 569
    intercession of, 248n.110, 326n.210, 522
    and water miracles, 173, 184, 253

Nestorius (bishop, Constaninople), 79

Nicenes, 69-74

Noah (patriarch), 222, 248, 248n.110, 250, 253, 258, 326n.210, 331, 443, 552

Novatian (schismatic bishop, Rome), 29, 33, 183n.101, 323n.189, 376, 380, 498, 604

Novatus (schismatic presbyter, Carthage), 372n.70, 373n.79, 380-81

Numidicus (presbyter, Carthage), 373n.79, 374n.94

Numitoria Saturnina (wife of Gaius Julius Serenus, Thaenae), 123, 128, 484

Nundinarius (deacon, Cirta), 393-95

Optatus (bishop, Thuburbo Minus), 3, 9

Optatus (Caecilianist bishop, Milevis), 101, 124, 197-99, 201, 216, 227, 287, 353, 363, 397-98, 414, 425, 529, 607-10, 621

Optatus (Donatist bishop, Thamugadi), 54, 89, 106, 124, 125, 160-62, 200, 396, 402, 591-92, 608

Optatus (subdeacon, Carthage), 371n.61

Origen (Christian theologian, Alexandria and Palestine), 12, 31-33

Orosius, Paul (Spanish presbyter), 95, 545

Parmenian (Donatist bishop, Carthage), 52, 53, 398, 414n.383, 601, 611
    ecclesiology of, 197-99, 201, 227, 282, 288, 292, 363, 428, 607, 609
    and Tyconius, 282, 607, 614

Patricius (father of Augustine), 502

Paul (apostle), 352, 539
    baptismal practice of, 168, 187, 192, 199, 217
    and marriage, 143, 444, 446, 457, 474
    and memorials to, 116, 118, 133, 135-36, 163, 531, 534, 538
    and penitential practice, 305, 310, 336, 347, 394, 561
    teaching of, 120, 244, 335, 510, 511, 546, 561, 576, 581
    writings of, 3, 192, 612n.63

Paul (imperial notary), 37, 49, 156n.285, 196, 332, 397, 527-29, 542

# Index of Places and Monuments

Nola (Italy), 71, 544, 545
Nova Germania, 409
Nova Petra, 528
Novara (Italy), 107
Novarum (basilica, Carthage), 71, 72,
88n.2, 135, 137, 138n.217
Numidia, 2, 4-6, 11, 23-25, 27, 36, 38, 41,
48n.61, 49, 53, 62-64, 66, 71, 80, 81, 89,
95, 108, 117, 160, 388, 391-94, 396, 409,
412, 413, 417-19, 452-53, 527, 534, 591,
609
Numidia Cirtensis, 36, 40, 41, 332, 389, 391,
392, 393
Numidia Militiana, 36
Numidia Proconsularis, 36, 155
Numitoria Saturnina (tomb mosaic, Thae-
nae), 123, 128, 484

Oea (Tripoli), 438n.378
Optatus (Thamugadi)
inscription, 162
tomb, 124, 125, 162
Ostia (port of Rome), 2, 48n.61, 504, 558
Oudna. *See* Uthina
Oued Ramel (Sainte Marie du Zit),
106n.98, 109, 111, 221
Oumcetren (on Cap Bon), 109, 111, 433
Oxyrhynchus (Egypt), 16

Pacis/Maior (basilica, Hippo Regius), 90,
92, 95, 96, 104, 108, 155, 156, 159
Palestine, 10, 57, 282, 429, 519, 534, 545
Pascasius (tomb, Lepti Minus), 124, 129,
432, 507
Paul (basilica, Carthage), 135, 163
Paulus (tomb, Sidi Abiche), 125, 129, 431,
433, 506
Perpetua, Felicity, and Companions (mo-
saic, Carthage), 117
Persia, 37, 45-46
Peter (basilica, Carthage), 135, 163
Peter and Paul (basilica, Tipasa), 118
Peter and Paul (memorial, Castellum
Tingitanum), 133
Peter and Paul (memorial, Uppenna), 531
Philadelphia (Egypt), 16
Phrygia, 1
Pompeia Maxima (tomb, Thabraca), 118,
130, 463, 465, 485, 508, 530, 544, 596
Prime, St. (chapel, Carthage), 141

Privata (tomb, Thabraca), 119, 121, 484,
485, 549
Privatus (tomb, Thabraca), 129, 431
Proconsular Africa. *See* Africa
Proconsularis
Protasius, Gervasius, and Tryphon (basil-
ica, Sufetula), 97, 101, 154, 163, 283
Punic stele (Thamugadi), 128, 508
Pupput (Hammamet), 433

Quiriacus (tomb, Taparura), 129-31, 236,
555, 596

Ravenna, 56, 63-65, 107n.101, 111n.114
Redemptus (chapel, Carthage), 106, 113,
122, 141, 147
Reparatus (epitaph, Castellum Tingita-
num), 100, 133
Restituta (basilica, Carthage), 71, 89, 96,
134, 136, 141-44
Rhine River, 35-36, 59, 62
Rome, 3-4, 12-13, 15, 17, 24, 26, 30, 44,
53-54, 59, 64-65, 78, 83-84, 147, 276, 373,
385, 391, 396, 423-24, 537-38, 566, 568,
587, 593
Lateran baptistery, 107n.110
Ruspe, 74, 125, 207

Sabratha (Tripolitana), 109, 112n.122,
413n.378
Salakta. *See* Sullecthum
Salsa, St. (basilica, Tipasa), 117, 118, 127,
530
Sardinia, 65
Saturn (temple, Carthage), 137n.214
Saturn (temple, Mactaris), 91
Saturn (temple, Simitthu), 91
Sbeitla. *See* Sufetula
Scilli, 39, 519, 534
Scillitan Martyrs (basilica, Carthage), 71,
96n.53, 134n.199, 135-38, 144, 531
Secundinus (sarcophagus, Lepti Minus),
121
Serapaeum (Alexandria), 13
Servus (Sufetula), baptistery, 109, 153
basilica, 91, 107, 108, 124, 152, 153,
210n.255, 223, 431
Severus (catacomb, Hadrumetum), 121,
459

Theadelphia (Egypt), 16
Thelepte (Medinet el Kdima), 109
Theodosiana (basilica, Carthage),
    135n.208, 137
Theogenes (basilica, Hippo), 95, 531, 535
Theoprepia (basilica, Carthage), 89, 136,
    143, 536n.110
Theotokos (basilica, Carthage), 76, 97, 141
Theveste (Tabessa), 93n.34, 95, 98, 99,
    100n.69, 106, 110, 112-14, 118, 133, 396,
    524-25, 530, 534
    baptismal font, 106, 110, 112
    basilica and plan, 114
    Crispina, basilica, 98, 106, 110, 112, 114-
        15, 160, 534
    shrine, 114
Thibari (Thibar), 29
Thibilis (Announa), 106n.99, 109
Thosbis (Egypt), 16
Thuburbo Maius (Henchir Kasbat), 91, 106,
    107, 109, 134n.197, 223, 355, 525n.32
    baptismal font, 106, 107, 109
    basilica and plan, 91, 106, 107, 223, 355
    Caelestis/Tanit, temple, 107
    Ceres, temple, 91n.27
Thuburbo Minus (Tebourba), 144n.245,
    525n.32
Thubursicu Numidarum (Khamissa), 409
Thugga (Dougga), 38n.13, 43, 91
    Capitoline, temple, 91
Thysdrus (El Djem), 4
Tiddis. See Castellum Tidditanorum
Tigzirt. See Iomnium
Timgad. See Thamugadi
Tipasa (Tipaza), 50, 94, 95, 98, 104, 106,
    108, 109, 114, 117-18, 125-27, 223, 431, 432,
    466, 506, 528, 530, 532
    Alexander, basilica, 94, 125-27, 431-32,
        506, 530, 532
    baptismal font, 104, 106, 109
    basilica and plan, 98, 106, 108, 223
    Matares, necropolis, 127

mausoleum, 114, 118, 530
    *mensa* mosaic, 94, 126, 127, 506, 530
    Peter and Paul, basilica, 118
    St. Salsa, basilica, 117, 118, 127, 530
Tricliarum (basilica, Carthage), 136-37
Tripolitana, 1, 2, 5, 36, 64, 103n.90, 108, 109
Tryphon, Gervasius, and Protasius (basil-
    ica, Sufetula), 97, 101, 154, 163, 283
Tunisia, 2, 38n.13, 99n.66, 103, 147, 261
Twenty Martyrs (basilica, Hippo), 95, 531,
    532

Unapompei (Diocese of Hippo Regius),
    405n.306
Uppenna (Henchir Chigarnia), 95n.50,
    109-10, 113, 116, 121-23, 125, 128-29, 130,
    131n.188, 431-32, 433n.510, 508, 531
    Baleriolus, tomb, 116, 125, 131n.118, 431-
        32, 433n.510, 531
    baptismal font, 110
    basilica plan, 116
    Crescentius, tomb, 116, 122-23, 432, 508
    Faustina, tomb, 116, 125, 129
    Honorius, tomb, 116, 125, 131n.188, 431,
        432, 433n.510, 531
    Peter and Paul, memorial, 531
    tomb mosaic, 116, 531
Uthina (Oudna), 4
Utica (Utique), 394-95
Uzalis (El Alia), 53, 213, 502, 505, 545n.180,
    546

Varia Victoria (dedication, Hadrumetum),
    130, 459, 460n.149, 484
Victor (tomb, Thabraca), 131, 433, 508
Victoria (tomb, Thabraca), 119, 121, 485,
    549
Vitalis (Sufetula), baptismal font, 104, 106,
    110-11, 113, 152, 221-23, 433, 531
    basilica, 150
Vitalis (tomb, Furnos Minus), 111, 122, 128

# Index of Subjects

Acolyte, 371, 403

Adultery, 295, 305, 308, 313, 319, 335, 454n.100, 458. *See also* Sin, adultery, idolatry, and murder

Africa, 1-3
  Arab, 84-85
  Byzantine, 75-84
  provinces of, 36-37
  reconquest of, 64-65, 75-77
  religions of, 1, 37-59
  revolts in, 52-54, 57, 59, 63-64, 76-77, 84, 160
  Vandal, 61-75

*Agapē,* 234, 240-41, 269, 365, 367-68, 555
  as eucharist, 102n.80, 234n.5, 235, 240-41, 251-52, 289-90
  for household, 246, 251-52, 287, 289-90
  and *stibadium,* 241

Almsgiving, 262n.211, 308, 567, 570-81, 598
  among Christians, 574, 577, 605, 620
  communal, 571-72
  for benefit of dead, 501-2, 512, 579
  and fasting, 338, 565, 567
  as penitential, 315-16, 338, 570, 572, 574, 579
  and prayer, 579
  and tithing, 578

Altar, 102, 157, 197, 234, 250, 259, 287-88, 377, 397
  as *altare,* 102, 255, 287, 287n.428, 290

as *ara,* 102, 238n.41, 255, 287, 287n.428, 290
coverings of, 101, 265, 287
for eucharistic ritual, 211, 235, 250, 262-66, 283, 288, 292, 298
heavenly, 147n.260, 283, 288, 560, 617
placement of, 98, 101, 114-15, 138-162 *passim,* 211, 283, 288, 293
relics under, 101, 113, 117, 122, 154, 530, 537
symbolism of, 252, 257, 259, 281, 292
wooden, 101, 157, 234, 287, 333

Anointing, in baptism. *See* Baptismal ritual, anointings in
in ordination, 243, 414

Antichrist, 11, 59, 71

Apostasy, 13, 20, 70, 182, 328, 390, 486, 525, 588, 595, 606-9
of bishops, 20, 198, 214, 332-33, 378, 389-90, 393-94, 610, 621
by equivocation, 15, 17, 307, 321, 358
by flight, 167n.9, 585
as forgivable, 73, 188, 197-98, 324, 356, 492, 497, 573, 575
and the Holy Spirit, 192, 196, 227, 385, 391
by schism, 55, 200, 225, 329, 331, 333, 390n.217, 391
by *traditio,* 195, 200, 214, 277n.369, 392, 526, 590, 607, 609

Apse, 97-102, 116, 133, 153-54

and altar, 97, 101, 114, 122, 149, 154, 162, 288

and baptistery, 104, 106, 140, 152, 223

burials in, 124-26, 133, 149, 151, 152, 162, 431-33

*cathedra* in, 102, 158, 262, 283, 288, 292, 407, 431-32

in *consignatorium*, 108, 210

counter or doubled, 97, 99-100, 116, 132-34, 138, 149, 151, 162, 531

orientation of, 99, 132-33, 151

and place in basilica, 98, 132, 157, 160-61

*presbyterium* in, 98, 151, 157

*synthronon* in, 102, 157, 262, 288, 407, 432

Ascension of Christ, 174, 207, 278, 378, 509

Ashes, 297, 315, 570

Astrology, 503n.86, 582, 595

Avarice, 336, 572, 576, 579, 581

Banquets, 234, 235, 240-42, 247, 261, 269, 562

for the dead. *See* Burial, and meals at tombs; Feast, funeral

heavenly, 245, 250, 253, 258

*See also Agapē*

Baptism

age at, 168, 171, 180, 212

and bathing, 170, 208, 223n.324, 274

as birth, 170, 185, 190, 199, 218, 222

and charity, 220, 227-29, 275

and circumcision, 180, 230

and *clinicus,* 183

and *competentes,* 204-5

and death of Jesus, 175, 184, 222

as dedication to Christ, 215-17, 219-20, 225, 229, 275-76, 281, 477-78, 612-13

delaying of, 168, 176, 213, 309-10, 354, 516

in emergency, 171-72, 182-83, 202, 213, 492, 497. *See also* Death, baptism before

and forgiveness of sins. *See* Baptism, and sanctification

in heresy, 173-74, 186-90, 192-95, 216-19, 225-26

and the Holy Spirit, 169-70, 173-74, 177-78, 191-93, 210, 226-28, 275

and idolatry. *See* Idolatry, renunciation of

of infants, 168, 179-80, 212-13, 229-30

of Israel. *See* Israel, baptism of

of John the Baptist. *See* John the Baptist

as joining the church, 165, 179, 225, 226, 230

and martyrdom, 169, 175, 182, 193, 256, 257, 302

minister of. *See* Minister of Ritual

and orders, 228, 243, 275, 290

and original sin, 176, 180, 190, 213, 230

pollution by, 181, 188, 196

preparation for, 167-68

and priesthood, 170, 210, 243

recipient of, 192-93, 196, 216, 220, 276, 609

repeated, 29-30, 174-75, 187-90, 196-97, 217, 220, 224-26, 275

repentance in. *See* Repentance, baptismal

salvation by, 168, 171, 176, 192-93, 204, 230, 502

and sanctification, 179, 186-90, 215-16, 219, 226-29, 275, 612-13

in schism, 178, 184, 186-90, 193-94, 199-200, 215-20, 225, 229, 275

of Spirit, 174, 192-94, 229

sponsors in, 168, 171, 209

and tattoo, 215, 275, 277

of water, 172-73, 177-78, 189, 191-94, 229

Baptismal ritual, 169-70, 177-79, 198, 208, 219. *See also* Catechumen; Neophytes

anointings in, 169, 170, 172, 178, 210, 213, 223-24

and the *cilicium,* 205, 209, 222

clothing for, 210, 211, 223

and creed. *See* Creed

deacon's role in, 171, 182, 209-10, 223

and the eucharist, 170, 179, 181, 203, 211-12, 219

exorcism in, 169, 177, 205-6, 219, 223, 280, 372

by fire, 174, 192

by immersion, 170, 172, 177, 209, 222-23

and imposition of hands. *See* Imposition of hands, in baptismal ritual

invocation in, 169-70, 177, 191, 193, 198-99, 209-10, 609

with milk and honey, 170, 179, 244

and oath to Christ, 166, 168, 178, 192, 209, 215, 219, 225, 603 presbyter's role in, 105, 171, 182, 209-10, 214

and profession of church, 170, 178, 220

and profession of faith, 170, 176, 178, 191, 198-99, 209, 212, 220

and renunciation of Satan, 166, 169, 174, 178, 206, 208, 219, 221-23, 225, 304, 328, 581

salt in, 202-3

scrutiny in, 205, 206

and sign of the cross, 178, 202-3, 209

space for, 172, 184, 219, 224, 292

and sprinkling with water, 183, 190, 193, 497

time of, 172, 204, 208

and washing of feet, 161, 179, 210, 212

water in, 169, 172-73, 178, 183, 184, 209, 219

Baptistery, 93, 103-13, 141, 143, 149-53, 159, 161

ciborium over. *See* Font, covered by ciborium

design of, 92, 106-8, 150, 152-53, 159

font for. *See* Font

multiple baptisteries in one location, 105-6, 223-24

at pilgrimage sites, 105, 139-40

placement of, 106-10, 147

Basilica. *See* Church building

Binding and loosening. *See* Forgiving power

Bishop, 89, 189-90, 364, 375-79, 407-9

as agent of Christ, 379, 428, 436

apostate, 391, 392

Apostles as, 428, 435, 437-38

as civil magistrate, 52, 408

election of, 375, 393, 400, 411, 413

as *episcopus*, 283, 288, 292, 407

governing, 389, 429, 430

installation of, 375, 392, 413, 414

as judge, 378, 379, 382, 429

lists of, 80, 89, 189, 376, 418

as mediator, 428, 607, 609

as presider, 252

property of, 407, 416

removal of, 377, 378, 389

as *sacerdos*, 283, 288, 292, 375, 379, 407

sanctifying power of, 178, 180-81, 186-90, 216, 226, 391, 603, 604-5, 607

in schism, 390, 391

seniority of, 388, 408

as symbolized by Peter, 384

transfer of, 413

unworthy, 377, 430, 605, 608

Burial, 120-31. *See also* Catacomb; Cemetery; Necropolis

*ad sanctos*, 118-20, 125, 530, 543-45

anniversary of, 494, 506, 512

cemeteries for, 124-26, 503, 514

in church buildings, 124-26, 132-33, 149-52, 161, 504

and cremation, 493, 514, 517

and decoration of tombs, 122, 128-31, 506-7

inscriptions for, 116-17, 122-23, 507

and meals at tombs, 120-21, 126-31, 493, 505-6, 508

and *mensa*, 120, 126-28, 145, 512, 530

and mosaics for, 96, 119, 125-26, 128-31, 432-33, 465, 484-85

ritual of, 492-94, 496-98, 503-4

in sarcophagus, 161, 463, 485, 507

Candles, 101, 111, 117, 122, 130, 221, 265, 287, 508

Catacomb, 43n.36, 121, 459-60

Catechist, 169, 202, 205

Catechumen, 203n.201, 248, 262, 265, 280

Catechumenate, 168-69, 183, 202-5

Cemetery, 6, 88n.3, 121-22, 124-26, 463, 496, 498, 504-8, 512, 514

access to, 23, 24, 43n.36, 496

as *area*, 6, 30, 88n.3, 94, 144

as meeting place, 41n.25, 88, 393n.232

shrines in. *See* Church building, in cemetery

Chancel. *See* Church building, chancel of

Charity. *See also* Baptism; Church; Forgiving power; Holy Spirit; Marriage; Sanctification

and marital affection, 474, 475, 483, 486, 487

as power to forgive, 216, 217-18, 219, 227

Chrism, 178, 210n.258, 214n.287

Christ

ascension of, 174, 207, 278, 378, 509

crucifixion and death of, 46, 110, 173, 193, 222, 239, 240n.51, 539, 556, 564, 566-67, 569 flesh of, 238n.38, 246, 252, 276-79, 286, 615

as head of church, 278-82, 292, 611, 614

as mediator, 282-83, 292, 428-29, 617

passion of, 111, 174, 175, 193, 208, 250, 253, 270, 277n.371, 561n.100

priesthood of, 254-55, 282-83, 290, 617

resurrection of, 110, 111, 174, 211, 260, 270, 299, 327, 357, 509, 564, 616

as Whole, 278-83, 291, 292, 428-29, 606, 614, 615, 618

as the Word of God, 278, 509, 614-16

Christogram, 119, 122, 128, 129, 151, 152, 155, 161, 209, 485, 514

Church, 87, 473, 607

as body of Christ, 218, 220, 227, 259, 277, 280, 428, 429, 430, 436, 607, 615, 617, 620

as body of Trinity, 170, 225, 602, 603

boundary of, 165, 166, 218, 226

as bride, virgin, and widow, 442, 443, 449, 455, 477, 479, 481, 482, 483, 488

and charity, 611, 613, 615

as *ecclesia mater*, 87, 119, 128, 134, 185, 287

as *ecclesia sancta*, 133

endowments of, 197, 199, 201, 226, 227

holiness of, 328, 330, 354, 601-2, 611

and the Holy Spirit, 611, 613, 615, 618

in houses, 43, 87-88, 88n.2

intercession of, 309, 312, 315, 331, 353, 602-3

as mediator, 189, 230, 330, 602, 604, 620

as mother, 87, 185, 190, 218, 222, 451

peace of, 295, 309, 312, 319, 341

and power to sanctify, 198, 216, 225-30, 305-6, 604-5, 610, 612-13. *See also* Forgiving power, church's

profession of, 170, 178, 207, 220, 602, 604

reconciliation to, 302, 312-14

unity of, 217-20, 250, 610, 611, 616

Church building, 131-63

altar in. *See* Altar, placement of

ambulatory in, 107, 113, 117, 140, 141, 143, 148

apse of. *See* Apse

architrave of, 98, 114

atrium of, 106, 114, 115, 138, 139, 146, 161

baptistery in. *See* Baptistery

for bishop's residence, 92, 143, 153, 156

Byzantine, 138, 140-44, 154, 160

and cathedrals, 141-43, 155-56, 160-61

in cemetery, 92, 94, 115-16, 124-26, 135-40, 144, 146-47, 153, 514

chancel of, 100, 142, 149, 154, 158, 160, 211, 219

chancel screen of, 101, 142, 151, 152, 160, 234, 262, 266, 268, 283, 342

ciborium in, 115, 117, 138, 151, 154

cistern in, 113, 127, 143, 157, 158, 172

clerestory of, 87, 98

colonnade in, 1, 98, 106, 132, 139, 141, 143, 161

complex of, 92, 99, 114, 139, 141, 150-52, 155-62

*consignatorium* of, 92, 108, 153, 159, 210

construction of, 87-91, 95-96

crypt of, 93, 113, 115, 132, 152, 158

dating of, 95, 97, 132, 138-39, 153

design of, 97-100, 149-51, 158, 160-61

dome of, 97, 98, 100, 107, 137, 140, 141, 153

gallery of, 97, 98, 100, 132, 133, 150, 158

nave of. *See* Nave

orientation of, 91, 99, 132, 149, 157, 209n.243

ownership of, 50, 88-89, 96, 136-37, 142

peristyle of, 91, 106, 150

for pilgrimage, 92, 94, 99, 138-41, 143, 145, 162

sacristy of, 92, 98, 146, 154, 160

*solea* of, 149, 151

using *opus africanum*, 76, 97

Vandal, 95-96, 134, 139, 142, 162

vault of, 97, 98, 107, 122, 153, 154, 158, 159

Church furnishings

altar. *See* Altar

ambo, 98, 157, 163, 262, 263, 287, 292

candles, 101, 111, 117, 122, 130, 221, 265, 287, 508

decoration, 132-34, 140, 143, 151, 156-58

*pulpitum,* 102, 287, 292

reliquary, 115, 122, 223

Clergy, 242, 252, 366, 415

age of, 412

appointment of, 379, 410-12, 428

burial of, 431-32. *See also* Burial, in church buildings

civil exemptions of, 44, 392

clothing of, 381, 415, 433
discipline of, 380, 420-24, 428
governance of, 430, 434, 435
holiness of, 254, 257, 284, 291
housing of, 92, 143, 153, 156
marriage of, 243, 365, 366, 412
penance for. *See* Penitential ritual, for
  clergy
place during rituals, 262, 283, 287-88, 432
as presiders, 250, 259, 287, 289
priesthood of, 282-83, 292
property of, 415, 416
qualifications of, 365, 380, 390, 412, 461
ranks of, 364, 370, 391-92
sanctifying power of, 430, 434, 435
in schism, 390, 398-401, 426, 436-37,
  613, 617
secular business of, 365, 381, 412
shortage of, 412-13
stipend of, 373, 380
Concubinage, 457-58
Conference of Carthage in 411: 37, 56, 95,
  286, 396, 400, 425, 526, 592, 611
Confessing Christ, 581-96, 599
  necessity of, 584, 585, 586-87
  by avoiding oaths, 585-86, 594
Confessor of Christ, 303, 317, 356-57, 382
  as clergy, 368n.38, 380
  as delegate of martyr, 303, 325
  forgiveness of sins by, 323, 356
  intercession by, 303, 308, 352, 382, 435,
    522
Continence, 453, 456, 473, 567
  of clergy, 412, 464
  in marriage, 444, 448-50, 456-58, 469-
    71, 476, 483, 486
*Conuiuium,* 126, 234n.5, 239, 241n.59,
  242n.75, 245, 247n.97, 251, 259, 555n.15
Conversion, divine grace, 348-49
Councils, episcopal, 27-30, 378, 385, 386-
  87, 396-97, 417-19, 429, 434, 437
  at Arles in 314: 48, 201, 275, 332, 334, 391,
    397, 402, 438, 541, 590-91, 610-11
  at Bagai in 393: 54, 200, 201, 333, 395,
    396
  at Carthage in the 220s: 4, 176, 187, 224,
    225
  at Carthage in 251: 17-18, 27, 28, 386
  at Carthage in 252: 28, 29, 387
  at Carthage in 253: 29, 387, 427

at Carthage in 256 (spring): 387
at Carthage in 256 (September): 5, 44,
  148, 191, 200, 387
at Carthage in 336: 196n.164, 396
at Carthage in 345-48: 396
at Carthage in 390: 397, 464
at Carthage in 393: 395, 396
at Carthage in 397: 202n.195, 398, 420,
  537
at Carthage in 398: 403n.293, 482n.311
at Carthage in 401 ( June): 399, 419, 427
at Carthage in 401 (September): 114, 273,
  400, 422
at Carthage in 403: 55
at Carthage in 407: 400, 409, 419
at Carthage in 408: 56n.109
at Carthage in 410: 56
at Carthage in 411. *See* Conference of
  Carthage in 411
at Carthage in 416: 57, 418-19
at Carthage in 418: 56, 58, 417
at Carthage in 419: 148-49, 417,
  419n.427, 420
at Carthage in 525: 74, 96n.55, 139, 142,
  267n.269, 273
at Carthage in 535: 78, 141
at Carthage in 550: 79
at Cebarsussi in 393: 8, 54n.96, 198n.176,
  200, 333, 395, 396
at Chalcedon in 451: 58, 78, 82, 83, 84
at Cirta in 303: 41, 526, 591
at Constantinople in 553: 79
at Constantinople in 680: 84n.142
Donatist in 418-19: 396
at Ephesus in 431: 58, 62
at Hippo in 393: 273, 397, 398, 417, 418,
  419-20, 427, 503
at Hippo in 427: 397, 418, 419
at Milevis in 402: 419
at Milevis in 416: 57, 418-19
at Nicaea in 325: 58, 198n.178, 390-91,
  401n.288, 411, 423-24, 438
at Rome in 386: 398-99
at Sardica in 343: 58
at Thelensis in 418: 399n.270
at Theveste in the 360s: 396
at Thuysdrus in 417: 418n.20
Creed, 178, 191, 194, 205-7, 219-20, 330, 334,
  602, 604
Cross. *See* Sign of the cross

Crucifixion and death of Christ, 46, 110, 173, 193, 222, 239, 240n.51, 539, 556, 564, 566-67, 569

Deacon(s), 25, 27, 44, 131, 262, 340, 364-65, 372-73, 404-5, 427-28, 433
    in baptismal ritual, 159, 171, 182, 187, 209-10, 223, 364
    discipline of, 81, 321-23, 332, 393, 405, 409n.344, 418, 421-24, 465-66
    in eucharistic ritual, 258, 262, 263, 265, 266, 268, 529, 587
    marriage of, 365, 370, 405, 412, 415, 458-59, 461-62, 465-66
    as minister, 183, 363-64, 370, 372-73
    number of, 6, 23, 391, 392, 405
    in penitential ritual, 320
Dead, the (Christian), 130, 494-85, 499-500, 509-11, 515, 605
    almsgiving for, 512, 579
    and awareness of the living, 512, 513, 546-47
    prayer for, 495, 512, 515-16, 544-45
    purification of, 495, 499, 511, 512-13, 515-16
    reward and punishment of, 495, 499, 509
Death, 180, 219, 303, 312, 483, 491-517
    age at, 92, 126, 129, 462, 507
    baptism before, 171, 180, 182-83, 202, 212-13, 218, 268, 296, 497, 502, 510
    ending marriage, 443-44, 448-50, 459, 476-77, 482, 485, 487, 488, 491, 602-3
    and generation, 442, 471, 473, 486
    and mortality, 210, 472, 483, 501-2
    reconciliation before, 256, 259, 280, 315-16, 319-20, 328, 331, 340-41, 347-49, 355, 358, 497-98, 503, 604
    and sin, 180, 190, 230, 442, 450, 496, 501, 513-14
    symbolic, 103, 110, 113, 222
Decalogue, 306, 335, 461, 602
*Defensor ecclesiae,* 410
Demons, 165, 177, 305, 470, 540, 561, 606, 607n.44, 581, 582
*Deo laudes,* 82, 100, 130
*Dis Manibus Sacrum (DMS),* 460n.149, 484, 514
Divorce, 443, 444, 448-50, 455
Doorkeeper, 402

Easter, 20, 27, 29, 76, 158, 172, 204, 206, 211, 236, 279, 290, 457, 566, 593
    date of, 33, 418
    season of, 172, 203, 204, 236, 270, 555, 563, 565, 566
    vigil of, 204, 208-11, 219, 269-70, 445
Elders, lay, 369-70, 383-84, 392-94, 409-10, 433
Election, divine, 286, 291
End of time, 556, 557
Episcopal college, 189, 197, 349, 389, 408, 429, 437-38, 605-6
    holiness of, 201, 227, 291, 385, 605, 610
    origin of, 180, 186, 216, 384-85, 428
    power of, 187, 216, 226-28, 330-31, 389, 437, 605
    standing in, 181, 217, 331, 376
    unity of, 186, 187, 216, 227, 228, 384
Episcopate, organization of, 417-24, 429
Eucharist
    and baptism, 181, 257, 274-77, 279-83
    as *cena,* 234n.5, 239, 365n.10
    and church as the body of Christ, 276-80
    communion in, 233, 249-50. *See also* Reconciliation, to church
    as danger to the unworthy, 258
    and death of Christ, 250, 254, 256, 260-61, 274, 289
    exclusion from, 245, 252, 256-57, 268, 280, 295-98, 308, 313-17, 339, 342, 348, 458
    as *figura,* 238
    as flesh and blood, 238, 246, 250, 252, 277-80, 286-87, 616
    and Holy Spirit, 279-81, 377-78, 613-14
    for immortality, 238, 256
    and martyrdom, 255-56, 258, 289
    as necessary for salvation, 245, 246, 256-57, 290, 296, 319, 330, 331, 341, 604.
    *See also* Death, reconciliation before
    and Passover, 250, 252, 258
    pollution of, 244-45, 257, 276
    as prefigured, 250, 253, 255, 290
    and reserved bread, 235n.9, 238, 244, 246, 250, 251, 258, 268, 282
    as sacrifice, 237-38, 242-43, 246, 250, 253-54, 256, 258, 260, 289, 290
    saints in, 277, 279-81, 286-87, 292
    and sanctification, 276-77, 279, 281

in schism, 251-52, 255, 257, 261, 274, 276, 281, 290

and unity of the congregation, 246, 252-61, 274-77, 279-80, 290

and universal church, 274-82, 290

and the Whole Christ, 276-78, 281-82, 290, 292, 616

Eucharistic ritual, 234-44, 262, 289

as *agapē. See Agapē*

and altar for. *See* Altar

with bread and wine, 265-66, 277, 279, 281, 289

commemorations in, 240, 250, 253, 254, 260, 267, 289-90

distribution during, 239, 244, 250, 266-68, 289

in the evening, 87, 234, 239, 243-47, 251-53, 259-61, 273-74

fasting before. *See* Fasting, eucharistic

for full assembly, 236, 239, 242, 245-47, 251, 259, 277, 289, 299, 605

furnishings for, 234, 242, 262, 265, 287

and heavenly banquet, 245, 250, 253, 258

at homes, 87, 237, 239, 241-42, 251

Lord's Prayer in, 236, 249

as Lord's Supper, 233, 234, 253, 261, 267, 273

in the morning, 87, 233, 235, 239, 241-46, 251-53, 255, 259-61, 269, 273-74, 286

as offering, 237-39, 249-50, 252, 260, 265-68, 283, 287-88

petitions in, 248-49, 265

posture during, 236, 242, 247, 248, 251, 262, 263-64, 266, 268, 272, 283

and prayer, 236, 250, 266

and preaching, 235, 248, 263-65

and preface dialogue, 250, 266, 290

presider at, 239, 241-42, 250, 252, 253, 254, 260, 263, 273, 276, 291

reading during, 235, 247, 263, 269-70

secrecy of, 238n.35, 265, 267, 289

singing in, 234, 240, 243, 245-46, 262, 263, 266, 268, 269, 284

time of, 239, 269

wine and water in, 244, 246, 250-54, 259, 266n.252, 280n.390, 289, 290

Exile during persecution, 528, 572, 588

Exorcism, 169, 177, 205-6, 219, 223, 280, 367, 372

Exorcist, 367, 371-72

Family, 444, 470

in burial practice, 462-63, 484-85

and children, 460, 474

head of, 444, 452, 460-61

inheritance in, 407, 460, 512, 574, 580, 581, 619

as obstacle, 443, 451-52, 461, 470, 474, 486

slaves in, 459, 461

Fasting, 240, 243, 280, 297, 563-69, 598

and almsgiving, 338, 565, 567, 569

and bathing, 204, 243, 564

eucharistic, 235-37, 239, 244, 268-69, 273-74, 564

and kiss of peace, 204n.14, 237, 239n.50, 554n.7, 555, 564

during Lent, 566-67

penitential, 297, 308, 315, 563, 565, 569

petitionary, 565, 569

time of, 563-64, 565, 566, 567

as *xerophagia,* 243, 564

Feast, funeral, 305-6, 335, 343, 367, 445, 446, 452, 455-56, 493, 505-6, 514

at anniversaries of death, 494, 506, 508, 513

for martyrs, 506, 530

Feet, washing of, 161, 179, 210, 212

Festivals, 146-47, 155, 409, 535-38, 548-49, 562

Font(s), 93, 161, 209-10, 221-24

covered by ciborium, 106, 107, 110, 138, 143, 150, 153, 159, 161, 209, 223

decoration of, 111-12, 150, 152, 159, 161, 221-22

design of, 108-12, 150, 152, 161, 222-23

multiple, 105-6, 223-24

Forgiveness of sins

in baptism. *See* Baptism, and sanctification; Penance; Penitential ritual

among Christians, 249, 298, 337, 338, 341, 511, 616, 620

by church, 296, 319, 353

by God, 296, 300, 302, 306, 313, 318, 319, 341, 348, 353

through martyrdom, 302

through rebuke, 337, 338, 339, 342

prayer for, 297, 561

Forgiving power, 186, 295, 356

as agent, 311, 356

by authority, 311, 312, 356, 425, 427, 429

of bishop, 326-28, 339, 350, 353, 357, 425
through charity, 345, 348, 350, 353, 357,
    399, 427, 428, 612, 613
of Christ, 356, 435
of church, 301, 305, 310-11, 324-28, 342,
    347-50, 356, 424-25, 426-27
of episcopal college, 186-87, 189, 216,
    226-27, 327
by Holy Spirit, 334, 350, 428, 616
of laity, 187, 216, 339, 349-50, 357, 612,
    613, 616
Petrine, 310, 326, 327, 349-50, 357, 616

Generation of children, 448, 456, 457, 469,
    471-74
to increase human race, 471, 472, 486
in Israel, 473
in Paradise, 471, 472
to preserve human race, 442, 471, 473,
    486
as unnecessary for Christians, 441, 443,
    450, 453, 471, 473, 475, 486
Grace, 286, 291
Gravedigger, 6, 372, 392

Hades, 494-95, 499, 503
Hell, 165, 300, 346, 507
Heresy, 28, 54, 57, 58, 78, 81, 83, 217, 306,
    461, 511, 621. See also Baptism, in heresy
Holiness
    of clergy, 254, 257, 283, 284, 291
    of laity, 243, 254, 257, 258, 283
Holy Spirit, 611
    in baptism. See Baptism, and Holy Spirit
    and body of Christ, 47, 218, 279, 280,
        281, 282, 351, 480, 611, 615
    and charity, 216-20, 275, 292, 334, 341,
        350-53, 428, 431, 471, 611-13, 618
    and forgiveness of sins, 176, 180, 186-87,
        193, 215-19, 226-27, 327, 334, 350, 428,
        616

Idolatry, 198, 306-7, 312, 328, 333, 335, 491-
    92, 553, 582-86, 588-89, 601-3. See also
Sin: adultery, idolatry, and murder
    celebrations of, 583, 585, 593
    in civic office, 167, 584
    cleansing from, 166-69, 593
    in contracts, 167, 570
    and eucharistic exclusion, 167, 245

forgivable by the church, 26-29, 313-14,
    318-20, 324, 381
minor forms of, 306, 307
renunciation of, 166-69, 175-78, 188, 202,
    225
and schism, 225, 226
in theatre, 582, 593
Immortality, 495, 501, 510, 514
Imposition of hands, 275, 334
    in baptismal ritual, 105, 108, 177-79,
        182-83, 187-89, 191-95, 202-10, 213, 219,
        229, 605
    in ordination ritual, 398n.265, 414
    in penitential ritual, 178, 220, 275, 314,
        318, 320, 332, 334, 341, 357, 360, 381,
        398n.267
    for reception of schismatics, 183, 186-89,
        193, 194, 198, 275, 336, 344, 372, 390-
        91, 399
Incense, 177, 266, 379, 493, 582-83
Intercession, 304, 326, 513
    of church, 297, 298, 299, 301, 306, 315,
        499
    of laity, 298, 360, 516, 547, 574
    of martyrs. See Martyr(s), intercession
        of
Israel, 175, 368, 394, 443, 470, 473, 483, 606
    baptism of, 217
    priests of, 377, 379, 414, 477, 617
    sacrifices of, 283, 290-91, 554, 617

Keys, power of. See Forgiving power,
    church's; Forgiving power, Petrine
Kiss of peace, 179, 237, 239, 249, 267,
    554n.7, 555, 564
Lectionary, 269-70
Lector, 367, 371, 391-92, 403-4

Lent, 204-5, 219, 265, 270n.308, 271, 273-
    74, 457, 534n.83, 566-67
Libation, 254n.162
Lord's Prayer, 236, 249, 267, 338, 554, 555,
    558, 559
    in baptismal ritual, 207-8
    and forgiveness, 212, 218, 324, 337, 597
Lust, 448, 470, 474n.247, 475, 510

Marriage, 441-46, 448-49, 451-52, 455-63,
    468-78
    bond of, 475

charity in, 474, 475, 476, 483, 486, 487
of Christ and his church, 477-78, 487, 618
and concubinage, 457-58
as *coniugium,* 458, 460
and *coniunx,* 459, 460, 485
as *contubernium,* 458, 459, 460, 484
and death. *See* Death, ending marriage
fidelity in, 448, 456, 457, 475-76, 477,
    483, 486-88
for generation. *See* Generation of
    children
and *maritus,* 459, 460, 485
to non-Christian, 444-46, 448, 450
in resurrection, 442, 449, 463, 474, 485,
    487
sacramentality of, 477-78
of slaves, 444, 458-60, 462, 484-85
spousal fidelity in. *See* Sex, fidelity in
and unity of humanity, 470, 471
Marriage ritual, 445, 446, 451, 456
and blessing, 445
and *tabulae nuptiales,* 445, 446
Martyr(s), 70, 356-57, 515-16, 521-22
commemoration of, 498-99, 505-6, 521,
    533
cult of, 113-20, 136, 140, 146, 163, 523,
    528-33, 538, 548
glory immediate for, 494-95, 499, 509,
    515, 520, 522
and Holy Spirit, 303, 368
and identity with Christ, 303
intercession of, 118, 186, 303, 325-26,
    329, 352, 511-12, 520, 528, 532, 538-39,
    544-50
in the military, 11, 524, 528, 529n.53
and miracles of healing, 545-47, 550
and penitential ritual, 227, 303, 308, 317,
    325-26, 356-57, 381-82, 435, 521-23
relics of. *See* Relics
shrines of. *See* Martyrium
and victory over demons, 533, 539-40,
    549, 551
Martyrdom, 302, 496-97, 526, 584, 592
and *acta,* 8-10, 247, 263, 270, 520, 523,
    524-29, 535, 538
and baptism, 169, 175, 182, 193, 256, 257,
    302
and eucharist, 255-56, 258, 289
and forgiveness of sins, 175, 302, 323,
    327n.220, 368

in private, 522, 540, 551, 595-96
in schism, 8, 257, 541-42
and unity of the church, 523, 541-43,
    550
voluntary, 527, 528, 529, 534, 550,
    592n.351
Martyrium, 88, 92, 94-95, 113-20, 138-40,
    144-47, 153-55, 514, 530-31, 533
Minister of ritual, 171, 173-74, 213-15, 220,
    228, 242-43, 289
as agent of Christ, 215, 218, 227, 612, 613,
    617
as agent of the church, 617
competence of, 209n.247, 215, 257
holiness of, 201, 214, 216, 276, 330, 353,
    426, 427
from laity, 171, 176, 228, 229, 242-43,
    366-67, 492
qualifications of, 171-73, 176, 178, 180-82,
    197-98, 227
unworthy, 180-82, 186-88, 194, 196-99,
    201, 214, 215, 217
Miracles, 546-47, 550, 574
accounts of, 117, 213, 282, 493n.13, 502
at shrines, 163n.313, 213, 272, 502, 519,
    532, 535, 538, 545-50
*Mitra,* 463n.177, 464, 465, 479
Monastery, 92, 93-94, 156
Monogamy, 365-67, 443, 449-50, 451
Monothelitism, 82-84
Montanism, 4, 8, 51, 55, 243, 253, 369, 601.
    *See also* New Prophecy
Mortality. *See* Death, and mortality
Mourning, 118, 123, 491, 492, 498, 502, 504,
    505-6, 513
Murder, 42, 310, 335, 342, 343, 352n.400,
    450. *See also* Sin: adultery, idolatry, and
    murder

*Natalicium,* 127, 508
Nave (of church building), 91, 97-98, 101-2,
    132-62 *passim,* 210, 219, 262-63, 292-93,
    341, 345, 432-33
altar in. *See* Altar, placement of
ambo in, 98, 157, 292, 301, 303, 306, 308,
    311, 358
burials in, 115, 125, 132-33, 152, 158, 161
Necropolis, 115, 118, 119, 122, 127, 147
Neophytes, 170, 179, 210-12, 219, 220, 223,
    279-80, 288

New Prophecy, 4, 226, 239-40, 243-44, 304-11, 359-60, 443-49, 564, 589
Novatianism, 29, 46, 51, 58, 376, 377, 498, 604

Orarium, 130, 131, 433, 508
Orders, clerical, 424-30
   and baptism, 210n.260, 228, 243, 275, 290
   ranks of. See Clergy, ranks of
   sacramental, 397-98, 425, 434, 436, 477
   schismatic, 257n.190, 275
Ordination, 44, 176, 178, 228, 275, 345, 363, 376, 397-98, 411-15
   by apostate, 390
   of primate bishop, 48n.61, 414n.383
   ritual of, 210n.260, 275, 345, 360, 398n.265, 403n.293, 407, 414-15, 418
   as sacramental, 44, 176, 363, 398, 425-28, 434, 436
   in schism, 50, 275, 390-91, 398-402

Paenula, 131, 433, 508
Paraclete, 311, 359, 449
Paradise, 111, 130, 184, 331, 475, 477, 483, 510
   martyrs of, 3, 9, 175, 494, 495, 509, 520, 522
   original, 442, 469, 471-74, 475, 477, 483, 510n.143
   rivers of, 140, 184, 331
Parentalia, 126, 505
Passion of Christ, 111, 174, 175, 193, 208, 250, 253, 270, 277n.371, 561n.100
Peace of the church, 295, 319, 341. See also Death, reconciliation before; Eucharist, necessary for salvation
   and Pax, 122, 130, 133, 155n.284, 460n.149, 463
   and vixit in pace, 123n.162, 124, 129, 151n.273, 152n.276
Penance
   absolution after, 299
   allowed once, 300, 304, 307, 308, 310, 320, 340-43, 352, 358, 359
   and forgiveness, 309
   and satisfactory works, 329, 340
Penitent, 297
   admission to status of, 314-15
   exclusion of, 245, 247, 256, 265, 268, 280

supported by church, 298, 301, 306, 309, 316, 348-49
Penitential ritual, 297-301, 307, 312, 314-18, 339-45, 352, 360
   for clergy, 322, 323n.189, 332-33, 397-98, 425-26, 608
   confession of sin in. See Penitential ritual, exomologesis in
   for deserters, 344, 401, 426
   duration of, 298, 316, 340, 355
   for dying. See Death, reconciliation before
   exomologesis in, 297, 317, 319-22, 328, 339, 343, 359, 574
   imposition of hands in. See Imposition of hands, in penitential ritual
   place of, 298, 316, 354
   in private, 342-43, 354, 359. See also Repentance, in private
   in public, 299, 314, 317, 339, 354
   for schismatics. See Imposition of hands, for reception of schismatics
   use of, 318, 321-22, 359
Pentecost, 172, 193, 236, 554, 555, 564-66, 618
Persecution, 7-26, 39-42, 69-75
   apostates in, 19-20, 41-42
   decrees of, 15-16, 40
   flight to avoid, 17-18, 29, 347, 380, 382, 585, 588-89, 603
   implementation of, 16-18, 24-26, 40-41
   and lapsi, 17, 101n.99. 316n.138
   libellatici in, 12, 14-17, 28, 321, 451, 587
   and sacrificati, 15, 18, 19-20, 257, 316, 322-23, 377, 452, 572, 587, 603
   and stantes, 18, 247n.101, 316n.138
Persecutors
   Caracalla, 11
   Constans, 37, 49-50, 89, 196, 527, 542, 590-91, 609
   Decius, 12-20, 38, 177, 181-83, 186-88, 233, 246, 252, 254n.162, 255, 256, 289
   Diocletian, 37, 39-42, 88, 234, 291, 523-27, 590-91
   Gallus, 20-22
   Geiseric, 69-72
   Huneric, 46, 72-73, 137
   Julian, 50-51, 88n.6, 533
   Septimius Severus, 8-11
   Thrasamund, 74

in imperial law, 447, 449

Repentance, 299, 348, 351, 357, 360, 499
  by apology, 338, 351, 360, 462
  baptismal, 167-68, 174, 176, 192-95, 216,
    275, 296
  post-baptismal, 193, 245, 257, 296, 310,
    343-44
  in private, 268, 301-2, 304-6, 309, 319,
    321-22, 341-43
  ritual of. *See* Penitential ritual

Resurrection of Christ, 110, 111, 174, 211,
  260, 270, 299, 327, 357, 509, 564, 616
  death and, 110, 199, 254, 299, 509
  symbolized, 180, 222, 247n.98

Resurrection of Christians, 207, 319, 450,
  463, 491, 493-96, 501, 513-17, 520, 548-
  49, 609, 617
  time between death and, 118, 280, 496,
    499-500, 507-13, 515-16, 605
  and judgment, 300, 378, 515, 605, 618
  and marriage, 449, 474, 476, 485, 487,
    515, 556

Rich, the, 444n.28, 476, 509, 576-78, 580-
  81, 619-20

Sackcloth, 205, 255, 297, 315, 570

Sacrifice, 283, 290
  eucharist as. *See* Eucharist, as sacrifice
  of Israel. *See* Israel, sacrifices of
  as *sacrificium,* 238n.41, 239

Saints
  as body of Christ, 279, 615
  and eucharist, 277, 279-81, 286-87, 292
  in identity with Christ, 218, 282, 429, 436
  and power to sanctify, 218, 220, 227-28,
    282, 291, 351, 429, 612, 614
  unity of, 217, 218, 220, 437, 612, 613, 614

Salvation, 511
  by baptism, 168, 171, 176, 192-93, 204,
    230
  by church incorporation, 295-96, 319-20,
    331, 341, 355-56

Sanctification, 226, 295
  by agency, 215, 226, 285-86
  baptismal. *See* Baptism, and
    sanctification
  by charity, 227, 292, 436
  and episcopal college, 186-90, 227, 435
  by Holy Spirit, 176, 186-87, 193, 216-20,
    226, 377-78, 436

Satisfaction (works of), 228, 296, 297, 308,
  314-15, 345, 346, 353-54
  adequacy of, 317-18
  objectives of, 301, 330
  in private, 343
  in public, 300
  as showing repentance, 315, 318, 327, 329

Schism, 27-28, 188-89, 257, 333, 606, 608,
  609. *See also* Baptism, in schism; Eucharist, in schism

Scripture, 235, 263
  interpretation of, 271, 606
  reading of, 235, 247, 263, 269-70

Scrutiny. *See* Baptismal ritual, scrutiny in

Secrecy, 206, 238n.35, 265, 266n.252, 267,
  279n.387, 289, 445

*Seniores. See* Elders, lay

Sex
  abstinence from. *See* Continence
  differentiation of, 469-70, 474, 486
  fidelity in, 475, 486, 487
  as intercourse, 449, 450, 456, 469, 471-
    72, 487

Shrine. *See* Martyrium; Miracles, at shrines

Sign of the cross, 178, 202-3, 209, 267, 554,
  559

Sin, 297, 300
  of action, 299, 319, 321
  of adultery, idolatry, and murder, 245,
    295-96, 301, 303, 306, 308, 311, 358
  in daily living, 295, 307, 324, 337
  as forgivable through the church, 305,
    335
  as forgivable without the church, 304-5,
    307, 336
  against God, 295, 301, 306, 319
  against humans, 295, 305, 306
  as imperial crime, 342, 354
  of intention, 299, 300, 319
  as unforgivable, 304, 305, 336, 351, 358

Sin, original, 57n.119, 190, 205, 230, 469,
  470
  guilt of, 176, 180, 180n.85, 190, 212, 230,
    514
  lust from, 469, 472, 474n.247, 475, 483,
    510
  mortality from, 230, 346, 471-73, 486,
    489, 496, 501, 513-14

Slaves, 444n.28, 458, 459n.144-46, 461-62,
  461n.157

Subdeacon, 6, 370, 371, 391-93, 404, 412,
415-16, 590
and discipline, 322, 421, 424n.463, 466
and marriage, 404, 412

Temples, 90, 99
*cella* of, 91, 107, 109, 153, 223
transformation of, 90-91, 149, 152
Theater, 2, 52, 68, 202n.196, 204n.214, 306,
351, 559n.62, 582, 586, 593-94
*Three Chapters,* 78-80, 83
Toleration, religious, 42-52, 71-73
*Traditio,* 48, 526, 607, 610
Treasure, heavenly, 575, 579, 620
*Triclinium,* 87, 156, 241
Trinity, 192n.145, 194, 199, 201, 227

Vengeance, 147, 338, 522, 539n.138, 560, 597
*Vidua,* 131, 464n.186, 467, 485
Vigil, 567, 594
of Cyprian, 146, 535-36
of Easter, 172, 204, 208-11, 219, 269, 270,
445
for prayer, 167, 205, 262n.209, 555, 556,
562, 565
Virgins, consecrated, 367, 443, 446, 452-
54, 463-67, 473, 478-81, 595

age of, 412, 464
consecration of, 464, 479
and integrity of body, 478-80, 487, 602
and integrity of faith, 479, 488, 617
pride of, 480, 488
and relation to Christ and church,
464n.180, 479, 481-83, 487-88
as *sanctimoniales,* 466
veiling of, 237, 446, 464, 487
*Virtus (imperium),* 311, 356, 357

Widows, consecrated, 443, 446-47, 454-55,
467-68, 481-83, 487-488, 595
age of, 454, 467
and continence, 481, 602
as former concubines, 458n.134, 468
poverty of, 454, 468, 488
and relation to Christ and church, 477,
481-83, 488, 617
remarriage of, 446, 465, 467, 481-82,
488, 617
single marriage of, 454, 467
status of, 479, 481-82, 488
vow of, 467-68, 488
Widows and widowers, 242, 365, 405,
444, 447, 449, 455, 475, 480, 488, 493-
94, 515